CANADA

MAINE

Augusta

Burlington
Montpelier
N.H.
VT.
Portland

Concord

Manchester

L. Superior

Duluth

MICHIGAN

L. Huron

Albany

Boston

NEW YORK

MASS.

Providence

Hartford

CONN.

R.I.

MINNESOTA

St. Paul

Minneapolis

WISCONSIN

L. Michigan

Milwaukee

Madison

Lansing

Detroit

L. Erie

Buffalo

Allegheny R.

Newark

New York

PENNSYLVANIA

Trenton

NEW JERSEY

Philadelphia

IOWA

Chicago

Gary

Cleveland

Pittsburgh

Harrisburg

Baltimore

Dover

Wabash R.

OHIO

Wheeling

MD.

DELAWARE

Des Moines

Columbus

Annapolis

WASHINGTON D.C.

Omaha

ILLINOIS

INDIANA

WEST
VIRGINIA

Potomac R.

Springfield

Indianapolis

Cincinnati

Charleston

Richmond

Lincoln

Missouri R.

Ohio R.

Louisville

Frankfort

VIRGINIA

Norfolk

Kansas City

St. Louis

KENTUCKY

Roanoke R.

Jefferson City

Cumberland R.

Raleigh

MISSOURI

Nashville

Knoxville

NORTH CAROLINA

APPALACHIAN MOUNTAINS

Charlotte

Atlantic Ocean

Memphis

TENNESSEE

Cape Fear R.

ARKANSAS

Tennessee R.

SOUTH
CAROLINA

Little Rock

Columbia

Oklahoma City

Chattahoochee R.

Santee R.

Birmingham

Atlanta

Charleston

MISSISSIPPI

ALABAMA

GEORGIA

Altamaha R.

Jackson

Montgomery

Alabama R.

LOUISIANA

Sabine R.

Red R.

Jacksonville

Tallahassee

Baton Rouge

New Orleans

FLORIDA

Houston

Trinity R.

Gulf of Mexico

Miami

BAHAMAS

Elevation

Feet	Meters
9,843	3,000
6,562	2,000
3,281	1,000
1,640	500
656	200
0	0
Below sea level	Below sea level

Atlantic
Ocean

67°

66°

San Juan

PUERTO RICO

18°

Ponce

Caribbean Sea

0   50

Miles

CUBA

200   400

Miles

95°   90°   85°   80°   75°

Political divisions as of January 1, 1993

RUSSIAN FEDERATION

SWEDEN
FINLAND
LITH. EST.
RUSS LAT.
POLAND
BELARUS
CZ. REP.
SLOV.
UKRAINE
AUS. HUNG.
ROMANIA
MOL.
CRO.
YUG. BULG.
B.H.
ALB.
MAC.
GREECE
TURKEY
GEORGIA
ARM.
AZER.
TUNISIA
CYPRUS
LEB.
SYRIA
IRAQ
ISRAEL
JORDAN
KUWAIT
QATAR
U.A.E.

KAZAKHSTAN

MONGOLIA

OZBEKISTAN
KYRGYZSTAN
TURKMENISTAN
TAJIKISTAN
AFGHANISTAN
PAKISTAN
NEPAL
BHUTAN
CHINA

N. KOREA
S. KOREA
JAPAN

IRAN

LIBYA
EGYPT
SAUDI
ARABIA
OMAN
YEMEN
ERITREA
DJIBOUTI

CHAD
SUDAN

CAMEROON
CENTRAL
AFRICAN
REPUBLIC
ETHIOPIA
SOMALIA
GABON
CONGO
ZAIRE
UGANDA
RWANDA
BURUNDI
KENYA
TANZANIA
MALAWI
SEYCHELLES
COMOROS

INDIA

BANGLADESH
MYANMAR
(BURMA)
LAOS
VIET NAM
THAILAND
CAMBODIA

TAIWAN

PHILIPPINES

SRI
LANKA

MALDIVES

SINGAPORE
MALAYSIA

BRUNEI

Pacific Ocean

NORTHERN
MARIANAS (U.S.)
GUAM (U.S.)

MARSHALL
ISLANDS

FEDERATED STATES
OF MICRONESIA

KIRIBATI

NAURU

INDONESIA

PAPUA
NEW
GUINEA

SOLOMON
ISLANDS

TUVALU

VANUATU

ANGOLA
ZAMBIA
NAMIBIA
ZIMBABWE
BOTSWANA
MOZAMBIQUE
MADAGASCAR
REUNION
(FR.)
MAURITIUS

Indian
Ocean

FIJI

NEW
CALEDONIA
(FR.)

SOUTH
AFRICA
SWAZILAND
LESOTHO

AUSTRALIA

NEW
ZEALAND

Arctic Ocean

20° 40° 60° 80° 100° 120° 140° 160°

▢ Nations with nuclear weapons

▢ Nations thought to have nuclear weapons programs*

▢ Other nations

*Iran, Iraq, and Libya, as signatories of the Nuclear Non-Proliferation Treaty (expires 1995), are subject to periodic inspections by the International Atomic Energy Agency of the United Nations.

ANTARCTICA

Entirely new, the *Student Guide* is designed to help students improve their performance in the course. Not only will their comprehension of the textbook and their confidence in their abilities be advanced through its conscientious use, but they will develop better learning skills and study habits. The guide begins with an introduction by Gerald J. Goodwin on how to study history. Each chapter includes a summary of the essential facts and ideas of the text chapter, with fill-in questions; the timeline from the textbook with short explanations of the significance of each event; a glossary; skill-building exercises based on a map, table, or figure from the textbook; exercises for the American Voices documents and the American Lives and New Technology essays; and a self-test.

Instructor's Resource Manual

by Clifford Egan (University of Houston), Kendall Staggs (Oklahoma Panhandle State University), Thomas R. Frazier (Baruch College), and Linda Moore (Eastern New Mexico University)

The *Instructor's Resource Manual* contains an abundance of material to aid instructors in planning the course and enhancing student involvement. For each chapter of the textbook the resources include chapter themes, a brief summary, the timeline from the textbook with additional details, lecture suggestions, class discussion starters, and topics for writing assignments. In addition, the manual includes sixteen historiographic essays on a variety of topics by outstanding scholars in these fields. For courses with a topical focus, special documents sets (modules) are provided for constitutional, southern, and diplomatic history, as well as the history of African-Americans, Latinos, and women. The *Instructor's Resource Manual* also includes a guide to writing about history by Gerald J. Goodwin, a guide to the uses of computers in teaching history by James B. M. Schick (Pittsburg State University), and a film and video guide by Stephen J. Kneeshaw.

Test Bank

by Thomas L. Altherr and Adolph Grundman (Metropolitan State College of Denver)

There are 70 to 80 questions in various formats for each chapter, including multiple-choice factual and analytical questions, fill-ins, map questions, and short and long essay questions. Computerized test-generation systems are also available.

Documents Collection

by Douglas Bukowski (University of Illinois, Chicago), Thomas E. Terrill (University of South Carolina), Maurice Isserman (Hamilton College), David Hammack (Case Western Reserve University), Barry D. Karl (University of Chicago), David Steigerwald (Ohio State University, Marion), and Katherine G. Aiken (University of Idaho)

The *Documents Collection*, containing 300 key documents, is packaged with the textbook (if required) or available separately. Each document is preceded by a brief introduction and followed by questions to help students understand its context and significance.

Transparencies

A set of 110 full-color acetate transparencies includes maps, charts, tables, fine art, and the thematic timelines from the textbook, along with teaching suggestions.

Acknowledgments

We are extremely grateful to the many scholars and teachers who reviewed manuscript chapters of the second edition at various stages. Their comments and suggestions often challenged us to rethink or justify our interpretations and always provided a useful check on accuracy down to the smallest detail.

Katherine G. Aiken, *University of Idaho*

Sara Alpern, *Texas A&M University*

Thomas L. Altherr, *Metropolitan State College of Denver*

Anne Bailey, *Georgia Southern University*

Paula Baker, *University of Pittsburgh*

Ronald Bayor, *Georgia Institute of Technology*

Eugene H. Berwanger, *Colorado State University*

W. Roger Biles, *Oklahoma State University*

Thomas Blantz, *University of Notre Dame*

Frederick Blue, *Youngstown State University*

John B. Boles, *Rice University*

Howard Brick, *University of Oregon*

William Brinker, *Tennessee Technological University*

Jane Turner Censer, *George Mason University*

Martin B. Cohen, *George Mason University*

John Cooper, *University of Wisconsin, Madison*

George H. Daniels, *University of South Alabama*

Wayne K. Durrill, *University of Cincinnati*

Henry Ferrell, *East Carolina University*

Robert Fishman, *Rutgers University, Camden*

Dan Flores, *Texas Technological University*

Dee Garrison, *Rutgers University, New Brunswick*

Adolph Grundman, *Metropolitan State College of Denver*

Benjamin Harrison, *University of Louisville*

Herman M. Hattaway, *University of Missouri, Kansas City*

Margot A. Henriksen, *University of Hawaii at Manoa*

Joan Hoff, *Indiana University*

Herbert T. Hoover, *University of South Dakota*

Elizabeth Jameson, *University of New Mexico*

John Jameson, *Kent State University*

David A. Johnson, *Portland State University*

Maxine Jones, *Florida State University*

Lawrence Kelly, University of North Texas

Jeffrey P. Kimball, *Miami University (Ohio)*

Nancy McLean, *Northwestern University*

Samuel T. McSeveney, *Vanderbilt University*

John Muldowny, *University of Tennessee, Knoxville*

Edward Muller, *University of Pittsburgh*

Barbara Posadas, *Northern Illinois University*

Howard N. Rabinowitz, *University of New Mexico*

Leo Ribuffo, *George Washington University*

Jere Roberson, *Central State University (Oklahoma)*

Jerome L. Rodnitzky, *University of Texas, Arlington*

Naomi Rogers, *University of Alabama, Tuscaloosa*

Joy Scime, *Ohio State University*

Sharon Seager, *Ball State University*

Judith Sealander, *Wright State University*

Judith Stanley, *California State University, Hayward*

Mark Summers, *University of Kentucky*

Thomas E. Terrill, *University of South Carolina, Columbia*

Richard Turk, *Allegheny College*

David Walker, *University of Northern Iowa*

John Wilson, *University of South Carolina, Columbia*

Randall B. Woods, *University of Arkansas, Fayetteville*

We would also like to thank Jennifer Sutherland, our main editor at Worth Publishers, for holding us to her high and exacting standards, Toni Ann Scaramuzzo, George Touloumes, and Stacey Alexander for guiding *America's History* through production, and Paul Shensa, Anne Vinnicombe, and Bob Worth for their valuable suggestions and unflagging encouragement and support. Their contributions, and those of Carol Bullock, Rory Dicker, Jeannie Jhun, Patricia Lawson, Demetrios Zangos, and many other members of the fine staff at Worth Publishers, have helped make this a more accessible and intellectually stimulating book.

Finally, we wish to state clearly that this is a collaborative work. For the past three years, the four of us have read and commented on each other's draft chapters, meeting periodically to thrash out differences on matters large and small—from organizational issues, to what topics should be covered, to how to turn a phrase. We believe this collaboration has strengthened each part of the book and afforded a greater cohesiveness to the whole. We hope that the students we introduce to America's history will develop an interest in some aspect of our nation's past and the skills to think critically about historical issues that will last long after the course is over.

James A. Henretta
W. Elliot Brownlee
David Brody
Susan Ware

January 1993

America's History

Volume 2 SINCE 1865

John Kane *From My Studio Window, 1932,* Oil on canvas
The Metropolitan Museum of Art

John Kane (1860–1934), born in Scotland of Irish parentage, arrived in Pennsylvania in 1879. He made his way as a laborer in the coal mines and steel mills of western Pennsylvania until he lost his leg below the knee in a railroad accident. Forced to take up less strenuous work, he became a watchman, house painter, and carpenter, drawing and sketching in his spare time. He achieved sudden fame as an artist in 1927, when the Carnegie International Exhibition showed one of his works, and he devoted the rest of his life to painting.

Kane painted this scene from his studio above a shoemaker's shop on Fifth Avenue in Pittsburgh. It combines views from both the front and side windows.

SECOND EDITION

America's History

Volume 2 SINCE 1865

James A. Henretta
University of Maryland

W. Elliot Brownlee
University of California, Santa Barbara

David Brody
University of California, Davis

Susan Ware
New York University

Worth Publishers

America's History, Volume 2 Since 1865, *Second Edition*

Copyright © 1993 by Worth Publishers, Inc.

All rights reserved.

Manufactured in the United States of America

Library of Congress Catalog Card Number: 92-61800

ISBN: 0–87901–629–9

Printing: 1 2 3 4 5 — 97 96 95 94 93

Development editor: Jennifer Sutherland

Design: Malcolm Grear Designers

Art director: George Touloumes

Production editor: Toni Ann Scaramuzzo

Production supervisor: Stacey B. Alexander

Layout: Patricia Lawson

Picture editor: Deborah Bull/Photosearch

Picture researcher: Joanne Polster/Photosearch

Line art: Demetrios Zangos

Advisory editor for cartography: Michael P. Conzen

Cartography: Mapping Specialists, Ltd.

Composition and separations: TSI Graphics

Printing and binding: R. R. Donnelley & Sons Company

Cover and frontispiece: John Kane, *From My Studio Window* (detail), 1932. The Metropolitan Museum of Art, Bequest of Miss Adelaide Milton de Groot (1876–1967).

Illustration credits begin on page IC-1, and constitute an extension of the copyright page.

Worth Publishers
33 Irving Place
New York, New York 10003

For our families

Contents in Brief

Contents

Chapter Features

★

★

──────────────★──────────────

TABLES

──────────────★──────────────

AMERICAN LIVES

Preface

At the core of *America's History* stands a vision of a "democratic" history, one not confined to the deeds of the great and powerful but concerned also with the experiences of ordinary women and men. We present political and social history in an integrated way, using each perspective to make better sense of the other. We believe that there is a continual interaction between the lives of ordinary people and the practice of politics—and that both are shaped by the political institutions, economic conditions, and moral values of the times. *America's History* thus offers a balanced and comprehensive narrative of our nation's past, from government and politics, diplomacy and war, to society, the economy, popular culture, and intellectual life. Just as important, it consistently places American history in a global context—for example, explaining the increasing role of overseas markets in America's prosperity at the end of the nineteenth century, and exploring the impact of American ideals, popular culture, and military power on the wider world today.

Organization

As history casts its net to draw in ever more diverse aspects of human experience, the need to organize and make sense of this abundance of disparate material for the student becomes more and more imperative. We have reorganized *America's History* to provide a clear chronology and a strong conceptual framework. The book is now divided into three Parts, corresponding to three distinct phases of the country's development. The Part breaks reflect not only the obvious turning points of revolution and war but also more gradual changes in the economy and society and the dynamic forces that produced them. Each Part begins with a two-page overview: first, a **Thematic Timeline** highlights the key developments in government, the economy, society, culture, and foreign affairs; then these themes are summarized in a brief Part essay. The Part essays focus on the crucial engines of historical change—in some eras primarily economic, in others political—that created new conditions of life and transformed social relations. The essays and the Part organization will help students understand the major themes and periods of American history, to see that bits and pieces of historical data acquire significance as part of the larger, interconnected pattern of development.

Part 4, "A Maturing Industrial Society, 1877–1914," explores the emergence of heavy industry and large-scale enterprise and describes their impact on how people lived and how they made a living. Part 5, "The Modern State and Society, 1914–1945," focuses on the formation of modern government and the emergence of a national culture—strong centralizing forces that gradually undermined earlier patterns of regionalism and local autonomy. Part 6, "America and the World, 1945 to the Present," describes how the Cold War drove government decision making, resulting in a massive military-industrial complex, and, by highlighting Americans' image of themselves as the defenders of democracy abroad, advanced the struggle for equality at home fought by African-Americans, Hispanics and other minorities, and women.

In telling this complex story, we have given equal attention to historical actors and to historical institutions, customs, and forces—writing what the historian Lawrence Stone has called the "new narrative history." At the center of our narrative are the actions of individual Americans: we show how the people of all classes and groups make their own history. But we also make clear how people's choices are influenced and constrained by the circumstances of their lives and times. Such a narrative not only conveys the rich diversity of life in the past but also will help students understand their own potential for purposeful action in the present and future.

Changes in the Second Edition

Those familiar with the first edition will notice changes on virtually every page. In particular, we now devote a full chapter to the settling of the West (17), including a new section on California and its important Hispanic and Asian communities. American diplomacy in the late nineteenth and early twentieth centuries is the subject of a new foreign policy chapter, "An Emerging World Power, 1877–1914" (22). We retain two full chapters (25 and 26) on the Great Depression and the New Deal, but they have been extensively reorganized and rewritten. And the entire post-1945 section has been reorganized and refocused to place more emphasis on the dominant influence of the Cold War on foreign relations, domestic politics, the economy, and society. Finally, the last chapter, on the Reagan and Bush years through the 1992 election, is almost entirely new.

To enhance clarity and interest, we have strengthened the narrative line, added subheads on important topics, and enlivened the story with telling illustrations and examples. And, reflecting current scholarly interest, we have expanded the treatment of a variety of social groups, from newly emancipated slaves, immigrant factory workers and steel and railroad magnates in the nineteenth century, to women bureaucrats in the New Deal and religious fundamentalists today. We think our text captures the quite remarkable social and cultural diversity of the United States even as it describes the evolution of America's political institutions and national identity.

Features

America's History contains a wealth of special features, all closely tied to the main text. In keeping with our emphasis on the experiences of individual Americans we include two new features, **American Voices** and **American Lives**. Each chapter contains two or three American Voices, contemporary first-person accounts from letters, diaries, autobiographies, and public testimony that paint a vivid portrait of the social or political life of the time. And most chapters include an American Lives essay, a short biography of a representative individual or group—from controversial generals to ardent social reformers and icons of popular culture. Four major essays on **New Technology** focus on the technical aspects of innovations and how discoveries affected everyday life: what people ate, how they made a living, how they fought in battle. Together, these documents and essays will help students enter into the life of the past and see it from within.

At the end of each chapter a **Summary** and an expanded **Timeline** provide a convenient review. In addition, for courses that require a research paper, each chapter includes a **Topic for Research** (a broad topic that can be explored in a variety of short papers), and a **Bibliography**.

We have significantly expanded our illustration program. The text now has 275 photographs, many from unusual sources. There are now 56 maps, 14 entirely new and 42 redrawn to improve readability or provide additional information. We have added 3 new figures and redrawn the remaining 17. We have increased the number of tables, adding useful lists to help students disentangle complicated sequences of events, such as the legislative cornucopia of the New Deal. At the end of the text, in addition to lists of presidential elections, Supreme Court justices, population data, and economic statistics, we include two special charts: (1) lists of the ten largest American cities at selected dates from 1700 to 1990, and (2) a currency conversion chart that enables readers to convert any historic pound Sterling or U.S. dollar amount into a roughly equivalent amount in 1990 U.S. dollars.

Supplements

Student Guide

by Thomas R. Frazier (Baruch College), and Linda Moore (Eastern New Mexico University)

About the Authors

James A. Henretta is Priscilla Alden Burke Professor of American History at the University of Maryland, College Park. He received his undergraduate education at Swarthmore College and his Ph.D. from Harvard University. Professor Henretta has taught at the University of Sussex, England; Princeton University; UCLA; Boston University; as a Fulbright lecturer in Australia at the University of New England; and in 1991–92 at Oxford University as the Harmsworth Professor of American History. His publications include *The Evolution of American Society, 1700–1815: An Interdisciplinary Analysis; "Salutary Neglect": Colonial Administration Under the Duke of Newcastle; Evolution and Revolution: American Society, 1600–1820; The Origins of American Capitalism;* and important articles in early American and social history. He is presently working on a study of *The Rise and Decline of the Liberal State in America, 1800–1930.*

W. Elliot Brownlee is Professor of History at the University of California, Santa Barbara, and Chair of the Academic Senate of the University of California. He is a graduate of Harvard University, received his Ph.D. from the University of Wisconsin, Madison, and specializes in U.S. economic history. He has been awarded fellowships by the Charles Warren Center, Harvard University, and the Woodrow Wilson International Center for Scholars. He has been a visiting professor at Princeton, and was Bicentennial Lecturer at the U.S. Department of the Treasury. His published works include *Dynamics of Ascent: A History of the American Economy; Progressivism and Economic Growth: The Wisconsin Income Tax, 1911–1929; Women in the American Economy: A Documentary History, 1675–1929* (with Mary M. Brownlee); and *The Essentials of American History* (with Richard N. Current, T. Harry Williams, and Frank Freidel). His current projects include a history of the financing of World War I.

David Brody is Professor of History at the University of California, Davis. He received his B.A., M.A., and Ph.D. from Harvard University. He has taught at the University of Warwick in England, at Moscow State University in the former Soviet Union, and at Sydney University in Australia. He is the author of *Steelworkers in America; Workers in Industrial America: Essays on the 20th Century Struggle;* and, forthcoming, *Main Chapters in American Labor History: From Origins to the Present.* He has been awarded fellowships from the Social Science Research Council, the Guggenheim Foundation, and the National Endowment for the Humanities. He is past president (1991–92) of the Pacific Coast Branch of the American Historical Association. His current research is on industrial labor during the Great Depression.

Susan Ware is Associate Professor of History at New York University, where she specializes in twentieth-century U.S. history and the history of American women. She received her undergraduate degree from Wellesley College and her Ph.D. from Harvard University. Ware is the author of *Beyond Suffrage: Women in the New Deal; Holding Their Own: American Women in the 1930s; Partner and I: Molly Dewson, Feminism, and New Deal Politics; Modern American Women: A Documentary History;* and the forthcoming *Still Missing: Amelia Earhart and the Search for Modern Feminism.* She serves on the national advisory boards of the Franklin and Eleanor Roosevelt Institute and the Schlesinger Library of Radcliffe College and has been a historical consultant to numerous documentary film projects.

America's History

Volume 2 SINCE 1865

Robert B. Elliott

Robert B. Elliott (1842–1884) was an African-American born in
Boston and educated there, and in Jamaica and England. After
studying law and serving in the U.S. Navy during the Civil War,
he moved to Charleston. He won election to the South Carolina
legislature (1868–1870), to two terms in Congress (1871–1874),
and to Speaker of the House in South Carolina (1874–1876). He
is pictured in this 1874 lithograph entitled, *The Shackle Broken
by the Genius of Freedom,* addressing his fellow state legislators
on civil rights. With the end of Reconstruction he left politics and
moved to New Orleans where he practiced law.

CHAPTER **16** *The Union Reconstructed, 1865–1877*

When the Confederacy collapsed in the spring of 1865, President Lincoln hoped that he could achieve a swift reconciliation between the triumphant North and the shattered South. In his second inaugural address Abraham Lincoln had spoken of the need to "bind up the nation's wounds." But many questions remained unanswered. Who would control the rebuilding of the Union—the president or Congress? How long should the rebuilding last? How far should it go—should it exclude former Confederates from politics and reward freedmen with land confiscated from their former masters?

At the end of the war, most Republican leaders defined the task of rebuilding simply as *restoration*. These moderates wanted to establish loyal, pro-Union state governments and restore the southern states' representation in Congress. But the freedmen, former abolitionists, and some Republican politicians favored a more radical plan—one requiring a degree of *reconstruction* of the South. In their view, steps should be taken to ensure a measure of political and even economic equality for the freed slaves and to prevent the return to power of unrepentant planters. For radicals, the key to reconstructing the South was to make the Republican party dominant there.

When northern Republicans adopted a policy of radical reconstruction in 1867, ex-Confederates and their Democratic sympathizers in the North maintained that their goal should be the *redemption* of the South. They claimed that the Union's victory had defeated democracy in the South, depriving southerners of control over their economic, social, and political systems. The Union would be rebuilt, the redeemers claimed, only when white southerners had regained power over their own affairs.

The Reconstruction Era—the years from 1865 to 1877—was shaped by continuous struggles among the groups holding these differing views. It was a time of unparalleled peacetime turmoil and violence. In the struggles, every kind of tactic was brought to bear—the assassination of one president and the impeachment of another; the adoption of three amendments to the Constitution and a welter of new legislation; the use of violence, including nighttime terrorism by robed whites in the South; the creation of new institutions by African-Americans; and the conventional compromises and deals by politicians on all sides.

Presidential Restoration

Lincoln and his successor, Andrew Johnson, took the initiative for rebuilding the Union. Both presidents believed that the southern states had never legally left the Union; that rebuilding the nation was simply a process of restoring state governments loyal to the Union; and that this political process could take place quickly, largely under presidential direction. This moderate approach put the presidents on a collision course with those Republicans in Congress who sought a reconstruction of southern society.

Restoration Under Lincoln

The process of rebuilding had actually begun during the war as President Lincoln tried to subvert the southern war effort. Lincoln thought that a policy of moderation and reconciliation in those portions of the South occupied by federal troops would induce the Confederates to abandon the rebellion. In implementing his restoration plan, Lincoln relied on his power as military commander-in-chief. Lincoln assumed that states could not legally secede and that reorganizing the Union was purely an administrative matter. (In 1869, in *Texas v. White*, the Supreme Court accepted Lincoln's constitutional interpretation, ruling that secession was impossible under the Constitution.)

Lincoln's Plan. In December 1863, Lincoln announced his restoration plan. He offered a general amnesty to all Confederate citizens except high-ranking civil and military officials. Citizens of states seeking to reconstitute their governments would have to take an oath pledging their *future* loyalty to the Union and accepting the Union's wartime acts and proclamations concerning slavery. When 10 percent of the number of voters in 1860 had taken the loyalty oath, those individuals could organize a new state government.

President Lincoln aimed his plan at former southern Whigs, many of whom he had known well as former political allies. Under his plan, they would step forward, declare allegiance to the Union, and take charge of southern state governments. This is what happened in three states under military occupation—Louisiana, Arkansas, and Tennessee. The former Whigs who organized loyal governments under Lincoln's supervision often retained their economic power. In Louisiana, for

example, Whig sugar planters who declared their loyalty to the Union received help from Generals Benjamin F. Butler and Nathaniel P. Banks, who used their troops to enforce labor discipline, transforming slaves into wage laborers and enabling the former Whigs to save their plantations.

Radical and Moderate Republicans. Many members of his own party, including some of his fellow moderates, disapproved of Lincoln's plan. Their opposition was based, in part, on a different constitutional interpretation. They argued that the southern states *had* left the Union and were now the equivalent of conquered provinces with territorial status. As such, they were subject to congressional rule rather than the president's executive authority.

The most strenuous criticism came from a group of radical Republicans, some of whom had abolitionist backgrounds. Led by Senator Charles Sumner of Massachusetts and Representative Thaddeus Stevens of Pennsylvania, the radicals wanted a harder, slower peace. In Stevens's words, the federal government should "revolutionize Southern institutions, habits, and manners." He declared that "the foundations of their institutions . . . must be broken up and relaid, or all our blood and treasure will have been spent in vain."

Stevens, Indiana congressman George W. Julian, and African-American leaders, including Frederick Douglass, staked out the most radical definition of what reconstruction should mean. The core of their program was an economic one—confiscation and redistribution of southern plantations to the freed slaves and white farmers who had been loyal to the Union. The program was meant to answer the dreams of the former slaves, whose expectations had been raised by emancipations,

Radical Republicans

Lincoln's readmission plan was harshly criticized by radical Republicans. One of their leaders was Thaddeus Stevens (front row, second from left) pictured here with fellow members of Congress in a photograph taken by Mathew Brady. Stevens outlined a radical economic plan that called for a redistribution of land in the South. He believed that the former slaves needed more than the vote to control their fate—they needed land. He was unable to muster support for this radical plan.

and even of the poor white farmers of the South. To the former slaves, emancipation and freedom meant control over their lives. But to control their fate in an agricultural economy, they knew they needed more than the vote—they needed to own land. But Stevens and Julian were unable to recruit other members of Congress to support a large-scale redistribution of land in the South. The majority of radical Republicans regarded such a plan as a violation of the Constitution's protection of property rights and a threat to the capitalist order.

The radical Republicans did agree on three key points: (1) The leaders of the Confederacy should not be allowed to return to power in the South; (2) Steps should be taken to establish the Republican party as a major, even dominant, force in southern political life; (3) The federal government should ensure that African-Americans participated in southern society with full *civil* equality by guaranteeing their voting rights. The last point was especially important. As Frederick Douglass declared in May 1865, "Slavery is not abolished until the black man has the ballot."

Moderate Republicans in Congress shared the radicals' view that Lincoln's program was too lenient, and they endorsed the first two points of the radical program. But as a group they hesitated in going further to support black suffrage and civil equality. Like virtually all conservative Republicans and Democrats, some moderates were profoundly racist and believed that African-Americans could never become responsible citizens. Other moderates, like Lincoln, had confidence in blacks' abilities. But they wanted to avoid the violent resistance that southern whites might offer to drastic changes in the relationship between the races.

The Wade-Davis Bill. In 1864 the radical and moderate Republicans in Congress devised an alternative to Lincoln's program, based on the two reconstruction principles on which they could agree. In the Wade-Davis bill, passed by Congress on July 2, 1864, they prescribed harsher conditions for former Confederate states to rejoin the Union. A *majority* of the state's adult white men would have to swear an oath of allegiance to the Union. The state could then hold a constitutional convention—but no one could vote in the election for delegates or serve as a delegate unless he could swear that he had never carried arms against the Union or aided the Confederacy in any way. Requiring this pledge, which became known as the *ironclad oath*, would exclude most southern whites, therefore leaving the task of constitution-making to those white men who had overtly opposed the Confederacy. Finally, the bill required slavery to be prohibited and Confederate civil and military leaders to be permanently disfranchised.

The Wade-Davis bill proposed going further than Lincoln's plan in punishing ex-Confederates, especially those who had led the South in rebellion. Despite this difference, Lincoln seemed ready to compromise with the congressional Republicans. Rather than openly challenging Congress by vetoing the Wade-Davis bill, he executed a "pocket" veto by not signing it before Congress adjourned. At the same time he initiated informal talks with members of Congress aimed at producing a compromise solution when the war ended. He even suggested that he might support the radical program of establishing federal control over race relations in the South and guaranteeing the vote to African-Americans there. In the last speech he ever delivered, on April 11, 1865, Lincoln demonstrated that he was moving pragmatically to endorse freedmen's suffrage, beginning with those who had served in the Union army.

The Assassination of Lincoln. Whether Lincoln and his party could have forged a unified approach to reconstruction is one of the great unanswered questions of American history. On April 14, 1865—Good Friday—Lincoln was shot in the head at Ford's Theater in Washington by an unstable actor named John Wilkes Booth. Ironically, Lincoln might have been spared if the war had dragged on longer, for Booth and his Confederate associates had originally plotted to kidnap the president to force a negotiated settlement. After Lee's surrender, Booth became desperate for revenge. In the middle of the play, he entered Lincoln's box, shot him at close range, stabbed a member of the president's party, and fled. Booth was hunted down and killed by Union troops. Eight people were eventually convicted as accomplices by military courts, and four of them were hanged.

Lincoln never regained consciousness and died on April 15. The Union—and the hundreds of thousands of African-Americans for whom his name had become synonymous with freedom—went into profound mourning. Even Lincoln's critics suddenly conceded his greatness. Millions of Americans honored his memory by waiting in silence to watch the train bearing his body back to Illinois for burial.

Lincoln's death dramatically changed the prospects for a moderate reconstruction. At one stroke, John Wilkes Booth had sent Lincoln to martyrdom, convinced many northerners that harsher measures against the South were necessary, and forced the presidency into the hands of Vice-President Andrew Johnson.

Restoration Under Johnson

Andrew Johnson was a self-made man and former slaveholder from the hills of eastern Tennessee. A Jacksonian Democrat, he saw himself as the champion of ordinary people. He hated what he called the "bloated, corrupt aristocracy" of the Northeast, and he blamed

Andrew Johnson
The president was not an easy man. This photograph of Andrew Johnson (1808–1875) conveys some of the personal qualities that contributed so centrally to his failure to reach agreement with Republicans on a program of moderate Reconstruction.

southern planters for the Civil War. His political career had led from the Tennessee legislature to the U.S. Senate, where he remained, loyal to the Union, after Tennessee seceded. He served as military governor of his home state after federal forces captured Nashville. In 1864 the Republicans gave him the vice-presidency in an effort to promote wartime political unity and to court the support of southern Unionists.

Like Lincoln, Johnson believed that the southern states had retained their constitutional status and that reunification was exclusively an executive matter. During the summer of 1865, when Congress was not in session, Johnson unilaterally executed his own plan of restoration. He insisted only that the states revoke their ordinances of secession and ratify the Thirteenth Amendment, which abolished slavery. He offered amnesty and a return of all property except slaves to almost all southerners if they took an oath of allegiance to the Union. Those southerners who were excluded from amnesty—high-ranking Confederate military officers and civil officials, and persons with taxable property of more than $20,000—could petition Johnson personally. By December 1865 all of the former Confederate states had functioning governments and had met Johnson's requirements to rejoin the Union.

Johnson's plan would not become complete until Congress accepted the senators and representatives from the former Confederacy. Under the Constitution, Congress is "the judge of the elections, returns and qualifications of its own members" (Article I, Section 5), and it would not convene again until December 1865. This step need not have been a problem for Johnson. While most moderate Republicans in Congress hoped to make changes in Johnson's program to bring it closer to the Wade-Davis bill, they supported the basic outline of his program. Perhaps most important, they agreed with Johnson that the federal government ought not to protect African-American suffrage or civil equality. Even most radicals were optimistic. They liked the stern treatment of Confederate leaders, and they hoped that the new southern governments would respond positively to Johnson's conciliatory attitude and offer the vote at least to those African-Americans who were literate and owned property—probably no more than 10 percent of adult African-American men.

During the summer and fall, however, Johnson lost any support from radical Republicans. They first became angered over a telegram that Johnson had sent in August to the provisional governor of Mississippi, who was presiding over the state's constitutional convention. Johnson urged that the vote be given to literate African-Americans—on the grounds that "the radicals, who are wild upon negro franchise, will be completely foiled." The telegram also embarrassed Republican moderates, who had hoped to win the support of the radicals as well as Johnson for a compromise program.

During the fall of 1865, news reports of conditions in the South alarmed the moderates and further outraged the radicals. They learned that ex-Confederates were frequently attacking freedmen and white Union supporters; that the new provisional governments were making no effort to enfranchise African-Americans; and that ex-Confederates had taken control of southern governments. Southern voters elected to Congress nine men who had served in the Confederate Congress, seven former officials of Confederate state governments, four generals and four colonels from the Confederate army, and even the vice-president of the Confederacy, Alexander Stephens. It turned out that Johnson had been exceedingly liberal in pardoning ex-Confederate leaders. He seemed less interested in punishing them than in humbling them by making them submit to his personal power.

As radical Republicans increased their attacks on Johnson, he shifted away from his strongly bipartisan stance. He began to believe he could build a coalition of white southerners, northern Democrats, and conservative Republicans to support the creation of a democracy for white southerners. To avoid embarrassing potentially supportive Republicans or ex-Whigs in the South, his banner would be "National Union." Democrats in both the North and South praised Johnson as the leader they needed to restore their party on a national basis. As the president warmed to Democratic applause, he granted more and more pardons to wealthy southerners—an average of a hundred a day in September.

The president's movement toward the Democrats further agitated radical Republicans and dismayed the moderates. By December 1865, when Congress convened, the moderates had become convinced that they had to join with the radicals in order to protect the Republican party. It would be necessary, they concluded, to take action to guarantee the civil rights of former slaves and to establish the Republican party in the South.

The Republican party acted quickly to reject the newly elected southern representatives and propose that Johnson work with Congress on a new program for reconstructing the South. A House-Senate committee— the Joint Committee on Reconstruction—was formed to develop that program in cooperation with the president.

The Joint Committee conducted public hearings on conditions in the former Confederacy and publicized alarming reports from army officers, federal officials, and white and black southerners. The testimony augmented the newspaper reports by revealing an astonishing level of violence, and by providing disturbing details on how southern planters and southern legislatures were attempting to resubjugate the freed slaves. Although most moderates were still not ready to impose black suffrage on the South, almost all were shocked by what they regarded as a movement to circumvent the Thirteenth Amendment.

Acting on Freedom

While congressmen discussed conditions in the South, African-Americans were already far advanced in acting on their idea of freedom. Exultant and hopeful, their main concern was economic independence, which they assumed was necessary to be truly free. During the Civil War they had acted on this assumption throughout the South, whenever Union armies drew near. But many officers actively sympathized with the planters, allowing planters who expressed loyalty to the Union to retain control of their plantations and their former slaves. Other officers wished to destroy the power of the planters but preserve a class system in the South. General Lorenzo Thomas, for example, devised a plan in 1863 to lease plantations in the Mississippi Valley to loyal northern men who would hire African-American laborers under conditions set by the army.

During the final months of the war, when the Union directed its military operations against civilians, the freedmen found greater opportunities to win control of land. Most visibly, General William T. Sherman reserved vast tracts of coastal lands in Georgia and South Carolina—the Sea Islands and the abandoned plantations within 30 miles of the coast—for African-American settlers and gave them "possessory titles" to 40-acre tracts. Sherman had little use for radicals or freedmen; he only wanted to relieve the pressure that African-American refugees placed on his army as it marched across the lower South. But the freedmen assumed that Sherman's order meant that the land would be theirs—a reasonable expectation after one of Sherman's generals told a large group of freedmen "that they were to be put in possession of lands, upon which they might locate their families and work out for themselves a living and respectability."

The resettlement of freedmen was organized by the Bureau of Refugees, Freedmen, and Abandoned Lands, which Congress created in March 1865. Known as the Freedmen's Bureau, it was charged with feeding and clothing war refugees of both races, renting confiscated land to "loyal refugees and freedmen," and drafting and enforcing labor contracts between freedmen and planters. The Freedmen's Bureau also worked with the large number of northern voluntary associations that sent missionaries and teachers to the South to establish schools for former slaves.

Schoolhouse, Port Hudson, Louisiana

This was probably the first schoolhouse built for freedmen by Union forces. In front, African-American soldiers from the Port Hudson "Corps d'Afrique" pose with their textbooks. In 1865 and 1866, most new schools in the South were established by blacks forming societies and raising money among themselves.

AMERICAN VOICES

Report on the Freedmen's Bureau *Eliphalet Whittlesey*

In October 1865, Colonel Eliphalet Whittlesey, an assistant commissioner for the Freedmen's Bureau in North Carolina, wrote the following report on the activities of the Bureau. He was later promoted to general and served as a trustee of the national Freedman's Savings Bank in Washington, D.C. He was typical of many Freedmen's Bureau officials in that he saw his role as one of mediating between two worthy groups—former slaves and former masters.

On the 22d of June I arrived at Raleigh with instructions . . . to take the control of all subjects relating to "refugees, freedmen, and the abandoned lands" within this State. I found these subjects in much confusion. Hundreds of white refugees and thousands of blacks were collected about this and other towns, occupying every hovel and shanty, living upon government rations, without employment and without comfort, many dying for want of proper food and medical supplies. A much larger number, both white and black, were crowding into the towns, and literally swarming about every depot of supplies to receive their rations. My first effort was to reduce this class of suffering and idle humanity to order, and to discover how large a proportion of these applicants were really deserving of help. . . .

It was evident at the outset that large numbers were drawing rations who might support themselves. . . . orders were issued that no able-bodied man or woman should receive supplies, except such as were known to be industrious, and to be entirely destitute. . . . The homeless and helpless were gathered in camps, where shelter and food could be furnished, and the sick collected in hospitals, where they could receive proper care. . . .

Suddenly set free [the freedmen] were at first exhilarated by the air of liberty, and committed some excesses. To be sure of their freedom, many thought they must leave the old scenes of oppression and seek new homes. Others regarded the property accumulated by their labor as in part their own, and demanded a share of it. On the other hand, the former masters, suddenly stripped of their wealth, at first looked upon the freedmen with a mixture of hate and fear. In these circumstances some collisions were inevitable. . . .

. . . [M]any freedmen need the presence of some authority to enforce upon them their new duties. . . . The efforts of the bureau to protect the freedmen have done much to restrain violence and injustice. Such efforts must be continued until civil government is fully restored, just laws enacted, or great suffering and serious disturbance will be the result.

Contrary to the fears and predictions of many, the great mass of colored people have remained quietly at work upon the plantations of their former masters during the entire summer. . . . In truth, a much larger amount of vagrancy exists among the whites than among the blacks. . . .

The report is confirmed by the fact that out of a colored population of nearly 350,000 in the State, only about 5,000 are now receiving support from the government. . . . Our officers . . . have visited plantations, explained the difference between slave and free labor, the nature and the solemn obligation of contracts. The chief difficulty met with has been a want of confidence between the two parties.

. . . Rev. F. A. Fiske, a Massachusetts teacher, has been appointed superintendent of education, and has devoted himself with energy to his duties. . . . the whole number of schools . . . is 63, the number of teachers 85, and the number of scholars 5,624. A few of the schools are self-supporting, and taught by colored teachers, but the majority are sustained by northern societies and northern teachers. The officers of the bureau have, as far as practicable, assigned buildings for their use, and assisted in making them suitable; but time is nearly past when such facilities can be given. The societies will be obliged hereafter to pay rent for school-rooms and for teachers homes. The teachers are engaged in a noble and self-denying work. They report a surprising thirst for knowledge among the colored people—children giving earnest attention and learning rapidly, and adults, after the day's work is done, devoting the evening to study. . . .

Source: Report of the Joint Committee on Reconstruction, 39th Cong., 1st sess. (Washington, D.C.: Government Printing Office, 1866), II: 186–92.

By the end of the war, the army and the Freedmen's Bureau had resettled about ten thousand families on half a million acres of "Sherman" land in Georgia and South Carolina. Reports of such actions inspired many African-American families to stay on their old plantations in the hope that they would own some of the land after the war. When South Carolina planter Thomas Pinckney returned home, his freed slaves told him, "We ain't going nowhere. We are going to work right here on the land where we were born and what belongs to us."

One Georgia freedman offered to sell to his former master the share of the plantation he expected to receive after the federal redistribution.

Andrew Johnson's amnesty plan allowed pardoned Confederates to recover their land if Union troops had confiscated or occupied it. In October, Johnson ordered General Oliver O. Howard, head of the Freedmen's Bureau, to tell Sea Island blacks that they did not hold legal title to the land and that they would have to come to terms with the white landowners. When Howard reluctantly obeyed, the dispossessed farmers protested: "Why do you take away our lands? You take them from us who have always been true, always true to the Government! You give them to our all-time enemies! That is not right!" When some of the Sea Islanders refused to deal with the restored white owners, Union soldiers forced them to leave or work for their old masters.

The former slaves resisted efforts to remove them. Often led by African-American veterans of the Union army, they fought pitched battles with plantation owners and bands of ex-Confederate soldiers. Whenever possible, landowners attempted to disarm and intimidate the returning soldiers. One of them wrote from Maryland: "The returned colard Solgers are in Many cases beten, and their guns taken from them, we darcent walk out of an evening. . . . they beat us badly and Sumtime Shoot us." In this warfare, federal troops often backed the local whites, who generally prevailed in recapturing their former holdings.

A New Labor System. Throughout the South, high postwar prices for cotton prompted returning planters not only to reclaim land but also to establish a labor system that was as close to slavery as they could make it. On paper, emancipation had cost the slaveowners about $3 billion—the value of their capital investment in former slaves—a sum that equaled nearly three-fourths of the nation's economic production in 1860. The *real* losses of planters, however, depended on whether they lost control of their former slaves. Planters attempted to reestablish that control and to substitute low wages for the food, clothing, and shelter that their slaves had previously received. They also refused to sell or rent land to blacks, hoping to force them to work for low wages.

The freedmen resisted the new wage system, as well as the loss of land. During the growing seasons of 1865 and 1866, thousands of former slaves abandoned their old plantations and farms. Many freedmen sought better lives in the towns and cities of the South. Those who remained in the countryside either refused to work in the cotton fields or tried to reduce the amount of time they worked there. When they could, freedmen developed their own garden plots, therefore, guaranteeing themselves a subsistence level of rations during the postwar disruptions. The freedmen who did return to work in the white-owned cotton fields refused to submit to the grueling gang system that had been the major tool of economic exploitation under slavery. Now they wanted a pace of work and independence that reflected their new status. What was freedom all about if not to have a bit more leisure time, to work less intensely than they had as slaves, and to work for themselves and their families?

Wage Labor of Ex-Slaves

This photograph, taken in South Carolina shortly after the Civil War, shows former slaves being led from the cotton fields. Although they now worked for wages, they were probably organized into a gang not far removed from the earlier slave gangs. Their plug-hatted crew leader is dressed much as his slave-driving predecessor would have been.

The Black Codes. The efforts of former slaves to control their own lives ran counter to deeply entrenched white attitudes. Emancipation had not destroyed the racist assumptions and fears that the planters had fostered in order to maintain and defend slavery. The former slaveowners and many of the poorer whites who looked to them for leadership attempted to maintain the South's caste system. Beginning in 1865, southern legislatures enacted sets of laws—known as Black Codes—that were designed to keep African-Americans in a condition close to slavery.

The codes varied from state to state, but virtually all required the arrest of blacks for vagrancy if they were found without employment. In most cases they could not pay the fine, and the county court would then hire them to an employer, who could hold them in slavery-like conditions. Several state codes established specific hours of labor, spelled out the duties expected of laborers, and declared that any laborer who did not meet these standards was a vagrant. The codes usually restricted black employment opportunities outside agriculture by requiring licenses for those who wished to pursue skilled work or even "irregular job work."

The state legislatures went even further, sanctioning the efforts of local governments to circumscribe narrowly the lives of blacks. Localities set curfews, required black agricultural workers to obtain passes from their employers, insisted that blacks who wished to live in town obtain white sponsors, and, in an effort to prevent political gatherings, sharply regulated meetings of blacks, including those held in churches. Fines and forced labor were the penalties for violators.

Congressional Initiatives

Reports of southern repression aroused moderate Republicans in Congress. They decided they must provide for some guarantees of the civil rights of freedmen. The moderates first drafted a bill to extend the life of the Freedmen's Bureau and enlarge its powers, including the authority to establish courts to protect the rights of freedmen.

The news from the South had not, however, convinced Republicans that they should confiscate land and give it to the freedmen. A large majority of Republicans voted down an amendment to the Freedmen's Bureau bill proposed by Thaddeus Stevens that would have made "forfeited estates of the enemy" available to freedmen. Still, Republicans were now willing to go further in creating opportunities for land ownership. Thus the Freedmen's Bureau bill countermanded Johnson's order to Howard to evict the freedmen from the confiscated lands on the Sea Islands. Also, two days after the bill's passage, the House passed another bill, sponsored by George Julian, that became the Southern Homestead

Act of 1866. It designated about 45 million acres of public land in Alabama, Arkansas, Florida, Louisiana, and Mississippi for 80-acre grants to settlers who cultivated the land for five years. Congress prohibited anyone who had supported the Confederacy from filing a claim until 1867. Although Republicans were unwilling to violate planters' property rights, they offered freedmen the same chance to acquire land that northerners had enjoyed since the passage of the Homestead Act of 1862.

Republicans approved the Freedmen's Bureau bill almost unanimously, but in February 1866 Johnson vetoed it. The bill was unconstitutional, he argued, because the Constitution did not authorize a "system for the support of indigent persons" and because the states most directly affected by its provisions were not yet represented in Congress. His veto, implying that *any* Reconstruction legislation passed without southern representation was unconstitutional, enraged moderate Republicans. They tried to override the veto but failed, just barely, to hold the votes of enough conservative Republicans to collect the necessary two-thirds majority.

Democrats applauded Johnson's firmness. To celebrate the veto, and Washington's Birthday, a group of Democrats went to the White House to serenade him. The president emerged to deliver an impromptu, impassioned speech that suggested to many listeners that he was drunk. Accusing the radical Republicans of being traitors, he likened Stevens and Sumner to Confederate leaders because they all were "opposed to the fundamental principles of this Government." He mentioned himself two hundred times in the speech and suggested that the radicals were plotting to assassinate him.

The First Civil Rights Bill. Johnson's veto and his Washington's Birthday speech pushed the moderate Republicans close to a complete break with him. But they still expected his cooperation on their second major piece of legislation, a civil rights bill. Passed in March 1866, it defined the citizenship rights of the freedmen—for example, the rights to own and rent property, to make contracts, and to have access to the courts. And, it authorized federal authorities to bring suit against those who violated these rights and guaranteed that appeals in such cases could be heard in federal courts. The moderate Republicans were prepared to expand federal protection of civil rights, though they were still not ready to guarantee black suffrage.

Against the advice of his cabinet, Johnson vetoed the civil rights bill. He restated his constitutional point about absent southern representation and added a new objection, with the votes of Democratic wards in the large cities in mind. The bill, he argued, discriminated against whites by providing immediate citizenship for newly freed slaves. Under federal law, he pointed out, immigrants had to wait five years.

Johnson's veto was the last straw for almost all moderate Republicans. They now agreed with the radicals that Congress must take charge of Reconstruction. In April moderates engineered an override of Johnson's veto, and in July—after watering down the Freedmen's Bureau bill by requiring freedmen to buy the confiscated land on the Sea Islands—they won the votes of enough conservative Republicans to pass the Freedmen's Bureau bill over a second veto.

The Fourteenth Amendment. The central part of the independent plan that moderates and radicals now undertook was to provide freedmen with constitutional as well as legislative protection. In April the Joint Committee on Reconstruction drafted and submitted to Congress a proposal for a fourteenth amendment to the Constitution. It did not provide what the radicals wanted—a guarantee of black suffrage—but it went beyond the Civil Rights Act of 1866.

Section 1 declared that "all persons born or naturalized in the United States" were citizens. No state could abridge "the privileges or immunities of citizens of the United States" or deprive "any person of life, liberty, or property, without due process of law" or deny anyone "the equal protection of the laws." The drafters intended these phrases to be vague, but they hoped that their force would increase over time, especially since Section 5 gave Congress the power to enforce the amendment.

Section 2 penalized any state that denied suffrage to any adult male citizens. A state's representation in the House of Representatives would be reduced by the percentage of adult male citizens who were denied the vote.

Rising violence against African-Americans throughout the South clinched the support of moderates for the amendment. Most dramatic were three days of race rioting in Memphis in May. Forty-six blacks and two whites were left dead, and hundreds of black houses, churches, and schools were looted and burned. In June 1866, Congress forwarded the Fourteenth Amendment to the states for ratification.

President Johnson attacked the Fourteenth Amendment. Even its moderate provisions went too far in protecting African-Americans for his taste, and he wanted to create an issue for the 1866 elections. At his urging, ten ex-Confederate states, joined by Delaware and Kentucky, all turned it down, denying the amendment the necessary approval of three-fourths of the states. Among the former states of the Confederacy, only Tennessee approved the amendment, and it was formally readmitted to the Union in July 1866.

The Congressional Elections of 1866. Johnson planned to attack the Fourteenth Amendment and advance his National Union movement during the congressional elections of 1866. In July a National Union Convention

Resistance in the South

The engraving, subtitled "Verdict, 'Hang the D--- Yankee and Nigger,'" appeared in *Harper's Weekly* in March 1867. It may have led readers to recall the killing of the Republicans who attended the black suffrage convention in New Orleans the previous summer. We have no reliable estimates of the total number of Republicans, white and black, killed by ex-Confederates during Reconstruction.

met for the purpose of uniting his supporters from around the nation. But the Republican and Democratic politicians in attendance were unwilling to share power across party lines, and the convention did not attempt to create a new national party. Another problem for Johnson's movement was a major race riot in the South, just two weeks before the convention assembled. A white mob in New Orleans attacked the delegates to a black suffrage convention and, aided by the local police, killed forty people, including thirty-seven blacks. Popular support in the North for radical Reconstruction seemed to grow instantly.

In August and September, Johnson tried to win back support in a disastrous "swing around the circle"—a railroad tour from Washington to Chicago and St. Louis and back. It was unprecedented for a president to campaign personally, and Johnson made matters worse by engaging in shouting matches with hecklers and insulting members of the hostile crowds. His message was consistent: Congress had acted illegally by approving the Fourteenth Amendment without the participation all of the southern states, southerners were now loyal to the Union, and the real traitors were the radical Republicans who were delaying restoration of the Union.

Moderate and radical Republicans responded by escalating their attacks on Democrats. They charged that ex-Confederates wanted to resume the Civil War, and, in a practice that became known as "waving the bloody shirt," they charged that the Democratic party had caused the Civil War and then sided with the traitors. Indiana's Republican governor, Oliver Morton, described the Democratic party as "a common sewer and loathsome receptacle, into which is emptied every element of treason North and South, every element of inhumanity and barbarism which has dishonored the age."

The 1866 congressional elections brought a humiliating defeat for the president, who still had two years left to serve. The Republicans won a three-to-one majority in Congress (margins of 42 to 11 in the Senate, and 143 to 49 in the House) and gained control of the governorship and legislature in every northern state, as well as West Virginia, Missouri, and Tennessee. The moderate Republicans interpreted the election results as a clear call for radical Reconstruction, rather than mere restoration, of the South. The most important policy shift was the moderates' acceptance of the radicals' proposition that the federal government must guarantee the vote for black men.

Radical Reconstruction

In the months following the 1866 elections, moderates and radicals in Congress joined together to take control of Reconstruction. They agreed on a more radical program than even the one proposed in the Wade-Davis bill.

The Congressional Program

In March, Congress passed the Reconstruction Act of 1867, which was designed to implement the radical plan. It organized the South as a conquered land, dividing it (with the exception of Tennessee) into five military districts, each under the command of a Union general. Each commander was ordered to register all adult black men in his district but was given considerable discretion in registering former Confederates. After the registration, the commander was to supervise the election of a convention to write a state constitution and to make certain that the constitution include guar-

antees for black suffrage. Congress would readmit the state to the Union if its voters ratified the new constitution, if that document proved acceptable to Congress, if the new state legislature approved the Fourteenth Amendment, and if enough states had already ratified the Fourteenth Amendment to make it part of the Constitution. Johnson vetoed the act, but Congress overrode the veto. During 1868, six states—North Carolina, South Carolina, Florida, Alabama, Louisiana, and Arkansas—met the requirements and were readmitted to the Union.

These measures were radical, but a few radical Republicans argued that even more dramatic measures were needed to guarantee racial equality. They pressed for the distribution of land to former slaves, federal support for black schools, and disfranchisement of ex-Confederates. Congressman George Julian warned that "the power of the great landed aristocracy in these regions, if unrestrained by power from without, would inevitably assert itself." But even the most extreme of the radicals accepted the new Reconstruction policies as all they could get in 1867.

The Tenure of Office Act. Republicans also acted to check the power of President Johnson to undermine their Reconstruction plan. At the same time the Reconstruction Act of 1867 became law, Congress passed the Tenure of Office Act, which required congressional consent for the removal of any official whose appointment had required Senate confirmation. Congress chiefly wanted to protect Secretary of War Edwin M. Stanton, a Lincoln appointee and the only member of Johnson's cabinet who favored radical Reconstruction. In his position Stanton could do much to prevent Johnson from frustrating the goals of Reconstruction. Congress also required the president to issue all orders to the army through its commanding general, Ulysses S. Grant, also a supporter of radical Reconstruction. In effect, Congress was attempting to reconstruct the presidency as well as the South.

Johnson appeared to cooperate with Congress at first, appointing generals recommended by Stanton and Grant to command the five military districts in the South. But he was just biding his time. In August 1867, after Congress had adjourned, he "suspended" Stanton until Congress reconvened and replaced him with Grant on a temporary basis, believing that Grant would act like a good soldier and follow orders. Next Johnson replaced four Republican generals who commanded southern districts, including Philip H. Sheridan, Grant's favorite cavalry general.

Johnson, however, had misjudged Grant, who wrote a letter protesting the president's thwarting of Congress and then deliberately leaked it to the press. When the Senate reconvened in the fall, it intensified the political drama by overruling Stanton's suspension. Grant increased the pressure on Johnson by resigning so

Stanton could resume his office. Johnson overreacted, publicly protesting Grant's resignation. Grant responded by becoming an open enemy of the president.

The Impeachment of Johnson. Johnson decided to challenge the constitutionality of the Tenure of Office Act. In February 1868 he formally dismissed Stanton. This time Stanton barricaded the door of his office, refusing to admit the replacement Johnson had appointed. Three days later, on February 24, the House of Representatives struck out against Johnson using the power granted by the Constitution to impeach—to charge federal officials with "Treason, Bribery, or other high Crimes and Misdemeanors." The House overwhelmingly (128–47) brought eleven counts of criminal misconduct, nine of which dealt with violations of the Tenure of Office Act, against the president.

The trial in the Senate, which the Constitution empowers to act as a court in impeachment cases, lasted eleven weeks and was presided over by Chief Justice Salmon P. Chase. On May 16 thirty-five senators voted for conviction—one vote short of the two-thirds majority required. Seven moderate Republicans had broken ranks, voting for acquittal along with twelve Democrats. The reluctant moderates were overwhelmed by the drastic nature of impeachment and conviction; Congress had removed federal judges from office, but never before had it seriously considered removing a president. While these moderates agreed that Johnson had broken the law, they felt the real issue was a disagreement between Congress and the president over a matter of policy. They feared that a conviction based on a policy dispute would establish a dangerous precedent and undermine the presidency. The Civil War had demonstrated to them the need for a strong federal government administered by a powerful executive. These moderates doubted that the nation could preserve internal unity, advance the Republican economic program, and defend itself against foreign enemies without a strong presidency.

The radical Republicans had failed to convict Johnson, but they had defeated him politically. For the remaining ten months of his term, Johnson was forced to allow Reconstruction to proceed under congressional direction.

The Elections of 1868. The impeachment controversy made Grant, already the North's most popular war hero, a hero of Reconstruction as well. He easily won the Republican presidential nomination. In the fall campaign he supported radical Reconstruction and "waved the bloody shirt," but he also urged reconciliation between the sections. His Democratic opponent was Horatio Seymour, a former governor of New York and Peace Democrat who almost declined the nomination, certain that Grant would win. In the face of rising violence in the South, Seymour and the Democrats received little support for their claim that the government should let southern state governments reorganize on their own. Grant won about the same share of the northern vote (55 percent) that Lincoln had in 1864, collected a majority of the national popular vote, and received 214 out of 294 electoral votes, including those of six of the eight reconstructed states. The Republicans also retained two-thirds majorities in both houses of Congress. The Republicans were convinced they had a strong popular mandate for their program of radical Reconstruction.

The Fifteenth Amendment. The Republicans quickly produced the last major piece of Reconstruction legislation—the Fifteenth Amendment. Intended to guarantee black manhood suffrage, the amendment forbade states to deny their citizens the right to vote on the grounds of race, color, or "previous condition of servitude."

Some radical Republicans would have preferred more aggressive protections of black citizenship, such as prohibiting state governments from using property ownership or literacy tests to disqualify blacks as voters. But Republican moderates did not want to ban tactics that northern and western states might want to employ to deny immigrants the vote. Massachusetts and Connecticut used literacy as a requirement for voting, as did California, which sought to deny the vote to Chinese immigrants. Even though it failed to prohibit such tactics, the Fifteenth Amendment was much more effective than the Fourteenth in promoting African-American suffrage. The amendment was passed in February 1869, and Congress required the unreconstructed states of Virginia, Mississippi, Texas, and Georgia to ratify it before they were readmitted to the Union.

The Issue of Suffrage for Women

Radical Reconstruction could have changed the legal status of women. Instead, by referring to adult "male citizens," the Fourteenth Amendment wrote the term "male" into the Constitution for the first time and, in effect, sanctioned the denial of the suffrage for women. Under the Fourteenth Amendment, suffrage limitations based on gender—alone among all the possible restrictions on suffrage—would not reduce a state's representation in Congress.

Former abolitionists such as Elizabeth Cady Stanton and Susan B. Anthony were deeply disappointed. They had organized a massive petition drive that collected almost 400,000 signatures in support for the Thirteenth Amendment; they believed that their male collaborators would reciprocate by supporting universal suffrage. In fact, many did, but most assumed that the public was not ready for the idea. As Wendell Phillips told women leaders, "One question at a time. This hour belongs to the Negro."

The leaders of the women's movement did not oppose ratification of the Fourteenth Amendment. They accepted defeat at the federal level and focused on the reform of state constitutions. Through a new organization, the American Equal Rights Association—which they formed in 1866, at their first women's rights convention since the Civil War—they launched a campaign to win *universal* suffrage at the state level.

The Fifteenth Amendment wounded those who sought the vote for women even more deeply; it made no reference to gender and thus permitted states to deny suffrage to women. In response, Stanton and Anthony concluded that feminists should develop a program independent of any political party. They broke with Republican abolitionists and refused to support the Fifteenth Amendment unless it was accompanied by a new amendment enfranchising women. Stanton argued that ratification of the Fifteenth Amendment alone would create an "aristocracy of sex." She declared, "All manhood will vote not because of intelligence, patriotism, property or white skin, but because it is male, not female." In promoting a new amendment, she made a special appeal to women of the business class:

> American women of wealth, education, virtue and refinement, if you do not wish the lower orders of Chinese, Africans, Germans and Irish, with the low ideas of womanhood to make laws for you and your daughters . . . to dictate not only the civil, but moral codes by which you shall be governed, awake to the danger of your present position and demand that woman, too, shall be represented in the government!

Other advocates of woman suffrage—including

Lucy Stone and Frederick Douglass—saw the politics of suffrage differently. The Fifteenth Amendment had opened up a schism in the ranks of the women's movement. In 1868, Stone and Douglass broke with the American Equal Rights Association of Stanton and Anthony and formed a new group, the New England Woman Suffrage Association. Their goal was to maintain an alliance with Republicans and to support the Fifteenth Amendment. They believed that this was the best way to enlist Republican support for women's suffrage after Reconstruction issues had been settled.

The differences between the two groups increased in the postwar years. In 1869 the American Equal Rights Association renamed itself the National Woman Suffrage Association and elected Stanton as its first president. It concentrated on mobilizing local suffrage societies in communities around the country. Meanwhile, the New England Woman Suffrage Association reorganized itself as the American Woman Suffrage Association. Its members elected Henry Ward Beecher, a prominent Brooklyn minister, as president and cultivated strong ties with Republicans and men who had been abolitionists.

For twenty-one years, the two national organizations competed for the leadership of the women's movement. The "American" association tended to focus on suffrage, while the "National" association developed a more comprehensive reform posture. While the split weakened the movement in the short run, the formation of the "National" association meant that a major part of the women's movement had broken away from abolitionism and Republicanism and was free to develop independent political strategies.

A Woman Suffrage Quilt, Made Around 1875
Home-made quilts provided funds and a means of persuasion for the temperance and antislavery movements. But woman suffrage quilts, such as this detail from "The Suffragette Quilt" (c. 1860–1880), picturing a women's rights lecturer, were rare. The leaders of the woman suffrage movement usually regarded quilts and needlework as representing the domestic subjugation of women.

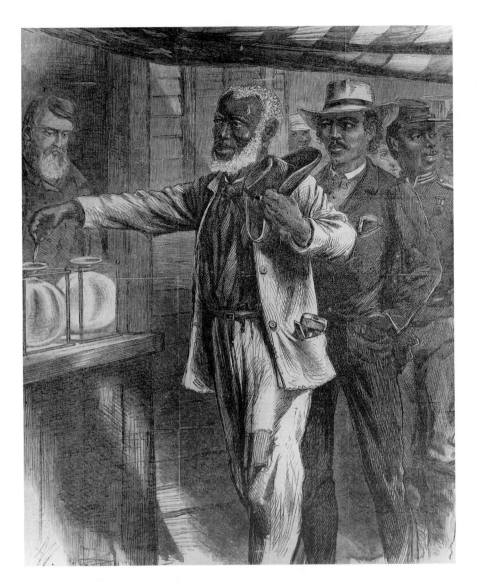

The South During Radical Reconstruction

Between 1868 and 1871 all the southern states met the stipulations of Congress and rejoined the Union. The Reconstruction governments under Republican control remained in power for periods ranging from a few months for Virginia to nine years for South Carolina, Louisiana, and Florida. African-Americans were at the center of forming and maintaining these Republican governments. In Alabama, Florida, South Carolina, Mississippi, and Louisiana, they constituted an outright majority of all the registered voters. They provided the votes for Republican victories there and in Georgia, Virginia, and North Carolina as well where they accounted for nearly half the registered voters. But the Republican governments were more than African-American regimes; they also drew support from whites who had not owned slaves and from white northerners who moved south after the war.

Democratic ex-Confederates satirized and stereotyped the Republicans who dominated the reconstructed state governments. They mocked and scorned black Republicans as ignorant field hands who could only play at politics, and they ridiculed whites who became Republicans as *scalawags*—an ancient Scots-Irish term for underfed, runty, worthless animals. White settlers who had come from the North they denounced as *carpetbaggers*—transient exploiters who carried all their property in cheap suitcases called carpetbags. Carpetbaggers held more than half the Republican governorships in the South and almost half of its seats in Congress.

Actually, few southern Republicans conformed to these stereotypes. Some of the carpetbaggers did come south to seek personal profit, but they also brought capital and skills to invest in the region's future. Most were former officers of the Union army who had fallen in love with the South—its climate, people, and economic

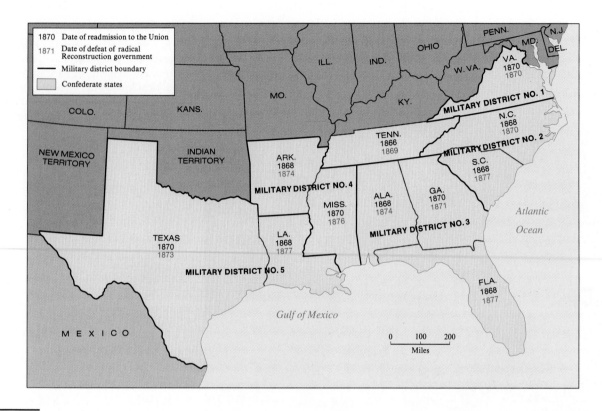

MAP 16.1

Reconstruction

The federal government organized the Confederate states into five military districts during radical Reconstruction. For each state the first date indicates when the state was readmitted to the Union; the second date is when radical Republicans lost control of the state government. All the ex-Confederate states rejoined the Union from 1868 to 1870, but the periods of radical rule varied widely. Radicals lasted only a few months in Virginia; they held on until the end of Reconstruction in Louisiana, Florida, and South Carolina.

opportunities. Many carpetbaggers were professionals and college graduates. The scalawags were even more diverse. Some were wealthy ex-Whigs and even former slaveowners. Some of these groups saw Republicanism as the best way to attract northern capital to southern railroads, mines, and factories. Immigrant workingmen and farmers were often found among the Republicans. The largest such group were the Germans in southwest Texas. They sent to Congress Edward Degener, an immigrant and San Antonio grocer, whom Confederate authorities had imprisoned and whose sons had been executed for treason. But most numerous among the scalawags were yeoman farmers from the backcountry districts. They wanted to rid the South of its slaveowning aristocracy, and scalawags had generally fought against, or at least refused to support, the Confederacy. They believed that slavery had victimized whites as well as blacks. "Now is the time," a Georgia scalawag wrote, "for every man to come out and speak his principles publickly and vote for liberty as we have been in bondage long enough."

African-American Political Leadership. The Democrats' stereotypes of black political leaders were just as false. Until 1867 most African-American leaders in the South, attracted to the movement for black suffrage, came from the elite that had been free before the Civil War. When Congress began to organize Republican governments in 1867, this diverse group of ministers, artisans, shopkeepers, and former soldiers reached out to the freedmen. African-American speakers, some financed by the Republican Congressional Committee, fanned out into the old plantation districts and drew ex-slaves into political leadership. Still, few of the new leaders were field hands; most had been preachers or artisans. The literacy of one ex-slave, Thomas Allen, who was a Baptist minister and shoemaker, helped him win election to the Georgia legislature. "In my county," he recalled, "the colored people came to me for instructions, and I gave them the best instructions I could. I took the *New York Tribune* and other papers, and in that way I found out a great deal, and I told them whatever I thought was right."

Many of the African-American leaders who emerged in 1867 had been born in the North or spent many years there. They moved south when congressional Reconstruction began to offer the prospect of meaningful freedom. Like white migrants, many were veterans of the Union army; some had fought in the antislavery crusade; some were employed by the Freedmen's Bureau or northern missionary societies; a few were from free families and had gone north for an education. Others had escaped from slavery and were now returning home, such as Blanche K. Bruce, who became one of two black U.S. senators from Mississippi. He had received tutoring on the Virginia plantation of his white father. During the war Bruce escaped to Kansas from Missouri, where his father had moved, and then returned to Missouri, establishing a school for African-Americans in Hannibal. He arrived in Mississippi in 1869 and entered politics; in 1874 he became the second African-American elected to the Senate and the first elected to a full term until 1966.

Although the number of African-Americans who held office during Reconstruction never reflected their share of the electorate, they held positions of importance throughout the South, and their significance increased in every state under Republican rule. Sixteen African-Americans served in the U.S. House of Representatives in the Reconstruction Era. In 1870, Mississippi sent Hiram Revels, a minister born in North Carolina, to the Senate as its first African-American member. In 1868, African-Americans won a majority in one house of the South Carolina legislature; subsequently they won half of the state's eight executive offices, elected three members of Congress, and won a seat on the state supreme court. Over the entire course of Reconstruction, twenty African-Americans served as governor, lieutenant governor, secretary of state, treasurer, or superintendent of education, and more than six hundred served as state legislators. Almost all the African-Americans who became state executives had been freemen before the Civil War, while most of the legislators had been slaves. Because these African-Americans represented the districts that large planters had dominated before the Civil War, they embodied the potential of Reconstruction for revolutionizing class relationships in the South.

The Radical Program. Southern Republicans believed that the South needed to be fundamentally reconstructed. They wanted to end the South's dependence on cotton agriculture and unskilled labor and create an economy based on manufacturing, capital investment, and skilled labor. Southern Republicans fell far short of making this vision a reality. But they accomplished much more of it than their critics gave them credit for.

Southern Republicans made their societies more democratic. They repealed Black Codes and rejected new

Hiram R. Revels

In 1870 Hiram R. Revels (1822–1901) was elected to the U.S. Senate from Mississippi to fill Jefferson Davis's former seat. Revels was a free black from North Carolina who had migrated North and attended Knox College in Illinois. He recruited blacks for the Union army and, as an ordained Methodist minister, served as chaplain of a black regiment in Mississippi, where he settled after the war.

proposals for enforcing labor discipline. They modernized state constitutions, extended the right to vote, and made more offices elective. They established hospitals, penitentiaries, and asylums for orphans and the insane. South Carolina purchased medical care for the poor, while Alabama provided them with free legal counsel. Republican governments built roads in areas where roads had never existed. They supervised the rebuilding of the region's railroad network and subsidized investment in manufacturing and transportation. They undertook major public works programs. And they did all this without federal financing. To pay for their ambitious programs they introduced the taxes that northern states had relied on since the Jacksonian era. These were general property taxes that taxed not only real estate but the trappings of wealth—personal property such as furnishings, machinery, tools, and even cash. The goal was to force planters to pay their fair share of taxes and to force uncultivated land onto the market. In many plantation counties, especially in South Carolina, Louisiana, and Mississippi, former slaves served as tax assessors and collectors, administering the taxation of their onetime owners.

A Freedmen's School
An 1866 sketch from *Harper's Weekly* of a Vicksburg, Mississippi, school run by the Freedmen's Bureau illustrates the desire for education by ex-slaves of all ages. Because most southern blacks were farmers, schools commonly offered night classes that left students free for field work during the day.

The most important accomplishments of the southern Republicans came in education. The Republican state governments viewed schooling as the foundation for a democratic order in the South. Led by both black and white superintendents of education, many of whom had served in the Freedmen's Bureau, the Reconstruction governments built public schools that served more people, black and white, than had ever been reached by free education in the South. African-Americans of all ages rushed to attend the newly established schools, even when they had to pay tuition. One elderly man in Mississippi explained his desire to go to school: "Ole missus used to read the good book [the Bible] to us . . . on Sunday evenin's, but she mostly read dem places where it says, 'Servants obey your masters.' . . . Now we is free, there's heaps of tings in that old book we is just suffering to learn." By 1875 about half of all the children in Florida, Mississippi, and South Carolina were enrolled in school.

Virtually all the new schools were segregated by race; only Louisiana attempted to establish an integrated system. But most African-Americans seemed to agree that segregation was an issue for a later day; most shared Frederick Douglass's judgment that what was most important was the fact that separate schools were "infinitely superior" to no schools at all.

Social Institutions in Freedom. The building of schools was part of a larger effort by African-Americans to fortify the institutions that had sustained their spirit during the days of slavery. Most important, they strengthened their family life as the cornerstone of new communities. Families moved away from the slave quarters, usually building homes scattered around or near their old plantations and farms. Sometimes they established entirely new all-black villages. Husbands, wives, and children who had been separated by the slave trade often reunited, sometimes after journeys of hundreds of miles. Couples stepped forward to record marriages that had been unrecognized under slavery. As slavery crumbled, mothers rescued their children from the control of planters and overseers. Many women refused to work in the fields. Instead, they insisted on tending gardens, managing households, and bringing education and religion to their children. Many wives asserted their independence, opening individual bank accounts, refusing responsibility for their husbands' debts at country stores, and bringing complaints of abuse and lack of child support to the Freedmen's Bureau.

Christianity had played a central role in nineteenth-century slave society, and freed slaves buttressed their new communities by founding their own churches. Rather than participate in biracial congregations in which they had only second-class status, requiring them to worship in segregated balcony pews and denying them rights in church ownership or governance, they purchased land and built their own churches. These churches joined together to form African-American versions of the Southern Methodist and Southern Baptist denominations. The largest new denominations were the National Baptist Convention and the Colored Methodist Episcopal Church. The vigorous new churches served not only as places of worship but as schools, social centers, and political meeting halls. The ministers were community leaders and often held political offices during Reconstruction. Charles H. Pearce, a

Methodist minister in Florida, declared that "A man in this State cannot do his whole duty as a minister except he looks out for the political interests of his people." The religious message of black ministers, who called for a recognition of the brotherhood of man and a special destiny like that of the "Children of Israel," provided a powerful religious bulwark for the Republican politics of their congregations.

The Counterrevolution of the Planters

Even if radical Reconstruction had been adopted right at the end of the Civil War, it would have sparked southern resistance to federal power. But coming after Johnson's lenient policy of restoration, which had enabled ex-Confederates to resume control of the South, their reaction was especially intense. Former slaveowners were the most bitter opponents of the Republican program, especially the effort to expand political and economic opportunities for African-Americans, because it threatened their vested interest in traditional agriculture and their power and status in southern society. Led by former slaveowners, the ex-Confederates staged a massive counterrevolution—one designed to "redeem" the South by regaining control of southern state governments.

The former slaveowners united under the Democratic banner to oppose the Republicans. In the eight southern states where whites formed a majority of the population—all except Louisiana, Mississippi, and South Carolina—planters sought to return ex-Confederates to the rolls of registered voters. They appealed to racial solidarity and southern patriotism; they attacked black suffrage as a threat to the social status of whites. Relying primarily on conventional, albeit unsavory, means of political competition, Democrats recovered power in Tennessee in 1869 and Virginia in 1870.

But the Democrats were prepared to go far beyond conventional techniques. Throughout the deep South, and almost everywhere that Republicans and Democrats were nearly equal in number, planters and their supporters engaged in terrorism against people and property. They organized secret societies to frighten blacks and Republican whites from voting or taking other political action.

The Ku Klux Klan. The most widespread of these groups, the Ku Klux Klan, was organized in Tennessee in 1865 and quickly spread throughout the South. The Klan's first leader was Nathan Bedford Forrest, a former Confederate general. A skilled and ferocious leader, Forrest was notorious in the North for an incident at Fort Pillow, Tennessee, in 1864, when his troops killed

Klan Portrait, 1868
Two armed Klansmen from Alabama posed proudly in their disguises. Northern audiences saw a lithograph based on this photograph in *Harper's Weekly* in December 1868.

African-American soldiers holding the fort after they had surrendered. Forrest based the initial organization of the Klan on Confederate army units and openly threatened to kill Republicans if they tried to suppress the Klan.

By 1870 the Klan was operating almost everywhere in the South as a military force serving the Democratic party. The Klan murdered and whipped Republican politicians, burned black schools and churches, and attacked party gatherings. In October 1870, a group of Klansmen assaulted a Republican rally in Eutaw, Alabama, killing four African-Americans and wounding fifty-four. For three weeks in 1873, Klansmen laid siege to the small town of Colfax, Louisiana, defended by black veterans of the Union army who were holding the county seat after a contested election. On Easter Sunday, armed with a small cannon, the whites overpowered the defenders and slaughtered fifty blacks and two whites after they had surrendered under a white flag. Such terrorist tactics enabled the Democrats to seize power in Georgia and North Carolina in 1870 and make substantial gains elsewhere. An African-American politician in North Carolina wrote that "Our former masters are fast taking the reins of government."

AMERICAN VOICES

The Intimidation of Black Voters *Harriet Hernandes*

The following testimony was given in 1871 by Harriet Hernandes, a black resident of Spartanburg, South Carolina, to the Joint Congressional Select Committee investigating conditions in the South. The terrorizing of black women through rape and other forms of physical violence were among the means of oppression used by the Ku Klux Klan.

Question: How old are you?

Answer: Going on thirty-four years. . . .

Q: Are you married or single?

A: Married.

Q: Did the Ku-Klux come to your house at any time?

A: Yes, sir; twice. . . .

Q: Go on to the second time. . . .

A: They came in; I was lying in bed. Says he, "Come out here, sir; come out here, sir!" They took me out of bed; they would not let me get out, but they took me up in their arms and toted me out—me and my daughter Lucy. He struck me on the forehead with a pistol, and here is the scar above my eye now. Says he, "Damn you, fall." I fell. Says he, "Damn you, get up." I got up. Says he," Damn you, get over this

fence!" and he kicked me over when I went to get over; and then he went on to a brush pile, and they laid us right down there, both together. They laid us down twenty yards apart, I reckon. They had dragged and beat us along. They struck me right on top of my head, and I though they had killed me; and I said, "Lord o' mercy, don't, don't kill my child!" He gave me a lick on the head, and it liked to have killed me; I saw stars. He threw my arm over my head so I could not do anything with it for three weeks, and there are great knots on my wrist now.

Q: What did they say this was for?

A: They said, "You can tell your husband that when we see him we are going to kill him. . . ."

Q: Did they say why they wanted to kill him?

A: They said, "He voted the radical ticket [slate of candidates], didn't he?" I said, "Yes," that very way. . . .

Q: When did [your husband] get back home after this whipping? He was not at home, was he?

A: He was lying out; he couldn't stay at home, bless your soul!. . .

Q: Has he been afraid for any length of time?

A: He has been afraid ever since last October. He has been lying out. He has not laid in the house ten nights since October.

Q: Is that the situation of the colored people down there to any extent?

A: That is the way they all have to do—men and women both.

Q: What are they afraid of?

A: Of being killed or whipped to death.

Q: What has made them afraid?

A: Because men that voted radical tickets they took the spite out on the women when they could get at them.

Q: How many colored people have been whipped in that neighborhood?

A: It is all of them, mighty near.

Source: Report of the Joint Select Committee to Inquire into the Condition of Affairs in the Late Insurrectionary States, House Reports, 42d Cong., 2d sess. (Washington, D.C.: Government Printing Office, 1972), Vol. 5, South Carolina, December 19, 1871.

Congress responded to the Klan-led counterrevolution by passing the Force Acts in 1870 and 1871, which included the Ku Klux Klan Act (1871). The acts authorized the president to use federal prosecutions, military force, and martial law to suppress conspiracies to deprive citizens of the right to vote, hold office, serve on juries, and enjoy the equal protection of the laws. For the first time, the government had made private criminal acts violations of federal law.

Federal agents penetrated the Klan and gathered evidence that provided the basis for thousands of arrests. Federal grand juries indicted more than three thousand Klansmen. In South Carolina, where the Klan was most deeply entrenched, federal troops occupied nine counties, made hundreds of arrests, and drove as many as

two thousand Klansmen from the state. The U.S. attorney general brought several dozen notorious Klansmen to trial and sent most to jail. Elsewhere, victories were only temporary. Justice Department attorneys usually faced all-white juries, and the department lacked the resources to prosecute effectively. Only about six hundred Klansmen were convicted under the Force Acts, and only a small fraction of them served significant prison terms.

The Grant administration's war against the Klan raised the spirits of southern Republicans, but if they were going to prevail, they required what one carpetbagger described as *"steady, unswerving power from without."* In particular, to defeat the well-armed paramilitary forces of the ex-Confederates, they needed sustained federal military aid. However, after seeming to defeat the Klan, northern Republicans increasingly lost enthusiasm for fighting—let alone enlarging—what amounted to a guerrilla war. Republican leaders continued to "wave the bloody shirt," but with each election it had less appeal for voters. Northerners grew weary of the financial costs of Reconstruction and the continuing bloodshed it seemed to produce. Moreover, they became preoccupied with the severe depression that began in 1873. Racism played a role as well; many moderate Republicans in the North began to conclude that Republican defeats in the South reflected the incompetence of black politicians. Because of the diminishing federal help, Republican governments in the South eventually found themselves overwhelmed by ex-Confederate politicians during the day and by terrorists at night. Democrats overthrew Republicans in Texas in 1873, in Alabama and Arkansas in 1874, and in Mississippi in 1875.

The defeat in Mississippi demonstrated the crucial role of federal aid. As elections neared in 1875, paramilitary groups such as the Rifle Clubs and Red Shirts operated openly. Often local Democratic clubs paraded armed, as if they were militia companies. They identified African-American leaders in assassination lists called "dead-books"; broke up Republican meetings; provoked rioting that left hundreds of African-Americans dead; and threatened voters, who still lacked the protection of the secret ballot. Mississippi's Republican governor, Adelbert Ames, a Congressional Medal of Honor winner from Maine, appealed to President Grant for federal troops, but he refused, fearing damage to Republicans in northern elections and lacking the heart for more bloodshed. Ames then contemplated organizing a state militia but decided against it, believing that only African-Americans would join. Rather than escalate the fighting and turn it into a racial war, he conceded victory to the terrorists.

By 1877, Republican governments, along with token U.S. military units, remained in only three states—Louisiana, South Carolina, and Florida. Southern Republicans had done their best to reconstruct southern society, but the ex-Confederates had exhausted the northern Republicans, who finally abandoned the southern members of their party.

The Economic Fate of the Former Slaves

The greatest failure of radical Reconstruction was in not redistributing land, along with the resources required to cultivate it, from the planters to the former slaves. The only major federal program enabling freedmen to obtain land, the Southern Homestead Act, turned out to provide little assistance. Although the land was free, very few freedmen had the capital to move their families and buy the necessary seed, tools, and draft animals to get in their first crop. Fewer than seven thousand ex-slaves claimed land, and only about a thousand eventually qualified for ownership, most of them in sparsely populated areas of Florida. Compounding the problem, state governments rarely had the resources to help freedmen buy and settle land. Alone among all the Republican state governments, South Carolina purchased land from planters and resold it to former slaves on long-term credit. Between 1872 and 1876, the South Carolina land commission enabled more than 14,000 African-American families (accounting for about one-seventh of the state's black population) to purchase homesteads.

Sharecropping

This sharecropping family seems proud of their new cabin and their crop of cotton, which they planted in every available bit of ground. But the presence of their white landlord in the background suggests the forces that led families like this one into debt peonage.

Nathan Bedford Forrest

Nathan Bedford Forrest (1821–1877) became a hero by defending the honor of his family at the age of twenty-four. Armed with only a pistol and a bowie knife, he fought off four men who had a grudge against his uncle, a merchant in the hamlet of Hernando, Mississippi. The uncle died from a bullet meant for his nephew, but young Forrest had shown that he could meet violence with violence. He soon used his pistol again, facing down a well-armed planter who had just killed a friend of Forrest's. The local citizens rewarded Forrest's courage by making him town constable and county coroner, and a respectable young woman from Hernando agreed to marry him.

Forrest's father had been a yeoman farmer and blacksmith who followed the frontier from North Carolina to Tennessee, where Bedford, the eldest child of eleven, was born. His family moved to northern Mississippi in 1834, but three years later, when he was only sixteen, his father died, leaving Bedford the primary breadwinner. He had no more than six months of schooling in his life, but he supported the family, working on their small farm and then joining an uncle's horse-trading business. At the age of twenty-one, when his mother remarried, he left home for Hernando.

Recognized and respected in Hernando, the hard-driving young Forrest was able to scratch his way up the social ladder in the booming cotton economy. He took over his uncle's store, ran a stagecoach service between Hernando and Memphis, opened a brickyard, again traded horses and cattle, and then turned to buying and selling slaves. By 1850 he owned three of his own. In 1851, Forrest's ambition took him and his family to nearby Memphis, Tennessee. In this Mississippi river town he became one of the largest interstate slave traders and entered the ranks of the planter class. He purchased large land holdings, including a Mississippi plantation of more than 3,000 acres worked by dozens of slaves. He even entered politics, winning election to the Memphis Board of Aldermen in 1857.

The Civil War created new opportunities for Forrest. His reputation for boldness and shrewdness, as well as his riding and shooting skills, won him an appointment from the governor of Tennessee as a lieu-

Nathan Bedford Forrest

In his often violent career Forrest was a farmer, slave trader, planter, politician, cavalry general, Grand Wizard of the Ku Klux Klan, and railroad entrepreneur. This portrait was done by Nicola Marshall c. 1866. (Collection Tennessee State Museum)

tenant colonel. He organized a cavalry regiment and, after distinguishing himself at Shiloh, was promoted to brigadier general in July 1862. In the course of the war he became the premier cavalry officer of the Confederacy—perhaps the best on either side. The Confederate government failed to make the best use of Forrest and his troops, but he almost always carried out his missions with dramatic success, protecting Confederate armies in retreat, raiding Union lines of communications, and attacking Union posts, often deep within enemy lines.

Forrest's intimate knowledge of the countryside and the people of the Mississippi, Tennessee, and Cumberland river valleys, his superb organizational skills, his powerful tactical sense of when to use bluff and deception, his sobriety, and his ability to inspire his troops served him well. He had a ferocious temper, and he used it to good advantage in combat—turning a zest for fighting into enraged fury whenever his honor, or the honor of his troops, seemed at stake. He counted thirty Union soldiers that he had killed personally—one more than the number of horses shot out from under him. And he was wounded by saber cut or gunfire several times, including once by a junior Confederate officer whom Forrest quickly stabbed to death.

Forrest's code of honor, his readiness for violence, his racism, and his commitment to slavery, all honed and hardened by war, have suggested to many that Forrest played a role in the slaughter of black troops at Fort Pillow, Tennessee, on April 12, 1864. Forrest approached the assault on Fort Pillow with a combination of anger and contempt for the garrison there—largely white pro-Union Tennesseans and former slaves. The war in western Tennessee had taken a bitter turn in 1864, involving civilians more directly in combat, and Forrest was outraged at rumors that the garrison had been harassing local whites loyal to the Confederacy. Although Forrest's direct role in the slaughter remains uncertain, it is clear that his troops believed they were acting as he wished, that they experienced the same fury he usually displayed in battle, and that he accepted the outcome with equanimity.

The war left Forrest exhausted but determined to recreate as much of his old life as possible. This meant adapting to the new economic system and, when necessary, to the reality of Union victory. In 1866, to restore his plantation labor force, he rented his Mississippi land to seven former Union officers and worked closely with the Freedmen's Bureau, writing some of the highest-wage contracts. He drew on some of his old slave-trading skills to bring in workers from as far away as Georgia. At the same time he moved into new enterprises—provisioning the reorganized plantations, selling fire and life insurance, and contracting for paving the streets of Memphis and for laying railroad track. In building the Memphis and Little Rock Railroad, Forrest used labor supplied by the Freedmen's Bureau. Meanwhile, he sought a pardon from President Johnson, which was granted in 1868.

But Forrest was unprepared to accept a radical Reconstruction. As conflicts between ex-Confederates and coalitions of former Unionists and freedmen intensified, Forrest's ambition and loyalty to his comrades—a sense of honor defined by shared wartime experiences—led him to support the effort to restore the social world of 1860. In 1867 he joined secret organizations in Memphis and Nashville that became chapters of the Ku Klux Klan. He soon became the Klan's Grand Wizard and turned the organization into a major force throughout most of the South. Under cover of his insurance business, Forrest corresponded with perhaps thousands of Confederate veterans and traveled to neighboring states to confer with other ex-generals.

In 1868 the Republican governor of Tennessee, "Parson" William G. Brownlow, threatened to organize a militia of eastern Tennessee Unionists to root out the Klan. Forrest told his former troops to prepare for civil war, warning a reporter from the Cincinnati *Commercial* that he could "raise 40,000 men in five days, ready for the field." Forrest's intimidation worked, as it had so often in the past. Brownlow resigned in early 1869 to take up a seat in the U.S. Senate, and his replacement sought to appease the Democrats and the Klan. Victorious in Tennessee and hoping to reduce pressure from Washington on the Klan, Forrest ordered its members to destroy their regalia and moderate their excesses, such as whippings and jail breaks. Forrest knew full well that he had no power to implement such an order.

Forrest may have continued a secret life within the Klan, but after his political victory he appeared to devote his full attention to his businesses. He tried to combine northern capital with new sources of cheap labor. Marketing bonds in New York, he established the Selma, Marion, and Memphis Railroad. He promoted Chinese immigration to the South and made extensive use of convict labor on his railroad and plantation crews. But he achieved only modest success in the depression of the 1870s. In 1877 he died of a debilitating intestinal illness, perhaps related to his wartime wounds. Shortly before, he ended his litigation, which had grown massive in the years since the Civil War. He told his lawyer: "My life has been a battle from the start. . . . I have seen too much of violence, and I want to close my days at peace with all the world. . . ."

Without guaranteed economic independence, the content of freedom depended largely on thousands of conflicts between freedmen, acting individually and collectively, and the planter class. Here too the federal government failed to assist the freedmen in a significant way. The vast majority of army officers and federal marshals held the racist assumption that had been behind the Black Codes—that former slaves were suited only for agricultural labor. If these agents of the federal government had different ideas at first, they usually came to support the economic interests of the planters. One Louisiana freedman described the process as follows: "Whenever a new Provost Marshall comes he gives us justice for a fortnight or so; then he becomes acquainted with planters, takes dinners with them, receives presents; and then we no longer have any rights, or very little." In disputes between employers and laborers, federal marshals generally sided with the planters and sustained their authority. Army commanders complied with the requests of planters for help in forcing African-Americans to work. They expelled former plantation workers from towns and cities and punished them for disobedience, theft, vagrancy, and erratic labor.

Even agents of the Freedmen's Bureau often supported the planters. Many Bureau officials interpreted their mandate to promote a transition to free labor as meaning that they should teach former slaves to be industrious, reliable agricultural workers. They preached the gospel of work to African-Americans. To discourage labor violence, they warned that it was better "to suffer wrong than to do wrong." They urged former slaves to vindicate the cause of abolition by staying at home and working even harder than they had under slavery. One Bureau official told some freedmen that their former master "is not able to do without you, and you will . . . find him as kind, honest, and liberal as other men" and that "you can be as free and as happy in your old home, for the present, as anywhere else in the world." The agents of the Freedmen's Bureau who did side with African-Americans were stymied by northern racism, lack of funds, understaffing, poor coordination within the Bureau, and uncooperative military authorities.

Sharecropping. The Freedmen's Bureau helped change, however, the way planters controlled the labor of their former slaves. It encouraged, even compelled, planters and freedmen to agree on written contracts through a formal bargaining process. The labor contract system was a poor substitute for land ownership, but it assisted the freedmen in attaining something else they greatly desired: the elimination of gang labor.

As early as 1865, written contracts between freedmen and planters provided that the former slaves would

MAP 16.2

The Barrow Plantation

Comparing the map of this central Georgia plantation with the 1881 map reveals the changing patterns of black residence and farming. In 1860 the slave quarters clustered near the planter's house, which sat above them on a small hilltop. The free sharecroppers of 1881 built their cabins along the spurs or ridges of land between the streams, scattering their community over the plantation. A black church and school were built by this date. A typical sharecropper on the plantation earned most of his income from growing cotton.

work for wages. But, the contracts also provided for less supervision, a slower pace of work, and more free time than had been typical under slavery, as well as the elimination of drivers and overseers. By 1866 the process of bargaining between planters and freedmen had become more difficult, partly because a shrinking money supply reduced the amount of cash available to pay wages. To resolve the growing number of conflicts over labor contracts, Freedmen's Bureau agents introduced a form of compensation that was common, though not typical, in northern agriculture—payment of agricultural workers in shares of the crop rather than in wages. This system was known as *sharecropping*. While it came to involve many poor whites in the South, it was far more important for blacks. For them, sharecropping was the dominant mode of agricultural labor.

At first, freedmen were enthusiastic about sharecropping. It increased their control over working conditions and allowed them to improve their standard of living. Under typical sharecropping contracts, sharecroppers turned over between half and two-thirds of their harvested crops to their landlord. The owner's share was not necessarily excessive, because the landlord commonly provided land, seed, fertilizer, tools, and assistance in marketing.

The sharecropping system joined laborers and owners of land and capital in a common sharing of risks and returns. But it produced little upward mobility. By the end of Reconstruction, only a fraction of sharecroppers, no more than one-quarter of the total, had managed to save enough to rent land with cash payments, as most landless whites did. Even though these so-called "tenant farmers" could now sell their crops directly to market, they remained impoverished.

Land Ownership. Virtually all African-American farmers struggled long and hard to buy the land they tilled, and some of the cash renters gradually succeeded. They were willing to pay exorbitant prices for land just for the sake of being independent. But the system was stacked against them. African-American renters had far less access to land ownership than did their white counterparts. Planters made agreements among themselves to drive up the price of land to blacks or even refuse to sell to them. Some planters used the Ku Klux Klan to intimidate blacks who tried to buy land. Despite the adversity, by 1910 black farmers owned nearly a third of the land they cultivated. But black farm-owners usually occupied marginal land—in the coastal swamps of Georgia and South Carolina, for example—and the land had usually cost far more than its productivity warranted.

Debt Peonage. The financial condition of all African-American farmers was extremely difficult. Sharecropping, cash-renting of land, and land ownership enabled former slaves to raise their incomes but also increased their financial needs. They wanted more food and better clothing than they had received under slavery; they often needed more farm supplies than their landlords were willing to provide; and renters and owners had to purchase all their seed, fertilizer, and equipment. The purchase of major farm supplies almost always required borrowing. But southern banks were reluctant to lend money to black farmers, whom they saw as bad risks, and cash was generally in short supply.

The owners of country stores stepped in. Eager to lend money, they furnished everything the black farmers needed and extended credit for the purchases. The country merchants took advantage of the weak bargaining power of the former slaves, especially the sharecroppers, by charging unusually high prices and interest rates. In effect, these storekeepers became rural loan sharks.

Once African-American sharecroppers accepted credit from the country merchants, high interest rates made it difficult for them to settle their accounts. At best, after paying their debts they broke even. Most sharecroppers fell deeper and deeper into debt.

Throughout the South, when Democrats regained control of state governments, they passed laws that gave force to this economic system by providing merchants with the right to take liens on crops. Merchants could take crops to settle sharecroppers' debts and seek criminal prosecution of sharecroppers who could not pay the full amount of the interest they owed. Indebted African-American farmers faced imprisonment and forced labor unless they toiled on the land according to the instructions of the merchant-creditor. Increasingly, merchants and landlords cooperated to maintain this lucrative system, and many landlords themselves became merchants. The former slaves had become trapped in the vicious circle of *debt peonage,* which tied them to the land and robbed them of their earnings.

In sum, despite the odds against them, the freedmen won some modest economic gains. But their gains came only within the restrictions of the system of debt peonage that replaced slavery. Thus, most African-Americans and many whites remained mired in an agricultural poverty created by racism and economic forces.

The North During Reconstruction

Although the Republicans in Congress failed to break the hold of the planter elite on the South, they did reconstruct the economy of the North. They enacted nearly all of their nationalizing economic program—national banking, tariff protection, and subsidies for internal improvements—despite resistance from the Democrats. The Republican program promoted unprecedented economic growth and industrial development.

A Dynamic Economy

The Civil War disrupted the nation's economic life, yet by the 1870s Americans had become more productive than ever before. Northeastern industry led the way. Production of iron more than doubled between the end of the Civil War and 1870; it doubled again by 1880. Steel production grew even more rapidly, increasing fivefold between 1865 and 1870 and then nearly twenty times by 1880. The era began an *age of capital*—a period that lasted until World War I and was marked by great increases in investment in factories and railroads. It also began the era of big business, which was characterized by the rise of giant corporations.

The Republican Economic Program. During Reconstruction, Republicans expanded the ambitious economic program they had enacted during the war. The broad support that middle-class northerners gave to the program indicated that they now largely shared business-class values.

The scope of the Republican economic program was vast. Republicans strengthened government regulation of the banking system, winning praise from investors who appreciated a more predictable economic environment. Republican Congresses expanded subsidies to national rail systems and chartered new railroads; they expanded the national postal system; and they financed major river and harbor development throughout the North. They also funded the cavalry forces who fought the nation's wars against the Indians in the Great Plains (see Chapter 17). In fact, military spending accounted for 60 percent of the federal budget by 1880. Republicans used the Homestead Act of 1862 to subsidize the settling of the Great Plains.

Revenues raised from the Civil War tax system paid for these programs. Postwar Congresses kept the high tariffs, which had proven lucrative and appealed to average Republicans because they seemed to protect against foreign workers. Congress also retained the "emergency" wartime taxes on alcohol and tobacco, which were popular among many Republicans because they taxed "sin."

The tariffs and "sin" taxes not only funded programs but also provided money to pay back the Americans who had bought Union bonds during the war. Because the taxes increased the cost of everyday items, average Americans were paying a far higher share of their income for debt repayment than were the wealthy. Moreover, the repayment was going largely to the wealthy, who owned a disproportionate share of Civil War bonds. Republicans were self-consciously redistributing wealth from the poor to the rich, who were more

likely to save and invest, as a way of increasing the supply of capital and accelerating the rate of economic growth.

The most popular Republican economic program was the Civil War pension program, which the government extended and broadened virtually every year. It provided disabled veterans and the widows and children of Union veterans with generous benefits, which were particularly welcome during the severe depressions of the 1870s and 1890s. At the same time, the pensions solidified the Republican loyalties of the families of the men who had served in the Union army.

An ideological shift also contributed to the Republicans' success in enacting their economic program. The Civil War had led many Americans to relax their traditional suspicion of concentrations of power—in both business and government. This was particularly true of the men and women who had served in the Union army and the Sanitary Commission. The war had given them their first direct experience of living and working within modern bureaucracies—elaborate hierarchies imposing a high degree of job specialization and rigorous discipline. Wartime service also had taken them, usually for the first time, far from home and placed them in intimate contact with people who came from distant places and yet served in the same cause. And the Union had won the war. This disciplined, collective, national—and successful—experience predisposed northerners to accept American business, the Republican party, and the federal government as the central agencies of national economic development.

Republican Foreign Policy

Some Republican leaders were alert to new possibilities for expansion abroad. The most important advocate of expansion was William H. Seward, Lincoln and Johnson's secretary of state. Believing in the importance of foreign commerce to the long-term health of the republic, Seward promoted the acquisition of colonies that could be used as trading bases in the Caribbean and the Pacific. But Seward was ahead of his time. During the Reconstruction Era, most Americans wanted to concentrate on the development of their own territory.

Seward inherited his most pressing foreign policy issues from the Civil War. In Mexico, Napoleon III's puppet government under Archduke Maximilian was still in power; the threat this European regime posed to American interests in the Southwest was especially great since it might draw die-hard Confederate soldiers to its support. "On to Mexico," Grant only half-jokingly told an aide just a day after he accepted Lee's surrender at Appomattox. It was a good guess as to where the next war might take place. Within a year, president Johnson and Seward sent General Philip Sheridan with 50,000 battle-hardened Union veterans to the Mexican border, while Seward negotiated the withdrawal of French troops. The threat of force worked. The French left in 1867, abandoning Maximilian to a Mexican firing squad.

The American government was also troubled over another Civil War issue: Great Britain's allowing the *Alabama* and other Confederate cruisers to sail from British shipyards to raid Union commerce. Seward claimed that Britain had violated international laws of neutrality and owed compensation for damages. Britain, fearing that Americans might build ships for British enemies in some future war, accepted Seward's legal point and agreed to submit the *Alabama* claims to arbitration. However, Charles Sumner, chairman of the Senate Foreign Relations Committee, insisted that the compensation cover "indirect" damages. Including lost shipping revenue and the costs of Britain's prolonging the war, his cost estimates reached more than $2 billion. Sumner was angry over English aid to the Confederacy during the war, and he wanted to acquire Canada as part of the financial deal with Britain. In 1866, Congress restricted Canadian trade and fishing privileges in an attempt to force Canadians to support annexation. However, with the stakes so high, the British refused to agree to a settlement during Johnson's presidency.

Meanwhile, American expansionist ambitions in the Caribbean and the Pacific met with only mixed success. Supporting the U.S. Navy's demands for a base in the Caribbean, Seward negotiated a treaty with Denmark to purchase the Virgin Islands, but Congress rejected the $7.5 million price. Congress also turned down his proposal to annex Santo Domingo (now the Dominican Republic), which had won independence from Spain in 1865. Seward did persuade Congress to annex the small Midway Islands west of Hawaii, after his effort to acquire the Hawaiian Islands had failed. Most important, Seward convinced the Senate, in 1867, to ratify a treaty to buy Alaska from Russia and to appropriate the $7.2 million for the purchase. Critics referred to Alaska as "Johnson's Polar Bear Garden" and "Seward's Folly," but its acquisition promised to obstruct any British ambitions in North America. Also, the price was reasonable when weighed against even the low estimates that Congress made of Alaska's fish, fur, lumber, and mineral resources.

When Ulysses S. Grant became president in 1869, he took up the cause of expansion in the Caribbean. He was influenced by American investors and adventurers in Santo Domingo, including Orville E. Babcock, his former military aide, who became his personal secretary in the White House. Grant proposed a treaty to annex the country as a colony for freed slaves dissatisfied with Reconstruction. The Senate defeated Grant's imperial ambition in 1870. Leading the attack was Charles Sumner, who feared that annexation would threaten the independence of the neighboring black republic of Haiti. "These islands by climate, occupation, and destiny . . . belong to the colored people," he declared.

Grant's secretary of state was genteel Hamilton Fish, a former Whig who had been governor of New York and a U.S. senator. Fish had less interest than Seward in acquiring new territory and concentrated on settling differences with Britain. Part of his goal was to strengthen the ties of capital and commerce between the two nations. Interest in annexing Canada still remained high, but Fish finally persuaded Grant that the British North America Act of 1867, uniting Canada in a confederation (the Dominion of Canada) and providing for greater self-government, had removed any serious Canadian interest in annexation. Fish then quickly negotiated the Treaty of Washington in 1871, which submitted for arbitration all the outstanding issues between the two countries, including the *Alabama* claims. In 1873, the British government obeyed the ruling of an international tribunal established under the treaty and presented a $15.5 million check to the United States government. A period of unprecedented good will between America and Britain followed.

The Politics of Corruption and the Grant Administration

During the Grant administration, the Democratic party, seeking to reestablish its national base of power, made the Republican economic program its primary target. Since the key elements of Republican policy had wide support, the Democrats avoided attacking specific programs. Instead, they renewed their traditional assault on "special privilege."

Democrats warned that Republican programs were creating islands of privilege, enabling wealthy individuals to buy favors from the federal government and the Republicans to buy support from the people their programs served. The result, Democrats charged, was increasing concentration of wealth and power in the hands of the wealthy and corruption of the republic. By stressing corruption, the Democrats tried to appeal to Americans who valued honesty and still cherished the Jeffersonian ideal—a society composed of independent and virtuous farmers, artisans, and small entrepreneurs. The Democrats claimed that they would restore a competitive economy, one that they said had been lost during the Industrial Revolution and the Civil War.

Dissident Republicans. Some Republicans joined the Democratic chorus condemning Grant's policies. These dissidents included radicals on Reconstruction like Charles Sumner but most numerous and influential were men like Charles Francis Adams—wealthy, well-educated members of established northeastern families—who resented the critical role professional politicians had come to play in the party. They attacked Grant for turning the Republican party into a self-serving bureaucracy, with too many professional politicians in executive positions, especially cabinet posts. And they faulted their party for requiring government workers to pay a portion of their salaries into the party's treasury.

The dissidents coined the term *Grantism* to describe this new system of party patronage. To counter it they endorsed a program of civil service reform, beginning with a *merit system* to replace the spoils system established under Jackson. A civil service commission would administer competitive examinations as the basis for appointments.

The Liberal Republicans and the Election of 1872. When the dissident Republicans failed to replace Grant as the party's nominee in 1872, they called themselves the Liberal Republicans and formed a new party. The name reflected their commitment to liberty, competition, and limited government. Their platform emphasized civil service reform and—in an appeal for Democratic support—amnesty for all former Confederates and removal of troops from the South. For president they nominated Horace Greeley, the influential editor and publisher of the *New York Tribune*. In an attempt to steal the Liberals' thunder, the Democrats nominated Greeley too, but with little enthusiasm. Although Greeley now supported reconciliation with ex-Confederates, he had earlier favored a radical approach to Reconstruction, and he supported high tariffs, which conflicted with the views of the Democrats.

In the election of 1872, Grant won an even larger percentage of the popular vote—56 percent—than in 1868. In fact, this was a higher percentage of the popular vote than any candidate had won since Andrew Jackson in 1828. Grant carried every northern state and, because of support for him among African-American voters and the distaste of ex-Confederates for Greeley, he carried all of the states of the former Confederacy except Tennessee, Georgia, and Texas.

Crédit Mobilier and the Whiskey Ring. During Grant's second term, the issue of corruption in the Republican party erupted again. In 1873 a congressional committee confirmed newspaper reports of a complicated deal in which high-ranking Republicans appeared to have cheated the taxpayers. The scandal centered on Crédit Mobilier, a construction company that contracted for

"Grantism"

Grant was lampooned on both sides of the Atlantic for the scandalous behavior of his administration. The British magazine *Puck* showed Grant only barely defying gravity in protecting corrupt members of his administration. Despite the scandals, the British public welcomed Grant with admiration on his triumphal foreign tour in 1877.

work on the Union Pacific Railroad. It turned out that Crédit Mobilier was a dummy corporation. Union Pacific stockholders had formed it and made enormous purchases from it, sometimes for services that were never delivered, to be paid to the corporate conspirators in Union Pacific stock and federal subsidies. In an attempt to prevent a congressional investigation, the insiders had sold Crédit Mobilier stock at a discount to several members of Congress.

An even more dramatic scandal, which reached into the White House itself, involved the Whiskey Ring, a network of large whiskey distillers and Treasury agents who defrauded the Treasury of millions of dollars of excise taxes on liquor. The ring was organized by a Union general, John A. McDonald, whom Grant had appointed to the post of supervisor of internal revenue in St. Louis. Grant's private secretary, Orville Babcock, kept a protective eye on McDonald's activities and funnelled some of the spoils into the campaign chests of the Republican party. The game was up in 1875 when Benjamin Bristow, an upright and ambitious secretary of the Treasury, exposed the ring and brought indictments against more than 350 distillers and government officials. Babcock was later acquitted, but more than a hundred men, including McDonald, went to prison.

The Whiskey Ring scandal ruined Grant's second term in office and crushed whatever prospects Grant might have had for a third term. Grant had ordered Bristow to "Let no guilty man escape," but Grant protected his good friend Babcock with extraordinary measures, possibly even perjuring himself in a deposition he gave in the presence of Chief Justice Morrison Waite.

The Depression of 1873–1877. These scandals occurred in the midst of the worst depression the nation had ever endured. By 1876 nearly 15 percent of the labor force was unemployed, and thousands of farmers had gone bankrupt. The precipitating event was the Panic of 1873, which involved the bankruptcy of the Northern Pacific Railroad and its major investor, Jay Cooke. Both Cooke's privileged role as a financier of the Civil War and the extensive Republican subsidies to railroads suggested to many suffering Americans that Republican financial manipulations had caused the depression.

To Americans who had suffered economic loss or even ruin, the Grant administration seemed unresponsive. Especially troublesome was an important money issue: how much paper money should be in circulation. Rapidly decreasing prices hurt small farmers and all others who were heavily in debt. Forced to repay debts with dollars that were swiftly increasing in value, they called on the federal government to increase the nation's money supply—action that they hoped would stop prices from falling. The Grant administration ignored the debtors' pleas for relief and further angered them by insisting that Civil War bondholders be fully repaid in gold, even though they had bought their bonds with greenbacks and had received only the guarantee that the interest on the bonds would be paid in gold. In 1874, the Democrats gained sufficient support from Republicans to push through Congress a bill that would have increased the number of greenbacks in circulation, and eased the money pinch. But President Grant vetoed it, fueling Democratic charges that Republicans served only the special interests of capitalists. In the election of 1874, the Democrats rode their criticism of Grant's leadership to gains in both houses of Congress and a majority in the House of Representatives—for the first time since secession.

Before the new Congress met, however, the lame-duck Republicans passed the Specie Resumption Act of 1875. This law provided that the federal government would exchange gold for greenbacks, thus making federal paper money as "good as gold." It put the nation's money supply squarely on the gold standard, which increased the confidence of investors in the economy and helped foreign trade. But, by increasing the value of greenbacks, the act induced wealthy Americans to hoard them, reducing the amount of money in circulation, pushing prices up more sharply, and increasing still more the burden of debts. The severe financial pain felt by many Americans worsened even further the political prospects of the Grant administration.

The Political Crisis of 1877

Republican leaders approached the 1876 presidential campaign with a sense of foreboding. If they were to thwart the Democrats, they had to shake themselves free of the atmosphere of scandal and special privilege that had come to surround President Grant. They turned to the electoral-vote-rich state of Ohio for a candidate—Governor Rutherford B. Hayes, who had won three closely contested races. His scandal-free terms had won him a reputation for honesty; he had a good Civil War record; and he was a supporter of civil service reform. He was a moderate on Reconstruction and a former Whig, whose election strategy included an appeal to southern conservatives—especially former southern Whigs.

The Democrats concentrated on the Grant scandals. They nominated Governor Samuel J. Tilden of New York, a well-known fighter of corruption who had helped break the control of the infamous Tweed Ring over New York City politics. Their platform emphasized reform, especially of the civil service, promising to save the nation from "a corrupt centralism which has honeycombed the offices of the Federal government itself with incapacity, waste, and fraud."

The Election of 1876. On election night, the outcome seemed clear; headlines announced that Tilden had won. The Democrats celebrated, and the Republicans plunged into gloom. In Ohio, Hayes went to bed convinced that he had been defeated. Tilden had won a bare majority of the popular vote—51 percent. The Democrats had made deep inroads in the North, carrying New York, New Jersey, Connecticut, and Indiana, and they had apparently swept the southern states.

But by dawn two or three sleepless politicians at Republican headquarters in New York City had woven together a daring strategy. Republicans still controlled election procedures in three southern states—Louisiana, South Carolina, and Florida. If they could argue that Democratic fraud and intimidation had affected the election results in those states, they could certify Republican victories and report Republican electoral votes. Of course, newly elected Democratic officials in the three states would send in electoral votes for Tilden. As a result, there would be two sets of electoral votes from those states when Congress counted them early in 1877. If Congress accepted all the Republican votes, Hayes would have a one-vote electoral majority. The auda-

BALLOTS FOR REPUBLICANS!

BULLETS FOR DEMOCRATS!!

VOTE FOR HAYES!

LATEST FROM CHARLESTON.

DEATH TO COLORED DEMOCRATS!

ADMINISTRATION REFORM.

SOUTHERN LIBERTY.

BLACK SUPREMA

Anti-Republican Sentiment, 1876
This Democratic cartoon portrays
Union soldiers, with bayonets fixed, co-
ercing African-Americans to vote Republican. The carpetbag in the foreground identifies the politics of the
civilian at the voting table. To the far
left, the individual casting a watchful
eye on the proceedings is probably an
ex-planter, supposedly powerless in the
new politics of the South.

cious announcement came: Hayes had carried the three
southern states and won the election.

The Compromise of 1877. The Constitution had established no method to resolve this unprecedented dispute
over the validity of electoral votes, and the long period
of uncertainty between the election in November and
the inauguration the following March were filled with
rumors: There might be a violent coup by Democrats if
the Republicans tried to steal the election; President
Grant might use the military to prevent Tilden from
taking office; there might be a new election, or even a
new civil war. While the rumors flew, various interests
tried to gain some advantage from the situation. Railroad promoters jockeyed for new federal subsidies,
promising to deliver blocs of support in Congress to the
party that made the best promises. Politicians on all
sides flirted with the opposition, hoping for rewards.

In the end, political compromise and accident won
out. Congress decided to appoint an electoral commission to settle the question. The commission would include seven Republicans and seven Democrats. The
fifteenth and deciding vote would go to Justice David
Davis of the Supreme Court, a man with a reputation

for being free of party loyalty. But Justice Davis resigned from the Court at the crucial moment to accept
election to the Senate from Illinois and the deciding vote
fell to Joseph P. Bradley, a lifelong Republican. When
the commission completed its careful investigation of
the election results in Florida, Louisiana, and South
Carolina, the decision on each state was made by a
straight party vote of eight to seven.

It remained to be seen whether Congress would accept the result. The Senate was controlled by the Republicans, the House by the Democrats. Southern
Democrats held the balance of power, and Hayes's representatives sought their support. Some of these southerners were convinced that Hayes had made various
promises to the "negotiators"—to confine federal
troops to their barracks throughout the South, to appoint Democrats to major offices, and to support the
construction of a railroad across Texas to the Pacific.
Whether or not such promises were actually made,
enough southerners in the House accepted the commission's findings to make Hayes president.

This sequence of events is often referred to as the
Compromise of 1877, but historians remain uncertain
as to whether any kind of deal was really struck. During

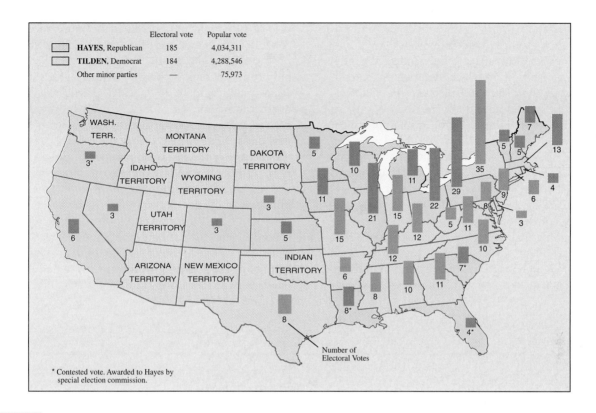

MAP 16.3

The Election of 1876

Tilden made such inroads in northern states that Hayes could not win without the contested votes of three states in the deep South.

his campaign Hayes had promised to end the military occupation of the South. He had also planned to appoint a few Democrats to his cabinet. And his faction of the Republican party did not support the Texas railroad scheme. The alleged compromise may have been a fiction created by southern Democrats to justify their votes for Hayes.

The End of Reconstruction. The only certainty was that Reconstruction had ended. The outcome was mixed and unclear; no single position emerged tri-

umphant. In 1877 political leaders on all sides were ready to say that what Lincoln had called "the work" was complete. But for many Americans, especially the freed slaves, the work had clearly not been completed. To be sure, they had won three amendments to the Constitution, established public schools for African-American children, and gained some access to land for former slaves. But any work toward further improvement in the condition of African-Americans had been abandoned and left to the slow, frustrating, and imperfect processes of history.

Summary

In 1865, after the Civil War ended, the Thirteenth Amendment made slavery unconstitutional. President Abraham Lincoln's plan for quickly restoring the Union encountered opposition from radical Republicans in Congress, who believed that freedmen must vote, and moderate Republicans, who wished to punish the South

and establish their party in southern states. Lincoln was assassinated before he could negotiate a unified Republican position.

Possibilities for a swift sectional reconciliation continued into the administration of Andrew Johnson, but he could not satisfy both moderate Republicans and the defeated Confederacy. His difficulties in working with Congress deepened the contest for the control of Reconstruction and resulted in an erratic policy that intensified the South's resistance to federal power.

Congressional Reconstruction extended the civil rights of former slaves through the Fourteenth Amendment, protected their suffrage through the Fifteenth Amendment, and encouraged the formation of southern state governments in which freedmen played crucial roles. Northern Republicans, however, failed to equip these governments to defeat the old planter elite, which managed to regain control through political appeals to racial solidarity and by means of terror and intimidation. By 1877 all the Reconstruction state governments had been overturned. The freedmen also won some modest economic gains during Reconstruction, but without access to land ownership they became ensnared in a system of debt peonage and once again found themselves dependent on the planters, who were now their landlords.

The Republicans proved to be more successful in consolidating the power of industrial capitalism than in reconstructing the South. Democrats attacked the Republican economic program with a Jeffersonian and Jacksonian critique of "special privilege," but most northerners came out of the Civil War more receptive to concentrations of power and to the values of the business class. Many believed that the Republican program was necessary for sustained prosperity and a strong nation. Although scandals during the Grant administration inflamed opposition to the Republicans, the Republicans took the election of 1876 by capitalizing on the South's hunger for an end to Reconstruction and for some influence in national politics. What is sometimes called the Compromise of 1877 kept the Republicans in control of the federal government by cementing an alliance between the northern business class and southern economic elites.

TOPIC FOR RESEARCH

The Overthrow of Radical Reconstruction

One by one, the Reconstruction state governments fell to counterrevolutions. This text has surveyed the general reasons for the victories of the Democratic "redeemers" over the Republicans, but the timing and particular circumstances differed from state to state. Choose one of the states of the former Confederacy and investigate how and why Reconstruction came to an end there. You should explore the methods of the redeemers, examining the extent to which they relied on conventional methods of political persuasion and organization as opposed to terrorism and guerrilla warfare. You should also consider the role of divisions among the various groups of Republicans—African-Americans, carpetbaggers, and scalawags—in the party's defeat. And, finally, examine the role of the federal government and the Union army. Could greater effort and commitment in Washington have saved the Republicans? General books on Reconstruction, such as Eric Foner, *Reconstruction: America's Unfinished Revolution, 1863–1877* (1988), have bibliographies listing books, articles, and other sources on the individual states. Be alert to the possibility of consulting the documents compiled by Congress as it struggled to understand the problems of Reconstruction. Especially fascinating, for example, are the hearings on the Ku Klux Klan: *Testimony Taken by the Joint Committee to Enquire into the Condition of Affairs in the Late Insurrectionary States*, indexed as 42d Cong., 2d sess., H. Rept. 22.

BIBLIOGRAPHY

Among the best general studies are three older works: W. E. B. Du Bois, *Black Reconstruction* (1935), the first to challenge traditional racist interpretations of Reconstruction; John Hope Franklin, *Reconstruction: After the Civil War* (1965); and Kenneth M. Stampp, *The Era of Reconstruction* (1965). More modern studies are Eric Foner, *Reconstruction: America's Unfinished Revolution* (1988), currently the best survey of Reconstruction, and James M. McPherson, *Ordeal by Fire: The Civil War and Reconstruction* (1982).

Presidential Restoration

For important studies of presidential efforts to rebuild the Union see the books on Abraham Lincoln listed in Chapter 15 and the following works on Andrew Johnson: Albert Castel, *The Presidency of Andrew Johnson* (1979); Eric L. McKitrick, *Andrew Johnson and Reconstruction* (1960), which initiated scholarly criticism of Johnson; and James Sefton, *Andrew Johnson and the Uses of Constitutional Power* (1979). Books that focus more closely on Congress include LaWanda Cox and John H. Cox, *Politics, Principle, and Prejudice, 1865–1867* (1963); David Donald, *The Politics of Reconstruction, 1863–1867* (1965); and William B. Brock, *An American Crisis: Congress and Reconstruction, 1865–1867* (1963). For insight into developments in the South, see Dan T. Carter, *When the War Was Over: The Failure of Self-Reconstruction in the South, 1865–1867* (1985). Michael Perman, *Reunion Without Compromise: The South and Reconstruction, 1865–1868* (1973), analyzes how the South manipulated Johnson.

Radical Reconstruction

For studies of Congress's role in radical Reconstruction, see Michael Les Benedict, *A Compromise of Principle: Congressional Republicans and Reconstruction* (1974); William Gillette, *Retreat from Reconstruction, 1863–1879* (1979); and Hans L. Trefousse, *Impeachment of a President: Andrew Johnson, the Blacks, and Reconstruction* (1975). William S. McFeely, *Grant: A Biography* (1981), deftly explains the politics of Reconstruction. Study of the South during radical Reconstruction should begin with the wealth of literature on the experience of blacks. Among the most useful works are Ira Berlin et al., *Freedom: A Documentary History of Emancipation, 1861–1867, The Wartime Genesis of Free Labor: The Lower South* (1990); Robert Cruden, *The Negro in Reconstruction* (1969); Jacqueline Jones, *Labor of Love, Labor of Sorrow: Black Women, Work, and the Family from Slavery to the Present* (1985); and Leon F. Litwack, *Been in the Storm So Long: The Aftermath of Slavery* (1979). The economic condition of the freedmen and the postwar South is the focus of Robert Higgs, *Competition and Coercion: Blacks in the American Economy, 1865–1914* (1977); Jay Mandle, *The Roots of Black Poverty: The Southern Plantation Economy After the Civil War* (1978); Roger L. Ransom and Richard Sutch, *One Kind of Freedom: The Economic Consequences of Emancipation* (1977); Jonathan M. Wiener, *Social Origins of the New South: Alabama, 1860–1885* (1975); and Gavin Wright, *The Political Economy of the Cotton South* (1978). Specialized studies of African-Americans and race relations, often focused on particular states, include John Blassingame, *Black New Orleans, 1860–1880* (1973); Barbara Fields, *Slavery and Freedom on the Middle Ground: Maryland During the Nineteenth Century* (1985); Thomas Holt, *Black over White: Negro Political Leadership in South Carolina During Reconstruction* (1977); Peter Kolchin, *First Freedom: The Responses of Alabama's Blacks to Emancipation and Reconstruction* (1972); Howard N. Rabinowitz, *Race Relations in the Urban South, 1865–1890* (1977); Willie Lee Rose, *Rehearsal for Reconstruction: The Port Royal Experiment* (1964); and Joel Williamson, *After Slavery: The Negro in South Carolina During Reconstruction, 1861–1877* (1965). Other instructive state studies of Reconstruction politics appear in Otto Olsen, ed., *Reconstruction and Redemption in the South* (1980). The best study of carpetbaggers is Richard N. Current, *Those Terrible Carpetbaggers: A Reinterpretation* (1988). On yeoman farmers, consult Steven Hahn, *The Roots of Southern Populism: Yeoman Farmers and the Transformation of the Georgia Upcountry, 1850–1890* (1983). The most thorough study of the Ku Klux Klan is Allen W. Trelease, *White Terror: The Ku Klux Klan Conspiracy and Southern Reconstruction* (1972). Biographies of Nathan Forrest include: Brian S. Wills, *A Battle from the Start: The Life of Nathan Bedford Forrest* (1992), and John A. Wyeth, *That Devil Forrest: A Life of General Nathan Bedford Forrest* (1989). To survey Reconstruction politics in the South consult Michael Perman, *The Road to Redemption: Southern Politics, 1869–1879* (1984).

TIMELINE

1864	Wade-Davis Bill
1865	Freedmen's Bureau established
	Lincoln assassinated; Andrew Johnson succeeds as president
	Joint Committee on Reconstruction formed
1866	Civil Rights Act passed over Johnson's veto
	Memphis and New Orleans riots
	American Equal Rights Association founded
	Johnson defeated in congressional elections
1867	Reconstruction Acts
	Tenure of Office Act
	Purchase of Alaska
1868	Impeachment crisis
	Fourteenth Amendment ratified
	Ulysses S. Grant elected president
1870	Ku Klux Klan at peak of power
	Fifteenth Amendment ratified
1873	Panic of 1873 ushers in depression of 1873–1877
1875	Whiskey Ring scandal undermines Grant administration
1877	Compromise of 1877; Rutherford B. Hayes becomes president
	Reconstruction ends

The North During Reconstruction

On state politics in the North, see Eugene H. Berwanger, *The West and Reconstruction* (1981), and James Mohr, ed., *The Radical Republicans in the North: State Politics During Reconstruction* (1976). Studies on national politics that extend beyond Reconstruction include Paul H. Buck, *The Road to Reunion, 1865–1900* (1937), and Morton Keller, *Affairs of State: Public Life in Late Nineteenth-Century America* (1977). The best studies of classic liberalism and liberals during the Reconstruction Era are John G. Sproat, *"The Best Men": Liberal Reformers in the Gilded Age* (1968), and Robert Kelley, *The Transatlantic Persuasion: The Liberal-Democratic Mind in the Age of Gladstone* (1968). On the monetary difficulties of the 1870s, see Walter T. K. Nugent, *The Money Question During Reconstruction* (1967). On the Compromise of 1877, see K. I. Polakoff, *The Politics of Inertia: The Election of 1876 and the End of Reconstruction* (1973), and C. Vann Woodward, *Reunion and Reaction* (1956).

P A R T 4

A Maturing Industrial Society,

1877–1914

THEMATIC TIMELINE

	Economy	Politics	Society	Culture	Diplomacy
	The triumph of industrialization	**From inaction to progressive reform**	**Racial, ethnic, and gender divisions**	**The rise of the city**	**An emerging world power**
1877	Andrew Carnegie launches modern steel industry Knights of Labor becomes national movement (1878)	Election of Rutherford B. Hayes ends Reconstruction	Defeat of the struggle for black equality End of nomadic Indian life High tide of women's "separate sphere"	Commercialization of leisure: National League founded (1876) Dwight L. Moody pioneers urban revivalism	U.S. becomes a net exporter
1880	Gustavus Swift pioneers vertically integrated firm American Federation of Labor founded (1886)	Ethnocultural issues dominate state and local politics Civil service reform (1883)	Chinese Exclusion Act (1882) Dawes Severalty Act divides tribal lands (1887)	Electrification transforms city life First *Social Register* defines high society (1888)	Diplomacy of inaction Naval build-up begins
1890	U.S. surpasses Britain in iron and steel output Economic depression (1893–97) Great merger movement	Populist party founded (1891) William McKinley wins presidency; defeats Bryan's free silver crusade (1896)	Black disfranchisement and racial segregation in the South Immigration from southeastern Europe rises sharply	Settlement houses spread progressive ideas to cities Hearst's *New York Journal* pioneers yellow journalism	Social Darwinism and Anglo-Saxonism promote expansionism Spanish-American War (1898–99); conquest of the Philippines
1900	Industry recruits immigrants for factory work Industrial Workers of the World founded (1905) Ford builds first automobile assembly line	Progressivism in national politics Theodore Roosevelt attacks the trusts Hepburn Act establishes government's regulatory power over railroads (1906)	Women take leading roles in social reform Revival of the struggle for civil rights Immigration restriction movement launched	Muckraking journalism Movies begin to overtake vaudeville	Panama cedes Canal Zone to United States (1903) Roosevelt Corollary of Monroe Doctrine (1904) Root-Takahira agreement (1908)
1910	U.S. business seeks foreign markets	Election of Woodrow Wilson (1912) New Freedom legislation creates Federal Reserve, FTC	NAACP founded (1910) Women win the right to vote in western states World War I ends the great European migration	Urban liberalism	Taft's Dollar Diplomacy promotes American business Woodrow Wilson proclaims U.S. neutrality in World War I

While the nation's attention had been riveted on the political dramas of Reconstruction, few people noticed an equally momentous watershed in American economic life. For the first time, as the decade of the 1870s passed, farmers no longer constituted a majority of working Americans. Henceforth, the nation's future would be linked irrevocably to its development as an industrial society.

The effects of accelerating industrialization were felt, first of all, in the manufacturing sector itself. As heavy industry emerged and the railroad system was completed, the modern techniques of industrial management took shape. Enterprise came increasingly to be carried on by big, nationwide firms. The trade union movement became firmly established, and, as immigration surged, the foreign-born and their children came to make up America's industrial workforce. What had been partial and limited became general and widespread as America turned into a land of factories, of great corporate enterprise, and of restless workers.

Second, the demands of industrialism largely drove the final surge of settlement across the Great Plains. Industry needed the West's mineral resources, while cities called for new sources of food. In the struggle for their way of life, the Plains Indians were ultimately defeated not so much by the rifles of army troopers as by events taking place far off in the nation's industries and cities. Rural America was likewise locked into the advancing Industrial Revolution. The distress American farmers experienced in this period resulted from their imperfect integration into the modern industrial order. They remained small-scale operators in an economic world increasingly dominated by far-flung railroads and giant corporations.

Third, industrialization transformed the physical and human make-up of the nation's cities. By 1900, one in five Americans lived in cities. That was where the jobs were—as workers in factories, as clerks and salespeople in offices and department stores, as members of a new salaried middle class of managers, engineers, and professionals, and, at the apex, as a wealthy elite of property owners and entrepreneurs. But the city was more than just a place to make a living. It provided a setting for an urban way of life unlike anything seen before in the United States.

Fourth, politics too marched in step with the industrial order. In the years of unprecedented economic expansion between 1877 and 1893, there seemed little need for government intervention. The major parties were robust and active, but their vitality stemmed from a political culture of popular participation, from ethnocultural conflicts linked to party loyalties, and from the informal functions the parties performed as highly organized political machines. Economic crisis during the 1890s triggered a major challenge to the political status quo, first, through the formation by the nation's distressed farmers of the Populist party, and then, as economic troubles spread across the land, over the explosive issue of free silver. The election of 1896 turned back that challenge. Still unresolved, however, was another economic concern—the enormous concentration of business power that had accompanied the nation's corporate development. This issue dominated the national politics of the Progressive Era years. Moreover, the nation belatedly began to address its social ills. From their bases in the settlement houses, women progressives took the lead in the struggle to make life better for America's urban masses. African-Americans, oppressed by disfranchisement and segregation, found allies among white progressives, and launched a new drive for racial equality.

Fifth and finally, the dynamism of America's economic development forced a decisive shift in the country's world relations. In the decades after the Civil War, America remained inward-looking, its indifference to global affairs reflected in an inactive diplomacy and a neglected navy. The economic crisis of the 1890s, however, brought home to American leaders the urgent need for secure access to overseas markets for the nation's surplus products. In short order, the United States fought a brief war with Spain, acquired an overseas empire, and forcefully asserted its national interests in Latin America and Asia. There was now no mistaking America's standing as a Great Power, nor, as World War I approached, any way to evade the responsibilities and entanglements that came with that exalted status.

California Cornucopia of the World

In the 1880s there was a burst of publicity about the charms
of Southern California. Eager for business, the Southern
Pacific Railroad was responsible for this promotion.

CHAPTER **17** *The American West, 1865–1890*

During the last third of the nineteenth century, American society seemed to be at odds with itself. From one angle the nation looked like an advanced industrial society, with great factories and mills and enormous, crowded cities. But from another angle America still seemed to be a frontier country, with settlers streaming westward on to the Great Plains, repeating the old dramas of "settlement" they had been performing over and over ever since Europeans had first set foot on the continent. Not until the 1890 census would the federal government declare that the frontier no longer existed: the country's "unsettled area has been so broken into . . . that there can hardly be said to be a frontier line."

That same year, 1890, the country surpassed Great Britain in the production of iron and steel. Newspapers told about Indian wars and labor strikes in the same editions. The army's massacre of Indians at Wounded Knee, South Dakota, the final tragedy in the suppression of the Plains tribes, occurred only eighteen months before the great Homestead steel strike of July 1892.

This combination of events from the distant worlds of factory and frontier did not occur by accident. The final surge of westward settlement across the Great Plains was powered primarily by the dynamism of American industrialization. The Industrial Revolution likewise shaped the history of agricultural America in these years. Farmers had one foot in the Jeffersonian past and the other in the industrial age. They remained small-scale operators in an economic world increasingly dominated by far-flung railroads and giant corporations. They were producing for international markets but thinking as family farmers. The distress they experienced during this period resulted basically from their

imperfect integration into the modern industrial order. Rural America could no longer be understood on its own terms. Its history had become linked ever more tightly to the larger industrial society.

The Great West

Before the Civil War, the vast lands west of the Mississippi seemed of little importance. Accustomed to woodlands and ample rainfall, farmers hung back from the dry country of the Great West. They saw it much as did Horace Greeley on his way to California in 1859: "a land of starvation," "a treeless desert," with a "terrible" climate of baking heat in the daytime and "chill and piercing" cold at night.

The Great West began at the edge of the prairie country several hundred miles west of the Mississippi River. Farther west, at roughly the ninety-eighth meridian running down from what are now North and South Dakota through central Texas, the tall grass of the prairies gave way to the short buffalo grass of the semiarid country. The land of buffalo grass, the Great Plains, extended to the Rocky Mountains. Beyond the mountains lay a high, arid plateau that spread to the Sierra and Cascade ranges. Schoolbooks referred to the Great Plains as the Great American Desert. Major Stephen H. Long, after exploring the region west of the ninety-eighth meridian in 1820, had declared it "almost wholly unfit for cultivation, and of course uninhabitable by a people depending upon agriculture for their subsistence."

Indians of the Great Plains

Whites generally considered the Great Plains best left to the native American inhabitants—the Apache and Comanche in the Southwest; Arapaho and Pawnee on the central plains; and, to the north, Crow, Cheyenne, and the great Sioux nation. The Sioux, who had been spared the epidemics of smallpox and measles that had ravaged many of the rival tribes, became the dominant power on the northern Great Plains.

Originally, the Sioux had been eastern prairie people occupying semipermanent settlements in the lake country of northern Minnesota. Under pressure from the better-armed Ojibwa, and with dwindling sources of fish and game, some Sioux tribes began to drift westward during the early eighteenth century. Around 1760, they began to cross the Missouri River into the vast short-grass country. From tribes to the south and west, the Sioux acquired horses. Now mounted, they became hunters of the buffalo herds that ranged the Great Plains. The Sioux became a seminomadic people, living in portable skin tepees and claiming the entire Great Plains north of the Arkansas River as their hunting grounds. By the early nineteenth century, they had built an essentially new and robust Indian culture based on the horse, the buffalo, and the open land.

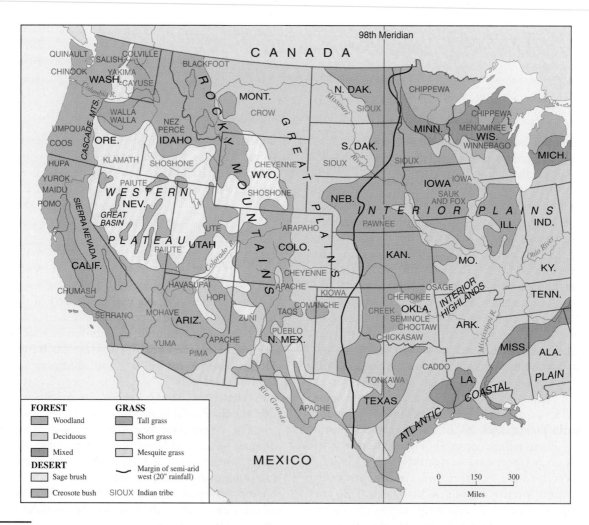

MAP 17.1

The Natural Environment and Peoples of the West

As settlers pushed into the Great Plains beyond the line of semiaridity, they sensed the overwhelming power of the natural environment. In a landscape without trees for fences and barns, without adequate rainfall, farmers had to relearn their business. The native Americans peopling the plains and mountains were also part of the western "environment," but ultimately they were easier to overcome than natural barriers. Pioneering whites never doubted that their country had the power to crush Indian resistance to the invasion of their ancestral lands.

The Teton Sioux. The westernmost Sioux—they called themselves the Teton people—made up a loose confederation of seven tribes: Oglala, Brulé, Hunkpapa, Minneconjou, Sans Arc, Two Kettle, and Blackfoot. In the winter months these tribes broke up into small bands, but each spring they would assemble and prepare for the summer hunt. Survival through the winter depended on the success of the buffalo hunt. This was conducted with much ritual, and required a high degree of organization. Summer was also the season for making war. Mostly, raiding parties of thirty or forty warriors went forth intent on capturing ponies and taking scalps, but larger, well-organized territorial campaigns were sometimes also mounted against rival tribes. The Sioux, it must be remembered, were an invading people. Warfare was the means by which they drove out or subjugated longer-settled tribes and made the Teton Sioux the dominant power on the Great Plains.

A society that celebrates the heroic virtues is likely to define gender roles sharply. Before the Sioux mastered the use of the horse, chasing down buffalo and antelope had been a group enterprise. The entire community—women as well as men—worked collectively to construct a "pound" and channel the herds in the right direction. Once on horseback, the male buffalo hunters were on their own, and gender roles became more distinct. The men did the fighting, hunting, and trading, while the women prepared the skins, made the clothing, and moved the camp. White observers frequently described Sioux women as "beasts of burden." Fanny Kelly, who had been a Sioux captive, considered "their life a servitude"; but she noticed also that Sioux women were "very rebellious, often displaying ungovernable and violent temper." Subordination to the men was not how Indian women understood their unrelenting labor; this was their allotted share in a partnership on which the proud, nomadic life of the Teton Sioux depended.

Living so close to nature, depending on its bounty for survival, the Sioux saw sacred meaning in every manifestation of the natural world. Unlike the white man, they conceived of God not as a supreme being, but (in the words of the ethnologist Clark Wissler) as "a controlling power or series of powers pervading the universe." The most sacred of these powers were the *wakan tanka*. First came the sun, Wi; then came Skan, the sky; Maka, the earth; Inyan, the rock. Below these came the moon, wind, buffalo, down through a hierarchy embodying the perceived natural order. The central experience of Sioux religion was to establish a bond with those mysterious powers through visions induced by prayer and fasting in some isolated place. Medicine men provided instruction, but the religious experience was essentially an individual matter, open both to women and men. The vision, when a supplicant achieved it, attached itself to some object—a feather, the skin of an animal, or a shell—which was tied up into a sacred bundle and became the Indian's lifelong talisman. For the tribe as a whole, Sacred Pipe bundles served as the symbolic and ceremonial core of Sioux religion. In the Sun Dance, the entire tribe engaged in the rites of coming of age, of fertility, of the hunt and combat, followed by four days of fasting and dancing in supplication to Wi, the sun.

The world of the Teton Sioux was not self-contained. From the very start of their westward trek, they had been traders, exchanging beaver and buffalo skins for the agricultural products of the sedentary eastern plains Indians, such as the Mandan. They soon extended these exchanges to the white traders who had appeared on the upper Missouri River during the eighteenth century and a substantial commerce in furs developed. Although the buffalo provided most of the essentials of life—not only food but clothing, shelter, fuel, carrying bags, and a variety of bone implements— the Sioux came to rely as well on the traders' pots, kettles, blankets, knives, and firearms. Sophisticated as this trade economy became, it was integrated into the Sioux way of life and indeed depended on the survival of the Great Plains as the Sioux had found it, wild grassland on which the antelope and buffalo ranged free.

Intruders

In 1834, Congress had formally created a permanent Indian country in the Great West. The army built border forts from Lake Superior to Fort Worth, Texas, to keep the Indians in and white settlers out. In 1838 the commanding general of the area, Edmund Gaines, recommended that the forts be constructed of stone because they would be there forever. The creation of an Indian country supported the contemporary belief that the Great American Desert could serve only as home, in the words of the explorer Zebulon M. Pike, "to the wandering and uncivilized aborigines of the country."

Though solemnly committed to the Indians, the Great West was put to new, more profitable uses almost immediately. The first encroachment came with the migration of settlers to Oregon and California during the 1840s. Instead of serving as a buffer against the British and the Mexicans, the Indian country became a bridge to the Pacific. The first wagon train headed west for Oregon from Missouri in 1842. Thousands of emigrants then traveled the Oregon Trail to the Willamette Valley or, cutting south beyond Fort Hall, down into California. Approaching that juncture in 1859, it seemed to Horace Greeley as if "the white coverings of the many emigrant and transport wagons dott[ing] the landscape" gave "the trail the appearance of a river running through great meadows, with many ships sailing on its bosom." Only these "ships" left behind not a trailing wake of foam, but a rutted landscape, devoid of grass and game, and littered with the debris of abandoned wagons and rotting garbage.

The migrants had no interest in the land they crossed; they considered it barren ground. But their journey marked the intrusion of the modernizing world on the habitat of the western Indians. And where the wagons came, the railroads were sure to follow.

As early as 1853, the federal government began surveying railway routes to the Pacific. A sectional stalemate over the proposed transcontinental route delayed railroad construction for a decade. Wagon freight lines, stagecoaches, and the horseback riders of the Pony Express furnished the first regular links between East and West. A telegraph line reached San Francisco in 1861. The tracks of the Union Pacific and Central Pacific railroads finally converged at Promontory Point, Utah, in 1869, uniting the continent by rail. A burst of western railway building followed. By 1883, two more continental routes had reached California—the Southern Pacific line from New Orleans and the Santa Fe from Kansas City—while the Northern Pacific linked Portland, Oregon, to St. Paul, Minnesota.

Hydraulic Mining in the Boise Basin, Idaho
Hydraulic mining, invented in the California gold fields in 1853, was a highly efficient method that yielded profits even with low-grade concentrations of gold. The technology was simple—it used high-pressure water jets to wash away hillsides of gold-bearing soil. Although building the necessary reservoirs, piping systems, and sluices required heavy investment, the profits from the hydraulic process helped transform western mining into big business. But, as Mary Brown's painting of 1875 suggests, hydraulic mining was environmentally disastrous.

The Mining Frontier. On the heels of the wagon traffic across the plains and mountains came the exploitation of the mineral wealth of the Great West. The rush to California had been triggered in 1848 by the discovery of gold in the foothills of the Sierras. By the mid-1850s, as easy pickings in the California gold country diminished, disappointed prospectors began to pull out and spread across the Great West in hopes of striking it rich elsewhere. Gold was discovered on the Nevada side of the Sierras, in the Colorado Rockies, and along the Fraser River in British Columbia. New strikes occurred

MAP 17.2

The Development of the West, 1860–1890

The first organized settlements—Mormons around Salt Lake, farmers in Oregon, ranchers and miners in California—were far from other populated areas. Mining sprang up in scattered places wherever gold and silver was discovered. The transportation routes of wagon trains, cattle trails, and railroads crossed wide expanses of open land. The final phase of western settlement thus broke from the earlier pattern of a frontier line moving westward and instead resembled a series of incursions that gradually enveloped an entire region.

in Montana and Wyoming during the 1860s, in the Black Hills of South Dakota in the 1870s, and in the Coeur d'Alene region of Idaho during the 1880s.

As the news of each gold strike spread, a wild, remote area turned almost overnight into a mob scene of prospectors, traders, gamblers, prostitutes, and saloon keepers. At least a hundred thousand fortune seekers flocked to the Pikes Peak area of Colorado in the spring of 1859. Always trespassers on government or Indian land, the prospectors made their own law. The mining codes, devised at community meetings, limited the size

of a mining claim to what a person could reasonably work. This kind of informal law-making also became an instrument for excluding or discriminating against Mexicans, Chinese, and African-Americans in the gold fields. And it turned into hangman's justice for the many outlaws who infested the mining camps.

The heyday of the prospectors was always very brief. They were equipped only to skim gold from the surface of the earth and from streambeds. To extract the metal locked in the underground lodes required mine shafts and crushing mills, which took capital, technology, and business organization. The original claim holders quickly sold out after exhausting the surface gold or when a generous bidder came along. At every gold-rush site, the prospector soon gave way to entrepreneurial development and large-scale mining. Rough mining camps turned into cities.

Virginia City. Nevada's Virginia City was a case in point. It started out as a bawdy, ramshackle mining camp. But within a few years of the opening of the Comstock lode in 1859, Virginia City boasted a stock exchange, five newspapers and, in short order, ostentatious mansions for the mining kings, fancy hotels, opera, even Shakespearean theater. The underlying characteristics of a boom town persisted, however. In 1870, the ratio of men to women was two to one, and children made up only 10 percent of the population. There were a hundred saloons, and brothels lined D Street. Virginia City was a magnet for desperate job seekers of both sexes: the men who became miners and gambled their lives below ground for $4 a day, the working-class women who became dance-hall entertainers and prostitutes because that was the best chance offered many of them by Virginia City's bonanza economy. Nowhere among today's major cities, notes the leading sociologist of the subject, is prostitution "so central to community life" as it was in the miners' world of Virginia City.

When James Galloway arrived on February 4, 1875, from California, however, he brought his family with him, and so did many other miners. By 1880 there were as many women and children as men in Virginia City. Galloway's diary indicates a family life not out of the ordinary in its recording of church going, picnics, the purchase of a lot for a small house. But Galloway was infected by Virginia City's pervasive gambling fever: he speculated regularly in mining stock and always lost money. In the end, he fell victim of the extraordinary hazards of hard-rock mining. He was killed when his sleeve got caught in the gears of a mine machine. He might have survived had he agreed to having his arm hacked off, but he took a long chance on being cut loose and coming out whole, and lost.

Industrialization of Western Mining. In its final stage, the mining frontier passed into the industrial world. At some sites, gold and silver proved less important than the commoner metals with which they were intermixed. Beginning in the mid-1870s, copper mining thrived in the Butte district of Montana, especially after the opening of the fabulous Anaconda mine. It also flourished in the Globe and Copper Queen fields of New Mexico and Arizona. In the 1890s, following earlier finds at Leadville, Colorado, the Coeur d'Alene silver district became the nation's main source of lead and zinc.

The industrial order swiftly took hold of these remote places in the Great West. Entrepreneurs raised capital, built rail connections, devised the technology for treating the lower-grade copper deposits, constructed smelting facilities, and recruited a labor force. As elsewhere in American industry, trade union organization appeared among the miners (see Chapter 18). And, as elsewhere in corporate America, the western metal industries went through a process of consolidation. The Anaconda Copper Mining Company and other Montana mining firms came under the control of the Amalgamated Copper Company in 1899. That same year, the American Smelting and Refining Company brought together the bulk of the nation's lead-mining and copper-refining properties. Still Blackfoot and Crow country in the 1860s, the Butte copper district was a center of industrial capitalism barely thirty years later.

The Cattle Frontier. As with copper and lead mining in the mountain country, the demands of a growing industrial economy spurred the relentless exploitation of the Great Plains. For years, Indians had been selling buffalo hides to whites at the trading posts that dotted the Great Plains. In the early 1870s, eastern tanneries conducted successful experiments in curing buffalo hides, and a ready market developed among shoe and harness manufacturers. Parties of professional hunters, armed with high-powered rifles, swept across the plains and began a systematic slaughter of the buffalo. The great herds, already diminished by the spread of horses and cattle, almost vanished within ten years. Many people spoke out against this mass killing, but no method existed to curb people bent on making a quick dollar. Besides, as General Philip H. Sheridan assured the Texas legislature, the extermination of the buffalo brought benefits: the Indians would be starved into submission and feeding grounds would open up for a more valuable commodity, the Texas longhorn.

Since the eighteenth century, these tough Spanish cattle had spread westward across Texas from the grasslands between the Rio Grande and the Nueces River. About 5 million longhorns roamed the region in 1865, largely untended and unclaimed, and hardly worth bothering about because they could not be profitably marketed. That year, however, the Missouri Pacific Railroad reached Sedalia, Missouri. At that terminal, connecting as it did to hungry eastern markets, the $3 longhorn might command $40. This realization by Texas ranchers set off the famous Long Drive. Cowboys began to herd Texas cattle a thousand miles or more north to the railroads that were pushing west across Kansas.

At Abilene, Ellsworth, and, beginning in 1875, Dodge City, the stockmen sold the cattle and the trail-weary cowboys went on a binge. Like the mining

The Cowboy at Work

Open-range ranching, where cattle from different ranches grazed together, gave rise to distinctive traditions. At the roundup, cowboys separated the cattle by owner and branded the calves. The cowboy, traditionally a colorful figure, was really a kind of farmhand on horseback, with the skills to work on the range. He earned twenty-five dollars a month, plus his food and a bed in the bunkhouse, for long hours of grueling, lonesome work.

camps, the wide-open cattle towns captured the nation's imagination as symbols of the Wild West. The reality was much more ordinary. The cowboys, perhaps a third of them African-Americans and Hispanics, were in fact farm hands on horseback, working long hours under harsh conditions for small pay. Colorful though it seemed, the Long Drive was actually a makeshift method of bridging a gap in the developing transportation system. As soon as railroads reached the Texas range country during the 1870s, stockmen abandoned the hazardous and wasteful Long Drive for a more settled kind of ranching.

Others, meanwhile, introduced longhorns to the northern ranges and found that the cattle could survive the harsh winter climate. In hardly a decade, starting in the late 1860s, the Great Plains changed into ranching country. The land itself was treated as a free commodity, available to anyone who seized it and put it to use. Hopeful ranchers would spot a likely area along a creek and claim as much land as they could qualify for as settlers under federal homesteading laws, plus what might be added by the fraudulent claims taken out by one or two ranch hands. By a common usage that quickly became established, the rancher had a "range right" to all the adjacent land rising up to the divide—the point

where the land sloped down to the next creek. As they improved the scrawny longhorns through crossbreeding with Hereford and Angus cattle, and as the herds multiplied, ranchers quickly became substantial operators. But they remained very much pioneers in relying on themselves and, through stock-raisers' associations, on each other to protect their rights as ranchers.

A cattle boom during the early 1880s hastened the end of open-range ranching. Eastern and British investors rushed in to benefit from the high profits. Overgrazing depleted the grasslands. Cattle prices had begun to slump at the Chicago stockyards in 1882, and they collapsed as stockmen dumped stricken cattle on the market during the cold weather and drought of 1885–1886. The following winter, the most terrible in memory, wiped out vast herds. Open-range ranching came to an end. Cattle ranchers built fences around their land and laid in hay crops for winter feed. No longer would cattle be left to fend for themselves on the open range. The Great Plains turned into ordinary ranch country. Sheep raising, previously scorned as unmanly work and resisted as a threat to the grass, now became respectable. Some ranchers even sold out to the despised "nesters"—those who wanted to try farming the Great Plains.

Buffalo Bill and the Wild West

Scott County, Iowa, was still frontier country when William F. Cody was born there on February 26, 1846. Kansas, where his family moved in 1854, was even wilder, for it was not only frontier country but racked by bloody conflict between proslavery and free-soil settlers. Bill's father, Isaac Cody, was active on the free-soil side, serving in the Topeka legislature and frequently in harm's way from neighboring southern sympathizers and marauding Border Ruffians. One of Bill's first exploits was a wild gallop, with proslavery men in hot pursuit, to warn his father of a trap set for him near the family farm. Isaac Cody was less an idealist, however, than a typical enterprising westerner on the lookout for the main chance. He had been an Indian trader, a farm manager, a stagecoach operator, and, in Kansas, a land speculator around Grasshopper Falls. When he died suddenly in 1857, Cody left the family with a lot of land titles but little money.

Bill, never much for schooling anyway, had to find work. Only eleven, he was taken on by Majors and Waddell, the firm that freighted goods from Fort Leavenworth to army posts west of the Missouri River. Bill worked as a messenger boy, livestock herder, and teamster helper on the freight wagons going west. When his employers (now Russell, Majors, and Waddell) organized the short-lived Pony Express in 1860, Cody became a stocktender and occasional rider in the Colorado-Nebraska division. Most of this was hard and tedious labor, but there were flashes of excitement—scrapes with Indians and bandits (at fifteen, Bill killed one), buffalo stampedes, and brief encounters with Wild Bill Hickock and other tough western characters on which to model himself. In the early part of the Civil War, Cody was somewhat at loose ends. Among other things he engaged in some horse-thieving disguised as guerrilla activity in Missouri, and he became a heavy drinker. After a stint in the Seventh Kansas Cavalry and a half-hearted effort to settle down after the war (and an unhappy marriage), Cody got his lucky break in 1867.

Buffalo Bill's Wild West Show
(Buffalo Bill Historical Center)

The Kansas Pacific Railroad was building a line through Indian country to Sheridan, Kansas. To provision the work crews, the contractors hired Cody at $500 a month—excellent pay—to bring in twelve buffalo a day for the cooks. Cody was a crack shot, an excellent horseman, and he knew buffalo hunting. This assignment was duck soup for him, and the aplomb with which he carried it off soon gave him the name "Buffalo Bill."

The next summer, 1868, Indian war broke out in Kansas, and Cody got his second claim to fame. He was hired as chief scout for the U.S. Fifth Calvary. Cody knew the Kansas landscape intimately, he seemed to have a remarkable instinct for following a trail, and he was absolutely intrepid in the face of danger. At the height of the fighting in 1868-1869, Cody saw repeated action. In the climactic Battle of Summit Springs, his scouting played a decisive role and he himself shot the Cheyenne chief Tall Bull. Although the legends later built up around Buffalo Bill (and the claims of others) have inclined scholars to be skeptical, Buffalo Bill was in fact an authentic hero. Perhaps the best testimony was the extra $100 awarded him by the normally tight-fisted army "for extraordinarily good services as a trailer and fighter in the pursuit of hostile Indians."

Out of these promising materials there began to emerge a mythic figure. In July 1869, the dime novelist Ned Buntline (Edward Zane Carroll Judson) came through Kansas, met Cody, and, after returning to New York, wrote *Buffalo Bill, the King of the Border Men*—the first of some 1,700 potboilers to feature Cody's name and exploits. Then there were the buffalo hunting parties of the rich and famous that Cody periodically led, including a royal hunt in 1872 with the Grand Duke Alexis of Russia that had the entire country agog. With his white horse, buckskin suit, crimson shirt, and broad sombrero, Buffalo Bill began to play his part to the hilt. "He realized to perfection the bold hunter and gallant sportsman of the plains," wrote one appreciative participant. In 1872 Cody was persuaded to appear as himself in a play Ned Buntline proposed to put on in New York. Buntline was said to have dashed off *The Scouts of the Prairie* in four hours, and as a play critics pronounced it "execrable." But Buffalo Bill, who mostly ad-libbed, was a great hit, and so was the production. Cody was launched on his career as a showman.

From then on, the lines between reality and make-believe began to blur. Not only did Buffalo Bill draw on his past exploits when he went on stage, but he had the stage in mind when he returned to the real world. During the Sioux wars of 1875-1876, Cody was again out

Buffalo Bill Cody

in the field as an army scout. (Fortunately, the fighting took place during the theatrical off-seasons in the East.) Shortly after the annihilation of Custer's troops at Little Big Horn, Cody gained a measure of vengeance in a famous skirmish in which he killed and scalped a Sioux chief named Yellow Hand. Cody rode into that engagement wearing his stage *vaquero* outfit—black velvet and scarlet with lace—so that when he reenacted the mayhem on stage, he could say he was wearing the very clothes in which he had seen action. Over time, with some help from Cody, the fight with Yellow Hand assumed legendary proportions, becoming a formal duel, with a challenge laid down by the Indian chief, and troopers and Indian warriors lined up on opposing sides watching Buffalo Bill and Yellow Hand fight it out.

The mythic West Cody was creating became full-blown in his Wild West Show. Modeled on the circus and rodeo, it was first staged in 1883. It was an open-air extravaganza, with displays of horsemanship, sharpshooting by Little Annie Oakley, real Indians (in one season Chief Sitting Bull toured with the company), and reenactments of stagecoach robberies and great events like Custer's Last Stand. The Wild West toured the country every year—and was a smashing success in Europe as well.

Buffalo Bill had been keen enough to see the hunger of city people for a legendary West. He traded on his talents as a showman, but he relied as well on his grasp of the authentic world behind the make-believe. When Cody died in 1917, that world had long gone, but his Wild West Show kept it alive in legend, where it still remains in the mythic figures of cowboys and Indians that populate our movies and television screens.

The Impact on the Indians

And what of the Indians who had inhabited the Great West? Basically, their fate has been told in the foregoing account of western settlement. "The white children have surrounded me and have left me nothing but an island," lamented the great Sioux chief Red Cloud in 1870, the year after the completion of the transcontinental railroad. "When we first had all this land we were strong; now we are all melting like snow on a hillside, while you are grown like spring grass." Francis A. Walker, a knowledgeable government official, expressed that hard truth from the whites' point of view: "The freedom of territorial and industrial expansion, which is bringing industrial greatness to the nation, to the Indian brings wretchedness, destitution, beggary."

Every advance of the whites—the Oregon-bound wagon train, the railroad, the buffalo hunter, the miner, the cattle rancher, the farmer—intruded on the Indians' world. No historical equation could have been more precise: the progress of the settlers meant the end of the Indian's way of life.

The provision for a permanent Indian country, written into federal law and into treaties with various tribes, was swept away in the westward march of the settler. By 1860 all the resettled eastern tribes, treaties notwithstanding, had been forced to cede their lands and move farther west. The nomadic tribes presented a more formidable barrier. As miners and other pioneers thrust into Indian lands from the late 1850s on, they fought running battles with the Indians all along the frontier—from the Apache in the Southwest, to

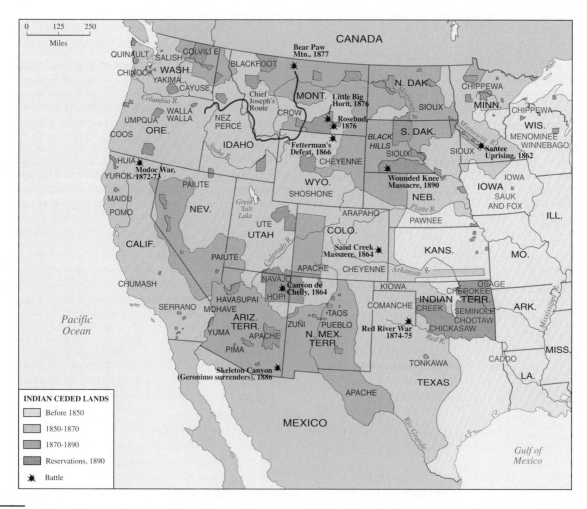

MAP 17.3

The Indian Frontier

As settlement pushed on to the Great Plains after the Civil War, the Indians put up bitter resistance, but ultimately to no avail. Over a period of decades, they ceded most of their lands to the federal government, and by 1890 they were confined to scattered reservations where most could expect an impoverished and alien way of life.

the Cheyenne and Arapaho in Colorado, to the Sioux in the Wyoming and Dakota territories. Fighting ferociously between 1865 and 1867, the Sioux prevented a wagon road from being built through their prized Powder River hunting grounds to the booming mining town of Bozeman in eastern Montana.

The Reservation Solution. This fierce resistance led to the formulation in 1867 of a new policy for dealing with the western Indians. Few whites questioned the necessity of moving the Indians out of the path of settlement, nor the idea that the Indians should be placed on reservations. This process had already begun intermittently. Now it would be pushed to a conclusion. And to it would be linked something new: a planned approach for weaning the Indians from their nomadic way of life. Under the guidance of the Office of Indian Affairs, they would be wards of the government until they learned "to walk on the white man's road."

The government set aside two extensive areas for the Indians. It allocated the southwestern quarter of the Dakota Territory—present-day South Dakota west of the Missouri River—to the Teton Sioux tribes. And it assigned what is now Oklahoma to the southern Plains Indians, as well as to the Five Civilized Tribes—the Choctaw, Cherokee, Chickasaw, Creek, and Seminole—and other eastern Indians already there. Scattered reservations went to the Apache, Navaho, and Ute in the Southwest and to the mountain Indians in the Rockies and beyond.

As in the past, the transfer of land went through the legal process of treaty making. And, as in the past, the whites bribed and tricked the Indian chiefs and in the end forced the chiefs to accept what they could not prevent. In 1868, the western Sioux tribes signed a treaty ceding all their land outside the Dakota reservation but explicitly retaining their hunting grounds in the Powder River country. "We have now selected and provided reservations for all, off the great road," concluded the western commanding general in September 1868. "All who cling to their old hunting-grounds are hostile and will remain so till killed off."

The Plains Indians, despite the treaties, inevitably tried to hold on to their way of life. Their subjugation was equally inevitable. The U.S. Army was thinly spread, having been cut back after the Civil War to a total of 27,000 for the entire country. But these were veteran troops, including 2,000 black cavalrymen of the Ninth and Tenth regiments, whom Indians called with grim respect "buffalo soldiers." Technology also favored the army. Telegraph communications and railroads enabled the troopers to be quickly concentrated; repeater rifles and Gatling guns increased their fire power against the Indians. As fighting in the mid-1870s intensified, a reluctant Congress made appropriations

to augment the western troopers. Tribal rivalries prevented the Indians from ever concentrating their united power against a common enemy; on the contrary, the army generally counted on the help of friendly Indians in its campaigns. But the worst disadvantages facing the Indians derived less from a formidable U.S. Army or their own disunity than from the overwhelming impact of white settlement on their capacity to carry on the struggle.

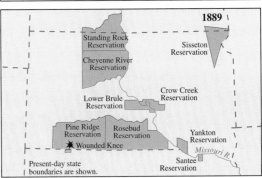

MAP 17.4

The Sioux Reservations in South Dakota, 1868–1890

When they bent to the demand in 1868 that they move on to the reservation, the Sioux thought they had gained secure rights to a substantial part of their ancestral hunting grounds. As they learned to their sorrow, however, fixed boundary lines only increased their vulnerability to the land hunger of the whites and sped up the process of expropriation.

Resisting the reservation solution, the Indians fought on for years—in Kansas in 1868–1869, in the Red River Valley of Texas in 1874, sporadically in New Mexico among the Apache until the capture of Geronimo in 1886. On the northern plains the crisis came in 1875, when the Indian Office—notwithstanding the treaty of 1868—ordered the Sioux to vacate their Powder River hunting grounds and withdraw to the reservation.

Led by Sitting Bull, Sioux warriors began to gather on the Little Big Horn River just to the east of the Powder River country. In a typical concentrating maneuver, army columns from widely separated forts converged on the Little Big Horn from three sides. The commanding general, Alfred H. Terry, sent Colonel George A. Custer ahead with a small force to locate the Sioux encampment, with orders to block the Indians from escaping into the Big Horn Mountains before the main army forces arrived. Instead, the reckless Custer sought out battle on his own. On June 25, 1876, he advanced on what he thought was a minor Indian encampment. This turned out to be the main Sioux force of 2,500 warriors. They surrounded and annihilated Custer and his 256 men. It was a great Indian victory, but not a decisive one. The day of reckoning was merely postponed. Weakened by unrelenting military pressure and increasing physical privation, the Sioux bands one by one gave themselves up and moved on to the reservation. Last to come in were Sitting Bull's followers. They had retreated to Canada, but in 1881 after five hard years they recrossed the border and surrendered at Fort Buford, Montana.

The Indians had no chance against the relentless white occupation of the land. Homesick bands of southern Cheyenne learned this bitter truth in 1878 when they escaped from their reservation in the Indian Territory of Oklahoma. Along the route to their native grounds in the Wyoming Territory lay three railroads, numerous telegraph lines, and ranchers and homesteaders eager to report the Cheyenne's movements. The Indians made their way through Kansas and Nebraska, but the army eventually caught up with and captured them. The surviving remnants declared that they preferred death to returning to the reservation. The government relented and permitted them to stay on their native land.

It was the whites, not the Indians, who wrecked the reservation policies of 1867. Prospectors began in 1873 to dig gold in the Black Hills, part of the Sioux reservation in Dakota. Unable to hold back the prospectors or to buy out the Indians, the government opened up the Black Hills to gold seekers at their own risk and then, when war with the Sioux broke out, forced the cession of the western third of the Sioux reservation.

The Indian Territory of Oklahoma met the same fate. Two million acres in the heart of the territory had not been assigned to any tribe, and white homesteaders coveted the fertile land of this area. The "Boomer" movement, stirred up initially by railroads running across the Indian Territory during the 1880s, agitated tirelessly to open this so-called Oklahoma District to settlers. In 1889, the government gave in and placed the Oklahoma District under the Homestead Act. On April 22, 1889, a horde of homesteaders rushed in and staked

The Cherokee Strip

This photograph captures the wild race into the Cherokee Strip in the northern part of Oklahoma Territory on September 16, 1893, the second such "run" that opened the region to white settlement. The winners staked out their claims under the Homestead Act, and looked forward to a prosperous future on some of the richest farmland in America. Those who lost out hoped for better luck as other parts of the territory opened up. The Indians who had lived on that land had nothing to hope for, because this process spelled the end of their way of life.

out the entire district within a few hours. Two tent cities—Guthrie with 15,000 people and Oklahoma City with 10,000—were in full swing by nightfall.

Severalty. The completion of the land-grabbing process was hastened, ironically, by the avowed friends of the native Americans. The Indians had never lacked sympathizers, especially in the East. After the Civil War, reformers created the Indian Rights Association. The movement got a big boost from Helen Hunt Jackson's powerful book *A Century of Dishonor* (1881), which told the story of the unjust treatment of the Indians. The reformers, however, had little sympathy for the tribal way of life. They could think of no other future for the Indian than assimilation into white society.

During the 1870s, the Indian Office had developed a program to train Indian children for farming and manual work and to prepare them for citizenship. Some attended reservation schools, while the less lucky were sent to boarding schools distant from family and home. The reformers approved of this educational program. They also favored the deliberate efforts by the Office of Indian Affairs to undercut tribal authority. In particular, they highly esteemed private property as a "civilizing" force.

The resulting policy was called *severalty:* the division of reservation lands into individually owned parcels. Notwithstanding that private ownership was a notion alien and repugnant to the Indians, or that earlier experiments with land allotments had failed dismally, the reformers remained unshaken in their faith that private property would transform the Indians into prudent, hard-working members of white society. With their blessing, the Dawes Severalty Act of 1887 authorized the president to divide tribal lands, giving 160 acres to each family head and smaller parcels to other individuals. The land would be held in trust by the government for twenty-five years, and the recipients would become U.S. citizens. Remaining reservation lands would be sold off, with the proceeds to be placed in an Indian education fund.

The Last Battle: Wounded Knee. The Sioux were among the first to feel the full effect of the Dawes act. According to the proposed allotments, roughly half their Dakota lands would become "surplus" and available for white settlement. The government drew up a plan breaking up the Sioux reservation into six smaller ones, and once again began the familiar process of negotiating assent from the unwilling Indians. This time the Sioux were determined not to be taken in: they would not bargain, they would simply say no. But once again they ultimately succumbed to coercion, golden promises, and division in their own ranks.

On February 10, 1890, the federal government announced that it had gained the required number of Sioux signatures (three quarters of the population) and threw the ceded land open to white settlement. But no surveys had yet been made for the reservation boundaries, nor any provision for land allotments for the Indians living in the ceded lands. On top of these signs of bad faith, there came drought that wiped out the Indians' crops. It seemed beyond endurance. They had lost their ancestral lands. They faced a future as sedentary farmers that was alien to all their traditions. And immediately confronting them was a hard winter of starvation.

But news of salvation had also come. An Indian Messiah, a holy man who called himself Wovoka, was preaching a new religion on a Paiute reservation in Nevada. In a vision, Wovoka had gone to heaven and received God's word that the world would be regenerated. The whites would disappear, all the Indians of past generations would return to earth, and life on the Great Plains would go back to the time of the roaming buffalo. All this would come to pass in the spring of 1891. Preparatory to that great day, the Indians should follow Wovoka's commandments and practice the Ghost Dance. This daylong submersion in dancing and praying brought participants into trancelike states during which their spirits rose to heaven. Wovoka's teachings were nonviolent and not specifically antiwhite, but among Wovoka's Sioux adherents the new religion took a belligerent and increasingly threatening turn toward white settlers. As the frenzy of the Ghost Dance swept through some of the Sioux encampments in the fall of 1890, resident whites became alarmed and called for army intervention.

Tragedy was almost inescapable. Confined as they were within their shrunken reservations, the Sioux had no hope of prevailing against the rapid military build-up. But neither did it seem possible to pacify them without letting loose a bloodbath. When Indian police backed by federal troops tried to arrest Sitting Bull on December 14, a gun battle broke out, killing the old chief and at least twelve others. Worse was to come. Among the Minneconjou, the medicine man Yellow Bird had stirred up a fervent Ghost Dance following. But, with their chief Big Foot desperately sick with pneumonia, they had given up and come in under military escort to an encampment at Wounded Knee Creek on December 28. The next morning, when the soldiers attempted to disarm the Indians, a battle exploded in the midst of the encampment. In the document on page 528, Black Elk describes what happened. Among the U.S. troopers, 25 died; among the Indians, 153 men, women, and children perished, plus probably 20 or more whose bodies were not found.

AMERICAN VOICES

Wounded Knee: "Something terrible happened. . . ."
Black Elk

Black Elk, an Oglala Sioux holy man, was at Wounded Knee when the killing happened. This is his account, as he recollected the event forty years later.

It was in the evening when we heard that the Big Foots were camped over there with the soldiers. . . . In the morning [December 29, 1890] I went out after my horses, and while I was out I heard shooting off toward the east, and I knew from the sound that it must be wagon guns [cannon] going off. The sounds went right through my body, and I felt that something terrible would happen. . . .

A little way ahead of us, just below the head of the dry gulch, there were some women and children who were huddled under a clay bank, and some cavalrymen were there pointing guns at them. . . .

I had no gun, and when we were charging, I just held the sacred bow out in front of me with my right hand. The bullets did not hit us at all. . . .

After the soldiers marched away, I heard from my friend, Dog Chief, how the trouble started, and he was right there by Yellow Bird when it happened. This is the way it was:

In the morning the soldiers began to take all the guns away from the Big Foots. Soldiers were on the little hill and all around, and there were soldiers across the dry gulch to the south and over east along Wounded Knee Creek too. The people were nearly surrounded, and the wagon-guns were pointing at them.

Some had not yet given up their guns, and so the soldiers were searching all the tepees, throwing things around and poking into everything. There was a man called Yellow Bird, and he and another man were standing in front of the tepee where Big Foot was lying sick. They had white sheets around and over them, with eyeholes to look through, and they had guns under these. An officer came to search them. He took the other man's gun, and then started to take Yellow Bird's. But Yellow Bird would not let go. He wrestled with the officer, and while they were wrestling, the gun went off and killed the officer. As soon as the gun went off, Dog Chief told me, an officer shot and killed Big Foot who was lying sick inside the tepee.

Then suddenly nobody knew what was happening, except that the soldiers were all shooting and the wagon-guns began going off right in among the people.

Many were shot down right there. The women and children ran into the gulch and up west, dropping all the time, for the soldiers shot them as they ran. There were only about a hundred warriors and there were nearly five hundred soldiers. The warriors rushed to where they had piled their guns and knives. They fought soldiers with only their hands until they got their guns. . . .

It was a good winter day when all this happened. The sun was shining. But after the soldiers marched away from their dirty work, a heavy snow began to fall. The wind came up in the night. There was a big blizzard, and it grew very cold. The snow drifted deep in the crooked gulch, and it was one long grave of butchered women and children and babies, who had never done any harm and were only trying to run away.

Source: John G. Neihardt, ed., *Black Elk Speaks: The Legendary 'Book of Visions' of an American Indian* (1932; New York: William Morrow and Co., 1971), pp. 216–23.

In December 1890, U.S. soldiers massacred about one hundred seventy-five Sioux men, women and children in the Battle of Wounded Knee in South Dakota. It was the last big fight on the northern plains between the Indians and the whites. Black Elk, a Sioux holy man, related that "after the soldiers marched away from their dirty work, a heavy snow began to fall . . . and it grew very cold." The body of Yellow Bird lay frozen where it had fallen.

Wounded Knee was the final episode in the long war of suppression of the Plains Indians, but not the end of their story. The process of severalty now proceeded without hindrance. On the Dakota lands, the Teton Sioux fared relatively well, and many of the younger generation settled down as small farmers and stock grazers. In general, however, the Indians gained little profit from the land to which they received title as individuals. Their vulnerability spawned an industry of land-leasing scams, followed by sale of their land once the twenty-five year trustee period forbidding the transfer of legal title expired. On the Indian reservations of the Oklahoma Territory, where this process went on with wild abandon, expropriation took scarcely two decades. When Oklahoma became a state in 1907, Indians made up a scattered minority of 70,000 among a million whites. As an Oklahoma editor put it in the year of statehood: "Sympathy and sentiment never stand in the way of the onward march of empire."

California and the Far West

In 1860, when the Great Plains was still Indian country, the booming state of California already had 300,000 residents, 57,000 of them in the bustling metropolis of San Francisco. California never conformed very closely to the prevailing conception of a "frontier" settlement. For one thing, California was not empty of "civilization" when the Americans began to arrive in significant numbers during the 1840s. Settled as an outpost of the Spanish empire in the late eighteenth century, California had roughly 8,000 Spanish-speaking inhabitants and a functioning ranching economy at the time that it was seized in 1848 by the United States from Mexico as part of the spoils of war. Moreover, although many Americans came overland, there was always sea access to California, and maritime commerce crucially shaped its growth from the outset. Finally, Indian resistance was nothing like what settlers had encountered farther east. Already subdued by half a century of Spanish rule, the California Indians lacked a tribal structure, a warrior tradition, or the farming skills of other sedentary Indians. These tribes were easy prey for the aggressive miners and settlers flooding into California, who, in short order, virtually exterminated them. Of the 100,000 Indians who had been living in California in the 1840s, scarcely 15,000 remained by 1900 in remote and barren reservations.

California was the anchor of two distinct far western regions. First, it joined with the present-day states of Oregon and Washington to form the Pacific slope. And second, by climate and Hispanic heritage, it was linked to the Southwest, which today includes Arizona and New Mexico.

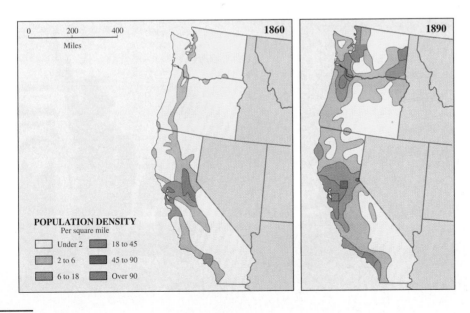

MAP 17.5

The Settlement of the Pacific Slope
In 1860 the settlement of the Pacific Slope was remarkably uneven—fully underway in northern California, scarcely begun anywhere else. By 1890, a new pattern had begun to emerge, with the swift growth of southern California already foreshadowed and the settlement of the Pacific Northwest well-launched.

Hispanics, Chinese, Anglos

The Hispanic Southwest. California was the westernmost end of a crescent of Spanish-speaking communities that extended across the American Southwest as far as San Antonio, Texas. The oldest and most stable settlements were along the upper Rio Grande Valley in New Mexico around Santa Fe, an adobe town that was over two hundred years old in 1860 and contained at that time 4,635 residents. The economy of this entire Hispanic crescent consisted primarily of cattle and sheep raising with some small-scale mining and trading. The social order was highly stratified and traditional. At the top was an aristocracy of large landowners; at the bottom, with little in between, was a Mexican peasantry that served as herders and farm hands on the big ranches or lived as subsistence farmers in small villages.

The survival of this Spanish-Mexican crescent after its incorporation into the United States depended very much on the rate of Anglo immigration. In New Mexico, which was off the beaten track before the arrival of railroads in the 1880s, the old culture more than held its own, incorporating through intermarriage and partnerships the Anglo newcomers into the Hispanic elite of Santa Fe. As the army broke the resistance of the warlike Navaho, Apache, and Ute tribes, moreover, New Mexican settlement expanded up into Colorado, and along the rivers and valleys into Texas and Arizona.

Most active in this Hispanic expansion were the New Mexico peasantry. The robustness of their subsistence culture stemmed from a division of labor that gave women a central productive role in the village economy. Women raised much of the family food in small gardens, engaged in village bartering trade, made the clothes, and plastered the adobe houses. When the Anglo economy pressed in during the 1880s, the men began to leave the villages seasonally to work on the railroads or in the Colorado mines and sugar-beet fields, thereby earning crucial dollars while leaving the village economy ever more firmly in their wives' hands.

Vaqueros in a Corral
On California cattle ranches, owners relied on Mexican cowhands—*vaqueros*—whose skills as riders and rope handlers were unexcelled. This striking painting was done in 1877 by the artist James Walker, who came from New York City but had a special enthusiasm for southwestern scenes. (The Thomas Gilcrease Institute)

When Texas cattle ranchers forced their way into an area known as the Las Vegas Grant, the Mexicans long settled there, *los pobres* (the poor ones), organized themselves into masked night-riding raiders and in 1889 and 1890 mounted an effective campaign of harassment against the Anglo interlopers. A vigorous Hispanic culture, with its hub around Santa Fe, thus stubbornly held its own within the American Southwest.

In California, on the other hand, the Spanish-speaking society was rapidly overwhelmed by the flood of Yankee migrants. The expropriation of the great ranchos was relentless, accomplished partly by legal challenges to the authenticity of the land grants, partly by the spendthrift ways of the *Californios* themselves. By the 1880s just a handful of the original families—the Dominguezes near Los Angeles, for example—managed to hold on to their Mexican land grants.

Only in the slow-growing southern part of the state did Hispanic communities retain a significant foothold. Overwhelmingly Spanish-speaking in the early decades, Los Angeles still counted 20 percent with Spanish surnames among its 11,000 inhabitants in 1880. Partly the remnants of the *Californio* working people, partly more recent migrants from Mexico, these Angelenos were mostly manual laborers and poor artisans, and they already formed what was identifiably a *barrio*—a distinct ethnic neighborhood—in the old downtown. At that point, an Anglo influx into southern California suddenly began, but so, more slowly, did the migration from old Mexico.

Mexican Immigrants. All along the Southwest borderlands, economic activity was picking up. Railroads were being built, copper mines were opening in Arizona, cotton and vegetable agriculture were developing in south Texas, and irrigated fruit growing was being introduced in southern California. There is no way of knowing precisely how many Mexicans migrated to the work thus created, since the borders were open until 1917 and few bothered to register when they entered the United States. But clearly their numbers were increasing from the 1880s onward; one estimate puts the number of immigrants arriving in 1900 at between 60,000 and 100,000. Some came as contract workers for railway track gangs and harvest labor; virtually all were relegated to the lowest-paying and most backbreaking work; and everywhere they were discriminated against and reviled by higher-status Anglo workers. Mostly the Mexicans came as short-term and casual workers, not as permanent settlers, but some remained and swelled the numbers and resources of the Mexican-American communities of the Southwest borderland cities from El Paso to Los Angeles.

What stimulated the Mexican immigration, of course, was the enormous need for labor by a region undergoing explosive economic development. Hence the exceptionally high numbers of immigrants generally in the California population of this era: between 1860 and 1890, roughly one-third were foreign-born, more than twice the level for the country as a whole. Many came from Europe; most numerous were the Irish, then the Germans and British. But there was also another group that was unique to the West—the Chinese.

The Chinese in California. Attracted first by the California gold rush of 1849, over 200,000 Chinese migrated to the United States over the next three decades. In those years they constituted a considerable minority of California's population—around 9 percent—and because virtually all were economically active, they represented a much larger proportion of the state's labor force—probably a quarter in 1870. The coming of the Chinese to California was not an isolated event, but part of a larger, world-wide pattern of Asian migration that began in the mid-nineteenth century. Driven by poverty from their overpopulated lands, Chinese went to Australia, Hawaii, and Latin America, Indians to Fiji and South Africa, and Javanese to Dutch colonies in the Caribbean. Most of these Asians migrated under the system of indentured or coerced servitude. That was not true of the Chinese who came to America. Contrary to the stubborn popular image of a "coolie trade," theirs was an essentially voluntary movement, mostly financed by a *credit-ticket system*. Under this system, migrants merely borrowed passage money from a broker; unlike indentured servants, they retained their personal freedom and the right to choose their employer.

Building the Central Pacific
Chinese laborers at work on the great trestle spanning the canyon at Secrettown in the Sierra Nevada.

Market Scene, Sansome Street
This exuberant painting by William Hahn captures downtown San Francisco as he
saw it in 1872, a veritable boiling pot of races (note the black woman at left, the
Chinese group at right) and classes (note, in the midst of the market bustle, the proper
lady at far left, with her Lord-Fauntleroy son). It was its role as metropolis for the entire Far West that gave San Francisco the great vitality conveyed in this painting.
(Crocker Art Museum)

Once they arrived, however, Chinese immigrants
normally entered the orbit of the Six Companies—the
powerful confederation of Chinese merchants in San
Francisco's Chinatown. Most of the arrivals were unat-
tached males eager to earn a stake and return to their
native villages in Canton province. The Six Companies
acted not only as an employment agency, but provided
them with all the social and commercial services they
needed to survive in an alien world. The small number
of Chinese women—the male/female ratio was thirteen
to one—worked mostly as prostitutes, sad victims
drawn from the bottom of the world of poverty that
drove the Chinese to America. Some were sold by
impoverished parents; others had been enticed into
fraudulent marriages or kidnapped by procurers and
smuggled into American ports.

Until the early 1860s, when surface mining played
out, Chinese men labored mainly in the gold fields—as
prospectors where the white miners permitted it, as laborers and cooks where they did not. Then, when the
transcontinental railroad was started in 1865, the Central Pacific began to recruit Chinese workers. Eventually they constituted four-fifths of the railroad's entire
labor force. With as many as 11,000 working at any
one time, the Chinese accomplished by their sheer
physical labor the extraordinary feat of thrusting the
railroad across the High Sierras. The Central Pacific
perfected a system of contract labor for employing the
Chinese. Many were recruited directly from around
Canton by labor agents and worked as labor gangs
under the control of "China bosses," who not only supervised but fed, housed, paid, and often cheated them.

When the transcontinental railroad was completed in 1869, the Chinese scattered. Some continued to work in construction gangs for the railroads, others labored on swamp-drainage and irrigation projects in the Central Valley and then became agricultural workers. Chinese settlements could be found across the Far West, but most Chinese remained in California. In San Francisco many of them became factory workers. The Chinese were excluded from higher-wage trades, but they soon dominated certain industries—such as cigar-making—that competed with eastern products and could survive only with cheap labor. "Wherever we put them, we found them good," remarked Charles Crocker, one of the Big Four of the Central Pacific. From the standpoint of employers, "their orderly and industrious habits make them a very desirable class of immigrants."

The Anti-Chinese Agitation. White workers, however, did not share this enthusiasm for Chinese labor. Why they should have taken so venomous a view of the Chinese has never been easy to explain. It involved, most certainly, a sense of unfair economic competition that pitted them against "Chinamen's wages" and "Chinamen's living conditions." But the hatred clearly went deeper. In other parts of the country, popular racism was directed against African-Americans; in California (where blacks were few in number) it found a target in the Chinese. They were "an infusible element" who could not be assimilated into American society, wrote the young journalist Henry George in a famous 1869 letter that made his reputation as a spokesman for California labor. "They practice all the unnameable vices of the East. [They are] utter heathens, treacherous, sensual, cowardly and cruel." Sadly, this vicious racism was intertwined with labor's republican ideals. The Chinese, argued George, would drive out free labor, "make nabobs and princes of our capitalists, and crush our working classes into the dust . . . substitut[ing] . . . a population of serfs and their masters for that population of intelligent freemen who are our glory and our strength."

The anti-Chinese agitation climaxed in San Francisco in the late 1870s when mobs ruled the streets, at one point threatening to burn the docks of the Pacific Mail Steamship Company from which the Chinese arrivals disembarked. The principal agitator, an Irish teamster named Denis Kearney, quickly became a dominant figure in the California labor movement. Under the slogan "The Chinese Must Go!" Kearney led a Workingmen's party which strongly challenged the state's major parties. Both of those parties, however, had already jumped on the anti-Chinese bandwagon—the Democrats enthusiastically, eager to recover their popularity after the Civil War, the Republicans more reluc-

tantly, in the face of an issue too potent to resist. Finally, after renegotiating an end to the free-immigration provision of the Burlingame Treaty (1868) with China, Congress in 1882 adopted the Chinese Exclusion Act, which barred the further entry of Chinese laborers into the country.

Chinese immigration effectively came to an end, but not the demand for cheap labor that had drawn the Chinese to America in the first place. If anything, California's need intensified because its agriculture was shifting from wheat, the state's first great cash crop, to fruits and vegetables. These row crops needed lots of workers: stoop labor, meagerly paid, and mostly seasonal. This was not, as one San Francisco journalist put it, "white men's work."

That ugly phrase serves as a touchstone for California agricultural labor as it would thereafter develop—a kind of caste labor system, always drawing downtrodden, foot-loose whites into it, yet basically defined along color lines. But if not the Chinese, then who? First, Japanese immigrants, who came in increasing numbers and by the early twentieth century constituted half the state's agricultural labor force. Then, when rising anti-Japanese agitation closed off that population flow as well in 1908, Mexico became the next, essentially permanent, provider of migratory workers for California's booming commercial agriculture.

The irony of the state's social evolution is painful to behold. Here was California, the last, best hope of the American Dream, a land of limitless opportunity, boastful of its democratic egalitarianism. Yet simultaneously, and from its very birth, it was a racially torn society, at once exploiting and despising the Hispanic and Asian minorities whose hard labor helped make California the enviable land it was.

The Golden West

Had gold not been discovered at Sutter's mill in 1848, California's history would certainly have been very different. At that time it was a remote place, hard to get to, with a semiarid climate uninviting to American farmers. "The country is hilly and mountainous," noted a U.S. Navy officer in 1849. "Great dryness prevails during the summer, and occasionally excessive droughts parch up the soil." California, he concluded, would never be "susceptible of supporting a very large population." In fact, Oregon's Willamette Valley had been for the westward-bound settlers of the 1840s much the preferred place. And, but for gold rush, California's early development would likely have been very like that of the

Willamette Valley—an economic backwater, lacking markets for its products, slow to attract newcomers. In 1870, a decade after it had achieved statehood, Oregon still had scarcely 90,000 residents.

The hundreds of thousands of fortune seekers who descended on California changed everything. Mineral wealth poured in, first from the gold country, then from Nevada's Comstock Lode, and finally from mining sites up and down the Far West. Railroad building accelerated. Agriculture boomed. And so, as they found a market in California, did the timber industry, fisheries, and farms of Oregon and Washington. During the 1880s, both states grew prodigiously. By 1890, Oregon had 318,000 people, while Washington (which became a state in 1889) had a population of 357,000, and was by then finally linked to the east by the Northern Pacific and Great Northern railroads.

California counted over a million residents that year, fully a quarter of whom lived in San Francisco. Life in California offered all that the modern world of 1890 had to offer—a cosmopolitan city, comfortable travel, a high living standard, colleges and universities, even resident painters and writers.

And yet California was still remote from the rest of America, still a long journey away and, of course, differently and spectacularly endowed by nature. Location, environment, and history all conspired to set California somewhat apart from the American nation. And so, in certain ways, did the Californians.

California Culture. What Californians sought, first of all, was a cultural tradition of their own. Closest to hand was the bonanza era of the Forty-Niners. California had the great good fortune of attracting to its parts one Samuel Clemens. Clemens arrived in the Nevada Territory in 1861, did a bit of prospecting, became a reporter in Nevada City, adopted the pen name Mark Twain, and moved in 1864 to San Francisco, where he became a newspaper columnist writing about what he pronounced to be "the livest, heartiest community on our continent."

Exiled briefly in 1865 to Angel's Camp in the Sierra foothills because his sharp pen had made him some dangerous enemies, Twain listened to the tales of the old miners from the neighborhood. One he jotted in his notebook, as follows:

> Coleman with his jumping frog—bet stranger $50— stranger had no frog, and C. got him one:—in the meantime stranger filled C's frog full of shot and he couldn't jump. The stranger's frog won.

In Twain's hands, this fragment was transformed into a marvelous tall tale that caught the imagination of the country and made his reputation as a humorist. What "The Celebrated Jumping Frog of Calaveras County" had somehow encapsulated was the entire world of make-or-break optimism in the mining camps.

In such short stories as "The Luck of Roaring Camp" and "The Outcasts of Poker Flat," Twain's fellow San Franciscan Bret Harte developed this theme in a more literary fashion and firmly implanted it in California's memory. Other writers—among them amateur historian Charles Howard Shinn in his *Mining Camps: A Study in American Frontier Government* (1885)— gave a more serious gloss to California's bonanza origins. Even so, this past was too raw, too suggestive of the tattered beginnings of so many of the state's leading citizens—in short, too disreputable—for an up-and-coming society.

Then, in 1884, Helen Hunt Jackson published her novel *Ramona*. In this story of a half-caste girl caught between two cultures, Jackson intended to advance the cause of the Indians, but she placed her tale in the evocative context of Old California, and that rang an immediate bell. By then, the Spanish missions—disestablished by the Mexican government back in 1833, long before the arrival of the Yankees—had fallen into total disrepair and the padres were wholly forgotten, their Indian acolytes scattered and in dire poverty. Now that lost world of "sun, silence and adobe" became all the rage. Sentimental novels and histories appeared in abundance. There was a movement to restore the missions (though not with aid to the Indians in mind). The Spanish-Mexican dons of the great ranchos became larger in death than they had ever been in life. Many communities began to stage Spanish fiestas, and the mission style of architecture enjoyed a great vogue among developers. In its Spanish past California found the cultural traditions it needed. Very much the same kind of discovery was taking place elsewhere in the Southwest, although, in the case of Santa Fe and Taos, with considerably more authenticity.

Land of Sunshine. All this enthusiasm was of course strongly tinged with commercialism. And this was even more true of a second distinctive feature of California's development. The southern part of the state was neglected, thinly populated and too dry for anything more than grazing and some chancy wheat growing. What it did have, however, was an abundance of sunshine. At the beginning of the 1880s there burst upon the country amazing publicity about the charms of southern California. "There is not any malaria, hay fever, loss of appetite, or languor in the air; nor any thunder, lightning, mad dogs . . . or cold snaps." This was mostly the work of the Southern Pacific Railroad, which had reached Los Angeles in 1876 and was anxious for business.

When the Santa Fe arrived in 1885, a furious rate war broke out, and it became possible to travel all the way from Chicago or St. Louis to Los Angeles for $25 or less. Thousands of people, mostly midwesterners, poured in; a dizzying real estate boom developed, along with the frantic building of such resort hotels as San Diego's opulent Hotel del Coronado. Los Angeles County had less than 3 percent of the state's population in 1870; it had 12 percent by 1900. Although the real estate bubble collapsed at the end of the 1880s, by then southern California had firmly established itself as the land of sunshine and orange groves. It had found a way to translate climate into riches.

The Great Outdoors. That California was specially favored by nature some Californians knew even as its great stands of redwoods and sugar pine were being hacked down, the soil depleted by the relentless cycle of wheat crops, the streams polluted, and the hills torn apart by reckless mining techniques. Back in 1864 influential Americans who had seen it prevailed on Congress to grant to the state of California "the Cleft, or Gorge in the granite peak of the Sierra Nevada Mountain, known as Yosemite Valley," which would thereafter be reserved "for public pleasuring, resort, and recreation." When the young naturalist John Muir arrived in California four years later, he made straight for Yosemite. Its "grandeur . . . comes as an endless revelation," he wrote. Muir, and others like him, became devoted to studying the High Sierras, and protecting them from "despoiling gain-seekers . . . eagerly trying to make everything immediately and selfishly commercial." One result was the creation of California's national parks in 1890—Yosemite, Sequoia, King's Canyon. Another was the formation in 1892 of the Sierra Club, which became a powerful voice for the defenders of California's wilderness.

They won some and lost some. In particular, there was an uphill battle against the advocates of water-resource development, who insisted that California's irrigated agriculture and thirsty cities could not grow without tapping the abundant snowpack of the Sierras. By the turn of the century, Los Angeles faced a water crisis that threatened its further growth. The answer was a 238-mile aqueduct to the Owens River in the southern Sierra. A bitter controversy blew up over this immense project, driven by objections by local residents and preservationists to the damming up of the beautiful Owens Valley. More painful yet was the defeat suffered by John Muir and his allies in their battle to save the Hetch-Hetchy gorge north of the Yosemite National Park. In 1913, after years of controversy, the federal government approved the damming of Hetch Hetchy to serve the water needs of San Francisco.

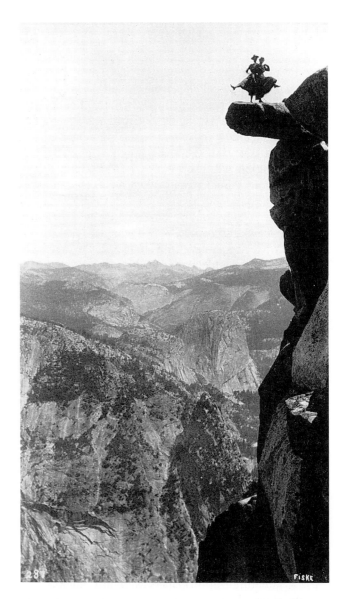

Kitty Tatch and Friend on Glacier Point, Yosemite
From the time the Yosemite Valley was first set aside in 1864 as a place for "public pleasuring, resort, and recreation," it attracted a stream of tourists eager to experience the grandeur of the American West. As is suggested by this photograph taken sometime in the 1890s, the magic of Yosemite was enough to set even staid young ladies a-dancing.

When the development stakes became high enough, nature lovers like John Muir generally came out on the short end. Even so, something original and distinctive had been added to California's heritage—the linking of a society's well-being with the preservation of its natural environment.

The Agricultural Interest

In certain grain-growing areas, as in California's Central Valley until the 1890s, farmers might be large-scale, even corporate, operators. In the South after Reconstruction, the typical farmer was a tenant or sharecropper. Elsewhere, and most generally, farmers were independent freeholders, operating their own family farms. The freeholder tradition was deeply rooted in the Jeffersonian ideal of a nation of virtuous yeomen farmers and was enshrined in the policy of free land for the settler. Generation after generation of farmers had joined the westward movement aspiring to this freeholder ideal. In the face of the treeless Great Plains, however, they had hesitated, permitting miners and ranchers to precede them. Then, in the 1870s, they overcame the mental barrier created by the notion of a Great American Desert.

The Farmers' Last Frontier

As the midwestern states filled up, farmers began to look hungrily farther west. Farmers in Europe, especially in Scandinavia, also were eager to find a place in America. Land speculators, steamship lines, and the western states and territories all encouraged settlement of the Great Plains. Railroads, anxious to sell their huge land holdings and develop traffic for their routes, became especially active sponsors of settlement programs.

Federal land policy also offered a strong attraction. Under the Homestead Act of 1862, settlers could obtain 160 acres of public land free, except for a filing fee, if they lived on it for five years. Aliens who had taken out their first naturalization papers were also eligible. Although married women could not file claims, widows and single women had the same rights as men. In fact, according to the land-office records for Colorado and Wyoming, 12 percent of the homestead filers were women. Beginning in 1873, with the passage of the Timber Culture Act, settlers could claim an additional 160 acres if they planted trees on at least a fourth of the land.

None of these forces, however, could have pushed the agricultural frontier far out on to the plains without the intervention of a highly inventive society. The notion of a Great American Desert, illusion though it was, did point to a plain truth: the grasslands could not be worked by the methods known to American farmers at the time.

Consider the absence of trees. Determined pioneers could manage the problem of shelter by cutting dugouts in the sides of hills. Then they built sod houses, using strips of turf cut from the ground. These crude homes served—often for years—until the settler had earned enough money to buy lumber for a proper house and barn. But what about fencing to protect the crops? A furious patent race developed to meet this crucial need. In 1874 Joseph F. Glidden, an Illinois farmer, invented barbed wire, which provided a cheap, effective barrier against roaming cattle.

The dry climate presented a tougher problem. The eastern, high-grass prairie received enough rain for grain crops. But west of the ninety-eighth meridian the annual rainfall averaged less than 20 inches. The Mormons living in the area near the Great Salt Lake had demonstrated how irrigation could turn a wasteland into a garden. But the Great Plains lacked the surface water needed for irrigation. The answer lay in dry-farming methods, which involved deep planting to bring subsoil moisture to the roots and quick harrowing after rainfalls to turn over a dry mulch that slowed evaporation.

Dry farming produced a low yield per acre. To be profitable, a semiarid farm had to operate on a scale much larger than an eastern farm. Therefore it had to rely much more on machinery. Western mechanized farming developed most fully on the corporate farms that covered up to 100,000 acres in the Red River Valley in the Dakota Territory. But even family farms, which remained the norm elsewhere, could not operate with less than 300 acres of cereal crops and so required machinery for plowing, planting, and harvesting. Such basic inventions as the McCormick reaper had

Homesteading on the Great Plains
This was what their homestead looked like when Peter Widvey, a Swedish Lutheran minister, and his family were starting out in 1891. At the upper lefthand corner is the dugout in which they lived before their house was built and a farm carved out of this bleak landscape north of Round Valley, Custer County, Nebraska.

AMERICAN VOICES

Swedish Emigrant in Frontier Kansas *Ida Lindgren*

Like many emigrants, Ida Lindgren did not find it easy to adjust to the harsh new life on the frontier. Her diary entries and letters home show that the adjustment for the first generation was never complete.

15 May 1870 [Lake Sibley, Nebraska]

What shall I say? Why has the lord brought us here? Oh, I feel so oppressed, so unhappy! Two whole days it took us to get here and they were not the least trying part of our travels. We sat on boards in the work-wagon packed in so tightly that we could not move a foot, and we drove across endless, endless prairies, on narrow roads; no, no, not roads, tracks like those in the fields at home when they harvested grain. No forest but only a few trees which grow along the rivers and creeks. And then here and there you see a homestead and pass a little settlement. The Indians are not so far away from here, I can understand, and all the men you see coming by, riding or driving wagons, are armed with revolvers and long carbines, and look like highway robbers.

No date [probably written July 1870]

Claus and his wife lost their youngest child at Lake Sibley and it was very sad in many ways. There was no real cemetery but out on the prairie stood a large, solitary tree, and around it they bury their dead, without tolling of bells, without a pastor, and sometimes without any coffin. A coffin was made here for their child, it was not painted black, but we lined it with flowers and one of the men read the funeral service, and then there was a hymn, and that was all.

August 25, 1874 [Manhattan, Kansas]

It has been a long time since I have written, hasn't it? . . . when one never has anything fun to write about, it is no fun to write . . . We have not had rain since the beginning of June, and then with this heat and often strong winds as well, you can imagine how everything has dried out. There has also been a general lamentation and fear for the coming year. We are glad we have the oats (for many don't have any and must feed wheat to the stock) and had hoped to have the corn leaves

to add to the fodder. But then one fine day there came millions, trillions of grasshoppers in great clouds, hiding the sun, and coming down into the fields, eating up *everything* that was still there, the leaves on the trees, peaches, grapes, cucumbers, onions, cabbage, everything, everything. Only the peach stones still hung on the trees, showing what had once been there.

July 1, 1877 [Manhattan, Kansas]

. . . It seems so strange to me when I think that more than seven years have passed since I have seen you all . . . . I can see so clearly that last glimpse I had of Mamma, standing alone amid all the tracks of Eslov station. Oliva I last saw sitting on her sofa in her red and black dress, holding little Brita, one month old, on her lap. And Wilhelm I last saw in Lund at the station, as he rolled away with the train, waving his last farewell to me . . . .

Source: H. Arnold Barton, ed. *Letters from the Promised Land.* Minneapolis: University of Minnesota Press, 1975, 143–145, 150–156.

appeared before the Civil War; but only later did the farm-equipment industry pick up speed in response to the demand of western farmers.

Despite barbed wire, dry-farming methods, and harvesting machines, the push into the semiarid lands required a great deal of wish fulfillment. The Great Plains happened to experience a wet cycle between 1878 and 1886. "As the plains are settled up we hear less and less of drouth, hot winds, alkali and other bugbears that used to hold back the adventurous," remarked one Nebraska man. Some settlers attributed the increased rainfall to soil cultivation and tree planting, which somehow generated air moisture and caused more rain. Others credited God. As one settler on the southern plains remarked, "The Lord just knew we needed more land an' He's gone and changed the cli-

mate." But no matter how they explained it—and no matter how much scientists warned otherwise—settlers moved westward convinced that the increased rainfall was permanent.

No amount of optimism, however, could take away the hardships of that migration, which seemed to fall disproportionately on the women. "That last separating word *Farewell!* sinks deeply into the heart," one pioneer woman recorded in her diary, thinking of family and friends left behind. Emigrants had always taken parting as a kind of death, with reunion unlikely "on this side of the dark river." But then came the treeless land, more alien and frightening than anything previously encountered in the westward settlement. "Endless, endless prairies," wrote the Swedish woman Ida Lindgren from her covered wagon in Kansas; or, from a

Nebraska-bound woman, "such an air of desolation"; and, from the Texas plains, "such a lonely country." There was a liberating side to frontier life as well, of course—the breakdown of gender roles as women shouldered men's work on new farms; for many, a heightened sense of self-reliance in the face of danger and hardship; and, as new communities sprang up, opportunities to teach school, run boardinghouses, participate in church and town affairs. Yet, one can surmise from Ida Lindgren's letters how hard life was for settlers, with the unrelenting round of toil, the harsh climate and primitive sod-house living, the crushed hopes when the rains failed or the grasshoppers swept in, and, of course, the loneliness.

Nothing, at any rate, seemed in the least to discourage the final frontier thrust across the continental United States. More land came under cultivation between 1870 and 1900 than in the previous 250 years. More than a million people went west from the settled

Midwest during the 1880s. "Hardly anything else was talked about," recalled the short-story writer Hamlin Garland about his Iowa neighbors. "Every man who could sell out had gone west or was going. . . . Farmer after farmer joined the march to Kansas, Nebraska, and Dakota. . . . The movement . . . had . . . become an exodus, a stampede."

The Exodusters. For some southern blacks, Kansas briefly represented something even more precious—the modern land of Canaan. Blacks from Kentucky and Tennessee had been migrating to Kansas all through the 1870s. Then in the spring of 1879, with Reconstruction over and federal protection withdrawn, religious enthusiasm for Kansas swept through the terror-stricken black communities of Louisiana and Mississippi. Within a month or so, some 6,000 blacks arrived via St. Louis, most of them with nothing more than the clothes on their backs and faith in the Good Lord. How many of these Exodusters remained it is hard to say, but the 1880 Census reported 40,000 blacks in Kansas, by far the largest African-American concentration in the Great West aside from Texas, whose expanding cotton frontier attracted hundreds of thousands of black migrants during the 1870s and 1880s.

On the northern plains European immigration contributed a mighty share. At the peak of the "American fever" in 1882, over 105,000 Scandinavians emigrated to the United States. Swedish and Norwegian became the primary languages of entire areas of Minnesota and Dakota.

By 1880, Kansas was home to 850,000 people. Dakota, which had been very thinly settled when it became a territory in 1861, had 20,000 inhabitants in 1873. Its population jumped to 135,000 in 1880 and all the way to 550,000 in 1885. The dry years that followed reduced the population of North and South

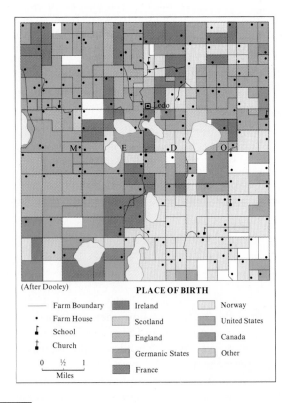

(After Dooley)

PLACE OF BIRTH

— Farm Boundary   ▪ Ireland   ▪ Norway
• Farm House   ▪ Scotland   ▪ United States
⚐ School   ▪ England   ▪ Canada
⚐ Church   ▪ Germanic States   ▪ Other
   ▪ France

0   ½   1
    Miles

MAP 17.6

The Rural Ethnic Mosaic: Blue Earth County, Minnesota, 1880

What could have been more natural for emigrants like Ida Lindgren, in light of the isolation and hardship she describes (see document on page 537) than to settle next to others sharing common ties to a homeland? This map of Medo township reveals that in rural America, no less than in the cities, ethnicity determined where people lived.

Exodusters

Driven by terror raids from their homes, these southern blacks camped out on a Mississippi levee on the way to Kansas.

Dakota (they had become states in 1889) to 500,000 by 1890, and a comparable departure of drought-stricken farmers occurred up and down the Great Plains. But that vast region, where buffalo herds had thrived a few decades earlier, had been conquered. By 1900 about half the nation's cattle and sheep, a third of its cereal crops, and nearly three-fifths of its wheat came from the newly settled lands.

The Farming Business

With the settlement of the Great Plains, the regional patterns of American agriculture became well defined. The wheat belt lay on the western edge of the Midwest, from North Dakota down to Kansas and into northern Texas. Wheat had long been a virgin crop, the first to be planted when new land opened up. As the frontier

moved on, wheat growing moved steadily westward. Wheat farming settled on the Great Plains, partly because of the suitability of the land and partly because of the arrival of hardy Russian varieties. Russian wheat prospered in the harsh plains climate and produced a bread flour superior to that from the soft wheat of milder regions. From Iowa eastward ran the corn belt, which devoted most of its product to feeding livestock. North of the corn belt, the dairy belt stretched from Minnesota as far east as New York and New England. It produced the nation's milk, butter, and cheese. In California, wheat raising gave way to orange groves and a wide variety of fruits and vegetables. In the South, cotton dominated, spreading steadily westward during the last third of the nineteenth century, from the old Cotton Kingdom into Texas to the semiarid line and northward up into Oklahoma and Arkansas.

American farmers stood at the center of a vast and

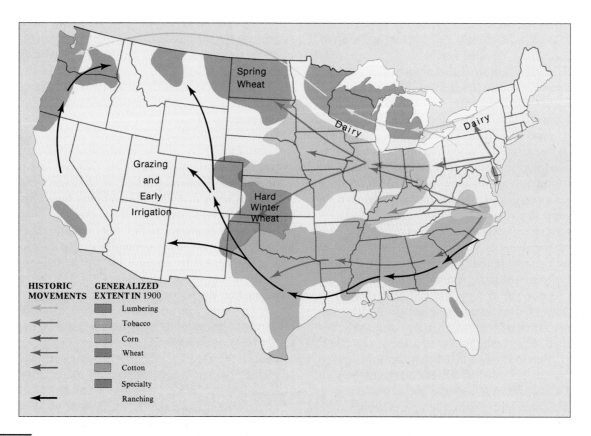

MAP 17.7

Agricultural Regions, 1900

The development of agricultural regions reflected the commercial bent of American agriculture—that is, farmers raised crops for market rather than for home consumption. Regional specialization matched climate and soil to the most suitable crops. The westward movement carried crops westward, of course. Wheat, generally a first crop choice in frontier areas, concentrated finally on the northern and central Plains and in the Northwest. By 1900, the basic pattern of crop specialization was well established in the United States.

complex system of trade. They depended on the railroads to carry their crops to market. A highly sophisticated network of commodity exchanges determined prices and found buyers throughout the country and beyond. Great processing industries turned wheat into flour, livestock into dressed meat, and fruit and vegetables into canned goods. Only through this modern commercial system could farmers gain access to the expanding urban markets in the United States and overseas. About 20 percent of American agricultural production went abroad during the late nineteenth century.

American farmers were likewise well supplied with modern goods and services. They met their credit needs through mortgage companies that drew on eastern and European capital. The McCormick Reaper Company, John Deere and Company, and other manufacturers sold them labor-saving farm machinery. Other industries supplied an increasing share of household and farming needs. "The old rule that a farmer should produce all he required is part of the past," noted a farm journal. "Agriculture, like all other business, is better for its subdivisions, each one growing that which is best suited for his soil, skill, climate and market, and with its proceeds purchasing his other needs."

Farmers eagerly followed this advice. True, subsistence farming persisted in infertile, hilly areas; and general farming, in which no crop represented as much as 40 percent of a farm's total production, went on throughout rural America. But farmers everywhere tended to concentrate on a cash crop, although—excepting in the cotton South—not to the exclusion of some gardening and small-stock raising. As a result, a high degree of regional specialization developed in American agriculture.

This agricultural specialization served as the best indicator of the commercial path taken by American farmers. But there were many other signs as well, such as the attitude toward land. Americans had little of the passionate identification with the soil that tied European peasants to their inherited plots. In 1910 more than half the farmers lived on different land than they had inhabited five years earlier. Farmers saw their acreage as a commodity—to be bought and sold, and to be valued for the price it could bring on the market. In developing areas, farmers believed they could earn as much profit, if not more, from the appreciation of the land's value as from the crops it produced. This attitude fostered the willingness to operate on borrowed capital. In boom times, farmers rushed into debt to extend their land holdings.

The commercial spirit also made farmers enthusiastic about the innovations of the industrial age. Between 1850 and 1900 farm machinery cut production costs for the leading crops by about half. The railroad, especially the prospect of local rail service, delighted the western pioneers. They happily supported whatever inducements might be necessary, such as the public purchase of railway bonds, to lure the line to their towns. And they developed an agricultural system of amazing abundance; farm output more than tripled between 1860 and 1900. To an Austrian observer, the surplus produced seemed "the greatest event of modern times."

Agrarian Distress

Family farms predominated throughout rural America in the late nineteenth century. The average farm comprised about 150 acres and employed an average of fewer than one hired hand. Farm ownership also was widespread. In 1880 owners occupied 75 percent of Iowa's farms. In an age of trusts and corporations, farmers succeeded as did no other group in retaining the *forms* of economic individualism. But their *functions* took them far from the self-sufficient yeoman farmer of Jeffersonian America. They had been fully inducted into the modern economic order.

Farmers participated eagerly in this market economy; they embraced its entrepreneurial spirit. Yet they found themselves more victims than beneficiaries of the modern economy. The late nineteenth century was a time of deep agricultural discontent. For thirty years, as farmers nursed their grievances, protest movements swept across the farm belt.

Farm Life. Part of the farmers' discontent stemmed from the harshness of rural life. No one labored longer or harder. Farmers worked an average of sixty-eight hours a week in 1900, twelve hours longer than industrial workers; in 1850 the difference had been only six hours. Mechanization did not actually reduce work loads on farms, as it generally did in factories. Crop acreage tended to increase in step with more efficient planting and harvest machinery. Most other chores remained on the farmer's shoulders.

For farm women too the burdens increased. Larger harvests meant more field hands for whom to cook and clean up. At the same time, work in the kitchen remained almost unaffected by the conveniences and appliances already commonplace in many urban homes. Laundry was "the most trying" of all household chores, long hours spent lugging and boiling water, bent over wash tubs and rubbing boards. Even on well-equipped farms, one Michigan woman observed, "the women must still do the work much as their mothers did before." "I have in mind a small, delicate woman," wrote another from Pennsylvania, "with a family of small children who does all her own housework, milks four or five cows, cooks for extra help, carries from the spring all the water—no time to read a paper or book. . . . Yet neither [her husband] nor she has any idea they could make her burden easier."

Laundry Day
Of all women's work on the farm, doing the wash was "the most trying . . . ."

On northern farms, women normally did not work in the fields after the pioneering days, although substantial numbers of widows and single women ran farms on their own—300,000 were recorded in the 1900 census. In the South, especially among tenant farmers, both black and white, wives did commonly go into the fields, making "a full hand at whatever the occasion demands—plowing, hoeing, chopping, putting down fertilizer, picking cotton."

Throughout rural America children, as soon as they were old enough, pitched in with the farm chores and field work. "Many a time a shudder has passed through the mother heart of me," said a Missouri woman, "at the sight of some little fellow struggling with the handles of a plow, jerking and stumbling over cloddy ground from daylight till dark. Boys 'making a full hand,' 'helping Pa.'" Farm children in 1900 attended school only two-thirds as many days as did city children, and they left school at an earlier age. In an era of rapidly advancing urban education, farm children still attended gloomy, ungraded one-room schools—hardly the little red schoolhouses of popular mythology.

Farm families may have accepted how hard they labored, how the men and women were worn out and the children sacrificed, for the living they wrested from the soil. It was harder to swallow the widening discrepancy in the quality of life between farm and city. Electricity, indoor plumbing, and paved roads had not yet come to the farm. The rural diet consisted of salt pork, bread, and potatoes for much of the year. Farm sanitation remained primitive. On two-thirds of all farms, according to a survey in 1918 by the U.S. Public Health Service, the water supply was threatened by "potentially dangerous contamination from privy contents."

Hardest to bear was the sense of isolation. On the Great Plains, with its cruel winters and the long, empty distances, loneliness was hard on everyone, but especially on the Scandinavian immigrants.

> Life in the fatherland was hard and toilsome [wrote one critic of dispersed American farming practices], but it was not lonesome. Think for a moment how great the change must be from the white-walled, red-roofed village on a Norway fiord . . . to an isolated cabin on a Dakota prairie, and say if it is any wonder that so many Scandinavians lose their mental balance.

Farm life everywhere, however, tended to be isolated and circumscribed. Rural neighborhoods, even in long-settled areas, totaled 3 or 4 square miles where perhaps a dozen families lived. As one writer remarked, "the end of the neighborhood was almost the end of the world." Hamlin Garland and other authors of the late nineteenth century wrote powerfully about the dullness of the countryside and the lure of the city. "I hate farm life," grumbled one of Garland's heroines. "It's nothing but fret, fret and work the whole time, never going any place, never seeing anybody but a lot of neighbors just as big fools as you are. I spend my time fighting flies and washing dishes and churning. I'm sick of it all."

Understandably, when farmers formed organizations they provided for social activity first of all. This was true of the National Grange of the Patrons of Husbandry, whose local granges spread by the thousands across rural America in the early 1870s. The Grange became the social center for farm families through its fraternal ceremonies and its dances, picnics, and lectures. Women and men joined on an equal footing. Oliver H. Kelley, the government clerk who founded the Grange in 1867, hoped that participation by "the young folks of both sexes . . . will have a tendency to instill in their

Granger Poster

This poster conveys all the longing for community and uplift that drove farmers to organize themselves in the late nineteenth century. It speaks as well of the underlying basis for the outrage they felt as victims of an exploitative economic order: that, as the farmer who produces the society's material wealth, "I pay for it all."

minds a fondness of rural life, and prevent in great measure so many of them flocking to the cities."

Economic Problems. The hunger for social activity cemented organizational ties, but the dynamism of agrarian movements came from economic grievances. The farmers' basic problem was their imperfect participation in the economic transformation of the late nineteenth century. They remained individual operators in a business world that was becoming ever more complex and highly organized. And they were, in certain ways, acutely aware of their predicament.

Farmers understood, for example, the disadvantages they faced as individuals dealing with the big businesses that supplied them with machinery, arranged their credit, and marketed their products. Cooperative activity, especially through stores and creameries, had started before the Civil War. The Grange took up the cooperative idea in a big way by organizing bulk pur-

chasing from manufacturers, along with scattered cooperative banks, insurance companies, grain elevators, and processing plants. In Iowa, the state Grange started to manufacture farm implements in 1873.

Unfortunately, the cooperative record listed many more failures than successes. The opposition by private business was too unrelenting, cooperative managers too unskilled, and the pooled resources of the farmers too thin. Residual benefits did remain, among them an efficient mail-order business that emerged from farmers' hostility to middlemen. In 1872, Montgomery Ward and Company was founded specifically to "meet the wants" of Grange members for everything from clothes to toys and household goods by direct mail order. The early marketing cooperatives also led to more permanent institutions, especially for dairy farmers and fruit growers. Cooperative stores, grain elevators, and telephone exchanges became familiar parts of the countryside throughout rural America. As a solution to the organizational weakness of the late-nineteenth-century farmer in the marketplace, however, cooperative movements had to be accounted a failure.

Another solution was for farmers to enlist the power of government against economic monopoly. Western farmers, generally served by only one grain elevator or railroad, felt continually cheated on storage charges and wheat grading. They also complained about having to pay freight rates higher than those farther east. The Grange was itself strictly a social-educational organization, but it encouraged the formation of independent political parties during the early 1870s that ran on antimonopoly platforms. In a number of states, these parties won control of the legislatures and passed so-called Granger laws regulating grain elevators, fixing maximum railroad rates, and prohibiting discriminatory practices against small and short-haul shippers. In *Munn v. Illinois* (1877), the Supreme Court upheld these laws on the ground that such enterprises involved the public interest and were subject to the police powers of the states. But ten years later a more conservative Supreme Court drastically reduced the scope of state regulatory powers by invoking the interstate commerce clause of the U.S. Constitution. The Court declared that states exceeded their powers when they tried to regulate economic activity that was interstate in character. On that basis, *Wabash v. Illinois* (1886) voided an Illinois law prohibiting long- and short-haul rate discrimination. By then, however, a movement had started for federal regulation of the railroads. The Interstate Commerce Act (1887) created the Interstate Commerce Commission—the first federal regulatory agency—and made railroad regulation a permanent part of national public policy, although, for the next twenty years, not with very much practical effect.

Relief, at least in the short run, came mainly as the

TABLE 17.1

Freight Rates for Transporting Crops

Grand Island to Omaha (150 miles)				Grand Island to Chicago (650 miles)			
Date effective	Corn	Wheat (In cents per hundredweight)	Oats	Date effective	Corn	Wheat (In cents per hundredweight)	Oats
January 1, 1883	18	19½	18	January 7, 1880	32	45	32
April 16, 1883	15	16½	15	September 15, 1882	38	43	38
January 10, 1884	18	19½	18	April 5, 1887	34	39	34
March 1, 1884	17	19½	17	November 1, 1887	25	30	25
August 25, 1884	20	20	20	March 21, 1890	22½	30	25
April 5, 1887	10	16	10	October 22, 1890	22	26	22
November 1, 1887	10	12	10	January 15, 1891	23	28	25

Source: Sigmund Diamond, ed., *The Nation Transformed* (New York: George Braziller, 1963), p. 352.

result of further economic development. After the 1870s, as improved technology reduced operating costs and the volume of western traffic increased, rail freight rates fell steadily and East-West differentials narrowed (see Chapter 18).

Farmers turned to cooperatives and government regulation out of a deep sense of organizational disadvantage. But this disadvantage, real as it was, did not really account for the unprofitability of farming in these years. Manufacturers and banks lacked the degree of market control ascribed to them by angry farmers. The much-maligned mortgage companies actually could not rig credit markets in the western states. Their interest rates matched those in the rest of the country. Nor, for the period from 1865 to 1890, could manufacturers establish a relative price advantage over agriculture. In fact, the wholesale price of all commodities fell at a slightly faster rate than did farm prices during those years.

The Wheat and Cotton Belts. The impact of this general fall in prices, or *deflation,* did have dire consequences for certain kinds of farmers, however. First, there were those whose crops were subject to wider, more unpredictable price swings. Of these crops two—both world-traded commodities—were especially prominent: cotton and wheat. The second category of farmers at risk in deflationary periods were those in debt, since falling prices meant they had to pay back more in real terms than they had borrowed. And who was most deeply in debt? The same two groups: cotton and wheat farmers.

The nature of their indebtedness was of course different. For the tenant farmers growing cotton, the debt

was short-term, lasting only for a single season, but nevertheless painfully hard if they had to repay debt on earnings reduced by falling cotton prices. For the wheat farmer, indebtedness was a more deep-seated and entangling problem. This was because, in the nineteenth century, wheat was characteristically a virgin-land crop. Settling new land meant going into debt to start up—to pay for machinery, fencing, a new house, and so on. So wheat farmers were frequently debtors and hence under constant pressure when price levels dropped. And if, as commonly happened in frontier areas, a speculative spirit took hold and land prices were bid up, the debt levels of newly mortgaged farmers could become insupportable.

This happened for example in Harrison Township, Nebraska, which was first settled in 1872. Land that sold for $8 an acre in 1880 brought $25 and up a few years later. Given the price for wheat in the late 1880s, an investigator noted, no one taking out a mortgage to buy land at $25 an acre could hope to meet the payments, at 6 percent interest. "One is almost tempted to draw the moral that the would-be purchaser . . . had almost better throw his money away than invest it in farming operations in Nebraska."

In the 1870s the major wheat-growing states had been Illinois, Wisconsin, and Minnesota. These states had been at the center of the Granger agitation of that decade. By the 1880s wheat had moved on to the Great Plains. Among the indebted wheat farmers of Kansas, Nebraska, and the Dakotas, along with the tenant farmers of the cotton-growing South, the deflationary economy of the 1880s made for stubbornly hard times. All it would take was a sharp drop in world prices for wheat and cotton to bring on a real crisis.

Summary

In 1860 the Great Plains was still ancestral home to no-madic Indian tribes who had built a vibrant society based on the horse and the buffalo. By 1890 the Indians had been crowded onto reservations and forced to sub-mit to the white man's notion that they should abandon their tribal way of life. The surge across the Great Plains and the Rockies, the final phase of America's westward movement, was strongly driven by the nation's eco-nomic development. Industry needed the West's mineral resources; the cities demanded agricultural products; and the railroad, barbed wire, and other symbols of an industrial age made the conquest of the West relatively easy. Doomed by the swift penetration of their lands, the western Indians were ultimately victims of events that occurred far off in the nation's industries and cities.

Anchor both to a crescent of Hispanic-Mexican set-tlement stretching into the Southwest and to the Pacific slope region reaching up into the Northwest, California never experienced in its American settlement the fron-tier process that characterized the rest of the country. The discovery of gold set off a huge migration that overwhelmed the thinly spread Hispanic inhabitants and swiftly transformed California into a populous state with a large urban sector. California developed a distinctive culture that capitalized on its rediscovered Hispanic heritage and on its climate and natural envi-ronment. The treatment of the Chinese, Japanese, and Mexicans who provided the state's cheap labor, how-ever, infused a dark streak of racism into its society.

The settlement of the Great West completed the agricultural development characterized by regional crop specialization. American farming became integrated into the modern industrial order. However, that integra-tion was imperfect—in particular because farming re-mained a family operation in an economy increasingly dominated by large-scale enterprise. Most aggrieved were the cotton farmers of the South and wheat farmers of the Great Plains.

TOPIC FOR RESEARCH

Women on the Frontier

Until recently historians paid little attention to the expe-rience of women in the westward movement. When they did, they relied on a few well-worn stereotypes of the frontier woman as Victim, dragged down by a harsh and lonesome frontier life, or as Heroic Civilizer, uplift-ing by her example a raw frontier society. A number of recent books provide a more realistic and complex por-trait of women on the frontier: Julie Roy Jeffrey, *Fron-tier Women: The Trans-Mississippi West, 1840–1880* (1979); Sandra L. Myres, *Westering Women and the Frontier Experience, 1800–1915* (1982); Glenda Riley, *Women and Indians on the Frontier, 1825–1915* (1984) and *The Female Frontier: A Comparative View of the Prairie and the Plains* (1988). Sarah Deutsch, *No Sepa-rate Refuge: Culture, Class, and Gender on an Anglo-Hispanic Frontier in the American Southwest, 1880–1940* (1987) focuses on Hispanic women. An-other kind of frontierswoman—prostitutes—are dis-cussed in Marion S. Goldman, *Gold Diggers and Silver Miners; Prostitution and Social Life on the Comstock Lode* (1981).

Choose one of these books to help you answer some of the questions posed by Sandra L. Myres:

What preconceptions did women have about the fron-tier? How did they view the physical wilderness? What preconceptions did they have about Indians, Mexican-Americans, and other groups they would en-counter in the West? How, if at all, were these ideas changed by life on the frontier? . . . Did women's ideas about their role in the family and the community change as a result of the westering experience? Did women take on new roles in the West . . . ? In what ways did women's reactions and adaptations to the frontier differ from those of men?

Since the books cited above seek to answer these ques-tions through the voices of women themselves, they rely heavily on diaries and other contemporary writings, some of which have been published and may be avail-able in college libraries. For a more ambitious paper, consult one or more of these primary sources in addi-tion to a secondary work. The place to begin is with the notes and bibliographies of the books cited above.

BIBLIOGRAPHY

The Great West

A recent treatment of the West for this period is Rodman Paul, *The Far West and the Great Plains in Transition, 1859–1900* (1988). The liveliest general introduction is Robert V. Hine,

The American West (2nd ed., 1984). An important revisionist history, which emphasizes the hardships and costs of westward expansion, is Patricia N. Limerick, *The Legacy of Conquest: The Unbroken Past of the American West* (1987). The seminal 1893 statement on the significance of the frontier is in Frederick Jackson Turner, *The Frontier in American History* (1950). Another highly influential work is Walter P. Webb, *The Great Plains* (1931), which stresses the settlers' adaptation to the western climate and environment. The best book on western mining is Rodman Paul, *Mining Frontiers of the Far West: 1848–1880s* (1963). On railroad development, see Oscar O. Winther, *The Transportation Frontier: The Trans-Mississippi West, 1865–1890* (1964), and on the cattlemen, Lewis Atherton, *The Cattle Kings* (1961), and Robert R. Dykstra, *Cattle Towns* (1968). Cowboys receive full treatment in Joe B. Frantz and Julian Choate, *American Cowboy: Myth and Reality* (1955).

A useful introduction to native American history is William T. Hagan, *American Indians* (1961). More specific to the coverage of this chapter is Robert M. Utley, *The Indian Frontier of the American West, 1846–1890* (1984). Two valuable collections by deans of the subject are Wilfred E. Washburn, ed., *Indian and White Man* (1964), and Francis Paul Prucha, *Indian Policy in the United States: Historical Essays* (1981). Ralph K. Andrist, *Long Death: Last Days of the Plains Indians* (1964), and Francis Utley, *The Last Days of the Sioux Nation* (1963), eloquently retell that tragic story. On the religious life of the Plains Indians, see Howard L. Harrod, *Renewing the World: Plains Indians Religion and Morality* (1987). The best study of white attitudes is Richard Drinnon, *Facing West: The Metaphysics of Indian-Hating and Empire-Building* (1980).

California and the Far West

The best general history of California is Andrew F. Rolle, *California, A History* (2nd ed., 1969). Two valuable regional histories are Earl Pomeroy, *The Pacific Slope: A History of California, Oregon, Washington, Idaho, Utah, and Nevada* (1965), and Donald W. Meinig, *Southwest: Three Peoples in Geographical Change, 1600–1970* (1971). A very imaginative recent treatment of the New Mexican frontier is Sarah Deutsch, *No Separate Refuge* (1987). An important local study is Mario T. Garcia, *Desert Immigrants: The Mexicans of El Paso, 1880–1920* (1981). Leonard Pitt, *The Decline of the Californios: A Social History of the Spanish-Speaking Californians, 1846–1890* (1960) offers a narrative history of that subject, with an emphasis on the fate of the large ranchers. Two more recent studies focus on the Chicano peasantry: Albert Camarillo, *Chicanos in a Changing Society: From Mexican Pueblos to American Barrios in Santa Barbara and Southern California, 1848–1930* (1979), and Richard Griswold del Castillo, *The Los Angeles Barrio, 1850–1890* (1979). On the Chinese, the standard work is Gunther Barth, *Bitter Strength: A History of the Chinese in the United States, 1850–1870* (1964), which can be supplemented by a thorough recent study: Sucheng Chan, *This Bittersweet Soil: The Chinese in California Agriculture, 1860–1910* (1986). Labor's opposition to the Chinese is skillfully treated in Alexander

Saxton, *The Indispensable Enemy: Labor and the Anti-Chinese Movement in California* (1971). On John Muir and the California wilderness, see Michael L. Smith, *Pacific Visions: California Scientists and the Environment, 1850–1915* (1987).

The Agricultural Interest

The standard works are Fred A. Shannon, *The Farmer's Last Frontier, 1860–1897* (1945), and Gilbert C. Fite, *The Farmer's Frontier, 1865–1900* (1966). For the farming pioneers, see Everett Dick, *Sod-House Frontier* (1954). On semiarid farming, see Mary W. M. Hargreaves, *Dry-farming in the Northern Great Plains, 1900–1925* (1957). A more far-ranging study of the impact of insufficient rainfall on the West is Donald Worster, *Rivers of Empire: Water Aridity and the Growth of the American West* (1985). On the black migration to Kansas, see the vivid treatment in Nell Irvin Painter, *Exodusters: Black Migration to Kansas after Reconstruction* (1976). The flavor of farm life can best be captured in fiction: Hamlin Garland, *Main-Travelled Roads* (1891), Willa Cather, *My Antonia* (1918), and O. E. Rölvaag, *Giants in the Earth* (1927). For women and the West, see the citations in the Topic for Research.

TIMELINE

1862	Homestead Act
1865	Long Drive of Texas longhorns begins
1867	Patrons of Husbandry (the Grange) founded
	U.S. government adopts Reservation policy for Plains Indians
1869	Union Pacific–Central Pacific transcontinental railroad completed
1874	Barbed wire invented
1876	Battle of Little Big Horn
1877	San Francisco anti-Chinese riots
	Munn v. Illinois
1879	Exoduster migration to Kansas
1882	Chinese Exclusion Act
1886	Dry cycle begins on the Great Plains
	Wabash v. Illinois
1887	Dawes Severalty Act
	Interstate Commerce Act
1889	Oklahoma opened to white settlement
1890	Indian massacre at Wounded Knee, South Dakota
	U.S. Census declares end of the frontier

Montgomery Ward & Co, Chicago

In 1872 Aaron Montgomery Ward began selling
goods to rural customers through mail order cata-
logs. By the 1890s Montgomery Ward was one of
the emerging retail and mail order giants along with
Sears, Roebuck and Company.

CHAPTER **18** *Capital and Labor in the Age of Enterprise, 1877–1900*

The year 1877 marked the end of Reconstruction. That year also marked the conclusion of the first great crisis of the emerging system of industrial capitalism. Four years earlier, in 1873, the great banking house Jay Cooke & Co. had failed, triggering a financial panic. In the severe depression that followed, 47,000 firms went under. Wholesale prices fell about 30 percent. Railroad building ground almost to a halt. Orders for industrial goods disappeared. And with unemployment running as high as 25 percent, hundreds of thousands of workers lost their jobs. Suffering was widespread. Across the country workers demanded "bread for the needy, clothing for the naked, and houses for the homeless." Before long, the very foundations of the social order began to shake.

On July 16, 1877, railroad workers in West Virginia went on strike against the Baltimore and Ohio system to protest wage cuts. In railway towns along the B&O tracks, crowds cheered as the strikers attacked company property and prevented trains from running. The strike spread quickly to other lines. In Pittsburgh, the Pennsylvania Railroad roundhouse went up in flames on July 21, followed by the Union Depot the next day. Rioters and looters roamed freely. For nearly a week, riotous strikes swept other cities, including San Francisco, St. Louis, Omaha, and Chicago. President Rutherford B. Hayes called up the National Guard, which gradually restored order. On August 15, the president wrote in his diary: "The strikers have been put down *by force*." The Great Strike of 1877 had been crushed. But never had the nation edged so close to social revolution.

And then recovery came. Within months the economy was booming again. The march toward industrial power resumed. The physical output of manufactured goods increased over 150 percent between 1877 and 1890. The vitality of industrial capitalism renewed America's confidence in the future. "Can there be any doubt that cheapening the cost of necessaries and conveniences of life is the most powerful agent of civilization and progress?" asked a railroad president in 1888. "History and experience demonstrate that . . . material progress must come first and . . . upon it is founded all other progress."

Industrial Capitalism Triumphant

Economic historians speak of the late nineteenth century as the age of the Great Deflation. Prices fell steadily worldwide, including in the United States. Following a brief upturn after 1877, wholesale prices declined by almost 30 percent between 1880 and 1892. Normally, falling prices are a sign of economic stagnation: there is not enough demand for the goods and services that are available. But that was not America's experience in these years. Because of increasing efficiencies in production and distribution, manufacturers were able both to cut prices *and* to earn profits and invest in better equipment. So that while in England the Great Deflation did indeed signal economic decline, in the United States it was associated with industrial expansion and technological progress.

MAP 18.1

The Westward Movement of Iron and Steel Production

Before the Civil War, the iron industry was concentrated in eastern Pennsylvania and northern New Jersey. With the development of steel and the shift westward of population and industry, production moved first to western Pennsylvania, then to Ohio, Indiana, and Illinois, and also southward into Alabama. The specific locations—Pittsburgh, Youngstown, Chicago, Birmingham—were dictated by the rail network, new sources of coal and iron ore, and the markets for metal.

Basic Industry

By the 1870s, manufacturing already had a long history in America. But the early industries were an outgrowth of the larger agricultural economy. They processed farm and forest materials and relied on traditional sources of hand and water power. The goods they produced—textiles, boots and shoes, paper and furniture—were primarily consumer goods that could be substituted for existing home-made or artisan-made products. Gradually, however, a different kind of demand developed. This was the result of the surging economic growth of the country. Railroads needed locomotives, new factories called for machinery, and the expanding cities required vast quantities of building materials for trolley lines, sanitation systems, and commercial buildings. Locomotives, machinery, and construction materials were *capital* goods—that is, goods that themselves added to the productive capacity of the economy. And it was the manufacture of capital goods, as distinct from consumer products, that increasingly characterized America's industrial sector.

Central to this development was iron making. An extensive industry already existed, producing large quantities of wrought iron. This was a soft and malleable metal, ideally suited for use by country blacksmiths and farmers. But wrought iron was expensive—it was produced in small batches by skilled puddlers and rollers—and did not stand up well for heavy use as railway track. In 1856, the English inventor Sir Henry Bessemer perfected a new process for refining iron. Unlike the puddling furnaces that made wrought iron, Bessemer converters produced steel—a harder, more durable metal—and did so in large amounts with little labor. Others took up this invention, but it was Andrew

Carnegie who demonstrated its revolutionary importance.

Andrew Carnegie and American Steel. Carnegie had arrived from Scotland in 1848 at the age of twelve with his poverty-stricken family. He became a telegraph operator, then went to work for the Pennsylvania Railroad and rapidly ascended the managerial ladder. Having become wealthy from a series of successful speculations, Carnegie resigned in 1865 to become an iron manufacturer. His main customers were his former associates in the railroad business.

Keenly aware of the possibilities of the Bessemer converter, Carnegie embarked in 1872 on a venture aimed at the fullest exploitation of the new refining process. He built a massive steel-rail mill outside Pittsburgh that utilized the most advanced equipment of the day. Equally important, the mill integrated all the stages of production—smelting, refining, and rolling—into a single operation that began with iron ore and ended with finished steel rails. Carnegie's mill, which he named the Edgar Thompson Works after his admired former boss at the Pennsylvania Railroad, fully repaid its investment in a few years and became a model for the modern steel industry.

Large, integrated steel plants swiftly replaced the older blast furnaces and puddling mills. At first, steel went mostly into railroad building. Steel rails made up nearly three-quarters of the total output in 1885. But thereafter, as railroad building slowed, the demand became more diversified. More and more steel went into bridges, skyscrapers, machinery, and a host of other industrial uses such as piping and tubing, sheet steel and wire, and armor for the nation's new navy.

TABLE 18.1

Increasing Output of Heavy Industry, 1870–1910

	Bituminous Coal (in thousands of tons)	Rolled iron and steel (in thousands of tons)	Copper (tons)	Industrial Machinery (in millions of dollars)
1870	20,471	850*	14,112	110.4†
1880	50,757	3,301	30,240	98.6‡
1890	111,302	6,746	129,882	185.6
1900	212,318	10,626	303,059	347.6
1910	417,111	24,216	544,119	512.4

*Approximate total.
†Data for 1869.
‡Data for 1874.

The Corliss Engine
The symbol of the Philadelphia Centennial in 1876 was the great Corliss engine, which towered over Machinery Hall and powered all the equipment on exhibit there. Yet the Corliss engine also signified the incomplete nature of American industrialism at that time; it soon became obsolete. Westinghouse turbines generating electricity would be the power source for the nation's next great World's Fair in Chicago in 1893.

The production of copper and other nonferrous metals went through a similar development. Before the Civil War, copper had been employed mainly in the manufacture of kettles, pots and pans, and other household products. Now it became a key ingredient in oil refining equipment, electric generators, and other new products such as telephone cable. Copper output grew at a phenomenal rate, increasing from 14,000 tons in 1870 to 130,000 tons in 1890.

The growth of the metal industries depended on the intensive exploitation of the country's mineral resources. Major discoveries of rich iron ore deposits occurred from the 1850s onward, first in upper Michigan and then in the huge Mesabi Range of Minnesota. These ores were readily shipped down the Great Lakes to the growing steel-making centers in Illinois, Ohio, and Pennsylvania.

Coal mining, a minor enterprise before 1850, grew rapidly thereafter, first in the anthracite region of eastern Pennsylvania and then in the soft-coal Appalachian fields of western Pennsylvania and Ohio. Coal production, scarcely half a million tons in 1860, reached 270 million tons in 1900.

It was the insatiable energy needs of American industrialism that spurred this remarkable expansion in coal mining. Carnegie's blast furnaces and Bessemer convertors burned prodigious amounts of coal. Coal-burning steam engines drove locomotives and ships, and increasingly became the power source for factories. Steam was as important as water power for running machinery by 1880, and six times as important twenty years later. At the Philadelphia Centennial Exhibition of 1876, visitors gazed in wonder at the enormous Corliss reciprocating engine, with a flywheel 30 feet in diame-

ter and the capacity to drive all the other exhibits in Machinery Hall. Steam power became increasingly efficient, first through refinements in the reciprocating engine, then, in the 1880s, because of the steam turbine. The turbine was an inherently superior design because it utilized continuous rotation rather than the back-and-forth motion of the reciprocating engine. These advances in turn laid the basis for the next major innovation—the coupling of the steam turbine to the electric generator. After 1900 factories rapidly converted from steam to electric power.

Thus, in the decades following the Civil War, the modern metal-producing industries were established, the nation's mineral resources came under intensive exploitation, and energy was harnessed to the manufacturing system. All these basic elements of modern industrialism—steel, coal, and energy output—grew after 1870 at rates far exceeding that of manufacturing production itself.

NEW TECHNOLOGY *Iron and Steel*

Iron was not a product new to the nineteenth century in the sense that plastic was new to the twentieth century. Early Europeans made iron tools and weapons at least a thousand years before Christ. Nor did the underlying processes change, for they are dictated by the nature of iron metallurgy. Iron ore must be *smelted* into metal; the raw metal must be *refined* to acquire desired properties such as malleability or hardness; and the refined iron must be *shaped* into useable forms. What did begin to change, slowly at first, were the techniques for carrying out these processes. Only as iron became available in large quantities and at low cost could the Industrial Revolution proceed.

Metallurgical innovation took place in two great waves. The first began in smelting late in the Middle Ages, when blast furnaces appeared in Belgium around 1340. Ore was melted in a charcoal-burning furnace to which limestone had been added. A blast of air then set off a combustion process that combined carbon from the charcoal with the molten iron while its impurities combined with the limestone to form a slag. The slag was drawn off from the top of the furnace while the molten iron was tapped from the bottom into sand forms resembling piglets feeding from a sow—hence the term "pig iron."

By the eighteenth century, the shortage of wood for charcoal had become acute in England. The substitution of coke, made by superheating coal, broke this bottleneck in iron production. An improved refining furnace, with separate chambers for the fuel and iron, was also developing. In 1784, Henry Cort invented the puddling furnace. Molten iron collected in the hollowed-out bottom, where it worked with a long bar or paddle by hand from the outside. The resulting product was a malleable iron called *wrought iron*. Cort also made a crucial advance in the finishing stage at this time. For the laborious hammering process, he substituted the rolling mill, which shaped iron as it passed through grooved rolls.

This iron technology—blast furnace, puddling furnace, and rolling mill—formed the metallurgical basis for England's Industrial Revolution in the first half of the nineteenth century. Endowed with ample forests, the United States was slow to adopt the coke-using technology, but by 1860 it had caught up fairly well with England technologically and was producing nearly a million tons of iron annually. The iron industry, as it had developed to this point, met America's needs very well. Wrought iron was admirably suited for farm use because it was malleable and easily worked, and was also suitable for the localized machine- and engine-building characteristic of early industrialism. But wrought iron was too soft for the increasingly heavy service it received as railroad track. The search for a harder, more durable metal resulted in the invention in 1856 of an entirely different refining process by Henry Bessemer, an Englishman.

The Bessemer converter was a pear-shaped vessel open at the top, with a bottom perforated by many holes. Molten pig iron flowed into the top while the converter was tilted on its side. Air was blasted at great force through the perforated bottom, and the converter then swung back to its upright position. The resulting combustion set off a spectacular display of flame and smoke. Within fifteen minutes, the impurities in the molten iron had burned off and the flames died down. The converter was again tilted on its side and, after manganese and other chemicals had been added, the purified iron was emptied into ingot molds.

The refined metal, called steel, was harder than wrought iron and ideally suited for use as railroad track. The Bessemer process had one significant drawback: it operated successfully only with expensive, low-phosphorous iron. The open-hearth method, developed shortly after the Bessemer process, could handle low-quality iron and was more economical and flexible. By World War I, the open-hearth method was rapidly becoming the dominant refining process. But the Bessemer converter had given life to the modern steel industry.

The device that Bessemer had invented to produce a better metal also proved vastly more efficient than the hand-operated puddling furnace. The Bessemer converter turned out great quantities of steel with virtually

The Railroads

A transportation system capable of welding the nation into a vast, unified market had been developing since early in the nineteenth century. Until around 1850, the major advances had been in the improvement of water transportation. But while suitable for bulky raw materials, canal barges and riverboats could not provide the year-round, on-time service demanded by the growing industrial economy. Railroads performed this task far no labor. This forced changes up and down the line. To feed the converters' appetite for pig iron, blast furnaces grew even larger and, with the introduction of the hot blast, much more efficient. To handle the flow of steel from the converters, rolling mills became increasingly mechanized and automatic, so that the steel could move continuously through progressively narrower rolls set in tandem. By means of a variety of metal-handling devices, the stages of production became integrated, enabling the iron to proceed "with perfect regularity" from the blast furnace to the Bessemer converter to its emergence from the rolling mill as a finished rail or girder. The integrated steel plant of 1900, capable of producing 2,500 tons or more a day, was vastly more efficient than the small blast furnaces and iron mills of 1860.

The revolution in steelmaking changed the face of American industrialism. The geographic concentration of industrial activity intensified. The places best located in relation to raw materials, transportation, and markets—Pittsburgh, the steel towns along the Great Lakes, and Birmingham, Alabama—became the great centers of steel production.

A second result involved the scale of business enterprise. The principal steel companies evolved into vertically integrated firms that controlled their own raw materials, some of their transport facilities, and the marketing of their products. For the workers, the effects were no less sweeping. The skills of the puddler, heater, and hand roller became obsolete; gang labor was largely replaced by ore- and metal-handling equipment; and face-to-face relationships with employers disappeared. The typical steelworker of 1900 was a machine-tender in an impersonal, bureaucratic business organization.

Steel made possible dramatic changes in transportation and construction. With steel rails capable of withstanding heavy traffic, and steel locomotives capable of ever greater pulling power, the railroads became the primary carriers of the nation's enormous volume of goods. The efficiency of the railroads rose nearly 70 percent between 1870 and 1900, and freight charges

The Bessemer Steel Furnace

per ton-mile fell by almost the same amount—thanks largely to the use of steel for rails and equipment. In the growth of America's cities, steel played a key role in the construction of skyscrapers, trolley lines, and subways, and the vast underground complexes of pipe that supplied the urban millions with water and gas and carried away their sewage. Steel battleships asserted the nation's new role as a world power. Without steel, the emerging automobile industry would not have grown, nor a host of other American industries. It is no wonder that historians have called the last decades of the nineteenth century America's Age of Steel.

better. They had started in the 1830s as feeders linking river and canal traffic to inland towns and cities but quickly grew into a system rivaling water transportation. By the 1860s, with a network of tracks covering the states east of the Mississippi, the dominance of the

railroads was assured for both goods and passengers.

Between 1877 and 1893, in a remarkable burst of building activity, over 100,000 miles of new track were laid. The rail network doubled in size, mainly as a result of construction west of the Mississippi and in the South.

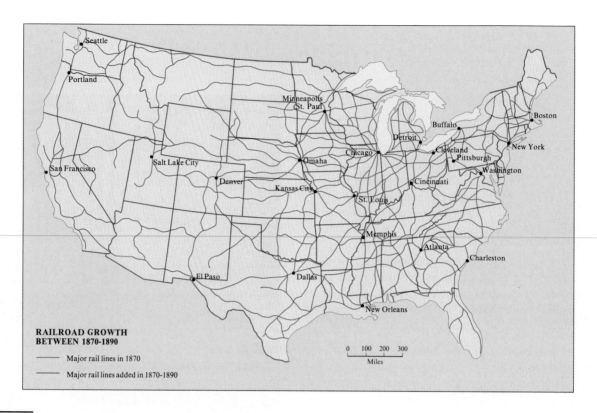

MAP 18.2

The Expansion of the Railroad System, 1780–1890

In 1870, the nation had 53,000 miles of rail track; in 1890, 167,000 miles. That burst
of construction essentially completed the nation's rail network, although there would
be additional expansion for the next two decades. The main areas of growth were in
the South and west of the Mississippi. The Great Plains and Far West accounted for
over 40 percent of all construction in this period.

By the early twentieth century, the American network,
with more railway track than the rest of the world combined, brought virtually every populated area in the
country within reach of railroad service.

Accompanying this physical growth was the rising
efficiency of railway transportation. The early system,
built by competing local companies, had been a jumble
of discontinuous segments. Gauges of track—the width
between the tracks—varied widely and at terminal
points railroads were not physically connected. Many
rivers lacked railroad bridges. Also, each railroad company reserved the use of its track exclusively for its own
equipment. As late as 1880, a shipment of heavy textile
machinery had to go through eight transfers en route
from Massachusetts to South Carolina.

Beginning with the Civil War years, however, pressures increased for integration of the railroads. Track
was hastily laid through Philadelphia, Richmond, and
other cities to speed the huge shipments of troops and
equipment. The postwar economy, as it grew more
complex and interdependent, demanded a better-orga-
nized rail system. Much railroad integration took place

through the expansion of such great trunk lines as the
Pennsylvania, New York Central, and Illinois Central
connecting different regions of the country. By the end
of the 1880s, a standard track gauge (4 feet, 8½ inches)
had been adopted across the country. Through the use
of fast-freight firms and standard accounting procedures, the railroad network served shippers as if it were
a single unit, moving their goods without breaks in
transit, freight transfers between cars, or other delays
that had once bedevilled smooth rail service.

At the same time, railroad technology was advancing. The key innovation was the shift to steel rails,
which could bear much heavier loads than wrought-
iron rails. Locomotives became heavier and more powerful, freight cars progressively larger, and freight trains
longer. The Consolidation-type locomotive, with four
sets of driving wheels, nearly tripled the pulling power
of freight trains. To control the great mass and length of
the new freight trains, the inventor George Westinghouse perfected the automatic coupler, the air brake,
and the friction gear for starting and stopping a long
line of cars.

Integrated service and advancing technology increased the efficiency of the railroads. Costs per ton-mile fell by 50 percent between 1870 and 1890, resulting in a steady drop in freight rates for shippers.

The railroads brilliantly met the transportation needs of the maturing industrial economy. However, this achievement did not stem from any orderly plan or design; it sprang from the competitive energy of a free-wheeling market economy. True, especially before the 1870s, federal, state, and city governments had provided financial assistance in the form of land grants, loans, and tax breaks. But the actual enterprise of building railroads remained, with a few early exceptions, entirely in private hands.

The Railroad Magnates. Railroad construction required, more than anything else, enormous amounts of capital. That was why, long before other businesses did so, the railroads organized themselves as corporations capable of raising funds from the public through the sale of stocks and bonds. Finance became the central entrepreneurial activity in railroading.

The key figures were those with access to capital—their own or that of others. For example, John Murray Forbes, a Bostonian who had made his fortune in the China trade, went on to develop the Chicago, Burlington and Quincy Railroad into the preeminent midwestern system. A more aggressive figure was Cornelius Vanderbilt, who left the steamboat business in 1863 to invest his fortune in the New York Central Railroad. Vanderbilt and his son William built the Central into an East-West trunk line rivaled only by the Pennsylvania Railroad. Forbes and the Vanderbilts aimed at creating well-constructed, well-financed railroad systems.

Jay Gould, a very different kind of entrepreneur, started out as a stock-market speculator. Gould earned early notoriety by his amazing attempt to corner the New York gold market. In 1869 he tried to acquire so much of the gold supply as to be able to force up gold prices almost at will. Many people at the time—and historians long after—considered Gould a *robber baron*, someone who loots commerce and gives nothing in return. But Gould did give something in return. His great talent lay in gaining control over weak properties—the Erie, the Union Pacific, the Wabash, and the Southwest lines during the 1880s—and making them turn a profit. Gould cared little for improving his properties, but he was a fierce competitor—for good reason. Gould's railroads generally were heavily in debt, and only a high volume of traffic enabled them to meet the interest charges. His wealthier rivals, such as Forbes and the Vanderbilts, bitterly resented his ruthless rate-cutting tactics, but shippers and consumers benefited from the lower transportation fees. In the free-market economy in which American railroads grew, even a buccaneer like Jay Gould made a positive contribution.

Railroad development in the United States was often sordid, fiercely competitive, and subject to boom and bust. When the Panic of 1893 hit, fully a third of the industry (by track mileage) went bankrupt. Yet vast sums of capital had been raised, an integrated, highly advanced rail system built, and the transportation needs of the nation amply met.

Mass Markets and Large-Scale Enterprise

The railway network, in turn, sparked a revolution in the distribution and marketing of goods. Until well into the industrial age, business firms were typically small. Most manufacturers produced goods in limited quantities, mainly for nearby markets. And they left the marketing to wholesale merchants and commission agents. Products normally passed through numerous hands on their way from the factory to final sale to the consumer.

Then after the Civil War the scale of economic activity began to grow dramatically. "Combinations of capital on a scale hitherto wholly unprecedented consti-

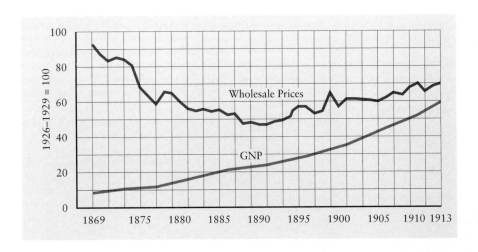

FIGURE 18.1

Business Activity and Wholesale Prices, 1865–1900

tute one of the remarkable features of modern business methods," the economist David A. Wells wrote in 1889. He already could see "no other way in which the work of production and distribution can be prosecuted." The increasing scale of enterprise seemed "not voluntary on the part of the possessors and controllers of capital, but necessary or even compulsory."

What was there about the nation's economic activity that led to Wells's sense of inevitability? The dynamic features of American growth—availability of capital, receptivity to technology, and the emergence of a heavy industrial base—certainly played a part. But the key to large-scale enterprise lay in the American market. Immigration and a very high birth rate swelled the population from 40 million in 1870 to over 60 million in 1890. People flocked to the cities, and the railroads brought these dense consuming markets within the reach of distant producers. The telegraph, in widespread use by the Civil War, eliminated communication barriers. Unlike Europe, America was not carved up into many national markets; no political frontiers impeded the flow of goods across the continent. Mean-

while, high tariffs protected American industry from foreign competition. Nowhere else did manufacturers have an internal market so vast and accessible for their products.

Gustavus Swift and Vertical Integration. The meat packing industry was a case in point. Before the Civil War, Cincinnati and Chicago had become great centers for the processing of preserved products like salt pork and smoked beef. But fresh meat remained the province of local butchers and slaughterhouses whose practices had scarcely changed since the preindustrial era. Fresh meat was a luxury item, and the diet of city dwellers, especially the poor, depended heavily on salt pork.

The coming of the railroads brought big changes to the fresh-meat business. Cattle raising shifted to the grazing ranges of the Great Plains and to the feed lots of the corn belt. Chicago, the rail terminal for the upper Midwest, became the hub of the American meat trade once the Union Stock Yards opened in 1865. Cattle were shipped by railroad from Chicago to eastern cities, where, as before, they were slaughtered in local

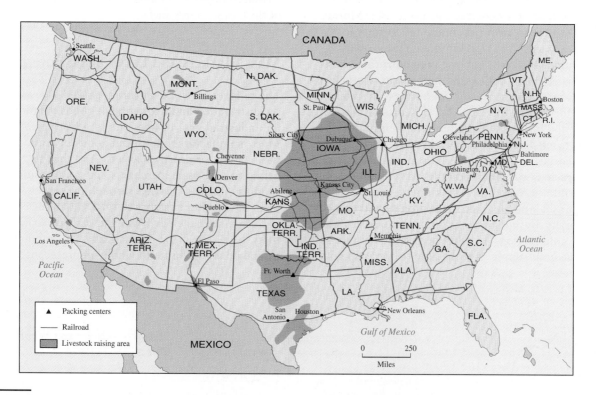

MAP 18.3

The Dressed Meat Industry

No industry better reveals than meat packing how transportation, supply, and demand combined to foster the growth of the American industrial economy. The main centers of beef production in 1900—Chicago, St. Paul, Kansas City, Fort Worth— were great rail hubs with connections westward to the cattle growing regions and eastward to the great cities hungry for cheap supplies of meat. Vertically integrated enterprise sprang from these elements, linked together by an efficient and comprehensive railroad network.

"butchertowns." By means of regional specialization and an efficient rail network, the meat trade serviced an exploding urban population and, without further development, might have done so indefinitely.

Gustavus F. Swift, a shrewd Massachusetts cattle dealer who settled in Chicago in 1875, saw the future differently. The system of marketing fresh meat seemed inefficient to him. Livestock in cattle cars deteriorated en route to the East, and local slaughterhouses were too small to utilize waste by-products and cut high labor costs. If a way could be found to keep the dressed beef fresh in transit, then processing operations could be concentrated in Chicago. Primitive refrigeration already enabled Chicago pork-packing plants to operate year-round. The problem was how to apply this technology to a railroad freight car. After Swift's engineers had figured out an effective system of air circulation, he built a fleet of refrigerator cars and constructed a central beef-processing plant at the Chicago stockyards.

This was only the beginning of Swift's activities. Since no refrigerated warehouses existed in the cities to which he shipped chilled beef, Swift had to build his own network of branch houses. Next, he established a fleet of wagons to distribute his products to retail butcher shops. Swift constructed additional facilities to process the fertilizer, chemicals, and other usable by-products from his slaughtering operations. He also added to his line of business other perishable commodities, including dairy products, so he could fully utilize his refrigerated cars and branch houses. As the demand grew, Swift built more packing houses in other stockyard centers, such as Kansas City, Fort Worth, and Omaha.

Step by step, Swift had created a new kind of enterprise, the *vertically integrated* firm—that is, a national company capable of handling within its own structure all the functions of an entire industry. In effect, Swift and Company replaced a large number of small specialized firms that had operated locally. Several other Chicago companies that had started as preserved pork packers—Armour and Company was the most prominent—followed Swift's lead. By the end of the 1890s five firms, all of them nationally organized and vertically integrated, produced nearly 90 percent of all the meat shipped in interstate commerce.

The Birth of Mass Marketing. The development of the refrigerator car had made all this possible in the fresh-meat trade. In most other fields, no such single event was so decisive. But other manufacturers did share Swift's insight that the essential step was to identify a mass market and then develop a national enterprise capable of serving it. In the petroleum industry, John D. Rockefeller built the Standard Oil Company partly by taking over rival firms; but he also developed a national distribution system to reach the enormous market for

kerosene as a fuel for lighting and heating homes. The Singer Sewing Machine Company formed its own sales organization, using both retail stores and door-to-door salesmen. The McCormick Harvesting Machine Company set up a network of franchise dealers. Through such distribution systems, manufacturers provided technical information, credit, and repair facilities for their products. Like the meat packers, these companies became vertically integrated firms that served a national market.

To gain the benefits of mass distribution, retail business went through comparable changes. Montgomery Ward and Sears, Roebuck developed into national mail-order houses for rural consumers. From Vermont to California, farm families selected identical goods from mail-order catalogues, and became part of the nationwide consumer market. In the cities, mass distribution followed different strategies. Department stores, a form of retailing pioneered by John Wanamaker in Philadelphia, spread to every large city in the country. Sometimes this growth occurred through the efforts of a wholesale merchant, but more often—as with R. H. Macy of New York—it came through the

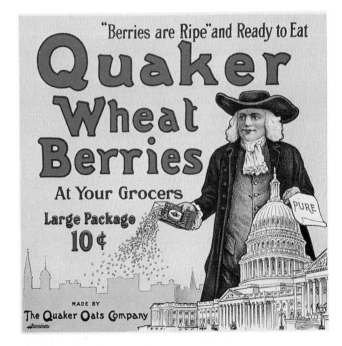

Quaker Oats

Like crackers, sugar, and other nonperishable foods, oatmeal had traditionally been marketed to consumers in bulk from barrels. In 1882, the grain merchant Henry P. Cowell completed the first continuous-process mill for oatmeal, cutting production costs and greatly increasing output. He also struck on the idea of selling oatmeal in boxes of standard size and weight to a national market. Broadsides showing the Quaker Oats man soon appeared in every American town, advertising a product of reliable quality and uniform price. (National Museum of American History, Smithsonian Institution) addition of departments to a dry goods store. The most important innovators in this field were such Jewish families as the Strauses of New York, the Lazaruses of Columbus, Ohio, and the Mays of Colorado, most of whose founders had started as peddlers or small dry good proprietors. An alternative route to urban distribution was the establishment of extensive chain store systems, which was the strategy of the Great Atlantic and Pacific Tea Company (A & P) and the F. W. Woolworth Company.

American society prepared citizens to be consumers of the standardized goods produced by national manufacturers and sold by mass marketers. The high rate of geographic mobility broke down loyalties to local custom and regional distinctiveness that were so strong in Europe. And social class in America, though by no means absent, was blurred at the edges. Equally important, it did not call for distinguishing ways of dressing. Foreign visitors often noted that ready-made clothing made it difficult to tell sales girls from debutantes on the city streets.

The American consumer's receptivity to standardized goods should not be exaggerated. Gustavus Swift, for example, encountered great resistance to his Chicago beef. How could it be wholesome weeks later in Boston or Philadelphia? Cheap prices helped, but advertising perhaps had a greater influence. Modern advertising was born during the late nineteenth century, bringing brand names and an urban landscape increasingly cluttered by billboards and signs. By 1900, advertisers were spending more than $90 million annually for space in newspapers and magazines. Advertisements urged readers to bathe with Pears' soap, to munch Uneeda biscuits, to sew on a Singer machine, and to snap pictures with a Kodak camera. The active molding of demand for brand names became a major function of American business.

The Managerial Revolution

At one time, observed the railroad expert Marshall M. Kirkman in 1896, it had been thought "practically impossible to manage a great railway effectively." On the early roads, "management had been personal and autocratic; the superintendent, a man gifted with energy and clearness of perception, moulded the property to his own will. But as the properties grew, he found himself unable to give his personal attention to everything. Undaunted, he sought to do everything and do it well. He ended by doing nothing."

It is not hard to understand the mistake of the early railroad superintendent. How could he know that methods which had worked brilliantly in the past would not work in the future? And where, in a world of small businesses, was there a model for running an enterprise other than by personal and direct control over its activities? How else could a business be run? No problem was harder to see clearly or, once discovered, more taxing on the business imagination. Nor was any industrial success, once achieved, fated to have more enduring consequences than the mastery of the techniques of modern management.

As trunk lines thrust westward from Baltimore, Philadelphia, and New York before the Civil War, they came up against a managerial crisis that had not troubled shorter roads. In 1856, in a classic statement of the problem, the Erie Railroad official Daniel C. McCallum compared a 50-mile road and a 500-mile road. On the short road, the superintendent could personally attend to every detail, "and any system, however imperfect, may prove comparatively successful." But not on long roads: "I am fully convinced that in the want of a system lies the true secret of their failure." McCallum's crucial insight was in realizing the need for a *system*—a formal administrative structure—for the successful operation of large-scale, complex enterprises. He knew he was working in the dark: "We have no precedent or experience upon which we can fully rely."

The railroads were the most complex form of nineteenth-century enterprise. They had to raise huge amounts of capital, and their properties stretched over ever greater distances. They employed armies of workers—nearly 50,000 on the Pennsylvania system by 1890. And, unlike the leisurely traffic on the canals, trains had to be precisely scheduled and closely coordinated. Even with telegraph communication, train accidents took a heavy toll.

Step by step, always under the prod of necessity, the early trunk lines pioneered in the main elements of modern business administration. They divided overall management from day-to-day operations and created separate departments along functional lines—maintenance of way, rolling stock, and traffic. Then they carefully defined the lines of communication from the operating divisions upward to the central office. When Albert Fink perfected his cost-accounting system for the Louisville and Nashville Railroad after the Civil War, managers at last had precise data on which to assess the performance of their roads. By the end of the 1870s, the managerial crisis on the railroads had been resolved.

As industrial enterprises became comparably complex, they confronted the same kind of managerial problems. However, manufacturers benefited from the experience of the railroads. Sometimes there was a direct link. Andrew Carnegie, for example, drew on his early career with the Pennsylvania Railroad. Whether by learning from the railroads or by trial and error, large companies everywhere moved toward a modern management structure and solved the problems of administering far-flung business empires.

By the beginning of the twentieth century, the main lines of managerial strategy had taken hold throughout large-scale American industry. With few exceptions, vertically integrated firms followed a centralized, functionally departmentalized plan (see Figure 18.2, below). The central office housed a number of departments, each charged with the overall responsibility for a specific area of activity—purchasing, auditing, production, transportation, or sales. These functionally defined departments provided "middle management," and they represented the heart of the managerial revolution in American industry. Middle managers were the key innovators; in matters of business practice they were equivalent to engineers who improved technology.

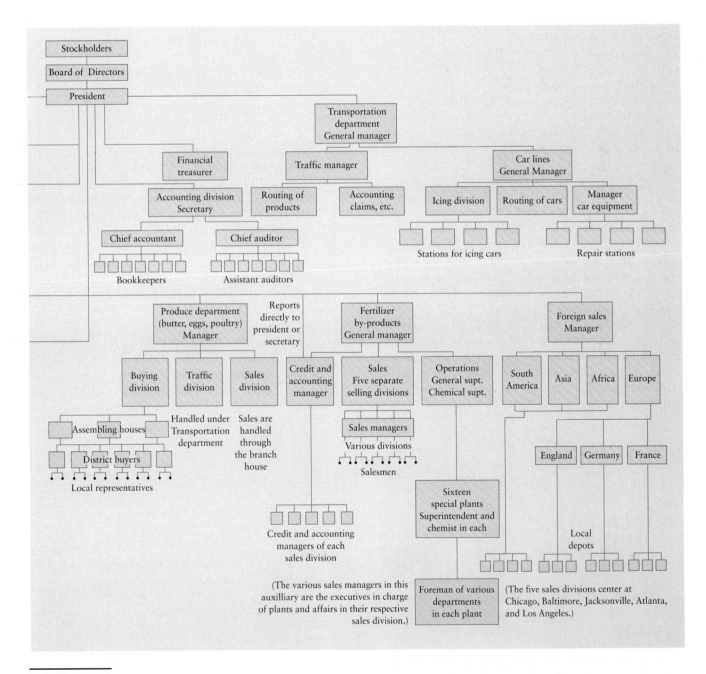

FIGURE 18.2

The Organization of Armour & Company in 1907

Their superiors, the top executives, could not claim such a complete achievement. The firms that developed through internal growth had been built by individual entrepreneurs—Gustavus Swift, Phillip D. Armour, and Cyrus McCormick. The successors, often their sons, were generally reluctant to surrender the tight supervision with which the founding fathers had developed their companies. In 1907, J. Ogden Armour spent his days reading operational reports and issuing orders to his buying, processing, and selling departments. All middle managers reported directly to him. Priding himself on his knowledge of the company and absorbed in the details of its operation, Armour had neither the time, the staff, nor the inclination to engage in long-term strategic planning or systematic evaluation of his firm's performance. Armour typified an entire generation of owner-managers. Brilliant in creating the subordinate administrative structure, they normally were slow to apply managerial principles to their own tasks.

The New South

"Shall we dethrone our idols?" This was a question that southerners had to ask themselves as they enviously observed the tremendous burst of economic activity in the North. For many, the answer was a resounding yes. Nostalgia for the glories of Old South became the chief target of the advocates of southern economic development. The South, they argued, had always given "the places of trust and honor" to "warriors and orators," forgetting that "what it would most need was the practical wisdom of businessmen." Led by Henry W. Grady of the Atlanta *Constitution,* an influential group of publicists made the "practical wisdom of businessmen" the credo of a "New South."

Catching up with the North was of course no easy task. The plantation economy of the Old South had strongly impeded industrial development. In 1860, railroad building lagged far behind, and there were few cities, a primitive distribution system, and not much manufacturing. After the devastation of the Civil War, this modest infrastructure was quickly restored. In 1879, with both Reconstruction and the economic depression ended, outside capital flowed in and a railroad boom developed. Track mileage doubled in the next decade and, at least by that measure, the South became nearly competitive with the rest of the country.

But the South remained overwhelmingly an agrarian society; two of every three persons wrested a livelihood from the soil. Farming and poverty are not necessarily linked. But in the South they were. Sharecropping, which required a cash crop (see Chapter 16), committed the South inflexibly to cotton, despite soil depletion and unprofitable prices. With leases on a year-to-year basis, neither tenant nor owner had an incentive to invest in long-term improvements. At a time of rapid advances in northern agriculture, cotton growing remained tied to the mule, the plow, and the hoe.

The result was a stagnant agricultural system. Low productivity and low cotton prices translated into low-wage agriculture. The price for southern farm labor fell steadily, until in South Carolina and Georgia it stood at scarcely half the national average by the 1890s—roughly 75 cents a day without board for a farm laborer.

Southern Industry. This low agricultural wage turned out to be the salvation of the South's hopes for industrialization. Consider, for example, how southern textile mills got started in the Piedmont upcountry of North Carolina, South Carolina, and Georgia in the mid-

A Model Mill.

The Industrial South

No development so buoyed the hopes of New South proponents as the success of the region's textile industry. After 1877, new mills sprung up in South Carolina, North Carolina, and Georgia. Investors received a high rate of return—average profits ran at 22 percent in 1882—and publicists boasted that new jobs were created for "the necessitous masses of poor whites." This 1887 engraving of a "model" mill at Augusta, Georgia, conveys the South's sense of pride in its new industrial prowess.

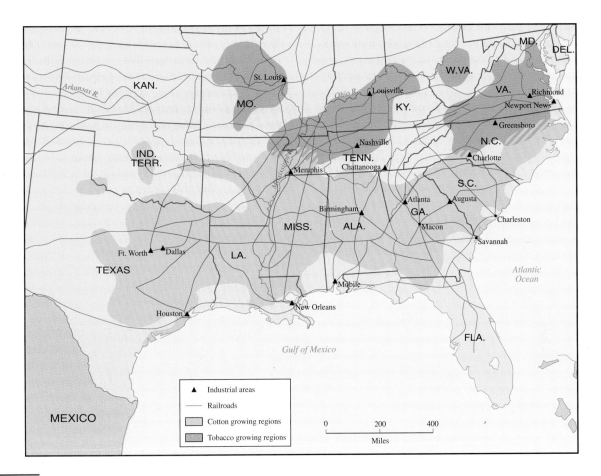

MAP 18.4

The New South, 1900

The economy of the Old South had concentrated heavily on the raising of staple crops—above all, cotton and tobacco. In the New South, staple agriculture continued to dominate, but there was marked industrial development as well. Industrial regions developed, producing textiles, coal and iron, and wood products. By 1900, the South's industrial pattern was well-defined.

1870s. Capital was raised locally, subscribed by investors large and small in an atmosphere of intense public boosterism. Workers were recruited mostly from the surrounding countryside, from the hardscrabble hill farms where people struggled to make ends meet. To attract them, mill wages had to be higher than their farm earnings, but wage-setting was pegged to that agricultural standard. And since the agricultural wage was so low in the South, the new mills had a great competitive advantage over the long-established New England industry. An 1897 report estimated the cost of cotton-mill labor as 40 percent lower in the South than in New England.

The labor system that evolved likewise reflected southern agrarian society. To begin with, it was a family system. "Papa decided he would come because he didn't have have nothing much but girls and they had to get out and work like men," recalled one woman. It was not Papa, in fact, but his girls whom the mills wanted, for work as spinners and loom tenders. Only they could not be recruited individually: no right-thinking parent would have permitted that. There was, on the other hand, no reason to object to hiring by families; after all, everyone had been expected to work on the farm. And so the family system of mill labor developed, in which half or more of the operatives were women, and in which, overall, the work force was very young. Fully a quarter of all southern textile workers in the 1880s were under fifteen years of age; three-quarters were twenty-four or younger.

The hours were long—twelve hours a day was the norm—but life in the mill villages was, in the words of one historian, "like a family." Employers tended to be highly paternalistic, providing company housing and a variety of services. The mill workers themselves built close-knit, supportive communities. However, mill jobs were for whites only. Blacks found occasional work as day laborers and janitors, but hardly ever as operatives inside the mills.

Cheap, abundant labor might have been termed the South's most valuable natural resource. But the South was rich in other natural resources. From its rich soil came tobacco, the region's second cash crop. Processing the leaf had always been southern work, and so had been much of the handicraft manufacture of chewing and smoking tobacco. When cigarettes became the fashion in the 1880s, the young North Carolina entrepreneur James B. Duke seized the new market by taking advantage of a southern invention—James A. Bonsack's machine for producing cigarettes automatically. Blacks retained the manual tasks of stemming and stripping the leaf that they had always performed, but, as in the textile mills, machine tending was restricted exclusively to white women.

Lumbering, on the other hand, was largely integrated, with a labor force evenly divided between black and white men. The extensive pine forests of the South were rapidly—*heedlessly* is perhaps the better word—exploited in these years. Finally, there were the rich coal and iron ore deposits of Alabama. These were vigorously developed from the late 1870s onward, so that by 1890 nearly a million tons of pig iron were being produced in the Birmingham district.

Contrary to the high hopes it raised for an emergent New South, this burst of industrial development did not lift the region out of poverty. Industrial output increased impressively, at a more rapid rate than in the North, but not enough to challenge the dominance of the agricultural sector. In 1900 two-thirds of all southerners made their living from the soil, just as they had in 1870. Moreover, the industries that did develop were usually extractive, such as forestry and mining. Nearly two-thirds of the South's labor force worked in the production of raw materials, compared with hardly one-eighth in the Middle Atlantic and New England states. Processing rarely went beyond coarse, semifinished goods, even in textiles. Industry by industry, the key statistic—the value added by manufacturing—showed the South consistently behind the North.

Southerners tended to blame the North. Theirs was a "colonial" economy controlled by New York and Chicago. There was something to this, certainly. Much of the capital—by no means all—did come from the North and from Britain. And the integrating processes of the economy did subordinate regional to national interests. When the railway network moved to a standard gauge, it was of course the southern railroads that had to conform to the national standard. In 1886, in one massive effort, the entire South converted to the 4 feet 8

½ inch standard of the North. Nor was there any lack of instances where northern interests used their muscle to maintain the interregional status quo. Railroads, for example, charged different freight rates for raw materials and finished goods, making it cheap for southern cotton and timber to flow out and northern manufactured goods to flow in.

Yet in the end the South's economic backwardness was mostly of its own making. There was a crowning irony here. The great advantage of the South was its cheap labor. But this also acted as a brake on its capacity to develop into a more technologically advanced economy. First, low wages discouraged employers from replacing workers with machinery. Second, low wages attracted labor-intensive industry, such as textiles. Third, a cheap labor market inhibited investment in education. (In its way, this was a rational choice: the better educated workers would flee to higher-wage markets and the investment in them would be lost).

What was special about the southern labor market was that it was *insulated* from the rest of the country: the normal flow of workers back and forth did not occur and wage differentials did not narrow. And so long as this condition persisted, the South would remain a tributary economy, a supplier on unequal terms to the advanced industrial heartland of the North.

TABLE 18.2

Comparison of South and Non-South Value-Added per Worker, 1910

Type of Industry	South	Non-South
Lumber and timber products	820	1020
Cotton goods	544	764
Cars and general shop construction by steam railroad companies	657	746
Turpentine and resin	516	—
Tobacco manufactures	1615	1394
Foundry and machine shop products	1075	1307
Printing and publishing	1760	2100
Cotton seed oil and cake	1715	—
Hosiery and knit goods	461	724
Furniture and refrigerators	732	1052
Iron and steel	1182*	1433
Fertilizer	1833	1947

*Partially estimated

Source: Gavin Wright, *Old South, New South: Revolutions in the Southern Economy Since the Civil War* (New York: Basic Books), 1986, p. 163.

The World of Work

In a free enterprise system, profit drives the entrepreneur. But the industrial order is not populated only by profit makers. It includes—in vastly larger numbers—wage earners. What is done for profit always acts directly and powerfully on those working for wages. Never did those actions have more profound consequences than in the late nineteenth century. During that period, the modern factory system transformed the lives of American workers.

Autonomous Labor

No one supervised the nineteenth-century coal miner. He was a tonnage worker, paid for the amount of coal he produced. He provided his own tools, worked at his own pace, and knocked off early when he chose. Such autonomous craft workers—almost all of them men—flourished in many branches of nineteenth-century industry. They were mule spinners in cotton mills; puddlers and rollers in iron works; molders in stove making; and machinists, glass blowers, and skilled workers of many other types.

Within the shop, they abided by the *stint*, a limit placed by the workers themselves on the amount that they would produce each day. This informal system of limitation on output infuriated efficiency-minded engineers. But to the worker it signified personal dignity and "unselfish brotherhood" with his fellow employees. The male craft worker took pride in a "manly" bearing, both toward his fellows and toward the boss. One day a shop in Lowell, Massachusetts, posted regulations requiring all employees to be at their posts in work clothes at the opening bell and remain, with the shop door locked, until the dismissal bell. A machinist promptly packed his tools and quit, declaring that he had not "been brought up under such a system of slavery."

Underlying this ethical code was a keen sense of the craft group, each with its own history and customs. Hat finishers, masters of the art of applying fur felting to top hats and bowlers, had a language of their own. When a hatter was hired, he was "shopped"; if fired, he was "bagged"; when he quit work, he "cried off"; and when he took an apprentice, the boy was "under teach." The hatters, most of whom worked in Danbury, Connecticut, or Orange, New Jersey, formed a distinctive, self-contained community.

The craft worker's skills were crucial to nineteenth-century production. He was valued also for the responsibilities he assumed. He hired his own helpers, supervised their work, and paid them out of his earnings. In an era when the scale of production was expanding, autonomous craft workers relieved their employers of the mounting burdens of shop-floor management. Many factory managers tried to shift responsibility to employees. A system of inside contracting developed in metal-fabricating firms that did precise machining and complex assembling. Contractor-employees hired and paid their own men and supervised them completely.

The skilled worker was one central figure of nineteenth-century industry; the common laborer was another. Great numbers of laborers had been needed to dig canals, lay railroad tracks, and build cities. They were equally important in heavy industry. Until the last years of the century, virtually all hauling of materials was done by hand. In the steel mills, a third or more of the workers shoveled coal and iron ore from freight cars and pushed filled wheelbarrows to the furnaces. They also handled the tons of metal that passed through the mill daily at every stage of steel production. They worked in gangs, completely under the charge of the foreman or gang boss. He hired them, told them what to do, and disciplined and fired them.

Dispersal of authority was thus characteristic of nineteenth-century industry. The aristocracy of the workers—the craftsmen, the inside contractors, and the foremen—had a high degree of autonomy. However, their subordinates often paid dearly for that independence. The opportunities for abuse were endless. Any worker who paid his helpers from his own pocket might be tempted to exploit them. In the Pittsburgh area, foremen were known as "pushers," notorious for driving their gangs mercilessly. On the other hand, industrial labor in the nineteenth century was still on a human scale. People dealt with each other face-to-face and often developed cohesive ties within the shop. Striking craft workers commonly received the support of helpers and laborers, and labor gangs sometimes walked out on behalf of a popular foreman.

Labor Recruits

Wherever in the world industrialism took hold, it set people in motion. Artisans moved into factories. Farm folk migrated to manufacturing centers. An industrial labor force emerged. These events took place in all industrializing nations. But the United States built its work force in a distinctive way. Unlike European countries, it could not rely primarily on its own population.

For one thing, the demand for labor was enormous. American industry required nearly three times as many workers in 1900 as in 1870. No less important, people born in the United States after the 1850s could no

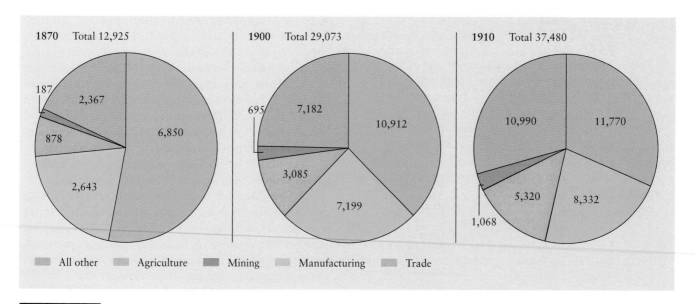

FIGURE 18.3

Changes in the Labor Force, 1870–1910

The numbers represent thousands of people (i.e., 12,925 = 12,925,000). They reveal both the enormous increase in the total labor force between 1870 and 1910 and the dramatic shift from agriculture to industry and other nonagricultural jobs.

longer be attracted into factories. It was not that rural people, who still made up about 75 percent of the population in 1870, refused to leave their land. Indeed, many went westward—but they remained farmers. About half of those leaving farms did move to cities, but they tended to avoid factory work. The desirable jobs—those of puddlers, rollers, molders, and machinists—required industrial skills not held by rural Americans. They did have a basic education. They could read and calculate, and they understood American institutions and ways of doing things. City-bound white Americans found their opportunities in the multiplying white-collar jobs in offices and retail stores rather than in the nation's factories.

As for rural blacks, even the lowest factory job probably seemed better than sharecropping or day labor on a farm. A trickle of blacks began to migrate northward and westward—roughly 80,000 between 1870 and 1890 and another 200,000 from 1890 to 1910. Most of them settled in cities, but they encountered in northern factories racial barriers just as impenetrable as those in the South. The great majority of the black men ended up as casual laborers and janitors, the women as maids and laundresses. Only 7 percent of all African-American men worked in industry in 1890. Industrial employers were able to exclude blacks because of an apparently limitless supply of foreign workers on which they could draw.

Immigrant Labor. The exodus from the Old World had started in the 1840s when the potato famine sent more than a million Irish peasants fleeing to America. During the following years, other traditional rural economies began to break down. As agriculture shifted to cash crops, peasant families lost their self-sufficiency. Increasing populations meant there was not enough land to go round. The erosion of peasant economies struck first in Germany and Scandinavia. Then later in the nineteenth century it spread east into Austria-Hungary and Russia, and south into Italy and the Balkans. In industrial districts of Europe, the forces of economic change also cut loose many workers in the declining artisan trades and obsolete occupations such as hand-loom weaving. A total of about 25 million European immigrants arrived in America between 1870 and 1914.

Ethnic origin largely determined the kind of work that the immigrants found in their new country. Many Western Europeans were seasoned artisans and industrial workers. They generally sought the same types of jobs they had held in the Old World. The nineteenth-century occupational structure took on an ethnic character: the Welsh worked as tin-plate workers, the English as miners, the Germans as machinists and traditional artisans, the Belgians as glass workers, and the Scandinavians as seamen on Great Lakes boats. For common labor, employers had long counted on the brawn of rural immigrants to dig canals, lay railroad

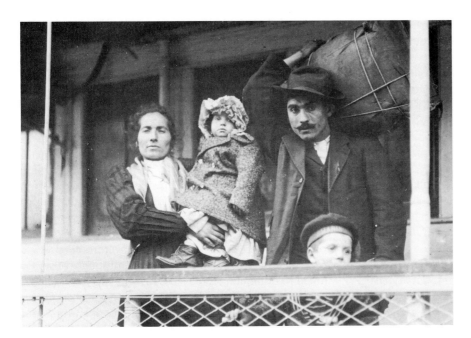

Immigrant Workers

Many native-born Americans resented the influx of peasant immigrants from eastern and southern Europe that began in the 1880s. In fact, however, the newcomers, more than any other group, manned the machines, laid the railroad tracks, and did the heavy construction labor that built the nation's cities. They were, in truth, Europe's gift—its most vigorous and hard-working people.

tracks, and provide unskilled labor in factory and construction gangs.

As industrialization advanced, the demand for unskilled workers increased and the nation's dependence on European craft skills moderated. These developments helped trigger the remarkable shift in immigration away from northern Europe that started in the 1880s. More than 9 million people migrated to America from eastern and southern Europe between 1900 and 1914. Italian and Slavic immigrants, almost wholly lacking in industrial skills, flooded into the lowest rungs of American industry. Heavy, low-paid factory labor became the domain of the recent immigrants. Blast-furnace jobs, a job-seeking investigator heard, were "Hunky work," not suitable for him or any other American.

Factors other than skills determined where immigrants ended up in American industry. Although most of the newcomers arrived alone, they moved within well-defined networks. The immigrants followed relatives or fellow villagers already in America, joined their households as family members or boarders, and relied on them to find a job. A high degree of ethnic clustering resulted, even within a single factory. At the Jones and Laughlin steel works in Pittsburgh, the carpentry shop was German, the hammer shop Polish, and the blooming mill Serbian. Distinctive ethnic characteristics also determined the jobs that immigrants found. For example, men from Italy preferred outdoor work to factory labor, and they were already accustomed to the form of gang labor under a *padrone* (boss) under which they performed construction and road work in America.

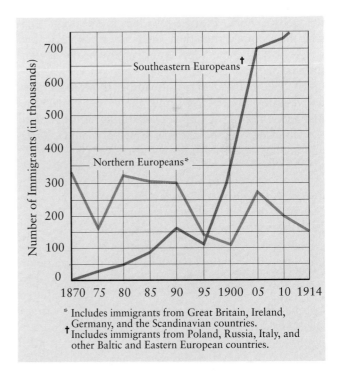

* Includes immigrants from Great Britain, Ireland, Germany, and the Scandinavian countries.
† Includes immigrants from Poland, Russia, Italy, and other Baltic and Eastern European countries.

FIGURE 18.4

American Immigration, 1870–1914

The immigrants entered a modern industrial order, but they saw their surroundings through peasant eyes. With the disruption of the traditional rural economies of Eastern and southern Europe, many peasants had begun to lose their land. This meant an intolerable decline into the class of dependent, propertyless servants. Peasants could avoid such a bitter fate only if they had money to buy property. In Europe, job-seeking peasants commonly tried seasonal agricultural labor or temporary work in nearby cities. America represented merely a larger leap, made possible by cheap and speedy steamship transportation across the Atlantic. The peasant immigrants, most of them young and male, came with the purpose of earning enough money to buy land and then returning to their native villages.

As long as the work lasted, peasant workers were rarely inclined to protest against low wages, harsh conditions, or the hardships of their lives. When work ran out, as it almost always did, there was a safety valve. In depression years, they flooded back to Europe. As many as half of the new immigrants returned to their homelands. No one knows how many saved enough money to fulfill their peasant goals and how many left simply for lack of work. Clearly, however, the peasants' reasons for coming, and their tendency to leave in bad times, made them an ideal labor supply for the new industrial order.

A few fields, such as railroading, employed mostly native-born workers. Overall, however, immigrants manned American industry, constituting well over half the labor force of the nation's principal manufacturing and mining industries after the turn of the century.

Working Women

Between 1870 and 1900 the number of American women grew by half, but the number in wage-earning jobs jumped by almost two-thirds. Women became increasingly important to the industrial economy, and by 1900 they made up more than a fourth of the total nonfarm labor force. The role they found as wage earners was shaped by the fact that they were women. Contemporary beliefs about womanhood largely determined which women entered the work force and how they were treated once they became wage earners.

Wives were not supposed to hold jobs. In 1890 less than 5 percent of all married white women worked outside their homes. Black married women had a much higher labor participation rate, over 30 percent. Before marriage young women generally did go to work, at least those below the respectable middle class; indeed, in most working-class families they had no choice. The majority of all employed women in 1890 were from sixteen to twenty-four years old. When older women worked, remarked one observer, it "was usually a sign

that something had gone wrong"—their husbands were gone, jobless, or incapacitated.

Since women were considered to be inherently different from men, it followed that they should not be permitted to do "men's work." And regardless of the value of their labor, they could not be paid at men's rates. The dominant view was that a woman did not require a "living wage" because, as one investigator reported, "it is expected that she has men to support her." Moreover, the occupation that served as the baseline for all women's jobs was domestic service, always very poorly paid, or, in a woman's own home, not paid at all. And because virtually all occupations employed either women or men exclusively, the job opportunities for women were always limited and overcrowded.

The sex-typing of occupations, although certainly linked to dominant stereotypes of women's lesser capacities, is not easy to explain. There were some originally male occupations, such as telephone operators and store clerks, that by the 1890s became female. In each case, as an occupation became feminized, it also became characterized as having female attributes, even though very similar or even identical work had been done by men. Once a job became identified with women, it became unsuitable for men. There were, literally, no male telephone operators by 1900.

At the turn of the century, women workers fell into three roughly equal categories. A third worked as maids or other types of domestic servants. Another third held "female" white-collar jobs in teaching, nursing, sales, and office work. Sex-typing affected the third of the women in industrial occupations as well. Few worked as supervisors, fewer in the crafts, nearly none as day laborers. Most female industrial workers were classified as *operatives*—machine tenders and hand workers. Women were heavily concentrated in the garment trades and textile mills but could be found throughout industry in "light" occupations—as packers, inspectors, assemblers, or as sausage stuffers in packing houses.

As with male workers, ethnicity and race played a big part in the distribution of women's jobs among particular groups. Exclusion from all but the most menial of jobs applied as rigidly to black women as to black men. White-collar jobs were reserved for the native-born, although in the cities these were often the second-generation daughters of immigrants. And, as with men, ethnicity created clustering patterns in the jobs held by wage-earning women, or, as in the case of Italian families, restricted them to subcontracting tasks like sewing that could be done at home.

But gender also mattered crucially. Women's identity give their work distinctive meaning. Department store clerks, for example, developed a work culture and language just as robust as that of the hard-drinking hatters of South Orange, New Jersey. Most important was the fact that wage-earning women were young and un-

1907-J.Byron Photo.

Switchboard Operators

Telephone work offers a prime historical example of the process of sex-typing in American employment. When the first telephone exchange was set up in Boston in 1878, it was manned by teen-age boys, following the practice in the telegraph industry. During the 1880s, however, young women increasingly replaced the boys, and by 1900 switchboard operation was defined strictly as women's work. In this photograph of a telephone exchange in Columbus, Ohio, in 1907, the older woman at left has risen to be supervisor, but it is the two men in the picture who are clearly in charge. The other major occupations in this new industry—telephone installation and line maintenance—were just as strictly male as switchboard operation was female, but, of course, on a much higher pay scale.

married. For many, the first job was also the first escape from family discipline. It was an opportunity to gain some independence, to form friendships with other young women, and to experience, however briefly, a fun-loving time of nice clothes, dancing, and other "cheap amusements."

To some degree, these preoccupations made it easier to overlook or accept the miserable terms under which they worked. But working young women also developed a sense of group solidarity and self-respect. Fashionable clothes might appear frivolous to the casual observer, but they also conveyed the message that the working girl considered herself as good as anyone. And there were occasions, as with the Jewish garment workers of New York and the Irish-American telephone operators of Boston, when the rebellious youth culture united with feelings of job grievance to produce astonishing strike movements among working women.

Sex-typing of work was legitimized by the sentimental view of women as the weaker sex. But powerful interests also played a role. Craft workers protected their male domain, and employers profited from cut-rate work. Wherever they worked, women earned wages below those of the lowest male occupations. At the turn of the century, the weekly wage of women factory workers came to roughly $7—$3 less than unskilled males and $5 less than the average for all industrial employees.

The objection to working wives, also expressed in sentimental and moral terms, was likewise based on

solid necessity. From the standpoint of the industrial economy, the basic economic unit consisted of the individual employee. For workers, however, the family was the economic unit. In this family economy, the wife contributed crucially. Cooking, cleaning, and tending the children were not income-producing or reckoned in terms of money. But everyone knew that the family household could not function without the wife's contribution. Therefore, her place was in the home.

Working-class families, however, found the going hard on a single income. Only among the highly skilled workers, wrote an investigator of the family budgets of coal and iron workers in the early 1890s, "was it possible for the husband unaided to support his family." For most working-class families, the hardest period came during the child-bearing years, when there were many mouths to feed and only the earnings of the father. Thereafter, the family income began to grow. Not only unmarried sons and daughters but the younger children as well contributed their share. In 1900, one of every five children below the age of sixteen worked, including probably a quarter of a million below the age of ten. "When the people own houses," remarked a printer from Fall River, "you will generally find that it is a large family all working together."

Obstacles to child labor, however, began to appear. By the 1890s, all the northern industrial states had passed laws prohibiting the employment of young children and regulating the work hours of teen-agers. Most of those states also required children from eight to four-

Breaker Boys

In the anthracite districts of eastern Pennsylvania, giant structures called breakers processed the coal as it came out of the mines, crushing it and sorting it by size for sale as domestic fuel. The boys shown in this photograph had the job of picking out the slate and refuse as the processed coal came down the shutes, working long hours in a constant cloud of coal dust for less than a dollar a day. Breaker boy was the the first job, often begun before the age of ten, in a lifetime in the mines. The photograph does not show any old men, but sick and disabled miners often ended their careers as breaker boys—hence the saying among coal diggers, "twice a boy and once a man is the poor miner's life."

teen years of age to go to school for a certain number of weeks each year. Working-class families continued to rely on second incomes, but this money was more and more likely to come from the wife than from the children. After 1890 the proportion of working married women crept steadily upward. For working-class women, entry into the labor market went forward especially rapidly. About a fifth of the wives of unskilled and semiskilled men in Chicago held jobs in 1920. Wage-earning wives, many with children, were on their way to becoming a primary part of America's labor force.

Systems of Control

As technology advanced and modern management emerged, controls over the work process increased.

Workers might have preferred the older systems of autonomous work, but they had no choice. They increasingly lost the proud independence that had characterized nineteenth-century craft work.

When mine owners introduced undercutting machines in the 1880s, they deprived the coal miners of the pick work that was their most prized skill. "Anyone with a weak head and a strong back can load machine coal," grumbled one Kentucky miner. "But a man has to think and study every day like you was studying a book if he is going to get the best of the coal when he uses only a pick." Similar complaints came from many other craft workers as their skills fell victim to machinery—from hand-loom weavers early in the nineteenth century to glass-blowers a hundred years later.

What was primarily at work in this de-skilling process was a new system that we call *mass production*. This system applied to products that became standardized and found high-volume markets. Consider, for example, the great advances that accompanied the creation of a national market for dressed beef in the 1870s. The huge packing houses that sprang up in Chicago shifted from the traditional reliance on skilled butchers to a highly specialized division of labor. At the Armour plant, workers performed seventy-eight distinct jobs, working extremely efficiently and at high speed as the carcasses moved along, hooked to overhead conveyors. In a ten-hour day, a gang of 157 workers could handle 1,050 cattle, many more per employee than if one skilled butcher did everything. Machinery did not replace workers; rather, a minute division of labor vastly increased workers' output.

In most cases, however, the division of labor did lead to mechanization. This was because once jobs had been subdivided into simple, repetitive tasks, it was generally possible to design machines that could do those tasks. The greatest opportunity came in the manufacture of products assembled from standardized, interchangeable parts—such as agricultural implements, sewing machines, typewriters, bicycles, and, after 1900, the automobile. In all these cases, machine tools that cut, drilled, and ground the metal parts had originally been manned by skilled machinists. But as machine tools became more specialized, they became *dedicated* machines, that is, set up to do the same job over and over again, and the need for skilled operatives disappeared.

"A man never learns the machinist's trade now," a craft worker complained in 1883. In the manufacture of sewing machines, "the trade is so subdivided that a man is not considered a machinist at all. One man may make just a particular part of a machine and may not know anything whatever about another part of the same machine." Such a worker, noted an observer, "cannot be master of a craft, but only master of a fragment."

AMERICAN VOICES

The Impact of Mechanization *John Morison*

John Morison, a machinist, describes to a Senate investigating committee in 1883 what technological progress has meant to him and his fellow skilled workers.

Q. Is there any difference between the conditions under which machinery is made now and those which existed ten years ago?

A. A great deal of difference.

Q. State the differences as well as you can.

A. Well, the trade has been subdivided and those subdivisions have been again subdivided, so that a man never learns the machinist's trade now. Ten years ago he learned, not the whole of the trade, but a fair portion of it. Also, there is more machinery used in the business, which again makes machinery. In the case of making the sewing-machine, for instance, you find that the trade is so subdivided that a man is not considered a machinist at all. Hence it is merely laborers' work and it is laborers that work at that branch of our trade. Machinery is produced a great deal cheaper than it used to be formerly, and in fact, through this system of work, 100 men are able to do now what it took 300 or 400 men to do fifteen years ago.

Q. Have you noticed the effect upon the intellect of this plan of keeping a man at one particular branch?

A. Yes. It has a very demoralizing effect upon the mind throughout. The man thinks of nothing else but that particular branch; he knows that he cannot leave that particular branch and go to any other; he has got no chance whatever to learn anything else because he is kept steadily and constantly at that particular thing, and of course his intellect must be narrowed by it.

Q. And does he not finally acquire so much skill in the manipulation of his particular part of the business that he does it without any mental effort?

A. Almost. In fact he becomes almost a part of the machinery.

Q. What is the social condition of the machinists in New York and the surrounding towns and cities?

A. It is rather low compared to what their social condition was ten or fifteen years ago.

Q. Do you remember when it was better?

A. When I first went to learn the trade a machinist considered himself more than the average workingman; in fact he did not like to be called a workingman. He liked to be called a mechanic. Today he recognizes the fact that he is simply a laborer the same as the others. Ten years ago even, he considered himself a little above the average workingman; he thought himself a mechanic, and felt he belonged in the middle class; but today he recognizes the fact that he is simply the same as any other ordinary laborer, no more and no less.

Q. What is the social air about the ordinary machinist's house? Are there evidences of happiness, and joy, and hilarity, or is the general atmosphere solemn, and somber, and gloomy?

A. To explain that fully, I would state first of all, that machinists have got to work ten hours a day in New York, and that they are compelled to work very hard. In fact the machinists of America are compelled to do about one third more work than the machinists do in England in a day. . . . Of course when a man is dragged out in that way he is naturally cranky, and he makes all around him cranky; so, instead of a pleasant house it is every day expecting to lose his job by competition from his fellow workmen, there being so many out of employment, and no places for them, and his wages being pulled down through their competition, looking at all times to be thrown out of work in that way, and staring starvation in the face makes him feel sad, and the head of the house being sad, of course the whole family is the same, so the house looks like a dull prison instead of a home . . . .

Q. Where do you work?

A. I would rather not have it in print. Perhaps I would have to go Monday morning if I did. We are so situated in the machinist's trade that we daren't let them know much about us. If they know that we open our mouths on the labor question, and try to form organizations, we are quietly told that "business is slack," and we have got to go.

Source: U.S. Senate, Committee on Education and Labor, *Report on the Relations between Labor and Capital* (1885), I, 755–59.

The Killing Floor
To the modern eye, the labor process depicted in this 1882 engraving of a Chicago meat-packing plant seems primitive and inefficient, but in fact it contains the seeds of America's mass-production revolution. At the far left, the steer has already been stunned by one specialist, killed by a second, and attached to a chain that will lift it on to the overhead conveyor. The division of labor is already in place (each of the workers on the line does a single repetitive task) and the process is continuous. It would be only a small step from the killing floors of the Chicago packing plants to Henry Ford's assembly line.

Technology also took hold of the pace of operations. The machine, not the worker, determined how fast production would go. "If you need to turn out a little more," boasted a superintendent at Swift and Company, "you speed up the conveyor a little and the men speed up to keep pace." Complaints about speed-ups were a sure sign of workers' loss of control over their jobs.

Frederick W. Taylor and Scientific Management. The impact of machinery on workers was essentially unintentional, a by-product of decisions made for technological reasons. Employers doubtless recognized that mechanization would better enable them to discipline their workers. But this was only an incidental benefit added to the efficiencies that came from the machinery itself. Gradually, however, employers came to realize that managing workers might itself be a way of reducing the cost of production.

The pioneer in this field was Frederick W. Taylor. Taylor had made a name for himself as an expert on metal-cutting methods. In 1895 he published a landmark essay, "A Piece Rate System," that proposed a strategy for getting the maximum work from the individual worker. Taylor suggested two basic reforms. The first would eliminate the brain work from manual labor. Managers would assume "the burden of gathering together all of the traditional knowledge which in the past has been possessed by the workmen and then of classifying, tabulating, and reducing this knowledge to rules, laws, and formulae." The second reform, a logical consequence of the first, would deprive workers of the authority they had normally exercised on the shop floor. Workers would "do what they are told promptly and

without asking questions or making suggestions . . . . The duty of enforcing . . . rests with the management alone."

Once they had the knowledge and power, according to Taylor, managers would put labor on a "scientific" basis. This meant subjecting each task to a *time-and-motion study*, by which an engineer with a stopwatch analyzed and timed each job. A personnel office would hire and train the right person for each job. Workers would be paid at a differential rate—that is, a certain amount if they met the stopwatch standard, a higher rate for any greater output. Taylor claimed that his techniques would guarantee the optimum level of worker efficiency. His simplistic assumption was that only money mattered to workers, and that they would be automatically responsive to the lure of higher earnings.

Taylor called his method *scientific management*. It was not, in practice, a roaring success. His reforms called for a total restructuring of factory administration. No company ever adopted Taylor's entire system, and the few that tried to do so paid dearly for the effort. The differential-rate method, which was widely used, met stubborn resistance. "It looks to me like slavery to have a man stand over you with a stopwatch," complained one iron molder. A union leader insisted that "this system is wrong, because we want our heads left on us."

Yet Taylor, a brilliant publicist, achieved something of fundamental importance. He and his disciples spread his scientific-management teachings throughout American industry. Taylor's successors moved beyond his simplistic economic psychology, creating the new professions of personnel administration and industrial psychology that purported to know how to extract more and better work from workers. A threshold had been crossed into the modern era of labor management.

So the circle closed on American workers. With each advance, the quest for efficiency cut deeper into their cherished autonomy. Mechanization, scientific management, and the growing scale of industrial activity diminished workers and cut them down to fit the production system. The process occurred unevenly. For textile workers, the loss had come early. Miners and iron workers felt it much more slowly. Others, such as craft workers in the building trades, escaped the process almost entirely. But increasing numbers of workers found themselves in an environment that crushed any sense of mastery or even understanding.

The Labor Movement

Wherever industrialization has taken hold, workers have organized and responded collectively. However, the movements they built have varied from one industrial society to another. In the United States, workers were especially uncertain about the path they wanted to take. Only in the 1880s did the American labor movement settle into a fixed course.

Reformers and Unionists

In 1883, a New York wagon driver named Thomas B. McGuire testified before a Senate committee. He had saved $300 from his wages, "so that I might become something of a capitalist eventually." But he soon failed. "A man in the express business today owning one or two horses and a wagon cannot even eke out an existence from the business," McGuire complained. "The competition is too great from the Adams Express Company and all those other monopolies." McGuire's prospects seemed no better in the hack (hired carriage) business:

> Corporations usually take that business themselves. They can manage to get men, at starvation wages, and put them on a hack, and put a livery on them with a gold band and brass buttons, to show that they are slaves—I beg pardon; I did not intend to use the word slaves; there are no slaves in this country now—to show that they are merely servants.

Slave or liveried servant, the symbolic meaning was the same to McGuire. He was speaking of the crushed aspirations of the independent American worker.

Labor Reform and the Knights of Labor. What would satisfy the Thomas McGuires of the nineteenth century?

Only the restoration of a republican society in which all members were social and political equals and in which everyone might hope to become independent. To recapture the republican virtues did not require returning to the agrarian past but, rather, moving forward beyond the selfishness of the existing industrial order to a time when no distinction would exist between capitalists and workers. All would be "producers" laboring together in what was commonly called the "cooperative commonwealth." This ideal inspired wave after wave of labor-reform movements, going back to the workingmen's parties of the 1830s and culminating after the Civil War in the Noble and Holy Order of the Knights of Labor.

The Knights of Labor was founded in 1869 as a secret society of Philadelphia garment cutters. The organization gradually spread to other cities and by 1878 had become a national movement. Led by Grand Master Workman Terence V. Powderly, the Knights boasted an elaborate ritual and ceremony that appealed strongly to the fraternal spirit of the nineteenth-century worker. The Knights of Labor typified the American labor-reform tradition. The goal was to "give voice to that grand undercurrent of mighty thought, which is today [1880] crystallizing in the hearts of men, and urging them on to perfect organization through which to gain the power to make labor emancipation possible."

But how was "emancipation" to be achieved? The Knights tried a number of solutions, including cooperation. Funds would be raised to set up cooperative factories and shops that would be owned and run by the employees. As these cooperatives flourished and spread, American society would be transformed into a cooperative commonwealth. But little was actually done. In reality, the Knights concentrated mainly on "education." Powderly regarded the organization as a vast labor lyceum that almost anyone could join. The cooperative commonwealth would arrive in some mysterious way as more and more "producers" became members and learned the group's message from lectures, discussions, and publications. Social evil would not end in a day, but "must await the gradual development of educational enlightenment."

Trade Unionism. The labor-reform movement expressed the higher aspirations of American workers. Another kind of organization—the trade union—tended to their day-to-day needs. Unions had long been central to the lives of craft workers. Apprenticeship rules regulated entry into a trade, and the *closed shop*— by reserving all jobs for union members—kept out lower-wage and incompetent workers. Union rules specified the terms of work, sometimes in minute detail. Above all, trade unionism defended the craft worker's traditional skills and rights.

A Railroad Brotherhood

Locomotive firemen, who fed the boilers on nineteenth-century steam engines, ranked below the engineers, but still considered themselves a privileged occupation. This union certificate conveys the respectable values to which the locomotive firemen adhered and, as depicted in the scenes on the right-hand side—the need they felt to protect their families (through the affordable insurance provided by their union) in the event of accidents that were so much a part of the dangerous trade they followed.

The union also symbolized the social identity of a craft. Hatters took pride in their drinking prowess, an on-the-job privilege jealously guarded, and their unions sometimes resembled drinking clubs. More often, however, the craft union had an uplifting character. A Birmingham iron puddler claimed that his union's "main object was to educate mechanics up to a standard of morality and temperance, and good workmanship." Because operating trains was a high-risk occupation, the railroad brotherhoods stressed mutual aid, providing accident and death benefits and encouraging members to assist one another. On the job and off, the unions played a big part in the lives of craft workers.

The earliest unions were local groups of workers in the same trade. Many of them, especially among German workers, organized initially along ethnic lines. These local bodies grew into national unions. The first to survive, the International Typographical Union, was formed in 1852. By the 1870s, molders, iron workers, bricklayers, and about thirty other trades had formed national unions.

The protection of job interests might have seemed a far cry from the reform idealism of the Knights of Labor. But both kinds of motives arose from a single workers' culture. Seeing no conflict, many workers carried membership cards in both the Knights of Labor and a trade union. The careers of many labor leaders, including Powderly, likewise embraced both kinds of activity. For many years even the functional lines were indistinct. At the local level, little separated a trade assembly of the Knights from a local trade union; both engaged in fraternal and bargaining activities.

Trade unions generally barred women, and so had the Knights until, in 1881, women shoe workers in Philadelphia struck in support of their male co-workers and won the right to form their own local assembly. By 1886 probably 50,000 women belonged to the Knights of Labor. Their courage on the picket line prompted Powderly's rueful remark that women "are the best men in the Order." For a handful, like the hosiery worker Leonora M. Barry, the Knights provided a rare chance to take up leadership roles as organizers and officials. For many others, the liberation was more modest, but very real: "timid young girls—girls who have been overworked from their cradle—stand[ing] up bravely . . . swayed . . . by the wrongs heaped upon their comrades, talk[ing] nobly and beautifully of the hope of redress to be found in organization." Similarly, the Knights of Labor grudgingly expanded the opportunity for black workers to join up, recognizing the need for solidarity and, just as important, in deference to the Order's egalitarian principles. The Knights could rightly boast that their "great work has been to organize labor which was previously unorganized."

The American Federation of Labor

In the early 1880s the Knights began to act increasingly like a trade union. Boycott campaigns against the products of "unfair" employers achieved impressive results. With the economy booming and workers in short supply, the Knights began to win strikes, including a major victory against Jay Gould's Southwestern railway system in 1885. Workers flocked into the organization, and its membership jumped from 100,000 to perhaps 700,000 in less than a year. For a brief time, the Knights stood poised as a potential industrial-union movement capable of bringing all workers into its fold.

AMERICAN VOICES

On Strike *H. J. Thomas*

H. J. Thomas, a Welsh iron worker, writes home about a strike wave in the iron mills and coal mines of the Pittsburgh region. Note the mixture of labor dignity, craft pride, and ethnic identity that informs his account. Thomas is a Welshman, but in America he does not consider himself a "foreigner"—that term is reserved for the unskilled Swedish and Bohemian "rubbish" brought in to break the strike.

June 27, 1882 [Pittsburgh, Pennsylvania]

As yet there is no expectation that the strike wounds will be healed and there is little change in the situation. It is true that some mills are working, one in Cleveland, Ohio, one in Apollo, Armstrong County, Pennsylvania, and another near the city of Allegheny. These mills are worked by nonunion and unskilled labor, the sweepings of foreign countries, Swedes and Bohemians, who, it seems, were brought here to make good the shortage by the aristocratic elements for the purpose of bringing down the American workman to the low level in the European countries. No doubt much of this rubbish left their own lands for the good of those countries. Who knows but that the transporting of unskilled foreigners to this country, who undermine the rights of our workmen and help their oppressors to rob them of their just wages for their work and lower the dignity of the American workman, may provide the opportunity for someone in the federal government to put forward a law that will be second to the Chinese bill to prevent foreigners from emigrating to this country for ten or fifteen years.

Let the masters remember that the balance of power is in the hands of the sons of toil by the ballot box. It is a pity that someone does not whisper in the ears of the masters that there are breakers ahead. But this strike is not confined to the iron workers but also to a large number of the coal miners. Two thousand of them have been on strike since the 1st of last April. They are trying to get four cents a bushel for mining coal. . . .

Many of these miners are camping out in harmony like the Apostles long ago. They have two aims for adopting the gypsy life, thrift and to prepare tents if the masters throw them out of their cottages. Remember that the dignity of the workman in the United States is higher than on the Continent of Europe as the division between the rich John and the poor David is lower. . . .

On Saturday, 17th of this month, there was a majestic procession by different branches of industry. There were about thirty thousand in the procession but the rain fell in a flood and half of them fell out. Their banners were many and their mottoes showed their spirit. On one there was the outline of a male skeleton with the following words: "This is all of the man that works for nothing all day. All we ask is enough to make some stuffing." And another was "Competence obtained by honest labor is a blessing. Genius is gold in the mines. Talent is a miner who works and brings it out." Another was "Capital without labor like faith without works is dead."

P.S. Warn our nation from emigrating at this time for the strike is spreading rapidly. It would be too much to forecast what is in store for the sons of toil.

Source: Sigmund Diamond, ed., *The Nation Transformed* (New York: George Braziller, 1963), pp. 26–67.

The rapid growth of the Knights of Labor frightened the national trade unions. They tried to keep their local branches away from the Knights, but without success. The unions then began to insist on a clear separation of roles, with the Knights confined strictly to the field of labor reform. This was partly a battle over turf, but it reflected also a deepening divergence of labor philosophies.

This divergence is perhaps best seen in the debate over the shorter workday. For labor reformers, the need for more leisure arose from the duties workers had "to perform as American citizens and members of society." More leisure for workers was a precondition for a healthy republican society. Increasingly, however, the issue was seized by trade unionists, and they gave the demand for the eight-hour day a more practical bent: it was a way of spreading the available jobs among more workers, of protecting against overwork, and (like higher wages) of providing workers with a better life. "Eight hours for work, eight hours for rest, eight hours for what we will" was the slogan of the trade unions, not the Knights of Labor.

The Haymarket Square Riot. The trade unions set May 1, 1886, as the deadline for achieving the eight-hour day. As the time approached, a wave of strikes and demonstrations broke out. In Chicago, a battle on May 3 at the McCormick agricultural-implement works resulted in the deaths of four strikers. Chicago was a hotbed of American *anarchism*—the revolutionary advocacy of a stateless society—and local anarchists, most of them German immigrants, called a protest meeting the next evening at Haymarket Square. The meeting went off peacefully, but when police moved in at the end to break it up, someone threw a bomb and several policemen were killed or wounded. The anarchist organizers of the rally were charged wtih criminal conspiracy, a legal doctrine so broad as to require no proof of direct involvement in the bombing to justify a finding of guilt. There was, in fact, no evidence linking them to the bombing. Four men were executed, one committed suicide, and the others received long prison sentences. They were victims of one of the great miscarriages of American justice.

Seizing on the popular antiunion hysteria set off by the Haymarket affair, employers took the offensive against the campaign for an eight-hour day. They broke strikes violently, compiled blacklists of defeated strikers, and forced others to sign *yellow-dog contracts* (guarantees that, as a condition of employment, they would not join a union). If trade unionists needed any further confirmation of the tough world in which they lived, they found it in Haymarket and its aftermath.

Samuel Gompers and the AFL. In December 1886, having failed to prevail on the Knights of Labor to desist from union activity, the national trade unions formed the American Federation of Labor (AFL). The AFL embodied the belief of the national unions that they constituted a distinctive movement. The federation, in effect, locked into place the trade-union structure as it had evolved by the 1880s. Underlying this structure was the conviction that workers had to take the world as it was, not as they dreamed it might be.

The architect of the American Federation of Labor, and its president for nearly forty years, was Samuel Gompers. Gompers, a cigar maker from New York City, hammered out the philosophical position that would define American "pure and simple" unionism. First, there would be a steady focus on concrete, short-term gains. Second, unions would rely on economic power rather than politics. Third, they would limit their membership to workers, organized on strictly occupational lines. Finally, the unions strongly rejected the theories and grand schemes that had excited the labor reformers. "No matter how just a cause is," Gompers argued, "unless the cause is backed up with power to enforce it, it is going to be crushed and annihilated."

The steady growth of the trade unions after the formation of the AFL seemed to justify Gompers's confidence that he had hit on the correct formula for the American labor movement. The Knights of Labor faded away. The organization had been hard hit by the antilabor reaction to the Haymarket affair, and after a series of disastrous strikes, it retreated from the trade-union field. Grand Master Workman Powderly turned back to the rhetoric of labor reform. But the appeal to wage earners had disappeared. In its declining years, the Knights survived mainly in small-town America, no longer a workers' movement.

Industrial War

The Homestead Strike. Of America's workers, few had more reason to be satisfied with their lives than the skilled steelworkers of Homestead, Pennsylvania. They earned good wages, lived comfortably, and generally owned their own homes. The town was very much their community, with a municipal government run by officials elected from their own ranks. And in Andrew Carnegie the Homestead workers thought they had a truly sympathetic employer: for had not Good Old Andy said in a famous magazine article that the right of workers to combine was no less sacred than that of capitalists? Or that workers held a kind of moral claim on their jobs that forbade the use of strikebreakers by employers?

Carnegie, however, had other plans. In his view, the union had become too expensive. It deprived his steel company of the full benefits of the advanced machinery he was introducing; and with that machinery, the skills of his workers counted for less. Lacking the stomach for the hard battle ahead, Carnegie hid himself away in his remote castle in Scotland. But he left behind a second-in-command eminently qualified for the job at hand. This was Henry Clay Frick, a former coal baron with a deservedly fearsome reputation as an enemy of trade unionism.

After some perfunctory bargaining, Frick announced that, effective July 1, 1892, the company would no longer deal with the Amalgamated Association of Iron and Steel Workers. If the employees wanted to work, they would have to return on an individual basis. Frick's strategy was already clear. Preparations had been made to fortify the plant so that strikebreakers could be brought in to resume operations and defeat the union. At stake now was not just wage cuts but the defense of an entire way of life. To preserve their "workers' republic," Homesteaders thought they had the right to deny the company access to the plant, and town authorities turned away the county sheriff when he tried to take possession of the plant on behalf of the company. The entire community—women no less than men—mobilized in defense of the union.

At dawn on July 6, two bargeloads of Pinkerton guards were spied approaching Homestead up the Monongahela River. Behind hastily erected barricades, the strikers opened fire, and a bloody battle ensued. When the Pinkertons finally surrendered, they were mercilessly pummeled by the enraged women of Homestead as they retreated to the railway station. Frick appealed to the governor of Pennsylvania, who mobilized the state militia. Homestead was placed under martial law, strike leaders and town officials were arrested on charges of riot, murder, and treason, and the great steelworks was taken over and opened to strikebreakers.

The defeat at Homestead marked the beginning of

the end of trade unionism in the iron and steel industry. Ended too were any lingering illusions about the sanctity of workers' communities such as Homestead. "Men talk like anarchists or lunatics when they insist that the workmen of Homestead have done right," asserted one conservative journal. Nothing could be permitted to interfere with private property or threaten law and order. The Homestead strike ushered in an era of strife in which working people found arrayed against them not only the formidable power of corporate industry but the even more formidable power of their own government.

The Great Pullman Boycott. The fullest demonstration of that hard reality had its origins at a place that seemed an even less likely site for class warfare than Homestead. Pullman, Illinois, was a model factory town, famous for the amenities it offered to workers and the beauty of its landscaping and city plan. The town was named for its creator, George M. Pullman, who had made a great fortune as the inventor and manufacturer of the Pullman sleeping cars that brought comfort and luxury to railway travel. Still, when the Panic of 1893 struck, business fell off and the Pullman Company cut wages. But the rents for company housing, always higher than elsewhere, were not cut, and for many workers take-home pay shrank to pitiful levels.

When a committee finally called on him in May 1894 to present the workers' grievances, Pullman refused to budge. There was no connection between his role as employer and landlord, he insisted. In addition, he fired the committee members.

The strike that ensued might have become no more than a footnote in American labor history but for one thing—the Pullman workers belonged to the American Railway Union (ARU), a rapidly growing industrial union of railroad workers recently formed by the labor leader Eugene V. Debs. In response to the strikers' plea, the ARU directed its members not to handle Pullman sleeping cars, which were operated by the railroads but were owned and serviced by the Pullman Company. This was a classic example of a *labor boycott*, in which force is applied at a secondary point (the railroads) as a way to bring pressure on the primary target (Pullman). Railroad officials, already fearful of the growing power of the ARU, saw the Pullman boycott as their chance to break the union. The General Managers' Association, which represented the railroads serving Chicago, insisted on running the Pullman cars. Since ARU members refused to operate trains with Pullman cars, a far-flung rail strike soon spread across the country and threatened to disrupt the entire economy.

Quite deliberately, the railroad managers maneuvered to bring the federal government into the dispute. Their hook was the U.S. mail cars, which they took care to attach to every train hauling Pullman cars. When strikers tried to stop these trains, the General Managers' Association appealed to President Cleveland to send in troops to protect the U.S. mails and halt the growing violence. It so happened that in Attorney-General Richard Olney, a former railroad lawyer, the General Managers' Association had a direct link to the president. Overriding the protests of the liberal Illinois gov-

The Pullman Strike
Chicago was the hub of the midwestern railwork network, and the strategic center of the battle between the Pullman boycotters and the trunkline railroads. For the strikers, the crucial thing was to keep trains with Pullman cars attached from running, for the railroads, it was to get the trains through at any cost. The stage was thus set for violent confrontation, as is evident in this contemporary drawing of a standoff between armed railroad guards and angry strikers.

ernor, John P. Altgeld, Cleveland sent in federal troops. When this tactic failed to quell the popular resistance, Olney got court injunctions prohibiting the ARU leaders from conducting the strike. Debs and his subordinates refused to obey; they were held in contempt of court and jailed. Now leaderless and totally uncoordinated, the strike quickly disintegrated.

But no one could doubt what had defeated the great Pullman boycott of 1894: it had been crushed by the naked use of government power on behalf of the railroad companies.

American Radicalism in the Making

Oppression does not radicalize all its victims, but for some, it does. And when social injustice is most painfully felt, when the underlying power realities stand most openly revealed, the process of radicalization speeds up. Such was the case during the depression years of the 1890s. Out of the industrial strife of that decade emerged the main forces of twentieth-century American radicalism.

Eugene Debs and American Socialism. Very little in Eugene Debs's background suggested that he would one day become the nation's preeminent socialist. Born in 1855 of middle-class French-Alsatian parents, Debs grew up believing in the essential goodness of American society as he found it in his home town of Terre Haute, Indiana, a prosperous midwestern railroad center. Active in the Democratic party and very popular in the community, Debs might have made a career in politics or business. Instead, he returned to the railway yards where he had worked as a boy, became involved in the local labor movement, and in 1880, at the age of twenty-five, was elected national secretary-treasurer and journal editor of the Brotherhood of Locomotive Firemen.

This was one of the craft unions that had emerged to represent the skilled operating trades on the railroads. It was highly conservative, opposed to strikes, and indifferent to the well-being of the mass of low-paid track and yard laborers. This began to bother Debs, and in 1892 he unexpectedly resigned from his comfortable union post to devote himself to a new organization—the American Railway Union—that would organize all railroad workers irrespective of skill, that is, an *industrial union.*

The Pullman boycott, as it developed into a life-and-death struggle, visibly changed Debs. It had become "a contest between the producing classes and the money power of the country," Debs declared. Debs was sentenced to six months in the federal penitentiary—not

for having violated any specific law, but for refusing to obey court orders he knew to be trumped-up and prejudicial. He came out of jail an avowed radical, committed to a lifelong struggle against a system that enabled employers to enlist the powers of government to enforce their arbitrary rule over working people. Initially Debs identified himself as a Populist, but he quickly gravitated toward the Socialist camp.

German refugees had brought the ideas of Karl Marx, the German radical philosopher, to America after the failed 1848 revolutions in Europe. Marx offered a powerful economic critique of capitalism. His prescription for revolution through class struggle inspired the most durable of radical movements throughout the industrial world. Although little noticed in most parts of American society, Marxist socialism struck deep roots in the growing German-American communities of Chicago and New York. In 1877 the Socialist Labor Party was formed, and from that time onward Marxist socialism maintained a continuing, if narrowly based, presence in American politics.

When Eugene Debs appeared in their midst in 1897, the Socialists were in a state of crisis. Their leader, Daniel De Leon, was a brilliant theorist but a poor political manager. He preferred an ideologically pure party to one that tried to appeal for the popular vote. De Leon's rigid beliefs prompted a revolt within the Socialist Labor Party, in which Debs joined. When the rival Socialist Party of America was formed in 1901, it was with the aim of building a broad-based political movement.

A spellbinding campaigner, Debs was a superb spokesman for his party. He had the common touch, and he attracted a devoted national following. Debs talked socialism in an American idiom, making Marxism understandable and persuasive to many ordinary Americans. Under him the new party began to break down ethnic barriers and attract American-born voters. Many trade unionists, disillusioned as Debs himself had been by the events of the 1890s, went through the same kind of radical evolution and joined up in large numbers. In Texas, Oklahoma, and Minnesota, socialism exerted a powerful appeal among cotton and wheat farmers. The party was also highly successful at attracting women activists. Inside of a decade, with a national network of branches and state organizations, the Socialist party had become a force to be reckoned with in American politics.

Western Radicalism. In the meantime, a different brand of American radicalism was taking shape in the West. After many years of mostly friendly labor relations, the situation in the western mining camps turned ugly during the 1890s. Powerful new corporations were taking over, and they wanted to be rid of the miners' union, the Western Federation of Miners (WFM). Moreover, silver and copper prices became increasingly unprofitable in the early 1890s, bringing pressure to cut the miners' wages. When strikes resulted, they took a particularly violent turn.

In 1892 at Coeur d'Alene, a silver-mining district in northern Idaho, striking miners engaged in gun battles with company guards, sent a car of explosive powder careening into the Frisco Mine, and threatened to blow up processing plants. Martial law was then declared, federal troops came in, the strikers were crowded into "bullpens" (enclosed stockades), and the strike was broken. Similarly violent strikes took place at Cripple Creek, Colorado, in 1894, at Leadville, Colorado, in 1896, and again in Coeur d'Alene in 1899.

In these western strikes, government intervention was particularly naked and unrestrained. This was partly a reaction to the level of violence, but it stemmed also from the character of politics in the lightly settled western states: either the miners would dominate state politics—as they did in coalition with the Populists during their successful strike at Cripple Creek in 1894—or, as was increasingly true, the mine owners would dominate, with disastrous consequences for the miners.

The union leaders—Ed Boyce, Charles Moyer, "Big Bill" Haywood—all served their time in the bullpens or on the barricades. And they drew the appropriately grim conclusions. Initially their radicalism led them, like Debs, into the Socialist party. But they also were strongly inclined toward direct action. In 1897, WFM President Boyce called on all union miners to arm themselves with rifles, and his rhetoric—that the wage system was "slavery in its worst form"—had a very hard edge. Any lingering faith in the political process died in the Colorado state elections of 1904, after the suppression of bitterly fought strikes across the state in the previous two years. The miners thought they had defeated their archenemy, the Republican governor James H. Peabody, only to have the Colorado Supreme Court overturn the election results and reinstall Peabody (who, by prearrangement, resigned in favor of his lieutenant governor).

In 1905 the Western Federation of Miners led the way in creating a new radical labor movement, the Industrial Workers of the World. Although the IWW initially had links to the Socialist party, it swiftly repudiated political action and settled on its own radical course. The Wobblies, as IWW members were called, fervently supported the Marxist class struggle—but strictly in the industrial field. By action at the point of production and by an unending struggle against employers—ultimately by a general strike—they believed that the workers themselves would bring about a revolution. A workers' society would emerge, run directly by the workers through their industrial unions. The term *syndicalism* describes this brand of workers' radicalism.

In both its major forms—the politically oriented Socialist party and the syndicalist IWW—American radicalism flourished after the crisis of the 1890s, but only on a limited basis. Socialists and Wobblies lived, in a sense, on the tolerance of society. They would later be crushed without ceremony. Nevertheless, they served a larger purpose. American radicalism, by its sheer vitality, bore witness to what was exploitative and unjust in the new industrial order.

Summary

American industrialism took its modern shape during the last decades of the nineteenth century. Heavy industry developed in these years, producing in vast quantities the capital goods and energy required by an expanding manufacturing economy. An efficient railway system provided access to national markets. The scale of enterprise grew very large, and the vertically integrated firm became the predominant form of business organization. A managerial revolution enabled entrepreneurs to gain mastery over the complex business organizations they were building. Only in the South did prevailing conditions—in particular, its insulated, low-wage labor market—retard the growth of an advanced industrial economy.

Workers felt these developments most strongly in the loss of control over the labor process. Mass production, the high-volume output of standardized products, had the effect of de-skilling workers and replacing them with machinery. Scientific management, the brainchild of Frederick W. Taylor, cut further into the traditional autonomy of American workers. The enormous demand for labor in the meantime led to a great influx of immigrants into the industrial economy, making ethnic diversity a distinctive feature of the American working class. Gender likewise defined occupational opportunity. Women joined the labor force in growing numbers, but almost universally they were subjected to a sex-typing process that relegated them to "women's work," always at wage rates below those of men.

The late nineteenth century gave rise to the American labor movement in its modern form. In the Knights of Labor, anticapitalist labor reform enjoyed one final surge during the mid 1880s, then succumbed to the "pure and simple" unionism of the American Federation of Labor. The bitter industrial warfare of the 1890s, however, stirred new radical impulses, leading on the one hand to the political socialism of Eugene Debs and on the other to the industrial radicalism of the IWW.

TOPIC FOR RESEARCH

The Making of the Modern Labor Movement

For much of the nineteenth century, American workers debated a defining question: What should be the goal of the labor movement? By the 1880s two answers had emerged: *labor reform*, the demand of the Knights of Labor for fundamental change in the economic system, and *pure-and-simple unionism*, the efforts of the American Federation of Labor to extract the best possible terms for workers from the existing system. Choose either the Knights or the AFL as the subject of your investigation. What were the organization's main goals, and why did it adopt those positions? What were some of the steps it took to achieve its goals, and how successful was it? For a more ambitious paper, compare and contrast both organizations, and explain why the "pure-and-simple" strategy of the AFL eventually prevailed.

The standard book on the struggle between labor reform and trade unionism is Gerald N. Grob, *Workers and Utopia, 1865–1900* (1961). For the Knights of Labor, it should be supplemented by Leon Fink, *Workingmen's Democracy: The Knights of Labor and American Politics* (1983), which captures the cultural dimensions of labor reform not seen by earlier historians. The pioneering work on the American labor movement is John R. Commons et al., *History of Labor in the United States* (4 vols., 1918–1935); volumes 2 and 4 cover the period of this chapter. The most recent survey, incorporating much of the latest scholarship, is Bruce Laurie, *Artisans Into Workers: Labor in Nineteenth Century America* (1989). The clash of ideas, however, is best understood through the words of the two leading exponents, Terence V. Powderly of the Knights, and Samuel Gompers of the AFL. Both have left autobiographies—Powderly, *The Path I Trod* (1940), and Gompers, *Seventy Years of Life and Labor* (2 vols., 1925). Moreover, the letters and papers of Gompers are being published in an authoritative multivolume edition by Stuart B. Kaufman. The volumes covering the 1880s have appeared, and they contain a rich documentary record of the dispute. In Melvyn Dubofsky and Warren Van Tine, eds., *Labor Leaders in America* (1986), there are excellent brief biographies of Powderly and Gompers, with up-to-date bibliographical guides for further reading.

You may prefer to examine the views of the Knights and the AFL on another issue: the place of women and blacks in the labor movement. The starting points are two books by Philip S. Foner, *Women and the American Labor Movement From Colonial Times to the Eve of World War I* (1979), and *Organized Labor and the Black Worker* (1974).

BIBLIOGRAPHY

A Maturing Industrial Economy

The most useful introduction to the economic history of this period is Edward C. Kirkland, *Industry Comes of Age, 1860–1897* (1961). A more sophisticated analysis can be found in W. Elliot Brownlee, *Dynamics of Ascent* (rev. ed., 1979). For essays on many of the topics covered by this chapter, consult Glenn Porter, ed., *Encyclopedia of American Economic History* (3 vols., 1980).

On railroads, a convenient introduction is John F. Stover, *American Railroads* (1970). The growth of the railroads as an integrated system has been treated in George R. Taylor and Irene D. Neu, *The American Railway Network, 1861–1890* (1956). Thomas Cochran, *Railroad Leaders, 1845–1890* (1953), is a pioneering study of the industry's entrepreneurs. Julius Grodinsky, *Jay Gould: His Business Career, 1867–1892* (1957), is a complex study demonstrating the contributions this railroad buccaneer made to the transportation system. Books like Cochran's and Grodinsky's have gone a long way to resurrect Gilded Age businessmen from the debunking tradition first set forth with great power in Matthew Josephson, *Robber Barons: Great American Fortunes* (1934). Peter Temin, *Iron and Steel in the Nineteenth Century* (1964), is the best treatment of that industry. Joseph F. Wall, *Andrew Carnegie* (1970), is the definitive biography of the great steelmaster. Equally definitive on the oil king is Allan Nevins, *A Study in Power: John D. Rockefeller* (2 vols., 1953). Harold C. Passer, *The Electrical Manufacturers, 1875–1900* (1953), treats both the entrepreneurial and technological aspects of this emergent industry. On the development of mass production, the key book is David A. Hounsell, *From the American System to Mass Production, 1800–1932* (1984).

On the emergence of modern management, the magisterial work is Alfred D. Chandler, *The Visible Hand: The Managerial Revolution in American Business* (1977), not an easy book but one that will amply repay the labors of the interested student. Also worth reading is Chandler's earlier *Strategy and Structure: Chapters in the History of Industrial Enterprise* (1962). On the monetary system, the definitive book is Milton Friedman and Anna J. Schwartz, *Monetary History of the United States, 1867–1960* (1963).

On the New South, the standard work has long been C. Vann Woodward, *Origins of the New South, 1877–1913* (1951). A brilliant reinterpretation of the causes of the South's economic retardation is Gavin Wright, *Old South, New South: Revolutions in the Southern Economy Since the Civil War* (1986).

The World of Work

To understand the impact of industrialism on American workers, three collections of essays make the best starting points: Herbert G. Gutman, *Work, Culture and Society in Industrializing America* (1976); David Montgomery, *Workers' Control in America* (1979); and Michael S. Frisch and Daniel J. Walkowitz, eds., *Working-Class America: Essays on Labor, Community and American Society* (1983). On the introduction of Taylorism, the most useful book is Daniel Nelson, *Managers and Workers: Origins of the New Factory System* (1975). The impact of Taylorism on American workers is treated with great insight in David Montgomery, *The Fall of the House of Labor: The Workplace, the State, and American Labor Activism, 1865–1925* (1987). For a sweeping analysis of long-term change in American labor relations, see David M. Gordon et al., *Segmented Work, Divided Workers: The Historical Transformation of Labor in the United States* (1982). There are two valuable recent collections of essays on immigrant workers: Richard Ehrlich, ed., *Immigrants in Industrial America* (1977), and Dirk Hoerder, ed., *American Labor and Immigration History, 1877–1920: Recent European Research* (1983). David Brody, *Steelworkers in America: The Nonunion Era* (1960), examines workers in a single industry. John Bodnar, *Immigration and Industrialization: Ethnicity in an American Mill Town* (1977), is an important case study of a single community. On women workers, the best introduction is Alice Kessler-Harris, *Out to Work* (1982). Leslie Woodcock Tentler, *Wage-Earning Women: Industrial Work and Family Life, 1900–1930* (1979), and Mary H. Blewett, *Men, Women, and Work: Class, Gender, and Protest in the New England Shoe Industry, 1780–1910* (1988), are thoughtful treatments of the impact of industrial work on female identity. On black workers, the best introduction is William H. Harris, *The Harder We Run: Black Workers Since the Civil War* (1982).

The Labor Movement

The history of the Knights of Labor and the AFL can be studied in the books cited in the Topic for Research. The founder of the AFL is the subject of a lively brief biography by Harold Livesay, *Samuel Gompers and Organized Labor in America* (1978). Among the many books on individual unions, Robert

---

TIMELINE

1869	Knights of Labor founded in Philadelphia
1872	Montgomery Ward, first mail-order house, founded
	Andrew Carnegie starts construction of Edgar Thompson steel works near Pittsburgh
1873	Panic of 1873 ushers in economic depression
1875	John Wanamaker establishes first department store in Philadelphia
1878	Gustavus Swift introduces refrigerator car
1886	Haymarket Square bombing in Chicago American Federation of Labor (AFL) founded
1890	U.S. passes Britain in producing iron and steel
1892	Homestead strike crushed
1893	Panic of 1893 starts depression of the 1890s
1894	President Cleveland sends troops to break Pullman boycott
1895	Frederick A. Taylor explains scientific management in "A Piece Rate System" essay
	Southeastern European immigration exceeds northern European immigration for the first time
1901	Eugene V. Debs helps found Socialist party
1905	Industrial Workers of the World (IWW) founded

Christie, *Empire in Wood* (1956), best reveals the way pure-and-simple unionism worked out in practice. On industrial conflict, the most vivid book is Robert V. Bruce, *1877: Year of Violence* (1959). Stanley Buder, *Pullman: An Experiment in Industrial Order and Community Planning, 1880–1930* (1967), provides an informed account of the great Pullman strike and places it in its local context. The best book on the IWW is Melvyn Dubofsky, *We Shall Be All* (1969). On socialism, David Shannon, *The Socialist Party of America* (1955), remains the standard account. There is, however, a fine biography of that party's leader that supersedes previous studies: Nick Salvatore, *Eugene V. Debs: Citizen and Socialist* (1982). A dimension of American radicalism long neglected has recently received sensitive attention in Mari Jo Buhle, *Women and American Socialism, 1870–1920* (1982).

Bandanna, 1888 Election Memorabilia

During the late nineteenth century, politics became a
vibrant part of America's culture. Party paraphernalia, like
the bandanna above, flooded the country. (Museum of
American Political Life)

CHAPTER **19** *The Politics of Late Nineteenth-Century America*

In times of national ferment, as a rule, public life becomes magnified. Leaders emerge. Electoral campaigns debate great issues. The powers of government expand. That had certainly been true of the Civil War era. During the crises of Union and Reconstruction, the nation's public institutions had been tested to the utmost. The final challenge had occurred over the contested presidential election of 1876. In 1877, with the Republican Rutherford B. Hayes safely settled in the White House and the last federal troops withdrawn from the South, the era of sectional crisis finally ended. Political life went on, but was drained of its earlier drama. In the 1880s there were no Lincolns, no great national debates, and little exercise of governmental power. Public life was vigorous in other ways—highly organized and rife with cultural conflict—but not through the formal, public processes by which a nation confronts its central concerns. The politics of the status quo had arrived.

The Politics of the Status Quo (1877–1893)

The National Scene

There were five presidents from 1877 to 1893: Rutherford B. Hayes (Republican, 1877–1881), James A. Garfield (Republican, 1881), Chester A. Arthur (Republican, 1881–1885), Grover Cleveland (Democrat,

1885–1889), and Benjamin Harrison (Republican, 1889–1893). All were estimable men. Hayes, Garfield, and Harrison boasted distinguished war records. Hayes had served well as governor of Ohio for three terms, and Garfield had been a congressional leader for many years. Arthur, despite his cloudy reputation as a machine politician, had demonstrated fine administrative skills as head of the New York Customs House. Cleveland had made his mark as reform mayor of Buffalo and governor of New York. None was a charismatic leader, and only Cleveland, the lone Democrat of the lot, was an assertive public figure. But circumstances more than personal qualities explain why these presidents did not make a larger mark on history.

Their biggest job was to dispense political patronage. Under the spoils system, government appointments were treated as rewards for those who had served the victorious party. Reform of this system became a national issue after Charles Guiteau, a disappointed office seeker, assassinated President Garfield in 1881. The Pendleton Act of 1883 created a list of civil-service jobs to be filled on the basis of examinations administered by the new Civil Service Commission. The list originally included only 10 percent of all federal jobs. But each president added to it—generally at the close of his term in order to safeguard some of his appointees. But handling patronage remained a preoccupation in the White House. When the Democrats regained the presidency in 1884 for the first time in nearly thirty years, the pent-up hunger for jobs by the party faithful nearly overwhelmed Grover Cleveland. He was known to complain bitterly about the "damned, everlasting clatter for

Grover Cleveland
In the years after Reconstruction, Americans did not look
for charismatic personalities or dramatic leadership in their
presidents. They preferred men who accepted the limits of
executive power, men of "sound conservatism." Grover
Cleveland fitted this bill to perfection. For political reformers, Cleveland had the additional virtues of independence and
personal integrity. He best represented the late nineteenth-
century ideal of the American president.

office." The standards of public administration did rise
measurably, but there was no American counterpart to
the elite professional civil services taking shape in England and Germany in these years.

Other than dispensing patronage, presidents did
not have a lot to do. As late as 1897, White House staff
consisted of half a dozen assistants, plus a few clerks,
doorkeepers, and messengers. The president exerted little control over the federal bureaucracy. Budgetary matters were not his province, but Congress's, and federal
agencies accordingly paid much more heed to Capitol
Hill and the key money-dispensing committees than to
the White House.

The functions of the executive branch were, in any
event, very limited in these years. Of the 100,000 federal employees in 1880, fully 56 percent worked for the
Post Office. The largest item of expenditure—over a
third of the 1890 federal budget—went for veterans'
pensions. During the 1880s, the important government
departments—Treasury, State, War, Navy, Interior—
were sleepy places carrying on largely routine duties.
Virtually all federal income came from customs duties
and the excise tax on liquor and tobacco. These sources
produced more money than the government spent. The
problem of how to reduce the federal surplus ranked as
one of the most troublesome issues of the 1880s.

As for setting a national agenda, this was—unlike
in Lincoln's day, or our own—not to be looked for
from the White House. "The office of President is essentially executive in nature," Cleveland insisted, not policy making. In fact, as a Democratic president facing a
hostile Republican Senate, Cleveland did begin to assert
himself on policy matters, but in an entirely negative
way: in his first term, he vetoed three times as many
bills as did all the previous presidents combined.

Congressional Government.   On matters of national
policy, the presidents took a back seat to Congress. But
Congress was not well set up to do its work. In the
House of Representatives, the rules had grown so complicated and numerous that they frequently brought
business to a standstill. Party leaders were unable to
exert discipline over the members of either house, and
neither party ever stayed in power long enough to push
through a coherent legislative program. From 1877 to
1893, neither Democrats nor Republicans controlled
both houses for more than a single two-year term. Most
of the time, the Democrats controlled the House, and
the Republicans the Senate. Consequently, the ability of
Congress to take forceful action was extremely limited.

Neither party, moreover, had much stomach for
taking strong positions. Historically, they represented
somewhat different traditions—the Democrats favoring states' rights and limited government, the Republicans supporting government encouragement of economic development. But after Reconstruction neither
party was eager to translate these differences into well-
defined positions. On most leading issues of the day—
civil-service reform, the currency, and regulation of the
railroads—the divisions occurred within the parties, not
between them. The laws Congress passed could not be
clearly identified as either Democratic or Republican.

The tariff was something of an exception. From
Lincoln's day onward, high duties protected American
industry against imported goods. It was an article of
Republican faith, as President Harrison said in 1892,
that "the protective system . . . has been a mighty instrument for the development of the national wealth."

The Democrats, free traders by tradition, regularly attacked Republican protectionism.

Actually, however, the parties disagreed only about the degree of protection. Congressmen voted according to their constituents' interests on tariffs, regardless of party rhetoric. As a result, every tariff bill was a patchwork of bargains among special interests. In 1887, President Cleveland made a mighty effort to sharpen the battle. He devoted his entire annual message to Congress to the need for tariff reform and campaigned for reelection on that issue. His narrow defeat seemed to confirm the political wisdom of evading big issues. "They told me it would hurt the party," he later wrote. "Perhaps I made a mistake from the party standpoint; but damn it, it was right. I had at least that satisfaction."

Electoral Politics. The major parties treated issues gingerly partly because they feared each other. The Democrats, in retreat immediately after the Civil War, quickly regrouped and, by the end of Reconstruction, stood on virtually equal terms with the Republicans. Every presidential election from 1876 to 1892 was decided by a thin margin, and neither party gained commanding control over Congress. Political caution seemed wise; any false move on national issues might tip the balance to the other side.

The Englishman James Bryce, accustomed to the philosophical divisions between Tories and Liberals, grumbled about the indistinctness of American politics. "Neither party has any principles, any distinctive tenets," he wrote in *The American Commonwealth* (1888). Perhaps Lord Bryce exaggerated when he added, "All has been lost, except office or the hope of it." But electoral success had unquestionably taken precedence over party principle.

This was evident particularly in the way the Republican party treated its Civil War legacy. The major unfinished business after 1877 involved the needs of the former slaves in the South. The Blair Education bill, which would have appropriated federal funds to combat illiteracy, was on the Republican agenda at the end of the 1880s, but did not pass into law. More threatening to the South was the Lodge Election bill, which would have provided federal protection for black voters in southern congressional elections. This last gasp of Reconstruction politics died in 1890. The Republican administrations, more interested in building white support in the South, back-pedaled on the race issue and gradually abandoned the blacks to their fate.

The Republicans were not so willing to abandon their identification with the Civil War itself, however. In every election campaign Republican orators "waved the bloody shirt" against the "treasonous" Democrats. Service in the Union army gave candidates a strong claim

The Plumed Knight

In the fierce party politics of the Gilded Age, the political cartoon became a polished art form, and its high priest was Thomas Nast. In this cartoon, Nast pillories James G. Blaine, celebrated as the "Plumed Knight" among his Republican supporters, but fatally damaged in his ambitions to become president by reports that as Speaker of the House of Representatives he had taken bribes from an Arkansas railroad. Nast depicts the "knight" Blaine jousting in a tournament, with this ironic comment: "The 'Great American' Game of Public Office for Private Gain."

to public office. One-third of the Republican congressmen of the 1880s had a war record, and veterans' benefits always stood high on the Republican agenda. The Democrats played the same game in the South as the defenders of the Lost Cause. Bryce criticized American politicians for "clinging too long to outworn issues and neglecting . . . the problems which now perplex the country."

Alternatively, campaigns could descend into sideshows. In the hard-fought election of 1884, the personal reputations of the candidates overshadowed everything else. Was it more important that Grover Cleveland, a man of impeccable public honor, had years earlier fathered an illegitimate child? Or that James G. Blaine, perhaps the most gifted Republican of his generation, had taken favors from the railroads? In the midst of all the mudslinging, the issues got lost.

The characteristics of public life in the 1880s—the inactivity of the federal government, the evasiveness of both political parties, and the absorption in politics for its own sake—derived ultimately from the conviction that little was at stake in public affairs. In 1887, President Cleveland vetoed a small appropriation for drought-stricken Texas farmers with the remark that "though the people support the Government, the Government should not support the people." Government activity was in itself considered a bad thing. All that the state can do, said Republican Senator Roscoe Conkling, "is to clear the way of impediments and dangers, and leave every class and every individual free and safe in the exertions and pursuits of life." Conkling was expressing the political corollary to the doctrine of *laissez faire*—the mainstream belief of the late nineteenth century that that government was best which governed least.

The Ideology of Individualism

In 1885 at the height of the Knights of Labor, the cotton manufacturer Edward Atkinson gave a talk to the textile workers of Providence, Rhode Island. They had, he told them, no cause for discontent. "There is always plenty of room on the front seats in every profession, every trade, every art, every industry . . . There are men in this audience who will fill some of those seats, but they won't be boosted into them from behind." (There were certainly women as well in the audience—at least half of the Rhode Island labor force was female—but, as was characteristic of his times, Atkinson assumed economic opportunity to be of interest only to men.) Every man, Atkinson continued, gets what he deserves. For example, Cornelius Vanderbilt had amassed a fortune of $200 million by building the New York Central Railroad. Atkinson went through some rapid calculations. Every person in the audience consumed about a barrel of flour a year. In 1865, it had cost $3.45 to ship that barrel from Chicago to Providence. In 1885, the New York Central carried it for 68 cents, taking 14 cents as profit, while the workingman saved nearly $3. "Wasn't Vanderbilt a cheap man for you to employ as a teamster?" Atkinson asked. "Do you grudge him the fourteen cents?"

Atkinson's homely talk went to the roots of conservative American thought—that any man, however humble, could rise as far as his talents would carry him; that every person received his just reward, great or small; and that the success of the individual, so encouraged, contributed to the progress of the whole. How persuasive the workers listening to Atkinson found his message we have no way of knowing. But the confidence with which Atkinson presented his case is evidence of the continuing appeal of the ideology of individualism in the age of industrial expansion.

Facing the World

The cover of this Horatio Alger novel (1893) captures to perfection the myth of opportunity that Edward Atkinson extolled to his audience of textile workers. Our hero "Harry Vane" is a poor but earnest lad, valise packed, ready to make his way in the world and, despite the many obstacles thrown in his path, sure to succeed. In some 135 books, Horatio Alger repeated this story, with minor variations, for an eager reading public in the millions.

A wide variety of popular writings trumpeted the individualist creed, from the rags-to-riches tales of Horatio Alger to the stream of success manuals with such titles as *Thoughts for the Young Men of America, or a Few Practical Words of Advice to those Born in Poverty and Destined to be Reared in Orphanages* (1871). It was a lesson celebrated in the lives of such self-made men as Andrew Carnegie, whose book *Triumphant Democracy* (1886) paid homage to a nation in which a penniless Scottish child could rise from bobbin boy to steel magnate.

From the pulpit came the assurances of the Episcopal bishop William Lawrence of Massachusetts that "Godliness is in league with riches." In American Protestantism, there was a venerable tradition going back to the Puritans that linked success in one's earthly calling to the promise of eternal salvation. This link enabled a conservative ministry to make morally reassuring the furious acquisitiveness of industrial America. "To secure wealth is an honorable ambition," intoned the Baptist minister Russell H. Conwell in his lecture "Acres of Diamonds." "Money is power. Every good man and woman ought to strive for power, to do good with it when obtained." This notion of *stewardship*— that wealth carried with it a social obligation—Andrew Carnegie elevated into a formal doctrine that he called "the gospel of wealth." Carnegie argued that it was the responsibility of the rich to put their money to good use. This should be done not by coddling the less privileged, Carnegie said, but by providing the libraries, education, and cultural and scientific institutions by which they might prepare themselves for life's challenges.

Social Darwinism. American individualism drew strong intellectual support from the most important scientific theory of the age. In his great book *On the Origin of Species* (1859), the English naturalist Charles Darwin had presented a bold hypothesis to explain the evolution of plants and animals. In nature, Darwin wrote, all living things struggle and compete. Particular members of a species are born with characteristics that better enable them to survive. Future generations inherit these characteristics, and the species evolves. This process of evolution, which Darwin called *natural selection,* created a revolution in biological science.

Although not intended by Darwin, his theory also had an enormous impact on the study of human society. Drawing on Darwin, the British philosopher Herbert Spencer developed an elaborate analysis of how society evolved through constant competition and "the survival of the fittest." Social Darwinism, as Spencer's ideas became known, was championed in America by William Graham Sumner, a Yale sociology professor. Competition, said Sumner, is a law of nature that "can no more be done away with than gravitation." Furthermore, "if we do not like the survival of the fittest, we have only one possible alternative, and that is the survival of the unfittest. The former is the law of civilization; the latter is the law of anti-civilization." And who are the fittest? "The millionaires . . . They may fairly be regarded as the naturally selected agents of society. They get high wages and live in luxury, but the bargain is a good one for society."

Social Darwinists also argued that social processes must be permitted to take their course. "The great stream of time and earthly things will sweep on just the same in spite of us," Sumner wrote in his famous essay "The Absurd Attempt to Make the World Over" (1894). "That is why it is the greatest folly of which a man can be capable to sit down with a slate and pencil to plan out a new social world." As for the government, it had "at bottom . . . two chief things . . . with which to deal. They are the property of men and the honor of

women. These it has to defend against crime." The political meaning of Social Darwinism was clear. As Sumner put it: "Minimize to the utmost the relations of the state and industry."

The Supremacy of the Courts. This antigovernment appeal not only paralyzed political initiative. It also shifted power away from the executive and legislative branches. "The task of constitutional government," declared Sumner, "is to devise institutions which shall come into play at critical periods to prevent the abusive control of the powers of a state by the controlling classes in it." Sumner meant the judiciary. From the 1870s onward, the courts increasingly took the role that he assigned to them.

During this period the states, rather than the federal government, took primary responsibility under their police powers for regulating the economy. So it was against the states that the courts began a concerted attack. The number of decisions striking down state social welfare and regulatory laws rose markedly in the 1880s.

The Supreme Court's crucial weapon in this campaign was the Fourteenth Amendment (1868), which prohibited the states from depriving "any person of life, liberty, or property, without due process of law." The due-process clause had been intended to protect the civil rights of the former slaves. But due process protected the property rights and contractual liberty of "any person," and the Supreme Court expanded the meaning of person" to include corporations. So understood, the Fourteenth Amendment became an effective means of preventing the states from regulating business activity.

The Supreme Court erected similar barriers against the federal government through narrow interpretations of the Constitution. It ruled in 1895 that the federal power to regulate interstate commerce did not cover manufacturing and that the federal power to tax did not extend to personal incomes. And where federal power was undeniable—as in the regulation of railroads—the Supreme Court narrowly limited the exercise of that power. It reserved for itself the oversight of decisions that invaded property interests, such as how much railroads could charge their customers. With increasing aggressiveness, the courts took over the shaping of public policy on economic affairs.

Power conferred status. The legal profession and the courts, not politics, attracted the ablest people and held the public's esteem. A Wisconsin judge boasted: "The bench symbolizes on earth the throne of divine justice . . . . Law in its highest sense is the will of God." Judicial supremacy reflected the degree to which the ideology of individualism had become dominant in industrial America; it testified also to the low esteem to which American politics sank after Reconstruction.

Cultural Politics

Yet, for all the criticism leveled against it, politics still figured centrally in the nation's life. Proportionately more voters turned out in presidential elections from 1876 to 1892 than at any other time in American history. Party loyalty ran high, with little change from one election to the next. This loyalty manifested itself in high rates of party membership. Among Republican voters in New York City, a fourth were dues-paying party members. National conventions attracted huge crowds. "The excitement, the mental and physical strains," remarked an Indiana Republican after the 1888 convention, "are surpassed only by prolonged battle in actual warfare, as I have been told by officers of the Civil War who later engaged in convention struggles." The convention he described had nominated the colorless Benjamin Harrison on a routine platform. What was all the excitement about? Why did politics mean so much to late nineteenth-century Americans?

For one thing, politics had become a vibrant part of the nation's culture. The journalist George M. Towle told an English audience that America "is a land of conventions and assemblies, where it is the most natural thing in the world for people to get together in meetings, where almost every event is the occasion for speechmaking." Spellbinding orators like Herbert G. In-

gersoll drew enormous crowds at Republican rallies. During the election season, the party faithful marched in impressive torchlight parades. Party paraphernalia flooded the country—handkerchiefs, mugs, posters, and buttons emblazoned with the Democratic donkey or the Republican elephant, symbols that had been adopted in the 1870s. In 1888, pictures of the presidential hopefuls appeared on cards, like baseball players, packed into Honest Long Cut tobacco. The campaigns had the suspense of baseball pennant races plus the excitement of the circus coming to town. In an age before movies and radio, politics ranked as one of the great American forms of mass entertainment.

Party loyalty was a deadly serious matter, however. Civil War emotions lasted a long time in both North and South. The Ohio Republican party, recalled the urban reformer Brand Whitlock, was "a synonym for patriotism, another name for the nation. It was inconceivable that any self-respecting person should be a Democrat." The two parties did, in fact, represent different sorts of people. Republicans tended to have higher incomes, and they prided themselves on being the respectable elements of northern society. Senator George F. Hoar of Massachusetts described them as the people "who do the work of piety and charity in our churches . . . administer the school systems, own and till their own farms . . . perform the skilled labor in the shops."

The Presidential B.B. Club (1888)
On the left, Grover Cleveland is the baseman; at center Benjamin Harrison is at bat; and, on the right, Cleveland tags Harrison out—not, alas, the right prediction, since Harrison won the 1888 election.

Ethnocultural Politics. More important than class, however, were religion and ethnic background. The two parties drew on different ethnic and cultural segments of society. Statistically, Democrats outside the South tended to be foreign-born and Catholic, while Republicans tended to be native-born and Protestant. Among Protestants, the more pietistic the theology—that is, the more personal and direct the person's relationship to God—the more likely he or she was to be a Republican. In political terms, this translated into a party policy favorable to using the powers of the state to legislate public morality and regulate individual behavior. The Democrats, on the other hand, favored "the largest individual liberty consistent with public order."

During the 1880s ethnic tensions began to build up in many cities. Education became an arena of bitter conflict. One issue was the place of foreign languages in schools. Immigrant groups, especially the Germans, wanted their children taught in their own language. However, native-born Americans pushed through laws making English the language of instruction. In St. Louis, a heavily German city, the long-standing policy of teaching German to all students was overturned after an acrimonious campaign.

Religion was an even more divisive school issue. The use of the King James Version of the Bible in school angered Catholics. They also fought a losing battle over public aid for parochial schools. By 1900 such aid had been prohibited by twenty-three states. In Boston a furious controversy broke out in 1888 over the use of an anti-Catholic history text. When the school board withdrew the offending book, angry Protestants mounted a campaign to throw the moderates off the board and put the text back into the curriculum.

Similar tensions developed over the regulation of public morals. Evangelical Protestants renewed their efforts to enforce the so-called blue laws, which restricted activity on Sundays. When Nebraska banned Sunday baseball, the state supreme court approved the law as a blow struck in "the contest between Christianity and wrong." But German and Irish Catholics, who saw nothing evil in a bit of fun on Sunday, considered blue laws a violation of their personal freedom.

The same kind of ethnocultural conflict flared over the liquor question. In a speech introducing the first constitutional amendment for national prohibition in 1876, Senator Henry W. Blair of New Hampshire laid down a challenge to his ethnic opponent: "Upon discussion of this issue Irishman and German will in due time demonstrate that they are Americans." Although the Blair amendment languished, the antiliquor movement intensified. Many states adopted strict licensing and local-option laws governing the sale and consumption of alcoholic beverages. Indiana permitted drinking, but only joylessly in rooms containing "no devices for amusement or music . . . of any kind."

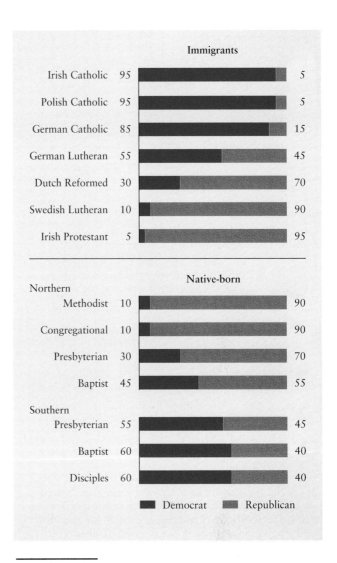

FIGURE 19.1

Ethnocultural Voting Patterns in the Midwest, 1870–1892

The hottest issues of the day—education, the liquor question, and observance of the Sabbath—were contested along ethnic and religious lines. Because they were also party issues—more so than tariffs, currency, or civil-service reform—they gave deep significance to party affiliation. Crusading Methodists thought of Republicans as the party of morality. For embattled Irish or German Catholics, the Democratic party was the defender of their freedoms. These cleavages occasionally surfaced in national elections. For example, when a Republican clergyman accused the Democrats in 1884 of being the party of "Rum, Romanism, and Rebellion," he undermined Republican efforts to woo the Irish-American vote and may have cost James G. Blaine the presidency. But the battles over public education and the liquor question were fought mostly at the state and local levels, mostly in the North. (In the South, which recieved few immigrants, politics lacked this ethnocul-

Carry Nation Under Arrest
Opponents of alcohol had traditionally advocated temperance; that is, self restraint. The Women's Christian Temperance Union took a more coercive approach. It demanded legal prohibition of alcohol. Some prohibitionists turned to direct action. Carry Nation became famous for her ax-wielding attacks on saloons. She meant to draw attention to the struggle, and so gladly went to jail—where she is headed in this photograph, taken in Enterprise, Kansas, in 1901.

tural dimension.) In the North ethnocultural issues gave a significance to party politics that would scarcely have been apparent to anyone looking only at the national scene.

Organizational Politics

Political life was also important because of the remarkable organizational activity that it generated. By the 1870s, both of the major parties had evolved a formal, well-organized structure. At the base lay the precinct or ward, whose meetings could be attended by all party members. County, state, and national committees ran the ongoing business of the parties. Conventions determined party rules, adopted platforms, and selected the party's candidates for public office.

At election time the party's main job was to get out the vote. In the South, where the Democratic nomination was equivalent to election, little organized effort went into election day. As a result, fewer people voted in southern states than anywhere else in the country. In states or communities with hard-fought elections, however, the parties mounted intensive efforts organized down to the individual voter. In Indiana, for example, the Republicans appointed 10,000 "district men" in 1884, each responsible for turning out a designated group of voters. The Pennsylvania Republican party maintained a list of 800,000 voters, classified according to degree of voting reliability.

Only professionals could manage such a highly organized political system. The German sociologist Max Weber remarked that Americans regarded "politics as a vocation." This factor, above all else, gave American politics its special character. The distinguishing trait of American politicians, James Bryce observed, was "that their whole time is more frequently given to political work, that most of them draw an income from politics . . . that they . . . are proficient in the arts of popular oratory, of electioneering, and of party management." The party system required professionals, and professionalism created careers. Politics, like professional sports and trade unionism, served as an avenue of upward mobility for many who, because of ethnic or class background, lacked the more conventional opportunities open to other Americans.

Machine Politics. Party administration was, on the face of it, highly democratic. In theory, all power derived from the party members in the precinct and ward organizations. In practice, however, the professionals ran the parties. They did this through unofficial, internal organizations called *machines*, which consisted of insiders willing to accept discipline and do work in exchange for getting on the public payroll or pocketing bribes and other profitable forms of "graft." The machines tended toward one-man rule, though this was based more on consensus than on dictatorship. Each state party had a "boss," such as, in New York, the Republican Thomas C. Platt and the Democrat David B. Hill. Sometimes the state leader held public office, generally as a U.S. senator, because it was the party-dominated state legislatures that chose senators until the adoption of the Seventeenth Amendment in 1913. But public office was not necessary for the boss to do his job.

Machine control affected the tone of party politics. Absorbed in the tasks of power brokerage, the machine boss tended to see public issues as somewhat irrelevant. The Republicans fought bitterly among themselves after President Grant left the White House in 1877. For the next six years, the party was divided into two warring factions—the Stalwarts, who followed Senator Roscoe Conkling of New York, and the Halfbreeds, led by James G. Blaine. The split resulted from a personal feud

The Levi P. Morton Association
The top-hatted gentlemen depicted in this photograph constituted the local Republican party organization of Newport, Rhode Island, named in honor of Levi P. Morton, Republican leader and vice president during the Benjamin Harrison administration (1889-1893). The maleness of party politics veritably leaps from the photograph and asserts more clearly than a thousand words why the suffragist demand for the right to vote was met with ridicule and disbelief.

between Conkling and Blaine, and it lasted because of a furious struggle over patronage. The Halfbreeds represented a newer Republican generation, more inclined to pay lip service to political reform and less committed to the old Civil War issues. But issues had little to do with the war between Stalwarts and Halfbreeds. They were really fighting over the spoils of the machine system.

And yet the record was by no means wholly negative. Machine politics raised the standards of government in certain ways. As seasoned machine politicians rose to higher office, their professionalism and party discipline measurably improved the performance of state legislatures and Congress. More important, the party machines filled a void in the nation's public life. They did informally much of what the governmental system left undone, especially in the cities (see Chapter 20).

The Mugwumps. For all its effectiveness, machine politics never managed to win public legitimacy. The social elite—professionals, intellectuals, well-to-do businessmen, and old-line families—deeply resented a politics that left little room for public service by people like themselves—the "best men." There was, too, a genuine clash of values. Political reformers called for "disinterestedness" and "independence"—the opposite of the self-serving careerism and party regularity fostered by the machine system. Many of them had earned their spurs as Liberal Republicans fighting the reelection of President Grant back in 1872.

In 1884, Carl Schurz, Edwin L. Godkin, and Charles Francis Adams, Jr., split from the Republican party again because they could not stomach its presidential candidate, James G. Blaine, whom they associ-

ated with corrupt party politics. Mainly from New York and Massachusetts, these Republicans became known as Mugwumps—a derisive bit of contemporary slang, supposedly of Indian origin, referring to pompous or self-important persons. The Mugwumps threw their support to the Democrat Grover Cleveland. After the 1884 election, something of a national reform movement sprang up, spawning good-government campaigns across the country. Although they won some municipal elections, the Mugwumps achieved greater importance as the nation's opinion molders. They controlled the respectable newspapers and journals and occupied a strategic place in the urban world.

Most of all, the Mugwumps defined the terms of political debate. They denounced the machine system for its violation of American political values. The potency of their attack was most evident in their campaign for the secret ballot, which had been used for the first time in Australia in 1857. Under this reform citizens would, in the privacy of a voting booth, mark an official ballot listing the candidates of all the parties instead of submitting in public view a party-supplied ticket at the polling place. The Australian ballot, adopted throughout the United States in the early 1890s, freed the voters from party surveillance as they exercised their right to vote.

The Mugwumps were reformers, but not on behalf of social justice. They had little sympathy for the problems of working people, nor any enthusiasm for using the powers of the state to alleviate the suffering of the poor and needy. As far as they were concerned, that government was best which governed least. Theirs was the brand of "reform" perfectly in keeping with a politics of the status quo.

Women's Political Culture

The young Theodore Roosevelt, an up-and-coming Republican state politician in 1884, referred to the Mugwump reformers contemptuously as "man-milliners." The sexual slur was not accidental. In attacking organizational politics, the Mugwumps were challenging one of the great bastions of male society of the late nineteenth century. Party meetings and conventions were occasions not only for carrying on the business of politics but also for performing the satisfying rituals of male sociability amidst cigar smoke and whiskey. Moreover, politics was identified with manliness. It was brutally competitive. It dealt in the commerce of power. It was frankly self-aggrandizing. Party politics, in short, was no place for a woman.

So it was no wonder that the woman suffrage movement met with serious opposition in these years. Susan B. Anthony succeeded in getting a constitutional amendment introduced in 1878, but the cause of woman suffrage made little headway through Congress. Suffragists mounted campaigns at the state level, but before 1900 women gained the right to vote in only four western states—Wyoming, Idaho, Colorado, and Utah. In other states, the most that women could win was the right to vote for school boards or on tax issues.

"Men are ordained to govern in all forceful and material things, *because they are men*," asserted one antisuffrage resolution, "while women, by the same decree of God and nature, are equally fitted to bear rule in a higher and more spiritual realm, where the strong frame and the weighty brain count for less"—that is to say, not in politics. Yet this same invocation of the doctrine of "separate spheres"—that men and women had different natures, and that women's nature fitted them for "a higher and more spiritual realm"—did open a channel for women to enter public life. "Women's place is Home," acknowledged the journalist Retha Childe Dorr. "But Home is not contained within the four walls of an individual house. Home is the community. The city full of people is the Family . . . . And badly do the Home and Family need their mother." So believing, socially conscious women had from the early nineteenth century onward engaged in charitable and reform activities. Women's organizations fought prostitution, assisted the poor, agitated for the reform of women's prisons, and tried to improve educational and job opportunities for women. Since many of these goals required state intervention, women's organizations of necessity became politically active, but not, they stressed, with any desire to participate in partisan politics or gain the ballot. Quite the contrary: women were bent on creating their own political sphere.

Thus in 1869, Sorosis, a women's professional club in New York City, convened a Women's Parliament in the hope of launching a parallel government responsible for public matters especially of concern to women.

Nothing came of the Women's Parliament, but it did indicate the degree to which women's sphere had taken on a political dimension. If not a parallel government, the social activism of women certainly did give rise to a female political culture that made itself powerfully felt in the public life of late nineteenth-century America.

The Women's Christian Temperance Union. No issue joined home and politics more poignantly than the liquor question. Just before Christmas in 1873, the women of Hillsboro, Ohio, began to hold vigils and prayer meetings in front of the town's saloons, pleading with the owners to close down and end the suffering of families of hard-drinking fathers. Thus began a spontaneous uprising of women that spread across the country and, it was estimated, closed 3,000 saloons. The temperance movement had been inactive for twenty years. Now, from this groundswell of public agitation, came the Women's Christian Temperance Union, which after its formation in 1874, rapidly blossomed into the largest organization of women in the country. The WCTU put the liquor question back on the public agenda.

The WCTU quickly came to exemplify the vitality of women's political culture. It had a powerful consciousness-raising effect on its members and, because it was limited to women, created a whole generation of new leaders. Under the skilled guidance of Frances Willard, who became president in 1879, the WCTU broadened its concerns and adopted a "Do-Everything" policy. For one thing, women recognized that alcoholism was not so much a cause as a symptom of more deep-seated social problems. But just as important, Willard's "Do-Everything" strategy would attract members who had no particular interest in temperance. Local bodies were encouraged to undertake causes important for their own communities. By 1889, the WCTU had thirty-nine departments concerned with labor, social purity, health, international peace, as well as temperance.

Most important, the WCTU was drawn to woman suffrage. This was necessary, Willard argued, "because the liquor traffic is entrenched in law, and law grows out of the will of majorities, and majorities of women are against the liquor traffic." Women needed the vote, said Willard, in order to fulfill their social responsibilities *as women*. This was very different from the claim made by the suffragists—that the ballot was an inherent right of all citizens *as individuals*—and much less threatening to masculine culture. Not much changed in the short run. The WCTU was in fact internally divided on the suffrage issue and did not become a major participant in the later struggles for women's right to vote. But by linking women's social concerns and women's political participation, the WCTU helped lay the groundwork for a fresh, much broader attack on the bastion of male electoral politics in the early twentieth century.

AMERICAN VOICES

The Case for Women's Political Rights *Helen Potter*

In 1883, Helen Potter came to testify before the Senate Committee on Education and Labor about the sanitary conditions of the poor in New York City. But in the course of her testimony she was swept into a powerful indictment of the unequal treatment of women that speaks volumes about the evolving women's political culture of the late nineteenth century.

The Witness. It is really an important question—this of the condition of women in our community. When I was a young girl I had some ambition, and when I heard a good speaker, or when I read something written by a good writer, I had an ambition to do something of that kind myself. I was exceedingly anxious to preach, but the churches would not have me; why, they said that a woman must not be heard. . . .

Q. I suppose you have an idea that women might abolish some of the tricks of the politician's trade?

A. Well, sir, it would take them a long time to learn to dare to do those things that men do in the way of politics—to sell and buy votes. . . .

Q. What would be the effect of conferring suffrage upon women? Would not the effect be injurious to the moral character and high influence of woman, if she should devote herself to the tricks of the politician's trade, which you very properly criticize so severely?

A. . . . I certainly think it would clean our streets, and I think it would purify politics, at least for the next two hundred years. It would take about that time to get women to understand the tricks of politicians as at present practiced. I do not think that women would be injured by it. Men and women are raised in the same family, they go to school together, they marry together, they go to church together, and why they should separate just at that point I do not quite see. . . . This Government is based upon the will of the people—women are "people," yet we have not a word to say about the laws. You will hear women in the course of your acquaintance say they wish they were men; I never heard a man say he wished he was a woman.

Q. Do you think the only reason for that is that they want the suffrage?

A. Yes, sir. They want the power, and I do not blame them.

Q. Why do you think that the suffrage is not extended to women by men—what is the true reason, the radical reason, why men do not give up one half their political power to women?

A. Well, it may arise from a false notion of gallantry. I think most men feel like taking care of, and protecting the ladies. They do not stop to think that there are in New England alone 150,000 unmarried women, who can have no help, as things are. It would be all very well, perhaps, if all women had representatives, and if all had a generous, straightforward honorable man to represent them. But take the case of a good woman who has a drunken husband; how can he represent her? He votes for liquor and for everything he may happen to want, even though it may ruin her and turn her out of doors, and even though it may ruin her children. If the husband is a bad man would it not be better for that woman to represent herself?

Q. If she could vote, wherein would anything be changed?

A. I think the children raised would be better in every way. The mother could have something to say as to whether she should have a liquor saloon on each side of her home, so that her children would not have this terrible temptation constantly before them from the time they are brought into the world until they are grown up. If she had a vote she would have nine out of ten of these places put out of the way. . . .

Q. What effect do you think the extension of the suffrage to women would have upon their material condition, their wage-earning power and the like?

A. They would get equal pay for equal work of equal value. I do not think a woman ought to be paid the price of an expert, when she is not herself an expert, but I believe there would be a stimulus for a woman to fit herself for the very best work. What stimulus is there for woman to fit herself properly, if she never can attain the highest pay, no matter what sort of work she does? If women had a vote I think larger avenues of livelihood would be opened for them and they would be more respected by the governmental powers.

Source: U.S. Senate, Committee on Education and Labor, *Report upon Relations Between Labor and Capital* II, (1885), 627, 629–32.

The Crisis of American Politics: The 1890s

For a decade and more after the end of Reconstruction in 1877, the overriding characteristic of national politics had been the stalemate between two evenly balanced national parties. Such an equilibrium was, however, bound to break down sooner or later. In fact this began to happen at the end of the 1880s. The immediate cause was the intensification of debate over the tariff. The Republicans, in power after Benjamin Harrison defeated the incumbent Grover Cleveland in the 1888 presidential election, pushed through the highly protectionist McKinley Tariff of 1890. The unpopularity of this measure gave a strong edge to the Democrats in the 1890 elections. They gained 76 seats in the House of Representatives and won state offices in Pennsylvania, Massachusetts, and other normally Republican states. Two years later, Cleveland regained the presidency; in command of both the Congress and the White House, the Democrats seemed to have established a firm lock on national politics.

Had everything else remained equal, the events of 1890 and 1892 might have inaugurated a long period of Democratic supremacy. But everything else did not remain equal. On May 3, 1893, the stock market crashed. Even before the crash, there had been signs of economic trouble in the increasing number of railroad bankruptcies and reports of economic distress among farmers. Now the Panic of 1893 struck, followed by a deepening depression. Before the end of the year, 16,000 firms and hundreds of banks had failed. In Chicago, 100,000 jobless workers walked the streets; nationwide, the unemployment rate soared to over 20 percent; as always in hard times, suffering and unrest mounted alarmingly.

As the economic crisis of the 1890s set in, which party would prevail, and on what platform, became very much an open question. The first challenge swept up from the West and South in the form of the Populist party.

The Populist Revolt

Farmers were, of necessity, joiners. They needed organization to overcome their social isolation and to provide them with crucial economic services based on the cooperative principle. By the end of the 1880s, two great regional concentrations had emerged—the Southern Farmers' Alliance along with the Colored Farmers' Alliance and the Farmers' Alliance of the Northwest. The first was strongest among the cotton farmers of the Deep South, the second among the wheat growers of Kansas, Nebraska, and the Dakotas. The alliances were originally nonpolitical, but as economic conditions worsened, they were drawn into politics.

The Populist Program. How that happened is perhaps best seen in Texas, where the Southern Alliance had originated. Its great achievement had been the establishment of the Texas Exchange, a massive cooperative that marketed the crops of cotton farmers and provided them with cheap credit. When cotton prices fell sharply in 1891, the Texas Exchange failed. The Texas Alliance then proposed a new scheme—a *subtreasury system* that would enable farmers to store their crops in public warehouses. Farmers would be able to borrow against those crops from a federally supplied fund at low interest rates until prices rose enough so their cotton could be profitably marketed. The subtreasury plan would provide the same credit and marketing functions as had the defunct Texas Exchange, but with this crucial difference: now it was the federal government that would play the key role. The subtreasury plan was thus a *political* proposal, and when it was rejected by the Democratic party as being too radical, the Texas Alliance saw no choice but to strike out in politics independently.

A similar process—first economic failure, then a proposal political solution, and finally rejection by the established parties—turned Alliancemen across the South and West to political action. In 1890, third parties won control of the Nebraska and Kansas legisla-

Mary Elizabeth Lease

As a political movement, the Populists were short on cash and organization, but long on rank-and-file zeal and tub-thumping oratory. No one was more rousing on the stump than Mary Elizabeth Lease, who came from a Kansas homestead and pulled no punches. "What you farmers need to do," she proclaimed in her speeches, "is to raise less corn and more *Hell!*"

tures, and in the South they captured several governorships as well as eight state legislatures. These successes led to the formation of the national People's (Populist) party. In the 1892 election, with the veteran antimonopoly campaigner James B. Weaver as their presidential candidate, the Populists captured a million votes and carried four western states. For the first time agrarian protest had truly challenged the national two-party system.

The challenge went, however, beyond the contest for political office. Populism contained a strong radical bent. The problems afflicting farmers, Populists felt, could stem only from some basic evil. They identified this evil as the control of the "money power" over the levers of the economic system. "There are but two sides," proclaimed a Populist manifesto. "On the one side are the allied hosts of monopolies, the money power, great trusts and railroad corporations . . . . On the other are the farmers, laborers, merchants and all the people who produce wealth . . . . Between these two there is no middle ground."

This reasoning identified farmers and workers as a single producer class. Populists made a strong effort to ally themselves with the labor movement. Their best successes came in Colorado, among the metal miners, and in Illinois, where the union leadership favored independent labor politics. In its explicit class appeal—in recognizing that "the irrepressible conflict between capital and labor is upon us"—populism differed fundamentally from the two mainstream parties.

Equally distinguishing was the prominent role that women played in the Populist movement. The organizational basis of the established parties, the local political clubs, were for men only. Populism, on the other hand, had its roots in a network of suballiances that had formed for largely social purposes and that welcomed women without discrimination. Only a handful of women achieved high office either in the Alliances or in the Populist party structure. But they did participate actively and served prominently as speakers and lecturers. Most indefatigable was the fiery Mary Elizabeth Lease, who became famous for calling on farmers "to raise less corn and more hell." Populism brought women into politics to a degree unprecedented at that time. "No other movement in history—not even the antislavery cause," commented the writer Hamlin Garland, "appealed to the women like this movement here in Kansas."

In an age dominated by laissez-faire doctrine, what most distinguished Populism from the major parties was its positive attitude toward the state. The Populist platform declared: "We believe that the powers of government—in other words, of the people—should be expanded as rapidly and as far as the good sense of an intelligent people and the teachings of experience shall justify, to the end that oppression, injustice and

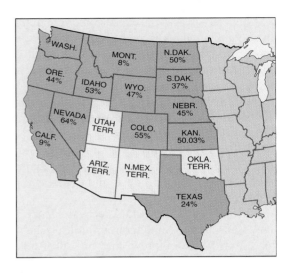

MAP 19.1

The Heyday of Western Populism, 1892
This map shows the percentage of the popular vote won by James B. Weaver, the People's party candidate, in the presidential election of 1892. Except for California and Montana, the Populists won broad support across the West and genuinely threatened the established parties in that region.

poverty should eventually cease in the land." The Populist program called for nationalization of the railroads and communications; protection of the land, including natural resources, from monopoly and foreign ownership; a graduated income tax; the creation of postal savings banks; and the Southern Alliance's subtreasury plan. In addition, the Populists adopted resolutions supporting organized labor, veterans' pensions, and such political reforms as the secret ballot and the direct election of senators. Finally, the Populists called for the free and unlimited coinage of silver. From a comprehensive program, the silver question quickly emerged as the overriding issue of the Populist party.

Free Silver. Cotton and grain farmers were especially vulnerable to falling commodity prices (see Chapter 17, page 543). In the early 1890s the bottom fell out of the market for cotton, wheat, and corn, wreaking havoc among those growers and making them the strongest supporters of Populism. They were strongly attracted to inflationary solutions to their problems. Increasing the money supply would raise farm prices and, since farmers would be paying back their loans in cheaper dollars, also lighten the burden of farm debt. But how to increase the money supply? One way was to get the government to issue paper dollars. This was one feature of the subtreasury plan: the funds lent to farmers on the collateral of their stored crops would be new money issued by the federal government.

But free silver—the expansion of the money supply by the unlimited coinage of silver—quickly became the more attractive alternative. For one thing, it was much the simpler course and, given the far-reaching nature of the subtreasury plan, much more likely to be implemented. In addition, free silver would bring in hefty contributions to the Populist party by silver-mining interests. These mine operators, scornful though they might be of the Populist program, yearned for the day when the government would buy at a premium price all the silver they could produce, and to that end they were prepared to support the Populists.

Urban social democrats such as Henry Demarest Lloyd of Chicago, and agrarian radicals such as Georgia's Tom Watson pleaded that free silver not be made the leading Populist issue. It would undercut the broader Populist program, they argued, and alienate wage earners, who had no particular enthusiasm for inflationary measures. Any chance of a farmer-labor alliance that might transform Populism into an American version of a social-democratic party would be doomed. As Lloyd complained, free silver was "the cowbird of reform," stealing in and taking over the nest that others had built.

Although fiercely debated within the party, the outcome was never in doubt. The practical appeal of free silver was simply too great. But once Populism made that choice, its capacity to maintain an independent existence was fatally compromised. For free silver was not an issue over which the Populists held any monopoly. It was, on the contrary, a question at the very center of mainstream politics in the 1890s.

Money and Politics

In a rapidly developing economy such as nineteenth-century America's, the money supply is bound to be a big political issue. The money supply has to increase rapidly enough to meet the economy's needs, or growth will be stifled. How fast the money supply should grow, however, is a question that creates sharp divisions. Borrowers and those suffering from low prices for their products want a larger money supply: more money in circulation inflates prices and reduces the real cost of borrowing. The "sound money" people—creditors, people on fixed incomes or in the slower-growing sectors of the economy—have an opposite interest. Touching people in the pocketbook as it does, the clash of interests can be very explosive.

Although the federal government always issued its own coins, the main source of the nation's money supply before the Civil War was the bank notes issued by several thousand state banks. Although more or less subject to state regulation, these banks issued their notes entirely in their private role as providers of credit

to their customers. The notes given to borrowers circulated as money until presented for redemption at the originating bank. Economists tell us the burgeoning economy's need for money was amply met by the state banks, although the goodness of the bank notes—the ability of the issuing banks to stand behind their notes and redeem them at par—was always uncertain. During the Civil War, this freewheeling system came to an end. Bank notes still existed, but (under the National Banking Act of 1863) only to the extent that they were backed by U.S. government bonds.

The effects of the act were threefold. First, the money supply became inadequate for the country's needs. Second, the ensuing economic troubles—the deflation of prices and the scarcity of credit—magnified public debate over the money question. Finally, since solutions now depended so exclusively on the currency role of the federal government, the money question became much more politicized.

The constitutional power of the federal government to issue money was in theory unlimited. The Lincoln administration had not hesitated to pay for the Civil War largely by printing paper money—greenbacks, so-called—backed by nothing more than the government's declaration that the greenbacks were legal tender. The prevailing policy, however, going back to the founding years of the Republic, was to base the federal currency on the amount of *specie*—i.e., gold and silver—held by the U.S. Treasury.

Under the bimetallic standard, silver and gold were fixed in value at a ratio of sixteen to one: sixteen ounces of silver equaled one ounce of gold. Silver, however, had become scarce relative to the supply of gold after mid-century. As silver rose in market price, it became more valuable as metal than as money and disappeared from currency circulation. In 1873 silver was officially dropped as a medium of exchange. Soon thereafter, great silver discoveries occurred in Nevada, Arizona, and elsewhere in the West. With this new supply, silver prices dropped swiftly. If the government resumed the coinage of silver at the ratio of sixteen to one, silver would flow into the Treasury and greatly expand the volume of currency. It would also, of course, greatly enrich the silver-mining interests.

With so much at stake for so many people, the currency question became one of the staple issues of post-Reconstruction politics. Twice the prosilver coalition in Congress won modest victories. First, under the Bland-Allison Act of 1878, the U.S. Treasury was required to purchase and coin between $2 and $4 million worth of silver each month. Then, in the more sweeping Sherman Silver Purchase Act of 1890, 4.5 million ounces of silver bullion were to be purchased monthly to serve as the basis for new issues of U.S. Treasury notes. These legislative battles over silver coinage, although hard-fought, cut across party lines in a way that was wholly characteristic of the cautious party politics of the 1880s.

But in the early 1890s this situation changed. Silver now became a defining issue between the parties; in particular, it had a radicalizing effect on the Democratic party.

The Cleveland Administration and the Silver Question.

When the Panic of 1893 hit, the Democrats were in power in Washington. The party in office usually gets blamed if the economy falters, but President Cleveland made things worse for the Democrats. When jobless marchers arrived in Washington in 1894 to agitate for federal relief, Cleveland's response was to disperse them forcibly and arrest their leader, Jacob S. Coxey. Cleveland's brutal handling of the Pullman strike further alienated the labor vote. Nor was he able to deliver on his campaign promise to reverse the protectionist McKinley Tariff of 1890. In a signal failure of presidential leadership, Cleveland lost control of the congressional battle for tariff reform. The resulting Wilson-Gorman Tariff of 1894, which he allowed to pass into law without his signature, caved in to special interests and cut average tariff rates only slightly.

Cleveland's worst failure, however, was his stand on the silver question. Cleveland was a committed sound-money man who had repeatedly denounced "the dangerous and reckless experiment of free, unlimited, and independent silver coinage." Nothing that happened after the depression set in—not collapsing prices, not the suffering of farmers, not the groundswell of support for free silver within his own party—budged Cleveland from that position.

Economic pressures, in fact, soon pushed him in the opposite direction. The problem was a persistent drain on U.S. gold reserves. This was caused partly by transfers of gold overseas to make up an unfavorable balance of international payments and partly by heavy redemptions of gold by holders of U.S. Treasury notes. To help stem the gold outflow, Cleveland persuaded Congress in 1893 to repeal the Sherman Silver Purchase Act, effectively sacrificing the country's painfully crafted effort at maintaining a partial bimetallic standard.

As his administration's difficulties deepened, Cleveland turned in 1895 to a syndicate of private bankers led by J. P. Morgan to finance the gold purchases needed to replenish the Treasury's depleted gold reserves. The administration's secret negotiations with Wall Street, once discovered, raised a furor among Democrats, and completed Cleveland's isolation from his own party.

William Jennings Bryan and the Election of 1896.

In 1896, at their national convention in Chicago, the Democrats repudiated Cleveland and turned left. The leader of the triumphant silver Democrats was William Jennings Bryan of Nebraska. Bryan was truly a political phenomenon. Only thirty-six years old, he had already served two terms in Congress and become a passionate advocate of free silver. He was a consummate politician and, no less important, an inspiring public speaker. Bryan, remarked the journalist Frederic Howe, was "pre-eminently an evangelist . . . . He was a missionary . . . the *vox ex cathedra* of the Western self-righteous missionary mind." Bryan spoke with a Christian fervor that swept up his audiences, and he did so again when he joined the debate on free silver at the Democratic convention. He had been quietly building up delegate support while keeping a distance between himself and convention politicking. Bryan locked up the presidential nomination when he electrified the convention with his stirring attack on the gold standard: "You shall not press down upon the brow of labor this crown of thorns, you shall not crucify mankind on a cross of gold."

Bryan's nomination meant that the Democrats had identified themselves as the party of free silver; his "cross of gold" speech meant he would turn the money question into a national crusade.

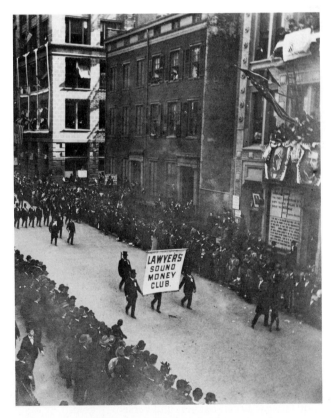

Lawyers March for the Gold Standard

Presidential campaigns of the late nineteenth century were always hard-fought, and none more so than the 1896 election. Big issues were at stake. Would the country stay on the gold standard, or drastically expand the money supply through the free coinage of silver? Lawyers paraded in the streets of New York City to demonstrate their conviction that the nation's fate hung on *sound money* and on the election of the Republican William McKinley.

AMERICAN VOICES

The Nomination of William Jennings Bryan *Edgar Howard*

Edgar Howard, a member of the Nebraska delegation, provides an eyewitness account of the heady idealism that swept the Democratic convention and launched William Jennings Bryan on his Free Silver crusade.

I have been asked by many friends to tell the convention story. I cannot do it. In common with countless thousands I was so overjoyed by the triumph of the people over the cohorts of Wall Street and monopoly that for once in my life I am unable to find words which will fittingly portray the scenes incident to this greatest convention in our country's history. I say it was the greatest convention of modern times because it was the only great political gathering in recent years which was not controlled by the representatives of the monied interests in our land, and to me there is no grander day than that in which the people rise in their majesty and break the cords which bind them to the enemy of mankind—the power of gold.

I frankly confess that we of the Nebraska delegation did not go to Chicago with strong hopes for success. We were ready to plead, pray or fight for Bryan, and yet we scarce dared hope that our pleas, prayers or our fights would avail. It has been said that Bryan could never have secured a nomination had he not made a speech. I am frank to admit that his speech went far to push him on to victory, but I also know that several states had resolved to support him before he made his speech, and I firmly believe he would have been nominated if he had never opened his mouth. He was not a candidate in an active sense. He refused to permit his friends to urge his name, begged the Nebraska delegates not to wear Bryan badges, and persistently refused to let us place his name before the convention, or before the delegates in hotel headquarters. He argued that if the People wanted him as their candidate they would call him to the leadership. . . . In short he was in

Chicago the same, noble, clean, Christian gentleman that he has ever been in Nebraska, spurning all proffers of place and power, the receiving of which would be repugnant to his high sense of honor.

But about Bryan's great speech. There are no words in our language to picture the effect it produced upon the vast multitude which heard it. . . . At Bryan's first utterance all was still. The silence was broken at the close of his first beautiful paragraph by a powerful wave of approval which made the great iron building quiver. It was the polished effort of the day, and yet so plain and clear that the most untutored hearer could understand. Again and again the convention broke forth into the wildest demonstrations of approval, ceasing only when the speaker begged for opportunity to proceed. Then the thousands would be silent, every ear being bent to hear the wonderful flow of words, every eye straining to see the majestic man who was hurling defiance in the teeth of the money power. . . . At the conclusion of his speech—well, there's no use of a country editor like me trying to tell you about it. For ten seconds a death-like silence prevailed. Then like a great cloud that monster assemblage rose to its feet. The cheers were deafening. . . . The demonstration continued nearly half an hour, only ceasing when the participants became exhausted. . . .

When we went out upon the streets that night the air was full of Bryan enthusiasm, and especially among the laboring classes, who had already memorized his immortal words in his closing sentence: "You shall not press down this crown of thorns on labor's brow; you shall not crucify mankind upon a cross of gold." At our hotels we had hundreds of callers who begged us to get out a band and make a Bryan demonstration on the streets. . . .

At last the balloting began. . . . Bryan gained steadily from the start, reaching the necessary two-thirds on

As this ironic portrait of him suggests, Bryan's special genius as a politician was to place himself above politics and to identify his cause with moral values deep in the American psyche.

the fifth ballot, and was later declared the unanimous choice of the convention. Throughout the balloting there were wild demonstrations of approval at every mention of Bryan's name. And when victory came at last the scenes following the great speech were enacted over again. . . . It was not a stampede. Bryan was in the hearts of all the delegates who were not controlled by Wall street.

Source: William E. Christenson, ed., "The Cross of Gold Reburnished: A Contemporary Account of the 1896 Democratic Convention," *Nebraska History* 46 (September 1965), 225–33.

No campaign since Reconstruction evoked such a sharp division over issues. The silver Republicans bolted from their party; the gold Democrats went for a splinter Democratic ticket or supported the Republican party; even the Prohibition party split into gold and silver wings. The Populists, meeting after the Democratic convention, accepted Bryan as their candidate. The free silver issue had become so vital that they could not do otherwise. Despite their best efforts, the Populists found themselves, for all practical purposes, absorbed into the Democratic silver crusade.

The Republicans took up the challenge. Their key party leader was Mark Hanna, a wealthy Cleveland ironmaker, who was a brilliant political manager and an exponent of the new industrial capitalism. Hanna's candidate, William McKinley of Ohio, personified the virtues of Republicanism, standing solidly for prosperity, high tariffs, and honest money. While Bryan broke

with tradition and criss-crossed the country in a furious whistle-stop campaign, the dignified McKinley received delegations at his home in Canton, Ohio. As Bryan orated with passionate moral fervor, McKinley talked of industrial progress and a full dinner pail.

Not since 1860 had the United States witnessed such a hard-fought election, and over stakes that loomed so high. The nation's currency had exceptional social significance in American life. For the middle class, sound money meant the soundness of the social order. With jobless workers tramping the streets and bankrupt farmers up in arms, Bryan's fervent assault on the gold standard struck fear in many hearts. Republicans denounced the Democratic platform as "revolutionary and anarchistic." They called Bryan's supporters "social misfits who have almost nothing in common but opposition to the existing order and institutions." The formidable party machinery was pumped up to the

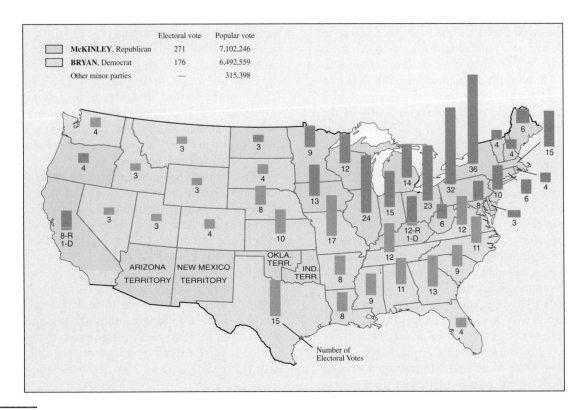

MAP 19.2

The Election of 1896

The 1896 election was one of the truly decisive elections in American history. The Republican party won by its largest margin since 1872. More important, the Republicans established a firm grip on the key midwestern and Middle Atlantic states—especially New York, Indiana, Ohio, and Illinois—that had been the decisive states in every national election since Reconstruction. The 1896 election broke a party stalemate of twenty years' duration and began a period of Republican domination that would last until 1932.

limit. Contributions flowed in from businessmen in record amounts. Hanna's network kept close tabs on the race in every state; and about 1,400 Republican speakers went out on the hustings. The political debate reached a level of intensity and significance unequaled since the days of the Lincoln-Douglas debates.

Although little noticed at the time, ethnocultural issues also figured strongly in the campaign. The Republicans, it will be recalled, had in the 1880s been the party of morality, appealing to native-born and evangelical Protestants on such issues as temperance and Sunday laws, but as a consequence alienating the foreign-born and Catholic vote. The Democrats had capitalized on these tensions in making their bid for electoral dominance in 1890 and 1892. Now, in 1896, the Republicans beat a strategic retreat from the politics of morality. McKinley himself had represented a mixed district of northeastern Ohio in Congress. In appealing to his immigrant and working-class constituents, he had learned the art of easy tolerance, as expressed in his phrase "live and let live." Of the two candidates, the prairie orator Bryan, with his biblical rhetoric and moral righteousness, presented the more alien image to traditional Democratic voters in the big cities.

McKinley won handily, with 271 electoral votes to Bryan's 176. He kept the Republican ground that had been regained in the 1894 mid-term elections and pushed into Democratic strongholds, especially in the cities. Boston, New York, Chicago, and Minneapolis, all taken by Cleveland in 1892, went for McKinley in 1896. Bryan ran strongly only in the South, in silver-mining states, and in the Populist West. The gains his evangelical style brought him in some Republican rural areas fell far short of what he lost in traditionally Democratic urban districts.

The paralyzing equilibrium of American politics ended in 1896, and the Republicans emerged as the majority party. The Republican party accomplished this victory by exploiting both the economic and the cultural aspects of party allegiance. The Republicans persuaded the nation that they were the party of prosperity, and they reduced their liability of being perceived as the party of moral intolerance. In 1896, too, electoral politics regained its place as an arena for national debate, setting the stage for the reform politics of the Progressive Era after 1900.

The Decline of Agrarian Radicalism. As for Populism, it simply faded away. Fusion with the Democrats in 1896 deprived the party of its identity and undermined its organizational structure. After the election, the issue on which populism had staked its fate—free silver—likewise vanished. During the 1890s, gold was discovered in South Africa, Colorado, and the Yukon, while the new cyanide refining method greatly increased ore yields.

The newly abundant gold supply did for the embattled farmers just what they had hoped to accomplish through free silver, ending the long deflation and easing their debt burdens. Wheat went from 72 cents a bushel in 1896 to 98 cents in 1909, corn from 27 cents to 57 cents, and cotton from 6 cents to 14 cents a pound. The world market for these products also turned more favorable. Farm prices rose faster than prices of other products, and as a result, so did the real income of farmers. A new spirit of prosperity and optimism took hold in the "golden age" of American agriculture before World War I.

The farmers' sense of inferiority and deprivation—that they were "rubes" and "hicks" and that life was inherently better in the city—began to subside after 1900. The new prosperity meant that more farmers could afford labor-saving home appliances and farm machinery to lighten field work. New inventions helped ease the isolation and monotony of rural life. The telephone became commonplace, not so much because of the spread of commercial service but through the determined efforts of farmers themselves. Telephone cooperatives were the most common type of farm cooperatives in the early twentieth century. The automobile, especially the Ford Model T, gave rural Americans a mobility they had never before known. The Country Life Commission, formed in 1908, took a sunny view of farm society: "There has never been a time when the American farmer was as well off as he is today, when we consider not only his earning powers but the comforts and advantages he may secure."

The farmer's self-conception also underwent an irreversible transformation. As long as farmers remained in the majority, they naturally considered themselves as representative Americans. They could readily regard their own economic distress as a general disorder of the entire nation. Pushed far enough, they might seek to mobilize their fellow producers—farmers and workers—to seize political power. In short, they could become Populists. But by the opening of the twentieth century, farmers no longer composed a majority of the population. In 1900 only a little more than a third of the labor force earned a living from the soil, and with each succeeding census, the numbers would become fewer and fewer.

There would be times in the twentieth century when distressed farmers would turn again to insurgent politics, but never with the potency generated by the Populist party. It was as an organized interest group, not as a political movement, that farmers in the future would advance their cause.

Agriculture had long been at the heart of American life. In the twentieth century, agriculture became just one more economic interest—an important one, but now subordinate in the larger scheme of the modern industrial order.

Race and Politics in the South

When Reconstruction came to an end in 1877, so did the hopes of African-Americans that they would enjoy the equal rights of citizenship promised them by the Fourteenth and Fifteenth amendments. In education there was strict segregation. Access to jobs, to justice, and to social welfare, was racially determined and unequal. And in 1883 the Supreme Court struck down the Civil Rights Act of 1875, exempting the discriminatory practices of private citizens—owners of restaurants, theaters, hotels—from the strictures of the Fourteenth Amendment. However, southern state laws did not yet *require* the exclusion or segregation of black patrons. After Reconstruction, segregation in public accommodation was general but not absolute: streetcars, for example, seem to have been largely integrated.

In politics, the picture was even more mixed. Blacks were routinely subject to white intimidation—but with the aim of controlling black participation, not eliminating it. In all southern states, blacks continued to vote in large numbers. In the black belt areas, where African-Americans sometimes constituted a majority, they claimed a share of the local offices and sent representatives to the state legislatures and, in Mississippi and the Carolinas, to Congress as well.

Whatever glimmer of hope blacks entertained for better things, however, was soon exploded by a terrible burst of racist terrorism and repression. What made this outcome so peculiarly tragic was that it had started as a positive effort to overcome racial divisions in the South. Black disfranchisement and rigid segregation stemmed directly from the crisis of the 1890s and, in particular, from a political upheaval that briefly challenged the southern status quo.

The Failure of Biracial Politics

Under normal conditions American politics serves to balance, or at least to give voice to, contending economic and social interests. In the New South the party system lacked that integrating capability. For one thing, there was no genuine competition between the parties. With the Republicans wholly discredited in southern eyes by Radical Reconstruction, the South became a one-party region. Whoever controlled the Democratic party controlled southern politics. This dominating group turned out to be, overwhelmingly, a business elite of new entrepreneurs and older plantation owners committed to southern economic development.

Because the Reconstruction struggle had been about home rule, the Democrats could portray themselves as the party of southern patriotism. In seizing control of the Democratic party, the economic elite thus had enormous advantages. Not only was there no effective opposition party, but those who controlled the Democratic party could cloak themselves in the mantle of the Lost Cause and present themselves as the champions of southern "redemption" from black Republican rule. The conservative Democrats, in fact, are most readily identified as the Redeemers.

White Supremacy Versus Class Solidarity. The crucial success of the Redeemers was their ability to exclude competing interests from the public arena. Class antagonism, although often muted, was never absent from southern society. There had been long-smoldering differences between hill-country farmers and the planters. Fresh sources of conflict now arose from the tenant-farmer system—which increasingly included whites as well as blacks—and from an emerging industrial working class. The Redeemers were occasionally challenged—for example, by the Readjuster movement, which after 1877 resisted the full repayment of discounted bonds issued by the Reconstruction state governments. On the whole, however, the Redeemers skillfully utilized the white-supremacist order to keep dissent in check.

"The white laboring classes here," wrote an Alabamian in 1886, "are separated from the Negroes, working all day side by side with them, by an innate consciousness of race superiority. This . . . excites a sentiment of sympathy and equality on their part with the classes above them, and in this way becomes a healthy social leaven." White workers expressed this "innate consciousness of race superiority" by claiming privileged rights above the blacks. Blacks were systematically driven from the many skilled jobs they had held after the Civil War; and they were excluded, except as janitors, from textile work, from the new factory jobs in cigarette manufacture, and in general from the opportunity to rise up in the industrial ranks.

The segregation and deference imposed on blacks were the social marks of their inferiority, asserting that "the lowest white man counts for more than the highest Negro." The pressure for a rigid system of social segregation came primarily from poor whites. "The best people of the South do not demand this separate [railroad] car business," wrote a North Carolina black man. By accepting segregation, he declared, they were "pandering to the lower instincts of the worst class of whites in the South."

In times of economic distress, however, the logic of class solidarity strongly challenged the doctrine of white supremacy. Blacks and whites worked together in many places, such as coal mines and timber camps and on the waterfronts of southern seaports. There they sometimes organized together into trade unions and even went on strike side by side. During the mid-1880s, the Knights of Labor preached the message of interracial unionism with considerable effect.

More significant in the predominantly agricultural South, was the fact that distressed white farmers showed some willingness to work with black farmers to achieve their common goals. "They are in the ditch just like we are," asserted a white Texan. Beginning in 1886, white dirt farmers began to agitate for agrarian reform through the Southern Alliance. Black farmers formed a separate organization, the Colored Farmers' Alliance, but the two bodies worked together. Once the farmers' movement entered politics around 1890, this formal racial division began to be overcome.

Unable to capture the Democratic party, the Southern Alliance formed independent parties or, as in North Carolina, fused with the Republicans. The southern Populists needed the black vote. "The accident of color can make no difference in the interest of farmers, croppers, and laborers," stated the Populist leader Tom Watson of Georgia. "You are kept apart that you may be separately fleeced of your earnings." By organizing interracially as a third party representing southern dirt farmers, the Populists endangered the structure of conservative southern politics.

The Repudiation of Racial Equality. The Populist challenge was put down, but at a terrible cost to racial justice in the South. In the contest for the black vote, the conservative Democrats had the advantages of money, power, and paternalistic influence over many blacks. The Redeemers also attacked the Populists at their most vulnerable point—that they were courting "Negro domination." When all this did not suffice, fraud at the polls enabled the Democrats to defeat the Populist challenge. Thus the Mississippian Frank Burkitt's bitter attack on the conservatives: they were "a class of corrupt office-seekers" who had "hypocritically raised the howl of white supremacy while they debauched the ballot

boxes . . . disregarded the rights of the blacks . . . and actually dominated the will of the white people through the instrumentality of the stolen negro vote."

What was Burkitt's solution? A state constitutional convention to eliminate black Mississippians from politics! Thus, out of Populist frustration came the first decisive move to deprive blacks of their right to vote. And where it was the Populists who benefited from the black vote, as in North Carolina, the conservatives took much the same view. Black disfranchisement came through the constitutional adoption, beginning with Mississippi in 1890, of literacy tests, property requirements, and poll taxes.

The race issue had been instrumental in bringing down the Populists; now it served to reconcile them to defeat. Embittered poor whites, deeply ambivalent all along about interracial cooperation, turned their fury on the blacks. And southern conservatives, chastened by the Populist show of strength, encouraged this anger.

The poor whites favored disfranchisement as an expression of militant white supremacy. Their own voting rights were partially protected from the literacy tests by lenient enforcement and constitutional loopholes—such as Louisiana's grandfather clause, which exempted those entitled to vote on January 1, 1867, together with their sons and grandsons. But poor whites were not at all protected from property and poll-tax requirements. They might have objected more had they not been given a voice within the Democratic party.

From the 1890s onward, a new brand of southern politician spoke for the poor whites. He appealed now not to their class interests but to their racial prejudices. Tom Watson, the fiery Georgia Populist, rebuilt his political career as a brilliant practitioner of race baiting. Starting in the early 1900s, he and other racial demagogues thrived throughout the Deep South.

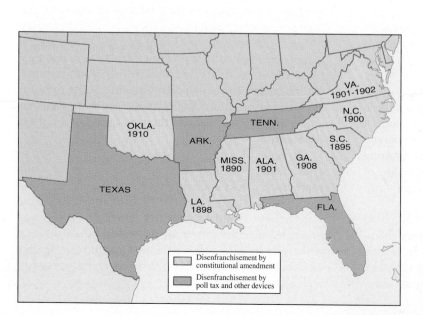

MAP 19.3

Disfranchisement in the South

In the midst of the Populist challenge to Democratic one-party rule in the South, a movement to deprive blacks of the right to vote spread from Mississippi across the South. By 1910 every state in the region except Tennessee, Arkansas, Texas, and Florida had made constitutional changes designed to prevent blacks from voting, and these four states accomplished much the same result through poll taxes and other exclusionary devices. For the next half-century, the political process in the South would be for whites only.

The Ascendancy of Jim Crow. The Populist struggle, tragically, produced a brand of white supremacy more virulent and impenetrable than anything the blacks had faced since Emancipation. The color line, hitherto incomplete, became rigid and comprehensive. Starting in Florida in 1887, state after state in the South passed laws requiring segregated seating in trains and other public accommodation. Such racial legislation, known as Jim Crow laws, soon applied to every type of public facility. In the 1890s, the South became for the first time a fully segregated society by law.

The Supreme Court of the United States soon ratified the South's decision. In the case of *Plessy v. Ferguson* (1896), the Court ruled that segregation was not discriminatory—that is, it did not violate black civil rights under the Fourteenth Amendment—provided that blacks had accommodations equal to those of whites. The "separate but equal" doctrine of course had little regard for the realities of southern life: segregated facilities were rarely if ever "equal" in any material sense, and segregation was itself intended to underscore the inferiority of blacks. With a similar disregard for the realities, the Supreme Court in *Williams v. Mississippi* (1898) validated the disfranchising devices of the southern states: so long as race was not a specified criterion for disfranchisement, the Fifteenth Amendment was not being violated—never mind that the practical effect was the virtually total exclusion of blacks from politics in the Deep South.

Race hatred became an accepted part of southern life, manifested in a wave of lynchings and race riots and in the public vilification of blacks. For example, Benjamin R. Tillman, governor of South Carolina and after 1895 a senator, excoriated blacks as "an ignorant and debased and debauched race." This ugly racism came from several sources, including intensified competition between whites and blacks during the depression of the 1890s and the reaction of whites against the less submissive black generation born after slavery. The nationwide spread of a pseudoscientific theory of racial inferiority played a part, as did American imperialism and its subjugation of Filipinos, Hawaiians, and Hispanics. Recent scholarship also suggests more deep-seated psychological causes for this unreasoning and often murderous racism, in which the rage against blacks served as a way of reasserting a traditional sense of southern "manhood" that was under siege in industrializing America.

But what had triggered the antiblack offensive was the crisis over Populism. From then on, white supremacy propped up the one-party system that had emerged from Reconstruction. If the southern elite had to share political power with demagogic poor white leaders like Tom Watson and James K. Vardaman, this sharing would be on terms agreeable to them—the exclusion from the political process of any serious challenge to the economic status quo.

The Black Response

Where did this leave blacks? In 1890, African-Americans comprised more than half the population of Grimes County, a cotton-growing area of east Texas. They had managed to keep the local Republican party going after Reconstruction and regularly sent black representatives to the Texas legislature during the 1870s and 1880s. More remarkable yet, the local Populist party that appeared in 1892 among white farmers proved immune to the Democrats' taunts of "black rule." A Populist-Republican coalition swept the county elections in 1896 and 1898, surviving well after the collapse of the national Populist movement.

In 1899 defeated Democratic office seekers and prominent citizens of Grimes County organized the secret White Man's Union. Armed men prevented blacks from voting in town elections that year. The two most important black county leaders were shot down in cold blood. Night riders terrorized both white Populists and black Republicans. When the Populist sheriff proved incapable of enforcing the law, the game was up. The White Man's Union, now out in the open, became the county Democratic party in a new guise. The Democrats won Grimes County by an overwhelming vote in 1900. The day after the election, members of the Union laid siege to the Populist sheriff's office. They killed his brother and a friend and drove the sheriff, badly wounded, out of the county forever.

The White Man's Union ruled Grimes County for the next fifty years. The whole episode was the handiwork of the county's "best citizens," suggesting how respectable the use of terror had become in the service of white supremacy. The Union intended, as one of its leaders said, to "force the African to keep his place." After 1900, blacks could survive in Grimes County only if they tended to their own business and stayed out of trouble with whites.

Like the blacks of Grimes County, southern blacks in many places resisted white oppression as best they could. When Georgia adopted the first Jim Crow law applying to streetcars in 1891, Atlanta blacks declared a boycott, and over the next fifteen years there were boycotts against segregated streetcars in at least twenty-five cities. "Do not trample on our pride by being 'jim crowed,'" the Savannah *Tribune* urged its readers: "Walk!" Ida Wells-Barnett emerged as the most outspoken crusader against lynching, so enraging the Memphis white community by the editorials in her newspaper *Free Speech* that she was forced in 1892 to leave the city. And there were individual blacks such as Robert Charles who, driven beyond endurance, struck back, at the inevitable sacrifice of their own lives.

Like Charles, some were drawn to the back-to-Africa movement. It was a sign of their despair that once again Africa was seen as the place of black salvation.

Robert Charles: Black Militant

The trouble began in an ordinary way. The two black men were sitting quietly on the steps of a house on Dryades Street in New Orleans, between Washington and 6th Street. It was Monday evening, July 24, 1900. One of the two was nineteen-year-old Leonard Pierce, the other an older man named Robert Charles. They were waiting for a friend of Charles's, Virginia Banks, and her roommate to return from a day at Baton Rouge. Around 11 P.M., three policemen approached Pierce and Charles and began to question them roughly. When Charles stood up, Officer Mora grabbed him. A scuffle followed, and Mora began to beat Charles about the head with his billy club. Charles, a big man, broke away. There was an exchange of gunfire, wounding both in the thigh, Officer Mora more seriously. In a hail of bullets, Charles ran off.

"In any law-abiding community Charles would have been justified in delivering himself up immediately to the properly constituted authorities and asking for a trial by a jury of his peers," wrote the antilynching crusader Ida Wells-Barnet in her pamphlet on what followed. "Charles knew that his arrest in New Orleans, even for defending his life, meant nothing short of a long term in the penitentiary, and still more probable death by lynching at the hands of a cowardly mob." Those must have been Charles's thoughts. He made his way back to the room he shared with Pierce on 4th Street, took down his Winchester rifle, and got ready to fight.

In the meantime, Pierce had been brought to the police station, where Charles's name and address were soon "sweated" out of him. Captain John T. Day, a local hero who had rescued fourteen people from a hotel fire, led a squad to bring Charles in. The entrance to his room was along an alley. When the police arrived, Charles swung open the door, shot Day through the heart, then turned and fatally wounded a second officer. The other two policemen cowered along the wall and slipped into another house, where they hid in the dark. The officers on the street refused to enter the unlit alley. When reinforcements arrived at 5 A.M., Charles had slipped away, and the manhunt commenced.

Robert Charles
This is the only known picture of Charles, an engraving done for the cover of Ida Wells-Barnet's pamphlet on Charles' slaying.

The New Orleans newspapers labeled Charles a "fiend incarnate." No one who had known him would have said so. Robert Charles was one of thousands of rural blacks in this period who had sought to escape from grinding poverty by migrating to southern cities. Robert Charles was born just after the end of slavery, in 1865 or 1866, in Copiah County, Mississippi. His parents were sharecroppers, and he was one of ten children. He worked as a day laborer on the railroads and, after arriving in New Orleans around 1894, at a variety of odd jobs. In July 1900, he was unemployed. Charles was unmarried, rather stylish in his dress, favoring a brown derby hat. Acquaintances remembered him as quiet and intelligent. He had received little education, but in his room were the well-thumbed books and papers of a studious man. One other thing about Charles: he ardently believed that blacks should return to Africa.

The back-to-Africa movement, which enjoyed a revival in these hard years, reflected the despair that poor blacks like Robert Charles felt about life in America. Africa was their only salvation, preached Bishop Henry M. Turner, the combative leader of the movement. "I see no other shelter from the stormy blast, from the red tide of persecution, from the horrors of American prejudice." Charles was a reader of Bishop Turner's fiery paper *Voice of Missions,* and in 1899 he began to sell subscriptions. He also became a local agent for the International Migration Society, working on commission to sign up members who would secure transportation to Liberia if they contributed a dollar a month for forty months.

Recent events fortified Charles's conviction that blacks had no hope in America. He was said to have been infuriated by the most infamous lynching of the era, the burning and dismemberment of Sam Hose in Georgia in 1899. In Louisiana, moreover, blacks had been disfranchised in 1898, and a crisis was brewing in state politics. As 1900 elections approached, the Democrats vowed that on no account would they allow the Republicans and Populists to emerge as winners. In Charles's pocket was a newspaper clipping about an opposition leader calling upon his supporters to "*oil up their Winchesters* and prepare to fight" if Democrats tried to steal the election. In *Voice of Missions* there was a similarly desperate message: in one editorial Bishop Turner had urged that "Negroes Get Guns" in self-defense.

Charles, in fact, did habitually carry a Colt .38 revolver; it was in his belt when Officer Mora accosted him. There is no knowing what went through his mind when he chose not to submit to the policeman's abuse. But, having drawn his gun, Charles had stepped across the line. From then on, until his inevitable death, he was making a political statement.

That was how the whites of New Orleans saw Charles too: he was challenging the white power structure. As a leader of the mob that gathered in the streets on Wednesday put it:

> The only way you can teach these niggers a lesson and put them in their place is to go out and lynch a few of them as an object lesson. String up a few of them, and the others will trouble you no more. . . . On to the Parish Prison and lynch Pierce!

The mob couldn't get at Pierce, but they took their fury out on any other unfortunate black they encountered as they surged through the city. In the next two days, at least six people were killed, and dozens of others brutally beaten. Only late Thursday did the police and militia restore a semblance of law and order to New Orleans. But Charles remained at large. Then, on Friday afternoon, July 27, the police got a tip that he was hiding in a small house on Saratoga Street.

Springing from a back closet, Charles shot down the two police who came to investigate, then made his way up to the second story. A great crowd soon surrounded the house, peppering it with bullets. Dodging from window to window, Charles returned their fire for nearly two hours. In grudging admiration, one reporter wrote of his "diabolical coolness" and his "wonderful marksmanship [that] never failed him for a moment." More than twenty of his attackers were hit, three fatally. As dusk began to fall, the building was set ablaze, and Charles was forced out. Still defiant, he almost made it across the courtyard when he was felled by a bullet and went down. The crowd was at him in an instant, firing dozens of shots into him, stomping on his head. His body was carried off in a police wagon, his battered head hanging grotesquely from the back. Later that night, the mob broke loose again, burning buildings and murderously attacking six more blacks.

It would have meant certain death for any New Orleans black to say out loud that Robert Charles had done right. But Ida Wells-Barnet, writing from the safety of Chicago, insisted that he had. "The white people of this country may charge that he was a desperado, but to the people of his own race Robert Charles will always be regarded as the hero of New Orleans." Five weeks after Charles's burial in a potter's grave, a neighbor of Fred Clark's on South Ramparts Street came up behind Clark, put a gun to his head and shot him dead. Fred Clark was the black man who had given away Charles's hiding place to the police.

But emigration was not a real choice, and, like the blacks of Grimes County, African-Americans everywhere had to bend to the raging forces of racism and find a way to survive.

The Atlanta Compromise. Booker T. Washington, the foremost black leader of the South of his day, responded to that grim reality in a famous speech in Atlanta in 1895. Washington marked out a line of retreat from the defiant stand of an older generation of black abolitionists exemplified by Frederick Douglass, who died the same year that the Atlanta speech launched Washington into national prominence. Washington was conciliatory toward the South; it was a society that blacks understood and loved. He considered "the agitation of the question of social equality the extremest folly." Washington accepted segregation, provided that blacks had equal facilities. He accepted educational and property qualifications for the vote, provided that they applied equally to blacks and whites.

Washington's doctrine came to be known as the Atlanta Compromise. His approach was "accommodationist," in the sense that it avoided any direct assault on white supremacy. Despite the humble face he put on before white audiences, however, Washington did not concede the struggle. Behind the scenes, Washington did his best to resist Jim Crow laws and disfranchisement. More important, his Atlanta Compromise, while abandoning the field of political protest, opened up a second front of economic struggle.

Washington sought to capitalize on a southern dilemma about the economic role of the black population. Racist dogma dictated that blacks be kept down and that they conform to their image as lazy, shiftless workers. But for the South to prosper, it needed an efficient labor force. Washington made this need the target of his efforts. As founder of the Tuskegee Institute in Alabama in 1881, Washington advocated *industrial education*—that is, manual and agricultural training. He preached the virtues of thrift, hard work, and property ownership. Washington's industrial education program won generous support from northern philanthropists and businessmen and, following his Atlanta speech, applause from progressive supporters of the New South.

Washington assumed that black economic progress would be the key to winning black political and civil rights. He regarded members of the white southern elite as his crucial allies, because ultimately only they had the power to act. More important, they could see "the close connection between labor, industry, education, and political institutions." When it was in their economic interest, and when they had grown dependent on black labor and black enterprise, white men of business and property would recognize the justice of black rights. As Washington put it, "There is little race prejudice in the American dollar."

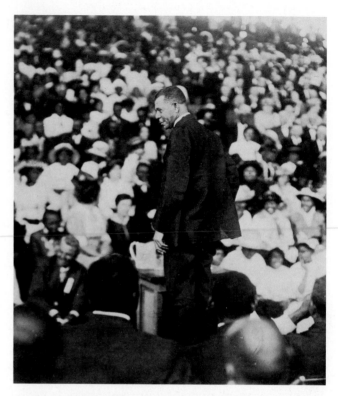

Booker T. Washington

In an age of severe racial oppression, Washington emerged as the acknowledged leader of black people in the United States. He was remarkable both for his ability as spokesman to white Americans and his deep understanding of the aspirations of black Americans. Born a slave, Washington suffered the indignities experienced by all blacks after Emancipation. But, having been befriended by several whites as he grew to manhood, he also understood what it took to gain white support—and maneuver around white hostility—in the black struggle for equality.

Do the facts suggest that Washington was right? Or, to put the question as an economist might: was it the impersonal market or race prejudice that most determined the economic treatment of blacks? For southern industry, the answer seems mixed. Employers did not discriminate very much over wage rates—that is, they did not pay whites higher wages than blacks for the same work. But racial barriers certainly prevented blacks from moving up into better-paid and more highly skilled jobs. This hard truth is made graphically clear in the comparative wage distributions of whites and blacks shown in Figure 19.2. In agriculture, too, the picture is mixed. The opportunity for black farmers to advance themselves clearly did exist. The proportion who became landowners inched slowly upward to roughly 25 percent in 1900; and they were able to achieve this at a slightly younger age than earlier. But the racial gap remained very wide, with whites almost three times as likely to be landowners as blacks.

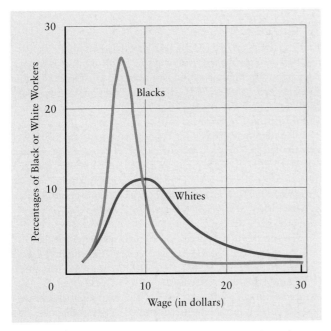

Source: Gavin Wright, *Old South, New South: Revolutions in the Southern Economy Since the Civil War* (New York: Basic Books, 1986), p. 184.

FIGURE 19.2

Wage Distributions of Black and White Workers in Virginia, 1907

To what extent black self-help—hard work, industrial education, the husbanding of small resources—might counterbalance the barriers thrown up by race prejudice was the nub of Booker T. Washington's problem. Where the almighty dollar reigned there was some hope of progress. Elsewhere, as Washington saw it, there was none.

For twenty years after his Atlanta address, Washington dominated organized black life in America. He was the authentic voice of black opinion in an age of severe racial oppression. No black dealt more skillfully with the leaders of white America or wielded more political influence. The black community knew him as a hard taskmaster. Intensely jealous of his authority, he did not regard opposition kindly. Black politicians, educators, and editors stood up to him at their peril.

Even so, a crack began to appear after 1900, especially among younger, educated blacks. They thought Washington was conceding too much. He instilled black pride, but of a narrowly middle-class and utilitarian kind. What about the special genius of blacks that W. E. B. DuBois celebrated in his collection of essays called *The Souls of Black Folk* (1903)? And what of the "talented tenth" of the black population whose promise could only be stifled by industrial education? Blacks also became increasingly impatient with Washington's silence over segregation and lynchings. By the time of his death in 1915, Washington's approach had been superseded by a strategy that relied on the courts and political leverage, not on black self-help and accommodation (see Chapter 21).

★

Summary

After Reconstruction ended in 1877, national politics became less issue-oriented and, as a formal process, less important in American life. This situation resulted from weaknesses in governmental institutions, from the prevailing philosophy of *laissez faire*, and from the paralysis of evenly matched political parties. Yet the politics of the years after 1877 had great vigor, evident in the high levels of popular participation. For one thing, politics was the arena in which the nation's ethnic and religious conflicts were largely fought out. Equally important, the party machines were very powerful and performed crucial functions that properly belonged to, but were still beyond the capacity of government institutions. Finally, despite the slow headway toward woman suffrage, women's organizations carved out for themselves a broadening public sphere of social reform activity.

During the 1890s, national politics again became an important arena. Threatened by the rise of Populism, the Democratic party committed itself to free silver and made the election of 1896 a contest over issues of real significance. The Republicans won decisively, ending the paralyzing party stalemate that had lasted for twenty years and assuring themselves of political dominance for the next thirty years. At the same time, the 1890s saw, in the failure of Populism, the last great challenge to the mainstream two-party system. And in the South the Populist failure turned into a grim reaction that disfranchised African-Americans, completed a rigid segregation system, and let loose a terrible cycle of racial hatred and violence. Blacks resisted, but had to bend to overwhelming white power. The accommodationist philosophy of Booker T. Washington seemed to be the best strategy for survival in an age of extreme racism.

TOPIC FOR RESEARCH

The Mugwump Critique of American Politics

In the years after the Civil War, the Mugwumps mounted a powerful critique of American party politics. What kind of people were the liberal reformers? What did they find objectionable in the machine system of politics? What was their attitude toward the immigrants who sustained the machine system? What was their attitude toward universal manhood suffrage? What kind of politics did they advocate, and what was their impact on the political process of the late nineteenth century? Among the many books that explore these questions, the most useful are Geoffrey T. Blodgett, *Gentle Reformers: Massachusetts Democrats in the Cleveland Era* (1966), John G. Sproat, *The "Best Men": Liberal Reformers in the Gilded Age* (1965), Gerald W. McFarland, *Mugwumps, Morals and Politics, 1884–1920* (1975), and Ari Hoogenboom, *Outlawing the Spoils: The Civil Service Reform Movement, 1865–1883* (1961). A good introduction to the subject, with ample notes on sources, is Chapter 3 in Michael E. McGerr, *The Decline of Popular Politics: The American North, 1865–1928* (1986). The Mugwumps were highly literate men, and they left an ample record of their views. You can find representative essays in 1880s issues of such journals as *The Nation, The North American Review,* and *Atlantic Monthly,* copies of which are available in many college libraries. Other accessible sources are the books or collected letters of many Mugwumps, such as Simon Sterne, Moorfield Storey, George William Curtis, and Henry Adams. (Citations to many of these published works can be found in McGerr's notes to Chapter 3 of his *Decline of Popular Politics.*) Adams's satirical novel *Democracy* (1880) conveys in lively fictional form the Mugwump critique of machine politics.

BIBLIOGRAPHY

The Politics of the Status Quo

The best introduction to American politics in the late nineteenth century is John A. Garraty, *The New Commonwealth, 1877–1890* (1968). Much more detailed is Morton Keller, *Affairs of State: Public Life in Late Nineteenth-Century America* (1977). Various aspects of national politics are discussed in Robert D. Marcus, *Grand Old Party: Political Structure in the Gilded Age* (1971), J. Rogers Hollingsworth, *The Whirligig of Politics: The Democracy of Cleveland and Bryan* (1963), H. Wayne Morgan, *From Hayes to McKinley: National Party Politics, 1877–1896* (1969), and David J. Rothman, *Politics and Power: The Senate, 1869–1901* (1966). On the development of public administration, see Leonard D. White, *The Republican Era, 1869–1901* (1958), and Stephen Skowronek, *Building a New American State: The Expansion of National Administrative Capacities* (1982).

The ideological basis for conservative national politics is fully treated in Robert L. Bannister, *Social Darwinism: Science and Myth* (1979), Sidney Fine, *Laissez Faire and the General Welfare State, 1865–1901* (1956), Richard Hofstadter, *Social Darwinism in American Thought* (rev. ed., 1955), and Robert G. McCloskey, *American Conservatism in the Age of Enterprise* (1951).

On the popular sources of political participation, see especially Michael E. McGerr, *The Decline of Popular Politics: The American North, 1865–1928* (1986), and Paul Kleppner, *The Third Electoral Party System, 1853–1892: Parties, Voters, and Political Cultures* (1979). The ethnocultural dimensions of party politics have been studied in Paul Kleppner, *The Cross of Culture: A Social Analysis of Midwestern Politics* (1970), and in Richard Jensen, *The Winning of the Midwest, 1888–1896* (1971). On the Mugwump reformers, see the citations in the Topic for Research. The existence of women's political culture in the late nineteenth century can be traced in Carl N. Degler, *At Odds: Women and the Family from the Revolution to the Present* (1979). A valuable book setting the stage is Ellen Carol DuBois, *Feminism and Suffrage: The Emergence of an Independent Women's Movement in America, 1848–1869* (1978).

The Crisis of the 1890s

The standard work on Populism is John D. Hicks, *The Populist Revolt* (1931). Richard D. Hofstadter, *The Age of Reform* (1955), stresses the darker side of Populism, in which intolerance and paranoia figure heavily. Hofstadter's thesis, which dominated debate among historians for some years, has now given way to a much more positive assessment. The key book here is Lawrence Goodwyn, *Democratic Promise: The Populist Moment in America* (1976), which argues that it was a broadly based, radical response to industrial capitalism. While Goodwyn stresses the southern roots of Populism, an earlier book makes a similar, but less complex, case for the radicalism of northwestern Populism: Norman Pollack, *The Populist Response to Industrial America* (1962). A highly stimulating book that traces the evolution of other strands of Populism into twentieth-century agrarian conservatism is Grant McConnell, *The Decline of Agrarian Democracy* (1953).

The money question is elucidated in Walter Nugent, *Money and American Society, 1865–1880* (1968), and Allan Weinstein, *Prelude to Populism: Origins of the Silver Issue* (1970). On the politics of the 1890s, see especially Peter H. Argesinger, *Populism and Politics: William A. Peffer and the People's Party* (1974), Robert F. Durden, *Climax of Populism: The Election of 1896* (1965), and Paul W. Glad, *McKinley, Bryan, and the People* (1964).

Race and Politics in the South

On southern politics, the seminal book for the post-Reconstruction period is C. Vann Woodward, *Origins of the New South, 1877–1913* (1951), which still defines the terms of discussion among historians. Two recent books stress the continuities between the Old South planters and the post–Civil War South: Dwight B. Billings, *Planters and the Making of "New South": North Carolina, 1865–1900* (1979), and Jonathan M. Wiener, *Social Origins of the New South: Alabama, 1860–1885* (1978). The standard book on New South thought is Paul M. Gaston, *The New South Creed: A Study of Southern Myth-Making* (1973). Gaston's book can profitably be read in conjunction with a much older study, Paul M. Buck, *The Road to Reunion, 1865–1900* (1937).

The classic book on segregation is C. Vann Woodward, *The Strange Career of Jim Crow* (2nd ed., 1968), but it should be supplemented by Howard N. Rabinowitz, *Race Relations in the Urban South, 1865–1890* (1978). A powerful analysis of southern racism, stressing its psychosocial roots, is Joel Williamson, *A Rage for Order: Black/White Relations in the American South Since Emancipation* (1986). Disfranchisement is treated with great analytic sophistication in J. Morgan Kousser, *The Shaping of Southern Politics: Suffrage Restriction and the Establishment of the One-Party South, 1880–1910,* (1974) and as an aspect of progressivism in Jack Temple Kirby, *Darkness at the Dawning: Race and Reform in the Progressive South* (1972). Rayford W. Logan, *The Betrayal of the Negro* (1965), is the standard history of blacks after Reconstruction. August Meier, *Negro Thought in America, 1880–1915* (1963), is a key analysis of black accommodation and protest. The preeminent exponent of accommodation is the subject of a superb two-volume biography by Louis B. Harlan, *Booker T. Washington: The Making of a Black Leader* (1973), and *Wizard of Tuskegee* (1983).

TIMELINE

1874	Women's Christian Temperance Union (WCTU) founded
1877	Rutherford B. Hayes inaugurated; end of Reconstruction
1881	President James A. Garfield assassinated
1883	Pendleton Civil Service Act
1884	Mugwump reformers bolt the Republican party to support Grover Cleveland, first Democrat elected president since 1856
1887	Interstate Commerce Act creates the Interstate Commerce Commission (ICC) to regulate railroads
1890	McKinley Tariff Mississippi becomes first state to adopt literacy test to disfranchise blacks
1892	People's (Populist) Party founded
1893	Panic of 1893 leads to national depression Repeal of Sherman Silver Purchase Act (1890)
1894	Coxey's Army
1895	Booker T. Washington sets out the Atlanta Compromise
1896	Election of William McKinley; free silver campaign crushed *Plessy v. Ferguson* upholds constitutionality of "separate-but-equal" facilities
1897	Economic depression ends

The Bowery at Night, 1895

This painting by W. Louis Sonntag, Jr., shows the
Bowery crowded with shoppers and pleasure
seekers. It was during this time that it gained its
raffish reputation. (Museum of the City of New
York)

CHAPTER **20** *The Rise of the City*

For the first two hundred years of its history, America remained a land of farmers. In 1820 barely 5 percent of the people lived in cities with a population of ten thousand or more. But after that, decade by decade, the urban population swelled, turning into a flood after mid-century. A comparable process was occurring in Europe, but at a slower pace. During the nineteenth century, the percentage of Europeans living in towns increased threefold, while in the United States the increase was sevenfold.

By 1900 one of every five Americans lived in an urban center of one hundred thousand or more residents. The greatest growth had taken place in the major metropolitan cities. Nearly a tenth of the nation—6.5 million persons—lived in cities of over a million. The late nineteenth century, an economist remarked in 1899, "was not only the age of cities, but the age of great cities."

The growth of the cities had enormous implications for American society. The city was the arena of the nation's vibrant economic life. Here the factories went up, and here the multitudes of working people settled. New immigrants swelled the ranks of the working class. At the turn of the century upwards of 30 percent of the residents of major cities in the United States were foreign-born. Here, too, lived the millionaires and a growing urban middle class of white-collar workers and businessmen. For all these people, the city was more than a place to make a living. It provided the setting for an urban culture unlike anything seen before in the United States. City people, although differing vastly among themselves, became distinctively and recognizably urban.

Urbanization

The march to the cities seemed inevitable to nineteenth-century Americans. "The greater part of our population must live in cities—cities much greater than the world has yet known," declared the Congregational minister and social critic Josiah Strong in 1898. "In due time we shall be a nation of cities." There was "no resisting the trend," said another writer. Urbanization became inevitable because of its link to another inevitability that gripped America—industrialization.

The Sources of City Growth

Until the Civil War, cities had been centers primarily of commerce, not industry. Located strategically along transportation routes, they were the places where merchants bought and sold goods for distribution into the interior or for shipment out to the world market. Early industrialism, on the other hand, was distinctly a rural phenomenon. Mills and factories needed water power from streams and rivers, ready access to sources of fuel and raw materials, and workers drawn from the surplus farm population. Of the nation's fifteen largest cities in 1860, only five reported as much as 10 percent of the labor force engaged in manufacturing activity.

After mid-century, industry began to abandon the countryside. With the arrival of steam power, mill operators no longer needed to locate along streams. In the iron industry, coal replaced charcoal as the primary fuel, so iron makers did not have to be near forests. Improved transportation, especially the railroads, gave entrepreneurs a greater choice in selecting the best sites in relation to supplies and markets. The result was the geographic concentration of industry. Iron makers gravitated to Pittsburgh because of its access not only to supplies of coal and iron ore but also to markets for iron and steel products. Chicago, ideally located between livestock suppliers and consuming markets, became a great meat-packing center in the 1870s.

Many smaller industrial cities depended on a high degree of economic specialization. Youngstown, Ohio, and Johnstown, Pennsylvania, specialized in iron and steel; Brockton and Haverhill, Massachusetts, in boots and shoes; Troy, New York, in collars and cuffs; East Liverpool, Ohio, in pottery. Other cities processed the raw materials of their regions. Sacramento canned fruits and vegetables, Richmond made cigarettes, Minneapolis milled grain, and Memphis handled lumber and produced cottonseed oil.

This geographic concentration of industry was one source of urban growth in the late nineteenth century.

Another was the increasing scale of production that became characteristic of modern industry. A factory that employed thousands of workers instantly created a small city in its vicinity. The result was often a company town—Aliquippa, Pennsylvania, for example, became body and soul the property of the Jones and Laughlin Steel Company. Many firms set up their plants near a large city so they could draw on its labor supply and transportation facilities. George Pullman located his sleeping-car works and model town southwest of Chicago, and George Westinghouse built his electrical plant just east of Pittsburgh. Sometimes the nearby metropolis spread and absorbed the smaller city, as happened with Pullman, Illinois. Elsewhere, as in northern New Jersey or south of Chicago and across the state line into Indiana, smaller communities merged and formed an extended urban-industrial area. The same process could be seen in Europe, where industrial regions were emerging in northeastern France around Lille and in Germany's Ruhr Valley.

The established commercial cities also grew significantly in this era. They benefited from the tendency of a

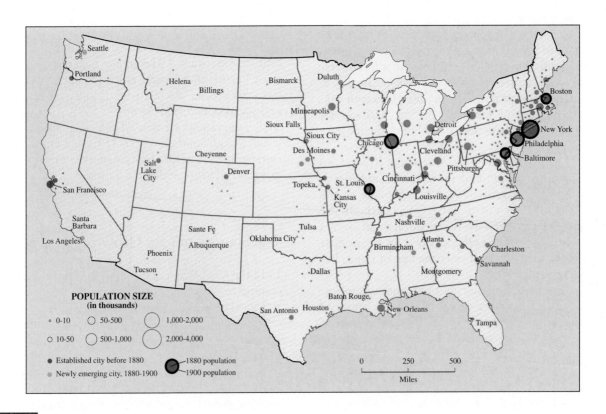

MAP 20.1

The Growth of America's Cities, 1880–1900
The number of Americans living in urban places more than doubled between 1880 and 1900. The most dramatic increases occurred in the largest metropolitan centers. New York went from 1.2 million to 3.4 million, Chicago from 0.5 million to 1.7 million. Notable among newly emerging cities—places that had been small towns or minor cities in 1880—were Los Angeles, Seattle, Birmingham, Omaha, and Atlanta.

maturing industrial economy to create complex marketing and administrative structures. The greatest centers—New York and Chicago—became headquarters for corporations operating across the country. Finance, publishing, distribution, advertising, and fashion were concentrated in the metropolitan centers.

These commercial centers also attracted certain kinds of industries. They had warehouse districts that could readily be converted to small-scale manufacturing, and they offered ample transportation and services. In addition, they could supply abundant cheap labor because they served as gateways for immigrants. Boston, Philadelphia, Baltimore, and San Francisco became hives of small-scale, labor-intensive industrial activity. New York's enormous pool of immigrant workers made it a magnet for the garment trades, cigar making, and diversified light industry. Preeminent as a city of trade and finance, New York also ranked as the nation's largest manufacturing center.

By 1870, a core industrial region had formed from New England down through the Middle Atlantic states to Maryland. In this region, the percentage of people living in urban places was twice the national average. Forty years later, in 1910, the original industrial core was nearly three-quarters urbanized. It had also thrust westward to include the Great Lakes states, which became America's industrial heartland. Important new centers for steel making, manufacturing, and food processing sprang up in this region. Pittsburgh, Cleveland, Detroit, Milwaukee, Minneapolis—all of them small cities or modest commercial centers in 1870—had by 1910 grown into major industrial cities ranging from 300,000 to well over half a million inhabitants.

TABLE 20.1

Ten Largest Cities by Population, 1870 and 1910

	1870		1910
City	Population	City	Population
1. New York	942,292	New York	4,766,883
2. Philadelphia	674,022	Chicago	2,185,283
3. Brooklyn*	419,921	Philadelphia	1,549,008
4. St. Louis	310,864	St. Louis	687,029
5. Chicago	298,977	Boston	670,585
6. Baltimore	267,354	Cleveland	560,663
7. Boston	250,526	Baltimore	558,485
8. Cincinnati	216,239	Pittsburgh	533,905
9. New Orleans	191,418	Detroit	465,766
10. San Francisco	149,473	Buffalo	423,715

*Brooklyn was consolidated with New York in 1898.
Source: U.S. Census data.

City Building

How would so many people move around, communicate, and satisfy their physical needs? "The only trouble about this town," wrote Mark Twain on arriving in New York in 1867, "is that it is too large. You cannot accomplish anything in the way of business, you cannot even pay a friendly call, without devoting a whole day to it. . . . The distances are too great." Finding ways of moving nearly a million New Yorkers around was not as hopeless an undertaking as it might have seemed to Twain, but it did pose daunting challenges to city builders. The city demanded innovation no less than did industry itself and, in the end, compiled an equally impressive record of technological achievement.

The preindustrial city had been a compact place, densely settled around a harbor or along a river. As late as 1850, when it had 565,000 people, greater Philadelphia covered only 10 square miles. From the foot of Chestnut Street on the Delaware River, a person could walk to almost anywhere in the city within forty-five minutes. Thereafter, however, Philadelphia—and, indeed, all American cities—tended to spread out and become less compact as they developed.

A downtown area emerged, usually in what had been the original commercial city. Downtown, in turn, broke up into shopping, financial, warehousing, manufacturing, hotel and entertainment, and red-light districts. Although somewhat fluid at their edges, all these districts were well-defined areas of specialized activity. Moving out from the center, industrial development tended to follow the arteries of transportation—railroads, canals, and rivers—and, at the city's outskirts, to spread out into complexes of heavy industry. At the same time the middle class moved in large numbers to new suburban areas.

The contrast with continental Europe was very marked. There, even rapidly growing cities remained physically compact, with boundaries that broke sharply at the surrounding countryside. In America, cities constantly expanded, spilling beyond the formal city boundaries and forming what the federal census began to designate in 1910 as *metropolitan areas*. While there was much congestion at the center, the population density of American cities was actually much below that of European cities—22 persons per acre for fifteen American cities in the 1890s, for example; 157.6 for a comparable group of German cities. It followed, of course, that the development of efficient urban transportation had a much higher priority in the United States than in Europe.

Mass Transit. The first step toward mass transit, dating back to the 1820s, was the omnibus, an elongated version of the horse-drawn coach. The omnibus was a con-

Traffic Jam in Downtown Chicago, 1905
The purpose of urban transit systems was to move masses of people rapidly and efficiently through the city. However, better transportation brought more congestion as well, like this scene of temporary gridlock at Randolph and Dearborn streets in Chicago.

venience, but it did not do much to relieve congestion; downtown, people could walk just as fast. Much more effective was the horsecar. The key thing was that it ran on iron tracks, so that it could carry more passengers, move them at a faster clip through congested city streets, and reach out into the residential areas. But it took a refinement of the railroad track—the invention in 1852 of a grooved rail that was flush with the pavement—to make the horsecar practical. For the next forty years, horsecars became the mainstay of urban transit across America, accounting for 70 percent of the traffic in 1890.

The horse was not, of course, an ideal source of locomotion. It moved slowly, had limited pulling power, and left piles of manure behind. Among various early improvements was the cable car, which was pulled by an underground cable set in below the tracks. The first cable cars ran in San Francisco in 1873, and more than twenty other cities used them during the 1880s. But the cable car could run only at a slow, unvarying speed; systemwide breakdowns occurred frequently.

Then came the electric trolley car. Its development was the work primarily of Frank J. Sprague, an electrical engineer once employed by the great inventor Thomas A. Edison. In 1887, Sprague designed an electric-driven system for Richmond, Virginia: a "trolley" carriage running along an overhead power line was attached by cable to streetcars equipped with an electric motor—hence the name trolley car. After Sprague's success, the electric trolley swiftly displaced the horsecar and became by 1900 the primary means of public transportation in most American cities.

MAP 20.2

The Expansion of Chicago
In 1865 Chicagoans, depended on slow horsecar transport to get around town. By 1900 the city limits had expanded enormously, accompanied by equally dramatic extension of streetcar service, by then all electrified. Elevated trains also now helped ease congestion in the urban core. New streetcar lines, some beyond the city limits, were important to suburban development in coming years.

In the great metropolitan centers, however, mounting congestion led to demands that public transit be moved off the streets. The railroad had long been used by well-to-do suburbanites to commute to the city. The problem was how to harness railway technology to serve the needs of ordinary city dwellers. In 1879, the first elevated lines went into operation on Sixth and

Ninth avenues in New York City. Powered at first by steam engines, the "els" converted to electricity following Sprague's success with the trolley. Chicago developed elevated transit most fully. New York, on the other hand, turned to the subway. Although Boston opened a short underground line in 1897, the completion in 1904 of a subway running the length of Manhattan demonstrated the full potential of underground rapid transit. Thinly settled areas of northern Manhattan and the Bronx, predicted the *New York Times*, would soon boast "a population of ten million . . . housed comfortably, healthfully and relatively cheaply." The subway would especially delight "all who travel with the sole purpose of 'getting there' in the least time possible." Mass transit had become *rapid* transit.

Nowhere else in the world was the demand for mass urban transit so acute. In 1890 the number of passengers carried on American street railways was more than 2 billion per year, over twice that of the rest of the world combined. Berlin, which boasted the best system in Europe, had a per capita usage that was exceeded by twenty-one American cities. In England, the horsecar remained dominant long after it had disappeared from American streets. In Tokyo, the biggest Asian city, the horsecar was not even introduced until 1882, while the first electric streetcar appeared only in 1903.

The Skyscraper. If urban transit evolved in response to the geographic expansiveness of the American city, advances in construction techniques answered the need to create more space in the downtown business districts. New building materials made it possible to construct commercial buildings of greater height, interior space, and fire resistance. With the availability by the 1880s of steel girders, mass-produced durable plate glass, and the passenger elevator, a wholly new way of construction opened up. A steel skeleton would support the building, and the walls, hitherto weight-bearing, would serve as curtains enclosing the structure. The sky, so to speak, became the limit.

The first "skyscraper" to be built on this principle was the ten-story Home Insurance Building (1885) in Chicago. Although this pioneering effort was conventional in appearance—it looked just like the other commercial buildings in the downtown district—the steel-girdered structure swiftly liberated the aesthetic perceptions of American architects. A Chicago school sprung up, dedicated to the design of buildings whose form expressed, rather than masked, their structure and function. The masterpiece of the Chicago school was Louis Sullivan's Carson, Pirie, Scott and Company department store (1904). Chicago pioneered in skyscraper construction, but New York, with its unrelenting need for prime downtown space, took the lead after the mid-1890s. The climax of New York's construction surge came with the completion in 1913 of the fifty-five story

Manhattan's First Skyscraper
The Tower Building at 50 Broadway was completed in 1889. To the modern eye, this first New York skyscraper seems modest and old-fashioned. Compared with its squat neighbors, however, it was a revolutionary building based on new principles of slender, soaring architecture. (Museum of the City of New York)

Woolworth Building. Aptly called the "Cathedral of Commerce," the Woolworth Building towered over its neighbors and marked the beginning of the modern Manhattan skyline.

Bridges. Rivers, in earlier times the lifeline of trade, now became barriers that interrupted rail traffic and hindered city expansion. The second half of the nineteenth century became the great age of bridge construction. Hundreds of iron and steel bridges went up during this period. Some—including the Eads Bridge (1873) spanning the Mississippi River at St. Louis and the Brooklyn Bridge (1883) over New York's East River—are still in use. The Brooklyn Bridge, linking Brooklyn and Manhattan, took fifteen years to build. A giant suspension structure, the Brooklyn Bridge was not only an engineering marvel but the symbol of a new kind of functional architecture—"the first product of the age of coal and iron to achieve completeness of expression," wrote the architectural critic Lewis Mumford.

The Electric City. If the railroad was the economic lifeline of the industrial city, electricity was the source of its quickening tempo. Charles F. Brush's electric arc lamps, first installed in the windows of the Wanamaker department store in Philadelphia in 1878, soon replaced gaslight in stores and hotel lobbies and on city streets throughout the country. The following year, Thomas Edison created the first commercially practical incandescent lamp, which brought electric lighting into American homes. Before electricity had any significant effect on industry, it lifted and lowered elevators and powered streetcars and subway trains. No other invention so transformed America's urban life. Meanwhile the telephone, patented by Alexander Graham Bell in 1876, speeded up communication beyond anything imagined previously. Twain's complaint of 1867 that it was impossible to carry on business in New York had been answered: all he needed to do now was pick up the phone. By 1900, 1.5 million telephones were in use, linking urban activity into a network of instant communication.

The Private City

City building was very much an exercise in private enterprise. The great innovations—the trolley car, the skyscraper, the elevator, electric lighting, and the telephone—had been spurred by the lure of profit. So was urban real-estate development. The investment opportunities looked so tempting that new cities sprang up almost overnight from the ruins of the Chicago fire of 1871 and the San Francisco earthquake of 1906. Likewise, real-estate interests, anxious to develop subdivisions, were often partly instrumental in pushing streetcar lines outward from the central districts of cities.

Mass transit became big business. In the early 1880s, Peter A. B. Widener and William L. Elkins teamed up to unite much of Philadelphia's streetcar system within the Philadelphia Traction Company. They did the same in alliance with Charles T. Yerkes in Chicago and with William C. Whitney and Thomas Fortune Ryan in New York. By 1900 their syndicate controlled streetcar systems in more than a hundred cities and had expanded to include utilities supplying gas and electricity to urban customers. The city, like industry, became an arena for enterprise and profit.

This was a matter of choice, however. Under the law, cities had extensive powers of self-development. In a key decision in 1897, the New York state courts authorized New York City to build a municipally owned subway. There could be "no complete definition of 'a city purpose.'" Cities had to determine their needs and then carry out those responsibilities as they saw fit. If a city chose to have services provided by others, it did so by, in effect, turning a private corporation into a municipal instrumentality. Even the use of privately owned land was subject to whatever regulations the city might choose to impose.

But in sharp distinction from Europe, American cities generally hesitated to use the broad municipal powers granted them by the courts. America produced what the urban historian Sam Bass Warner has called "the private city"—one shaped primarily by the actions of many private individuals. All these persons pursued their own goals and tried to maximize their own profit. The prevailing belief was that the sum of such private activity would far exceed what the community could accomplish through public effort. This meant that the city itself handled only functions that could not be undertaken efficiently or profitably by private enterprise.

In that public realm, American cities actually compiled an impressive record of achievement in the late nineteenth century. Nowhere in the world were there more massive public projects: water aqueducts, sewage systems, street paving, bridge building, extensive park systems. Though by no means free of the corruption and wastefulness of earlier days, city governments became markedly more centralized in these years, better administered and more professional, and, above all, more expansive in the functions they undertook. How else could they have gathered the resources and built the infrastructure on which the modern industrial city depended? Massive though it was, however, this public contribution did not undercut the prevailing conception of the city as an arena for private enterprise.

The nation paid an enormous price for such unrestricted development. A century later, we are still adding up the costs in terms of the quality of American urban life.

The Urban Environment. Some of those costs could be seen right away. In 1879 an English visitor observed the blight that spread along streets on which elevated trains operated:

> The nineteen hours and more of incessant rumbling day and night from the passing trains; the blocking out of a sufficiency of light; the full, close view passengers on the cars can have into rooms on the second and third floors.

Skyscrapers also shut out the light, and added to downtown congestion. People regarded such conditions as sad but inevitable costs of progress.

Other consequences were more clearly the result of deliberate choice. Priority went to projects considered vital to a city's economic development. Thus bridge construction flourished. Grand public buildings, symbols of a city's eminence, enjoyed great popularity. Philadelphia's City Hall, said one critic, had been "projected on a scale of magnificence better suited for the capitol of an empire than the municipal building of a debt-burdened city." On the other hand, the condition of the streets, mainly a matter of convenience for the people, often remained scandalously bad. "Three or four days of warm spring weather," remarked a New York journalist, would turn Manhattan's garbage-strewn, snow-clogged streets into "veritable mud rivers."

A visitor to Pittsburgh noted "the heavy pall of smoke which constantly overhangs her . . . until the very sun looks coppery through the sooty haze." As for the lovely hills rising from the rivers, "they have been leveled down, cut into, sliced off, and ruthlessly marred and mutilated, until not a trace of their original outlines remain." Pittsburgh presented "all that is unsightly and forbidding in appearance, the original beauties of nature having been ruthlessly sacrificed to utility."

These failings resulted not only from the low value placed on the quality of urban life. The city's dynamism confounded efforts to provide adequate services. New York's Croton aqueduct, when completed in 1842, was hailed as "more akin in magnificence to the ancient and Roman aqueducts [than anything] achieved in our times." Yet less than a decade later, water consumption was outstripping the capacity of the aqueduct. In 1885, New York started to build a second, larger aqueduct. When that one also failed to meet the city's needs, New York built still another aqueduct a hundred miles away in the Catskill Mountains. Each new facility and innovation seemed to fall short, not merely outstripped by the rising demand, but also contributing further to that demand. This occurred with urban transportation, high-rise building, and modern sanitation systems. They attracted more users, created new necessities, and caused additional crowding and shortages.

It was not that America lacked an urban vision. On the contrary, an abiding rural ideal had exerted a powerful influence on American cities for many years. Frederick Law Olmsted, who designed New York's Central Park before the Civil War and many other city parks in later years, wanted cities that exposed people to the beauties of nature. One of Olmsted's projects, the Chicago World's Fair of 1893, gave rise to the influential "City Beautiful" movement. The results included larger park systems, broad boulevards and parkways, and after the turn of the century, zoning laws and planned suburbs.

Cities usually heeded urban planners too little and far too late. "Fifteen or twenty years ago a plan might have been adopted that would have made this one of the most beautiful cities in the world," the Kansas City Park Commissioners reported in 1893. At that time, "such a policy could not be fully appreciated." Nor, even if Kansas City had foreseen its future, would it have shouldered the "heavy burden" of trying to shape its development. The American city had placed its faith in the dynamics of the marketplace, not the restraints of a planned future.

Housing. The most disastrous impact of dynamic urban growth was on the living conditions of the poor. In the preindustrial city, low-income people had lived on a makeshift basis. They occupied small wooden structures in the alleys and back streets and, increasingly, in the subdivided homes of more prosperous families who had fled to other neighborhoods. When rising

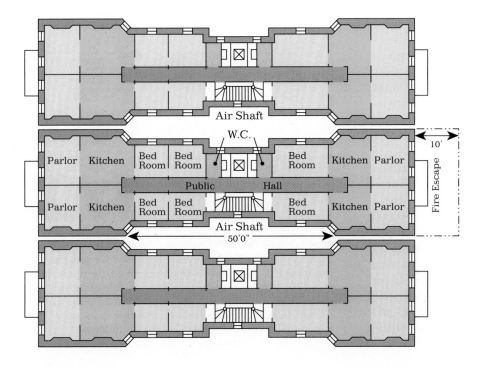

FIGURE 20.1

Floor Plan of a Dumbbell Tenement

land values after the Civil War made this practice un-economical, speculators began to build housing specifically designed for the urban masses. In New York City, the dreadful result was the "dumbbell" tenement, so shaped as to utilize nearly all the standard 25 by 100–foot lot. A five-story building of this type could house twenty families in cramped, airless apartments (see Figure 20.1). In New York's Eleventh Ward, an average of 986 persons occupied each acre, a density matched only in Bombay, India. In other cities, the pressure for space was not quite as severe. Chicago, Boston, and St. Louis relied on two- and three-story buildings for low-income housing, while Philadelphia and Baltimore made do with dingy row houses.

But people everywhere considered these districts to be blights on the city. Here is how one investigator described Chicago's Halsted Street in 1896:

> The filthy and rotten tenements, the dingy courts and tumble-down sheds, the foul stables and dilapidated outhouses, the broken sewer pipes, the piles of garbage fairly alive with diseased odors, and . . . children filling every nook, working and playing in every room, eating and sleeping in every windowsill, pouring in and out of every door, and seeming literally to pave every scrap of "yard."

Reformers recognized the problem but seemed unable to solve it. Some favored model tenements financed by public-spirited citizens willing to accept limited dividends on their investments. When such private philanthropy failed to make much of a dent on the problem, cities tried to impose basic housing codes. The most advanced of these was New York's Tenement House Law of 1901, which applied stringent requirements for open courts, indoor toilets, and stronger fire safeguards on new housing, but did little to improve existing housing stock. Enforcement of housing standards was, moreover, always problematic. Commercial development had pushed up land values in downtown areas. Only high-density, cheaply built housing could earn a sufficient profit for the landlords of the poor. This basic economic fact defied nineteenth-century solutions.

A Balance Sheet: Chicago and Berlin. In 1902 Chicago and Berlin had virtually equal populations—1.8 million each. Their histories were, however, profoundly different. Seventy years earlier, when Chicago was just a muddy frontier outpost, Berlin already housed 250,000 people and had been for centuries the seat of the Hohenzollerns of Prussia. With German unification in 1871, the imperial authorities set about rebuilding Berlin on a grander scale. "A capital city is essential for the state, to act as a pivot for its culture," proclaimed the Prussian historian Heinrich von Treitschke, and Berlin served that national purpose—"a center where

[Germany's] political, intellectual, and material life is concentrated, and its people can feel united." Chicago had no such pretensions. It was strictly a place of business, made great by virtue of its strategic grip on the commerce of America's industrial heartland. Nothing in Chicago evoked the grandeur of Berlin's boulevards or its monumental palaces and public buildings, nor were Chicagoans ever witness to the pomp and ceremony of the imperial parades through the Brandenburg Gate and up broad, tree-lined Unter den Linden to the national cathedral.

Yet as a functioning city Chicago was in many ways clearly superior to Berlin. For instance, Chicago's waterworks pumped 500 million gallons of water a day, providing 139 gallons of water per person, while a Berliner had to make do with 18 gallons. Flush toilets, a rarity in Berlin in 1900, could be found in 60 percent of Chicago's homes. Its streets were lit by electricity while Berlin was still relying mostly on gas lamps. Chicago had a much more extensive streetcar system, twice as much acreage devoted to parks, and a public library containing many more volumes than Berlin's. And Chicago had just completed an amazing sanitation project to protect its water supply in Lake Michigan. By

Hester Street, New York City
As cities grew, land values in core areas skyrocketed. For the immigrant poor, with nowhere else to go, the result was incredible crowding in tenement housing. Life necessarily spilled out into the streets. The streets offered a place to transact business, a bit of fresh air, a chance to socialize with neighbors, and playing space for the children.

means of the new Sanitary and Ship Canal, the course of the Chicago River had been reversed so that its waters—and the city's sewage—would flow away from the lake and southward down into the Illinois and Mississippi rivers. To create the giant canal, over 30 million cubic yards of dirt had had to be excavated. This was the greatest earth-moving project in municipal history up to that time.

Giant sanitation projects were one thing, an inspiring urban environment something else. "We are enormously rich," admitted the journalist Edwin L. Godkin, "but . . . what have we got to show? Almost nothing. Ugliness from an artistic point of view is the mark of all our cities." This, then, was the urban balance sheet: a utilitarian infrastructure superb by nineteenth century standards, but "no municipal splendors of any description, nothing but population and hotels."

City People

The city symbolized energy and enterprise, with its soaring skyscrapers, rushing subways and jostling traffic, and hum of business activity. When the budding writer Hamlin Garland and his brother arrived in Chicago from rural Iowa in 1881, they knew immediately that they had entered a new world: "Everything interested us. . . . Nothing was commonplace, nothing was ugly to us." In one way or another, every city-bound migrant, whether from the American countryside or a foreign land, experienced something of this exhilaration and wonder.

But with the opportunity and boundless variety came profound disorder and uncertainty. The urban world was utterly unlike the rural communities that the newcomers had left. In the countryside every person had been known to his or her neighbors. Mark Twain found New York "a splendid desert, where a stranger is lonely in the midst of a million of his race. A man walks his tedious miles through the same interminable streets every day, yet never seeing a familiar face, and never seeing a strange one the second time. . . . Every man rushes, rushes, rushes, and never has time to be companionable—never has any time at his disposal to fool away on matters which do not involve dollars and duty and business." If rural roles and obligations had been well understood, in the city the only predictable relationships were those dictated by the marketplace.

The newcomers could never recreate in the city the worlds they had left behind. But new ways developed to meet the social needs of urban dwellers—to give them a sense of their place in the community; to teach them how to function in an impersonal, heterogeneous environment; and to make the complex, dynamic city understandable. An urban culture emerged, and through it there developed a new breed of American entirely at home in the modern city.

Immigrants

At the turn of the century upwards of 30 percent of the residents of New York, Chicago, Boston, Cleveland, Minneapolis, and San Francisco were foreign-born. Except in the South, America's cities had attracted large numbers of immigrants for many years. In 1900 the dominant groups still represented mainly the older migration from northern Europe. The biggest ethnic group in Boston was Irish; in Minneapolis, Swedish; in most other northern cities, German. But by 1914 the influx from southern and Eastern Europe had changed the ethnic complexion of many of these cities. In Chicago, Poles and Russians (mostly Jewish) took the lead; in New York, Italians were second to Russians; in San Francisco, Italians became the largest foreign-born group.

For all of these immigrants—old and new—ethnic identity played a crucial role in forming an urban community. All of them carried experiences and customs from the homeland that shaped their lives in the new world. But for the later arrivals from southern and Eastern Europe, there was less intermingling with the older populations than had been possible in the earlier "walking cities." Beginning in the 1880s, observers invariably reported that only foreign-born people lived in the poorer downtown areas of the great eastern and midwestern cities. "One may find for the asking an Italian, a German, a French, African, Spanish, Bohemian,

TABLE 20.2

Foreign-Born Population of Philadelphia, 1870 and 1910

	1870	1910
Irish	96,698	83,196
German	50,746	61,480
Austrian	519	19,860
Italian	516	45,308
Russian	94	90,697
Hungarian	52	12,495
Foreign-born population	183,624	384,707
Total population	674,022	1,549,008

Source: Allen F. Davis and Mark Haller, *The Peoples of Philadelphia* (Philadelphia: Temple University Press, 1973).

MAP 20.3

The Lower East Side, New York City

Jews from Eastern Europe concentrated in Manhattan's Lower East Side and, within that area, settled among others from their home regions. The feeling of group identity led to a remarkable flowering of institutions built by Jewish immigrants to meet their educational, cultural, and social needs.

Jewish Ethnic Concentrations

- Hungarian
- Romanian
- Galician
- Mixed Levantine and Romanian
- Russian

Neighborhood Institutions

1. Newspaper Row
2. Chatham Square Library
3. Beth Israel Hospital
4. Israel Elchanan Yeshiva
5. Educational Alliance
6. Henry Street Settlement
7. Machzike Talmud Torah
8. Hebrew Sheltering House
9. Hebrew Technical School for Girls
10. Home for the Aged
11. Jewish Maternity Hospital
12. Beth Hamedrash Hagadol
13. Yiddish Rialto
14. Thalia Theater
15. People's Bath
16. Police Headquarters
17. Public School 63
18. Music School Settlement
19. Asch Building
20. Astor Library
21. Hebrew Technical School for Boys
22. Labor Temple

The Economy of the Ghetto

Downtown immigrant neighborhoods would not have struck the casual observer as industrial districts. But tucked away in the tenements were commercial lofts and small workshops. An entire ready-made clothing industry flourished within the ghettoes of large cities, drawing especially on the young women of the neighborhoods to do the low-paid sewing tasks.

Russian, Scandinavian, Jewish, and Chinese colony," remarked the Danish-American journalist Jacob Riis in his study of lower New York in 1890. "The one thing you shall vainly ask for in the chief city of America is a distinctively American community."

The foreign-born had little choice about where they lived: they needed to be near their jobs and could not afford better housing. Some gravitated to the factory districts; others settled in the congested downtown ghettoes. The immigrants did not arrive randomly in these districts, however. Even where this seemed to happen, as in Philadelphia, closer study revealed that ethnic groups clustered in certain houses and portions of blocks. More commonly, as Riis discovered, an ethnic group took over an entire neighborhood. In New York, Italians crowded into the Irish neighborhoods west of Broadway, and Russian and Polish Jews pushed the Germans out of the Lower East Side. A dense colony of Hungarians lived around Houston Street, and Bohemians occupied the Upper East Side between Fiftieth and Seventy-sixth streets.

Within ethnic groups, one could also spot clusterings of people from the same province or even the same village. Among New York Italians, for example, Neapolitans and Calabrians populated the Mulberry Bend district, while Genoese lived on Baxter Street. Other northern Italians occupied the Eighth and Fifteenth wards west of Broadway, while southern Italians moved into "little Italy" far up in Harlem. In 1903, along a short stretch of Elizabeth Street, lived several hundred families from a single Sicilian fishing town, Sciacca.

Capitalizing on the feeling of companionship that drew ethnic groups together, a variety of institutions

(After K. Conzen)

0   ½   1
Mile

Milwaukee River

Laborers

"Good class"

"Good class"

Mechanics and laborers

Menominee River

Lake Michigan

Artisans and laborers

Artisans and laborers

Laborers

	1850	1890
Native		
German		
Irish		
Polish		
Scandinavian		
Black		
Mixed (both dates)		

Central business district (1890)

Industrial zone (1890)

MAP 20.4

The Urban Ethnic Mosaic: Milwaukee, 1850–1890

Neighborhoods in American cities developed strong class and ethnic identities in the second half of the nineteenth century. Core areas near downtown Milwaukee expanded outward as immigrant populations increased and new residents arrived. Artisans and laborers tended to settle near their places of work in and near the industrial zone. The "good class" (upper and middle classes) and German residents have remained dominant in certain areas throughout Milwaukee's history.

sprang up to meet their needs. Wherever substantial numbers of immigrants lived, newspapers appeared. In 1911 the twenty thousand Poles in Buffalo, New York, supported two Polish-language daily papers. Immigrants throughout the country avidly read *Il Progresso Italo-Americano* and the Yiddish-language *Jewish Daily Forward*, both published in New York City. Conviviality could always be found on street corners, in barbershops and club rooms, and in saloons. A 1905 survey showed that Chicago had as many saloons as grocery stores, meat markets, and dry-goods stores together. Italians marched in saint's day parades, Bohemians gathered in singing societies, and New York Jews patronized a vibrant Yiddish theater. To provide help in times of sickness and death, the immigrants organized mutual-aid societies. The Italians of Chicago had sixty-six of these organizations in 1903, composed mainly of

people from particular provinces and towns. Immigrants built a rich and functional institutional life in urban America, to an extent unimagined in their native villages.

Urban Blacks. The vast majority of African Americans—85 percent in 1880—lived in the rural South. In the ensuing years some of them migrated to the modestly growing southern cities. By 1900 blacks constituted roughly a third of the South's total urban population, ranging from 20 percent in Louisville and Dallas to absolute majorities in Memphis and Charleston.

The great African-American migration to northern cities was just beginning. The black population of New York increased by 30,000 between 1900 and 1910, making it second only to Washington, D.C., as a black urban center. Still, the 91,000 blacks in New York in 1910 represented fewer than 2 percent of the population, as did Chicago's 45,000 black residents, and Cleveland's 6,000.

Despite their relatively small numbers, urban blacks could not escape becoming targets of the fierce racism of the age. In northern cities generally, residential segregation was intensifying, and the scattered black neighborhoods were giving way to concentrated ghettoes—Chicago's Black Belt on the south side, for example, or the early outlines of New York's Harlem. Job opportunities were likewise narrowing. While 26 percent of Cleveland's blacks had been skilled workers in 1870, only 12 percent were by 1890, and entire occupations like barbering (at least for a white clientele) disappeared. Two-thirds of all Cleveland's blacks in 1910 worked as domestic and day laborers, with little hope of pushing their way up the job ladder.

In the face of segregation and economic discrimination, urban blacks built their communities. They created a flourishing press, fraternal orders, a vast array of women's organizations, and a middle class of doctors, lawyers, and small entrepreneurs who catered to their needs. Above all, there were the black churches—twenty-five in Chicago in 1905, mainly Methodist and Baptist. More than any other institution, remarked one scholar in 1913, it was the church "which the Negro may call his own. . . . A new church may be built . . . and . . . all the machinery set in motion without ever consulting any white person. . . . [It] more than anything else represents the real life of the race." As in the southern countryside, the church was the central institution for city blacks, and the preacher—"a leader, a politician, an orator, a 'boss,' an intriguer, an idealist," as W. E. B. Du Bois described him—the most important local citizen. Manhattan's Union Baptist Church, housed like many others in a storefront, attracted the "very recent residents of this new, disturbing city" and, ringing with spirituals and fervent prayer, made Christianity come "alive Sunday mornings."

Ward Politics

Race and ethnicity tended to divide newcomers to the city and turn them inward. Politics acted in the opposite direction, serving as a powerful instrument for integrating immigrants and blacks into the larger urban society. The basic unit of city governance was the *ward*, each one entitled to its representative on the city council or board of aldermen. Whether realizing it or not, every migrant to an American city automatically belonged to a ward, and by virtue of residence on a particular street immediately acquired a spokesman at city hall. In earlier days, the aldermen had been the dominant figures in urban politics, but that was no longer the case in the late nineteenth century. Power had largely passed to the mayor's office and the various citywide administrative agencies. But the city council still represented the parochial interests of the wards, and immigrants learned very quickly that if they needed anything from city hall, the alderman was the person for them. That was how streets got paved, or water mains extended, or a variance granted—so that, for example, in 1888, Vito Fortounescere could "place and keep a stand for the sale of fruit, inside the stoop-line, in front of the northeast corner of Twenty-eighth Street and Fourth Avenue" in Manhattan, or that the parishioners of Saint Maria of Mount Carmel could set off fireworks at their Fourth of July picnic.

Interlinked with this formal representation was the pervasive presence of the party machines in the immigrant and black neighborhoods. Machine control of political parties existed at every level of American politics (see Chapter 19). The system flourished most luxuriantly, however, in the big cities. Most famous was Tammany Hall, the political machine that dominated Manhattan's Democratic party; but the major parties of most large cities—Democratic or Republican—had their versions of Tammany. The power of the urban machines depended on a loyal party constituency. This meant organization down to the grass roots. The wards were divided into election districts of a few blocks, each with a district captain who reported to the ward boss (who might or might not also be the alderman). It was the main job of these functionaries to be accessible and, as best they could, to serve the needs of the party's constituents.

The machine performed a similar function for the business community. Entrepreneurs of many kinds wanted something from the city. Contractors sought city business; gas companies and streetcar lines wanted licenses and privileges; manufacturers needed services and not-too-nosy inspectors; and the liquor trade and numbers racket relied on a tolerant police force. All of them turned to the machine boss and his lieutenants. In addition to these everyday functions, the machine continually mediated among conflicting interests and oiled the wheels of city government. The machines filled a void in the public life of the nineteenth-century city. They did informally much of what the municipal system left undone. "Nowhere else in the world," remarked the journalist Henry Jones Ford, "has party organization had to cope with such enormous tasks . . . and its efficiency in dealing with them is the true glory of our political system."

Of course, the machine exacted a price for all these services. The tenement dweller gave his vote. The businessman wrote a check. Those who became the machine's beneficiaries enabled it to function. Corruption permeated this informal system. Some portion of the money that changed hands almost inevitably ended up in the pockets of the machine politicians. This boodle could take the form of outright corruption—kickbacks by contractors, protection money from gamblers, saloonkeepers, and prostitutes, payoffs from gas and trolley companies. The Tammany ward boss George Washington Plunkitt, however, insisted that he had no need for kickbacks and bribes. He favored what he called "honest graft," the easy profits that came to political insiders from sure-fire investment—for example, by purchasing a vacant lot he knew would soon be needed for a city project—and the inside track on city contracts. Plunkitt himself made most of his money building wharves on Manhattan's waterfront. One way or another, legally or otherwise, machine politics rewarded its supporters.

For the young and ambitious, this was reason enough to favor the machine system. American society celebrated personal achievement but denied economic opportunity to poor immigrants. Not only did they lack the means to get started in business, remarked Robert A. Woods about the inhabitants of Boston's South End, "but they have to meet strong prejudices of race and religion. Politics, therefore, is for them apparently the easiest way to success in life." In the mid-1870s, over half of Chicago's forty aldermen were foreign-born, sixteen of them Irish immigrants. In 1885 the first Italian was elected to the board, and in 1888, the first Pole, followed in the 1890s by Czechs and Scandinavians. Blacks did not manage to get on to Chicago's board of aldermen until after 1900; but in Baltimore an African-American represented the Eleventh Ward from 1890 onward, and Philadelphia had three black aldermen by 1899. As a ladder for social mobility, machine politics (like professional sports, entertainment, and organized crime) was the most democratic of American institutions.

For most tenement dwellers, however, the machine had a more modest value. It acted as a rough-and-ready social service agency, providing jobs for the jobless, a helping hand for a bereaved family, and intercession against an unfeeling city bureaucracy. As a Boston ward boss remarked, "There's got to be in every ward somebody that any bloke can come to—no matter what he's done—and get help. *Help, you understand; none of your law and justice, but help.*" Tammany ward boss Plunkitt had a "regular system" when fires broke out in his district. "Any hour of the day or night, I'm usually there . . . as soon as the fire engines. If a family is burned out I don't ask whether they are Republicans or Democrats, and I don't refer them to the Charity Organization Society. . . . I just get quarters for them . . . and fix them up till they get things runnin' again. It's philanthropy, but it's politics, too—mighty good politics. . . . The poor look up to George W. Plunkitt as a father, come to him when they are in trouble—and don't forget him on election day."

Plunkitt was an Irishman, and so, indeed, were most of the ward politicians controlling Tammany Hall. But by the 1890s, Plunkitt's Fifteenth District was filling up with Italians and Eastern European Jews. In general, the New York Irish had no love for these newer immigrants. But Plunkitt played no favorites. On any given day (as recorded in a diary) he might be attending an Italian funeral in the afternoon and a Jewish wedding in the evening, and at each probably conveyed his respects with a few choice Italian words or a bit of Yiddish.

"Think what New York is and what the people of New York are," remarked Richard Croker, the powerful head of Tammany during the 1890s, and Plunkitt's boss.

> One half, more than half, are of foreign birth. . . . They do not speak our language, they do not know our laws, they are the raw material from which we have to build up the state. . . . [Tammany] looks after them for the sake of their vote, grafts them upon the Republic, makes citizens of them, in short. . . . Who else would do it if we did not? . . . There is not a mugwump in the city who would shake hands with the [immigrant voter].

The Mugwump reformer (see pp. 587) would doubtless have retorted that the nation could do without citizens whose notion of politics was only what was in it for themselves. But Croker spoke a powerful truth. In an era when so many forces acted to isolate the ghetto communities, politics served an *integrating* function, cutting across ethnic lines and giving immigrants and blacks a stake in the larger urban order.

Religion and Ethnic Identity

Among immigrant groups, religion was an abiding concern and so intertwined with ethnic identity as to be inseparable from the story of how the newcomers adapted to the American city.

Eastern European Jews. When Jews from Eastern Europe began their mass migration in the 1880s, about 250,000 Jews, mostly of German origin, were already living in America. The German Jews, well established and increasingly prosperous, had long since begun to embrace Reform Judaism. Reform Jews abandoned religious practices "not adapted to the views and habits of modern civilization." They practiced a form of Judaism very remote from the orthodoxy of Yiddish-speaking Jews. The Eastern Europeans founded their own Orthodox synagogues, often in vacant stores and ramshackle buildings. The number of synagogues in the United States jumped from 270 in 1880 to 1,901 in 1916.

Many Jews found it difficult to adhere to the traditional forms of their religion. In the isolated villages of Eastern Europe, Judaism comprised not only worship and belief but an entire way of life. Not even the closely confined urban American ghetto could re-create the communal environment essential for strict religious observance. "The very clothes I wore and the very food I ate had a fatal effect on my religious habits," confessed the hero of Abraham Cahan's novel *The Rise of David Levinsky* (1917). "If you . . . attempt to bend your religion to the spirit of your surroundings, it breaks. It falls to pieces." Levinsky shaved off his beard and plunged into the Manhattan clothing business. Orthodox Judaism survived this shattering of faith, but only by sharply reducing its claims on the lives of the faithful.

Catholic Immigrants. Catholics faced much the same problem. The issue, explicitly defined within the Roman Catholic Church as "Americanism," turned on how far Catholicism should respond to American society. Catholics fought out the question on many fronts. Should Catholic children attend parochial or public schools? Should they intermarry with non-Catholics? Should the traditional education for the clergy be changed? Bishop John Ireland of St. Paul, Minnesota, felt that "the principles of the Church are in harmony with the interests of the Republic." But traditionalists, led by Archbishop Michael A. Corrigan of New York, denied the possibility of such harmony. They argued, in effect, for insulating the church from a hostile environment.

In 1895, Pope Leo XIII announced his support of the traditionalists. In America, with its tradition of religious pluralism and sharp separation of church and state, was not "to be sought the type of the most desirable status of the Church." The pope regretted the absence of the benefits that came from state support and urged Catholics "to prefer to associate with Catholics, a course which will be very conducive to the safeguarding of their faith." Catholicism, because of its hierarchical structure, had a better chance than Judaism to resist American influences.

AMERICAN LIVES

Big Tim Sullivan: Tammany Politician

Timothy D. Sullivan was born on July 23, 1863, near the Hudson River docks in Lower Manhattan. His parents were Irish immigrants, part of the mass migration of potato famine victims that flooded into New York in the 1840s. Four years later Tim's father died, leaving the young widow Catherine Connelly Sullivan with four small children. Soon thereafter Catherine married Lawrence Mulligan, an Irish laborer, and the family moved to the notorious Five Points district on the Lower East Side. There the 1870 census found them, a household of ten (including three boarders), living in an overcrowded tenement at 25 Baxter Street (see Map 20.3, which can be consulted to trace the urban geography of Sullivan's career).

Tim had a harsh childhood. His stepfather drank heavily and regularly beat his wife and children. To make ends meet, Catherine took in washing, and Tim went to work at age seven bundling paper for $1.50 a week on Newspaper Row across from City Hall. Tim got through grammar school, but his family needed his earnings too much for him to go on to high school. "Free as it was," he later remarked, "it was not free enough for me to go there." Instead—Horatio Alger-style—he pushed his way up in the newspaper business and by age eighteen was well established as a wholesale newspaper dealer. He soon became the proprietor of two saloons and, in his early twenties, was ready for politics. Sullivan was a big fellow, over six feet tall, handsome, and quick with his fists. He gained a local reputation by thrashing a tough he had encountered on the street beating up a woman. True or not, the story helped him win the Democratic nomination at age twenty-three for the New York State Assembly from the Second District.

In 1889, Sullivan opposed a bill granting Manhattan's police virtually unlimited powers to detain people with jail records. The champion of the bill was Thomas F. Byrnes, chief inspector of the New York Police Department and the most celebrated detective in the country. Byrnes did not take kindly to opposition from small-time politicians. He raided Sullivan's saloons, arrested two barkeepers for excise tax violations, and denounced Sullivan as a consorter with criminals. Against the advice of friends, Sullivan took the Assembly floor to answer the charge. In tearful tones, Sullivan cast himself as an "honest Bowery boy," describing his impoverished childhood, his saintly mother, his struggle to rise in the world. "When, at the conclusion [so a reporter recorded], he asked if he had any time or money to spend with thieves, there was a 'No' on nearly every member's lips." It was the making of the obscure assemblyman. Although he gained a notoriety with uptown New Yorkers that would dog him throughout his career, he won the hearts of his own constituents, who revelled in the success story of one of their own. They thought "Big Tim" a fine fellow, and so did the Tammany leaders.

When the Tammany machine swept into power in the 1892 elections, Boss Richard Croker tapped Sullivan to run the new Third Assembly District centering around the Bowery. Sullivan swiftly consolidated his power. His inner circle was all Irish, but for election district captains he appointed Jews, Italians, and Germans who were well-connected in the immigrant communities that populated his fiefdom. Sullivan became famous for his summer "chowders," when he transported his constituents by riverboat to the country for a rowdy day of picnicking. At Christmas there was a fine dinner for all who were in need. And in February Sullivan handed out wool socks and shoes—always with the sentimental tale of how a teacher had given him free shoes one cold winter. Big Tim also attended assiduously to the nitty-gritty business of running a political machine. He got jobs for his supporters, visited the jails regularly to offer bail and other aid to the inmates, and, on election day, made sure his strong-arm crews patrolled the polling places. Sullivan's district became the best organized in the city, and Tammany hailed him as "the most popular man on the East Side."

In the meantime, Sullivan was making his fortune. His particular form of "honest graft" was commercial entertainment. In his bones Big Tim knew how important a good time was to city people. Besides, the main street of his district, the Bowery, was the gaudy center of low-life entertainment for the entire city, lined with burlesque houses, concert saloons, restaurants, and cheap hotels. In the mid-1890s he formed a partnership with two theatrical producers and began to invest in vaudeville houses. He contributed not only money and a shrewd head but the political contacts that assured lax enforcement of building codes and easy access to liquor licenses. Sullivan also became involved in professional boxing, horse racing, and, more illicitly, the gambling dens that dotted his district.

Sullivan was accused of trafficking in East Side prostitution, but this he indignantly denied. "Nobody who knows me well will believe I would take a penny from any woman, much less from the poor creatures who are more to be pitied than any other human beings on earth. I'd be afraid to take a cent from a poor woman of the streets for fear my old mother would see me. I'd a good deal rather break into a bank and rob the safe. That would be a more manly and decent way of getting money."

When Boss Croker resigned in 1902, Sullivan might have succeeded him, but Big Tim preferred his own district and threw his support to Charles F. Murphy, who ruled Tammany for the next twenty-two years. Sullivan served briefly in Congress, made a lot more money investing in the early movie industry and in vaudeville syndicates across the country, and, in the final phase of

Big Tim Sullivan

his career, became a champion of progressive social legislation in the New York State Senate. In 1912, Sullivan suffered a severe mental breakdown, possibly caused by tertiary syphilis. A year later he died under the wheels of a freight train while trying to escape from his brother's house outside New York. His funeral procession down the Bowery was one of the largest in memory and brought out an immense crowd from every stratum of New York society, from statesmen to prizefighters and scrubwomen.

Immaculate Heart of Mary Church, 1908

In the crowded immigrant neighborhoods, only the church rose from the undistinguished mass to assert the centrality of religious belief in the life of the community. The photograph is a view of Immaculate Heart of Mary Church from Polish Hill in Pittsburgh taken in 1908.

The Church's traditional wing had the support of immigrant Catholics, who wanted to preserve their religion as they had known it in Europe. But the needs of the immigrants extended beyond purely religious matters. They wanted the Church also to be an expression of their ethnic identities. Newly arrived Catholics wanted their own parishes, where they could celebrate their own customs and holidays, speak their own languages, and educate their children in their own parochial schools. When they became numerous enough, they also demanded their own bishops. German Catholics had pressed these ethnic claims for years, and so did the southern and Eastern Europeans who flocked to America from the 1890s onward.

The Church had difficulty responding. The demands of its immigrant congregations seemed to challenge the Catholic hierarchy, which was dominated by Irish Catholics, and, more important, to challenge the integrity of the Church itself. The desire for ethnic parishes did more than divide Catholics; it also led to demands for local control of Church property. In addition, if the Church appointed bishops with jurisdiction over specific ethnic groups, this would mean disrupting the diocesan structure that unified the Church.

The severity of the conflict depended partly on the religious traditions of each ethnic group. Italians, for example, had a strong anticlerical feeling, much strengthened by the papacy's opposition to the unification of Italy. Italian men also had a tradition of religious apathy. On the other hand, the Church played such an important part in the lives of Polish immigrants that they sometimes tolerated no interference from the Catholic hierarchy. In 1907, fifty parishes formed the Polish National Catholic Church of America, which adhered to Catholic ritual without recognizing the pope's authority.

On the whole, however, the Church reconciled its authority with the ethnic needs of the immigrant faithful. It met the demand for representation in the hierarchy by appointing Polish and other immigrant priests as auxiliary bishops within existing dioceses. Before World War I, American Catholics worshiped in more than two thousand foreign-language churches and in many others that were bilingual. The Catholic Church thus became a central institution for the expression of ethnic identity in urban America.

Urban Protestantism. For the Protestant churches, the city posed different, but not easier, challenges than those faced by the largely immigrant Jewish and Catholic faiths. With the surge of immigration from southern and Eastern Europe, urban populations were becoming increasingly non-Protestant. At the same time, Protestant congregations were abandoning the older residential neighborhoods. Many formerly prosperous churches found themselves stranded in bleak working-class districts. During the twenty years after 1868, seventeen Protestant churches moved out of Lower Manhattan, as the area below Fourteenth Street filled up with immigrants.

Nearly every major city retained great downtown churches where wealthy Protestants worshiped. Some of these churches, richly endowed, took pride in nationally prominent pastors, including Henry Ward Beecher of Plymouth Congregational Church in Brooklyn and Phillips Brooks of Trinity Episcopal Church in Boston.

AMERICAN VOICES

The Salvation Army at Work

Maud Ballington Booth, daughter-in-law of the founder of the Salvation Army, describes the efforts of the Army's Slum Brigade in 1894.

When the Salvation Army launched out upon its work of raising and helping the outcast, it . . . reached, and is now reaching the poor, otherwise untouched by religious influence. Street loungers, drunkards, wife-beaters, wild, reckless youths, and fallen women, were attracted to its halls, by the hundreds of thousands, by the open-air procession, and through the lively and enthusiastic character of its services. . . .

It is now five years since we began the Slum Brigade work in New York City. . . . Perhaps the duty which absorbs the greatest part of their time is . . . the systematic house-to-house and room-to-room visitation of all the worst homes in their neighborhood. The visits paid in saloons and dives are naturally of a different character. There it has to be personal, dealing face to face with the people upon the danger of their wild lives, and the sorrow and misery that is coming to them. Sometimes it has to be very straight and earnest talk to some drunken man. At others gentle, affectionate pleading with some poor outcast girl, down whose painted cheeks the tears of bitter remorse fall. . . . Our women work entirely without escort, and this very fact appeals to the spark of gallantry in the hearts of those rough, hardened men, and if anyone dared to lay a finger upon the "Slum Sisters," or say an insulting word to them, champions would arise on every hand to defend them. . . . These visits are often lengthened into prayer-meetings, which include singing and speaking, to a more interested audience, and certainly a more needy one, than can be found within the walls of many a church. . . .

Street work is another phase of their mission. . . . In this they deal with the people whom they have not found within the saloons . . . many of them being sailors and members of the floating population. . . . They are talked to in a friendly and yet very practical way during the evening hours, when there is a great deal of street lounging. . . .

Yet another means of reaching these people is the gathering of them into our halls or meeting places. . . . The audiences are chiefly composed of men, very often young men such as from the toughest gangs in downtown sections of the city. . . . The bright, lively songs of the Salvation Army, the ever changing phases of the meetings, and the thorough bond of sympathy between the speakers on the platform and the roughs in the hall make these meetings a source of great power and interest. Of course, there are occasionally fights among the audience, chairs are upset every now and then, windows are broken . . . and yet through it all a deep, powerful wave of influence carries into the hearts of the people the sincerity and truth of things spiritual.

Source: Maud Ballington Booth, "Salvation Army Work in the Slums," *Scribner's Magazine* 17 (January 1895), pp. 103, 110–112, reprinted in Bayrd Still, *Urban America: A History with Documents* (Boston: Little, Brown, 1974), pp. 299–300.

The eminence of these churches, with their fashionable congregations and imposing edifices, emphasized the growing remoteness of Protestantism from much of its urban constituency. "Where is the city in which the Sabbath day is not losing ground?" lamented a minister in 1887. The families of businessmen, lawyers, and doctors could be seen in any church on Sunday morning, he noted, "but the workingmen and their families are not there."

To counter this decline, the Protestant churches responded in two ways. They evangelized among the unchurched and indifferent, for example, through the Sunday-school movement that blossomed in these years. Protestants also made their churches instruments of social uplift. Starting in the 1880s, many city churches provided reading rooms, day nurseries, clubhouses, and vocational classes. Sometimes the churches linked evan-gelism and social uplift. The Salvation Army, which arrived from England in 1879, spread the gospel of repentance among the urban poor and built up an assistance program that ranged from soup kitchens to homes for former prostitutes. When all else failed, the down-and-outers of American cities knew they could count on the Salvation Army.

The Young Men's and Women's Christian Associations attracted large numbers of the young single people flocking into the cities. Originating in England, the two organizations had arrived in the United States before the Civil War, and both grew prodigiously in the late nineteenth century. By the mid-1880s, virtually every large city had a YMCA equipped with gymnasiums, auditoriums, and dormitories. Housing for single women was an especially important mission of the YWCAs. No other organizations better met the needs of young adults for physical recreation, education, or companionship, or so effectively combine these services with an evangelizing appeal in the form of Bible classes, nondenominational worship, and a religious atmosphere.

The need of many people to unite religion with social uplift could be seen in the enormous popularity of a book called *In His Steps* (1896). The author, the Congregational minister Charles M. Sheldon, told the story of a congregation that resolved to live by Christ's precepts for one year. "If the church members were all doing as Jesus would do," Sheldon asked, "could it remain true that armies of men would walk the streets for jobs, and hundreds of them curse the church, and thousands of them find in the saloon their best friend?"

Urban Revivalism. The most potent form of urban evangelism—revivalism—said little about social uplift. From its beginnings in the eighteenth century, revivalism had steadfastly focused on the individual and had stressed personal redemption. The solution of earthly problems would follow the conversion of the people to Christ. Beginning in the mid-1870s, revival meetings swept the cities.

The pioneering figure was Dwight L. Moody, a former Chicago shoe salesman and YMCA official. After preaching in England for two years, Moody returned to America in 1875. With his talented chorister and hymn writer, Ira D. Sankey, Moody staged revival meetings that drew thousands of people. He preached an optimistic, uncomplicated, nondenominational message. Eternal life could be had for the asking, Moody shouted as he held up his Bible. His listeners needed only "to come forward and take, TAKE!"

Many other preachers followed in Moody's path. The most notable was Billy (William Ashley) Sunday, a hard-drinking outfielder for the Chicago White Stockings who mended his ways and found religion. Like Moody and other city revivalists, Sunday was a farm boy. His rip-snorting cries against "Charlotte-russe Christians" and the "booze traffic" carried the ring of rustic America. By realizing that many people remained villagers at heart, revivalists had found a key for bringing city dwellers back into the church fold.

In a larger sense, however, revivalism was expressive of a more general Fundamentalist movement seeking to preserve old-time religion against the increasing complacency and the doctrinal liberalism of mainstream Protestantism. Just as Methodism had arisen to challenge the Church of England in the eighteenth century, so now in the late nineteenth century new churches arose against Methodism. The Holiness evangelical movement was at first nondenominational, but then it began to spawn such new denominations as the Church of the Nazarene (1908). Out of the Holiness Revival came the still more radical Pentecostal movement, which by 1914 had brought together many local bodies into the Assemblies of God.

Luna Park, Coney Island
Luna Park was the Disneyland of the Industrial Age, but more unbuttoned and casual, intended to lift city dwellers out of their work-a-day lives for a few hours. The view is down the main thoroughfare looking toward the entrance.

Leisure in the City

City people divided life's activities into separate units, setting workplace apart from home, and working time apart from free time. Leisure became a defined function, marked by the clock and enjoyed in distinctive ways and at designated places. In the impersonal, anonymous world they inhabited, urban dwellers increasingly found themselves the paying customers of commercial entertainment. A new class of entrepreneurs emerged whose business it was to give the public what it wanted.

Amusement parks—Boston's Paragon Park, Philadelphia's Willow Grove, Atlanta's Ponce de Leon Park, Cleveland's Euclid Beach, San Francisco's The Chutes—went up at the end of trolley lines in cities across the country. Most remarkable perhaps was Luna Park at New York's Coney Island—"an enchanted, storybook land of trellises, columns, domes, minarets, lagoons, and lofty aerial flights. . . . It was a world removed—shut away from the sordid clatter and turmoil of the streets." In fact, that escape from everyday urban life was the lure of the amusement parks. The creators of Luna Park intended it to be "a different world—a dream world, perhaps a nightmare world—where all is bizarre and fantastic—crazier than the craziest parts of Paris—gayer and more different from the every-day world."

Theatrical entertainment likewise attracted huge audiences. Chicago had six vaudeville houses in 1896, and twenty-two in 1910. Evolving from cheap variety and minstrel shows, vaudeville moved from boisterous beer halls into grand theaters. It cleaned up its routines, making them suitable for the entire family, and turned into thoroughly professional entertainment handled by national booking agencies. With its standard program of nine acts of singing, dancing, and comedy, vaudeville attained enormous popularity just as the movies began to appear. The first primitive films, a minute or so of humor or glimpses of famous people, appeared in 1896 in penny arcades and as filler in vaudeville shows. Within a decade, millions of city people were watching story films of increasing length and artistry at nick-elodeons (after the five-cent admission charge) across the country.

For young unmarried workers, the cheap amusements of the city created a new social space. "I want a good time," one New York clothing operator told an investigator. "And there is no . . . way a girl can get it on $8 a week. I guess if anyone wants to take me to a dance he won't have to ask me twice." Hence the widespread ritual in the urban working class of "treating." The girls spent what they had looking stylishly pretty; their beaus were expected to pay for the fun. Parental control over courtship broke down, and amid the bright lights and lively music of the dance hall and amusement park, working-class youth forged a more easy-going culture of sexual interaction and pleasure seeking.

Baseball. Of all forms of male diversion, none was more specific to the city, nor so spectacularly successful, as professional baseball. The game's promoters decreed that baseball had been created in 1839 by Abner Doubleday in the village of Cooperstown, New York. Actually, baseball was neither of American origin—it developed from the English game of rounders—nor a product of rural life.

Organized play began in the early 1840s in New York City, where a group of gentlemen enthusiasts competed among themselves on an empty lot. During the next twenty years, the aristocratic tone of baseball disappeared. Clubs sprang up across the country, and intercity competition developed on a scheduled basis. In 1868 baseball became openly professional, following the example of the Cincinnati Red Stockings in signing players to contracts at a negotiated salary for the season.

Big-time commercial baseball came into its own with the launching of the National League in 1876. The team owners were profit-minded businessmen who carefully shaped the sport to please the fans. Wooden grandstands gave way to the concrete and steel stadiums of the early twentieth century, such as Fenway Park in Boston, Forbes Field in Pittsburgh, and Shibe Park in Philadelphia.

For the urban multitudes, baseball grew into something more than an occasional afternoon at the ball park. By rooting for the home team, fans found a way of identifying themselves with the city they lived in. Amid the diversity and anonymity of urban life, the common experience and language of baseball acted as a bridge among city people.

Students of the game have suggested that baseball was peculiarly attuned to city life. It followed strict, precise rules, which suggested an underlying order to the chaotic city. Far from respecting the rules, however, the players tried to get away with whatever they could in order to win. Did this not match the competitive scramble of urban life? The blue-coated umpire, the symbol of authority, was scorned by players and derided by fans. What better substitute for the resentment against the powers-that-be who ruled the lives of city

The National Pastime

This lithograph celebrates the opening game of the 1889 season, with the Boston Base-Ball Club taking on the New York Base-Ball Club. The National League was then scarcely twelve years old. The fielders played barehanded, but otherwise the game remains today much as the artist pictured it a century ago, even down to the umpire's characteristic stance.

people? Baseball, like many other emerging urban institutions, served as a mechanism for inducting people into the life of the modern city.

Newspapers. The press undertook this task in a clear-eyed, calculated way. Ever since Benjamin H. Day had established the *New York Sun* in 1833, American newspapers had aimed for a broad audience. James Gordon Bennett, founder of the *New York Herald*, wanted to "record the facts . . . for the great masses of the community." Journalism defined the news to be whatever interested city readers. The *Herald* covered crime, scandal, and sensational events. After the Civil War, *Sun* editor Charles A. Dana added the human-interest story, which made news of ordinary, insignificant happenings. Newspapers also targeted specific audiences. A women's page offered recipes and fashion news, separate sections covered sports and high society, and the Sunday supplement helped fill the spare weekend hours.

Newspaper wars erupted periodically, as when Joseph Pulitzer, the owner of the *St. Louis Post-Dispatch*, invaded New York in 1883 by buying the *World*. In 1895, William Randolph Hearst, who owned the *San Francisco Examiner*, bought the *New York Journal* and challenged the *World*. Hearst developed a sensational style of newspaper reporting and writing that became known as *yellow journalism*. The term de-

rived from the first comic strip to appear in color, "The Yellow Kid" (1895). In his combative zeal, Hearst often abandoned the journalistic canon of telling the truth. The *Journal*'s sensational reporting of the civil war in Cuba enabled Hearst's paper to win its circulation battle with the *World*; it also helped bring on the Spanish-American War of 1898 (see Chapter 22).

"He who is without a newspaper," said the great showman P. T. Barnum, "is cut off from his species." Barnum was speaking of city people and their hunger for information. By meeting this need, newspapers revealed their sensitivity to the public they served.

Upper Class/Middle Class

Wealth, more than anything else, has determined social class in the United States. By that measure, American society was highly stratified during the nineteenth century. The top 1 percent of Americans held about a quarter of all wealth, and the upper 5 percent owned fully a half. The middle class, who made up the next 30 percent, owned most of the rest of the nation's wealth. The bottom half of the population owned virtually nothing. This sharply unequal division of wealth emerged early in America's Industrial Revolution and continued well into the twentieth century with little change. Income levels were likewise sharply unequal. In 1890 wage earners in manufacturing averaged $439 a year, clerical workers in manufacturing made twice that—$848 a year—while solidly middle-class people like doctors, lawyers, editors, and managers earned between $3,000 and $5,000. In the topmost ranks, of course, were those whose incomes came largely from investments rather than from salaries and wages. Given the great concentration of wealth at the top, America's wealthy necessarily enjoyed magnificent incomes.

In the compact preindustrial city, people had not defined their social position by where they lived. Class distinctions had been expressed by the way men and women dressed, how they behaved, and the deference they demanded from or granted to others. As the industrial city grew, these interpersonal marks of class began to lose their force. In the anonymity of a large city, recognition and deference no longer served very well as mechanisms for conferring status. Instead, people began to rely on external signs. These included conspicuous display of wealth, exclusive association in clubs and similar social organizations, and above all, choice of neighborhood.

People's place of residence had previously depended primarily on the location of their work. For the poor, that continued to be true. But for higher-income urbanites, where to live became much more a matter of personal means and social preference.

Joseph Pulitzer
Pulitzer (1847–1911) left Hungary at seventeen because he wanted to be a soldier and his best chance was with the Union Army in America. He ended up the greatest newpaper publisher of the century, extraordinary for his instincts as to what an urban reading public wanted from a newspaper, and extraordinary also because he came to this task as a foreigner, without English as his mother tongue and without native roots in the society.

The Urban Elite

As early as the 1840s, Boston merchants took advantage of the new railway service to move out of the congested central city. Fine rural estates appeared in Milton, West Roxbury, Newton, and other outlying towns. By 1848 roughly 20 percent of Boston's businessmen were making the long trip from the countryside to their downtown offices. They traveled on 118 scheduled trains that served stations within 15 miles of the center of Boston. Ferries that plied the harbor between Manhattan and Brooklyn or New Jersey served the same purpose for New Yorkers.

As commercial development engulfed downtown residential areas and as transportation services improved, the exodus from cities by the well-to-do spread across America. In Cincinnati, wealthy families settled on the scenic hills rimming the crowded, humid tableland that ran down to the Ohio River. On those hillsides, a traveler noted in 1883, "the homes of Cincinnati's merchant princes and millionaires are found . . . elegant cottages, tasteful villas, and substantial mansions, surrounded by a paradise of grass, gardens, lawns, and tree-shaded roads." Residents of the area, called Hilltop, founded several country clubs, the Cincinnati Riding Club, the New England Society, five downtown gentlemen's clubs, and many other institutions that assured an exclusive social life for Cincinnati's elite.

Despite the temptations of country life, many of the very richest people preferred the heart of the city. Chicago had its Gold Coast; San Francisco, Nob Hill; Denver, Quality Hill; and Manhattan, Fifth Avenue. The New York novelist Edith Wharton recalled how the comfortable mid-century brownstones—"all so much alike that one could understand how easy it would be for a dinner guest to go to the wrong house"—gave way to the "'new' millionaire houses," which then spread northward beyond Fifty-ninth Street and up Fifth Avenue along Central Park. Great mansions, reminiscent of European aristocratic houses and filled with Old World artifacts, lined Fifth Avenue at the turn of the century.

By carving out fashionable areas in the heart of a city, the rich visibly demonstrated the power of money in American society. But great fortunes did not automatically mean high social standing. An established elite stood astride the social heights even in such relatively raw cities as San Francisco and Denver. It had taken only a generation—and sometimes less—for money made in commerce or real estate to shed its tarnish and become "old" and genteel. In more venerable cities, such as Boston, wealth passed intact through several generations. A high degree of intermarriage occurred there among the so-called Brahmin families. By withdrawing from trade, and by asserting a high cultural and moral code, the proper Bostonians kept moneyed newcomers at bay. Elsewhere, urban elites tended to be

The Breakers
The favorite summering place of the New York elite was the historic colonial port of Newport, Rhode Island. The opulent mansions there were known as "cottages." The Breakers was built in 1892 at a cost of $5 million for Cornelius Vanderbilt II. Designed in the style of an Italian palace, the Breakers had seventy-three rooms, thirty-three of them to house the small army of servants. The ornate dining room is shown in this photograph.

more open, but only to the socially ambitious who were prepared to make visible and energetic use of their money.

New York's Metropolitan Opera was one of the products of this ongoing struggle among the wealthy. The Academy of Music, home to the city's opera since 1854, was controlled by the Livingstons, the Bayards, the Beekmans, and other old New York families. Frustrated in their efforts to purchase boxes at the Academy, the Vanderbilts and their allies determined to sponsor a rival opera house. In 1883, with its glittering opening to the strains of Gounod's *Faust*, the Metropolitan proclaimed its ascendancy in the opera world and, in due course, won the patronage of even the Beekmans and Bayards. During this battle of the opera houses, the Vanderbilt circle achieved social recognition.

"High Society." New York became the home of a national elite. The most successful people gravitated from everywhere to this preeminent center of American economic and cultural life. Manhattan's extraordinary vitality, in turn, kept the city's high society fluid and relatively open. The tycoon Frank Cowperwood, in Theodore Dreiser's novel *The Titan* (1914), reassured his unhappy wife that if Chicago society would not accept them, "there are other cities. Money will arrange matters in New York—that I know. We can build a real place there, and go in on equal terms, if we have money enough." New York thus came to be a magnet for millionaires. The city attracted them not only by its importance as a financial center, but also by the opportunities it offered for display and social recognition.

From Manhattan an extravagant life of leisure radiated outward to such resort centers as Saratoga Springs, New York; Palm Beach, Florida; and Newport, Rhode Island. Newport featured a grand array of summer "cottages," crowned by the Vanderbilts' Marble House and The Breakers. To these resorts, and elsewhere, the affluent traveled in great comfort by private railway car. A style of living emerged that was incredible for its lavish excess, ranging from yachting and horseracing to huge feasts at such luxurious restaurants as Sherry's and Delmonico's. "Our forefathers would have been staggered at the cost of hospitality these days," remarked one New Yorker.

This infusion of wealth shattered the older elite society of New York. Seeking to be assimilated into the upper class, the flood of moneyed newcomers simply overwhelmed it. There followed a curious process of reconstruction, a deliberate effort to define the rules of conduct and identify those who properly "belonged" in New York society.

The key figure in this process was Ward McAllister, a southern-born lawyer who had made a quick fortune in gold rush San Francisco and then devoted himself to a second career as arbiter to New York society. McAllister compiled the first *Social Register* in 1888, to serve as a "record of society, comprising an accurate and careful list" of all those deemed acceptable to participate in New York society. McAllister instructed the socially ambitious on how to select guests, set a proper table, arrange a ball, and launch a young lady into society. McAllister fostered an ordered social round of assemblies, balls, and dinners that defined the boundaries of an elite society. The key lay in the creation of associations sponsored by established social leaders, "organized social powers, capable of giving a passport of society to all worthy of it." To top things off, McAllister came up with the idea of "the Four Hundred"—the true cream of New York society. His list corresponded to those invited to Mrs. William Astor's great ball of February 1, 1892.

Social registers, coming-out balls for debutantes, and lesser versions of Ward McAllister soon popped up in cities throughout the country. In this fashion, the socially ambitious struggled to master the fluidity at the height of the social order.

Americans were adept at making money, noted the journalist Edwin L. Godkin in 1896, but they lacked the European traditions for spending it. "Great wealth has not yet entered our manners," Godkin remarked. "No rules have yet been drawn to guide wealthy Americans in their manner of life." In their struggle to find the rules and establish the manners, the moneyed elite made an indelible mark on urban life. If there was magnificence in the American city, it was mainly their handiwork. And if there was conspicuous waste and vulgarity, it was likewise their doing. In a democratic society, wealth finds no easier outlet than through public display.

The Middle Class

The middle class left a smaller imprint on the public and cultural faces of urban society. Its members, unlike the rich, preferred privacy and retreated into the domesticity of suburban comfort and family life.

The emerging corporate economy spawned a new middle class. Bureaucratic organizations required managers, accountants, and clerks. Advancing technologies needed engineers, chemists, and designers. The distribution system sought salesmen, advertising executives, and buyers. These salaried ranks increased sevenfold between 1870 and 1910, much faster than any other occupational group. The traditional business class that had emerged in the first stages of industrialization before the Civil War—independent businessmen and professionals—also grew, but only at a third of the rate of salaried personnel. Nearly 9 million people held white-collar jobs in 1910, more than a fourth of all employed Americans.

The middle class, particularly its salaried portions,

AMERICAN VOICES

Throwing a Great Party During Hard Times

Frederick Townshend Martin

Gilded Age society was known for the magnificence of its parties. Here Frederick Townshend Martin describes the lavish affair his brother and sister-in-law put on for the cream of New York society in 1897 during a severe national depression.

Every year my brother Bradley and his wife spent their winters in New York, when they entertained largely. One morning at breakfast my brother remarked—

"I think it would be a good thing if we got up something; there seems to be a great deal of depression in trade; suppose we send out invitations for a concert."

"And pray, what good will that do?" asked my sister-in-law, "the money will only benefit foreigners. No, I've a far better idea; let us give a costume ball at so short notice that our guests won't have time to get their dresses from Paris. That will give an impetus to trade that nothing else will."

Directly Mrs. Martin's plan became known, there was a regular storm of comment. . . .

We were besieged by reporters, but my brother and his wife invariably refused to discuss the matter. Threat-ening letters arrived by every post, debating societies discussed our extravagance, and last, but not least, we were burlesqued unmercifully on the stage. . . .

I think every one anticipated a disturbance, but nothing of the kind took place, and the evening passed without any untoward incident.

The best way I can describe what is always known as the "Bradley Martin Ball," is to say that it reproduced the splendour of Versailles in New York, and I doubt if even the Roi Soleil himself ever witnessed a more dazzling sight. The interior of the Waldorf-Astoria Hotel was transformed into a replica of Versailles, and rare tapestries, beautiful flowers and countless lights made an effective background for the wonderful gowns and their wearers. I do not think there has ever been a greater display of jewels before or since; in many cases the diamond buttons worn by the men represented thousands of dollars, and the value of the historic gems worn by the ladies baffles description.

My sister-in-law personated Mary Stuart, and her gold embroidered gown was trimmed with pearls and precious stones. Bradley, as Louis XV, wore a Court suit of brocade, and I represented a gentleman of the period.

The whole thing appealed most strongly to my imagination. . . .

The power of wealth with its refinement and vulgarity was everywhere. It gleamed from countless jewels, and it was proclaimed by the thousands of orchids and roses, whose fragrance that night was like incense burnt on the altar of the Golden Calf.

I cannot conceive why this entertainment should have been condemned. We Americans are so accustomed to display that I should have thought the ball would not have been regarded as anything very unusual. Every one said it was the most brilliant function of the kind ever seen in America, and it certainly was the most talked about.

After the ball the authorities promptly raised my brother's taxes quite out of proportion to those paid by any one else, and the matter was only settled after a very acrimonious dispute. Bradley and his wife resented intensely the annoyance to which they had been subjected, and they decided to sell their house in New York and buy a residence in London.

Source: Bulkley S. Griffin, ed., *Offbeat America* (Cleveland: World Publishing, 1967) pp. 221–24.

was an urban population. Some lived within the city, in the row houses of Baltimore or Boston, or in the comfortable apartment houses of New York or other metropolitan centers. But far more preferred to escape from the clamor and congestion of the city. They were attracted by a persisting rural ideal. They agreed with the landscape architect Andrew Jackson Downing, who thought that "nature and domestic life are better than the society and manners of town." With the extension of rapid transit service from the city center, middle-class Americans followed the wealthy into the countryside. All sought what a Chicago developer promised of his North Shore subdivision in 1875: "qualities of which the city is in a large degree bereft, namely, its pure air, peacefulness, quietude, and natural scenery." And advanced building techniques—mass-produced materials and balloon-frame construction—made suburban housing broadly affordable by the American middle class.

Cincinnati Suburb
The lives of the people inhabiting these neat homes were woven into the dynamic capitalism of a major industrial metropolis, including the children lounging on the corner. They were most certainly being educated for service in the new economic order. Looking at the bucolic setting of this Cincinnati street, no one would have thought so, and that was just the illusion which the suburb was intended to create: that Americans still partook of a rural ideal and could hold at bay the modern industrial order of which they were not a part. (The Cincinnati Historical Society)

No major American city escaped rapid suburbanization during the last third of the nineteenth century. City limits everywhere expanded rapidly. By 1900, more than half of Boston's people lived in "streetcar suburbs" outside the original city. The U.S. Census of 1910 reported that nationwide about 25 percent of the urban population lived in suburbs outside the city limits.

On the European continent, by contrast, cities remained highly concentrated and it was the poor, not the well-to-do, who inhabited the margins. Unlike their American counterparts, the European middle class was not attracted (except in England) to the rural ideal and valued urban life for its own sake. In Europe, mass transit developed much more slowly; more efficient balloon-frame construction techniques were not adopted; and there was little of the free-wheeling real-estate development that so powerfully encouraged American suburbanization. Nor, finally, did the culturally homogeneous European cities give rise to the impulse felt by middle-class Americans to escape the racially and ethnically diverse urban masses who occupied the city centers.

American suburbs were middle-class territory. But the middle class was not monolithic. It ranged from prosperous business proprietors and lawyers to clerks and traveling salesmen who earned no more than foremen and craft workers. Close in to the city, indeed, the suburbs increasingly took on a working-class character.

The geography of the suburbs was truly a map of class structure in America, because where a family lived told where it ranked. The farther the distance from the center of the city, the finer the houses and the larger the lots. This arrangement reflected the ability to pay and the work situations that went with varying income levels. The well-to-do had the leisure and flexible schedules to travel the long distance into town. People closer in wanted a direct transit line convenient to home and office. Lower-income suburbanites were likely to have more than one wage earner in the family, less security of employment, and jobs requiring movement around the city. They needed easy access to crosstown transit lines, which ran closer in to the city center.

Divisions within suburbs, although always a precise measure of economic ranking, never became rigidly fixed. People in the city center who wanted to better their lives moved to the cheapest suburbs. Fleeing from these newcomers, those already settled pushed the next higher group farther out in search of space and greenery.

Suburbanization was the sum of countless individual decisions. Each move represented an advance in living standards—not only more light, air, and quiet but also better housing than the city afforded. Suburban housing had more space and better design, as well as indoor toilets, hot water, central heating, and, by the turn of the century, electricity. Even people living in the inner suburbs came to regard these amenities as standard comforts. The suburbs also restored a basic opportunity that had seemed sacrificed by rural Americans when they moved to the city. In the suburbs, home ownership again became a norm. "A man is not really a true man until he owns his home," propounded the Reverend Russell H. Conwell in his famous sermon on the virtues of making money, "Acres of Diamonds."

The small town of the rural past had fostered community life. Not so the suburbs. The grid street pattern, while efficient for laying out lots and providing utilities, offered no natural focus for group life. Nor did stores and services that lay scattered along the trolley-car streets. Not even schools and churches were located to make them the centers of community life. Suburban development conformed to the economics of real estate and transportation, and so did the thinking of middle-class home seekers entering the suburbs. They wanted a house that gave them good value and convenience to the trolley line.

The need for community had lost some of its force

(1974). The struggle to reshape the chaotic nineteenth-century city can be explored in Laura Wood Roper, *FLO: A Biography of Frederick Law Olmsted* (1973); William H. Wilson, *The City Beautiful Movement in Kansas City* (1964); and David Schuyler, *The New Urban Landscape: The Redefinition of City Form in Nineteenth-Century America* (1986).

City People

Much has been written on immigrants and the city. Among the leading books are Moses Rischin, *The Promised City: New York's Jews, 1870–1914* (1962); Joseph Barton, *Peasants and Strangers: Italians, Rumanians, and Slovaks in an American City, 1890–1950* (1975); and Humbert S. Nelli, *The Italians in Chicago, 1860–1920* (1970). On blacks in the city, see Gilbert Osofsky, *Harlem: The Making of a Ghetto, 1890–1930* (1966); Allan H. Spear, *Black Chicago, 1860–1920* (1966); and Kenneth L. Kusmer, *A Ghetto Takes Shape: Black Cleveland, 1870–1930* (1976). The encounter of Protestantism with the city is treated in Henry F. May, *Protestant Churches and Urban America* (1949); Aaron I. Abell, *The Urban Impact on American Protestantism* (1943); and William G. McLoughlin, *Modern Revivalism* (1959). On the Catholic Church, see Robert D. Cross, *The Emergence of Liberal Catholicism in America* (1958), and Cross, ed., *Church and City, 1865–1910* (1967). Aspects of an emerging city culture are studied in Gunther Barth, *City People: The Rise of Modern City Culture in Nineteenth-Century America* (1982); Susan Porter Benson, *Counter Cultures: Saleswomen, Managers, and Customers in American Department Stores, 1890–1940* (1986); John F. Kasson, *Amusing the Million: Coney Island at the Turn of the Century* (1978); Roy Rosenzweig, *Eight Hours for What We Will: Workers and Leisure in an Industrial City, 1870–1920* (1983); and Kathy Peiss, *Cheap Amusements: Working Women and Leisure in Turn-of-the-Century New York* (1986).

Upper Class/Middle Class

Urban social mobility is the focus of Stephan Thernstrom, *The Other Bostonians: Poverty and Progress in an American City, 1880–1970* (1973), which contains also a useful summary of mobility research on other cities. On the social elite, see Frederic C. Jaher, *The Urban Establishment: Upper Strata in Boston, New York, Charleston, Chicago, and Los Angeles* (1982); Dixon Wecter, *The Saga of American Society* (1937); and, for a personal account, Ward McAllister, *Society as I Have Found It* (1890). Two recent books greatly advance our understanding of the urban middle class: Stuart S. Blumin, *The Emergence of the Middle Class: Social Experience in the American City, 1760–1900* (1989) and Olivier Zunz, *Making Corporate America, 1870–1920* (1990). Aspects of middle-class life are revealed in Richard Sennett, *Families Against the City: Middle Class Homes of Industrial Chicago, 1872–1890* (1970); Kathryn Kish Sklar, *Catharine Beecher: A Study of Domesticity* (1973); Margaret Marsh, *Suburban Lives* (1990); Gwendolyn Wright, *Moralism and the Model Home: Domestic Architecture and Cultural Conflict in Chicago, 1873–1913* (1980); Susan Strasser, *Never Done: A History of American Housework* (1983); and, on the entry of immigrants into the middle class, Andrew R. Heinze, *Adapting to Abundance: Jewish Immigrants, Mass Consumption, and the Search for American Identity* (1990). Contemporary notions of sexuality are skillfully captured in John S. Haller and Robin M. Haller, *The Physician and Sexuality in Victorian America* (1980). Whether those views actually applied to the private world of the middle class is strongly questioned in Karen Lystra, *The Searching Heart: Women, Men, and Romantic Love in Nineteenth-Century America* (1989). On the fostering of high culture in the American city, see Daniel M. Fox, *Engines of Culture: Philanthropy and Art Museums* (1963). The best introduction to intellectual currents in the emerging urban society is Alan Trachtenberg, *The Incorporation of America: Culture and Society, 1865–1893* (1983).

TIMELINE

1871 Chicago fire

1873 Mark Twain and Charles Dudley Warner publish *The Gilded Age*

1875 Dwight L. Moody launches urban revivalist movement

1876 Alexander Graham Bell patents the telephone
National Baseball League founded

1878 Electric arc-light system installed in Philadelphia

1879 Thomas Edison's incandescent light bulb
Salvation Army arrives from England

1883 New York City's Metropolitan Opera founded
Brooklyn Bridge opens
Joseph Pulitzer purchases the *New York World*

1885 William Jenney builds first steel-framed structure, Chicago's Home Insurance Building

1888 First electric trolley line constructed in Richmond, Virginia

1893 Chicago World's Fair

1895 The comic strip "The Yellow Kid" appears

1897 Boston's subway

1900 Theodore Dreiser publishes *Sister Carrie*

1901 New York Tenement House Reform Law

1906 San Francisco earthquake

1913 Woolworth Building, New York City

The Cliff Dwellers

The 1913 painting by George Bellows shows a poor
tenement neighborhood in New York's Lower East Side.
(Los Angeles County Museum of Art)

for middle-class Americans. Two other attachments assumed greater importance. One was work; the other was family.

Families

The family had been the primary productive unit in the preindustrial economy. Farmers, merchants, and artisans had carried on their work within a family setting, and the value of family members could be reckoned by their economic contribution. The family circle included not only blood relatives but all others living and working within the household. As industrialism progressed, the family gradually lost its function as a productive unit. For the middle class in particular, the family became disassociated from economic activity. The father left the home to earn his living; clothing was bought ready-made; food came increasingly in cans and packages; and the children spent more years in school. Families became smaller and excluded all but nuclear members. The typical middle-class family of 1900 consisted of husband, wife, and three children.

Within this small circle, relationships became intense and affectionate. "Home was the most expressive experience in life," recalled the literary critic Henry Seidel Canby of his growing up in the 1890s. "Though the family might quarrel and nag, the home held them all, protecting them against the outside world." In a sense, the family served as a refuge from the competitive, impersonal business world. The suburbs provided a fit setting for such middle-class families. The quiet, tree-lined streets created a domestic world insulated from the hurly-burly of commerce and enterprise.

The Wife's Role. The burdens of this domesticity fell heavily on the wife. It was nearly unheard of for her to seek an outside career; that was her husband's role. She had the job of managing the household. "The woman who could not make a home, like the man who could not support one, was condemned," Canby remembered. But with better household technology, greater reliance on purchased goods, and fewer children, the wife's workload declined. Moreover, servants still played an important part in middle-class households. In 1910 there were about two million domestic servants, the largest job category for women.

As the physical burdens of household work eased, higher-quality homemaking became the new ideal. This was the message of Catharine Beecher's best-selling book *The American Woman's Home* (1869) and of such magazines as the *Ladies' Home Journal* and *Good Housekeeping*, which first appeared during the 1880s. The wife did more than make sure that food was on the table, that clothes were washed and mended, and that the house was kept clean. She had the higher calling of bringing sensibility, beauty, and love to the household. "We owe to women the charm and beauty of life," wrote one educator. "For the love that rests, strengthens and inspires, we look to women." In this idealized view, the wife made the home a refuge for her husband and a place of nurture for their children.

Womanly virtue, even if a happy marriage depended on it, by no means put the wife on equal terms with her husband. Although the legal status of married women—the right to own property, to control separate earnings, to make contracts and bring suit, to get a divorce—improved markedly during the nineteenth cen-

Middle-Class Domesticity

For middle-class Americans, the home was a place of nurture, a refuge from the world of competitive commerce. Perhaps that explained why their residences were so heavily draped and cluttered with bric-a-brac, every space filled with overstuffed furniture. All of it emphasized privacy, and pride of possession. The young woman shown playing the piano symbolizes another theme of American domesticity—wives and daughters as ornaments, and as bearers of culture and refinement. (Mrs. Leoni's Parlor, 1894, Museum of the City of New York) tury, sufficient legal discrimination remained to establish their subordinate role within the family. More important, custom dictated the wife's submission to her husband. She relied on his ability as the family breadwinner and, despite her superior virtues and graces, ranked as his inferior in vigor and intellect. Her mind could be employed "but little and in trivial matters," wrote one prominent physician, and her proper place was as "the companion or ornamental appendage to man."

Bright, independent-minded women understandably rebelled against marriage. The marriage rate in the United States fell to its lowest point during the last forty years of the nineteenth century. More than 10 percent of all women of marriageable age remained single, and the rate was much higher among college graduates and professionals. Only half of the Mount Holyoke College class of 1902 married. "I know that something perhaps, humanly speaking, supremely precious has passed me by," remarked the writer Vida Scudder. "But . . . how much it would have excluded!" Married life "looks to me often as I watch it terribly impoverished, for women."

The strains of marriage were manifest in the substantial number of middle-class families that broke apart. Most of these domestic failures remained unrecorded because of the stigma attached to divorce. In a Chicago suburb in the 1880s, at a time when divorce was virtually unknown there, about 10 percent of the households had an absent spouse. The national divorce rate increased from 1.2 per thousand marriages in 1860 to 7.7 in 1900. It was more difficult to document the other ways women responded to marriages that denied their autonomy and downplayed their sexuality. Middle-class women became the principal victims of neurasthenia, a disorder whose symptoms included depression and general disability. Some unhappy housewives found "silent friends" in opium and alcohol, both often dispensed in well-laced patent medicines.

A happier release came through the companionship of other women. In an age that defined separate spheres for men and women, close ties commonly formed between schoolmates, cousins, and mothers and daughters. The intimacy and intensity of such attachments can be sensed in surviving letters of separated friends. Such enduring female ties yielded emotional gratification not often found in marriage. Husbands, absorbed in business, frequently played a secondary and remote role in the lives of their wives. Women's own sphere often filled that emotional vacuum.

Changing Views of Sexuality. The middle-class family had long faced a difficult dilemma. Many couples wished to limit the number of their children, but birth control was not an easy matter. Antipornography laws,

pushed through by the social-purity campaigner Anthony Comstock during the 1870s, banned the distribution of birth control information through the mail. Many states classified such material as obscene literature and prohibited its sale. Abortion became illegal except to save the mother's life. Although the practice of abortion was probably widespread, it was expensive and dangerous, and considered shameful. Family planning could be best achieved by delaying marriage and then by practicing abstinence. The repressed sexuality within the family resulted from practical necessity. A fulfilling sexual relationship could not be squared with the desire to limit and space childbearing.

The New Woman

John Singer Sargent's painting, *Mr. and Mrs. Isaac Newton Phelps Stokes* (1897), captures on canvas the essence of the "new woman" of the 1890s. Nothing about Mrs. Stokes, neither how she is dressed nor how she presents herself, suggests physical weakness or demure passivity. She confidently occupies center stage, a fit partner for her husband, who, indeed, is relegated to the shadows of the picture. (The Metropolitan Museum of Art)

Somewhere around 1890, change set in. Although the birth rate continued to decline, more young people married, and at an earlier age. These developments reflected the beginnings of a sexual revolution within the American middle-class family. With the growing acceptability of contraception—the Comstock laws notwithstanding—people no longer tightly linked sex and procreation. Experts began to abandon the notion, put forth by one popular medical text, that "the majority of women (happily for society) are not very much troubled by sexual feeling of any kind." In succeeding editions of his book *Plain Home Talk on Love, Marriage and Parentage*, the physician Edward Bliss Foote began to favor a healthy sexuality that gave pleasure to both women and men.

During the 1890s, the artist Charles Dana Gibson created the image of the "new woman" in his drawings for *Life* magazine. The Gibson girl was tall, spirited, athletic, and chastely sexual. Constricting bustles, hoop skirts, and hourglass corsets gave way to shirtwaists and other natural styles that did not hide or disguise the female form. In the city, moreover, women's sphere began to take on a more public character. Of the new urban institutions catering to women, the most important was the department store, which became a temple for their emerging role as consumers.

And the Children. The children of the middle class went through their own revolution. In the past, American children everywhere had been regarded chiefly as an economic asset—added hands for the family farm, shop, or counting house. That no longer held true for the urban middle class. Parents stopped treating their children as working members of the family. In the old days, remarked Ralph Waldo Emerson in 1880, "children had been repressed and kept in the background; now they were considered, cosseted, and pampered." There was such a thing as "the juvenile mind," lectured Jacob Abbott in his book *Gentle Measures in the Management and Training of the Young* (1871). The family had the responsibility of providing a nurturing environment in which the young personality could grow and mature.

Preparation for adulthood became increasingly linked to formal education. School enrollment went up one and a half times between 1870 and 1900. High school attendance, while still encompassing only a small percentage of teenagers, increased at the fastest rate. The years between childhood and adulthood began to stretch out, and a new stage of life—adolescence—emerged. Rooted in an extended period of family dependency, adolescence at the same time shifted much of the socializing role from parents to peer group. A youth culture—one of the hallmarks of American life in the twentieth century—was starting to take shape.

The Higher Culture

America's metropolitan centers, repositories of the nation's wealth, became the site for new institutions of higher culture. A hunger for the cultivated life did not, of course, originate in cities. Before the Civil War, the lyceum movement had sent lecturers to the remotest towns bearing messages of culture and learning. The Chautauqua movement, founded in upstate New York in 1874, carried on this work of cultural dissemination in the last decades of the nineteenth century. However, large cultural institutions such as museums, public libraries, opera companies, and symphony orchestras could flourish only in metropolitan centers.

The first outstanding art museum, the Corcoran Gallery of Art, opened in Washington, D.C., in 1869. New York's Metropolitan Museum of Art started in rented quarters two years later. In 1880 the museum moved to its permanent site in Central Park and launched an ambitious program of art acquisition. J. P. Morgan became chairman of the board in 1905, ensuring the Metropolitan's preeminence. The Boston Museum of Fine Arts was founded in 1876, and Chicago's Art Institute in 1879. By 1914 virtually every major city, and about three-fifths of all cities with more than a hundred thousand people, had an art museum.

Top-flight orchestras also appeared—first in New York under the conductors Theodore Thomas and Leopold Damrosch in the 1870s. Symphonies started in Boston and Chicago during the next decade. National tours by these leading orchestras planted the seeds for orchestral societies in many other cities. Public libraries grew from modest collections (in 1870 only seven had as many as fifty thousand books) into major urban institutions. The greatest library benefactor was Andrew Carnegie, who announced in 1881 that he would build a library in any city that was prepared to maintain it. By 1907, Carnegie had spent more than $32.7 million to establish about a thousand libraries throughout the country.

If the late nineteenth century was the great age of money making, it was also the great age of money *giving*. Surplus private wealth flowed in many directions, particularly to universities. These schools included Vanderbilt, Tulane, and Johns Hopkins universities, all named for their chief benefactors, and the University of Chicago, founded by John D. Rockefeller. Urban cultural institutions also received their share, partly as a matter of civic pride. To some extent patronage of the arts also served the need of the newly rich to establish themselves in society, as in the founding of the Metropolitan Opera in New York. But the higher culture, beyond being merely a commodity of civic pride and social display, also received support out of a sense of cultural deprivation.

"In America there is no culture," pronounced the English critic G. Lowes Dickinson in 1909. Science and the practical arts, yes, "every possible application of life to purposes and ends," but "no life for life's sake." Such condescending remarks received a respectful hearing in the United States because of a deep sense of cultural inferiority to the Old World. In 1873, Mark Twain and Charles Dudley Warner had published a novel, *The Gilded Age*, satirizing America as a land of money grubbers and speculators. This enormously popular book touched a nerve in the American psyche. Its title has, in fact, been appropriated by historians to characterize the late nineteenth century—America's "Gilded Age"—as an age of materialism and cultural shallowness.

Some members of the upper class, including the novelist Henry James, despaired of their country and moved to Europe. Others spent their lives in the kind of perpetual alienation that Henry Adams described in his caustic memoir *The Education of Henry Adams* (1907).

The more common response was to try to raise the nation's cultural level. The newly rich had a hard time of it. They did not have much opportunity to cultivate a taste for art, and a great deal of what they collected was mediocre and garish. On the other hand, George W. Vanderbilt, grandson of the rough-hewn Cornelius Vanderbilt, became a patron of the Art Students League in New York and an early champion of French Impressionism. And the coal and steel baron, Henry Clay Frick, built a brilliant art collection that still remains housed

as a public museum in his mansion in New York City. The enthusiasm of moneyed Americans—not always well directed—largely fueled the great cultural institutions that arose in many cities during the Gilded Age.

A deeply conservative idea of culture sustained this generous patronage. The aim was to embellish urban life, not to probe or reveal its meaning. "Art," says the hero of the Reverend Henry Ward Beecher's sentimental novel *Norwood* (1867), "attempts to work out its end solely by the use of the beautiful, and the artist is to select out only such things as are beautiful."

Culture had also become firmly linked to femininity. In America, remarked one observer, culture was "left entirely to women. . . . It is they, as a general rule, who have opinions about music, or drama, or literature, or philosophy. . . . Husbands or sons rarely share in those interests." Men represented the "force principle," said the clergyman Horace Bushnell, and women symbolized the "beauty principle."

Literature. The treatment of life, wrote one eminent editor, "must be tinged with sufficient idealism to make it all of a truly uplifting character. We cannot admit stories which deal with false or immoral relations. . . . The finer side of things—the idealistic—is the answer for us." The *genteel tradition*, as this literary school came to be called, dominated American cultural agencies, such as universities and publishing companies, from the 1860s on.

Rebellion against the genteel tradition sparked the main creative impulses of late nineteenth-century American literature. *Realism* became the rallying cry of a new generation of writers. Their champion, William Dean Howells, resigned in 1881 as editor of the *Atlantic Monthly*, a stronghold of the genteel tradition. He became editor of *Harper's Monthly* and called for literature that "wishes to know and to tell the truth" and seeks "to picture the daily life in the most exact terms possible." In a series of realistic novels—*A Modern Instance* (1882), *The Rise of Silas Lapham* (1885), and *A Hazard of New Fortunes* (1890)—Howells captured the world of the urban middle class.

Henry James, a far greater writer, also treated the novel as "a direct impression of life" and aimed above all at achieving "an air of reality." He wrote about the world of leisured Americans, and his central concern was the study of moral decay and regeneration. This concern, often set in motion by the confrontation of American innocence with European corruption, appears in *The American* (1877), *Portrait of a Lady* (1882), and *The Golden Bowl* (1904).

The nostalgia of urbanized Americans for their agrarian past helped sustain a vigorous literature of local color and regionalism. These writings included the mining camp stories of Bret Harte, the Uncle Remus tales of Joel Chandler Harris, the Indiana poetry of James Whitcomb Riley, and the New England fiction of Sarah Orne Jewett. Such literature fit comfortably within the genteel tradition, for it was generally sentimental, reassuring, and morally uplifting.

Mark Twain was an entirely different kind of regional writer. Starting as a western journalist and humorist, Twain avoided the influence of the eastern literary establishment. His greatest novel, *The Adventures of Huckleberry Finn* (1884), violated the custom of keeping "low" characters in their proper place for the amused inspection of the culturally superior reader. Huck, an outcast boy, seizes control of the story. The words are his, and so is the innocence with which he questions right and wrong in America. No other novel so fully engaged the themes of racism, injustice, and brutality in nineteenth-century America.

Although not graced with Twain's genius, other novelists did begin to come to grips with the hard realities of city life. Stephen Crane's *Maggie: A Girl of the Streets* (1893), privately printed because no publisher would touch it, told unflinchingly of the destruction of a slum girl. In another urban novel, Henry Blake Fuller's *The Cliff-Dwellers* (1893), the city itself occupied the author's imagination. This story traces the fortunes of the occupants—"cliff-dwellers"—of an immense Chicago office building. In *McTeague* (1899), Frank Norris captured the sights, sounds, and, most acutely, the smells of the city. One reviewer called the story "a study in stinks." Although the novel was set in San Francisco, Norris insisted that it "could have happened in any big city, anywhere."

These *naturalistic* novels stressed the insignificance of the individual, and his or her helplessness in the face of urban life and the inexorable logic of Darwin's survival of the fittest. Frank Norris's character McTeague, more animal than man, is the creature of his instincts and his environment, and he cannot escape coming to a bad end. In Norris's *The Octopus* (1901), the implacable force is the Southern Pacific Railroad; in *The Pit* (1903) it is the Chicago grain market. The city itself, however, was the most powerful influence on the naturalistic writers.

The best of these authors, Theodore Dreiser, surmounted the crude determinism of Frank Norris. But the city people in his great novels *Sister Carrie* (1900), *Jennie Gerhardt* (1911), *The Financier* (1912), and *The Titan* (1914) are no less hostage to an urban world they cannot understand or control. Dreiser sought to capture this world in all its detail, "to talk about life as it is, the facts as they exist, the game as it is played."

Visiting his fiancée's Missouri farm home in 1894, Dreiser had been struck by "the spirit of rural America, its idealism, its dreams." But this was an "American tradition in which I, alas!, could not share." Said Dreiser, "I had seen Pittsburgh. I had seen Lithuanians and Hungarians in their 'courts' and hovels. I had seen the girls of the city—walking the streets at night." The city had entered the American imagination. By the early 1900s, it had become a main theme of American art and literature, and also an overriding concern of the Progressive Era.

★

Summary

America, an agrarian society since its birth, became increasingly urbanized after the Civil War. By 1900 about 20 percent of the population was living in cities of a hundred thousand or more people. City growth stemmed primarily from industrialization—the concentration of industry at key points, the increasingly large scale of production, and the need for commercial and administrative services that were best located in urban centers. A burst of innovation, including mass transit systems, steel frame buildings, electric lighting, and the telephone solved the problems arising from the concentration of an extremely large population in a confined area. Although amply endowed with regulatory powers, American cities left decision-making as much as possible in the hands of private interests. The result was dramatic growth, but not much attention to the impact of growth on the urban environment.

Within the city, geography defined the social order of the population. The poor were found in the city centers and the factory districts, the middle class spread out into the suburbs, and the rich lived insulated either in exclusive central sections of the cities or beyond the suburbs. A distinctive urban culture emerged, drawing heavily on ethnic social institutions and new leisure activities, enabling city dwellers to accommodate themselves to the world of the city. For the wealthy, an elite society emerged, stressing an opulent life style and ex-clusive social organizations. The middle class, on the other hand, withdrew into the private world of the family. For the wives, the cult of domesticity reigned, but its more repressive features began to relax as a new conception of female sexuality took hold. The nurturance of children persisted, but as the years of dependent childhood lengthened, a new phase of adolescence began to emerge that would draw teenagers out of the family orbit.

The great cities of the United States became the sites of a higher culture, including art museums, opera companies, symphony orchestras, and libraries. A new literature emerged that took the urban world as its subject. From the late nineteenth century on, American life would increasingly be defined by what happened in the nation's cities.

TOPIC FOR RESEARCH

The City Boss

How did machine politics come to play the key role in governing the industrial cities of the late nineteenth century? There is a rich contemporary literature describing the boss system by critics looking in from the outside— for example, James Bryce, *The American Commonwealth* (1888); Josiah Strong, *Our Country* (1891); and (on Boston) Robert A. Woods, *The City Wilderness* (1898). Historical studies of the subject include Zane Miller, *Boss Cox's Cincinnati* (1968); Humbert S. Nelli, "John Powers and the Italians: Politics in a Chicago Ward, 1896–1921," *Journal of American History* (June 1970); David C. Hammack, *Power and Society: Greater New York at the Turn of the Century* (1982); and Bruce M. Stave, ed., *Urban Bosses, Machines, and Progressive Reformers* (1972). But how did the system look from the inside? How did the bosses themselves see their role? What values did they hold? How did they explain the loyalty they engendered in the immigrant wards? How did they justify the "graft" that rewarded them for their labors? One Tammany boss—George Washington Plunkitt—gave a series of interviews in which he candidly addressed these questions. See William L. Riordon, ed., *Plunkitt of Tammany Hall* (1948). You might want to compare Plunkitt's views with those of contemporary critics such as Bryce, Strong, or Woods, or try to place Plunkitt's views in a more analytical context by reading one or more historical accounts of city machine politics. Or Plunkitt might be compared to Big Tim Sullivan, whose biography appears on page 620 of this chapter. A full account of his life can be found in Daniel Czitrom, "Underworlds and Underdogs: Big Tim Sullivan and Metropolitan Politics in New York, 1889–1913," *Journal of American History* (September 1991), 536–58.

BIBLIOGRAPHY

Urbanization

Useful as introductions to urban history are Charles N. Glaab and A. Theodore Brown, *A History of Urban America* (1967); Arthur M. Schlesinger, *The Rise of the City* (1936), a pioneering study; and Blake McKelvey, *The Urbanization of America, 1860–1915* (1963). A sampling of the innovative scholarship that opened new historical paths can be found in Stephan Thernstrom and Richard Sennett, eds., *Nineteenth-Century Cities: Essays in the New Urban History* (1969).

Allan Pred, *Spatial Dynamics of U.S. Urban Growth, 1800–1914* (1971), traces the patterns by which cities grew. On the revolution in urban transit, see the pioneering book by Sam B. Warner, *Streetcar Suburbs: The Process of Growth in Boston, 1870–1900* (1962). In a subsequent work, *The Private City: Philadelphia in Three Periods* (1968), Warner broadened his analysis to show how private decision making shaped the character of the American city. Innovations in urban construction are treated in Carl Condit, *American Building Art: Nineteenth Century* (1969) and *Chicago School of Architecture* (1964); Robert C. Twombly, *Louis Sullivan* (1986); and Alan Trachtenberg, *The Brooklyn Bridge* (1965). The problems of meeting basic human needs are treated in Jon C. Teaford, *The Unheralded Triumph: City Government in America, 1870–1900* (1984); Eric H. Monkkonen, *Police in Urban America, 1860–1920* (1981); and David B. Tyack, *The One Best System: A History of American Urban Education*

CHAPTER **21** *The Progressive Era, 1900–1914*

On the face of it, the political ferment of the 1890s ended after the 1896 election. The bitter struggle over free silver left the victorious Republicans with no stomach for political crusades. The McKinley administration devoted itself to maintaining business confidence: sound money and high tariffs were the order of the day. The main thing, as party chief Mark Hanna said, was to "stand pat and continue Republican prosperity."

Yet beneath the surface a deep uneasiness was taking hold of the country. The depression of the 1890s had unveiled harsh truths not acknowledged in better days. One such discovery was the power of vested economic interests. In Wisconsin, for example, utility and transit companies had raised prices, reduced services, and received special tax relief—all at the expense of the public. This discovery of corporate arrogance launched movements in Wisconsin for tax reform, for municipal ownership of utilities, and for an end to boss-run party politics.

The labor unrest of the 1890s produced a similar response. The Cleveland administration had broken the great Pullman railway strike of 1894 by plotting with the railroad operators, issuing injunctions against the strike leaders, and sending in troops to get the trains moving again. The architect of this policy, Attorney General Richard Olney, took little satisfaction from his success in suppressing the strike. He asked himself what might be done in the future to avoid the need for such one-sided intervention. Olney began to advocate labor legislation, first expressed in the Erdman Mediation Act of 1898, that would regulate labor relations on the railroads and prevent crippling rail strikes. In such ways

did the crisis of the 1890s turn the nation's thinking to reform.

The problems themselves, however, were of much older origin. For more than half a century, Americans had been absorbed in the furious development of their nation. Now, at the beginning of the twentieth century, they paused, looked around, and began to add up the costs. Industrialization had led to a frightening concentration of economic power in corporate hands, and an equally troubling growth of a restless working class. The cities had spawned widespread misery and corrupt machine politics. The heritage of an earlier America seemed to be succumbing to the demands of the new industrial order.

These problems had troubled the reform-minded for many years, but the crisis of the 1890s had forestalled action. Only now, after the threat of Populism had subsided, did it seem safe to return to the nation's festering problems. Reform became a central and absorbing concern of Americans. It was as if social awareness had reached a critical mass around 1900 that set reform activity going as a major, self-sustaining phenomenon of early twentieth-century America. For this reason the years from 1900 to World War I have come to be known as the Progressive Era.

The Course of Reform

Historians have sometimes spoken of a progressive "movement." But progressivism was not a movement in any meaningful sense. There was no single progressive constituency, no agreed-upon agenda, and no unifying organization or leadership. At different times and places, different social groups became active. People who were reformers on one issue might be conservative on another. The term *progressivism* embraces a widespread, many-sided effort after 1900 to build a better society. Progressive reformers shared only this objective, plus an intellectual style that can be called "progressive."

The Intellectual Roots of Progressivism

Intellectual climates change. It is usually hard to explain why they change, but not so difficult to tell when new ideas take hold. Such a change of ideas clearly seemed to be in the wind as the twentieth century began.

A Sense of Mastery. The Progressive Era was an age of scientific investigation. The federal government launched massive statistical studies of immigration, women's and children's labor, and working conditions in many industries. Vice commissions studied prostitution, gambling, and other moral ills of American cities. Among private investigations, the classic was the multivolume *Pittsburgh Survey* (1911–1914). Financed by Margaret Olivia Sage and other New York City philanthropists, a team of investigators recorded in great detail living and working conditions of the steel district.

The facts were important because they formed the basis for corrective action. When the young journalist Walter Lippmann wrote *Drift and Mastery* (1914), he asserted the Progressive's confidence in people's ability to act purposefully and constructively. This sense of mastery expressed itself in many ways. For example, people had great faith in academic experts. In Wisconsin, the state university became a key resource for Robert M. La Follette's progressive administration. "The close intimacy of the university with public affairs explains the democracy, the thoroughness, and the scientific accuracy of the state in its legislation," boasted one La Follette supporter.

Scientific management exerted a particularly strong attraction on progressives. The original aim of scientific management had been to reorganize and rationalize work in factories (see Chapter 19). But its founder, Frederick W. Taylor, argued that his basic approach—the "scientific" analysis of human activity—offered solutions to waste and inefficiency in municipal government, in schools and hospitals, and even in homes and churches. "The fundamental principles of scientific management are applicable to all kinds of human activities," Taylor stressed, and could solve all the social ills that arise "through such of our acts as are blundering, ill-directed, or inefficient."

Attacking Nineteenth-Century Formalism. The essential thing, in the progressive view, was to resist intellectual formulations that denied people this sense of mastery. One of the worst offenders was the English philosopher Herbert Spencer, whose doctrine of Social Darwinism had exerted enormous influence on conservative American thought. Spencer argued that society developed "automatically," according to fixed laws that could not be changed. Spencer's intellectual approach was *formalistic*—that is, he based his conclusions on abstract theory rather than factual investigation. Critics of Spencer denied that the evolution of society was guided by absolute and unvarying rules. "It is folly," protested the Harvard philosopher William James, "to speak of the 'laws of history,' as of something inevitable, which science only has to discover, and which any one can then foretell and observe, but do nothing to alter or avert." Man could "shape environmental forces to his own advantage," argued the sociologist Lester F. Ward. Society could advance through "rational planning" and "social engineering."

A comparable attack on formalism took place in many academic disciplines. In classical economics, for example, scholars assumed that markets were perfectly competitive, and hence perfectly responsive to the laws of supply and demand. Such a system left no room for reform, which would only disrupt what could not be improved. Critics of classical economics—they called themselves "institutional economists"—denied that the market ever operated so perfectly. They conducted field research to determine how institutions and power relationships influenced the operation of the marketplace. In his *The Theory of the Leisure Class* (1899) and *The Instinct of Workmanship* (1914), the economist Thorstein Veblen lampooned the classical economists' abstract image of the economic man. In the real world, Veblen contended, people acted not out of pure economic calculation, but from complex motives ranging from vanity to pride in their work.

In legal thought, likewise, formalism had dominated the field. The courts treated the rights of property and liberty of contract as if these were eternal principles outside the realm of social reality. Thus in the famous *Lochner v. New York* decision (1905), the Supreme Court invalidated a law that would have limited the notoriously long hours of bakers in New York State. Such regulation, the Court concluded, violated the contractual rights of *both* employers and workers. Justice Oliver Wendell Holmes, the leading dissenter on the Supreme Court, objected; in his view, the *Lochner* decision was based on a fictional equality. If the choice was between working and starving, could it really be said that workers freely accepted jobs requiring that they labor fourteen hours a day? Or that state regulation limiting excessive working hours violated their liberty of contract in any meaningful sense?

Holmes had earlier asserted the essence of the progressive legal critique: "The life of the law has not been logic; it has been experience. The felt necessities of the time, even the prejudices which judges share with their fellow-men, have had a good deal more to do than [logic] in determining the rules by which men shall be governed." "Sociological jurisprudence," as Dean Roscoe Pound of the Harvard Law School termed it, called for "the adjustment of principles and doctrines to the human conditions they are to govern rather than assumed first principles."

In philosophy, it was William James who led the assault on formalism as an intellectual system. James denied the existence of absolute truths. His philosophy of *pragmatism* judged ideas by their consequences; ideas served as guides to action that produced desired results. Philosophy should concern itself with solving problems, said James, not with contemplating ultimate ends.

James's most important disciple was John Dewey. Like James, Dewey had a great interest in psychology, and was a pioneer in applying psychological insights to education. In his Laboratory School at the University of Chicago, Dewey broke from the rigid curriculum of traditional education and instead stressed problem solving and practical activity as the keys to children's educational growth. Children were encouraged to explore and discover for themselves rather than learning lessons by rote. Nowhere could the intellectual bent of progressivism in action be better seen than in Dewey's experiments. Fittingly, they came to be known as progressive education.

Idealism. Progressive reformers prided themselves on being tough-minded. They had confidence in people's capacity to take purposeful action. But there was another side to the progressive mind. It was deeply infused with idealism. Progressives framed their intentions in terms of high principle. The progressive cause, pronounced Theodore Roosevelt, "is based on the eternal principles of righteousness."

Much progressive idealism came from the American past. No American hero loomed larger in the minds of progressives than Abraham Lincoln. For many, like Jane Addams, the Great Emancipator served as a lifelong guide. Lincoln's example, in particular, inspired the battle for political reform. "Go back to the first principles of democracy; go back to the people," Robert La Follette told his audience when he first launched his attack on Wisconsin machine politics. Political reformers typically described theirs as a work of political restoration. They frequently said they had converted to reform after discovering how far party politics had drifted from the ideals of representative government.

Progressive idealism also derived from American radical traditions. Many progressives traced their conversion to a reading of Henry George's *Progress and Poverty* (1879), which asked why, in the midst of fabulous wealth, so many Americans should be condemned to want. George's answer—that private control of land siphoned the community's wealth into the hands of nonproductive landlords—led to a Single Tax movement that served as a school for many budding progressives. Others traced their awakening to Edward Bellamy's novel *Looking Backward* (1888), with its utopian vision of an ordered, affluent American socialism; or to the Chicago social democrat Henry Demarest Lloyd's *Wealth Against Commonwealth* (1894), with its powerful indictment of the Standard Oil trust. In later years, this radical tradition came to be transmitted mainly through the Socialist party, which flourished after 1900 under the leadership of Eugene Debs. Walter Lippmann and many other young reformers passed through socialism on their way to progressivism, while other reformers, like Charlotte Perkins Gilman, never left the socialist camp.

The most important source of progressive idealism, especially among social reformers, was religion. Within the Protestant churches, a new doctrine—the Social Gospel—took hold. The Baptist cleric Walter Rauschenbusch, its most influential exponent, had been deeply affected by his ministry near the squalid Hell's Kitchen section of New York City. Shocked by the conditions he found there, Rauschenbusch fought for more playgrounds and better housing in slum neighborhoods. The churches had to reassert the "social aims of Jesus," Rauschenbusch argued. The "Kingdom of God on Earth" would be achieved, he said, not by striving only for personal salvation but by struggling for social justice. The Social Gospel, increasingly heard from urban Protestant pulpits after the turn of the century, led to the formation of the Federal Council of Churches in 1908. The council aimed at "promoting the application of the law of Christ in every relation to human life."

The Social Gospel expressed the concerns of the Protestant ministry, but the underlying religious sentiment extended far beyond formal church boundaries. Progressive leaders of the Protestant faith characteristically grew up in families imbued with evangelical piety. Many went through a religious crisis, having sought and failed to experience a conversion, and ultimately settled on a career in social work, education, journalism, or politics. There they could translate inherited religious belief into modern secular action. Jane Addams, for example, had taken up settlement-house work with this intent. She believed that, by uplifting the poor in tenement districts, settlement workers would themselves be uplifted: they would experience "the joy of finding Christ" by acting "in fellowship" with those in need.

As a result, progressive thought contained a pervading Christian undercurrent. The philosopher John Dewey called democracy "a spiritual fact" and the "means by which the revelation of truth is carried on." Theodore Roosevelt launched his Progressive party in 1912 with the battle cry, "We stand at Armageddon and we battle for the Lord." His supporters at the party's national convention marched around the hall singing "Onward Christian Soldiers."

The Muckrakers. The progressive mode of thought—idealistic in intent and tough-minded in approach—nurtured a new kind of reform journalism. A growing urban audience had already given rise during the 1890s to a rash of popular magazines, including *Munsey's*, *McClure's*, and *Collier's*. Unlike the highbrow *Atlantic Monthly* or *Harper's*, these journals sold for only 10 cents and catered to a broad audience. Almost by accident—Lincoln Steffens's article "Tweed Days in St. Louis" in the October 1902 issue of *McClure's* is credited with getting things started—magazine editors discovered that what most excited their readers was the exposure of evildoing.

In a series of powerful articles, Steffens wrote about "the shame of the cities"—the corrupt ties between business and political machines. Ida M. Tarbell attacked Standard Oil, and David Graham Phillips told how money controlled the Senate. William Hard exposed industrial accidents in "Making Steel and Killing Men" (1907) and child labor in "De Kid Wot Works at Night" (1908). Others described prostitution, Wall Street abuses, and adulterated food. Hardly a sordid corner of American life escaped the scrutiny of these brilliant and tireless reporters. They were moralists as well. They made their writing powerful not only by uncovering facts, but also by telling the facts with great indignation.

President Roosevelt, among many others, thought they went too far. In a 1906 speech, he compared them to the man with the muckrake in *The Pilgrim's Progress*, by the seventeenth-century English preacher John Bunyan. The man was too absorbed with raking the filth on the floor to look up and accept a celestial crown. Thus the term *muckrakers* became attached to journalists who exposed the underside of American life. Their efforts were, in fact, health-giving. More than any other group, the muckrakers called the people to arms.

Political Reformers

Progressives infused their efforts with a deep sense of idealism. They were confident of the human capacity to take purposeful action. This much progressives had in common. But once in action, different groups took up different reforms, and to a greater or lesser degree, they did so out of self-interest. Nowhere were these crosscurrents stronger than in the battles for political reform.

Ida Tarbell Takes on Rockefeller

A popular biographer of Napoleon and Lincoln in the 1890s, Ida Tarbell turned her formidable journalistic talents to muckraking. Her first installment of "The History of the Standard Oil Company" appeared in *McClure's Magazine* in November 1902. John D. Rockefeller, she wrote, "was willing to strain every nerve to obtain for himself special and illegal privileges from the railroads which were bound to ruin every man in the oil business not sharing them with him." As Tarbell built her case, a crescendo of criticism rained down on Rockefeller. A more sympathitic cartoon in the magazine *Judge* pleads with Rockefeller's critics: "Boys, don't you think you have bothered the old man just about enough?"

AMERICAN VOICES

The Shame of the Cities *Lincoln Steffens*

One of the best-known muckraking journalists, Steffens aimed his pen at many aspects of city machine politics. In this article, published in *McClure's* in 1903, he describes corruption and bribe-taking—"boodling"—in St. Louis.

The convicted boodlers have described the system to me. There was no politics in it—only business. The city of St. Louis is normally Republican. . . . The State of Missouri, however, is normally Democratic, and the legislature has taken political possession of the city by giving to the governor the appointment of the Police and Election Boards. With a defective election law, the Democratic boss in the city became its absolute ruler.

This boss is Edward R. Butler, better known as "Colonel Ed," or "Colonel Butler," or just "Boss." He is an Irishman by birth, a master horse-shoer by trade, a good fellow—by nature, at first, then by profession. . . .

His method was to dictate enough of the candidates on both tickets to enable him, by selecting the worst from each, to elect the sort of men he required in his business. In other words, while honest Democrats and Republicans were "loyal to party" (a point of great pride with the idiots) and "voted straight," the Democratic boss and his Republican lieutenants decided what part of each ticket should be elected; then they sent around Butler's "Indians" (repeaters) by the vanload to scratch ballots and "repeat" their votes, till the worst had made sure of the government by the worst, and Butler was in a position to do business.

His business was boodling, which is a more refined and a more dangerous form of corruption than the police blackmail of Minneapolis. It involves, not thieves, gamblers, and common women, but influential citizens, capitalists, and great corporations. For the stock-in-trade of the boodler is the rights, privileges, franchises, and real property of the city, and his source of corruption is the top, not the bottom, of society. . . .

Butler organized and systematized and developed [boodling] into a regular financial institution, and made it an integral part of the business community. He had for clients, regular or occasional, bankers and promoters; and the statements of boodlers, not yet on record, allege that every transportation and public convenience company that touches St. Louis has dealings with Butler's combine. And my best information is that these interests were not victims. Blackmail came in time, but in the beginning they originated the schemes of loot and started Butler on his career. Some interests paid him a regular salary, others a fee, and again he was a partner in the enterprise, with a special "rake-off" for his influence. . . .

Boodling was safe, and boodling was fat. Butler became rich and greedy, and neglectful of politics. Outside capital came in, and finding Butler bought, went over his head to the boo-dle combines. These creatures learned thus the value of franchises, and that Butler had been giving them an unduly small share of the boodle.

Then began a struggle, enormous in its vile melodrama, for control of corruption—Butler to squeeze the municipal legislators and save his profits, they to wring from him their "fair share."

. . . Such then, is the boodling system as we see it in St. Louis. Everything the city owned was for sale by the officers elected by the people. The purchasers might be willing or unwilling takers; they might be citizens or outsiders; it was all one to the city government. So long as the members of the combines got the proceeds they would sell out the town. Would? They did and they will. If a city treasurer runs away with $50,000 there is a great haloo about it. In St. Louis the regularly organized thieves who rule have sold $50,000,000 worth of franchises and other valuable municipal assets. This is the estimate made for me by a banker, who said that the boodlers got not one-tenth of the value of the things they sold, but were content because they got it all themselves. . . .

Preposterous? It certainly would seem so; but watch the people of St. Louis as I have, and as the boodlers have—then judge.

Source: Lincoln Steffens, "The Shamelessness of St. Louis," *McClure's* 20 (March 1903), 546–53.

Municipal Reform. In many cities the demand for better government came from local businessmen. They complained that the economic burdens of old-fashioned party rule had become too heavy. Taxes went up while services fell short of business's growing needs. There had to be an end, as one manufacturer said, to "the inefficiency, the sloth, the carelessness, the injustice and the graft of city administrations." The solution, argued John Patterson of the National Cash Register Company, lay in putting "municipal affairs on a strict business basis." Cities should be run "not by partisans, either Republican or Democratic, but by men who are skilled in business management and social service."

In 1900 a hurricane devastated Galveston, Texas. Local businessmen took over and, in the course of rebuilding the city, replaced the mayor and board of aldermen with a five-member commission. The Galveston plan, although widely copied, had a serious flaw. It gave too much power to the individual commissioners. Dayton, Ohio, resolved this problem by assigning legislative duties to a nonpartisan commission and administrative functions to an appointed city manager. The commission-manager system aimed at running the American city "in exactly the same way as a private business corporation." Municipal political reform was chiefly the work of the business community, and overtly a matter of the balance sheet.

It was also a way of grabbing power. Municipal reformers favored citywide elections, nonpartisanship, and professional city administration. All these reforms attacked the ward politics that traditionally had given ethnic and working-class groups access to political power and influence. As a result, municipal control moved into the hands of the urban middle class. In fact, municipal reform contained a decidedly antidemocratic bias. "Ignorance should be excluded from control," said former Mayor Abram Hewitt of New York in 1901. "City business should be carried on by trained experts selected upon some other principle than popular suffrage."

A different kind of urban progressive opposed such elitist reform. Mayor Brand Whitlock of Toledo, Ohio, believed "that the cure for the ills of democracy was not less democracy, as so many people were always preaching, but more democracy." The prototype of this new breed of urban politician was shoe manufacturer Hazen S. Pingree, who led the Republicans to victory against the Democratic machine in Detroit in 1889. Although drafted by a business coalition, Pingree skillfully appealed for support from trade unions and ethnic groups.

His administration not only attacked municipal corruption and inefficiency but also concerned itself with the needs of Detroit's working people. An increasing number of other cities came under the leadership of such progressive mayors, including Samuel M. "Golden Rule" Jones in Toledo, Tom Johnson in Cleveland, and Mark Fagan in Jersey City. By combining popular programs and campaign magic, they won over the urban masses and challenged the rule of the entrenched machines.

State Politics. The major battleground for democratic political reform, however, was at the state level. Preeminent among state progressives was Robert M. La Follette of Wisconsin. La Follette was a seasoned politician. Born in 1855, he had followed a conventional party career—as a lawyer, a district attorney, and then a congressman for three terms—before breaking with the Wisconsin Republican machine in 1891 allegedly because of an attempt by the top party boss to bribe him. La Follette became a tireless exponent of political reform. "I was merely expressing a common and widespread, though largely unconscious, spirit of revolt among the people," La Follette said of his fight to unseat the Wisconsin Republican machine. At first, it was an uphill battle. But after a decade of unremitting campaigning, La Follette finally gained the Republican nomination and won the governorship in 1900 on a platform that demanded higher taxes for corporations, stricter utility and railroad regulation, and political reform.

La Follette's key proposal was a direct primary law, by which party candidates would be chosen through popular election rather than in machine-run conven-

Robert M. La Follette

La Follette was transformed into a political reformer when a Wisconsin Republican boss attempted to bribe him in 1891 to influence a judge in a railway case. As he described it in his *Autobiography,* "Out of this awful ordeal came understanding; and out of understanding came resolution. I determined that the power of this corrupt influence . . . should be broken." This photo captures La Follette at the top of his form, taking his case in 1897 to the people of Cumberland, Wisconsin.

tions. Pushed through by La Follette in 1903, this democratic reform both expressed his political ideals and suited his particular political talents. The party regulars opposing him were insiders, more comfortable in the caucus room than out on the hustings. But that was where La Follette excelled. A brilliant campaigner, La Follette aimed at dramatizing the issues and generating grass-roots support. The direct primary gave La Follette the means to maintain his control over the Republican party in Wisconsin. Through good times and bad, he kept it until his death twenty-five years later.

What was true of La Follette was more or less true of all successful progressive politicians. Albert B. Cummins of Iowa, Harold U'Ren of Oregon, and Hiram Johnson of California all espoused democratic ideals and made skillful use of the direct primary to win political power and push through reform programs. If they were newcomers—as was Woodrow Wilson when he left academic life to enter New Jersey politics in 1910—they showed a quick aptitude for politics and gained a solid mastery of the trade. Once in office, they asserted control over their parties and beat the political bossesat their own game. They practiced a new kind of popular politics. In a reform age, it could be a more effective way to power than the back-room techniques of the old-fashioned machine politicians.

Not even the most radical of progressive reforms— the initiative, the referendum, and the recall—quite lived up to their billings. All three reforms were intended to shift political power back to the people. The *initiative* empowered the voters to place issues on the ballot, the *referendum* enabled them to vote on those issues, while the *recall* empowered citizens to remove from office politicians who had lost the public's confidence. It very soon became clear, however, that direct democracy did not supplant organized politics but only gave it a different form. For initiative, referendum, and recall campaigns put a premium on organization, money, and expertise, and these were attributes not of the people at large but of private, well-organized interests. As with the direct primary, the initiative, referendum, and recall had as much to do with power relations as with democratic idealism.

The Woman Progressive

Reform movements arise through a process of *recruitment*. Why do people enlist in a great cause? Each reform group—like the progressive politicians just described—has its own particular history, mobilized to action by linkages of varying kinds to the evil crying out for correction. For middle-class women of the Progressive Era, the linkage was between their identity within women's domestic sphere—as wives and mothers—and the special responsibility this gave them for the social well-being of their communities.

There was nothing new about this linkage. It had been the basis of women's social reform movements for many decades (see Chapter 19). By the late nineteenth century women's clubs and reform organizations already occupied a broad public sphere. But the tempo of women's reform activity now manifestly increased, and attention focused above all on the nation's urban problems.

Middle-class women had long borne the burden of humanitarian work in American cities. Characteristically, they did most of the leg work for the charity organization societies that since the 1870s had sprung up to coordinate citywide private relief. As voluntary investigators, women visited needy families, assessed their problems, and referred them to the appropriate relief agencies.

After many years of such dedicated charity work, Josephine Shaw Lowell of New York City concluded that it was not enough to give assistance to the poor. "If the working people had all they ought to have, we should not have the paupers and criminals," she declared. "It is better to save them before they go under, than to spend your life fishing them out afterward." Lowell founded the New York Consumers League in 1890. Her goal was to improve the wages and working conditions of the female clerks in the city's stores. To bring pressure on reluctant merchants, the league issued a "White List"—a very short one at first—of shops that met its standards for a living wage and decent working conditions for clerks.

The league then expanded its interest beyond retail stores and spread to other cities. Most important, these women reformers came to recognize that voluntary action was insufficient, that only state action could meet the most pressing problems of the urban poor. Accordingly, they founded the National Consumers League in 1899 to push this struggle. Under the crusading leadership of Florence Kelley, formerly a chief factory inspector in Illinois, the league became a powerful lobby for protective legislation for women and children.

Among its achievements, none was more important than the *Muller v. Oregon* decision (1908), which upheld an Oregon law limiting to ten hours the workday of women workers. The Consumers League had pushed that law through the state legislature and recruited the brilliant Boston lawyer Louis D. Brandeis to defend the law before the Supreme Court. In his brief, Brandeis devoted a scant two pages to legal citations on the narrow constitutional issue—whether, under its police powers, Oregon had the right to regulate women's working hours. Instead Brandeis rested his case on a vast amount of data gathered by the Consumers League showing how long hours damaged women's health and family roles. The *Muller* decision, which accepted Brandeis's reasoning, was a signal victory for the new "sociological jurisprudence" (see p. 663) and cleared the way for a wave of protective laws across the country.

AMERICAN LIVES

Frances Kellor: Woman Progressive

From the day its doors opened in 1892, the University of Chicago was a major center of American learning. Financed by John D. Rockefeller, the university modeled itself on the great German research universities and, unlike Yale or Harvard, concentrated on graduate education. At Chicago and other American universities, modern social science was taking shape, breaking from its nineteenth-century links to moral philosophy and seeking a scientific foundation for the study of society. The disciplines that were emerging—economics, political science, sociology—demanded a rigorous course of study certified by the granting of the Ph.D. But if the social sciences were becoming professional and research-oriented, the motive force was not yet knowledge for its own sake, but social reform. The city of Chicago was, in fact, seen as a great laboratory within which the university would do its work. The students who came were being prepared (whether they knew it or not) to be in service to the American progressivism of the next decade. The University of Chicago, moreover, was receptive to the admission of women; and for them, in particular, the university was a breeding ground for careers as social reformers. Among the women entering in 1898 was Frances Alice Kellor, a recent graduate of Cornell.

Kellor was born in Columbus, Ohio, in 1873. Her father abandoned the family before she was two, and her mother made a hard living as a domestic and laundress. This was not the kind of privileged background from which most woman progressives sprang, but Kellor's experience came closer to the norm than her personal circumstances might have suggested. In 1875 her family moved to Coldwater, Michigan, a former abolitionist center (and station on the Underground Railroad) and a stronghold of Yankee culture. From the Coldwater community, with its high moral standards

and strong educational institutions, Kellor received the reformist values that other budding progressives learned from their families. Kellor, moreover, had a remarkable talent for finding patrons, gaining by her wits the financial means her fellow progressives were born to. Her first patrons were the well-to-do librarians of Coldwater, Mary and Frances Eddy, who befriended her and then took her into their home. Born Alice, Kellor began to call herself "Frances" as a sign that she considered herself adopted by the Eddy sisters. She graduated from high school, became a reporter for the *Coldwater Republican*, and then, with the backing of the Eddys, enrolled at Cornell in 1895. Highly athletic, she made her first mark as a fighter for equal rights on a sports issue: she led the campaign for a women's crew. She got a solid education in the social sciences at Cornell and decided to become a criminologist.

Sociology was still an infant discipline when Kellor arrived in Chicago in 1898, with little in the way of systematic theory, and much emphasis on high-minded investigations of social problems. Kellor's interest in crime was accordingly encouraged by the Chicago faculty. The prevailing theory of the time, advanced by the Italian Cesare Lombroso, was that criminality was an inherited trait. Criminals were born criminal, and this was manifest in their physical features. Skeptical, Kellor conducted a study of the female inmates of five midwestern prisons. Comparing them to a control group of college women, she could find no physical differences. Rather, it was social environment, economic disadvantage, and poverty that made for criminality. Kellor also rejected "the prevailing opinion that when women are criminal they are more degraded and more abandoned than men." People thought so only because of "the difference in the standards which we set for the two sexes." A second project on southern prisons drew Kel-

Frances Kellor
This photograph of Kellor was taken in her early twenties, when she was a student at Cornell University.

lor to similar, antiracist conclusions: she found no inherent criminal propensity among blacks, only dire poverty, the ravages of centuries of slavery, and an unfair judicial system that came down with extreme hardness on black offenders.

Kellor's landmark studies resulted in a series of major research articles and a book but did not launch her into an academic career. Despite her brilliant record she left the university in 1902 without a degree. The reasons are not altogether clear, but doubtless had something to do with a painful truth of which Kellor must have been aware: Chicago almost never placed its female graduate students in tenure-track teaching jobs. To be a professor, it seemed, was still a male prerogative. There was, however, also a positive side to Kellor's decision. Like many of her fellow students, she had fallen under the spell of Jane Addams. Kellor lived periodically at Hull House, joined the circle of social reformers that congregated there, and began to see her

future out among the disadvantaged rather than in the university. When she left Chicago, it was to do social research for New York's College Settlement Association.

Unemployment had hitherto been seen primarily as a personal problem afflicting the shiftless and incompetent. In her pioneering investigation *Out of Work* (1904), Kellor treated it as a social and economic phenomenon. She was especially concerned with the plight of jobless women and their exploitation by employment agencies. Representing the Women's Municipal League of New York, Kellor lobbied successfully for state regulatory legislation for these agencies. The combination of professional social investigation and robust political advocacy became the hallmark of Kellor's progressivism. Her next study, on the problems of immigrants in New York, led to the establishment of the state Bureau of Industries and Immigration in 1910. Kellor was chosen to be its head, the first woman to hold so major a post in New York state government.

The high point of Kellor's career came two years later, when Theodore Roosevelt launched the Progressive party. Convinced that social reform required strong government, Kellor was drawn to the New Nationalism. She linked it with her own fervent advocacy of women's political rights. Always a fighter, she was entirely at ease in the rough and tumble of partisan politics. After Roosevelt's defeat in 1912, the Progressive party set up the National Progressive Service, a kind of think tank to study social problems and formulate legislative proposals. The idea was mainly Frances Kellor's, and she was tapped to chair the Service. This was truly a pinnacle for a woman in American politics, at a time when women in most states could not vote in national elections. Unfortunately, Kellor's emphasis on scientific investigation put her at odds with the practical politicians, and she was forced out in early 1914. Hers was a brief run in national politics, exhilarating while it lasted and unique for a woman in that era.

Kellor never married. Like many other woman progressives, including Jane Addams, she found personal fulfillment in an enduring relationship with another woman. This was Mary Dreier, one of two wealthy sisters who played leading roles in New York progressivism. From the time Kellor moved into the Dreier home in Brooklyn Heights in 1904 until her death almost fifty years later, she and Mary were constant companions. Kellor's later professional life was devoted to a distinguished career as vice president of the American Arbitration Association.

Women's organizations became a mighty force in state legislatures and in Congress on behalf of women and children. Their victories included the first law providing public assistance for mothers with dependent children, in Illinois in 1911; the first minimum wage law for women and children, in Massachusetts in 1912; and the creation of the Children's and Women's bureaus in the U.S. Labor Department, in 1912 and 1920, respectively.

The Settlement Houses. A second thrust of women's urban activism, just as strong as public advocacy, aimed at direct engagement with the underprivileged. The settlement-house movement began in London in 1884, when Oxford University students founded Toynbee Hall. Inspired by that example, two young American women, Jane Addams and Ellen Gates Starr, established Hull House on Chicago's West Side in 1889. During the next fifteen years, scores of settlement houses sprang up in the slum neighborhoods of the nation's cities. The settlement houses served as community centers run by their middle-class residents, who acted as amateur social workers for the surrounding immigrant communities. Hull House had meeting rooms, an art gallery, clubs for children and adults, and a kindergarten. Jane Addams herself led battles for garbage removal, playgrounds, better street lighting, and police protection. At the Henry Street Settlement in New York City, Lillian D. Wald made visiting nursing a major service. Mary McDowell, head of the University of Chicago Settle-

ment, installed a bathhouse, a children's playground, and a citizenship school for immigrants.

Beyond the modest good they did in slum neighborhoods, the settlement houses served as a breeding ground for social reform. At least half the women residents went on to careers in some branch of social service. The settlement houses thus contributed significantly to the emerging profession of social work. To a remarkable degree, too, the leaders of social reform—both men and women—served apprenticeships in settlement houses.

For the middle-class residents, more deep-seated needs were also being satisfied. In a famous essay, Jane Addams spoke of the "subjective necessity" of the settlement house. She meant that it was as much a response to the desire of educated young women to serve as it was to the needs of slum dwellers. Addams herself was a case in point. She had grown up in a comfortable Illinois family and graduated from Rockford College. Then she faced an empty future, an ornamental wife if she married, a sheltered spinster if she did not. Hull House became her salvation. It gave her contact with what she thought was the real world plus a useful career and a sense of purpose and personal worth.

The Revival of the Struggle for Women's Rights. Almost imperceptibly, women activists like Jane Addams and Florence Kelley began to breathe new life into the suffrage movement. Why should a woman who was capable of running a settlement house or lobbying a bill

Saving the Children

In the early years at Hull House toddlers sometimes arrived for kindergarten tipsy from breakfasts of bread soaked in wine. To settlement-house workers, education in child care seemed the obvious answer to such ignorance, and so began the program to send visiting nurses into immigrant homes. They taught mothers the proper methods of caring for children—including, as this photograph shows, the daily infant bath, in a dishpan if necessary.

be denied the right to vote? Suffrage, moreover, became more firmly linked to social reform. If women had the right to vote, they and their male supporters argued, more enlightened legislation and better government would certainly result. Finally, by their activities among working-class women, the women progressives helped to broaden the social base of the suffrage movement.

Believing that working women should be encouraged to help themselves, social reformers founded the National Women's Trade Union League in 1903. Financed and led by wealthy supporters, the league organized women workers, played a considerable role in their strikes, and perhaps most important, developed working-class leaders. Rose Schneiderman, for example, became a union organizer among the garment workers in New York City; Agnes Nestor led the women glove workers in Illinois; and both were lobbyists for protective legislation. Such trade-union women identified their cause with the broader struggle for women's rights. When the state of New York held referenda on woman suffrage in 1915 and 1917, strong support came from the Jewish and Italian precincts inhabited by unionized garment workers.

Suffrage activity began to revive nationwide. Women won the right to vote in the state of Washington in 1910, in California in 1911, and in four more western states during the next three years. Women also altered their tactics. In England, suffragists had begun to picket Parliament, assault politicians, and go on hunger strikes in jail. This disruptive strategy, which infused the cause

Rose Schneiderman, 1913

In their battles for better conditions, women garment workers produced their own leaders, and none was more devoted to their cause, or more fiery on the platform, than Rose Schneiderman. The daughter of a widowed immigrant woman, Schneiderman went to work at thirteen, quickly became caught up in union activities, and fashioned for herself a lifetime career as a trade unionist, including becoming president of the National Women's Trade Union League.

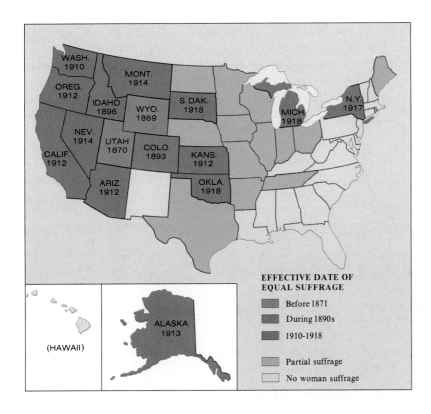

MAP 21.1

Woman Suffrage, 1869–1918

By 1909, after more than sixty years of agitation, only four lightly populated western states had granted women full voting rights. A number of other states granted partial suffrage, limited mostly to voting for school boards and such issues as taxes. Between 1910 and 1918, as the effort shifted to the struggle for a constitutional amendment, eleven states (and Alaska) joined the shortlist granting full suffrage. The most stubborn resistance was in the South.

Suffragists on Parade, 1912
After 1910 the suffrage movement went into high gear. Suffragist leaders decided to demand a constitutional amendment rather than relying solely on gaining the vote state by state. In 1912 they served notice on both parties that they meant business and, as in this suffragist parade in New York, made their demands a visible part of the presidential campaign.

of the English suffragists with new power, impressed their sisters in the United States.

Most important among the American converts was Alice Paul, a young Quaker who had lived in England and knew from firsthand experience how to apply the confrontational tactics of the English suffragists. Rejecting the slower route of enfranchisement by the states, Paul advocated a constitutional amendment that in one stroke would give women across the country the right to vote. In 1916, Paul organized the militant National Woman's party. The National American Woman Suffrage Association (NAWSA), from which Paul had split off, was also rejuvenated. Carrie Chapman Catt, a skilled political organizer from the New York movement, took over as national leader in 1915. Under her guidance, NAWSA brought a broad-based organization to the campaign for a federal amendment.

Feminism. In the midst of this suffrage struggle something new and more fundamental began to happen. A new generation of women activists was arising. They were college graduates or experienced trade unionists. Out in the world and self-supporting, these women were determined not to be hemmed in by the social constraints of women's "separate sphere." "Breaking into the Human Race" was the intention they proclaimed at a famous mass meeting in New York in 1914. "We intend simply to be ourselves," declared the chair Marie Jenny Howe, "not just our little female selves, but our whole big human selves."

The women at this meeting called themselves *feminists*, a term just then coming into use. In this, its first

incarnation, feminism meant freedom for full personal development, which in its specifics covered many things—freedom to follow a career, freedom from the double standard in sexual morality, freedom from social convention—but in a larger sense meant above all freedom from the stifling stereotypes of woman's separate sphere. Thus did Charlotte Perkins Gilman, famous for her advocacy of communal kitchens as a means of liberating women from homemaking, imagine the new woman: "Here she comes, running, out of prison and off pedestal; chains off, crown off, halo off, just a live woman."

Feminists were militantly prosuffrage; but unlike their more traditional suffragist sisters, feminists did not stake their claim on any presumed uplifting effect of women's vote on American politics. Rather, they demanded the right to vote because they considered themselves full equals to men. At the point that the suffrage movement was about to triumph, it was being overtaken by a larger revolution that redefined the struggle for women's rights as a battle against all the constraints that prevented women from achieving their full potential as human beings.

Urban Liberalism

The social evolution of the suffrage movement—in particular, the recruitment of working-class women to what had been a middle-class struggle—was entirely characteristic of how progressivism evolved more generally.

When Hiram Johnson first ran for governor of California in 1910, he was the candidate of the middle class and the countryside. Launched into prominence by his successful prosecution of the corrupt San Francisco political boss Abe Ruef, Johnson pledged to purify California politics and to curb the Southern Pacific Railroad, the dominating power in the state's economic and political life. By his second term Johnson was championing social and labor legislation. His original base of middle-class support had eroded and been replaced by the immigrant, working-class vote that kept him in power for years. These events illustrated the most enduring achievement of progressivism: the activation of America's working people as a force in reform politics.

The cities served as the main arena for this development. Historians have called the result *urban liberalism*: that is, a reform movement by city people for social protection attained by state intervention. In New York, the activating event was a tragic fire.

Thirty minutes before quitting time on Saturday afternoon, March 25, 1911, fire broke out at the Triangle Shirtwaist Company in downtown New York City. The flames trapped the workers, mostly young immigrant women. Forty-seven leaped to their deaths; another ninety-nine never made it to the windows. The tragedy caused a national furor and led, two months later, to the creation of the New York State Factory Commission.

In the next four years, the commission developed a remarkable program of labor reform: fifty-six laws dealing with fire hazards, unsafe machines, home work, and wages and hours for women and children. The chairman of the commission was Robert F. Wagner; the vice-chairman, Alfred E. Smith. Both were Tammany Hall politicians and Democratic party leaders in the state legislature. Wagner and Smith sponsored the resolution establishing the commission, participated fully in its work, and marshaled the party regulars to pass the proposals into law. All this the two men did with the approval of the Tammany machine (see Chapter 20). The labor code that resulted was the most advanced in the United States.

Tammany's reform role reflected a trend in American cities. Urban political machines increasingly recognized their limits as social agencies in the modern industrial age. Only the state could prevent future Triangle fires or cope with the evils of factory work and city life. Also, a new generation had entered machine politics. Al Smith and Robert Wagner, men of social vision, absorbed the lessons of the Triangle investigation. They formed durable ties with such middle-class progressives as the social worker Frances Perkins, who sat on the commission as the representative of the New York Consumers League.

For all their organizational strength, moreover, the urban machines could not ignore the voters' sentiments. In the successes of such middle-class reform politicians as Toledo's Sam Jones and Cleveland's Tom Johnson, the urban machines saw the appeal of progressive pro-

The Triangle Shirtwaist Fire

The doors were the problem. Most were locked (to keep the working girls from leaving early); the few that were open became jammed by bodies as the flames spread. When the fire trucks finally came, the ladders were too short. Compared to those caught inside, the girls who leaped to their deaths were the lucky ones. "As I looked up I saw a love affair in the midst of all the horror," a reporter wrote. A young man was helping girls leap from a window. The fourth "put her arms about him and kiss[ed] him. Then he held her out into space and dropped her." He immediately followed. "Thud—dead, Thud—dead . . . I saw his face before they covered it . . . . he was a real man. He had done his best."

grams in working-class wards. There was a threat from the left as well. The Socialist party was making significant headway in the cities, electing Milwaukee's Victor Berger as the nation's first socialist congressman in 1910, and challenging the status quo by winning municipal elections in towns and cities across the country. The political universe of the urban machines had changed, and they had to pay more attention to opinion in the precincts.

The Labor Movement. Always highly pragmatic in their operations, the city machines adopted urban liberalism without much ideological struggle. The same could not be said of the trade unions, the other institution that represented American working people. During its early years the American Federation of Labor (AFL) had strongly opposed state interference in labor's affairs. Samuel Gompers preached that workers should not seek from government what they could accomplish through their own initiative and activities. Economic power and self-help, not the state, would be the worker's salvation. *Voluntarism*, as trade unionists called this antistate doctrine, did not die out, but it weakened substantially during the progressive years.

Organized labor enlisted in the cause of urban liberalism partly for defensive reasons. In the early twentieth century the labor movement came under severe attack by antiunion employers, who had at their disposal powerful legal weapons. For one thing, they could sue unions under the Sherman Antitrust Act. In the *Danbury Hatters* case (1908), the Supreme Court found a labor boycott—a call by the Hatters' Union for people not to patronize the antiunion D. E. Loewe & Company—to be a conspiracy in restraint of trade and awarded triple damages to the company. Hundreds of union members stood to lose their homes and life savings until the labor movement stepped in and raised the money to pay the fines. More harmful to the economic power of the unions was the employers' routine use of injunctions during labor disputes. (An *injunction* was a court order prohibiting a union from carrying on a strike or boycott.) The justification was to prevent "irreparable damage" to an employer while the legality of a union's acts was being adjudicated; but the effect of this "temporary" measure was to immobilize and defeat the union, as had happened, for example, to the American Railway Union in the great Pullman boycott of 1894 (see p. 573).

Only a political response might blunt these assaults on labor's economic weapons. In its "Bill of Grievances" of 1906, the AFL demanded that Congress grant unions immunity from court attack. Rebuffed, the labor movement decided to become more politically active, adopting as its strategy support on a nonpartisan basis for candidates who favored labor's program. Hence-

forth, the AFL intended to "reward our friends and punish our enemies." The practical effect of this "nonpartisan" strategy was to draw labor closer to the Democratic party, since it was more responsive than the Republicans to labor's pleas for a curb on the courts.

Having breached the political barriers for defensive reasons, the labor movement had difficulty denying the case for social legislation. The AFL, after all, claimed to speak for the entire working class. When muckrakers exposed exploitation of women and children and middle-class progressives came forward with solutions, how could the labor movement fail to respond? Gompers served on the Triangle factory commission, and if—according to Frances Perkins—he was a less eager student than the Tammanyite members, learn he did. In state after state, organized labor joined the battle for progressive legislation and increasingly became its strongest advocate. Conservative labor leaders found some consolation by making a careful distinction: protective laws were for women and children, who lacked the ability to defend themselves. In practice, however, the trade unions became more flexible about legislative protections for men as well, and on the issue of workmen's compensation, they lobbied vigorously for new legislation.

Accidents took an awful toll in American factories and mines. Two thousand coal miners were killed every year, dying from cave-ins and explosions at a rate, for example, 50 percent higher than in Germany's mines. Liability laws, still governed by common-law principles, were archaic and so heavily favored the employer that victims of industrial accidents rarely got compensated. Nothing cried out more for reform than the plight of maimed workers and penniless widows. In Germany and England, state-funded accident insurance guaranteed compensation regardless of fault. Efforts to provide comparable protections for American workers quickly received the backing of the trade unions. Between 1910 and 1917, workers' compensation for industrial accidents went into effect in all the industrial states.

In Defense of Cultural Pluralism. The economic needs of working people were not the only forces shaping urban liberal politics. It was also influenced by a sharpening attack on the cultural values and way of life of immigrants. Old-stock evangelical Protestants had long agitated for laws imposing their moral and cultural norms on American society. During the Progressive period, these activities gained a new lease on life. The Anti-Saloon League, which called itself "the Protestant church in action," became a formidable force for Prohibition in many states. Prohibiting the sale of liquor linked up with other reform objectives: the saloon made for dirty politics, poverty, and bad labor conditions.

AMERICAN VOICES

Working for the Triangle Shirtwaist Company

Pauline Newman

Pauline Newman was an organizer and educational director for the International Ladies Garment Workers Union until her death in 1986. As a child she worked at the notorious Triangle Shirtwaist factory in New York. This is her account of what life was like for women garment workers in the early twentieth century.

A cousin of mine worked for the Triangle Shirtwaist Company and she got me on there in October of 1901. It was probably the largest shirtwaist factory in the city of New York then. They had more than two hundred operators, cutters, examiners, finishers. Altogether more than four hundred people on two floors. The fire took place on one floor, the floor where we worked. You've probably heard about that. But that was years later.

We started work at seven-thirty in the morning, and during the busy season we worked until nine in the evening. They didn't pay you any overtime and they didn't give you anything for supper money. Sometimes they'd give you a little apple pie if you had to work very late. That was all. Very generous.

What I had to do was not really very difficult. It was just monotonous. When the shirtwaists were finished at the machine there were some threads that were left, and all the youngsters—we had a corner on the floor that resembled a kindergarten—we were given little scissors to cut the threads off. It wasn't heavy work, but it was monotonous, because you did the same thing from seven-thirty in the morning until nine at night.

Well, of course, there were [child labor] laws on the books, but no one

bothered to enforce them. The employers were always tipped off if there was going to be an inspection. "Quick," they'd say, "into the boxes!" And we children would climb into the big boxes the finished shirts were stored in. Then some shirts were piled on top of us, and when the inspector came—no children. The factory always got an okay from the inspector, and I suppose someone at City Hall got a little something, too.

The employers didn't recognize anyone working for them as a human being. You were not allowed to sing. Operators would have liked to have sung, because they, too, had the same thing to do and weren't allowed to sing. We weren't allowed to talk to each other. Oh, no, they would sneak up behind if you were found talking to your next colleague. You were admonished: "If you keep on you'll be fired." If you went to the toilet and you were there longer than the floor lady thought you should be, you would be laid off for half a day and sent home. And, of course, that meant no pay. You were not allowed to have your lunch on the fire escape in the summertime. The door was locked to keep us in. That's why so many people were trapped when the fire broke out....

I stopped working at the Triangle Factory during the strike in 1909 and I didn't go back. The union sent me out to raise money for the strikers. I apparently was able to articulate my feelings and opinions about the criminal conditions, and they didn't have anyone else who could do better so they assigned me....

After the 1909 strike I worked with the union, organizing in Philadelphia and Cleveland and other places,

so I wasn't at the Triangle Shirtwaist Factory when the fire broke out, but a lot of my friends were. I was in Philadelphia for the union and, of course, someone from here called me immediately and I came back. It's very difficult to describe the feeling because I knew the place and I knew so many of the girls. The thing that bothered me was the employers got a lawyer. How anyone could have *defended* them— because I'm quite sure that the fire was planned for insurance purposes. And no one is going to convince me otherwise. And when they testified that the door to the fire escape was open, it was a lie! It was never open. Locked all the time. One hundred and forty-six people were sacrificed, and the judge fined Blank and Harris seventy-five dollars!

Conditions were dreadful in those days. But there was something that is lacking today and I think it was the devotion and the belief....

Even when things were terrible, I always had that faith.... Only now, I'm a little discouraged sometimes when I see the workers spending their free hours watching television—trash. We fought so hard for those hours and they waste them. We used to read Tolstoy, Dickens, Shelley, by candlelight, and they watch the "Hollywood Squares." Well, they're free to do what they want. That's what we fought for.

Source: Joan Morrison and Charlotte Fox Zabusky, eds., *American Mosaic: The Immigrant Experience in the Words of Those Who Lived It* (New York: E.P. Dutton, 1980), pp. 9–14. Copyright © 1980 by Joan Morrison and Charlotte Fox Zabusky. Reprinted by permission.

The moral-reform agenda expanded to include a new goal: restricting the immigration of southern and Eastern Europeans into the United States. "The entrance . . . of such vast masses of peasantry, degraded below our utmost concepts, is a matter which no intelligent patriot can look upon without the gravest apprehension and alarm," warned Francis A. Walker, the president of the Massachusetts Institute of Technology. These concerns were shared by many progressive academics—for example, by La Follette's close adviser Edward A. Ross of the University of Wisconsin, who denounced the "pigsty mode of life" of the immigrants. The danger, respected social scientists argued, was that the nation's Anglo-Saxon population would be "mongrelized" and its American civilization swamped by "inferior" Mediterranean and Slavic cultures. Feeding on this fear, the Immigration Restriction League spearheaded a movement to end America's historic open-door policy. Like Prohibition, immigration restriction was considered by its proponents to be a progressive reform.

Urban liberals thought otherwise. They bitterly resented the demands for Prohibition and immigration restriction as unwarranted attacks on the personal liberty and worthiness of urban immigrants. Prohibition, protested one Catholic academic, was "despotic and hypocritical domination." The Tammany politician Martin McCue accused the Protestant ministry of "seeking to substitute the policeman's nightstick for the Bible."

Urban liberal leaders championed both the economic needs of city dwellers and their right to follow their religious and cultural preferences. In many ways, certainly until the Great Depression of the 1930s, ethnocultural issues provided the stronger basis for urban liberal politics. And because the Democrats were the party identified with tolerance and diversity, they became the beneficiaries of the rise of urban liberalism. The growing size of the city vote destined the Democrats to become the majority party. The shift from Republican domination, although not completed until the 1930s, began during the Progressive Era.

Racism in an Age of Reform

The direct primary was the flagship of progressive politics—the crucial reform, as La Follette said, for defeating the party bosses and returning politics to "the people." The primary electoral system of nominating party candidates originated not in Wisconsin, however, but in the South, and by the time La Follette got his primary law in 1903, it was already operating in seven southern states. As in the North, the southern primary was celebrated as a democratizing reform, and its adoption was frequently the opening victory that brought reform administrations into power.

In the South, however, it was a *white* primary; black voters were excluded, and since the Democratic nomination was tantamount to election, to be excluded from the primary meant in effect to be disfranchised. The direct primary was a reform *intended* among other things to drive blacks out of politics. How could democratic reform and white supremacy be thus wedded together?

The answer is to be found in the racist thinking of the age. "A black skin means membership in a race of men which has never of itself succeeded to reason," pronounced Professor John W. Burgess of Columbia University in a 1902 book on Reconstruction, and for Congress to have granted blacks the vote after the Civil War was a "monstrous thing." Burgess was a southern-born historian, but he was confident that his northern audience saw the "vast differences in political capacity" between blacks and whites and approved of black disfranchisement in the South. Even the Republican party, once it reconciled itself to relying on "lily white" organizations in the South midway through Roosevelt's administration, had no quarrel with this view. Indeed, as president-elect in 1908, William Howard Taft applauded the southern laws as necessary to "prevent entirely the possibility of domination by . . . an ignorant electorate" and reassured southerners that "the federal government has nothing to do with social equality."

In the North, the Progressive Era was marked by growing racial tensions. Over 200,000 blacks migrated from the South between 1900 and 1910. Their arrival in northern cities invariably sparked white resentment. Attacks on blacks became widespread. The worst episode was a bloody race riot in Springfield, Illinois, in 1908. Even more indicative of the popular racism infecting the North was the huge success of D. W. Griffith's epic film *Birth of a Nation* (1915), with its crude depiction of Reconstruction as a moral struggle between rampaging, childlike blacks and a chivalrous Ku Klux Klan. Woodrow Wilson found the film's history "all so terribly true." His Democratic administration marked a sad low point for the federal government as ultimate guarantor of the principle of equal rights: during Wilson's tenure, segregation of the U.S. civil service would have gone into effect but for the outcry it raised among black leaders and a handful of influential white progressives.

The Revival of the Civil Rights Struggle. In these bleak years, a core of young black professionals, mostly northern-born, began to fight back. The key figure was William Monroe Trotter, the pugnacious editor of the-

Boston *Guardian* and an outspoken critic of Booker T. Washington (see Chapter 19). "The policy of compromise has failed," argued Trotter. "The policy of resistance and aggression deserves a trial." In this endeavor, Trotter was joined in 1903 by W. E. B. Du Bois, a Harvard-trained sociologist and the preeminent black intellectual of his day. In 1906 the two of them, having broken with Washington, called a meeting of twenty-nine supporters at Niagara Falls—but in Canada, because no hotel on the U.S. side would admit blacks. The Niagara Movement, which resulted from that meeting, had an impact far beyond the scattering of members and local bodies it organized. The principles it affirmed would thereafter define the struggle for the rights of African-Americans: first, encouragement of black pride by all possible means; second, an uncompromising demand for full political and civil equality. Above all, "We refuse to allow the impression to remain that the Negro-American assents to inferiority, is submissive under oppression and apologetic before insults."

The revival of black protest found a small echo within white progressivism. Going against the grain, a handful of reformers were drawn to the plight of African-Americans. Among the most devoted was Mary White Ovington. By upper-class background and social outlook, she very much resembled Jane Addams, except that Ovington came from a family of abolitionists and thought of herself as a socialist. Like Addams, Ovington became a settlement-house worker, but among urban blacks rather than in an immigrant neighborhood. News of the bloody Springfield race riot of 1908 changed her life. Convinced that her duty lay in the struggle for equal rights, Ovington called a meeting of sympathetic white progressives that led to the formation of the National Association for the Advancement of Colored People in 1909.

The Niagara Movement, torn apart by internal disagreements, was breaking up, and most of the black activists joined the NAACP. Its national leadership was in the early years dominated by whites, however. The one exception proved to be of crucial importance. Du Bois became the editor of the NAACP's journal *The Crisis*. With a passion that only a black voice could provide, Du Bois used that platform to proclaim the demands for black equality.

In the social welfare field, the principal concern during the Progressive Era was over the needs of black migrants arriving in northern cities. In 1911 the National Urban League united the principal organizations that had sprung up to assist black migrants. Like the NAACP, the Urban League was interracial, including white reformers like Ovington and black welfare activists like William Lewis Bulkley, the New York school principal who played the single most important role in the founding of the Urban League.

Progressivism was a house of many chambers. Most were infected by the respectable racism of the age, but not all. There was a saving remnant of white progressives who allied themselves with black activists and created, in the NAACP and the Urban League, the national institutions that would dominate the black struggle for a better life over the next half-century.

Editorial Office, The Crisis

In its early years, no activity undertaken by the NAACP was more important than publication of its journal, *The Crisis*, which under the brilliant editorship of W. E. B. Du Bois became the strongest voice for equal rights and black pride in the country. In this photograph of the magazine's editorial office, Du Bois is the balding man at the right rear.

Progressivism and National Politics

The gathering forces of progressivism reached the national scene only slowly. Reformers had been activated by immediate concerns—by problems that affected them directly, and by evils visible and tangible to them. Washington seemed remote from the battles they were waging in their cities and states. But progressivism was bound to come to the capital. In 1906, Robert La Follette moved from the governor's office in Wisconsin to the U.S. Senate. Other seasoned progressives, also ambitious for a wider stage, made the same move. By 1910, a highly vocal progressive bloc was making itself heard in both houses of Congress.

The crucial entry point of progressivism into national politics was not Congress, however, but the presidency. This was partly because the presidential office was a "bully pulpit"—to use Theodore Roosevelt's words—for mobilizing opinion and defining national issues. But just as important was the twist of fate that brought Roosevelt—the epitome of the progressive politician—to the White House on September 14, 1901.

The Making of a Progressive President

Except for his rather aristocratic background, Theodore Roosevelt was cut from much the same cloth as other progressive politicians. Born in 1858, he came from a wealthy, old-line New York family, attended Harvard, and might well have chosen the life of a leisured, literary gentleman. Instead, scarcely out of college, he plunged into Republican politics and in 1882 entered the New York state legislature. His reasons matched the high-minded motives of other budding progressives. Like most of them, Roosevelt had received a moralistic, Christian upbringing. A political career would enable him to act constructively on those beliefs. Roosevelt always identified himself—loudly—with the side of righteousness. On the other hand, he did not scorn power and its uses. He showed contempt for the amateurism of the Mugwumps— "those political and literary hermaphrodites," he called them—and much preferred the professionalism of party politics. Roosevelt rose in the New York party because he skillfully translated his moral fervor into broad popular support and thus forced himself on reluctant state Republican bosses.

After returning from the Spanish-American War as the hero of San Juan Hill (see Chapter 22), Roosevelt won the New York governorship in 1898. During his single term he clearly indicated his inclinations toward reform. Roosevelt pushed through civil-service reform and a tax on corporate franchises. He discharged the corrupt superintendent of insurance over the Republican party's objections and asserted his confidence in the government's capacity to improve the life of the people.

In an attempt to neutralize him, the party bosses promoted Roosevelt in 1900 to what normally would have been a dead-end job as William McKinley's vice-president. Roosevelt accepted reluctantly. But on September 6, 1901, an anarchist named Leon F. Czolgosz shot the president. When McKinley died eight days later, Roosevelt became president. It was a sure bet, groaned Republican boss Mark Hanna, that "that damn cowboy" would make trouble in the White House.

Roosevelt in fact moved cautiously at the outset. In his first official statement, he reassured the nation that he would "continue absolutely unbroken" McKinley's policies. The conservative Republican bloc in Congress greatly limited his freedom of action. He treated the Senate leader, Nelson W. Aldrich of Rhode Island, with kid gloves. Much of Roosevelt's energy was devoted to consolidating his position. He skillfully used the patronage powers of his office to gain control of the Republican party. But Roosevelt was also restrained by uncertainty about what reform role the federal government ought to play. At first, the new president might have been described as a progressive without a cause.

Even so, Roosevelt gave early evidence of his activist bent. An ardent outdoorsman, he devoted part of his first annual message to conservation. A national movement had begun in the late nineteenth century to protect the country's natural resources and scenic wonders against reckless exploitation. With the establishment of Yellowstone National Park in 1872, the national park system had been launched, and the Forest Reserve Act of 1891 began the process of withdrawing timberlands from unregulated commercial use.

Unlike John Muir (see Chapter 17), Roosevelt was not a preservationist broadly opposed to the exploitation of the nation's wilderness. Rather, Roosevelt aimed at *conserving* the nation's public resources. He was not against commercial development, so long as it was regulated and mindful of the public interest. Roosevelt added more than 125 million acres to the national forest reserve and brought mineral lands and water power sites into the reserve system. In 1902 he backed the Newlands Reclamation Act, which designated the proceeds from public land sales for irrigation development in arid regions. His administration strongly upgraded the management of public lands and, to the chagrin of some Republicans, energetically prosecuted violators of federal land laws. In the cause of conservation, Roosevelt demonstrated his enthusiasm for exercising executive authority and his disdain for those who sought profit "by betraying the public."

The same inclinations influenced Roosevelt's handling of the anthracite coal strike of 1902. Hard coal was the main fuel for home heating in those days. As cold weather approached with no settlement in sight, the government faced a national emergency. The United Mine Workers, led by John Mitchell, were willing to submit to arbitration, but the coal operators adamantly opposed any recognition of the union. Roosevelt's advisers told him there was no legal basis for federal intervention. Nevertheless, the president called both sides to a conference at the White House on October 1, 1902. When the conference failed, Roosevelt threatened the operators with a government take-over of the mines. He also persuaded the financier J. P. Morgan to use his considerable influence with them. At this point the coal operators caved in. The strike ended with the appointment by Roosevelt of an arbitration commission to rule on the issues, another unprecedented step. Roosevelt did not especially support organized labor, but he became infuriated by what he labeled the "arrogant stupidity" of the mine employers.

"Of all the forms of tyranny the least attractive and the most vulgar is the tyranny of mere wealth," Roosevelt wrote in his autobiography. He was prepared to deploy all his presidential authority against the "tyranny" of irresponsible business.

The Trust Problem. The economic issue that most concerned Roosevelt was a disturbing assault on the competitive market by big business. The drift toward large-scale enterprise had been under way for many years, as entrepreneurs sought the efficiencies of nationwide, vertically integrated operations (see Chapter 18). But building larger business units was also a way of limiting competition and controlling markets. The depression of the 1890s, which had driven down prices and caused staggering business losses, led to an astonishing scramble to merge rival firms once economic recovery began in 1897. These mergers—*trusts*, as they were called—greatly increased the degree of business concentration in the economy. Of the 73 largest industrial companies in 1900, 53 had not existed three years earlier. By 1910, 1 percent of the nation's manufacturers accounted for 44 percent of the total industrial output.

The sheer economic power of the new combines was not their only disturbing feature. Most of them were heavily *watered*—that is, the stocks and bonds they issued much exceeded the real value of the properties they controlled. For their underwriting services in launching the new trusts, moreover, investment bankers such as J. P. Morgan charged huge fees. Worse yet, financiers did not relinquish control over the combines they had fathered, for they sat on the boards of directors of the new firms and behind the scenes exerted heavy influence on the operating executives. Almost overnight, a "money power"—a handful of Wall Street bankers—seemed to have gained a stranglehold on the American economy.

Roosevelt's sense of the nation's uneasiness became evident as early as his first annual message, in which he referred to the "real and grave evils" of economic concentration. But what weapons could the president use in response?

The basic legal principles upholding free competition were already firmly established. Under the common law—the body of court-made legal precedents that America had inherited from England—it was illegal for anyone to conspire to restrain or monopolize trade; persons economically injured by such actions could sue for damages. These common-law rights had been enacted into statute law in many states during the 1880s, and then, because the magnitude of the problem exceeded

Jack and the Wall Street Giants

In this vivid cartoon from the humor magazine *Puck*, Jack (Teddy Roosevelt) has come to slay the giants of Wall Street. To the country, trust busting took on the mythic qualities of the fairy tale—with about the same amount of awe for the fearsome Wall Street giants and hope in the prowess of the intrepid Roosevelt. J. Pierpont Morgan is the giant leering at front right.

state jurisdictions, had been incorporated into the Sherman Antitrust Act of 1890 and become part of federal law.

Neither the Cleveland nor the McKinley administrations had been much inclined to enforce the Sherman Act, except against organized labor. Of the eighteen federal suits brought before 1901, half were against trade unions. Nor were the courts any more enthusiastic about attacking business. In *U.S. v. E. C. Knight* (1895), the Supreme Court ruled that manufacturing was not covered by the Constitution's commerce clause and hence lay beyond the reach of federal antitrust regulation. This ruling crippled the Sherman Act but did not kill it. The potential of the act rested, above all, in the fact that it incorporated common-law principles of unimpeachable validity. In the right hands, the Sherman Act could be a strong weapon against the abuse of economic power.

Trust Busting. Roosevelt made his opening move when he strengthened the government's capacity to enforce the law. In 1903, despite considerable opposition, Congress accepted Roosevelt's proposal for a Bureau of Corporations within the newly created Department of Commerce and Labor. Empowered to investigate business practices, the bureau provided the factual record on which the Justice Department could mount antitrust suits. The first suit had already been filed in 1902 against the Northern Securities Company, a combination of the railroad systems of the Northwest. In a landmark 1904 decision, the Supreme Court ordered Northern Securities dissolved. The next year, the Court reversed the *Knight* doctrine: it ruled that manufacturing fell within the commerce clause and was therefore subject to federal antitrust law.

In 1904, Roosevelt handily defeated a weak conservative Democratic candidate, Judge Alton B. Parker. Now president in his own right, Roosevelt stepped up the attack on the trusts. He took on forty-five of the nation's giant firms, including Standard Oil, American Tobacco, and DuPont. The president accompanied these actions with a rising crescendo of rhetoric. He became the nation's trust buster, a crusader against "predatory wealth."

Despite his rhetoric, Roosevelt was not antibusiness; he regarded large-scale enterprise as a natural result of modern industrialism. Only firms that abused their power deserved punishment. But how would those companies be identified? Under the common law, and under the Sherman Act as originally intended, it had been up to the courts to decide whether a given act in restraint of trade was "unreasonable"—that is, actually harmed potential competitors or damaged the public interest. This was a highly flexible approach, enabling the courts to evaluate the actions of corporations on a case-by-case basis. In 1897, however, the Supreme Court had

repudiated this "rule of reason" in the *Trans-Missouri* case. Now, even if the impact on the market was not harmful, actions that restrained or monopolized trade would automatically put a firm in violation of the Sherman law.

Little noticed when it was first decided, *Trans-Missouri* placed Roosevelt in an awkward position when he began to enforce the Sherman Act. Roosevelt had no desire to hamstring legitimate business activity. But he could not rely on the courts to distinguish between "good" and "bad" trusts. The only solution was for the executive to assume that responsibility. This the president could do because it was up to him—or his attorney general—to decide whether or not to initiate antitrust prosecutions in the first place.

That Roosevelt would use this discretionary power became clear in November 1904, shortly after the Bureau of Corporations began to investigate the United States Steel Corporation. The company chairman, Elbert H. Gary, asked for a meeting with Roosevelt. Gary proposed an arrangement: cooperation in exchange for preferential treatment. The company would open its books to the Bureau of Corporations. If the bureau found evidence of wrongdoing, the company would be

J. Pierpont Morgan

J. P. Morgan was the giant among American financiers. He had served an apprenticeship in investment banking under his father, a leading Anglo-American banker in London. A gruff man of few words, Morgan had a genius for instilling trust, and the strength of will to persuade others to follow his lead and do his bidding—qualities the great photographer Edward Steichen captured in this portrait. (The Museum of Modern Art, New York) advised privately and given a chance to set matters right. Roosevelt accepted this "gentlemen's agreement," which was followed by one with International Harvester the next year. J. P. Morgan controlled both firms. From the financier's standpoint, the arrangement seemed entirely sensible. Two great powers, one political and the other economic, would meet as equals and settle matters between them. For Roosevelt, the gentlemen's agreements eased a serious dilemma. He could accommodate the realities of the modern industrial order while maintaining his public image as the champion against the trusts.

Railroad Regulation. Abuse of economic power by the railroads posed a somewhat different kind of problem for Roosevelt. As quasi-public enterprises, the railroads had always been subject to public regulation. Initially, this had been the responsibility of the states, but with the passage of the Interstate Commerce Act of 1887, the federal government had entered the field, establishing in the Interstate Commerce Commission the nation's first federal regulatory agency. As with the Sherman Act, however, railroad regulation remained pretty much a dead letter in its early years. Restrained by a hostile Supreme Court, the ICC lapsed into a mere collector of statistics. Roosevelt was convinced, however, that the railroads needed firm regulation. The Elkins Act of 1903 empowered the ICC to act against discriminatory rebates—that is, reductions on published rates for preferred or powerful customers. Then, with the 1904 election behind him, Roosevelt made his push for a major expansion of railroad regulation.

The central issue was the setting of rates. Roosevelt considered it essential that the ICC have this power. Senator Nelson Aldrich and his conservative bloc opposed it just as firmly. In 1906, after nearly two years of wrangling, Congress passed the Hepburn Railway Act. This law empowered the ICC to set and put into effect maximum rates upon complaint of a shipper and gave it the authority to examine railroad books and prescribe uniform bookkeeping. But as a concession to the conservative bloc the courts retained broad powers to review ICC rate decisions.

The Hepburn Act stood as a testament to Roosevelt's skills as a political operator. He had maneuvered brilliantly against determined opposition and come away with the essentials of what he wanted. Despite grumbling by Senate progressives critical of any compromise, Roosevelt was satisfied. He had achieved a landmark expansion of the government's regulatory powers over business.

Consumer Protection. The regulation of consumer products, another hallmark of progressive reform, was very much the handiwork of muckraking journalists. In 1905 Samuel Hopkins Adams published a series of arti-

cles on the patent-medicine business in *Collier's*. The first paragraph opened with these riveting words:

> Gullible America will spend this year some seventy-five millions of dollars in the purchase of patent medicines. In consideration of this sum it will swallow huge quantities of alcohol, an appalling amount of opiates and narcotics, a wide assortment of varied drugs ranging from powerful and dangerous heart depressants to insidious liver stimulants; and, far in excess of all other ingredients, undiluted fraud. For fraud, exploited by the skillfullest of advertising bunco men, is the basis of the trade.

Numerous pure food and drug bills, introduced in Congress in 1905, had been stymied by industry lobbies. Then, in 1906, Upton Sinclair's novel *The Jungle* appeared. Sinclair had aimed at exposing labor exploitation in the Chicago meat-packing plants, but his graphic descriptions of rotten meat and filthy conditions excited—and sickened—the nation. President Roosevelt, hitherto not greatly concerned about consumer issues, now threw his weight into the legislative battle, initiating a federal investigation of conditions in the stockyards and threatening to make public its harsh findings unless Congress took swift action. The Pure

Campaigning for the Square Deal
When William McKinley ran for president in 1896, he sat on his front porch in Canton, Ohio, and received delegations of voters. That was not Theodore Roosevelt's way. He considered the presidency a "bully pulpit," and he used the office brilliantly to mobilize public opinion and to assert his leadership. The preeminence of the presidency in American public life begins with Roosevelt's administration. Here, at the height of his crusading powers, he stumps for the Square Deal in the 1904 election.

Food and Drug Act and the Meat Inspection Act passed within months. And another administrative agency was added to federal bureaucratic structure that Roosevelt was building—the Food and Drug Administration.

The Square Deal. During the 1904 presidential campaign, Roosevelt had taken to calling his program "the Square Deal." This kind of labeling was new to American politics. It introduced a political style that dramatized issues, mobilized public opinion, and asserted leadership. But the Square Deal meant something of substance as well. After many years of passivity and weakness, the federal government was reclaiming the large role it had abandoned after the Civil War. Now, however, the target had become the new economic order. When companies misused corporate power, the government had the responsibility for correcting matters and assuring ordinary Americans of a "square deal." Under Roosevelt's leadership, progressivism had come to national politics.

The Fracturing of Republican Progressivism

During his two terms as president, Theodore Roosevelt struggled to bring a modern corporate economy under control. He was well aware, however, that his Square Deal was built on nineteenth-century foundations; in particular, antitrust doctrine, which aimed at enforcing competition, seemed to Roosevelt inadequate to the demands of a large-scale industrial order. A better approach, he felt, would be to give the federal government the administrative powers to oversee and regulate big business. In his final presidential speeches, Roosevelt dwelt on the need for a reform agenda for the twentieth century. When he left office in 1909, he thought he had arranged matters so that there would be steady movement in that direction. He was mistaken. By the time Roosevelt returned from a year-long safari in Africa, turmoil reigned in Washington.

The Presidency of William Howard Taft. The agents of historical change sometimes take strange forms. A person out of tune with the times can, by the sheer friction he or she generates, serve as the catalyst for great events. Such became the fate of William Howard Taft, Roosevelt's hand-picked successor.

Taft's Democratic opponent in the 1908 campaign was William Jennings Bryan. This was Bryan's third—and last—try for the presidency, and he made the most of it. Eloquent as ever, Bryan showed again why he was known as the Commoner, the voice of the people. He attacked the Republicans as the party of the "plutocrats," and outdid them in urging stronger antitrust legislation, lower tariffs, stricter railway regulation, and

labor legislation so favorable to the unions as to gain the support of the officially nonpartisan AFL. Bryan's campaign moved the Democratic party into the mainstream of national progressive politics, but this was not enough to offset Taft's advantages as President Roosevelt's candidate. Taft won comfortably, if by a smaller margin than Roosevelt's smashing 1904 victory, and he entered the White House with a mandate to pick up where TR had left off.

William Howard Taft was an estimable man in many ways. He had been an able jurist and a superb administrator. He had served Roosevelt loyally and well as governor general of the Philippines and as secretary of war. He was an avowed Square Dealer. But he was not by nature a progressive politician. Taft was incapable of dramatizing issues or of stirring the people. He disliked the give-and-take of politics, he distrusted power, and he generally deferred to Congress. In fundamental ways, moreover, Taft was deeply conservative. He sanctified property rights, he revered the processes of the law, and unlike Roosevelt, he found it hard to trim his means to fit his ends.

By 1909, the ferment of reform had unsettled the Republican party. On the right, the conservatives were girding themselves against further losses. Under Senator Aldrich, they were still a force to be reckoned with both on Capitol Hill and within the party. On the other hand, progressive Republicans were rebellious. They had broad popular support—especially in the Midwest—and, in Robert La Follette, a fiery leader. They felt that Roosevelt had made too many concessions to business interests. With the resourceful Roosevelt gone from the White House, the Congressional progressives were determined to have their way. Reconciling these conflicting forces within the Republican party would have been a daunting task for the most accomplished politician. For Taft, it spelled disaster.

First there was the tariff. Progressives generally considered high tariffs to be a major cause for the decline of competition and the rise of the trusts. Taft had campaigned for a "sizable reduction." During the lengthy drafting process, however, he was won over by the conservative Republican bloc and gave his approval for the protectionist Payne-Aldrich Tariff Act of 1909, which favored eastern industry.

Next came the battle over "Uncle Joe" Cannon, Speaker of the House of Representatives. A dyed-in-the-wool conservative, Cannon virtually controlled the flow of legislation in the House. Progressives were determined to depose him. Taft abandoned them in exchange for Cannon's help on administration legislation. When a House revolt finally broke the Speaker's power in 1910, Cannon's defeat was regarded as a defeat for the president as well.

Equally damaging to Taft was the Pinchot-Ballinger affair. U.S. Chief Forester Gifford Pinchot, an ardent conservationist and a chum of Roosevelt's, accused Secretary of the Interior Richard A. Ballinger of conspiring to transfer public coal lands in Alaska to a private syndicate. When Pinchot made the charges public in January 1910, Taft fired him for insubordination. The fact that Taft was actually a dedicated conservationist some how did not matter. In the eyes of the progressives, the Pinchot-Ballinger affair marked Taft for life as a friend of the "interests" plundering the nation's resources.

Solemnly pledged to carry on in Roosevelt's tradition, Taft managed to work his way into the conservative Republican camp in less than two years. While doing so, he helped transform the reformers into a distinct faction of the Republican party. By 1910 they were calling themselves "Progressives" or, in more belligerent moments, "Insurgents." Taft responded by trying to purge them in the Republican primaries that year. This vendetta climaxed Taft's record of disastrous leadership.

The Progressive Insurgency. The Progressives emerged from the 1910 elections stronger and angrier than ever. In January 1911 they formed the National Progressive Republican League and began a drive to take control of the Republican party. La Follette was the Progressives' leader and their designated presidential candidate, but they knew that their best chance to win lay with Theodore Roosevelt.

Roosevelt, home from Africa, yearned to reenter the political fray. He was not easily reconciled to the absence of power and would have been troublesome for Taft under any circumstances. As it was, the president's handling of the Progressives fed Roosevelt's mounting sense of outrage. But Roosevelt was too loyal a party man to defy the Republican establishment, and too astute a politician not to recognize that a party split would benefit the Democrats. He could be spurred into rebellion only by the discovery of a true clash of principles. On the question of the trusts, such a clash materialized.

From the first, Roosevelt had been troubled by the Sherman Antitrust Act. To enforce competition seemed to him to fly in the face of the inevitable modern tendency toward economic concentration. By distinguishing between good and bad trusts, Roosevelt had managed to reconcile public policy and economic reality. But this was a makeshift solution, depending as it did on a president inclined to stretch his powers to the limit. Taft had no such inclination. His legalistic mind rebelled at the discretionary use of presidential authority over instituting antitrust suits. The Sherman Act was on the books. "We are going to enforce that law or die in the attempt," Taft promised grimly.

In its *Standard Oil* decision (1911), the Supreme Court eased Taft's dilemma by reasserting the common-law principle of the "rule of reason" on antitrust actions: once again, it would be up to the courts to distinguish between "good" and "bad" trusts. With that burden lifted from the executive branch, Attorney General George W. Wickersham stepped up the pace of antitrust actions.

The United States Steel Corporation immediately became a prime target. Among the charges against the Steel Trust was that it had violated the antimonopoly provision of the Sherman Act by acquiring the Tennessee Coal and Iron Company. The purchase had been made in 1907 from a banking house that had fallen into trouble and urgently needed to sell its TCI stock in order to raise capital. Roosevelt had personally approved the acquisition as a necessary step—so U.S. Steel representatives had explained it to him—to prevent a financial collapse on Wall Street. Taft's suit against U.S. Steel thus amounted to an attack on Roosevelt: he had as president entered into a private agreement with U.S. Steel to circumvent the Sherman Act. Nothing was better calculated to propel Roosevelt into action than an issue that was both an affair of personal honor and a question of broad principle.

The New Nationalism. The country did not have to choose between breaking up big business and submitting to corporate rule, Roosevelt argued. There was a third way. The federal government could be empowered to oversee big business to make sure it acted in the public interest. The tool would be a federal trade commission with powers comparable to those exerted by the Interstate Commerce Commission over the railroads. The nation's industrial corporations would be treated, in effect, as if they were natural monopolies or public utilities and placed under direct public oversight.

In a speech in Osawatomie, Kansas, in August 1910, Roosevelt made his case for what he called the New Nationalism. The central issue, he argued, was human welfare versus property rights. In modern society, property had to be controlled "to whatever degree the public welfare may require it." The government would become "the steward of the public welfare."

This formulation removed the restraints from Roosevelt's thinking. Ultimately, he did not stop short of advocating government price fixing for corporate industry. He took up the cause of social justice, adding to his program a federal child labor law, federal workmen's compensation, regulation of labor relations, and a national minimum wage for women. Most radical perhaps was Roosevelt's attack on the legal system. Insisting that the courts should not be making social policy, Roosevelt proposed sharp curbs on their powers, even raising the possibility of popular recall of court decisions.

Beyond these specifics, the New Nationalism presented a new political philosophy. The key source was a book by the journalist Herbert Croly, *The Promise of American Life* (1909), which called for a uniting of rival strains in the American political tradition. From Hamilton's federalism, Croly drew his emphasis on strong national government; from Jefferson's republicanism came Croly's enthusiasm for democracy and the primacy of the interests of the common citizen. The result, however, was a genuine break from America's political past. The New Nationalism offered a *statist* solution—an enormous expansion of the role of the federal government—to the problem of corporate power.

Early in 1912, Roosevelt announced his candidacy for the presidency and immediately swept the Progressive Republicans into his camp. A bitter and divisive party battle ensued. Taft proved to be a tenacious opponent. Roosevelt won the states that held primary elections, but Taft controlled the party organizations elsewhere. The party regulars dominated the national convention, and they threw the nomination to Taft.

Roosevelt, considering himself cheated out of the nomination, led his followers into a new Progressive party, soon nicknamed the "Bull Moose" party. In a crusading campaign, Roosevelt offered the New Nationalism to the people.

Woodrow Wilson and the New Freedom

While the Republicans battled among themselves, the Democrats were on the move. The scars caused by the free silver campaign of 1896 had faded, and in the 1908 campaign William Jennings Bryan had established the progressive credentials of the rejuvenated party. In the 1910 elections, the Democrats made dramatic gains, taking over the House of Representatives for the first time since 1892, winning ten Senate seats, and capturing a number of traditionally Republican governorships. After fourteen years as party standard-bearer, Bryan now reluctantly made way for a new generation of leaders.

The ablest, by all odds, was Woodrow Wilson of New Jersey. Wilson was an academic, a noted political scientist who, as president of Princeton, had brought it to the front rank of American universities. In 1910, without ever before running for public office, he left Princeton to accept the Democratic nomination for governor of New Jersey. Wilson compiled a brilliant record as governor and went on, in a bruising battle, to win the Democratic presidential nomination in 1912. He could identify himself as a reformer by his achievements in New Jersey—defeat of the boss system and passage of a direct primary law, workmen's compensation, and the regulation of railroads and utilities.

Wilson possessed, to a fault, the moral certainty

On to the White House

At the Democratic convention, Woodrow Wilson only narrowly defeated the front runner, Champ Clark of Missouri. *Harper's Weekly* triumphantly depicted Wilson immediately after his nomination—the scholar turned politician riding off on the Democratic donkey, his running mate, Thomas R. Marshall, hanging on behind. *Harper's* editor, George Harvey, had identified Wilson as of presidential timber as early as 1906, long before the Princeton president had thought of politics, and worked on his behalf ever since.

that characterized the progressive politician. A brilliant speaker, he almost instinctively assumed the mantle of righteousness and showed little tolerance for the views of his critics. Only gradually, however, did Wilson hammer out, in reaction to Roosevelt's New Nationalism, a coherent reform program, which he called the New Freedom.

It is important to recognize how much ground Wilson shared with Roosevelt. "*The old time of individual competition is probably gone by*," Wilson stressed. "We will do business henceforth, when we do it on a great and successful scale, by means of corporations." Like Roosevelt, Wilson opposed not bigness, but the abuse of economic power. Nor did Wilson think that the abuse of power could be prevented without a strong federal government. Where he parted company from Roosevelt was over *how* the authority of government should be used to restrain private power.

Direct control over corporations by the federal government as advocated by Roosevelt was an anathema to Wilson. As he warmed to the debate, Wilson cast the issue in the fundamental terms of slavery and freedom. "This is a struggle for emancipation," he proclaimed in October 1912. "If America is not to have free enterprise, then she can have freedom of no sort whatever." Wilson also scorned Roosevelt's social welfare program. It might be benevolent, he declared, but it also would be paternalistic and contrary to the traditions of a free people. The New Nationalism represented a future of collectivism, Wilson warned, whereas the New Freedom would conserve the political and economic liberties of the individual.

How, then, did Wilson propose to deal with the problem of corporate power? Court enforcement of the Sherman Act was Wilson's basic answer. His task was to figure out how to make that long-established antitrust approach work better. In this effort Wilson relied heavily on a new adviser, Louis D. Brandeis, famous as the "people's lawyer" for his public service in many progressive causes (including the landmark *Muller* case).

An expert on regulatory matters, Brandeis understood that an all-powerful trade commission was likely to end up not as the defender of the public interest but in a cozy relationship with the industries it was supposed to regulate. Nor did Brandeis believe that bigness meant efficiency. On the contrary, he argued that the trusts were inherently wasteful compared to firms vigorously competing in a free market. The main thing was to prevent the trusts from unfairly using their power to curb that free competition. The aim of public policy should be "so [to] restrict the wrong use of competition that the right use of competition will destroy monopoly."

The 1912 election fell far short of being a great referendum on the New Nationalism versus the New Freedom. The outcome turned on a more humdrum reality: Wilson was elected because he kept the traditional Democratic vote while the Republicans split between Roosevelt and Taft. Although he won by a landslide in the electoral college, Wilson received only 42 percent of the popular vote—115,000 fewer votes than Bryan had amassed against Taft in 1908.

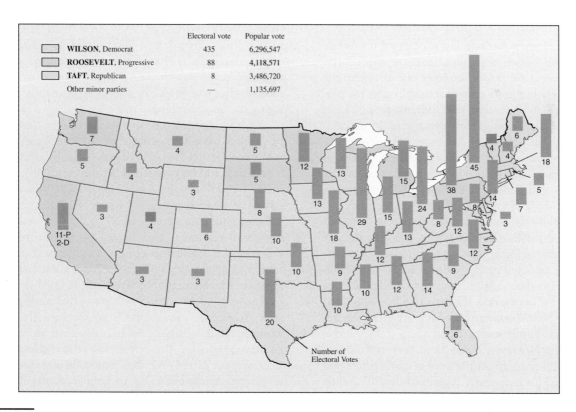

	Electoral vote	Popular vote
WILSON, Democrat	435	6,296,547
ROOSEVELT, Progressive	88	4,118,571
TAFT, Republican	8	3,486,720
Other minor parties	—	1,135,697

Number of Electoral Votes

MAP 21.2

The Election of 1912

The 1912 election reveals why the two-party system has been so strongly rooted in American politics. The Democrats, although a minority party, won an electoral landslide because the Republicans divided their vote between Roosevelt and Taft. The disastrous result indicated the enormous incentive for major parties against splintering. The Socialists, despite a record vote of 900,000, got no electoral votes at all. To vote Socialist in 1912 meant, in effect, to throw away one's vote.

Moreover, voter turnout fell substantially, from 65.4 percent of eligible voters in 1908 to 58.8 in 1912. If there was a beneficiary of the reform ferment sparked by the presidential campaign, it was not Wilson, but the Socialist candidate, Eugene V. Debs, who captured a record 900,000 votes, 6 percent of the total. At best it could be said that the 1912 election signified that the American public was in the mood for reform: only 23 percent, after all, had voted for the one candidate who stood for the status quo, President Taft. Woodrow Wilson's own reform program, however, had received no particular mandate from the people.

As anticlimactic as the 1912 election might seem, it proved to be a decisive event in the history of national reform. Out of the searching campaign debate between Roosevelt and Wilson there emerged in the New Freedom a program capable of resolving the crisis over corporate power that had gripped the nation for the whole of the previous decade. And, just as important, the election created a rare opportunity for decisive legislative action in Washington. Wilson became president with the Democrats in firm control of both houses of Congress and united in their eagerness to get on with the New Freedom.

The New Freedom in Action. Upon entering the White House, Wilson chose a flank attack on the central problem of economic power. So long out of office, the Democrats were hungry for tariff reform. From the prevailing average of 40 percent, the Underwood Tariff Act of 1913 pared rates down to an average of 25 percent. Targeting especially the trust-dominated industries, Democrats confidently expected the Underwood Tariff to spur competition and reduce prices for consumers by opening protected American markets to foreign products.

The administration then turned to the nation's banking system, whose key weakness was the absence of a central reserve bank. The main functions of a central bank are to regulate the private banks and back them up in case they cannot meet their obligations to their depositors. In practice, this role had been assumed by the major New York banks, which accepted the deposits of lesser banks and assisted them if they came under pressure. However, if the New York institutions themselves weakened, the entire system could totter and even collapse. This had nearly happened in 1907, when the Knickerbocker Trust Company failed and panic swept through the nation's financial markets.

The need for a reserve system became widely accepted, but the form it should take was hotly debated. Wall Street wanted a centralized system, controlled by

the bankers. Rural Democrats and their spokesman, Senator Carter Glass of Virginia, preferred a decentralized network of reserve banks. Progressives in both parties agreed that the essential feature should be public control over the reserve system. The bankers, already under severe criticism from a congressional investigation early in 1913, were on the defensive in this contest.

President Wilson, no expert to begin with, learned quickly and reconciled the reformers and bankers. The monumental Federal Reserve Act of 1913 gave the nation a banking system that was resistant to financial panic. The act delegated reserve functions to twelve district reserve banks, which would be controlled by the member banks. The Federal Reserve Board imposed public regulation on this regional structure. In one stroke, the act strengthened the banking system considerably and placed a measure of restraint on the "money trust."

The Clayton Act and the FTC. Having dealt with tariff and banking reform, Wilson turned at last to the central issue of corporate power: how to give full effect to the antitrust principles of the Sherman Act. Brandeis had already formulated two main approaches. One was to define with precision the prohibited practices—interlocking directorates, discriminatory pricing, and exclusive contracts that shut out competitors. The second approach was to create a new federal trade commission that would aid the executive branch in administering the antitrust laws.

In both approaches, there were knotty questions to be resolved. Was it feasible to be absolutely rigid in prohibiting illegal practices? Brandeis finally decided that it was not, and he persuaded Wilson to modify the definition of practices prohibited in the Clayton Antitrust Act of 1914 to apply only "where the effect may be to substantially lessen competition or tend to create a monopoly in any line of commerce." As for the trade commission, the problem was how much power and what functions it should have. Wilson was understandably sensitive on this matter, given his principled opposition to Roosevelt's conception of a powerful trade commission overseeing American business. Initially, Wilson wanted no more than an advisory and information-gathering agency. But ultimately the Federal Trade Commission (1914) received much broader powers to investigate companies and to issue "cease and desist" orders against unfair trade practices that violated antitrust law. FTC decisions, however, were subject to court review, so that Wilson's entire program was situated within the established judicial antitrust system based on the "rule of reason." As before, it would ultimately be up to the courts to decide which business practices were illegal.

Despite a good deal of commotion, an underlying consensus-building attended this arduous legislative process. Wilson himself had opened the debate in a conciliatory way. "The antagonism between business and government is over," he said, and the time was ripe for a program representing the "best business judgment in America." Afterward, Wilson felt he had brought the long controversy over corporate power to a successful conclusion. And, in fact, he had. Steering a course between Taft's conservatism and Roosevelt's radicalism, he had carved out a middle way—what the historian Martin J. Sklar has termed "corporate liberalism." This middle way brought to bear the powers of government without threatening the constitutional order; and it dealt in some measure with the abuses of corporate power without threatening the capitalist system.

Wilson's Social Program. On social policy, too, Wilson carved out a middle way. During the 1912 campaign he had denounced the social program of the New Nationalism as paternalistic. Compared to his dealings with big business, Wilson proved rather more resistant to special legislation for workers and farmers. He accepted cosmetic language in the Clayton Act stating that labor and farm organizations were not illegal combinations. But he rejected the exemptions they wanted from antitrust prosecution.

The labor vote had grown increasingly important to the Democratic party, however. As his second presidential campaign drew nearer, Wilson lost some of his scruples about prolabor legislation. In 1915 and 1916 he championed a host of bills beneficial to American workers. These included a model federal workmen's compensation law, a federal child labor law, the Adamson eight-hour law for railroad workers, and the landmark Seamen's Act, which eliminated age-old abuses of sailors aboard ship and granted them the individual rights held by all other workers. Likewise, after stubborn earlier resistance, Wilson approved in 1916 the Federal Farm Loan Act, providing the low-interest rural credit system long demanded by farmers.

Wilson encountered the same kind of dilemma that confronted all successful progressives—the claims of moral principle versus the unyielding realities of political and economic life. Progressives were high-minded but not radical. They saw evils in the system, but they did not consider the system itself evil. They also prided themselves on being realists as well as moralists. So it stood to reason that Wilson, like other progressives who achieved power, would find his place at the center.

Summary

A new chapter in American reform began at the start of the twentieth century. For decades, the problems resulting from industrialization and urban growth had been mounting. Now, after 1900, progressive activity sprang up and dominated the nation's public life until World War I. The unifying element in progressive reform was a common intellectual outlook, highly principled and idealistic as to goals, and confident of the human capacity to find the means.

Beyond this shared outlook, progressives broke up into diverse, often conflicting groups. Political reformers included business groups concerned chiefly with improving the efficiency of city government, while other progressives, such as Robert La Follette, opposed privilege and wanted to democratize the political process. Both groups worked to enhance their power at the expense of entrenched party machines.

Social welfare became very much the province of American women, and that effort in turn reinvigorated the struggle for women's rights. In the cities, working people and immigrants also became reform-minded and thereby set in motion a new political force, urban liberalism. While progressivism was sadly infected by the prevailing racism in American life, there was a reform wing that joined with black activists to forge the major institutions of black protest and uplift of the twentieth century, the National Association for the Advancement of Colored People and the Urban League.

At the national level, progressives focused primarily on controlling the economic power of corporate business. This overriding problem led to Theodore Roosevelt's Square Deal, then to his New Nationalism, and finally to Woodrow Wilson's New Freedom. The role of the federal government expanded dramatically, but in service to a cautious and pragmatic approach to the problems of the country.

TOPIC FOR RESEARCH

The Muckrakers

No group was more instrumental in stimulating reform activity than the muckraking journalists. They investigated political corruption, child labor, adulterated food, business fraud, racial conflict, prostitution, and many other evils. Arthur and Lila Weinberg, eds., *The Muckrakers* (1961) is a representative collection of the most important muckraking articles, and contains an extensive bibliography of other such articles. Important muckraking books include Lincoln Steffens *The Shame of the Cities* (1904), Ida M. Tarbell's *The History of the Standard Oil Company* (1904). Most famous of the muckraking novels is Upton Sinclair, *The Jungle* (1906). Others are Frank Norris, *The Octopus* (1901) and *The Pit* (1903); David Graham Phillips, *The Great God Success* (1901), *The Plum Tree* (1905), and *Susan Lenox* (1917); and Robert Herrick, *The Memoirs of an American Citizen* (1905). Finally, the ideas and experiences of the muckrakers might be explored through their autobiographies, the best of which is *The Autobiography of Lincoln Steffens* (1931).

BIBLIOGRAPHY

The Course of Reform

The most recent survey of the Progressive Era is John Milton Cooper, *Pivotal Decades: The United States, 1900–1920* (1990). Two older but still serviceable narrative accounts are George E. Mowry, *The Era of Theodore Roosevelt, 1900–1912* (1958), and Arthur S. Link, *Woodrow Wilson and the Progressive Era, 1910–1917* (1954). Harold U. Faulkner, *The Quest for Social Justice, 1898–1914* (1931), is a useful portrait of the social setting in which progressivism developed. A highly influential interpretation of progressive reform, still worth reading despite the effective refutation of its central arguments, is Richard Hofstadter, *Age of Reform* (1955). A radical critique that stresses the reforming role of big business is James Weinstein, *The Corporate Ideal in the Liberal State, 1900–1918* (1968). Robert H. Wiebe, *The Search for Order, 1877–1920* (1967), places progressive reform in a broader context of organizational development. On the historical debate over progressivism as a movement, see Daniel Rodgers, In Search of Progressivism," *Reviews in American History* 10 (1982).

The progressive mind has been studied from many different angles. The religious underpinnings are stressed in Robert M. Crunden, *Ministers of Reform: The Progressives' Achievement in American Civilization, 1889–1920* (1982). In *The*

New Radicalism in America, 1889–1963 (1965), Christopher Lasch sees progressivism as a form of cultural revolt. Samuel Haber traces the influence of Frederick W. Taylor in *Efficiency and Uplift: Scientific Management in the Progressive Era* (1964). On the intellectual basis for progressivism, the key book is Morton White, *Social Thought in America: The Revolt Against Formalism* (1975). For leading figures in this antiformalist tradition, see Samuel Konefsky, *The Legacy of Holmes and Brandeis* (1956), and David Riesman, *Thorstein Veblen* (1963). Most useful on political thinkers is Charles Forcey, *The Crossroads of Liberalism: Croly, Weyl, Lippmann, and the Progressive Era* (1961). A provocative study set in an international context is James T. Kloppenberg, *Uncertain Victory: Social Democracy and Progressivism in European and American Thought, 1870–1920* (1986). Clarke A. Chambers, *Paul U. Kellog and the Survey* (1971), treats one of the key social investigators. For the muckrakers, see David M. Chalmers, *The Social and Political Ideas of the Muckrakers* (1964) and Harold S. Wilson, *McClure's Magazine and the Muckrakers* (1970).

Political reform has been the subject of a voluminous literature. Wisconsin progressivism can be studied in David P. Thelen, *The New Citizenship: Origins of Progressivism in Wisconsin, 1885–1900* (1972) and *Robert La Follette and the Insurgent Spirit* (1976), and Robert S. Maxwell, *La Follette and the Rise of Progressivism in Wisconsin* (1956). Other important progressives are treated in Spencer C. Olin, *California's Prodigal Son: Hiram Johnson and the Progressive Movement* (1968); Robert F. Wesser, *Charles Evans Hughes: Politics and Reform in New York State, 1905–1910* (1967); and Richard Lowitt, *George W. Norris: The Making of a Progressive* (1963). On city reform, see Bradley R. Rice, *Progressive Cities: The Commission Government Movement* (1972); Jack Tager, *The Intellectual as Urban Reformer: Brand Whitlock and the Progressive Movement* (1968); and Melvin G. Holli, *Reform in Detroit: Hazen S. Pingree and Urban Politics* (1969).

The best treatment of the settlement-house movement is Allen F. Davis, *Spearheads of Reform* (1967). Allen F. Davis, *American Heroine: Jane Addams* (1973), and George Martin, *Madame Secretary: Frances Perkins* (1976), deal with leading woman progressives. The connection to working women is effectively treated in Nancy S. Dye, *As Equals and Sisters: Feminism, the Labor Movement, and the Women's Trade Union League of New York* (1980). Women garment workers, the key labor constituency for the woman Progressives, are studied with great skill and insight in Susan A. Glenn, *Daughters of the Shtetl: Life and Labor in the Immigrant Generation* (1990). On the ideology of women's suffrage, see Aileen Kraditor, *Ideas of the Women's Suffrage Movement, 1890–1920* (1965). Two path-breaking books on the origins of American feminism are Rosalind Rosenberg, *Beyond Separate Spheres: The Intellectual Origins of Modern Feminism* (1982), and Nancy F. Cott, *The Grounding of Modern Feminism* (1987).

The seminal essay on urban liberalism is J. Joseph Huthmacher,   Urban Liberalism and the Age of Reform," *Missis-*

sippi Valley Historical Review (September 1962). Huthmacher's ideas have been fully developed in John D. Buenker, *Urban Liberalism and Progressive Reform* (1973). The relationship to organized labor can be followed in Irwin Yellowitz, *Labor and the Progressive Movement in New York State* (1965). The rise of anti-immigrant sentiment has received authoritative treatment in John Higham, *Strangers in the Land* (1955). James H. Timberlake, *Prohibition and the Progressive Crusade* (1963) covers another important aspect of progressive moralism. On the South, see Jack Temple Kirby, *Darkness at the Dawning: Race and Reform in the Progressive South* (1972), and Dewey Grantham, *Southern Progressivism* (1983). The revival of black protest is vigorously described in Stephen R. Fox, *The Guardian of Boston: William Monroe Trotter* (1971).

Progressivism and National Politics

National progressivism is best approached through its leading figures. John Milton Cooper, *The Warrior and the Priest* (1983) is a provocative joint biography of Wilson and Roosevelt that emphasizes their shared worldview. Other good biographies include William Harbaugh, *Power and Responsibility: The Life and Times of Theodore Roosevelt* (1961); G. Wallace Chessman, *Theodore Roosevelt and the Politics of Power* (1969); John Morton Blum, *The Republican Roosevelt* (1954); Donald E. Anderson, *William Howard Taft* (1973); John Morton Blum, *Woodrow Wilson and the Politics of Morality* (1956); and Melvin I. Urofsky, *Louis D. Brandeis and the Progressive Tradition* (1981). Aspects of national progressive politics can be followed in James Penick, *Progressive Politics and Conservation: The Ballinger-Pinchot Affair* (1968); Robert Wiebe, *Businessmen and Reform* (1962); Gabriel Kolko, *The Triumph of Conservatism* (1963); James Holt, *Congressional Insurgents and the Party System* (1969); and David Sarasohn, *The Party of Reform: The Democrats in the Progressive Era* (1989). On the socialists, in addition to the books cited in Chapter 18, see Aileen S. Kraditor, *The Radical Persuasion, 1890–1917* (1981), and James Weinstein, *The Decline of American Socialism, 1912–1925* (1967). Naomai Lamoreaux, *The Great Merger Movement in American Business, 1895–1904* (1985), offers a sophisticated modern analysis of trust activity, and Thomas K. McCraw, ed., *Regulation in Perspective* (1981), contains valuable interpretative essays on the problems of trust regulation. Albro Martin, *Enterprise Denied: The Origins of the Decline of American Railroads, 1897–1917* (1971), assesses the impact of railway regulation. A comprehensive rethinking of the progressive struggle to fashion a regulatory policy for big business is offered in Martin J. Sklar, *The Corporate Reconstruction of American Capitalism, 1890–1916: The Market, the Law, and Politics* (1988).

TIMELINE

1889	Jane Addams and Ellen Gates Starr found Hull House
1893	Economic depression (until 1897)
1899	National Consumers League founded
1900	Robert M. La Follette elected Wisconsin governor First commission form of city government in Galveston, Texas
1901	President McKinley assassinated, Theodore Roosevelt succeeds
1902	President Roosevelt settles national anthracite strike
1903	National Women's Trade Union League
1904	Supreme Court dissolves the Northern Securities Company
1905	*Lochner v. New York* overturns law restricting length of the work day
1906	Hepburn Railway Regulation Act AFL adopts Bill of Grievances Upton Sinclair's *The Jungle*
1908	*Muller v. Oregon* upholds regulation of working hours for women Federal Council of Churches founded William Howard Taft elected president
1909	NAACP formed Herbert Croly's *Promise of American Life*
1910	Roosevelt announces the New Nationalism Woman suffrage movement revives; suffrage victory in Washington state
1911	*Standard Oil* decision restores "rule of reason" Triangle Shirtwaist fire
1912	Progressive party formed Woodrow Wilson elected president
1913	Federal Reserve Act Underwood Tariff
1914	Clayton Antitrust Act

Battle of Santiago de Cuba, 1898

James G. Tyler's dramatic painting of the final sea
battle of the Spanish-American War showcased
America's newest weapon of war, the battleship.
(Courtesy Franklin D. Roosevelt Library)

CHAPTER **22** *An Emerging World Power,*
1877–1914

In 1881, England sent a new envoy to Washington. He was Sir Lionel Sackville-West, son of an earl, brother-in-law of the Tory leader Lord Denby, but otherwise distinguished only as the steadfast lover of a celebrated Spanish dancer. His well-connected friends wanted to park Sir Lionel somewhere comfortable, but out of harm's way. So they made him minister to the United States.

Twenty years later such an appointment would have been inconceivable. All the major European powers had by then elevated their missions in Washington to embassies and routinely staffed them with top-of-the-line ambassadors. And they treated the United States, without question, as a fellow Great Power.

When Sir Lionel arrived in Washington in 1881, the United States scarcely cast any shadow on world affairs. As a military power the United States was puny, even comical. Its army was smaller than Bulgaria's, and its navy ranked thirteenth in the world—and was a threat mainly to the crews who manned its unseaworthy ships. Twenty years later, however, the United States was flexing its muscles. It had just made short work of Spain in a brief but decisive war, and acquired for itself an empire that stretched from Puerto Rico to the Philippines. America's standing as a rising naval power was manifest, and so was its aggressive assertion of national interest in the Caribbean and in the Pacific.

In practice, the United States acted as a regional power in the early twentieth century, but Europeans had become keenly aware of its capacity to cut a larger swath whenever it chose to do so. "Are we to be confronted by an American peril . . . before which the Old World is to go down to irretrievable defeat?" wondered

a former French foreign minister. The notion of an "American peril" became a lively topic after 1900 among Europeans surveying the industrial and military potential of the United States. No one could be quite sure what America's role would be, since the United States retained its traditional policy of nonalignment in European affairs. But in chanceries across the Continent, the importance of the United States was universally acknowledged and its likely response to every event carefully assessed.

How the United States emerged on to the world stage in the decades before World War I is the subject of this chapter.

The Roots of Expansionism

Diplomacy in the Gilded Age

In 1880 the United States had a population of 50 million and, by that measure, ranked easily with the great European powers. It was the world's leading producer of wheat and cotton. In industrial production, the United States was second only to Britain, and rapidly closing the gap. And if anyone doubted the military prowess of Americans, he or she only needed to recall the ferocity with which they had fought one another in the Civil War. The great campaigns of Lee, Sherman, and Grant entered the military textbooks and were closely studied by army strategists everywhere. In the encounter between the ironclads *Monitor* and *Merrimack* at Hampton Roads on March 9, 1862, the world had received its first example of modern naval warfare.

Nor, when its vital interests were at stake, had the United States shown itself to be lacking in diplomatic vigor. Both major crises with European powers arising from the Civil War had been settled to America's satisfaction. In 1867, France abandoned its imperial adventure in Mexico and withdrew its forces. And in 1871, Britain expressed its regrets for nonneutral acts against the Union during the war and agreed to the arbitration of the *Alabama* claims (see Chapter 16).

In the years that followed, the United States lapsed into diplomatic isolation, not out of inherent weakness, but for lack of any clear national purpose in world affairs. In this industrializing age, George Washington's warning against entangling alliances seemed as pertinent as it had when America was a thinly populated land of farmers. The business of building the nation's industrial economy absorbed Americans in these years and kept their attention inward-looking. And while the new international telegraphic cables provided the country with swift overseas communication after the 1860s, wide oceans still kept the world at a distance and gave Americans a sense of isolation and security. Nor did European power politics, which centered on Franco-German rivalry and on nationalistic conflict in the Balkans, seem to matter very much. As far as Cleveland's secretary of state Thomas F. Bayard was concerned, "we have not the slightest share or interest [in] the small politics and backstage intrigues of Europe . . . upon which we look with impatience and contempt."

As for the empire building in which the European powers were so avidly engaged, this expression of national prowess did not tempt the United States. Even so ardent an American nationalist as the young Theodore Roosevelt saw the folly of overseas expansion. "We want no unwilling citizens to enter our Union," he wrote in 1886. "European nations war for the possession of thickly settled districts which, if conquered, will for centuries remain alien and hostile to the conquerors; we, wiser in our generation, have seized the waste solitudes that lay near us."

In these circumstances, with no external threat to be seen, what was the point of maintaining a big navy? After making certain of the French departure from Mexico in 1867, the government began to dismantle the Civil War fleet. The ships that remained on duty gradually deteriorated. Of the 125 ships on the navy's active list, only about 25 were actually seaworthy at any one time. No effort was made to keep up with European advances in weaponry or battleship design. Indeed, the American fleet consisted mainly of sailing ships and obsolete ironclads.

During the administration of Chester A. Arthur (1881–1885), the navy began a modest upgrading program. New ships were put into service, standards for the officer corps were raised, and the Naval War College was founded. But the fleet remained small, and the squadrons lacked any unified naval command. The mission of the navy remained as before: to maintain coastal defenses and a modest cruising fleet capable of preying on enemy commerce at sea. An expenditure of 1 percent or less of the gross national product for the entire military establishment seemed entirely adequate in the 1880s.

The conduct of diplomacy was likewise small potatoes. Appointment to the foreign service was mostly through the spoils system. American ministers and consular officers were notoriously unskilled, and included an inordinate number of idlers and drunkards. Domestic politics, moreover, made it difficult to develop a coherent program. Although foreign relations was an executive responsibility, the U.S. Senate jealously guarded its right to give its "advice and consent" on treaties and diplomatic appointments. Partisan squabbling between Democrats and Republicans left the White House even less room for maneuver. For its part the State Department tended to be inactive, exerting little control either over policy making or over its missions abroad. It was remarkable how many actions (some of them subsequently repudiated or simply ignored by the State Department) were taken independently by ministers and naval officers out in the field. In the more remote parts of the world, the American presence was often primarily religious: the intrepid missionaries bent on Christianizing the native populations of Asia, Africa, and the Pacific islands.

Latin American Diplomacy. In the Caribbean, the United States remained the dominant power, but the expansionist enthusiasm of the Civil War era subsided. Nothing came of the grandiose dreams of William H. Seward, secretary of state under Presidents Lincoln and Johnson, for an American empire, perhaps with a capital in Mexico. President Grant's strongest efforts could not persuade the Senate to purchase Santo Domingo in 1870, and Congress likewise blocked later moves to acquire bases in Haiti, Cuba, and Venezuela. Nor did the United States pursue its long-expressed interest in an interoceanic canal in Central America. Despite its protests that no one else should build such a canal, the United States stood by when a French company headed by the builder of the Suez Canal, Ferdinand de Lesseps, started to dig across the Panama isthmus in 1880. That project failed after a decade—but the reason was bankruptcy, not American opposition.

On becoming secretary of state in 1881, James G. Blaine engaged in a flurry of diplomatic activity in Latin America. He got involved in a border dispute between Mexico and Guatemala, tried to settle a war Chile was waging against Peru and Bolivia, and called the first

Pan-American conference. Blaine's interventions in Latin American disputes proved disastrous, however, and the Pan-American conference seems mainly to have been a gesture to restore some lustre to his tarnished diplomatic reputation. Blaine had no particular strategic aims in mind. He was concerned mainly with his own political prospects at home, and, in any case, left office soon after sending out the invitations in late 1881. His successor canceled the conference. This was a characteristic instance of Gilded Age diplomacy, driven partly by partisan politics, and carried out without any clear sense of national purpose.

Pan-Americanism—the notion of a community of American states—took root, however, and in 1888 Congress requested President Cleveland to call a conference of American states to promote trade and peace in the Western Hemisphere. Blaine, returning in 1889 for a second stint at the State Department under the new Republican administration of Benjamin Harrison, took up the plans already laid for a new Pan-American conference. An impressive agenda called for a customs union, improved communications, and arbitration treaties. But the only result was the creation of an information agency in Washington, later renamed the Pan-American Union. Any Latin American goodwill garnered by Blaine's efforts was soon blasted by the humiliation he visited upon Chile because of a riot against American sailors in the port of Valparaiso in 1891. Threatened with war, Chile was forced to apologize to the United States and pay an indemnity of $75,000.

Pacific Episodes. In the Pacific, American interest centered on Hawaii. American missionaries had long been active among the Hawaiian islanders. With a climate ideal for raising sugar cane, Hawaii also attracted many American planters and investors. Nominally an independent nation with its own monarchy, Hawaii fell increasingly within the American orbit. In 1875 a treaty of commercial reciprocity opened the American market to Hawaiian sugar and declared that no Hawaiian territory could be ceded to a third power. A second treaty in 1887 granted the United States naval rights at Pearl Harbor.

Having encouraged the sugar economy in Hawaii, the United States abruptly withdrew Hawaii's trading advantages in the McKinley Tariff of 1890. All foreign sugar could now enter the United States duty free, while domestic producers received a special subsidy to compensate for the drop in sugar prices. Anxious to gain that benefit, American planters in Hawaii began to plot for annexation to the United States. Aided by the U.S. minister to Hawaii, and with American sailors conspicuously present, they revolted in January 1893 against Queen Liliuokalani. Within a month the provisional government they installed negotiated a treaty of annex-

ation with the Harrison administration. Before annexation could be approved by the Senate, however, Grover Cleveland returned to the presidency, and, following an investigation of the Hawaiian episode, withdrew the treaty. To annex Hawaii, he declared, would violate both America's "honor and morality" and its "unbroken tradition" against acquiring territory far from the nation's shores.

In the meantime, the American presence elsewhere in the Pacific was growing. In 1867 the United States had purchased Alaska from imperial Russia. The deal was at the behest of the Russians, who were anxious to unload (to their everlasting subsequent regret) a possession they considered militarily indefensible and economically unprofitable. For $7.2 million the United States got not only the huge territory of Alaska with its vast natural resources but an unlooked-for presence stretching across the northern Pacific.

Far to the south, with even less forethought, the United States became involved in the remote Samoan islands. In 1878 the United States secured the right to a coaling station in Pago Pago harbor—a key link on the route to Australia—and in exchange promised local Polynesian leaders to use its good offices in Samoa's relations with other foreign powers. An informal protectorate resulted. In the mid-1880s, Germany began to press its claims to the islands, and the United States, stung by German arrogance, responded with equal fervor. In 1889 naval warfare might have broken out but for a fierce hurricane that wrecked both the German and the American fleets. At that point, agreement on a tripartite protectorate (the third European power was Britain) averted further strife and left the United States with its rights at Pago Pago.

American diplomacy in these years has been characterized as a series of incidents, not the pursuit of a foreign *policy*. Many things happened, but intermittently and without a plan, driven by individuals and pressure groups, not by any well-founded and coherent conception of national objectives. This was possible because, as the Englishman James Bryce remarked in 1888, America still sailed "upon a summer sea." In the stormier waters that lay ahead, a different kind of American diplomacy would be required.

Economic Sources of Expansionism

"A policy of isolation did well enough when we were an embryo nation," remarked Senator Orville Platt of Connecticut in 1893. "But today things are different. . . . We are 65 million people, the most advanced and powerful on earth, and regard to our future welfare demands an abandonment of the doctrines of isolation."

The Singer Sewing Machine
The sewing machine was an American invention, but it swiftly found markets abroad. The Singer Company, the dominant firm, not only exported large quantities, but was producing 200,000 machines annually at a Scottish plant that employed 6,000 workers. Singer's advertising rightly boasted of its prowess as an international company and of a product that was "The Universal Machine."

Why America's future welfare demanded an abandonment of isolation was first of all a matter of economics. In a sense the greatest danger to the country seemed to arise from its very success as a productive economy. The gross national product quadrupled between 1870 and 1900, and industrial output quintupled. But were there sufficient markets to absorb the staggering volume of goods flowing from America's farms and factories? It was true that America itself constituted an enormous market. Over 90 percent of American output in the late nineteenth century was consumed at home. Even so, foreign markets were important. Roughly a fifth of the nation's agricultural output was exported, and for the major staple crops—cotton, wheat, tobacco—the percentage ranged much higher, up to 80 percent, for example, in the case of cotton.

As the industrial economy expanded, so did factory exports. Between 1880 and 1900, the industrial share of total exports jumped from 15 percent to over 30 percent. Although only 9 percent of manufactured output went overseas in 1900, the export share for key industries loomed much larger: 57 percent for petroleum products, 50 percent for copper, 25 percent for sewing machines, 15 percent for iron and steel.

The importance of foreign trade was evident in the efforts of major firms to develop overseas production and marketing facilities. As early as 1868, the pioneering Singer Sewing Machine Company established its first foreign plant in Glasgow, Scotland. Most prominent among American firms doing business abroad was Standard Oil. Beginning with the Anglo-American Oil Company in 1888, Rockefeller's trust created affiliates across Europe to operate its tankers, establish bulk stations, and distribute its kerosene to foreign retailers. In Asia, Standard Oil's kerosene cans, made over into utensils and roofing tin, became an infallible index of American market penetration. Brand names such as Kodak (cameras), McCormick (agricultural equipment), and later Ford (the Model T) became household words around the world.

Foreign trade was important partly for reasons of international finance. As a developing economy, the United States attracted a lot of foreign capital, but sent relatively little abroad—scarcely 1 percent of all the money Americans were investing in the late nineteenth century. The result was a heavy outflow of dollars from the United States in the form of interest and dividend payments to foreign investors. To balance this account, the United States needed to ship overseas more goods than it imported. In fact, a favorable import-export balance was achieved in 1876 and was sustained almost every year thereafter. But because of its status as a net importer of capital, America would have to be constantly vigilant about the health of its export trade.

FIGURE 22.1

Balance of U.S. Imports and Exports, 1870–1914

Even more important, however, was the relationship that many Americans perceived between foreign markets and the nation's social stability. In hard times, as we have seen, farmers took up radical politics and workers became militant strikers. The problem, many thought, was that the nation's capacity to produce was outrunning its capacity to consume. And when the economy slowed and domestic demand fell, the impact on farmers and workers was devastating, driving down farm prices and wages, and cutting a swath of layoffs and farm foreclosures across the country. The answer was to make sure that there would always be enough buyers for America's surplus products, and this meant, more than anything else, access to foreign markets.

Overseas Trade and Foreign Policy. The nub of the question was how these concerns over foreign markets linked up to America's foreign policy. The bulk of American exports in the late nineteenth century—over 80 percent—went to Europe and Canada. In these countries, the normal instruments of diplomacy sufficed. In Europe, for example, a major issue for the United States during the 1880s was the restrictions placed by France and Germany on imports of American pork, allegedly on health grounds. The United States protested vigorously, threatened to embargo the imports of countries discriminating against American meat products, and in 1890–1891 negotiated a settlement of the dispute.

But there was a second category of foreign markets that seemed to demand a more vigorous kind of American intervention. These were the countries of Asia, Latin America, and other "backward" (by Western definition) parts of the world. Here the United States found itself in competition with other industrial powers. It was true that Asia and Latin America represented a rather modest part of America's export trade—roughly

an eighth of the total in the late nineteenth century. Still, this trade was growing—it was worth $200 million in 1900—and parts of it mattered a great deal to specific industries, as, for example, the China market for American textiles.

Even more significant was the *potential* that these non-Western markets seemed to hold, because they, not Europe, constituted the future consumers of American goods. With its enormous population of potential customers, China exerted an especially powerful hold on the American mercantile imagination. Many felt that the China trade, although actually quite small, would one day be the key to American prosperity. Therefore, China and other beckoning markets must not be closed to the United States.

From the mid-1880s onward, with the surge of European imperialism, that feared prospect became more real. After the Berlin Conference of 1884, the African continent was rapidly carved up by the European powers. In the Far East, in a burst of modernizing energy, Japan transformed itself into a major power and began to challenge China's claims over Korea. In the Sino-Japanese war of 1894–1895, Japan won an easy victory and started a scramble among the great powers, including Russia, to carve China up into spheres of influence. In Latin America, U.S. interests began to be challenged more aggressively by Britain, France, and Germany. On the European continent, moreover, the free-trade liberalism of earlier years gave way after the 1870s to rising protectionism, threatening established European markets for American goods just at the point when empire building was closing off the likely new markets elsewhere. On top of all this came the Panic of 1893, setting in motion the movements of industrial and agrarian protest that many Americans, such as Cleveland's secretary of state Walter Q. Gresham, took to be "symptoms of revolution."

TABLE 22.1

Exports to Canada and Europe Compared with Exports to Asia and Latin America

Year	Exports to Canada and Europe	Percentage of Total	Exports to Asia and Latin America	Percentage of Total
1875	$ 494,000,000	86.1%	$ 72,000,000	12.5%
1885	637,000,000	85.8	87,000,000	11.7
1895	681,000,000	84.3	108,000,000	13.4
1900	1,135,000,000	81.4	200,000,000	14.3

Tables compiled from information in *Historical Statistics of the United States*, 1960; U.S. Department of Commerce, *Long Term Growth, 1860–1965*, 1966; National Bureau of Economic Research, *Trends in the American Economy in the Nineteenth Century*, 1960.

In these circumstances, with the nation's social stability seemingly at stake, securing the markets of Latin America and Asia became an urgent necessity, and from that urgent necessity sprang the expansionist diplomacy of the 1890s.

The Making of an Expansionist Foreign Policy

"Whether they will or not, Americans must now begin to look outward. The growing production of the country requires it." So wrote Captain Alfred T. Mahan, America's leading naval strategist, in his book *The Influence of Seapower upon History* (1890). An obscure naval officer posted to a rickety ship cruising Latin America in the mid-1880s, Mahan had spent his spare time reading history. In a library in Lima, Peru, he hit on the idea that great empires—first Rome and, in modern times, Great Britain—had depended for their power on the control of the seas. From this insight, Mahan developed a naval analysis that became the cornerstone of American strategic thinking.

The United States should no longer regard the oceans as barriers, Mahan argued, but as "a great highway . . . over which men pass in all directions." To traverse that highway required a robust merchant marine,

Alfred T. Mahan
Mahan's impressive theory of the influence of seapower on history, so he recalled, was sparked by reading he did on Roman history in a library in Lima, Peru, in 1885. His insight was personal as well as intellectual: embarrassed by the decrepit ships on which he served, Mahan thought the United States should have a modern fleet in which officers like himself could serve with pride (and with some hope of professional advancement).

which had fallen on hard times since its heyday in the 1850s, and a powerful navy to protect American commerce. "When a question arises of control over distant regions . . . it must ultimately be decided by naval power," Mahan advised. To sustain its navy and its commerce, the United States needed strategic overseas bases. Here technology played a part because, having converted to steam, navies required coaling stations far from home. Without such stations, Mahan warned, warships were "like land birds, unable to fly far from their own shores."

Mahan called first of all for a canal across Central America to connect the Atlantic and Pacific oceans. Such a canal would enable the eastern United States to "compete with Europe, on equal terms as to distance, for the markets of East Asia." The canal's approaches would need to be guarded by bases in the Caribbean Sea. And Hawaii would have to be annexed to extend American power into the Pacific—a step that Mahan called "natural, necessary, irrepressible." Mahan was defining a distinctive and limited form of colonialism—not the rule over large territories and native populations to which European empire-builders aspired, but control over strategic bases from which American power could be asserted where Americans wanted to trade.

What Mahan offered was a *coherent* foreign policy for the United States: first, the securing of foreign markets for the nation's surplus products; second, of equal importance, the nation's development as a naval power; and, sustaining both these goals, an expansionist strategy anchored on an interoceanic canal and bases in the Caribbean and Pacific.

Mahan's reasoning was most eagerly taken up by other exponents of a powerful America, including publishers like Whitelaw Reid of the *New York Tribune*, and such young politicians as Theodore Roosevelt and Senator Henry Cabot Lodge of Massachusetts. The influence of these men, few in number but strategically placed, increased during the 1890s. They pushed steadily for what Lodge called a "large policy." But mainstream politicians also accepted Mahan's underlying logic, and from the inauguration of Benjamin Harrison's administration in 1889 onward, a surprising consistency began to emerge in the conduct of American foreign policy.

Rebuilding the Navy. This consensus was most evident in the rethinking of American naval strategy. The crucial thing, Mahan argued, was to drop the reliance on shore defense and lightly armed cruising ships and create instead a battleship fleet capable of roaming the far seas and of striking a decisive first blow against an enemy. This was precisely the line that Benjamin F. Tracy, Harrison's secretary of the navy, took in his first annual report. Battleships might be expensive, but they were "the premium paid by the United States for the in-

The Battleship Oregon
The battleship was the centerpiece of naval strategy in the industrial age, and the key marker in the naval arms race among the Great Powers. Building a battleship fleet was America's ticket of entry into that race.

surance of its acquired wealth and its growing industries." In 1890 Congress made appropriations for the first three battleships in the two-ocean fleet envisioned by Secretary Tracy, and by the time the Harrison administration left office in 1893, American naval power—thirteenth or worse in 1889—stood seventh in the world. "The sea will be the future seat of empire," predicted Tracy. "And we shall rule it as certain as the sun doth rise."

The incoming Cleveland administration was less spread-eagled and, by canceling Harrison's scheme for annexing Hawaii, established its antiexpansionist credentials. But after a brief period of hesitation, the Democrat Cleveland picked up the naval program of his Republican predecessor, pressing Congress just as forcefully for more battleships (five were authorized) and making the same basic argument. The nation's commercial vitality—"free access to all markets," in the words of Cleveland's second secretary of state, Richard Olney—depended on its naval power.

While rejecting the colonial aspects of Mahan's thinking, Cleveland absorbed the underlying strategic arguments about where America's vital interests lay. That this was so explains the remarkable crisis that suddenly blew up in 1895 with Great Britain over Venezuela.

The Venezuela Crisis. For years a border dispute had simmered between Venezuela and British Guiana. In the past the United States had urged arbitration, only to be told by the haughty British that they did not submit their interests to the judgments of third parties. Now that answer could no longer be accepted. For one thing, Britain's aggressive claims, if they prevailed, would strongly enhance its position in the Caribbean. More-

over, the Venezuela dispute seemed part of a larger pattern of European aggressiveness in Latin America, including ominous moves against Nicaragua, Brazil, Trinidad, and Santo Domingo. European empire building was carving up Africa and Asia in this period. How could the United States be sure that Europe did not have similar designs on Latin America? Indeed, prompted by President Cleveland, Secretary of State Olney made just that point in the bristling note he sent to London on July 25, 1895, demanding that Britain accept arbitration, or face the consequences.

Invoking the Monroe Doctrine, Olney warned that the United States could not tolerate any European attempt to intimidate or overthrow the nations of the Western Hemisphere. "Today the United States is practically sovereign upon this continent, and its fiat is law upon the subjects to which it confines its interposition," Olney asserted. Olney's words sound bombastic, but they were intended to convey a clear message to Britain and the European powers that the United States would brook no challenge to its perceived vital interests in the Caribbean. (Note that these were America's vital interests, not those of Venezuela, which was not consulted and was virtually ignored during the entire dispute.)

Because the Venezuela crisis blew up so suddenly, because it seemed so out of proportion to the boundary issue itself, and because it created war hysteria in the United States—for these reasons historians have found it difficult to recognize that the pugnacious stand of the Cleveland administration was not an aberration but a logical step in the new outward thrust of American foreign policy. Once the British realized that Cleveland meant business, they backed off and agreed to the arbitration of the boundary dispute. Afterward, Secretary of State Olney remarked with satisfaction that, as a great industrial nation, the United States needed "to accept [its] commanding position" and take its place "among the Powers of the earth." And these countries would have to accommodate to the American need for access to "more markets and larger markets for the consumption and products of the industry and inventive genius of the American people."

The Ideology of Expansionism. As policy makers hammered out a new foreign policy, a sustaining body of ideology took shape as well. One source of expansionist thinking was the Social Darwinist theory that so dominated the political thinking of this era (see Chapter 19). If animals and plants evolved through the survival of the fittest, so did nations. "Nothing under the sun is stationary," warned the American social theorist Brooks Adams in *The Law of Civilization and Decay* (1895). "Not to advance is to recede." By this criterion, the United States had no choice; if it wanted to survive, it had to expand.

Linked to Social Darwinism was a spreading belief in the inherent superiority of the Anglo-Saxon "race." On both sides of the Atlantic, Anglo-Saxonism had come into great vogue. John Fiske, an American philosopher and historian, popularized Social Darwinism and Anglo-Saxonism by lecturing the nation on its future responsibilities. "The work which the English race began when it colonized North America," Fiske declared, "is destined to go on until every land on the earth's surface that is not already the seat of an old civilization shall become English in its language, in its religion, in its political habits, and to a predominant extent in the blood of its people."

Fiske entitled his famous lecture "Manifest Destiny." This term had been used half a century earlier to convey the sense of national mission—America's "manifest destiny"—to sweep aside the native American peoples and occupy continental America. Now, in the 1890s, that process of westward expansion was declared by the U.S. Census to have come to an end: there was no longer a frontier line beyond which land remained to be conquered. The psychological impact of that news on Americans was profound, spawning among other things a new interpretation of America's past that stressed the shaping importance of the frontier on the nation's character. In his landmark essay first setting out this thesis—"The Significance of the Frontier in American History" (1893)—the young historian Frederick Jackson Turner suggested a linkage between the closing of the frontier and overseas expansion. "He would be a rash prophet who should assert that the expansive character of American life has now entirely ceased," Turner wrote. "Movement has been its dominant fact, and, unless this training has no effect upon a people, the American energy will continually demand a wider field for its exercise." As Turner predicted, Manifest Destiny did indeed now turn outward.

Thus a strong current of ideas, deep-rooted in American experience and ideology, justified the new diplomacy of expansionism. The United States was eager to step onto the world stage. All it needed was the right occasion.

An American Empire

The Cuban Crisis

Ever since Spain had lost hold of its vast empire in South America in the early nineteenth century, Cubans had yearned to join their mainland brothers and sisters in freedom. Cuban movements for independence had sprung up repeatedly, most recently in a rebellion that lasted from 1868 to 1875. In February 1895, Cuba rose up once more against Spanish rule. This time a bloody standoff developed; the Spaniards controlled the towns, the insurgents the countryside. In early 1896, the newly appointed Spanish captain general, Valeriano Weyler, adopted a brutal policy of *reconcentration*. The Spaniards forced entire populations into armed camps and treated any Cuban on the outside as a rebel. The strategy, while militarily effective, took a dreadful toll on the Cubans. Out of a population of 1,600,000 at least 200,000 died of starvation, exposure, or dysentery.

A wave of sympathy for the Cuban rebels swept across the United States. Cuban exiles skillfully played on public opinion. They got help from a yellow press eager to capitalize on the situation. Locked in a circulation war, William Randolph Hearst's *New York Journal* and Joseph Pulitzer's *New York World* elevated the atrocities and skirmishes into front-page news. Across the country powerful sentiments were stirred, mixing humanitarian concern for the Cubans, a superpatriotism that was tagged *jingoism*, and increasing demands that the Cubans be made free. Responding to public opinion, Congress passed resolutions in 1896 for Cuban autonomy, and early the next year, for complete independence.

The White House took a cooler view of the situation. Cleveland was still in office when the Cuban rebellion broke out. As with Venezuela, concern about America's vital interests—"by no means of a wholly sentimental or philanthropic character," he told the Congress—guided Cleveland's thinking. First, there were economic interests at stake. The rebellion was disrupting the sizable trade between the two countries and destroying profitable American investments, especially in Cuban sugar plantations. More important, the United States could no longer tolerate instability in the Caribbean. It became alarmed that Spain's troubles might draw other European powers into the situation. A chronically unstable Cuba was not compatible with America's increasing strategic interests in the region, especially its plans for an interoceanic canal whose approaches would have to be safeguarded. If Spain could put down the rebellion, that was fine from Cleveland's point of view. But as Spain's impotence became clearer, he began to urge the Spanish government to make reforms and to warn that the United States would have to intervene unless there was a speedy resolution of the Cuban crisis.

McKinley and the Road to War. On that central matter there was an essential continuity between Cleveland and the McKinley administration that took office in March 1897. Both were guided by the conception of the United States as the dominant Caribbean power, with vital interests that had to be defended. McKinley, however, was inclined to take a tougher line with the Spanish. For one thing, he was more appalled by Spain's "uncivilized and inhumane conduct" in Cuba and not so indifferent as Cleveland to the aspirations of the rebels. In addition, McKinley had to contend with the rising jingoism within the Republican party. At the 1896 national convention the Republicans had adopted a bristling platform calling for Cuban independence and proclaiming a new American imperialism. But the notion, long held by historians, that McKinley was swept along against his better judgment by popular opinion and by a Republican war faction led by Theodore Roosevelt, Henry Cabot Lodge, and other aggressive advocates of a "large policy" is not true. McKinley was very much his own man. He was a skilled politician and a canny, if undramatic, president. He would not proceed until he sensed a broad national consensus for war. In particular, he was sensitive to business interests fearful of any disruption to an economy just recovering from a depression.

On September 18, 1897, the American minister in Madrid asked the Spanish government "whether the time has not arrived when Spain . . . will put a stop to this destructive war." If Spain could not give assurances of an "early and certain peace," he warned, the United States would take whatever steps it "should deem necessary to procure this result." At first the Spanish response sparked some hope. The conservative regime fell, and a liberal government, upon taking office in October 1897, moderated its Cuban policy. Spain recalled Weyler, eased reconcentration, and adopted an autonomy plan that would grant Cuba a degree of self-rule, but not independence. Madrid's incapacity soon became clear, however. In January 1898, Spanish loyalists in Havana rioted against the offer of autonomy. The Cuban rebels, encouraged by the prospect of American intervention, demanded full independence.

Relations between the United States and Spain worsened. On February 9, 1898, the *New York Journal* published a private letter of Dupuy de Lôme, the Spanish minister to the United States. De Lôme called President McKinley "weak" and "a bidder for the admiration of the crowd." What was probably worse, De Lôme suggested that the Spanish government was not taking the American demands for reform seriously.

A week later, the U.S. battleship *Maine* blew up and sank in Havana harbor, with the loss of 260 seamen. "Whole Country Thrills with the War Fever," proclaimed Hearst's *New York Journal*. But McKinley kept his head. He assumed the sinking had been accidental: what motive could the Spanish have had for attacking the *Maine*? A naval board of inquiry, however, submitted a more damaging report. The explosion had been

"Remember the Maine!"

In late January 1898, the *Maine* entered Havana harbor on a courtesy call. On the evening of February 15, a mysterious blast sent the U.S. battleship to the bottom. This dramatic lithograph conveys something of the impact of that tragic event on American public opinion. Although no evidence ever linked the Spanish authorities to the explosion, the sinking of the *Maine* fed the emotional fires preparing the nation for war with Spain.

caused by a bomb, not, as experts had suspected, by a boiler rupture on the *Maine.* No evidence linked the Spanish to the explosion, but they had failed to meet their responsibility to protect the American vessel from attack.

This was damning evidence that Spanish control over Cuba had broken down, and it was reinforced by a memorable speech by Senator Redfield Proctor of Vermont after a visit to Cuba. The account by this anti-imperialist senior Republican of the devastation in the Cuban countryside made a deep impression and led even the skeptical to the conclusion that Spain had lost its claim to rule Cuba.

President McKinley had no stomach for the martial spirit engulfing the country. He was not swept along by the calls for blood to avenge the sinking of the *Maine.* But he did heed the advice of business leaders, earlier hesitant, but now impatient for the dispute with Spain to come to an end. War was preferable to the unresolved Cuban crisis. On March 27, McKinley cabled to Madrid what was in effect an ultimatum: an immediate armistice for six months, abandonment of the practice of reconcentration, and, with the United States as mediator, peace negotiations with the rebels. A telegram the next day added that only Cuban independence would be regarded as a satisfactory outcome to these negotiations.

In response, Spain made a series of desperate concessions, climaxed on April 9 by a unilateral declaration of an armistice whose duration would be at the discretion of the Spanish military. But it rejected American mediation, as well as the American demand for an independent Cuba. There had never been any chance that the proud Spanish would voluntarily accept that final humiliation.

On April 11, McKinley sent a message to Congress asking for authority to intervene to end the fighting in Cuba. His motives were as he described them: "In the name of humanity, in the name of civilization, in behalf of endangered American interests which give us the right and the duty to speak and to act, the war in Cuba must stop." The war hawks in Congress—a mixture of Republican jingoists and western Democrats who sympathized with the cause of Cuban independence—were impatient with McKinley's cautious progress. But the president did not lose control of things. On the one crucial difference he had with the war hawks, McKinley prevailed. He beat back their effort to grant recognition to the rebel republican government, which would have greatly reduced the administration's freedom of action in dealing with Spain.

The war hawks did push through the Teller amendment, by which the United States disclaimed any intention of taking Cuba. Senator Henry M. Teller wanted to make it impossible for European governments to say that "when we go out to make battle for the liberty and freedom of Cuban patriots, that we are doing it for the purpose of aggrandizement for ourselves or the increasing of our territorial holdings." This had to be made clear with regard to Cuba, "whatever," Senator Teller added, "we may do as to some other islands."

Did McKinley have in mind "some other islands"? Was this really a war of aggression, secretly motivated by a desire to seize strategic territory from Spain? In a strict sense, almost certainly not. It was not *because* of expansionist ambitions that McKinley pressed Spain into a corner. On the other hand, once war came he saw it as an opportunity to be exploited. As he wrote privately after hostilities began: "While we are conducting war and until its conclusion, we must keep all we get; when the war is over we must keep what we want." Precisely what would be forthcoming, of course, would depend on the fortunes of battle.

The Spoils of War

Hostilities formally began when Spain declared war on April 24, 1898. The day before, President McKinley had called for 125,000 volunteers. Across the country, regiments began to form up. Theodore Roosevelt immediately resigned as assistant secretary of the navy, ordered a fancy uniform, and was commissioned lieutenant colonel in a volunteer cavalry regiment that became famous as the Rough Riders. Raw recruits poured into the makeshift bases around Tampa, Florida. Confusion reigned. Tropical uniforms did not arrive; the food was bad, the sanitation worse; and rifles were in short supply. No provision had been made for getting the troops to Cuba; the government hastily began to collect a miscellaneous fleet of yachts, lake steamers, and commercial boats. Fortunately, the small regular army was a disciplined, highly professional force, and its seasoned 28,000 troops provided a nucleus for the 200,000 civilians who had to be turned into soldiers inside of a few weeks.

The navy was in better shape and, as it turned out, the real key to the outcome of the war. On April 23, acting on plans already drawn up, Commodore George Dewey's small Pacific fleet set sail from Hong Kong for the Philippines. Here, at this Spanish possession in the far Pacific, not in Cuba, the decisive engagement of the war was fought. On May 1, the American ships cornered the Spanish fleet in Manila harbor and destroyed it. The victory produced euphoria in the United States. Immediately, part of the army being trained for the Cuban campaign was diverted to the Philippines. Manila, the Philippine capital, fell on August 13, 1898.

With Dewey's naval victory, American strategic thinking suddenly clicked into place. "We hold the other side of the Pacific and the value to this country is almost beyond imagination," declared Senator Lodge.

"We must on no account let the [Philippine] Islands go." President McKinley agreed, and so did his key advisers. An anchor on the western Pacific had long been coveted by naval strategists. At this time, too, the great powers were carving up China into spheres of influence. If American commerce wanted a place in that glittering market, the power of the United States would have to be projected into Asia. "With a strong foothold in the Philippine Islands, we can and will take a large slice of the commerce of Asia," asserted Senator Mark Hanna. "That is what we want . . . and it is better to strike while the iron is hot."

Once the decision for a Philippine base had been made, other decisions followed almost automatically. For one, the question of Hawaii was quickly resolved. In 1897 McKinley had reintroduced an annexation proposal in the Congress, but it had stalled. In July 1898, Congress pushed Hawaiian annexation through by joint resolution. Hawaii had suddenly acquired a crucial strategic value: it was a halfway station on the way to the Philippines. The navy pressed for a coaling base in the central Pacific; that meant Guam, a Spanish is-

land in the Marianas. There was need also for a strategically located base in the Caribbean; that meant Puerto Rico. By July, before the assault on Cuba, the full scope of McKinley's war aims had crystallized. Nor was there any question that he had the people behind him. In the wake of Dewey's victory, enthusiasm for colonial annexations swept the country and, so one close reader of the nation's press reported, was "getting so strong it will mean the political death of any man to oppose it pretty soon."

The campaign in Cuba, the main theater of operations, was something of an anticlimax. The Spanish fleet was bottled up in Santiago harbor, and the city itself became the strategic key to the military campaign. Half-trained and ill-equipped, the American forces moving on Santiago might have been checked by a determined opponent; but the Spaniards lacked the heart for battle. They would fight hard enough to maintain their honor, but they had no stomach for a real war against the Americans. There were two sharp engagements—the first at Las Guasimas on the road to Santiago, the second, on July 1, near the city on the heights

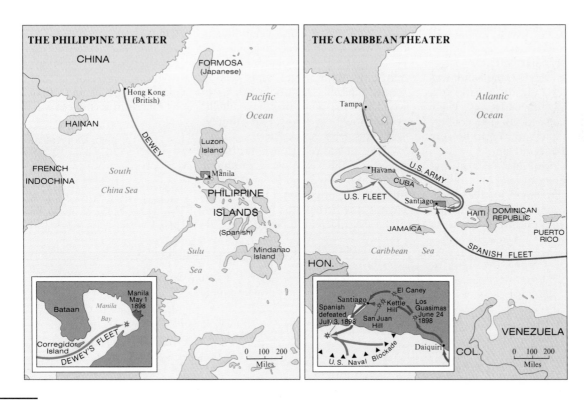

MAP 22.1

The Spanish-American War

The swift American victory in the Spanish-American War derived from overwhelming U.S. naval superiority. Dewey's destruction of the Spanish fleet in Manila harbor doomed the Spaniards in the Philippines. In Cuba, American ground forces won a hard victory on San Juan Hill, for they were ill-equipped and poorly supplied. With the United States in control of the seas, the Spaniards saw no choice but to give up the battle for Cuba.

AMERICAN VOICES

Black Soldiers in a White Man's War *George W. Prioleau*

The chaplain of the Ninth Cavalry regiment expresses his bitterness against the racism experienced by black troopers in the South on their way to battle in Cuba.

Hon. H. C. Smith
Editor, *Gazette*

Dear Sir:
The Ninth Cavalry left Chickamauga on the 30th of April for Tampa, Fla. We arrived here (nine miles from Tampa) on May 3. From this port the army will sail for Cuba. We have in this camp here and at Tampa between 7,000 and 8,000 soldiers, artillery, one regiment of cavalry (the famous fighting Ninth) and the Twenty-fourth and Twenty-fifth infantries. The Ninth Cavalry's bravery and their skillfulness with weapons of war . . . is well known by all who have read the history of the last Indian war. . . .

Yesterday, May 12, the Ninth was ordered to be ready to embark at a moment's notice for Cuba. . . . These men are anxious to go. The country will then hear and know of the bravery of these sable sons of Ham.

The American Negro is always ready and willing to take up arms, to fight and to lay down his life in defense of his country's flag and honor. All the way from northwest Nebraska

this regiment was greeted with cheers and hurrahs. At places where we stopped the people assembled by the thousands. While the Ninth Cavalry band would play some national air the people would raise their hats, men, women and children would wave their handkerchiefs, and the heavens would resound with their hearty cheers. The white hand shaking the black hand. The hearty "goodbyes," "God bless you," and other expressions aroused the patriotism of our boys. . . . These demonstrations, so enthusiastically given, greeted us all the way until we reached Nashville. At this point we arrived about 12:30 A.M. There were about 6,000 colored people there to greet us (very few white people) but not a man was allowed by the railroad officials to approach the cars. From there until we reached Chattanooga there was not a cheer given us, the people living in gross ignorance, rags and dirt. Both white and colored seemed amazed; they looked at us in wonder. Don't think they have intelligence enough to know that Andrew Jackson is dead. . . .

The prejudice against the Negro soldier and the Negro was great, but it was of heavenly origin to what it is in this part of Florida, and I suppose that what is true here is true in other parts of the state. Here, the Negro is not al-

lowed to purchase over the same counter in some stores that the white man purchases over. The southerners have made their laws and the Negroes know and obey them. They never stop to ask a white man a question. He (Negro) never thinks of disobeying. You talk about freedom, liberty, etc. Why sir, the Negro of this country is freeman and yet a slave. Talk about fighting and freeing poor Cuba and of Spain's brutality; of Cuba's murdered thousands, and starving reconcentra-does. Is America any better than Spain? Has she not subjects in her very midst who are murdered daily without a trial of judge or jury? Has she not subjects in her own borders whose children are half-fed and half-clothed, because their father's skin is black. . . . Yet the Negro is loyal to his country's flag. . . .

The four Negro regiments are going to help free Cuba, and they will return to their homes, some then mustered out and begin again to fight the battle of American prejudice. . . .

Yours truly,
Geo. W. Prioleau
Chaplain, Ninth Cavalry

Source: Cleveland *Gazette* (May 13, 1898), reprinted in Willard B. Gatewood, *"Smoked Yankees" and the Struggle for Empire, 1898–1902* (Urbana: University of Illinois Press, 1971), pp. 27–29.

commanded by San Juan Hill. Roosevelt's dismounted Rough Riders (there had been no room for horses on the transports) and four black regiments took the brunt of the fighting. In the battle of San Juan, which was actually a close call for the Americans, white observers grudgingly credited much of the victory to the "superb gallantry" of the black soldiers. On July 3, in a last futile gesture, the Spanish fleet in Santiago harbor made a

suicidal daylight attempt to run the American blockade—and was destroyed.

Three weeks later, Spain sued for peace. The two nations signed an armistice in which Spain agreed to give up Cuba and cede Puerto Rico and Guam to the United States. American forces would occupy Manila pending a peace treaty that would decide the fate of the Philippines.

The Battle of San Juan Hill
On July 1, 1898, the key battle for Cuba took place on heights overlooking Santiago. The brunt of the fighting was taken by African-American troops. Although generally overlooked, the black role in the San Juan battle is in fact done justice in this contemporary lithograph, and without the demeaning stereotypes by which blacks were normally depicted in an age of intensifying racism. Even so, the racial hierarchy is maintained. The blacks are the foot soldiers; their officers are white.

The Imperial Experiment

The big question was the Philippines. This was an archipelago of over 7,000 islands populated—as William R. Day, McKinley's secretary of state, put it with the characteristic racism of that era—by "eight or nine millions of absolutely ignorant and many degraded people." Not even the most avid of American expansionists had advocated colonial rule over such a population: that was European-style imperialism, not what Mahan and his followers had in mind. Both Mahan and Lodge initially advocated keeping only Manila as a western Pacific base. It gradually became clear, however, that Manila was not defensible without controlling the whole of Luzon, the large island on which the city is located.

McKinley and his advisers surveyed the options. One possibility would have been to return most of the islands to Spain, but the reputed evils of Spanish rule made that a "cowardly and dishonorable" solution. Another possibility would have been to partition the Philippines with one or more of the Great Powers. There would have been no dearth of takers, particularly Germany, whose ships were already prowling the nearby waters. But, as McKinley observed, to turn over valuable territory to "our commercial rivals in the Orient—that would have been bad business and discreditable."

Most plausible was the possibility of granting the Philippines independence. As in Cuba, Spanish rule had already stirred up a rebellion, led by the fiery patriot Emilio Aguinaldo. It would have been feasible to make an arrangement like the one being negotiated with the Cubans over Guantanamo Bay: the lease of a naval base to the Americans as a price for freedom. But after some hesitation McKinley was persuaded that "we could not leave [the Filipinos] to themselves—they were unfit for self-rule—and they would soon have anarchy and misrule over there worse than Spain's was."

The fact was that, having expended American lives and money on conquering the Philippines, the administration had no politically easy way of extricating itself. In October 1898, while the peace negotiations were in progress, McKinley made a two-week speaking tour of the Midwest to get a reading on public opinion. What he heard from the crowds confirmed his own belief that the United States would have to take the entire archipelago. On October 26 he cabled instructions to that effect to the American delegation in Paris. Afterward, to a visiting group of Methodist clergymen, McKinley provided a more sanctimonious explanation: after much prayer he had concluded "that there was nothing left for us to do but to take them all, and to educate the Filipinos, and uplift and civilize and Christianize them and by God's grace do the very best we could by them, as our fellow men, for whom Christ also died."

As for the Spaniards, they had little choice. In the Treaty of Paris, they ceded the Philippines to the United States for a payment of $20 million. The treaty encountered harder going at home. The seizure of the Philippines reawakened traditional antiexpansionist sentiment in the United States. An organized movement formed in many cities, starting with Boston, and grew into the formidable Anti-Imperialist League in October 1899. The Philippine issue delayed the treaty in the Senate for weeks. Senator George Hoar of Massachusetts protested that annexation violated the Constitution.

AMERICAN VOICES

Subduing the Filipinos — the Ideal

Major General Arthur MacArthur

In 1902 MacArthur, the commanding general of U.S. forces in the Philippines, appeared before a Senate committee investigating conditions there. In his presentation he expressed a widely held view of the necessity—and desirability— of American rule.

At the time I returned to Manila [May 1900] to assume the supreme command it seemed to me that we had been committed to a position by process of spontaneous evolution. . . . [o]ur permanent occupation of the islands was simply one of the necessary consequences in logical sequence of our great prosperity. . . . our conception of right, justice, freedom, and personal liberty was the precious fruit of centuries of strife; that we had inherited much in these respects from our ancestors, and in our own behalf have added much to the happiness of the world, and as beneficiaries of the past and as the instruments of future progressive social development we must regard ourselves simply as the custodians of imperishable ideas held in trust for the general benefit of mankind. In other words, I felt that we had attained a moral and intellectual height from which we were bound to proclaim to all as the occasion arose the true message of humanity as embodied in the principles of our own institutions. . . .

To my mind the archipelago is a fertile soil upon which to plant republicanism. . . . We are planting the best traditions, the best characteristics of Americanism in such a way that they never can be removed from that soil. That in itself seems to me a most inspiring thought. It encouraged me during all my efforts in those islands, even when conditions seemed most disappointing, when the people themselves, not appreciating precisely what the remote consequences of our efforts were going to be, mistrusted us; but that fact was always before me—that going down deep into that fertile soil were the imperishable ideas of Americanism.

AMERICAN VOICES

Subduing the Filipinos—the Realities

F. A. Blake and Richard T. O'Brien

MacArthur's voice was not the only one the Senate committee heard. News of battlefield atrocities reached them as well. This account by F. A. Blake, a Red Cross worker, for example, had appeared in the *San Francisco Call* on March 30, 1899.

I never saw such execution in my life and hope never to see such sights as met on all sides as our little corps passed over the field, dressing wounded legs and arms nearly demolished, total decapitation, horrible wounds in chest and abdomen, showing the determination of our soldiers to kill every native in sight.

Richard T. O'Brien, of M Company, 26th Infantry Volunteers, U.S. Army, told this story to the Senate Committee on the Philippines in 1902.

[H]ow the order started and who gave it I don't know, but the town was fired on. I saw an old fellow come to the door, and he looked out: he got a shot in the abdomen and fell to his knees and turned around and died. . . .
After that two old men came out, hand in hand. I should think they were over 50 years old, probably between 50 and 70 years old. They had a white flag. They were shot down. At the other end of the town we heard screams, and there was a woman there; she was burned up, and in her arms was a baby, and on the floor was another child. The baby was at her breast, the one in her arms, and this child on the floor was, I should judge, about 3 years of age. They were burned. Whether she was demoralized or driven insane I don't know. She stayed in the house.

"The power to conquer alien people and hold them in subjugation is nowhere expressly granted [and] nowhere implied," he protested. With only a vote to spare, the Senate approved the treaty on February 6, 1899.

War in the Philippines. Two days earlier, on February 4, fighting had broken out between American and Filipino patrols on the edge of Manila. Confronted by the prospect of American annexation, Aguinaldo asserted his nation's independence and turned his guns on the occupying American forces.

The ensuing conflict far exceeded in ferocity the war just concluded with Spain. Fighting tenacious guerrillas, the U.S. army resorted to the same tactics of reconcentration used by the Spaniards in Cuba, moving the people into the towns, carrying out indiscriminate attacks beyond the perimeters, and burning crops and villages.

Atrocities became commonplace on both sides. The American forces specialized in the "water cure"—forcing water into a person's stomach and then pounding it out—to force captured guerrillas to talk. In more than three years of warfare, forty-two hundred Americans and thousands of Filipinos died. The fighting ended in 1902, and Judge William Howard Taft, appointed governor in 1901, set up a civilian government. He intended to make the Philippines a model of American road building and sanitary engineering.

In the 1900 election, McKinley's convincing victory over William Jennings Bryan, an avid antiexpansionist, suggested popular satisfaction with America's overseas adventure. Yet a strong sense of misgivings was evident.

Emilio Aguinaldo

At the start of the war with Spain, U.S. military leaders brought the Filipino patriot Aguinaldo back from Singapore because they thought he would stir up a popular uprising that would help bring about the defeat of the Spaniards. Aguinaldo came because he thought the Americans favored an independent Philippines. These differing intentions—it has remained a matter of dispute as to what assurances Aguinaldo received—were the root cause of the tragic Filipino insurrection that proved far costlier in American and Filipino lives than the war with Spain that had preceded it.

Fighting the Filipinos

The United States went to war against Spain in 1898 partly out of sympathy with the Cuban struggle for independence. Yet the United States found it necessary to use very much the same brutal tactics to put down the Filipino struggle for independence as the Spaniards had used against the Cubans. Here the Twentieth Kansas Volunteers march through the burning village of Caloocan.

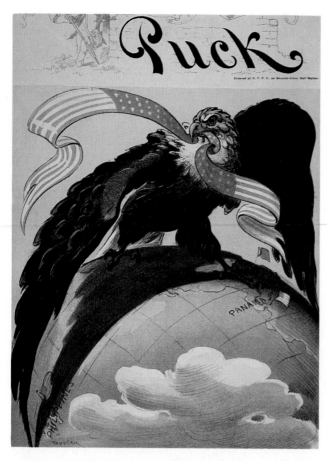

Second Thoughts About American Empire

After the shouting was over, and the United States had its empire, doubts began to creep in, as is evident in this *Puck* cover in celebration of July 4, 1904. There is the American eagle in all its glory, but with wings spreading far out to Philippines in one direction and Puerto Rico in the other, and grumbling: "Gee, but this is an awful stretch!"

Americans had not anticipated the brutal methods needed to subdue the Filipino guerrillas. "We are destroying these islanders by the thousands, their villages and cities," protested the philosopher William James. "No life shall you have, we say, except as a gift from our philanthropy after your unconditional surrender to our will. . . . Could there be any more damning indictment of that whole bloated ideal termed 'modern civilization'?"

There were, moreover, disturbing political issues to be resolved. Did the Constitution extend to the acquired territories? Did their inhabitants automatically become citizens? In 1901 the Supreme Court ruled negatively on both questions; these were matters for Congress to decide. In its report on administration for the Philippines, the special commission appointed by McKinley recommended ultimate independence after an indefinite pe-

riod of U.S. rule, during which the Filipinos would be readied for self-government. In 1916, the passage of the Jones Act formally committed the United States to granting Philippine independence, but set no date.

The ugly business in the Philippines rubbed off some of the moralizing gloss but left undeflected the global aspirations driving the United States. In a few years the United States had acquired the makings of a strategic overseas empire—Hawaii, Puerto Rico, Guam, the Philippines, and finally, in 1900, several of the Samoan islands that had hitherto been jointly administered with Germany and Britain. The United States, remarked the legal scholar John Bassett Moore in 1899, had moved "from a position of comparative freedom from entanglements into a position of what is commonly called a world power."

Onto the World Stage

A Power Among Powers

In Europe the flexing of America's muscles against Spain caused a certain amount of consternation. The assault on an ancient, if decayed, European state seemed to many government leaders the work of a country that was (in the words of the French envoy to Washington) "ignorant, brutal, and quite capable of destroying the complicated European structure." At the instigation of Kaiser Wilhelm II of Germany, the major powers had tried before war broke out to intercede on Spain's behalf—but tentatively, because no one was looking for trouble with the Americans. President McKinley had listened politely to the representations of their envoys on April 6, 1898, and had then, dismissively, proceeded with his war.

The decisive outcome confirmed what the Europeans already suspected. After Dewey's naval victory, the semiofficial French paper *Le Temps* observed that "what passes before our eyes is the appearance of a new power of the first order." And, in a long editorial, the London *Times* concluded: "This war must . . . effect a profound change in the whole attitude and policy of the United States. In the future America will play a part in the general affairs of the world such as she has never played before."

Anglo-American Amity. Precisely what that part would be in the European balance of power remained uncertain. Germany toyed briefly with the notion of an American alliance, but only Great Britain had a clear view of what it wanted from the United States. In the late nineteenth century, Britain's position in Europe had steadily worsened. It was being challenged industrially and militarily by a unified Germany. Clashing expansionist ambitions in North Africa and across Asia soured Britain's relations with France and Russia. And there was general European hostility toward British imperial policy in South Africa, a policy that resulted in the Boer War against the independent-minded Dutch settlers at the end of the 1890s. In its growing isolation, Britain turned to the United States. This explained why Britain had meekly bowed to American demands in the Venezuela dispute of 1895. From that time onward, after a century of cool relations (or worse) with its former colonies, Britain strove consistently for a *rapprochement* (literally, a "coming together") with the United States.

In the Hay-Pauncefote Agreement (1901) Britain gave up its treaty rights to joint participation in any Central American canal project, thereby clearing the way for a canal exclusively under U.S. control. And two years later the last of the vexing U.S.–Canadian border disputes, this one involving British Columbia and Alaska, was settled—again, to American satisfaction. The lone British member of the U.S.–Canadian tribunal cast the deciding vote awarding to the United States the Pacific inlets and ports that provided the only convenient access to the Klondike gold fields of the Canadian Yukon. No formal alliance was forthcoming, but Anglo-American friendship had been placed on a firm basis, so much so that beginning in 1901 the British admiralty designed its war plans on the assumption of a friendly U.S. navy. The assumption was that America was "a kindred state with whom we shall never have a parricidal war."

The Caribbean—An American Lake

If America's role in Europe remained uncertain, that was certainly not the case closer to home. An exuberant exponent of the "large policy" of overseas expansionism, Theodore Roosevelt had been thrust into the presidency in 1901 just as the United States was concluding its brief burst of imperialism by subduing the Filipino independence movement. The next step was to consolidate the resulting strategic gains in the Caribbean and the Pacific. This was Roosevelt's main foreign policy task, and he welcomed it.

"All the great masterful races have been fighting races," Roosevelt declared. Nothing would be worse for the United States, already too commercial for his aristocratic taste, than "slothful and ignoble peace." But a nation's power had to be used only for good ends and, in particular, to keep the world from sliding into anarchy. The international forces for disorder were such, Roosevelt maintained, as to "render it incumbent on all civilized and orderly powers to insist on the proper policing

of the world." This view licensed the United States to exert power as needed in the regions that, because of the country's overseas expansion, had fallen under its direct influence.

Roosevelt stated his foreign policy in the menacing phrase, "Speak softly and carry a big stick." By a "big stick" he meant above all naval power. Under Roosevelt, the battleship program went on apace. By 1904 the U.S. Navy stood fifth in the world, and by 1907, second. Roosevelt was a friend of Captain Mahan, and a close student of his geopolitical writings. Mahan's program called for a big navy and strategic bases—and, as a final step, a canal across Central America. Indeed, the Spanish-American War had demonstrated that strategic need in the most graphic way: the entire country had waited breathlessly as the battleship *Oregon* had sped for sixty days from the Pacific around the southern tip of Latin America to join in the final action against the Spanish fleet in Cuba.

The Panama Canal. A canal was at the top of Roosevelt's agenda. With Britain's treaty right to a joint canal enterprise surrendered in 1901, Roosevelt proceeded to more troublesome matters. For $40 million, the United States purchased from the New Panama Canal Company the assets of de Lesseps's earlier canal project. Panama was a province of Colombia, so the Roosevelt administration entered into negotiations with Colombia to lease the strip of land through which the canal would run. The Colombian legislature voted down the proposed treaty, partly because the company's rights would soon expire and the sale to the United States could then be renegotiated on terms more favorable to Colombia. Furious over what seemed to him a breach of faith, Roosevelt contemplated outright seizure of Panama but settled on a more devious solution.

The key intermediary in the sale of the de Lesseps assets, an engineer named Philippe Bunau-Varilla, let Roosevelt know that an independence movement was brewing in Panama. The United States in turn informed Bunau-Varilla that American ships were steaming toward Panama. The idea was that the Americans would provide cover for the expected uprising. There was a mix-up when the cruiser *Nashville* arrived at Colon, however, and the American commander failed to prevent 400 Colombian troops from disembarking at that small Atlantic port. Using their wits, the conspirators managed to keep these troops from proceeding to Panama City, and the bloodless revolution against Colombian rule went off on schedule. The next day, November 4, the United States recognized Panama. Less than two weeks later, with Bunau-Varilla serving as the representative of the new republic, Panama signed a treaty with the United States. The agreement granted the United States a perpetually renewable lease on a canal zone. These machinations were a dirty business, but they got Roosevelt what he wanted.

Roosevelt never regretted the victimization of Colombia, although the United States, as a kind of conscience money, paid Colombia $25 million in 1922. Building the canal was one of the heroic engineering feats of the century, involving a swamp-clearing project to rid the area of malaria and yellow fever, the construction of a series of great locks, and the excavation of 240 million cubic yards of earth. It took the U.S. Army Corps of Engineers eight years to finish the huge project. When it opened in 1914, the Panama Canal gave the United States a commanding commercial and strategic position in the Western Hemisphere.

Policeman of the Caribbean. Next came the task of making the Caribbean basin secure. The countries there, said Secretary of State Elihu Root, had been placed "in the front yard of the United States" by the

Panama Canal. Therefore, as Roosevelt put it, they had to "behave themselves."

In the case of Cuba, this was readily managed in the settlement following the Spanish-American War. Before the United States withdrew from Cuba in 1902, it reorganized Cuban finances and concluded a swampclearing program that eliminated yellow fever, a disease that had ravaged Cuba for many years (and killed probably four thousand of the occupying U.S. troops). As a condition for gaining independence, Cuba was required to include in its constitution a proviso called the Platt amendment. The amendment gave the United States the right to intervene if Cuban independence was threatened or if Cuba failed to maintain internal order. Cuba also granted the United States a permanent lease on Guantanamo Bay, where the U.S. Navy built a large base.

Roosevelt believed that instability in the Caribbean invited the intervention of European powers. For example, Britain and Germany blockaded Venezuela in

MAP 22.2

The American Empire

In 1890 Alfred T. Mahan wrote that the United States should regard the oceans as "a great highway" across which America would carry on world trade. That was precisely what resulted from the empire the United States acquired in the wake of the Spanish-American War. The Caribbean possessions, strategically located Pacific islands, and, in 1903, the Panama Canal Zone gave the United States commercial and naval access to a wider world.

The Panama Canal
The Canal Zone was acquired through devious means in which Americans could take little pride (and which led in 1978 to the Senate's decision to restore the property to Panama). But the building of the Panama Canal itself was a triumph of American ingenuity and drive. Dr. William C. Gorgas cleaned out the malarial mosquitoes that had earlier stymied the French. Under Col. George W. Goethels, the U.S. Army overcame formidable obstacles in a mighty feat of engineering. This photograph shows the massive effort under way in December 1904 to excavate the Culebra Cut so that ocean-going ships would be able to pass through.

1902–1903 for failing to meet its debt payments. In 1904, Roosevelt announced that the United States would act as "policeman" of the region, stepping in "however reluctantly, in flagrant cases . . . of wrong doing or impotence."

This policy became known as the Roosevelt Corollary to the Monroe Doctrine. It transformed what had been a broad principle of opposition against European expansionist ambitions in Latin America into an unrestricted American right to regulate Caribbean affairs. The Roosevelt Corollary was not a treaty with other states; it was a unilateral declaration sanctioned only by American power and national interest.

Under the Roosevelt Corollary the United States intervened regularly in the internal affairs of Caribbean states. In 1905, for example, American authorities took over the customs and debt management of the Dominican Republic. When similar financial intervention by the United States touched off a rebellion in Nicaragua in 1912, American marines landed and occupied the country.

Roosevelt's thinking was primarily strategic; his successor, William Howard Taft, took a more commercial view. American investments in the Caribbean region grew dramatically after 1900. The United Fruit Company owned about 160,000 acres in Central American countries by 1913, and U.S. investments in Cuban sugar plantations quadrupled in fifteen years. Taft quickly intervened when disorder threatened American property. But he also regarded business investment as a force for stability in underdeveloped areas. Taft spoke for *dollar diplomacy*—the aggressive coupling of American diplomatic and economic interests abroad.

The Open Door

In the Far East, commercial interests had always stood at the forefront of American policy—especially the huge China market. But by the late 1890s, Japan, Russia, Germany, France, and England had all moved into China, carved out spheres of influence, and instituted discriminatory trade practices in their zones. Fearful that the United States was being frozen out of China, Secretary of State John Hay in 1899 sent an "Open Door" note to the occupying powers: he wanted to establish the right of equal trade access—an Open Door—for all nations wanting to do business in China. Even with its control over the Philippines, the United States was in a weak position compared to the occupying powers on the scene. The best that Hay was able to achieve were responses that were ambiguous and highly conditional. But Hay chose to interpret them as accepting the American Open Door position.

When a secret society of Chinese nationalists launched the Boxer Rebellion in 1900, the United States sent 5,000 troops from the Philippines and joined the multinational campaign to raise the siege of the foreign legations in Beijing (Peking). America took the opportunity to assert a second principle to the Open Door: that China would be preserved as a "territorial and administrative entity." As long as the legal fiction of an independent China survived, so would American claims to equal access to the China market. The other powers gave their assent.

With a network of bases stretching across the Pacific, American power could now be projected into Asia. But here the United States faced formidable rivals.

The European powers had acceded to American claims to preeminence in the Caribbean, including the Roosevelt Corollary. In the Far East, however, Britain, Germany, France, and Russia were strongly entrenched, with no inclination to defer to American interests. The United States also confronted a strategically placed Asian nation—Japan—that had its own vital interests at stake.

The Japanese Challenge. Japan was a rising world power. It had unveiled its military strength in the Sino-Japanese War of 1894–1895, which had begun the dismemberment of China. With the signing of the Anglo-Japanese Alliance in 1902, the power balance in East Asia shifted in Japan's favor, giving Japan a freer hand in confronting Russia over their rival claims in Manchuria and Korea. In 1904, provoked by Russian demands for a military withdrawal from northern Korea, Japan suddenly attacked the tsar's fleet at Port Arthur, Russia's leased port in China. In a series of brilliant victories, the Japanese demolished the Russian military forces in Asia. Roosevelt, anxious to restore some semblance of a power balance, mediated a settlement of the Russo-Japanese War at Portsmouth, New Hampshire, in 1905. Japan emerged as the predominant power in East Asia.

Despite his robust rhetoric, Roosevelt took an accommodating stance toward Japanese expansionism. In exchange for Japanese acquiescence to American sovereignty over the Philippines, the United States approved of Japan's protectorate over Korea and raised no objection when this became full sovereignty in 1911. However, a surge of anti-Asian feeling in California complicated Roosevelt's efforts. In 1906 the San Francisco school board placed all Asian students in a segregated school, infuriating Japan. The "gentlemen's agreement" of 1907, in which Japan agreed to restrict immigration to the United States, smoothed matters over, but the periodic resurgence of racism in California led to continuing tensions with the proud Japanese.

Roosevelt meanwhile moved to balance Japan's military power by increasing American naval strength in the Pacific. American battleships visited Japan in 1908 and then made a global tour in an impressive display of sea power. Late that year, near the end of his administration, Roosevelt achieved his accommodation with Japan. The Root-Takahira Agreement confirmed the status quo in the Pacific, as well as the principles of free oceanic commerce and equal trade opportunity in China.

However, William Howard Taft entered the White House in 1909 convinced that the United States had been short-changed. An exponent of "dollar diplomacy," Taft pressed for a larger role for American bankers and investors in the Far East, especially in the railroad construction going on in China. Taft hoped that American capital could counterbalance Japanese power and pave the way for increased commercial opportunities. When the Chinese Revolution of 1911 toppled the ruling Manchu dynasty, Taft supported the Chinese Nationalists as a new counterforce to the Japanese. The United States thus entered a long-term conflict with Japan that would grow worse and end in war thirty years later.

The triumphant thrust across the Pacific lost some of its luster. The United States had become embroiled in a distant struggle that promised many future liabilities but little of the fabulous profits that had lured Americans to Asia. It was a chastening experience for an emerging world power.

The Japanese in California

The Japanese who flocked into California from 1890 onward made a mighty contribution to the state's agriculture, and by sheer hard work many of them became independent and highly productive farmers. But the prejudice against them was unrelenting, and when the San Francisco school board sought to segregate Japanese children in 1906, an international incident blew up. President Roosevelt got the segregation order rescinded, and Japan agreed to limit emigration to the United States voluntarily. Despite this so-called Gentlemen's Agreement, a festering wound had been opened in the relations between the two countries.

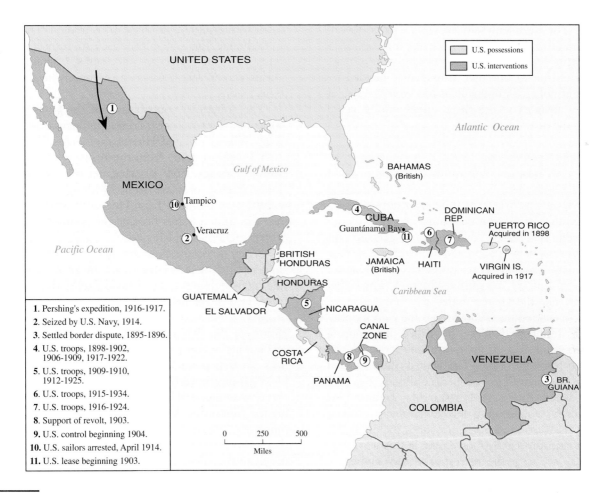

MAP 22.3

Policeman of the Caribbean, 1898–1917

After the Spanish-American War, the United States vigorously asserted its interest in
the affairs of its neighbors to the south. As the record of interventions shows, the
United States truly became the "policeman" of the Caribbean, and not only to
maintain stability in the region. In the Mexican intervention, the United States was
acting, at least in part, out of a sense that it had the right to impose its political values
on its neighbors.

Woodrow Wilson and Mexico

When Woodrow Wilson became president in 1913, he
was bent on reform in American foreign policy no less
than in domestic politics. William Howard Taft's dollar
diplomacy seemed to Wilson to be an extension abroad
of the arrogant business practices that he and other progressives were trying to curb at home. On the importance of economic development overseas, Wilson did
not really differ with his predecessors. He applauded
the "tides of commerce" that would arise from the
Panama Canal. But he was opposed to dollar diplomacy
that bullied weaker countries into inequitable financial
relationships and gave undue advantage to American
business. It seemed to Wilson "a very perilous thing to
determine the foreign policy of a nation in terms of material interest."

Within two weeks of taking office, Wilson demonstrated what he had in mind. American banks had
joined an international consortium to provide a loan to
China. When the investment banker J. P. Morgan
sought his approval, Wilson refused, on the grounds
that the terms of the loan threatened the independence
of the Chinese government. The plan "was obnoxious
to the principles upon which the government of our
people rests."

The United States, Wilson insisted, should conduct
its foreign policy in conformity with America's own democratic principles. He aimed to foster the "development of constitutional liberty in the world" and, above
all, to extend it to the nation's neighbors in Latin America. In a major policy speech in October 1913, he
promised those nations that the United States would
"never again seek one additional foot of territory by

conquest." The president said he would strive to advance "human rights, national integrity, and opportunity" in Latin America. To do otherwise would make "ourselves untrue to our own traditions." Guided by such a moral policy, future generations would arrive at "those great heights where there shines unobstructed the light of the justice of God."

The Mexican Intervention. Mexico became the primary object of Wilson's ministrations. A cycle of revolutions had begun there in 1911. The long dictatorship of Porfirio Diaz was overthrown by Francisco Madero, who spoke much as Wilson did about liberty and constitutionalism. But before Madero could get very far with his reforms, he was deposed and murdered in February 1913 by his chief lieutenant, Victoriano Huerta. Other powers quickly recognized Huerta's provisional government, but the United States had not yet acted when Wilson entered the White House the next month.

Wilson abhorred Huerta; he called his coup a "usurpation" and Huerta himself a murderer. Wilson pledged "to force him out." The United States denied recognition to Huerta's government, although this policy contradicted America's longstanding tradition of granting quick recognition to new governments. Wilson also subjected Mexico to other pressures, including the threatened use of force. By intervening in this way, Wilson insisted, "we act in the interest of Mexico alone. . . . We are seeking to counsel Mexico for its own good." Wilson meant that he intended to put the Mexican revolution back on the constitutional path started by Madero. Wilson was not deterred by the fact that American business interests, with enormous investments in Mexico, favored Huerta. On the contrary, that fact seemed to make Wilson all the more determined to get Huerta out.

The emergence of armed opposition to Huerta in northern Mexico under Venustiano Carranza strengthened Wilson's hand. Carranza's Constitutionalist movement, as it became known, gave Wilson some grounds for denying recognition to Huerta—his government did not fully control the country. More important, Carranza signified to Wilson the vitality of the reformist politics that he wanted to foster in Mexico.

But the Constitutionalists were ardent nationalists. They had no desire for American intervention in Mexican affairs. Carranza angrily rebuffed Wilson's efforts to bring about elections through a compromise between the rebels and the Mexican government. He also vowed to resist by force any intrusion of U.S. troops in his country. All he wanted from Wilson, Carranza asserted, was recognition of the Constitutionalists' belligerent

status so they could purchase arms in the United States. In exchange for vague promises to respect property rights and "fair" foreign concessions, Carranza finally got his way in 1914. American weapons began to flow to his troops.

The American contribution to the Constitutionalists' cause went well beyond selling them arms. For one thing, Wilson isolated Huerta diplomatically. Huerta's crucial support came from the British, who wanted to ensure a steady flow of Mexican oil for their fleet. Under intense pressure from Washington, the British withdrew recognition from Huerta in late 1913. In return the United States became the guarantor of British property interests in Mexico.

When it became clear that neither the loss of British support nor the supplying of Carranza would turn the tide against Huerta, the United States threw its own forces into the game. Using the pretext of a minor insult to the U.S. Navy at Tampico, Wilson ordered the occupation of the major port of Vera Cruz on April 21, 1914. This action cost 19 American and 126 Mexican lives. At that point, the Huerta regime began to crumble. Carranza nevertheless condemned the United States for intervening, and his own forces came close to engaging the Americans. When he entered Mexico City in triumph in August 1914, Carranza had some cause to thank the Yankees. But if any sense of gratitude existed, it was overshadowed by the anti-Americanism inspired by Wilson's insensitivity to Mexican pride and revolutionary zeal.

This sad chapter in Mexican-American relations had a chastening effect on Wilson. It revealed to him the difficulties of acting on, or even of living up to, well-meant ideals amid the confusion of war, revolution, and clashing national interests. Indeed, there were even more egregious examples on which he might have drawn: despite his anti-imperialist pronouncements, Wilson acted no differently than had his predecessors in sending in the U.S. Marines when law and order broke down in Haiti in 1915 and in the Dominican Republic in 1916.

The Gathering Storm in Europe

In the meantime, Europe had begun to drift toward a great world war. There were two main sources of tension. One derived from the deadly rivalry between Germany, the new military and economic superpower of Europe, and the European states threatened by Germany's might—above all France, which had been humiliated in the Franco-Prussian War of 1870 and forced to cede the Alsace-Lorraine provinces to Germany. The second danger zone was the Balkans, where the Ottoman Empire was disintegrating and where, in the midst of explosive ethnic rivalries, Austria-Hungary and Russia were competing for dominance. On the basis of these conflicts an alliance system had emerged, with Germany, Austria-Hungary and Italy (the Triple Alliance) on one side and France and Russia (the Dual Alliance) on the other.

The tensions within Europe were to some degree released by European imperial adventures—most of all by France in Africa and by Russia in Asia. These activities placed France and Russia in opposition to imperial Britain, effectively excluding the latter from the European alliance system. Fearful of Germany, however, England in 1904 composed its differences with France, and the two countries reached a friendly understanding, or *entente*. When England came to a similar understanding with Russia in 1907, the basis was laid for the Triple Entente, and the potential was thereby much magnified for a deadly confrontation between two great European power blocs.

In these European quarrels the United States had no obvious stake, nor any inclination (in the words of a cautionary Senate resolution) "to depart from the traditional American foreign policy which forbids participation . . . [in] political questions which are entirely European in scope." But, on becoming president, Theodore Roosevelt had taken a lively interest in European affairs, and he was eager, as the head of a great power, to make a contribution to the cause of peace there. In 1905 he got his chance.

The Anglo-French entente of the previous year had been based partly on an agreement dividing up spheres of influence in North Africa: the Sudan was conceded to Britain, Morocco to France. Now Germany suddenly challenged France over Morocco. It was a disastrous move, contravening Germany's self-interest in keeping France's attention diverted away from Europe by its colonial involvements overseas. Instead, the Morocco issue brought France into conflict with Germany and produced a great European crisis. Kaiser Wilhelm turned to Roosevelt for help. Finding in an obscure commercial treaty with Morocco the basis for American involvement, Roosevelt persuaded France to participate in an international conference, which was held in January 1906 at Algeciras, Spain. With U.S. diplomats playing a key role, the crisis was defused: Germany got a few token concessions, but France's dominance over Morocco was sustained.

Algeciras marked, in actuality, an ominous turning point, in which the power blocs that would become locked in battle in 1914 first squared off against one another. But at the time it looked like a diplomatic triumph, and Roosevelt's secretary of state, Elihu Root, boasted of America's success in "preserv[ing] world peace because of the power of our detachment."

Root's words prefigured how the United States would define its role among the great powers: it would be the apostle of peace, distinguished by its "detachment," by its lack of selfish interests in European affairs. But cutting athwart this internationalist impulse was the tenacious grip of America's traditional isolationism.

The Peace Movement. Enthusiasm ran high in America for the international peace movement that had been launched by the Hague Peace Conference of 1899. The Permanent Court of Arbitration it created offered new hope for the peaceful settlement of international disputes. Both the Roosevelt and the Taft administrations negotiated arbitration treaties with other countries pledging to submit their disputes to the Hague Court, only to see the treaties emasculated by a Senate unwilling to permit the nation's sovereignty to be compromised in any significant way. Nor was there any sequel to Roosevelt's initiative at Algeciras. It had been coolly received in the Senate and by the nation's press. Roosevelt's successor, William Howard Taft, was not inclined to transgress the doctrine of nonentanglement.

When Woodrow Wilson became president, he chose William Jennings Bryan to be his secretary of state. Bryan was a great apostle of world peace, and he devoted himself to negotiating a series of "cooling off" treaties with other countries—so-called, because the parties agreed to wait for one year while issues in dispute were submitted to a conciliation process. These bilateral agreements were admirable, but they were of no relevance to the explosive power politics of Europe. As tensions there reached the breaking point in 1914, the United States remained effectively on the sidelines.

Yet at Algeciras Roosevelt had rightly seen what the future would demand of America. So did the French writer Andre Tardieu, who remarked in 1908:

The United States is . . . a world power. . . . Its power creates for it . . . a duty—to pronounce upon all those questions that hitherto have been arranged by agreement only among European powers. These powers themselves, at critical times, turn toward the United States, anxious to know its opinion. . . . The United States intervenes thus in the affairs of the universe. . . . It is seated at the table where the great game is played, and it cannot leave it.

★

Summary

In 1877 the United States was, by any economic or population measure, already a great power. But America's orientation was inward-looking. The lax conduct of its foreign policy—and the neglect of its naval power—reflected the absence of significant overseas concerns. America's rapid economic development, however, began to force the country to look outward—in particular, because of the felt need for outlets for its surplus products. By the early 1890s a new strategic outlook had taken hold, best expressed in the writings of Alfred T. Mahan, that called for a battleship navy, an interoceanic canal, and overseas bases from which American naval power could be projected to ensure access to vital markets in Latin America and Asia. Accompanying this new expansionism were legitimating ideas drawn from Social Darwinism, Anglo-Saxon racism, and America's earlier tradition of Manifest Destiny.

With the Spanish-American War, the opportunity presented itself for acting on these imperialist impulses. On the one hand, America's traditional antiexpansionism was briefly silenced; on the other hand, swift victory enabled the United States to seize from Spain the key possessions it wanted. In taking the Philippines, however, the United States overstepped the bounds of the kind of colonialism palatable to the country—overseas bases, not the rule of alien populations. The result was a resurgence of anti-imperialist sentiment, deepened by Filipino resistance to annexation. Even so, the McKinley administration realized the strategic goals it had set for itself, and the United States entered the twentieth century poised to fulfill its destiny as a Great Power.

In Europe, the immediate consequences were few. Only in its *rapprochement* with England, and in Roosevelt's involvement in the Moroccan crisis, did the United States begin to depart from its traditional policy against European entanglements. Regarding its regional interests in the Caribbean and Asia, however, the United States moved much more decisively, building the Panama Canal, asserting its dominance over the nearby Latin states, and pressing for the Open Door in China. When Woodrow Wilson became president, he tried to bring the conduct of America's foreign policy into closer conformity with the nation's own political ideals, only to have the limitations of that new departure driven painfully home by his intervention in the Mexican revolution. That lesson was not so fundamental, however, as to stay Wilson's hand when a great world war engulfed Europe in 1914.

TOPIC FOR RESEARCH

The Anti-Imperialists (1898–1900)

During the 1890s, the attention grabbers were those advocating American expansionism. But America also had a long tradition of anti-imperialism—of opposition to the rule of other peoples by the United States—and this tradition was very much revived by the Spanish-American War and the sudden acquisition of an overseas empire. Although they had little political success, the anti-imperialists mounted a powerful critique of expansionism and, in particular, of the taking and subsequent bloody suppression of the Philippines. What were the ideas and arguments these anti-imperialists leveled against their nation's imperial adventure? The starting point for such an inquiry is Robert L. Beisner, *Twelve Against Empire: The Anti-Imperialists, 1898–1900* (1968), in particular the chapters on the philosopher William James, the industrialist Andrew Carnegie, the journalist E. L. Godkin (the editor of the *Nation*), and the Yankee businessman and historian Charles Francis Adams. A guide to the writings of these anti-imperialists is to be found in Beisner's "Note on Sources." Beisner links anti-imperialism to the Mugwump tradition. There were, however, many anti-imperialists outside that tradition. For labor, one might study the anti-imperialist Samuel Gompers; for a woman's perspective, Jane Addams; and, to see how humor was brought to bear on the pretensions of the expansionists, Mark Twain. As victims of American racism, African-Americans had particularly ambiguous feelings about the events of 1898–1900, and these might be explored in the writings of Booker T. Washington or in the contemporary black press. A useful source book is Philip S. Foner and Richard C. Winchester, eds., *The Anti-Imperialist Reader: A Documentary History of Anti-Imperialism in the U.S.* (1984).

BIBLIOGRAPHY

The Roots of Expansionism

Two useful surveys of late nineteenth-century diplomatic history are Foster R. Dulles, *Prelude to World Power, 1865–1900* (1965), and Charles S. Campbell, *The Transformation of American Foreign Relations, 1865–1900* (1976). Focusing more narrowly on the pre-expansionist era are

David M. Pletcher, *The Awkward Years: American Foreign Relations under Garfield and Arthur* (1963), and Milton Plesur, *America's Outward Thrust: Approaches to American Foreign Affairs, 1865–1890* (1971). Invaluable as an informed guide to recent scholarship is Robert L. Beisner, *From the Old Diplomacy to the New, 1865–1900* (2nd ed., 1986). Walter LaFeber's highly influential *The New Empire, 1860–1898* (1963) has placed economic interest—especially the need for overseas markets—at the center of scholarly debate over the sources of American expansionism. On American business overseas, the definitive work is Myra Wilkins, *The Emergence of the Multinational Enterprise: American Business Abroad from the Colonial Era to 1914* (1970). Other important books dealing with aspects of American expansionism are David Healy, *U.S. Expansionism: The Imperialist Urge in the 1890s* (1970); Robert Seager, *Alfred Thayer Mahan* (1977); Lester D. Langley, *Struggle for the American Mediterranean: United States–European Rivalry in the Gulf-Caribbean* (1976); and the early chapters of Akira Iriye, *Across the Pacific: An Inner History of American–East Asian Relations* (1967).

An American Empire

On the war with Spain and its settlement, see Lewis S. Gould, *The Spanish-American War and President McKinley* (1982); David S. Trask, *The War with Spain in 1898* (1981); Frank Freidel, *A Splendid Little War* (1958); and Julius W. Pratt, *The Expansionists of 1898: The Acquisition of Hawaii and the Spanish Islands* (1936). Lewis L. Gould, *The Presidency of William McKinley* (1980), emphasizes McKinley's strong leadership. Ernest R. May, *Imperial Democracy: The Emergence of America as a Great Power* (1961), exemplifies the earlier view—that McKinley was a weak figure, driven to war by jingoistic pressures—and is especially interesting because it shows the European view of America's emergence. On the Philippines, see Richard E. Welch, *Response to Imperialism: The United States and the Philippine-American War, 1898–1903* (1979), and, for the subsequent history, Peter Stanley, *A Nation in the Making: The Philippines and the United States, 1899–1921* (1974).

Onto the World Stage

On the European context, a useful introduction is to be found in the early chapters of Felix Gilbert, *The End of the European Era, 1890 to the Present* (4th ed., 1991), and, for a stimulating interpretation, L. C. B. Seaman, *From Vienna to Versailles* (1955). On American relations with Britain, the standard work is Bradford Perkins, *The Great Rapprochement: England and the United States, 1895–1914* (1968). On progressive diplomacy, the starting point remains Howard K. Beale, *Theodore Roosevelt and the Rise of America to World Power* (1956). There are keen insights into the diplomatic views of both Roosevelt and Wilson in John Milton Cooper, *The Warrior and the Priest* (1983). On the thrust into the Caribbean, see Walter LaFeber, *The Panama Canal* (1979); Dana G. Munro, *Intervention and Dollar Diplomacy in the Caribbean, 1900–1921* (1964); and David Healy, *The United States in Cuba, 1898–1902* (1963). America's Asian involvements are treated in Thomas J. McCormick, *China Market: America's Quest for Informal Empire, 1893–1901* (1967); Michael H. Hunt, *The Making of a Special Relationship: The*

United States and China to 1914 (1983); and Akira Iriye, *Pacific Estrangement: Japanese and American Expansion, 1897–1911* (1972). On the Mexican involvement, see P. Edward Haley, *Revolution and Intervention: The Diplomacy of Taft and Wilson with Mexico, 1910–1917* (1975). There is a lively and critical analysis of Wilson's misguided policies in Robert E. Quirk, *An Affair of Honor: Woodrow Wilson and the Occupation of Vera Cruz* (1962). The revolution as experienced by the Mexicans is brilliantly depicted in John Womack, *Zapata and the Mexican Revolution* (1968).

TIMELINE

1867	Purchase of Alaska
1871	Settlement of *Alabama* claims
1875	Reciprocity treaty with Hawaii
1876	United States achieves favorable balance of trade
1881	Secretary of State James G. Blaine inaugurates Pan-Americanism
1889	Conflict with Germany in Samoa President Harrison begins rebuilding U.S. Navy
1890	Alfred Thayer Mahan publishes *The Influence of Seapower on History*
1893	Annexation of Hawaii fails Frederick Jackson Turner's "The Significance of the Frontier in American History" Panic of 1893 ushers in economic depression (until 1897)
1894	Sino-Japanese war begins breakup of China into spheres of influence
1895	Venezuela crisis Cuban civil war
1898	Outbreak of Spanish-American War Hawaii annexed
1899	Treaty of Paris Guerrilla war in the Philippines "Open Door" policy in China
1901	Theodore Roosevelt becomes president; diplomacy of the "big stick"
1903	Panama Canal Treaty
1904	Roosevelt Corollary
1905	U.S. mediates Franco-German crisis over Morocco
1907	Gentlemen's Agreement with Japan
1908	Root-Takahira Treaty
1909	Taft becomes president; "dollar diplomacy"

PART 5

The Modern State and Society

1914–1945

THEMATIC TIMELINE

	Government	Diplomacy	Economy	Society	Culture
	The rise of the state	**From isolation to world leadership**	**Prosperity, depression, and war**	**Nativism, migration, and social change**	**The emergence of a mass national culture**
1914	Wartime agencies expand power of the federal government	U.S. enters World War I, 1917 Wilson's Fourteen Points, 1918	Agricultural glut	Southern blacks begin migration to northern cities	Silent screen; Hollywood becomes movie capital of the world
1920	Republican ascendancy Prohibition, 1920–33 Business-government partnership	Treaty of Versailles rejected by U.S. Senate, 1920 Washington Conference sets navy limits, 1922	Economic recession, 1920–21 Booming prosperity, 1922–29 Welfare capitalism	Rise of nativism National Origins Act (1924) Mexican-American immigration increases	The Jazz Age Advertising promotes consumer culture, supports radio and new magazines
1930	Franklin D. Roosevelt becomes president, 1933 The New Deal: unprecedented government intervention in economy, social welfare, arts	Roosevelt's Good Neighbor Policy toward Latin America, 1933 Abraham Lincoln Brigade fights in Spanish Civil War U.S. neutrality proclaimed, 1939	Great Depression, 1929–41 Rise of labor movement	Farming families migrate from Dust Bowl states to California and the West	Documentary impulse Federal patronage of the arts
1940	Government mobilizes industry for war production	U.S. enters World War II, 1941 Allies defeat Axis powers; bombing of Hiroshima, 1945	War moblization ends depression	Rural whites and blacks migrate to war jobs in cities Civil rights movement revitalized	Movies enlisted to aid war effort

No single event marked the birth of modern America in the twentieth century. But by 1914 industrialization, economic expansion abroad, and the growth of a vibrant urban culture had laid the foundations for a new, distinctly *modern* American society. The patterns of localism, autonomy, and isolation that had prevailed in industrializing America were being challenged by new forces of centralization and nationalism.

First, one of the strongest forces shaping modern American society was the rise of the state. The state came late to America, and it came haltingly, compared to Western European industrialized countries. Despite the trust-busting and worker protection laws of the Progressive Era, Americans remained uneasy about the idea of a strong national state. When the United States entered World War I, policymakers were wary of a permanent concentration of government power in Washington. State bureaucratic capacity expanded to fight the war, but the wartime agencies were quickly dismantled at the end of the conflict. During the 1920s the Republican administrations of Harding and Coolidge followed a philosophy of business-government partnership, which blurred the lines between public and private power but still relied heavily on private initiatives. Most Americans continued to believe that unrestricted corporate capitalism could provide adequately for the welfare of the American people. It took the Great Depression, with its uncounted business failures and unprecedented levels of unemployment and suffering, to overthrow that long-cherished idea. President Franklin D. Roosevelt's New Deal dramatically expanded federal responsibility for regulating the economy and guaranteeing the social welfare of ordinary citizens. While the New Deal resulted in a huge growth of federal power, an even greater expansion of the state came with the massive mobilization necessitated by World War II. Unlike the experience after World War I, the new state apparatus was not dismantled when the war ended.

Second, the United States was finally drawn, slowly and reluctantly, into the position of world leadership it still occupies today. In 1918, American troops provided the margin of victory for the Allies in World War I, and President Wilson helped shape the treaties that ended the war. But America was not prepared to embrace Wilson's internationalist vision and refused to join the League of Nations. America's self-imposed isolation from world events ended definitively in 1941, when the nation threw all its energies into defeating Germany and Japan. The United States became the leader of the alliance, and the dominant world power.

Third, by 1920 American society had been transformed by the great wave of European immigration and the migration from the farm to the cities. The growth of metropolitan areas gave the nation an increasingly urban tone, while geographic mobility broke down old regional differences. Many old-stock white Americans viewed these aspects of modern America with alarm; in 1924 nativists succeeded in all but eliminating immigration from the Eastern Hemisphere. But internal migration continued to change the human face of America, as African-Americans moved north to take up factory jobs and Dust Bowl farmers moved to the Far West in search of better land.

Fourth, a defining feature of modern America was the emergence of a mass national culture. Citizens were increasingly drawn into a web of interlocking cultural experiences. Advertising and the new entertainment media—the movies, radio, and magazines—disseminated the new values of consumerism. Not even the Great Depression could wean Americans from their desire for leisure, self-fulfillment, and consumer goods. The emphasis on consumption and a rising standard of living would define the American experience for the rest of the twentieth century.

Despite the many forces combining to centralize power and decisionmaking and nationalize American culture, modern America was still marked by great and deep-seated diversity. The lives of ordinary Americans were shaped by whether they lived in cities or rural areas, whether they were black or white, male or female, rich or poor, young or old. Describing the centralizing tendencies in modern American life while connecting them to the ongoing diversity of social experience offers clues to the complexity of America's history in the 1914–1945 period, and beyond.

America and the War Effort

Irving Berlin's 1918 songsheet captured the ambivalence surrounding American participation in World War I: soldiers were proud to serve, but it was still hard to get up in the morning.

CHAPTER 23 *War and the American State, 1914–1920*

"It would be the irony of fate if my administration had to deal chiefly with foreign affairs," Woodrow Wilson confided to a friend early in his first term. But the United States was no longer just a regional power—it was seated at the table of the "great game" of international politics. When war broke out in Europe in August 1914 Wilson had to play his hand. For more than two years he tried to mediate as an honest broker between two sides. Only when Germany's resumption of unrestricted submarine attacks posed an unacceptable threat to American lives and shipping did he reluctantly ask for a declaration of war.

When the United States entered the conflict in 1917, President Wilson led the country with the same idealistic rhetoric he had brought to domestic concerns during the Progressive Era. American participation would make the world "safe for democracy," "end all wars," and "bring peace and safety to all nations." In the first major U.S. intervention in Great Power politics, Wilson aimed for no less than a new international order based on democratic American ideals.

Despite Woodrow Wilson's rhetoric, the United States was not ready to wage a modern war in 1917. Entirely new arms of the federal bureaucracy had to be created to coordinate the efforts of business, labor, and agriculture, a process that hastened the emergence of a national administrative state. War meant new opportunities—for women, for blacks, and for other ethnic minorities. It also meant new divisions among Americans and new hatreds, first of Germans and Austrians and then of "Bolshevik" Reds. When the war ended, the United States confronted the legacy of deep class, racial, and ethnic divisions that had surfaced during wartime mobilization.

The Great War, 1914–1918

When the Great War erupted in August 1914 (few anticipated a second world war just a generation later), most Americans saw no reason to get involved in a struggle among Europe's imperialistic powers. No vital American interests were at stake; indeed America had good relationships with both sides. But a combination of factors—economic interests, neutrality rights, cultural ties with Great Britain and France, and German miscalculations—would finally draw the United States into the war on the Allied side in 1917.

War in Europe

Almost from the moment that the Triple Entente was formed in 1907 to counter the Triple Alliance (see Chapter 22), European leaders prepared for what they saw as an inevitable conflict. The spark that ignited war came in Europe's perennial tinderbox, the Balkans. As the Ottoman Empire slowly disintegrated, Austria-Hungary and Russia competed for the remains of its Balkan possessions. Austria's seizure of the provinces of Bosnia and Herzegovina in 1908 enraged Russia and its client, the independent state of Serbia, who had wanted the provinces for itself. Serbian terrorists recruited Bosnians to agitate against Austrian rule and on

June 28, 1914, one of their number assassinated Franz Ferdinand, the heir to the Austro-Hungarian throne, and his wife in the Bosnian town of Sarajevo.

After the assassination, the complex European alliance system that had for years maintained a fragile peace now quickly pulled all the major powers into war. When Serbia failed to respond to a harsh Austrian ultimatum, Austria declared war on Serbia on July 28. Russia, which had a secret treaty with Serbia, began preparations for war. Germany in turn declared war on Russia and Russia's ally France, and invaded Belgium. On August 4, Great Britain declared war on Germany, and two days later Russia and Austria-Hungary formally entered the conflict.

The combatants were divided into two rival blocs. The Allied Powers were composed of Great Britain, France, Japan, Russia, and in 1915, Italy. They were pitted against the Central Powers, initially Germany, Austria-Hungary, Turkey, joined by Bulgaria in 1915. Because of the alliance system, the fighting spread to parts of the world beyond Europe. The Austrians and Germans faced the Russians on the Eastern Front; Turkey squared off against Russian and British troops (including units from Australia, New Zealand, and India) in the Middle East and Mesopotamia; and the British, French, and Japanese quickly seized German overseas territories in Africa, China, and the South Pacific. The resulting carnage, especially in battles such as Gallipoli in the Dardanelles, confirmed the conflict's designation as a world war. World War I was also the first modern war to involve extensive harm to civilian populations.

Since the Franco-Prussian War in 1870, massive industrialization and an escalating arms race among the Great Powers had completely transformed the technology of war. In the hands of every World War I soldier was a long-range, high-velocity rifle that could reach a target at 1000 yards, a vast improvement over the 300-yard range of the rifle-musket of the American Civil War. Significantly, the mass production of rifles in Europe was made possible by the adoption of technology first developed in Connecticut factories. Another innovation, the machine gun, also had American roots. Its Maine-born inventor, Hiram Maxim, had moved to England in the 1880s, heeding a friend's advice: "If you want to make your fortune, invent something which will allow those fool Europeans to kill each other more quickly." And make his fortune he did.

The concentrated fire of rifles and machine guns gave a tremendous advantage to defensive positions. For four bloody years between 1914 and 1918, the Allies and Central Powers faced each other on the Western Front, a small swath of territory in Belgium and northern France riddled with approximately 25,000 miles of heavily fortified trenches, enough to circle the globe. Trench warfare produced unprecedented casualties. If either side tried to break the stalemate by venturing into the "no man's land" between, soldiers were mowed down by artillery fire or poison gas, first used by the Germans at the battle of Ypres in April 1915. Between February and December 1916, the French suffered 550,000 casualties and the Germans 450,000 as Germany tried to break through the French lines at Verdun. The front did not move.

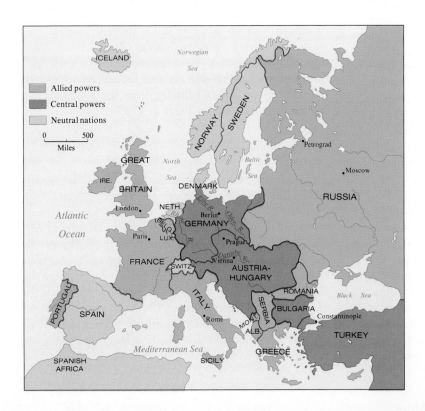

MAP 23.1

Europe at the Start of World War I
In early August 1914 a complex set of interlocking alliances drew the major European powers into war. At first the United States held aloof from the conflict. Not until April 1917 did the country enter the war on the Allied side.

The Landscape of War
World War I devastated the countryside: this was the battleground at Ypres in 1915.
The carnage of trench warfare also scarred the soldiers who served in these surreal
settings, causing the "burial-alive neurosis," "gas neurosis," and "soldiers' heart,"
all symptoms of shell-shock.

Military Technology. Military strategists struggled to find ways to break the stalemate on the Western Front. Tanks, first used in the battle of the Somme in the fall of 1916, proved effective against the machine gun and could crush through the barbed wire protecting enemy trenches, but they did not play the decisive military role they would in World War II. Nor did airplanes, despite the dramatic growth of aviation since the Wright brothers' 12-second, 120-foot flight at Kitty Hawk, North Carolina, in 1903. The technology of aerial bombardment was still primitive, so airplanes mainly flew photographic reconnaissance missions. An American Brigadier General marveled at the new perspective airplanes supplied on battle: a plane could cross the lines in a few minutes, survey enemy territory, and return quickly, "whereas the armies had been locked in the struggle, immovable, powerless to advance, for three years."

The Perils of Neutrality

Two weeks after the outbreak of war in Europe, President Wilson made the American position clear. In a widely publicized speech, the president called on Americans to be "neutral in fact as well as in name, impartial in thought as well as in action." Wilson wanted to keep out of war in order to play a larger, not a lesser, role in world affairs. The child of a Presbyterian minister, Woodrow Wilson approached foreign affairs with missionary zeal. He never doubted the superiority of the Christian values he had learned as a boy, nor did he question the chauvinistic belief that the United States was better than the rest of the world. Only if he kept America aloof from the European quarrel, Wilson reasoned, could he impartially arbitrate—and influence—its ultimate settlement.

The nation's divided loyalties also influenced President Wilson's neutrality policy. Many Americans, including Wilson himself, felt deep cultural ties to the Allies, especially Britain and France. And yet, most Catholic Irish-Americans fiercely resented the centuries-long British occupation of their home country and the cancellation of Irish Home Rule in 1914. On the other hand, 10 million immigrants had come from Germany or Austria-Hungary, and German-Americans made up the largest, best-established ethnic group in the United States. Many aspects of German culture, including classical music and Germany's university system, were widely admired. It would not have been easy for Wilson to rally the nation to the Allied side in 1914, had he chosen to try.

Many other Americans had no sympathy for either side. Pacifist sentiment was diffuse but broad. Progressive Republican senators, such as Robert La Follette of Wisconsin and George Norris of Nebraska, vehemently opposed American participation in the European conflict. Practically the entire political left, led principally by Eugene Debs and the Socialist party, condemned the war as imperialism. Pacifist groups, among them the American Union Against Militarism and the Women's Peace party founded in 1915, also mobilized popular opposition. Feminists Jane Addams and Crystal Eastman spoke out against war as an instrument of national policy. Prominent industrialists Andrew Carnegie and Henry Ford bankrolled antiwar activities. Ford spent almost half a million dollars in December 1915 to send more than a hundred men and women on a "peace ship" to Europe in the hope of negotiating an end to the war.

Conflict on the High Seas. With no stake in the territorial struggles among the European powers, the United States might well have remained neutral, had the conflict not spread to a new, undefined theater—the high seas. Here the United States initially had as many arguments with Britain as with Germany. The most troublesome issue concerned freedom of the seas and neutrality rights, that is, the freedom to trade with nations on both sides of a conflict.

By the end of August 1914, the British had succeeded in imposing a naval blockade on the Central Powers. The Allies were hoping to cut off military supplies and starve the German people into submission, but their action also effectively prevented neutral nations such as the United States from trading with Germany and its allies. American business was profiting handsomely from supplying food and arms to the combatants on both sides. The United States chafed at the British infringement of its neutrality rights, but chose to do little else, largely because the spectacular increase in trade with the Allies more than made up for the lost trade with the Central Powers. American trade with England and France grew from $824 million in 1914 to $3.2 billion in 1916, and by 1917, U.S. bankers had loaned the Allies $2.5 billion. In contrast, American trade with the Central Powers declined from $169 million in 1914 to $1 million in 1916.

To challenge British control of the seas, the German navy launched a devastating new weapon, the U-boat, short for *Unterseeboot* (undersea boat, or submarine). In February 1915, Germany announced its own naval blockade of Great Britain: German submarines would attack any ship transporting military supplies to the

Confrontation on the High Seas
These passengers and crew on a Spanish steamer have just been halted for inspection by a German submarine patrolling the North Sea in 1917. They are understandably nervous, since they know that the confrontation with the German sub could easily cost them their ship, and possibly their lives.

British Isles. Traditional rules of naval warfare required submarine commanders to warn and search a ship before it could be sunk. If a submarine surfaced to carry out this requirement, however, it lost its greatest advantage—surprise—and left itself vulnerable to attack. The Germans began sinking enemy ships, including passenger ships, without warning.

Although the Germans sank an American ship without warning on May 1, it was the sinking of a British luxury liner, the *Lusitania*, off the Irish coast on May 7, 1915, that brought the United States to the brink of war. When the *Lusitania* went down, 1,200 people died, including 128 Americans. The passenger ship, although unarmed, was carrying thousands of cases of ammunition, and passengers had been warned of the risk of attack. Yet many Americans shared the outrage of former president Theodore Roosevelt who characterized the attack as "an act of piracy." Newspapers called the loss of innocent civilian lives "mass murder." The National Security League intensified its calls for "preparedness," including a system of universal military training.

Woodrow Wilson sent a series of strongly worded notes to Germany protesting the assault on the freedom of nonbelligerents to travel on the high seas, although he did not take the additional precaution of banning Americans from traveling on the ships of Germany's enemies. The crisis continued until September when Germany announced that submarine commanders would not attack passenger ships without warning. (Eight months later the Germans halted, at least temporarily, attacks on merchant shipping.) For the Germans, the danger of drawing the United States into the war over neutrality rights and freedom of the seas far offset the benefits of attacking British ships. A temporary lull set into the naval war.

The *Lusitania* crisis divided Wilson's government into pro- and anti-British factions. Secretary of State William Jennings Bryan resigned in protest. Bryan could not support Wilson's harsh criticism of Germany's violation of neutrality rights, while the president remained silent about Britain's violation of American rights with its blockade. Throughout the stalemate years of 1915 and 1916, Wilson's attempt to mediate the European conflict came to naught.

The 1916 Election. The 1916 election failed to serve as a referendum on the American stance toward the European war. The Republicans passed over Theodore Roosevelt's prowar belligerence in favor of Justice Charles Evans Hughes of the Supreme Court, a former reform governor of New York. The Democrats renominated Woodrow Wilson. The foreign policies of the two candidates hardly differed, although the Democrats picked up votes with their widely circulated campaign slogan, "He kept us out of war." They won a narrow victory over a Republican party reunited after its 1912 split. Despite polling three million more votes than he had received in 1912, Wilson defeated Hughes by only about 600,000 popular votes and by 277 to 254 in the electoral college. This slender margin limited Wilson's options both in mobilizing the nation for war and planning the postwar peace.

Toward War. The events of early 1917 diminished whatever hopes Wilson had of staying out of the

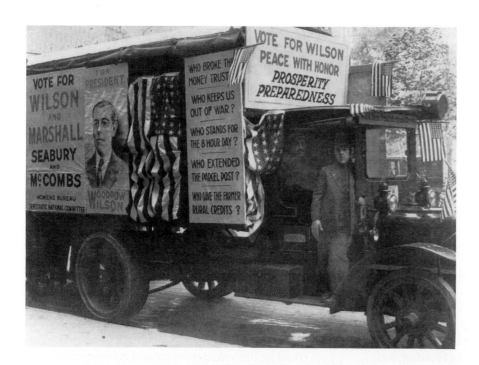

The 1916 Campaign

This campaign van sponsored by the Women's Bureau of the Democratic National Committee linked Woodrow Wilson to the themes of prosperity and preparedness. Note the variation on the popular slogan, "Who keeps us out of war?"

conflict. On January 31, Germany announced the resumption of unrestricted submarine attacks, a decision dictated by the impasse of the ground war. Germany planned boldly to sever the trade links between America and the Allies. Although the Germans knew the renewal of attacks would almost certainly bring the United States into the war, the German General Staff assured the government that their submarines could paralyze Allied shipping before the Americans could join the fighting. In response, President Wilson broke off diplomatic relations with Germany on February 3, and though he still held off requesting a declaration of war from Congress, he ordered the War Department to prepare for hostilities.

The release of the "Zimmermann telegram" in late February 1917 also moved the country closer to war. Newspapers published an intercepted communication from Germany's foreign secretary, Alfred Zimmermann, to the German minister in Mexico City, which contained conclusive evidence of German interference in Mexican affairs. In a direct challenge to the Monroe Doctrine, Germany urged Mexico to join the war against the United States, and in return, Germany promised to help Mexico recover "the lost territory of Texas, New Mexico, and Arizona." When the telegram was decoded and made public on February 27, this threat to the territorial integrity of the United States jolted both Congressional and public opinion, especially in the West where support for the war had lagged. Combined with the resumption of unrestricted submarine warfare, this telegram further inflamed anti-German sentiments.

Although the likelihood of Mexico reconquering the border states was slim, American policymakers took this threat seriously because the situation there remained highly fluid. In the final stage of the Mexican revolution, the Constitutionalist movement led by Venustiano Carranza consolidated its power over challenger Pancho Villa. But Villa continued to stir up trouble along the border, killing sixteen U.S. citizens in January 1916 and razing the town of Columbus, New Mexico, in March. As the Mexican civil war threatened to spill over the Rio Grande into the United States, Wilson sent troops led by General John J. Pershing into Mexico after the elusive Villa; soon Pershing's force resembled an army of occupation rather than a punitive expedition. Mexican public opinion demanded that Pershing withdraw immediately. At the brink of war, the two governments backed off and U.S. troops began to leave in early 1917. The Carranza government received official recognition from Washington on March 13, 1917, less than a month before the United States entered World War I.

Declaring War. Throughout March, U-boats attacked American ships without warning, sinking three U.S. ships on March 18 alone. On April 2, 1917, after con-

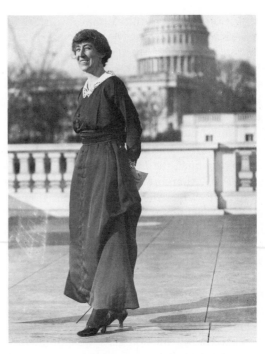

The First Woman in Congress
In 1916, Jeannette Rankin, a former suffrage organizer, became the first woman elected to Congress. Her vote against U.S. entry into World War I cost her the chance for election to the Senate in 1918. In 1940, Rankin once again won election to Congress from Montana. True to her lifelong pacifism, she cast the only vote against American entry into World War II.

sulting the Cabinet and his own conscience, Wilson appeared before a special session of Congress to ask for a declaration of war. "The world must be made safe for democracy," he stated, in a memorable phrase intended to ennoble the conflict. America had no selfish aims: "We desire no conquest, no dominion. We seek no indemnities for ourselves, no material compensation for the sacrifices we shall freely make. We are but one of the champions of the rights of mankind."

Four days later, on April 6, 1917, the United States declared war on Germany. Six senators and fifty members of the House voted against the action, including Representative Jeannette Rankin of Montana, the first woman elected to Congress. "I want to stand by my country," she declared, "but I cannot vote for war."

Over There

To native-born Americans especially, Europe was a great distance away, literally "over there," as the lyrics of a popular World War I song described it. After the declaration of war, many citizens were surprised to learn that the United States planned to send troops to Europe—they had assumed that the nation's participation could be limited to military and economic aid.

In May 1917, General John J. Pershing, recently returned from pursuing Pancho Villa in Mexico, set sail for London and Paris to determine how the Americans could best support the war effort. The answer was clear: as the French Marshall Joseph Joffre put it, "Men, men, and more men." The problem was that the United States had always avoided having a large standing army in peacetime. There were only about 200,000 soldiers, mostly life-time volunteers, on active duty in early 1917. To field a credible fighting force, the government turned to conscription.

Conscription. The passage of the Selective Service Act in May 1917 demonstrated the increasing impact of the state on ordinary Americans. Unlike the resistance to conscription during the Civil War, no major draft riots marred its implementation. The selective service system worked in part because it combined central direction from Washington with local administration and civilian control, and thus did not tread unnecessarily on traditions of individual freedom and local autonomy. On a single day, June 5, 1917, more than 9.5 million men between the ages of 21 and 30 were processed for military service at their local voting precincts. Draft registration demonstrated the potential bureaucratic capacity of the American state.

Although compliance was not universal, most male citizens went along with the draft's premise of service (a key Progressive word) as a responsibility of modern citizenship. By the end of the war, almost 4 million men, plus a few thousand female navy clerks and army nurses, were in uniform. Nearly 3 million men were inducted by a draft lottery; the rest volunteered. Over 300,000 men evaded the draft (they were called "slackers") and another 4,000 were classified as conscientious objectors.

President Wilson chose General Pershing to head the American Expeditionary Force (AEF), but the newly raised army did not have an immediate impact on the European fighting. The new recruits had to be trained and outfitted. Then they had to wait for one of the few available transport ships to take them thousands of miles across the submarine-infested Atlantic. By June 1917 only 15,000 AEF troops had arrived in France.

At first, the main contribution of the United States was to secure the safety of the seas. When the United States entered the war, German submarines were sinking Allied ships at the alarming rate of about 900,000 tons a month. The U-boats had seriously hampered the ability to send supplies and munitions to the Allies and threatened the transport of American troops to the European front. Adopting a plan that aimed for safety in numbers, the government began sending armed convoys across the Atlantic. The plan worked. No American soldiers were killed on their way to Europe. Allied shipping losses were cut to 400,000 tons a month by late 1917, to 200,000 tons by April 1918.

Call to Arms
To build popular support for the war effort, the government called on the services of such artists as Howard Chandler Christy, Charles Dana Gibson, and James Montgomery Flagg. This 1917 recruiting poster by Flagg was adapted from a June 1916 cover of *Leslie's Illustrated Weekly Newspaper*. The model was the artist.

Meanwhile, trench warfare continued its deadly grind on the Western Front. Allied commanders pleaded for American reinforcements to be assigned to their units, but Pershing was reluctant to put his independent fighting unit under non-American commanders. Because the AEF was not ready as a fighting force until May 1918, the brunt of the fighting continued to fall on the French and British, and Britain's imperial troops, primarily from Canada and Australia.

The Russian Revolution and the Collapse of the Eastern Front. On the Eastern Front, the strain of fighting the Germans had exposed the weaknesses of the Russian government headed by Tsar Nicholas II, and a general mutiny of the troops led to the overthrow of the monarchy in March 1917. The new provisional government headed by Prince George Lvov and socialist Alexander Kerensky promised democratic reforms, but it also insisted on continuing the war. Russian workers and peasants were sick of war—sick of the seemingly endless food shortages at home, sick of the horrendous casualties at the front. Conditions were ripe for a second revolution.

The communist theorist Vladimir Ilych Lenin, who had been living in exile in Switzerland when the March revolution took place, saw his chance. Lenin was a follower of Karl Marx, and he anticipated that a period of the "dictatorship of the proletariat" [workers] would be necessary to root out capitalism before a classless society could emerge. The Germans, hoping to promote internal strife in Russia, cannily arranged Lenin's safe passage home on a sealed railroad car. Lenin and a group of Bolshevik revolutionaries arrived in Petrograd (later Leningrad, and now St. Petersburg) in April 1917 and began their agitation against the provisional government. On November 6, Lenin directed a Bolshevik-led coup against the government and quickly consolidated his control by promising "peace, land, and bread" to the long-suffering masses.

The new Bolshevik government kept the first part of its promise. Russia agreed to a cease-fire with Germany and Austria-Hungary on December 15, 1917, and signed the Treaty of Brest-Litovsk on March 3, 1918. The Bolsheviks surrendered massive territories—Russian Poland, the Ukraine, the Baltic provinces, and Finland—in return for an end to hostilities. Yet instead of peace, the Russian people got three more years of war, a vicious, devastating civil war.

Allied Victory in the West. The plight of the new Soviet state would command the Allies' attention after the armistice. When hostilities ended with Russia, Germany turned its full fighting force to break the stalemate on the Western Front. On March 21, 1918, the Germans launched a major offensive and by May the German army had advanced to the Marne River within 50 miles of Paris. Allied leaders intensified their calls for fresh American troops, and Pershing, who was under orders to keep the AEF a separate fighting unit, relented a bit to help the Allies bolster their defenses. About 60,000 American soldiers helped the French repel the Germans in the battles of Château-Thierry and Belleau Wood in May and June.

American reinforcements now began to arrive in force. Fresh troops flooded the ports of Liverpool in England and Brest and Saint Nazaire in France—245,000 in May 1918, 278,000 in June, and 306,000 in July. From there they worked their way slowly to the front along the clogged French transportation system. The Allied force, augmented by 85,000 American troops, brought the German offensive to a halt in mid-July. At that point, a million American troops were in France, and the counteroffensive began. On July 18, the Allies with 270,000 American troops began a drive to push the Germans back from their position on the Marne, which was successful. Approximately 100,000 American soldiers helped the British push the Germans back north of the Somme River.

MAP 23.2

U.S. Participation on the Western Front, 1918

When American troops finally reached the European front in significant numbers in 1918, the Allied and Central powers had been grinding each other down in a war of attrition for almost four years. The influx of American troops and supplies broke the stalemate. Successful offensive maneuvers by the American Expeditionary Force included Belleau Wood, Château-Thierry, and the Meuse-Argonne campaign.

Mustard Gas *Frederick Pottle*

Frederick Pottle volunteered for service as an enlisted man in the Medical Corps. He describes here the effects of mustard gas during the battles of Belleau Woods and Château-Thierry in June of 1918.

Indeed, those dreadful mustard-gas cases were probably the most painful we had to witness in all our service. As a matter of fact, the majority were in much less serious plight than the wounded men. Mustard gas (it has nothing to with mustard) is a heavy liquid, which, though fairly volatile, will remain for some time clinging to grass and undergrowth, and will burn any flesh with which it comes in contact. It is especially adapted for use by a retreating army. By soaking down with mustard gas the area through which the pursuing American troops had to advance, the Germans made sure that a large number of the advancing force would be incapacitated. The soldier's clothing soon becomes impregnated with the stuff as he

brushes through the undergrowth, and the burns develop through the help of moisture. Those parts of the body subject to excessive perspiration are especially affected. The burns are extremely painful, but in general not fatal unless the gas has been inhaled, or (as with other surface burns) a third or more of the total skin area has been affected. A bad feature of mustard gas, however, is that it almost invariably produces temporary, but complete, blindness. Nothing demoralizes a man so much as the fear of losing his sight, and telling him that he will see again in a day or two generally fails to reassure him. The gas cases began to arrive at Juilly as early as June 12. Since most of them were immediately evacuable, we made temporary wards for them in the great cloisters which ran around two sides of the court in front of Wards F and G—the children's dormitories. By the sixteenth there were nearly seven hundred gassed men there, just out of the glare of the sunny court, lying fully dressed on blanket-

covered cots, some of them badly gassed in the lungs and fighting horribly for breath, which could be a little prolonged by giving them oxygen; nearly all blinded, many delirious, all crying, moaning, tossing about. For most of the patients there was nothing to do but renew frequently the wet dressings which relieved somewhat the smart of the burns, and to try to restore their lost morale. For those who had been gassed worst, nothing effectual could be done. They were spared much by being in general delirious, but it required the constant attention of several orderlies to keep some of them in bed. Later on, the hospital service was so organized that the gas cases were handled by special gas hospitals. After we left Juilly we almost never received gas victims unless they were also wounded.

Source: Frederick A. Pottle, *Stretchers: The Story of a Hospital Unit on the Western Front* (New Haven: Yale University Press, 1929), 117–118.

In mid-September 1918, General Pershing, leading 500,000 Americans and 100,000 French soldiers, launched an offensive aimed at closing a hole in Allied lines at Saint-Mihiel. After four days of heavy artillery shelling of German positions, the Germans, who had been preparing to evacuate the area, retreated. On September 26, Pershing launched the last major assault of the war, which pushed the enemy back across the Selle River near Verdun and broke the German defenses. This forty-seven-day Meuse-Argonne campaign represented the main American military contribution to the fighting.

The flood of American troops and supplies during the last six months of fighting provided the Allied margin of victory. In many ways, this American contribution was emblematic of the shift in international power

as European dominance declined and the United States emerged as a new world leader. World War I ended on November 11, 1918, when German representatives signed an armistice in the railway car of the French Marshall Foch.

The American Fighting Force

About two million American soldiers were in France when the war ended. Two-thirds of them had seen at least brief action on the western front, but most American "doughboys" escaped the horrors of sustained trench warfare that had sapped the morale of Allied and German troops. (The nickname may have derived from

AMERICAN LIVES

Edward Vernon Rickenbacker, Fighter Pilot

He was born Edward Rickenbacher in Columbus, Ohio, on October 8, 1890. Notice the slight but significant difference in the spelling: he adopted a less Germanic version of his last name, and added an English-sounding middle name, at the beginning of World War I. Even before his designation as the "American Ace of Aces" for shooting down more enemy craft than any other American pilot, Eddie Rickenbacker was front page news as a celebrity race car driver. He began racing at the age of sixteen, and in 1911 competed in the first Indianapolis 500 road race. The holder of the world speed record of 134 miles per hour, he earned the fabulous sum of $60,000 at the height of his racing career in 1916.

When the United States entered the war in 1917, Rickenbacker immediately enlisted. He was sent to France as a member of General John J. ("Black Jack") Pershing's motor car staff, although he was not Pershing's personal chauffeur, as legend sometimes has it. But his skills as a mechanic and a driver brought him to the attention of Colonel Billy Mitchell, one of Pershing's senior air staff, who helped arrange Rickenbacker's transfer to the Air Service. At that point, he had never flown a plane. He was originally told that at the age of twenty-eight he was too old to fly combat, but he proved the doubters wrong: his quick reflexes and competitive instincts from his racing career made him a superb pilot. Rickenbacker dutifully informed his mother about his change in assignment, telling her that flying was safer than race car driving because there was lots of room in the sky. She in turn cautioned him to be sure to fly slow and close to the ground.

In March 1918, Rickenbacker was posted to the 94th Aero Pursuit Squadron, the first all-American air squadron to go into action on the Western Front. The 94th was known as "hat-in-the ring," for the American custom of throwing a hat into the ring as an invitation to battle, and they adopted that representation as the insignia for their planes. But at first the American pilots did not have much of an impact on the fighting, hampered by antiquated French planes that did not even have machine guns. Only in August 1918 did the 94th get new planes, French-made SPADS, a single-seat pursuit fighter equipped with machine guns, which was fast and reliable.

When the war broke out, airplanes were used mainly for reconnaisance and artillery spotting, but the addition of machine guns transformed planes into offensive weapons. With guns mounted in front, combat pilots zoomed in on the tail of an enemy craft; to aim their machine gun, they simply aimed the plane at the intended target and poured bullets into both the plane and the pilot before beating a hasty retreat. French inventor Roland Garros made aerial combat possible by figuring out how to synchronize the firing of bullets with the rotation of the propeller.

Although German squadrons often hunted in packs (the so-called flying circus under the direction of Baron Manfred von Lichthofen, the German ace known as the "Red Baron"), American pilots preferred to sneak up on their targets one at a time. These pilots had great respect for each other's skills, and would often joust in the air for position until one of them ran out of fuel and headed for home. Eddie Rickenbacker remembered no personal animosity against his German foes and was always delighted to learn that a downed pilot had escaped with his life. (This rarely happened since few aircraft were equipped with parachutes.) But once locked in a dogfight, Rickenbacker remembered, "I had no regrets over killing a fellow human being. I do not believe that at that moment I even considered the matter. Like nearly all air fighters, I was an automaton behind the gun barrels of my plane. I never thought of killing an individual but of shooting down an enemy plane." He fought in 134 air battles in all, and narrowly escaped death on several occasions.

Flying Aces
One of America's best known aces was former professional race car driver Eddie
Rickenbacker (middle). Note the "hat-in-the ring" insigna on the plane.

In September 1918, Rickenbacker was named Commander of the 94th Squadron, and most of his victories came in the last two months of the war. In one encounter, for which he was later awarded the Congressional Medal of Honor, he singlehandedly took on seven German planes and downed two of them. He shot down fourteen enemy aircraft in the month of October alone, bringing his total to twenty-six confirmed victories and clinching his status as the American Ace of Aces. Under his leadership, the 94th "Hat in the Ring" Squadron became the most victorious American air unit of the war. Eddie Rickenbacker returned to the United-States a national hero, publishing a book about his war experiences, *Fighting the Flying Circus*, in 1919.

World War I dramatically accelerated the growth of aviation, both in its commercial and military applications. After the war, Eddie Rickenbacker dabbled in racing and automobile production before joining Eastern Airlines as its general manager in 1935; in1938 he became its president. As head of Eastern, then one of the flagships of modern aviation, Rickenbacker served as a spokesperson for commercial aviation until his retirement in 1963. Over the course of his lifetime (he died in 1973), this new industry grew up. Eddie Rickenbacker symbolized the fascination of early flight, even in the unlikely arena of war, and its possibilities for individual heroism. But just as significantly, he stood for the development of commercial aviation, which in the years after World War II would revolutionize world travel.

the buttons on the uniforms of American infantrymen, which resembled dumplings made of dough.) During the eighteen months that the United States fought in the war, 50,585 American servicemen were killed in action. Another 60,000 died from other causes, mainly the influenza epidemic that swept the world in 1918–1919. The nation suffered minimal casualties compared with the 8 million soldiers lost by the Allies and the Central Powers. The French lost far more soldiers in the siege of Verdun than the United States did in the entire war.

Although individual bravery grew increasingly anachronistic in the midst of modern warfare, the war generated its share of American heroes. Sergeant Alvin York singlehandedly killed twenty-five Germans and took 132 prisoners at the battle of Châtel-Chéhéry in the Meuse-Argonne campaign. Although air power played only a minor part in the actual conduct of the war, it captivated the popular imagination. One of America's best known aces was former professional race car driver Eddie Rickenbacker. The exploits of daredevil pilots, fighting it out in the skies like medieval knights in combat armor, provided a thrill that contrasted with the monotony of trench warfare. The popular fascination with Rickenbacker and York suggests a deep-seated need to annoint individual heroes in what had become an increasingly depersonalized and mechanized pursuit of war.

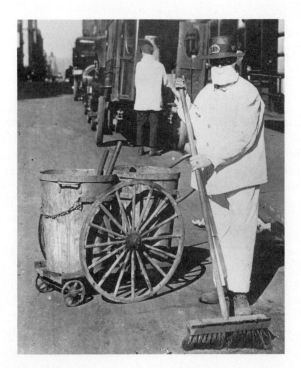

Fighting the Flu
The influenza epidemic of 1918–1919 strained the resources of a public health system already fully mobilized for the war effort. Here sanitation workers don protective masks to lessen their risk of contracting the often deadly disease.

Military Morality. High ideals set the tone for military service. Reformers urged the adoption of progressive solutions to the vices of alcohol and sex, and government and military officials agreed. Reflecting the anti-liquor fever taking hold in America, Secretary of the Navy Josephus Daniels declared navy ships dry. The army banned drinking by soldiers in uniform, and prohibited liquor on army bases and their surrounding localities.

The army also mounted an ambitious program of sex education. In an era when people rarely discussed sex in public, the army program brought the subject into the open. Concerned that venereal disease might sap the strength of the fighting men (antibiotics had not yet been developed), the army launched an anti-VD campaign. As soldiers ate dinner in their mess halls, they looked up at posters that proclaimed "A German Bullet is Cleaner than a Whore" or "How could you look the flag in the face if you were dirty with gonorrhea?" In France, the army continued its campaign against venereal disease, although it never totally stopped American soldiers from patronizing French prostitutes. Army-issue condoms and safety razors, a novelty that changed the shaving habits of an entire generation of men, were two of the souvenirs that American soldiers brought home from France.

Intelligence Testing. Intelligence testing joined the progressive belief in social science to wartime needs. To sort all the conscripts, the Army used the newly developed Stanford-Binet intelligence test. Army psychologists, who administered the test to all recruits, expressed shock at the level of illiteracy among draftees—as high as 25 percent. Racial and ethnic variations in the test scores reinforced stereotypes about the supposed intellectual inferiority of blacks and immigrants, who scored lower on the tests. But the lower scores stemmed from the cultural biases of the tests rather than innate differences in intelligence among ethnic groups. The army dropped the test in 1919, but revised versions of intelligence tests soon became a standard part of the American educational system.

Reformers expressed high hopes for the democratization and educational potential of military service. Theodore Roosevelt, whose offer to raise an independent regiment was politely but firmly refused by President Wilson, hoped that army duty would foster class unity. "The military tent where they all sleep side by side will rank next to the public school among the great agents of democratization," Roosevelt predicted. Yet the army reflected the same divisions found in American society. About a fifth of the American soldiers had been born in another country, leading some people to call the AEF the American Foreign Legion. Army censors had to be able to read forty-nine languages to check letters written home by American doughboys. The "Americanization" of even the American army remained imperfect at best.

Racism in the Armed Forces. African-American soldiers received the worst treatment. White Southerners became especially alarmed at training blacks to bear arms, and few whites from any part of the country would have consented to serve under a black officer. As a result, blacks were organized into rigidly segregated units, in all but a few cases under the control of white officers. In addition, blacks were always assigned to the most menial tasks, such as laborers, stevedores, and messboys. Although the policy of segregation minimized contact between black and white recruits, racial violence erupted at several camps. The worst incident occurred in Houston in August 1917, where black members of the Twenty-fourth Infantry's Third Battalion killed sixteen white soldiers and police officers after police beat up two black soldiers. The army immediately tried more than a hundred black soldiers in military courts, and disbanded the battalion. Thirteen black soldiers were executed within days, and six more were later hanged.

The black experience in World War I reflected the persistent gap between progressive rhetoric and reality. Over 400,000 black men served in the military, 13 percent of the armed forces; 92 percent were draftees, a far higher rate than for whites. In France, black soldiers found the French far more willing to socialize with them on an equal basis than many white American soldiers. Despite documented cases of extreme heroism, no black received the Congressional Medal of Honor, the nation's highest military award.

Demobilization. Just as it had taken months to get troops to Europe to join the fighting, similar delays, minus the U-boats, slowed demobilization at war's end. June 1919 was the peak month for returns, with 368,000 men—plus a few thousand women who had served in France as telephone operators, canteen workers, and nurses—arriving stateside to begin the process of readjusting to civilian life. When their ships sailed into New York harbor, many mouthed the old vaudeville saying, "If the Statue of Liberty wants to see my face again, she'll have to turn around" to emphasize that they had no desire to leave American shores again.

After the armistice, the war continued to live on in the minds of the men and women who had gone "over there" to serve. Spared the horror of sustained battle, many members of the AEF had experienced the war more as tourists than as soldiers. Before joining the army, recruits had barely traveled beyond their hometowns, and the journey across the ocean to Europe was a monumental, once-in-a-lifetime event. In 1919 a group of former AEF officers formed the American Legion "to preserve the memories and incidents of our as-

A Black Veteran Returns Home
Black soldiers received segregated and unequal treatment at every stage of their military service. When the war ended, black veterans faced hostility from many whites alarmed that blacks no longer "knew their place."

sociation in the great war." The word "legion" perfectly captured the romantic, almost chivalric memories that many veterans chose to hold of their wartime service. Only later did disillusionment over the contested legacy of World War I set in.

Mobilizing the Home Front

Fighting World War I required extraordinary economic mobilization on the home front. Business, the work force, and the public all cooperated to win the war. At the height of mobilization, a fourth of the gross national product went for war production. Business and government proved especially congenial partners, a collaboration which typified the pattern of statebuilding in America. Similarly, the rapid dismantling of this apparatus when the war ended confirmed the ongoing unease that Americans felt with a strong bureaucratic state.

Financial and Economic Mobilization

Even before the formal declaration of war, the United States had geared up as the arsenal for Allied supplies and financing. As tons of American grain and military supplies crossed the Atlantic, America reversed its historic debtor position and become a leading creditor nation when Allies paid for their purchases in gold. In addition, U.S. financial institutions increasingly provided capital for foreign investment on the world market now that the British pound sterling was diverted to the Allied war effort. This shift from debtor to creditor status, which would last until the 1970s, guaranteed the nation a major role in international financial affairs after the war and confirmed the new role of the United States as a world power.

Paying for the War. The monetary cost to the United States of World War I reached $33 billion, a huge sum for a government unaccustomed to large expenditures. The disruption in international trade after the outbreak of war in 1914 had reduced the revenues raised by tariffs, ordinarily a major source of federal revenues. Wilson's Treasury Secretary William McAdoo had two options: impose a national sales tax or increase income taxes. (The Sixteenth Amendment to the Constitution which allowed a federal income tax had been approved in 1913.) Wilson and McAdoo, in conjunction with progressive Democratic leaders in Congress, chose the second option. The resulting Revenue Acts of 1916 and 1917 transformed the previously limited income tax into the foremost instrument of federal taxation, surely one of the most lasting legacies of World War I. The Wilson administration rejected a mass-based income tax falling on wages and salaries in favor of placing the burden on wealthier individuals and corporations. The corporate excess profits tax signaled a direct and unprecedented intrusion of the state into the workings of corporate capitalism. By 1918, U.S. corporations were paying over $2.5 billion in excess-profits taxes per year, more than half of all federal taxes.

In all, the United States raised about a third of the cost of the war from taxes; the rest came from loans, especially the popular Liberty Loans that encouraged public support for the war effort. The government also helped pay for the war by using the Federal Reserve System to expand the money supply, which made it easier to borrow money. Even so, the federal debt increased from $1 billion in 1915 to $20 billion in 1920. Federal expenditures never again dropped to their prewar levels, but by the 1920s the federal budget was posting a surplus.

Wartime Economic Regulation. In addition to financing the war, mobilization required coordination of economic production. The government never seriously considered exercising total control over the economy, but the war hastened the creation of a centralized national administrative structure to match the consolidated power of the business and banking communities. For economic expertise, the government turned primarily to those who knew the capacities of the economy best—the nation's business leaders. Executives flocked to Washington, regarding war work as both a duty and an opportunity for professional advancement.

A series of boards and agencies tried to rationalize and coordinate the economy. A network of industrial committees linked war agencies to organizations in private industry, and government leaders utilized a combination of public and private power to enforce their decisions. This semi-voluntarist approach was an attempt to find a middle ground between total state control of the economy and letting business operate without direction. Like most compromises, it had mixed results.

The Fuel Administration, directed by President Harry Garfield of Williams College, allocated the coal resources necessary for operation of the nation's railroads and factories. Its task became more difficult during the severe winter of 1917–1918, when coal shortages occurred in major northeastern cities and industries. At one point, Garfield ordered all factories east of the Mississippi River to shut down for four days. By raising the price of coal to artificially high levels, the Fuel Administration stimulated production of coal from previously unprofitable mines to meet the nation's energy needs.

The Railroad War Board, under Secretary of the Treasury William G. McAdoo, coordinated the nation's sprawling transportation system by taking over the railroads in December 1917. (The army needed the railroads to move its troops.) The board guaranteed railroad owners a "standard return" equal to average earnings between 1915 and 1917, and promised that the carriers would be returned to private control no later than twenty-one months after the war. The government quickly fulfilled that pledge after the armistice.

Perhaps the most successful government agency was the Food Administration, created in August 1917 and led by future president Herbert Hoover, a Stanford-trained engineer. Using the slogan "Food will win the war," Hoover encouraged the expansion of domestic production of wheat and other grains from 45 million acres in 1917 to 75 million in 1919. The increased output not only fed the large domestic market, but also allowed a threefold rise in food exports to war-torn Europe. At no time did the government contemplate domestic food rationing; most consumers patriotically followed government propaganda to "Serve Just Enough" and "Use All Left-Overs." "Wheatless" Mondays, "Meatless" Tuesdays, and "Porkless" Thursdays and Saturdays resulted in substantial conservation of food resources. Hoover emerged from the war as one of the nation's most admired public figures.

The War Industries Board. The central agency for mobilizing wartime industry was the War Industries Board (WIB), established in July 1917. After a fumbling start that showed the limits of voluntarism in a national emergency, the Wilson administration reorganized the board under the centralized control of Bernard Baruch, a Wall Street financier, in March 1918. Baruch's financial experience and his ability to cajole American business to cooperate with the government contributed significantly to the success of the WIB.

The WIB reflected the ambivalent attitude of Americans towards government intervention in the economy. When Wilson elevated Baruch to a position of "industrial czar," he recognized the need for central authority in wartime, but he always saw the WIB as a temporary expedient. Baruch proceeded to organize the WIB around specific commodities and industries, whose administrators then negotiated such issues as market allocation with their equivalents in private industry. This frequent consultation blurred the lines between the needs of business and government, and often left patterns of private power undisturbed.

The WIB produced an unparalleled expansion of the economic powers of the federal government. The board allocated scarce resources, gathered economic data and statistics, controlled the flow of raw materials, ordered conversion of factories to war production, set prices, imposed efficiency and standardization procedures, and coordinated purchasing. The board had the authority to compel compliance, but Baruch preferred to win voluntary acceptance from business. He saw himself as a partner of business, not its enemy. To a large degree, business supported this government expansion because federal growth coincided with its interests so well. Despite higher taxes, corporate profits soared, aided by the suspension of antitrust laws, competitive bidding during wartime, and guaranteed profits on war work. War profits produced an economic boom that continued without interruption until 1920.

With the signing of the armistice in November 1918, the United States scrambled to dismantle its wartime controls. Wilson disbanded the WIB effective January 1, 1919, resisting suggestions that keeping the board in place at least briefly would help stabilize the economy during the period of demobilization. Wilson was determined to take "the harness off." Like most Americans, he could tolerate planning power in the hands of the government during an emergency, but not as a permanent feature of the American economy.

Although U.S. participation in the war lasted only eighteen months, it left an important legacy for the modern bureaucratic state. Entire industries had been organized as never before, linked to a maze of government agencies and executive departments. The contours of the modern system of progressive income taxation took shape. The partnership between business and government had been mutually beneficial, a lesson that both partners would put to use in the statebuilding that occurred in the 1920s and beyond.

Mobilizing American Workers

Wars are never won solely by armies and business and government leaders. Farmers, factory workers, indeed the entire civilian population have crucial roles to play. However, World War I produced fewer rewards for workers than for owners and managers.

Organized Labor. Labor's position improved during the war, although it remained a junior partner to business and government. Samuel Gompers, leader of the American Federation of Labor (AFL), traded labor's support of the war for a voice in government policy. This bargain proved acceptable to government and business leaders concerned with averting crippling strikes. Gompers represented labor's interests on the National Defense Advisory Commission. Also, the War Labor Policies Board, headed by Felix Frankfurter, a Harvard law professor, coordinated labor and welfare programs in government and industry. The United States Employment Service placed four million workers in war jobs.

The National War Labor Board. Far more important to workers was the National War Labor Board, established in April 1918, which arbitrated labor disputes. Comprised of representatives of labor, management, and the public, the NWLB was chaired by former President William Howard Taft, representing management, and Frank P. Walsh, a labor lawyer. In some ways, the NWLB functioned more as a judicial than an administrative body; labor leaders often called it "labor's Supreme Court."

The board's decisions favored labor more often than management, giving important federal support to the goals of the labor movement. During the eighteen months of the NWLB's existence, it arbitrated about 1,250 cases. The board established an eight-hour day for war workers, with time-and-a-half pay for overtime; it also endorsed equal pay for women workers. Workers were not allowed to disrupt war production through strikes or other disturbances; in return, the NWLB supported the right of workers to organize unions and required employers to deal with shop committees. The NWLB had ample power to enforce its decisions and intervene in unresolved disputes. For example, when the Smith and Wesson arms plant in Springfield, Massachusetts, flouted NWLB rules by discriminating against union employees, the federal government took over the firm.

After years of federal hostility toward labor, the actions of the National War Labor Board improved labor's status and power. From 1916 to 1919, AFL membership grew by almost a million workers, reaching over three million by the end of the war. Few of these wartime gains lasted, however. Wartime inflation ate up most of the wage hikes, and a virulent postwar anti-union movement drove union membership into a rapid decline that lasted until the 1930s. The labor movement did not yet have enough power to bargain on an equal basis with business and government.

Black and Mexican-American Workers. When soldiers go to war, jobs open up for workers normally excluded from them. Black men, for example, found jobs in northern defense industries that never would have accepted them in peacetime. The magnet of industrial jobs and an escape from the southern agricultural system lured between 400,000 and 450,000 blacks to northern and midwestern cities such as St. Louis, Chicago, Cleveland, and Detroit during the war. Henry Ford sent agents to the South to recruit black workers for his automobile plants and even provided special trains to bring them north. In Detroit blacks shared in the unprecedented five-dollar daily wage that Ford had instituted in 1914. The migration of blacks from the South, which began in World War I and continued until the 1970s, represented one of the most fundamental population shifts of the twentieth century.

Mexican-Americans in California, Texas, New Mexico, and Arizona also found new opportunities during the war. The disruption of immigration from abroad opened up industrial opportunities, as did the conscription of U.S. citizens. Many left farm labor for new industrial opportunities, often settling in segregated neighborhoods (*barrios*) in urban areas. Other Mexican-Americans, however, feared they would be drafted into the army, and returned to Mexico. The exodus of so many workers increased the labor shortage in agriculture. The government quickly exempted agricultural workers from the draft, whereupon the migration resumed. At least a hundred thousand Mexican-Americans entered the United States between 1917 and 1920.

Women and the War Effort

Women made up the largest group that took advantage of new opportunities in wartime. White women and, to a lesser degree, black and Hispanic women, found jobs open to them in factories and war industries as never before. About one million women joined the labor force for the first time. In addition, many of the nation's eight million women who already held jobs switched from low-paying fields, such as domestic service, to higher-paying industrial work. Americans soon got used to the novel sight of woman streetcar conductors, train engi-

Wartime Opportunities
Women took on new jobs during the war, working as mail carriers, police officers, drill-press operators, and farm laborers attached to the Women's Land Army. These three women clearly enjoyed the camaraderie of working in a railroad yard in 1918. When the war ended, women usually lost such employment.

neers, and defense workers. But everyone—including the women themselves—believed that these jobs would return to men after the war.

Professional women also found opportunities in government service. Mary Van Kleeck, an industrial sociologist and expert on the problems of woman workers, joined the Department of Labor to lobby for equal pay and better working conditions for woman workers. Pauline Goldmark, a social reformer from the National Consumers' League, acted as a women's rights advocate at the Railroad Administration. Mary Anderson, a trade unionist who had been Van Kleeck's assistant, became the first director of the Women's Bureau, established by the Labor Department in 1920. Women's groups failed, however, to get a woman named to the National War Labor Board.

World War I proved especially liberating for middle-class women outside the work force. Women's clubs and groups had grown steadily since the nineteenth century, and they turned much of their organizational energy to the war effort. Suffragist leaders such as Carrie Chapman Catt and Anna Howard Shaw mobilized women's support for the war through the Women's Committee of the Council of National Defense. Housewives played a crucial role in the success of Herbert Hoover's Food Administration. Other groups, including the American Red Cross and the Young Women's Christian Association (YWCA), sent volunteers to France, where they organized relief work and recreational activities in conjunction with the AEF.

Suffrage Victory. The war had an important impact on the battle for woman suffrage. The main suffrage organization, the National American Woman Suffrage Association (NAWSA), threw the support of its two million members solidly behind the Wilson administration. Carrie Chapman Catt, president of the organization, argued that women had to prove their patriotism in order not to jeopardize the suffrage movement. Only a small group of radical suffragists, led by Alice Paul and her Congressional Union, joined peace activists like Jane Addams in opposing the war.

Women's wartime contributions helped push their campaign for suffrage to its successful conclusion. Especially effective was a simple moral challenge: how could

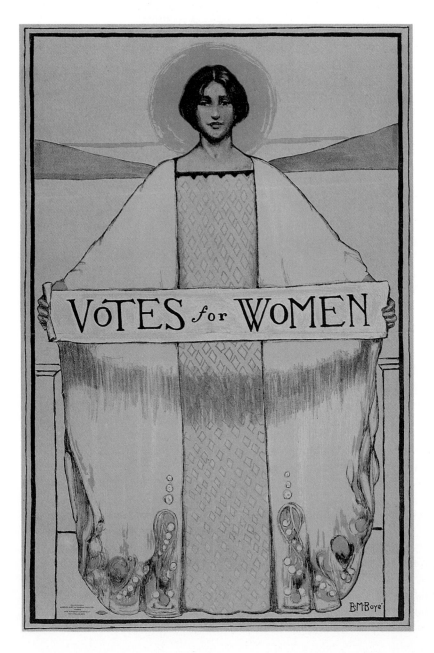

Votes for Women
Mass suffrage parades, introduced in the final stages of the campaign, provided an effective and eye-catching way to build popular support. Many of the banners and posters carried in the parades, such as this one by B. M. Boye, were in the suffrage colors of green, purple, or gold.

the United States fight to make the world safe for democracy while denying half its citizens their right to vote? Woodrow Wilson, who had accepted the Democratic platform's endorsement of woman suffrage in 1916 but preferred to leave the matter to the states, withdrew his opposition to a federal woman suffrage amendment in January 1918. The constitutional amendment quickly passed the House but took eighteen months to get through the Senate. Then came another year of hard work for ratification by the states. Finally, on August 26, 1920, Tennessee gave the Nineteenth Amendment the last vote it needed. The goal that had first been declared at the Seneca Falls convention in 1848 won approval seventy-two years later, partly because of women's contributions to the war effort.

Promoting National Unity

The course of American participation in World War I was fundamentally shaped by the Progressive period that preceded it. Reformers eagerly embraced American involvement as an opportunity to put Progressive ideals into practice. Educator and philosopher John Dewey, a staunch supporter of the war, argued that wars represented a "plastic juncture" when societies became more open to reason and new ideas. In the collective effort of fighting and winning a war, society could be improved. Dewey's optimistic view matched the spirit of the times. Unfortunately, a dissenting observation by Randolph Bourne, an outspoken pacifist and intellectual who had once been a pupil of Dewey's, came closer to reality. "If the war is too strong for you to prevent," Bourne asked, "how is it going to be weak enough for you to control and mold to your liberal purposes?"

Although the enactment of woman suffrage confirmed Dewey's prediction that social progress could occur in a war context, the excesses committed in the name of building national unity corroborated Bourne's warnings about the passions that could get out of control during wartime. Wilson had shared Bourne's foreboding: "Once lead this people into war, and they'll forget there ever was such a thing as tolerance." But the president also realized the need to manufacture support for the war. "It is not an army we must shape and train for war, it is a nation."

Wartime Propaganda. In April 1917, Wilson designated the Committee on Public Information (CPI) to promote public backing for the war, which was never a foregone conclusion. This government propaganda agency, headed by journalist George Creel, acted as a magnet for Progressive reformers and muckraking journalists, such as Ida Tarbell and Ray Stannard Baker. The CPI professed high-sounding goals, such as educating

A Human Statue of Liberty

Patriotic gestures knew no bounds, as demonstrated by the 18,000 soldiers at Camp Dodge in Iowa who formed a human replica of the Statue of Liberty. One wonders if the conscripts shared the photographer's enthusiasm for the project after what must have been a long, boring afternoon in the sun.

citizens about democracy, promoting national unity, Americanizing immigrant groups, and breaking down the isolation of rural life. Indirectly, it acted as a nationalizing force by promoting the development of a common national ideology.

The Committee on Public Information touched the lives of practically every American during World War I. It distributed seventy-five million pieces of patriotic literature. At local movie theaters before the feature presentation (which might be a CPI-supported film, such as *The Prussian Cur* or *The Kaiser, Beast of Berlin*) a volunteer called a "four-minute man" made a short speech supporting the war. Such speeches reached an audience estimated at more than three hundred million, three times the population of the United States at the time. But the CPI sometimes went too far. By early 1918, for example, the CPI was encouraging speakers to use inflammatory stories of alleged German atrocities to build support for the war effort.

The Climate of Suspicion. As a spirit of conformity pervaded the home front, many Americans found themselves the targets of suspicion. Local businesses donated ads to newspapers and magazines that asked citizens to report to the Justice Department "the man who spreads pessimistic stories, cries for peace, or belittles our efforts to win the war." Posters encouraged Americans to be on the lookout for German spies. One of the most popular posters, called "Spies and Lies," began by warning that "German agents are everywhere." An unintended byproduct of this wartime propaganda was the stimulation of the advertising industry, which became a major force in shaping patterns of consumption in the 1920s.

The CPI also urged ethnic groups to give up their old-world customs and become "Unhyphenated Americans." German-Americans bore the brunt of the Americanization campaign. In an orgy of hostility generated by propaganda about German militarism and war atrocities, everything German became suspect. German music, especially opera, was banished from the concert repertoire. Publishers removed pro-German references from textbooks, and many communities banned the teaching of the German language. Sauerkraut was renamed "liberty cabbage," and hamburgers transformed into "liberty sandwiches" or Salisbury steaks. Even the German measles got a new name, "liberty measles." Anti-German hysteria dissipated quickly when the war ended, in large part because German-Americans were one of the best integrated immigrant groups in American society.

More aggressive than propaganda were quasi-vigilante groups, such as the American Protective League. This organization mobilized about 250,000 self-appointed "agents" to spy on their neighbors, fellow workers, and innocent bystanders. The American Protective League (whose members were furnished with badges issued by the Justice Department) and groups including the Sedition Slammers and the Boy Spies of America staged violent raids against draft evaders and other war opponents in 1918.

Curbing Dissent. Law enforcement officials tolerated little criticism of American values and institutions in wartime. For example, the Washington, D.C. police moved in quickly to arrest militant suffragists from the Congressional Union who chained themselves to the White House fence and burned copies of President Wilson's speeches on democracy to protest their lack of the vote. The suffragists, charged with obstructing traffic and blocking sidewalks, were sentenced to seven months in jail. In protest, Alice Paul and other women prisoners went on hunger strikes and were forcibly fed. Public shock at their treatment made them martyrs and ultimately aided the suffrage cause. But the suffragists'

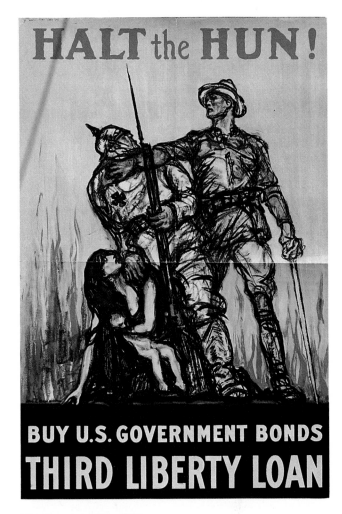

The Iconography of War

This poster made clear who the enemy was, and the proper patriotic American response. The iconography builds on traditional gender definitions, with the male American soldier pushing back the German Hun who is about to ravish a woman and her child, who stand for European civilization.

status as white middle-class women protected them from some of the harsher reprisals meted out to others who dared to criticize the government during wartime.

The main legal tools for curbing such dissent were the Espionage Act of 1917 and the Sedition Act of 1918. The espionage law set stiff penalties for antimilitary actions and empowered the federal government to ban treasonous material from the mails. The definition of treason was left to the discretion of the postmaster general. The sedition law went further, punishing anyone who might "utter, print, write or publish any disloyal, profane, scurrilous, or abusive language about the form of government in the United States, or the uniform of the Army or the Navy." More than a thousand people were convicted under these broad restrictions on freedom of speech in wartime.

AMERICAN VOICES

An Imprisoned Suffrage Militant *Rose Winslow*

Suffragist Rose Winslow smuggled out descriptions of the treatment she and Alice Paul, militant founder of the National Woman's Party, endured in Occuquan prison. The process of forcible feeding she mentions, which involved inserting a 20-inch-long tube through the nostril to the stomach while the patient was restrained, was excruciatingly painful as well as demeaning.

The women are all so magnificent, so beautiful. Alice Paul is as thin as ever, pale and large-eyed. We have been in solitary for five weeks. There is nothing to tell but that the days go by somehow. I have felt quite feeble the last few days—faint, so that I could hardly get my hair brushed, my arms ached so. But today I am well again. Alice Paul and I talk back and forth though we are at opposite ends of the building and a hall door also shuts us apart. But occasionally—thrills—we escape from behind our iron-barred doors and visit. Great laughter and rejoicing! . . .

Alice Paul is in the psychopathic ward. She dreaded forcible feeding frightfully, and I hate to think how she must be feeling. I had a nervous time of it, gasping a long time afterward, and my stomach rejecting during the process. I spent a bad, restless night, but otherwise I am all right. The poor soul who fed me got liberally besprinkled during the process. I heard myself making the most hideous sounds. . . . One feels so forsaken when one lies prone and people shove a pipe down one's stomach. . . .

We still get no mail; we are "insubordinate." It's strange, isn't it; if you ask for food fit to eat, as we did, you are "insubordinate"; and if you refuse food you are "insubordinate." Amusing. I am really all right. If this continues very long I perhaps won't be. I am interested to see how long our so-called "splendid American men" will stand for this form of discipline.

All news cheers one marvelously because it is hard to feel anything but a bit desolate and forgotten here in this place.

All the officers here know we are making this hunger strike that women fighting for liberty may be considered political prisoners; we have told them. God knows we don't want other women ever to have to do this over again.

Source: Doris Stevens, *Jailed For Freedom* (1920; rpt. New York: Schocken Books, 1976), 188–91.

The Justice Department also targeted the Industrial Workers of the World, or Wobblies (see Chapter 18). IWW organizers spoke out against militarism and threatened to disrupt war production in the western lumber and copper industries. In September 1917 the Justice Department arrested 113 top IWW leaders for interfering with the war effort. Vigilante groups contributed their own reprisals: a mob in Butte, Montana, dragged IWW organizer Frank Little through the streets and hanged him from a railroad trestle. By the end of the war, the Wobblies were decimated.

Socialists encountered similar attacks for criticizing the war and the draft. The postmaster general banned their publications from the mails. Party leader Eugene Debs drew ten years in jail for stating that the master classes caused wars while the subject classes fought them. Victor Berger, a Milwaukee Socialist, was twice prevented from taking his seat in the United States House of Representatives. Berger had served in the House from 1911 to 1913. He was reelected in 1918 and 1919, but the House refused to seat him because he had been jailed under the Espionage Act for his antiwar views. The Supreme Court reversed Victor Berger's sentence in 1921, and he served in the House again from 1923 to 1929.

The Supreme Court rarely overturned the wartime excesses. In *Schenck v. United States* (1919), Justice Oliver Wendell Holmes ruled in a unanimous decision that if an act of speech was uttered in circumstances that would "create a clear and present danger to the safety of the country," Congress could constitutionally restrict it. The defendant, the general secretary of the Socialist party, Charles T. Schenck, had been convicted for mailing pamphlets that urged draftees to resist induction. In *Abrams v. United States* (1919), the Court also upheld the sedition conviction of Jacob Abrams, a Russian anarchist and recent immigrant. Abrams had dumped Yiddish and English pamphlets from tenement windows in New York denouncing American military intervention in Russia. Holmes dissented in this case, seeing no clear threat to the conduct of the war. He and Justice Louis Brandeis made up the minority in the 7 to

2 decision. During a national war emergency, the Court upheld limits on freedom of speech that would not have been acceptable in peacetime.

An Unsettled Peace, 1919–1920

In January 1917, Woodrow Wilson had proposed a "peace without victory," since only "peace among equals" would be likely to last. His goal was "not a balance of power, but a community of power; not organized rivalries, but an organized common peace." With victory achieved, Wilson confronted the task of constructing the new moral international order he dreamed of. First he would have to win over a Senate openly hostile to the treaty he brought home. At the same time, ethnic and racial tensions that had smoldered during the war erupted in controversy and strife. And fears of domestic radicalism boiled over in the Red Scare.

The Treaty of Versailles

President Wilson scored an early victory when the Allies accepted his Fourteen Points as the basis for the peace negotiations that began in January 1919. First put forward in a speech to Congress in early 1918, the Fourteen Points represented Wilson's clearest articulation of his blueprint for the postwar world. The president called for open diplomacy, "absolute freedom of navigation upon the seas," removal of economic barriers to trade, an international commitment to territorial in-

tegrity, and arms reduction. The fifth point reaffirmed Wilson's long-standing commitment to national self-determination. He proposed redrawing national boundaries following the breakup of the Austro-Hungarian, Russian, and German empires, including the restoration of an independent Polish state. Essential to Wilson's vision was the creation of a multinational organization "for the purpose of affording mutual guarantees of political independence and territorial integrity to great and small States alike." This League of Nations became Wilson's obsession.

The Fourteen Points matched the spirit of Progressivism. Widely distributed as propaganda during the final months of the war, Wilson's declaration proposed to extend the benefits of the American way of life—democracy, freedom, and peaceful economic expansion—to the rest of the world. The League of Nations would serve as a mediator of international disputes so that future wars could be avoided and as a kind of Federal Trade Commission for the world. By pegging American involvement to such lofty goals, however, Wilson virtually guaranteed disappointment. When the Allies won the war, his ideals for world reformation were too far-reaching to be practical or attainable.

Many factors limited Wilson's ability to enforce his views of a just peace. Despite the president's plea to make the 1918 Congressional elections a referendum for his peace plan, American voters returned a Republican majority to Congress. Wilson shortsightedly failed to appoint even one Republican senator to the United States delegation to the peace conference, a political gaffe that later helped doom the treaty's chances for approval in the Senate.

Woodrow Wilson Triumphant
After the armistice, Woodrow Wilson toured Europe to tumultuous acclaim, such as here in Paris where citizens erected an electric sign saying "Vive [long live] Wilson." But his heady reception from the people contrasted sharply with the cool reception he received from the leaders of the major European powers.

The peace delegation sailed for Europe in December 1918. Wilson toured the major European capitals and received a tumultuous welcome. To European citizens the American president represented the hope for national self-determination that had become a major justification for the war. In Paris two million people lined the Champs-Élysées to pay tribute to "Wilson the Just." This reception encouraged Wilson to press ahead with his plans to dominate the peace conference.

Intervention in the U.S.S.R. The Allies deliberately excluded representatives of the new Bolshevik state from the peace conference. Wilson remained deeply disturbed by Lenin's calls for a proletarian revolution to liberate the world from capitalism and imperialism, a direct challenge to the Wilsonian international order. Not only did Wilson refuse to recognize Lenin's legitimacy, but he took steps to try to topple the Bolshevik regime. Under the ostensible excuse of helping 60,000 trapped Czechoslovakians who wanted to return to fight the Germans, Wilson deployed 5,000 American troops to Archangel in northern Russia in June 1918 and sent an additional 10,000 troops to Siberia in July. England and Japan also sent troops. The unstated purpose of this Allied military maneuver was to give support to anti-Bolshevik forces within Russia. American troops remained on Soviet soil until the spring of 1920, leaving a bitter legacy for American-Soviet relations.

Negotiating the Treaties. Twenty-seven countries sent representatives to the peace conference in Versailles, near Paris; like the Soviet Union, Germany was not invited. The Big Four—Wilson, Prime Minister David Lloyd George of Great Britain, Premier Georges Clemenceau of France, and Prime Minister Vittorio Orlando of Italy—did most of the negotiating. The three European leaders sought a peace that differed radically from Wilson's plan. They wanted to punish Germany through heavy reparations, and treat themselves to the spoils of war. In fact, Britain, France, and Italy had already made secret treaties to divide up territory of the defeated German empire before the conference began.

Territorial Settlements. It is a tribute to Woodrow Wilson that he managed to influence the peace agreement as much as he did. His presence at Versailles softened some of the harshest demands for reprisals against Germany. National self-determination, a fundamental American principle enunciated in Wilson's Fourteen Points, found fulfillment in the creation of the independent states of Austria, Hungary, Poland, Yugoslavia, and Czechoslovakia from the defeated empires of the Central Powers. The establishment of a *cordon sanitaire* (sanitary zone) of the new nations of Finland, Estonia,

Lithuania, and Latvia further served Wilson's determination to isolate the Soviet Union from the rest of Europe. Even though Lenin did not attend the peace conference, Allied leaders realized that the new Soviet state was changing the complexion of power in Eastern Europe—and the world.

The president won only limited concessions regarding the colonial empires of the defeated powers. The old Central and Eastern European empires were dismantled, but the overseas empires of the victorious allies were actually enlarged by the addition of colonies taken from the defeated powers. The colonies were placed under a mandate system of protectorates, assigned to various powers for administration as trustees. France and England received parts of the old Turkish and German empires in the Middle East and Africa, and Japan assumed responsibility for the former German colonies in the Far East. Germany's loss of all its colonies, and their transfer to other imperialist powers like England and Japan, hardly constituted a blow for national self-determination.

Wilson had to back down on many other issues in the Fourteen Points as well. The secret negotiating sessions held by the Big Four at Versailles mocked Wilson's call for "open covenants of peace openly arrived at." Certain topics, such as freedom of the seas and free trade, never even made the agenda because of Allied resistance. Wilson yielded to French and British demands for a "war guilt" clause, which provided the justification for the heavy restitution demanded from Germany. France was especially adamant about reparations, since the war on the Western Front had been fought primarily on French soil. The final figure, set in 1921, was $33 billion. Although lower than France's original demands for $100 billion, it was still far more than the crippled German economy could bear.

In the face of his many disappointments, Wilson consoled himself with the peace conference's commitment to his proposed League of Nations. He acknowledged that the treaty had defects, but he expressed confidence that they could be resolved by a permanent international organization that brought nations together for the peaceful resolution of disputes.

The Fate of the Treaty

German leaders reacted with dismay at the severity of the treaty, but with the nation reduced almost to starvation by the Allied blockade they had no choice but to accept it. On June 28, 1919, representatives of the participating nations and Germany gathered in the Hall of Mirrors in the Palace of Versailles to sign the treaty. Wilson sailed home immediately after the ceremony and presented the treaty to the Senate on July 10. The treaty was already in trouble, however, with support in the Senate far short of the two-thirds vote necessary for ratification. Would Wilson compromise? "I shall consent to nothing," he told the French ambassador. "The Senate must take its medicine."

Congressional Opposition. Opposition to the Versailles treaty came from several sources. One group, called the "irreconcilables," consisted of such Western progressives as William E. Borah of Idaho, Hiram W. Johnson of California, and Robert M. La Follette of Wisconsin. They disagreed fundamentally with the premise of permanent U.S. participation in European affairs symbolized by the League of Nations. Moreover, they were horrified at the harsh terms of the treaty toward Germany.

Less dogmatic, but more influential, was a group of Republicans led by Senator Henry Cabot Lodge of Massachusetts. They too expressed strong reservations about the break with American isolationism represented by membership in the League of Nations. Lodge's Republicans proposed a list of amendments that, scholars now agree, would not have seriously weakened the peace treaty. Most of these changes centered around Article X, the section of the League of Nations covenant calling for collective security measures if a member nation were attacked. Lodge correctly argued that this provision restricted Congress's constitutional authority to declare war. More importantly, Lodge and many other senators felt that the treaty imposed unacceptable restrictions on the freedom of the United States to pursue a unilateral foreign policy.

Wilson still refused to budge, especially to placate Lodge, his hated political rival. Hoping to mobilize support for the treaty, the president launched an extensive speaking tour to take his case to the American people. He brought large audiences to tears with his impassioned defense of the treaty. But the strain proved too much for the ailing sixty-two-year-old president, and he collapsed in Pueblo, Colorado, in late September. One week later in Washington, Wilson suffered a severe stroke that left him paralyzed on one side of his body.

Defeat. We will never know whether a healthy Wilson could have mobilized public support for the League of Nations and gained Senate ratification. Perhaps if he had allowed the Democrats to compromise, the treaty might have been saved. From his sickbed, however, Wilson ordered the Democratic senators to vote against all Republican amendments. The treaty came up for a vote in November 1919 and failed to be ratified. Another attempt several months later fell seven votes short of approval, and the issue was dead.

While his wife, Edith Galt Wilson, and his physician oversaw the routine business of government, Wilson slowly recovered. But he was never the same again. He had delusions of making the 1920 election campaign "a great and solemn referendum" on the League of Nations, and even hoped to run for a third term as president. Neither dream was a serious possibility. Woodrow Wilson died in 1924, "as much a victim of the war," David Lloyd George noted, "as any soldier who died in the trenches."

The United States never signed the Versailles treaty or joined the League of Nations. Many wartime issues remained only partially resolved, notably the future of Germany, the fate of colonial empires, and rising nationalist demands for self-determination. These unsolved problems played a major role in the coming of World War II.

Racial Strife

Woodrow Wilson spent only ten days in the United States between December 1918 and June 1919. This striking circumstance illustrates his total preoccupation with the peacemaking process at Versailles. For more than six months, Wilson was practically an absentee president. Unfortunately, many urgent domestic problems demanded his attention.

The immediate postwar period brought a severe decline in race relations throughout the country. The volatile mix of black migration, American imperialism, intensified segregation in the South, and black service in World War I all combined to exacerbate white hostility to blacks. In the South, the number of lynchings rose from forty-eight in 1917 to seventy-eight in 1919. Several blacks were lynched while still wearing their military uniforms. Northern blacks also faced hostility. Serious racial violence broke out in more than twenty-five cities, and the resulting death toll for the summer of 1919 reached 120.

The riots resulted from the northward migration set in motion by World War I. Superficially at least, northern cities promised new freedoms. But southern blacks faced a difficult readjustment to the diverse urban environment after the South's traditional patterns of deference to whites. In turn, white northerners reacted hostilely to this perceived onslaught of unwelcome newcomers, especially when competition for jobs was added to racism. Violence between blacks and whites erupted as early as 1917 in Houston and Philadelphia. In East St. Louis, Illinois, nine whites and more than forty blacks died in a riot sparked by competition over jobs at a defense plant.

Racial Violence in Chicago

Much of the violence perpetrated against blacks during the 1919 race riot was perpetrated by young white men, many of Irish descent, who belonged to gangs such as the "Dirty Dozen" and "Our Flag." A city commission later concluded that without the gang activities, "it is doubtful if the riot would have gone beyond the first clash."

Riots in Chicago. One of the worst race riots took place in Chicago in July 1919. It began at a Lake Michigan beach when a black teenager named Eugene Williams swam into an area of the lake customarily reserved for whites. Someone threw a rock that hit him on the head, and he drowned. The incident touched off five days of rioting in which twenty-three blacks and fifteen whites died.

Chicago on the eve of the riot was a tinderbox waiting to ignite. The arrival of fifty thousand black newcomers during the war years had strained the city's social fabric. In politics black voters often provided the balance of power in close elections. Blacks and whites competed for jobs, and the more heavily unionized white population deeply resented the blacks who became strikebreakers—white stockyard workers considered the words "Negro" and "scab" synonymous. Blacks and whites competed for scarce housing as well, and blacks soon overflowed the racially segregated South Side into Chicago's intensely ethnic neighborhoods. Even before that sultry July afternoon at the beach, tensions had erupted in bombings of black homes and other forms of harassment.

Chicago blacks did not sit meekly by as whites destroyed their neighborhoods. They fought back, both in self-defense and for their rights as citizens. World War I had an indirect effect on their actions. Many blacks had served in the armed forces. The rhetoric about democracy and self-determination raised their expectations, too.

Labor Unrest

Workers had similar hopes as a result of the war. The war years had provided important breakthroughs for many industrial employees, including higher pay, shorter hours, and better working conditions. Soon after the armistice, however, many employers returned to older patterns of hostility toward union activity. Many consumers blamed workers for the rising cost of living, and many native-born Americans continued to identify unions with radicalism and foreigners. Nevertheless, workers hoped to expand their wartime gains. The worst problem was rapidly rising inflation, which threatened to wipe out their wage increases. By 1919 the cost of living had risen 77 percent over its prewar level.

1919—A Year of Strikes. More than four million workers—one out of every five—went on strike in 1919, a proportion never since equalled. The year began with a walkout by shipyard workers in Seattle. Their action spread into a general strike that crippled the city. In the fall, the Boston police force struck. The idea of public employees trying to unionize shocked many Americans. Governor Calvin Coolidge of Massachusetts propelled himself into the political spotlight by declaring, "There is no right to strike against the public safety by anybody, anywhere, any time." The strike failed, and the entire police force was fired by Coolidge. The public supported this harsh reprisal, and Coolidge was rewarded with the Republican vice-presidential nomination in 1920.

The most extensive labor disruption in 1919 was the great steel strike. More than 350,000 steelworkers across the country walked off the job in late September. The main issue was union recognition, but strikers were also protesting such conditions as twelve-hour shifts and seven-day weeks. Elbert H. Gary, chairman of the United States Steel Corporation, refused to meet with representatives of the steelworkers' union to discuss their demands. The company hired Mexicans and blacks to break the strike and maintained steel production at about 60 percent of the normal level.

The continued high production rate doomed the strike. Striker solidarity began to slacken as winter approached; by January, the strike had collapsed. The union charged that U.S. Steel's "arbitrary and ruthless misuse of power" had crushed the strike. Just as important to the union's defeat was the lack of public support for the goals of organized labor. Unions had made important gains during the war, but they were unable to hold on to them.

The Eighteenth Amendment

Another issue demanding national attention as the war ended was the century-old campaign for Prohibition. On the eve of World War I, nineteen states had passed Prohibition laws and many more provided that communities could regulate liquor if they desired. Generally only highly industrialized states with large immigrant populations, such as New York, Massachusetts, Rhode Island, Illinois, and California, had resisted the trend towards alcohol restriction.

In early twentieth-century America, Prohibition was viewed as a progressive reform, not as a repressive denial of individual freedom. Urban reformers, concerned about good government, urban poverty, and public morality, supported a nationwide ban on drinking. Among the Progressive-Era leaders who campaigned for Prohibition were Supreme Court Justice Louis Brandeis, former presidents William Howard Taft and Theodore Roosevelt, and settlement leader Jane Addams.

The drive for Prohibition also picked up substantial backing in rural communities. Many people equated liquor with all the sins of the city—prostitution, crime, machine politics, and public disorder. In addition, the churches with the greatest strength in rural areas such as the Methodists, Baptists, and Mormons strongly condemned drinking. Protestants from rural areas dominated the membership of the Anti-Saloon League, which by the 1910s had supplanted the Women's Christian Temperance Union as the leading proponent of Prohibition.

Support for the right to drink existed primarily in the nation's heavily urbanized areas, places where immigrants had settled. Alcoholic beverages, especially

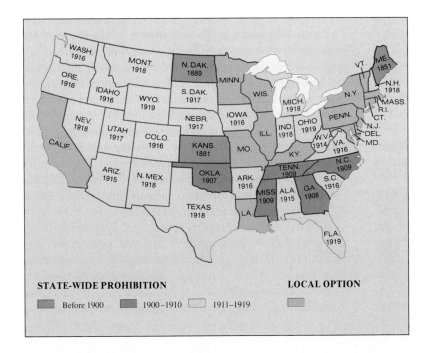

MAP 23.3

Prohibition on the Eve of the Eighteenth Amendment

Prohibition had already made strong headway in the states before the adoption of the Eighteenth Amendment in 1919. States such as Maine, North Dakota, and Kansas had been dry since the nineteenth century; by 1919, two-thirds of the states had already passed laws banning liquor. Most states that resisted the trend were industrial centers or had large immigrant populations.

beer and whiskey, played an important role in certain ethnic cultures, especially those of German- and Irish-Americans. Most saloons were in working-class neighborhoods and served as gathering places for workers at the end of the day. Machine politicians conducted much of their business in bars.

During World War I, those who supported a constitutional amendment to prohibit drinking had the political momentum. One spur to action was the intense anti-German hysteria of the war years. Because several major breweries (Pabst and Busch, for example) had German names, beer drinking became unpatriotic in many people's minds. As part of the drive to conserve food, Congress prohibited the use of food products to make distilled beverages. In December 1917 Congress passed the proposed Eighteenth Amendment prohibiting the manufacture, transport, or sale of intoxicating liquors. Every state with the exception of Connecticut and Rhode Island ratified it by 1919, and it went into effect on January 16, 1920. Among its few exemptions were alcohol prescribed for medicinal reasons and wine consumed for sacramental purposes.

The passage of the Eighteenth Amendent was another example of how "progressive" solutions to issues of purity, poverty, and public safety found success in the climate of war. It also amply demonstrated the widening influence of the state on matters of personal behavior. Yet the ethnic and urban-rural clashes over Prohibition also foreshadowed the ethnocultural debates after the war. Unlike woman suffrage, the other constitutional amendment that won wartime passage, Prohibition would never win general acceptance.

The Red Scare

Underlying and unifying many of the social tensions in the aftermath of World War I was fear of radicalism. Wartime hatred of the German Hun was quickly replaced by postwar hostility toward the Bolshevik Red. The Russian Revolution of 1917 set these fears in motion. The founding of the Third International (or Comintern) in 1919 to export revolution throughout the world threatened the Wilsonian vision of an international order based on democracy, capitalism, and harmony. As labor unrest increased, Americans suddenly began seeing radicals everywhere.

Ironically, as the public became increasingly concerned about domestic Bolshevism, American radicalism rapidly lost members and political power. No more than seventy thousand Americans belonged to the fledgling U.S. Communist party or the Communist Labor party in 1919. The IWW and the Socialist party had been weakened by wartime repression and internal dissension. Yet the public and the press continued to blame almost any disturbance, especially labor conflicts, on radicals. "REDS DIRECTING SEATTLE STRIKE—TO TEST CHANCE FOR REVOLUTION," warned a typical newspaper headline.

Then a series of bombings shocked the nation in early spring. "The word 'radical' in 1919," one historian observed, "automatically carried with it the implication of dynamite." Thirty-four mail bombs addressed to prominent government officials were discovered by alert postal workers before they exploded. Many people immediately suspected that the intended bombings had been timed to coincide with the communist celebration of International Labor Day on May 1. In June a bomb exploded outside the Washington townhouse of the recently appointed attorney general, A. Mitchell Palmer. His family escaped unharmed, but the bomber was blown to bits. Despite intensive efforts, law enforcement agencies never traced the origin of a single bomb.

As hysteria mounted in the fall of 1919, the federal government became involved. One aspect of the expansion of state power was increased surveillance of citizens and repression of dissent. President Wilson's debilitating stroke prevented him from providing decisive leadership, but Attorney General Palmer seized the moment. Angling for the presidential nomination, Palmer rode the crest of public hysteria about domestic radicalism into 1920.

The Palmer Raids. Palmer set up an antiradicalism division in the Justice Department and appointed a young government attorney named J. Edgar Hoover to direct it. Hoover's division shortly became the Federal Bureau of Intelligence. In November 1919, on the second anniversary of the Russian Revolution, the attorney general staged the first of what became known as "Palmer raids." Federal agents stormed the headquarters of radical organizations and captured such supposedly revolutionary booty as a set of drawings that turned out to be blueprints for an improved phonograph, not sketches for a bomb. The dragnet netted thousands of aliens who had committed no crime, but were suspect because of their anarchist or revolutionary beliefs or merely their immigrant backgrounds. Lacking the protection of U.S. citizenship, they faced deportation without formal trial or indictment. In December 1919 the U.S.S. *Buford*, nicknamed the "Soviet Ark," embarked for Finland and the Soviet state with a cargo of 294 deported radicals. Its passengers included two famous anarchists, Emma Goldman and Alexander Berkman.

The peak of Palmer's power came with his New Year's raids in January 1920. In one night, with the greatest possible newspaper publicity, Palmer rounded up six thousand radicals. Agents invaded private homes, union headquarters, and meeting halls. The government held both citizens and aliens without specific charges and denied them legal counsel, a violation of their civil liberties. Some prisoners were even forced to march through the streets handcuffed to one another. One of the few moments of comic relief came when "patriotic" prisoners in a Chicago jail rioted when ordered to share cells with arrested radicals. "There are some things at which even a Chicago crook draws the line," a local newspaper reported.

Palmer was riding high, and his ambitions for the presidency swelled. But then he overstepped himself. Palmer predicted that on May Day 1920 an unnamed conspiracy would attempt to overthrow the United States government. State militia units and police on twenty-four-hour alert guarded the nation against the threat of revolutionary violence. Not a single incident occurred. The hysteria of the Red Scare began to abate as the summer of 1920 passed without major labor strikes or renewed bombings.

The Sacco-Vanzetti Case. One dramatic episode kept the wartime legacy of antiradicalism alive well into the next decade. In May 1920, at the height of the Red Scare, Nicola Sacco, a shoemaker, and Bartolomeo Vanzetti, a fish peddler, were arrested for the robbery and murder of a shoe company paymaster in South Braintree, Massachusetts. Sacco and Vanzetti were self-proclaimed anarchists and Italian aliens who had evaded the draft; both were armed at the time of their arrest.

Sacco and Vanzetti were convicted in 1921 and sat on death row for six years while supporters tried unsuccessfully to appeal their verdicts. Regardless of their guilt or innocence, it is clear that they did not receive a fair trial from the American judicial system. Shortly before his execution in the electric chair on August 23, 1927, Vanzetti claimed triumph.

> If it had not been for these thing, I might have live out my life among scorning men. I might have die, unmarked, unknown, a failure. Now we are not a failure. This is our career and our triumph. Never in our full life can we hope to do such work for tolerance, for justice, for man's understanding of man, as now we do by an accident.
>
> Our words—our lives—our pains—nothing! The taking of our lives—lives of a good shoemaker and a poor fish-peddlar—all! That last moment belongs to us—that agony is our triumph.

This oft-quoted elegy captures the eloquence and tolerance of one victim caught in the last spasm of antiradicalism and fear that capped America's participation in World War I.

★

Summary

The outbreak of the Great War in 1914 posed the greatest challenge yet to American diplomacy. For more than two years, President Wilson kept the nation out of war, attempting to use American power and prestige to mediate between the two sides. The United States finally entered the war in 1917 because of violations of its neutrality rights at sea, but, more broadly, because the country's foreign policy reflected the same moral concerns that animated the domestic reform movement. On April 6, 1917, Congress declared war on Germany.

American participation in the war was brief but decisive. Two million freshly recruited "doughboys" turned the tide for the Allies on the Western Front in 1918. Flush with victory, Wilson sought a role in the peace commensurate with America's contribution. Yet the Versailles treaty only partially reflected the hopes of President Woodrow Wilson for such goals as freedom of the seas, peaceful economic expansion, and national self-determination. His postwar plans suffered a worse blow when the Senate refused to ratify the treaty, which included U.S. participation in the League of Nations.

As the Wilson administration put the nation on a war footing, Progressive reform energies were largely diverted to the war effort. An army had to be created almost from scratch, American agriculture and manufacturing had to be directed to produce for the Allies as well as the home market, and American workers had to be recruited for war work and kept on the job. All this absorbed the energies of a new group of professional experts turned government bureaucrats. World War I thus helped create the tools of the modern bureaucratic state which, laid aside temporarily at war's end, would be taken up again during the nation's greatest peacetime crisis, the Great Depression.

The government tried to mobilize the minds of the American people as well, but succeeded mainly in inflaming passions. Certain groups, such as woman suffragists, found success during the war. But others became targets of repression, including blacks who migrated to northern cities, labor activists who called widespread strikes, and Socialists and other radicals who criticized the government. Domestic tensions erupted in race riots in many northern cities, and in the Red Scare of 1919–1920.

Free Speech in Wartime

How far does the First Amendment go in protecting the right of free speech? Does the state have a legitimate interest in imposing stringent regulations on public expression during wartime? Carefully analyze the reasoning of the Supreme Court in the 1919 cases of *Schenck v. United States* (249 U.S. 47) and *Abrams v. United States* (250 U.S. 616). What are the facts in each case? How is the doctrine of "clear and present danger" presented? Why did Justices Oliver Wendell Holmes and Louis Brandeis vote with the unanimous majority in *Schenck* but dissent in the *Abrams* case? Is there an absolute right to free speech? If not, then what are acceptable limits in a democratic society?

For background, Zechariah Chaffee, Jr.'s classic *Free Speech in the United States* (1941) can be supplemented by Richard Polenberg, *Fighting Faiths: The Abrams Case, the Supreme Court, and Free Speech* (1987). For further historical context, consult Harold C. Peterson and Gilbert Fite, *Opponents of War, 1917–1918* (1968); Donald Johnson, *The Challenge to American Freedoms: World War I and The Rise of the American Civil Liberties Union* (1963); William Preston, Jr., *Aliens and Dissenters: Federal Suppression of Radicals, 1903–1933* (1963); and Harry Schreiber, *The Wilson Administration and Civil Liberties, 1917–1921* (1960).

BIBLIOGRAPHY

David M. Kennedy, *Over Here: The First World War and American Society* (1980) provides a comprehensive overview. For the links between the Progressive Era and the war, see Neil A. Wynn, *From Progressivism to Prosperity: World War I and American Society* (1986); John A. Thompson, *Reformers and War* (1987); and Robert M. Crunden, *Ministers of Reform: The Progressives' Achievement in American Civilization, 1889–1920 (1982)*. Ellis W. Hawley, *The Great War and the Search for a Modern Order, 1917–1933* (1979), stresses the continuities between the war years and the 1920s.

The Great War

On American entry into World War I, see John Coogan, *The End to Neutrality* (1981); Emily Rosenberg, *Spreading the American Dream* (1982); Ernest May, *The World War and American Isolationism* (1959); Ross Gregory, *The Origins of American Intervention in the First World War* (1971); Daniel Smith, *The Great Departure: The United States and World War I, 1914–1920* (1965); and Thomas A. Bailey and Paul

Ryan, *The Lusitania Disaster* (1975). There is a large body of material on the policies and personality of Woodrow Wilson, beginning with Arthur Link's five-volume biography (1947–1965), as well as his *Wilson the Diplomatist* (1957). See also Alexander L. George and Juliette L. George, *Woodrow Wilson and Colonel House: A Personality Study* (1956), and John M. Blum, *Woodrow Wilson and the Politics of Morality* (1956). Later studies of Wilson include Robert Ferrell, *Woodrow Wilson and World War I* (1985); John Milton Cooper, Jr., *The Warrior and the Priest: Woodrow Wilson and Theodore Roosevelt* (1983); and Edwin Weinstein, *Woodrow Wilson: A Medical and Psychological Biography* (1981).

For American participation in the war, Russell Weigley, *The American Way of War* (1973); Edward M. Coffman, *The War to End All Wars* (1968); and Harvey deWeerd, *President Wilson Fights His War* (1968), provide useful introductions. They can be supplemented by Laurence Stallings, *The Doughboys: The Story of the AEF, 1917–1918* (1963), and A. E. Barbeau and Florette Henri, *The Unknown Soldiers: Black Troops in World War I* (1974). John Whiteclay Chambers II, *To Raise an Army* (1987), covers the draft. Allan Brandt, *No Magic Bullet* (1985), discusses the anti-venereal disease campaigns in the army and on the homefront. Paul Chapman, *Schools as Sorters* (1988), describes the intelligence testing movement. Material on Eddie Rickenbacker and other wartime aces can be found in his *Fighting the Flying Circus* (1919) and his autobiography, *Edward Rickenbacker* (1967). See also Robert Jackson, *Fighter Pilots in World War I* (1977) and Christopher Campbell, *Aces and Aircraft of World War I* (1981).

Mobilizing the Home Front

Robert D. Cuff, *The War Industries Board: Business-Government Relations During World War I* (1973), provides an excellent case study of war mobilization. See also Stephen Skowronek, *Building a New American State: The Expansion of National Administrative Capacities, 1877–1920* (1982); Charles Gilbert, *American Financing of World War I* (1970); and David F. Noble, *America By Design* (1977). Valerie Jean Conner, *The National War Labor Board* (1983), covers federal policies towards labor. Jordan Schwarz, *The Speculator* (1981), is a biography of Bernard Baruch.

Maurine Greenwald, *Women, War, and Work* (1980), and Barbara Steinson, *American Women's Activism in World War I* (1982), provide good overviews of women's wartime experiences. Anne F. Scott and Andrew Scott, *One Half the People* (1975), and Eleanor Flexner, *Century of Struggle* (1959), cover the final stages of the woman suffrage campaign. For the peace movement, see C. Roland Marchand, *The American Peace Movement and Social Reform, 1898–1918* (1973); Charles Chatfield, *for Peace and Justice: Pacifism in America, 1914–1941* (1971); and Charles DeBenedetti, *Origins of the Modern Peace Movement* (1978). Allen F. Davis, *American Heroine* (1974), is a biography of Jane Addams.

Efforts to promote national unity are covered in Stephen Vaughan, *Holding Fast the Inner Lines: Democracy, Nationalism, and the CPI* (1980); William J. Breen, *Uncle Sam at Home* (1984); Paul L. Murphy, *World War I and the Origins of Civil Liberties* (1979); George Blakey, *Historians on the Homefront* (1970); and Frederick Luebke, *Bonds of Loyalty: German-Americans and World War I* (1974). For the experiences of Mexican-Americans, see Rodolfo Acuna, *Occupied America* (1980), and Wayne Cornelius, *Building the Cactus Curtain: Mexican Migration and U.S. Responses From Wilson to Carter* (1980).

An Unsettled Peace

For Wilson's diplomacy, see Lloyd Ambrosius, *Woodrow Wilson and the American Diplomatic Tradition* (1987); Arthur Walworth, *Wilson and the Peacemakers* (1986); and N. Gordon Levin, Jr., *Woodrow Wilson and World Politics* (1968). For more on Versailles and the League of Nations, see Thomas Bailey, *Woodrow Wilson and The Great Betrayal* (1945); Ralph A. Stone, *The Irreconcilables: The Fight Against the League of Nations* (1970); and Arno J. Mayer, *Politics and Diplomacy of Peacemaking: Containment and Counter Revolution at Versailles* (1967). See also William Widenor, *Henry Cabot Lodge and the Search for an American Foreign Policy* (1980), and John A. Garraty, *Henry Cabot Lodge* (1953). Anglo-American responses to revolution between 1913 and 1923 are covered in Lloyd C. Gardner, *Safe for Democracy* (1984). On American intervention in Russia, see George F. Kennan, *The Decision to Intervene* (1958); John L. Gaddis, *Russia, the Soviet Union, and the United States* (1978); and Peter Filene, *Americans and the Soviet Experiment, 1917–1933* (1967). Ronald Steel's fine biography, *Walter Lippmann and the American Century* (1980), offers another view of the Versailles conference.

Robert K. Murray, *The Red Scare* (1955), summarizes the antiradicalism of the postwar period. See also James Weinstein, *The Decline of Socialism in America, 1912–1923* (1967); John Higham, *Strangers in the Land* (1955); and Burl Noggle, *Into the Twenties* (1974). David Brody, *Labor in Crisis* (1965), describes the steel strike of 1919; for a more general overview, see David Montgomery, *The Fall of the House of Labor: The Workplace, the State, and American Labor Activism, 1865–1925* (1987). For race relations, see James R. Grossman, *Land of Hope: Chicago, Black Southerners, and the Great Migration* (1989); William M. Tuttle, Jr., *Race Riot: Chicago in the Red Summer of 1919* (1970); Robert V. Haynes, *A Night of Violence: The Houston Riot of 1917* (1976); and Elliot M. Rudwick, *Race Riot at East St. Louis, July 2, 1917* (1964). For an introduction to the complicated Sacco and Vanzetti case, see Louis Joughin and Edmund Morgan, *The Legacy of Sacco and Vanzetti* (1948), and Roberta Strauss Feuerlicht, *Justice Crucified* (1977).

TIMELINE

1914	Outbreak of war in Europe United States declares neutrality (1914)
1915	German submarine sinks *Lusitania*
1916	Wilson reelected
1917	U.S. enters World War I War Industries Board established Revenue Act of 1917 passed Selective Service Act passed Suffrage militancy East St. Louis race riot Espionage Act Passed Bolshevik Revolution
1918	Wilson proposes Fourteen Points Armistice ends War Eugene Debs imprisoned under Sedition Act U.S. troops intervene in Soviet Union
1919	Treaty of Versailles Steel Strike Red Scare and Palmer Raids League of Nations defeated in Senate Eighteenth Amendment (Prohibition)
1920	Nineteenth Amendment (woman suffrage)

Advertising Modernity

Artist Maxfield Parrish's yearly calendars for
General Electric, such as this 1920 "Prometheus"
for Mazda lamps, brought him widespread visibility and suggest the power of modern advertising.

CHAPTER **24** *Modern Times:*
The 1920s

In 1924 sociologists Robert Lynd and Helen Merrell Lynd arrived in Muncie, Indiana, to study the life of a small American city. They set about observing how citizens of Middletown (the fictional name they bestowed on the city, which had been chosen for its middle-of-the-road quality) went about their daily round of making a living, maintaining a home, educating the young, practicing religion, organizing community activities, and spending their leisure time. As the Lynds' field work proceeded, they were repeatedly struck by how much had changed over the past thirty-five years—the actual lifetime of a middle-aged Middletown resident. They decided to contrast the Muncie of the 1890s with the Muncie of the 1920s. When *Middletown* was published in 1929, this "study in modern American culture" became an unexpected bestseller.

Many characteristics of modern America were in place by the end of World War I. American participation in the war made the country a major player in the world economy; the foundations of the modern corporate economy were firmly established, as well as those of the modern state. The 1920s, rather than World War I, represented a watershed in the development of a mass national culture. The Protestant work ethic and the old values of self-denial and frugality gave way in the 1920s to a fascination with consumption, leisure, and self-realization, which is the essence of modern life. In economic organization, political outlook, and cultural values, the 1920s have more in common with the United States of today than with the industrializing America of the late nineteenth century.

The prosperity and economic innovation of the 1920s gave Americans the highest standard of living in the world, although not every American was lucky enough to benefit from this new way of life. Most farmers, urban blacks, and recent immigrants could not afford the new mass-produced consumer goods and sampled them only selectively, adapting them to their traditional lifestyles. Other Americans found that the new values conflicted with old religious and cultural ones. But despite ambivalence toward the changes under way, patterns of consumption that appeared during the "New Era" of the 1920s and ways of spending leisure time quickly became part of American life.

The Business-Government Partnership of the 1920s

The business-government partnership that accelerated during World War I expanded on an informal basis throughout the 1920s. The successful performance of the economy from 1922 to 1929 seemed to confirm its ability to regulate itself with minimal government intervention. The impulse toward reform that had animated the Progressive Era was gone, or had at least gone underground. Business leaders were no longer villains but respected public figures. President Warren Harding captured the prevailing political mood when he offered the American public "not heroics but healing, not nostrums but normalcy."

The Economy

America's transition from a wartime to a peacetime economy was not smooth. During the immediate post-war years, the worst problem was runaway inflation. Prices jumped by a third in 1919, accompanied by feverish economic activity. The postwar boom was less an indication of solid economic growth than a reflection of consumers' desire to buy before prices rose even higher. In an attempt to balance the budget, the Wilson administration sharply reduced federal expenditures and thus stopped the inflationary spiral. At the same time, in 1920, the Federal Reserve System tightened credit because its previous expansive money policies had encouraged people to borrow and spend, and thereby pushed prices even higher. The new policy resulted in a recession, demonstrating that the government had much to learn about how to achieve economic stability.

The recession of 1920–1921 was the sharpest short-term downturn the United States had ever faced. Unemployment reached 10 percent. Foreign trade dropped by almost half, from $13.5 billion in 1920 to less than $7 billion in 1921, as European nations returned to production after the disruptions of war. Prices fell so dramatically—more than 20 percent—that much of the inflation of World War I was wiped out. The recession lasted only a short time. By 1922 the economy had started to recover, and the recovery continued, broken only by brief, mild downturns, until 1929. Unemployment hovered around 3 or 4 percent and inflation was negligible. Between 1922 and 1929, the gross national product grew from $74.1 billion to $103.1 billion, approximately 40 percent. Per capita income rose proportionally from $641 in 1921 to $847 in 1929. Soon the

federal government was recording a budget surplus. The boom of the 1920s provided the backdrop for the partnership between business and government which bloomed in that decade.

An abundance of new consumer products, particularly the automobile, stimulated the recovery and prosperity of the 1920s. Manufacturing output expanded 64 percent during the decade, with industries churning out automobiles, appliances, chemicals, electric power, radios, aircraft, and movies. Behind this growth lay new management and mass production techniques, which resulted in a 40 percent increase in worker productivity. The value of total new construction increased from $6 billion in 1921 to $12 billion in 1927. The demand for goods and services kept unemployment low throughout the 1920s, but the expanded demand was not so strong that it produced inflation.

One sector of the economy that never fully recovered from the 1920 recession was agriculture. During the inflationary period of 1914 to 1920, farmers had borrowed heavily to finance mortgages and buy farm equipment as they expanded production in response to government incentives, increased demand, and rising prices. When the war ended and European countries resumed agricultural production, the world market was glutted with agricultural products. The price of wheat dropped 40 percent as the government withdrew wartime price supports. Corn fell 32 percent, hogs 50 percent, and farm income plunged.

Since American farmers produced mainly for the world market, one key to agricultural recovery was to prevent worldwide surpluses from further depressing domestic prices. Farmers turned for help to the political system. The McNary-Haugen bill, a far-reaching attempt to create federal price supports for agricultural

The Assembly Line

The success of the automobile industry contributed significantly to the prosperity of the 1920s, and mass production made automobiles affordable to ordinary citizens, not just the well-to-do. By 1929 there were more than 23 million cars on the road.

products, used the idea of a "fair exchange value" to guarantee that farmers earned back at least their production costs, no matter what price prevailed on the world market. A 1924 bill restricting this principle to grain failed in Congress, where Eastern Republicans and President Coolidge opposed it as special interest legislation. When Midwestern supporters of the bill added cotton, rice, and tobacco to win southern farm support, the measure passed, only to be vetoed by President Coolidge in 1927 and again in 1928. By the end of the decade, the farmers' share of the national income had plummeted from 16 percent in 1919 to 8.8 percent.

Besides agriculture, certain "sick industries," like coal and textiles, also missed out on the prosperity of the 1920s. These industries had expanded in response to World War I demands only to face overcapacity or unprofitability, and grew sluggishly, if at all, in the 1920s. This underside of economic life foreshadowed the Depression of the 1930s.

The Republican Ascendancy

Except for two terms under Woodrow Wilson, the national government had been controlled by the Republican party since 1896. With Wilson's progressive coalition floundering in 1918, the Republicans were in a position to regain their edge in the upcoming election. In 1920 the Democrats passed over the ailing Wilson in favor of Governor James M. Cox of Ohio, with Assistant Secretary of the Navy Franklin D. Roosevelt as the vice-presidential candidate. The Democratic platform called for ratification of U.S. participation in the League of Nations and a continuation of Wilsonian progressivism, while the Republicans, represented by Warren G. Harding and Calvin Coolidge, promised a return to normalcy, which meant a strong pro-business stance and conservative cultural values. Harding and Coolidge won in a landslide, marking the beginning of a new Republican era that lasted until 1932.

Hardly a towering national figure, President Harding had built an uninspiring record in Ohio state politics before winning election to the United States Senate in 1914. With a Republican victory almost a certainty in 1920, party leaders wanted a candidate they could dominate. Genial, loyal, and mediocre, "Uncle Warren" fit the bill.

Harding knew his limitations and tried to assemble a strong cabinet to help him guide the government. Charles Evans Hughes, former presidential candidate and Supreme Court justice, headed the State Department. As Secretary of Agriculture, Henry C. Wallace set up conferences between farmers and government agencies, such as the Bureau of Agricultural Economics. Financier Andrew W. Mellon ran the Treasury Depart-

ment, engineering a massive tax cut to reduce the federal surplus. Most of the benefits went to the wealthy, freeing up money for private investment, as Mellon intended.

By far the most active member of the Harding administration was Secretary of Commerce Herbert Hoover, who had successfully headed the food administration during the war. Hoover embodied the business-government cooperation of the 1920s, continuing the pattern of state-building begun during World War I. Unlike Secretary of the Treasury Mellon who sought to minimize government intervention, Hoover supported expansion of the federal government in what he called the spirit of "associationalism." Voluntary cooperation in the public interest, Hoover maintained, would stabilize prices and assure general economic stability in volatile sectors of the economy such as agriculture, construction, and mining. He used persuasion, educational conferences, and fact-finding commissions to accomplish his goals.

Hoover actively promoted trade associations as the key to "associated individualism." There were about two thousand of these instruments of voluntary cooperation, representing almost every major industry and commodity. Trade associations were supposed to lend stability to modern economic life through conferences, conventions, publicity, lobbying, and trade practice controls. Statistics gathered by the Commerce Department and by private groups, such as the National Bureau of Economic Research, were useful in corporate planning and in allocating investments and markets. Trade conferences organized by the Commerce Department provided a forum for the exchange of information. The Republican-dominated Federal Trade Commission conveniently ignored antitrust laws that forbade such restraints on trade, then approved the resulting agreements. Here it followed the lead of the Supreme Court, which in 1920 had dismissed the long-pending antitrust case against the United States Steel Corporation, ruling that the large size of a business was not in and of itself against the law as long as some competition remained.

Unfortunately, not all of Harding's appointees were as earnest as Hoover. Harding himself was an honest man, but some of his political associates lacked ethical standards. When Harding died suddenly in San Francisco in August 1923, evidence of widespread fraud and corruption in his administration had just started coming to light. The worst scandal concerned the government's leasing of oil reserves in Teapot Dome, Wyoming, and Elk Hills, California, to private companies. Secretary of the Interior Albert Fall was eventually convicted of taking $300,000 in bribes and became the first cabinet officer in American history to serve a prison sentence.

Following Harding's death, Vice-President Calvin

Coolidge moved to the White House. In contrast to Harding's political cronyism and outgoing style, Coolidge personified Vermont rectitude. As vice-president, "Silent Cal" often sat through official functions without uttering a word. His dinner partner once challenged him by saying, "Mr. Coolidge, I've made a rather sizable bet with my friends that I can get you to speak three words this evening." Coolidge replied, "You lose." Like Harding, Coolidge backed business and believed in limited government; he was said to have performed all his presidential duties in four hours a day. Coolidge's unimpeachable morality reassured voters in the wake of the Harding scandals, and he soon announced he would run for president in 1924.

The 1924 Election. The Democratic party found it difficult to mount an effective challenge to its more popular and better-financed rival, whose strength was drawn chiefly from the native-born Protestant middle class, augmented by small businesspeople, skilled workers, farmers, northern black voters, and wealthy industrialists. Democrats drew their support mainly from the South and from northern urban political machines, such as Tammany Hall in New York, but these were two constituencies whose interests often collided. Until the Democrats could build an effective national organization to rival the Republicans, they would remain a minority party.

When the Democrats gathered that year in the sweltering July heat of New York City, they were even more divided than usual. Their convention, the first to be broadcast live on national radio, lasted seventeen days, prompting the humorist Will Rogers to say, "This thing has got to come to an end. New York invited you people here as guests, not to live." The convention became hopelessly deadlocked between Governor Alfred E. Smith of New York, who had the support of northern urban politicians, and William G. McAdoo of California, Wilson's secretary of the treasury (and son-in-law), the western and southern choice. McAdoo had the backing both of former Progressives and a large faction of the Ku Klux Klan, causing opponents to jeer "Ku, Ku, McAdoo." After 103 ballots, the delegates compromised on candidate John W. Davis, a Wall Street lawyer who had served as a West Virginia congressman and ambassador to Great Britain. To attract rural voters, the Democrats chose as the vice-presidential candidate Governor Charles W. Bryan of Nebraska, brother of William Jennings Bryan.

The 1924 campaign also featured a third-party challenge by Senator Robert M. La Follette of Wisconsin, who ran on the Progressive ticket. His candidacy mobilized reformers and labor leaders, as well as disgruntled farmers. The Progressive party platform called for nationalization of the railroads, public ownership of utilities, and the right of Congress to overrule Supreme

Court decisions. The platform also favored election of the president directly by the voters, rather than by the electoral college.

The Republicans won an impressive victory, with Coolidge receiving 15.7 million popular votes to 8.4 million for Davis and a decisive victory in the electoral college. Despite La Follette's vigorous campaign, he could not draw many midwestern farm leaders away from the Republican party; his labor support also proved soft. La Follette got almost 5 million popular votes but only Wisconsin supported him in the electoral college.

Perhaps the most significant fact about the 1924 election was voter apathy. Only 52 percent of the electorate bothered to vote, compared with more than 70 percent who voted in the presidential elections of the late nineteenth century. The nation's newly enfranchised women were not to blame, however: it was the drop in voting by men that was responsible for the decline.

Women in Politics. Instead of resting after the suffrage victory, women expanded their political activism throughout the 1920s. Partisan women tried to break into party politics, but the Democrats and Republicans granted them only token positions on party committees. For women, political officeholding remained a "widow's game": about two-thirds of the women in Congress were named to finish out their late husbands' terms.

Women were more influential as lobbyists. The Women's Joint Congressional Committee, a Washington-based coalition of ten major women's organizations including the newly formed League of Women Voters and the National Consumers' League, lobbied for reform legislation. Its major accomplishment was winning the passage in 1921 of the Sheppard-Towner Federal Maternity and Infancy Act, the nation's first federally funded health care program. In an attempt to reduce the high rates of death associated with childbirth, Congress appropriated $1.25 million for medical clinics, educational prenatal programs, and visiting-nurse projects. The Sheppard-Towner law passed because politicians feared that if it didn't, women would vote them out of office. As one supporter noted, "If the members could have voted in the cloak room, it would have been killed." However, in 1929, when politicians had realized that women did not vote as a bloc, they cut off appropriations for the program.

At mid-decade the Republicans were in an enviable position. The scandals of the Harding years were behind them and the economy continued to be strong, seeming to support their policy of vesting primary responsibility for the well-being of the country in the hands of corporate capitalism. The informal business-government partnership worked—or so it seemed, until the depression.

Corporate Capitalism

A revolution in management that had been reshaping American business since the late nineteenth century triumphed in the 1920s. Large-scale corporate organizations with bureaucratic structures of authority replaced family-run businesses. Ownership was divorced from control of daily operations; what the eighteenth-century economist Adam Smith had called the "invisible hand" of market forces gave way to the visible hand of management.

There were more mergers in the 1920s—368 in 1924 and 1,245 in 1929—than at any time since the heyday of combinations in the 1880s and 1890s. The largest number occurred in such rapidly growing industries as chemicals (Du Pont), electrical appliances and machinery (Westinghouse and General Electric), and automobiles (General Motors). By 1930 the two hundred largest corporations controlled almost half the nonbanking corporate wealth in the United States. It was rare for a corporation to monopolize an entire industry; rather, oligopolies, in which a few large producers controlled the market of an industry, became the norm.

By 1920 many industries, especially manufacturing industries, had modern organizational structures. The multi-unit enterprise coordinated production and distribution through divisions organized by functions, such as sales, operations, and investment. Alfred P. Sloan, Jr., an engineer and mid-level manager at General Motors, whose innovative structure set the pattern for large companies in the 1920s and 1930s, further refined this structure by relieving top management of all day-to-day control of production, freeing them to concentrate on long-range planning, while autonomous, integrated divisions met short-range production goals.

More important, corporations greatly increased their commitment to research and development, using current earnings to finance future profits. Corporate mergers were an important source of capital for this purpose. By 1927 more than a thousand corporations had set up independent research programs, among them Bell Laboratories, the research arm of the American Telephone and Telegraph Company, formally incorporated in 1925.

Running these huge modern corporate structures called for a new breed of man: the professional manager. (Women found few opportunities in the corporate hierarchy until the 1970s.) Increasingly, corporations relied on graduate schools of business, such as Wharton and Harvard, to produce managers, consultants, and executives, many of whom had engineering training. The chief executives at General Motors, General Electric, Singer, Du Pont, and Goodyear in the 1920s had been engineering classmates at the Massachusetts Institute of Technology several decades before.

River Rouge

Industrial photographers in the 1920s celebrated the power and raw beauty of industrial technology. Charles Sheeler's 1927 photograph shows Henry Ford's River Rouge plant outside Detroit. But where are the workers? (University Art Museum, University of New Mexico)

The nation's financial institutions expanded and consolidated along with its corporations. Total bank assets rose from almost $48 billion in 1919 to $72 billion in 1929, largely because of rising deposits in savings accounts and business and loan associations, along with life insurance policies and accounts. Mergers between Wall Street banks enhanced the role of New York as the financial center of the United States and, increasingly, the world. In 1929, almost half the nation's banking resources were controlled by 1 percent, or 250, of the nation's banks.

Business leaders enjoyed enormous popularity and respect in the 1920s, their reputations often surpassing those of the era's rather lackluster politicians, who often drew parallels between business leadership and religion. President Calvin Coolidge solemnly declared, "The man who builds a factory builds a temple. The man who works there worships there." The secularization of religion, or glorification of business, reached its height in a book called *The Man Nobody Knows* (1924), by advertising executive Bruce Barton. The man of the title was Jesus Christ, whom Barton portrayed as the founder of modern business, writing that Christ, "picked up twelve men from the bottom ranks of business and forged them into an organization that conquered the world." Barton's parable became an instant best seller.

The most respected businessman of the decade was Henry Ford, whose rise from a poor farm boy to corporate giant symbolized the values of rural society and American individualism in a rapidly changing world. Ford's factories, especially the River Rouge plant in suburban Detroit, represented the triumph of mass production. Ironically, this American capitalist hero achieved great popularity in the Soviet Union, selling the Russians twenty-five thousand tractors between 1920 and 1926, when the United States and the Soviet Union had no formal diplomatic relations.

Labor and Welfare Capitalism

Workers also shared in the prosperity of the 1920s, although labor lagged behind business in reaping the benefits of technology. Workers were given higher wages deliberately to increase their buying power. With a shorter work week (five days and a half day on Saturday), workers had more leisure time. Large firms like International Harvester offered employees two weeks annual paid vacation. But the scientific management techniques implemented in the 1920s reduced labor's control over the work environment. Decisions from the extremely pro-business Supreme Court, led by Chief Justice William Howard Taft, also adversely affected workers. For example, in *Colorado Coal Company v. United Mine Workers* the court ruled that a striking union could be prosecuted for illegal restraint of trade. It also struck down federal legislation regulating child labor and the minimum wage for women workers in the District of Columbia.

The 1920s were also the heyday of "welfare capitalism," a system of labor relations that stressed management's responsibility for the well-being of its employees. Though tinged with paternalism, such systems provided benefits to workers at a time when unemployment compensation and old age pensions did not exist. Employee security was not, however, the primary concern of such corporate programs, which existed mainly as a deterrent to the formation of unions.

Welfare capitalism took several forms. Workers could increase their stake in the company by buying the stock below the market price. Some firms subsidized mortgages or contributed to employee savings funds; others set up insurance and pension plans. Many adopted programs for consultation between management and elected representatives of the workers. These employee representation schemes, another device to avert unionization, were called the American Plan, so as to establish the idea that unions were un-American. Management's long-term goals included control over the workplace, an open (nonunion) shop, and worker loyalty.

However, the system had serious defects, the worst being the lack of protection against unemployment. Welfare capitalism appeared in the largest, most prosperous firms, such as General Electric and U.S. Steel, and reached only a minority of workers. Furthermore, corporate profits often dictated the nature of the programs. The Proctor & Gamble Company guaranteed forty-eight weeks of employment a year to its soap-manufacturing workers, because of the steady public demand for soap, but workers who processed vegetable oils, which were subject to wild sales fluctuations, received no such guarantee.

Welfare capitalism represented a form of labor relations squarely in keeping with the values of the 1920s. It placed the responsibility for economic welfare on the private rather than the public sector, avoiding the specter of government interference in the workplace. It also satisfied management's desire to reverse the tide of unionization: union membership dropped from 5.1 million in 1920 to 3.6 million in 1929, about 10 percent of the nonagricultural work force. The number of strikes also fell dramatically from the 1919 level. Welfare capitalism seemed to represent the wave of the future in industrial relations.

Economic Expansion Abroad

As the domestic economy expanded, so did the nation's position on the international scene. During the 1920s, the United States was the most productive country in the world, with an enormous capacity to compete in foreign markets. There was a growing demand from abroad for American products such as radios, telephones, automobiles, and sewing machines. Just as important was the demand for U.S. capital. America's emergence as the world's largest creditor nation, a reversal of its pre-World War I status as a debtor, represented a significant shift of power in the world capital markets. American investment abroad more than doubled between 1919 and 1930. By the end of the 1920s, American corporations had invested $15.2 billion in foreign countries.

Manufacturers led the way in foreign investment. Electric companies, including General Electric, built new plants in Latin America, China, Japan, and Australia. Ford had major facilities throughout the British Empire, and General Motors took over such established firms as Vauxhall in England and Opel in Germany. The International Telephone and Telegraph Corporation, founded in 1920, employed ninety-five thousand workers outside the country, more than any other U.S. company.

Other U.S. companies invested internationally during the 1920s to take advantage of lower production costs or to procure raw materials or supplies, concentrating mainly on Latin America. The three major American meat packers—Swift, Armour, and Wilson—built packing plants in Argentina to capitalize on lower livestock prices. Fruit growers, such as the United Fruit Company, developed plantations in Costa Rica, Honduras, and Guatemala. American capital also dominated sugar plantations in Cuba and rubber plantations in the Philippines, Sumatra, and Malaya.

American companies also invested heavily in mining and oil, especially in South America and Canada. The Anaconda Copper Corporation owned Chile's largest copper mine. Standard Oil of New Jersey led American oil companies in the acquisition of oil reserves in Mexico and Venezuela. American involvement in the oil-rich Persian Gulf became significant only after World War II.

American banks supported U.S. enterprises abroad, focusing much of their attention on Europe. European countries, especially Germany, desperately needed private American capital to finance economic recovery after World War I. Germany needed to rebuild its economy and pay reparations to the Allies; Britain and France had to repay wartime loans. As late as 1930, the Allies still owed the United States $4.3 billion. American political leaders, responding to the disenchantment with the nation's costly participation in the war, insisted on payment. "They hired the money, didn't they?" scoffed President Coolidge.

European countries had trouble repaying their debts because the United States maintained high protective tariffs to keep foreign-made goods out. The Fordney-McCumber Tariff of 1922 followed the long-standing Republican policy of protectionism, and the Hawley-Smoot Tariff of 1930 took economic nationalism even further. American manufacturers favored such tariffs because they feared that foreign competition would reduce their profits. But the difficulty European nations had in selling goods in the United States made it harder for them to use dollars to pay off their debts.

Concerned about debt repayment, the American banking community and many U.S. corporations with European investments opposed excessively high tariffs and urged modification of the debt structure. They recognized that a rapidly recovering Europe and a freer trade environment would help American business, while a weak European economy might undermine long-term loans and investments.

In 1924 at the prodding of the United States, France, Great Britain, and Germany joined with the United States in a plan to promote European financial stability. The Dawes plan, named for Charles G. Dawes, a Chicago banker who negotiated the agreement, offered substantial loans to Germany and a reduction in the amount of reparations owed the Allies. But the Dawes plan did not provide a permanent solution. The international economic system, dependent on the flow of American capital to Germany, reparations payments from Germany to the Allies, and the repayment of debts to the United States, was inherently unstable. If the flow of capital from the United States slowed or stopped, the whole international financial structure could collapse.

Foreign Policy in the 1920s

Foreign affairs in the period between the wars are often viewed through the lens of isolationism—that is, the view that the United States, disillusioned after World War I, willfully retreated from involvement in world affairs. But the term isolationism masks the active role that the United States was taking in world affairs, both before and after the Great War. Economic expansion into new markets was a major component of the 1920s prosperity, and the United States ardently sought a peaceful and stable world order to facilitate American investments in Latin American, European, and East Asian markets. This expansion abroad was abetted by the appropriate branches of the federal government, such as the State and Commerce departments.

In the 1920s the United States continued its quest for peaceful ways to dominate the Western Hemisphere, economically and diplomatically, but retreated slightly from its pattern of unchecked military intervention in Latin American affairs. The United States withdrew troops from the Dominican Republic in 1924, but maintained military forces in Nicaragua almost continuously from 1912 to 1933. American troops also occupied Haiti from 1915 to 1934. Relations with Mexico remained tense as a legacy of U.S. intervention during the Mexican Revolution.

There was little popular or political support, however, for entangling diplomatic commitments to allies, European or otherwise. The United States never joined the League of Nations or the Court of International Justice (the World Court). International cooperation had to come through other forums.

The Washington Conference and the Kellogg-Briand Pact. The 1921 Washington Naval Arms Conference represented a milestone in the history of disarmament. By placing limits on naval expansion, policymakers hoped to encourage stability in areas such as the Far East and protect the fragile postwar world economy from excessive arms spending. They also wished security to contain Japan, whose expansionist tendencies were already seen as threatening two decades before the outbreak of World War II.

Led by Secretary of State Charles Evan Hughes, the three leading naval powers—Britain, the United States, and Japan—joined other countries in agreeing to halt construction of large battleships for ten years and to maintain current tonnage among Britain, the United States, Japan, Italy, and France at a ratio of 5: 5: 3: 1.75: 1.75. (This maintained parity among the big three, since the Japanese fleet operated only in the Pacific.) The conferees even agreed to scrap some existing warships, leading one commentator to exclaim that in a thirty-five-minute speech the Secretary of State had sunk "more ships than all the admirals of the world have sunk in a cycle of centuries."

In a similar spirit of international cooperation, the 1928 Kellogg-Briand Peace Pact condemned militarism as a tool for advancing national interests. In 1927, French foreign minister Aristide Briand had asked the United States to sign an agreement guaranteeing France's territorial integrity and outlawing war between France and the United States. Instead, Coolidge's Secretary of State Frank Kellogg proposed a broader treaty, by which participating countries agreed to "condemn recourse to war for the solution of international controversies, and renounce it as an instrument of national policy." Fifteen nations signed the pact in Paris in 1928, with forty-eight additional nations approving it later. The Kellogg-Briand pact enjoyed the enthusiastic support of U.S. peace groups such as the Women's International League for Peace and Freedom and the Conference on the Cause and Cure of War, passing the U.S. Senate 85-1. Yet critics claimed that it was nothing more than an "international kiss": lacking enforcement machinery, it was only as effective as its signers made it. For many who abhorred war, however, the pact's broad moral statement was an important contribution to the maintenance of peace.

In the end, fervent hopes and pious declarations were no cure for the massive economic, political, and territorial problems that World War I left behind. The United States vacillated, as it would in the 1930s, between wanting to play a large role in world events and fearing that treaties or responsibilities would limit its ability to act unilaterally. Rather than criticize as naive or misguided the diplomatic efforts of the 1920s, it is perhaps best to see them as honest yet ultimately inadequate efforts to find a will to peace.

A New National Culture

The 1920s represented an important watershed in the development of a mass national culture. Automobiles, paved roads, parcel post service, movies, radios, telephones, mass circulation magazines, brand names, and chain stores linked Americans—in the mill towns of the Southern Piedmont, to outposts on the Oklahoma plains, western mining settlements, and ethnic enclaves on the East and West coasts—in an ever-expanding web

The Roaring Twenties
Rarely has a decade been defined so predominantly in cultural clichés as the 1920s—flappers, bathtub gin, speakeasies, the Charleston, and gangsters shooting it out on the streets of Chicago. John Held, Jr.'s cover for *McClure's* magazine suggests how the decade got its name of the "Roaring Twenties." But most Americans were too concerned with earning a living and raising a family to learn the latest dance craze.

of national experience. A new emphasis on leisure, consumption, and amusement characterized the modern era, although its benefits were more accessible to the white middle class than to minorities and other disadvantaged groups.

Consumption and Advertising

In homes across the country during the 1920s, Americans sat down to a breakfast of Kellogg's corn flakes with toast prepared in a General Electric toaster. They got into the Ford Model T to go about their business—perhaps shopping at one of the new chain stores, such as Safeway or A. & P., which had sprung up across the country. In the evening, the family gathered to listen to radio programs, such as "Great Moments in History" and "True Story," read the latest issue of the *Saturday Evening Post*, *Reader's Digest*, or *Collier's*. On weekends they might hop into the car to take in the latest Charlie Chaplin film at the local movie theater. Millions of Americans now shared the same daily experiences.

The 1920s were a critical decade in the development of the American consumer society. Although not every family participated in this new lifestyle, consumption became a cultural ideal for most of the middle class, often providing the criterion for judging self-worth that was once supplied by character, religion, and social standing. Spending money became a form of self-fulfillment, a gratification of personal needs.

Yet participation in commercial mass culture did not necessarily mean a total sell-out to middle-class values. Buying a Victrola or a radio on credit and listening to the opera singer Enrico Caruso could be one way for Italian immigrants to keep their culture alive. Nor was owning a car simply a symbol of consumption. "I had bought a jalopy in 1924, and it didn't change me," remembered one Communist Party activist, "It just made it easier for me to function." One historian concluded, "Chicago's ethnic workers were not transformed into more Americanized, middle-class people by the objects they consumed. Buying an electric vacuum cleaner did not turn Josef Dobrowolski into 'True Story''s Jim Smith."

The unequal distribution of income limited some consumers' ability to buy the enticing new products. At the height of prosperity in the 1920s, about 65 percent of America's families had an income of less than $2,000 a year. The average family income for the bottom 40 percent of the population was $725. Of that amount, a family would spend about $290 a year for food, $190 for housing, and $110 for clothing, leaving only $135 for everything else.

Retailers and automobile manufacturers addressed this situation by selling on the installment plan. In those days "Buy now, pay later" was a revolutionary concept. Before World War I most urban families paid cash for everything except a house. Then, during the 1920s, the automobile was such an object of desire that consumers put aside their fears of buying on time. By 1927, two-thirds of the cars in the United States were being paid for on the installment plan. Once people saw how easy it was to finance a car, they bought radios, refrigerators, and sewing machines. "A dollar down and a dollar forever," a cynic remarked. By 1929 banks, finance companies, credit unions, and other institutions were extending consumers loans of over $7 billion a year, and consumer lending was the tenth largest business in the United States.

Consumers spent about $667 million for electric appliances in 1927. By 1930, 85 percent of the nation's nonfarm households had the electricity to run their favorite gadgets. Irons and vacuum cleaners were the most popular appliances, followed by phonographs, sewing machines, and washing machines. Radios,

Advertising on a National Scale

Refrigerators did not save as much time or labor as other appliances, such as electric irons and vacuum cleaners, but they did have advantages. For example, food stayed fresh longer, which reduced the need to shop every day and, as this ad from the *Saturday Evening Post* in August 1928 suggested, refrigerators made entertaining easier.

whose production increased twenty-five-fold in the 1920s, sold for around $75. One of the most expensive items was a refrigerator, which cost $900 at the beginning of the decade. Technology quickly brought the price down to $180, but many families still had to make do with an icebox.

Because much of the new technology was concentrated in the home, it had a dramatic impact on the lives of women. Domestic chores became less arduous. It was far easier to plug in an electric iron than it was to heat an iron on the stove, and quicker to use a vacuum cleaner than a broom and a rug beater. Paradoxically, however, all these conveniences made more work for women. Electric servants replaced human ones and more middle-class women began to do their own housework and laundry. Technology also raised standards of cleanliness so that a man could wear a clean shirt every day instead of just on Sunday, and a house could be vacuumed daily rather than weekly.

The Flapper
The flapper phenomenon was not limited to Anglos. This 1921 photograph of a young Mexican-American woman shows how American fads and fashions reached into Hispanic communities across the country.

Advertising became big business in the 1920s. By 1929 advertisers were spending an average of $15 annually for every man, woman, and child in the United States—a total of $2.6 billion—to entice them to buy automobiles, cigarettes, radios, and refrigerators. That year, the advertising industry, which one historian called the "town criers" of modernity, accounted for 3 percent of the gross national product, comparable to its share after World War II. Many of the major advertising firms relied on experts in the field of psychology. The prominent psychologist John B. Watson left Johns Hopkins University in 1920 to become vice-president of the J. Walter Thompson advertising agency, and the advertising pioneer Edward Bernays was the nephew of Sigmund Freud.

Few of the new consumer products could be considered necessities of life, so advertisements used psychology to stir desire in consumers. Advertisers often used a white-coated doctor to imply scientific approval of their products. They also appealed to people's social aspirations by projecting images of successful, elegant, sophisticated people, who smoked a certain brand of cigarettes or drove a recognizable make of car. Ad writers sold products by preying on people's insecurities. They came up with a variety of socially unacceptable diseases, including "sneaker smell," "paralyzed pores," "office hips," "ashtray breath," and the dreaded "B.O." (body odor). After the term *halitosis* was discovered in an obscure British medical journal, many consumers rushed out to buy Listerine mouth wash. Yet American consumers were hardly passive victims of advertisers— evil "captains of consciousness" manipulating their every whim. America gloried in its role as the world's first mass-consumption economy.

Many of these cultural images came together in the flapper, the emancipated woman of the 1920s. With her slim, boyish figure, bobbed hair, short skirt and rolled-down silk stockings, the flapper symbolized the personal freedom trumpeted by the movies, advertisements, and other elements of the emerging mass culture. The flapper wore makeup (previously associated with lower-class women out for sexual favors) and lit up her cigarettes in public, a shocking affront to ladylike decency, which suggested the new, looser morality of the times. Like so many cultural icons, the flapper represented only a tiny minority of women. Yet the image mass marketed the belief in women's postsuffrage emancipation.

The Automobile Culture

As the predominant symbol of the 1920s, the automobile typified the new consumer-based economy. "Why on earth do you need to study what's changing this country?" a Muncie, Indiana, resident asked sociologists Robert and Helen Lynd, who were studying American culture and values. "I can tell you what's happening in just four letters: A-U-T-O!" The showpiece of modern capitalism and the ultimate consumer toy, the automobile revolutionized the ways Americans spent their income and their leisure time. The isolation of rural life broke down in the wake of the automobile. New phrases, such as "filling station" (or, as they were known west of the Rockies, "service stations") entered the nation's vocabulary. The automobile even affected crime, providing gangsters with a "getaway car" and the possibility of "taking someone for a ride." Cars touched so many aspects of American life that the word *automobility* was coined to describe their revolutionary impact on production methods, the nation's landscape, and even American values.

The automobile stimulated the prosperity of the 1920s. Before the introduction of the moving assembly line in 1913, it took Ford workers twelve and a half

AMERICAN VOICES

The Automobile Culture *The Residents of "Middletown"*

In their study of community life in Muncie, Indiana, Robert and Helen Lynd found that the "horse culture" of the 1890s had been totally supplanted by the automobile culture of the 1920s. According to the sociologists, "ownership of an automobile has now reached the point of being an accepted essential of normal living," as these residents confirm.

"We'd rather do without clothes than give up the car. We used to go to his sister's to visit, but by the time we'd get the children shoed and dressed there wasn't any money left for carfare. Now no matter how they look, we just poke 'em in the car and take 'em along."

"We don't spend anything on recreation except for the car. We save every place we can and put the money into the car. It keeps the family together."

"No, sir, we've *not* got a car. *That's* why we've got a home."

"The Ford car has done an awful lot of harm to the unions here and everywhere else. As long as men have enough money to buy a second-hand Ford and tires and gasoline, they'll be out on the road and paying no attention to union meetings."

"We don't have no fancy clothes when we have the car to pay for. The car is the only pleasure we have."

"He don't like to go to church Sunday night. We've been away from church this summer more'n ever since we got our car."

"I'll go without food before I'll see us give up the car."

"An automobile is a luxury, and no one has a right to one if he can't afford it. I haven't the slightest sympathy for any one who is out of work if he owns a car."

Source: Robert S. Lynd and Helen Merrell Lynd, *Middletown: A Study In Modern American Culture*

hours to assemble an auto; it took ninety-three minutes on an assembly line. In 1927, Ford produced an auto every twenty-four seconds. Car sales climbed from 1.5 million in 1921 to 5 million in 1929, when Americans spent $2.58 billion on new and used cars. By the late 1920s, a new Ford Model T, which cost $1,000 in 1908, sold for only $295 (at a time when the average industrial worker earned about $5 a day). Lower cost and installment buying increased yearly car registrations from 8.5 million in 1920 to 23 million in 1929. By the end of the decade, Americans owned about 80 percent of the world's automobiles, with an average of one car for every five people.

The growth of the auto industry had a ripple effect on the American economy. In 1929, 3.7 million workers owed their jobs to the automobile, directly or indirectly. Auto production stimulated the steel, petroleum, chemical, rubber, and glass industries. Total U.S. demand for oil, mainly for gasoline, multiplied two and a half times in the United States between 1919 and 1929, and domestic oil production expanded to meet the need. (The United States was still the world's chief supplier of oil in the 1920s.) The advertising industry grew along with the automobile; cars and cigarettes were two of the most heavily marketed products of the decade. Highway construction became a billion-dollar-a-year enterprise financed by federal subsidies and state gasoline taxes. Car ownership also spurred the growth of suburbs and contributed to real estate speculation. It spawned the first shopping center, Country Club Plaza, in Kansas City in 1924. Not even the death of twenty-five thousand people a year in traffic accidents, 70 percent of them pedestrians, could cool America's passion for the automobile.

Nowhere was this more obvious than in the way Americans were spending their leisure time. They took to the roads, becoming a nation of tourists. The American Automobile Association, founded in 1902, reported that in 1929 about 45 million people—almost a third of the population—took vacations by automobile. Of the $10 billion spent on recreation in 1930, two-thirds went for cars and related expenses. People preferred the freedom of automobiles to the rigid timetables and predetermined routes of trains. With improved roads, mo-

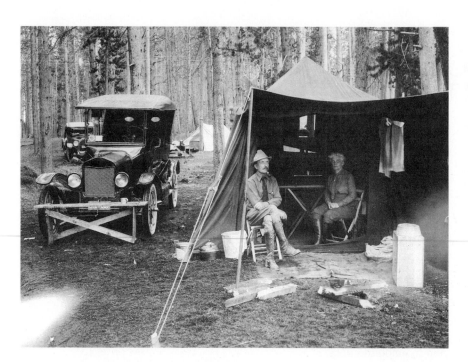

The Automobile Vacation
This contented couple was autocamping in Yellowstone Park in 1923. Autocamping was portrayed as a great liberation from seedy hotels and rigid railroad timetables. When farmers complained about auto tourists' tendency to camp right in their fields, towns instituted auto camps. When auto camps became associated with transients and hobos in the depression, tourist cabins (with a spot to park your car next to the cabin) became the vogue. By the 1940s, it was just a short step to the modern motel chain.

torists could average more than 45 miles per hour on their way to the "autocamps" and tourist cabins that were the forerunners of motels.

Young people embraced cars because they made it possible to escape parental supervision. Like movies and other products of the new mass culture, cars changed the dating patterns of young Americans. Contrary to many parents' views, sex was not invented in the back seat of a Ford, but a Model T offered more privacy and comfort than the family living room or front porch. City elders in Muncie, Indiana, overreacted by calling automobiles "prostitution on wheels."

The most popular car of the decade was the Model T. The Ford Motor Company manufactured over fifteen million Model T's between 1908 and 1927. "Tin Lizzies," as the dependable Model T's were called, required a driver who was mechanically inclined. The motorist had to handcrank the car to start it, and keep one hand on the accelerator and the other on the wheel while driving. There was no gas gauge—one had to remove the front seat and peer into the tank to see how much gas there was. As for color, Henry Ford said, "The customer can have a Ford any color he wants—so long as it's black." As late as 1919, only about 10 percent of the nation's cars had a roof.

Consumers eventually became discontented with the Model T and Ford faced stiff competition from General Motors. GM's five automobile divisions turned out cars for specialized markets: the luxury Cadillac cost the most and had the lowest volume of sales; the Chevrolet boasted the cheapest price tag and highest volume of sales; Oldsmobile, Pontiac, and Buick were geared to incomes in between. GM cars also featured self-starters and foot accelerators. Henry Ford finally

bowed to consumer demands when he introduced the Model A in 1927. More than a million New Yorkers visited the Ford showroom during the five days after the new model was unveiled. At prices ranging from $495 to $570, the Model A lived up to consumers' demands for different styles, more colors, and greater comfort, and helped make the automobile a permanent part of American culture.

The Movies and Mass Culture

The movie industry probably did more than anything else to disseminate common values and attitudes throughout the United States. Its growth coincided with America's transformation into a predominantly urban, industrial society. In contrast to Europe, where cinema developed as an avant-garde, highbrow art form, American movies were part of popular culture almost from the start—a mass entertainment industry that was both democratic and highly profitable.

The Silent Era. Movies began around the turn of the century in nickelodeons, where for a nickel the mostly working-class audience could see a one-reel silent film such as *The Great Train Robbery* (1903). Because the films, mostly comedies and melodramas, were silent, they could be understood by immigrants who did not yet speak English. The new medium grew in popularity and profitability.

During the first years of the twentieth century, most films were made in New York City or Fort Lee, New Jersey. After 1910, moviemakers like D. W. Griffith and Cecil B. DeMille moved to southern California, drawn

The Tramp

Charlie Chaplin did not invent the tragicomic figure of the tramp, but it soon became his trademark screen persona. Chaplin grew up poor in the London slums, but the movies brought him wealth and fame. In 1919 he joined Douglas Fairbanks, Mary Pickford, and D. W. Griffith to form United Artists.

by cheap land, plenty of sunshine, and varied scenery—mountains, deserts, cities, and the Pacific Ocean all within easy reach—and by Los Angeles's reputation as an anti-union town. Actors also flocked to California, especially to Hollywood, a fast-growing suburb of Los Angeles. The new movie stars—comedians Buster Keaton, Charlie Chaplin, and Harold Lloyd, Mary Pickford ("America's Sweetheart"), the dashing Douglas Fairbanks, and Clara Bow (the "It" girl)—became national idols.

Movies quickly outgrew their working-class origins and reached middle-class audiences. D. W. Griffith's racist epic *Birth of a Nation* (1915) was a milestone in establishing the feature film as popular entertainment. The outbreak of World War I in Europe eliminated competition from Italian and French moviemakers (the same chemicals used to produce celluloid for film were crucial for the manufacture of gunpowder). By the war's end, the United States was making 90 percent of the world's films, and Hollywood reigned as the movie capital of the world for the next several decades. Foreign distribution of Hollywood films stimulated the market for the American material culture so lavishly displayed on the screen.

Movies fed the desires of a mass consumption economy, and set national trends in clothing and hairstyles. They also served as a form of sex education. Rudolph Valentino, best known as the romantic hero of *The Sheik* (1921), symbolized passion on the screen. The message was not wasted on the nation's youth. "It was directly through the movies that I learned to kiss a girl on her ears, neck, and cheeks, as well as on the mouth," confessed one boy. Many girls noticed that actresses kissed with their eyes closed, and so they too closed their eyes. A sociologist concluded that movies made young people more "sex-wise, sex-excited, and sex-absorbed" than any previous generation. The impact of the movies on sexual attitudes and morality has remained strong ever since.

The Coming of Sound. Movies were big business. Power in the industry was concentrated in large studios such as United Artists, Paramount, and Metro-Goldwyn-Mayer, which were controlled mainly by Eastern European Jewish immigrants, like Adolph Zukor and Samuel Goldfish (later Goldwyn). These studios were out for maximum profitability, not for artistic expression or creativity. In 1926 they grossed $1.5 billion a year. With distribution as well as production tightly controlled, the movie industry represented an example of a vertically integrated monopoly.

Though most of the movies were made in Hollywood, the studios were financed by eastern banks. Such financial connections were strained in the late 1920s because all the major studios borrowed huge sums of money to convert from silent production to "talkies." The total cost of conversion reached $300 million, but the overwhelming success of the new films quickly paid back the investment.

Warner Brothers' *The Jazz Singer* (1927), starring Al Jolson, was the first feature-length film to offer sound. By 1929 all the major studios had completed the changeover to talkies. While no one had thought of movies as silent until talkies took their place, silent films soon became obsolete. By the end of the 1920s, the nation had almost twenty-three thousand movie theaters, many of them elaborate movie palaces built by the studios in major cities. Movie attendance rose from 60 million in 1927 to 90 million in 1930. By then, movies were thoroughly entrenched as the most popular—and probably the most influential—form of the new urban-based mass media.

AMERICAN LIVES

Clara Bow
The "It" Girl

When Clara Bow, the "It" Girl of the 1920s, was asked to define what "it" meant, she replied, "I ain't real sure." To most fans, "it" was synonymous with sex appeal, but Elinor Glyn, the British writer who coined the phrase, had a more convoluted definition: "To have 'It' the fortunate possessor must have that strange magnetism which attracts both sexes. 'It' is purely virile quality belonging to a strong character. . . . There must be physical attraction, but beauty is unnecessary. Conceit or selfconsciousness destroys 'It' immediately." Whatever "it" was, when Paramount released a movie in 1927 based on the Elinor Glyn novella and starring Clara Bow, the film grossed $1 million. Soon Clara Bow was receiving almost 35,000 fan letters a month, many addressed simply to "The 'It' Girl, Hollywood U.S.A." In 1927 she was all of twenty-two years old.

The thin plot of the film hardly seems capable of launching a national obsession, but it did. Clara Bow plays a department store clerk named Betty Lou Spense, who is out to catch her rich, handsome boss. He too is smitten, and when he calls on her in her modest home, he finds her minding a friend's baby. However, he jumps to the mistaken conclusion that she is an unmarried mother, and propositions her. She is indignant at the insult, but after several twists of the plot they resolve their differences. In the final scene they kiss on the store owner's yacht, *Itola*, with the embrace obscuring all but the first two letters of the yacht's name. That's right—IT!

"It" was typical of Hollywood's fascination with flapper themes in the 1920s. (The term *flapper* originated with women's fad of leaving galoshes unbuckled, which made them flap.) On screen and off the flapper was emancipated, urban, and young, befitting the worship of youth characteristic of the 1920s. She was a working girl with money to spend, time on her hands, and a wardrobe of mass-produced fashions, especially short skirts suitable for dancing and dating. On screen

Clara Bow—the Twenties' Sex Symbol

she was sensual, but not promiscuous, often marrying the male lead at the end. Hollywood stars Colleen Moore and Louise Brooks also played flapper roles.

Before Clara Bow became indelibly known as the "It" girl, her studio had tried to promote her as the "Brooklyn Bonfire." The name never stuck, but it revealed her background. Clara Bow was born on July 29, 1905, to an extremely poor family in Brooklyn, New York; her mother was mentally unstable and her father was often unemployed. She dropped out of school during the eighth grade. About the only place she found refuge from her grim family life was at the movies. Like so many other young girls, Clara Bow decided that she wanted to be an actress.

Her break came when she won a 1921 "Fame and Fortune" beauty contest sponsored by three movie magazines, which helped her land a bit part in *Beyond the Rainbow* (1922). Unfortunately, her scenes ended up on the cutting room floor, but they were restored after she became a hit. In 1923 she won a Hollywood contract, and by 1924 had made thirteen films, none memorable. Her roles improved when she signed with Paramount Studio in 1925; it was her performances in *Dancing Mothers* (1926) and *Mantrap* (1926), two movies with Jazz-Age themes, that led Elinor Glyn to pronounce that Clara Bow had "it" on the screen.

Clara Bow had an amazing screen presence. Studio executive B. P. Schulberg called her "the hottest jazz baby in films." Observed a young man who first saw her at age seventeen, "I've never taken dope, but it was like a shot of dope when you looked at this girl." Wrote the *New York Times* of her performance in *Mantrap*, "She could flirt with a grizzly bear." She had a boyish figure, and what one reviewer called "flirts eyes." She was especially known for her shock of red hair. (In the 1920s redheads were thought to be highly sexed. Just as the vamp of the 1910s had dark hair and the platinum blonde was the typical star of the 1930s, the 1920s was the decade of the redhead.) On screen, she never seemed to stay still.

Yet Clara Bow's career lasted less than five years after the success of *It*. Somewhat unstable emotionally, she had several nervous breakdowns. As she once said, "A sex symbol is a heavy load to carry when one is tired, hurt, and bewildered." She was also hurt by scandals in her personal life, including widely publicized affairs with Gary Cooper and director Victor Fleming and a legal dispute with a former secretary. Futhermore, like many silent stars she found the transition to talkies difficult. It was not simply a matter of her Brooklyn accent—voice lessons could smooth that out. But her whole style of acting, which was very emotional and involved constant movement around the set, was inimical to the early days of sound recording, where an actor had to stay close to a stationary microphone in order to speak dialogue.

In 1931, Clara Bow announced she was leaving Hollywood to live with Rex Bell, a Nevada rancher

"Rough-House Rosie"
A hand-painted poster was created for this 1927 film.

whom she married later that year. She returned briefly to make two films before declaring, "I've had enough" in 1933. She now devoted full time to her marriage, and her sons born in 1934 and 1938, but her emotional instability made it hard for her to find happiness and she and Bell eventually separated. She died in Los Angeles in 1965, long before her films had become cult classics. Said her son on seeing *It* for the first time in 1987, sixty years after its release, "If I ever saw Mother, I saw her in that movie. The tremendous facial expression. . . . It brought back so vividly what she was like." Or more likely, what she wished she was like.

Towards the end of her life, Clara Bow reflected on the differences between Hollywood in the 1920s and the 1960s in a way that makes clear where her sympathies lay. "We had individuality. We did as we pleased. We stayed up late. We dressed the way we wanted. Today, stars are sensible and end up with better health. But *we* had more fun."

All That Jazz
George E. Lee's Singing Novelty Orchestra was a popular Kansas City act. Part of the novelty was his sister Julia Lee, who was both pianist and singer.

Jazz. It is perhaps no coincidence that the first talkie was *The Jazz Singer*. Jazz was such a popular part of the new mass culture that the 1920s are often called "the Jazz Age." This music remains one of the most distinctive American art forms. An improvisational form whose notes are rarely written down, jazz originated in the bordellos of New Orleans' Storyville quarter around the turn of the century. The origin of the word is obscure, but many link it to a vulgar term for the sex act. With its roots in urban culture, and drawing on earlier African-American music, such as ragtime and the blues, jazz gave African-Americans an outlet for expression of dissent and opposition to white values.

All the early jazz musicians were black. As they left the South, they took jazz rhythms to Chicago, New York, Kansas City, Los Angeles, and other cities. Some of the best known were composer-pianist Ferdinand ("Jelly Roll") Morton, who wrote "Dead Man Blues" and "Black Bottom Stomp"; trumpeter Louis Armstrong, who got his start with Joseph ("King") Oliver's Creole Jazz Band in Chicago in the early 1920s; and singer Bessie Smith, "the empress of the Blues." One of the most creative jazz innovators, Edward "Duke" Ellington, came to New York in 1927, and performed at the Cotton Club in Harlem. Phonograph records, especially those made by Louis Armstrong in the late 1920s, spread the appeal of jazz by capturing its spontaneity; in turn, jazz boosted the infant recording industry. Soon this uniquely American art form had caught on in Europe, especially in France.

Journalism and Radio. Other instruments of mass media helped establish national standards of taste and behavior. In 1922 ten magazines claimed a circulation of at least 2.5 million, and twelve others sold a million copies of each issue. The *Saturday Evening Post*, the *Ladies' Home Journal*, *Collier's Weekly*, and *Good Housekeeping* could be found in homes throughout the country. *Reader's Digest*, *Time*, and *The New Yorker* all started up in the 1920s. Thanks to syndicated columns and features in newspapers, people could read the same articles everywhere in the United States. They also bought the same books, partly because the Book of the Month Club was founded in 1926.

Tabloid newspapers—sometimes called jazz journalism—also became part of the national scene in this period. In 1919, just two days before the signing of the Versailles treaty, publisher Joseph Medill Patterson introduced *The New York Illustrated Daily News*. Half the size of a regular newspaper, with bold headlines, large photographs, and short, preferably sensational stories, tabloids were meant to be read quickly—for instance, while riding the subway to work. All the country's major cities had at least one tabloid competing with more sedate newspapers by 1932. As journalist Simon Bessie noted, the tabloid reflected the tenor of the times: "excitement, candid interest in sex and crime, hurry and an intense application to diversion."

The newest instrument of mass culture was truly a child of the 1920s. On November 2, 1920, professional radio broadcasting began when station KDKA in Pittsburgh carried the presidential election returns. By 1929 about 40 percent of the nation's households had a radio. There were more than eight hundred stations, most affiliated with either the Columbia Broadcasting Service (CBS), formed in 1928, or the National Broadcasting Company (NBC), started in 1926, which had two networks, Red and Blue. (These corporations would dominate the next leap forward in mass communication: television.) Unlike European networks, which were government monopolies, American radio stations operated for profit. The U.S. government licensed the stations, but their revenue came primarily from advertisers and corporate sponsors.

Americans loved radio. They listened to the World Series and other sports events, and to variety entertainment shows sponsored by advertisers of major brand-name products, which featured such composers as the Cliquot Club Eskimos, the Lucky Strike Orchestra, and the A. & P. Gypsies. One of the most popular radio shows of all time, "Amos 'n' Andy," which premiered on the NBC network in 1928, featured two white actors playing stereotypical black characters. Soon fractured phrases from "Amos 'n' Andy," like "Check and double check," became part of everyday speech. So many people "tuned in" (another new phrase of the 1920s) that the country almost seemed to come to a halt during favorite programs.

New Patterns of Leisure

One of the most significant developments in modern life has been the growing freedom of workers from constant physical toil. As the work week shrank and workers won the right to paid vacations, Americans had more time—and energy—to spend at leisure. Like so much else in the 1920s, leisure was increasingly tied to consumption and mass culture.

Sports and Recreation. Public recreation flourished during the 1920s. Cities and suburbs built baseball diamonds, tennis courts, swimming pools, and golf courses for their residents. In the New York metropolitan area, city planner Robert Moses masterminded a vast system of parks, playgrounds, and picnic areas. His greatest achievement was Jones Beach on Long Island. Moses not only created the state park but built limited-access highways to it. Any New Yorker with a car—an important limit on freedom of consumption—could escape to a public beach in less than forty minutes.

People not only played sports, but had time and money to watch them as well. Professional sports became increasingly commercialized. People could watch a game in a comfortable stadium, listen to it on the radio, or see highlights of it in a newsreel at the local movie theater. One of the most widely followed sports was boxing; Jack Dempsey was one of the decade's celebrity athletes. Baseball drew between nine and ten million fans a year. Tarnished in 1919 by the "Black Sox" scandal when gamblers bribed Chicago White Sox players to throw the World Series, baseball bounced back with the rise of such heroes as Babe Ruth of the Boston Red Sox and the New York Yankees. Nicknamed the "Sultan of Swat," Ruth electrified crowds by hitting more home runs—and hitting them farther—than any other player up to that time. Yankee Stadium became known as the "house that Ruth built." Reflecting the racism found in sports and in society as a whole, black athletes played in Negro Leagues, which were formed in the 1920s.

Boxing Heroes

Painter George Bellows (1882–1925) often painted boxing scenes. *Dempsey and Firpo* (1924) depicts a heavyweight fight between Jack Dempsey, the "Manassas Mauler," and challenger Luis Firpo, the "Wild Bull of the Pampas." Dempsey is the one being unceremoniously knocked out of the ring. Boxing was one of the most popular sports in the sports-crazy 1920s. (Whitney Museum of American Art)

Newspapers, especially the tabloids, capitalized on popular interest in sports. Sports coverage, especially the latest scores or fight results, sold papers. College football games, such as the annual Harvard-Yale game and the Rose Bowl, received national coverage. Football fans followed the fortunes of the Four Horsemen of Notre Dame, the most famous backfield in college football history. In 1924 Red Grange of the University of Illinois became nationally known for scoring five touchdowns against the University of Michigan the first five times he carried the ball.

Other sports gave the public more heroes. Bobby Jones ranked as the decade's best golfer. Bill Tilden dominated men's tennis, while Helen Wills and Suzanne Lenglen reigned in the women's game. The decade's best-known swimmer, male or female, was Gertrude Ederle, who shattered all records in 1926 by swimming the English Channel in just over fourteen hours. Thanks to the attention of the media, the popularity of sports figures rivalled that of movie stars.

Without a doubt, the decade's most popular hero was aviator Charles Lindbergh, a former stunt flyer and airmail pilot from Minnesota. On May 20, 1927, Lindbergh made the first successful solo nonstop flight between New York and Paris. For the 3,610 mile, $33\frac{1}{2}$-hour flight, in *The Spirit of St. Louis*, Lindbergh took only five sandwiches and one day's worth of tinned rations, saying, "If I get to Paris, I won't need any more, and if I don't get to Paris, I won't need any more either." Lindbergh captivated America because he combined the mastery of new technology (the airplane) with the traditional American virtues of individualism, self-reliance, and hard work. His charm and boyish good looks didn't hurt, either. He was twenty-five years old at the time of his record-breaking flight, and in 1928 *Time* magazine chose him as its first Man of the Year.

Dissenting Values and Cultural Conflict

Many Americans were deeply disturbed by the secular values unleashed in the 1920s. To rural Americans, the new values were an affront to a more traditional way of life, rooted in small towns and farming communities of the nineteenth century. Cultural and political conflict broke out over such issues as immigration restriction, Prohibition, and race relations. Tension between city and country played a part in all these conflicts, but it was not the sole cause. Many city dwellers had been born and raised in the country and their memories were strong. Resistance to change and an ambivalence about modernity—feelings that transcended the urban-rural polarity—probably had a greater influence.

Urban Majority, Rural Minority

"The United States was born in the country and has moved to the city," the historian Richard Hofstadter observed. When the 1920 census revealed that for the first time city people outnumbered rural ones, Americans realized that a big change had taken place, rivalling the closing of the frontier in 1890. In 1920, 52 percent of the population lived in urban areas, compared with 28 percent in 1870, only fifty years earlier.

The 1920 census exaggerated the extent of urbanization by classifying as cities towns with only 2,500 people, but there was still no mistaking the trend. By 1929, ninety-three cities had a population of over 100,000. New York City exceeded 7 million in the 1920s, Chicago boasted close to 3 million, and the population of fast-growing Los Angeles doubled to more than 1.2 million. Outside the major cities, growth was even more impressive. Thanks to the availability of cheap land and better transportation—notably the automobile—metropolitan areas spread out and suburbs sprang up. This trend started long before the post-World War II suburban boom.

The conflict over values that had been building since the late nineteenth century took on special force in the 1920s. After the recession of 1920–1921, farmers continued to struggle, and rural communities lost people to the cities at an alarming rate. During the 1920s, about six million Americans left the farms for the cities, including many blacks who abandoned the South altogether for the seemingly greater freedom of the North. Political districts did not reflect this population shift, however, and rural areas still controlled most state legislatures. Battles over the equitable use of tax dollars, especially for city services, intensified the rural-urban political conflict.

Yet it would be wrong to describe this conflict as a last-ditch effort on the part of rural America to maintain political and cultural dominance. The lives of rural people, too, had been affected by the same forces that influenced urban life. Much of the new technology—especially electricity and automobiles—enhanced rural life. Rural people were tempted by the new materialistic values trumpeted by radio programs, magazines, and movies, and though they tried to resist, many found more to attract them than to repel them. The cultural conflicts in the 1920s may have been intensified by the realization, on the part of both rural and urban dwellers, of how far they had already strayed.

The Rise of Nativism

When native-born white Protestant Americans looked at their communities in 1920, they saw a different nation than the one they had been born into forty years earlier. During that time, more than 23 million immi-

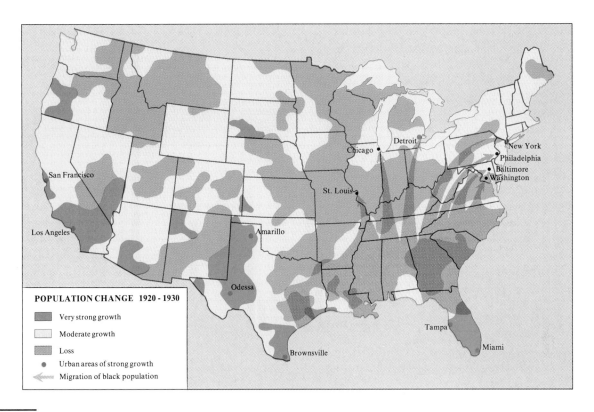

MAP 24.1

The Shift From Rural to Urban Population, 1920–1930

Despite the increasingly urban tone of modern America after 1920, regional patterns of population growth and decline were far from uniform. Cities in the South and West grew most dramatically, as southern farmers moved to more promising areas in familiar climates. One important component of the growth of northern cities, such as New York and Chicago, was the migration of southern blacks set in motion by World War I.

grants had come to America to seek a new life. Most of them came from peasant backgrounds, and many were Catholics or Jews. Senator William Bruce of Maryland called them "indigestible lumps" in the "national stomach," implying that the nation would be unable to absorb these immigrants from southeastern Europe and Russia. As President Coolidge said in 1924, "America must be kept American." Such sentiments, which were widely shared, came to be known as nativism.

These feelings were tapped in the 1920s to mount a successful drive against immigration. Originally, immigrants from Asia had been targets of restriction. In 1882 the Chinese were totally excluded, and Theodore Roosevelt negotiated a "gentleman's agreement" to limit Japanese immigrants in 1908. But now nativists demanded broader measures, aimed at European immigrants. In 1917 the United States required all immigrants to pass a literacy test, but it proved to be only a slight deterrent. If immigrants were determined to find a new life in America, they were willing to learn enough English to pass a simple test.

World War I and its aftermath had a direct impact on the immigration question. Nativists played up the

immigrants' association with radicalism and labor unrest—a legacy of the Red Scare. The super-patriotism of the war years, especially the emphasis on Americanization, also fed into nativism. When the end of the war made it possible to cross the Atlantic in safety again, many feared that it would bring a new wave of immigrants to America, and they would take jobs away from Americans and cause social unrest. In 1921, Congress passed an emergency bill limiting the number of immigrants to 3 percent of each national group, as counted in the 1910 census. President Wilson refused to sign the legislation, but it was reintroduced and passed under Warren Harding. The new law produced immediate results. In the twelve-month period ending in June 1921, 805,228 immigrants had entered the United States; in the next twelve months, the number dropped to 309,556.

For many Americans, this quota system was still a sieve with too many holes. The National Origins Act of 1924 cut immigration back to 2 percent of each nationality, as reflected in the 1890 census, which included relatively small numbers of people from the "undesirable" areas of southeastern Europe and Russia. This cut the

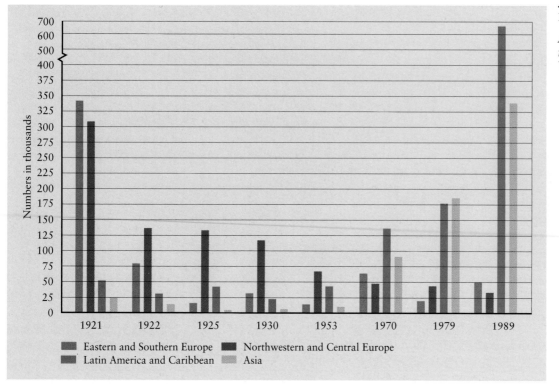

FIGURE 24.1

American Immigration since World War I

total immigration of 1924 to 164,000 persons, mostly from Great Britain, Ireland, and Germany. Japanese and Chinese immigrants continued to be excluded entirely.

In 1929 an even more restrictive quota went into effect, by which only 150,000 immigrants would be admitted each year, with national origins to be apportioned according to the 1920 census. President Herbert Hoover lowered the quota still further in 1931. The next year, during the depths of the Great Depression, more foreigners left the United States than entered. The last remaining loophole permitted unrestricted immigration from countries in the Western Hemisphere. This became increasingly significant over the years, as Central and Latin Americans crossed the border in increasing numbers, filling the places vacated by the cutoff of immigrants from Europe and the Pacific Rim.

Nativism took other forms as well during the 1920s. Many elite colleges instituted quotas to limit the enrollment of Jewish students, and many law firms refused to hire Jewish lawyers. Henry Ford spoke for many Americans when he warned of the menace of the "International Jew," referring to the supposed Jewish domination of international finance. Ford became so closely identified with anti-Semitism that some Jewish families could not bring themselves to buy one of his company's cars until decades later.

The New Klan. Another example of nativism in the 1920s was the revival of the Ku Klux Klan. Shortly after the premier in 1915 of *Birth of a Nation*, which glori-

fied the Klan, a group of southerners gathered on Stone Mountain outside Atlanta, Georgia, to revive the KKK. Encouraged by the superpatriotism of the war years, Klan leaders chose as their motto "Native, white, Protestant supremacy." The modern Klan appealed to both urban and rural people, but it was mainly an urban phenomenon. Spreading out from its southern base, it found significant support in the far West, Southwest, and the Midwest, especially Indiana, Oklahoma, and Oregon. Unlike its earlier incarnation after the Civil War, the Klan of the 1920s did not limit its harassment to blacks. Its targets were just as likely to be Catholics and Jewish immigrants. Its tactics, however, were the same: nightriding, arson, tarring and feathering, and other forms of physical intimidation, as well as very effective economic boycotts directed at Klan targets. At the height of its power in 1925, the Klan had over three million members, including a strong contingent of women who pursued their own political agenda, combining racism, nativism, and a commitment to equal rights for white Protestant women.

After 1925, the Klan declined rapidly. Battles between rival factions and disclosures of rampant corruption hurt its image. Especially damaging was the revelation that Grand Dragon David Stephenson, the Klan's national leader, had kidnapped and sexually assaulted his former secretary, driving her to suicide. Nativism, which was a legacy of World War I, began to decline and that, along, with the passage of the 1924 immigration act, robbed the Klan of its most potent issue.

AMERICAN VOICES

The Klan Comes to Kokomo *Robert Coughlan*

Robert Coughlan grew up in Kokomo, Indiana, and as a young boy he witnessed a Ku Klux Klan Konklave, or gathering. As Catholics living in a strong pro-Klan neighborhood, Coughlan's family had reason to feel uncomfortable on the hot July day in 1923 when the Klan came to central Indiana.

The Konklave was an important day in my life. I was nine years old, with a small boy's interest in masquerades and brass bands. But I was also a Catholic, the son of a Catholic who taught in the public schools and who consequently was the object of a good deal of Klan agitation. If anything worse was to come, the Konklave probably would bring it. Every week or so the papers had been reporting Klan atrocities in other parts of the country—whippings, lynchings, tar-and-feather parties—and my father and my family were logical game in our locality. . . .

As we sat on our front porch after watching the parade, we could see the Klansmen of our neighborhood trickling home. Some still wore their regalia, too tired to bother with taking it off before they came into sight. Others carried little bundles of white; they were the ones who still made some pretense of secrecy about being members. One of the last to come down the street was old Mrs. Crousore, who lived a few doors away. Her white robe clung damply, and her hood was pushed back. As she climbed her steps and sank solidly into a rocking chair on her porch, we could hear her groan, "Oh, my God, my feet hurt!"

Mrs. Crousore spoke with such feeling that her words seemed to summarize the whole day. My parents adopted her comment as a family joke. July 4, 1923, became for us the day when Mrs. Crousore's feet hurt. But it was clear to me when I grew a little older that my parents needed that joke

Women of the Klan

The Ku Klux Klan was so well integrated into the daily life of white Protestants that one woman from rural Indiana remembered her time in the KKK in the 1920s as "just a celebration . . . a way of growing up." Perhaps as many as 500,000 women joined the Women of the Ku Klux Klan (WKKK) in the 1920s, including these Indiana Klanswomen in August 1924.

as much as Mrs. Crousore needed her rocking chair. There were wild rumors in the town in the months that followed: Father Pratt, the pastor at St. Patrick's Church, was on the list for tar-and-feathering; the church was going to be burned; the Klan was going to "call" on the Jewish merchants; it was going to "get" my father and Miss Kinney, another Catholic who taught in the public schools. Considering all the violent acts committed by the Klan elsewhere in the country, it seemed quite possible that any or all of these notions might mature into action.

As it turned out none of them did. . . . Perhaps the answer lay in the dead level typicalness of the town; a population overwhelmingly white Protestant, with small, well-assimilated numbers of Catholics, Jews, foreigners, and Negroes, and an economy nicely balanced between farming and industry. There were few genuine tensions in Kokomo in 1923, and hence little occasion for misdirected hate to flame into personal violence.

It may be asked why, then, did the town take so wholeheartedly to the Klan, which made a program of misdirected hate? And the answer to that my be, paradoxically enough, that the Klan supplied artificial tensions. Though artificial, and perhaps never quite really believed in, they were satisfying. They filled a need—a need for Kokomo and all the big and little towns that resembled it during the early 1920s.

Source: Robert Coughlan, "Konklave in Kokomo," in Isabel Leighton, ed., *The Aspirin Age, 1919–1941* (New York: Simon & Schuster, 1976) 107, 110–11.

Religious Fundamentalism

The religious debate between modernist and fundamentalist Protestants that had been simmering since the 1890s came to a boil in the 1920s. Modernists, or liberal Protestants, tried to reconcile religion with scientific discoveries, such as Darwin's theory of evolution, while fundamentalists clung to a literal interpretation of the Bible. Most major Protestant denominations struggled with conflicts in the 1920s, especially the Baptists and the Presbyterians, with the losers frequently splitting off to form their own churches. The most conspicuous evangelical figures were outside the established denominations, however. Popular preachers like Billy Sunday and Aimee Semple McPherson used revivals, storefront churches, and open-air preaching to reach their followers with their own brands of charismatic fundamentalism.

The modernist-fundamentalist controversy soon entered the political arena. The scientific theories in Charles Darwin's *On the Origins of the Species* (1859) conflicted with the account of creation in the book of Genesis, and legislation was designed to prevent teaching evolution in schools. In 1925 Tennessee passed a law providing that "it shall be unlawful . . . to teach any theory that denies the story of the Divine creation of man as taught in the Bible, and to teach instead that man has descended from a lower order of animals." The newly formed American Civil Liberties Union (ACLU) challenged the constitutionality of the Tennessee law in a test case involving John T. Scopes, a high school biology teacher in Dayton, Tennessee, who had taught evolution to his class. The famous criminal lawyer Clarence Darrow defended Scopes. The prosecuting attorney was William Jennings Bryan, three-time presidential candidate, a spellbinding orator and a fundamentalist.

The Scopes trial in July 1925 became known as the "monkey trial," referring both to Darwin's theory that human beings and other primates shared a common ancestor and to the circus atmosphere that prevailed at the trial. More than a hundred journalists crowded into the sweltering Dayton courthouse, and Chicago radio station WGN broadcast the proceedings live.

The trial quickly turned to volatile questions of faith and scientific theory. The judge rebuffed defense efforts to call expert scientific witnesses on evolution, dismissing such testimony as hearsay because the scientists had not been present when lower forms of life evolved. Darrow countered by calling Bryan to the stand as an expert on the Bible. Under oath, Bryan asserted his belief that Jonah had been swallowed by a "big fish," Eve created from Adam's rib, and the world created by God in six days. He hedged, however, about whether the days were literally twenty-four hours long, an inconsistency which Darrow ruthlessly exploited.

Even so, the jury took only eight minutes to find Scopes guilty. Although the Tennessee Supreme Court overturned Scopes's sentence on a technicality, the reversal prevented further appeal of the case and the controversial law remained technically in force for more than thirty years. As the 1920s ended, science and religion were locked in a standoff.

Intellectual Currents and Crosscurrents

The Lost Generation. The most articulate and embittered dissenters from American life in the 1920s were the writers and intellectuals who were profoundly disillusioned by the horrors of World War I and its uncertain legacy and by the crass materialism of the new American consumer culture. Some of the artists felt so at odds with what they saw as the complacent, anti-intellectual, moralistic tone of American life that they settled in Europe—some temporarily, like the novelists Ernest Hemingway and F. Scott Fitzgerald, others permanently. The poet T. S. Eliot, who left the United States before the war, became a British citizen. His despairing poem *The Waste Land* (1922), with its images of fragmented civilization in ruins after the war, influenced a generation of writers. Other writers also made powerful antiwar statements: John Dos Passos, whose first novel, *The Three Soldiers* (1921), was inspired by the war, the novelist Edith Wharton, and above all, Ernest Hemingway. Hemingway described the dehumanizing consequences and futility of the war in the novels *In Our Time* (1924), *The Sun Also Rises* (1926), and *A Farewell to Arms* (1929), which drew on his experience as an ambulance driver in Italy during the war.

But artists and writers who migrated to Europe, particularly to Paris, were not just a "lost generation" fleeing America; they were also drawn to Paris as the cultural and artistic capital of the world in the 1920s. Paris, as Gertrude Stein put it, was "where the twentieth century was happening." The *modernist* movement in literature, art, and music, which was marked by skepticism and technical experimentation, was in full swing, and its vitality invigorated American writing abroad and at home. Whether they settled in Paris, visited frequently, as Dos Passos did, or remained in their home country, as the poets Wallace Stevens and Marianne Moore and the novelists Willa Cather and William Faulkner did, American writers entered the modernist movement.

This movement began before the war as intellectuals began to react to the cultural and social changes that scientific advances, industrialization, and urbanization had brought to the American landscape. In the 1920s the new culture of business and the corruption of the Harding years caused intellectuals to cast a more critical eye on American society. One of the sharpest critics of American life and politics was H. L. Mencken, a Baltimore journalist and literary critic who founded the *American Mercury* in 1922. Mencken directed his mordant wit against small-town America and its guardians of public morals, American mass culture, and the "Booboisie," his contemptuous term for the middle class. In the *American Mercury* Mencken championed such writers as Sherwood Anderson, Sinclair Lewis, and Theodore Dreiser who satirized the provincialism of American society.

In *Main Street* (1920) Lewis scathingly depicted the narrow-mindedness of a midwestern farming town and in *Babbitt* (1922) he satirized the stifling conformity of a middle-class businessman. Dreiser wrote his naturalistic masterpiece *An American Tragedy* in 1925, an indictment of the American myth of success and materialism, as was John Dos Passos's *Manhattan Transfer*. In the same year Fitzgerald wrote *The Great Gatsby*, which showed the consequences of the mindless pursuit of wealth.

The literary outpouring of the 1920s was varied and rich as writers responded to the intellectual excitement of the decade and produced a large number of classics. Poetry enjoyed a renaissance, as Robert Frost, Wallace Stevens, Marianne Moore, and William Carlos Williams gave new strength to the genre. The novelist Edith Wharton, who had published many well-known novels in the first decades of the century, produced *The Age of Innocence* in 1920, which won a Pulitzer Prize. Warton's novels explored the human psyche and described the changing social relationships in a society where a new class of wealth was being created. Influenced by Freudian psychology, William Faulkner began his exploration of the mind of the South. Faulkner's first critical success, the novel *The Sound and the Fury* (1929), is set in the fictional Mississippi county of Yoknapatawpha with characters who cling to the old values of the agrarian South as they try to adjust to modern industrial capitalism.

The dramatist Eugene O'Neill also employed Freudian psychology in his experimental plays, which had the aspects of Greek tragedy. O'Neill was a brilliant and prolific playwright, producing thirteen plays between 1920 and 1933, including *The Hairy Ape* (1922) and *Desire Under the Elms* (1924).

Although William Faulkner and Eugene O'Neill went on to produce major works in the 1930s and American poets continued to write, the creative energy of the literary renaissance of the 1920s was not matched in the 1930s. The Great Depression, social and ideological unrest, and the rise of totalitarianism reshaped the intellectual landscape.

Harlem Renaissance. A different kind of cultural affirmation took place in the black community of Harlem in the 1920s. In the words of Reverend Adam Clayton Powell, Sr., the pastor of the influential Abyssinian Bap-

The Harlem Renaissance
Artist Aaron Douglas left his childhood home of Topeka, Kansas, in the mid-1920s for Harlem, "the Mecca of the New Negro." Douglas, whose paintings and murals often drew on African motifs, became the painter most closely associated with the New Negro Movement. This Douglas painting dates from around 1930. (The Howard University Gallery of Art)

tist Church, Harlem loomed as "the symbol of liberty and the Promised Land to Negroes everywhere." In literature, its writers championed racial pride and cultural identity in the midst of white society. Poet Langston Hughes, who became a leading exponent of the Harlem Renaissance, captured its affirmative spirit when he asserted " I am a Negro—and beautiful."

The Harlem Renaissance was a creative group of young writers and artists who broke with the older genteel traditions of black literature to reclaim their cultural identity with its African roots. The intent of the movement was artistic, not political. The critic and teacher Alan Locke, editor of *The New Negro* (1926), an anthology that gave the writers of the Harlem Renaissance national exposure, summed up the character of the movement when he stated that through art, "Negro life is seizing its first chances for group expression and self-determination." Authors such as Claude McKay, Jean Toomer, Jessie Fauset, and Zora Neale Hurston explored the black experience and represented the "New Negro" in fiction. Countee Cullen and Langston Hughes turned to poetry, and Augusta Savage used sculpture to draw attention to black accomplishments. The outpouring of literary work showed the ongoing African-American struggle to find a way, as W. E. B. DuBois put it, "to be both a Negro and an American."

Jean Toomer, a writer passionately committed to African-American self-expression, wrote the influential novel *Cane* in 1923. With its poems, sketches, and stories about a northern black's discovery of the rural black South, it inspired other black artists and writers and was a stimulus to the movement. Langston Hughes drew on the black artistic forms of blues and jazz in *The Weary Blues* (1926), a groundbreaking collection of poems. Considered the most original of black poets and the most representative of African-American writers, Hughes also wrote novels, plays, and essays. Zora Neale Hurston, born in Florida to a family of poor tenant farmers, attended Howard University and won a scholarship to study anthropology at Barnard College. She spent a decade collecting folklore in the South and the Carribbean and incorporated this material into her short stories and novels. Her genius for storytelling and the tension between her rural folk education and her formal education, which she drew on in her writing, won her acclaim.

The vitality of the Harlem Renaissance was short-lived. Although the NAACP's magazine *The Crisis* was a forum for the Harlem Renaissance writers, the black middle class and intellectual elite in Harlem was relatively small and could not support the group's efforts. The movement was thus dependent on white patronage for support and access to publication. Many of the writers were ambivalent about this dependency as they struggled to attain an authentic black voice in their fiction. Langston Hughes became disillusioned with his white patron when she withdrew support for his work as he began to write about common black people in Kansas and New York rather than African themes. Claude McKay expressed the dilemma of black intellectuals in the novel *Home to Harlem*: how to be an intellectual and not lose the vitality and energy of the black heritage.

During the Jazz Age, when Harlem was very much in vogue in the public imagination, the publishing industry courted its writers, but the stock market crash of 1929 brought this interest to a sudden end. The movement waned in the 1930s as the depression continued. The writers of the Harlem Renaissance influenced a future generation of black writers when their works were rediscovered by black intellectuals during the civil rights movement of the 1960s.

Marcus Garvey and the UNIA. Although the cultural developments of the Harlem Renaissance had little impact on the African-American masses, other movements built racial pride and challenged white political and cultural hegemony. The most successful was the Universal Negro Improvement Association (UNIA), which championed black separatism under the leadership of Jamaican-born Marcus Garvey. Based in Harlem, the UNIA was the black working class's first mass movement. At its height it claimed four million followers, many of whom were recent migrants to northern cities. Like several nineteenth-century reformers, Marcus Garvey urged blacks to return to Africa because, he said, blacks would never be treated justly in countries ruled by whites. His wife, Amy Jacques Garvey, appealed to black women by combining her black nationalism with emphasis on women's contributions to culture and politics.

The UNIA grew rapidly in the early 1920s. It published a newspaper called *Negro World* and opened "liberty halls" in New York, Chicago, Detroit, Philadelphia, Pittsburgh, Cleveland, Cincinnati, and other northern cities. The UNIA also undertook extensive business ventures as part of its support for black capitalism. Its most ambitious project was the Black Star Line, a steamship company that would ferry cargo between the West Indies and the United States and take American blacks to Africa. The Black Star Line caused the downfall of the UNIA. Irregularities in fund raising led to Garvey's conviction on charges of mail fraud in 1925, and he was sentenced to five years in prison. President Calvin Coolidge paroled him in 1927, and Garvey was deported to Jamaica. Without his charismatic leadership, the movement soon collapsed.

Prohibition

The most notorious cultural debate of the 1920s was the battle over Prohibition. More than any other issue, Prohibition gave the decade its reputation as the Roaring Twenties. The Eighteenth Amendment, which took effect on January 20, 1920 (see Chapter 23), did make Americans drink less. Beer consumption declined the most, because beer was more difficult to manufacture and distribute illegally than hard liquor, but once people showed their willingness to flout the law, this effort to legislate private morality was doomed.

In major cities, support for Prohibition had always been limited. Before the law went into effect, the Yale Club of New York bought a fourteen-year supply of wine and hard liquor. Illegal saloons called speakeasies sprang up—more than 30,000 in New York City alone. People who preferred to drink at home and serve liquor to their guests emulated rural moonshiners and learned to distill their own "bathtub gin." Liquor smugglers op-

The Speakeasy

There aren't many photographs of speakeasies—after all, they were supposed to be private clubs tucked away beyond the reach of the law. Fancy hotels found themselves unable to compete with speakeasies once their bars were shut down, and many went out of business in the 1920s. But John Sloan's 1928 painting shows the rich enjoying themselves at New York's posh Lafayette Hotel. It is quite likely that these gentlemen and ladies had a flask concealed somewhere in the midst of their evening finery. (The Metropolitan Museum of Art)

erated with ease along borders and coastlines. Organized crime, already a factor in major cities, supplied a ready-made distribution network for bootleg liquor, and gangsters used "the noble experiment" to entrench themselves even more deeply in city politics. The decade's most notorious gangster, Al Capone, said "Everybody calls me a racketeer. I call myself a businessman. When I sell liquor, it's bootlegging. When my patrons serve it on a silver tray on Lake Shore Drive, it's hospitality."

By the middle of the decade, Prohibition was clearly failing. Government appropriations for the enforcement were woefully inadequate. The few highly publicized raids didn't make a dent in the liquor trade. In 1929, Attorney General William D. Mitchell conceded in 1929 that liquor could be bought "at almost any hour of the day or night, either in rural districts, the smaller towns, or the cities." Even a committee appointed by President Hoover in 1931 to study Prohibition only weakly urged that it be retained.

But Prohibition was in the Constitution, so the forces for repeal—the "wets," as opposed to the "drys," who continued to support the Eighteenth Amendment—undertook the long process of gaining the necessary majorities in Congress and state legislatures to amend the constitution once again. The Women's Organization for National Prohibition Repeal, headed by Pauline Sabin, a wealthy New York Republican, lobbied Congress and mobilized support from other national organizations.

The onset of the Great Depression hastened repeal. People argued that liquor production would provide jobs and prop up the faltering economy. On December 5, 1933, the Eighteenth Amendment was repealed. Ironically, drinking became more socially acceptable, although not necessarily more widespread, during Prohibition than it had been before.

The 1928 Election

Emotionally charged issues such as Prohibition, religious fundamentalism, and nativism eventually spilled over into national politics. The Democratic party, which drew on Protestant rural supporters in the South and West as well as ethnic voters from political machines in northern cities, was especially susceptible to the urban-rural conflicts of the 1920s. Four years earlier, the 1924 Democratic national convention had revealed a fissure between the party's urban forces and its rural wing.

Alfred E. Smith. The Democrats approached the 1928 campaign in somewhat better shape. The death of Senator Robert La Follette in 1925 ended the threat of another challenge by the Progressive party. William Jennings Bryan died the same year, just a week after his impassioned defense of fundamentalism in the Scopes trial, removing another potential spoiler from the field. Former contender William McAdoo was well into his sixties and considered too old for the nomination. As a result, Al Smith, who had just been elected to his fourth term as governor of New York, stood in a commanding position to win the Democratic nomination. In 1924 the Democrats had needed more than a hundred ballots to select a candidate, but in 1928 they nominated Smith on the first try.

Alfred E. Smith was the first presidential candidate to reflect the aspirations of the urban working classes. The grandson of Irish immigrants, and a Catholic, Smith had worked his way up in politics from Tammany Hall to the governor's mansion in Albany. He was proud of his urban background and adopted "The Sidewalks of New York" as his campaign song. Democrats hoped Smith would attract recent immigrants and workers who traditionally voted Republican. Belle Moskowitz, a New York social worker who served as Smith's political adviser, made Smith more attractive to women and liberal urban Jews.

But Smith had liabilities, too. He spoke in a heavy New York accent, sprinkling his speeches with "ain't" and "he don't," which did not play well on the radio. His early career in Tammany Hall troubled many voters, suggesting, unfairly, that he was little more than a cog in the political machine. Smith's stand on Prohibition alienated many voters. Although he promised, if elected, to enforce Prohibition, he made no secret of his support for repeal. Smith chose John J. Raskob, a wealthy entrepreneur and one of the nation's most ardent "wets," as head of the Democratic National Committee.

By far the most damaging handicap to Smith's campaign was his Catholicism. Protestant Americans were not ready for a Roman Catholic president in 1928. Although Smith insisted that his religion would not interfere with his duties as president, being Catholic cost him support from Democrats and Republicans alike. Protestant clergymen, who already opposed Smith because he had flouted Prohibition, led the drive against him. "No Governor can kiss the papal ring and get within gunshot of the White House," declared a Methodist bishop from Buffalo.

Herbert Hoover. Just as Smith marked a new kind of presidential candidate for the Democrats, so did Herbert Hoover as the Republican nominee. President Coolidge's unexpected decision not to run for reelection in 1928 opened the field, and Hoover led from the start. His popularity and power as secretary of commerce under Harding and Coolidge left no room for the other main contenders, Vice-President Charles G. Dawes and former Governor Frank O. Lowden of Illinois.

As a professional administrator and engineer, Hoover embodied the new managerial and technological elite. He had never been elected to any political office. During his campaign, in which he gave only seven speeches, Hoover promised that his vision of individualism and cooperative endeavor would banish poverty from the United States. Many voters considered him more progressive than Smith.

Hoover won a stunning victory. He received 58 percent of the popular vote to Smith's 41 percent, and 444 electoral votes to 87 for Smith. For the first time since Reconstruction, a Republican candidate carried Virginia, Texas, and North Carolina, largely because many Democratic voters refused to vote for a Catholic. The voter turnout rose from 52 percent in 1924 to 56.9 percent in 1928, partly due to extensive education campaigns undertaken by the League of Women Voters. The polling places were moved from their former location in saloons to schools and churches, which helped women feel more comfortable with their new role as citizens. Many Catholic and immigrant women voted for Smith, but even more native-born Republican women supported Herbert Hoover.

The 1928 election reflected important underlying

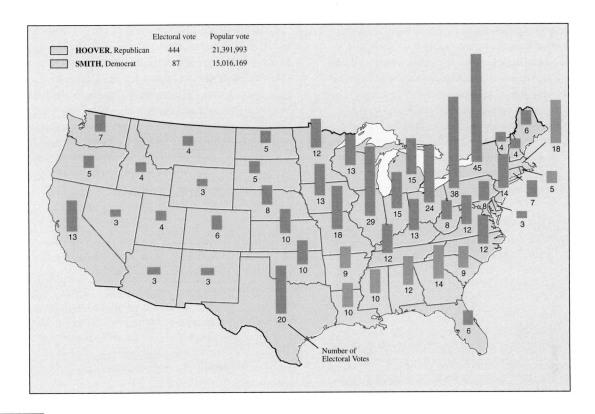

	Electoral vote	Popular vote
HOOVER, Republican	444	21,391,993
SMITH, Democrat	87	15,016,169

Number of
Electoral Votes

MAP 24.2

The Election of 1928

Historians still debate the extent to which 1928 was a critical election—that is, one that produced a significant realignment in voting behavior. Although Republican candidate Herbert Hoover swept the electoral college, Democrats were heartened that Alfred E. Smith won the heavily industrialized states of Rhode Island and Massachusetts. For the first time, the Democratic ticket carried the nation's twelve largest cities, garnering strong support from immigrants and urban dwellers.

political changes. The Democratic turnout, despite the party's overwhelming loss, increased substantially in urban areas. Smith won the heavily industrialized states of Massachusetts and Rhode Island, and carried the nation's twelve largest cities. The Democrats were on their way to a new identity as the party of the urban masses, including ethnic voters, a reorientation completed by the New Deal.

It is unlikely that any Democratic candidate, let alone a Catholic, could have won the presidency in

1928. With a seemingly prosperous economy, national consensus on foreign policy, and strong support from the business community, the Republicans were unbeatable. Herbert Hoover's victory put him in the unenviable position of leading the United States when the Great Depression struck in 1929. Having claimed credit for the prosperity of the 1920s, the Republicans found it difficult to escape blame for the depression. Twenty-four years passed before a Republican won the presidency again.

★

Summary

By the 1920s, modern America had arrived. The Republican party controlled the national government and cemented the partnership between business and government that had been accelerated by World War I. In foreign policy, the United States generally steered clear of European affairs, and concentrated on economic ex-

pansion abroad, especially in the Western Hemisphere. With the exception of the 1920–1921 recession, the economy performed well, although agriculture never recovered from the postwar slump and certain industries remained overextended following wartime expansion. The automobile industry typified the new mass production techniques that dominated economic life in the United States and revolutionized American society.

During the 1920s, a national culture began to develop. It was characterized by the wide diffusion of ideas and values through movies, radio, and other mass media, new ways of spending leisure time, and a heightened emphasis on consumption and advertising. The new lifestyles of the decade, often called the "Roaring Twenties" or the "Jazz Decade," captured the popular imagination but were limited to a minority of the population. Families had to enjoy at least a middle-class income to buy cars, radios, vacuum cleaners, and toasters. Those left outside the circle of prosperity included farmers, coal miners, textile workers, and minorities such as blacks and Hispanics.

Not everyone welcomed the new secular values of the 1920s. Conflicts arose over Prohibition, religion, race, and immigration. These cultural disputes spilled over into politics, disrupting the already fractured Democratic party. The 1928 election showed that the nation could not yet accept a Catholic as president. The Republican ascendancy continued under Herbert Hoover, who looked forward to a term filled with even greater prosperity and progress.

TOPIC FOR RESEARCH

Advertising Modernity

Nothing conveys the tone of modernity in the 1920s better than advertising, but ads (like movies) are not a simple mirror of society. Nonetheless, they are an excellent source for chronicling the emergence of a mass consumption economy. Pick a specific consumer good, such as the automobile, radio, an electrical appliance, cigarettes, or a hygiene product such as deodorant or mouthwash. Look for advertisements from the 1920s in a magazine like *The Saturday Evening Post, Ladies' Home Journal, Literary Digest, Fortune,* or *True Story.* How was the product marketed? Were any unusual stylistic or artistic devices used to sell the product? What was its audience? How representative of American society were the models or situations shown in the ads? What do the advertisements say about societal attitudes about race, class, and gender?

To place your own observations into a broader context, consult histories of advertising such as Roland Marchand, *Advertising the American Dream: Making Way for Modernity, 1920–1940* (1985), Daniel Pope, *The Making of Modern Advertising* (1983), and T. J. Jackson Lears, "From Salvation to Self-Realization: Advertising and the Therapeutic Roots of the Consumer Culture, 1880–1930," in Richard Wightman Fox and T. J. Jackson Lears, *The Culture of Consumption* (1983). Trade journals such as *Printers' Ink* and *Advertising Age* supply the industry perspective.

BIBLIOGRAPHY

General overviews of the 1920s are provided by Ellis Hawley, *The Great War and the Search for a Modern Order, 1917–1933* (1979); William Leuchtenburg, *The Perils of Prosperity* (1958); Frederick Lewis Allen, *Only Yesterday* (1931); and Geoffrey Perrett, *America in the Twenties* (1982).

Robert S. Lynd and Helen Merrell Lynd, *Middletown: a Study in Modern American Culture* (1929), remains a superb study of American life and values in the 1920s. John Braeman, Robert H. Bremner, and David Brody, eds., *The Twenties* (1968), offers interpretations of the decade's major trends.

The Business-Government Partnership of the 1920s

Alfred Chandler provides a stimulating introduction to business life in *Strategy and Structure* (1962) and *The Visible Hand* (1977). Further discussion of corporate developments can be found in Louis Galambos, *Competition and Cooperation* (1966); Robert Himmelberg, *The Origins of the National Recovery Administration: Business, Government, and the Trade Association Ideal, 1921–1933* (1976); and James Gilbert, *Designing the Industrial State* (1972). Irving Bernstein, *The Lean Years* (1960), David Brody, *Steelworkers in America* (1960) and *Workers in Industrial America* (1980), and David Montgomery, *The Fall of the House of Labor* (1987), cover labor developments.

The domestic and international aspects of the economy are treated in Jim Potter, *The American Economy Between the Wars* (1974); Mira Wilkins, *The Maturing of Multinational Enterprise* (1974); Emily Rosenberg, *Spreading the American Dream* (1982); and Joan Hoff Wilson, *American Business and Foreign Policy, 1920–1933* (1968) and *Ideology and Economics: U.S. Relations with the Soviet Union, 1918–1933* (1974). Interpretations of foreign policy include Warren Cohen, *Empire Without Tears* (1987); William Appleman Williams, *The Tragedy of American Diplomacy* (1962); L. Ethan Ellis, *Republican Foreign Policy, 1921–1933* (1968); and Stephen Randall, *U.S. Foreign Oil Policy, 1919–1948* (1986). Walter LaFeber, *Inevitable Revolutions* (1983) covers the United States involvement in Central America.

General introductions to politics in the 1920s are found in John D. Hicks, *Republican Ascendancy* (1960), and Robert Murray, *The Politics of Normalcy* (1973). Biographies of the decade's major political figures include Donald McCoy, *Calvin Coolidge* (1967); David Burner, *Herbert Hoover* (1979); Joan Hoff Wilson, *Herbert Hoover: Forgotten Progressive* (1975); and Paula Elder, *Governor Alfred E. Smith: The Politician as Reformer* (1983). On women in politics, see J. Stanley Lemons, *The Woman Citizen* (1973); Clarke A.

Chambers, *Seedtime of Reform* (1963); Nancy Cott, *The Grounding of Modern Feminism* (1987); and Elisabeth Israels Perry, *Belle Moskowitz* (1987).

A New National Culture

Daniel Boorstin, *The Americans: The Democratic Experience* (1973) provides an excellent introduction to the emerging mass culture. On movies, see Robert Sklar, *Movie-Made America* (1975); Lary May, *Screening Out the Past* (1980); Lewis A. Erenberg, *Steppin' Out* (1981); and Neil Gabler, *An Empire of Their Own: How the Jews Invented Hollywood* (1988). Material on Clara Bow can be found in David Stenn, *Clara Bow, Runnin' Wild* (1988) and Sumiko Higashi, *Virgins, Vamps and Flappers: The American Silent Movie Heroine* (1978). Erik Barnouw, *A Tower in Babel: A History of American Broadcasting in the United States To 1933* (1966), Susan Douglas, *Inventing American Broadcasting* (1987), and Philip Rosen, *The Modern Stentors: Radio Broadcasting and the Federal Government, 1920–1933* (1980), discuss radio. See also Melvin Patrick Ely, *The Adventures of Amos 'n' Andy: A Social History of an American Phenomenon* (1991). Stewart Ewen, *Captains of Consciousness* (1976), Daniel Pope, *The Making of Modern Advertising* (1983), Roland Marchand, *Advertising the American Dream* (1985), and Stephen Fox, *The Mirror Makers* (1984), cover advertising. Paula Fass, *The Damned and the Beautiful* (1977) and Beth L. Bailey, *From Front Porch to Back Seat* (1988), cover youth, while Susan Strasser, *Never Done* (1982), and Ruth Schwartz Cowan, *More Work For Mother* (1983), discuss white middle-class women's lives. Lizabeth Cohen, *Making A New Deal: Industrial Workers in Chicago, 1919–1939* (1990), suggests how working-class communities adapted mass culture for their purposes.

The impact of the automobile on modern American life is amply documented by James Flink, *The Car Culture* (1975) and *The Automobile Age* (1988); John Rae, *The American Automobile* (1965); Ed Cray, *Chrome Colossus: General Motors and Its Times* (1980); Bernard A. Weisberger, *The Dream Maker* (1979); and Reynold Wik, *Henry Ford and Grass Roots America* (1972). For women and the automobile, see Virginia Scharff, *Taking The Wheel* (1991). For sports, see Allen Guttmann, *A Whole New Ball Game* (1988); Harvey Green, *Fit For America* (1986); and Larry Englemann, *The Goddess and the American Girl: The Story of Suzanne Lenglen and Helen Wills* (1988). Good sources for Charles Lindbergh are his two accounts, *"We"* (1927), and *The Spirit of St. Louis* (1953).

Dissenting Values and Cultural Conflict

Paul Carter, *Another Part of the Twenties* (1977), outlines the decade's deeply felt cultural controversies; many of the essays in Isabel Leighton, *The Aspirin Age, 1919–1941* (1949), also cover those themes. Background on rural and urban life is provided by Don Kirschner, *City and Country: Rural Responses to Urbanization in the 1920s* (1970); Zane Miller, *The Urbanization of America* (1973); and Jon Teaford, *The Twentieth-Century American City* (1986). John Higham, *Strangers in the Land* (1955), and Maldwyn A. Jones, *American Immigration* (1960), describe immigration restriction. Richard K. Tucker, *The Dragon and the Cross: the Rise and*

TIMELINE

1920-1921	Recession
1920	First commercial radio broadcast Warren G. Harding elected president
1921	Sheppard-Towner Act Immigration Act passed Washington Conference on naval disarmament
1923	Calvin Coolidge succeeds Harding as president *Time* magazine founded
1924	Dawes Plan reschedules German War reparations Teapot Dome scandal National Origins Act passed
1925	Scopes ("Monkey") trial
1927	First "talkies" Charles Lindbergh's solo flight Ford Model A Kellogg-Briand pact
1928	Herbert Hoover elected president

Fall of The Ku Klux Klan in Middle America (1991), Kenneth Jackson, *The Ku Klux Klan in the City, 1915–1930* (1965), and David Chalmers, *Hooded Americanism* (1965), cover the KKK's rise and fall. Kathleen M. Blee, *Women of the Klan* (1991) offers a provocative discussion of racism and gender in the 1920s. Ray Ginger, *Six Days or Forever?* (1958), Norman F. Furniss, *The Fundamentalist Controversy, 1918–1933* (1954), George M. Marsden, *Fundamentalism and American Culture* (1980), and William G. McLoughlin, *Fundamentalism in American Culture* (1983), cover religion. Robert Crunden, *From Self to Society, 1919–1941* (1972), Roderick Nash, *The Nervous Generation: American Thought, 1917–1930* (1969), and Edmund Wilson, *The Twenties* (1975) cover intellectuals. For the Harlem Renaissance, see Jervis Anderson, *This Was Harlem, 1900–1950* (1982); Nathan Huggins, *Harlem Renaissance* (1971); and Gloria T. Hull, *Color, Sex, and Poetry: Three Women Writers of the Harlem Renaissance* (1987). David Cronin, *Black Moses* (1962), and Theodore Vincent, *Black Power and the Garvey Movement* (1970), describe Marcus Garvey. On prohibition, see Andrew Sinclair, *Prohibition: The Era of Excess* (1962); Joseph R. Gusfield, *Symbolic Crusade* (1963); and Norman Clark, *Deliver Us From Evil* (1976). The treatment of the 1928 election found in David Burner, *The Politics of Provincialism* (1967), and Oscar Handlin, *Al Smith and His America* (1958), should be supplemented by Kristi Andersen, *The Creation of a Democratic Majority, 1928–1936* (1979), and Allan J. Lichtman's quantitative study, *Prejudice and the Old Politics* (1979).

Employment Agency

Isaac Soyer's 1937 painting captures the resignation and despair of Americans searching for a job, any job, in the midst of the Great Depression. (Whitney Museum of American Art)

✦ ★ ✦

CHAPTER **25** *The Great Depression*

Flappers and movie stars in the 1920s, breadlines and hoboes in the 1930s: were the 1920s just "one long party" after which "everyone had a hangover—known as the depression—in the morning"? Did the country really go from unprecedented prosperity to the poorhouse practically overnight?

Obviously, the contrast between the flush times of the 1920s and the hard times of the 1930s is too starkly drawn. The vaunted prosperity of the 1920s was never as widespread or as firmly rooted as many believed at the time. Although America's mass-consumption economy was the envy of the world, many Americans lived on its margins. Nor was every American devastated by the depression of the 1930s. Those with secure jobs or fixed incomes survived the economic downturn in relatively sound shape—some people even managed to get rich in the decade. But few could escape contact with the wide-ranging social, political, and cultural developments of the depression.

Almost all of our impressions of the 1930s are black-and-white, in part because of the stark visual image of depression America etched on the popular consciousness through photographs taken by the Farm Security Administration. Although not every event of the 1930s should be viewed through the lens of the depression, more than any other factor, it provides the unifying theme for the decade.

The Coming of the Great Depression

Booms and busts are a permanent feature of the business cycle of capitalist economies. Since the beginning of the Industrial Revolution in the early nineteenth century, the United States had experienced recessions or panics at least every twenty years. The most recent downturn was the postwar recession of 1920–1921. But no slump was as severe and none lasted as long as the Great Depression.

The Causes of the Depression

The Great Depression began slowly and almost imperceptibly. After 1927, consumer spending declined, and housing construction slowed. Inventories piled up, and in 1928 and 1929 manufacturers began to cut back production and lay off workers. Reduced incomes and buying power reinforced the downturn. By the summer of 1929, the economy was clearly in a recession, although at that point not as severe as the one that had begun in 1920.

Stock Market Speculation and the Great Crash. Among the causes of the Great Depression, a flawed stock market played an important, but not dominant, role. By 1929 the market had become the symbol of the nation's prosperity and an icon in American business culture. Financier John J. Raskob captured this mentality in a *Ladies' Home Journal* article, "Everyone Ought to Be Rich." Invest $15 a month on sound common stocks, Raskob advised, and in twenty years the investment will grow to $80,000. Not everyone was playing the stock market, however. About four million Americans owned stock in 1929, representing about 10 percent of the nation's households. A mere 1.5 million had portfolios large enough to require the services of a stockbroker.

Wall Street, October 1929
When the stock market collapsed, Julius Rosenwald, the chairman of Sears, Roebuck
and Company, offered to guarantee the accounts of Sears employees who had bought
stocks on margin. Comedian Eddie Cantor jokingly asked for a job as a Sears office boy.

Stock market prices had been rising steadily since 1921, but in 1928 and 1929 they surged forward—the average price of stocks rising over 40 percent. All this economic activity was essentially unregulated. Margin buying, in particular, proceeded at a feverish pace: stockbrokers permitted many of their customers to borrow up to 75 percent of the purchase price of stocks. Such easy credit lured more speculators and less creditworthy investors into the market. The Federal Reserve Board warned member banks not to lend money for stock speculation—if prices dropped, many investors would not be able to pay their debts—but no one listened. As long as prices continued to soar, everyone felt like a winner. A noted economist proclaimed in mid-October 1929 that "stock prices have reached what looks like a permanently high plateau."

The stock market had been sliding since early September, but people ignored this warning. On "Black Tuesday"—October 29, 1929—the bubble burst. In frantic trading, more than 16 million stocks changed hands. Overextended investors, suddenly finding themselves heavily in debt, began to sell their stocks, inducing others to follow suit to protect their investments.

This set off waves of panic selling, and many stocks found no buyers at all. Practically overnight, stock values fell from a peak of $87 billion (at least on paper) to $55 billion. The precipitous decline of stock prices became known as the Great Crash.

The impact of "Black Tuesday" was felt far beyond the trading floors of Wall Street. The stock market crash intensified the course of the Great Depression in several ways. It wiped out the savings of thousands of Americans and hurt commercial banks that had invested heavily in corporate stocks. Less tangibly, it destroyed the optimism of people who had regarded the stock market as the crowning symbol of America's economic prosperity, causing a crisis of confidence that prolonged the depression.

However, the stock market crash alone does not account for either the severity or the length of the Great Depression, especially the deep plunge between 1931 and 1933. The drag of "sick" industries, the growing inequality of wealth, the unstable international financial situation, and the monetary policies of the Federal Reserve System—all of these contributed to the prolonged decline.

Structural Weaknesses. The crash exposed long-standing weaknesses in the American economy. Agriculture was in the worst shape; farmers had never recovered from the recession of 1920–1921. They faced high fixed costs for equipment and mortgages incurred during the inflationary war years. At the same time, prices fell owing to overproduction and the resulting surpluses, forcing farmers to default on mortgage payments and risk foreclosure. In 1929 the yearly income of a farmer averaged only $273, compared to $750 for other occupations. Because farmers accounted for about a fourth of the nation's gainfully employed workers in 1929, their difficulties weakened the general economic structure.

Certain basic industries also had economic troubles during the otherwise prosperous 1920s, many of them dating back to World War I or the depression of 1920–1921. The textile industry, for example, had steadily declined after the war. Textile firms abandoned New England for cheaper labor markets in the South but continued to suffer from decreased demand and excess capacity. The railroad industry also suffered, hit by shrinking passenger revenues, stagnant freight levels, and inefficient management. In addition, the railroads faced stiff new competition from truck transportation on publicly subsidized roads.

Mining and lumbering, which had expanded in response to wartime demands, produced too much during peacetime. Coal mining, especially, was battered by overexpansion, technological obsolescence, and a legacy of bitter labor struggles. New sources, including hydroelectric power, fuel oil, and natural gas, now competed with coal. As secretary of commerce, Herbert Hoover had plans to help these ailing industries, but the trade associations he promoted were ineffectual.

Unequal Distribution of Wealth. The country's unequal distribution of wealth also contributed to the severity of the depression. During the 1920s, the share of national income going to families already in the upper- and middle-income brackets increased. The tax policies of Secretary of the Treasury Andrew Mellon contributed to this concentration of wealth by easing personal tax rates, eliminating the wartime excess-profits tax, and expanding deductions that favored wealthy individuals and corporations. In 1929, the lowest 40 percent of the population received only 12.5 percent of the aggregate family personal income, while the top 5 percent got 30 percent. Once the depression had begun, not enough people could afford to spend the money necessary to revive the economy.

The Worldwide Depression. The economic problems of the United States had an impact on the rest of the world, and vice versa. The international economic system had been out of kilter since World War I. It could function only as long as American banks exported enough capital for European countries to repay their debts and continue to buy American manufactured goods and agricultural products. By the late 1920s, European economies were staggering under the weight of large debts and trade imbalances with the United States, which undercut the recovery that looked possible earlier in the decade. By 1931, most European economies had collapsed.

In an interdependent world, the downturn of the American economy had enormous repercussions. In 1929 the United States had produced over 40 percent of the world's manufactured goods, twice as much as Great Britain and Germany combined. When American companies cut back production, they also cut back purchases of raw materials and supplies abroad, which had a devastating effect on many foreign economies. American financiers reduced foreign investments and consumers cut down on European goods, making debt repayment even more difficult. As economic conditions worsened on the continent, European demand for American exports fell drastically. When the Hawley-Smoot Tariff of 1930 raised rates to all-time highs, foreign governments retaliated with their own trade restrictions, further limiting the market for American goods, especially agricultural products, and deepening the worldwide depression.

The Deepening Economic Crisis

The Great Depression became self-perpetuating. The more the American economy contracted, the longer people expected the depression to last and the longer they expected it to last, the more afraid they were to spend or invest their money (if they had any), which was exactly what was necessary to stimulate economic recovery. Business investment plummeted 88 percent from 1931 to 1933. The economy showed some signs of recovery in the summer of 1931 as many inventories were eliminated and low prices encouraged renewed consumption, but plunged again in late fall.

At this point, the chronically depressed agricultural sector put pressure on the commercial banking system, worsening the economic contraction. The nation's banks had already been weakened by the stock market crash. When agricultural prices and incomes fell even more steeply than usual in 1930, many farmers went over the edge into bankruptcy. Rural banks failed in alarming numbers—particularly in the cotton belt—after the harvest of 1930. By November and December, so many rural banks had defaulted on their obligations that urban banks, too, began to fail. The wave of bank failures frightened depositors into withdrawing their savings, further deepening the banking crisis.

Flawed Monetary Policy. A change in the nation's monetary policy in 1931 added to the banking problems. During the first phase of the depression, the Federal Reserve System had reacted cautiously. In October 1931 the system's managers took several gravely incorrect steps. The New York Reserve Bank significantly increased the discount rate—that is, the interest rate it charged to loan money to member banks—and cut back the amount of money it placed in circulation through the purchase of government securities. These actions of the Federal Reserve hampered the ability of the banking system to meet domestic demands for currency and credit. By March 1933, when the economy reached its lowest point, the money supply had fallen from its August 1929 level by about a third.

The inadequate money supply forced prices down and deprived businesses of investment funds. In the face of such a money shortage, only by spending faster could the American people have pulled the country out of the depression. But because of falling prices, rising unemployment, and a banking system in disarray, Americans preferred to save their dollars, stashing them under the mattress rather than in the bank, thereby limiting even further the amount of money in circulation.

International Repercussions. Adherence to the gold standard had long been the most sacrosanct principle in the international business community, because gold provided a fixed standard against which the value of currencies throughout the world could be pegged. Great Britain unilaterally decided to abandon the gold standard in 1931, striking another blow to the already shaky international economic system. Currencies no longer had a definite value in relation to gold, and thus to each other, but now "floated" according to supply and demand, depriving the world market of a system for the orderly adjustment of values of international currencies. By 1932, forty-one countries had followed Britain's example and fear spread in Europe that, despite Herbert Hoover's unswerving support for the gold standard, the United States would follow suit. Consequently, holders of dollars abroad began to demand gold, and gold flowed out of the United States. The Federal Reserve's decision in October 1931 to drive up short-term interest rates successfully attracted gold holders to U.S. investments, thereby saving the gold standard, at least temporarily.

President Herbert Hoover later blamed the severity of the depression in the United States on the international economic situation. No other major trading nation was hit as hard as the United States. Although domestic factors far outweighed international ones in causing America's protracted decline, Hoover had a point. During the depression, no single country stepped forward to provide leadership and stability for the world market, as Britain had done prior to World War

I. Instead, nations raised tariff barriers and imposed exchange controls to hoard precious gold, dollars, and pounds sterling, in a fit of economic nationalism that prolonged the depression. By 1933 the world economy finally showed signs of recovery, although progress remained uneven.

The Downward Spiral. Herbert Hoover personally chose the term *depression* to describe America's post-1929 economic downturn. He thought depression sounded less ominous than "panic" or "crisis." Whatever one calls the conditions of the American economy from 1929 to 1932, the statistics paint a stark picture.

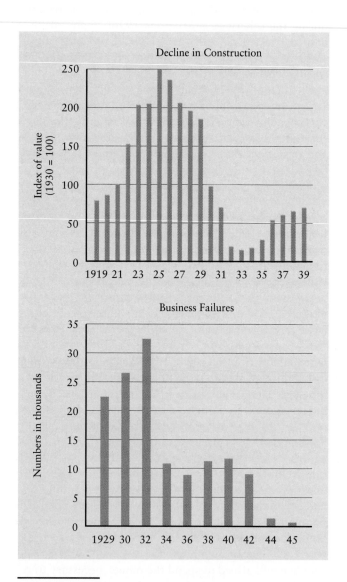

FIGURE 25.1

Statistics of the Depression

The top graph shows the decline in construction; bottom graph gives the numbers of business failures.

Source: Historical Statistics of the United States, Colonial Times to 1970, (Washington: Government Printing Office, 1975).

FIGURE 25.2

Unemployment, 1915–1945

From the height of the prosperity before the stock market crash in 1929 to the depths of the depression in 1932–1933, the gross national product dropped by almost half, declining from $103.1 billion to $58 billion in 1932; consumption expenditures dropped by 18 percent; construction fell by 78 percent; private investment plummeted by 88 percent; and farm income, already low, was more than cut in half. In this period, 9,000 banks either went bankrupt or closed their doors, and 100,000 businesses failed. The consumer price index declined by 25 percent, and corporate profits fell from $10 billion to $1 billion.

Most tellingly, unemployment rose from 3.2 percent to 24.9 percent, affecting approximately twelve million workers. The statistical measures at the time were fairly crude and unemployment was probably even higher. At least one of every four workers was out of a job. Even those who did have jobs faced wage cutbacks or the fear of being laid off. Their stories put a human face on the almost incomprehensible dimensions of this economic downturn.

Hard Times

"We didn't go hungry, but we lived lean." That sums up the experiences of many American families during the

Great Depression. The vast majority were neither very rich nor very poor. For most, the depression did not mean losing thousands of dollars in the stock market or pulling children out of an expensive boarding school. Nor did it mean going on relief or living in shanty-towns. In a typical family in the 1930s the husband had a job and the wife was a homemaker. Life was not easy, but it consisted of "making do" rather than stark deprivation.

The Invisible Scar

"You could feel the depression deepen," recalled the writer Caroline Bird, "but you could not look out the window and see it." Many people never saw a bread-line or a man selling apples on the street corner. The depression caused a private kind of despair that often simmered behind closed doors. "I've lived in cities for many months broke, without help, too timid to get in breadlines," the writer Meridel LeSueur remembered. "I've known many women to live like this until they simply faint on the street from privations, without saying a word to anyone. A woman will shut herself up in a room until it is taken away from her, and eat a cracker a day and be as quiet as a mouse."

"Mass unemployment is both a statistic and an empty feeling in the stomach," observed a perceptive

Unemployment
The rate of unemployment was staggering during the depression. And, as Reginald Marsh's 1933 painting *The Park Bench*, illustrates, unemployment's effects on individuals were devasting. (Sheldon Memorial Art Gallery)

historian. "To fully comprehend it, you have to both see the figures and feel the emptiness." The victims of the depression were a varied group. The depression did not create poverty; it merely publicized the conditions of the poor. People who had always been poor were joined by the newly poor. These formerly solid working-class and middle-class families strongly believed in the Horatio Alger ethic of upward mobility through hard work but suddenly found themselves floundering in a society that no longer had a place for them. They were proud people who felt humiliated by their plight, and many of the down-and-out blamed themselves for their own misfortune. "What is going to become of us?" asked an Arizona man. "I've lost twelve and a half pounds this last month, just thinking. You can't sleep, you know. You wake up at 2 A.M. and you lie and think."

Hard times were distressing for old people, who faced total destitution in their final years. Some lost their savings in bank failures. In a cartoon from the 1930s, a squirrel asks an old man on a park bench why

he had not saved for a rainy day. "I did," the old man replies listlessly. Children, on the other hand, often escaped the sense of bitterness and failure that gripped their elders. Some youngsters thought it was fun to stand in a soup line. Yet hard times made children grow up fast.

Downward mobility was especially hard for middle-class Americans. An unemployed Pittsburgh man told investigator Lorena Hickok, "Lady, you just can't know what it's like to have to move your family out of the nice house you had in the suburbs, part paid for, down into an apartment, down into another apartment, smaller and in a worse neighborhood, down, down, down, until finally you end up in the slums." Before a laid-off chauffeur started his relief construction job, he spent the day watching how the other men handled their picks and shovels so he could "get the hang of it and not feel so awkward." A wife broke into tears when her husband, formerly a white-collar worker, put on his first pair of overalls to go to work.

The key to surviving the depression was maintaining self-respect. One man spent two years painting his father's house (in fact, he painted it twice). Keeping up appearances, keeping life as close to normal as possible, was an essential strategy. Camaraderie and cooperation helped many families and communities survive, as people found that they were all in the same boat. When a truck driver "accidentally" dumped a load of oranges or coal off the back of his truck, he was probably contributing to the welfare of the neighborhood. Hoboes developed an elaborate system of sidewalk chalk marks to tell one another at which back doors they could get a meal, an old coat, or some spare change.

After savings and credit had been exhausted, many families faced the humiliation of going on relief. Seeking aid from the government hurt people's pride and disrupted the traditional pattern of turning to relatives, neighbors, churches, and mutual aid societies in time of need. A young caseworker tearfully remembered her embarrassment when investigating the homes of these proud people:

> The father was a railroad man who had lost his job. I was told by my supervisor that I really had to see the poverty. If the family needed clothing, I was to investigate how much clothing they had at hand. So I looked into this man's closet . . . he was a tall, gray-haired man, though not terribly old. He let me look into the closet—he was so insulted . . . He said, "Why are you doing this?" I remember his feeling of humiliation . . . this terrible humiliation. He said, "I really haven't anything to hide, but if you really must look into it . . ." I could see he was very proud. He was so deeply humiliated. And I was, too.

Even if families survived the demeaning process of being certified for state or local relief, the amount was a pittance: in New York State, for example, where benefits were among the highest in the nation, each family received only $2.39 per week.

Such hardships left deep wounds—the "invisible scar" described by author Caroline Bird. One elderly civil servant bought a plot of land outside Washington so that if the depression ever recurred, she would have the means to live. Labor organizer Larry Van Dusen described another common reaction: "The depression left a legacy of fear, but also a desire for acquisition—property, security. I now have twenty times more shirts than I need, because all during that time, shirts were something I never had." Virginia Durr, a white civil rights activist from Alabama, concurred: "The great majority reacted by thinking money is the most important thing in the world. Get yours. And get it for your children. Nothing else matters. Not having that stark terror come at you again." For many Americans, that was the Great Depression: "that stark terror" of losing control over their lives.

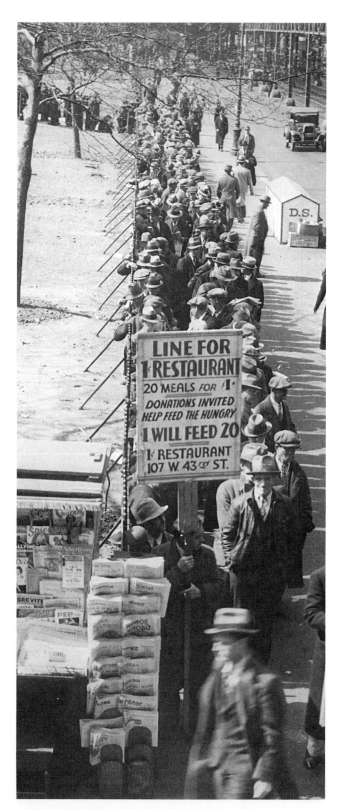

The Breadline

Some of the most vivid images from the depression were breadlines and men selling apples on street corners. Note that all the people in this breadline are men. Women rarely appeared in breadlines, often preferring to endure private deprivation rather than violate standards of respectable behavior for women.

The Family Faces the Great Depression

Sociologists who studied family life during the 1930s found that the depression usually intensified already existing behavior. For example, if a family had been stable and cohesive before the depression, it now pulled together to surmount the new obstacles. However, if a family had shown signs of disintegration, the depression made the situation worse. On the whole, researchers thought far more families hung together than broke apart.

In many ways, the depression disrupted women's lives less than men's. Millions of men lost their jobs, but few of the nation's 28 million homemakers lost their position in the home. In fact, women's domestic roles took on greater importance.

Men and women experienced the Great Depression differently, partly because of the traditional gender roles that governed male and female behavior in the 1930s. Men had been trained from childhood to be breadwinners for their families and they considered themselves failures if they could no longer support their families. Women, however, felt their self-importance increase as they struggled to keep their families afloat. The sociologists Robert and Helen Lynd noticed this phenomenon in their follow-up study of Middletown (Muncie, Indiana), published in 1937:

> The men, cut adrift from their usual routine, lost much of their sense of time and dawdled helplessly and dully about the streets; while in the homes the women's world remained largely intact and the round of cooking, housecleaning, and mending became if anything more absorbing.

Even if a wife took a job when her husband lost his, she still retained almost total responsibility for housework and childcare.

Women made many contributions to family survival during the depression years. With the national median annual income at $1,160, a typical woman had $20 to $25 a week to feed, clothe, and provide shelter for her family. Deflation had lowered the cost of living, so that milk sold for 10 cents a quart, bread 7 cents a loaf, and butter 23 cents a pound. Yet housewives still had to watch every penny. Two friends who often bought hamburger together split two pounds for 25 cents and took turns keeping the extra penny. Eleanor Roosevelt described the effect of the depression on these women's lives: "It means endless little economies and constant anxiety for fear of some catastrophe such as accident or illness which may completely swamp the family budget." The line between making do and doing without was often thin.

Despite the hard times, Americans managed to maintain a fairly high level of consumption. Continuing the pattern of the 1920s, households in the middle-income range, the 50.2 percent of American families with an income of $500 to $1,500 in 1935, did much of the buying. Several factors enabled these families more or less to keep up their former standard of living despite pay cuts or unemployment. Deflation lowered the cost of living almost 20 percent between 1929 and 1935. And families spent their reduced income differently. For example, telephone use and clothing sales dropped sharply during the depression, but people had a harder time giving up cigarettes, movies, radios, and newspapers, once considered luxuries but now regarded as necessities. An automobile proved to be one of the most depression-proof items in the family budget. Sales of new cars dropped, but gasoline sales stayed stable, suggesting that people bought used cars or kept their old models running longer.

Some families maintained their life-style in the 1930s through "deficit living"—that is, using installment payments and credit to stretch their income. This strategy added about 10 percent to a family income under $500, and 2 to 5 percent to a family in the $500 to $1,500 range. By 1936 consumer credit in the United States had increased by 20 percent over 1929 levels. A Middletown resident summed up the prevailing attitude toward installment buying: "Most of the families I know are after the same things today that they were after before the Depression, and they'll get them in the same way—on credit."

To maintain their families' life-style, housewives also substituted their own labor for goods and services they had formerly purchased. Women sewed their own clothes and canned fruits and vegetables. They practiced small economies such as buying day-old bread and heating several dishes in the oven at once to save fuel. Women who used to have servants now did their own housework. These economies helped pay for cars and movies, which could not be manufactured at home. Women generally accepted this new work stoically. "We had no choice," remembered one housewife. "We just did what had to be done one day at a time."

Demographic Trends

The depression directly affected demographic trends of the 1930s. The marriage rate fell from 10.14 per thousand persons in 1929 to 7.87 in 1932. The divorce rate dropped as well, because people could not afford the legal expense. Although marriage and divorce rates rebounded after 1933, postponement of marriage sometimes became no marriage at all. Elsa Ponselle, a Chicago schoolteacher who later became the principal of one of the city's largest elementary schools, recalled her experience:

Do you realize how many people in my generation are not married? . . . It wasn't that we didn't have a chance. I was going with someone when the Depression hit. We probably would have gotten married. He was a commercial artist and had been doing very well . . . Suddenly he was laid off. It hit him like a ton of bricks. And he just disappeared.

The birthrate was the demographic factor most affected by the depression. Since 1800 the birthrate had fallen steadily, but in the years from 1930 to 1933 it dropped from 21.3 live births per thousand population to 18.4, a 13 percent decrease. The 1933 level, if maintained, would have led to a population decline. The overriding concern was whether a couple could afford to raise a child. The birthrate rose slightly after 1934 but by the end of the decade had reached only 18.8. In contrast, at the height of the baby boom following World War II, the birthrate was 25 per thousand population.

Birth Control. The extensive limitation of births during the Great Depression meant that people had access to effective contraception. The production of diaphragms and condoms was one business that thrived in the 1930s. Abortion remained illegal, but the number of women who had abortions increased. Because many abortionists operated under unsafe or unsanitary conditions, between eight and ten thousand women died each year from these illegal operations.

The 1930s marked a significant stage in the long history of the birth control movement in America. In 1936 a federal court decision in the case of *United States v. One Package of Japanese Pessaries* struck down all federal bans on the dissemination of contraceptive information. Doctors now had wide discretion in prescribing birth control for married couples, which became legal in all the states except Massachusetts and Connecticut. Public support for birth control also increased: a 1936 Gallup poll found that 63 percent of those interviewed favored the teaching and practice of contraception.

Margaret Sanger played a major part in encouraging popular acceptance of birth control in America. She had started her career as a public health nurse in the slums of New York in the 1910s. Anxious immigrant women continually asked Sanger to tell them the "secret" of how to avoid having more babies. When a patient who had been referred to her died from the effects of a botched abortion, Sanger dedicated her life to birth control. At first, she joined forces with socialist movements aimed at the working class. In the 1920s and 1930s, however, she appealed to the middle class for support, identifying this as the key to the movement's success. Sanger also courted the medical profession, pioneering the establishment of birth control clinics staffed by doctors and winning the American Medical Association's endorsement of contraception in 1937. Birth control became less a feminist demand and more a medical issue.

Birth control had long been a private decision between individuals. Its public acceptance increased greatly during the 1930s because of the widespread desire to limit family size for economic reasons. In 1942 the American Birth Control League, an organization Sanger had founded in 1921, became Planned Parenthood, an organization that remains active today.

Women on the Job

One way for families to make ends meet in the 1930s was to send an additional member of the household into the work force. At the turn of the century, this additional family worker probably would have been a child or a young unmarried adult. In the 1930s, it was increasingly a married woman. Instead of expelling women from the work force, the depression solidified their position in it: the 1940 census reported almost 11 million women in the work force, approximately a fourth of the nation's workers and a small increase over 1930. The number of married women employed outside the home rose by 50 percent.

Working women, especially married ones, encountered sharp resentment and outright discrimination when they entered the depression workplace. After calculating that the number of employed women roughly equaled the 1939 unemployment total, editor Norman Cousins suggested this tongue-in-cheek remedy: "Simply fire the women, who shouldn't be working anyway, and hire the men. Presto! No unemployment. No relief rolls. No depression." A 1936 Gallup poll asked whether wives should work when their husbands had a job, and a resounding 82 percent of the people interviewed said no. From 1932 to 1937 the federal government would not allow a husband and wife to hold government jobs at the same time. Many states adopted laws that prohibited married women from working; such laws were especially widespread in the field of education. Yet the proportion of married female school teachers rose from 17.9 percent in 1930 to 24.6 percent in 1940.

The attempt to make women scapegoats for the depression rested on shaky moral and economic grounds. Most women worked because they had to. A sizable minority were the sole support of their families, their husbands having either left home or lost their jobs. Single, divorced, or widowed women had no husbands to support them. Moreover, women rarely took jobs away from men. "Few of the people who oppose married women's employment," observed one feminist in 1940, "seem to realize that a coal miner or steel worker cannot very well fill the jobs of nursemaids, cleaning women, or the factory and clerical jobs now filled by women." Custom, rather than law or economics, made crossovers rare.

The division of the work force by gender gave women a small edge during the depression. Many fields with large numbers of female employees, including clerical work, sales, and service and trade occupations, suffered less from economic contraction than the steel industry, mining, and manufacturing, which employed men almost exclusively. As a result, unemployment rates for women, although extremely high, were somewhat lower than for men. This small bonus came at a heavy price, however. The jobs women held reinforced the traditional stereotypes of female work. When the depression ended, women found themselves even more concentrated in low-paying dead-end jobs than when it began.

This gender advantage benefited white women at the expense of minority women. To make ends meet, white women willingly took jobs usually held by blacks or minority workers—entering domestic service, for example—and employers were quick to act on their preference for a white work force. White men also took jobs previously held by minority males.

During the Great Depression, there were few feminist demands for equal rights either at home or on the job. On an individual basis, women's self-esteem probably rose because of their importance to family survival. Both men and women, however, continued to believe that the two sexes should have fundamentally different roles and responsibilities, and that a woman's life-style should be shaped by her marriage and her husband's career. The substantial contributions by women in the 1930s actually reinforced their overall identification with the home, laying the foundation for the so-called feminine mystique of the 1950s.

Hard Times for Youth

The depression hit the nation's 21 million young people especially hard. Although children only dimly glimpsed the sacrifices of life in the 1930s, adolescents knew that "making do" usually meant "doing without." The writer Maxine Davis, who traveled 10,000 miles in 1936 interviewing the nation's youth, described them as "runners, delayed at the gun." She added, "The depression years have left us with a generation robbed of time and opportunity just as the Great War left the world its heritage of a lost generation." Studies of social mobility confirm that the young men who entered their twenties during the depression era had less successful careers than those before or since. About 250,000 young peo-

ple became so demoralized they simply took to the road as hoboes and "sisters of the road," as female tramps were called.

Because job prospects were so dim, some young people chose to stay in school longer. Public schools were free, and they were warm in winter. In 1930 less than half of the nation's youth attended high school, compared with three-fourths in 1940. This was partly due to increased attendance by boys, who had traditionally dropped out of school to work at an earlier age than girls.

College, on the other hand, remained the privilege of a distinct minority. About 1.2 million young people, or 7.5 percent of the population between eighteen and twenty-four, attended college in the 1930s, 40 percent of them women. After 1935 college became a little more affordable because of the National Youth Administration (NYA), which gave part-time employment to more than 2 million college and high school students. This government agency also provided work for 2.6 million out-of-school youths.

College students worked hard in the 1930s; financial sacrifices encouraged seriousness of purpose. The influence of fraternities and sororities declined on campus during the depression. Large numbers of students became involved in various political movements. Fueled by disillusionment with World War I, thousands took the "Oxford Pledge" never to support a war in which the United States might be involved. In 1936 the Student Strike Against War drew support from several hundred thousand students across the country.

Because young people spent more time in school, participating in organized athletics and extracurricular activities, adolescence became increasingly institutionalized in the 1930s, and teenagers developed their own values and patterns of behavior. Peers, rather than parents, influenced their values and tastes. Magazines and movies promoted a youth culture closely tied to an ethos of consumption. Teenagers throughout the country read the same comics, wore the same style clothes, and saw the same movies. They also experimented with necking, petting, and dating rituals that shocked their elders. The youth culture became a distinct feature of modern times.

Popular Culture

Popular culture played an important role in pulling the United States through the trauma of the Great Depression. As the novelist Josephine Herbst observed, there was "an almost universal liveliness that countervailed universal suffering." The mass culture that grew so dramatically in the 1920s flourished in the decade that followed.

Movie Palaces
In order to lure the more prosperous middle class to this new form of mass entertainment, movie theaters featured lavish interiors decorated to mimic European palaces. The recently restored Chicago Theatre shows the architectural grandeur of the picture palaces of the era.

Movies. The most popular form of entertainment during the 1930s was the movies. More than 60 percent of Americans saw at least one movie a week, with weekly attendance ranging from 60 to 75 million. In the 5,000 films made during the depression decade, moviegoers were transported to a world where hard times were practically unknown. Yet movies offered more than escapism. Hollywood in the 1930s, observed one film historian, "directed its enormous powers of persuasion to preserving the basic moral, social and economic tenets of traditional American culture."

Movies remained big business in the 1930s but the industry was not depression-proof. Although studios lowered admission prices from thirty cents to twenty, attendance dropped in the early 1930s, and by 1933 one-third of the nation's movie theaters were dark. Many of the major studios, dependent on Wall Street financing, were hurting. Not until 1934 did the industry begin to revive.

In many ways, films from the 1930s reflected the progress of the depression. In the grim early years gangster films were especially popular. Two of the most successful were *Little Caesar* (1930), starring Edward G. Robinson, and *The Public Enemy* (1931), in which James Cagney shoved a grapefruit in Mae Clark's face. These were replaced by extravagant Busby Berkeley musicals such as *Golddiggers of 1933,* suggesting an upswing in the public mood. The Marx brothers kept people laughing with such irreverent classics as *Animal Crackers* (1930) and *Duck Soup* (1933). Mae West titillated audiences with such lines as "It's not the men in my life, but the life in my men that counts" and "I used to be Snow White, but I drifted."

For some moviegoers, Mae West's sexual innuendoes went too far. To win back customers Hollywood made a highly publicized commitment to upholding ideals of decency and good taste. The Production Code Administration, headed by Joseph Breen, was Holly-

Dancing Cheek to Cheek

During the Great Depression, Americans turned to such in-expensive recreational activities as listening to the radio and going to the movies. One of the most popular attractions in Hollywood movies was the dance team of Fred Astaire and Ginger Rogers. Together Astaire and Rogers starred in ten movies.

wood's effort at self-censorship, an attempt to correct the perceived excesses of early talkies. Fearing a boycott from religious groups such as the Catholic Legion of Decency, studios in 1934 agreed to banish explicit sex, immorality, and violence from the screen. The standards promulgated were so narrow that censors barely permitted Rhett Butler to utter the famous last line of *Gone with the Wind*: "Frankly my dear, I don't give a damn." Critics charged that movies were cutting themselves off from reality, but the repressive standards held sway until the 1950s.

In part because of the Production Code, movies made after 1934 had a different feel than those made before. Sophisticated, fast-paced "screwball comedies" such as *It Happened One Night,* which swept the Oscars in 1934, epitomized Hollywood's new direction. Walt Disney emerged as a cultural mythmaker during the depression, producing 198 cartoons and such classics as *Snow White and the Seven Dwarfs* (1937), the first feature-length animated film. The 1940 Hollywood adaptation of John Steinbeck's novel *The Grapes of Wrath* was one of the few popular films to depict the depression. Otherwise, even the newsreels downplayed the depression in favor of heroes and heroines from the worlds of sport, entertainment, and popular culture.

At the height of the depression, movies continued to influence consumers. One of the decade's top box-office stars was a curly-headed little girl named Shirley Temple, who made twenty-one films by 1941. Shirley Temple dolls, books, and clothes flooded the market. Similarly, because of the popularity of such glamorous blondes as Jean Harlow, Carole Lombard, and Mae West, sales of peroxide hair rinse skyrocketed in the 1930s. Undershirt sales fell drastically after Clark Gable, a leading sex symbol of his day, took off his shirt in *It Happened One Night* and revealed his bare chest.

The Grapes of Wrath

John Steinbeck's bestselling 1939 novel became one of 1940's top movies, one of the few Hollywood films that tackled contemporary social problems. Ma Joad, played by Jane Darwell in the movie version, expressed the central message: "We're the people that live. They ain't gonna wipe us out. Why, we're the people—we go on."

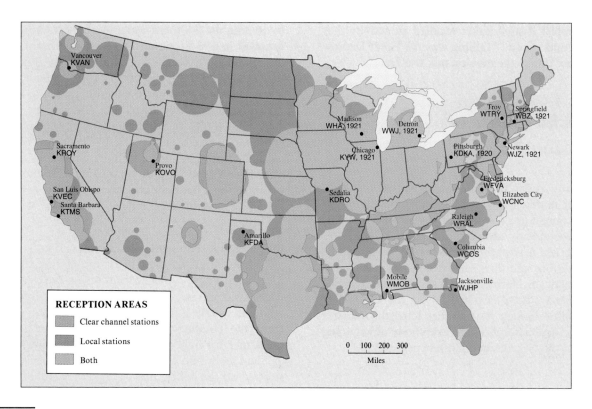

MAP 25.1

The Spread of Radio.

In 1938 more than 26 million American households, or about three-quarters of
the population, had a radio. The date of first transmission is given for the earliest
stations. By 1939 the period covered in this map, only a few sparsely populated
areas were beyond radio's reach.

Headline History. Although movies had the greatest influence on popular culture, newspapers and newsreels
provided quick coverage of world events. The kidnap-
ping of the twenty-month-old son of Charles and Anne
Morrow Lindbergh in 1932 instantly became a national
news story. Seventy-five days later, the child's body was
found in the woods near the Lindbergh home in New
Jersey. "BABY DEAD" ran the headlines, and everyone
knew what the two words meant. Other leading news
events of the depression years included the birth of the
Dionne quintuplets in Canada in 1934; the gunning
down of John Dillinger, "Public Enemy Number One,"
by the FBI in 1934; the abdication in 1936 of King Edward VIII of Great Britain to marry "the woman I
love," an American divorcee named Wallis Warfield
Simpson; the disappearance of aviator Amelia Earhart
on a round-the-world flight in 1937; and the fiery crash
of the Hindenburg, a German dirigible, at Lakehurst,
New Jersey, in 1937.

Radio Days. Radio occupied an increasingly large
place in popular culture during the 1930s. At the beginning of the decade, about 13 million households had a
radio set; by the end, 27.5 million owned one. Listeners
tuned in to daytime serials such as "Ma Perkins" or

picked up useful household hints on the "The Betty
Crocker Hour." Variety shows featured Jack Benny,
George Burns and Gracie Allen, and ventriloquist Edgar
Bergen and his impudent dummy, Charlie McCarthy.
Millions of listeners followed the adventures of the
Lone Ranger ("Hi-Ho Silver"), Superman, the Shadow,
and Dick Tracy.

Radio also brought music to depression-era audiences. Classical music devotees could listen to the Saturday afternoon broadcast of New York's Metropolitan
Opera (premiered in 1931) or the NBC Symphony Orchestra under the baton of Arturo Toscanini. On the
lighter side, people loved the new "swing" music of
Benny Goodman, Duke Ellington, and Tommy Dorsey,
which built on the jazz craze of the 1920s, and Cole
Porter songs such as "Begin the Beguine" and "Night
and Day" from Broadway hits. Radio increased the
consumer market for 78 r.p.m. phonograph records of
classical music, swing, and Broadway show tunes.

The depression also encouraged a return to traditional values. Church attendance rose slightly. The family again became a center of leisure activity, with an
evening at home by the radio providing a cheap form of
entertainment. Reading aloud from books borrowed
from the public library was another affordable diver-

sion. Columnist Russell Baker recalled an activity that everyone could afford: "Talking was the Great Depression pastime. Unlike the movies, talk was free."

The Social Fabric of Depression America

Much writing about the 1930s has focused on white working- or middle-class families who suddenly found themselves caught in a spiral of downward social mobility. For those already near the bottom, the depression had a much less devastating impact, both on their economic conditions and their self-esteem. For groups like African-Americans, farmers, and Mexican-Americans, times had always been hard and during the 1930s they just got a little harder. As the poet Langston Hughes noted, "The depression brought everybody down a peg or two. And the Negroes had but few pegs to fall."

Blacks and the Depression

Discrimination and limited opportunities had always been part of the lives of African-Americans, so they viewed the depression differently than most whites did. A black man didn't blame himself for his misfortune. "It didn't mean too much to him, the Great American Depression, as you call it," one remarked. "There was no such thing. The best he could be is a janitor or a porter or shoeshine boy. It only became official when it hit the white man." The novelist and poet Maya Angelou, who grew up in Stamps, Arkansas, recalled, "The country had been in the throes of the Depression for two years before the Negroes in Stamps knew it. I think that everyone thought the Depression, like everything else, was for the white folks."

Despite the pattern of black migration to northern cities begun in World War I, as late as 1940 more than 75 percent of all African-Americans were living in the South. Nearly all of the farmers who were black stayed in the South, their condition scarcely better than it was at the end of Reconstruction. Only 20 percent of black farmers owned their own land; the rest toiled on the bottom rung of the exploitative southern agricultural system, working as tenant farmers, farmhands, and sharecroppers. African-Americans rarely earned more than an average of $200 a year. The earnings of black women cotton pickers in one Louisiana parish averaged only $41.67 a year.

Throughout the 1920s southern agriculture had suffered from falling prices and overproduction. During the depression, an already desperate situation got worse. Some black farmers tried to protect themselves by joining the Southern Tenant Farmers Union (STFU), founded in 1934, one of the few southern groups that welcomed both blacks and whites. "The same chain that holds you holds my people, too," an elderly black farmer reminded whites on the organizing committee. "If we're chained together on the outside we ought to stay chained together in the union." Landowners, however, had a stake in keeping black and white sharecroppers from organizing, and they countered the STFU efforts with repression and harassment. In the end, the organization could do little to reform an agricultural system dependent on a single crop, cotton.

The Scottsboro Case. The Scottsboro case epitomized the harsh social and political discrimination that almost all blacks faced in the South during the 1930s. On March 25, 1931, a freight train pulled into Scottsboro, Alabama, carrying a number of hoboes and transients who had caught a free ride on the rails. Acting on a tip from the conductor, sheriff's deputies arrested nine black men for fighting with some of the white hoboes.

Suddenly, two white women wearing men's clothing stepped off the boxcar and claimed they had been raped by the nine blacks. The officers accepted without question the accusations of the women, Victoria Price and Ruby Bates, and barely restrained an angry white mob from lynching the men on the spot. Two weeks later, juries composed entirely of white men found the nine defendants guilty of rape and sentenced eight of them to death. (One defendant escaped the death penalty because he was a minor.) The U.S. Supreme Court overturned the sentences in 1932 and ordered new trials on the grounds that the defendants had been denied adequate legal counsel.

The youth of the Scottsboro defendants, their hasty trials, and especially their harsh sentences stirred public protest. The International Labor Defense (ILD), a labor organization closely tied to the Communist party, took over the defense of the so-called Scottsboro boys. The Communist party had targeted the struggle against racism as a priority in the early 1930s but was making little headway. "It's bad enough being black, why be red?" went a common retort. White southerners resented the interference of these radicals and also the fact that all those involved in the Scottsboro defense were northerners and Jews. In the words of a local solicitor, "Alabama justice cannot be bought and sold with Jew money from New York."

The case was complicated by the southern myth of the inviolate honor and chastity of white womanhood. The stories of the two women contained many inconsistencies, and Ruby Bates later recanted. However, in the South, when a white woman claimed to have been raped by a black man, she was taken at her word. As one court observer remarked, Victoria Price "might be a fallen woman, but by God she is a white woman."

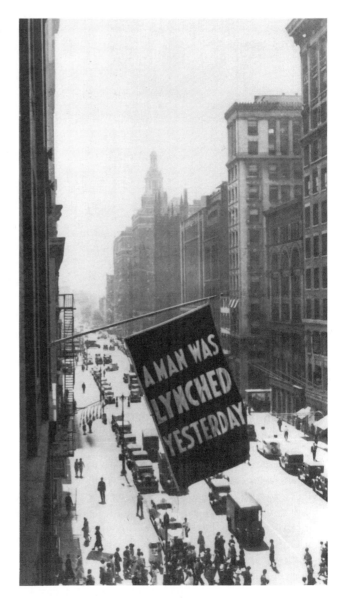

The Lynch Mob and Silent Witness
The threat of lynching remained a terrifying part of life for African-Americans in the 1930s, and not just in the South. The photograph on the left shows two young blacks who were lynched by an Indiana mob in 1930. Each day that a person was lynched, the NAACP hung a (right) banner outside the window of their New York office. NAACP appeals for federal anti-lynching legislation received little support from politicians, however.

The case dragged on through the courts for the next decade. In new trials held in 1936 and 1937, five of the defendants were convicted and sentenced to long prison terms. The charges against the other four were dropped in 1937. Four of the convicted men were paroled in 1944. The fifth escaped to Michigan, whose governor refused to return him to Alabama.

The Scottsboro case received wide coverage in black communities throughout the country. Along with the increase in lynching in the early 1930s (twenty blacks were lynched in 1930, twenty-four in 1933), it provided black Americans with a strong incentive to head for northern and midwestern cities. However, the lure of the North was offset by the lack of economic opportunities caused by the depression. About four hundred thousand black men and women left the South during the 1930s, only about half the number that left in the 1920s. By 1935 eleven cities had a black population of more than a hundred thousand. Two of the most popular destinations were the South Side of Chicago and Harlem in New York City.

Harlem in the 1930s. In the late nineteenth century, Harlem had been a neighborhood of wealthy white families—New York's first suburb. As late as 1900, blacks made up only a small minority of the Harlem population. Then World War I set in motion the great migration from the south. At the same time that blacks moved into Harlem, second-generation Italians and Jews began to move out.

Harlem reached the height of its fame in the 1920s, when it became a mecca for both whites and blacks. Adventurous New Yorkers associated Harlem with the Cotton Club and other glittering jazz palaces catering to white audiences. (Although the clubs featured African-American performers, they were white-only establishments, from which local blacks were excluded.) During the 1920s, the black population of New York City

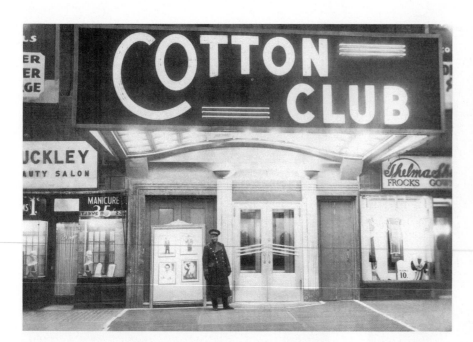

The Cotton Club

The Cotton Club, "the aristocrat of
Harlem" at Lenox Avenue and 142nd
Street, was home to such performers as
Duke Ellington, Ethel Waters, and Cab
Calloway. Even though blacks provided
the entertainment and were hired as
waiters and busboys at this swinging
nightclub, they were not admitted
as customers unless they were light-
skinned enough to pass as white.

increased by about 115 percent, straining Harlem's
housing facilities and community services. This once
prosperous middle-class community was on its way to
becoming a slum.

The depression aggravated the situation. Residential segregation kept blacks from moving elsewhere.
African-Americans paid excessive rents to unscrupulous
owners who allowed housing to deteriorate. Crowded
living conditions caused disease and death rates to
climb; tuberculosis became a leading cause of death in
Harlem. At the height of the depression, shelters and
soup kitchens staffed by the Divine Peace Mission,
under the leadership of charismatic black religious
leader Father Divine, provided 3,000 meals a day for
Harlem's destitute. Unemployment rose to 50 percent,
as whites now clamored for jobs traditionally held by
blacks—waiters, domestic servants, elevator operators,
and garbage collectors.

In March 1935 Harlem exploded in the nation's
only major race riot of the decade. Its residents were
angry about the lack of jobs, a slowdown in relief, and
pervasive economic exploitation of the black community. Although entirely dependent on black trade, white-
owned stores would not employ blacks. The arrest of a
teenage black shoplifter, followed by rumors that he
had been severely beaten by white police officers, triggered the riot. False reports of his death fueled the
panic, and the city mobilized five hundred police officers. Four blacks were killed, and property damage totaled $2 million.

However, the picture was not totally bleak for
blacks in the 1930s. The New Deal would channel significant amounts of relief money towards blacks outside
the South, partly in response to the 1935 riot but

mainly in return for growing black allegiance to the Democratic party (see Chapter 26). The National Association for the Advancement of Colored People continued
to publicly challenge the status quo of race relations.
Although calls for racial justice went largely unheeded
during the depression, World War II and its aftermath
would provide more fertile soil for the struggle for
black equality.

Dust Bowl Migrations

Distressed conditions in agriculture had been one of the
causes of the Great Depression. In the 1930s things only
got worse, especially for farmers on the Great Plains.
The decade became known as the "Dirty Thirties" because of the dust storms that blighted the land. The
worst drought in the country's history began in 1930
and lasted until 1941. Throughout the decade the three
words most often uttered by farmers were "if it rains."

Farmers who moved onto the semiarid Great Plains
after the 1870s had always risked the ravages of
drought (see Chapter 17). Even in wet years, the average rainfall was 20 inches or less—barely enough to
raise grain crops. But low rainfall alone did not create
the Dust Bowl. National and international market
forces, such as the demand for wheat during World War
I, caused farmers to push the farming frontier beyond
its natural limits, expanding onto increasingly marginal
land in order to capture a profit. After this land had
been stripped of its natural vegetation, the delicate ecological balance of the plains was destroyed. Nothing remained to hold the soil when the rains dried up and the
winds came.

AMERICAN VOICES

A Dust Bowl Diary *Ann Marie Low*

Born in 1912, Ann Marie Low kept diaries from 1927 to 1937 which describe the devastation wrecked by the drought and depression on her family's farm in the Badlands of southeastern North Dakota. They record both a young woman's coming of age and the harshness of life on the farm in the Dust Bowl.

April 25, 1934, Wednesday
Last weekend was the worst dust storm we ever had. We've been having quite a bit of blowing dirt every year since the drouth started, not only here, but all over the Great Plains. Many days this spring the air is just full of dirt coming, literally, for hundreds of miles. It sifts into everything. After we wash the dishes and put then away, so much dust sifts into the cupboards we must wash them again before the next meal. Clothes in the closet are covered with dust.

Last weekend no one was taking an automobile out for fear of ruining the motor. I rode Roany to Frank's place to return a gear. To find my way I had to ride right beside the fence, scarcely able to see from one fence post to the next.

Newspapers say the deaths of many babies and old people are attributed to breathing in so much dirt.

May 21, 1934, Monday
Ethel has been having stomach trouble. Dad has been taking her to doctors though suspecting her trouble is the fact that she often goes on a diet that may affect her health. The local doctor said he thought it might be chronic appendicitis, so Mama took Ethel by train to Valley City last week to have a surgeon there remove her appendix.

Saturday Dad, Bud, and I planted an acre of potatoes. There was so much dirt in the air I couldn't see Bud only a few feet in front of me. Even the air in the house was just a haze. In the evening the wind died down, and Cap came to take me to the movie. We joked about how hard it is to get cleaned up enough to go anywhere. . . .

May 30, 1934, Wednesday
Ethel got along fine, so Mama left her at the hospital and came to Jamestown by train Friday. Dad took us both home.

The mess was incredible! Dirt had blown into the house all week and lay inches deep on everything. Every towel and curtain was just black. There wasn't a clean dish or cooking utensil. . . It took until 10 o'clock to wash all the dirty dishes. That's not wiping them—just washing them. The cupboards had to be washed out to have a clean place to put them.

Saturday was a busy day. Before starting breakfast I had to sweep and wash all the dirt off the kitchen and dining room floors, wash the stove, pancake griddle, and dining room table and chairs. There was cooking, baking, and churning to be done for those hungry men. Dad is 6 feet 4 inches tall, with a big frame. Bud is 6 feet 3 inches and almost as big-boned as Dad. We say feeding them is like filling a silo.

Mama couldn't make bread until I carried water to wash the bread mixer. I couldn't churn until the churn was washed and scalded. We just couldn't do anything until something was washed first. Every room had to have dirt almost shoveled out of it before we could wash floors and furniture.

We had no time to wash clothes, but it was necessary. I had to wash out the boiler, wash tubs, and the washing machine before we could use them. Then every towel, curtain, piece of bedding, and garment had to be taken outdoors to have as much dust as possible shaken out before washing. The cistern is dry, so I had to carry all the water we needed from the well.

That evening Cap came to take me to the movie, as usual. Ixnay. I'm sorry I snapped at Cap. It isn't his fault, or anyone's fault, but I was tired and cross. Life in what the newspapers call "the Dust Bowl" is becoming a gritty nightmare.

Source: Ann Marie Low, *Dust Bowl Diary* (Lincoln, Nebraska: University of Nebraska Press, 1984), 95, 96–98.

Dust became a plague on everyday life throughout the Great Plains, but especially in Oklahoma, Texas, New Mexico, Colorado, Arkansas, and Kansas. When the clouds of dust rolled in, street lights blinked on as if night had fallen. Dust seeped into houses and "blackened the pillow around one's head, the dinner plates on the table, the bread dough on the back of the stove."

The dust storms were not confined to the Plains. In May 1934, the wind took dust clouds to Chicago, where filth fell like snow, dumping on the city the equivalent of 4 pounds of debris per person. Several days later, the same clouds blackened the skies and dirtied the streets of Buffalo, Boston, New York, and Washington. That winter red snow fell on New England.

NEW TECHNOLOGY *Rural Electrification*

In 1935, less than one-tenth of the nation's 6.8 million farms had electricity. For millions of farm families, this stark fact meant a life of unremitting toil made even harsher by the lack of simple conveniences. Farm families used an average of 200 gallons of water a day. Any chore requiring water—and most did—meant pumping the water from a distant well and carrying it to the house or barn in a pair of buckets weighing as much as 60 pounds full. Hot water had to be heated on a wood stove that required constant tending. Meeting a family's yearly water needs took sixty-three eight-hour days and involved carrying water a distance of 1,750 miles.

Rural women suffered especially from the lack of electricity. Canning, a necessity before refrigeration, kept women standing over steaming vats of fruit or vegetables, often in the worst summer heat before the freshly harvested produce spoiled. Washday, tradition-ally Monday, called for three large zinc washtubs for washing, rinsing, and bleaching. A week's wash consisted of at least four to eight loads, each requiring three washtubs of clean water hauled from the well. Few rural households could afford commercial soap, so women used lye, which barely got ground-in dirt out of soiled clothes and was very harsh on their hands.

If farm women dreaded Monday, they hated Tuesday even more. Tuesday was ironing day, another all-day job. The iron, a six- or seven-pound wedge of metal, had to be heated on the stove, and because it did not retain heat for more than a few minutes, it took several irons to do a single shirt. The women in Texas's Hill Country called them "sad irons."

A day that began in darkness and was given over to twelve hours of backbreaking toil brought few comforts come evening. Reading by kerosene lamps strained the

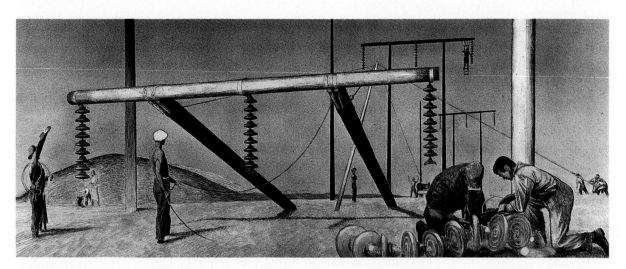

Electrification

While a woman and her two children watch, workers install the power lines that will bring electricity to their nearby homestead. This sketch by C. David Stone Martin was done for a mural in Lenoir City, Tennessee.

This ecological disaster caused a mass exodus from the land. Their crops ruined, their lands barren and dry, their homes foreclosed for debts they could not pay, thousands of farm families loaded all their belongings into their beat-up Fords and headed west along Route 66 to the promised land of California. The migrants were called "Okies" whether or not they were from Ok-lahoma. John Steinbeck's classic novel *The Grapes of Wrath* (1939) immortalized their journey. The Joads abandoned their land not only because of drought, but also as a result of economic forces changing American agriculture. Large-scale commercialized farming had spread to the plains, where people like the Joads still farmed with animals. After the bank foreclosed on their

"Blue Monday"
Laundry was one of women's hardest household chores. Although this woman did not have to haul water from an outdoor well, she still had to pump it by hand in order to do the wash because her home lacked electricity. She also had to wring out the wet clothes manually, another arduous task.

power companies balked at the prospect of electrifying the countryside. They claimed that it was economically unfeasible to run lines to individual farms. In 1935 the federal government made a commitment to bring power to rural America. The Rural Electrification Administration, an independent agency, promoted the formation of nonprofit farm cooperatives to bring electricity to their regions. For a $5 down payment, local farmers could join an association and become eligible for low-interest federal loans covering the cost of installing power lines. Each household was committed to a monthly minimum usage, usually about $3, but as usage increased, the rates came down. By 1940, 40 percent of the nation's farms had electricity; by 1950, the rate reached 90 percent.

Electricity brought relief from the drudgery and isolation of farm life. An electric milking machine saved hours of manual labor, most of it previously done, before dawn, by the faint glow of a kerosene lamp, so farmers could devote the daylight hours to outdoor chores. An electrically powered water pump lightened many chores, especially hauling water. Electric irons, vacuum cleaners, and washing machines eased the burden of women.

People's responses to rural electrification were poignant. A small child told his mother, "I didn't realize how dark our house was until we got electric lights." One farm woman remembered, "I just turned on the light and kept looking at Paw. It was the first time I'd ever really seen him after dark." Another family, caught unawares by the timing of the hookup, saw their house from a distance and thought it must be on fire. Schoolteachers noticed that children did better at school when they had light to do their homework by. Along with the automobile, electricity probably did more than any other technological innovation to break down the barriers between urban and rural life in twentieth-century America.

eyes. Children's eyes might be strong enough to read in the semidarkness, but few older folks could read without squinting. The absence of electricity also meant no radios, which meant no contact with the outside world, no bit of amusement to brighten the darkness.

Studies showed that farmers would find many uses for electricity and would make good customers, but

farm, a gasoline-engine tractor, the symbol of mechanized farming, plowed under their crops and demolished their house.

While powerful as fiction, the Joads' struggle does not convey the diversity of the westward migration, which was both a response to hard times and a part of the larger migration out of the nation's agricultural

heartland that began around World War I and continued through the 1970s. Not all Okies were destitute dirt farmers; perhaps one in six was a professional, a business proprietor, or a white collar worker. Many were participating in chain migrations—that is, following family members or friends to a specific place. For most the drive west was fairly easy: Route 66 was a paved

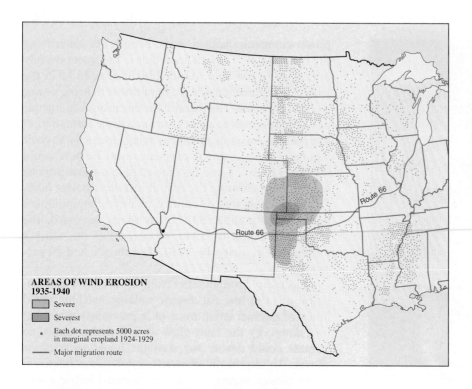

MAP 25.2

The Dust Bowl.
A U.S. Weather Bureau scientist called the drought of the 1930s "the worst in the climatological history of the country." Conditions were especially severe in the southern plains, where the dramatic increases in farming on marginal land had already strained production before the drought struck. Many farm families saw no choice but to follow Route 66, the highway that went straight west through Missouri, Oklahoma, and north Texas to California, the promised land.

Years of Dust
This 1936 Ben Shahn poster captured the despair and dislocation of the Dust Bowl years. Many farmers left their land to migrate to California.

two-lane road, and in a decent car, it took three to four days to make it from Oklahoma or Texas to California.

Before the 1930s California had already undergone changes that created a different type of agriculture from that practiced by southwestern and midwestern migrants. Farming in California was large-scale, intensive, and diversified. The state's wealth came from specialty crops whose staggered harvests required lots of transient labor for short picking seasons. The steady supply of cheap migrant labor provided by Chinese, Mexicans, Okies, and, briefly, even Hindustani made such farming economically feasible. Carey McWilliams, whose nonfiction *Factories in the Field* (1939) also focused national attention on migrant workers, noted that California agriculture was basically industrial in nature:

> Ownership is represented not by physical possession of the land, but by ownership of corporate stock; farm labor, no longer pastoral in character, punches a time clock, works at piece or hourly wage rates, and lives in a shack or company barracks, and lacks all contact with the real owners of the farm factory on which it is employed.

Encouraged by handbills promising good jobs in California, at least 350,000 southwesterners headed west during the 1930s. Some went to metropolitan areas, but about half settled in rural areas. White, native-born Americans had made up about 20 percent of the migratory farm labor force before the depression, but their proportion increased to more than 85 percent by the late 1930s. Since growers needed only 175,000 workers at the peak of the picking season, this surplus

Migrant Labor in California
By the 1930s, about 35,000 Filipinos were working as migrant laborers in California, including these lettuce workers in Salinas. At first, Filipinos were highly desired as migratory workers because they worked long hours for low wages. But they soon began to demand higher wages. In 1934, three thousand Filipino lettuce workers went on strike near Salinas. The strike was brutally broken, and many of the workers were driven from the community.

of labor assured them a cheap supply of labor, usually docile and willing to work at any price. That price was incredibly low in the 1930s. The average yearly family income for migrant farm workers in California ranged from $350 to $450, less than a third of the subsistence level. Yet what they earned in California was more than what they had left behind.

These migrants had a lasting impact on California culture. At first, they met outright hostility from old-time Californians, a demoralizing experience for these white, native-born Protestants, who were ashamed of the negative "Okie" stereotypes. But they stayed, filling important roles in the expanding California economy. Soon communities in the San Joaquin Valley—Bakersfield, Fresno, Merced, Modesto, Stockton—took on a distinctly Okie cast, identifiable by Southern-influenced evangelical religion and by the growing popularity of country music.

Mexican-American Communities

Mexican-Americans had a different experience in the west than Dust Bowl refugees did. In the depths of the depression, with fears about competition from foreign workers at their peak, perhaps a third of the Mexican-American population was deported or voluntarily relocated to Mexico. The 1930 census reported 617,000 Mexican-Americans; by 1940 the number had dropped to 377,000. A formal deportation policy instituted by the U.S. government was partly responsible for the decline, but many more Mexicans left voluntarily when work ran out, rather than be deported.

The deportation of Mexican-Americans was not in reaction to the arrival of migrants from the Dust Bowl. The largest number of Mexican-American deportations occurred under the Hoover administration, well before the Dust Bowl exodus reached its peak. Most deportations occurred in California and Texas, but Indiana, Illinois, and Colorado also repatriated unwanted workers. A one-way train ticket cost the equivalent of a week's relief allotment in 1932, and officials in many southwestern communities realized that it was cheaper to send migrant workers back to Mexico than to support them on relief during the winter, when there were no crops to pick. Pervasive racism and the proximity of Mexico made Mexicans the only immigrants targeted for deportation during the depression.

Mexican migration to the United States—legal and illegal—increased steadily throughout the twentieth century, except during the Great Depression and for short periods following the two world wars. The first *bracero* (day-laborer) program promoting Mexican immigration had been established during World War I to meet labor shortages. The importation of cheap Mexican labor continued throughout the 1920s. After being deported during the depression, Mexican workers found themselves being coaxed back again when World War II caused another labor shortage. The influx of Spanish-speaking migrants with their own distinct culture helped shape the patterns of life and work in the Southwest.

The experiences of his family as migrant workers during the 1930s influenced a Mexican-American named Cesar Chavez to become a farm union organizer. Chavez was a child of ten in 1934, when his father lost

Mexican-American Poverty in Texas
In 1937, Antonia and Pablo Martinez lived in a one-room house in San Antonio, Texas, with his parents and older brother. If either Pablo or Antonia was employed in 1937, it was probably in San Antonio's pecan-shelling industry, which depended heavily on the cheap labor of Mexican-Americans.

the family farm near Yuma, Arizona. The Chavez family joined the army of migrant workers that followed the crops in California. They experienced continual discrimination, even in restaurants where signs proclaimed "White Trade Only." Cesar's father became involved in several bitter labor struggles that hit the Imperial Valley in the mid-1930s. During 1933, thirty-seven major agricultural strikes occurred in California, including one in the San Joaquin Valley, which mobilized 18,000 cotton pickers. All these strikes failed, but they gave young Chavez a background in labor organizing, which he used to found a national farm workers' union in 1962.

Not all Mexican-Americans were migrant farm workers. A significant minority lived in cities and held industrial jobs. In 1930 Los Angeles was home to 150,000 Chicanos—people of Mexican birth or heritage—the largest concentration in the United States. By the 1930s, Mexican-Americans had spilled out of the downtown area known as "Sonoratown" into neighborhoods in East Los Angeles, where mutual aid societies, Spanish-language newspapers, and the Catholic Church fostered a sense of community.

In the cities, many Mexican-Americans found employment in fruit and vegetable processing plants, especially young single women who preferred cannery work to domestic service or farm labor. Corporate giants such as Del Monte (California Packing Corporation, or Cal

Pak) and Libby, McNeill, and Libby dominated California's food processing industry. In these plants Mexican-American women earned around $2.50 a day, while their male counterparts earned $3.50 to $4.50. So pervasive was the "cannery culture" that workers could say, "We met in spinach, fell in love in peaches, and married in tomatoes," and their friends would know they were referring to the harvests of March, August, and October.

In 1939 labor unions came to the canneries in the form of the United Cannery, Agricultural, Packing, and Allied Workers of America (UCAPAWA), an unusually democratic union in which women, who formed a majority of the rank-and-file workers, played leading roles. This heritage of activism from the 1930s, in the fields and in the factories, foreshadowed later Chicano labor militancy.

Herbert Hoover and the Great Depression

During the presidential campaign of 1928, Herbert Hoover predicted that "the poorhouse is vanishing from among us" and that America was "nearer to the final triumph over poverty than ever before in the history of any land." Once elected, Hoover planned to preside over an era of Republican prosperity and governmental restraint. Even after the stock market crash in 1929, Hoover stubbornly insisted that the downturn was only temporary. He greeted a business delegation in June 1930 with these words: "Gentlemen, you have come sixty days too late. The Depression is over." In 1931 and 1932, as the country hit rock bottom, Hoover finally acted, but by then it was too little, too late.

The Republican Response

In 1932 the journalist William Allen White wrote an article about the outgoing president entitled "Herbert Hoover—The Last of the Old Presidents, or the First of the New?" White concluded that Hoover had been a little of both, as have historians ever since. Hoover's early efforts to fight the depression are now seen as predecessors of many New Deal programs, and his reputation among historians has risen steadily over the years. Hoover, who lived until 1964, offered a simple explanation for the improvement in his historical stature, telling Chief Justice Earl Warren of the Supreme Court that he had simply managed "to outlive the bastards."

Hoover's approach to the Great Depression was shaped by his priorities as secretary of commerce: he turned to the business community. Hoover asked business to maintain wages voluntarily, keep up production, and work with the government to build confidence in the system.

Fiscal Policy. Hoover did not rely solely on public pronouncements. He also used public budgets and federal action to encourage recovery. Soon after the stock market crash, he cut federal taxes and called on state and local governments to increase capital spending in the "energetic yet prudent pursuit" of public construction. The 1929 Agricultural Marketing Act gave the federal government its largest role to date in a program of agricultural stabilization and farm relief. In 1930 and the first half of 1931, Hoover raised the federal public works budget to $423 million, a dramatic increase in an area not traditionally seen as the federal government's responsibility. Hoover also eased the international crisis by bringing about, early in the summer of 1931, a moratorium on the payment of Allied debts and reparations. The federal government's efforts to stimulate business activity were moderately effective, but the depression continued.

By 1931 more drastic action was required. However, Hoover faced a cruel dilemma that had been created by the Federal Reserve's contraction of the money supply. If he embraced deficit financing and encouraged recovery through increased government spending, interest rates would remain high, since the federal government would be competing for capital with corporations and private investors. Hoover decided that significantly higher interest rates posed the greater danger to recovery, so in December 1931 he asked Congress for a 33 percent tax increase to balance the budget. The Revenue Act of 1932 represented the largest peacetime tax increase in the nation's history. Like monetary restriction, higher taxes choked both consumption and investment, and contributed significantly to the severity of the Great Depression.

Not all the steps taken by the Hoover administration were so ill-conceived. The president pushed Congress to create a system of government home loan banks in 1932. He also supported the Glass-Steagall Banking Act of 1932, which made government securities available to guarantee Federal Reserve notes and thereby counter credit contractions from gold withdrawals. This step temporarily propped up the ailing banking system. The federal government under Hoover spent $700 million—an unprecedented sum for the time—on public works.

However, Hoover remained adamant in his refusal to consider any plan for direct federal relief for unemployed Americans. Throughout his career, he had believed that private organized charities were sufficient to meet social welfare needs. During World War I, Hoover had headed the Commission for Relief of Belgium, a private group that distributed 5 million tons of food to relieve the suffering of Europe's civilian population. In 1927 he coordinated a rescue and cleanup operation after a devastating Mississippi River flood left 16.5 million acres of land under water in seven states. This ef-fort involved private charities, including the Red Cross and the Rockefeller Foundation, as well as such government agencies as the U.S. Public Health Service and the National Guard. The success of these and other predominantly voluntary responses to public emergencies confirmed Hoover's belief that private charity, not federal aid, was the "American way." But charities and state and local relief agencies were unable to meet the growing needs of the unemployed.

The Reconstruction Finance Corporation. The centerpiece of Hoover's new initiative to combat the depression was the Reconstruction Finance Corporation (RFC), which Congress approved in January 1932. Modeled on the War Finance Corporation of World War I, and developed in collaboration with the business and banking communities, the RFC was the first federal institution that intervened directly in the economy during peacetime. It was designed to alleviate the credit crunch for business by providing federal loans to railroads, financial institutions, banks, and insurance companies, in a strategy that has been called *pump priming.* Money loaned at the top of the economic structure stimulates production, which in turn creates new jobs and increases consumer spending. Benefits thus "trickle down" to the rest of the economy.

Congress allocated $500 million for the RFC, but the agency's cautiousness in lending money limited its influence. In July 1932 Congress doubled this amount and authorized loans to the states for relief and public works. Once again the RFC acted far too cautiously, lending only $30 million by the end of 1932. It allocated and spent only 20 percent of the $1.5 billion appropriated for public works projects.

The Reconstruction Finance Corporation was a watershed in American political history and the rise of the state. When voluntary cooperation failed, the president turned to federal action to stimulate the economy. Yet Hoover's break with the past had clear limits. In many ways his support of the RFC was just another attempt to encourage business confidence. Compared with previous presidents, Hoover responded to the national emergency on an unprecedented scale. But the nation's needs during the Great Depression were also unprecedented, and federal programs failed to meet them.

Rising Discontent

As the depression deepened, many citizens came to hate Herbert Hoover. Once the symbol of business prosperity, Hoover became the scapegoat for the depression. His declarations that nobody was starving and that hoboes were better fed than ever before seemed cruel and insensitive. His apparent willingness to bail out business and banks while leaving individuals to fend

Hoovervilles
By 1930 shantytowns had sprung up in most of the nation's cities. In New York City, squatters camped out along the Hudson River railroad tracks, built makeshift homes in Central Park, or lived in the city dump. The two men in suits and hats are likely city inspectors or welfare officials.

for themselves added to his reputation for cold-heartedness. New terms entered the vocabulary: "Hoovervilles" (shanty towns where people lived in packing crates and other makeshift shelters), "Hoover flags" (empty pockets turned inside out), and "Hoover blankets" (newspapers). Columnist Russell Baker remembered his aunt's exaggerated recital of Hoover's faults:

> People were starving because of Herbert Hoover. My mother was out of work because of Herbert Hoover. Men were killing themselves because of Herbert Hoover, and their fatherless children were being packed away to orphanages . . . because of Herbert Hoover.

Signs of rising discontent and rebellion began to emerge as the country entered the fourth year of the depression. Farmers were among the most vocal groups, banding together to harass bank agents and government officers sent to enforce evictions and farm foreclosures, and protesting the low prices they received for their crops. Midwestern farmers had watched the price of wheat fall from three dollars a bushel in 1920 to barely thirty cents in 1932. Now they formed the Farm Holiday Association under the charismatic leadership of Milo Reno, the sixty-four-year-old former president of the Iowa Farmers' Union. Farmers barricaded local roads and dumped milk, vegetables, and other farm produce because the prices they would fetch on the market would not cover costs. Nothing better captured the cruel irony of underconsumption and maldistribution than farmers dumping food at a time when thousands of people were hungry.

The Bonus Army
During this July 1932 rally on the Capitol grounds, Brigadier General Pelham D. Glassford, superintendent of the Washington, D.C., police, has just asked the assembled veterans whether they were 100 percent Americans. The raised hands provide the overwhelming answer.

AMERICAN VOICES

The Despair of the Unemployed

In 1931 an unemployed tool and die designer wrote to the director of the President's Organization for Unemployment Relief (POUR), but his letter drew only this penciled response: "no use answering."

Detroit, Mich.
September 29, 1931

Mr. Walter Gifford
Dear Sir:

You and Pres. Hoover shows at times about the same degree of intelligence as Andy [of the "Amos & Andy" radio show] does. The other night Andy was going to send a fellow a letter to find out his address.

You have told us to spend to end the slump, but you did not tell us what to use for money, after being out of work for two years you tell us this, Pres. Hoover on the other hand tells the working man to build homes, and in face of the fact nearly every working man has had his home taken off him, "some more intelligence." This is a radical letter but the time is here to be radical. when an average of two a day has to take their own life right in the City of Detroit because they can not see their way out. right in the city where one of the worlds riches men lives who made last year 259 000 000 dollars. where hundreds of peoples are starving to death . . . Mr. Gifford why not come clean. and stop bluffing us tell us the truth. remember you have the all seeing eye of God over you. Tell us the reason of the depression is the greed of Bankers and Industrialist who are taking too great of amount of profits . . . . The other day our Pres. Hoover came to Detroit and kidded the soldier boys out of their bonus. Pres Hoover a millionaire worth about 12 000 000 dollars drawing a salary of 75 000 per year from the government asking some boys to forgo their bonus some of them have not 12 dollars of their own "Some more nerve."

Am I right when I say you and he shows the same degree of intelligence as Andy.

J. B.

Source: Quoted in Robert S. McElvaine, *Down & Out in the Great Depression* (Chapel Hill: University of North Carolina Press, 1983), 46–47.

Protest was not confined to rural America. Bitter labor strikes occurred in the depths of the depression, despite the threat that strikers could lose their jobs. In Harlan County, Kentucky, miners struck in 1931 over a 10 percent wage cut, only to see their union crushed by the mine owners and the national guard. At the Ford River Rouge factory outside Detroit in 1932, a demonstration provoked violence from police and Ford security forces, with the result that three demonstrators were killed and fifty seriously injured. Some 40,000 people viewed the coffins under a banner that charged "Ford Gave Bullets for Bread."

In 1931 and 1932, violence broke out in the nation's cities. Groups of unemployed citizens battled local authorities over inadequate relief; people staged rent riots and hunger marches. Fearing the consequences of trying to stop this civil disorder, Mayor Anton J. Cermak of Chicago challenged a congressional committee to send relief or troops.

Many of these urban actions were organized by the Communist party as a challenge to the American capitalist system. For example, the Communist party helped to organize "unemployment councils" that agitated for jobs and food. Communists coordinated a hunger march on Washington, D.C., in 1931. The marches were well attended, and often got results from local and federal authorities, but they did not necessarily win converts to communism. In the early 1930s, the Communist party was still a tiny organization, with only 12,000 members.

It was not radicals, but veterans who staged the most publicized—and tragic—protest. In the summer of 1932 the "Bonus Army," a ragtag group of about fifteen thousand unemployed World War I veterans, hitchhiked to Washington to demand that their bonuses, originally scheduled for distribution in 1945, be paid immediately. While they unsuccessfully lobbied Congress, members of the "Bonus Expeditionary Force" (parodying the wartime American Expeditionary Force) camped out in the capital, a visible reminder of the plight of the unemployed. "We were heroes in 1917, but we're bums now," one veteran remarked bitterly. When the marchers refused to leave their Anacostia Flats camp, Hoover called out riot troops led by General Douglas MacArthur, assisted by Majors Dwight D. Eisenhower and George S. Patton, to clear the area. MacArthur's forces burned the encampment to the ground, and in the fight that followed, more than a hundred bonus marchers were injured. Newsreel footage captured the deeply disturbing spectacle of the U.S. Army firing on U.S. citizens, and Hoover's popularity plunged even further.

The 1932 Election

Despite evidence of discontent the nation was not in a revolutionary mood as it approached the 1932 election. Despair and apathy, more than anger, characterized the feelings of most citizens. The Republicans, who could find no credible way of dumping an incumbent president, unenthusiastically renominated Herbert Hoover. The Democrats turned to Governor Franklin Delano Roosevelt of New York, who capitalized on that state's innovative record of relief and unemployment programs to win the nomination.

Roosevelt's route to the presidential nomination began on a Hudson River estate north of New York City. Born into a wealthy family in 1882, he attended the Groton School, Harvard, and Columbia Law

School. Roosevelt gave up his law career in 1910 for a seat in the New York legislature. He served as assistant secretary of the navy in the Wilson administration, which earned him the vice-presidential nomination on the losing Democratic ticket in 1920. Except for his allegiance to Democratic rather than Republican party ideology, he consciously modeled his career on that of his distant cousin Theodore Roosevelt, whose niece Eleanor he married in 1905.

Franklin Roosevelt was sidetracked in his path to the White House in 1921 by an attack of polio, which left him paralyzed in both legs for the rest of his life. Roosevelt fought back from his infirmity, emerging from the ordeal a stronger man. "If you had spent two years in bed trying to wiggle your toe, after that anything would seem easy," he said. Eleanor Roosevelt strongly supported her husband's return to public life, serving as his stand-in during the 1920s. She and Louis Howe, Roosevelt's devoted political aide, masterminded his reentry into Democratic politics. Roosevelt won the New York governorship in 1928 and the Democratic presidential nomination in 1932.

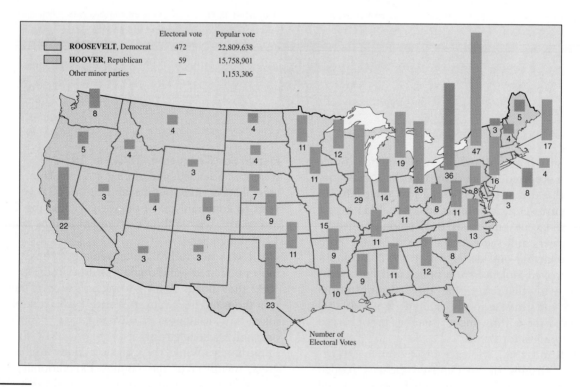

MAP 25.3

The Election of 1932.
Franklin Roosevelt's convincing electoral victory over Herbert Hoover in 1932 resulted from realignments in the Democratic party and dissatisfaction with the incumbent president. Even in the midst of the gravest crisis capitalism had ever faced, candidates of the Communist and Socialist parties received fewer than a million votes out of almost 40 million cast.

The 1932 campaign foreshadowed little of the New Deal. Roosevelt hinted at new approaches to the depression but stated his goals in vague terms. "The country needs and, unless I mistake its temper, the country demands bold, persistent experimentation," he said. Roosevelt won easily, receiving 22.8 million votes to Hoover's 15.7 million. Despite the economic collapse, Americans remained firmly committed to the two-party system. The Socialist party candidate, Norman Thomas, got fewer than a million votes. The Communist party drew only 100,000 votes for its candidate, party leader William Z. Foster.

The 1932 election marked a turning point in American politics: the emergence of a Democratic coalition that would dominate political life for the next four decades. In 1932 Roosevelt won with the support of the Solid South, which returned to the Democratic fold after defecting in 1928 because of Al Smith's religion and views on Prohibition. Roosevelt also drew substantial support in the West. An increasingly large urban vote continued the trend first noticed in the 1928 election, when the Democrats successfully appealed to recent immigrants and ethnic groups in the nation's cities. However, Roosevelt's election was hardly a mandate to reshape American political and economic institutions. Many people voted as much against Hoover as for Roosevelt.

The Interregnum. Having spoken, the voters had to wait until March 1933 before Roosevelt could put his ideas into action. (The interval between election and inauguration was shortened to the present January 20 by the Twentieth Amendment in 1933.) In the worst winter of the depression, Americans could do little but hope things would get better. According to the most conservative estimates, unemployment stood at 20 to 25 percent. The percentage was as high as 50 percent in Cleveland, 60 percent in Akron, and 80 percent in Toledo, all cities dependent on manufacturing jobs in industries that had basically shut down. The nation's banking system was so close to collapse that many state governors temporarily closed banks to avoid further panic.

By the winter of 1932–1933, the depression had totally overwhelmed public welfare institutions. Private charity and local public relief, whose expenditures had risen dramatically over earlier levels, still reached only a fraction of the needy. Hunger haunted cities and rural areas alike. When a teacher tried to send a coal miner's daughter home from school because she was weak from hunger, the girl replied, "It won't do any good . . . because this is sister's day to eat." In New York City, hospitals reported ninety-five deaths from starvation. This was the America that Roosevelt inherited when he took the oath of office on March 4, 1933.

★

Summary

The economic prosperity of the 1920s rested on shaky ground. After the stock market crash of 1929, the economy entered a downward spiral that did not bottom out until 1932–1933. In addition to the collapse of the stock market, the main causes of the depression were underconsumption, an unstable international situation, a legacy of "sick industries" and agricultural distress from the 1920s, and the flawed monetary policies of the Federal Reserve System. The Hoover administration authorized the first direct federal intervention in the economy during peacetime, the Reconstruction Finance Corporation, in an attempt to win business and public confidence. However, such measures did not end the Great Depression, and in 1932 the nation turned to Franklin D. Roosevelt and the Democrats.

The Great Depression left an "invisible scar" on many people who lived through the 1930s, especially on white middle-class Americans. Those who wanted to work blamed themselves if they could not find a job. The impact of the depression was less catastrophic for African-Americans and other minorities, for whom times had always been hard. But for farmers in the Midwest, things got even worse than they'd been in the 1920s. Drought and misguided agricultural practices created the Dust Bowl, forcing many farmers off their land.

Despite the devastating impact of the depression, many aspects of American life and culture continued to conform to traditional patterns. Families pulled together, with women taking on expanded roles—and often new jobs—to help support their households. Young people stayed in school longer. Families sought relief in popular culture, especially movies and radio programs. Only as the economy shifted towards war mobilization in the late 1930s did the depression finally ease.

TOPIC FOR RESEARCH

Remembering the Great Depression

One historian who studied the oral histories collected in the 1930s expressed surprise at how rarely people actually mentioned the Great Depression by name. "The Depression was not the singular event it appears in retrospect," she concluded. "It was one more hardship." On the other hand, the depression loomed larger in oral histories collected well after the event. As the years went by between hard times and the present, people's recollections of the depression's impact grew.

Test that hypothesis by comparing oral histories collected during the 1930s and those done later. Does the Great Depression take on an independent and different meaning as time goes by? How aware were people in the 1930s that they were living through "the Great Depression"? What does this tell us about the role historical memory plays in shaping our relation to the past? For an excellent introduction to Works Progress Administration (WPA) oral histories collected in the 1930s, see Ann Banks, ed., *First-Person America* (1980). Also of interest are the Federal Writers' Project, *These Are Our Lives* (1939), and Tom Terrill and Jerrold Hirsch, eds., *Such As Us: Southern Voices of the Thirties* (1978). The interviews Studs Terkel collected for *Hard Times: An Oral History of the Great Depression* (1970) provide an interesting counterpoint. See also Jeane Westin, *Making Do: How Women Survived the '30s* (1976). David Lowenthal's *The Past is a Foreign Country* (1985) discusses how the present influences our views of, and memories of, the past.

BIBLIOGRAPHY

Two useful overviews to begin the study of the Great Depression are John A. Garraty, *The Great Depression* (1987), and Robert S. McElvaine, *The Great Depression, 1929–1941* (1984).

The Coming of the Great Depression

Historians and economists continue to debate the causes of the Great Depression. See John Kenneth Galbraith, *The Great Crash* (1954); Milton Friedman and Anna Schwartz, *The Great Contraction, 1929–1933* (1965); Peter Temin, *Did Monetary Forces Cause the Great Depression?* (1976); and Michael Bernstein, *The Great Depression: Delayed Recovery and Economic Change in America, 1929–1939* (1988). For general overviews of economic developments, see Charles Kindelberger, *The World in Depression* (1974), and Jim Potter, *The American Economy Between the Wars* (1974). Irving Bernstein, *The Lean Years* (1960), offers a compelling portrait of hard times during the Hoover years.

Hard Times

A wealth of material brings the voices of the 1930s to life. The Federal Writers' Project, *These Are Our Lives* (1939); Tom Terrill and Jerrold Hirsch, eds., *Such As Us: Southern Voices of the Thirties* (1978); and Ann Banks, ed., *First-Person America* (1980), all draw on oral histories collected by the Works Progress Administration during the 1930s. See also Richard Lowitt and Maurine Beasley, eds., *One-Third of a Nation: Lorena Hickock Reports the Great Depression* (1981), and Robert S. McElvaine, ed., *Down & Out in the Great Depression* (1983), for first-hand accounts. Evocative secondary sources are Studs Terkel, *Hard Times: An Oral History of the Great Depression* (1970), and Caroline Bird, *The Invisible Scar* (1966).

Descriptions of family life in the 1930s include Robert and Helen Lynd, *Middletown in Transition* (1937); Mirra Komarovsky, *The Unemployed Man and His Family* (1940); and Roger Angell, *The Family Encounters the Depression* (1936). Russell Baker's autobiography, *Growing Up* (1982), provides an often humorous description of family life in the 1930s. Glen H. Elder, Jr., *Children of the Great Depression* (1974), looks at the long-term effects. For more on youth, see Maxine Davis, *The Lost Generation* (1936); Eileen Eagan, *Class, Culture, and the Classroom* (1981); Beth L. Bailey, *From Front Porch to Back Seat* (1988); and John Modell, *Into One's Own: From Youth to Adulthood, 1920–1975* (1989). Frederick Lewis Allen, *Since Yesterday* (1939), provides an impressionistic overview of the popular culture of the 1930s. Specific studies of movies and Hollywood include Robert Sklar, *Movie-Made America* (1975); Andrew Bergman, *We're in the Money* (1971); Molly Haskell, *From Reverence To Rape: The Treatment of Women in the Movies* (1974); Thomas Schatz, *The Genius of the System: Hollywood Film Making in the Studio Era* (1988); and Ed Sikov, *Screwball: Hollywood's Madcap Romantic Comedies* (1989).

Material on women in the 1930s is found in Susan Ware, *Holding Their Own* (1982); Winifred Wandersee, *Women's Work and Family Values, 1920–1940* (1981); Lois Scharf, *To Work and to Wed* (1981); and Alice Kessler-Harris, *Out to Work* (1982). For the special dimensions of white rural women's lives, see Margaret Hagood, *Mothers of the South* (1939). Jeane Westin, *Making Do: How Women Survived the '30s* (1976), is a lively account drawn from interviews. The birth control movement is surveyed in Linda Gordon, *Woman's Body, Woman's Right* (1976); James Reed, *From Private Vice to Public Virtue* (1978); and Estelle Freedman and John D'Emilio, *Intimate Matters: A History of Sexuality in America* (1988). See also *Margaret Sanger: An Autobiography* (1938).

The Social Fabric of Depression America

Developments in the black community during the 1930s are covered in Gilbert Osofsky, *Harlem: The Making of a Ghetto* (1966); Gunnar Myrdal, *An American Dilemma* (1944); David Lewis, *When Harlem Was in Vogue* (1981); Jervis Anderson, *This Was Harlem, 1900–1950* (1982); and Robert Weisbrot, *Father Divine and the Struggle for Racial Equality*

(1983). Dan T. Carter, *Scottsboro* (1969), remains the classic description of the case. Donald Grubbs, *Cry From Cotton* (1971), tells the story of the Southern Tenant Farmers Union. Robin D. G. Kelley, *Hammer and Hoe* (1990), is an excellent account of Alabama communists during the Great Depression.

For material on rural electrification, see D. Clayton Brown, *Electricity for Rural America* (1980), and Marquis Childs, *The Farmer Takes a Hand* (1952). The first volume of Robert Caro's biography of Lyndon Johnson, *The Path To Power* (1982), contains a moving portrait of the harshness of farm life before electricity.

Donald Worster, *Dust Bowl* (1979), evokes the plains during the "dirty thirties," as does Ann Marie Low's memoir, *Dust Bowl Diary* (1984). James N. Gregory, *American Exodus: The Dust Bowl Migration and Okie Culture in California* (1989), treats the experiences of the migrants in, and their impact on, California culture and the economy.

The experiences of Mexican-Americans during the 1930s are treated in Rodolfo Acuna, *Occupied America* (1981); Wayne Cornelius, *Building the Cactus Curtain* (1980); Mark Reisler, *By the Sweat of Their Brow* (1976); Abraham Hoffman, *Unwanted Mexican-Americans in the Great Depression: Repatriation Pressures, 1929–1939* (1974); and Francisco Balerman, *In Defense of La Raza: The Los Angeles Mexican Consulate and the Mexican Community, 1929–1936* (1982). For Mexican-American women's lives, see Vicki Ruiz, *Cannery Women, Cannery Lives: Mexican Women, Unionization, and the California Food Processing Industry, 1930–1950* (1987), and Patricia Zavella, *Women's Work and Chicano Families* (1987).

Herbert Hoover and the Great Depression

Hoover's response to the depression is chronicled in Alfred Romasco, *The Poverty of Abundance* (1965), and Jordan Schwartz, *The Interregnum of Despair* (1970). See also David Burner, *Herbert Hoover* (1978); Joan Hoff Wilson, *Herbert Hoover: Forgotten Progressive* (1975); and William Barber, *Herbert Hoover, the Economists, and American Economic Policy, 1921–1933* (1986). Eliot Rosen, *Hoover, Roosevelt, and the Brain Trust* (1977), treats the transition between the two administrations, as does Frank Freidel, *Launching the New Deal* (1973). For the 1932 election and the beginnings of the New Deal coalition, see David Burner, *The Politics of Provincialism* (1967); Samuel Lubell, *The Future of American Politics* (1952); and John Allswang, *The New Deal in American Politics* (1978).

TIMELINE

1929	Stock Market Crash
1930	Drought begins Hawley-Smoot Tariff
1931	Scottsboro case
1932	Reconstruction Finance Corporation Bonus Army
1933	Franklin Delano Roosevelt becomes President Birthrate drops to lowest level
1934	Southern Tenant Farmers Union *It Happened One Night* sweeps Oscars
1935	Rural Electrification Administration Harlem race riot
1936	Margaret Mitchell's *Gone with the Wind* Birth control legalized
1937	Amelia Earhart disappears
1939	John Steinbeck's *The Grapes of Wrath*

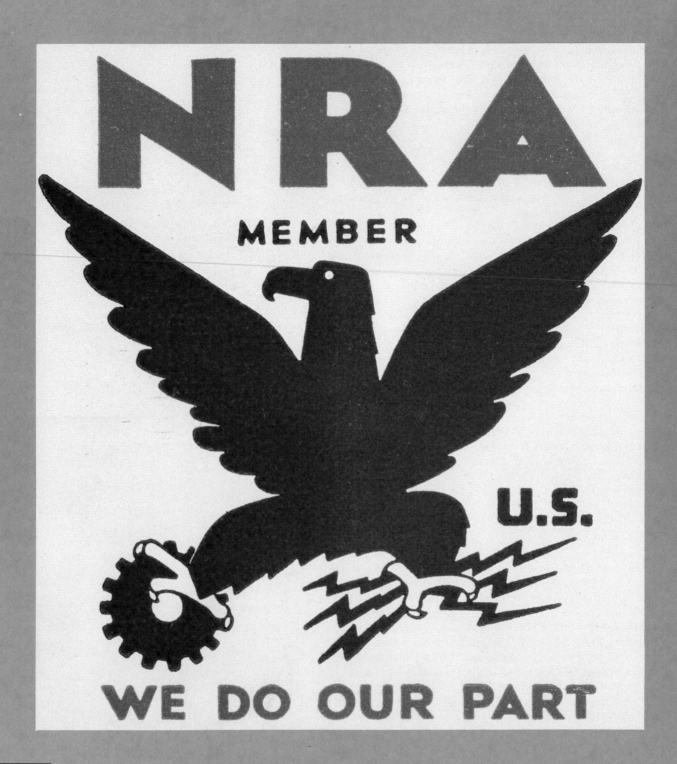

NRA Poster

Displaying the Blue Eagle and the slogan "We Do
Our Part" symbolized compliance with the National
Recovery Administration, one of the early programs
of the New Deal.

26 *The New Deal,*
1933–1939

In his bold inaugural address on March 4, 1933, President Franklin Delano Roosevelt declared, "The only thing we have to fear is fear itself." This memorable phrase rallied a nation that had already endured almost four years of the gravest economic contraction in its history, with no end in sight.

With his demeanor grim and purposeful, Franklin Roosevelt preached his first inaugural address like a sermon. He spoke of the economic and social problems the nation faced and their possible solutions only in the most general terms. Promising "a leadership of frankness and vigor," Roosevelt issued ringing declarations of his vision of governmental activism: "This Nation asks for action, and action now." Roosevelt repeatedly employed the analogy of fighting a war to combating the depression. The most explicit parallel was his willingness to ask Congress for "broad Executive power to wage a war against the emergency, as great as the power that would be given to me if we were in fact invaded by a foreign foe." Such a conception of presidential leadership was well suited to Roosevelt's self-confident personality and pragmatic political style.

In the end, however, Roosevelt intended not to scare the American people but to reassure them. The democratic system was basically sound, he told them, and hard times could be overcome, but only if a dispirited nation chose not to wallow in lethargy. On that cold March day in 1933, Roosevelt urged his fellow citizens to return to the values of hard work, cooperation, and sacrifice that had made the country great in the past. Roosevelt's restoration of hope and confidence was perhaps his greatest contribution to American life during the Great Depression of the 1930s.

The New Deal Takes Over, 1933–1935

When Franklin Roosevelt first used the term *New Deal* in his acceptance speech at the Democratic National Convention of 1932, he hardly realized that he had named his era. Plucked from deep in the speech by the newspaper cartoonist Rollin Kirby, the term came to stand for the Roosevelt administration's response to the depression. The federal government dominated political and economic life so thoroughly during the 1930s that the term *New Deal* is often used as a synonym for the decade itself.

The Roosevelt Style of Leadership

Every president since the 1930s has lived in the shadow of FDR. Few of his successors have matched his raw political talent; none had to face and surmount the twin crises of depression and war. "I have no expectation of making a hit every time I come to bat," he disarmingly told critics. "What I seek is the highest possible batting average." Roosevelt parlayed this experimental tone into a highly effective political and governmental style.

The New Deal represented many things to many people, but one unifying factor was the personality of its master architect, Franklin Roosevelt. The New Deal was "a very personal enterprise." Roosevelt, a superb and pragmatic politician, crafted his administration's program in response to shifting political and economic conditions, rather than by following a set ideology or plan. He experimented with one idea, and if it did not

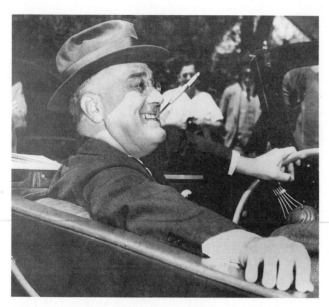

FDR
President Franklin Delano Roosevelt was a consummate politician who loved the adulation of a crowd. He consciously
adopted a cheerful mien to keep people from feeling sorry for
him because of his infirmity, knowing he could not be a
successful politician if the public pitied him.

work, he tried another. Roosevelt juggled advice in the
same way. Senator Huey Long of Louisiana complained, "When I talk to him, he says 'Fine! Fine! Fine!'
But Joe Robinson [the Senate majority leader] goes to
see him the next day and again he says 'Fine! Fine!
Fine!' Maybe he says 'Fine!' to everybody."

President Roosevelt established an unusually close
rapport with the American people. "Mr. Roosevelt is
the only man we ever had in the White House who
would understand that my boss is a son of a bitch," remarked one worker. Many ordinary citizens credited
him with the positive changes in their lives, saying "He
gave me a job" or "He saved my home." Roosevelt's
masterful use of the new medium of radio, typified by
the sixteen "fireside chats" he broadcast during his first
two terms, fostered this personal identification. More
than 450,000 letters poured into the White House in
the week after the inauguration, and an average of
5,000 to 8,000 arrived weekly for the rest of the decade.
One person had handled public correspondence during
the Hoover administration, but it took a staff of fifty
under Roosevelt. Understanding the importance of
communicating with the public, Roosevelt became the
first president to engage a press secretary.

Franklin Roosevelt continued the expansion of
presidential power that dated to the administrations of
Theodore Roosevelt and Woodrow Wilson. From the
beginning, Roosevelt centralized decision making in the
White House and dramatically expanded the role of the
executive branch in initiating policy. For policy formulation, he turned to his talented cabinet, which included

Interior Secretary Harold Ickes, Frances Perkins at
Labor, Henry A. Wallace at Agriculture, and old friend
Henry Morgenthau, Jr., who served as secretary of the
Treasury. During the interregnum, he relied so heavily
on the advice of Columbia University professors Ray-
mond Moley, Rexford Tugwell, and Adolph A. Berle,
Jr., that the press dubbed them the "Brains Trust."

When searching for new ideas and fresh faces, Roosevelt was just as likely to turn to advisers and administrators scattered throughout the New Deal bureaucracy.
Eager young people flocked to Washington to join the
New Deal—"men with long hair and women with short
hair," wags quipped. Lawyers in their mid-20s fresh out
of Harvard found themselves drafting legislation or
being called to the White House for strategy sessions
with the president. Paul Freund, a Harvard Law School
professor who worked in the Reconstruction Finance
Corporation and the Department of Justice, remembered, "It was a glorious time for obscure people."
Many young New Dealers, who went on to distinguished careers in government or public service, later
recalled that nothing matched the excitement of the
early New Deal.

The Hundred Days

The first problem that the new president confronted
was the banking crisis. Since the stock market crash,
about 9 million people had lost their savings, a total of
$2.5 billion. On the eve of his inauguration, thirty-eight
states had closed their banks, and banks operated on a
restricted basis in the rest. This collapse, far more than
the stock market crash, brought the depression home to
the middle class. Senator "Cotton Ed" Smith of South
Carolina began carrying his cash in a money belt on the
Senate floor rather than entrust it to a bank.

On March 5, the day after the inauguration, the
president declared a national "bank holiday," a eu-
phemism for closing all the banks and hurriedly called
Congress into special session. On March 9, Congress
passed Roosevelt's proposed banking bill, which permitted banks to reopen beginning on March 13, but
only if a Treasury Department inspection showed they
had sufficient cash reserves to operate on a sound basis.
The House approved the plan after only thirty-eight
minutes of debate.

Emergency Banking Act. The Emergency Banking Act,
developed in consultation with banking leaders, was a
conservative document. Herbert Hoover could have
proposed it. The difference was the public's reaction.
On the Sunday evening before the banks reopened,
Roosevelt made his first "fireside chat" to a radio audience estimated at 60 million. In simple terms, he reassured the people that the banks were now safe—and
they believed him. When the banks reopened on Monday morning, deposits exceeded withdrawals. "Capital-

ism was saved in eight days," observed Raymond Moley, who had served as Roosevelt's speechwriter in the 1932 campaign. The banking bill did its job: more than four thousand banks failed in 1933, but only sixty-one closed their doors in 1934.

The Banking Act was the first of fifteen pieces of major legislation enacted by Congress during the opening months of the Roosevelt administration. This legislative session, which came to be called the "Hundred Days," remains one of the most productive ever. Congress created the Home Owners Loan Corporation to refinance home mortgages threatened by foreclosure, and 20 percent of the nation's homeowners took advantage of it. A second banking law, the Glass-Steagall Act, curbed speculation by separating investment from commercial banking, and created the Federal Deposit Insurance Corporation (FDIC) which insured bank deposits up to $2,500. The Civilian Conservation Corps (CCC) sent 250,000 young men to live in camps where they performed reforestation and conservation work. The Tennessee Valley Authority (TVA) received legislative approval for its imaginative plan of government-sponsored regional development and public power. The price of electricity in the seven-state Tennessee Valley area soon dropped from ten cents a kilowatt hour to three cents. And in a move that lifted public spirits immeasurably, Roosevelt legalized beer in April. Full repeal of prohibition came eight months later, in December 1933.

The Agricultural Adjustment Act. The Roosevelt administration targeted three pressing problems: curbing agricultural overproduction, stimulating business recovery, and providing for the unemployed. Roosevelt considered a farm bill "the key to recovery." The Agricultural Adjustment Act (AAA) was developed by Secretary of Agriculture Henry A. Wallace, Assistant

The CCC

The Civilian Conservation Corps (CCC) was one of the most popular New Deal programs. Over ten years, it enrolled 2.75 million young Americans who worked for a dollar a day on such projects as soil conservation, disaster relief, reforestation, and flood control. The CCC was limited to men only, although a few camps benefited out-of-work young women.

Secretary Rexford Tugwell, and agricultural economist M. L. Wilson, in close collaboration with leaders of major farm organizations. A domestic allotment system for seven major commodities (wheat, cotton, corn, hogs, rice, tobacco, and dairy products) gave cash subsidies to farmers in return for cutting production; these benefits were financed by a tax on processing (such as, milling of wheat), which was passed on to consumers. New Deal planners hoped prices would rise in response to the federally subsidized scarcity, and thus spur more general recovery.

The AAA stabilized the farm situation, but its benefits were distributed unevenly. The subsidies for reducing production went primarily to large and medium-sized farm owners, who in turn cut production by often reducing the acreage of their renters and sharecroppers but continued to farm their own land. In the South this strategy had a racial component, because many sharecroppers were black and the land owners and government administrators were white. As many as two hundred thousand black tenant farmers were displaced from their land by the AAA. Thus New Deal agricultural policies fostered the migration of marginal farmers in the South and Midwest to Northern cities and California and consolidated the economic and political clout of larger landholders.

TABLE 26.1

American Banks and Bank Failures, 1920–1940

Year	Total Number of Banks	Total Assets	Bank Failures
1920	30,909	$53.1 billion	168
1929	25,568	72.3	659
1931	22,242	70.1	2,294
1933	14,771	51.4	4,004
1934	15,913	55.9	61
1940	15,076	79.7	48

Source: Historical Statistics of the United States: Colonial Times to 1970, (Washington, D.C.: U.S. Government Printing Office, 1975), pp. 1019, 1038–1039.

NRA. The New Deal attacked the problem of economic recovery with the National Industrial Recovery Act, which created the National Recovery Administration (NRA). This agency drew on the World War I experience of Bernard Baruch's War Industries Board and extended the reliance on trade associations of the Coolidge and Hoover administrations. The NRA set up a system of industrial self-government to handle the problems of overproduction, cutthroat competition, and price instability. To achieve its objectives, the NRA established codes of fair competition, tailored to prevent the specific practices within each industry that had forced prices downward. In effect, these legally enforceable agreements suspended the antitrust laws. Each code also contained provisions covering working conditions. For example, the codes established minimum wages and maximum hours and outlawed child labor completely. One of the most far-reaching provisions, Section 7(a), guaranteed workers the right to organize and bargain collectively "through representatives of their own choosing," which dramatically spurred the growth of the labor movement.

General Hugh Johnson, a colorful if somewhat erratic administrator, headed the NRA. He oversaw negotiations for more than six hundred NRA codes, ranging from large industries such as coal, cotton, and steel, to dog food, costume jewelry, and even burlesque theaters. The code process theoretically included equal input from management, labor, and consumers, but business trade associations basically set the terms. Because large companies dominated the trade associations, the code-drafting process further solidified the power of large businesses at the expense of smaller enterprises. Labor had little input, consumer interests almost none. An extensive public relations campaign, complete with plugs in Hollywood films such as *Gold Diggers of 1933* and stickers with the NRA slogan, "We Do Our Part," attempted to sell this program to skeptical consumers and businesspeople.

Unemployment. The early New Deal also addressed the critical problem of unemployment. The total exhaustion of private and local sources of charity made some form of federal relief essential in this fourth year of the depression. Roosevelt moved reluctantly toward federal responsibility for the unemployed. The Federal Emergency Relief Administration (FERA), set up in May 1933 under the direction of Harry Hopkins, a New York social worker, offered federal money to the states for relief programs. It was designed to keep people from starving until other recovery measures had a chance to take hold. Hopkins distributed $5 million in his first two hours in office. When told that some of the projects he had just authorized might not be sound in the long run, Hopkins replied, "People don't eat in the long run—they eat every day." During its two-year existence, the FERA spent $1 billion.

Roosevelt always maintained a strong distaste for the dole. Wherever possible, his administration promoted work relief, no matter how makeshift, over cash subsidies; it also consistently favored relief jobs that did not directly compete with the private sector. The Public Works Administration (PWA), under Secretary of the Interior Harold L. Ickes, received a $3.3 billion appropriation in 1933 for a major public works program. However, Ickes's cautiousness in starting up projects limited the PWA's effectiveness in spurring recovery or providing jobs. In November 1933, Roosevelt assigned $400 million in PWA funds to a new agency, the Civil Works Administration (CWA), headed by Harry Hopkins. Within thirty days, the CWA put 2.6 million men and women to work; at its peak in January 1934, it employed 4 million. CWA workers received fifteen dollars a week for jobs such as repairing bridges, building highways, constructing public buildings, and setting up community projects. The CWA, regarded as a stopgap measure to get the country through the winter of 1933–1934, lapsed the next spring after spending all its funds.

Many of the emergency measures of the first hundred days were deliberately inflationary—that is, they were designed to trigger price rises thought necessary to stimulate recovery and halt the steep deflation. Another element of this strategy was Roosevelt's April 18 executive order to abandon the gold standard and let gold rise in value, just like any other commodity. As the price of gold rose, so too would agricultural prices, a key to general recovery. Budget director Lew Douglas warned that abandoning the gold standard would lead to "the end of Western civilization." That did not happen, but neither did it have much impact on the domestic economy. Its main significance lay in the adoption of a flexible currency system in which the value of the dollar could be manipulated by the Federal Reserve system according to economic conditions, rather than tied to a fixed standard. This action represented an important shift in control over the economy to the public sector.

When an exhausted Congress recessed in June 1933, much had been accomplished. Rarely had a president so dominated a legislative session. A mass of "alphabet agencies," as the New Deal programs came to be known, flowed from Washington. They gave the impression of action, but despite a slight economic upturn, they had not turned the economy around.

Nevertheless, Americans saw a ray of hope. In April 1933, at the height of the excitement over the Hundred Days, Walt Disney released a cartoon film called *Three Little Pigs*. Echoing FDR's assertion that they had nothing to fear but fear itself, many people hummed the cartoon's theme song, "Who's Afraid of the Big Bad Wolf?" as they started down the road toward renewed confidence.

Consolidating the Hundred Days

If the measures taken during Franklin Roosevelt's first hundred days had cured the Great Depression, the rest of the New Deal probably would not have occurred. When the Depression stubbornly persisted, FDR and Congress turned to more far-reaching structural reform rather than the emergency recovery measures of 1933.

Reforming Wall Street. One obvious target for reform was Wall Street, where insider trading, fraud, and other abuses had contributed to the 1929 crash. In 1934 Congress established the Securities and Exchange Commission (SEC) to regulate the stock market. The commission had the power to regulate buying stocks on credit, or margin buying, and to restrict speculation by those with inside information on corporate plans. The Public Utilities Holding Company Act of 1935 limited the widespread practice of pyramiding holding companies on top of utilities for the sole purpose of issuing stock and inflating profits.

The banking system came under scrutiny as well. The Banking Act of 1935 represented a significant consolidation of federal control over the nation's banks. The law authorized the president to appoint a new Board of Governors of the Federal Reserve System. This reorganization placed control of interest rates and other money market policies squarely at the federal level

rather than with regional banks. By requiring all large state banks to join the Federal Reserve System by 1942 in order to use the federal deposit insurance system, the law further encouraged the centralization of the nation's banking system.

Roosevelt was not hostile toward business. He heartily accepted the capitalist system but realized that modern industrial life required more explicit federal control to limit some of capitalism's excesses. "To preserve we had to reform," Roosevelt commented succinctly. Even though he styled himself as the savior of capitalism, he provoked strong hostility from many well-to-do Americans. To the wealthy, Roosevelt became simply "That Man," a traitor to his class. Business leaders and conservative Democrats formed the Liberty League in 1934 to lobby against the New Deal and its "reckless spending" and "socialist" reforms.

The conservative majority on the Supreme Court also disagreed with the direction of the New Deal. On "Black Monday," May 27, 1935, the Supreme Court unanimously ruled that the National Industrial Recovery Act was an unconstitutional delegation of legislative power to an administrative agency in the case of *Schechter v. United States.* The so-called sick-chicken case concerned a Brooklyn, New York, firm convicted of violating NRA codes by selling diseased poultry. In the case, the court also held that the NRA was regulating commerce *within* an individual state and that the constitution limited federal regulation to *interstate* commerce. Roosevelt publicly protested that the Court's narrow interpretation would return the Constitution "to the horse-and-buggy definition of interstate commerce," but he could only watch helplessly as the court threatened to invalidate the entire New Deal.

Challenges from the Left

Other citizens thought the New Deal had not gone far enough. Francis Townsend, a Long Beach, California, doctor, spoke for the nation's elderly. Many Americans feared poverty in old age because few had pension plans. In 1933, Townsend proposed an Old Age Revolving Pension Plan, which would give $200 a month to citizens above the age of sixty. To receive payment, people would have to retire from their jobs, thereby opening the positions to others, and agree to spend the money within a month. Townsend Clubs soon sprang up throughout the country, with special strength in the Far West.

Father Charles Coughlin also challenged Roosevelt's leadership and attracted a large following, especially in the Midwest. Coughlin, a parish priest in the Detroit suburb of Royal Oak, had turned to the radio in the mid-1920s to enlarge his pastorate. In 1933 about 40 million Americans listened regularly to the "Radio

"Gulliver's Travels"
So many new agencies flooded out of Washington in the 1930s that you almost needed a scorecard to keep them straight. Here a July 1935 *Vanity Fair* cartoon by William Gropper substitutes Uncle Sam for Captain Lemuel Gulliver, tied to the ground by Lilliputians, in a parody of Jonathan Swift's satire *Gulliver's Travels.*

Priest." In many Roman Catholic neighborhoods during the summer, Coughlin's sermon could be heard blaring from open windows. At first he supported the New Deal but soon broke with Roosevelt over the president's refusal to support nationalization of the banking system and expansion of the money supply. Coughlin organized the National Union for Social Justice in 1935 to promote his views as an alternative to "Franklin Double-Crossing Roosevelt." As a Catholic priest who had been born in Canada, Coughlin could not run for president, but his rapidly growing constituency became a factor in the 1936 election.

The most direct political threat to Roosevelt came from Senator Huey Long. In a single term as governor of Louisiana, the flamboyant Long had achieved stunning popularity in his backward state. Voters applauded his attacks on big business, as he lowered their utility bills and increased the share of taxes paid by corporations. And Long's ambitious program of public works, which included the construction of new highways, bridges, hospitals, and schools, benefited all Louisianans and created many new jobs. But Long's accomplishments came at a price: to push through his reforms he seized almost dictatorial control of the state government. He maintained control over Louisiana's political

The Kingfish
Huey Long, the Louisiana governor and senator, ranks as one of the most controversial figures in American political history. He took his nickname of the "Kingfish" from a character in the popular radio show "Amos 'n' Andy." Long inspired one of the most powerful political novels of all time, Robert Penn Warren's *All the King's Men*, which won a Pulitzer Prize in 1946.

machine even after his election to the U.S. Senate in 1930. Long supported Roosevelt in 1932 but made no secret of his own presidential ambitions.

In 1934, Senator Long broke with the New Deal, arguing that its programs did not go far enough. Like Father Coughlin, he established his own national movement, the Share Our Wealth Society which had over 4 million followers in 1935. Long argued that the unequal distribution of wealth in the United States was the fundamental cause of the depression. Long's solution was to tax 100 percent of all incomes over $1 million and all inheritances over $5 million, and distribute the money to the rest of the population. Every family would be guaranteed about $2,000 annually, he predicted. Huey Long's rapid rise in popularity suggested a potentially large volume of public dissatisfaction with the Roosevelt administration. The president's strategists feared that Long might join forces with Coughlin and Townsend to form a third party, enabling the Republicans to win the 1936 election.

The Second New Deal, 1935–1939

By 1935, Roosevelt had abandoned his hope of building a classless coalition of rich and poor, workers and farmers, and rural and urban dwellers. Pushed from the left to do more, and bitterly criticized by the right for what he had already done, the president had no choice but to abandon the middle ground. For both political and ideological reasons, and with an eye fixed firmly on the 1936 election, Roosevelt moved dramatically to the left. Historians use the term *Second New Deal* to describe the outpouring of legislation that followed.

Legislative Accomplishments

The first beneficiary of Roosevelt's change of direction was the labor movement. The rising number of strikes in 1934, about eighteen hundred involving a total of 1.5 million workers, reflected a growth of rank-and-file militancy. After the Supreme Court declared the NRA unconstitutional, labor demanded legislation that would protect its rights to organize and bargain collectively. That year, Senator Robert F. Wagner of New York, one of labor's staunchest supporters in Congress, introduced legislation to replace the ineffective (and now inoperative) Section 7(a) of the NRA. Only when Congress was on the verge of passing Wagner's bill did Roosevelt reluctantly support the legislation; he signed the National Labor Relations Act, also known as the Wagner Act, on July 5, 1935.

The Wagner Act placed the weight of the federal government on labor's side in the struggle to organize. Most importantly, it upheld the right of workers to join

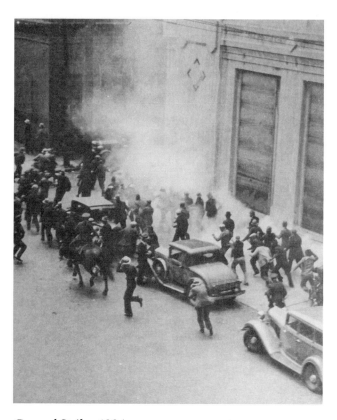

General Strike, 1934
San Francisco's general strike began with the longshoremen and soon spread to almost every union member (and some middle-class supporters as well) in the city. Here the strikers are battling police. On July 19, union leaders voted to accept government arbitration, and the strike ended.

unions. The law also outlawed many unfair labor practices used by employers to squelch unions, such as spying on workers, requiring yellow-dog contracts (where workers had to agree not to join a union in order to be hired), and firing or blacklisting workers because of union activities. The act established the nonpartisan National Labor Relations Board (NLRB) to protect workers from employer coercion, to supervise representation elections, and to enforce the guarantee of collective bargaining. If a union won a majority of the votes in a secret election, usually conducted by the NLRB, it was entitled to recognition as the sole bargaining agent for all the employees in a factory or other appropriate bargaining unit. The NLRB had the authority to force employers to comply.

Social Security. The Social Security Act, signed by President Roosevelt on August 14, 1935, was the second major piece of legislation in this phase of the New Deal. The law was a response to the political mobilization of the nation's elderly through the Townsend and Long movements. It also reflected the prodding of social reformers such as Grace Abbott, head of the Children's

Bureau, and Secretary of Labor Frances Perkins. The Social Security Act provided pensions for most workers in the private sector through a federal-state pension fund to which both employers and employees contributed. Roosevelt's advisers decided to fund this program with payroll deductions, rather than general tax revenues, in order to insulate it from political attack. The act also established a joint federal-state system of unemployment compensation, funded by an unemployment tax on employers and employees.

The Social Security Act represented a milestone in the creation of the modern welfare state. With this law, the United States joined such industrialized countries as Great Britain and Germany in providing old-age pensions and unemployment compensation benefits to its citizens. (The Roosevelt administration chose not to push for national health insurance, even though most other industrialized nations offered such protection.) The law also mandated categorical assistance, such as aid to the blind, deaf, and disabled, and to dependent children. These recipients were the so-called "deserving poor," people who could not support themselves through no fault of their own. The categorical assistance programs grew dramatically after the 1930s. Aid to Dependent Children covered only 700,000 youngsters in 1939; by 1974, its successor, Aid to Families with Dependent Children, enrolled 10.8 million Americans. Programs that had formed merely a small part of the New Deal gradually expanded through the years until they bore most of the burden of the American welfare system.

The WPA. Franklin Roosevelt was never enthusiastic about large expenditures for social welfare programs. As he said in January 1935, the government "must and shall quit this business of relief." But 10 million Americans were still out of work in the sixth year of the depression, a pressing political and moral issue for FDR and the Democrats. The Works Progress Administration (WPA), the main federal relief agency for the rest of the Depression, addressed the needs of the unemployed. Harry Hopkins, who had run the Federal Emergency Relief Administration from 1933 to 1935, took command of the new agency. Whereas the FERA had supplied grants to the states for relief programs, the WPA put relief workers on the federal payroll. Between 1935 and 1943 the WPA employed 8.5 million Americans and spent $10.5 billion. The agency constructed 651,087 miles of roads, 125,110 public buildings, 8,192 parks, 853 airports, and built or repaired 124,087 bridges.

The WPA, although an extravagant operation by the standards of the 1930s (it gave new meaning to the word "boondoggle" and inspired such nicknames as "We Putter Around"), never reached more than a third of the nation's unemployed. Its average wage of $55 a month, well below the government-defined subsistence

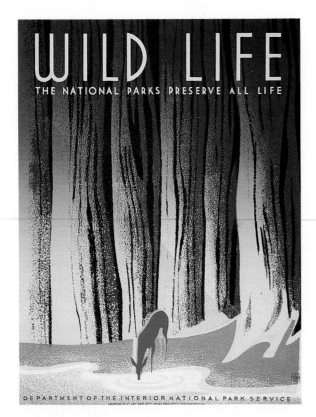

Posters of the WPA
During its eight-year existence, the WPA produced two million posters from 35,000 designs. WPA posters such as this one designed for the National Park Service to support wildlife conservation show the vitality of American graphic design in the 1930s.

level of $100 a month, enabled workers to eke out only a bare living. The government cut back the program severely in 1941 and ended it in 1943, when the WPA was no longer needed in the full-employment economy resulting from World War II.

The Revenue Act of 1935 showed Roosevelt's willingness to push reforms considered too controversial earlier in his presidency. Much of the business community had already turned violently against Roosevelt in reaction to such measures as the NRA, the Social Security Act, the Wagner Act, and the Public Utilities Holding Companies Act. In 1935 he antagonized the wealthy further by proposing a tax reform bill that called for federal inheritance and gift taxes, higher personal income tax rates in the top brackets, and increased corporate taxes. Conservatives quickly labeled this legislation an attempt to "soak the rich." Roosevelt, seeking to defuse the popularity of Huey Long's Share Our Wealth plan, was just as interested in the political mileage of the tax bill as in its actual results. The final version of the bill increased revenues by only $250 million a year.

The 1936 Election

As the 1936 election approached, the broad range of New Deal programs brought many new voters into the Democratic coalition. Many had been personally helped by federal programs; others benefited because their interests had found new support in the expanded functions of the government. Roosevelt could now count on a potent urban-based coalition of workers, organized labor, northern blacks, white ethnic groups, Catholics, Jews, liberals, intellectuals, progressive Republicans, and middle-class families concerned about old-age dependence and unemployment. The Democrats also held on, though somewhat uneasily, to their traditional strength among white southerners.

The Republicans realized they could not compete directly with President Roosevelt's popularity and his potent New Deal coalition. To run against Roosevelt, they chose the progressive governor of Kansas, Alfred M. Landon, who accepted the general precepts of the New Deal. But Landon and the Republicans stridently criticized the inefficiency and expense of many New Deal programs, and even accused FDR of harboring dictatorial ambitions.

Roosevelt's victory in 1936 was one of the biggest landslides in United States history. The assassination of Huey Long in September 1935 had deflated the threat of a serious third party challenge; the candidate of the combined Long-Townsend-Coughlin camp, Congressman William Lemke of North Dakota, garnered fewer than 900,000 votes (1.9 percent) for the Union party ticket. Roosevelt received 60.8 percent of the popular vote and carried every state except Maine and Vermont; Landon received 36.5 percent. Landon fought such an uphill battle that columnist Dorothy Thompson quipped, "If Landon had given one more speech, Roosevelt would have carried Canada." The New Deal was at high tide.

Stalemate

"I see one-third of a nation ill-housed, ill-clad, ill-nourished," the president declared in his second inaugural address in January 1937. Roosevelt's frank appraisal suggested that he was considering the further expansion of the welfare state that had begun to form late in his first term. However, retrenchment, controversy, and stalemate, not further reform, marked the second term.

The Supreme Court Fight.   Only two weeks after his inauguration, Roosevelt stunned Congress and the nation by asking for fundamental changes in the structure of the Supreme Court. He believed a grave constitutional crisis called for this drastic judicial reorganization.

After the Supreme Court found the NRA unconstitutional in the 1935 *Schechter* decision, it proceeded to strike down the Agricultural Adjustment Act, the Guffey-Snyder Coal Conservation Act, and New York's minimum wage law in the early months of 1936. With the Wagner Act, the TVA, and Social Security coming up on appeal, the whole future of New Deal reform legislation appeared in doubt.

In response, Roosevelt proposed adding one new justice to the Court for each one over the age of seventy. This scheme, which Roosevelt tried to pass off as concern for the workload of the elderly justices, would have increased the number of justices from nine to fifteen. Roosevelt's opponents quickly accused him of trying to "pack" the Court with justices favorable to the New Deal. The president's proposal was also regarded as an assault on the principle of separation of powers. The issue became moot when the Supreme Court, in what journalists called "a switch in time that saved nine," upheld several key pieces of New Deal legislation, including Washington state's minimum wage law and the Wagner Act.

Charitably, one could say that Roosevelt had lost a skirmish but won the war. In the spring of 1937 one conservative justice, Willis Van Devanter, resigned and other resignations soon followed. Within four years, Roosevelt reshaped the Supreme Court to suit his liberal philosophy with seven new appointments, including Hugo Black, Felix Frankfurter, Stanley F. Reed, and William O. Douglas. Yet his handling of the Court issue was a costly blunder at a time when he was vulnerable to the lameduck syndrome that often afflicts second-term administrations. No one yet suspected that FDR would break tradition to seek a third term.

Congressional conservatives had long opposed the direction of the New Deal, but the Court packing episode galvanized their opposition by demonstrating that Roosevelt was no longer politically invincible. Throughout Roosevelt's second term, a conservative coalition in Congress, composed mainly of southern Democrats and Republicans from rural areas, blocked or impeded further social legislation. Two pieces of reform legislation that did manage to win passage were the National Housing Act of 1937, which mandated the construction of low-cost public housing, and the Fair Labor Standards Act of 1938, which made permanent the minimum wage, maximum hours, and anti-child labor provisions first tried in the NRA codes.

Roosevelt's attempts to reorganize the executive branch met a different fate. In both 1937 and 1938 Congress refused to consider a Roosevelt plan that would have consolidated all independent agencies into cabinet-rank departments, extended the civil service system, and created the new position of auditor general. Conservatives effectively played on lawmakers' fears that centralized executive management would dramatically reduce congressional power. Opponents also linked Roosevelt's attempt to reorganize the executive branch with popular fears about fascism and dictatorship abroad. Roosevelt eventually settled for a weak bill in 1939, which allowed him to create the Executive Office of the President and name six administrative assistants to the White House staff. The White House also took control of the all-important budget process by moving the Bureau of the Budget to the Executive Office from its old home in the Treasury Department.

The Roosevelt Recession. The "Roosevelt recession" of 1937–1938 dealt the most devastating blow to the president's political standing in the second term. Until that point, the economy had made steady progress. From 1933 to 1937, the gross national product grew at a yearly rate of about 10 percent, and industrial output finally reached 1929 levels in 1937, as did real income. Unemployment declined from 25 percent to 14 percent, which meant that almost half the people without a job in 1933 had found one by 1937. Many Americans agreed with Senator James F. Byrnes of South Carolina that "the emergency has passed."

The steady improvement cheered Roosevelt. Reflecting his basic fiscal conservatism, he had never overcome his dislike of large deficits and huge federal expenditures for relief. Accordingly, Roosevelt slashed the federal budget in 1937. Congress cut the WPA's funding in half between January and August, which caused layoffs of about 1.5 million WPA workers. Moreover, the $2 billion withheld from workers' paychecks to initiate the new Social Security system further reduced purchasing power. Finally, the Federal Reserve, fearing inflation, tightened credit. The stock market promptly collapsed, and unemployment soared to 19 percent, which translated into more than 10 million workers without a job. Roosevelt found himself in the same situation that had confounded Hoover. Having taken credit for the recovery between 1933 and 1937, he now had to take the blame for the recession.

Roosevelt shifted gears and spent his way out of the downturn. Large WPA appropriations and a resumption of public works poured enough money into the economy to snap it out of the recession by early 1938. Roosevelt and his economic advisers were groping toward the general theories being advanced by John Maynard Keynes, a British economist. Keynes proposed that governments use deficit spending to stimulate the economy when private spending proved insufficient. But Keynes's theories would not be conclusively proved until the dramatic increase in federal defense spending for World War II finally ended the Great Depression.

As the 1938 election approached, Roosevelt decided to try to "purge" some of his most conservative opponents from the Democratic party. In the spring primaries, he campaigned against members of his own

TABLE 26.2

Major New Deal Legislation

Agriculture

1933	Agricultural Adjustment Act (AAA)
1935	Resettlement Administration (RA)
	Rural Electrification Administration
1937	Farm Security Administration (FSA)
1938	Second Agricultural Adjustment Act

Business and Industry

1933	Emergency Banking Act Glass-Steagall (FDIC)
	National Industrial Recovery Administration (NIRA)
1934	Securities and Exchange Commission (SEC)
1935	Public Utilities Holding Company Act
	Banking Act of 1935
	Revenue Act (wealth tax)

Conservation and the Environment

1933	Tennessee Valley Authority (TVA)
	Civilian Conservation Corps (CCC)
1963	Soil Conservation and Domestic Allotment Act

Labor and Social Welfare

1933	Section 7(a) NIRA
1935	Wagner Act
	National Labor Relations Board (NLRB)
	Social Security Act
1937	National Housing Act
1938	Fair Labor Standards Act (FLSA)

Relief

1933	Federal Emergency Relief Administration (FERA)
	Civil Works Administration (CWA)
	Public Works Administration (PWA)
1935	Works Progress Administration (WPA)
	National Youth Administration (NYA)

party who had blocked legislation in Congress and generally proven hostile or unsympathetic to New Deal initiatives. The purge failed abysmally (not one of his targets was unseated), and only served to widen the liberal-conservative rift in the Democratic party. In the general election, Republicans capitalized on the "Roosevelt recession" and the Court-packing backlash to pick up 8 seats in the Senate, 81 in the House, and gain 13 governorships.

By 1938 the New Deal had basically run out of steam. It had no climax; it simply withered away. For six years Franklin Roosevelt had inspired public confidence that hard times could be overcome. Roosevelt showed himself to be a superb politician, successfully balancing demands for more government programs with his own assessment of what was politically feasible. Throughout the New Deal, however, President Roosevelt always demonstrated clear limits on how far he was willing to go. His instincts were basically conservative, not revolutionary; he saved the capitalist economic system by reforming it. This new activism represented a major step beyond the informal (and one-sided) business-government partnership of the previous decade, but only because the emergency of the depression pushed Roosevelt in that direction. Under normal circumstances, he would have served out his second term and a new president would have been elected in 1940. Franklin Roosevelt won election to a third term (and eventually a fourth) primarily because the outbreak of World War II in Europe made Americans reluctant to risk a change in leadership during such perilous times.

The New Deal's Impact on Society

The New Deal was, as one historian put it, "somehow more than the sum of its parts." To understand its impact on society, we must look beyond the new federal programs coming out of Washington to consider broader changes in American political and social life. The New Deal set in motion dramatic growth in the federal bureaucracy. The Roosevelt administration opened unprecedented opportunities for women, African-Americans, and labor in public life. Its programs and priorities had an enormous impact on the public landscape, and it also laid the groundwork for the modern welfare system that shapes American life today.

Bureaucratic Growth

The New Deal accelerated the expansion of the federal bureaucracy that had been underway since the turn of the century. The number of civilian government employees increased 80 percent in just a decade, exceeding a million in 1940. The number of federal employees who worked in Washington grew at an even faster rate, doubling between 1929 and 1940. Power increasingly centered in the nation's capital, not in the states. In 1939 a British observer summed up this new orientation: "Just as in 1929 the whole country was 'Wall Street conscious,' now it is 'Washington conscious.'"

The new bureaucrats administered federal budgets

of unprecedented size. In 1930 the Hoover administration had spent $3.1 billion and had a surplus of almost $1 billion. With the increase in federal programs to fight the depression, federal expenditures grew steadily—$4.8 billion in 1932, $6.5 billion in 1934, and $7.6 billion in 1936. In 1939, the last year before war mobilization affected the federal budget, expenditures hit $9.4 billion. Government spending outstripped receipts throughout this period, producing yearly deficits of about $3 billion. Roosevelt had come close to balancing the budget in 1938, but he triggered a major recession. The deficit climbed toward $3 billion again the following year.

The beginnings of big government and bureaucracy have often been associated with the Roosevelt years, but many of the problems commonly ascribed to the New Deal belong to later eras. The real step toward big government spending came during World War II, not the depression. Federal outlays routinely surpassed $95 billion in the 1940s, and deficits grew to $50 billion. Although the deficit declined in the postwar era, government expenditures never returned to their pre–World War II levels.

Women and the New Deal

In the experimental climate of the New Deal, unprecedented numbers of women accepted positions in the Roosevelt administration, both as policy-makers and as middle-level bureaucrats. Frances Perkins served as Secretary of Labor throughout all four Roosevelt terms, the first woman in the cabinet. Molly Dewson, a social reformer-turned-politician, headed the Women's Division of the Democratic National Committee where she pushed an issue-oriented program that supported New Deal reforms. Roosevelt's appointments included the first woman director of the mint, head of a major WPA division, and judge of the Circuit Court of Appeals. Many of these women were close friends as well as professional colleagues, and they cooperated in an informal network to advance both feminist and reform causes.

Eleanor Roosevelt exemplified the growing prominence of women in public life. In the 1920s she worked closely with other reformers to increase women's power in political parties, labor unions, and education, an invaluable apprenticeship for the White House years. Franklin and Eleanor's marriage represented one of the most successful political partnerships of all time. He was a pragmatic politician, always aware of what could be done. She was an idealist, a gadfly, always pushing him—and the New Deal—to do more. Eleanor Roosevelt observed in her autobiography,

He might have been happier with a wife who was completely uncritical. That I was never able to be, and he had to find it in other people. Nevertheless, I think I sometimes acted as a spur, even though the spurring was not always wanted or welcome. I was one of those who served his purposes.

Eleanor Roosevelt underestimated her influence. She served as the conscience of the New Deal.

Although Franklin Roosevelt's expansion of the personalized presidency had roots in the administrations of Theodore Roosevelt and Woodrow Wilson, the nation had never seen a First Lady like Eleanor Roosevelt. She held press conferences for woman journalists, wrote a popular syndicated news column called "My Day," and traveled extensively throughout the country. Some people wondered why the First Lady could not stay home at the White House like a good wife. But a Gallup poll in January 1939 showed that 67 percent approved of Eleanor Roosevelt's conduct, a higher approval rate than the president's at that time. In 1938 *Life* magazine hailed her as the greatest American woman alive.

Without the vocal support of prominent women such as Eleanor Roosevelt, Molly Dewson, and the rest of the female political network, women's needs during the depression might have been totally overlooked. Grave flaws still marred the treatment of women in New Deal programs. For example, a fourth of the NRA codes set a lower minimum wage for women than for men performing the same jobs. New Deal agencies such as the Civil Works Administration or Public Works Administration provided jobs almost exclusively to men, mainly because construction work was considered unsuitable for women; only 7 percent of the Civil Work Administration workers were female. The Social Security Act and Fair Labor Standards Act did not cover major areas of female employment, such as domestic service. The Civilian Conservation Corps excluded women entirely, leaving critics to ask, where is the "she-she-she"?

Women fared somewhat better under the Works Progress Administration. At the WPA's peak, 405,000 women were on its rolls. The Women's and Professional Projects Division of the WPA, headed by Ellen Sullivan Woodward, a Mississippi social worker, created hundreds of programs to put women to work. Still, at a time when women accounted for about 23 percent of the labor force, they comprised only between 14 percent and 19 percent of the WPA workers. For the most part, progress for women did not come from specific attempts to single them out as a group. It occurred as part of the broader effort to improve the economic security of all Americans.

AMERICAN LIVES

Frances Perkins, New Deal Reformer

How should the first woman to serve in the cabinet be addressed, the press wanted to know? "Miss Perkins," came her no-nonsense reply. But the press said "Mr. Secretary" to the Secretary of State—how were they to address a woman who was the Secretary of Labor? After consultation with Speaker of the House Henry Rainey and *Robert's Rules of Order*, the verdict came down: Frances Perkins was to be addressed as "Madam Secretary." As usual, the first woman in the cabinet took the attention to her sex in stride. She kept a deliberately low profile, dressing conservatively in black dresses and always wearing a distinctive tricorne hat. When asked later if being a woman had ever been a handicap, she replied matter-of-factly, "Only in climbing trees."

Frances Perkins's career shows the continuities between Progressive Era activism and New Deal reform. Born in 1880 in Massachusetts, Perkins took advantage of the new opportunities for higher education for women to graduate from Mount Holyoke College in 1902. She then worked in the settlement movement, in the woman suffrage campaign, and with reform groups trying to pass a fifty-four-hour work week bill for New York women and children. Her service on the commission set up to investigate New York factory conditions in the wake of the 1911 Triangle Shirtwaist Fire, which killed 146 female garment workers, confirmed her commitment to legislative solutions for social problems. "I'd much rather get a law passed than organize a union," she later said. That orientation shaped her priorities as Secretary of Labor.

In 1913, at the age of thirty-three, Frances Perkins married Paul C. Wilson, an economist and reformer. She kept her given name, and continued to work after her daughter Susanna was born in 1916. As she later recalled, "I suppose I had been somewhat touched by feminist ideas and that was one of the reasons I kept my maiden name. My whole generation was, I suppose, the first generation that openly and actively asserted—at

least some of us did—the separateness of women and their personal independence in the family relationship." In 1918 her husband became seriously ill and spent the rest of his life in and out of mental institutions. Out of necessity, Perkins became the family breadwinner.

Perkins moved into government service in 1918 when newly-elected governor Alfred E. Smith, whom she had met during the Triangle investigation, appointed her a member of the New York State Industrial Commission. Smith appointed Perkins to the State Industrial Board in 1922, and made her its chairperson in 1926. In 1928, she became New York's industrial commissioner under Smith and then Franklin D. Roosevelt, who replaced Smith as governor that year. These positions made Perkins one of the highest-ranked women in state government in the immediate postsuffrage period.

When Franklin Roosevelt ran for president in 1932, talk began to circulate that Perkins might be offered a spot in the cabinet, a rumor which she dismissed as a "pipe dream." But to politicians like Molly Dewson, whose background in social welfare paralleled that of Perkins, Roosevelt's election offered an unprecedented opportunity for women to serve on the national level. Dewson set about convincing Roosevelt of the wisdom of choosing Perkins, and also overcoming Perkins's own doubts. Perkins was loathe to leave New York and a job she loved, she feared the effect of unwanted publicity on her husband and her teenage daughter, and the job would cause financial hardship. Molly Dewson blithely dismissed all these objections, emphasizing the importance of the appointment to the nation's women. "After all, you owe it to the women," Dewson argued repeatedly. "You probably will have this chance and you must step forward to do it." At other times, Dewson's pressure was less subtle. "Don't be such a baby. Frances, you do the right thing. I'll murder you if you don't!"

Duty to her sex finally carried the day. As Perkins later explained to suffrage leader Carrie Chapman Catt, "The overwhelming argument and thought which made on the chair that was offered, and so establish the right of others long hence and far-distant in geography to sit in the high seats." Franklin Roosevelt announced Perkins's appointment on February 28, and she was sworn in five days later. Of Roosevelt's original cabinet, only Perkins and Secretary of the Interior Harold Ickes served for all four terms.

As secretary of labor, Frances Perkins took as her mandate the promotion of the general welfare of American workers rather than specific advocacy of the interests of organized labor. She built the Department of Labor into a smoothly functioning bureaucracy, and attracted many talented men and women to Washington. She played an important role in drafting the 1935 Social Security Act and the 1938 Fair Labor Standards Act. She did not ignore the labor movement, however, and after a period of initial doubt, labor leaders realized that Madam Secretary was an important ally in the turbulent era of union mobilization in the 1930s.

An important key to Perkins's success was her strong personal rapport with Franklin Roosevelt, who unlike many male politicians felt comfortable working with strong-minded women. (He, of course, was married to one, and he met many of the talented women he brought into the New Deal administration through Eleanor.) Perkins called Franklin Roosevelt the most complicated human being she had ever met, but she emphatically asserted that he had never let her down. In 1946 she published *The Roosevelt I Knew*, an autobiographical account of her participation in the New Deal which many believe offers the most perceptive account of the elusive Roosevelt personality.

After Roosevelt's death, Perkins served on the Civil Service Commission under President Harry Truman. When the Republicans regained power in 1952, she left government service for a fulfilling career as a lecturer, maintaining an affiliation with the Cornell School of Industrial and Labor Relations. Perkins died in 1965. Her role in laying the foundation for the modern welfare state was her greatest legacy, but just as important was her demonstration of the contributions that public-spirited women could make to politics and government.

Secretary of Labor
Frances Perkins being greeted by workers of the Carnegie Steel Company in Pittsburgh.

AMERICAN VOICES

The Great Depression in Harlem *Nora Mair*

Nora Mair and her husband Jack, both Jamaican immigrants, lived in Harlem throughout the 1930s. She worked in a linen shop on Madison Avenue, and he struggled to find employment of any kind. Like many other Americans, black and white, the WPA was their salvation.

We were poor. We didn't pretend. But our gas bill was always paid. Our rent bill was always paid. And we always knew where our next meal was coming from. We shopped on Eighth Avenue. We had everything there. We moved out of West Harlem to 100th Street and Madison Avenue in 1933 because the rent was less than half of what we were paying in West Harlem. We were paying thirty-two dollars a month for a five-room apartment. In Harlem, we would have paid sixty-five dollars, and we had a lovely landlord who painted our house every year. It was a lovely neighborhood—a potpourri of many nationalities. . . .

My husband worked in the day and went to school nights. He graduated from Mechanical Institute in

1928, and right after that the Depression came, and he couldn't get work in his profession. In the meantime he drove a cab. It was no living at all as a taxi driver. I've known him to work around the clock and only make a dollar and a half.

He would come in in the morning and eat his dinner for his breakfast and then go to bed. I've known him to be so cold, because in those days the cabs only had three doors, that he'd come in and all he would take off was his hat, his shoes, and his overcoat and then into the bed until he was warm. Those things I did resent, because he had more to offer. He met so many people on the cab line—people he knew from Jamaica. He met professors who were driving cabs and couldn't get a job. First it was color. Then it was color and Depression.

There was nothing my husband did not do to make a living. He did not want welfare, and he wanted to be independent. But he couldn't get work as a draftsman. Once, while he was driving a cab, he saw an ad in the paper for a draftsman. He went down-

town to this office, and there was the receptionist. She didn't even look up. She waved him around the back, so he thought to himself, "She didn't ask what I wanted. She just motioned me to the back of the building. What kind of office could be back there?"

When he got back there, a white man with a pail and a mop said to him, "There is the pail and the mop."

"Pail and the mop for what?"

And said Mr. White Man, "Well, that's what you're here for, isn't it? A porter's job?"

Well, I won't tell you what my husband said when he came home, because he came home frothing at the mouth, and told me what he told him.

When the WPA came in, that was the first time he got to work in his profession. He worked on theaters, schools. They did everything, and it meant a lot that he was finally able to work in his field.

Source: Jeff Kisseloff, *You Must Remember This: An Oral History of Manhattan from the 1890s to World War II* (New York: Schocken, 1989), 326–327, 328.

Blacks and the New Deal

African-Americans had a similar experience. They benefited more from the general social and economic programs of the New Deal than from any concerted commitment to promote civil rights. There were striking parallels between the situation of blacks and women. (For black women, race proved more important than gender in determining treatment from the New Deal.) Mary McLeod Bethune, an educator who ran the Office of Minority Affairs of the National Youth Administration, headed the "black cabinet." This informal network worked for fairer treatment of blacks by New Deal agencies in the same way that the women's network advocated feminist causes. Both groups benefited greatly from the support of Eleanor Roosevelt. The First Lady's promotion of equal treat-

ment for blacks in the New Deal ranks as one of her greatest legacies.

The vast majority of the American people did not regard civil rights as a legitimate object for federal intervention in the 1930s. The New Deal provided little specific aid for blacks, for whom hard times were a permanent feature, not just a product of the 1930s. Many New Deal programs reflected prevailing racist attitudes. CCC camps segregated blacks, and many NRA codes did not protect black workers. Most tellingly, Franklin Roosevelt repeatedly refused to support a federal anti-lynching bill, claiming it would antagonize southern members of Congress whose support he needed for passage of New Deal measures.

At the same time, blacks received enormous benefits from New Deal relief programs directed toward poor Americans regardless of race or ethnic background.

Eleanor Roosevelt and Civil Rights
One of Eleanor Roosevelt's greatest legacies was her commitment to civil rights. For example, she publicly resigned from the Daughters of the American Revolution (DAR) in 1939 when the group refused to let the black opera singer Marian Anderson perform at Constitution Hall. Eleanor Roosevelt developed an especially close working relationship with Mary McLeod Bethune of the National Youth Administration, shown here at a conference on black youth in 1939.

Public works projects channeled funds into black communities. Blacks made up about 18 percent of the WPA's recipients, although only 10 percent of the population. The Resettlement Administration, established in 1935 to help small farmers buy land and to aid in resettlement of sharecroppers and tenant farmers to more productive land, fought for the rights of black tenant farmers in the South, that is, until angry southerners in Congress cut its appropriations drastically. Still, many blacks reasoned that the tangible aid coming from Washington outweighed the discrimination that marred many federal programs.

Help from the WPA and other New Deal programs, and a belief that the White House—at least Eleanor Roosevelt—realized their plight, caused a dramatic change in blacks' voting behavior. Since the Civil War, blacks had voted Republican, a loyalty resulting from Abraham Lincoln's freeing of the slaves. As late as 1932, black voters in northern cities overwhelmingly supported Republican candidates.

Then, in fewer than four years, blacks turned Lincoln's portrait to the wall and substituted that of Franklin Roosevelt. Because of the harshness of the depression, national politics assumed a new relevance for black Americans outside the South. They gave Roosevelt 71 percent of their votes in 1936. In Harlem, where relief dollars increased dramatically in the wake of the 1935 riot (see Chapter 25), the support was an extraordinary 81.3 percent. Black voters have remained overwhelmingly Democratic ever since.

The Rise of Organized Labor

During the 1930s, labor relations became a legitimate arena for federal action and intervention, and organized labor claimed a place in national political life. Labor's dramatic growth in the 1930s represented one of the most important social and economic changes of the decade, an enormous contrast to its demoralized state at the end of the 1920s.

Several factors encouraged the growth of the labor movement: the inadequacy of welfare capitalism in the face of the Depression, New Deal legislation such as the Wagner Act, the rise of the Congress of Industrial Organizations (CIO), and the growing militancy of rank-and-file workers. By the end of the decade, the number of unionized workers had tripled to almost 9 million, covering 23 percent of the nonfarm work force. Union strength grew rapidly in manufacturing, transportation, and mining. Organized labor won not only the battle for union recognition, but also higher wages, seniority systems, and grievance procedures. Labor also greatly expanded its political involvement.

The CIO served as the cutting edge of the union movement. It did so by promoting industrial unionism—that is, it organized all the workers in an industry, both skilled and unskilled, into one union. John L. Lewis, leader of the United Mine Workers and a founder of the CIO, was the leading exponent of industrial unionism. His philosophy put him at odds with the American Federation of Labor, which favored organiz-

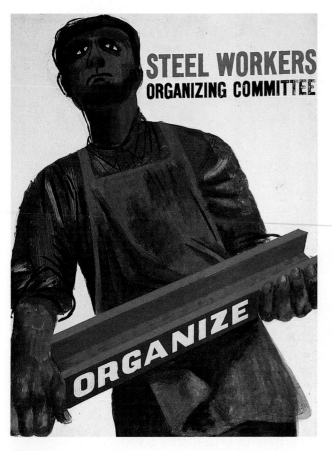

Organize

The Steelworkers' Organizing Committee was one of the most vital labor organizations contributing to the rise of the CIO. Note that artist Ben Shahn chose a male figure to represent the American labor movement in this poster designed in the late 1930s. Such iconography reinforced the notion that the typical worker was male, despite the large number of women who joined the CIO.

ing workers on a craft-by-craft basis. Lewis began to detach himself from the AFL in 1935, and the break became complete by 1938. Although the CIO generated much of the excitement on the labor front during the 1930s, the AFL gained more than a million new workers between 1935 and 1940.

The CIO scored its first major victory in the automobile industry. On December 31, 1936, General Motors workers in Flint, Michigan, staged a sit-down strike. They vowed to stay at their machines until management agreed to bargain collectively with them. The workers lived in the factories and machine shops for forty-four days before General Motors recognized the United Automobile Workers (UAW). The CIO soon won a second major victory, this time at the U.S. Steel Corporation. Despite a long history of bitter opposition to unionization (as demonstrated in the 1919 steel strike), "Big Steel" capitulated without a fight and recognized the Steel Workers Organizing Committee (SWOC) on March 2, 1937.

The victory in the steel industry was not complete, however. A group of companies known as "Little Steel" chose not to follow the lead of U.S. Steel in making peace with the CIO. Steelworkers struck the Republic Steel Corporation plant in South Chicago. On Memorial Day afternoon, May 31, 1937, strikers and their families gathered for a holiday picnic and rally outside the plant gates. Tension mounted, rocks were thrown, and the police fired on the crowd, killing ten protesters. All were shot in the back. A newsreel photographer recorded the scene, but Paramount Pictures considered the film of the "Memorial Day Massacre" too inflammatory for distribution. The road to recognition for labor, even with New Deal protections, was often still violent and protracted. Workers in Little Steel did not win union recognition until 1941.

The Sit-Down Strike

These members of the United Auto Workers helped to pioneer the sit-down tactic at a General Motors plant in Flint, Michigan in 1937. In their 44-day siege, workers made use of the car seats awaiting final assembly in GM cars while they passed the time. To avoid any taint of immorality, union leaders asked all women workers in the Flint plant to voluntarily leave once the sit-down strike began, and the women complied.

AMERICAN VOICES

Labor Militancy *Genora Johnson Dollinger*

During the Flint, Michigan, sit-down strike, Genora Johnson Dollinger, the wife of a General Motors striker and the mother of two small children, organized the Women's Emergency Brigade. Women like Dollinger played a major role in the Flint victory.

I was twenty-three years old on December 30, 1936, when the strike started. It lasted forty-four days, a very dramatic forty-four days, until February 11, 1937.

It was New Year's Eve when I realized women had to organize and join in the fight. I was on the picket lines when the men's wives came down. They didn't know why their husbands were sitting inside the plant. Living in a company town, you see, they got only company propaganda through the press and radio. So when they came down on New Year's Eve, many were threatening to divorce their striking husbands if they didn't quit and get back to work to bring home a paycheck.

I knew then that union women must organize on their own in order to talk with these wives. . . .

This was an independent move. It was not under the direction of the union or its administrators—I just talked it over with a few women—the active ones—and told them this is what we had to do.

Women might, after all, be called upon to give their lives. That was exactly the appeal I made while we were forming the brigade—I told the women, "Don't sign up for this unless you are prepared. If you are prone to hysteria or anything like that you'd only be in our way." I told them they'd be linking arms and withstanding the onslaughts of the police and if one of our sisters went down shot in cold blood there'd be no time for hysteria.

Around 500 women answered that call. We bought red berets and made arm bands with the white letters "EB" for Emergency Brigade. It was a kind of military uniform, yes, but it was mainly identification. We wore them all the time so we'd know who to call on to give help in an emergency. I had five lieutenants—three were factory women. I chose them because they could be called out of bed at any hour, if necessary, or sleep on a cot at the union hall. Mothers with children couldn't answer calls like that—although they did sign up for the brigade. Even a few grandmothers be-

came brigadiers and, I remember, one young girl only sixteen.

We had no communication system to speak of. Very few people had telephones so we had to call one woman who was responsible for getting the messages through to many others.

We organized a first aid station and child care center—the women who had small children to tend and couldn't join the EB took care of these jobs.

Listen, I met some of the finest women I have ever come across in my life. When the occasion demands it of a woman and once she understands that she's standing in defense of her family—well, God, *don't fool around with that woman then.* . . .

It's a measure of the strength of those women of the Red Berets that they could perform so courageously in an atmosphere that was often hostile to them. We organized on our own without the benefit of professional leadership, and yet, we played a role, second to none, in the birth of a union and in changing working families' lives forever.

Source: Genora Johnson Dollinger, quoted in Jeane Westin, *Making Do* (Chicago: Follett Publishing, 1976), 223, 225–226, 229.

The 1930s were one of the most active periods of labor solidarity in American history. The sit-down tactic spread rapidly. In March 1937, 167,210 workers staged 170 sit-down strikes. Labor unions called nearly five thousand strikes that year and won favorable terms in 80 percent of them. Yet large numbers of middle-class Americans felt alienated by sit-down strikes, which they considered attacks on private property. The Supreme Court agreed, upholding a law that banned the practice in 1939.

The CIO attracted new groups to the union movement. Blacks, for example, found the CIO's commit-

ment to racial justice a strong contrast to the AFL's long-established patterns of exclusion and segregation. About eight hundred thousand women workers also found a limited welcome in the CIO. Women participated in major CIO strikes and served as union organizers, especially in textile organizing drives in the South. Few blacks and women held union leadership positions, however.

Women found other ways beside joining a union to participate in the labor movement. During the Flint sit-down strike against General Motors in 1937, the Women's Emergency Brigade, a group of wives, sisters, and girlfriends of striking workers, supplied food and first aid. Wearing distinctive red berets and armbands, they picketed, demonstrated, and occasionally resorted to such tactics as breaking windows to dissipate the tear gas used against the strikers. After the strike, however, UAW leaders politely but firmly told the women to go back home where they belonged.

Labor's new vitality spilled over into political action. The AFL had always stood aloof from partisan politics, but the CIO quickly allied itself with the Democratic party. Through Labor's Nonpartisan League, the CIO gave $770,000 to Democratic campaigns in 1936. Labor also provided one of the few solid lobbies behind President Roosevelt's plan to reorganize the Supreme Court. In the 1940s the CIO's Political Action Committee became a major contributor to the Democratic war chest.

Despite the breakthroughs of the New Deal, the labor movement never developed into as dominant a force in American life as had seemed possible in the heyday of the late 1930s. Roosevelt never made the growth of the labor movement a high priority, and many workers remained indifferent or even hostile to calls for unionization. Although the Wagner Act guaranteed unions a permanent place in American industrial relations, it did not revolutionize actual working conditions. The important gain of collective bargaining did not redistribute power in American industry; it merely granted labor a measure of legitimacy. Management even found that unions could be a useful buffer against rank-and-file militancy. New Deal social welfare programs also diffused some of the pre-1937 radical spirit

by channeling significant economic benefits to workers, whether they belonged to unions or not. In the 1940s, the labor movement entered a period of consolidation and then stagnation that continued for several decades.

Other New Deal Constituencies

The growth of the federal government in the 1930s increased the potential impact that its decisions (and its spending) had on various constituencies. The New Deal considered a broader cast of the population worthy of inclusion in the political process, especially if they were organized into pressure groups. Politicians realized the importance of satisfying the concerns of certain blocs of voters in order to cement their allegiance to the Democratic party. As a result, women, blacks, and labor received more attention from the federal government and had a higher visibility in public life than ever before.

But what about groups who were not politically mobilized or recognized as key components of the New Deal coalition? The New Deal's impact on their communities often came down to whether they had sympathetic government administrators in Washington to promote their interests.

Native Americans made up one of the nation's most disadvantaged and powerless minorities. Their annual average income in 1934 totaled only $48, and their unemployment rate was three times the national average. Concerned New Deal administrators, such as Secretary of the Interior Harold Ickes and Commissioner John Collier of the Bureau of Indian Affairs, tried to correct

New Deal Murals
Social realist painter William Gropper portrayed the contributions of labor to modern industry in the heroic, dynamic style that was typical of public art during the depression. His mural, *Construction of a Dam*, was commissioned in 1937 for the Department of the Interior Building in Washington, D.C. (National Museum of American Art)

some of these inequalities. The Indian Reorganization Act of 1934 reversed the Dawes Severalty Act of 1887 by promoting more extensive self-government through tribal councils and constitutions. The government also reversed the policy of forced integration into American society by pledging to help preserve Indian languages, arts, traditions, and other tribal heritages. The economic problems of native Americans were so severe, however, that these changes in federal policy produced only marginal results.

Hispanic Americans, scattered throughout the West in rural areas and urban barrios, had no such advocates within the New Deal bureaucracy. Too diverse to speak as an organized constituency, Hispanics found little help from the New Deal. Major legislation such as the Social Security Act and the Fair Labor Standards Act excluded agricultural workers, a major source of Hispanic employment. The Wagner Act did not cover farm workers' unions. And Mexican-Americans faced discrimination and prejudice, indeed the threat of deportation, when applying for relief (see Chapter 25). In part because Mexican-Americans were not mobilized politically in the 1930s, they did not know how to attract the attention—and federal dollars—of an increasingly activist state. Whatever benefits came their way were the result of generalized attacks on poverty and unemployment, rather than specific reforms addressed to the needs of Hispanic Americans.

The New Deal and the Land

Concern with the land was one of the dominant motifs of the New Deal, and the shaping of the public landscape was among its most visible and enduring legacies. Franklin Roosevelt brought to the presidency a love of forestry and a conservation ethic nurtured on his Hudson River estate. New Deal administrators like Interior Secretary Harold Ickes were avid conservationists. The expansion of federal responsibilities in the 1930s, especially the need to put the unemployed to work on public projects, created a climate conducive to action. So too did public concern heightened by the dramatic images of drought and devastation of the Dust Bowl. The resulting national resources policy stressed scientific management of the land, conservation over commercialism, and the often aggressive use of public authority to safeguard land that was either privately or publicly held.

The most extensive New Deal environmental undertaking was the Tennessee Valley Authority. The need for dams to control flooding and erosion in the Tennessee River Basin, a seven-state area with some of the country's heaviest rainfall, had been recognized as far back as World War I. During the 1920s progressives led by Senator George Norris of Nebraska pushed for the construction of a dam at Muscle Shoals on the Tennessee River, but utility companies successfully blocked the project. In the first hundred days of the Roosevelt administration in 1933, the Tennessee Valley Authority finally won approval to develop the region's resources under public control. The TVA was the ultimate watershed demonstration area, with its integrated plans for flood control, reforestation, and agricultural and industrial development, including a chemical fertilizer plant. Its hydroelectric grid provided cheap electrical power for the valley residents. The TVA was admired worldwide and became one of the most popular destinations for foreign visitors to the United States.

The Dust Bowl helped to focus attention on land use management and ecological balance. Agents from the Soil Conservation Service in the Department of Agriculture taught farmers the proper technique for tilling hillsides. (Quipped journalist Alistair Cooke, the New Deal's conception of the common man was someone who could "take up contour plowing late in life.") Government agronomists also worked to remove marginal land from cultivation and prevent soil erosion through better agricultural practices. One of their most widely publicized programs was the Shelterbelts, the planting of a line of some 220 million trees to run roughly along the ninety-ninth meridian from Abilene, Texas, north to the Canadian border. Planted as a wind break, these trees also prevented soil erosion. Shelterbelts were a personal favorite of Franklin Roosevelt's.

Sometimes political reality dictated specific legislation affecting the environment, such as the Soil Conservation and Domestic Allotment Act of 1936. This legislation filled the void created when the Supreme Court ruled the Agricultural Adjustment Act unconstitutional. Under the act, farmers received payments for cutting commercial production of crops like wheat and cotton, which depleted the soil, and planting instead soil-building grasses and legumes such as clover and soybeans. Not coincidentally, wheat and cotton were major surplus commodities, and the law provided a way to cut production as well as encourage soil conservation. The Agricultural Adjustment Act of 1938 continued the policy of price supports and payments to farmers to limit production and established soil conservation as a permanent program.

Another priority of the Roosevelt administration was helping rural Americans stay on the land. The Rural Electrification Administration established in 1935, which brought power to the nation's farms (see Chapter 25), was part of this attempt to improve the quality of rural life. The New Deal also encouraged urban dwellers to move back to rural areas. This "back to the land" motif animated many New Deal projects, especially those planned by the Resettlement Administration under the direction of Rexford Tugwell. Some of

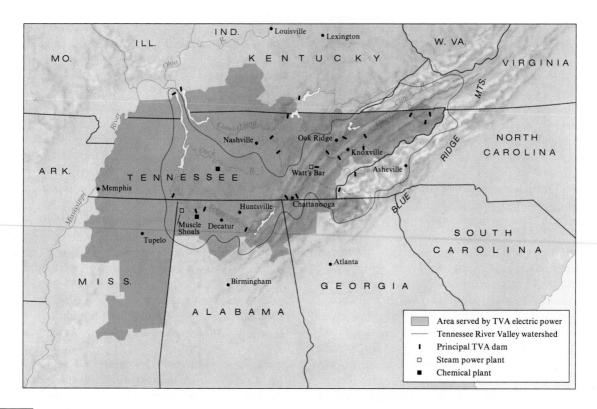

MAP 26.1

The Tennessee Valley Authority

The Tennessee Valley Authority was one of the New Deal's most far-reaching
environmental projects. Between 1933 and 1952, the TVA built twenty dams and
improved five others. The cheap hydroelectric power generated by the dams brought
electricity to more local residents than ever before.

the best known examples were planned cooperative
communities in rural areas, such as Arthurdale in West
Virginia, or the "Greenbelt" residential towns outside
Washington, D.C., Cincinnati, and Milwaukee.

Although the TVA, Shelterbelts, and Greenbelt
towns were primarily environmental programs, they
also put large numbers of the unemployed to work. The
Civilian Conservation Corps, the so-called Tree Army,
planted some 2 billion trees by 1941, a dozen for every
American citizen at the time. Not only was this sound
conservation, but it gave the 2.5 million CCC workers a
job to do. Similarly, many WPA projects fulfilled conservation and recreational goals.

New Deal construction projects affecting the nat-
ural environment are all around us, artifacts from the
depression era. CCC and WPA workers built the Blue
Ridge highway, the consummate parkway of the 1930s,
connecting the Shenandoah National Park in Virginia
with the Great Smoky Mountain National Park in
North Carolina. Government workers built the San
Francisco Zoo, Berkeley's Tilden Park, and the canals of
San Antonio; the CCC helped to complete the East
Coast's Appalachian Trail and the West Coast's Pacific

Crest Trail through the Sierras. In state parks throughout the country, cabins, shelters, picnic areas, lodges,
and observation towers were built in a style that has
been called "government rustic." All these projects
shared the New Deal ethos of leisure and recreation co-
existing with nature.

What was the long-term impact of the New Deal on
land use and conservation? On the Great Plains, probably not very much. Without proper care, many of the
shelterbelts deteriorated, and dust storms once again
struck in the 1950s. When the Civilian Conservation
Corps and the Works Progress Administration lost
funding in the early 1940s, maintenance work lapsed.
But many of these facilities still exist today, relics of the
conservation ethic and the need to put citizens to work.

Although the New Deal was ahead of its time in its
attention to conservation, its legacy to later environmental movements is more mixed. Many of the tactics
of the New Deal projects—damming rivers, blasting fire
roads, altering the natural landscape with buildings and
shelters—would now be seen as too intrusive. The TVA
especially came under attack in the 1970s for its
overzealous application of technology, its longstanding

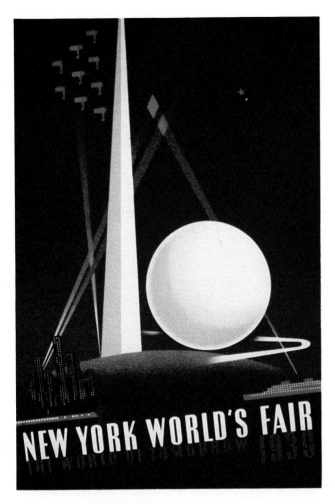

The New York World's Fair
The theme of the 1939 World's Fair was "Building the World of Tomorrow." After grimly struggling for a decade to overcome hard times, many Americans were more than ready to embrace a rosy future of social harmony, interdependence, and material progress. Joseph Binder's prize-winning poster featured the Trylon and Perisphere, the fair's instantly recognizable symbols. (The Queens Museum of Art)

practice of strip mining, and the pollution caused by its power plants and chemical factories. Because of environmental concerns, a project as massive as the TVA probably could never be built today, an ironic conclusion to what was hailed at the time as an enlightened use of government power for the public good.

The Legacies of the New Deal

The New Deal set in motion far-reaching changes, notably the growth of a modern state of significant size. For the first time, people experienced the federal government as a concrete part of everyday life. During the decade, more than a third of the population received

direct government assistance from such new federal programs as Social Security, farm loans, relief, and mortgage guarantees. Furthermore, the government made a concrete commitment to intervene in the economy when private instruments of power proved insufficient to guarantee economic stability. New legislation regulated the stock market, reformed the Federal Reserve system by placing more power in the hands of Washington policy-makers, and brought many practices of modern corporate life under federal regulation. The New Deal thus continued the pattern begun during the progressive era of using federal regulation to bring order and regularity to modern economic life.

The New Deal also laid the foundations of America's welfare state, that is, the federal government's acceptance of primary responsibility for the individual and collective welfare of the people. Although the New Deal offered more benefits to American citizens than they had ever received before, its safety net had many holes, especially in comparison to the far more extensive welfare states found in Western Europe. The greatest defect of the emerging welfare system was its failure to reach a significant minority of American workers. For example, the Social Security program excluded domestic servants and farm workers entirely for many years. And since state governments administered the programs, benefits varied widely from state to state, with the South consistently providing the lowest amounts. Not until the Great Society programs of President Lyndon Johnson in the 1960s did social welfare programs reach significant numbers of America's poor.

To its credit, the New Deal recognized that poverty was a structural economic problem, not a matter of personal failure. New Deal reformers assumed that once the Depression was over, full employment and an active economy would take care of welfare needs, and poverty would simply wither away. It did not. When later administrations confronted the persistence of inequality and unemployment, they grafted welfare programs onto the modest jerrybuilt system left over from the New Deal. Thus the American welfare system would always be marked by its birth during the crisis atmosphere of the Great Depression.

New Deal Coalition. Even if the early welfare system set some ill-advised precedents, it was brilliant politics. The Democratic party courted the allegiance of citizens who benefited from New Deal programs. Organized labor aligned itself with the administration that had promoted it as a legitimate force in modern industrial life. Blacks voted Democratic in direct relation to the economic benefits that poured into their communities. The Women's Division mobilized eighty thousand women at the grassroots level who supported what the New Deal had done for their communities. The unemployed also looked kindly on the Roosevelt administration. According to one of the earliest Gallup polls, 84 percent of those on relief voted the Democratic ticket in 1936.

The Democratic party did not attract only the down and out. Franklin Roosevelt's magnetic personality and the dispersal of New Deal benefits to families throughout the social structure brought middle-class voters, many of them first- or second-generation immigrants, into the Democratic fold. The New Deal thus completed the transformation begun in the 1920s toward a Democratic party reflecting the interests of ethnic groups, city dwellers, organized labor, blacks, and a broad cross section of the middle class. These voters provided the backbone of the Democratic coalition for decades to come.

Yet even in the 1930s, the New Deal coalition contained lurking, potentially fatal, contradictions, mainly over the issue of race. Because Franklin Roosevelt depended on the support of southern white Democrats for passage of New Deal legislation, he was unwilling to challenge the economic and political marginalization of blacks in the South. At the same time, New Deal programs were themselves changing the face of southern agriculture by undermining the sharecropping tenant system and encouraging the migration of southern blacks to northern and western cities. Outside the South, blacks could vote, thus guaranteeing that civil rights would enter the national agenda. The resulting fissures would eventually weaken the coalition that had seemed so invincible at the height of Franklin Roosevelt's power.

Culture and Commitment

Many American artists redefined their relationship to society in response to the Depression. Never had there been a decade, noted critic Malcolm Cowley in 1939, "when literary events followed so closely on the flying coat-tails of social events." Political engagement replaced the personal alienation of the 1920s, as world events like the rise of fascism demanded intellectuals' energy. Although not all art in the decade was federally funded, the New Deal helped to foster creative expression in the 1930s with a wide-ranging, and controversial, experiment in federal patronage of the arts.

New Deal Culture

The depression had dried up traditional sources of private patronage and creative artists, like most Americans, had nowhere to turn except Washington. The WPA project known as "Federal One" put unemployed artists, actors, and writers to work. Federal One's spirit and purpose extended far beyond mere relief. New Deal administrators wanted to redefine the relationship between artists and the community, so that art no longer would be consumed only by the elite. "Art for the millions" became a popular New Deal slogan.

The Federal Art Project (FAP) gave work to many of the twentieth century's leading painters, muralists, and sculptors at a point in their careers when the lack of

Relief Blues
Between 1934 and 1939, an Italian immigrant O. Louis Guglielmi, found work on the Federal Art Project of the WPA, to which he submitted this painting in 1938. Entitled *Relief Blues*, it represents the social concern and urban realism prominent in American painting during the 1930s. The starkness of the room and its occupants is intensified by the bright red slippers, the pink rose on the floor, and the red lipstick and nail polish of the woman on the left. (National Museum of American Art)

AMERICAN VOICES

Artists on Relief *Anzia Yezierska*

Anzia Yezierska's powerful descriptions of immigrant life, particularly *Hungry Hearts* (1920) and *Bread Givers* (1925), brought her fame and a Hollywood movie contract in the 1920s, but she found herself penniless once the depression hit. The Federal Writers' Project was her salvation.

FOUR BILLION DOLLARS FOR JOBS . . . One after another picked up the newspaper, disbelieving. Perhaps because they had fought so hard for it they were stunned. It was too good to be true. And when they were finally convinced that their dream was about to be realized, the discussion became a joyous shouting celebration.

A new world was being born. A world where artists were no longer outcasts, hangers-on of the rich, but backed by the government, encouraged to produce their best work.

The President said so.

People who no longer hoped or believed in anything but the end of the world began to hope and believe again.

In the weeks that followed, radios boomed with it. Everywhere—at grocers, cigar stores, lunch counters, in the streets—people were discussing the President's plan to end unemployment. Every day we read announcements in the newspapers of the prominent men and women appointed by the President to direct the various departments of W.P.A.

One morning as I was in the kitchen of my rooming house fixing breakfast, the radio broadcast a special news item about W.P.A.: a headquarters had just been set up for the new Writers' Project. I hurried to the address, eager to work. Ever since I had marched with the unemployed I was full of ideas for stories. All I needed to begin writing again was the security of a W.P.A. wage to get my typewriter out of the pawnshop. . . .

Each morning I walked to the Project as lighthearted as if I were going to a party. The huge, barracks-like Writers' Hall roared with laughter and greetings of hundreds of voices. As we signed in, we stopped to smoke, make dates for lunch and exchange gossip. Our grapevine buzzed with budding love affairs, tales of salary raises, whispers of favoritism, the po-litical maneuvers of the big shots, and the way Barnes told off Somervell over the phone. There was a hectic camaraderie among us, although we were as ill-assorted as a crowd on a subway express—spinster poetesses, pulp specialists, youngsters with school-magazine experience, veteran newspaper men, art-for-art's-sake literati, and the clerks and typists who worked with us—people of all ages, all nationalities, all degrees of education, tossed together in a strange fellowship of necessity. . . .

"Thank God for the depression!" a tall, gaunt man spouted. "The depression fathered W.P.A.!" His tattered coat hung loose on his shrunken body. A safety pin fastened the frayed collar of his shirt. Unaware of his rags, his ghastly appearance, he fixed his eyes on me. "Roosevelt will go down to posterity as the savior of art in America."

"The savior of art!" I laughed. "At the bargain price of $23.86 per artist."

Source: Anzia Yezierska, *Red Ribbon on a White Horse* (New York: Charles Scribner's Sons, 1950; reprint, Persea Books, 1981), 150, 156, 165.

---

private patronage might have prevented them from continuing their artistry. Jackson Pollack, Alice Neel, Willem de Kooning, and Louise Nevelson all received support. Under the direction of Holger Cahill, an expert on American folk art, the FAP commissioned murals for public buildings and post offices throughout the country. Huge WPA murals covered the walls and ceilings of terminals at the newly constructed La Guardia airport in New York. In the 1940s and 1950s as artistic tastes changed, most of La Guardia's murals were painted over, but those at its Marine Air Terminal have since been restored to their original splendor.

Under the direction of Nicholas Sokoloff, the conductor of the Cleveland Symphony Orchestra, the Federal Music Project employed fifteen thousand musicians. Government-sponsored orchestras toured the country, presenting free concerts of classical and popular music. Like many other New Deal programs, the Music Project emphasized American themes. Composer Aaron Copland wrote his *Billy the Kid* and *Rodeo* suites for the WPA, compositions that specifically incorporated western folk melodies. Musicologist Charles Seeger, and his wife, composer Ruth Crawford Seeger, catalogued the American folk tradition.

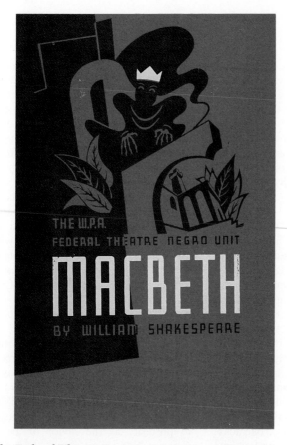

The Federal Theatre Project
The New Deal's Theatre Project promised "free, adult, un-censored theatre." One of the most popular plays was the version of Shakespeare's *Macbeth* produced by John House-man and directed by Orson Welles. This 1936 production drew on the talents of Harlem's Federal Theatre Project, one of sixteen "Negro Units" across the country. (Poster by Anthony Velonis)

Former journalist Henry Alsberg headed the Federal Writers' Project (FWP), which employed about five thousand writers at its height. Young FWP writers who later achieved fame included Saul Bellow, Ralph Ellison, Tillie Olsen, and John Cheever. The black folklorist and novelist Zora Neale Hurston finished three novels while on the Florida FWP, among them *Their Eyes Were Watching God* (1937). Richard Wright won the 1938 *Story* magazine prize for the best tale by a WPA writer and used his spare time on the project to complete *Native Son* (1940).

The Federal Writers' Project produced more than a thousand publications. It collected oral histories of Americans in many walks of life, including a set of two thousand narratives of former slaves. Its most ambitious project was a set of state guidebooks. Fifty-one state and territorial guides, city guides, and twenty regional guides, including *U.S. One: Maine to Florida*, were published, mostly by commercial presses. Combining tourism, folklore, and history, they reflected

the resurgence of interest in everything American. The guides became widely popular, but the choice of subjects occasionally annoyed politicians and state boosters. For example, the 675-page Massachusetts guide gave only fourteen lines to the Boston Tea Party and five to the Boston Massacre, while allotting thirty-one to the Sacco-Vanzetti case.

Of all the federal creative programs, the Federal Theatre Project (FTP) was the most ambitious. American drama thrived in the 1930s, the only time that the United States has had a federally supported national theater. Under the gifted direction of Hallie Flanagan, former head of Vassar College's Experimental Theater, the Theatre Project reached an audience of 25 to 30 million in the four years of its existence. Talented directors, playwrights, and actors, including Orson Welles, John Huston, and Arthur Miller, offered their services.

The Theatre Project's most successful productions included T. S. Eliot's *Murder in the Cathedral*, Mark Blitzstein's *The Cradle Will Rock*, William Shakespeare's *Macbeth* with an all-black cast in a Haitian voodoo setting, and the *Swing Mikado*, a jazz rendition of the Gilbert and Sullivan operetta. Sinclair Lewis's anti-fascist *It Can't Happen Here* opened simultaneously in eighteen cities across the country, including productions in Spanish and Yiddish. Also popular were mini-plays called "living newspapers," among them *Triple A Plowed Under*, about farm problems, and *Power*, concerning public ownership of utilities.

The theater was one of the most politically committed fields of American creative life in the 1930s. However, Congress proved unwilling to appropriate federal funds for its often controversial productions, and the Federal Theatre Project was terminated in 1939. Federal One limped on under federal-state sponsorship until 1943, when wartime priorities dealt it a final blow.

The Documentary Impulse

The WPA arts projects were influenced by a broad artistic trend called the *documentary impulse*. Combining social relevance with distinctively American themes, this approach characterized artistic expression in the 1930s. The documentary, probably the decade's most distinctive genre, influenced practically every aspect of American culture—literature, photography, art, music, film, dance, theater, and radio.

The documentary impulse was the communication of real life, the presentation of actual facts and events in a way that aroused the interest and emotions of its audience. Emphasizing observation and narration without relying on overembellished prose for impact, this technique exalted the ordinary, finding beauty and emotion in subjects not usually considered the province of art. It tried to make you, the audience, experience the subject as though you were actually on the scene.

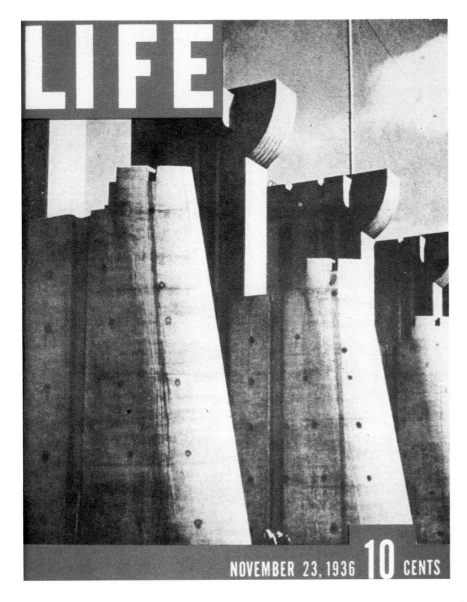

NOVEMBER 23, 1936   10 CENTS

Life

Margaret Bourke-White's photograph of the Fort Peck Dam, with the two human figures in the foreground establishing its huge scale, graced the inaugural cover of *Life* magazine in 1936. Fort Peck was part of a series of dams the WPA was constructing in the Columbia River Basin for flood control. *Life*'s first issue also contained a photo essay about the town nearest to the Fort Peck Dam, which was named, appropriately, New Deal, Montana.

The documentary impulse is evident in John Steinbeck's fiction and in John Dos Passos's *U.S.A.* trilogy, which used actual newspaper clippings, dispatches, and headlines throughout its fictional story. The *March of Time* newsreels, which movie audiences saw before the feature film, presented images of the world for the pre-television age. The standard opening of radio news broadcasts, "We now take you to . . . ," did the same thing. Filmmaker Pare Lorentz commissioned the composer Virgil Thompson to create music that set the mood for documentary movies such as *The Plow that Broke the Plains* (1936) and *The River* (1936). The new photojournalism magazines, including *Life* and *Look*, founded in 1936 and 1937, respectively, reflected this documentary approach. So did many creative works of the New Deal, from the living newspapers of the Federal Theatre Project to the American Guide series and oral history interviews prepared by the Federal Writers'

Project. The New Deal actually institutionalized the documentary impulse. It sent investigators, such as journalist Lorena Hickok and writer Martha Gellhorn, into the field to report on conditions of people on relief.

The camera was the prime instrument of the documentary impulse. The use of cameras to document social conditions dated back to the probing photography of Jacob Riis and Lewis Hines at the turn of the century. When the nation entered another period of intense social and economic questioning in the 1930s, photographers revived and updated this technique. With their haunting images of sharecroppers, Dust Bowl migrants, and the urban homeless, photographers Dorothea Lange, Walker Evans, and Margaret Bourke-White permanently shaped the image of the Great Depression.

The federal government played a leading part in compiling the photographic record of the 1930s. In 1935 Roy Stryker, a Columbia economics instructor who had been a teaching assistant under brains trust member Rexford Tugwell, took charge of the Historical Section of the Resettlement Administration. He had a mandate to document and photograph the American scene for the government. Stryker gathered a talented group of photographers for this massive task, including Evans, Lange, Ben Shahn, Arthur Rothstein, and Marion Post Wolcott. The government hired these photographers solely for their professional skills, not to provide relief like Federal One's creative projects. The photographs collected by the Historical Section, which in 1937 became part of the newly created Farm Security Administration (FSA), rank as the best visual representation of life in the United States during the depression decade.

Intellectuals and the Popular Front

By the mid-1930s, the rise of fascism in Europe and the Far East called for new forms of political engagement by writers and other intellectuals. Many literary figures participated in a broad leftist movement dedicated to stopping the spread of fascism throughout the world. The Communist party played a leading role in rallying intellectuals against the fascist threat.

The period from 1935 to 1939 marked the Communist party's greatest appeal in American society. Marxism, having predicted the collapse of capitalism, provided an alternative vision of social and economic organization. Communists were scattered throughout all walks of life in the 1930s—working-class activists, intellectuals, housewives, union organizers, farmers, blacks, and even a few New Deal administrators. No longer a small sectarian group, party membership peaked at about a hundred thousand members.

The Communist party exerted an especially powerful influence on American writers in the 1930s. Although some intellectuals joined the Communist party, many others considered themselves "fellow travelers." They sympathized with the party's objectives, wrote for the *Daily Worker* and other party newspapers, and associated with organizations sponsored by the party. Author Mary McCarthy recalled the fascination that the party held for her and other intellectuals: "For me, the Communist Party was *the* party, and even though I did not join it, I prided myself on knowing that it was the pinnacle."

The Rise of Fascism in Europe. The courting of intellectuals was part of an important shift in Communist party tactics in response to the rise of fascism. Benito Mussolini had established the first fascist regime in Italy in 1922, but fascism did not become a worldwide threat until Adolf Hitler and the National Socialist party seized power in Germany in 1933 and began a program

The Abraham Lincoln Brigade
In the Spanish Civil War, most Americans sympathized with the Loyalists, who were fighting against Franco. This 1937 song by Lewis Allen shows how American volunteers associated their fight against fascism in Spain with the figure of Abraham Lincoln, symbol of American democracy and human rights.

of massive rearmament and expansion of the German state (see Chapter 27).

Fearful of a world war set in motion by fascist aggression, the Soviet Union attempted to mobilize support in democratic countries. In Europe and the United States, communist parties called for a "popular front" and welcomed cooperation with any group concerned about the threat of fascism to such areas as civil rights, organized labor, and world peace. As part of the popular front, the American Communist party adopted the slogan "Communism is 20th Century Americanism" and worked for President Roosevelt's reelection in 1936; Eleanor Roosevelt, once depicted as a slave of the ruling class, was lauded for her humanitarianism. This alliance with American liberal groups at mid-decade represented the height of the party's impact in the United States.

The Spanish Civil War. The popular-front strategy became even more urgent with the outbreak of the Spanish Civil War in 1936. Army forces led by Generalissimo Francisco Franco led a rebellion against the elected coalition government. Franco received strong support from the fascist regimes in Germany and Italy.

Only the Soviet Union and Mexico backed the Spanish government forces, called the Loyalists. The governments of the United States, Great Britain, and France sympathized with the Loyalists but stayed neutral. In the United States strict neutrality legislation in 1935, 1936, and 1937 forbade arms shipments to either side. Because Franco was receiving substantial military aid from Germany and Italy, the neutrality policy doomed the Loyalists.

Most American activists and intellectuals, overcoming their general distaste for war, expressed shock at the policy of nonintervention. The Spanish Civil War became the most vital issue of their generation. "People of my sort," observed writer Malcolm Cowley, "were more deeply stirred by the Spanish Civil War than by any other international event since the World War and the Russian Revolution." Ernest Hemingway immortalized the Spanish conflict in his novel *For Whom the Bell Tolls* (1940).

Approximately 3,200 American men and women volunteered to fight on the Loyalist side. Calling themselves the Abraham Lincoln Brigade, they formed part of an international force of soldiers, ambulance drivers, and support personnel. Years later, survivors recalled the struggle as the "good fight." Despite assistance from the Soviet Union, the Loyalists were outnumbered and inadequately supplied and in March 1939 the Spanish Republic fell to Franco's forces. More than half the American volunteers died in the carnage, which claimed over 700,000 lives altogether.

Although American intellectuals applauded the Soviet Union's active support of the Spanish Loyalists, many literary figures began to feel uncomfortable in leftist circles. The Communists remained suspicious of intellectuals, many of whom were too independent to submit to party discipline. A number of writers found it increasingly difficult to satisfy both their artistic urges and the party's demand for fiction that reflected working-class concerns. They were also deeply distressed by mounting evidence of Soviet leader Joseph Stalin's widespread political repression.

The Nazi-Soviet Pact. The final blow to the popular front came in August 1939, when the Soviet Union, eager to avoid war, signed a nonaggression pact with Nazi Germany. Stalin's willingness to deal with Hitler devastated many supporters of the popular front. Diehard party members loyally accepted Stalin's about-face, but others left the party in disgust. The heyday of American Communism ended abruptly.

With the signing of the Nazi-Soviet pact, the world again stood on the brink of war. Although many Americans considered themselves isolationists and hoped the United States could remain aloof from the coming European conflict, they began to realize that the nation faced a greater enemy than the economic problems that had gripped the country for the past decade. Barely twenty years after the war to end all wars, the United States prepared once again to enter a worldwide struggle for the survival of democracy.

Summary

The New Deal offered a broad-based program of political and economic reform, but its programs were hardly revolutionary. President Hoover had taken the first steps toward involving the federal government more actively in economic life, a trend Roosevelt continued. The New Deal never did cure the depression, but it restored confidence that hard times could be overcome. And it provided a measure of economic security against the worst depression in American history by greatly relieving many of the tragic effects of the depression.

The New Deal dramatically expanded the size and power of the federal government, continuing a trend which had begun in the late nineteenth and early twentieth centuries. Decisions made in Washington now touched millions of individual lives. The New Deal provided new opportunities and a larger role in public life for blacks, women, and the labor movement. In politics, the Democratic coalition of white Southerners and the urban working class that had begun to emerge in the 1920s reached its climax in the landslide victory of 1936. By 1938, however, the New Deal had run out of steam and hard times were far from over.

The collapse of the economy encouraged a reassertion of American values in literature and the arts. This artistic flowering was partly supported by a unique experiment in government patronage of the arts through the WPA. Many writers blended artistic concerns with intense political commitment. This activism culminated in the popular front, where liberals and Communists joined together to oppose the spread of fascism, especially in the Spanish Civil War. The brief alliance ended in 1939 when the Soviet Union signed an agreement with Nazi Germany, bringing the world to the brink of war again.

TOPIC FOR RESEARCH

The New Deal and Your Community

Historians say that the New Deal affected virtually every locality in the country—what did it mean to yours? Find examples of the impact of New Deal projects on your local area. Likely candidates include buildings, highways, or public works projects funded by the WPA; post office murals painted by the Federal Arts Project or Treasury Department; a nearby state park or recreation area, including playgrounds and golf courses; forestry or Shelterbelt projects, perhaps in connection with a CCC camp; and a traveling art project or theatrical performance funded by the WPA. As you play historical detective, consider these questions: What did it mean to the community to have the federal government enter its life? Did the federal presence mean different things to different segments of the community?

Several overviews suggest the kinds of places to start looking. Phoebe Cutler, *The Public Landscape of the New Deal* (1985), cites examples throughout the country. Marlene Park and Gerald Markowitz, *Democratic Vistas: Post Offices and Public Art in the New Deal* (1984), surveys New Deal murals and art. Carl Fleischhaeuer and Beverly Brannan, *Documenting America, 1935–1943* (1988) samples New Deal photography. For your community, visit the local historical society or library, check for town records and old newspaper clippings from the 1930s, and seek out senior citizens. If your town does not have enough material, investigate the New Deal's impact on a large urban area such as New York or San Francisco.

BIBLIOGRAPHY

Comprehensive introductions to the New Deal include Robert S. McElvaine, *The Great Depression* (1984); William E. Leuchtenburg, *Franklin D. Roosevelt and the New Deal* (1963); Barry Karl, *The Uneasy State* (1983); John A. Garraty, *The Great Depression* (1987); and Roger Biles, *A New Deal For the American People* (1991). Other useful surveys include Albert Romasco, *The Politics of Recovery* (1983); Paul Conkin, *The New Deal* (1967); and Harvard Sitkoff, ed., *Fifty Years Later: The New Deal Evaluated* (1985). Arthur M. Schlesinger, Jr., *The Age of Roosevelt* (3 vols., 1957–1960), and Frank Freidel, *Franklin D. Roosevelt: A Rendezvous With Destiny* (1990), examine the era and its leading protagonist in detail.

The New Deal Response

The New Deal has inspired a voluminous bibliography. Frank Freidel, *Launching the New Deal* (1973) covers the first hundred days in detail. Monographic studies include Bernard Bellush, *The Failure of the NRA* (1975); Thomas K. McCraw, *TVA and the Power Fight* (1970); John Salmond, *The Civilian Conservation Corps* (1967); Jerold Auerbach, *Labor and Liberty* (1966); Susan Kennedy, *The Banking Crisis of 1933* (1973); Michael Parrish, *Securities Regulation and the New Deal* (1970); Mark Leff, *The Limits of Symbolic Reform: The New Deal and Taxation, 1933–1939* (1984); James Olson, *Saving Capitalism: The Reconstruction Finance Corporation and the New Deal, 1933–1940* (1988); and Bonnie Fox Schwartz, *The Civilian Works Administration, 1933–1934* (1984). Ellis Hawley, *The New Deal and the Problem of Monopoly* (1966), provides a stimulating account of economic policy. Agricultural developments are covered in Theodore Saloutos, *The American Farmer and the New Deal* (1982); Richard S. Kirkendall, *Social Scientists and Farm Politics in the Age of Roosevelt* (1966); David Conrad, *The Forgotten Farmers* (1965); Paul Mertz, *The New Deal and Southern Rural Poverty* (1978); and Sidney Baldwin, *Poverty and Politics: The Rise and Decline of the Farm Security Administration* (1968). Alan Brinkley, *Voices of Protest* (1982), describes the Coughlin and Long movements; see also T. Harry Williams, *Huey Long* (1969), and Leo Ribuffo, *The Old Christian Right: The Protestant Far Right From the Great Depression to the Cold War* (1983). Roy Lubove, *The Struggle for Social Security*, and J. Joseph Huthmacher, *Senator Robert Wagner and the Rise of Urban Liberalism* (1968), cover major initiatives from the Second New Deal.

The second term has drawn far less attention than the 1933–1936 period. James MacGregor Burns, *Roosevelt: The Lion and the Fox* (1956), provides an overview, as does Barry Karl, *The Uneasy State*. For the Supreme Court fight, see Joseph Alsop and Turner Catledge, *168 Days* (1938), and Leonard Baker, *Back to Back* (1967). The growing opposition to the New Deal is treated in James T. Patterson, *Congressional Conservatism and the New Deal* (1967), and Frank Freidel, *FDR and the South* (1965). See also Richard Polenberg, *Reorganizing Roosevelt's Government* (1966), and Barry Karl, *Executive Reorganization and Reform in the New Deal* (1963). James T. Patterson, *The New Deal and the States* (1969), examines changing patterns of federalism, while Charles Trout, *Boston: The Great Depression* (1977), examines the impact of the New Deal on one city.

The New Deal's Impact on Society

Katie Louchheim, ed., *The Making of the New Deal: The Insiders Speak* (1983), provides an engaging introduction to some of the men and women who shaped the New Deal. See also Peter Irons, *New Deal Lawyers* (1982). On women in the New Deal, see Susan Ware, *Beyond Suffrage* (1981). Joseph

Lash, *Eleanor and Franklin* (1971), provides a comprehensive account of Eleanor Roosevelt's activities, which can be supplemented by her autobiographies, *This Is My Story* (1937), and *This I Remember* (1949). George Martin, *Madam Secretary* (1976), covers the career of Frances Perkins. Also of interest is Perkins's memoir, *The Roosevelt I Knew* (1946).

For minorities and the New Deal, see Harvard Sitkoff, *A New Deal For Blacks* (1978); Raymond Wolters, *Negroes and the Great Depression* (1970); John B. Kirby, *Black Americans in the Roosevelt Era: Liberalism and Race* (1980); Robert Zangrando, *The NAACP Crusade Against Lynching, 1909–1950* (1980); and Nancy J. Weiss, *Farewell to the Party of Lincoln* (1983).

Irving Bernstein, *The Turbulent Years* (1970) and *A Caring Society: The New Deal, the Worker, and the Great Depression* (1985), chronicle the story of the labor movement in compelling detail through 1941. Additional studies include Peter Friedlander, *The Emergence of a UAW Local* (1975); Melvin Dubofsky and Warren Van Tine, *John L. Lewis* (1977); Sidney Fine, *Sit-Down: The General Motors Strike of 1936–1937* (1969); David Brody, *Workers in Industrializing America* (1980); Ronald Schatz, *The Electrical Workers* (1983); David Milton, *The Politics of U.S. Labor: From the Great Depression to the New Deal* (1980); and Lizabeth Cohen, *Making A New Deal: Industrial Workers in Chicago, 1919–1939* (1990).

For Indian policy, see Donald Parman, *Navajoes and the New Deal* (1976); Laurence Hauptman, *The Iroquois and the New Deal* (1981); Laurence C. Kelly, *The Assault on Assimilation: John Collier and the Origins of Indian Policy Reform* (1983); and Kenneth Philp, *John Collier's Crusade for Indian Reform, 1920–1945* (1977).

The creation of the New Deal's welfare system is treated in James T. Patterson, *America's Struggle Against Poverty* (1981), which carries the story through 1980. See also Michael Katz, *In the Shadow of the Poorhouse: A Social History of Welfare in America* (1986); John Garraty, *Unemployment in History* (1978); and Otis Graham, *Towards a Planned Society: From Roosevelt to Nixon* (1976). Margaret Weir, Ann Shola Orloff, and Theda Skocpol, eds., *The Politics of Social Policy in the United States* (1988), and Amy Gutmann, ed., *Democracy and the Welfare State* (1988), provide perspectives from political science. For the enduring impact of Franklin Roosevelt on the political system, see William Leuchtenburg, *In the Shadow of FDR* (1983).

Culture and Commitment

The various New Deal programs have found their historians in Jerry Mangione, *The Dream and the Deal: The Federal Writers' Project, 1935–1943* (1972); Monty Penkower, *The Federal Writers' Project* (1977); Richard McKinzie, *The New Deal For Artists* (1973); and Jane DeHart Mathews, *The Federal Theater, 1935–1939* (1967). General studies of cultural expression include William Stott, *Documentary Expression and Thirties America* (1973); Richard Pells, *Radical Visions*

TIMELINE	
1933	Banking crisis
	Agricultural Adjustment Act
	National Industrial Recovery Act
	Roosevelt's first fireside chat
	Tennessee Valley Authority
1934	Securities and Exchange Commission
	Indian Reorganization Act
1935	National Labor Relations (Wagner) Act
	Social Security Act
	Works Progress Administration
	Huey Long assassinated
	CIO formed
1936	Roosevelt reelected
	Black Cabinet
1936–1939	Spanish Civil War
1937–1938	Recession
1937	Supreme Court reorganization fails
	Sitdown strikes
1938	Fair Labor Standards Act
1939	Nazi-Soviet Pact

and American Dreams (1973); and R. Alan Lawson, *The Failure of Independent Liberalism, 1933–1941* (1971). See also Karen Becker Ohrn, *Dorothea Lange and the Documentary Tradition* (1980) and F. Jack Hurley, *Portrait of a Decade: Roy Stryker and the Development of Documentary Photography in the Thirties* (1972).

Daniel Aaron, *Writers on the Left* (1961), provides an overview of literary currents in the decade. For selections from the 1930s, see Harvey Swados, ed., *The American Writer and the Great Depression* (1966), and Charlotte Nekola and Paula Rabinowitz, eds., *Writing Red: An Anthology of American Women Writers, 1930–1940* (1987). See also Paula Rabinowitz, *Labor and Desire: Women's Revolutionary Fiction in Depression America* (1991). Material on the relationship between intellectuals and the Communist party is in Harvey Klehr, *The Heyday of American Communism* (1984), and Irving Howe and Lewis Coser, *The American Communist Party* (1957). Warren Susman provides a provocative analysis of culture and commitment in the 1930s in *Culture as History* (1984). See also Alice Goldfarb Marquis, *Hopes and Ashes: The Birth of Modern Times, 1929–1939* (1986), and David P. Peeler, *Hope Among Us Yet: Social Criticism and Social Solace In Depression America* (1987).

UNITED WE WIN

United We Win

This poster captured the spirit of unity and sacrifice
needed to win World War II. At the same time it
reminded Americans of the contributions blacks
were making to the war effort, a spur to civil rights.

27 *The World at War, 1939–1945*

On a Sunday night in October 1938, actor Orson Welles's "Mercury Theater of the Air" broadcast a modern version of *The War of the Worlds* (1898) by the English writer H. G. Wells. Using fictional news bulletins interspersed with simulated on-the-spot reports, Orson Welles convinced large numbers of people that Martians had landed near Princeton, New Jersey, and were invading the countryside. Even though the radio broadcast included four announcements that the attack was just a dramatization, many people fled from their homes. No one doubted the power of radio anymore.

One reason that so many people believed Orson Welles's fictional invasion may have been that during September 1938, radio programs had been repeatedly interrupted by ominous news bulletins about a possible European war. Even the news on September 30 of the Munich Agreement between England, France, and Germany, which prevented war for another year, did not ease public fears of imminent catastrophe.

By the late 1930s, popular culture, as represented by the "War of the Worlds" hoax, increasingly reflected America's involvement in international, if not cosmic, events. The coming of World War II would intensify this involvement. When radios announced on December 7, 1941, that the Japanese had attacked Pearl Harbor, Americans realized that this news flash was no hoax.

World War II ranks with the New Deal as a crucial period of political and economic change in America. Mobilization pumped money and confidence into the economy, ending the Great Depression. The task of fighting a global war increased government influence on American life and caused dramatic social changes on the home front. But the most far-reaching impact was the decision by the United States following the war to accept a leading, and continuing, role in world affairs.

The Road to War

The rise of fascism in Europe and Asia in the 1930s threatened the fragile world peace that had prevailed since the end of World War I. The League of Nations set up by the Versailles treaty, which the United States never joined, proved too weak to deal with threats to world peace. As early as 1936, Roosevelt foresaw the possibility of America's participation in another European war, but he bowed to the isolationist sentiment predominant in the country. By 1939, however, he was leading the nation toward war.

Depression Diplomacy

During the early years of the New Deal, America's involvement in international affairs remained limited. Roosevelt put national interests first, reasoning that only when the United States regained a stable economy at home could it be an effective international leader. His message to the 1933 London Economic Conference stating that the United States would not participate in plans to stabilize world currency killed any hope of common action. One of Roosevelt's few diplomatic initiatives was formal recognition of the Soviet Union in November 1933.

The Good Neighbor Policy. During his first term, Franklin Roosevelt followed the lead of the Republican administrations of the 1920s, working to consolidate American influence in the Western Hemisphere. His diplomatic strategy, which combined both political and economic goals, became known as the Good Neighbor Policy. Under the Reciprocal Trade Agreements Act of 1934, the president was empowered to raise or lower tariffs, without congressional approval, in return for reciprocal concessions from other nations. As a corollary to economic expansion, the United States also voluntarily renounced the use of military force and armed intervention in the Western Hemisphere. At the Pan-American Conference in Montevideo, Uruguay, in December 1933, Secretary of State Cordell Hull proclaimed that "no state has the right to intervene in the internal or external affairs of another." The U.S. Congress agreed in 1934 to repeal the Platt Amendment, a relic of the Spanish-American War, which had asserted the United States' right to intervene in the internal affairs of Cuba. The Navy still kept its major base at Cuba's Guantanamo Bay, a symbol of the American presence.

Isolationism. Although most Americans wished to steer clear of foreign entanglements during the early to mid-1930s, Roosevelt disagreed. An internationalist at heart, he wanted the United States to play a prominent role in an international economic and political system that would foster the long-term prosperity necessary for a lasting peace. But FDR was hampered in his wish for international action by the isolationism prevalent in Congress and the nation.

Isolationism had been building throughout the 1920s, as a product of disillusionment with American participation in World War I, and was fueled by the revelations of the Nye Committee in 1934 and 1935. Gerald P. Nye, a Republican senator from North Dakota, conducted a congressional investigation into the profits of munitions makers during World War I, and then widened the investigation to determine the influence of economic interests on America's decision to declare war. Nye's committee concluded that profiteers, whom it called "merchants of death," had maneuvered the United States into the war for financial gain.

Most of the Nye Committee's charges were dubious or simplistic, but they added momentum to the growing isolationist movement. In late 1934, President Roosevelt revived a proposal supported by the Republican administrations of the 1920s for the United States to join the World Court, a mild internationalist gesture of symbolic rather than real importance. In January 1935 the Senate rejected it.

The Neutrality Act of 1935 pushed the United States further along an isolationist course. The passage of this legislation showed the political power of such prominent isolationists as Nye, William Borah, Burton K. Wheeler, and Hiram Johnson in the senate, in addition to Joseph P. Kennedy, the Ambassador to Great Britain. Explicitly designed to prevent a recurrence of the events that had pulled the United States into World War I, the Neutrality Act imposed an embargo on arms trade with countries at war and declared that American citizens traveled on belligerent ships at their own risk.

In 1936, Congress expanded the Neutrality Act to ban loans to belligerents and, in 1937, it adopted a "cash and carry" provision. That is, if a country at war wanted to purchase nonmilitary goods from the United States, it had to pay for them in cash and pick them up in its own ships. The point of this restriction was to protect American commercial ships from attack. Roosevelt did not like it, because it gave him no discretion to decide whether some belligerents, such as the Spanish Loyalists, deserved American support. But he realized how strong the spirit of isolationism was and accepted the verdict of Congress. It would not be very long before the neutrality policy would be put to the test.

Aggression and Appeasement

World War II had its roots in the settlements of World War I. Germany deeply resented the international order laid down by the Treaty of Versailles, while other nations, notably Japan and Italy, revived their dreams of overseas empire after the war, in ways that fundamentally challenged the status quo. The League of Nations, the collective security system set up at Versailles, proved unable to stop aggression. After 1931, those who wanted to upset the status quo used force, but those who wanted to maintain it didn't.

The first challenge came from Japan. To develop as an industrial power, Japan needed raw materials and markets for its goods. By 1930 the country was under the leadership of an ultranationalist, militaristic regime, with designs on dominating the entire Pacific basin in a Greater East Asia Co-Prosperity Sphere. In 1931 the Japanese army occupied Manchuria, the northernmost province of China. China appealed to the League of Nations, which found Japan at fault, but imposed no sanctions and took no action. Japan simply resigned from the League of Nations.

Japan's defiance of the League encouraged a dictator half a world away, in Italy: Benito Mussolini. Mussolini had seized power in 1922, and introduced the system of *fascismo*. Fascism, in Italy and, later, in Germany, rested on an ideology of state control of economic affairs, the subordination of individual rights to the "collectivity," suppression of the labor movement and the Left, and in general a cult of the state, race, and war. Above all, fascism called for a strong, almost dictatorial leader. Parliamentary government and democratic guarantees were superseded by what Mussolini called, far too benevolently, a "dictatorship of the State over many classes cooperating."

Mussolini had long been unhappy with the provisions of the Versailles treaty, which did not give Italy any former German or Turkish colonies. Also, the Italians had never forgotten their stinging defeat by Abyssinia (modern Ethiopia) in 1896, the first time that Africans successfully defended themselves against white imperialists. In 1935, Italy invaded Ethiopia, one of the few independent countries left in Africa. The Ethiopian emperor Haile Selassie went before the League of Nations, which condemned the Italian action as aggression, and this time it imposed sanctions. However, member nations could not agree to include the vital sanction on oil, so the League's action had little effect. By 1936, Italian subjugation of Ethiopia was complete.

Not Italy but Germany presented the gravest threat to world order in the 1930s. The Weimar Republic of the 1920s was fundamentally unstable, saddled with huge reparations payments and a guilt clause for World War I that inflamed nationalist passions. Runaway inflation, fear of communism, labor unrest, and rising unemployment were conditions that Adolf Hitler and his National Socialist Party (Nazis) skillfully exploited. On January 20, 1933, Hitler became chancellor of Germany, and the *Reichstag* (legislature) soon gave him dictatorial powers. Hitler took the title of *Führer* (leader),

proclaimed the Third Reich, and outlawed all other political parties. Hitler's goal was nothing short of world domination, which he made clear in his book *Mein Kampf*. He would seek to overturn the territorial settlements of the Versailles treaty, "restore" all the Germans of Central and Eastern Europe to a single greater German fatherland, and annex large areas of Eastern Europe to provide "living space" for Germans. "Inferior races," such as Jews and Slavs, would have to make way for the "master race."

Hitler's strategy was to provoke a series of crises which presented England and France with no alternative but to let him have his way. Hitler withdrew from the League of Nations in 1933; two years later he announced that he planned to rearm Germany in violation of the Versailles treaty. No one stopped him. In 1936, Germany reoccupied the Rhineland, which, under the treaty, had been declared a demilitarized zone, and once again France and Britain took no action. Later that year, Hitler and Mussolini joined forces in the Rome-Berlin Axis, a political and military alliance. After the Spanish Civil War broke out in 1936, Germany and Italy supplied the Spanish fascists.

To help him fulfill his global strategy, Hitler needed an Asian ally. The obvious choice was Japan. On November 26, 1936, Japan entered into the Anti-Comintern pact with Germany. The announced purpose was to oppose communism, but the pact was really a military alliance between Japan and the Axis, which was formalized in 1940. In 1937, Japan launched a full-scale invasion of China. Once again, the League of Nations was helpless to stop the aggression.

Hitler

Adolf Hitler seized power in Germany in 1933, and embarked on a plan for world domination. Here he addresses followers at a Nazi rally in Nuremberg in 1938. Note the swastika—the Nazi symbol—prominently displayed on the uniforms of the soldiers and on the *Führer* himself.

The Failure of Appeasement. Within Germany, persecution of the Jews escalated, and Hitler's ambitions grew. In 1938 he sent troops into Austria and annexed it, proclaiming an *Anschluss* (union) between Germany and Austria. France and Great Britain hoped he would go no further, as they had been hoping since he started on his road of conquest. But the German dictator was already scheming to seize part of Czechoslovakia, the keystone of Eastern Europe. Because Czechoslovakia had an alliance with France, war seemed imminent. At the Munich Conference in September 1938, Prime Minister Neville Chamberlain of Britain and Prime Minister Edward Daladier of France capitulated to Hitler, agreeing to let Germany annex the Sudetenland, the German-speaking border areas of Czechoslovakia, in return for Hitler's pledge that he would seek no more territory.

Within six months, Adolf Hitler overran the rest of Czechoslovakia and threatened to march into Poland, exposing the folly of Chamberlain's pronouncement that the Munich agreement guaranteed "peace with honor . . . peace for our time." Britain and France realized that their policy of appeasement wouldn't work and prepared to take a stand. In August 1939, Hitler signed a nonaggression pact with the Soviet Union, shocking Popular Front supporters but protecting Germany from having to wage war on two fronts. German troops attacked Poland on September 1, 1939, and two days later Britain and France declared war. World War II had begun.

American Neutrality, 1939–1941

Two days after the war started, the United States officially declared its neutrality. Roosevelt made no secret of his sympathies, however. He pointedly rephrased Woodrow Wilson's declaration in 1914, "This nation will remain a neutral nation, but I cannot ask that every American remain neutral in thought as well." The overwhelming majority of Americans supported the Allies over the Nazis—84 percent to 2 percent, with 14 percent neutral, according to a 1939 poll—but most Americans did not want to be drawn into another world war.

So began what *Time* magazine would later call America's "thousand-step road to war." After a bitter battle in Congress, Roosevelt won a modification of the neutrality laws in November 1939. The Allies could now buy weapons from the United States, but only on the same "cash and carry" basis established for nonmilitary goods by the 1937 Neutrality Act. To avoid a repetition of the conflicts that drew the United States into World War I, Congress authorized the president to restrict Americans and American ships from entering combat zones and to prevent merchant ships from carrying cargo to combatants' ports.

After the German conquest of Poland in September

1939, a false calm settled over Europe. This "phony war" lulled many Americans into the belief that supplying the Allies with arms would be enough to defeat Germany. Hitler soon shattered their complacency. In a few hours on April 9, 1940, Nazi tanks overran Denmark. Norway fell to the Nazi *blitzkrieg* (lightning war) next, and the Netherlands, Belgium, and Luxembourg soon followed. Then the Germans stormed into France, flanking the fixed defenses of the Maginot line and making short work of the combined English and French troops. On June 22, 1940, France fell. Only England stood between the United States and Hitler's plans for world domination.

Intervention Gains. During the summer and fall of 1940, German planes bombarded England mercilessly in the Battle of Britain, while in America the debate between interventionists and isolationists continued. Journalist William Allen White and the Committee to Defend America by Aiding the Allies led the interventionists. Isolationists, including aviator Charles

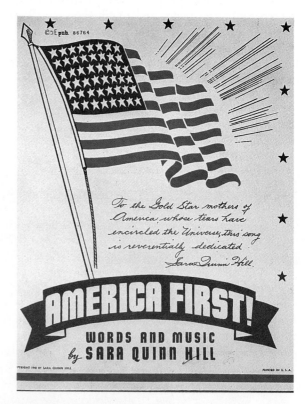

America First

In rallies, radio broadcasts, newspaper advertisements, and even in music (such as this 1940 songsheet by Sara Quinn Hill), the America First Committee expressed its opposition to U.S. entry into World War II. The movement was strongest in the Midwest, least successful in the South. After Pearl Harbor, however, the America First Committee pledged full support to the war effort.

Lindbergh, Senator Gerald Nye, and former NRA administrator Hugh Johnson, formed the America First Committee in 1940, to keep the nation out of the war. The *Chicago Tribune*, the Hearst newspapers, and other conservative publications, especially in the Midwest, gave full support to the isolationist cause.

Despite the efforts of America Firsters, in 1940 the United States moved closer to involvement. After the fall of France, the number of Americans who believed that a German victory would threaten national security increased from 43 percent (in March 1940) to 69 percent. Roosevelt began putting the economy and the government on a defense footing by creating the National Defense Advisory Commission and the Council of National Defense in May 1940. In June, he brought two prominent Republicans, Henry Stimson and Frank Knox, into his cabinet as the secretaries of war and navy, respectively, to give a bipartisan character to the war preparations. During the summer, the president traded fifty World War I destroyers to Great Britain for the right to build military bases on British possessions in the Atlantic, circumventing the 1939 neutrality legislation by an executive order. In October, a bipartisan majority in Congress approved a big increase in defense spending and instituted the first peacetime draft registration and conscription in American history. Another draft law, which came up in August 1941, lengthening draftees' service from one year to two and a half years, passed by a single vote.

The 1940 Election. In the midst of the deteriorating situation in Europe, the United States prepared for the 1940 election. Would Roosevelt seek an unprecedented third term? He had not designated a successor, and the Nazi *blitzkrieg* in the spring of 1940 convinced him that he should run again. He submitted to a "draft" at the Democratic National Convention. Although the delegates acclaimed Roosevelt's renomination, they balked at his choice for vice-president: liberal Secretary of Agriculture Henry A. Wallace, to replace John Nance Garner of Texas, a conservative who had long since broken with the New Deal. Wallace's nomination went through only after Eleanor Roosevelt flew to the convention in Chicago and asked the delegates to put politics aside in a national crisis.

The Republicans nominated a political newcomer, Wendell Willkie of Indiana, a lawyer and president of the Commonwealth and Southern Electric Utilities Company. Willkie, a former Democrat, supported many of the New Deal's domestic and international policies, including Roosevelt's destroyers for military bases deal with Britain. Trying to compete against the charismatic Roosevelt, Willkie portrayed himself as a man of the people, provoking crusty Secretary of the Interior Harold Ickes to call him "a simple barefoot Wall Street lawyer." The platforms of the two parties differed only slightly. Both pledged aid to the Allies but stopped short of calling for American participation in the war.

Initially Willkie conducted his campaign in a bipartisan spirit, but as the election approached, Republican leaders pressured him to go on the offensive. Charging that Roosevelt was leading the country into war, Willkie promised that he would not send "one American boy into the shambles of another war." Roosevelt's reply on October 28, 1940, probably clinched his victory: "I have said this before, but I shall say it again and again and again: Your boys are not going to be sent into foreign wars." Of course, if America was attacked, it would no longer be a foreign war. Willkie was a stronger contender than the Democrats had anticipated, and his spirited campaign resulted in a closer election than 1932 or 1936, but Roosevelt and the vital Democratic coalition won 55 percent of the popular vote and a lopsided victory in the electoral college.

Lend-Lease. The United States virtually entered the war when Congress passed the Lend-Lease Act in March 1941. This legislation enabled the nation to serve, in Roosevelt's words, as "the great arsenal of democracy." Great Britain, already at war for eighteen months and being bombed nightly by the German air force, could no longer afford to pay cash for arms. Roosevelt decided to "get away from the dollar sign." In a fireside chat to build support for Lend-Lease, Roosevelt used the analogy of lending a neighbor a garden hose to put out a fire: "I don't say to him, . . . 'Neighbor, my garden hose cost me fifteen dollars; you have to pay me fifteen dollars for it.' . . . . I don't want fifteen dollars—I want my garden hose back after the fire is over." Under the Lend-Lease Act, the president was empowered to "lease, lend, or otherwise dispose of" arms and other equipment to any country whose defense was considered vital to the security of the United States. In Roosevelt's view, the survival of Britain was the key to American security, so anything that helped Britain's defense was crucial to that of the United States. To administer the Lend-Lease program, Roosevelt turned to former relief administrator Harry Hopkins, who became one of his most trusted advisers during the war years.

Roosevelt's determination to aid Britain was reinforced by the personal rapport he was developing with British leader Winston Churchill. The two leaders communicated regularly. In January 1941, Roosevelt sent Harry Hopkins to meet with Churchill to lay the basis for the Anglo-American partnership. In August 1941, Roosevelt and Churchill, accompanied by the ever-present Hopkins, met secretly aboard a cruiser off the Newfoundland coast to discuss goals and military strategy. Defeating Germany was their top priority, especially since Germany had invaded the Soviet Union in June 1941, abandoning the Nazi-Soviet pact of two years earlier.

As in World War I, when Americans started supplying the Allies, the Germans attacked American and Allied ships. By September 1941, Nazi submarines and American vessels were fighting an undeclared naval war in the Atlantic, unbeknownst to the American public. In October, Congress authorized the arming of merchant vessels. However, without an actual enemy attack, Roosevelt still hesitated to ask for a declaration of war against Germany.

The Attack on Pearl Harbor

The final provocation came from Japan, not from Germany. Conflict between Japan and the United States had been building throughout the 1930s. Japanese military advances in China upset the balance of political and economic power in the Far East, where the United States had long enjoyed the economic benefits of the Open Door policy, especially control over the raw materials and large markets of China. After the Japanese invasion of China in 1937, Roosevelt denounced "the present reign of terror and international lawlessness," suggesting that aggressors like Japan be "quarantined" by peace-loving nations. But he deliberately left the meaning of "quarantine" vague, a political necessity when isolationism was so strong in the land.

Even when directly provoked, the United States avoided taking a stand. In 1937 the Japanese sank an American gunboat, the *Panay*, in the Yangtze River near Nanking. The United States allowed Japan to apologize and accepted more than $2 million in damages, and the incident was quickly forgotten.

Japanese intentions soon became more expansionist. In 1940, Japan signed the Tri-Partite Pact with Germany and Italy. By the fall of 1941, Japanese troops occupied the north part of French Indochina. The United States retaliated by effectively cutting off trade with Japan, including vital oil shipments. (At this time, the United States was producing two-thirds of the world's oil.) Before its supplies ran down, Japan had to decide whether to go forward into war or accept the demand of the American Secretary of State Cordell Hull that it cease its expansionist activities in Asia. In July 1941, Japanese troops occupied the rest of Indochina, and Roosevelt froze all Japanese assets in the United States.

In September 1941, the government of Prime Minister Hideki Tojo began secret preparations for war against the United States. By November, American military intelligence knew that Japan was planning an attack, but did not know where it would come. In fact, Japan had decided to mount simultaneous surprise attacks on all the principal British and U.S. naval bases in the Western Pacific. Early on Sunday morning, December 7, 1941, Japanese bombers attacked Pearl Harbor, killing more than 2,400 Americans. Eight battleships, three cruisers, three destroyers, and almost two hundred airplanes were destroyed or heavily damaged. There were no aircraft carriers in port at the time—vessels that were far more important in the war to come. The Japanese also failed to knock out Pearl Harbor's oil reserves, which would have stranded the navy in Hawaii until oil shipments arrived from the West Coast, thousands of miles away. From a military standpoint, the Japanese attack was actually something of a failure.

Pearl Harbor

The U.S. destroyer *Shaw* exploded into flames and smoke after receiving a direct hit during the surprise Japanese attack on Pearl Harbor on December 7, 1941. It was early Sunday morning and many of the servicemen were still asleep. More than 2,400 Americans were killed; the Japanese suffered only light losses.

But the psychological impact was devastating. Pearl Harbor Day is etched in the memories of millions of Americans, who remember precisely what they were doing when they heard about the Japanese attack. Many were relieved that the period of indecision was over. The next day, President Roosevelt went before Congress and, calling December 7 "a date which will live in infamy," asked for a declaration of war against Japan. The Senate unanimously voted for war, and the House concurred by a vote of 388 to 1. The lone dissenter was Jeannette Rankin of Montana, who had also opposed American entry into World War I. Three days later, Germany and Italy declared war on the United States, and the United States in turn declared war on Germany and Italy.

Mobilizing for Victory

The task of fighting a global war accelerated the growing influence of the state on all aspects of American life. Coordinating the changeover from civilian to war production, raising an army, and assembling the necessary work force taxed government agencies to their limits. Mobilization on such a scale demanded cooperation between business executives and political leaders in Washington, solidifying the partnership that had been growing since World War I. But the most dramatic expansion of power occurred at the presidential level, when Congress passed the War Powers Act of December 18, 1941, giving President Roosevelt unprecedented authority over the conduct of the war.

Defense Mobilization

Defense mobilization did more than end the Great Depression: it caused the economy to more than double. In 1940, the gross national product stood at $99.7 billion; it reached $211 billion by the end of the war, in 1945. After-tax profits of American business companies rose from $6.4 billion in 1940 to $10.8 billion in 1944. Agricultural output grew by a third.

During the war, the federal government spent $186 billion on war production, sometimes as much as $250 million a day. The peak of mobilization occurred in late 1943, when two-thirds of the economy was directly involved in the war effort, as opposed to only one quarter in World War I. By 1945, the United States had turned out 86,000 tanks, 296,000 airplanes, 15 million rifles and machine guns, 64,000 landing craft, and 6,500 ships. Mobilization on this gigantic scale gave a tremendous boost to the economy and, after years of depression, restored faith in the capitalist system.

The federal bureaucracy also grew far more than it had during the eight years of the New Deal. The number of civilians employed by the government increased almost fourfold, to 3.8 million. The government gave the civil service exam two or three times a day at the height of wartime hiring. The federal budget of $9.4 billion in 1939 was ten times that in 1945 at $95.2 billion. The national debt grew sixfold, topping out at $258.6 billion in 1945. Along with these astronomical federal budgets came greater acceptance of Keynesian economics—that is, the use of fiscal policy to spur economic growth.

Financing the War. Taxes paid about half the cost of the war, compared with 30 percent of the cost of World War I. The Revenue Act of 1942 continued the income tax reform begun during World War I by widening the system to reach beyond wealthy individuals and corporations to average citizens. The number of people paying income tax grew from 3.9 million in 1939 to 42.6 million in 1945; tax collections rose from $2.2 billion to $35.1 billion. This mass-based tax system, a revolutionary change in the financing of the modern state, was sold to the taxpayers as a way to express their patriotism. The system of payroll deductions and tax withholding was instituted in 1943 by the federal government to facilitate collection. Bond drives and war loans gave people the opportunity of putting their savings at the disposal of the government by buying long-term Treasury bonds, which financed the remaining cost of the war. War bonds had the side benefit of withdrawing money from circulation, which helped hold down inflation.

Roosevelt turned to business leaders to run the war economy, as had Woodrow Wilson during World War I. Defense preparations had been under way since 1940; 25 percent of the economy was already devoted to war production before Pearl Harbor. In January 1941, Roosevelt established the Office of Production Management under William Knudsen, the president of General Motors. After the Japanese attack, Roosevelt disbanded that agency and replaced it with the War Production Board (WPB), headed by Donald Nelson, a former Sears, Roebuck executive.

The War Production Board was a powerful, comprehensive agency that awarded defense contracts, evaluated military and civilian requests for scarce resources, and oversaw the conversion of industries to military production. Many business leaders, the depression still fresh in their minds, were reluctant to invest in plant expansion or new production, so as a spur, the government granted generous tax write-offs for plant construction. It also approved contracts with cost-plus provisions that guaranteed profits and promised that industries could keep the factories after the war.

In the interest of efficiency and maximum production, the WPB found it easier to deal with major corporations than with small businesses. The fifty-six largest corporations held three-fourths of the war contracts, with a full third going to the top ten. This system of allocating contracts, along with the suspension of antitrust prosecution during the war, hastened the trend toward large corporate structures. In 1940 the largest hundred companies manufactured 30 percent of the nation's industrial output; by 1945, their share had grown to 70 percent. These same corporations formed the core of the military-industrial complex of the postwar years (see Chapters 28 and 29).

The Office of Price Administration and Civilian Supply (OPA) oversaw the domestic economy, allocating resources and trying to keep inflation down. By February 1942 retail prices were rising rapidly at 2 percent a month. In April the OPA froze most prices and rents at their March 1942 level. When loopholes, especially regarding food prices, undermined the effort, Congress passed the Anti-inflation Act, which stabilized prices, wages, and salaries. The Consumer Price Index rose 28.3 percent between 1940 and 1945, but most of the inflation occurred before 1943.

Roosevelt remained unsatisfied with the mobilization effort; there were too many government agencies and they often overlapped. In October 1942 Roosevelt persuaded Justice James F. Byrnes to resign from the Supreme Court and head the Office of Economic Stabilization and, after 1943, the Office of War Mobilization. Byrnes soon became the second most powerful person in the administration and finally brought order to production goals for civilian and military needs. The results were remarkable.

Shipbuilding showed American productive capacity at full strength. By 1941, the German navy had crippled transatlantic transport, sinking about 12 million tons of Allied shipping—mainly U.S. built—in the North Atlantic. Producing replacement vessels became a high priority. By turning out easy-to-build but clunky Liberty ships, which Roosevelt, an experienced sailor, called "ugly ducklings," the United States produced 19 million tons of merchant shipping by 1943, up from a million tons just two years earlier.

Henry J. Kaiser, a West Coast shipbuilder, performed shipyard production miracles. Using the mass production techniques of the automobile industry, Kaiser cut the time needed to build a transport ship from three hundred days to seventeen. He motivated workers through high pay and fringe benefits, including one of the country's first prepaid medical programs.

Kaiser's name became synonymous with getting things done fast. Although not all industries could boast such relative freedom from snafus (an acronym coined during the war from the expression "situation *n*ormal, *a*ll *f*ouled *u*p"), business and government compiled an impressive record. As in World War I, industry played a significant role in the military victory.

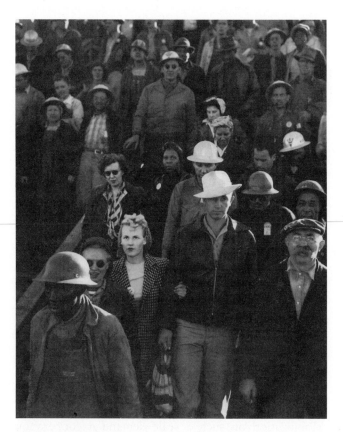

Wartime Workers
Photographer Dorothea Lange captured these shipyard construction workers coming off their shift at a factory in Richmond, California, in 1942. Note the large number of women workers, and also the presence of minority workers. Several of the workers are prominently wearing union buttons. (The Oakland Museum)

Mobilizing the American Fighting Force

Going to war meant mobilizing human resources, both for the battlefield and on the home front. During World War II, the armed forces of the United States numbered more than 15 million men and women. The army enlisted the most—about 10.5 million, including those who served in the Army Air Force—but almost 4 million served in the Navy, 600,000 in the Marines, and 240,000 in the Coast Guard.

Draft boards registered about 31 million men between the ages of eighteen and forty-four and ordered physical examinations for about a sixth of the male population. More than half the men failed to meet the physical standards: a height of 5 feet; weight of 105 pounds; correctable vision; at least half the number of natural teeth; no flat feet, hernia, or venereal disease. Defective teeth and eyes caused the greatest number of rejections. The military's attempts to screen out homosexuals were ineffectual. Once in the services, homosexuals found opportunities to participate in a gay subculture unavailable in civilian life.

Class distinctions and racial discrimination prevailed in the armed forces, mainly directed against the approximately seven hundred thousand blacks in uniform. Blacks served in all branches of the armed forces, but they were assigned the most menial duties; a great number served as messmen on navy ships, for example. The army segregated black and white blood banks, a practice without genetic or scientific merit. The NAACP and other civil rights groups chided the government with such reminders as "A Jim Crow army cannot fight for a free world," but the military remained rigidly segregated.

Women in Military Service. About 350,000 American women, both black and white, enlisted in the armed services and achieved permanent status in the military establishment. There were about 140,000 WACS (Women's Army Corps), 100,000 WAVES (Women Appointed for Volunteer Emergency Service in the Navy), 23,000 members of the Marine Corps Women's Reserve, and 13,000 SPARs (for *Semper Paratus*, or *Always Ready*, the Coast Guard motto) in the Coast Guard. In addition, about 1,000 WASPs (Women's Airforce Service Pilots) ferried planes and supplies in noncombat areas. A third of the nation's registered nurses volunteered for military duty: about 60,000 served in the army, and 14,000 in the navy.

The armed forces limited the types of duty assigned to women, as it did with blacks. Women were barred from combat, although nurses and medical personnel sometimes served close to the front lines, risking capture. Most jobs reflected stereotypes of women's roles in civilian life—clerical work, communications, and health care. The pin-ups of Betty Grable in a bathing suit, Rita Hayworth in a flimsy nightgown, and, for the black soldiers, the tempestuous singer Lena Horne, which were widely distributed to the troops, were probably closer to the average GI's view of women than a WAC or a WAVE was.

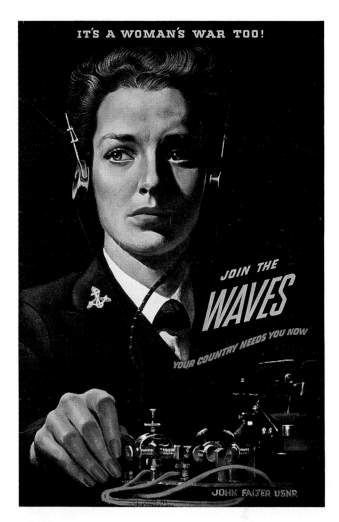

Join the Waves
Government ads pitched patriotic appeals to join the military, and women eagerly enlisted. As the poster said, "It's a Woman's War Too." Once in the navy, a WAVE would likely find herself stateside, working at jobs traditionally held by women, like clerical work. Not until 1944 were WAVES permitted to serve overseas.

Women and the War Effort

When millions of citizens entered military service, a huge hole opened in the American work force. The backlog of Depression-era unemployment quickly disappeared, and the United States faced a critical labor shortage. The nation's defense industries provided jobs for about seven million new workers, including great numbers of women and blacks, who found employment opportunities for the first time.

Government planners "discovered" women while casting about for workers to fill the jobs vacated by departing servicemen. The recruiting campaign drew on patriotism. One poster urged, "Longing won't bring him back sooner . . . GET A WAR JOB!" Recruiters promised that women would take to riveting machines and drill presses "as easily as to electric cake-mixers and vacuum cleaners." The artist Norman Rockwell supported the campaign by creating his famous "Rosie the Riveter" cover for the *Saturday Evening Post.*

Although the government directed its propaganda at housewives, women who were already employed gladly abandoned low-paying "women's" jobs as domestic servants or file clerks for higher-paying jobs in defense factories. Suddenly the nation's factories were full of women, working as riveters, welders, blast furnace cleaners, and drill press operators. Women made up 36 percent of the labor force in 1945, compared with 24 percent at the beginning of the war. When the war ended, an overwhelming majority said they wanted to keep their jobs.

Women Aviators
WASPs piloted every type of military aircraft, from the huge B-29 bombers to sleeker fighter craft. Barred from combat duty, women pilots mainly ferried planes and supplies throughout the United States and Canada. As the smile on this aviator's face shows, the women were just glad to be able to fly at all. Because women pilots never achieved full military status, they were ineligible for military and veterans' benefits when the war ended.

However, government planners regarded women as just filling in while the men were away. Employers rarely offered such benefits as day care or flexible hours. Government child care programs set up by the 1940 Lanham Act reached only 10 percent of those who needed them. Because women were responsible for home care as well as for their jobs, they had a higher absentee rate than men did. Often, the only way to get shopping done or take a child to the doctor was to skip work. Women war workers also faced discrimination on the job. In shipyards, women with the most seniority and responsibility earned $6.95 a day, while the top men made as much as $22 a day.

When the men came home from war and the plants returned to peacetime operations, Rosie the Riveter was out of a job. However, many women refused to put on an apron and stay home. Women's participation in the labor force dropped temporarily when the war ended, but rebounded steadily for the rest of the 1940s.

Organized Labor

The labor movement also grabbed opportunities during the wartime mobilization effort. No dramatic changes occurred, but the war confirmed the industrial breakthroughs of the 1930s. By the end of the war, almost fifteen million workers—a third of the nonagricultural labor force, up from nine million at the end of the previous decade—belonged to unions.

Organized labor responded to the war with an initial burst of patriotic unity. On December 23, 1941, representatives of major unions made a "no strike" pledge—albeit nonbinding—for the duration of the war. To maintain industrial peace, in January 1942, President Roosevelt set up the National War Labor Board (NWLB), composed of representatives of labor, management, and the public. The board established wages, hours, and working conditions and had the authority to order government seizure of plants that did not comply. Forty plants were seized during the war.

During its tenure, the NWLB handled 17,650 disputes affecting 12 million workers. It faced two controversial issues: union membership and wage increases. Union organizers favored either the union shop or the closed shop, but management preferred the open shop. (In a union shop, the employees must belong to a certain union, or join it within a specified period. In a closed shop, the employer may hire only workers who are already members of a union. In an open shop, the employer usually uses only nonunion workers.) As a compromise, the NWLB imposed the principle of maintenance of membership. Workers did not have to join a union, but those already in a union had to maintain their membership during the life of the contract.

Agitation for wage increases caused a more serious disagreement. In contrast to the deflation of the depression, inflation pushed prices up throughout the war. Because management wanted to keep production (and profits) running smoothly, it was willing to pay the higher wages demanded by workers. However, such raises would conflict with the OPA policy of keeping inflation as low as possible. In 1942 the NWLB established the "Little Steel Formula," which granted a 15 percent wage increase to match the increase in the cost of living since January 1, 1941. Although the NWLB froze hourly wages in principle, it allowed them to rise another 24 percent by 1945. Actually, incomes rose as much as 70 percent because workers earned overtime pay, which was not covered by wage ceilings. The tremendous increase in output during World War II was largely because people worked overtime.

Although incomes were higher than anyone in the depression would have dreamed possible, many union members felt cheated as they watched corporate profits soar while their wages remained frozen. The high point

AMERICAN VOICES

"Rosie the Riveter" *Helen Studer*

Helen Studer was forty-four years old, and had a son in the armed forces, when she went to work at Douglas Aircraft in 1942. Overcoming blatant age discrimination, she eventually fought for a promotion to an inspection job before returning to full-time homemaking when the war ended.

We didn't train in the plant; we trained someplace else. You had classes and somebody'd be talking and get you familiar with what the process was going to be. We didn't get right down to basic working for, oh, probably three weeks or more. Then we went out to the plant.

I was awed, really awed. It is so huge. Well, you can imagine how big it would be to have that big airplane. And all these fluorescent lights. The place was just like daylight. Really, it takes you several hours almost to quit looking. I had never been inside anything like that. And the noise was absolutely terrible. There were times that the noise was just so bad, you'd have to really lay your tools down and walk outside. I wore earplugs a lot of times. . . .

I was going to work on the wing section; I was going to be a riveter or bucker. The one that drove the rivets had to have the drill and a whole set of different-sized bits, 'cause you never knew what size you were going to use. I didn't do a whole lot of bucking because I wasn't that strong. They furnished you with a rivet gun, but you had to have your own drill, your own hammer, your own flashlight. Small things.

They assigned you your job according to what they thought you could do. My husband's cousin's granddaughter, she went to work out there at the same time. She didn't rivet, either. She got a job with inspection right off the bat. Young and beautiful, see. An old lady didn't get anything like that. I was assigned to this wing section on the C-47. There were usually two of you paired together, and you stay with what you were doing, and then they'd have an inspector come along.

The men really resented the women very much, and in the beginning it was a little bit rough. You had to hold your head high and bat your eyes at 'em. You learned to swear like they did. However, I made myself stop because I don't think it's too ladylike. The men that you worked with, after a while, they realized that it was essential that the women worked there, 'cause there wasn't enough men and the women were doing a pretty good job. So the resentment eased. However, I always felt that they thought it wasn't your place to be there.

But some of the characters they had working there was just something else. We had a leadman and that was more or less a disaster. He was a young fellow, about the same age as my son who was overseas in the war—that was a primary reason to work, because I had a son that was in the service. Anyhow, this young fellow, they lived in Santa Ana and they were quite well-to-do people and his father bought him off. Got him a job in the defense plant so he was deferred. Boy, was he useless. He didn't know as much as we girls did. Time and time again, I've gone around the side of the plane, and he'd be sitting there playing mumblety-peg. And we women working our heads off! Just goes to show the politics.

Source: Sherna Berger Gluck, *Rosie the Riveter Revisited: Women, the War, and Social Change* (Boston: Twayne, 1987), 186–88.

of dissatisfaction came in 1943. First a nationwide railroad strike was narrowly averted. Then John L. Lewis led more than half a million United Mine Workers out on strike, demanding wages higher than the Little Steel Formula allowed. Lewis won concessions, but he alienated Congress, and by defying the government, he became one of the most disliked public figures of the 1940s.

Congress countered Lewis's action by overruling Roosevelt's veto of the Smith-Connally Labor Act of 1943, which required a thirty-day cooling-off period before a strike and prohibited strikes in defense industries entirely. Nevertheless, about fifteen thousand strikes occurred during the war. Less than one tenth of a percent of working hours were lost to strikes, but the public perceived the disruptions as far more costly. Labor unions won acceptance during the war years, but also provoked increased hostility.

Politics in Wartime

At a press conference late in 1943, President Roosevelt playfully announced that "Dr. Win the War" had replaced "Dr. New Deal." During the 1940s, Roosevelt rarely pressed for further social and economic change, thus placating conservative members of Congress whose support he needed to conduct the war in a bipartisan spirit. With little protest, he agreed to drop several popular New Deal programs. In 1942 the Civilian Conservation Corps was dismantled, followed in 1943 by the National Youth Administration and the Works Progress Administration. Severe budget cuts crippled the Farm Security Administration, which had represented the interests of poor farmers. The speed with which the government terminated these agencies suggested that they had been more a response to the crisis of the depression than a commitment to promoting the general welfare through federal programs. Such programs as Social Security remained untouched, however.

The war years brought a significant decline in the reform spirit that had flourished in Washington during the 1930s. Few public figures talked about using the war to bring about social change, as they did in World War I. One exception was the reform of the tax system. Business executives replaced the reformers and social activists who had staffed New Deal relief agencies in the 1930s. These executives became known as "dollar-a-year men" because they volunteered for government service while remaining on their corporate payrolls.

Roosevelt had hoped politics could be shelved for the duration of the war, but that expectation proved unreasonable. The Republicans picked up seats in both houses of Congress and increased their share of state governorships in the 1942 election. These gains reflected the general tendency of the party out of power to improve its position in off-year elections. The Republicans also benefited from a low voter turnout. Relocations, caused by enlistment, and residency requirements contributed to the low turnout.

Roosevelt himself did not give up politics for the duration. After concluding that continuation of the war made a fourth term necessary, Roosevelt went on a mild offensive to attract Democratic voters. In his state of the union address in 1944, the president called for a second Bill of Rights. As the basis of postwar prosperity, he pledged such rights as a job, adequate food and clothing, a decent home, proper medical care, and an education.

The president's sweeping commitment remained largely rhetorical. Congressional support for this vast extension of the welfare state did not exist in 1944. It was possible, however, to win some of these rights for a special group of American citizens: the veterans. The GI Bill of Rights, passed in 1944, provided education, job training, medical care, pensions, and mortgage loans for men and women who had served in the armed forces during the war.

The Election of 1944. "I am an old campaigner and I love a good fight," Franklin Roosevelt had said during the 1940 election. He approached the 1944 campaign with the same verve, but the years had taken their toll. Concern about Roosevelt's health and need for a succes-

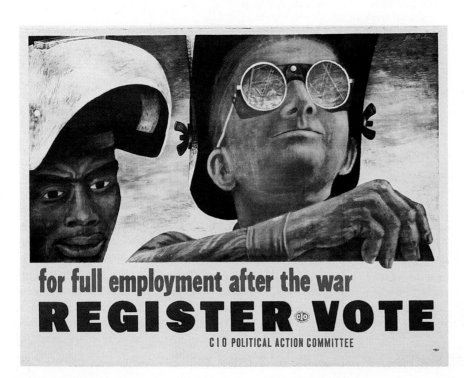

Labor and Politics
The CIO Political Action Committee was formed to harness the political power of new recruits for labor's postwar agenda, especially full employment. Artist Ben Shahn's vivid 1944 poster reinforced the CIO's commitment to racial equality. (The Museum of Modern Art, New York)

sor prompted the Democrats to drop Vice-President Henry Wallace, whose outspoken support for labor, civil rights, and domestic reform was too extreme for many party leaders. In Wallace's place, they chose Senator Harry S. Truman of Missouri.

Truman, a World War I veteran and Kansas City haberdasher whose business had failed in the 1920–1921 recession, found success in politics. Sponsored by Thomas Pendergast, the Democratic boss in Kansas City, he was elected to the Senate in 1934 and reelected in 1940. Truman became known for heading a Senate investigation of government waste and inefficiency in defense contracts during the war.

The Republicans nominated New York Governor Thomas E. Dewey. Only forty-two years old, Dewey had won fame fighting organized crime as a U.S. attorney. He accepted the broad outlines of the welfare state and belonged to the internationalist wing of the Republican party. The 1944 election was the closest since 1916. Roosevelt received 53.5 percent of the popular vote. The Democrats lost ground among farmers, but most ethnic groups remained solidly Democratic. Roosevelt got his customary support from the South, augmented by the overwhelming allegiance of members of the armed forces, who voted by absentee ballot. His margin of victory came from the cities. In urban areas with more than a hundred thousand people, the president drew 60 percent of the vote.

Roosevelt also received strong support from organized labor. Under the prodding of CIO leaders Sidney Hillman and Philip Murray, labor contributed more than $1.5 million, or about 30 percent of the Democratic party's election funds. The CIO's Political Action Committee canvassed door-to-door and conducted voter registration campaigns. Organized labor continued to play a significant role in the Democratic party after the war.

Life on the Home Front

In contrast to World War I, there was almost no domestic opposition to the nation's role in World War II. Americans fought for their way of life and for the preservation of democracy against the forces of Nazi and Japanese totalitarianism. Because the enemies seemed so evil, and America's will to fight was so strong, many remember it as the "good war." But those words have an ironic meaning for certain groups of Americans, notably Japanese-Americans.

"For the Duration"

Although the United States did not suffer the physical devastation that ravaged much of Europe and the Far East, the war affected the lives of those who stayed behind. Every time a family with a loved one overseas saw the Western Union boy on his bicycle, they were afraid it meant a telegram from the War Department telling them that their son or husband or father would not be coming home. Other Americans tolerated small deprivations daily. "Don't you know there's a war on?" be-

Wartime Prosperity
War mobilization brought prosperity to many American households. This photograph, taken in 1942, shows the Hall family of Sheffield, Alabama, in their comfortable home, part of a defense housing project connected with the TVA. The picture looks posed, but the new levels of consumption and affluence it represented were true for many Americans like the Halls.

came the standard reply to a request that could not be fulfilled. People accepted the fact that their lives would be different "for the duration."

Just like the soldiers in uniform, people on the home front had a job to do. They worked on civilian defense committees, performed volunteer work, donated blood, collected old newspapers and scrap material, and served on local rationing or draft boards. Advertising campaigns displaying the popular "V for Victory" slogan stressed patriotism. All seven war loan drives were oversubscribed. "Victory gardens" in about 20 million homes produced 40 percent of the vegetables grown in the United States.

However, many Americans remember the war years as much for the return of prosperity as for anything else. Unemployment disappeared and per capita income rose from $691 in 1939 to $1,515 in 1945. Despite geographical dislocations and shortages of various items, about 70 percent of the population admitted midway through the war that they had personally experienced "no real sacrifices." A Red Cross worker put it bluntly: "The war was fun for America. I'm not talking about the poor souls who lost sons and daughters. But for the rest of us, the war was a hell of a good time."

During the war years, demographic patterns rebounded from their depression-induced declines. Young people could afford to marry, and the imminent departure of men for military service induced many couples to take the step sooner rather than later. Not all these marriages survived the strain of separation or wartime relocation, and the divorce rate also rose. The birth rate went up, with many babies being conceived before their fathers went off to war. In effect, the wartime birth patterns marked the beginning of the pro-family "baby boom" that characterized American culture in the postwar period.

Popular Culture. Popular culture, especially the movies, reinforced the connections between the home front and the troops serving overseas. Hollywood escaped the restrictions and cutbacks that affected other industries, in part because studio heads argued that movies built morale. Many Hollywood directors leant their services to the military. Director Frank Capra's "Why We Fight" series, a documentary produced for the War Department, explained war aims to new soldiers and sailors. John Huston provided an intensely realistic portrayal of men in combat in *The Battle of San Pietro* (1944).

The average weekly movie attendance soared during the war, to over 100 million. Demand was so high that many theaters operated around the clock to accommodate defense workers on the swing and night shifts. Many movies had patriotic themes, and such films as *Wake Island* (1942) and *Thirty Seconds over Tokyo*

Entertaining the Troops

The original Stage Door Canteen opened in the basement of a Broadway theater in 1942. It served servicemen coffee, doughnuts, and big-time entertainment volunteered by Broadway and Hollywood stars. The canteen's popular weekly radio show was the inspiration for the 1943 movie *Stage Door Canteen*.

(1945) portrayed life in the armed services. Dramas about struggles on the home front were also popular. In the box-office hit *Since You Went Away* (1943), Claudette Colbert took a war job after her husband went off to fight; Oscar-winning Greer Garson played a courageous British housewife in *Mrs. Miniver* (1942). Newsreels accompanied feature films and kept the public up-to-date on the war, as did on-the-spot radio broadcasts by commentators such as Edward R. Murrow. Thus popular culture reflected America's new international responsibilities at the same time as it built up home front morale.

Rationing. During the war, almost anything that Americans ate, wore, or used was subject to rationing or regulation. The first major scarcity was rubber. The Japanese conquest of Malaya and the Netherlands East Indies cut off 97 percent of America's imports of natural rubber, an essential raw material for war production. An entire new industry, synthetic rubber, was born, and by late 1944 the United States was producing 762,000 tons of it a year, mostly for the war effort.

Meanwhile, to conserve rubber, the government rationed tires, a hard sacrifice for the nation's 30 million car owners. Many people put their cars up on blocks for the duration. If people walked instead of drove, they wore out their shoes. In 1944 shoes were rationed to two pairs per person a year, barely half the average number people bought before the war.

The government also rationed gasoline and fuel oil. Shortages of fuel oil forced schools and restaurants to shorten their hours; home thermostats were lowered to 65 degrees. Gasoline rationing, introduced in December 1942, was both a response to depleted domestic gasoline supplies and an attempt to save wear on precious rubber tires. To further discourage gasoline consumption, Congress imposed a nationwide speed limit of 35 miles per hour, and highway death rates dropped dramatically.

People found it harder to cut back on eating. Among the many food items that were in short supply during the war, sugar disappeared quickly from grocery shelves. The government soon rationed it at the rate of 8 to 12 ounces per person a week. However, the manufacturers of such products as Coca-Cola and Wrigley's chewing gum received unlimited quantities of sugar by convincing the government that their products helped the morale of the men and women in the armed forces.

By 1943 the amount of meat, butter, and other foods Americans could buy was regulated by a complicated system of rationing points and coupons. Most people cooperated with the restrictions, but almost a fourth occasionally bought items on the black market.

Shortages of other consumer products also hit the home front. With the economy growing, people finally had enough money to buy refrigerators, cars, and radios, but the components of these items—such as rubber, copper, and steel—had been earmarked for war production. The last Ford rolled off the assembly line in 1942 and automobile plants converted to bomber production. To placate consumers, many companies ran advertisements promising delayed gratification. After the war, they told the public, you can buy that new house and fill it with all the appliances you dreamed of.

But some purchases just could not wait. One of the most sought-after items on the black market was women's stockings. In the 1930s, women had worn silk stockings, but when the war with Japan cut off imports of silk they switched to nylon stockings. Unfortunately for women, nylon was essential to war production: thirty-six pairs of nylons equaled one parachute. Many women began wearing slacks in public, a dramatic fash-

ion change of the 1940s. The strict rationing of food and other items eased in the summer of 1944, when victory appeared on the horizon.

Migration and Family Life. The war caused people to move from one part of the country to another in unprecedented numbers. When men volunteered or were drafted into the armed services, their families often followed them to training bases or points of debarkation. The lure of high-paying defense jobs encouraged others to move. About 15 million Americans changed their residences during the war years, half of them moving to another state. The pace of urbanization increased, but this movement was not simply an exodus from rural to urban areas. About 5.4 million people left farms, but 2.5 million moved onto them. A million southerners, black and white, went north, but 600,000 migrants moved south. The greatest number of people went west.

As a center of defense production, California was affected by wartime migration more than any other state. During the war, one-tenth of all federal dollars went to California, and the state turned out one-sixth of the total war material. California welcomed nearly 3 million new residents during the war, a 53 percent population growth. They went where the defense jobs were—to Los Angeles, San Diego, and the San Francisco Bay Area. Some towns grew practically overnight. In just two years after the Kaiser Corporation opened a shipyard in Bay-area Richmond, the population quadrupled.

Migration and relocation often caused strains. Many towns with defense industries had scarce housing, inadequate public transportation, and tensions between old-timers and newcomers over public space and recreation. Of special concern were young people whom the war had set adrift from traditional community restraints. Newspapers were filled with stories of "latchkey" children, home alone while their mothers were at work in defense plants. Adolescents were even more of a problem. Teenage girls who hung around army bases looking for a good time were known as "victory girls."

In 1942 and 1943, juvenile delinquency seemed to be reaching epidemic proportions. In Los Angeles, male Hispanic teenagers organized *pachuco* (youth) gangs, dressing in broad felt hats, pegged trousers, and clunky shoes, wearing long slicked-down hair, and carrying pocket knives on gold chains. (This style was especially suitable for the jitterbug craze.) Such youths became known as "zoot suiters." Although this style was most popular among Hispanics, it was also taken up by blacks and by a few white working-class teenagers in Los Angeles, Detroit, New York, and Philadelphia. To adults, and many Anglos, the Zoot Suit came to symbolize wartime juvenile delinquency.

Zoot Suits

Zoot suit fashions gained wide popularity among young Americans during the war. In 1943, this well-dressed teenager greased his hair in a ducktail and wore a loosely cut coat with padded shoulders ("fingertips") that reached mid-thigh, baggy pleated pants cut tight ("pegged") around the ankles, and a long gold watch chain.

In Los Angeles, white hostility toward the Mexican-American community had been smoldering for some time, and zoot suiters became the targets. In July 1943 rumors that a Hispanic gang had beaten a white sailor set off a four-day riot, during which white servicemen entered Mexican-American neighborhoods and attacked zoot suiters, taking special pleasure in slashing the pegged pants of their victims. The attacks occurred within full view of white police officers, who did nothing to stop the violence.

Rising Winds of Change for African-Americans

"A wind is rising throughout the world of free men everywhere," Eleanor Roosevelt wrote during the war, "and they will not be kept in bondage." Unlike Mexican-Americans, for whom the war did little to bring about lasting change, African-Americans felt such a rising wind in the 1940s. The war disrupted a number of traditional patterns, and many barriers to racial equality tottered or fell.

Even before Pearl Harbor, there was evidence that the war might encourage greater black activism. In 1940 only 240 of the nation's 100,000 aircraft workers were black, and most of them were janitors. Black leaders demanded that the government require defense contractors to integrate their work forces. When the government took no action, A. Philip Randolph, head of the Brotherhood of Sleeping Car Porters, a black union, announced plans for a "March on Washington" in the summer of 1941. Roosevelt was not a strong supporter of civil rights, but he feared the embarrassment of such a massive public protest. Even more, he feared a disruption of war preparations. The president agreed to take action, and Randolph canceled the march.

In June 1941, Roosevelt issued an executive order declaring it to be the policy of the United States "that there shall be no discrimination in the employment of workers in defense industries or government because of race, creed, color, or national origin." To oversee the policy, the president established the Fair Employment Practices Committee (FEPC) in the Office of Production Management.

This federal commitment to black employment rights was unprecedented, but still limited in scope. For instance, it did not affect segregation in the armed forces. Moreover, the FEPC, which could not require compliance with its orders, often found that the needs of defense production took precedence over fair employment. The FEPC received more than eight thousand complaints, of which it resolved about a third. Blacks made up 8 percent of the defense workers in 1944, probably because of the labor shortage more than the FEPC prodding. Nevertheless, they got symbolic satisfaction from the federal action against discrimination in the work force.

Spurred by the new economic opportunities in defense and factory work, blacks migrated from the South in increasing numbers after the temporary slowdown of the depression. More than a million African-Americans moved to defense centers in California, Illinois, Michigan, Ohio, and Pennsylvania. Their need for jobs and housing led to racial conflict in several cities.

Some of the worst racial violence took place in Detroit, the new home of a large number of southern migrants, both black and white. Competition over scarce housing caused many of the disputes. Early in 1942, black families encountered resistance and intimidation when they tried to move into the Sojourner Truth housing project in the Polish community of Hamtramck. Similar tensions erupted into violence in June 1943, when a major race riot in Detroit left thirty-four people dead, including twenty-five blacks. Racial conflicts broke out in forty-seven cities throughout the country during 1943.

A new mood of militancy appeared among the nation's minorities during the war years. Black leaders pointed out parallels between anti-Semitism in Germany and racial discrimination in America. Civil rights leaders pledged themselves to a "Double V" campaign: victory over Nazism abroad and victory over racism and inequality at home.

Encouraged by the ideological climate of the war years, black organizations increased their membership. The NAACP grew ninefold, to 450,000 in 1945. In 1942, A. Philip Randolph helped found the Congress of Racial Equality (CORE). Unlike the NAACP, which favored lobbying and legal strategies, CORE was more aggressive; its tactics included demonstrations and sit-ins. In 1944, CORE forced several restaurants in Washington, D.C., to serve blacks after picketing them with signs that read "Are You for Hitler's Way or the American Way? Make Up Your Mind."

An awareness of civil rights was heightened in other ways as well. The Swedish sociologist Gunnar Myrdal wrote a monumental study of race relations, *An American Dilemma: The Negro Problem and Modern Democracy* (1944), focusing white Americans' attention on the issue for the first time. In 1944 the Supreme Court ruled in *Smith v. Allwright* that Texas's all-white primary election, a common device used to disfranchise blacks in southern states, was unconstitutional. Following the Court's decision, Congressman Wright Patman of Texas vowed that blacks in his district would vote "over my dead body." Soon, however, Patman was courting black voters at church picnics and other social events in his reelection campaigns. These wartime developments laid the groundwork for the civil rights revolution of the 1950s and 1960s.

Japanese Relocation

Although racial confrontations and Zoot Suit riots recalled the widespread racial tensions of World War I,

the mood on the home front was generally calm in the 1940s. German culture and German-Americans did not come under suspicion, nor did Italian-Americans. Leftists and Communists were left alone mainly because after Pearl Harbor, the Soviet Union became an ally of the United States. There was one glaring exception to this record of tolerance: the internment of Japanese-Americans on the West Coast. The prejudice and hysteria directed at Japanese-Americans is a reminder of the fragility of civil liberties in wartime.

Immediately after Pearl Harbor, the West Coast remained calm. Then partly as a reflection of the region's vulnerability to attack, coastal residents began to demand protection against supposed Japanese spies. California had a long history of antagonism toward both Japanese and Chinese immigrants. The Japanese-Americans, who clustered together in highly visible communities, were a small, politically impotent minority. Unlike German- or Italian-Americans, the Japanese stood out. "A Jap's a Jap," an army general stated. "It makes no difference whether he is an American citizen or not."

Mounting fears on the West Coast brought a far-reaching decision from Washington in early 1942. President Roosevelt approved a War Department plan to intern Japanese-Americans in relocation camps for the duration of the war. In March 1942, Milton Eisenhower, a career civil servant and the brother of General Dwight D. Eisenhower, took over the War Relocation Authority, a civilian agency created to carry out the policy. Few public leaders opposed the plan. The Supreme Court upheld its constitutionality as a legitimate exercise of power during wartime in *Hirabayashi v. United States* (1943) and *Korematsu v. United States* (1944).

The relocation announcement shocked Japanese-Americans, more than two-thirds of whom were native-born American citizens. (They comprised the *Nisei* generation, the children of the foreign-born *Issei* generation.) The government gave families only a few

Japanese Internment

A Japanese-American family arrives at their new "home" in Heart Mountain, Wyoming, after being relocated from the West Coast military zone. The average internee spent 900 days—more than two and a half years—confined behind the barbed wire, which is not visible in this picture.

AMERICAN VOICES

The Insult and Injury of Internment *Peter Ota*

Peter Ota's father had come from Okinawa in 1904 and had built up a successful fruit and vegetable business in the Los Angeles area. Here the son, a member of the *Nisei* generation, remembers his family's internment during World War II. When Peter turned draft age, he was inducted into the army, even though his father and sister remained in the relocation camp for the duration of the war.

It was just my sister and myself. I was fifteen, she was twelve. In April, 1942, we were evacuated to Santa Anita. At the time we didn't know where we were going, how long we'd be gone. We didn't know what to take. A toothbrush, toilet supplies, some clothes. Only what you could carry. We left with a caravan.

Santa Anita is a race track. The horse stables were converted into living quarters. My sister and I were fortunate enough to stay in a barracks. The people in the stables had to live with the stench. Everything was communal. We had absolutely no privacy. When you went to the toilet, it was communal. It was very embarrassing for women, especially. . . .

We had orders to leave Santa Anita in September of 1942. We had no idea where we were going. Just before we left, my father joined us . . . . I can still picture it to this day; to come in like cattle or sheep being herded in the back of a pickup truck bed. We were near the gate and saw him come in. He saw us. It was a sad, happy moment, because we'd been separated for a year.

He never really expressed what his true inner feelings were. It just amazes me. He was never vindictive about it, never showed any anger. I can't understand that. A man who had worked so hard for what he had and lost it overnight. There is a very strong word in Japanese, *gaman*. It means to persevere. Old people instilled this into the second generation: you persevere. Take what's coming, don't react.

He had been a very outgoing person. Enthusiastic. I was very, very impressed with how he ran things and worked with people. When I saw him at Santa Anita, he was a different person.

We were out on a train, three of us and many trains of others. It was crowded. The shades were drawn. During the ride we were wondering, what are they going to do to us? We Niseis [first generation Japanese Americans] had enough confidence in our government that it wouldn't do anything drastic. My father had put all his faith in this country. This was his land.

Oh, it took days. We arrived in Amache, Colorado. That was an experience in itself. We were right near the Kansas border. It's a desolate, flat, barren area. The barracks was all there was. There were no trees, no kind of landscaping. It was like a prison camp. Coming from our environment, it was just devastating . . . .

When I think back to my mother and father, what they went through quietly, it's hard to explain. [Cries.] I think of my father without ever coming up with an angry word. After all those years, having worked his whole life to build a dream—an American dream, mind you—having it all taken away, and not one vindictive word. His business was worth more than a hundred thousand. He sold it for five. When he came out of camp, with what little money he had, he put a down payment on an apartment building. It was right in the middle of skid row, an old rooming house. . . . He died a very broken man.

Source: Studs Terkel, *"The Good War:" An Oral History of World War Two* (New York: Pantheon, 1984), 29–30, 32–33.

---

days to dispose of their belongings and prepare for relocation. Businesses that took a lifetime to build were liquidated overnight, and speculators snapped up Japanese real estate for a fraction of its value. A Japanese-American piano teacher got only $30 for her treasured piano. Another woman, rather than accept $17.50 from a secondhand dealer for her family's heirloom porcelain, broke every piece of it. The government later estimated that the total financial loss to Japanese-Americans was $400 million, but Congress appropriated only $38 million in compensation after the war. (Partial restitution came decades later, in 1988, when Congress voted to issue a public apology, and $20,000 in cash, to the 60,000 surviving internees.)

Relocation took place in two stages. First the government sent the Japanese-Americans to temporary assembly centers, such as the Santa Anita racetrack in Los Angeles, where they lived in stables that horses had occupied a few days earlier. Then they were moved to ten permanent camps away from the coast. These intern-

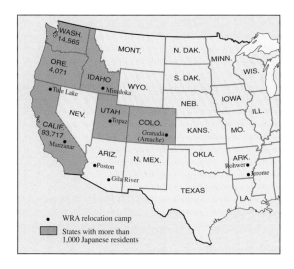

MAP 27.1

WRA Relocation Camps

In 1942 the government ordered 112,000 Japanese-Americans living on the West Coast into internment camps in the nation's interior because of their supposed threat to public safety. Some of the camps were as far away as Arkansas.

ment camps, located in California, Arizona, Utah, Colorado, Wyoming, Idaho, and Arkansas, "were in places where nobody had lived before and no one has lived since," one historian commented. Milton Eisenhower had hoped the relocation camps would resemble the CCC youth camps of the New Deal, but the barbed wire and enforced communal living mocked his hopes. Although sometimes compared to Nazi concentration camps, the relocation centers more closely resembled Indian reservations.

All ten camps were in hot, dusty places, and their communal bathroom and dining facilities made family life nearly impossible. Eight people often lived in a space measuring 25 by 20 feet. No one had any privacy and boredom was a major problem. Generational differences between the Issei, with an average age of fifty-five, and the Nisei, with an average age of seventeen, added to the tensions.

Almost every Japanese-American in California, Oregon, and Washington—a total of approximately 112,000 people—was involuntarily detained for some period during World War II. Ironically, the Japanese-Americans who made up one-third of the population of Hawaii, and presumably posed a greater threat because of their numbers and closer proximity to the Far East, were not affected. They were less vulnerable to detention, in part because of the island's multiracial heritage. More important, Japanese provided much of the un-

skilled labor on the island, and the Hawaiian economy could not function without them.

Cracks soon appeared in the relocation policy. Japanese-Americans had played an important role in California agriculture, and, even with stepped-up recruitment of Mexican-Americans through the *bracero* program, the labor shortage in farming led the government to furlough seasonal Japanese-American agricultural workers as early as 1942. In addition, about 4,300 young people who had been in college when the relocation order came through were allowed to stay in school—if they transferred out of the West Coast military zone. Another route out of the camps was enlistment in the armed services. The 442nd Infantry Combat Team, a segregated unit composed entirely of Nisei volunteers, became the most decorated unit in all the armed forces for its bravery in the European theater of operations.

Most Japanese-Americans accepted relocation stoically. They hoped that by proving their loyalty, they could reenter society after the war. Many Japanese-Americans of the third generation, called the *Sansei*, some of whom were born in the internment camps, and the fourth generation, the *Yonsei*, think their elders should have protested more strongly. With each generation, the memory of internment grows dimmer, but this shameful episode is burned into the national conscience.

Fighting and Winning the War

The Second World War was "the largest single event in human history, fought across six of the world's seven continents and all of its oceans," noted a military historian. "It killed fifty million human beings, left hundreds of millions of others wounded in mind or body and materially devastated much of the heartland of civilization." Dropping the atomic bomb on Hiroshima and Nagasaki in 1945 was the final stage in this most destructive and awesome of human conflicts.

Wartime Goals and Strategies

The Allied coalition was composed of Great Britain, the United States, the Soviet Union, and China. France, under German occupation until 1944, played a lesser role, although it was represented in Big Power discussions by Free French resistance leader General Charles De Gaulle. To America's dismay, Chinese leader Jiang Jieshi (Chiang Kai-shek) seemed more interested in fighting the communist revolution in his country (see Chapter 28) than in mobilizing the Chinese people to expel the Japanese invaders.

AMERICAN LIVES

The Quiet Diplomacy of Harry Hopkins

Winston Churchill called Harry Hopkins "Lord Root of the Matter" for his ability to dissect complex problems. President Franklin D. Roosevelt told Wendell Willkie that all presidents needed somebody like Hopkins "who asks for nothing except to serve you." Roosevelt put it more directly at the Teheran conference when he said simply, "Dear Harry, what would we do without you?"

In many ways, Hopkins's wartime service represented an unexpected career twist for this professional social worker. Born in Iowa in 1890, the son of a harness maker, he graduated from Grinnell College in 1912. Following in the footsteps of his older sister Adah, he became a social worker in New York, where he proved himself a competent and humane administrator. After the onset of the Great Depression, Hopkins became head of New York State's Temporary Emergency Relief Administration under Governor Franklin Roosevelt, whom he followed to Washington in 1933. During the New Deal, Hopkins headed emergency work relief programs such as the Civilian Works Administration (CWA), the Federal Emergency Relief Administration (FERA), and the Works Progress Administration (WPA), and served briefly as commerce secretary. He also made a run for the 1940 Democratic nomination, an unsuccessful foray into partisan politics that is universally regarded as the nadir of his career.

If Hopkins's government service had ended in 1940 (at the time he had severe health problems, which would continue until his death in 1946), he would be remembered as "the minister of relief." But Hopkins proved a remarkably quick learner when it came to diplomacy and international affairs, despite a total lack of background in these fields. In early 1941 Roosevelt sent him off as a special envoy to assess British morale and to offer assurance to Winston Churchill that American aid would be forthcoming. The two week trip stretched to six, and cemented Hopkins's relationship with Churchill. Hopkins modestly described his role as that of a "catalytic agent between two prima donnas,"

but from then on he proved indispensible to FDR. Later that year Hopkins undertook another mission of personal diplomacy: he went to the Soviet Union to reassure Russian leader Joseph Stalin that the United States would send military supplies to help the Soviets avoid defeat by Germany. In 1941, Hopkins also played a role in the administration of Lend-Lease aid to the Allies before the United States officially entered the war.

The kind of ad hoc arrangements that had characterized policy formulation during the New Deal continued after Pearl Harbor, and Hopkins found many opportunities to use his skills of crisis management. He always preferred troubleshooting and problem solving to being tied down in a bureaucratic chain of command; his only official position in the wartime bureaucracy was on the relatively minor Munitions Assignments Board. Instead, ensconced in a suite at the White House where he lived, he operated under the implied mantle of presidential authority. The key to Hopkins's unmatched working relationship with the president was his uncanny ability to anticipate FDR's views. But while Hopkins gave advice and counsel, Roosevelt always made up his own mind, especially on matters of military strategy.

The specter of illness haunted Hopkins's years of government service. Associates described him as a "bundle of energy," a chain-smoking workaholic, the worst possible lifestyle for a man plagued by stomach and digestive disorders. Because of his ongoing health problems, he often was forced to conduct government business from his White House suite dressed in his pajamas. The pajamas were usually silk—for a government bureaucrat, Hopkins had expensive tastes. He loved horse racing, fine dining, and first-class accomodations; he found it impossible to hold onto money and had trouble fulfilling his family obligations (he was married three times). But on the job Hopkins was scupulously honest and fair, and he inspired loyalty and high levels of performance from those who worked with him.

Hopkins's greatest contribution to the war effort came at the Teheran Conference in 1943, where he and Roosevelt tried to ensure Allied unity against competing Russian, British, and French demands. Functioning practically as the American secretary of state at Teheran since Roosevelt had not asked Cordell Hull to attend, Hopkins played an especially key role in convincing a reluctant Churchill to support the proposed invasion of France in 1944.

But at the height of Hopkins's power, illness once again struck. From January to July of 1944, Hopkins was out of Washington's (and FDR's) orbit entirely as he recuperated from surgery in Florida. Mounting one final comeback in late 1944, he regained his role as Roosevelt's chief adviser and confidante, in part by opposing Treasury Secretary Henry Morgenthau's postwar plans for German reorganization. In January 1945, Roosevelt tapped him for another major overseas assignment—meeting with French and English officials to review the plans for a postwar peace—before joining the American delegation at the Yalta conference in February.

By the time that Hopkins reached the Crimea, he was seriously weakened by the effects of wartime travel on his fragile system. His declining health prevented him from enjoying the personal triumphs he had experienced at Teheran: he attended only the major plenary sessions and instead used his dwindling energy to work with his staff in his quarters. He never doubted that Stalin's goal was to dominate Eastern Europe, but he still saw Yalta as the "dawn of a new day" for postwar cooperation. When he parted from FDR at the end of the conference (Hopkins was so ill he chose to fly home, rather than take the longer sea voyage with the president and his staff), it was the last time the two men saw each other. While Hopkins recuperated at the Mayo Clinic, he learned of Roosevelt's death. He performed one final act of government service by undertaking a personal mission to Moscow for Harry Truman before the Potsdam Conference, but ill health and his close identification with Franklin Roosevelt limited Hopkins's utility to the new president, and he declined Truman's invitation to join the official U.S. delegation.

In temporary retirement, Hopkins, who was only fifty-five, planned to rebuild his health and write his memoirs to provide financial stability for his family, but within eight months of Franklin Roosevelt, he too was dead. Appropriately for one who had contributed so much to the Anglo-American partnership during World War II, his last letter was to Winston Churchill.

Harry Hopkins and Joseph Stalin

While on his diplomatic mission to Moscow in 1941, Harry Hopkins took time-out from his discussions of the war situation to be photographed with Stalin at the Kremlin. The photo appeared in *Life* magazine.

The overall strategy for winning the war came out of give-and-take discussions among the dominant personalities of the Grand Alliance: Franklin Roosevelt, Prime Minister Winston Churchill of Great Britain, and Joseph Stalin, premier of the Soviet Union. Roosevelt's unswerving commitment to Britain's survival provided the basis for a strong, if not always smooth, relationship with Churchill. Stalin, however, was something of a mystery. He and Roosevelt did not even meet until late in 1943. Although the United States and Great Britain disagreed on such issues as the postwar fate of colonial empires, the potential for conflict with the Soviet Union was far greater. This uncertainty affected both the conduct of the war and the plans for the postwar peace.

The Atlantic Charter, drafted aboard ship during the Churchill-Roosevelt rendezvous off the Newfoundland coast in August 1941, provided the ideological foundation of the Allied cause and of the peace to follow, even before the Japanese attack on Pearl Harbor. It bore many similarities to Wilson's Fourteen Points of 1918. Calling for postwar economic collaboration and guarantees of political stability to ensure freedom from want, fear, and aggression, the Atlantic Charter supported free trade and condemned territorial gains achieved as the spoils of victory. It also supported the principle of collective security.

The Allied commitment to national self-determination was the most striking element of continuity with Wilson's Fourteen Points and presented the three leaders with their thorniest problem. Roosevelt's hope for self-determination in Eastern Europe conflicted with Stalin's desire for a band of Soviet-controlled satellite states to protect his western border. The fate of British colonies like India, where an independence movement had already begun, caused friction between Roosevelt and Churchill, though to a lesser degree. Despite such conflicts, Roosevelt hoped that the Allies could maintain friendly relationships, the basis of a constructive postwar system.

These long-term goals coexisted with the military necessities of fighting a global war. Defeating Germany always occupied top military priority, with the defeat of Japan in second place. One way to wear down the Germans was to open a second front on the European continent, preferably in France. The Russians strongly argued for this strategy, because it would draw German troops away from Russian soil. Roosevelt assured Stalin informally that such a front would be opened in 1942.

However, a combination of military priorities and British opposition caused a two-year delay in opening a second front. In 1942, the Allies did not have the necessary equipment, notably landing craft, to mount a successful invasion of the heavily defended French coast. Churchill adamantly opposed the invasion, fearing that the Allies would be trapped in a destructive ground war in France, as they had been in World War I.

The repeated delays in opening the second front proved damaging to harmony among the Allies. The issue came up so many times that Soviet Foreign Minister Vyacheslav Molotov was said to know only four English words: "yes," "no," and "second front." The delay meant that for most of the war, the Soviet Union bore the brunt of the land battle against Germany. Roosevelt and Churchill's unfulfilled pledges angered Soviet leaders, who were already suspicious about American and British intentions. This mistrust and bitterness carried over into the postwar world.

The War in Europe

During the first six months of 1942, the military news was so bad that it threatened to swamp the alliance completely. The Allies suffered severe defeats throughout Europe and on the Atlantic. German armies pushed deeper into Soviet territory, reaching the outskirts of Moscow and Leningrad, and simultaneously started an offensive in North Africa, aimed at seizing the Suez Canal. At sea, German submarines were crippling convoys of American supplies to Europe. Since the United States was the main supplier of oil for the Allies, these attacks went to the heart of the war effort, which was increasingly dependent on petroleum-based military technology such as tanks and airplanes.

The major turning point of World War II in Europe occurred in the winter of 1942–1943, when the Soviets halted the German advance in the Battle of Stalingrad. The Germans had taken most of the city in house-to-house fighting when the Soviets suddenly counterattacked. The Germans lost 330,000 soldiers and twenty-two divisions. Then came the task of pushing the Germans back through eastern Europe. By October 1943, Soviet armies stood on the east bank of the Dnieper River, ready to drive through the Ukraine into Romania. At the same time, the Allies launched a major offensive in North Africa, Churchill's substitute for a second front in France. Between November 1942 and May 1943, Allied troops under the leadership of Generals Dwight D. Eisenhower and George S. Patton defeated Germany's crack Afrika Korps led by General Erwin Rommel. From Africa the Allied command followed Churchill's strategy of attacking Europe through what he called its "soft underbelly": Sicily and the Italian mainland. In July 1943 the fascist regime of Benito Mussolini fell. The Allies invaded Italy the following fall, but encountered such heavy resistance from German troops that they did not enter Rome until June 1944.

D-Day. The long-awaited invasion of France came on D-Day, June 6, 1944. That morning, after an agonizing delay caused by bad weather, the largest armada ever

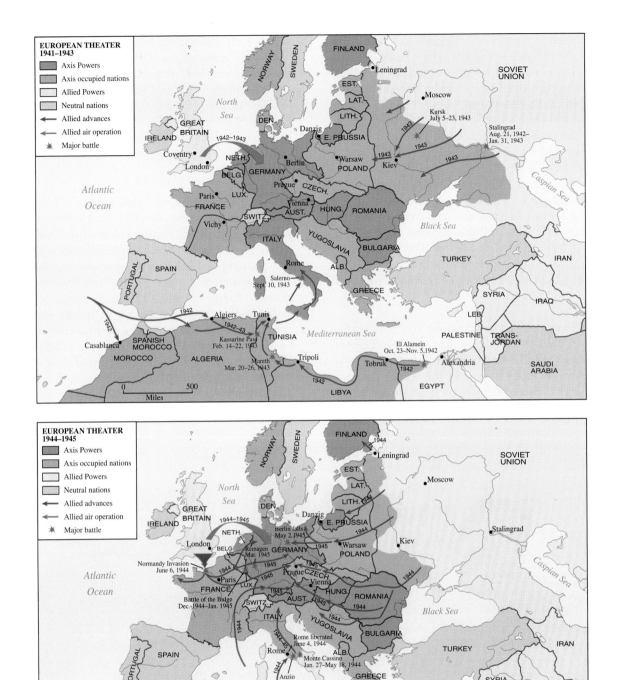

MAP 27.2

War in Europe

a. 1941–1943 Hitler's Germany reached its greatest extent in 1942, when Nazi forces finally stalled at Leningrad and Stalingrad. The tide of battle turned in the fall, when the Soviet army launched a massive counterattack at Stalingrad and Allied forces began to drive the Germans from North Africa. In 1943 the Allies invaded Sicily and the Italian mainland. *b. 1944–1945* On June 6, 1944 (D-Day), the Allies finally invaded France. It would take almost a year for the Allied forces to close in on Berlin—the Soviets from the east and the Americans, British, and French from the west. Germany surrendered on May 8, 1945.

assembled moved across the English Channel. The beaches of Normandy where the Allies landed—Utah, Omaha, Juno, Gold, and Sword—soon became household words in the United States. Under the command of General Dwight D. Eisenhower, more than 1.5 million soldiers crossed the channel over the next few days. In August, allied troops helped liberate Paris and by September, they had driven the Germans out of most of France and Belgium.

By the autumn of 1944, the German military situation looked hopeless. All that year, long-range Allied bombers had made daring daylight raids, damaging Nazi military and industrial installations and pulverizing cities such as Dresden and Berlin. The air campaign killed some 305,000 people and wounded 780,000, civilians and soldiers alike. No one remained free from attack.

Victory in Europe. The Germans were still not ready to give up. In December 1944, German forces in Belgium mounted an attack that began the Battle of the Bulge, so called because it made a dent in the Allied defenses. After ten days of heavy fighting in what turned out to be the final German offensive of the war, the Allies re-

gained their momentum and pushed the Germans back across the Rhine River. Their goal was to take Berlin, the German capital. American and British troops led the drive from the west, and Soviet troops advanced from the east through Poland. On April 30, with much of Berlin in rubble from Allied bombing, Hitler committed suicide in his bunker. Germany surrendered on May 8, 1945, which became known as V-E (Victory in Europe) Day.

The Holocaust. When Allied troops advanced into Germany in the spring of 1945, they came face to face with Adolf Hitler's "final solution of the Jewish question": the extermination camps where 6 million Jews had been put to death as well as another 6 million Poles, Slavs, gypsies, and other "undesirables" such as homosexuals. Pictures from Nazi death camps at Buchenwald, Dachau, and Auschwitz, of bodies stacked like cords of wood, and survivors so emaciated they were barely alive, horrified the American public and the world. It is not as if no one knew about the existence of the camps before the German surrender. The Roosevelt administration, for example, had reliable information about the death camps as early as November 1942.

Hitting the Beach at Normandy
These American reinforcements landed on the Normandy beach two weeks after D-Day, June 6, 1944. More than a million Allied troops came ashore during the next month. The Allies liberated Paris in August and pushed the retreating Nazi forces back behind the German border by September.

The Living Dead
When Allied troops advanced into Germany in the spring of 1945, they came face to face with what had long been rumored—concentration camps, Adolf Hitler's "final solution of the Jewish question." Margaret Bourke-White was one of the first photographers on the scene. This haunting image from the Buchenwald death camp appeared in *Life* magazine soon after.

The lack of response by the U.S. government to the systematic annihilation of European Jewry ranks as one of the gravest failures of the Roosevelt administration. So few Jews got out because the United States, and the rest of the world, would not take them in. Strict State Department policies allowed only 21,000 refugees to enter this country during the war. The War Refugee Board, established in 1944 with little support from the Roosevelt administration, eventually helped save about 200,000 Jews. Several things combined to inhibit U.S. action: anti-Semitism; fears of economic competition from a flood of refugees in a country just recovering from the depression; the failure of the media to grasp the magnitude of the story and publicize it accordingly; and the failure of religious leaders, Jews and non-Jews alike, to speak out.

In justifying the American course of action, President Roosevelt claimed that winning the war would be the strongest contribution America could make to liberating the camps. But it is hard to escape the conclusion that the United States could have done more—much more—to lessen the Holocaust's terrible human toll.

The War in the Pacific

The United States still had to defeat Japan. At the beginning of 1942, the news from the Pacific was uniformly grim. In the wake of Pearl Harbor, Japan had scored quickly with seaborne invasions of Hong Kong, Wake Island, and Guam. Japanese forces conquered much of Burma, Malaya, and the Philippines, as well as the Solomon Islands, and threatened Australia and India. Japan managed this huge territorial expansion in only three months. One of the few boosts for American morale came on April 18, 1942, when Colonel James H. Doolittle led sixteen American bombers on the first air raid on Tokyo, but the attack had little military value.

The more significant battles were far to the south. On May 7–8, 1942, in the Battle of the Coral Sea near southern New Guinea, American naval forces halted the Japanese offensive against Australia. Then in June, at the Island of Midway, the Americans inflicted serious damage on the Japanese fleet. Dive bombers and fighters, launched from the aircraft carriers *Enterprise*, *Hornet*, and *Yorktown*, provided the margin of victory in both battles. For the first time, major sea battles were waged—and decided—primarily by planes launched from aircraft carriers that never even came in sight of each other. Submarines also played an important role in the naval battles, but the human cost was high: 22 percent of American submariners lost their lives during the war, the highest death rate of any branch of the armed services.

After the Battle of Midway, the American military command, under General Douglas MacArthur and Admiral Chester W. Nimitz, took the offensive in the Pacific. For the next eighteen months, American forces advanced arduously from one island to the next, winning major victories at Tulagi and Guadalcanal in the Solomon Islands and at Tarawa and Makin in the Gilberts. They reached the Marshall Islands in early 1944. In October 1944, MacArthur began the reconquest of the Philippines by winning the Battle of Leyte Gulf, a massive naval encounter, in which the Japanese lost practically their entire remaining fleet, and the Americans suffered only minimal losses.

AMERICAN VOICES

The War in the Pacific *Anton Bilek*

Anton Bilek was taken prisoner when the Japanese overran the Bataan penisula of the Philippines in April 1942. He describes here the infamous "Bataan Death March" and its aftermath.

The next morning, we got orders to get rid of all our arms and wait for the Japanese to come. General King had surrendered Bataan. They came in. First thing they did, they lined us up and started searchin' us. Anybody that had a ring or a wristwatch or a pair of gold-rimmed spectacles, they took 'em. Glasses they'd throw on the floor and break 'em and put the gold rims in their pockets. If you had a ring, you handed it over. If you couldn't get it off, the guy'd put the bayonet right up against your neck. Fortunately I never wore a ring. I couldn't afford one.

They moved us about on the road. Here was a big stream of Americans and Filipinos marchin' by. They told us to get in the back of this column. This was the start of the Death March. (A long, deep sigh.) That was a sixty-mile walk. Here we were, three, four months on half-rations, less. The men were already thin, in shock. Undernourished, full of malaria. Dysentery is beginning to spread. This is even before the surrender. We had two hospitals chuck-full of men. Bataan peninsula was the worst malaria-infected province of the Philippines.

The Japanese emptied out the hospitals. Anybody that could walk, they forced 'em into line. You found all kinda bodies along the road. Some of 'em bloated, some had just been killed. If you fell out to the side, you were either shot by the guards or you were bayoneted and left there. We lost somewhere between six hundred and seven hundred Americans in the four days of the march. The Filipinos lost close to ten thousand. At San Fernando, we were stuffed into boxcars and taken about thirty-five miles further north. The cars were closed, you couldn't get air. In the hot sun, the temperature got up there. You couldn't fall down because you were held up by the guys stacked around you. You had a lot of guys blow their top, start screamin'. From there, they marched us another seven, eight miles to Camp O'Donnell, which was built hurriedly for the Philippine army. It was built like the huts were built, of native bamboo and *nipa* and grass. There must've been about nine thousand of us and about fifty thousand Filipinos. Americans in one camp, Filipinos in the other. We had to leave after a month and a half. The monsoon season was starting. A hurricane blew down two of the barracks. Eighty men were killed. Just crushed.

I went blind, momentarily. It scared the hell out of me. I was at the hospital for about two weeks, and the doctor, an American, said, "There's nothing I can do with you. Rest is the only thing. Eat all the rice you can get. That's your only medicine." That's the one thing that pulled me through. He said, "You won't have to go on details." The Japanese were comin' in and they'd take two, three hundred and start 'em repairing a bridge that was blown up. We were losin' a lot of men there. They couldn't work any more. They were dyin'.

Every room at the hospital was full. They were built on stilts. It was cool underneath, where I was put. I started to swell. I got beriberi. Lack of vitamin B-1. Your kidneys stop functioning. The fluids just stay in your body. You blow up like a balloon. I was seein' guys die all around me. Americans, at 50 a day. Filipinos, around 350. We buried close to 2,000 Americans at Camp O'Donnell. They buried between 28,000 and 30,000 Filipinos.

They moved us to another camp at Cabanatuan, about fifty miles away. I rode on the back of a truck.... I was naked from the waist down. It was some ride....

In camp, from the beginning to the end, you never talked of women. You never talked of sex. You never told stories. First thing you talked about is what you wanted in your stomach. Guys would tell stories about how their mother made this. Men would sit and listen very attentively. This was the big topic all the time.

I remember vividly this old Polack. One guy always wanted him to talk about how his mother made the cabbage rolls, the *golabki*. He had a knack of telling so you could almost smell 'em. He would say when he would be comin' home from school, he knew what he was gonna have to eat. When his mother made these *golabki,* he could smell 'em a block away. Oh, they'd get all excited. You'd see some of the fellas just lickin' their lips. Tasting it. You know?

I'm back home. It's all over with. I'd like to forget it. I had nothin' against the Japanese. But I don't drive a Toyota or own a Sony. . . . A lotta friends I lost. We had 185 men in our squadron when the war started. Three and a half years later, when we were liberated from a prison camp in Japan, we were 39 left. It's them I think about. Men I played ball with, men I worked with, men I associated with. I miss 'em.

Source: Studs Terkel, *"The Good War": An Oral History of World War Two* (New York: Pantheon, 1984), 85, 90–91, 95–96.

MAP 27.3

War in the Pacific

a. 1941–1942 After the attack on Pearl Harbor in December 1941, the Japanese rapidly extended their domination in the Pacific. The Japanese flag soon flew as far east as the Marshall and Gilbert Islands and as far south as the Solomon Islands and parts of New Guinea. Japan also controlled the Philippines, much of Southeast Asia, and parts of China, including Hong Kong. American naval victories at Coral Sea and Midway finally stopped further Japanese expansion.

b. 1943–1945 Allied forces retook the islands in the Central Pacific in 1943 and 1944 and the Philippines in early 1945. The capture of Iwo Jima and Okinawa put U.S. bombers in position to attack Japan itself. The Japanese offered to surrender on August 10, after the United States dropped atomic bombs on Hiroshima and Nagasaki.

Throughout the war, the Japanese were far more hated than the Germans. While Americans often differentiated between evil Nazi leaders and ordinary "good Germans," forced to go along with Nazi excesses, they lumped all Japanese together. Racial epithets like "slant eyes" and "yellow monkeys" were widely used in con-versation, and even respected magazines like *Time, Life,* and *Newsweek* routinely referred to the enemy as "Japs." Between American attitudes towards Japan, and Nazi atrocities against the Jews, racism was a constant undercurrent of World War II.

By early 1945, victory over Japan was in sight. The

A New Type of Naval Warfare
The battles of Coral Sea and Midway in 1942 marked a revolution in naval warfare. For the first time, major sea battles were waged—and decided—primarily by planes launched from aircraft carriers. This panorama shows the vastness of these naval encounters.

campaign in the Pacific moved slowly towards an anticipated massive and costly invasion of Japan. For a successful assault on the main Japanese island, the Americans needed to capture Iwo Jima and Okinawa. Airstrips there would put U.S. planes within striking distance of Tokyo. American Marines won the battles for Iwo Jima (February 1–March 20, 1945) and Okinawa (April 1–June 10) in some of the fiercest fighting of the war. At Iwo Jima, the Marines sustained more than 20,000 casualties, with 6,000 dead; at Okinawa, the toll reached 7,600 dead and 32,000 wounded.

By mid-1945, Japan's land troops, navy, and air force had suffered devastating losses. American bombing of the mainland had killed about 330,000 civilians and crippled the Japanese economy, which had difficulty functioning once oil imports were cut off. In a last-ditch effort to stem the tide, Japanese pilots began

kamikaze (suicide) missions, crashing their planes and boats into American ships. This desperate action, combined with the Japanese military leadership's refusal to surrender, suggested that Japan would keep up the fight despite overwhelming losses. American military commanders grimly predicted millions of casualties in the upcoming invasion.

The American GIs

During the war, 292,000 Americans were killed and 671,000 wounded in the global fighting. Although stationed in deserts, jungles, and tropical rain forests, American service personnel faced no more risk of death from disease than they would have at home. Because of medical advances, including new drugs such as penicillin and sulfa, the death rate was half that of World War I. The casualties represented less than half of 1 percent of the U.S. population. In contrast, the Soviets counted as many as 20 million military and civilian dead during the war, about 8 percent of their people.

War correspondents such as John Hersey and Ernie Pyle (who was killed in a foxhole on Iwo Jima by a Japanese bullet) reported on the GIs (short for "government issue") for readers back in the United States. Cartoonist Bill Mauldin created two scruffy infantrymen named Willie and Joe for the armed service newspaper *Stars and Stripes*. "Do retreatin' blisters hurt as much as advancin' blisters?" Willie asked Joe during the Italian campaign. American movies stressed the ethnic and racial diversity of the American forces. A film critic noted that almost every war movie featured "one Negro, one Jew, a Southern boy, and a sprinkling of second-generation Italians, Irish, Scandinavians and Poles."

War reporters often portrayed the GIs as ordinary boys doing their patriotic duty. "When you looked into the eyes of those boys, you did not feel sorry for the Japs: you felt sorry for the boys," John Hersey wrote of some Marines in Guadalcanal in 1944. "They were ex-grocery boys, ex-highway laborers, ex-bank clerks, ex-schoolboys, boys with a clean record . . . not killers." But, of course, soldiers were trained to kill. Another Marine who fought at Guadalcanal remembered it as a matter of simple survival: "The only way you could get it over with was to kill them off before they killed you. The war I knew was totally savage."

By the spring of 1945, soldiers who had finished their military duty, which averaged sixteen months, were beginning to return home. Fighting had been a dirty, bloody job, a far cry from their visions of saving democracy or stopping fascism. Dreams of marriage, a house in the suburbs, and a new car sustained many soldiers through the horror and tedium of the war. In 1947, veterans and their families made up a fourth of the American population.

The Big Three at Yalta
With victory in Europe at hand, Roosevelt journeyed to Yalta, on the Black Sea, in February 1945, to meet one last time with Churchill and Stalin. It was here they discussed the problems of peace settlements. The Yalta agreements mirrored a new balance of power and set the stage for the Cold War.

Wartime Diplomacy

Throughout the war, the three leaders of the Grand Alliance continued to meet to discuss military strategy and plan the postwar peace. In January 1943 Roosevelt and Churchill met in Casablanca, Morocco; Stalin could not attend because the Soviet Union's battle against the Germans had reached a crucial point. The main outcome of the Casablanca conference was the Allied demand for unconditional surrender as a condition for victory. In November 1943, Roosevelt, Churchill, and Chiang Kaishek of China met in Cairo to discuss military operations in the Pacific theater, a conference designed to keep China in the war as a major ally.

Traveling directly from Cairo to Teheran, Iran, Roosevelt finally met Stalin for the first time. As usual, Harry Hopkins was at Roosevelt's side. At the Teheran conference, Roosevelt and Churchill agreed to Stalin's demand for a second front within six months. In return, Stalin promised to join the fight against Japan after the war in Europe ended. Churchill and Roosevelt also agreed tacitly to Stalin's demand that Poland's borders be redrawn to give the Soviet Union more territory. The three men disagreed sharply, however, about who

should control the rest of Poland and the other eastern European states. Roosevelt still expressed confidence that the personal rapport he developed with Stalin would aid postwar relations among the superpowers.

Yalta. The three leaders held their last conference in February 1945 at Yalta, a Black Sea resort. Victory in Europe was in sight, but no agreement had been reached on the shape of the peace to come. Roosevelt remained concerned about maintaining Allied unity after the war. Stalin had become increasingly inflexible on the issue of Eastern Europe, insisting that he needed governments there that were well disposed to the Soviet Union to provide a buffer for national security. Roosevelt acknowledged the legitimacy of this demand, but he also hoped for democratically elected regimes in Poland and the neighboring countries.

The compromise reached at Yalta was open to multiple interpretations. Admiral William D. Leahy, Roosevelt's chief military aide, described the agreement as "so elastic that the Russians can stretch it all the way from Yalta to Washington without technically breaking it." At Yalta, Roosevelt and Churchill agreed in principle to the idea of a Soviet sphere of influence in Eastern Europe, but they left its actual dimensions deliberately vague. In return, Stalin pledged to hold "free and unfettered elections" at an unspecified time. (These elections never took place.) Stalin also reaffirmed his commitment to enter the war against Japan.

The Yalta conference also proceeded with plans to divide Germany into four zones, to be controlled by the United States, Great Britain, France, and the Soviet Union. Berlin, which lay in the middle of the Soviet zone, would also be partitioned among the four powers. The issue of German reparations remained unsettled.

The Big Three made further progress towards a postwar international organization: the United Nations. Roosevelt, determined to avoid Woodrow Wilson's mistakes, had already cultivated congressional support; realizing that such an organization would be impotent without the Soviets' participation, he cultivated their support as well. British, American, and Soviet representatives had already met at Dumbarton Oaks, an estate in Washington, D.C., in September 1944 to begin planning the structure of the organization. At Yalta, the Big Three agreed that the Security Council of the United Nations should consist of the five major Allied powers—the United States, Britain, France, China, and the Soviet Union—plus six elected nations on a rotating basis. They also decided that the permanent members of the Security Council should have veto power over decisions of the United Nations General Assembly, in which all nations would be represented. Roosevelt, Churchill, and Stalin announced that the United Nations would convene in San Francisco on April 25, 1945.

Hiroshima
This was all that remained of Hiroshima's Museum of Science and Industry on August 6, 1945. The shell of the building later became the center of Hiroshima's memorial to those who had died in the atomic blast.

Roosevelt returned to the United States in February, visibly exhausted from his 14,000 mile trip. When he reported to Congress on the Yalta agreements, he made an unusual acknowledgment of his physical infirmity. Referring to the heavy steel braces he wore on his legs, he asked Congress to excuse him if he gave his speech sitting down. The sixty-three-year-old president was by now a very sick man, suffering from heart failure and hypertension. On April 12, 1945, during a short visit to his vacation home in Warm Springs, Georgia, the president suffered a cerebral hemorrhage and died. Many Americans could not imagine any leader other than Franklin Roosevelt in the White House. Those who reached adulthood in the 1930s and 1940s had never known another president.

V-E Day came less than a month after Roosevelt died and Harry Truman succeeded to the presidency. The war in the Pacific ended after Truman ordered the dropping of atomic bombs on two Japanese cities, Hiroshima on August 6, and Nagasaki on August 9. Many later questioned why the United States did not provide advance warning about the attack or choose a noncivilian target; the rationale for dropping the second bomb was even less clear. At the time, however, the belief that Japan's military leaders would never surrender unless their country was utterly devastated convinced policymakers that they had no choice but to deploy the new weapon. The atomic bombs killed a hundred thousand people at Hiroshima and sixty thousand at Nagasaki. Tens of thousands more Japanese died slowly of radiation poisoning. Japan offered to surrender on August 10 and signed a formal treaty of surrender on September 2, 1945. World War II had ended, but the atomic age of insecurity had just begun.

The Onset of the Atomic Age

The development of the atomic bomb was closely linked to wartime military strategy. In December 1938, German scientists had discovered that the nuclei of atoms could be split into yet smaller particles, a process called fission. With materials prepared from uranium, a chain reaction of nuclear fission would release tremendous amounts of energy. American scientists like Enrico Fermi and Leo Szilard, many of them refugees from Fascist Italy and Nazi Germany, produced the first controlled chain reaction on December 2, 1942, at the University of Chicago.

Scientists soon began working frantically to harness such nuclear reactions for military purposes. Their goal was the development of an atomic bomb for possible use against Germany or, later, Japan. The secret research, called the Manhattan Project, cost $2 billion, employed 120,000 people, and involved the construction of thirty-seven installations in nineteen states under the direction of General Leslie R. Groves of the U.S. Army Corps of Engineers. In the final stages, a team consisting of most of the country's top physicists assembled the bomb at an isolated desert site in Los Alamos, New Mexico. All of this was hidden from Congress, from the American people, even from Vice-President Truman. The secrecy and scope of this alliance between science and government is one of the most dramatic examples of how much the power of the state grew during wartime.

President Roosevelt followed the bomb's progress closely. He and his advisers planned to deploy the bomb to end the war without the dreadful number of American casualties that had been predicted for an invasion of

Japan. At the same time, policymakers hoped that merely possessing such a powerful weapon—the "master card," in the words of Secretary of War Henry Stimson—would enhance American power in the postwar world. Instead, the new weapon became the first step in a deadly arms race between the United States and the Soviet Union that characterized the postwar period.

Until the last moment, the scientists did not know if the atomic bomb would work. On July 16, 1945, near Alamogordo, New Mexico, they watched in wonder as the test bomb exploded into a huge mushroom cloud. President Truman received news of the successful detonation in Potsdam, near Berlin, where he was about to meet with Churchill and Stalin in the final wartime conference about the shape of postwar Europe. Truman, who had not even known about the bomb before he became president, was ecstatic about its potential. After the bombing of Hiroshima, he told aides, "This is the greatest thing in history." Others were not so sure. J. Robert Oppenheimer, one of the leading scientists on the Manhattan Project, watched the test on that early July morning in the New Mexico desert. Overwhelmed by its frightening power, he recalled the words from the *Bhagavad Gita*, the Hindu bible: "I am become Death, Destroyer of Worlds."

Summary

With the rise of fascism and totalitarianism in Germany, Italy, and Japan, the international situation deteriorated rapidly throughout the 1930s, and the world was again at war by 1939. Although most Americans opposed participation, clinging to strong isolationist sentiment, President Roosevelt began mobilizing public opinion for intervention. The Japanese attack on Pearl Harbor on December 7, 1941, brought the nation into World War II.

Defense mobilization ended the Great Depression. As had happened during World War I, mobilization led to a dramatic expansion of the state. On the home front, the war resulted in rationing and shortages of many items. Geographical mobility increased as labor shortages opened job opportunities for women, blacks, and Mexican-Americans. The ideological climate of fighting Nazism aided the cause of civil rights. However, Japanese-Americans on the West Coast suffered a devastating denial of civil liberties when the government moved them into internment camps.

World War II was a global war, consisting of massive military campaigns in both Europe and the Pacific. The war news was bleak at first, but by 1943 the Allies had started to move toward victory. At the same time, Roosevelt attempted to maintain harmony among the United States, Great Britain, and the Soviet Union. Many of the disagreements over wartime diplomacy turned into major problems in the postwar world. Of all the major powers that fought in World War II, only the United States emerged physically unharmed. And at the end of the war, only the United States had the powerful new weapon, the atomic bomb.

TOPIC FOR RESEARCH

Hollywood Goes to War

After Pearl Harbor, the Office of War Information asked Hollywood to concentrate on six subjects as part of the war effort: the enemy, the Allies, the armed forces, war production, the homefront, and the issues. Choose a film made during the war, either a popular film or a documentary, and analyze it as a document about American participation and attitudes about the war. How useful is it as a historical source? Is its historical accuracy, or lack thereof, less important than its role in boosting patriotism and morale? Films about the armed services include *Wake Island* (1942), *Guadalcanal Diary* (1943), *So Proudly We Hail* (1943), *Lifeboat* (1944), *Thirty Seconds Over Tokyo* (1945), and *Keep Your Powder Dry* (1945). Frank Capra's *Why We Fight* series and John Huston's *Battle of San Pietro* (1944) are powerful documentaries. The best homefront film is probably *Since You Went Away* (1943). A cult classic like *Casablanca* (1942) looks different when watched through the lens of wartime America.

John E. O'Connor, ed., *Image as Artifact: The His-*

torical Analysis of Film and Television (1990) is an excellent introduction to using films as historical sources. For Hollywood in the 1940s, see Clayton R. Koppes and Gregory D. Black, *Hollywood Goes to War: How Politics, Profits, and Propaganda Shaped World War II Movies* (1987). See also Douglas Gomery and Robert Allen, *Film History: Theory and Practice* (1985), and David Bordwell, Janet Staiger, and Kristin Thompson, *The Classical Hollywood Cinema: Film Style and Mode of Production to 1960* (1985).

BIBLIOGRAPHY

John Morton Blum, *V Was For Victory* (1976), offers a good introduction to American politics and culture during the war years. Also useful are Richard Polenberg, *War and Society* (1972); Geoffrey Perrett, *Days of Sadness, Years of Triumph* (1973); and Richard Lingeman, *Don't You Know There's a War On?* (1970). A powerful and provocative oral history of the war is Studs Terkel, *"The Good War"* (1984). John Keegan, *The Second World War* (1990) offers the best one-volume account of the battlefront aspects.

The Road to War

Depression and wartime diplomacy are effectively covered in Robert Dallek, *Franklin D. Roosevelt and American Foreign Policy, 1932–1945* (1979). For more on American policy between the wars, see Lloyd Gardner, *Economic Aspects of New Deal Diplomacy* (1964), and Selig Adler, *The Uncertain Giant* (1966). William L. Langer and S. Everett Gleason provide a detailed chronology of American entry in *The Challenge to Isolation, 1937–1940* (1952) and *The Undeclared War, 1940–1941* (1953); see also Robert Divine, *The Reluctant Belligerent* (1965). For American isolationism, see Wayne Cole, *Roosevelt and the Isolationists, 1932–1945* (1983) and *Charles S. Lindbergh and the Battle Against American Intervention in World War II* (1974); Selig Adler, *The Isolationist Impulse* (1957); and Manfred Jonas, *Isolationism in America* (1966). Warren T. Kimball, *The Most Unsordid Act* (1969), describes the Lend-Lease controversy of 1939–1941. Roberta Wohlstetter, *Pearl Harbor* (1962), Herbert Feis, *The Road to Pearl Harbor* (1950), and Gordon W. Prange, *At Dawn We Slept* (1981), describe the final chain of events that led to American entry. George McJimsey, *Harry Hopkins* (1987), covers both the New Deal and Hopkins's wartime contributions. See also the rich portrait supplied by former Roosevelt speechwriter Robert E. Sherwood in his *Roosevelt and Hopkins* (1948).

Mobilizing for Victory

George Flynn, *The Mess in Washington* (1979); Bruce Catton, *War Lords of Washington* (1964); Donald Nelson, *Arsenal of Democracy* (1946); Gerald T. White, *Billions for Defense* (1980); and Harold G. Vatter, *The U.S. Economy in World War II* (1985), discuss America's economic mobilization. David Brinkley, *Washington Goes to War* (1988), offers an engaging journalistic perspective. Alan Winkler, *The Politics of Propaganda* (1978), covers the Office of War Information. On labor's role during war, see Joel Seidman, *American Labor From Defense to Reconstruction* (1953); Nelson Lichtenstein, *Labor's War at Home: The CIO in World War II* (1982); Howell Harris, *The Right to Manage* (1982); and Paul Koistinen, *The Hammer and the Sword: Labor, the Military, and Industrial Mobilization, 1920–1945* (1979). James C. Foster, *The Union Politic* (1975), details the CIO's political involvement. For more on politics in wartime, see James McGregor Burns, *Roosevelt: The Soldier of Freedom* (1970).

Women's roles in wartime are covered by Susan Hartmann, *The Home Front and Beyond* (1982); Karen Anderson, *Wartime Women* (1980); Leila J. Rupp, *Mobilizing Women for War* (1978); William H. Chafe, *The American Woman* (1972); Ruth Milkman, *Gender at Work* (1987); and Sherna B. Gluck, *Rosie the Riveter Revisited: Women, the War, and Social Change* (1987).

Life on the Home Front

Additional material on America during the war can be gleaned from Richard Polenberg, ed., *The War at Home* (1968), and Lester Chandler, *Inflation in the United States, 1940–1948* (1951). Alan Clive, *State of War* (1979), provides a case study of Michigan during the war. See also Gerald D. Nash, *The American West Transformed: The Impact of the Second World War* (1985), and Marc Scott Miller, *The Irony of Victory: World War II and Lowell, Massachusetts* (1988). The experience of black Americans is treated by Albert Russell Buchanan, *Black Americans in World War II* (1977); Neil Wynn, *The Afro-American and the Second World War* (1975); and Louis Ruchames, *Race, Jobs, and Politics* (1953). For racial tensions, see Dominic Capeci, Jr., *Race Relations in Wartime Detroit* (1984), and Mauricio Mazan, *The Zoot Suit Riots* (1984). August Meier and Elliott Rudwick, *CORE* (1973), describes the founding of this important civil rights organization. Richard Dalfiume, *Desegregation of the U.S. Armed Forces* (1969), covers black soldiers in the military. Alan Berube, *Coming Out Under Fire* (1990), is an oral history of gay men and lesbians in the military; see also John D'Emilio, *Sexual Politics, Sexual Communities* (1983), for the impact of the war on gay Americans. Maurice Isserman,

Which Side Were You On? (1982), analyzes the American Communist party during the war. Two compelling accounts of Japanese relocation are Audre Girdner and Anne Loftus, *The Great Betrayal* (1969), and Roger Daniels, *Concentration Camps, U.S.A.* (1972). See also John Tateishi, ed., *And Justice for All: An Oral History of the Japanese-American Detention Camps* (1984), and Peter Irons, *Justice at War: The Story of the Japanese-American Internment Cases* (1983).

Fighting and Winning the War

Extensive material chronicles the American military experience during World War II. Albert Russell Buchanan, *The United States and World War II* (1962), and Russell F. Weigley, *The American Way of War* (1973), provide overviews; Ronald Schaffer, *Wings of Judgement: American Bombing in World War II* (1985), and Bradley F. Smith, *The Shadow Warriors: OSS and the Origins of the CIA* (1983) are more specialized. Cornelius Ryan, *The Last Battle* (1966), and John Toland, *The Last Hundred Days* (1966), describe the end of the fighting in Europe. David S. Wyman, *The Abandonment of the Jews* (1984), devastatingly describes the lack of American response to the Holocaust from 1941 to 1945. For the Far East, see John W. Dower, *War Without Mercy: Race and Power in the Pacific War* (1986); Ronald H. Spector, *Eagle Against the Sun: The American War With Japan* (1984); John Toland, *Rising Sun: The Decline and Fall of the Japanese Empire* (1970); William Manchester, *American Caesar* (1979) on General Douglas MacArthur; and Barbara Tuchman, *Stillwell and the American Experience in China* (1971).

American diplomacy and the strategy of the Grand Alliance are surveyed in Dallek, *Franklin D. Roosevelt and American Foreign Policy*; William McNeill, *America, Britain, and Russia, 1941–1946* (1953); and Gaddis Smith, *American Diplomacy During the Second World War* (1965). The relationship between the wartime conferences and the onset of the Cold War are treated by Walter LaFeber, *America, Russia, and the Cold War* (6th ed., 1990); Stephen Ambrose, *Rise to Globalism* (5th ed., 1988); John L. Gaddis, *The United States and the Origins of the Cold War* (1972); and Herbert Feis, *Between War and Peace* (1960). Richard Rhodes, *The Making of the Atomic Bomb* (1987); McGeorge Bundy, *Danger and Survival* (1988); and Martin Sherwin, *A World Destroyed* (1975), provide compelling accounts of the development of the bomb. See also Gar Alperowitz, *Atomic Diplomacy* (1965), and Gregg Herken, *The Winning Weapon* (1980). John Hersey, *Hiroshima* (2nd ed., 1985), on the aftermath of the bombing, retains its power forty years after its original publication.

TIMELINE

1935–1937	Neutrality Acts
1938	Munich agreement "War of the Worlds" broadcast
1939	World War II breaks out in Europe
1940	Conscription reinstated
1941	Lend-Lease Fair Employment Practices Commission Atlantic Charter Japanese attack Pearl Harbor
1942–1945	Rationing
1942	Women recruited for war industries Japanese relocation Revenue Act of 1942
1943	Race riots in Detroit and Los Angeles Fascism falls in Italy Teheran Conference
1944	D-Day (June 6) Reconquest of Philippines GI Bill
1945	Germany surrenders (May 8) Battles of Iwo Jima and Okinawa Yalta Conference Harry S. Truman becomes president upon Roosevelt's death United Nations Atomic bombs dropped on Hiroshima and Nagasaki Japan surrenders (September 2)

P A R T   6

America and the World

1945 to the Present

Diplomacy	Government	Economy	Society	Culture
The Cold War Era— and after	**Redefining the role of the state**	**Rise and fall of *Pax Americana***	**Social movements and demographic diversity**	**A consumer society**
1945 Truman Doctrine (1947) Marshall Plan (1948) NATO founded (1949)	Truman's Fair Deal liberalism Employment Act	Bretton Woods system established: World Bank, IMF, GATT	Migration to cities accelerates Armed forces desegregated	End of wartime rationing Rise of television
1950 Permanent mobilization: NSC-68 (1950) Korean War (1950–53) McCarthyism	Eisenhower's modern Republicanism Interstate Highway Act (1956) Warren Court activism	Rise of military-industrial complex Labor movement at peak strength Service sector expands	*Brown v. Board of Education* (1954) Montgomery bus boycott SCLC founded	Growth of suburbia Baby boom Shopping malls spread
1960 Cuban missile crisis (1962) Nuclear Test-ban Treaty (1963) Gulf of Tonkin Resolution (1964);Vietnam War escalates	Kennedy and politics of expectation High tide of liberalism: the Great Society, War on Poverty Nixon ushers in conservative era	Kennedy-Johnson tax cut, military expenditures fuel economic growth	Student activism Civil Rights Act; Voting Rights Act Revival of feminism	Baby boomers swell college enrollments Youth counterculture
1970 Nixon visits China (1972) SALT initiates détente (1972) Paris Peace Accords (1973)	Watergate scandal; Nixon resigns (1974) Deregulation begins under Ford and Carter	Arab oil embargo (1973–74); inflation surges Deindustrialization begins	First Earth Day (1970) *Roe v. Wade* (1973) New Right urges conservative agenda	Gasoline shortages hit commuters, travel industry Apple introduces first personal computer (1977)
1980 Reagan arms buildup INF treaty Berlin Wall falls	Reagan Revolution Supreme Court conservatism	Reaganomics Budget and trade deficits soar Savings and loan bailout	Televangelists mobilize evangelical Protestants New Hispanic and Asian immigration	MTV debuts Wall Street greed AIDS epidemic
1990 War in the Persian Gulf U.S.S.R. disintegrates; end of the Cold War	Democratic party adopts "moderate" policies	Recession	Earth Summit (1992) Third wave of feminism	Health-care crisis Standard of living declines

Few years marked such a definitive turning point as 1945. In that year Americans celebrated the end of World War II and mourned the death of Franklin D. Roosevelt, who had led the country longer than any other president. The task of setting the goals for the United States in the postwar world fell to Harry S. Truman.

First, it was Truman and his advisers who shaped the diplomacy of the postwar world. With Germany and Japan prostrate in defeat and Britain and France severely weakened by six years of war, the normal balance of power was shattered. The United States, the most powerful country in the world, now played a hegemonic role in global affairs. The price of American hegemony was a permanent commitment to engagement in the international arena. When the Soviet Union challenged America's vision of postwar Europe, the Truman administration responded by crafting the policies and alliances that came to define the Cold War. American policymakers came to interpret almost every international event as a conflict between communism and the free world. The Cold War spawned two long "hot" wars, in Korea and Vietnam, and a terrifying direct confrontation between the two superpowers in the Cuban missile crisis. Although the policy of détente pursued by Richard Nixon and later presidents succeeded in easing tensions, the cold war mentality held sway until the final collapse and disintegration of the Soviet Union in 1991.

Second, thanks to the growth of a military-industrial complex of enormous size and the expansion of consumer culture, the quarter century after 1945 represented the heyday of American capitalism, an economic *Pax Americana*. Economic dominance abroad translated into years of unparalleled affluence at home. In the early 1970s competition from other countries began to challenge America's economic supremacy. And Americans learned that overseas commitments could have a severe and direct impact on their lives, as when the Arab nations cut off oil exports to the United States to retaliate for America's support for Israel.

Third, America's global commitments had dramatic consequences for American government and politics. Until the national consensus fractured over the Vietnam War, liberals and conservatives agreed on keeping the country in a state of permanent mobilization and maintaining a large and well-equipped military establishment. And all administrations, Republican or Democratic, were willing to intervene in the economy when private initiatives could not maintain steady economic growth. But liberals also pushed for a larger federal government role in the area of social welfare. Under Truman, John F. Kennedy, and especially Lyndon Johnson, the government went beyond the New Deal to erect an extensive federal and state apparatus to provide for the social well-being of the people. During Nixon's and, above all, Reagan's presidencies, conservatives cut back on many of the major programs but failed to eliminate any of them completely.

Fourth, the victory over fascism in World War II led to renewed calls for America to make good on its promise of liberty and equality for all. In great waves of protests in the 1950s and 1960s, African-Americans, then women, Hispanics, and other minorities challenged the political domination of elite white men. The resulting hard-won reforms dramatically expanded the democratic system, although the promise of full equality remains unfulfilled.

Today, half a century after the end of World War II, Americans are living in an increasingly interwoven mesh of national and international experience. Outside events shape ordinary lives in ways that would have been inconceivable a century earlier. As the Cold War Era fades into history, the outlines of a new world order are beginning to emerge. The United States remains the sole military superpower, but it shares economic leadership in the new interdependent global economy. Will international cooperation—to preserve the environment and alleviate hunger, to stop nuclear proliferation, civil strife, and regional conflicts—replace the old cold war patterns of confrontation? Or will the United States pull back from its global commitments to focus on domestic renewal? The next chapter of America's history remains to be written.

Danger and Survival

With its first successful test of a hydrogen bomb
in 1952, America entered into the nuclear age.

28 *Cold War America, 1945–1960*

When Harry Truman was summoned to the White House on April 12, 1945, after learning of Roosevelt's death, he asked the president's widow, "Is there anything I can do for you?" Eleanor Roosevelt responded with another question, "Is there anything we can do for you? For you are the one in trouble now."

Harry Truman inherited the presidency at one of the most important, and perilous, watersheds in modern American history. World War II ended two centuries of relative isolation from world diplomatic affairs and brought about a revolution in American foreign policy. The United States emerged from the war as the most powerful country in the world, and it deliberately set about to create conditions that maintained this global supremacy. Only the Soviet Union posed a real obstacle to American hegemony. Soon the two superpowers were locked in a Cold War that took economic, political, and military forms.

The dramatic shift in American foreign relations after 1945 had important domestic repercussions. In keeping with the centralization of American life and culture throughout the twentieth century, decisions made in Washington, and in other capitals across the world, now had an impact on ordinary lives. Reflecting the blurring of the lines between international and domestic events that characterized the postwar world, America's new global commitments fostered a climate of fear and suspicion about internal subversion at home. But the fruits of internationalism also fostered a period of unprecedented affluence and prosperity which gave the United States the highest standard of living in the world (see Chapter 29). America's global hegemony lasted through the early 1970s.

The Origins of the Cold War

The defeat of Germany and Japan did not bring stability to the world. Even before the end of World War II, the grand alliance among the United States, Britain, and the Soviet Union was disintegrating over differences in interpreting the Yalta and Potsdam agreements. Within two years the United States and the Soviet Union would be engaged in a global ideological and strategic struggle that historians call the Cold War. Cold war assumptions fundamentally shaped American and Soviet priorities for the next four decades.

Descent into Cold War, 1945–1946

Franklin Roosevelt had hoped that the establishment of the United Nations would provide a forum to help resolve postwar conflicts. When Roosevelt died in April 1945, American support for the United Nations became in part a memorial to the late president's hopes for the postwar peace. Avoiding the disagreements that had doomed American participation in the League of Nations after World War I, the Senate approved American participation in the United Nations by a margin of 80 to 2. One of the United Nations' most tireless supporters—and a member of the U.S. delegation from 1946 to 1953—was the president's widow, Eleanor Roosevelt.

Although Roosevelt heartily supported the United Nations, he also believed it was essential for the United States to continue good relations with the only other power whose strength realistically rivaled that of the

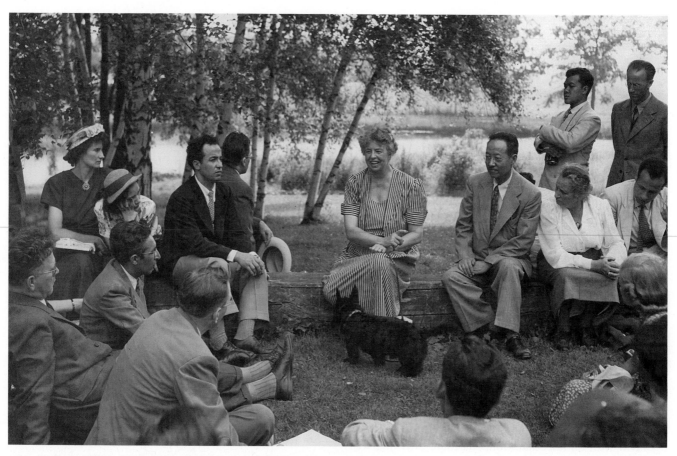

Eleanor Roosevelt, U.N. Representative

Eleanor Roosevelt won over her fellow members of the United Nations delegation by
doing her homework and standing firm on her convictions. Republican John Foster
Dulles admitted to her later, "I feel I must tell you that when you were appointed I
thought it terrible and now I think your work here has been fine!" Eleanor Roosevelt
was proudest of her role in drafting the 1948 Universal Declaration of Human Rights.
Here she entertains delegates from UNESCO at her home in Hyde Park, New York,
accompanied by the Roosevelt dog, Fala.

United States in 1945, the Soviet Union. Yet events in
the immediate postwar period proved far too controversial to be settled amicably between the two great
powers. Within twenty-four hours of taking over the
presidency, Harry Truman questioned whether the
United States could cooperate with its former wartime
ally. "We must stand up to the Russians," he stated privately.

Why did the Grand Alliance fall into disarray so
quickly in the immediate postwar period? Events in
Eastern Europe caused the most bitter conflicts among
the former allies. As the Soviet army drove the Germans
out of Russia and back through Romania, Bulgaria, and
Hungary, Soviet-sponsored, provisional governments
were established in those countries. At the Yalta conference, both American and British diplomats, including
President Roosevelt, had in effect agreed to recognize
this Soviet "sphere of influence" in the region occupied

by the Red Army along its borders. But as soon as the
war ended, Truman backed away from the Yalta
pledges. The new president berated Soviet Foreign Minister V. M. Molotov for imposing a Soviet-controlled
government on Poland. Molotov had never "been
talked to like that in my life," he told Truman. "Then
keep your agreements!" Truman retorted. The Soviets
had already gutted them anyway, by reneging on their
pledge to allow free elections, suppressing democratic
parties, and installing puppet governments.

No country so embodied the different visions that
the United States and the Soviet Union had for the postwar world than Germany. At Yalta, the defeated German state had been divided into four occupation zones
controlled by the United States, France, England, and
the Soviet Union. By 1946, the United States was encouraging the gradual reindustrialization of the German
industrial heartland within its zone as part of its general

goal of reviving the European economy. For its part, the Soviet Union began to develop the industrial capacities of its zone. The economic base was thus laid for what eventually became the political division into East and West Germany.

A critical source of tension in 1946 was the question of atomic weapons. The United States enjoyed the sole possession of the atomic bomb, and while leaders were willing to consider international control of atomic energy in the long run, they were loathe to give up their immediate advantage. In a plan submitted to the United Nations, the United States proposed a system of international control that relied on mandatory inspection and control but preserved the American monopoly. The Soviets rejected the plan categorically. This climate of mutual suspicion and distrust undercut any hope for international cooperation to develop atomic energy for peaceful purposes.

Former British prime minister Winston Churchill articulated the deepening pessimism about the Soviet Union shared by American diplomats by 1946. Out of power and eager for a platform to put forward his views, Churchill accepted an invitation from President Truman to deliver a major policy address in March 1946 in Fulton, Missouri. Churchill had gone along with plans for a Soviet sphere of influence in Eastern Europe at Yalta, but now had second thoughts, warning ominously about the "expansive tendencies" of the Soviet Union: "From Stettin in the Baltic to Trieste in the Adriatic, an Iron Curtain has descended across the Continent." If the West hoped to preserve peace and freedom in the face of the Soviet challenge, Churchill declared, it must remember that "there is nothing they [the Soviets] admire so much as strength, and there is nothing for which they have less respect than for weakness, especially military weakness."

Churchill's widely publicized "Iron Curtain speech" helped convince many Americans that the Soviet Union posed a dangerous threat to national security. This shift represented a return to the American hostility towards Bolshevism first articulated by Woodrow Wilson after the 1917 revolution, a distrust that had delayed recognition of the Soviet Union until 1933. The wartime collaboration necessitated by the common fight against fascism receded quickly from memory. For the next forty years, the popular rhetoric adopted by American and Soviet leaders painted international relations in harsh ideological terms—democracy versus totalitarianism, the free world versus the Iron Curtain, capitalism versus communism.

The strident dichotomies of the Cold War mask a more complex global reality, however. As the dominant player in the world system after World War II, it was in the self-interest of the United States to make the world more unitary, more interdependent, more open to capitalist penetration. The domination of the Soviet Union over Eastern Europe violated this goal; so too did political instability or underdevelopment in third world countries. Behind American rhetoric about democracy, free trade, and anticommunism lay a commitment to fostering a world economy that provided the most conducive conditions for the major industrial countries like the United States to flourish. The integration of a reindustrialized Japan into the Asian economy, the creation of a revitalized common European market, and the Cold War isolation of the Soviet bloc were all goals designed to maintain American hegemony. This global context provides important background for understanding many of the key conflicts of the postwar world.

From the Truman Doctrine to NATO, 1947–1949

By 1947 a new American policy—called containment—was taking shape. Although its precepts were widely shared in Washington policymaking circles, containment is usually associated with George F. Kennan, an intense, scholarly diplomat who had devoted his entire career to the study of the Soviet Union. Kennan first articulated containment's basic premises in February 1946 in an eight-thousand-word cable from his post at the U.S. Embassy in Moscow to his superiors in Washington, where it was widely circulated. He expanded on these ideas in an influential article in the journal *Foreign Affairs* in July 1947. According to Kennan (who was identified only as "X"), the Soviets moved "inexorably along the prescribed path, like a persistent toy automobile wound up and headed in a given direction, stopping only when it meets unanswerable force." To stop this expansionism, it was necessary to pursue a policy of "firm containment, designed to confront the Russians with unalterable counterforce at every point where they show signs of encroaching upon the interests of a peaceful and stable world."

Kennan's initial formulation envisioned economic and diplomatic means as the way to enforce containment, but the policy soon took on a military cast. In one version or another, containment defined the foreign policy of every subsequent administration, both Democratic and Republican, well into the 1980s. It served at least three purposes. Identifying an evil, expansionist enemy, the containment doctrine called on Americans to unite behind the president in order to counter the threat; it justified the creation of a vast peacetime military machine; and it masked other objectives of American foreign policy in the economic arena and the Third World.

AMERICAN LIVES

The Wise Men

They were, as their biographers Walter Isaacson and Evan Thomas neatly tallied it up, two bankers (W. Averill Harriman, Robert Lovett), two lawyers (Dean Acheson, John McCloy), and two diplomats (Charles Bohlen, George Kennan). These six friends were among the main architects of the containment policy which dominated American foreign policy from the 1940s through at least the 1960s. Individually their names are not that well known—certainly not in comparison to the presidents and military leaders of the time—but collectively they had an enormous impact on postwar developments. They represent a cross section of what British journalist Henry Fairlie first called in 1955 "the establishment." In 1965, presidential aide McGeorge Bundy dubbed these senior statesmen "the wise men," and the name stuck.

At first glance, the social profile of the six men, all born between 1893 and 1904, suggests that the foreign policy elite was synonymous with the rich and the powerful in the United States. W. Averill Harriman was the son of the founder of the Union Pacific Railroad and

Robert Lovett's father was the elder Harriman's second-in-command. Dean Acheson was the son of the Episcopal bishop of Connecticut, and Charles Bohlen was descended from the first American ambassador to France. But the establishment was more of a meritocracy than a closed club: John McCloy came from a poor family in Philadelphia and George Kennan was an outsider from Milwaukee. Access to education at the elite Eastern institutions that trained generations of leaders—prep schools like Groton and St. Paul, colleges such as Harvard, Yale, or Princeton—was crucial to membership. Averill Harriman taught Dean Acheson to row crew at Groton, they went off to Yale together, and their lives remained linked until they died.

After graduation from college, these privileged young men embarked on careers, mainly on Wall Street or in Washington. Charles Bohlen went into the foreign service, and became a specialist in Soviet affairs; he was assigned to the first United States mission to that country in 1934. George Kennan was also a foreign service officer in Moscow during the 1930s. Dean Acheson

President Truman (far left) confers with Secretary of State Robert Lovett and State Department aides George Kennan and Charles Bohlen (from left to right). In the photo on the right, Averill Harriman (left) and President Harry Truman (right) greet Secretary of State Dean Acheson on his return from a NATO conference in 1952. McCloy is not shown.

spent most of the 1920s and 1930s in private legal practice, as did John McCloy; W. Averill Harriman devoted his attention to business, and Robert Lovett worked with the banking firm of Brown Brothers, which merged with the Harriman empire in 1931.

One common thread among the six lives in the 1920s and 1930s was extensive contact with European affairs, including familiarity with the Soviet Union. The result was a collective internationalism which stood in stark contrast to the prevailing isolationism of the 1930s. Not surprisingly, all six ended up in Washington during World War II, a period when their personal and professional relationships coalesced. McCloy and Lovett served as assistant secretaries of war, where they were known as "the Heavenly Twins"; Harriman was ambassador to the Soviet Union, where one of his advisors was George Kennan; Acheson became assistant secretary of state for economic affairs; and Bohlen served as the State Department's chief translator and expert in Soviet affairs, accompanying Roosevelt to Teheran and Yalta.

When the war ended, the six men all joined the Truman administration and embarked on seven years of extraordinary power and influence at one of the most critical moments in modern American history: the onset of the Cold War, and the formulation of the policy of containment of the Soviet Union through diplomacy or force. Although containment is associated with George Kennan, its underlying assumptions were shared by all six. They fervently believed that the United States had a moral destiny to provide world leadership in the struggle against communism. The Truman Doctrine and the Marshall Plan epitomized the sweeping commitments they were willing to undertake to promote this world view.

The policy-making process in the Truman administration was fairly intimate and decentralized, and hence amenable to the kind of behind-the-scenes power these members of the establishment thrived on. Acheson was the most influential of the group, serving as undersecretary of state from 1945 to 1947 and then secretary of state from 1949 to 1953. Charles Bohlen was his special assistant, until Bohlen was named minister to France in 1949. George Kennan also served in various capacities in the State Department before being named ambassador to the Soviet Union in 1951. Averill Harriman joined the cabinet as secretary of commerce, and then became a special assistant to the president, where he played a key role in setting strategy for the conduct of the Korean war. John McCloy served as president of the World Bank and became a vigorous proponent of the Marshall Plan; in 1949 Truman named him U.S. high commissioner for Germany.

These six men wielded power individually, but their impact was enhanced by how they functioned as a group. They shared much in common, especially their belief in the Cold War ideology of containment. Just as important was their commitment to public service: remarkably free of personal ambition, they saw themselves as public servants above the fray of partisan politics. However, their pattern of moving in and out of government to lucrative positions on Wall Street suggests that they had no trouble reconciling public service with private gain.

Dwight Eisenhower's election sent most of the Wise Men into temporary retirement from public service, but the election of John Kennedy in 1960 called them in from what their biographers called "the wilderness years." Now generally in their fifties and sixties, this older generation served the young president in a variety of capacities—Bohlen and Kennan as ambassadors to France and Yugoslavia, respectively; Harriman as assistant secretary of state for Far Eastern affairs; McCloy, Lovett, and Acheson as advisers. Their service demonstrates the continuity of the postwar foreign policy elite from World War II through the 1960s.

After Kennedy's assassination, Lyndon Johnson continued to seek their counsel, especially as the Vietnam War escalated. But these six men, who had so forcefully supported standing up to communism in the 1940s and 1950s, now began to doubt the American commitment in Southeast Asia. One by one, they dropped their support for the war and some like Kennan, who was now a professor at Princeton's Institute for Advanced Study, criticized it publicly. At a March 1968 meeting of the Wise Men, even Dean Acheson, the epitome of the establishment, told Johnson that the United States had to get out of Vietnam. The defection of the foreign policy elite, those who had framed the Cold War, played a major role in Johnson's decision to begin negotiations to end the Vietnam War.

The Wise Men proved to be a hardy bunch, with Harriman, Lovett, and McCloy living into their nineties. They shared the experience of shaping America's Cold War policy and overseeing the dramatic expansion of American power and influence in the 1950s and 1960s. But of those who had been "present at the creation" (Acheson's modestly titled memoirs), only George Kennan was still alive to see the end of the Cold War and the dissolution of the Soviet Union. These events would no doubt have astounded, and pleased, the "wise men" who had so tirelessly served their country in the post war years.

The emerging policy of confronting the Soviets with counterforce crystallized in 1947 over the situation in Greece. Local communist-inspired guerrillas, whom American advisers mistakenly believed were controlled by Moscow, had fought for control of Greece since the end of 1944. After postwar elections installed the royalist Popular Party in the spring of 1946, several thousand communist guerrillas launched a full-scale civil war against the government and the British occupation authorities. In February 1947 the British informed Truman that they could no longer afford to assist the Greek anticommunists. "If Greece was lost," Truman argued, Stalin "would then direct the communist parties of Italy and France to grab for power" and thus threaten to bring the industrially developed regions of Western Europe into the Soviet sphere. Of more serious and immediate concern to the administration was the threat that potential Soviet domination posed to American and European influence in the eastern Mediterranean and the Middle East, especially in strategically located Turkey, and the oil-rich state of Iran.

To counter this perceived menace, the president announced what became known as the Truman Doctrine. In a speech to Congress on March 12, asking military and economic assistance to Greece and Turkey, President Truman called for all Americans to fight communism on a global level and "to support free peoples who are resisting attempted subjugation by armed minorities or by outside pressures." To win popular support for this unprecedented change in the U.S. stance toward the rest of the world, and to squeeze money out of a stingy Congress, the president followed the advice of Republican Senator Arthur Vandenberg "to scare the hell out of the country." Not just Greece, but freedom itself, was at issue, Truman declared: "If we falter in our leadership, we may endanger the peace of the world—and we shall surely endanger the welfare of our own Nation." Despite the open-endedness of this military and political commitment, Congress in a show of bipartisan support quickly approved Truman's request for $300 million in aid to Greece and $100 million for Turkey. This appropriation reversed the postwar policy of sharp cuts in foreign spending.

The Marshall Plan. Two weeks after Congress approved aid to Greece and Turkey, Secretary of State George Marshall proposed a plan to provide economic as well as military aid to Europe. European economies had been devastated by the war, and conditions worsened in the terrible winter of 1947. Only a massive influx of outside capital could begin the process of rebuilding and revitalization. Speaking at the Harvard University commencement in June 1947, George Marshall urged the nations of Europe to work out a comprehensive recovery program and then ask the United States for aid. "Any government that is willing to assist

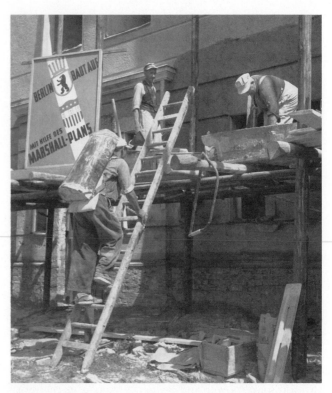

The Marshall Plan in Action
Between 1948 and 1951, the European Recovery Program, popularly known as the Marshall Plan for Secretary of State George C. Marshall, contributed over $13 billion toward its objective of "restoring the confidence of the European people in the economic future of their own countries and of Europe as a whole." Here a sign prominently announces that Berlin is being rebuilt with help from the Marshall Plan.

in the task of recovery," he promised, "will find full cooperation . . . on the part of the United States government." In Truman's words, the Marshall Plan was "the other half of the walnut." By bolstering European economies devastated by the war, Marshall and Truman believed, the United States could forestall the economic dislocation thought to give rise to communism. American economic self-interest was also a contributing factor—a revitalized Europe centered on a strong West German economy would provide a stronger market for U.S. goods and a European common market could serve as a model for economic multilateralism and interdependence.

Within the Congress, however, significant opposition remained to President Truman's pledge of economic aid to European economies. Republicans called the Marshall Plan a huge "international W.P.A.," a "European T.V.A.," and a "bold Socialist blue-print," none of which was meant as a compliment. In an election year, Republicans were loathe to give the Democratic president a major foreign policy triumph, but not all Republicans were opposed. Senator Vandenberg, the

Republican isolationist-turned-internationalist who chaired the Senate Foreign Relations Committee, supported the Marshall Plan, just as he had favored the appropriations for Greece and Turkey under the Truman Doctrine. In general, despite the continued influence of an isolationist wing of the Republican party, foreign policy in the 1940s and 1950s proceeded with bipartisan support.

In the midst of this stalemate came the communist coup in Czechoslovakia in March 1948, with its reminder of the menace of Soviet expansion in Eastern Europe. Czechoslovakia had been one of the few Eastern European countries to hold elections after the war ended. The Communists won 38 percent of the vote in the May 1946 elections, necessitating a coalition government; neither President Eduard Beneš nor Foreign Minister Jan Masaryk, who were both greatly admired in the West, were Communists. By early 1948 the fragile coalition had faltered, and the Communists took control in a coup on February 25, 1948. Two weeks later the Communist leadership assassinated Masaryk, an event which Truman said "sent a shock throughout the civilized world." To prevent similar situations in the rest of Europe, Truman argued, the Marshall Plan was imperative.

Congress agreed, overwhelmingly approving funds for the program in March of 1948. Historian Thomas J. McCormick calls the Marshall Plan "arguably the most innovative piece of foreign policy in American history." Over the next four years the United States contributed nearly $13 billion to a highly successful recovery effort. Western European economies revived and industrial production increased 64 percent, opening new areas for international trade. The Marshall Plan did not specifically exclude Eastern Europe or the Soviet Union, but it did require that all participating nations exchange economic information and work toward the mutual elimination of tariffs and other trade barriers. Soviet leaders denounced these conditions as attempts to draw Eastern Europe into the American orbit and forbade their satellites such as Czechoslovakia, Poland, and Hungary to participate.

The Berlin Airlift. Differing Soviet and American visions for postwar Germany continued to fuel the deepening Cold War. The United States wanted a unified, reindustrialized Germany that would be integrated into the European and world market. The Soviets feared the reemergence of a powerful German state, which had twice invaded the Soviet Union in the twentieth century. Especially troublesome was the fate of the city of Berlin, which lay deep within the Soviet zone of occupation and had been deemed so important that it was divided into four zones just like the country as a whole. The Soviet Union demanded control over the entire city, but the Allies refused. When Western nations took steps to revive the Berlin economy in the spring of 1948, the Soviet Union imposed a blockade on all highway, rail, and river traffic to West Berlin in June.

In this tense situation, Truman replied with an airlift. For nearly a year, American and British pilots, who had been dropping bombs on Berlin only four years earlier, flew in 2.5 million tons of food and fuel, nearly a ton for each Berlin citizen. On May 12, 1949, Stalin lifted the blockade, which by then had made West Berlin a symbol of resistance to communism.

The Berlin Airlift

For 321 days American planes like this DC-6 flew 272,000 missions to bring food and supplies to Berlin after the Soviet Union had blocked all surface routes into the city. The blockade was finally lifted on May 12, 1949.

MAP 28.1

Cold War Europe, 1955

In 1949 the United States sponsored the creation of the North Atlantic Treaty Organization (NATO), an alliance of ten European nations, the United States, and Canada. West Germany was formally admitted to NATO membership in May 1955. A few days later the Soviet Union and seven other Communist nations established a rival alliance, the Warsaw Pact.

NATO. The Berlin airlift and the coup in Czechoslovakia led to another dramatic turning point in U.S. diplomatic history. In April 1949, for the first time since the American Revolution, the United States entered into a peacetime military alliance with Western Europe and Canada—the North Atlantic Treaty Organization (NATO). To back up America's new stance, Truman asked Congress for $1.3 billion in military assistance to NATO. Under the pact, the United States, Britain, France, Italy, Belgium, the Netherlands, Luxembourg, Denmark, Norway, Portugal, Iceland, and Canada agreed that "an armed attack against one or more of them in Europe or North America shall be considered an attack against them all." In May 1949 these nations also agreed to the creation of the Federal Republic of Germany (West Germany). All assumed that it would join NATO, which it did in 1955.

Distressed by the aggressive American effort to promote a new economic and political order in Western Europe and the presence of substantial numbers of American troops in Western Europe as part of the NATO commitment, the Soviet Union tightened its grip on Eastern Europe. It created a separate government for East Germany in October 1949, which became the German Democratic Republic. The Soviets also sponsored an economic association, the Council for Mutual Economic Assistance or COMECON (1949), and a military alliance for Eastern Europe, the Warsaw Pact (1955). The postwar division of Europe was nearly complete.

The "Fall" of China

Containment was developed primarily to prevent Soviet expansion beyond its sphere of influence in Eastern Europe. As the mutual suspicion between the United States and the Soviet Union deepened, cold war doctrines influenced the American stance toward Asia as well. Here China, rather than the Soviet Union, was the main counterweight to American influence. The developing American policy toward Asia was informed by the recognition of Asia's importance in the world economy as well as the desire to contain communism. For eighteen of the thirty years between 1945 and 1975, the United States was involved in Asian wars.

A civil war had been raging in China since the 1930s. Communist forces led by Mao Zedong (Mao Tse-tung) and Zhou Enlai (Chou En-lai) contended for power with conservative Nationalist forces under Jiang Jieshi (Chiang Kai-shek). Jiang had strong connections with the Chinese business community and with the western world. His wealthy wife had been educated at Wellesley College in Massachusetts. In contrast, Mao was the son of struggling peasants, a tough, uncompromising leader who inspired loyalty in his associates. Mao won the devotion of China's overtaxed, land-hungry peasants, whom Jiang had alienated with the widespread corruption of his regime and his suppression of agrarian reforms. The Communists also won support for their resistance against the Japanese forces occupying their country. By 1944 Mao's forces were gaining the upper hand.

The Truman administration stuck with its Nationalist allies almost until the bitter end. Between 1945 and 1949, the United States provided more than $2 billion to Jiang's forces, to no avail. In 1947, General Albert Wedemeyer, who had tried to work with Jiang, reported to President Truman that "until drastic political and economic reforms" were undertaken by the "corrupt, reactionary, and inefficient Chinese National government, United States aid cannot accomplish its purpose." When these reforms did not occur, the United States cut off aid to the Nationalists in August of 1949, sealing their fate. The People's Republic of China was formally established on October 1, 1949, and what was left of Jiang's government fled the Chinese mainland to the island of Formosa (Taiwan).

Many Americans viewed Mao's success as a defeat for the United States. The Republican statesman John Foster Dulles, who became Secretary of State under Eisenhower, called the communist victory in China "the worst defeat the United States has suffered in its history." A pro-nationalist "China lobby," supported by such Republicans as Senators Karl Mundt of South Dakota and William S. Knowland of California, protested that the State Department under Secretary of State Dean Acheson was responsible for the "loss of China." Publisher Henry R. Luce, born in China to missionary parents, spread these accusations through his magazines, including *Time* and *Life*. Bowing to pressure from the China lobby, most of the State Department's experts on the Far East were forced to resign for supposedly having been too sympathetic to the Chinese Communists. The United States refused to recognize the new communist state, instead giving diplomatic recognition to the Nationalists ensconced on Taiwan. The United States also used its influence to block China's admission to the United Nations. For almost twenty years afterward, U.S. administrations acted as if mainland China, the world's most populous country, did not exist.

Containment Militarized: NSC-68

September 1949 brought another shock to U.S. policymakers. American military intelligence detected a rise in radioactivity in the atmosphere, proof that the Soviet Union had set off an atomic bomb. The United States' atomic monopoly, which some military and political advisers had argued would last for decades, had ended in less than four years. In combination with the Communist takeover in China, the world looked even more threatening now that the Soviets had the bomb.

The end of the American atomic monopoly forced a major reassessment of the nation's foreign policy. To devise a new blueprint for diplomatic and military priori-

ties, Truman turned to the National Security Council (NSC), an advisory body charged with assisting the president to set defense and military priorities. The NSC formed part of the unified military establishment set up by the National Security Act of 1947, which created a single Department of Defense to replace the previous Departments of War and the Navy. The recently established Joint Chiefs of Staff coordinated army, navy, and air force policy. And a new Central Intelligence Agency (CIA) gathered and analyzed military intelligence. These bureaucratic structures were a concrete reminder of the rise of the state.

In April 1950 the National Security Council delivered its report to President Truman. This document, known as NSC-68, reflected the bleak assumptions that American policymakers held about the Soviet Union: "It is quite clear from Soviet theory and practice that the Kremlin seeks to bring the free world under its dominion by the methods of the cold war." Because Moscow possessed tremendous military power that enabled the Soviet Union to "back up infiltration with intimidation," policymakers predicted an "indefinite period of tension and danger." In the immediate postwar period, the containment policy had relied primarily on economic and diplomatic means to counter Soviet expansionism and influence, but it became increasingly dependent on military force. The new stance thus pointed to far greater militarization of the Cold War.

NSC-68 made several specific recommendations. It favored development of a hydrogen bomb, an advanced weapon that was a thousand times more destructive than the atomic bombs that had destroyed Hiroshima and Nagasaki. (The United States exploded its first hydrogen bomb in November 1952, and the Soviet Union followed suit in 1953.) It supported increases in U.S. conventional forces and a strong system of alliances. Most importantly, it called for an increase in taxes to finance "a bold and massive program of rebuilding the West's defensive potential to surpass that of the Soviet world." NSC-68 envisioned defense budgets totaling up to 20 percent of the gross national product, four times their level at the time. The United States would function in a state approaching permanent mobilization, whether the country was officially at war or not.

The call for increased defense spending was linked directly to the end of atomic supremacy. The United States had been relying too heavily on atomic deterrence at the expense of its conventional military arsenal. Now that the nation's atomic monopoly had been broken, a general buildup of the American military arsenal was needed. The Korean War, which began just two months after NSC-68 was completed, provided the impetus to put this new policy into practice. Before 1950 the military budget stood at $13.5 billion. In just six months, Truman more than tripled it to nearly $50 billion.

The Korean War

Although Truman acknowledged that communist success in China raised urgent questions for American foreign policy, he recognized the limits of American power in Asia. In December 1949 Secretary of State Dean Acheson clarified American policy. The United States, he said, would help Asian nations realize their own aspirations but would consider itself bound to protect only a "defensive perimeter" that ran from the Aleutian Islands in Alaska to Japan, the Ryukyus (a chain of small islands that stretch from Japan to Taiwan), and the Philippines. If an attack occurred outside this perimeter—on Korea, Taiwan, or Southeast Asia, for example—"the initial reliance must be on the people attacked to resolve it and then upon . . . the United Nations."

A test of this new policy came quickly in Korea, a country whose artificial division after World War II contained seeds for later conflict. Both the United States and the Soviet Union had troops in Korea at the end of fighting in 1945, and neither side was willing to leave because of the peninsula's enormous strategic importance. As a compromise, the country was divided at the 38th parallel. Both occupying forces remained until 1948, when a Communist government led by Kim Il Sung took power in North Korea while Syngman Rhee, backed by the United States, took over in South Korea.

In 1950 the North Korean Communists decided to attempt to reunify the country. Whether the Soviet Union or the North Korean government initiated the action remains in dispute. Truman believed the attack to be Soviet-inspired, but in many ways the conflict was closer to a civil war. On June 25, North Korean troops launched a surprise attack across the 38th parallel. North Korean leaders may have expected Truman to ignore this armed challenge, but the president immediately asked the United Nations Security Council to authorize a "police action" against the invaders. Because the Soviet Union was temporarily boycotting the Security Council to protest the exclusion of the People's Republic of China from the U.N., it could not veto Truman's request, and the Security Council voted to send a peacekeeping force. Three days later Truman ordered General Douglas MacArthur, who was heading the American army of occupation that remained in Japan until 1951, to send American troops to help Rhee.

The outbreak of the Korean War further tipped the balance of foreign policy formulation from Congress to the president. When isolationist Republican Senator Robert A. Taft of Ohio objected that the president should have obtained congressional approval before committing American troops to Korea, Truman boldly insisted that he already had all the power he needed as commander-in-chief of the armed forces and as execu-

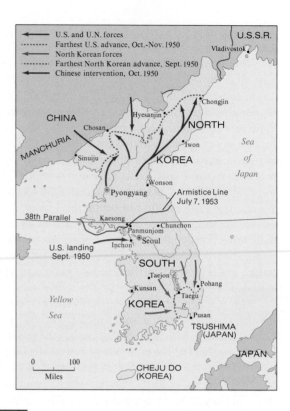

MAP 28.2

The Korean War, 1950–1953

The first months of the Korean War featured dramatic shifts in control up and down the 600-mile peninsula. From June to September 1950, North Korean troops overran most of the territory south of the 38th parallel. On September 15, U.N. forces under General Douglas MacArthur counterattacked behind enemy lines at Inchon and pushed north almost to the Chinese border. Massive Chinese intervention forced the U.N. troops to retreat to the 38th parallel in January 1951, and the war became a stalemate for the next two years.

tor of the treaty binding the United States to the United Nations. The Truman administration enjoyed widespread popular support for this action: a July 1950 poll showed 77 percent approved of U.S. intervention in South Korea.

Fighting the War. The rapidly assembled United Nations army in Korea remained overwhelmingly American, even though fourteen other non-Communist members sent troops, including Australia, Canada, and Great Britain. At the request of the Security Council, President Truman named General MacArthur to head the U.N. forces. At first, the North Koreans held an overwhelming advantage, controlling practically the entire peninsula except the Pusan beachhead. Then on September 15, 1950, MacArthur launched a brilliant amphibious attack at Inchon, far behind the lines of the North Korean invasion. Within two weeks, the U.N. forces controlled Seoul, the South Korean capital, and almost all the territory up to the 38th parallel.

Encouraged by this success, General MacArthur sought authority to lead his forces across the 38th parallel into North Korea itself. Truman's initial plan had been to restore the 1945 border; now he agreed to the broader goal of creating "a unified, independent and democratic Korea." The Chinese government in Beijing warned repeatedly that such a move would provoke its retaliation, but American officials failed to take these warnings seriously. MacArthur's troops drove rapidly northward, reaching the Chinese border at the Yalu River by the end of October. Just after Thanksgiving, however, a massive Chinese counterattack of almost 300,000 troops forced a retreat to the 38th parallel. On January 4, 1951, Communist troops reoccupied Seoul. "They really fooled us when it comes right down to it, didn't they?" a senator later asked Secretary of State Acheson. "Yes, sir," he replied.

Two months later, the American forces and their allies counterattacked, regained Seoul, and pushed back to the 38th parallel. Then a stalemate set in. Public support in the United States dropped after Chinese intervention increased the likelihood of a long war. By early January 1951, 66 percent thought the United States should withdraw, and 49 percent felt it was a mistake to have gone in in the first place.

Given those domestic and international constraints, Truman and his advisers in Washington decided to work for a negotiated peace. They did not wish to tie down large numbers of U.S. troops in a remote corner of Asia, far from what they considered more strategically important trouble spots in Europe and the Middle East. As Dean Acheson had said just before the Korean War broke out, "We cannot scatter our shots equally all over the world. We just haven't got enough shots to do that." If the Korean War had become a general war with China, reasoned General Omar N. Bradley, chairman of the Joint Chiefs of Staff, it would have been "the wrong war, at the wrong place, at the wrong time, and with the wrong enemy."

The Fate of MacArthur. MacArthur disagreed. Headstrong, arrogant, and brilliant, he fervently believed the nation's future opportunities lay in Asia, not in Europe. Disregarding Truman's instructions, General MacArthur traveled to Taiwan and urged the Nationalists to join in an attack on communist China. He pleaded for American use of the atomic bomb against targets in China. In an inflammatory letter to the House Minority Leader, Republican Joseph J. Martin of Massachusetts, he denounced the Korean stalemate. "We must win," MacArthur declared. "There is no substitute for victory."

Martin released MacArthur's letter on April 6, 1951, as part of a concerted Republican campaign to challenge President Truman's conduct of the war. The strategy backfired. On April 11, Truman relieved MacArthur of his command in Korea and Japan, accusing him of insubordination. "MacArthur left me no choice," Truman later insisted. "Even the Joint Chiefs of Staff came to the conclusion that civilian control of the military was at stake. . . . I didn't let it stay at stake very long."

The Korean War

The American GI's who fought in Korea were often the younger brothers of the men who had served in World War II. Unlike their older brothers, Korean War soldiers served in integrated units. Here members of a U.S. Combat Engineers battalion sweep a mountain trail for mines and booby traps.

MacArthur's Return From Korea
General Douglas MacArthur received a tumultuous welcome
in San Francisco in 1951, the first time the popular general
had set foot on the American mainland in fourteen years.
The public outcry over President Truman's dismissal of
MacArthur for insubordination reflected frustration with
the stalemated Korean War.

Truman's decision was highly unpopular. According
to a Gallup poll, 69 percent of the American people
supported MacArthur rather than Truman. The allure
of decisive victory under a charismatic military leader
temporarily pushed aside doubts about the war. The
general returned to tumultuous receptions in San Francisco, Chicago, and New York. In Washington, he delivered an impassioned address to a joint Congressional
session that ended with a line from an old West Point
ballad, "Old soldiers never die, they just fade away."
But when the shouting died down, Truman had the last
word. Failing to get the Republican presidential nomination in 1952, MacArthur did indeed fade from public
view.

The war dragged on for more than two years after
MacArthur's dismissal. Truce talks began in Korea in
July 1951, but a final armistice was not signed until July
1953. Approximately 45 percent of American casualties

were sustained in this period. The final settlement left
Korea divided very near the 38th parallel in place when
the war broke out, with a demilitarized zone dividing
the two countries. North Korea remained firmly allied
with the Soviet Union; South Korea signed a mutual defense treaty with the United States in 1954, allying itself
to the American sphere of influence in the Pacific and
playing host to large numbers of American troops stationed there. During the next thirty years, American
and Japanese investments helped South Korea rapidly
expand its economy.

The Impact of the Korean War. The Korean War had
only a limited domestic impact on the United States.
The government did not control the economy to the extent it had during World War II, although the military
budget nearly quadrupled over the course of the war.
Limited mobilization stimulated the economy and reduced unemployment, contributing to the general prosperity that characterized the 1950s.

Few soldiers felt the patriotic fervor that had characterized service during World War II. Struggling
against heavy snow and subzero cold, the men grew to
hate the endless fighting and "those damned hills of
Korea." One griped, "You march up them but there's always the sinking feeling you are going to have to march
right back down." A corporal from Chicago asserted,
"I'll fight for my country, but I'm damned if I see why
I'm fighting for this hell-hole." Showing the lack of engagement on the home front, when an Oregon newspaper prominently ran the same news dispatch from
Korea two days in a row, not a single reader called the
repetition to its attention.

Conditions did improve for black soldiers in Korea
compared to the discrimination they faced in the service
during World War II. President Truman had signed an
executive order desegregating the armed forces in 1948,
but little progress had been made before the war began.
During the rapid mobilization, demands for quick processing of draftees outweighed such customary practices
as keeping black and white draftees separate, thus
speeding up integration. The generally successful experience of an integrated armed services during the Korean War hastened the emergence of the civil rights
movement later in the 1950s.

The Korean War was costly for the United States:
54,200 American soldiers died, 103,000 were wounded,
and military expenditures totaled $54 billion. It reminded
Americans that global responsibilities required a heavy,
ongoing commitment. In contrast to the triumphs on
World War II battlefields, however, the protracted stalemate proved frustrating. "If we are so powerful," many
asked, "why can't we win?" When the armistice was finally signed in 1953, there were few public celebrations.
Similar frustration surfaced little more than a decade
later over American intervention in Vietnam.

Harry Truman and the Fair Deal

Harry S. Truman brought a complex character to the presidency. Alternately humble and cocky, he had none of Roosevelt's patrician ease. Yet he handled affairs with an assurance and crisp dispatch that has endeared him to later generations. "If you can't stand the heat, stay out of the kitchen," he liked to say of presidential responsibility. The major domestic issues that he faced were reconversion to a peacetime economy and the fears of communist infiltration and internal subversion generated by the Cold War, fears which his own administration played a part in fanning. Truman kept the New Deal coalition alive by proposing new federal programs to advance the interests of its constituencies, and his "Fair Deal" shaped the Democratic party's agenda for the next twenty years.

The Challenge of Reconversion

Harry Truman never intended to be just a caretaker president for a Roosevelt fourth term. On September 16, 1945, just fourteen days after Japan surrendered and World War II ended, Truman staked his claim to domestic leadership with a plan for expanded federal responsibilities that he named the Fair Deal. Anticipating a period of affluence rather than the austerity that had shaped the New Deal, Truman phrased his proposals in terms of the rights of individual citizens—the right to a "useful and remunerative" job, protection from monopoly, good housing, "adequate medical care," "protection from the economic fears of old age," and a "good education." Later President Truman added support for civil rights as well.

When Truman took over the presidency, Americans welcomed him with an initial approval rate of 87 percent, according to Gallup polls. Within a year, his popularity had dropped to 32 percent, and new phrases such as "To err is Truman" had entered the political language. What had happened? New to the presidency, Truman had to oversee the complex conversion of a war economy to a peacetime one. In part because government planners had not known about the atomic bomb, they had assumed that reconversion could be phased in while the country went through the long process of winning a land war in Japan, which was expected to last through 1946. Instead the war ended before adequate reconversion plans were in place.

The main fear on the public's mind in 1945 was that the depression would return once war production ended. The specter of mass unemployment was very real to those who had lived through the grim sacrifices of the 1930s, as well as older Americans who remembered the recession that had followed World War I. To their relief, the economy managed to escape this fate. Despite

a drop in government spending after the war, consumer spending increased, because workers had amassed substantial wartime savings that they were eager to spend. The Servicemen's Readjustment Act of 1944, popularly known as the GI Bill, also put money into the economy by providing a wide range of educational and economic assistance to returning veterans. Finally, despite some temporary dislocations as war production shifted back to civilian uses and veterans were reabsorbed into the workforce, unemployment did not soar. The most visible layoffs were the "Rosie the Riveters" who had taken on high-paying defense jobs during the war and were now forced to find jobs in traditional areas of women's employment at much lower pay.

But the transition was hardly trouble-free. One historian has called it the "morass of reconversion." The main domestic problem was inflation. Consumers wanted an end to wartime restrictions and price rationing, but Truman feared economic chaos if all controls were lifted immediately. In the summer of 1945, he eased industrial controls but retained the wartime Office of Price Administration. When the OPA was disbanded and almost all controls lifted in November 1946, prices soared. That year saw an annual inflation rate of 18.2 percent. The persistence of shortages of food and products also irritated consumers.

Helen Gahagan Douglas
Representative Helen Gahagan Douglas of California, a former Broadway and film star, illustrated a 1947 speech supporting the reestablishment of price controls by bringing a shopping basket of food to a press conference. Douglas served in Congress from 1944 until 1950, when she was defeated in a bid for the Senate by Representative Richard M. Nixon. In their bitterly fought campaign Nixon linked her with communism by calling her "pink."

With the Employment Act of 1946, the federal government began to develop mechanisms to pursue a coherent economic policy. The legislation formally integrated Keynesian ideas into American economic policy, proposing federal fiscal planning on a permanent basis, not just in times of crisis such as the Great Depression. Besides supporting the use of government spending to spur economic growth, the Employment Act envisioned the use of tax policy as a tool for managing the economy—cut taxes to spur economic growth, or raise taxes to slow inflation. Yet the legislation failed to establish clear economic priorities, such as the proper weight between the commitment to full employment and the need for a balanced budget. And the new three-member Council of Economic Advisers, appointed by the president and directly responsible to the White House, played only an advisory role. On balance, however, the Employment Act of 1946 marked an important turning point toward federal responsibility for the performance of the economy.

Postwar Strikes. The rapidly rising cost of living prompted demands for higher wages by the nation's workers. By 1945 the number of union members had swelled to more than 14 million—two-thirds of all workers in the mining, manufacturing, construction, and transportation industries. The labor movement had held the line on wages during the war but now was angered as corporate profits doubled while real wages declined due to the end of wartime overtime pay. Determined to make up for their war-induced sacrifices, workers mounted strikes in major sectors of the economy, crippling the automobile, steel, and coal industries. By the end of 1946, 5 million workers had idled factories and mines for a total of 107,476,000 work days.

Truman never doubted his proper course of action. Even if it meant alienating organized labor, an important component of the Democratic coalition, Truman felt it was the president's job to ensure economic stability. "If you think I'm going to sit here and let you tie up this whole country, you're crazy as hell," Truman told leaders of a nationwide railroad strike in the spring of 1946. Truman used his executive authority to place the nation's railroad system under federal control and asked Congress for power to draft striking workers into the army, a move that infuriated labor but pressured strikers back to work nonetheless. Three days later the president took a tough stand against labor leader John L. Lewis and the striking United Mine Workers by seizing control of the mines. Such actions won Truman support from Americans fed up with labor disruptions, but he incurred the enmity of organized labor.

The Election of 1946. These domestic upheavals did not bode well for the Democrats at the polls. In the 1946 elections Republicans capitalized on popular dissatisfaction with the myriad reconversion problems with the simple slogan, "Had enough?" (The original version was, "Have You Had Enough of the Alphabet?", a reference to the "alphabet soup" of New Deal agencies. Less was definitely more.) The Republicans gained control of both houses of Congress for the first time since 1928. Truman and the Democrats seemed thoroughly repudiated.

The Taft-Hartley Act. The Republican Congress elected in 1946 was determined to undo the New Deal's social welfare measures, and it singled out labor legislation as a special target. In 1947, Congress passed the Taft-Hartley Act, a direct challenge to several provisions of the 1935 National Labor Relations Act. This law outlawed the closed shop and restricted the political power of unions by prohibiting the use of union dues for political activity. It allowed the president to declare an 80-day cooling-off period in strikes with national impact. Unions especially disliked Section 14b of the act, which allowed states to pass "right to work" laws to prohibit the union shop. Truman issued a ringing veto of the Taft-Hartley bill in June 1947, calling it "bad for labor, bad for management, and bad for the country." Congress easily overrode Truman's veto, but his action brought labor back into the Democratic fold.

The 1948 Election

Most observers believed that Truman faced an impossible task in the presidential campaign of 1948. The Republicans were united and well led. They maintained the loyal support of most middle- and upper-income Protestants outside the South, and many farmers and skilled workers. Eager to attract votes from traditional Democratic constituencies, they nominated a moderate, Governor Thomas E. Dewey of New York. A well-known prosecuting attorney, Dewey had demonstrated his attractiveness as a national candidate in his 1944 campaign against Roosevelt. To increase their appeal in the West, the Republicans nominated Earl Warren, governor of California, for vice-president. Their brief platform promised to continue most New Deal reforms and supported a bipartisan foreign policy.

Truman, in contrast, led a party in severe disarray. Both the left and right wings of the Democratic party split off and nominated their own candidates. Henry A. Wallace, a former New Deal liberal whom Truman had fired as secretary of commerce in 1946 because he was

Taft-Hartley

No legislation angered organized labor more than the 1947 Labor-Management Relations Act, popularly known as Taft-Hartley, which rolled back many of the gains made by labor under the New Deal. The message to President Truman from these union members assembled at an American Federation of Labor rally at Madison Square Garden in 1947 is clear, even if they inverted the name of the bill to Hartley-Taft. Truman did veto the bill, but his veto was overridden by the Republican-controlled Congress.

perceived as too "soft" on communism, ran as the candidate of the new Progressive party. Wallace advocated increased government intervention in the economy, more power for labor unions, and greater cooperation with the Soviet Union.

Southern Democrats bolted the party over the issue of civil rights. At the Democratic national convention, leaders such as Mayor Hubert H. Humphrey of Minneapolis and gubernatorial candidate Adlai E. Stevenson of Illinois had pushed through a platform calling for the repeal of Taft-Hartley, the establishment of a permanent Fair Employment Practices Commission, and federal antilynching and anti-poll tax legislation. Many southerners would grudgingly support a greater role for the government in the economy, but they would not tolerate federal interference in race relations. Three days after the convention, southern Democrats met in Birmingham, Alabama, to set up the States' Rights, or Dixiecrat, party. They nominated Governor J. Strom Thurmond of South Carolina for president.

Truman responded to these challenges with one of the most effective presidential campaigns ever waged. He dramatically called Congress back into summer session to give the Republicans a chance to enact their platform into law. When, predictably, they failed to do so, he launched a strenuous cross-country speaking tour, hitting out at the "do-nothing Republican Congress." He also hammered away at the Republicans' support for the antilabor Taft-Hartley act and their

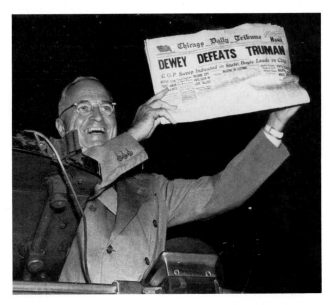

Truman Triumphant

In one of the most famous photographs in American political history, Harry S. Truman gloats over an inaccurate headline in the *Chicago Tribune*. Pollsters had predicted an overwhelming victory for Thomas E. Dewey. Their primitive polling techniques did not reflect the dramatic surge in support for Truman during the last days of the campaign.

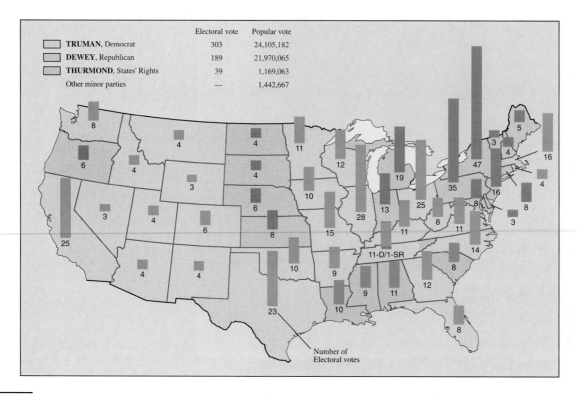

MAP 28.3

The Election of 1948

Political adviser Clark Clifford planned Truman's successful electoral strategy in 1948, arguing that the president should concentrate his campaign in urban areas where the Democrats had their greatest strength. In an election marked by low turnout, Truman held onto enough support from the Roosevelt coalition of blacks, union members, and farmers to defeat Dewey by more than 2 million votes.

opposition to full-parity price supports for farmers. Truman struck just the right chord. At his rallies enthusiastic listeners took up the cry, "Give 'em hell, Harry!"

Truman won a remarkable victory, receiving 49.6 percent of the vote to Dewey's 45.1 percent. Strom Thurmond and the Dixiecrats carried four southern states. Henry Wallace failed to win a single state. The Democrats also regained control of both houses of Congress. As a commentator in *The New Republic* observed, "Harry Truman won this election because Franklin Roosevelt had worked so well." Truman retained the support of organized labor and Jewish and Catholic voters in the big cities; the allegiance of northern black voters to the Democratic party offset the southern losses to the Dixiecrats. (The discovery that the Democrats could capture the presidency without the Solid South paved the way for later civil rights legislation.) Most importantly, Truman appealed effectively to people like himself who hailed from the farms, towns, and small cities in the nation's heartland. He had grasped something the pollsters had missed: "Everybody's against me but the people."

Fair Deal Liberalism

Truman's Fair Deal represented the essentials of postwar liberalism. Liberals' conception of the state was an expansive, Keynesian one, based on a willingness to use the fiscal powers of the federal government to stimulate economic growth, redress imbalances, and encourage social progress. With a rhetorical commitment to civil rights and economic abundance for all, liberalism committed the modern state to extending the benefits of capitalism to ever wider numbers of citizens. Postwar liberalism thus built on and surpassed the reforms begun during the New Deal.

Truman's ambitious agenda ran up against a generally hostile Congress. Despite its Democratic majority, the Senate and the House contained a fair number of conservatives of both parties. This same conservative coalition had blocked Roosevelt in his second term and dismantled or cut popular New Deal programs during wartime. With the exception of Taft-Hartley, the Truman administration forestalled any wholesale attacks on the New Deal. On the other hand, only parts of the

Fair Deal won adoption. The minimum wage was raised from forty cents an hour to seventy-five; the Social Security system was extended to cover 10 million new workers and its benefits raised by 75 percent. The National Housing Act of 1949 declared as public policy "the goal of a decent home and a suitable living environment for every American family" and called for the construction of 810,000 units of low-income housing.

Civil Rights. The Truman record on civil rights shows the combination of progress and stalemate that characterized most aspects of the Fair Deal. Civil rights became a national political issue in the 1940s. Black expectations had been raised by wartime opportunities as well as symbolic postwar victories, such as Jackie Robinson of the Brooklyn Dodgers breaking the color barrier in major league baseball in 1947. In addition, Truman realized that black voters played an increasingly large role in the Democratic party as they migrated from the South, where they were effectively disenfranchised, to northern cities. Finally, Truman was sensitive to the world's view of American treatment of blacks, especially since the Soviet Union often compared segregation of southern blacks with the Nazis' treatment of the Jews.

Lacking a popular mandate, Truman resorted to a variety of means to advance the cause of civil rights. In 1946 he appointed a National Civil Rights Commission; their 1947 recommendations called for an expanded federal role in civil rights that foreshadowed much of the legislation of the 1960s. He ordered the Justice Department to prepare *amicus curiae* (friend of the court) briefs in Supreme Court cases such as *Shelley v. Kraemer* (1948), which struck down as unconstitutional restrictive covenants designed to enforce residential segregation. By a 1948 executive order, he began the process of desegregating the armed forces which was hastened by the Korean War. And in 1949, safely after the election, the administration proposed a federal antilynching law, federal protection of voting rights (such as an end to poll taxes), and a permanent federal agency to guarantee equal employment opportunities. A filibuster by southern conservatives effectively blocked such legislation in Congress, however.

Interest groups successfully opposed other key items on the Fair Deal agenda. The American Medical Association squashed the movement for national health insurance by denouncing it as the first step toward "socialized medicine." Catholics successfully opposed any aid-to-education proposal that omitted subsidies for parochial schools. Farmers refused to join labor in supporting the outright repeal of Taft-Hartley. In general, the Truman administration failed to mobilize popular and congressional support for dramatically enlarged federal responsibilities in the economic and social spheres.

Two further factors limited the Fair Deal's chances for legislative success. One was the outbreak of the Korean War in 1950. The other was the nation's growing fear of internal subversion. The anticommunist crusade was just one manifestation of the increasing preoccupation with the cold war that was seeping into all facets of American life. Truman's own administration played a major role in fueling these domestic tensions.

The Great Fear

The deterioration of relations with the Soviet Union after 1945 underlay the fear of communism and the resulting domestic repression that gripped the country in the late 1940s and early 1950s. Americans often call this phenomenon "McCarthyism," after Senator Joseph R. McCarthy of Wisconsin, the decade's most vocal anticommunist. But this "great fear" was broader than the work of just one man. It built on the distrust of radicals and foreigners that had manifested itself in earlier periods such as the 1850s and the Red Scare after World War I. Worsening cold war tensions intersected with such deep-seated insecurities to spawn an obsessive concern over internal subversion, especially fears about how spies might pass the "secret" of the atomic bomb to the Soviet Union. Few spies or Communists were actually found in positions of power; far more Americans became innocent victims of the false accusations and innuendoes that flourished in the postwar climate of fear.

In the 1930s liberals and Communists had cooperated in a "popular front" against fascism. By the mid-1940s, however, Stalin's repressive dictatorship and fears of Russian expansionism into Eastern Europe and beyond made the Soviet Union seem as large a threat as fascism had been a decade earlier. Some postwar liberals, notably Henry Wallace and his followers in the Progressive party, continued to seek cooperation with the Soviet Union and were not disturbed by the presence of communist activists in their political movement. But many other liberal groups, particularly the Americans for Democratic Action, founded in 1947, broke from the popular front by including strident anticommunist planks in their political platforms.

Similarly, Communists had been active in the labor-organizing drives of the 1930s, and their contributions were welcomed, if not openly acknowledged. By the late 1940s, however, the labor movement reversed itself in the growing climate of fear and suspicion and suddenly purged Communists from its membership. CIO president Phillip Murray denounced communist sympathizers as "skulking cowards . . . apostles of hate." Unions that refused to oust their left-wing leaders, such as the United Electrical, Radio and Machine Workers of America, were expelled from the CIO.

The federal government also undertook its own an

Testifying before the House Committee on Un-American Activities *Pete Seeger*

Pete Seeger, a folk singer and song-writer, was one of many performers and artists called to testify before HUAC. This grilling by staff member Frank S. Tavenner, Jr., and Chairman Francis E. Walter was typical of the way investigators tried to force witnesses to divulge information against their will. After his 1955 appearance before the committee, Seeger and his group, the Weavers, were blacklisted.

Mr. Tavenner: When and where were you born, Mr. Seeger?

Mr. Seeger: I was born in New York in 1919.

Mr. Tavenner: What is your profession or occupation?

Mr. Seeger: Well, I have worked at many things, and my main profession is a student of American folklore, and I make my living as a banjo picker— sort of damning, in some people's opinion. . . .

Mr. Tavenner: You said that you would tell us about the songs. Did you participate in a program at Wingdale Lodge in the State of New York, which is a summer camp for adults and children, on the weekend of July Fourth of this year? [Witness consulted with counsel.]

Mr. Seeger: Again, I say I will be glad to tell what songs I have ever sung, because singing is my business.

Mr. Tavenner: I am going to ask you.

Mr. Seeger: But I decline to say who has ever listened to them, who has written them, or other people who have sung them.

Mr. Tavenner: Did you sing this song, to which we have referred, "Now Is the Time," at Wingdale Lodge on the weekend of July Fourth?

Mr. Seeger: I don't know any song by that name, and I know a song with a similar name. It is called "Wasn't That a Time." Is that the song?

Chairman Walter: Did you sing that song?

Mr. Seeger: I can sing it. I don't know how well I can do it without my banjo.

Chairman Walter: I said, Did you sing it on that occasion?

Mr. Seeger: I have sung that song. I am not going to go into where I have sung it. I have sung it many places. . . .

Chairman Walter: I direct you to answer the question. Did you sing this particular song on the Fourth of July at Wingdale Lodge in New York?

Mr. Seeger: I have already given you my answer to that question, and all questions such as that. I feel that is improper to ask about my associations and opinions. I have said that I would be voluntarily glad to tell you any song, or what I have done in my life.

Chairman Walter: I think it is my duty to inform you that we don't accept this answer and the others, and I give you an opportunity now to answer these questions, particularly the last one.

Mr. Seeger: Sir, my answer is always the same.

Source: Eric Bentley, ed., *Thirty Years of Treason: Excerpts From Hearings Before the House Committee on Un-American Activities, 1938–1968* (New York: Viking, 1971), 686, 690.

tisubversion campaign, which further inflamed the mounting hysteria. In March 1947, President Truman outraged many supporters by using an executive order to initiate a comprehensive investigation into the loyalty of all federal employees. More than 6 million individuals were subjected to security checks, and 14,000 underwent intensive FBI investigation. The case of Dorothy Bailey, a forty-one-year-old graduate of Bryn Mawr College and the University of Minnesota, was typical of the two thousand federal workers who were forced out of government service. A fourteen-year veteran of the U.S. Employment Service, Bailey lost her job because an unidentified informer claimed she was a Communist and associated with known Communists. Brought before the District of Columbia regional loyalty board, she denied the charge. No evidence against her was introduced and no witnesses testified to support the charges, but she lost her job anyway.

Following the lead from Washington, many state and local governments, colleges and universities, and private institutions and businesses undertook their own antisubversion campaigns. All 11,000 faculty members at the University of California were required to take a loyalty oath; UCLA alone fired 157 who refused to do so. In Hollywood, ex-FBI agents circulated a list of actors, directors, and writers whose names had been mentioned in congressional investigations or whose associations and friends had been described as dubious. Industry executives denied the existence of any such blacklist, but for ten years, hundreds of people were shut out of work in the entertainment industry. The Weavers, a popular group of folk singers, were blacklisted, and politically active actors such as Zero Mostel and John Garfield had difficulty finding work. One day actress Jean Muir headlined the popular radio show "The Aldrich Family"; the next she was out of a job— fired, the network said, not because she was a Communist but because gossip about her had made her too "controversial."

HUAC. The House Committee on Un-American Activities (HUAC) played an especially active role in fanning the anticommunist hysteria. HUAC had been ferreting out supposed Communists in government since its 1938 investigation into the Federal Theatre Project. In 1947, HUAC intensified its crusade by holding widely publicized hearings on communist infiltration in the film industry. A group of writers and directors, soon dubbed the "Hollywood Ten," went to jail for contempt of Congress when they cited the First Amendment rather than testify about their past associations.

HUAC next took up, with a vengeance, the case of Alger Hiss, a former New Deal State Department official who had accompanied Franklin Roosevelt to Yalta. The case against Hiss rested on the 1948 testimony of former Communist Whittaker Chambers, a senior editor at *Time*. Chambers claimed that Hiss had passed him classified documents in the 1930s as part of his duties as a member of a secret communist cell in the government, a charge that Hiss categorically denied. Congressman Richard M. Nixon of California orches-

trated the HUAC investigation of Hiss, which culminated in the dramatic release of the so-called Pumpkin Papers, microfilm that Chambers had hidden in a pumpkin patch on his Maryland farm. (This supposedly incriminating cache, when declassified, contained only Navy Department documents on life rafts and fire extinguishers.) Because the statute of limitations on espionage had expired by 1949, Hiss was charged instead with perjury for denying Chambers's charges before HUAC. The first trial resulted in a hung jury; the second in early 1950 found Hiss guilty of perjury and sentenced him to five years in federal prison. The conviction of Hiss increased the paranoia about a communist conspiracy in the federal government.

The Rise and Fall of McCarthy. The hysteria soon intensified. Senator Joseph McCarthy, a Marine Air Corps veteran, had won election in the 1946 Republican landslide with the slogan, "Wisconsin Needs a Tail Gunner in the Senate." In late 1949, McCarthy discovered that a speech attacking a liberal Madison, Wisconsin, newspaper brought him favorable attention. In a February 1950 speech in Wheeling, West Virginia, he launched what one columnist later called his string of "multiple untruths" by declaring, "I have here in my hand a list of the names of 205 men that were known to the Secretary of State as being members of the Communist Party and who nevertheless are still working and shaping the policy of the State Department." McCarthy never revealed the names on his list, later changing the number to 81, then to 57. The public was so responsive to his charges that these inconsistencies failed to dent his momentum.

McCarthy's political genius was his ability to make his name synonymous with the cause of uncovering sub-

The Army-McCarthy Hearings
These 1954 hearings contributed to the downfall of Senator Joseph McCarthy by bringing his reckless accusations, bullying tactics, and sneering innuendoes to huge television audiences day after day. Some of the most heated exchanges took place between McCarthy (on right) and Joseph Welch (seated, on left), the lawyer representing the Army. When an exasperated Welch asked, "Have you no decency left, sir?", McCarthy merely shrugged. But the audience broke into applause because someone finally had the courage to stand up to the senator from Wisconsin.

versives in government. Politicians who attacked him exposed themselves to charges of being soft on communism, the kiss of death in the postwar political climate. At first McCarthy's supporters were more visible than his detractors; Democratic congressman John F. Kennedy of Massachusetts thought "McCarthy may have something." But President Truman called McCarthy's charges "slander, lies, character assassination," although he could do nothing to curb them. Even when Republican Dwight D. Eisenhower was elected president in 1952, he did not publicly challenge his party's most outspoken senator.

The momentum of international events allowed McCarthy to retain credibility, despite his failure to identify a single Communist in government. Alger Hiss was convicted in 1950. The Korean War broke out soon after, embroiling the United States in a frustrating fight against communism in a faraway land. And in a sensational but isolated case in 1951, Julius and Ethel Rosenberg were accused and convicted of passing atomic secrets to the Soviet Union. Despite conflicting evidence, they were executed in 1953.

In 1954, McCarthy finally overreached himself by launching an investigation into possible subversion in the U.S. Army. The lengthy televised hearings brought McCarthy's smear tactics and leering innuendoes into the nation's living rooms, and support for him declined. Later that year, the Senate voted 67 to 22 to censure McCarthy. He died three years later at the age of forty-eight, his name forever attached to a period of political repression of which he was only the most flagrant manifestation.

Modern Republicanism

The 1952 election occurred in the midst of the Korean stalemate and at the height of the Great Fear. The newly elected president, Dwight D. Eisenhower, worked quickly to end the Korean War; the grip of McCarthyism lasted longer. Eisenhower set the tone for the modern Republican party by emphasizing a slowdown, but not a dismantling, of federal responsibilities; his low-key style of governing was well suited to these seemingly prosperous and confident times. In foreign policy, the Republicans continued to see the world in Cold War polarities while expanding the defense buildup begun during the Korean War.

The Soldier Becomes President

The Republican party's greatest strength lay in the largely Protestant and rural states of the Midwest. Since only a third of the nation's registered voters were Re-

publicans, however, the party had to find a candidate who could attract Democrats and independents. Republican leaders quickly realized that General Dwight D. Eisenhower would be just such a candidate.

Eisenhower's status as a war hero was his greatest political asset. Born in 1890 and raised in Abilene, Kansas, he graduated from the United States Military Academy at West Point in 1915. General Douglas MacArthur chose him as his aide in the early 1930s, and Eisenhower rose quickly through the ranks. After Pearl Harbor, he came to Washington under the sponsorship of a second mentor, General George C. Marshall. General Eisenhower oversaw the Allied invasion of North Africa in 1942, and in 1944 became Supreme Commander of Allied Forces in Europe, where he had the mammoth task of coordinating the D-Day invasion of France. To hundreds of thousands of soldiers, and to the millions who followed the war on newsreels, he was simply "Ike," the best known and best liked of the nation's military leaders.

Eisenhower had placed himself in a superb position for a presidential campaign. After serving as president of Columbia University from 1948 to 1950, he returned to active duty as the commander of NATO forces in Europe, serving at Truman's request. As a professional military man, he could insist that he stood "above politics." While in the army, in fact, he had never voted because he felt that such political activity would represent an intrusion of the military into civilian affairs. Many Democrats had hoped to make him their candidate for president in 1948, and again in 1952. Eisenhower did want the office, but as a Republican.

When conservative candidate Senator Robert A. Taft of Ohio did well in the early primaries of 1952, Eisenhower resigned his military position to campaign. He quickly proved an effective politician, winning several primaries and taking delegates away from Taft in a tough fight at the Republican National Convention. Eisenhower then asked Senator Richard M. Nixon of California to be his running mate. Young, tirelessly partisan, and with a strong anticommunist record from his crusade against Alger Hiss, Nixon brought an aggressive campaign style, as well as regional balance, to the ticket.

The Democrats never seriously considered renominating Harry Truman, who by 1952 was a thoroughly discredited leader. During the last two years of his presidency, his public approval rating had never risen above 32 percent and at one point had plunged to 23 percent. Lack of popular enthusiasm for the Korean War dealt the severest blow to Truman's support, but a series of widely publicized scandals involving federal officials in bribery, kickback, and influence-peddling schemes caused voters to complain about the "mess in Washington." With a certain relief, the Democrats turned to Governor Adlai E. Stevenson of Illinois, who enjoyed

They Liked Ike

In the 1952 election, Eisenhower's immense personal popularity, captured in the campaign slogan, "I Like Ike," propelled him to the largest popular vote of any candidate to that date. Here delegates show their enthusiasm at the Republican National Convention that year.

the support of respected liberals such as Eleanor Roosevelt and of organized labor. To appease southern voters who feared Stevenson's liberal agenda, the Democratic convention nominated Senator John A. Sparkman of Alabama for vice-president.

Throughout the 1952 campaign, Stevenson advocated New Deal–Fair Deal policies with an almost literary eloquence, but Eisenhower's artfully unpretentious speeches proved more effective with the voters. Eager to get maximum support from a broad electorate, Eisenhower played down specific questions of policy. Instead, he attacked the Democrats with the "K_1C_2" formula— "Korea, Communism, and Corruption." In a campaign pledge that clinched the election, he vowed to go to Korea to end the stalemated war if elected. Stevenson lamely quipped, "If elected, I shall go to the White House."

The only slip in the Republican campaign was the revelation that wealthy Californians had set up a secret "slush fund" for Richard Nixon. While Eisenhower contemplated dropping him from the ticket, Nixon adroitly used a televised speech to appeal directly for voters' sympathy, asserting that he had not misused campaign funds. Whereas Truman appointees had accepted mink coats from contractors—a reference to a widely reported case involving a loan examiner for the Reconstruction Finance Corporation—his wife wore only a "Republican cloth coat." Nixon did admit accepting one gift, a puppy his young daughters named Checkers. That gift he would not give back, he declared earnestly. Nixon's televised pathos turned an embarrassing incident into an advantage, as sympathetic viewers flooded Republican headquarters with telegrams and phone calls in his support. Outmaneuvered, Repub-

The "Checkers" Speech
Illustrating the power of the new medium of television, vice-presidential candidate Richard Nixon's "Checkers" speech kept him on the 1952 ticket despite allegations of an illegal campaign slush fund. Seen today, the half-hour speech seems stilted and amateurish, but viewers in 1952 were so impressed by Nixon's earnest delivery that they flooded Republican headquarters with telegrams demanding that he stay on the ticket.

lican leaders had no choice but to keep him on the ticket. The "Checkers speech" showed how the mass media—particularly television—were fundamentally changing the political process.

The Republican campaign paid off handsomely, with Eisenhower winning 55 percent of the popular vote. He carried all the northern and western states and won majorities in four southern states. Although Eisenhower won a great personal victory, Republican candidates for Congress ran far behind him. They won control of the House of Representatives by a slender margin of four seats and regained the Senate. In 1954 Democrats would regain control of both houses, an advantage they held even when the enormously popular Eisenhower won an easy reelection over Adlai Stevenson in 1956.

The Hidden-Hand Presidency

Seeking a middle ground between liberalism and conservatism, Eisenhower offered "modern Republicanism" as an alternative to the Democrats' liberal agenda. He did his best to set a quieter national mood, lessening the need for federal activism on social and economic issues. As columnist Richard L. Strout observed in *The New Republic*, "The less he does the more they love him. Here is a man who doesn't rock the boat." The nation's voters put it more simply in a popular slogan: "I Like Ike."

Yet Eisenhower was no stooge as president. Several historians have characterized his style of leadership as the "hidden-hand presidency." They point out that Eisenhower maneuvered deftly behind-the-scenes while maintaining a public demeanor of not concerning himself with partisan questions. They also cite the president's skillful handling of the press. When his press secretary, James Hagerty, asked what he would say at a press conference about a tricky foreign policy issue, Eisenhower replied, "Don't worry, Jim. If that question comes up, I'll just confuse them." He proved just as adept in personnel situations. In a characteristic move, Eisenhower recognized the outspoken anticommunism of Clare Booth Luce, an author, playwright, and former Republican member of Congress from Connecticut, by making her the nation's second woman ambassador. At the same time, by sending Luce to Italy, he removed her strident opinions from the Washington scene.

Eisenhower's presidential style deliberately avoided confrontation. He refused to speak out publicly against Senator Joseph McCarthy. Likewise, he displayed little leadership in the emerging area of civil rights. Inadvertently, though, he contributed to the advance of the black cause. In September 1953 he named Governor Earl Warren of California as chief justice of the Supreme Court. Warren's quiet persuasion convinced the Court to rule unanimously in *Brown v. Board of Education of Topeka* (1954) that racial segregation in the public schools was unconstitutional (see Chapter 31). Eisenhower remained disturbed by the decision, asserting, "I don't believe you can change the hearts of men with laws or decisions." Nonetheless, in 1957 he sent federal troops to enforce the integration of Central High School in Little Rock, Arkansas. He also signed the Civil Rights Act of 1957, a Democratic-inspired bill which though weak was the first national civil rights legislation passed since Reconstruction.

Eisenhower presided over other cautious increases in federal activity. When the Soviet Union launched the first satellite *Sputnik*—or "earth traveler"—in 1957, Eisenhower supported a U.S. space program to catch up with the Russians. Arguing that the Cold War required more scientists and experts on foreign affairs, he persuaded Congress to appropriate additional money for college and university scholarships and to increase support for research and development in universities and industry. He also yielded to demands of interest groups to increase federal outlays for veterans' benefits, unemployment compensation, housing, and Social Security. The minimum wage was raised from seventy-five cents an hour to a dollar. The creation of the new Department of Health, Education, and Welfare (HEW) confirmed the federal commitment to social welfare programs. When HEW head Oveta Culp Hobby, the second woman to hold a cabinet position, suggested that it would be "socialized medicine" for the government to

Sputnik

Given the size of the spacecraft that now take astronauts into space, we forget how tiny the original Soviet satellite was—a mere 184 pounds and 22 inches in diameter. Here a replica hangs in a Moscow exhibit hall—a symbol of pride for Soviet citizens, and in the Cold War atmosphere of 1957, an acute embarrassment for the United States government. When the American navy tried and failed to launch a satellite two months later (it only lifted six inches off the ground before exploding), newspaper headlines savagely pronounced, "Kaputnik!"

offer free distribution of the new Salk polio vaccine, she was forced from office by the adverse public reaction.

Under the Eisenhower administration, the government undertook new commitments on a more massive scale. It cosponsored with Canada the construction of the St. Lawrence Seaway to link the Great Lakes with the Atlantic Ocean, a project which had been under discussion since the 1930s. In a move that drastically altered the American landscape and favored the trend toward privately owned automobiles rather than mass transit, the Interstate Highway Act of 1956 authorized $26 billion over a ten-year period for the construction of a nationally integrated highway system. (This network of highways was also promoted to speed civilian

evacuation in the event of nuclear attack.) Projects such as the St. Lawrence Seaway and interstate highways were the largest public works programs to date, surpassing anything the New Deal had undertaken. They confirmed the permanent role that federal spending now played in American life, even under Republican administrations.

President Eisenhower realized that the vast federal budget, which reached almost 23 percent of the gross national product by the late 1950s, gave the government a major responsibility for the overall health of the nation's economy. The president made the fight against inflation, not full employment, his top economic priority. Eisenhower and his advisers believed their policies would encourage business confidence and lead to prosperity, but the economy grew only at the modest rate of 2.9 percent per year between 1953 and 1960—too slowly to absorb all those who sought work. The unemployment rate fluctuated from a low of 2.9 percent in 1953 to a high of 6.8 percent in 1958. Furthermore, Eisenhower's drive for a balanced budget and stable prices contributed to the recessions of 1953–1954, 1957–1958, and 1960–1961.

Modern Republicanism, it turned out, resisted the unchecked expansion of the state but did not cut federal power back in any tangible fashion. The responsibilities now accepted by the federal government—social welfare programs inherited from the New Deal, Keynesian intervention in the economy, and increased defense expenditures necessitated by the United States' larger role abroad—foreclosed any return to the limited Republican government that had prevailed in the 1920s. When Eisenhower retired from public life in 1961, the federal government had become an even greater presence in everyday life than when he took office.

Alliances and Arms

Dwight Eisenhower had earned a reputation for excellent judgment in military and diplomatic affairs during his years in the armed forces. One of his first acts as president was to put that skill to use to negotiate an end to the Korean War. As he had pledged in the campaign, he visited Korea in December 1952. The final settlement was signed in July 1953 at Panmunjom after a compromise on the tricky issue of prisoner exchange was reached. Once the Korean matter had been settled, Eisenhower's attention turned back to Europe. Secretary of State John Foster Dulles played an important role in defining the administration's foreign policy. Dulles, an experienced international lawyer and diplomat, was an outspoken critic of "atheistic communism." Rather than just limiting further Soviet expansion, he argued, the United States ought to promote the "liberation" of the "captive nations" of Eastern Europe.

The Soviet Union Under Khrushchev. At the beginning of the Eisenhower administration, the Soviet Union briefly appeared more interested in better relations. Joseph Stalin died in March 1953, and Georgi Malenkov, who adopted a more conciliatory tone toward the West, assumed his duties. After an intraparty struggle that lasted until 1956, Nikita S. Khrushchev emerged as Stalin's successor. He soon startled Communists throughout the world by denouncing Stalin as "a distrustful man, sickly and suspicious," and detailing publicly for the first time Stalin's "crimes" and "tortures" of the 1930s and 1940s. Khrushchev likewise surprised Westerners by calling for "peaceful coexistence" between communist and capitalist societies. He also seemed more willing to tolerate different approaches to communism, such as that developed by Yugoslavia's Marshal Tito or Poland's Wladislaw Gomulka. When Gomulka, who had once been jailed in a Stalinist purge, insisted that his nation's Communists be allowed to work out Poland's problems in their own way, Khrushchev agreed.

On the other hand, Khrushchev made certain that Russia's Eastern European satellites did not deviate too far from the Soviet path. When a nationalist revolt erupted in Hungary in 1956, Soviet tanks rapidly moved into Budapest. Demonstrating their willingness to use massive force to retain control in Eastern Europe, the Soviets crushed the revolt and installed a puppet regime. Despite Dulles's rhetoric, there was little the United States could do beyond loosening immigration quotas for Hungarian refugees.

A Web of Alliances. The Soviet repression of the Hungarian revolt confirmed that American policymakers had few, if any, options to "roll back" Soviet power in Eastern Europe short of going to war with the U.S.S.R. An alternative strategy, already in force, sought to limit communism through a permanent alliance structure. Truman, Marshall, and Acheson had established key military alliances in Europe, such as NATO. In 1954, Dulles negotiated bilateral defense treaties with South Korea and the nationalist Chinese regime on Taiwan, and orchestrated the creation of the Southeast Asia Collective Defense and Treaty Organization (SEATO). In 1955 the United States sponsored, but did not join, the Baghdad Pact, a defensive alliance between Turkey and Iraq that was important to national security because of those countries' strategic location on the borders of the Soviet Union.

U.S. policymakers also displayed a tendency to support stable governments, no matter what their politics, as a bulwark against the supposed threat of communism. As a result, some of America's staunchest allies—the Philippines, Iran, Nicaragua, and the Dominican Republic—were military dictatorships or governments lacking broad-based popular support. The secretary of state regarded the establishment of these overtly anti-communist alliances as an imperative. "Neutrality," Dulles maintained, was not only "obsolete" but "immoral."

CIA Activities. Firm in the righteousness of his cause, Dulles did not shrink from covert interventions against governments that were, in his opinion, too closely aligned with communism. For such tasks, he used the Central Intelligence Agency, which was headed by his brother, Allen Dulles. During the Eisenhower administration, the CIA moved beyond its original mandate of intelligence gathering to active, if secret, involvement in the internal affairs of foreign countries where such covert action suited American objectives.

In the 1950s the CIA successfully directed the overthrow of several foreign governments. When Iran's nationalist premier, Mohammad Mossadegh, seized British oil properties in 1953, CIA agents helped the young shah, Mohammad Reza Pahlevi, depose him. Using both economic leverage and a repressive secret police, the shah soon solidified his power within Iran. In 1954 the CIA supported a coup in Guatemala against popularly elected Jacobo Arbenz Guzman, who had expropriated 250,000 acres held by the American-owned United Fruit Company and accepted arms from the communist government of East Germany. The CIA also tried, unsuccessfully, to overthrow Achmed Sukarno of Indonesia in 1958 and Fidel Castro of Cuba in 1961. Eisenhower specifically approved these efforts. "Our traditional ideas of international sportsmanship," he wrote privately in 1955, "are scarcely applicable in the morass in which the world now flounders."

The "New Look" in Foreign Policy. Although Eisenhower strongly opposed communism, he hoped to keep the cost of containment at a manageable level. His "New Look" in foreign policy tried to encourage the nation's allies to bear some of the responsibility for maintaining large armed forces, mainly through the extensive system of defense pacts. One byproduct was an increased role for the CIA, an agency that was relatively cheap as a foreign policy tool. (Another advantage was its ability to work covertly, removed from public scrutiny.) The administration also increased the flow of American military aid. Truman had emphasized economic assistance over military aid, but Eisenhower reversed the priorities.

As part of the "New Look," Eisenhower and Dulles also embraced the policy of "massive retaliation." They believed the United States could economize by developing an effective nuclear deterrent rather than relying solely on expensive conventional armed forces. Nuclear weapons delivered "more bang for the buck" in the words of Defense Secretary Charles E. Wilson. If the nation's major foreign enemy were a worldwide commu-

Testing An Atomic Bomb
Throughout the 1950s, the Atomic Energy Commission conducted above-ground tests of atomic and hydrogen bombs. Thousands of soldiers were exposed to fallout during the tests, such as this one at Yucca Flat, Nevada, in April 1952. The AEC, ignoring or suppressing medical evidence to the contrary, mounted an extensive public relations campaign to convince local residents that the tests did not endanger their health.

nist movement led by Moscow, they reasoned, the United States did not need to keep a large number of soldiers under arms, because atomic weapons could threaten the Soviet Union directly and force it to back down. To this end, the Eisenhower administration expanded its commitment to the hydrogen bomb, including extensive atmospheric testing in the South Pacific and Western states such as Nevada, Colorado, and Utah. To improve U.S. defenses against an air attack from the Soviet Union, the administration supported research to develop the long-range bombing capabilities of the Strategic Air Command and installed the Distant Early Warning (DEW) line of radar stations in Alaska and Canada in 1958.

These efforts did little to improve the nation's security, as the Soviets matched the United States weapon for weapon in an escalating arms race. The Soviet Union carried out its own atmospheric tests of hydrogen bombs between 1953 and 1958 and developed a fleet of long-range bombers. It briefly won the race to build an intercontinental ballistic missile (ICBM), but the United States launched its own ICBM in 1958. In 1960 an American nuclear submarine was the first to launch an atomic-tipped Polaris missile. Soviet leaders raced to produce equivalent weapons.

Although the Soviet Union viewed the Eisenhower and Dulles policies of anticommunist alliances and massive deterrence as inherently hostile, Eisenhower continued to work toward a negotiated arms limitation agreement. President Eisenhower was deeply disturbed by the implications of a nuclear policy that was based on the premise of annihilating your enemy, even if your own country was destroyed—the aptly named acronym MAD (Mutual Assured Destruction). Although preliminary discussions with Soviet leaders between 1955 and 1957 had not yielded the "open skies" mutual arms inspection treaty he had wanted, they did produce plans for a summit meeting with Khrushchev in May 1960. Then, on May 5, an American spy plane was shot down over Soviet territory. With Eisenhower's admission that he had authorized this and other secret flights by high-flying U-2 reconnaissance aircraft over the Soviet Union, his last chance to negotiate an arms agreement evaporated.

AMERICAN VOICES

An Atomic Bomb Veteran Remembers *George Mace*

George Mace's life was changed by his participation in atomic testing in the Pacific in the 1950s. He blames his ongoing health problems on the over thirty-five atomic and hydrogen bomb blasts he witnessed there. He became involved in the National Association of Atomic Veterans, founded in 1979, which has pressured the federal government to release the full story of what happened during the tests of the 1940s and 1950s.

I graduated from high school in 1953 and enlisted in the Air Force in 1955 to gain a trade. I originally went into communications as a teletype repairman, and by the last year of my enlistment I was a crypto and typographical equipment instructor at Lackland Air Force Base in San Antonio. In 1957, orders came down assigning me to Joint Task Force 7 on the Enewetak atoll in the Marshall Islands of the South Pacific. Initially it was for six months. So I took my wife and baby daughter back home to Hagerstown and left for Enewetak. I was twenty-two. . . .

Enewetak was so small that at first, I couldn't find it from the air; but then a single concrete airstrip came into view and it was as if we had landed on an aircraft carrier. Immediately we were briefed on the island's facilities and its very tight security. I remember being told that we couldn't write home about anything we saw or did and that our mail would be checked and edited. All of our standard uniforms were exchanged for khaki shorts, short sleeved shirts, and blue baseball caps. We wore that uniform all the time when we were on the island, for the next nine months. . . .

We were never told that a shot was going to occur until the day of the event. And every day there was a shot, they'd march us out to the beach and make us sit there with our backs to the lagoon. At the time, I always asked how far we were away from it, and I was always told about fifty miles. But in 1979, when I got the declassified documents, I found out that I was only five to fifteen miles from the bombs—never more than fifteen miles! So there was a clear deception on the part of the government.

Watching the shots got to be kind of pointless after a while; there was no follow-up study of us at all. They were just preparing the troops for the age of atomic war. We were never told about any effects of radiation, and being young and ignorant, I had no fear of it. But I *did* fear the tremendous strength of each blast. The enlisted men would sit on the sand with their heads on their knees, and the officers faced the bombs with dark goggles—welder's goggles really. We'd cover our eyes until the fireball passed. A few seconds after the explosion went off you would see this tremendous flash, and then a tremendous wave of heat you could feel like the sun coming up on your back. The biggest one I ever saw—code named Oak—got to the point of being uncomfortable.

The Oak explosion was nine megatons. I will never forget it; we sandbagged the island beforehand, because it was only seven feet above sea level. When it went off there was this wink of light that I sensed through my closed eyes and hands, just like a flashbulb behind me. And when I turned to see the column of water rising out of the lagoon, it was so tremendous that no one spoke. You could hear the sound waves bouncing off the island—Boom! Boom! And when the sound wave hit Enewetak, the whole island shook and a hot wind blew our baseball caps off.

The column was surrounded by ragged haloes of white shock waves which produced an electrical field. I actually experienced an electrical field passing through me; my hair stood up and there was a cracking sensation all through me that was as much felt as heard.

And that thing just continued to build and grow until it had risen about sixty or seventy thousand feet. The mushroom covered the entire island chain. Fifteen miles of islands were all shadowed by this terrifying, magnificent thing. I remember talk of an evacuation, but it never occurred.

After fifteen or twenty minutes, the water in the lagoon began to recede until the bottom was exposed for about two hundred yards. We could see sunken PT boats and equipment that was normally covered by fifteen or twenty feet of water. I really thought that they had cracked the earth and that the water was running into it! I mean, it had to go somewhere, right? But finally, the water stopped receding and it just stood there like a wall for a minute. Then it started coming back. I got a hell of a feeling then, because here we were on this dinky little island, not even half a mile wide, and here comes the whole ocean. It hit the island and sprayed up over the sandbags—all day long, the water kept seesawing back and forth like that. The column of water had just sucked it all up from fifteen miles away. I will never forget that.

After that shot the water was off limits for swimming for three days. But the ironic part of it was that the ocean was the source of our drinking water after it went through the desalinization plant. I didn't have any knowledge of radiation, so I wasn't afraid of it. They did give us dosimeters to wear sometimes to measure the gamma rays, but that was just another badge to take care of. I wasn't worried—I trusted my country. In 1958, I really did. To be truthful with you, I was proud to be there.

Source: Sam Totten and Martha Wescoat Totten, *Facing the Danger: Interviews with 20 Anti-Nuclear Activists* (Trumansburg, N.Y.: The Crossing Press, 1984), 52–56.

The Emerging Third World

Though preoccupied with the Soviet Union throughout the postwar period, American policymakers faced another challenge: developing a coherent policy toward the new nations that were rapidly emerging from the disintegrating European empires in Africa, Asia, and the Middle East. In the interests of global capitalism, it was imperative that such nations develop stable market economies which could be integrated into the world system. Also important was the commitment to national self-determination that had shaped American participation in both world wars. Third World political problems generally remained low priority, however, unless a short-term crisis demanded U.S. attention. And in certain areas, such as Latin America, traditional patterns of American penetration and dominance played a far larger role in determining United States policies than global politics.

Nationalism, socialism, and religion had already inspired powerful anticolonial movements before World War II; such forces intensified and spread, especially in the Middle East, Africa, and the Far East, during the 1940s and 1950s. Between 1947 and 1962, the British, French, Dutch, and Belgian empires all but disappeared. The British withdrawal from India in 1947, and the subsequent creation of the states of India (predominantly Hindu) and Pakistan (predominantly Muslim), was an especially important milestone.

The end to colonial empires fulfilled a goal the United States had sought in vain after World War I, and the nation in general welcomed the independence of the new states. At the same time, both the Truman and Eisenhower administrations were so caught up in the polarities of the Cold War that they often failed to recognize that indigenous nationalist or socialist movements in these emerging nations had their own goals and were not always under the strict control either of local communists or the Soviet Union. This failure to appreciate the complexity of local conditions limited the effectiveness of American policy toward the emerging Third World.

The Middle East, an oil-rich area that was playing an increasingly central role in strategic planning, presented one of the most complicated challenges. Zionism, the Jewish nationalist movement, had long encouraged Jews to return to their ancient homeland. After World War II, many of the Jews who had survived the Nazi extermination camps resettled in Palestine, still controlled by Britain under a World War I mandate. On November 29, 1947, the United Nations general assembly voted for the partition of Palestine into Jewish and Arab states. On May 14, 1948, the British mandate ended and Zionist leaders proclaimed the state of Israel. The Arab League states rejected the U.N. partition and invaded Israel. Israel survived, but the planned Palestinian state never came into existence, creating a large number of Palestinian refugees who now had no homeland. President Truman quickly recognized Israel, alienating the Arabs but winning crucial support from Jewish voters in the tight 1948 election.

Britain had been the dominant foreign power in the

The Birth of Israel, 1948
Prime Minister David Ben-Gurion reads Israel's Declaration of Independence to the new country's assembled officials.

Persian Gulf since the nineteenth century, and its withdrawal from Palestine in 1947 created a power vacuum in this already unstable area. When Gamal Abdel Nasser came to power in Egypt in 1954, two years after independence from Britain, he pledged to lead not just his country but the entire Middle East out of its dependent, colonial relationship through a form of pan-Arab socialism. Nasser obtained arms and promises of economic assistance from the Soviet Union in return for Egyptian cotton. When the Soviets offered to finance a dam on the Nile River at Aswan, Secretary of State Dulles countered with an offer of American assistance. Nasser refused to distance himself from the Russians, however, and in July 1956, Dulles abruptly withdrew the U.S. offer.

A week later Nasser retaliated against the withdrawal of Western financial aid by nationalizing the Suez Canal, over which Britain had retained administrative authority. Nasser said he would use the tolls from the canal to build the dam himself. After several months of fruitless negotiation, Britain and France, in alliance with Israel, attacked Egypt and retook the canal. When Eisenhower and the United Nations condemned this action, they reluctantly pulled back, although Israel retained the Gaza strip temporarily. In the end the Suez crisis increased Soviet influence in the Third World and produced dissension among the leading members of the NATO alliance.

In January 1957, showing concern that the Soviet Union might step into the vacuum created by the British withdrawal, the president persuaded Congress to approve the "Eisenhower Doctrine." This policy stated that American forces would assist any Middle Eastern nation "requiring such aid, against overt armed aggression from any nation controlled by International Communism." Invoking the doctrine, Eisenhower sent the U.S. Sixth Fleet to the Mediterranean Sea to aid King Hussein of Jordan in 1957. A year later, Eisenhower landed 8,000 troops to back up a pro-United States government in Lebanon.

The attention that the Eisenhower administration paid to developments in the Middle East in the 1950s demonstrated how the desire for access to steady supplies of oil increasingly affected strategic foreign policy considerations. (By 1955, two-thirds of the traffic through the Suez Canal was petroleum.) More broadly, attention to the Middle East confirmed that American policymakers no longer believed that containment of Soviet power in Eastern Europe was enough to guarantee American national security. Now the United States had to be concerned about communism and nationalism globally, especially in emerging Third World countries, for both economic and geopolitical reasons. The case of the small country of Vietnam, which won its independence from France in 1954, would show that localized wars for national liberation could be just as troubling for American foreign policy as the threat of worldwide Soviet domination.

Eisenhower's Farewell Address

When President Eisenhower left office in January 1961, he used his final address to warn the nation of a "military-industrial complex" that already employed 3.5 million Americans and whose "total influence—economic, political, even spiritual—is felt in every city, every statehouse, every office of the Federal Government." Even though his administration had fostered this growth in the defense establishment, Eisenhower was still gravely concerned about its implications for a democratic people:

> In the councils of government we must guard against the acquisition of unwarranted influence whether sought or unsought, by the military-industrial complex. . . . We must never let the weight of this combination endanger our liberties or democratic processes. We should take nothing for granted. Only an alert and knowledgeable citizenry can compel the proper meshing of the huge industrial and military machinery of defense with our peaceful methods and goals so that security and liberty may prosper together.

With those words, Dwight Eisenhower showed how well he understood the major transformations that the Cold War had brought to American life.

Summary

American foreign policy shifted dramatically at the end of World War II. The United States took the leading role in world affairs and tried to shape the structure of international relations and trade to further its own interests.

A resurgent Soviet Union with its own agenda stood in the way of American goals, and the resulting clash between the two superpowers brought about the Cold War. Containment originally emerged in response to Soviet pressure on Eastern Europe, but that doctrine was expanded by succeeding administrations to include resistance to communism and left-wing revolution wherever they appeared. A cold war mentality shaped U.S. foreign policy well into the 1980s.

America's new international role had strong domestic repercussions. The new importance of foreign affairs enhanced the power of the president. Tension about communism abroad fostered a period of domestic repression and fear at home. Growing defense expenditures took up an ever-larger part of the gross national product. Besides paying for defense through taxes and growing deficits, American citizens now lived in a world where small foreign wars were a constant possibility and fear of nuclear attack became part of daily life.

The Democratic party set much of the legislative agenda for the postwar period, expanding the reforms first introduced by Franklin Roosevelt in the 1930s. Harry Truman's Fair Deal won only limited legislative victories but added civil rights to the national political agenda. The Republican administration of Dwight Eisenhower did not seek to roll back the New Deal and, in fact, presided over cautious increases in federal power.

TOPIC FOR RESEARCH

Truman and the Polls

The first Gallup polls appeared just before the 1936 election, and they have been a prominent aspect of political life ever since. For historians as well as politicians, polls offer a chance to sample a range of public opinion ("Americans believe . . .") on a wide variety of issues. Yet polls have proved imperfect sources, especially in their early days.

The Truman administration offers many cases to test the usefulness of public opinion polls as sources. The most obvious example is the 1948 election, where polls widely predicted a Dewey victory. Also of interest are the dramatic fluctuations in Truman's popularity and the seeming contradiction between popular dissatisfaction with the Korean War and public support for General Douglas MacArthur. What can polls tell us about political events? How useful are they for forming assessments of the Truman presidency? How closely can you correlate historical events with popular reaction? Conversely, can you show how public opinion shaped the course of political events and history?

Gallup polls from the 1940s have been collected in three volumes in George Gallup, *The Gallup Poll: Public Opinion, 1935–1971* (New York: Random House, 1972). Alonzo Hamby, *Beyond the New Deal: Harry S. Truman and American Liberalism* (1973) is a good overview of the Truman administration. For the 1948 election, see Irwin Ross, *The Loneliest Campaign* (1968) and Jules Abels, *Out of the Jaws of Victory* (1959).

BIBLIOGRAPHY

The Origins of the Cold War

The two best overviews are Walter LaFeber, *America, Russia, and the Cold War, 1945–1990* (6th edition, 1990), and Stephen Ambrose, *Rise to Globalism* (5th ed., 1988). Thomas J. McCormick, *America's Half-Century* (1989) places the United States in the modern world-system. See also John Lewis Gaddis, *Strategies of Containment* (1982), plus his earlier *The United States and the Origins of the Cold War* (1972); Bernard Weisberger, *Cold War, Cold Peace* (1984); Thomas Paterson, *Meeting the Communist Threat* (1988); and Lloyd Gardner, *Architects of Illusion* (1970). Daniel Yergin, *Shattered Peace* (1977), focuses on the rise of the national security state. For perspectives critical of American aims, see Joyce and Gabriel Kolko, *The Limits of Power* (1970) and Robert J. Maddox, *The New Left and the Origins of the Cold War* (1977). Specialized studies include Laurence S. Kaplan, *The United States and NATO* (1984); Imanuel Wexler, *The Marshall Plan Revisited* (1983); Richard Freeland, *The Truman Doctrine and the Origins of McCarthyism* (1972); and Richard J. Barnet, *The Roots of War* (1972).

The descent into Cold War can also be viewed through individual policymakers. Indispensable are George F. Kennan, *American Diplomacy, 1900–1950* (1952) and *Memoirs, 1925–1950* (1967); and Dean Acheson's modestly titled *Present at the Creation* (1970). Walter Isaacson and Evan Thomas, *The Wise Men* (1986) traces the impact of John McCloy, Averill Harriman, Charles Bohlen, George Kennan, Dean Acheson, and Robert Lovett on postwar foreign policy. Walter Lippmann, *The Cold War* (1947) can be supplemented by Ronald Steel's fine biography, *Walter Lippmann and the American Century* (1980). Adam Ulam presents the Soviet point of view in *The Rivals: America and Russia Since World War II* (1971).

McGeorge Bundy, *Danger and Survival* (1989); Martin J. Sherwin, *A World Destroyed* (1975); and Gar Alperowitz, *Atomic Diplomacy* (1965) cover the impact of atomic weapons on policy formulation. For general discussion of America and nuclear weapons, see Paul Boyer, *By the Bomb's Early Light* (1985); Richard G. Hewlett and Jack Hall, *Atoms for Peace and War, 1953–1961* (1989); Gregg Herken, *Counsels of War* (1985); and Howard Ball, *Justice Downwind* (1986).

For developments in Asia, Akira Iriye, *The Cold War in Asia* (1974) is a good starting point. See also Warren I. Cohen, *America's Response to China* (2nd ed., 1980); Kenneth Shewmaker, *Americans and the Chinese Communists* (1971); and Michael Shaller, *The United States and China in the Twentieth*

Century (1979). E. J. Kahn, Jr., *The China Hands* (1975) and Ross Y. Kuen, *The China Lobby In American Politics* (1974) cover the domestic repercussions. On Japan, see Michael Schaller, *The American Occupation of Japan* (1985).

There has been a recent explosion of scholarship on the Korean War, including Clay Blair, *The Forgotten War* (1988); Max Hastings, *The Korean War* (1987); Callum McDonald, *Korea: The War Before Vietnam* (1987); Burton Kaufman, *The Korean War* (1986); and Rosemary Foot, *The Wrong War* (1985). Especially influential are the two volumes of *The Origins of the Korean War* by Bruce Cumings: *Liberation and the Emergence of Separate Regions, 1945–1947* (1981) and *The Roaring of the Cataract, 1947–1950* (1990). Earlier studies include Joseph C. Gouldens, *Korea* (1962); David Rees, *Korea: The Limited War* (1964); and Ronald J. Caridi, *The Korean War and American Politics* (1969). William Manchester, *American Caesar* (1979) and Michael Schaller, *Douglas MacArthur* (1989) offer stimulating biographies of a leading figure of the war.

Harry Truman and the Fair Deal

Two lively introductions to politics in the postwar period are William E. Leuchtenberg, *A Troubled Feast: American Society Since 1945* (1979) and John Patrick Diggins, *The Proud Decades: America in War and Peace, 1941–1960* (1988). Harry Truman's *Memoirs* (1952–1962) tell his story in characteristically pointed language; see also Merle Miller's oral history, *Plain Speaking* (1980). General accounts of the Truman presidency are found in Robert J. Donovan, *Tumultuous Years: The Presidency of Harry S Truman, 1949–1953* (1982), plus his earlier *Conflict and Crisis* (1977); Eric F. Goldman, *The Crucial Decade and After—America, 1945–1960* (1961); Donald R. McCoy, *The Presidency of Harry S Truman* (1984); William Pemberton, *Harry S Truman* (1989). Critical perspectives are presented in Barton J. Bernstein, ed., *Politics and Policies of The Truman Administration* (1970). Arthur M. Schlesinger, Jr., states the case for Fair Deal liberalism in *The Vital Center* (1949).

More specialized studies of the Truman years include Gary Reichard, *Politics as Usual* (1986); Andrew J. Dunar, *The Truman Scandals and the Politics of Morality* (1984); Jack Stokes Ballard, *The Shock of Peace: Military and Economic Demobilization After World War II* (1983); Stephen K. Bailey, *Congress Makes a Law* (1957) (the Employment Act of 1946); Allen J. Matusow, *Farm Policies and Politics in the Truman Years* (1967); Susan Hartmann, *Truman and the 80th Congress* (1971). The story of the Democratic coalition can be traced in Samuel Lubbell, *The Future of American Politics* (1965); V. O. Key, *Politics, Parties, and Pressure Groups* (1964); and Everett C. Ladd and Charles Hadley, *Transformations of the American Party System* (1978). On the Wallace

challenge to Truman, see Norman D. Markowitz, *The Rise and Fall of the People's Century* (1973). Joseph P. Lash, *Eleanor: The Years Alone* (1972) describes the former First Lady's continuing work for liberal causes. James T. Patterson, *Mr. Republican: A Biography of Robert A. Taft* (1972), covers Truman's chief Republican critic.

The literature on McCarthyism is voluminous and intense. Two recent overviews are Richard Fried, *Nightmare in Red: The McCarthy Era in Perspective* (1990) and Stephen J. Whitfield, *The Culture of the Cold War* (1991). David Caute, *The Great Fear* (1978), provides another introduction, which can be supplemented by Victor Navasky, *Naming Names* (1980) and Athan Theoharis, *Spying on Americans* (1978). Two biographies are Thomas C. Reeves, *The Life and Times of Joe McCarthy* (1982), and David Oshinsky, *A Conspiracy So Immense* (1983); but Richard Rovere's *Senator Joseph McCarthy* (1959) still commands attention. Michael P. Rogin, *The Intellectuals and McCarthy* (1967), analyzes McCarthy's base of support, while Robert Griffith, *The Politics of Fear* (1970), and Richard Fried, *Men Against McCarthy* (1976), look at the politics involved. Ellen Schrecker, *No Ivory Tower* (1986) treats McCarthyism in academia, while Lary Ceplair and Steven Englund, *The Inquisition in Hollywood* (1983) looks at the impact on the film industry.

Allen Weinstein, *Perjury* (1978), covers the still-debated Hiss case. Walter and Miriam Schneir, *Invitation to an Inquest* (1965), and Ronald Radosh and Joyce Milton, *The Rosenberg File* (1983), cover the Rosenberg case. Lillian Hellman offers her biting, and not always reliable, memoir of the period in *Scoundrel Time* (1976). Eric Bentley, ed., *Thirty Years of Treason* (1971), collects excerpts from testimony before the House Committee on Un-American Activities. For the FBI and its controversial leader, see Richard Gid Powers, *Secrecy and Power: The Life of J. Edgar Hoover* (1987) and Athan Theoharis and John Stuart Case, *The Boss: J. Edgar Hoover and the Great American Inquisition* (1988).

Modern Republicanism

Two standard overviews of the Eisenhower administration, Herbert S. Parmet, *Eisenhower and the American Crusades* (1972), and Charles C. Alexander, *Holding the Line* (1975), can be supplemented by Fred I. Greenstein, *The Hidden-Hand Presidency* (1982) and Stephen Ambrose, *Eisenhower the President* (1984). Blanche Wiesen Cook, *The Declassified Eisenhower* (1984) contrasts the covert activities of the administration with its public image. Robert F. Burk, *The Eisenhower Administration and Black Civil Rights* (1984) looks at what the administration did, and did not, do. For scientific developments, consult James R. Killian, Jr., *Sputnik, Scientists, and Eisenhower* (1976). Richard M. Nixon, *Six Crisis* (1962) offers the perspective of the vice-president.

For the complex foreign policy of the 1950s, consult LaFeber, *America, Russia, and the Cold War,* Ambrose, *Rise to Globalism,* and McCormick, *America's Half Century.* Other overviews are Robert Divine, *Eisenhower and the Cold War* (1981), and Ronald Steel, *Pax Americana* (1967). An excellent book on the CIA is Victor Marchetti and John D. Marks, *The CIA and the Cult of Intelligence* (1974). For developments linking economics, corporations, and the defense industry, see Mira Wilkins, *The Maturing of Multinational Enterprise* (1974); Richard Barnet and Ronald Muller, *Global Reach* (1974); and Paul Hammond, *Organizing For Defense* (1971). Gabriel Kolko, *Confronting the Third World, 1945–1980* (1988), offers an opinionated overview; specific studies include Bruce Kuniholm, *The Origins of the Cold War in the Near East* (1980) and Michael Stoff, *Oil, War, and American Security* (1980).

On specific policy situations in the 1950s, see Robert Divine, *Blowing in the Wind: The Nuclear Test Ban Debate, 1954–1960* (1978); Robert Stookey, *America and the Arab States* (1975); John Snetsinger, *Truman, the Jewish Role and the Creation of Israel* (1974); Hugh Thomas, *Suez* (1967); and Melanie Billings-Yun, *Decision Against War: Eisenhower and Dien Bien Phu, 1954* (1988). Of interest for his later career are Henry Kissinger, *Nuclear Weapons and Foreign Policy* (1957) and *The Necessity of Choice* (1961).

TIMELINE

1945	Yalta and Potsdam conferences
	Harry S. Truman succeeds Roosevelt as president
	End of World War II
1946	Employment Act
1947	Taft-Hartley Act
	Truman Doctrine
	Marshall Plan
1948	Desegregation of armed forces
	State of Israel created
	Berlin airlift
1949	North Atlantic Treaty Organization (NATO) founded
	People's Republic of China established
	National Housing Act
1950–1953	Korean War
1950	Alger Hiss convicted of perjury
	NSC-68 (National Security Council report) calls for permanent mobilization
1952	Dwight D. Eisenhower elected president
	U.S. detonates hydrogen bomb
1954	Army-McCarthy hearings
	Brown v. Board of Education of Topeka
1956	Suez crisis
	Interstate Highway Act
1957	Eisenhower Doctrine
	U.S.S.R. launches *Sputnik*
1959	St. Lawrence Seaway completed

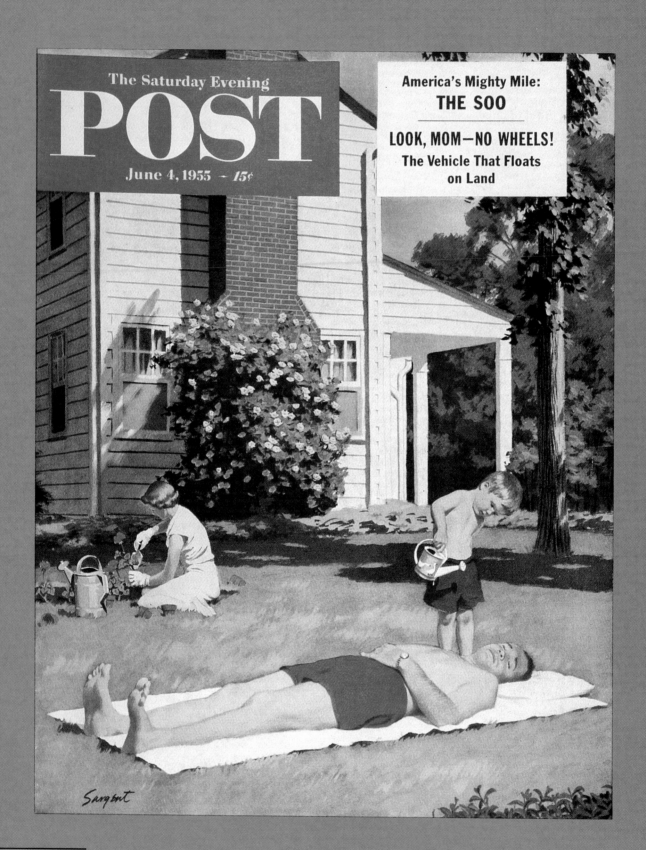

The Saturday Evening

POST

June 4, 1955 ~ 15¢

America's Mighty Mile:
THE SOO

LOOK, MOM—NO WHEELS!
The Vehicle That Floats
on Land

Sargent

Life in the Suburbs

During the 1950s the *Saturday Evening Post* celebrated the surburban ideal—family, leisure, and
nurturing wife and mother.

CHAPTER **29** *Affluence and Its Contradictions, 1945–1965*

In 1959, Vice-President Richard M. Nixon traveled to Moscow to open the American National Exhibition. It was the height of both the Cold War and the postwar baby boom. After sipping from bottles of Pepsi-Cola, Nixon and Soviet Premier Nikita Khrushchev got into a heated debate about the relative merits of Soviet and American societies. But instead of debating rockets, submarines, and missiles, they talked dishwashers, toasters, and televisions. Both the subject of the animated conversation and its site (it took place in the kitchen of a model American home) led to its popular designation as the "kitchen debate."

The Moscow exhibition was designed to showcase American consumer and leisure goods. Its main attraction was a full scale model of a six-room, ranch-style house, filled with labor-saving appliances and devices that supposedly were typical of an American family back home. Over the next three weeks, more than 3 million Russians toured the exhibit, no doubt struck by, and the Americans hoped, jealous of all the gadgets and consumer appliances unavailable in Soviet society.

What was so striking about the kitchen debate was the way that affluence and mass consumption were enlisted in the service of American cold war politics. The suburban lifestyle trumpeted in the exhibit symbolized the superiority of capitalism over communism. The American way of life could win the Cold War.

After 1945, American citizens enjoyed the highest standard of living in the world, but this affluence was never as widespread as the Moscow exhibit implied. Moreover, the strong performance of the American economy was due in part to the relative weakness of all its competitors, who emerged from the war in far less secure economic shape than the United States. When the world economy returned to a more normal pattern in the 1960s and 1970s, the United States would face strong challenges to its postwar hegemony.

Technology and Economic Change

At the end of 1945, war-induced prosperity had made the American people the richest in the world. Over the next two decades, the gross national product more than tripled, and affluence reached a wider segment of society than anyone would have dreamed possible during the dark days of the depression. Industrial workers in the largest smokestack industries found their unions accepted at last, which translated into rising wages and expanding benefits. Employees of the successful large corporations—New York accountants, Georgia factory managers, Chicago engineers, San Francisco advertising executives, and Dallas office managers—were able to move their families into new homes in the suburbs. At the heart of this postwar prosperity lay the involvement of the federal government in national economic life. Federal outlays for defense and domestic programs, combined with galloping consumer spending, seemed to promise a continually rising standard of living.

The Economic Record

The impact of war mobilization laid the foundations for postwar economic success. The United States enjoyed overwhelming political and economic advantages at the end of World War II. Unlike the Soviet Union, which had lost more than 20 million citizens, or Western Europe and Japan, whose cities, factories, and population had been devastated by the fighting, the United States emerged physically unscathed from the war. Consumers had accumulated wartime savings of $140 billion, which created a strong market for the consumer goods that had been unavailable during the war. Business quickly applied the scientific and technological innovations developed for war production, such as plastics and synthetic fibers, to the production of consumer goods. The federal government eased conversion to a peacetime economy by allowing businesses to buy factories built for the war effort at a fraction of their cost.

The period from World War II through the late 1960s and early 1970s represented the heyday of modern American capitalism. U.S. corporations and banking institutions so dominated the world economy that the period has been called the *Pax Americana*. This American global supremacy rested on an institutional structure created at a United Nations economic conference held in Bretton Woods, New Hampshire, in July 1944. Its two key components were the International Bank for Reconstruction and Development (known commonly as the World Bank) and the International Monetary Fund (IMF), both founded in 1944. The World Bank provided private loans for the reconstruction of war-torn Europe as well as for developing Third World countries. The IMF was set up to stabilize currencies so that trade could function without fluctuations and devaluations. It did so by encouraging fixed exchange rates, which facilitated the free convertibility of currencies to gold or the currency of other trading nations; the strong U.S. dollar served as the benchmark. In 1947 multinational trade negotiations resulted in the General Agreement on Tariffs and Trades (GATT), which became the international body of rules and practices governing fair trade.

The World Bank, the IMF, and GATT were the cornerstones of the so-called Bretton Woods system that guided the world economy after the war. The United States in effect controlled the World Bank and the IMF, because it subscribed the most capital to them and because the dollar was designated as the principal reserve for world financial systems. Thus the independent international organizations worked along lines that favored American-style internationalism, rather than economic nationalism or autarky (self-sufficiency), adopting policies that encouraged stable prices, the liberalization of trade barriers and reduction of tariffs, flexible domestic markets, and free trade based on fixed exchange rates. As long as the dollar remained the strongest currency in the world, the Bretton Woods system effectively served America's global economic interests, paralleling many of the diplomatic goals the United States pursued in the Cold War.

This American hegemony abroad translated into affluence at home. The country's gross national product grew from $213 billion in 1945 to more than $500 billion in 1960; in 1970 the GNP approached $1 trillion. To working Americans, the steady economic growth meant a 25 percent rise in real income between 1946 and 1959. Most Americans rightly felt they had more money to spend than ever before. In 1940, 43 percent of American families owned their homes; by 1960, 62 percent did. But while the standard of living was rising, there was no redistribution of income—the top 10 percent still earned more than all the people in the bottom 50 percent put together.

One reason ordinary Americans felt better off was that inflation finally had been brought under control by the 1950s, a boon to both investors and individuals on fixed incomes. After the immediate postwar reconversion period, inflation slowed to 2 to 3 percent annually during the 1950s. It stayed low until 1965, when the increased military spending for the Vietnam War set off an inflationary spiral.

Despite high rates of economic growth, a rise in real income, and low inflation, there was an unevenness to the postwar economy that limited the rosy picture of economic success and affluence. Not all Americans shared in the general prosperity: the economy was plagued by periodic recessions accompanied by high unemployment. The permanently unemployed, the aged, female heads of households, and nonwhites all found themselves at a significant disadvantage. In *The Affluent Society* (1958), economist John Kenneth Galbraith

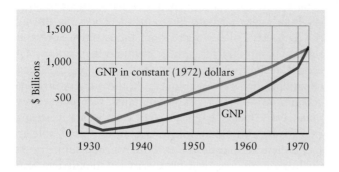

FIGURE 29.1

Gross National Product (GNP), 1929–1972
After a sharp dip during the Great Depression, the Gross National Product rose steadily in both real and constant dollars.

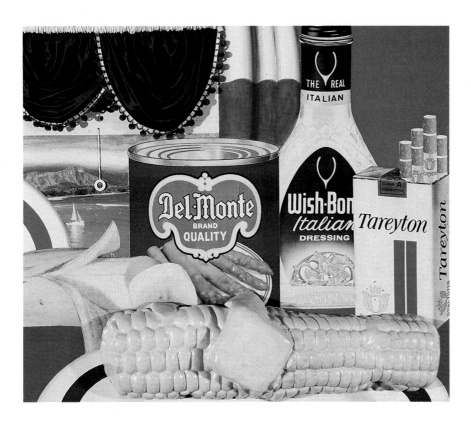

Consumer Culture
This 1962 painting by Tom Wesselmann mocks the consumer culture that it so lavishly illustrates with a table well stocked with brand-name goods. Realistic painting in the 1960s took on an air of cynicism, especially as practiced by artists such as Andy Warhol. Wesselman's *Still Life #24* treats the most ordinary objects of American life as icons, hinting at the new power of consumerism in popular culture. (The Nelson Atkins Museum of Art)

argued that the poor were only an "afterthought" in the minds of economists and politicians, who assumed that poverty was well on its way to extinction. Yet, as Galbraith noted, more than one family out of thirteen in the 1950s had a cash income of less than a thousand dollars.

The Military-Industrial Complex

An important linchpin of postwar prosperity was increased defense spending. The military-industrial complex that President Eisenhower identified in his 1961 farewell address had its immediate roots in the business-government partnerships of both world wars. But the massive commitment of government dollars to defense industries in the postwar era was unprecedented, a concrete reminder of how much the state had grown since the 1930s. Even though the country was technically at peace, the economy and government operated practically on a war footing—in a state of permanent mobilization.

In the late 1940s and 1950s, cold war mobilization and the Korean War led to a major expansion of the military establishment. Defense-related industries and the scientists and engineers they employed entered into a long-term relationship with the federal government in the name of national security. The Defense Department became practically a state within the state, with its headquarters at the sprawling Pentagon in Arlington, Virginia.

Certain companies did so much of their business with the government that they became almost exclusive vendors of the Defense Department. By the mid-1960s, Boeing and General Dynamics received 65 percent of their income from military contracts, Raytheon 60 percent, Lockheed 81 percent, and Republic Aviation 100 percent. The Pentagon reinforced the concentration of economic power at the top by awarding contracts to the largest firms. In 1967 the hundred largest corporations got 65 percent of the government contracts, while the top ten alone received more than 30 percent.

The impact of federal spending went deeper than just military contracts: science, corporate capitalism, and the federal government became increasingly intertwined in the postwar period. According to the National Science Foundation, federal money underwrote 90 percent of the cost of research on aviation and space, 65 percent on electricity and electronics, 42 percent on scientific instruments, and 24 percent on automobiles. With the government footing part of the bill, corporations transformed new ideas into useful products faster than ever before. After the Pentagon backed IBM's investment in integrated circuits in the 1960s, the new devices, crucial to the computer revolution, were in commercial production within three years.

The Pentagon

The Pentagon, so named because it has five sides, was the world's largest building when it was constructed in 1942. When the Department of Defense was established in 1947, the Pentagon became its sprawling headquarters, a symbol of America's postwar global responsibilities.

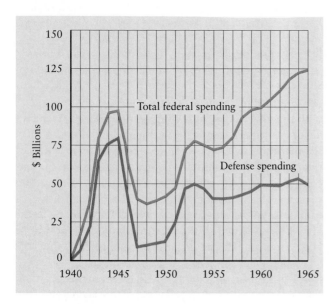

FIGURE 29.2

National Defense Spending, 1940–1965

In 1950 the defense budget was $13 billion, less than a third of the total federal outlays. In 1961 defense spending reached $47 billion—fully half of the federal budget and almost 10 percent of the nation's GNP.

The growth of this military-industrial establishment reflected a dramatic shift in national priorities. Military spending took up a greater percentage of national income as measured by the gross national product. Between 1900 and 1930, except for the two years that the United States fought in World War I, the country spent less than 1 percent of its GNP for military purposes. By 1960 the United States was regularly devoting close to 10 percent of its GNP to military spending.

The expansion of the military-industrial complex had a direct and ongoing impact on the American people. Channeling money into national security limited the resources available for domestic social needs. Critics of military spending added up the trade-offs—the cost of a subway system for Washington, D.C., equaled a nuclear aircraft carrier and support ships; sixty-six units of low-income housing matched the cost of one Huey helicopter.

The defense buildup also meant jobs, however, and lots of them. In 1966, 17 percent of California's workers were employed in jobs directly generated by defense contracts. Taking into account the multiplier effect, which measures the indirect benefits of such employment (the additional jobs created to serve and support the defense workers), perhaps as many as one worker in seven nationally owed his or her job to the military-industrial complex. This dependence of individual jobs on defense spending illustrates how the growth of a vast bureaucratic state, especially one committed to worldwide military responsibilities, affected daily life in the postwar period.

NEW TECHNOLOGY ## *The Computer Revolution*

The first modern computers—that is, information-processing machines capable of storing and manipulating data according to specified programs—appeared in the 1940s. During World War II, engineers and mathematicians at the University of Pennsylvania developed a general-purpose, programmable electronic calculator called ENIAC (Electronic Numerical Integrator and Computer), which could add 5,000 ten-digit decimal numbers in one second. It stood 8 feet tall, measured 80 feet long, and weighed 30 tons; it used 18,000 vacuum tubes for computations. When it performed complex mathematical computations, one scientist noted, ENIAC sounded "like a roomful of ladies knitting." Although ENIAC lacked a central memory and could not store a program, it was the bridge to the modern computer revolution.

Six computers were under construction by 1947, including UNIVAC (Universal Automatic Computer), the first commercial computer system. The word "UNIVAC" was synonymous with computer to the general public in the 1950s. UNIVAC was basically a data-processing system that could be tailored to individual customers' needs. In 1951 the U.S. Census Bureau bought the first UNIVAC. Soon CBS-TV signed on, using a UNIVAC to predict the outcome of the 1952 presidential election. At 9 P.M., only after the East Coast polls had closed and with only 7 percent of the votes counted, UNIVAC predicted that Dwight D. Eisenhower would sweep the election with 438 electoral votes. CBS programmers and network executives, who had expected a closer election, got jittery and altered the program to give Eisenhower a far narrower margin. When the final tally gave him 442 electoral votes, only four votes off the original projection, commentator Edward R. Murrow observed, "The trouble with machines is people."

Computers are essentially collections of switches, and programs tell the computer which switches to turn on and off. The puzzle that early computer scientists had to solve was how to increase the speed while lowering the cost of this basic operation. The first generation of computers need vacuum tubes for computation power and the use of punched cards for writing programs and analyzing data. Such computers were huge, room-sized machines, and programming them could take several days because programmers manually had to set thousands of switches in the On or Off position.

The vacuum tubes were the weakest part of early computers; burnout of just a few tubes could shut down the entire system. Furthermore, vacuum tubes gave off enormous amounts of heat, necessitating noisy and cumbersome air-conditioning units wherever computers operated. After a critical signal relay stopped one early program, scientists finally located the problem—a dead moth trapped in the apparatus, the origin of the term "debugging."

The 1948 invention of the transistor, a development that revolutionized computers and also the whole field of electronics, made possible the second generation of computers. Transistors, like vacuum tubes, served as on-off switches, but they did not generate heat, burn out, or consume vast quantities of energy. They also were inexpensive to manufacture. The invention of integrated circuits (IC) in 1959 ushered in the third computer generation, (1965), characterized by greater sophistication in miniaturization, meant that the number of transistors that could be crammed on a silicon chip increased dramatically, with a corresponding increase in computational power. The fourth computer generation arrived in 1971 with development of the microprocessor, the entire central processing unit (CPU) of a computer on a single silicon chip about the size of the letter "O" on this page, soon followed. Miniaturization progressed so rapidly that by the mid-1970s, a $1 chip provided as much processing power as the ENIAC of 30 years earlier. Computers and computer technology have become so much a part of modern life that it is hard to remember how recent the origins of this technological revolution are.

This early computer-data processing center featured an IBM704 computer.

America's military responsibilities overseas had another effect on the lives of ordinary citizens: permanent mobilization meant a peacetime draft. In the past, the armed forces had shrunk dramatically to a skeleton volunteer force at the end of each war or foreign engagement. But when World War II ended, the draft was kept in place to meet the military commitments associated with the Cold War. Suddenly every neighborhood seemed to have a boy in the service; many made the military a career. By the late 1960s, more than 1.5 million military personnel were stationed in a hundred foreign countries.

Corporate Strategies

The Cold War and the growth of the state brought major changes to American life, hastening the concentration of power in ever larger economic and political structures. Successful corporate managers adopted flexible strategies to take advantage of the postwar economic climate. They tapped federal money for research and development, diversified their range of products, expanded their multinational operations, and sought to improve their ability to plan.

Diversification. Diversification was the most important corporate strategy of the postwar era. The classic corporation of the early twentieth century had produced a single line of products. After World War II, the most successful managers developed new product lines and moved into new markets. Because the largest corporations could afford research laboratories, they diversified more easily. CBS, for example, hired the Hungarian inventor Peter Goldmark, who perfected color television during the 1940s, long-playing records in the 1950s, and a video recording system in the 1960s. As head of CBS Laboratories, Goldmark patented more than a hundred new devices.

Postwar managers also diversified through mergers and acquisitions, creating larger firms to compete in the expanding world market. The nation's third great merger wave (the first two had taken place during the 1890s and the 1920s) reached its peak during the 1960s. International Telephone and Telegraph became a diversified conglomerate by acquiring Continental Baking, Sheraton Hotels, Avis Rent-a-Car, Levitt and Sons home builders, and Hartford Fire Insurance. Ling-Temco-Vought, another conglomerate, simultaneously produced steel, built ships, developed real estate, and brought cattle to market. In 1947 the largest two hundred corporations accounted for 30 percent of all value added by manufacturing, but by 1972 the largest two hundred, now heavily diversified, accounted for 43 percent of this sum.

Expansion into foreign markets also helped managers build giant corporations. At a time when "made in Japan" still meant shoddy workmanship, American products were the best made in the world. International strategies enabled American business to enter new areas when domestic markets became saturated or when American recessions cut into sales. By the 1970s, such corporations as Gillette, IBM, Mobil, and Coca-Cola earned more than half their profits from sales of their products abroad. ITT had a worldwide payroll of 425,000 workers in seventy countries.

In their effort to direct large organizations through the uncertainties of the postwar economy, managers placed more emphasis on planning. Top executives were increasingly recruited for their business-school training, their ability to manage information, and their skill in corporate planning, marketing, and investment. As a result, corporate managers found themselves working more closely with their counterparts in other corporations, large banks, investment firms, law firms, economic research organizations, the federal government, and such international agencies as the World Bank and the International Monetary Fund.

The New Oligopolies. The predominant thrust of modern corporate life after 1945 continued to be consolidation of economic and financial resources in oligopolies, where a few large producers controlled the national and, increasingly, the world market. In 1970 the top four U.S. firms produced 91 percent of all motor vehicles in the domestic market; the top four in tires produced 72 percent, in cigarettes 84 percent, and in detergents 70 percent. Despite laws restricting branch banking to a single state, in 1970 the four largest banks held 16 percent of the nation's banking assets; the top fifty banks held 48 percent.

A case study of the beer industry illustrates this growing concentration of economic power. Beer has always been a highly profitable, high-volume business. At the end of World War II, the United States had about 450 breweries. Each produced a distinctive-tasting brand of beer, due to variations in the local water and differences in brewing techniques. This pattern of competing products and regional diversity changed dramatically in the 1950s. Large corporations went after the national market that had been created in part by advertising on network television, especially for sports events. National companies such as Anheuser-Busch developed a beer that could be manufactured anywhere in the country, no matter what the local water was like. They then used modern marketing techniques to push this homogenized product.

Soon the national brands were driving out local competition. Whereas the seven leading breweries in 1946 had accounted for barely 20 percent of national

Enjoy the game with light refreshing Ballantine!

THAT'S ALE, BROTHER!

P. BALLANTINE & SONS, NEWARK, N. J.

No other ale...no beer...has such
refreshing flavor, yet is so light

NO WONDER BALLANTINE LEADS ALL ALES IN SALES!

Enjoy some soon...
Ask the man for **Ballantine ale**

Cheers
The growth of national brands of beer such as Ballantine Ale
went hand in hand with the popularity of television, especially sports, in the 1950s. These sports fans seem a bit over-
dressed, however, for an afternoon watching the game with
their buddies.

sales, by 1970 the ten largest breweries had captured 70
percent of the beer market. American consumers could
find the beer advertised on their favorite television programs at local supermarkets, but they were choosing
among a much smaller selection of beers with much
blander taste. Only in the economic climate of the
1980s did micro-breweries discover that small companies could compete in a national consumer market, at
least in the beer industry.

The Changing World of Work

For most of the nineteenth century and the first half of
the twentieth, the United States had been a nation of
goods producers, but by 1956 a majority of Americans
were white-collar workers. The shift of American workers from heavy industry and manufacturing into
commerce, government, service industries, and the professions was as significant a watershed as the closing of

the frontier in 1890. In 1940 two-thirds of all workers
held industrial jobs that required them to use physical
strength and skills to make products. From 1947 to
1957 the number of factory workers dropped 4 percent,
while the ranks of clerical workers rose 23 percent and
those of salaried middle-class workers jumped 61 percent. Instead of producing products, American workers
increasingly provided services, the essence of a service
economy.

The sociologist C. Wright Mills captured the new
white-collar world in this riveting image: "What must
be grasped is the picture of society as a great salesroom,
an enormous file, an incorporated brain, a new universe
of management and manipulation." Soon panelists on
the popular quiz show "What's My Line?" learned to
ask their mystery guests this question: "Do you deal in
services?"

The new hierarchy of work altered old patterns of
status and class. In the late nineteenth century, an office
job as a secretary was a badge of upward social mobility and respectability for a working woman, as well as
an opportunity for increased pay. By the 1950s the jobs
of office workers were not too different from those of
factory operatives—narrow, repetitive, and lacking in
control and autonomy. Confounding the old formula
that work with your brain counted for more than work
with your hands, many unionized factory workers had
higher incomes than those in such occupations as teaching and social work.

Many of these new workers in the service economy
were women: twice as many women were at work in
1960 as in 1940. Because of the structural needs of the
economy, there was a demand for workers in fields traditionally filled by women, such as clerical work, a predominantly female field that expanded as rapidly as any
other white-collar sector in the economy. Teachers to
staff the nation's burgeoning school systems were also
in demand. Growing sectors of the economy such as
restaurant and hotel work, hospitals, and beauty care
offered low-paying jobs to women, jobs that have been
called the "pink-collar ghetto." Nonwhite and working-
class women predominated in such jobs.

Occupational segmentation remained a fundamental characteristic of women's work in the postwar period. More than 80 percent of all working women held
jobs in stereotypical "women's work," as salespersons,
health-care technicians, waitresses, flight attendants,
domestic servants, receptionists, telephone operators,
and secretaries. In 1960 women represented only 3.5
percent of all lawyers (many top law schools did not
admit women at all) and 6.1 percent of all physicians,
but 97 percent of the nurses, 85 percent of the librarians, and 57 percent of the social workers. Along with
women's jobs went women's pay, which averaged 60
percent of men's in 1963.

The New Middle Class. America's transformation from a society of producers to one of white-collar workers created a new middle class. Corporate managers and salaried professionals, such as teachers, professors, and researchers, formed its core. They earned a salary, which distinguished them from self-employed entrepreneurs and from service and blue-collar workers who earned an hourly wage. The members of the new middle class had taken advantage of the great expansion of high school and college education after the 1920s, and the explosion of universities after 1945, to make themselves much better educated than their elders. Such skills enabled them to advance more quickly, and at a younger age, than previous generations.

As young managers and professionals advanced in their careers, they changed jobs frequently. Atlas Van Lines estimated in the 1950s that corporate managers moved an average of fourteen times—once every two and a half years—during their careers. Perpetually mobile IBM managers joked that the company's initials stood for "I've Been Moved." A building contractor and future multimillionaire summed up the fifties' mobility this way: "If you had a college diploma, a dark suit, and anything between the ears, it was like an escalator; you just stood there and moved up." (He was talking only about men—women were still generally excluded from these careers.) Such advancement usually led them through the giant corporate structures—big business, government agencies, universities, and other bureaucratic organizations—that came to dominate the latter half of the twentieth century.

Switching jobs, or even careers, necessitated personality traits such as adaptability and the ability to get along in a variety of situations. Corporate managers worked hard, sometimes with the assistance of the resident corporate psychologist, to be "well adjusted." Their philosophy was "Evade, don't confront." In *The Lonely Crowd* (1950), sociologist David Reisman contrasted the stern, formal small business and professional types of earlier years with the new managers of the postwar world. He concluded that members of the new middle class were "other-directed," more concerned about their relations with immediate associates than about adherence to fundamental principles. Sociologist William Whyte painted a more somber picture of "organization men" who left the home "spiritually as well as physically to take the vows of organization life."

Many commentators worried that the conformity demanded by marching off each day in gray flannel suits to work in huge corporations at interchangeable middle-management jobs was stifling men's creativity. Men were also weighted down by their responsibilities as breadwinners for the consumption-oriented family life-style that was the goal of many members of the new middle class. Such heightened expectations put enormous pressure on these men. In fact, it was in the 1950s

Organization Men (and a Few Women)
What happened when the 5:57 discharged commuters in Park Forest, Illinois, a suburb of Chicago? This was the subject of William H. Whyte's *The Organization Man* (1956). Were these hordes of commuters thinking about their stressful day at the office, or the martini waiting for them when they walked in the door of their suburban home?

that cardiologists first sounded the alarm about the role of stress in coronary heart disease. Fueled in part by death rates three times as high for men as for women from heart attacks and strokes, it looked like work was in fact dangerous for men's health.

Challenges for the Labor Movement

The changing structural composition of the work force and the shifting nature of work itself posed challenges for the labor movement in the postwar world. Labor unions reached the peak of their strength immediately after World War II. The schisms of the 1930s had healed enough by 1955 that Walter P. Reuther of the United Auto Workers led the CIO back into an alliance with the AFL. This merger created a single organization, the AFL-CIO, that represented more than 90 percent of the nation's 17.5 million union members.

George Meany, a New York building-trade unionist, headed this organization from 1955 to 1979.

New priorities shaped labor-management relations after the war. Postwar inflation and changing patterns of consumption produced demands for higher incomes. Management agreed to contracts that brought many workers secure, predictable, and steadily rising incomes. In exchange, union leaders promised labor peace and stability—that is, fewer strikes. In 1950 General Motors and the United Automobile Workers signed a contract containing two novel provisions: an escalator clause providing that wages would be adjusted to reflect changes in the cost of living, and a productivity clause guaranteeing that wages would rise as productivity in the industry increased. Autoworkers won a guaranteed annual wage in 1955.

These contracts shared a common tendency to emphasize union members' status as consumers rather than workers. George Meany accepted the thrust of government-subsidized business prosperity; his goal was to ensure that labor got its share. Workers paid for these improved wages not only by limiting the number and duration of strikes, but also by putting aside their traditional claims for control over the pace of work. In return for higher wages and fringe benefits, workers allowed technologically minded managers to exert increasing control over their lives on the job.

But labor still had to fight for legitimacy in postwar society. The 1947 Taft-Hartley Act, which chipped away at some of the protections guaranteed by the 1935 National Labor Relations Act, represented the most virulent attack. Taft-Hartley showed that the New Deal labor reforms remained controversial a decade after their passage.

The Impact of Automation. Mechanization had long threatened skilled workers, but, in the 1950s, new technology affected the jobs of unskilled factory workers as well, many of them union members. In 1977, 400,000 workers in the steel industry produced twice as much steel as 600,000 had in 1947. Similar patterns held in coal mining and in the automobile industry, which had pioneered the assembly line. The Ford Motor Company introduced automatic drilling machines at a Cleveland engine plant in 1952, enabling 41 workers to do a job that formerly required 117.

When labor leader Walter Reuther inspected one of these automated engine plants, a Ford manager kidded him: "Well, you won't be able to collect dues from all these automated machines." "You know," Reuther replied, "that is not what is bothering me. What is bothering me is, how are you going to sell cars to all of these machines?" Reuther's reply was right on the mark. Without workers earning sufficient income to continue buying consumer goods, the American economy would falter.

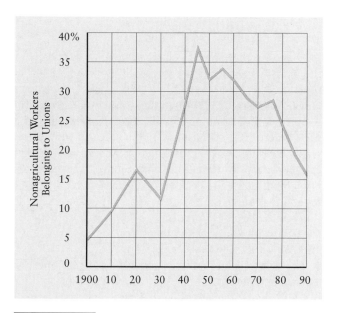

FIGURE 29.3

Labor Union Strength, 1900–1990
Labor unions reached their peak strength immediately after World War II. For thirty years they consistently represented more than a quarter of the nonfarm workforce. But labor union influence declined dramatically after 1975. (*Source:* AFL-CIO Information Bureau, Washington.)

New Recruits. These structural changes affected the labor movement in the postwar period. During the momentous 1930s and 1940s, unions had organized heavy industries such as mining, manufacturing, and transportation, but these sectors were no longer growing. The labor movement had to look elsewhere for new recruits, such as the less skilled, often black or Hispanic, workers in the lower-paying service and agricultural sectors or the millions of secretaries and file clerks in the nation's offices, who were predominantly women. The union movement needed to expand its industrial midwestern base into southern and western states, areas of rapid economic growth that were traditionally anti-union. Organized labor also had to woo younger workers who now saw unions as part of management, rather than as advocates of the rank and file. Finally, it had to branch out to organize white-collar employees in such previously untapped professions as teaching, nursing, and municipal services.

Organized labor met some, but not all, of these new challenges. By the mid-1950s, the labor movement had stalled. The unionized percentage of the nonagricultural work force peaked at 35.5 percent in 1946 and held level until 1954. Then union membership began a steady decline. This erosion of the labor movement stood in stark contrast to labor's vitality at the end of the New Deal.

The Agricultural Revolution

No sector of the economy changed more dramatically in the postwar period than agriculture. As late as 1945, a fourth of the American work force consisted of farmers. During the next twenty-five years, however, 25 million people left rural America; in 1969 only 5 percent of the population lived on farms. This farm-to-city migration was the result of two interrelated trends—a technological revolution in agriculture that reduced the need for labor, and the steady decline of the small family farm. A federal task force on rural development called this shift "one of the largest migrations of people in recorded history," rivaling European immigration to the New World and America's westward expansion.

The new technology that reduced the need for labor also contributed to an astonishing increase in agricultural productivity after 1945. Before the war, the typical American farm had been a small, modestly equipped family enterprise where horses and mules outnumbered tractors. In 1935 an hour of labor produced about 2 1/2 pounds of cotton, 2 bushels of wheat, just over 1 bushel of corn, 33 pounds of milk, or 3 chickens. During the postwar period, new machines and agricultural methods, including improved chemical fertilizers and pesticides, revolutionized farming. By 1978 a single hour's labor produced 50 pounds of cotton, 11 bushels of

wheat, 25 bushels of corn, 250 pounds of milk, or 100 chickens. But mechanization required major capital investments. Between 1940 and 1955, the cost of fuel, fertilizer, and repairs for farm machines quadrupled, and total operating costs tripled. Family farms often lacked the capital to compete with the large, technologically advanced farm units in such areas as California and the Midwest, further disadvantaging the small farmer in an increasingly corporate economy.

The technological revolution transformed the lives of many of the farmers who remained on the land. They now managed specialized organizations—small factories that poured industrial materials into the land and extracted raw products for immediate sale. They relied on outside industrial sources for fertilizer, feed, seed, and pesticides and for the energy needed to run the expanding array of gasoline-powered equipment. Farm families purchased consumer goods from commercial sources, rather than producing them at home. These ties made farmers, like other businesspeople, increasingly dependent on national and international market conditions, on scientific and technological developments, and on the actions of the expanding federal bureaucracy.

Farmers' fortunes were especially tied to federal farm policies, further confirmation of the impact of the bureaucratic state on postwar American life. There was no such thing as a free market in agriculture: all farms operated under a complicated system of government price supports, subsidies, and loans, which were linked both to domestic needs and to exports for the world market. In 1956 the federal farm program cost $2.5 billion. As it had during the New Deal, this federal largesse tended to benefit larger farms. According to figures gathered in 1954 by Secretary of Agriculture Ezra Taft Benson, sixty-four large corn, wheat, and cotton operators received more than $100,000 each in government loans, including one $1.27 million loan on cotton bales to the Delta and Pine Land Corporation of Mississippi. In contrast, the average cotton grower in that state only received $372 in loan payments.

The fuller integration of farmers into the national economy, and the diminishing number of Americans who made farming their occupation, greatly reduced the differences between rural and urban life. Farmers, once a major force in political life, no longer wielded as much clout in electoral politics except in the United States Senate, where a bloc of farm states still affected national policy. Agribusiness took its place as part of corporate America. Measurable farm income, which ranged from only 40 to 60 percent of the national average between the 1930s and 1950s, rose above 80 percent—and briefly to 110 percent—in the 1970s. As farming came to resemble other occupations, those who remained on the farm increasingly shared the experiences, views, and aspirations of other Americans.

TABLE 29.1

Trends in American Farming, 1935–1990

	Number of farms (thousands)	Farm population (thousands)	Percent of total population
1935	6,814	32,161	25.3%
1940	6,350	30,547	23.1
1945	5,967	24,420	17.5
1950	5,648	23,048	15.2
1956	4,514	18,712	11.1
1960	3,963	15,635	8.7
1965	3,356	12,363	6.4
1970	2,949	9,712	4.7
1975	2,521	8,864	4.2
1980	2,428	6,051	2.7
1985	2,293	5,355	2.4
1990*	2,143	4,801	2.1

*Data unavailable for 1989.
Source: Gilbert Fite, *American Farmers* (Bloomington: Indiana University Press, 1981), 101; *U.S. Statistical Abstract* (1991).

Cities and Suburbs

In the postwar years, Americans lived predominantly in metropolitan areas, largely because most jobs and housing were concentrated there. Economic activity in the twenty-five largest metropolitan areas picked up considerably after 1945. This growth did not occur in the central cities, which lost 300,000 jobs, but in the surrounding suburban areas, which gained an astounding 4 million jobs. By the late 1960s, suburbs surpassed cities in the number of jobs they offered. Only in white-collar office work did inner-city employment rise.

These patterns of employment and economic growth reinforced the growing gap between city dwellers and their suburban neighbors. Metropolitan areas developed a striking pattern of residential segregation that persists to this day. Poorer people, many of them nonwhites, clustered in the decaying inner cities, while the more prosperous middle class—whites and nonwhites—flocked to the suburbs.

Metropolitan Life

As early as 1880, demographers had noticed the appearance of sprawling metropolitan areas centered around one or more large cities and including scattered suburbs and satellite towns. That year, the U.S. Census identified twenty-five such regions, ranging in size from New York–Brooklyn–Newark, with 6,500,000 people, to Portland, Oregon, with 215,000. In 1920 the Census Bureau announced that urban population had surpassed rural for the first time, a major turning point in the modern era. At that time, a dozen metropolitan areas—located on the Atlantic Coast, near the Great Lakes or the Ohio River, or in California—had at least a million people each. Pilots flying along the East Coast

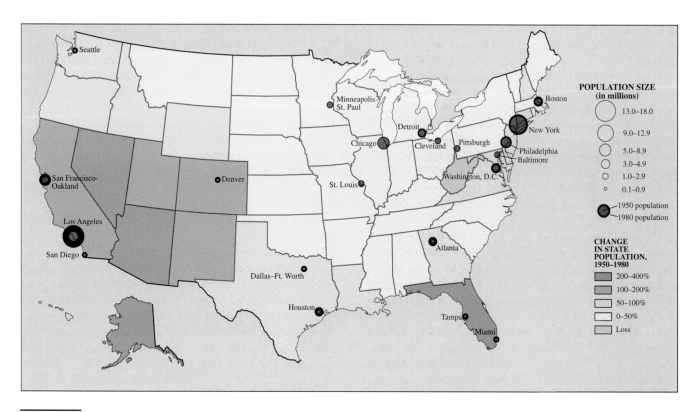

MAP 29.1

Metropolitan Growth, 1950–1980

A metropolitan area is generally defined as a central city which, in combination with its surrounding territory, forms an integrated economic and social unit. The U.S. Census Bureau introduced the "Standard Metropolitan Statistical Area" in 1950, but later changes in the definition of what comprises an SMSA make it difficult to generalize from the 1950 figures. This map compares the population of central cities in 1950 with population figures for the more broadly defined metropolitan areas in 1980 to illustrate the extent and geographic distribution of metropolitan growth in the postwar period.

at night began to notice that they could no longer distinguish one city from the next; a continuous strand of light stretched from Newport News, Virginia, past New York and up to Boston.

Urban migration, which had slowed to a trickle during the Great Depression, accelerated during the 1940s. In the years after World War II, metropolitan regions became the dominant form of settlement, providing a home for two-thirds of all Americans in 1960.

The Sun Belt. The growth of new metropolitan areas was most striking in the South and West, where large portions of the population had traditionally been rural and impoverished. Florida added 3.5 million people, many of them older or retired Americans, between 1940 and 1970. Texas cities grew as the petrochemical industry expanded rapidly after 1945; the oil and gas industries, together with the banks and law firms that served them, concentrated in Houston. Other expanding cities included Atlanta, Baton Rouge, Long Beach, Mobile, and Phoenix. Boosters heralded the booming metropolitan economies of the "Sun Belt." Overall, the South and West grew twice as fast as the Northeast between 1940 and 1970.

California was the most dramatic example of this new growth, with its climate and job opportunities acting as magnets to pull people from all parts of the country. California absorbed 2.6 million people in the 1940s and added 3.1 million more in the 1950s. Much of this growth was spurred by the expansion of defense industries, such as aircraft and electronics. In 1970, California had about a tenth of the entire U.S. population, and in 1972 it replaced New York as the state with the largest number of electoral votes.

During the postwar era, professional sports mirrored the new patterns of geographical and sectional growth, heralding a broader definition of a "big-league city." St. Louis had long been the westernmost baseball city. In 1958 baseball's Brooklyn Dodgers moved to Los Angeles and the New York Giants went to San Francisco. Teams in other professional sports also followed the sprawling metropolitan population. The New England Patriots played football in Foxboro, Massachusetts, halfway between Boston and Providence; the Detroit Lions moved to Pontiac, Michigan; and the Los Angeles Rams played in suburban Orange County.

The Northeast. While the older metropolitan areas in the Northeast grew less rapidly than the new Sunbelt centers, they experienced fundamental changes in their economies. Boston and nearby Lowell, Lawrence, and Salem, Massachusetts, lost most of their textile and manufacturing jobs, but high-technology industries that produced Polaroid instant cameras and Digital and Wang computers gave new life to the New England economy. So many companies built their corporate headquarters outside Boston along Route 128, one of the first peripheral highways to bypass downtown congestion, that it became known as the Technology Highway. New York City lost many of its garment-making and printing jobs, but outlying areas profited from the relocation of corporate headquarters to suburbs such as White Plains, New York, and Stamford, Connecticut. Reflecting the impact of military needs for defense production, Grumman and Northrop developed an important airplane and weapons-manufacturing industry on Long Island and the Electric Boat division of General Electric made submarines in Groton, Connecticut.

Blurring of Regional Differences. This redistribution of population, income, and economic activity gave metropolitan regions less sharply defined social and economic profiles than had prevailed in the late nineteenth and early twentieth centuries. The advent of metropolitan economies and the dramatic decline in small-scale farming caused by the agricultural revolution enabled people in the southern and western states to have incomes similar to those earned elsewhere in the nation. The migration of poor blacks and whites out of rural areas such as Appalachia into northern cities provided a further equalizer by relocating rural poverty to urban areas. Regional economic inequalities that had persisted since Reconstruction finally began to fade. But they were replaced by inequalities *within* regions, most notably between the central cities and their outlying suburban areas.

The Growth of Suburbia

At the end of World War II, many cities had pastures and working farms on their outskirts. Just five or ten years later, these cities were surrounded by tract housing and shopping centers. Between 1950 and 1960, the population of fourteen of the nation's fifteen largest cities shrank, while the suburbs surrounding these cities grew dramatically. New York lost 2 percent of its population in the 1950s, but its suburbs grew by 58 percent. Lakewood, California, had not even existed in 1950, but in 1960 this Los Angeles suburb counted more than 50,000 residents. Other areas that underwent rapid growth included San Mateo County, south of San Francisco; Cook and DuPage counties, north and west of Chicago; and Prince Georges County in Maryland, outside Washington, D.C. By 1960 more people lived in suburbs than in cities.

The Housing Boom. People flocked to the suburbs in part because they followed the available housing. Very little new housing had been built during the depression

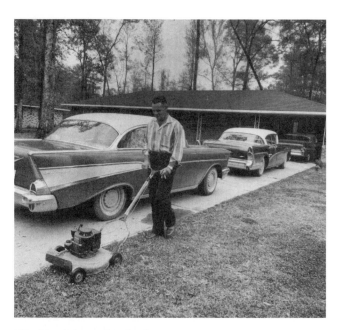

The Trappings of Suburbia
With a ranch house, three cars in the driveway, and a rotary lawn mower, this homeowner in Baton Rouge, Louisiana, embodied the middle-class suburban lifestyle.

or war years, and the returning World War II veterans and their families faced a critical housing shortage. The late 1940s and 1950s witnessed a dramatic surge in construction. A fourth of all housing in the country in 1960 had been built during the preceding decade. Most of it was single-family, owner-occupied homes.

The suburban housing market was revolutionized by a Long Island building contractor named Arthur Levitt, who applied mass-production techniques to home construction. His company could build as many as 150 homes a week, a rate of one every sixteen minutes. Levitt's basic four-room house, complete with kitchen appliances and an attic that could be finished on weekends by a handy homeowner into two additional bedrooms, was priced at less than ten thousand dollars in 1947. Levitt did not really need to advertise; word of mouth brought more customers than the firm could handle.

Levitt built planned communities in New York, New Jersey, and Pennsylvania (all named, not surprisingly, Levittown). The developments contained few old people and even fewer unmarried adults. Even the trees were young. Owners had to agree to cut their lawns once a week between April and November and not to hang out the laundry on weekends. (Reflecting cold war sentiments, Levitt asserted: "No man who owns his own house and lot can be a Communist. He has too much to do.") When residents complained that the streets and the houses were so similar that they could

not find their way home, the developer added more variety in style and site placement. Soon other developers were snapping up cheap farmland surrounding urban areas, further hastening the exodus from both the farm and the central city.

Many families financed their homes with mortgages from the Federal Housing Administration and the Veterans' Administration. Before World War II, banks, primarily the savings and loan industry that served this fairly stable market, usually demanded a 50 percent down payment for homeowner's loans and granted no more than ten years to pay back the balance. After the war, the Federal Housing Administration required only a 5 to 10 percent down payment and gave homeowners up to thirty years to pay back mortgages at the modest rate of 2 to 3 percent. The Veterans' Administration was even more lenient, requiring only a token one-dollar down payment from qualified veterans. In 1955 these two agencies wrote 41 percent of all nonfarm mortgages. Such lending demonstrated the quiet, yet revolutionary, way in which the federal government was entering and influencing daily life.

These suburban developments—and much of the savings and loan and VA money—were almost exclusively for whites. Levittown homeowners had to sign a covenant with a restrictive clause prohibiting occupation "by members of other than the Caucasian Race." (*Shelley v. Kraemer* [1948] only made restrictive covenants unenforceable in court; the custom was still prevalent until the civil rights laws of the 1960s banned private discrimination.) Not until 1960 did Levitt sell houses directly to blacks. Even then, the company carefully screened black families and made sure that no two black families lived next door to each other. Restrictive covenants also applied in other communities to such groups as Jews and Asians.

While suburbia was often portrayed as a homogeneous, even bland, environment, there were strong cultural and class variations among the suburbs. Older, wealthy suburbs already occupied the most pleasant locations, including the hills north and west of Los Angeles, Chicago's North Shore, and the heights well to the east of Cleveland's industrial Cuyahoga Flats. When less affluent firefighters, plasterers, machine-tool makers, or sales clerks moved to the suburbs, they were far more likely to move to a modest Levittown than to an upper-middle-class suburb such as Winnetka, Illinois, or Shaker Heights, Ohio. Blacks shut out of white suburbs established their own communities, such as Lincoln Heights, outside Cincinnati; Robbins, on the edge of Chicago; and Kinloch, near St. Louis. In well-equipped living quarters at bargain prices, working-class and black families could share in the ultimate postwar suburban dream "to give every kid an opportunity to grow up with grass stains on his pants."

Parade of Champions in Levittown

Levittown

So popular were Levittown homes that 1,400 contracts were signed in one day in 1949. The three models advertised here were the "Rancher" (the basic), the "Jubilee" (slightly larger), and the "Country Clubber" (the luxury edition). Homeowners especially enjoyed the privacy and space that such homes provided.

Cars and Highways. Automobiles and highways were essential to this dramatic suburban growth. Suburbanites needed cars to get to work or to take children to school and piano lessons. About 90 percent of suburban families owned cars, and 20 percent had more than one. Whereas 25 million cars had been registered in 1945, the number rose to 52 million in 1955 and increased to 75 million in 1965.

The car culture that had first emerged in the 1920s expanded dramatically during the 1950s, with cars becoming personal metaphors for status and success. With gas plentiful and cheap at fifteen cents a gallon, no one cared about fuel efficiency (8 miles to the gallon for the biggest gas guzzlers!). American cars became heavier and bigger, a disparity in size compared to Japanese or European models that remains to this day, even after American cars were downsized during the energy crisis of the 1970s.

More cars required more highways, which were funded largely by the federal government. In 1947, Congress authorized the construction of 37,000 miles of highway; the Interstate Highway Act of 1956 increased its commitment by another 42,500 miles. One of the largest civil engineering projects of world history, the new roads would be at least four lanes wide and

would link the entire country in an integrated interstate system. Gas taxes and user fees for commercial vehicles provided the necessary funds.

The interstate system changed both the cities and the countryside. It rerouted traffic through rural areas, bypassing old main roads like Route 1 on the eastern seaboard and the cross-country Route 66, and creating new communities of gas stations, fast-food outlets, and motels at anonymous cloverleaf exchanges. In urban areas, new highways cut wide swaths through old neighborhoods. Cities were soon plagued by the problems that cars brought to modern life—air pollution and traffic jams. Critics now complained about "autosclerosis," a hardening of the urban arteries.

Highway construction had far-reaching effects on patterns of consumption and shopping. Instead of taking a train into the city or walking to a corner grocery store, people now hopped into their cars and drove to suburban shopping malls and supermarkets. Although the first mall had appeared in the 1920s, there were only eight in 1945; by 1960 the number mushroomed to almost four thousand. When a 110-store complex at Roosevelt Field on suburban Long Island opened in 1956, it was conveniently situated at an expressway exit and offered parking for eleven thousand cars. Downtown retail areas and department stores declined accordingly.

The federally constructed highways threatened the demise of mass transit. Los Angeles, a city now largely dependent on freeways, had a viable mass transit system as late as the 1940s. The Highway Trust Fund set up in 1956 specifically prohibited use of its collected fees to promote urban mass transit. By 1960, two-thirds of all Americans drove to work each day. The percentage was even higher—between 80 and 95 percent—in such places as Los Angeles, Albuquerque, and Phoenix.

State and Local Government

The task of governing cities and suburbs fell to state and local governments. The average citizen lived under multiple layers of government—local, county, state, and federal—but local governments often had the greatest impact on people's daily lives. They ran the schools, supplied fire and police protection, picked up the trash, and cleaned the streets. State governments licensed the services of workers ranging from beauticians to lawyers, enforced building and health codes, and protected workers through child-labor laws and workers' compensation.

Like the federal government, state and local governments experienced rapid growth in the postwar period. In fact, their expenditures and payrolls increased faster

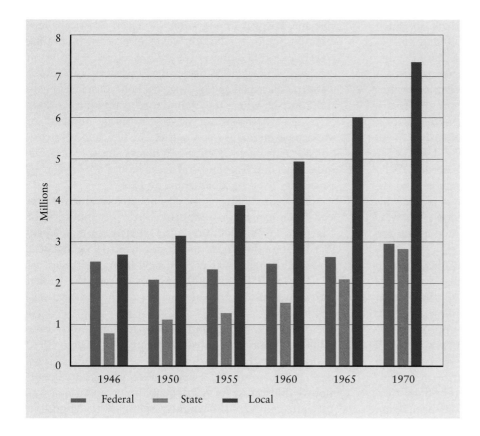

FIGURE 29.4

Federal, State, and Local Government Employees, 1946–1970
Although every level of government added employees in this period, the most dramatic growth took place in local government— counties, cities, and towns.

than the nondefense activities of the federal government during this time. State and local expenditures totaled $14 billion in 1946; in 1970 they had risen to almost $150 billion. Employment climbed correspondingly. In 1970, roughly one of seven Americans in the labor force worked for a government bureaucracy, yet another example of the rise of the state.

State and local revenues came from a variety of taxes. During the 1950s, state and local governments relied on property and sales taxes for almost half their revenues; state and city income taxes, and federal aid, were much less significant sources of revenue. State and local governments spent more money on education than on any other item, with expenditures for education in 1965 taking up approximately one-third of state and local budgets. The rest of the state and local budget went to welfare and social services (the second largest category), highways, health and hospitals, and other services.

Central cities and their surrounding suburban areas often had grossly unequal resources to meet local needs. Since the property tax provided a sizable part of local budgets, a wealthy community such as Grosse Pointe in suburban Detroit could far more easily provide funds for first-rate schools and adequate police departments than could Detroit, whose tax base shrank as businesses and middle-class residents relocated to the suburbs.

Although many of the problems of urban life— sewage, traffic, pollution, and police and fire protection—were shared by the cities and their surrounding areas, existing forms of government did not readily allow for cooperation. Political fragmentation was the rule. There were more than a thousand governmental units in the Chicago area, and fourteen hundred in the New York City region. Suburban communities remained reluctant to surrender their fiscal independence, to say nothing of the tradition of local self-rule, to the huge cities with their myriad social and economic problems.

City Dwellers and New Arrivals

Cities had always counted a heterogeneous population, one shaped by economic, religious, cultural, and racial diversity that changed neighborhood to neighborhood, sometimes from block to block. Migrants from other parts of the country and a new—if small—wave of immigration from abroad added to the postwar ethnic diversity of the nation's urban population.

Postwar Immigration. Until 1965 the United States immigration policy still followed the national origins quota system set up in 1924, whose purpose was generally to keep immigrants out, not let them in. Such restrictions, for example, had made it difficult to win entrance for Jews fleeing Hitler's Holocaust. But the dislocations caused by the war and its aftermath led to a slight loosening of the law. The Chinese Exclusion Act was repealed in 1943, a recognition of America's wartime alliance with China and a growing realization that the racism embodied in the total exclusion of all Asians was no longer tenable. The 1952 McCarran-Walter Act ended the former exclusion of certain racial and ethnic groups from immigration and naturalization. One impetus behind the change was a need inspired by the Cold War to strengthen the world's view of the United States as the symbol of democracy in the fight against communism.

Foreign policy shaped immigration priorities in other ways. In 1945 Congress passed the War Brides Act, which allowed the entrance and naturalization of the wives and children of Americans, mainly servicemen, abroad. As a result of the Korean War, approximately 17,000 Koreans entered the United States between 1950 and 1965, the vast majority war brides. In recognition of the independence of the Philippines from American control on July 4, 1946, this group received its own quota. The major increase in immigration from Asian countries would not occur until after 1965, however.

Changes in the immigration laws could have a large impact on the composition of immigrant communities. On the eve of World War II, the Chinatowns in the nation's major cities were populated primarily by Chinese men. Many of these men were married, but their wives had remained in China. The opening wedge of the 1943 legislation, coupled with the granting of the right of naturalization to Chinese already here, encouraged Chinese men to bring their wives to America. This increase of female immigrants led to a more balanced sex ratio, a pattern also seen in the Filipino-American and Japanese-American communities. There were approximately 135,000 men and 100,000 women of Chinese origin living in the United States in 1960, the majority in either New York State or California.

Proposals to admit displaced persons and refugees from Europe were more controversial. Many Americans feared being swamped with immigrants from devastated Europe, including displaced Jews who could or would not return to their former homelands. (In fact, most Jews headed to Israel once it became independent in 1948, one of the few alternatives open to them.) The 1948 Displaced Persons Act allowed approximately 415,000 Europeans to enter the United States before it expired in 1952. Among those who entered were a sizable number of Germans who had collaborated with the Nazis but whose expertise, in fields like rocketry, was deemed essential to national security.

Hispanic Postwar Immigration. Mexican-Americans represented one of the largest waves of postwar migrants. Nearly 275,000 came in the 1950s, almost 444,000 in the 1960s. They came primarily to western and southwestern cities such as Los Angeles, Long Beach, El Paso, and Phoenix, where they found jobs as migrant workers or in the expanding service sector. Large numbers of Mexican-Americans also settled in Chicago, Detroit, Kansas City, and Denver. Whereas most Mexican-Americans had lived in rural areas before World War II, a majority lived in urban areas by 1960.

The United States government actively sought Mexican-American labor under the *bracero* (temporary, or "day worker") program with Mexico during World War II labor shortages, then again from 1951 to 1964, when the Korean War created new labor shortages. At its peak in 1959, 450,000 braceros entered the United States, accounting for one-quarter of the nation's seasonal workers.

Another major group of Hispanic migrants came from the American-controlled territory of Puerto Rico. Residents of this island had been American citizens since 1917, and in 1952 Puerto Rico was granted commonwealth status. As such, their coming and going was not affected by the immigration laws. Migration increased dramatically after World War II, as Puerto Ricans were lured by the promise of better economic opportunities and social services. The inauguration of cheap, direct air service between San Juan and New York City (in the 1940s the fare was about $50, two weeks' wages) made Puerto Ricans this country's first group to immigrate by air, not by sea.

Most of the Puerto Rican migrants went to New York, where they settled first in East ("Spanish") Harlem and then in other areas throughout the city's five boroughs. This massive migration, which grew from 70,000 in 1940 to 613,000 just twenty years later, transformed the ethnic composition of the city. More Puerto Ricans now lived in New York City than in San Juan. They faced conditions common to all recent immigrants—crowded and deteriorating housing, segregation, unemployment or restriction to menial jobs, poor schools, and the problems of a bilingual existence.

Cuban refugees comprised the third large group of Hispanics. Nearly half a million people fled Cuba in the wake of Fidel Castro's seizure of power in 1959. The Cuban refugee community was so large and vigorous that it turned Miami into a cosmopolitan, bilingual city almost overnight. Unlike most new migrants to urban America, Miami's Cubans prospered, in large part because they had arrived with more resources. As the Castro regime consolidated its position, thus foreclosing prospects of returning home, Cuban-Americans increased their stakes in the United States. They differed

"West Side Story"

In 1961, United Artists released the movie version of Leonard Bernstein's 1957 Broadway hit, "West Side Story." The plot recast Shakespeare's "Romeo and Juliet" to a Hispanic neighborhood on New York's West Side in the 1950s. Confrontations between members of youth gangs and adult figures of authority, such as pictured here in a still from the movie, were set to highly stylized song and dance routines.

from most other Hispanics as they were predominantly middle class and politically conservative.

Internal Migration. Internal migration also brought large numbers of people to the nation's cities, especially African-Americans, continuing a trend begun during World War I. Black migration was hastened by the transformation of southern agriculture. New Deal agricultural policies and the development of synthetic fibers such as rayon and Dacron after World War II caused cotton acreage in the South to decline from 43 million acres in 1929 to fewer than 15 million in 1959. In addition, the mechanization of farming drastically reduced the demand for farm labor. The mechanical cotton picker, introduced in 1944, fatally undermined the sharecropper system; it could pick 1,000 pounds an hour compared to 20 pounds by an experienced hand. As a result, the southern farm population fell from 16.2 million in 1930 to 5.9 million in 1960. Although both whites and blacks left the land, the starkest decline was among black farmers. By 1990 there were only 69,000 black farmers in the entire nation, just 1.5 percent of the country's farmers.

Where did they go? Some of the migrants settled in southern cities, where they obtained industrial jobs. White Southerners from Appalachia moved north to "hillbilly" ghettoes such as Cincinnati's Over the Rhine neighborhood or Chicago's Uptown. In the most dramatic population shift, as many as 3 million blacks headed to cities such as Chicago, New York, Washington, D.C., Detroit, and Los Angeles between 1940 and 1960. Certain sections of Chicago seemed like the Mis-

sissippi Delta transplanted, so pervasive were the migrants. The nation's cities saw their nonwhite populations swell at the same time that whites were flocking to the suburbs. From 1950 to 1960, the nation's twelve largest cities lost 3.6 million whites while gaining 4.5 million nonwhites. In 1960 about half of the African-American population was living outside the South.

Urban Neighborhoods, Urban Poverty

By the time that blacks, Mexican-Americans, and Puerto Ricans moved into the inner cities, urban America was in poor shape. Housing continued to be a crucial problem. One common response on the part of city planners, politicians, and real estate developers to the problem of deteriorating inner-city housing in the 1950s was *urban renewal*, razing blighted urban neighborhoods and replacing them with modern buildings. Local residents were rarely consulted about whether they wanted their neighborhoods "renewed." Urban renewal often produced grim high-rise housing projects that destroyed feelings of neighborhood pride and created combat zones for street crime. Between 1949 and 1961, urban renewal projects demolished almost 150,000 buildings and displaced 500,000 people. By 1967 the number of razed structures topped 400,000, and 1.4 million urban dwellers had been forced to relocate.

Urban renewal projects often benefited the wealthy at the expense of the poor. Many downtown "revitalization" projects supplanted established ethnic neighborhoods with expensive rental housing or shiny office

Harlem: Dream and Reality *Claude Brown*

Claude Brown's *Manchild in the Promised Land* (1965) graphically described the conditions that awaited blacks when they journeyed to the promised land of Harlem in the postwar period. Brown dedicated the book to Eleanor Roosevelt, a benefactor of the Wiltwyck School for Boys, which helped troubled youth like Claude Brown break out of the ghetto.

Everybody I knew in Harlem seemed to have some kind of dream. I didn't have any dreams, not really. I didn't have any dreams for hitting the number. I didn't have any dreams for getting a big car or a fine wardrobe. I bought expensive clothes because it was a fad. It was the thing to do, just to show that you had money. I wanted to be a part of what was going on, and this was what was going on.

I didn't have any dreams of becoming anything. All I knew for certain was that I had my fears. I suppose just about everybody else knew the same thing. They had their dreams, though, and I guess that's what they had over me. As time went by, I was sorry for the people whose dreams were never realized.

When Butch was alive, sometimes I would go uptown to see him. He'd be sick. He'd be really messed up. I'd give him some drugs, and then he'd be more messed up than before. He wouldn't be sick, but I couldn't talk to him, I couldn't reach him. He'd be just sitting on a stoop nodding. Sometimes he'd be slobbering over himself.

I used to remember Butch's dream. Around 1950, he used to dream of becoming the best thief in Harlem. It wasn't a big dream. To him, it was a big dream, but I don't suppose too many people would have seen it as that. Still, I felt sorry for him because it was his dream. I suppose the first time he put the spike in his arm every dream he'd ever had was thrown out the window. Sometimes I wanted to shout at him or snatch him by the throat and say, "Butch, what about your dream?" But there were so many dreams that were lost for a little bit of duji. . . .

I used to feel that I belonged on the Harlem streets and that, regardless of what I did, nobody had any business to take me off the streets.

I remember when I ran away from shelters, places that they sent me to, here in the city. I never ran away with the thought in mind of coming home. I always ran away to get back to the streets. I always thought of Harlem as home, but I never thought of Harlem as being in the house. To me, home was the streets. I suppose there were many people who felt that. If home was so miserable, the street was the place to be. I wonder if mine was really so miserable, or if it was that there was so much happening out in the street that it made home seem such a dull and dismal place.

When I was very young—about five years old, maybe younger—I would always be sitting out on the stoop. I remember Mama telling me and Carole to sit on the stoop and not to move away from in front of the door. Even when it was time to go up and Carole would be pulling on me to come upstairs and eat, I never wanted to go, because there was so much out there in that street.

You might see somebody get cut or killed. I could go out in the street for an afternoon, and I would see so much that, when I came in the house, I'd be talking and talking for what seemed like hours. Dad would say, "Boy, why don't you stop that lyin'? You know you didn't see all that. You know you didn't see nobody do that." But I knew I had.

Source: Claude Brown, *Manchild in the Promised Land* (New York: Macmillan, 1965), 427–429.

buildings where suburban commuters worked. Boston's West End, a flourishing, if poor, Italian community, was razed by a private developer between 1958 and 1960 to build Charles River Park, an apartment complex whose rents were far too steep for the old-time residents. West Enders were forced into less desirable parts of the city, cut off from the vitality of their former neighborhood. The 575,000 units of public housing nationwide built by 1964 came nowhere near to filling the need for affordable housing in urban America.

Despite pockets of urban "gentrification," postwar cities were increasingly becoming a place of last resort for the nation's poor. Unlike earlier immigrants, for whom cities were gateways to social and economic betterment, inner-city residents in the postwar period faced diminishing hopes for improvement. Lured by the promise of plentiful jobs, migrants found that many of these supposed opportunities had relocated to the suburban fringe. Steady employment was out of reach for those who needed it most.

That the poor were increasingly trapped in the cities was also due to racism. Migrants to the city, especially blacks, faced racial hostility and institutional barriers to mobility. Two separate Americas were emerging—a white society located in suburbs and peripheral areas and an inner city made up of blacks, Hispanics, and other disadvantaged groups. This widespread metropolitan segregation remains one of the most striking and disturbing aspects of modern urban life.

American Society During the Baby Boom

One of the most distinctive characteristics of the immediate postwar period was its family orientation. Couples, especially the white middle class, flocked to the new suburban developments, where they had children, lots of them. The effects of the postwar baby boom are still felt. In the 1950s children provided plenty of patients for doctors and dentists, and students for elementary teachers. In the 1960s the baby-boom generation swelled college enrollments, and not coincidentally, the ranks of student protesters. By the 1970s, when the baby-boom generation entered the workplace, it had to compete for a limited number of jobs in what had become a stagnant economy. In the 1980s the delayed marriages and later childbearing of the career-oriented baby-boomers temporarily caused the birthrate to rise again. In the 1990s baby boomers, now in their forties,

took up positions of leadership in business, politics, and cultural life. The decisions made by many couples in the immediate postwar period to have large families will continue to ripple through American life well into the twenty-first century.

Consumer Culture

As we have seen, prosperity and affluence characterized much of postwar American life. In some respects, the consumer culture of the 1950s seemed like a return to the 1920s—an overabundance of new gadgets and appliances, the expansion of consumer credit and advertising, more leisure time, the growing importance of the automobile, and the development of new types of mass media. Yet there was a significant difference. The postwar economy was far better balanced than that of the 1920s; no depressed agricultural sector detracted from the prosperity and no Great Depression lurked on the horizon. By the 1950s consumption had become integral to middle-class culture. Due to rising incomes, even blue-collar families had discretionary income to spend on consumer goods.

As in the 1920s, though, the postwar prosperity was helped along by a dramatic increase in consumer credit, which enabled families to stretch their incomes. Between 1946 and 1958 short-term consumer credit rose from $8.4 billion to almost $45 billion. A hefty portion of this increase involved financing for the purchase of automobiles on the installment plan. The Diners Club credit card, introduced in 1950 and followed by the American Express card and Bank Americard in 1959, was initially geared toward the business traveler. But by the 1970s, the ubiquitous plastic credit cards had revolutionized personal and family finances. One casualty of the consumer credit phenomenon was the pawnshop, which no longer found much call for its services.

Advertising. Along with expanded consumer spending came a spurt in advertising, another example of the booming service sector. In 1951 businesses spent more on advertising ($6.5 billion) than taxpayers did on primary and secondary education ($5 billion); advertising expenditures topped $10 billion in 1960. The 1950s gave Americans the Marlboro Man; M & M's that melt in your mouth, not in your hand; the Hathaway eyepatch; Wonder Bread building strong bodies in twelve ways; and the "does she, or doesn't she?" Clairol woman. Motivational research delved into the subconscious to suggest how these messages should be pitched. The ads of the period reflected an uncritical view of American life that suggested, falsely, that all Americans were white and middle class, all women homemakers, and all families nuclear and intact.

Automobiles continued to be the most heavily advertised item in the 1950s, but advertising also promoted a variety of new consumer appliances to fill the suburban home. Production of some of these appliances had been halted during the war; others were new to the postwar market. In 1946 automatic washing machines replaced the old machines that required wringing out clothes by hand, and electric dryers came on the market that same year. In 1955, 1.2 million dryers were sold, twice the 1953 total, and commercial laundries across the country struggled to stay in business. Another new item on the market was the home freezer, which enabled families to eat seasonal foods, such as fruits and vegetables, all year and encouraged the dramatic growth of the frozen-food industry. Due in part to the purchases of electrical gadgets for the home, consumer use of electricity doubled during the 1950s.

Leisure Time. Consumers had more time to spend money than ever before. In 1960 the average worker put in a five-day week, with eight paid holidays each year (double the 1946 standard) plus a paid two-week vacation. The travel industry grew rapidly during the 1950s, with Americans devoting a seventh of the gross national product to spending on leisure and entertainment. Americans made use of the interstate highway system to travel domestically, encouraging the dramatic growth in motel chains, roadside restaurants, and fast-food eateries. (The first McDonald's restaurant opened in 1954 in San Bernardino, California; the Holiday Inn

Landmark for Hungry Americans
Conveniently located on major highways and in shopping centers, Howard Johnson's Motor Lodges and Restaurants (colloquially referred to as HoJo's) were instantly recognizable by their bright orange roofs. Like McDonald's Golden Arches, these roofs became familiar roadside beacons for travelers and suburbanites alike. (Henry Ford Museum & Greenfield Village)

motel chain started in Memphis in 1952.) Popular destinations were national and state parks, and Disneyland, the original theme park which opened in Anaheim, California, in 1955. Aided by the strong U.S. dollar and the introduction of jet air travel in 1958, families flooded Europe each summer, earning the unflattering epithet of "ugly Americans" for expecting things to be just like home.

Television

One of the most widespread leisure activities was watching television. TV's leap to cultural prominence was swift and overpowering. There were only ten broadcasting stations in the entire country in 1947, and a meager 7,000 sets in American homes. But in 1948 the CBS and NBC radio networks began offering regular programming on television. Just two years later, Americans had purchased 7.3 million TV sets. By 1955, 66 percent of American families had at least one television set; by 1960, 87 percent. More Americans owned a TV than a refrigerator.

In other countries, television developed as a government-controlled or subsidized service, but in the United States it emerged as private enterprise geared towards entertainment. Although stations were licensed by the Federal Communications Commission after 1941, television, like radio, depended entirely on advertising and corporate sponsorship for profits. Even though the radio networks, especially the corporate leaders NBC and CBS, played a large role in making TV happen, television soon supplanted radio as the chief diffuser of popular culture. Movies, too, lost the cultural predominance that they had enjoyed from the 1920s through the 1940s. Movie attendance shrank throughout the postwar period, and studios relied increasingly on overseas distribution of American films for their profits.

At first the novelty of television brought people together, at a neighbor's home or perhaps in a local tavern to watch the World Series or a political convention, but it soon had the opposite effect of isolating and atomizing leisure in the private home. Television fostered a mass national culture in a way similar to, but far more completely than, radio's effect in the 1920s. It promoted homogeneity and reduced regional and ethnic differences by its national network programming (the first live nationwide broadcast, the signing of the Japanese Peace Treaty ending the American military occupation, occurred in 1951). Viewers had only three or four channels to choose from; public television did not begin until 1967, and cable was a phenomenon of the 1980s.

Television encouraged the consumerism and advertising that has characterized mass culture since the 1920s. Like the golden era of radio in the 1920s and 1930s, corporations produced and sponsored major television shows, such as the "Texaco Star Theater" with Milton Berle, the "Camel News Caravan" with John Cameron Swayze, and the "General Electric Theater," hosted by Ronald Reagan. New items entered the home, such as frozen TV dinners of turkey, peas, and mashed potatoes, first introduced in 1954. Now a family could eat a meal in front of the television without having to talk. *TV Guide*, founded in television's breakthrough year of 1948, became the most successful new periodical of the 1950s. Television even affected city services. In 1954 the Toledo water commissioner wondered why water consumption rose dramatically during certain three-minute periods. The answer? All across Toledo, TV watchers flushed their toilets during commercials.

"The Honeymooners"
Sewer worker Ed Norton (left, played by Art Carney) and bus driver Ralph Kramden (Jackie Gleason) joust in an episode from the popular television series "The Honeymooners." Should Alice Kramden (played by Audrey Meadows) try to get a word in edgewise, Ralph's reply was likely to be, "One of these days, Alice, one of these days, pow! Right in the kisser!"

What Americans saw on television, besides the omnipresent commercials, was an overwhelmingly white, Anglo-Saxon world of nuclear families, suburban homes, and middle-class life. Shows like "The Honeymooners," starring Jackie Gleason as a Brooklyn bus driver, or "Life With Reilly" were rare in their treatment of working-class lives. Minorities appeared mainly as servants, such as Jack Benny's Rochester. Far more typical was "Father Knows Best," starring Robert Young and Jane Wyatt. We never knew what Father actually did for a living, except that he left home each morning wearing a suit and carrying a briefcase. Mother was a full-time housewife, always available and actively interested in her three children, but also prone to stereotypical female behavior such as bad driving and bursting into tears.

Probably the most popular situation comedy of the 1950s was "I Love Lucy," which revolved around the adventures of a wacky housewife and her Cuban-born bandleader husband, as portrayed by Lucille Ball and Desi Arnaz. Married in real life as well as on television, the show even incorporated Lucy's first pregnancy into the storyline. Twice as many Americans—44 million, the figure courtesy of the new sampling firm of A. C. Neilson—watched the 1956 show where Lucy had her baby as did the inauguration of President Dwight Eisenhower the next day.

The television genres developed in the 1950s still shape broadcasting today. Taking over a popular radio and movie category, television offered some thirty westerns on the air by 1959, including "Gunsmoke," "Have Gun, Will Travel," and "Bonanza," the first color show. National television coverage made professional sports big-time entertainment and big business. Programming geared to children, such as Walt Disney's Mickey Mouse Club, Howdy Doody, and Captain Kangaroo, meant that 1950s children were the first generation to grow up glued to the tube. The appeal of perennially popular quiz shows such as "Twenty-One" and "The $64,000 Question" was untarnished even when a scandal in 1959 revealed that contestants had been given the questions in advance. Although the new medium did offer some serious programming, notably live theater and documentaries, Federal Communications Commissioner Newton Minow concluded in 1963 that television was "a vast wasteland."

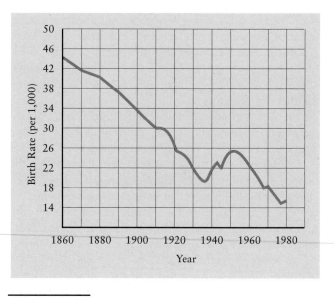

FIGURE 29.5

The Declining American Birthrate, 1860–1980
When viewed over more than a century, the postwar baby boom was clearly an aberration.

The Baby Boom

The dislocations of the depression and war years made both men and women yearn for a return to traditional family values. A popular 1945 song was "Gotta Make Up for Lost Time," and Americans did just that. The postwar generation approached life with an optimism and confidence notably absent from the depression cohort of the 1930s. The GI Bill and other federal programs aided their quest for unprecedented levels of material security, as did the general prosperity of the postwar era. As usual, these options were far more available to members of the white middle class than to minorities.

Such individual life choices were taking place against the backdrop of the Cold War. Just as the Marshall Plan and the Truman Doctrine were two halves of the same walnut, so too were cold war ideology and the 1950s emphasis on domesticity. One historian used the phrase "cold war, warm hearth" to capture how home and family seemed to offer a secure private retreat from the Cold War and the atomic age. (Note the semantic ironies of the *nuclear* family in the *nuclear* age.) As Richard Nixon argued in the "kitchen debate" with Nikita Khrushchev, stable suburban families (sexual "containment," no less) would provide the bulwark against the Soviet threat.

Two things were noteworthy about the men and women who formed families between 1940 and 1960. First, their marriages were remarkably stable. Not until the mid-1960s did the divorce rate begin to rise sharply. Second, they were strongly pronatal. Everyone expected to have at least several children—it was part of adulthood, almost a citizen's responsibility. "I'd like six kids," announced one young man. "It just seems like a minimum production goal." After a century and a half of declining family size, the birthrate shot up: more babies were born between 1948 and 1953 than in the previous thirty years. As a result, the American population rose dramatically, from 140 million in 1945 to 179 million in 1960, and 203 million in 1970.

There are several reasons for this twenty-year upsurge that demographers call the *baby boom*. Because a sustained rise in the birthrate did not occur in all the countries affected by World War II, it was not simply a response to the losses of war. Much more important was the drop in the marriage age, a trend that had begun during the war. The average age of marriage dropped to twenty-two for men, twenty for women; in 1951 a third of all women were married by the time they reached nineteen.

While younger couples were having babies earlier, they were not necessarily having huge numbers of children. Women who came of age in the 1930s had an average of 2.4 children; their counterparts in the 1950s averaged 3.2 children. What made the baby boom happen was that *everyone* was having children, and having them at the same time. This explosion in fertility peaked in 1957, and remained at a high level until the early 1960s. Since the 1960s the birthrate has generally declined, returning to more longstanding patterns. The postwar baby boom thus represents an aberration.

Increased Life Expectancy. In addition to the rising birthrate, the declining death rate contributed to the population growth. Life expectancy at birth had improved steadily over the first half of the twentieth century, from forty-seven years in 1900 to sixty-three years in 1940. Continued improvements in diet, public health, and surgical practices further lengthened the life span. So did "miracle drugs," such as penicillin, introduced in 1943, streptomycin (1945), and cortisone (1946). When Dr. Jonas Salk perfected a polio vaccine in 1954, he became a national hero. The free distribution of Salk's vaccine in the nation's schools, followed in 1961 by Dr. Albert Sabin's oral polio vaccine, demonstrated the potential of government-sponsored public health programs. The conquest of polio made the children of the 1950s one of the healthiest generations ever.

Scientific Child Rearing. For rearing all these baby boom children and keeping them healthy, middle-class parents increasingly relied on the advice of experts. Dr. Benjamin Spock's best-selling *Baby and Child Care* sold a million copies a year after its publication in 1946. Dr. Spock urged mothers to abandon the rigid feeding and baby-care schedules of an earlier generation. New mothers found Spock's common-sense approach liberating, but it did not totally soothe their insecurities. If mothers were too protective of their children, they might hamper their adjustment to a normal adult life. If they wanted to work outside the home, they felt guilty about neglecting their family. Dr. Spock could only recommend that mothers be constantly available to respond to their children's needs.

The baby boom had a broad and immediate impact on American society. The consumer needs of all those babies fueled the economy as families bought food, diapers, toys, and clothing for their expanding broods. Family spending on consumer goods joined federal expenditures on national security as the basis for the unparalleled prosperity and economic growth that characterized American society in the 1950s and 1960s.

The baby boom also encouraged a major expansion of the nation's educational system. The new middle class, America's first college-educated generation, placed a high value on education. To make schools into showplace community centers, suburbanites approved 90 percent of the proposed school bond issues during the 1950s. School expenditures accounted for 7.2 percent of the gross national product by 1970, double the 1950 level.

Polio Pioneers

These Provo, Utah, children each received a "Polio Pioneer" souvenir button for participating in the trial of the Salk vaccine in 1954. Dr. Jonas Salk's announcement the next year that the vaccine was safe and effective made him a national hero.

Elvis Presley
The young Elvis Presley (shown here on the cover of his first album in 1956) embodied cultural rebellion against the conservatism and triviality of adult life, but by the 1960s his music had lost its edge. He still remained enormously popular, however, especially after a 1968 comeback. After his death in 1977 from an accidental drug overdose, Elvis impersonators abounded and a major cult developed. Graceland, his home in Memphis, attracts more visitors each year than Mount Vernon.

Youth Culture

In 1956, only partly in jest, CBS radio commentator Eric Sevareid questioned "whether the teenagers will take over the United States lock, stock, living room, and garage." The centrality of youth culture to modern times, a trend first noticed in the 1920s and expanding ever since, had its roots in the democratization of education, the growth of peer culture, and what one historian has called the "burgeoning consumer independence" of teenagers in an age of affluence. Like so much else in the 1950s, the youth culture came down to money.

Market research convinced advertisers of the existence of a distinct teen market in the 1950s. A 1951 *Newsweek* story noted with awe that the $3 average weekly spending money of the typical teen was enough to buy 190 million candy bars, 130 million soft drinks, and 230 million sticks of gum. In 1956 advertisers projected an adolescent market of $9 billion for items such as transistor radios (first introduced in 1952), 45 rpm records, clothing, and fads such as silly putty (1950) and hula hoops (1958). Increasingly advertisers targeted their appeal to the young, both to capture their spending money and also for their influence on family spending patterns. Note the changing slogans for Pepsi-Cola: "Twice as much for a nickel" (1935); "Be Sociable—Have a Pepsi" (1948); "Now it's Pepsi for those who think young" (1960); and, finally, "The Pepsi Generation" (1965).

Hollywood movies played a large role in fostering, and legitimizing, this separate teenage culture. At a time when general movie attendance was declining because of competition from television, young people made up the largest audience for motion pictures. Soon Hollywood studios were catering to this youth orientation with such films as *The Wild One* (1951), starring Marlon Brando, and *Rebel Without A Cause* (1955), starring James Dean, Natalie Wood, and Sal Mineo. "What are you rebelling against?" a waitress asks Brando in *The Wild One*. "Whattaya got?" he replies.

What really defined this generation, however, was music. Just as wartime "bobby soxers" swooned over popular singers like Frank Sinatra, teenagers in the 1950s had rock and roll. Rock and roll developed from white country and western music, and what had been black-inspired music known as rhythm and blues. Cleveland disk jockey Alan Freed played a large role in introducing white America to the new black-influenced sound by playing what was known as "race" records when he came to primetime radio in 1954. Soon the record companies realized the size of the market. Between 1953 and 1959 record sales increased from $213 million to $603 million, with rock and roll as the driving force. The market for stereos and transistor radios rose accordingly.

The breakthrough year for rock and roll was 1956, thanks largely to Elvis Presley. "If I could find a white man who had the Negro sound and the Negro feel, I could make a billion dollars," said the owner of a record company. Presley, born in 1935 in Tupelo, Mississippi, in a working-class family, proved an instant sensation with his hits "Hound Dog" and "Heartbreak Hotel." In 1956 his records sold 10 million copies, more than 10 percent of all popular records sold that year. Between 1956 and his induction into the army in 1958 (the long arm of the state reached even the most popular teen idol), Presley had fourteen consecutive million-copy selling hits.

Many adults were appalled. They saw in music, movies, and magazines like *Mad* (introduced in 1952) an invitation to rebellion, disorder, and juvenile delinquency. They found the new music especially troubling. A noted psychiatrist called rock and roll "a communicable disease" and "a cannibalistic and tribalistic kind of music." When Elvis Presley appeared on the "Ed Sullivan Show," television cameras showed the teen idol only from the waist up, censoring his skin-tight pants and gyrating pelvis. Young people got the message anyway.

Contradictions in Women's Lives

"The suburban housewife was the dream image of the young American woman," feminist Betty Friedan has said of the 1950s. "She was healthy, beautiful, educated, concerned only about her husband, her children, and her home." Friedan herself gave up a psychology fellowship and a career as a journalist to marry, move to the suburbs, and raise three children. "Determined that I find the feminine fulfillment that eluded my mother . . . I lived the life of a suburban housewife that was everyone's dream at the time," she said.

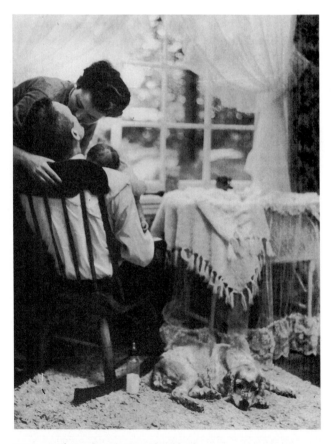

Home Life in the 1950s: The Ideal
This photograph reflects an idealized picture of family life in the 1950s. Taken in Long Island in 1958, it suggests the theme of "togetherness," a word coined by *McCall's* magazine in 1954. Many popular magazines promoted the notion of an idyllic home life for women who made a full-time career of homemaking, regardless of family size.

AMERICAN VOICES

The Feminine Mystique *Betty Friedan*

Betty Friedan drew on her own experiences as a suburban housewife to write her best-selling *The Feminine Mystique* (1963). This piece, published in 1974, describes her memories of "the way we were—1949."

I felt that I would never again, ever, be so happy as I was living in Queens. The floors were parquet, and the ceilings were molded white plaster, no pipes, and the plumbing worked. The rent was $118.50 a month, for four and one-half rooms, and we thought that was enormous. And now our friends were the other couples like us, with kids at the nursery school who squealed at each other from the baskets of the grocery carts we wheeled at the supermarket. It was fun at first, shopping in those new supermarkets. And we bought barbecue grills, and made dips out of sour cream and dried onion soup to serve with potato chips, while our husbands made the martinis as dry as in the city and cooked hamburgers on the charcoal, and we sat in canvas chairs on our terrace and thought how beautiful our children looked, playing in the twilight, and how lucky we all were, and that it would last forever.

There were six families in our group, and if your child smashed his finger in the manhole cover and you weren't home one of the others would take him to the doctor. We had Thanksgiving and Christmas and Passover Seders as a joint family, and in the summer rented houses together, on Lake George and Fire Island, that we couldn't afford separately. And the support we gave each other hid the cracks in our marriages—or maybe kept them from getting serious. As it

is, of the six families, three couples are now divorced, one broken by suicide.

Having babies, the Care and Feeding of Children according to Doctor Spock, began to structure our lives. It took the place of politics. But the mystique was something else—that college graduates should make a *Career* of motherhood, not just one or two babies, but four, five, six. Why even go to college? . . .

Besides, the reality of the babies, the bottles, the cooking, the diapering, the burping, the carriage-wheeling, the pressure cooker, the barbecue, the playground, and doing-it-yourself was more comfortable, more safe, secure, and satisfying—that year and for a lot of years thereafter—than that supposedly glamorous "career" where you somehow didn't feel wanted, and where no matter what you did you knew you weren't going to get anywhere. There was a guilty feeling, too: it was somehow your fault, *pushy* of you, to want that good assignment for yourself, want the credit, the by-line, if the idea, even the writing, had been yours. *Pushy*, too, if you felt rejected when the men went out to lunch and talked shop in one of those bars where women were not allowed—even if one of those same men asked you out to lunch, alone, in the other kind of restaurant, and held your hand, or knee, under the tablecloth. It was uncomfortable, unreal in a way, working in that kind of office with "career" still driving you, but having no words to deal with, even *recognize*, that barrier that you could never somehow break through, that made you invisible as a person, that made them not take you seriously, that made you feel so basically unimportant, almost unnec-

essary, and—buried very deep—so angry.

At home, you *were* necessary, you were important, you were the boss, in fact—the mother—and the new mystique gave it the rationale of career. . . .

Shortly after 1949, I was fired from my job because I was pregnant again. They weren't about to put up with the inconvenience of another year's maternity leave, even though I was *entitled* to it under my union contract. It was unfair, *wrong* somehow to fire me just because I was pregnant, and to hire a man instead. I even tried calling a meeting of the people in the union where I worked. It was the first personal stirring of my own feminism, I guess. But the other women were just embarrassed, and the men uncomprehending. It was my own fault, getting pregnant again, a *personal* matter, not something you should take to the union. There was no word in 1949 for "sex discrimination."

Besides, it was almost a relief: I had begun to feel so guilty working, and I really wasn't getting anywhere in that job. I was more than ready to embrace the feminine mystique. I took a cooking course and started studying the suburban real-estate ads. And the next time the census taker came around, I was living in that old Charles Addams house we were fixing up, on the Hudson River in Rockland County. And the children numbered three. When the census taker asked my occupation, I said self-consciously, virtuously, with only the faintest stirrings of protest from that part of me I'd turned my back on—"housewife."

Source: Betty Friedan, "The Way We Were—1949," *New York Magazine* (1974), in Friedan, *It Changed My Life* (New York: Dell, 1976), 33–37.

The 1950s were characterized by a pervasive, indeed pernicious, insistence that women's proper place was in the home. There was nothing new about this idea. What Betty Friedan tagged the *feminine mystique* of the 1950s—that "the highest value and the only commitment for women is the fulfillment of their own femininity"—bore remarkable similarities to the nineteenth-century's cult of true womanhood. But women's lives had changed dramatically since the nineteenth century, due to increased access to education and jobs, a declining birthrate, and the greater availability of consumer goods and services. It was much harder to convince women to stay in their homes in the 1950s than it had been in the 1850s. In fact, the shrillness with which the message of domesticity was trumpeted may have been in inverse relation to how far women had already strayed from total identification with the home.

The updated version of the cult of domesticity drew on new elements of twentieth-century science and culture, even Freudian psychology, to give it more force. Television, popular music, films, and advertising depicted career women as social and sexual misfits. As the postwar consumer culture took off, the media emphasized that women's primary role was to buy appliances and other consumer goods for home and family. "Love is said in many ways," ran an ad promoting a brand of toilet paper. Asked another, "Can a woman ever feel right cooking on a dirty range?"

While the feminine mystique held cultural sway in the postwar period, not all housewives were as unhappy or neurotic as Friedan later implied in her 1963 bestseller. Many women found constructive outlets for their energy in groups like the League of Women Voters, the PTA, the Junior League, and church women's groups. Blue-collar housewives proudly filled in census forms with "occupation: housewife"; unlike their mothers and unmarried sisters, they did not have to take routine employment outside the home. More fundamentally, not all American families could, or did, live by these norms. The ideals of suburban domesticity were out of reach, or totally irrelevant, to many minorities, inner-city residents, recent immigrants, rural Americans, and those on the margins of mainstream American culture, such as homosexuals. Once again, there was a large gap between popular culture and the reality of American lives.

Women at Work. Another way to widen our view beyond a domestic-bound 1950s is to confront the interesting and somewhat contradictory fact that at the height of the feminine mystique more than one-third of American women held jobs outside the home. As the service sector expanded, there was a steady demand for workers in fields traditionally filled by women. Economist Eli Ginzberg called the dramatic rise in the number

Home Life: One Reality
This young mother in New Rochelle, a suburb of New York City, was photographed in 1955. Her frenzied situation hints at why 24,000 American women responded to a 1960 *Redbook* magazine article entitled "Why Young Mothers Feel Trapped."

and kind of women who worked for pay outside the home "the single most outstanding phenomenon of our century."

The increase in the number of working women was paralleled by another change of equally significant proportion—the dramatic rise in the number of older, married, middle-class women who took jobs. At the turn of the century, the average female worker was a young recent immigrant who worked only until she married. By mid-century, the average woman worker was in her forties, married, and had children in school. In 1940 only 15 percent of all wives worked. This percentage had doubled by 1960 and reached 40 percent by 1970.

Many women entered the paid labor force to supplement their family income. Changing consumption habits increasingly required two incomes to maintain a certain standard of living. The wages that many men earned even in the prosperous 1950s and 1960s could not pay for all the necessities of new middle-class life—cars, houses, vacations, and a college education for their children. For minority households, multiple wage earners were often necessary just to get by.

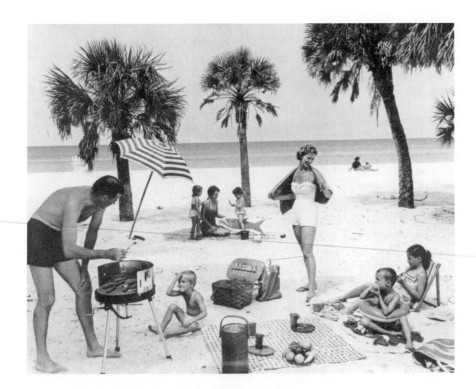

At the Beach

This 1958 photograph of Longboat Key, Florida, by Joe Steinmetz is packed with so many cultural clichés about family life in the 1950s that it is hard to know whether it is real or fake.

How could the society of the 1950s so steadfastly uphold the domestic ideal while an increasing number of wives and mothers took jobs? In many ways, the dramatic increase was kept invisible by the women themselves. Fearing public disapproval of their decisions, such women usually interpreted their work in very individual or family-oriented terms: "Of course I believe a woman's place is at home, but I took this job to save for college for our children." Moreover, when women took on jobs outside the home, they invariably maintained full responsibility for child care and household management, which allowed families and society to avoid the full implications of women's new roles. As one overburdened woman noted, she now had "two full-time jobs instead of just one—underpaid clerical worker and unpaid housekeeper." The absence of an active feminist movement in the 1940s and 1950s meant that few public figures or organizations paid attention to this major demographic and social shift. Similarly, few popular heroines from movies, television, or popular culture encouraged women's autonomy—quite the contrary. Women were left to cope on their own.

The Fifties: The Way We Were?

Like the 1920s, the 1950s are defined almost entirely in cultural terms. But once again, this emphasis on affluence, popular culture, and consumption is too super-ficial for understanding such a complex period of economic and social transformation. The popularized view of the "happy days" of the 1950s (a "decade" which really stretched from 1945 to the early 1960s) reflects only a tenuous rendering of reality.

In the popular mind the 1950s often represents the norm of American society. Families were close-knit and intact; children were happy; the economy was growing; and, despite the fear of nuclear annihilation, the United States was secure in its position as the strongest country, both economically and morally, in the world. Given all that has happened since the 1950s, changes in American family, political, and social life are often seen as declines from this ideal.

But perhaps the fifties were the aberration, not the norm—the result of a unique congruence of circumstances that would have been difficult to sustain on a permanent basis. The postwar baby boom was certainly an aberration in a two-hundred year trend toward smaller families. The stability of marriages in the 1940s and 1950s was also atypical in light of the liberalization of social mores in the 1920s and 1930s and the increasing divorce rates after the mid-1960s. Scarred by memories of war and depression-era dislocations, and scared by the ambiguities of living in the atomic age, this postwar generation embraced family life with a vengeance. When conditions changed, this profamily orientation slipped back more in line with the diversity and pluralism of the rest of the century.

Perhaps the greatest aberration, and the reason why

our view of the 1950s as the norm is so pernicious, is that the economic base on which this affluence rested was predicated on a set of international economic conditions that could not continue indefinitely. When the war-devastated economies of Japan and West Germany were rebuilt, they took advantage of new technology to compete, and eventually challenge, American economic supremacy in one industry after another: steel, rubber, automobiles, electronics, footwear, and textiles. So too did emerging industrial centers in the Pacific Rim, such as Korea, Hong Kong, and Singapore. Unfortunately, since the economic abundance and hegemony of the 1950s is taken as the norm, any decline is seen as a disturbing loss of American power and economic strength, rather than a return to a more normal state of economic affairs.

There are other ways that the stereotypes of the 1950s are misleading, if not downright false. The picture painted in popular culture of affluence unbounded hides, indeed makes invisible, those Americans who did not share equally in this postwar American dream. Many people—displaced factory workers, destitute old people, female heads of households, blacks and Hispanics—watched the affluent society from the outside and wondered why they were not permitted to share in its bounty. Not until the publication of Michael Harrington's *The Other America* in 1962 did Americans begin to realize that, in the richest country of the world, more than a quarter of the population was poor.

The contrasts between suburban affluence and the "other America," between the lure of the city for the poor and minorities and the grim reality of its segregated existence, between a heightened emphasis on domesticity and widening opportunities for women, would spawn protest and change in the turbulent 1960s. Amid the booming prosperity of the late 1940s and 1950s, however, these fundamental social and economic contradictions were barely noticed.

★

Summary

Postwar affluence rested on several foundations, especially the global hegemony enjoyed by the United States in the immediate postwar period. Federal intervention in the economy, especially in the form of defense spending, fueled prosperity, as did spending for consumer-goods. Consumer spending played an especially important role in the reconversion to a peacetime economy. Technological change stimulated productivity, notably in agriculture and industry.

Much of the economic activity in the postwar period concentrated in the growing metropolitan areas, especially in their expanding suburbs. Metropolitan areas exhibited a striking dichotomy, as poor migrants settled in the inner city while the more affluent took their families to the suburbs. For the new middle class, the postwar period brought a higher standard of living and access to an array of new consumer goods. Blacks, Puerto Ricans, and Mexican-Americans rarely shared in this affluence, however.

The structural changes transforming the American economy had a strong impact on individual Americans. White-collar workers now outnumbered blue-collar employees, and more women joined the work force. The labor movement could not maintain its momentum from the 1930s. Many of the smoldering contradictions of the postwar period—an unequally shared affluence, institutionalized racism that limited opportunities for nonwhite Americans, and tensions in women's lives— soon surfaced in the social protest movements of the 1960s.

TOPIC FOR RESEARCH

Poverty in the Age of Affluence

In 1962, Michael Harrington published *The Other America*, which described the persistence of poverty in postwar America. Assume you have been asked to review this book for a newspaper in 1962. You suspect that most of your readers will be surprised to learn that more than one-quarter of the population live in poverty and that the majority of the poor are white. Describe the findings of the book and analyze how successful it is in presenting its argument. How can you reconcile Harrington's picture with the general view of the 1950s as a period of unbounded affluence? Reflect on why the poor are so invisible and why modern capitalist societies, even those with welfare states, have been unable (or unwilling) to address the persistence of poverty.

For general background, sources on the history of poverty and social welfare include Michael B. Katz, *In the Shadow of the Poorhouse* (1986); Frances Fox Piven and Richard A. Cloward, *Poor People's Movements* (1977) and *Regulating the Poor* (1971); James Patterson, *America's Struggle Against Poverty, 1900–1980* (1981); and Oscar Lewis, *La Vida: A Puerto Rican Family in the Culture of Poverty* (1965). The classic text on the age of affluence in the 1950s remains John Kenneth Galbraith, *The Affluent Society* (1958).

BIBLIOGRAPHY

General introductions to postwar society include John Diggins, *The Proud Decades: America in War and Peace, 1941–1960* (1988); Elaine Tyler May, *Homeward Bound: American Families in the Cold War Era* (1988); William E. Leuchtenberg, *A Troubled Feast* (1979); James Gilbert, *Another Chance* (2nd ed., 1986); and William O'Neill, *American High* (1986).

Technology and Economic Change

For overviews on the economic changes of the postwar period, see W. Elliot Brownlee, *Dynamics of Ascent* (1979); David P. Calleo, *The Imperious Economy* (1982); and Harold G. Vatter, *The U.S. Economy in the 1950s* (1963). Robert Kuttner, *The End of Laissez-Faire* (1991) provides ample background on the Bretton Woods system. Herman P. Miller, *Rich Man, Poor Man* (1971) and Gabriel Kolko, *Wealth and Power in America* (1962), discuss inequality in income distribution. Michael Harrington, *The Other America* (1962), documents the persistence of poverty. John Kenneth Galbraith's lively books, *American Capitalism* (1952), *The Affluent Society* (1958), and *The New Industrial State* (1967), shaped much of the public discussion of the economy in the period. Robert L. Heilbroner, *The Limits of American Capitalism* (1965), is equally readable and more critical.

John L. Shover, *First Majority–Last Minority* (1976), analyzes the transformation of rural life in America. It can be supplemented by Willard W. Cochrane and Mary E. Ryan, *American Farm Policy, 1948–1973* (1976), and Gilbert C. Fite, *American Farmers: the New Minority* (1981). David Brody, *Workers in Industrial America* (1980); David Montgomery, *Workers' Control in America* (1979); and James R. Green, *The World of the Worker* (1980), provide overviews of labor in the twentieth century. On the impact of technology and automation, see Elting E. Morison, *From Know-how to Nowhere* (1974), and David F. Noble, *Forces of Production: A Social History of Industrial Automation* (1984). Harry Braverman, *Labor and Monopoly Capital* (1974) looks at the degradation of work from a Marxist perspective. In Studs Terkel's superb oral history, *Working* (1974), people from all walks of life talk about what they do and how they feel about it.

The most influential study of the new middle class remains David Reisman, with Nathan Glazer and Ruel Denney, *The Lonely Crowd* (1950). William H. Whyte, *The Organization Man* (1956), provides a similar perspective. See also the

work of C. Wright Mills, especially *White Collar* (1951) and *The Power Elite* (1956). Samuel Lubbell describes middle-class voting patterns in *The Future of American Politics* (1956) and *Revolt of the Moderates* (1956).

Alfred D. Chandler, *The Visible Hand* (1977), is the definitive history of American corporate structure and strategy. Myra Wilkin, *The Maturing of Multinational Enterprise* (1974), and Richard J. Barnet and Ronald E. Muller, *Global Reach* (1974), describe American business abroad. See also Robert Sobel, *The Age of Giant Corporations* (1972), and the early sections of Barry Bluestein and Bennett Harrison, *The Deindustrialization of America* (1982).

Cities and Suburbs

Zane L. Miller, *The Urbanization of Modern America* (1973); Blake McKelvey, *The Emergence of Metropolitan America, 1915–1966* (1968); Jon C. Teaford, *The Twentieth Century American City* (1986); and Kenneth Fox, *Metropolitan America: Urban Life and Urban Policy in the United States, 1940–1980* (1985), are strong overviews of the growth of urban areas. See also Sam Bass Warner, Jr., *The Urban Wilderness* (1972), for a more interpretive view.

Kenneth Jackson, *Crabgrass Frontier* (1985), provides an overview of suburban development, which can be supplemented by Jon C. Teaford, *City and Suburb: The Political Fragmentation of Metropolitan America, 1850–1970* (1979) and Robert Fishman, *Bourgeois Utopias* (1987). Michael N. Danielson, *The Politics of Exclusion* (1976) describes how blacks were kept out of suburbia. Zane Miller, *Suburb* (1982), is a case study of Forest Park, Ohio. Herbert Gans, *The Levittowners* (1967), describes the two years he spent as a participant-observer in that New Jersey community. Bennett M. Berger, *Working-Class Suburb* (1960), and Scott Donaldson, *The Suburban Myth* (1969), question the homogeneity of the suburban experience. Mark H. Rose, *Interstate* (1979) describes the politics of building the highway system.

Nicholas Lemann offers an overview of postwar black migration in *The Promised Land* (1991). Herbert J. Gans, *The Urban Villagers* (1962), tells the story of an Italian community in Boston displaced by urban renewal. Jane Jacobs, *The Death and Life of Great American Cities* (1961), is an opinionated look at urban problems. Stephen Thernstrom, *The Other Bostonians* (1973), suggests why blacks in urban areas did not find upward social mobility. Robert A. Caro's biography of Robert Moses, *The Power Broker* (1974), provides a case study of the impact of highways on the landscape of metropolitan New York City through his career. Books that treat the rise of the Sunbelt are Kirkpatrick Sale, *Power Shift* (1975), and Richard Bernard and Bradley Rice, eds., *Sunbelt Cities* (1983).

American Society During the Baby Boom

Books that highlight social and economic developments in the 1950s include Godfrey Hodgson, *America In Our Time* (1976); Carl Degler, *Affluence and Anxiety* (1968); and David Potter, *People of Plenty* (1954). See also Douglas T. Miller and Marion Nowak, *The Fifties: the Way We Really Were* (1977);

Jeffrey Hart, *When the Going Was Good! American Life in the Fifties* (1982); and Paul Carter, *Another Part of the Fifties* (1983).

For popular culture, George Lipsitz, *Time Passages: Collective Memory and American Popular Culture* (1991) surveys postwar television, music, film, and popular narrative. Eric Barnouw, *The Image Empire* (1970), chronicles the impact of television. Other treatments of the mass media include Marshall McLuhan, *Understanding Media* (1964); Todd Gitlin, *Inside Prime Time* (1983); Frank Mankiewicz and Joel Swerdlow, *Remote Control: Television and the Manipulation of American Life* (1978); and Edward J. Epstein, *News From Nowhere* (1973). Robert Sklar, *Movie-Made America* (1975), shows how movies reacted to the threat from television. See also Peter Biskind, *Seeing Is Believing: How Hollywood Taught Us to Stop Worrying and Love the Fifties* (1983). Vance Packard's influential unmasking of the advertising industry, *The Hidden Persuaders* (1957), can be supplemented by Stephen Fox, *The Mirror Makers* (1984).

Richard Easterlin, *American Baby Boom in Historical Perspective* (1962), and *Birth and Future: The Impact of Numbers on Personal Welfare* (1980), analyze the demographic changes, as does Landon Y. Jones, *Great Expectations: America and the Baby Boom Generation* (1980). See also Michael P. Nichols, *Turning Forty in the Eighties* (1986). Developments in medicine are treated in James Bordley and A. McGehee Harvey, *Two Centuries of American Medicine* (1967) and Jane S. Smith, *Patenting the Sun: Polio and the Salk Vaccine* (1990). Diane Ravitch describes education from 1945 to 1980 in *The Troubled Crusade* (1983). James Gilbert, *A Cycle of Outrage* (1986), looks at juvenile delinquency in the 1950s.

Elaine May's *Homeward Bound* is the best introduction to postwar family culture. See also Wini Breines, *Young, White, and Miserable: Growing Up Female in the Fifties* (1992). Betty Friedan, *The Feminine Mystique* (1963), provides a witty perspective on the lives of educated suburban women, which should be contrasted with Mirra Komarovsky, *Blue Collar Marriage* (1962). William H. Chafe, *The American Woman* (1972), and Carl Degler, *At Odds* (1982), survey women's public and private roles. Alice Kessler-Harris, *Out to Work* (1982), concentrates on women at work. Glenna Matthews, *Just A Housewife* (1987), and Susan Strasser, *Never Done* (1982), look at housewives and housework, respectively. Eugenia Kaledin surveys women in the 1950s in *Mothers and More* (1984), and Barbara Ehrenreich, *Hearts of Men* (1983), offers a provocative view of men's lives in the decade.

TIMELINE

1944	Bretton Woods economic conference World Bank and International Monetary Fund (IMF) founded
1946	Dr. Benjamin Spock publishes *Baby and Child Care*
1947	Levittown, New York, built General Agreement on Tariffs and Trade (GATT) UNIVAC computer developed
1948	Television's breakthrough year; CBS and NBC begin regular programming
1954	Polio vaccine developed by Dr. Jonas Salk First McDonald's opens
1955	AFL and CIO reunited Disneyland opens in Anaheim, California
1956	Interstate Highway Act Elvis Presley popularizes rock and roll
1957	Peak of postwar baby boom
1958	Brooklyn Dodgers move to Los Angeles Jet air travel introduced
1959	Nixon and Khrushchev's "Kitchen Debate"
1963	California passes New York as most populous state
1965	Immigration Act abolishes national quota system

Turbulent Sixties

Robert Rauschenberg's 1963 oil and silkscreen canvas *Kite*,
prefigures the turmoil that rocked America during the 1960s,
both on the domestic front and internationally with Vietnam.
(©Robert Rauschenberg/VAGA New York)

30 *Kennedy, Johnson, and the Liberal Consensus, 1960–1968*

As Franklin Roosevelt had reassured a nation that there was nothing to fear but fear itself in 1933, so did John Fitzgerald Kennedy seem to speak to a desire for national purpose in his 1961 inaugural address. "Let the word go forth from this time and place, to friend and foe alike, that the torch has been passed to a new generation of Americans, born in this century, tempered by war, disciplined by a hard and bitter peace, proud of our ancient heritage." He challenged his audience: "Ask not what your country can do for you, ask what you can do for your country." Without offering any radical or sweeping programs, John Kennedy fostered an atmosphere conducive to challenging the status quo, a climate that has been called the "politics of expectation." The social and political changes set in motion by this expansive national mood provide the focus for the next two chapters. This chapter examines the Kennedy and Johnson administrations and the American experience in Vietnam through 1968; Chapter 31 looks at the civil rights movement, the youth rebellion, and the revival of feminism.

The expansion of New Deal social welfare programs and the continuation of the Cold War were the twin pillars of postwar liberalism. The liberal conception of the state embraced government spending as a positive good. According to Keynesian economics, such spending served as a stimulus to economic growth. In addition, it also worked as a means toward social progress, spreading the abundance of a mass consumption economy to ever wider numbers of the citizenry. In essence, liberalism aimed to use the fiscal powers of the state to redress the imbalances of the private economy without directly challenging capitalism.

During the first half of the 1960s, the Democratic administrations of John Kennedy and Lyndon Johnson orchestrated the completion of much of the New Deal/Fair Deal agenda while also maintaining an activist stance abroad. A burst of legislation in 1964–1965 represented the high tide of postwar liberalism. Soon after, however, the growing American involvement in Vietnam began to crowd all other issues off the domestic and international stage. As the country tried simultaneously to wage, in historian Garry Wills's apt phrasing, a "welfare" and a "warfare" state, it found itself embroiled in domestic controversy that irrevocably shattered the liberal consensus.

John Kennedy and the Politics of Expectation

Franklin Roosevelt's enormously successful years in office had heightened expectations for presidential leadership, and by the 1960s citizens increasingly looked to Washington and the president for solutions to international, national, and local problems. Few presidents came to Washington more primed for action than John Fitzgerald Kennedy. Yet the accomplishments of what Kennedy speechwriter Theodore Sorenson first called the "New Frontier" were rather meager. Much of the Kennedy presidency was reactive and improvisational, far too often responding to events and crises rather than steering a clear ideological course.

The New Politics and the 1960 Campaign

The 1960 campaign marked the introduction to the national scene of political practices called the *new politics*. Charisma, style, and personality, rather than issues and platforms, were the hallmarks of the new politics. Although this new political style had roots in the nineteenth century, it took on new force when joined with the power of the modern media in the twentieth. Politicians paid special attention to the ability of television to reach individual voters. (By 1960, 88 percent of the nation's households owned at least one TV set.) Professional media consultants now advised candidates on their proper image, and professional pollsters not only told candidates whether they were leading their opponents, but also what issues to stress in order to get elected.

Originally developed in California in the late 1940s and early 1950s, this political style was well suited to a state that was growing so fast that it did not have entrenched political machines or active party organizations. The spread of the new politics contributed to a decline in the role of traditional political party organizations at the national level. Candidates now targeted their appeal to enthusiastic amateurs outside the traditional party organization, rather than to the ward bosses, state committee officials, and party machines that once delivered the votes on election day. By using the media, campaigns could bypass the party structures to touch, if only with a 30-second commercial, the ordinary citizen.

Running such campaigns took money, however, and the required funds often far exceeded those available through the traditional party coffers. Once candidates began to seek campaign funds from other sources, such as wealthy donors or mass mailings, the influence of political parties diminished even further. In addition, party loyalty declined as growing numbers of voters identified themselves as independents, a major shift from patterns of highly partisan political behavior in the nineteenth and early twentieth centuries. These factors set the context for the 1960 election.

The Republicans Choose Nixon. The crucial question for the Republicans in 1960 was whether they could hold on to the presidency without the popular Dwight D. Eisenhower. The Twenty-second Amendment now limited a president to two terms. A Republican-controlled Congress had passed the measure in 1951 to prevent another long-term presidency such as Franklin Roosevelt's. Ironically, it precluded another Eisenhower term.

The Republicans turned without opposition to Vice-President Richard M. Nixon, who, like a good 1950s junior executive, had patiently waited for his turn at the top. Nixon campaigned for an updated ver-

sion of Eisenhower's policies, carefully staking out a position between the Republican conservative wing, now led by Senator Barry M. Goldwater of Arizona, and the liberal wing represented by New York Governor Nelson A. Rockefeller. Nixon was hampered, however, by the lukewarm support he received from Eisenhower. Asked whether Nixon had helped make any major policy decisions in his administration, Eisenhower replied, "If you give me a week I might think of one."

The Democrats Select Kennedy. After two unsuccessful tries with Adlai Stevenson as their candidate, the Democrats turned to Senator John Fitzgerald Kennedy of Massachusetts, who beat out Senators Hubert Humphrey of Minnesota and Lyndon Johnson of Texas

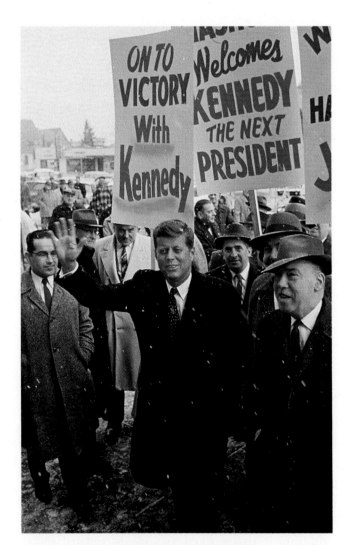

The New Politics Comes to New Hampshire
John Fitzgerald Kennedy, the first Catholic ever elected president, was also the first Democratic presidential nominee from New England in over one hundred years. Here the Massachusetts senator campaigned in neighboring New Hampshire, whose primary he won handily in February 1960.

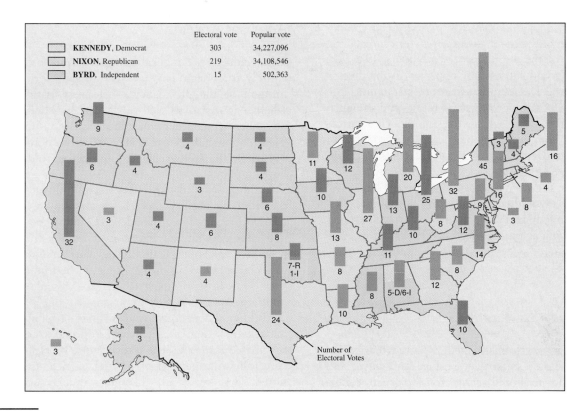

	Electoral vote	Popular vote
KENNEDY, Democrat	303	34,227,096
NIXON, Republican	219	34,108,546
BYRD, Independent	15	502,363

MAP 30.1

The Election of 1960

The Kennedy-Nixon contest produced the closest popular vote since 1884. Kennedy won 12 states, including Illinois, by less than 2 percent of the two-party vote tally; he lost 6 others, including California, by a similarly small margin. Fifteen electors cast their votes for the Independent Democrat, Harry F. Byrd. Despite his razor-thin margin of victory, Kennedy won 303 electoral votes, the same number as Truman in 1948, showing how the electoral college vote can be a misleading indicator of popular support.

for the nomination. Johnson joined the ticket as the vice-presidential nominee. Kennedy, an alumnus of Harvard and a World War II hero, had inherited his love of politics from his grandfathers, both of whom had been colorful Irish-Catholic politicians in Boston. His wealthy father, Joseph P. Kennedy, had headed the Securities and Exchange Commission and served as ambassador to Great Britain under Roosevelt. First elected to Congress in 1946, John Kennedy moved to the Senate in 1952. Ambitious, hard-driving and deeply aware of style, the forty-three-year-old candidate made full use of his many advantages to become, as novelist Norman Mailer put it, "our leading man." Besides his youth, Kennedy's main liability was his Catholicism: at that point, the United States had never elected a Catholic president.

Candidate Kennedy took the new politics to the national level in 1960, and his campaign altered the nature of American presidential contests. His family's wealth and the contributions he raised from sources outside traditional party donors paid for this expensive campaign. For example, his campaign bought its own airplane. Thanks to his media advisers and to his youthful and attractive personality, he projected a superb television image. His mastery of this method enabled him to appeal directly to voters, rather than just through the Democratic party.

A series of four televised debates between the two principal candidates, a major innovation of the 1960 campaign, reflected how important the media was becoming to political life. Nixon, a far less photogenic personality than Kennedy and at an added disadvantage because he was recovering from a minor illness, looked sallow and unshaven under the intense studio lights. Kennedy, in contrast, looked vigorous, cool, and self-confident on the TV screen, and he dispelled voters' doubts that he was not as well prepared for the presidency as the former vice-president. Public reaction demonstrated that appearances swayed political perceptions: voters who listened to the first debate on the radio concluded that Nixon had won, whereas TV viewers judged in Kennedy's favor.

Despite the ground Kennedy picked up in the debates, he won only the narrowest of victories, receiving 49.7 percent of the popular vote to Nixon's 49.5 percent. Kennedy had successfully appealed to the diverse elements of the Democratic coalition, attracting large proportions of Catholic voters and blacks and strengthening his party's appeal to the middle class; vice-presidential nominee Lyndon Johnson brought in southern white Democrats. Yet only 120,000 votes out of a total of 69 million cast separated the two candidates, and the shift of a few thousand votes in key states such as Illinois would have reversed the election results. Although Kennedy had campaigned on a promise to get America moving again, the electoral results hardly gave him a mandate for sweeping change.

The Kennedy Style

Unlike Eisenhower, John Kennedy believed the federal government should be strong, visible, and active, and that the president should set the tone for such leadership. Kennedy's activist bent attracted unusually talented and ambitious people to his administration. Robert S. McNamara, former president of the Ford Motor Company, introduced modern management techniques to the Department of Defense. Republican banker C. Douglas Dillon brought a corporate manager's desire for expanded markets and stable economic growth to the Department of the Treasury. The president's younger brother Robert took over the Department of Justice as attorney general, and his brother-in-law Sargent Shriver headed the popular Peace Corps. A host of "honorary Kennedys," trusted advisers and academics from leading universities, flocked to Washington to join the New Frontier. These advisers, dubbed "the best and the brightest" by journalist David Halberstam, also played a major role in plotting the Vietnam war.

The Kennedy administration, christened "Camelot" by the admiring media after the mythical realm of King Arthur in the popular musical of the same name, projected an aura of youth and energy. Secretary of State Dean Rusk recalled that Kennedy was "on fire, and he set people around him on fire." Vigor was one of Kennedy's favorite words, and he expected his appointees to move quickly. "The deadline for everything is the day before yesterday," exclaimed one cabinet member. House Speaker Sam Rayburn remained skeptical about this vigorous approach to government. Kennedy's people "might be every bit as intelligent as you say," he told his old friend Lyndon Johnson, "but I'd feel a whole lot better about them if just one of them had run for sheriff once."

Activism Abroad

John Kennedy's inaugural address was devoted almost entirely to foreign affairs, suggesting the priorities he brought to the presidency. "Let every nation know, whether it wishes us well or ill, that we shall pay any price, bear any burden, meet any hardship, support any friend, oppose any foe to assure the survival and success of liberty." Kennedy remained a resolute Cold Warrior. Foreign policy, not domestic affairs, captured the attention of most of those who flocked to Washington to join the New Frontier.

During the 1960 presidential campaign, Kennedy had charged that the Eisenhower administration had permitted the Soviet Union to develop superior nuclear capabilities. Once in office, however, he found that no such "missile gap" existed. In fact, Eisenhower had built up America's nuclear arsenal at the expense of conventional weapons. In his first national security message to Congress, Kennedy proposed a new policy of *flexible response*. The nation must be prepared "to deter all wars, general or limited, nuclear or conventional, large or small." Congress quickly acceded to Kennedy's military requests, boosting the number of combat-ready army divisions from eleven to sixteen and authorizing the construction of ten Polaris nuclear submarines and other warships. As Kennedy intended, the result was a major expansion of the military-industrial complex, as thousands of workers were recruited to build new weapons systems and military equipment.

These measures were designed to deter nuclear or conventional attacks by the Soviet Union. But what about the new kind of warfare, the wars of "national liberation" that had broken out in many Third World countries? Kennedy had a plan for these too: he adopted the new military doctrine of *counterinsurgency*. U.S. Army Special Forces, called the Green Berets for their distinctive headgear, received intensive training on how to repel the random and small-scale attacks typical of guerrilla warfare. The Vietnam war soon provided a testing ground for counterinsurgency techniques.

The Peace Corps. The New Frontier program that most captured the public imagination was the Peace Corps. The idea, Kennedy explained on March 1, 1961, was to create "a pool of trained American men and women" to be sent "overseas by the United States government or through private organizations and institutions to help foreign countries meet their urgent needs for skilled manpower." Thousands of idealistic Americans, many of them recent college graduates, responded to the call, agreeing to devote two or more years to teaching English to Philippine schoolchildren or helping African villagers obtain adequate supplies of water.

Kennedy also won congressional support for his ex-

AMERICAN VOICES

A Peace Corps Veteran Remembers *Thaine Allison*

The Peace Corps was the Kennedy program that most captured the nation's, and the world's, attention. Volunteers in parts of Africa were called *Wakina Kennedy* ("one who walks with Kennedy") and *los hijos de Kennedy* ("children of Kennedy") in Latin America. Thaine Allison and his wife spent from 1962 to 1964 in Borneo as Peace Corps volunteers.

When I was a kid, my parents took me to the YMCA to hear some missionaries speak about their experiences working and living in China. Their stories were fascinating. That's where I first started thinking that I might like to live in another country someday. When I went to college, I got involved with the Methodist Church youth movement and the option came up to work overseas as a missionary. But I didn't want to proselytize.

When the Peace Corps was announced, it just felt like the right thing to do after graduation. I had just gotten married and my wife wanted to get out of Iowa, where she'd lived all her life. At Chico State there were five graduates that year from the brand-new school of agriculture. Three of us went into the Peace Corps. The department chair was a bit upset that we were turning down real jobs.

When we found out we were going to Borneo, my dad said, "You guys quit running around. You sound like the wild man from Borneo."

My wife was assigned to teach English at a village school and I was an agricultural extension agent. I was told what the British colonial government was trying to do for agricultural development in my area and instructed to just go do it. "If you screw up," the Peace Corps said, "we'll see what we can do about it. Write us once a month and let us know how you're coming along." We were four hours by boat from the nearest volunteer.

I worked with Chinese and Muslim farmers. About a third of them were doing fairly well in that they had enough to eat: a lot of rice, some fresh fish, and sometimes dog or monkey. The rest grew just enough food to survive. I learned to speak Malay in training but it didn't help when I visited the Chinese farmers. They would say, "You Yankee Red dog, you come to talk to me and you don't even know my language." I took lessons in Mandarin Chinese from a school principal in the area and then went back to the Chinese farmers. They said, "You Yankee Red dog, since our language is obviously too difficult for you, why don't you just speak in English to us?"

I tried to tell the poorer farmers about ways to irrigate their crops, about the benefit of planting paddy rice instead of hill rice, and helped start some vegetable gardens. But much of the time, I never felt like I really knew what was happening. It seemed like it was more important that I show up in the villages for ceremonial purposes, rather than for any-

thing I was able to do. These were people who wore loincloths and were barely able to grasp the notion that I had come from far away to help them, and there I was—asking them to plant their rows straight.

I took my wife with me to one village where they had never seen a white woman before. The women gathered around her and wanted to talk to her and touch her. I asked some of them to watch after her while I went to look at some crops and she had fifty women and kids following after her. She couldn't have gotten lost if she tried. In many of the villages, they'd never seen anyone with hairy arms before so they all liked to pet my arms.

Why my wife and I didn't have children was totally baffling to them. When we first got there, we used the excuse that we had just gotten married. But after we'd been there awhile and my wife obviously wasn't pregnant, they began asking questions. I knew I had gotten pretty good speaking Malay when I could tease them about Americans being like elephants, which take three years to gestate. When the time came for us to go on vacation, a group of women showed up at our door and gave my wife some money. They said, "We don't know what you have but we want some because we don't want any more babies."

Source: Karen Schwarz, *What You Can Do for Your Country: An Oral History of the Peace Corps* (New York: Morrow, 1991), 38, 44–45.

panded program of economic aid to foreign countries. The State Department's Agency for International Development coordinated foreign aid for the Third World, and its Food for Peace program distributed surplus agricultural products to developing nations. In March 1961

the president proposed "a ten-year plan for the Americas" called the Alliance for Progress, a $100 billion partnership between the United States and the republics of Latin America designed to reduce the appeal of communism in that region.

Reflecting his activist approach to presidential leadership, Kennedy often turned for foreign policy advice to a small circle of personal aides rather than relying on formal Pentagon and State Department channels. Taking the institutional changes of the 1947 National Security Act a step further, Kennedy enhanced the authority of the National Security Council by moving its chief directly into the White House. Such shifts further concentrated foreign policy initiation in the presidency.

The Bay of Pigs Invasion. The nation's strengthened military arsenal and streamlined defense establishment failed to bring Kennedy the universal diplomatic success he had anticipated. In April 1961, Kennedy confronted his first crisis. Its immediate roots lay in the January 1961 statement by Soviet Premier Nikita Khrushchev that conflicts in Vietnam, Cuba, and elsewhere were "wars of national liberation" worthy of Soviet support. Kennedy took Khrushchev's words as a challenge, especially as they applied to Cuba.

Ever since Cuba had won its independence in the Spanish-American War, it had been economically and politically dominated by its powerful neighbor to the

north. In 1956, American companies owned 80 percent of Cuba's utilities, 90 percent of its mining operations, and 40 percent of its sugar plantations. On New Year's Day in 1959, Fidel Castro overthrew the unpopular dictatorship of Fulgencio Batista and called for a revolution to reshape Cuban society. He nationalized all its banks and industries, prompting the United States to embargo all exports to Cuba.

Concerned about Castro's growing friendliness with the Soviet Union, in early 1961 Kennedy used plans originally drawn up by the Eisenhower administration to dispatch Cuban exiles to foment an anti-Castro uprising. The invaders had been trained by the Central Intelligence Agency, but they were ill prepared for their task. After landing at Cuba's Bay of Pigs on April 17, the tiny force of 1,600 men was crushed by Castro's troops. Symptomatic of the inept CIA planning, pilots in Nicaragua who were supposed to provide air cover for the landing forces forgot to set their watches ahead to Cuban time and arrived at the beach an hour too soon. The anticipated rebellion never occurred.

The Bay of Pigs fiasco blighted the new administra-

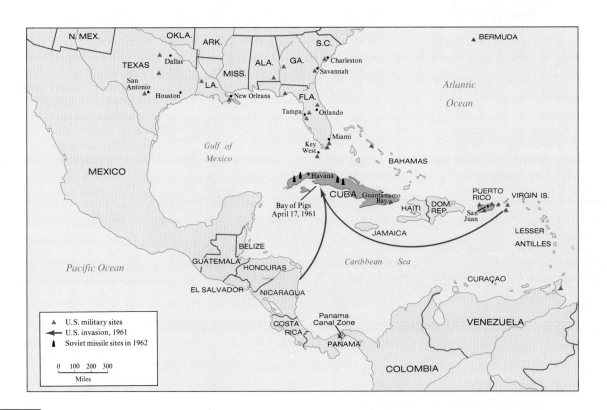

MAP 30.2

The United States and Cuba, 1961–1962
Fidel Castro's takeover in Cuba in 1959 soon brought cold war tensions to the Caribbean basin. In 1961 the United States tried unsuccessfully to overthrow Castro's regime by supporting an invasion of Cuban exiles launched from Nicaragua. In 1962 a major confrontation with the Soviet Union occurred over Soviet missile sites in Cuba. The Soviets removed the missiles after President Kennedy ordered a naval blockade of the island, which lies just 90 miles south of Florida.

tion with an embarrassing failure and cast doubts on Kennedy's activist approach to international affairs. It also affected U.S.-Soviet relations. Soviet leader Khrushchev interpreted the invasion as evidence of the United States's intent to launch a full-scale invasion of Cuba and stepped up military aid to Castro to protect against this contingency. A more subtle legacy was Khrushchev's view that he did not have to take the new American president seriously as an adversary.

The Berlin Wall. Kennedy's military response to the threat of a communist regime just 90 miles to the south confirmed how Cold War assumptions shaped foreign policy in the early 1960s, both in the Western Hemisphere and elsewhere. Kennedy never lost his preoccupation with the Soviet Union. In June 1961, weakened by the botched Cuban invasion, he met with Khrushchev in Vienna to discuss a test ban treaty, the civil war in Laos, and the status of Berlin. At the meeting, both men were truculent, especially about Berlin, which was part of a larger and longstanding disagreement about the status of Germany in postwar Europe. Khrushchev wanted it declared a "free city," which would mean the withdrawal of both Soviet and Western occupation forces, but he did not get his way.

Just days after this meeting, Khrushchev heightened international tensions by deploying soldiers to sever East Berlin from the western sector of the city. Determined to confront the Soviets publicly, Kennedy declared in a televised speech to the nation on July 25 that Berlin was the "great testing place of Western courage and will" and announced that he would ask Congress for large increases in military spending, a massive fallout shelter program, and the authority to mobilize the National Guard, call up reserves, and extend enlistments in response to this and future international crises. In mid-August, the East Germans under Soviet supervision erected the Berlin wall to stop the exodus of East Germans to the West and began policing the border with guards instructed to shoot to kill those trying to escape. Kennedy later visited the Berlin wall, where he invoked the solidarity of the free world by declaring "Ich bin ein Berliner" ("I am a Berliner"). The Berlin Wall stood as the supreme symbol of the Cold War until the fall of 1989 when it, and Soviet domination of Eastern Europe, crumbled.

The Cuban Missile Crisis. Tensions between the superpowers soon erupted again: for thirteen days in October 1962 the United States and the Soviet Union stood at the brink of war. The Soviets had stepped up their aid to the Castro regime after the Bay of Pigs invasion of the previous year, including sending 43,000 troops to join the 270,000 well-trained Cuban forces already assembled. In early October, American U-2 reconnaissance aircraft photographed Soviet bases under construction in Cuba, complete with missiles that, when assembled, would be able to reach U.S. targets as far as 2,200 miles away. It was later disclosed that the Soviets had supplied Havana with short-range nuclear weapons and that Soviet military commanders in Cuba were authorized to use them in the event of an American invasion.

Rather than work through State Department or diplomatic channels, Kennedy publicly confronted the Soviet Union over its actions in a somber televised address on Monday, October 22, 1962. The United States would use its newly enlarged navy to quarantine Soviet shipping to Cuba until the missiles were removed. Both the United States and the Soviet Union went on full military alert and the world held its breath—would this blockade lead to World War III? On the following Sunday, after one of the most harrowing weeks of the nuclear age, Kennedy and Khrushchev reached an agreement that the blockade would be lifted when the Soviets had removed their missiles from Cuba. "We're eyeball to eyeball," Secretary of State Dean Rusk observed, "and I think the other fellow just blinked." To allow Khrushchev to save face, the United States dismantled some outdated missiles in Turkey.

Although the risk of nuclear war was more grave during the Cuban missile crisis than at any other time in the postwar period, in retrospect it marked a turning point in U.S.-Soviet relations. In the words of presidential adviser McGeorge Bundy, "having come so close to the edge, the leaders of the two governments have since taken care to keep away from the cliff."

The Berlin Wall
A West Berlin resident walks alongside a section of the Berlin Wall in 1962, a year after its construction. Note the two border guards on the East Berlin side, plus the numerous loud speakers, which East German communists used to broadcast propaganda over the barricade that divided the city.

The Beginnings of Détente. Sobered by the Cuban missile crisis and the threat of nuclear annihilation, Kennedy began to seek ways to reduce international tensions. He turned away from the cold war rhetoric that had characterized his campaign and the first two years of his presidency and began to strive for world peace. In a notable speech at American University in June 1963, he stressed the need to "make the world safe for diversity." Russians and Americans alike, he observed, "inhabit this small planet. We all breathe the same air. We all cherish our children's future. And we are all mortal." Soviet leaders, also chastened by the confrontation over Cuba, were now willing to talk. In August 1963 the three nuclear powers—the United States, the Soviet Union, and Great Britain—agreed to ban the testing of nuclear weapons in the air or in the seas. Underground testing, however, was allowed to continue. The test-ban treaty was ratified by the Senate in the fall of 1963.

Kennedy's desire for peaceful coexistence with the Soviet Union resulted in a new foreign policy approach that came to be called *détente* (from the French word for a relaxation of tensions). Unlike containment, which called for confronting Soviet initiatives around the globe, détente accepted the Soviets as an adversary with whom the United States could negotiate and bargain. Mutual accommodation and coexistence was the ultimate goal. One concrete symbol was the establishment of a Washington-Moscow telephone "hotline" in 1963 so that leaders could quickly contact each other during potential crises.

But no matter how often American leaders talked about opening channels of communication with the Soviets, the obsession with the potential Soviet military threat to American national security remained a cornerstone of U.S. policy. Nor did Soviet leaders moderate their concern over the threat they believed the United States posed to the survival of the U.S.S.R. The two nations would maintain cold war tensions—and the escalating arms race that accompanied them—for another twenty-five years.

Kennedy's Thousand Days

The expansive vision of presidential leadership that Kennedy and his advisers brought to the White House worked less well at home than abroad. Kennedy, who was hampered by his lack of a popular mandate in the 1960 election, could not mobilize public support for the domestic agenda of the New Frontier. A conservative coalition of southern Democrats and western and midwestern Republicans effectively stalled most liberal initiatives.

One domestic program that did win both popular and congressional support was increased funding for space exploration. Seven astronauts had been chosen for America's Mercury space program in 1958. On May 5, 1961, just three months after Kennedy took office, Alan Shepard became the first American launched into space; on February 2, 1962, John Glenn became the first American to orbit the earth. (Soviet cosmonaut Yuri Gagarin held the distinction of being the first person in space with his 108-hour flight in April 1961.) At the height of American fascination with space, Kennedy proposed in 1961 that "this nation should commit itself to achieving the goal, before this decade is out, of landing a man on the moon and returning him safely to earth." To accomplish this mission, achieved in July 1969, he greatly increased the budget of the National Aeronautics and Space Administration (NASA), established in 1958.

Economic Policy. Kennedy's most striking domestic achievement was his use of modern economics to shape fiscal policy. Initially Kennedy had shared the belief of many business leaders that the federal government could best contribute to economic growth by reducing the national debt and balancing the budget. However, at the urging of Walter Heller, chairman of the Council of Economic Advisers, Kennedy decided on a different course. Rather than increase federal spending to stimulate the economy, he proposed a cut in the taxes paid by businesses and the public. A tax cut, he argued, would leave more money in the hands of taxpayers, enabling them to increase their investments and purchases, and thus bring about economic growth by creating more wealth and jobs. For a time, federal expenditures would exceed federal income, but after a year or two, the expanding economy would raise taxpayers' incomes, leading in turn to higher tax revenues.

Congress predictably balked at this unorthodox proposal. But Lyndon Johnson pressed for it after Kennedy's assassination and signed it into law in February 1964. The Kennedy-Johnson tax cut of 1964 marked a milestone in the purposeful use of the federal budget—fiscal policy—to encourage steady economic growth. Although economic expansion started before the effects of the tax cut could be felt, Kennedy and his economic advisers got credit for it anyway. The gross national product grew at a rate of 5 percent during the 1960s, nearly twice the rate of the Eisenhower years. Much of this growth, however, was fueled by massive defense expenditures linked to the growth of the military-industrial complex, as well as spending for the escalating Vietnam War.

A Limited Agenda. Kennedy's interest in stimulating economic growth did not include a corresponding commitment to spending for domestic social needs, although he did not entirely ignore the liberal legislative agenda Franklin Roosevelt and Harry Truman had set for the Democratic party. Kennedy proposed federal aid to elementary and secondary schools, civil rights legislation, federal investment in mass transportation, medical insurance for the elderly funded through Social Security, and wilderness preservation. But he failed to define any of these proposals in terms satisfactory to a majority in Congress and all were defeated.

Dissension within the Democratic coalition was particularly evident in the case of aid to education. Most northern Democrats favored such aid, but they disagreed about important details. Civil rights advocates insisted that federal school aid go only to desegregated schools, while Catholics insisted that federal assistance be extended to parochial systems. After great effort, Kennedy persuaded black leaders to accept a school aid plan that ignored existing segregation, but he told southern whites that federal aid would not be guaranteed to segregated schools in the future. Because Kennedy was himself a Catholic, however, he feared angering Protestants if he proposed a bill that permitted aid to parochial schools. In the absence of a bill acceptable to all these groups, the education proposal died in committee.

Kennedy failed to provide decisive leadership in other domestic fields. He appointed fewer women to federal positions than Eisenhower or Truman had, and made only a token attempt to address women's issues with the establishment of the Presidential Commission on the Status of Women in 1961. Most tellingly, he never made civil rights a top priority (see Chapter 31). He believed he would need the votes of southern whites to win reelection in 1964, and he sought to hold them in the Democratic coalition by delaying the civil rights reforms he had promised during the 1960 campaign. He doubted such measures would pass in any case. "There is no sense in raising hell," he insisted, "and then in not being successful."

The Warren Court. Some of the most controversial policies of the early 1960s came not from the Kennedy administration, but from the Supreme Court. Unlike the New Deal years, when the Supreme Court played an obstructionist role, during the postwar period it often acted as a catalyst for sweeping social change. So much of this judicial activism was linked to Earl Warren, the chief justice from 1953 to 1969, that the Supreme Court of these years is often referred to as the Warren Court.

The decisions of the Warren Court arguably had an equal or greater impact on American society than anything proposed by the president or the Congress. The most important decision of the Court, *Brown v. Board of Education*, requiring desegregation of public schools, had been handed down in 1954 during the Eisenhower administration (see Chapter 31). In the 1960s, the Court followed up with landmark decisions in the areas of defendants' rights and separation of church and state. In *Gideon v. Wainwright* (1963), *Escobedo v. Illinois* (1964), and *Miranda v. Arizona* (1966), the Supreme Court greatly expanded the rights of suspects accused of crimes. Tackling the issue of reapportionment of state legislatures in *Baker v. Carr* (1962) and *Reynolds v. Sims* (1964), the Court put forth the doctrine of "one person, one vote," which substantially increased the representation of both the suburbs and urban areas, with their concentration of black and Hispanic residents, at the expense of rural regions. Perhaps the most controversial decision was *Engel v. Vitale* (1962), which banned prayer in public schools as a violation of the First Amendment's injunction that "Congress shall make no law respecting an establishment of religion." President Kennedy, like President Eisenhower before him, pledged to uphold these decisions, even when he disagreed with the scope or content of this judicial activism.

The Kennedy Assassination

In the first two years of his presidency, Kennedy realized little of his promise. But in 1963 many political observers felt that he was maturing as a leader and was on the verge of even stronger presidential leadership. On November 22, 1963, Kennedy went to Texas, a state he needed to win for reelection in 1964, to heal divisions in the party organization there. As he rode in an open car past the Texas School Book Depository in Dallas, he was shot and killed. (Whether accused killer Lee Harvey Oswald, a twenty-four-year-old loner who had spent three years in the Soviet Union, was the sole gunman remains the source of considerable controversy.) Before Air Force One left Dallas to take the president's body back to Washington, a grim-faced Lyndon Johnson was sworn in as president. Kennedy's stunned widow, Jacqueline, still wearing a bloodstained pink suit, looked on.

By 1 P.M. Dallas time, just thirty minutes after the shooting, 68 percent of adults in the United States, about 75 million people, knew that Kennedy had been shot. By late afternoon, the proportion had risen to 99.8 percent, showing how within a few hours, the mass media could reach virtually every person in the nation. As on Pearl Harbor Day in 1941, people never forgot what they were doing when they first heard Kennedy had been shot. The shock that greeted the assassination reflected the personal identification that ordinary Americans now felt with the occupant of the White House, quite a change from the muted reaction to the last assassination of an American president, William McKinley, in 1901.

Americans suspended normal activities for four days as they sought reassurance in ceremonies of grief

Burying a President
A grief-stricken Jacqueline Kennedy walked behind her slain husband's casket at his 1963 funeral. To her left is brother-in-law Robert Kennedy, who himself would be assassinated five years later.

symbol of a tragic flaw in the democratic system. The argument that there was something wrong with the nation gained credence two days after the assassination, when Jack Ruby, a local nightclub owner, gunned down Lee Harvey Oswald in the basement of the Dallas police station. Since the television networks were covering Oswald as the police escorted him to another jail, his shooting by Ruby was shown live across the nation. Chief Justice Earl Warren warned ominously about "forces of hatred and malevolence" that made such acts possible, and newspapers and magazines asked, "What sort of nation are we?" Later in the 1960s, many Americans overwhelmed by the social conflict of the decade looked back on November 22, 1963, as the day when things began to come apart.

Lyndon Johnson and the Great Society

Lyndon Johnson, a seasoned politician who was best at negotiating in the backrooms of power, was no match for the Kennedy style, and he knew it. But less than a year after assuming office, Johnson won the 1964 presidential election in a landslide that far surpassed Kennedy's meager mandate in 1960. Johnson then used his astonishing energy and genius for compromise to bring to fruition many of Kennedy's stalled programs, and more than a few of his own. These legislative accomplishments are referred to as the Great Society, Johnson's own phrase to describe his commitment to end poverty and racial injustice. It was the Great Society, not the much less ambitious New Frontier, that fulfilled the New Deal liberal agenda of the 1930s.

The Great Coalition Builder

Lyndon Johnson brought to the presidency far more legislative experience than any modern president, and he used his talent to great effect. Born in the central Texas hill country in 1908, Johnson had served in Washington since 1932 as a congressional aide, New Deal administrator, congressman, senator, senate majority leader, and finally vice-president. A man of singular force, he often got his way by using what one journalist called the "Johnson treatment." Approaching unsuspecting colleagues, he moved "in close, his face a scant millimeter from his target, his eyes widening and narrowing, his eyebrows rising and falling. From his pockets poured clippings, memos, statistics. Mimicry, humor, and the genius of analogy made the Treatment an almost hypnotic experience." Johnson invariably left his targets overwhelmed and bruised—and willing to go along with his requests.

and continuity. The three television networks canceled their regular programs, and an estimated television audience of 100 million collectively mourned the slain president. Shared television images, such as the dignity of Jacqueline Kennedy as she and her two young children walked behind the casket, bound the American people together at a time of national grief.

Kennedy's buoyant youth, the trauma of his assassination, and the collective sense that Americans had been robbed of a promising leader contributed to a powerful Kennedy mystique. Only forty-six at the time of his death, he was the first president born in this century. The Kennedy mythologizing process had begun even before his tragic death. In June 1963 about 59 percent of the people surveyed claimed to have voted for Kennedy, a big jump over the 49.7 percent who actually had; after the assassination, this figure rose to 65 percent. A British journalist called it "a posthumous landslide."

The Kennedy assassination set off a national wave of self-examination. Americans debated whether the murder of the president had been an isolated act or the

The "Johnson Treatment"

Lyndon B. Johnson, a shrewd and adroit politician, learned many of his legislative skills while serving as majority leader of the Senate from 1953 to 1960. Here he zeroed in on Senator Theodore Francis Green of Rhode Island. After assuming the presidency, Johnson remarked, "They say Jack Kennedy had style, but I'm the one who's got the bills passed."

The Election of 1964. If 1964 was a year of liberal triumph in Congress, it was a year of conservative retrenchment within the Republican party. The Republican nominee for president in 1964 was Senator Barry Goldwater of Arizona. Goldwater, who was determined to offer "a choice, not an echo," campaigned against the expansion of federal power in such areas as the economy and civil rights. Goldwater's crisp speeches rejected Republican efforts to build a moderate coalition. "Extremism in the defense of liberty is no vice," he stated. "Moderation in the pursuit of justice is no virtue."

President Johnson easily won his party's nomination. Reaffirming his commitment to the liberal Democratic agenda, but putting some distance between himself and the Kennedy clan, Johnson passed over Robert F. Kennedy for vice-president in favor of Senator Hubert H. Humphrey of Minnesota, who in 1948 had introduced the controversial civil rights plank that split the party. An attempt by an avowed segregationist, Governor George C. Wallace of Alabama, to exploit a white backlash against civil rights showed early strength but then fizzled. The Johnson-Humphrey ticket won by one of the largest margins in history, receiving 61.1 percent of the popular vote. It surpassed even the 1936 landslide of that great coalition builder, Franklin D. Roosevelt, Johnson's political idol and mentor. Johnson's sweeping victory brought with it Democratic gains in Congress and state legislatures.

The Civil Rights Act of 1964. With characteristic energy and determination, Johnson seized the initiative almost as soon as Kennedy's assassination thrust him into the presidency. As a memorial to the slain president, he called for rapid passage of New Frontier proposals, especially the tax cut and civil rights legislation. Dramatically reminding Congress that he himself, a white southerner, had supported civil rights in 1957 and 1960, he urged Congress "to enact a civil rights law so that we can move forward to eliminate from this nation every trace of discrimination and oppression that is based upon race or color."

By June, black pressure and Johnson's surehanded tactics had their impact. Breaking a southern filibuster, the Senate approved the most far-reaching civil rights legislation since Reconstruction. The 1964 Civil Rights Act guaranteed equal access to public accommodations and schools and prohibited discrimination by employers and unions. It granted new powers to the U.S. attorney general to enforce these guarantees and designated the Equal Employment Opportunity Commission to prevent job discrimination by race, religion, national origin, or sex.

The 1964 Campaign

Barry Goldwater's 1964 Republican campaign produced some very creative political memorabilia, such as bumper stickers that proclaimed "AuH_2O" (the symbols for gold and water) and this gold elephant wearing glasses like the candidate's.

Enacting the Liberal Agenda

Like John Kennedy, Lyndon Johnson held an expansive view of presidential leadership. The 1964 election gave him the popular mandate, and more importantly, the filibuster-proof legislative majorities, to push forward legislation to achieve his "Great Society." "Hurry boys, hurry," he urged his staff. "Get that legislation up to the Hill and out. Eighteen months from now ol' Landslide Lyndon will be Lame-Duck Lyndon."

The Eighty-ninth Congress enacted more social-reform measures than any session since Roosevelt's first term, offering legislation for every important element of the Democratic coalition. Responding to growing black demands, Johnson increased federal support for civil rights. The Voting Rights Act of 1965 authorized the attorney general to send federal examiners to the South to register voters. In 1963 only a fourth of all southern blacks were registered to vote; when Johnson left office in 1969, their proportion had risen to two-thirds.

Johnson also found a way to break the congressional deadlock on aid to education. The Elementary and Secondary Education Act of 1965 authorized $1 billion in federal funds to benefit impoverished children, including Catholic children in parochial schools, rather than aiding the schools themselves. With his flair for the dramatic, he signed the education bill in the one-room Texas schoolhouse he had attended as a child.

The Eighty-ninth Congress also gave Johnson the votes to enact the federal health insurance legislation first proposed by Truman. Realizing that it could no longer block some form of federal health insurance, the American Medical Association now proposed that federal funds be used to pay doctors as well as hospitals. The result was two new programs: Medicare, a plan for the elderly funded from a surcharge on Social Security payroll taxes, and Medicaid, a health plan for poor recipients paid for by general tax revenues.

Administration programs did not just aid the poor—the middle class benefited too. Federal urban renewal and home mortgage assistance aided those who could afford to live in single-family homes or in modern apartments. Medicare assistance went to every elderly person covered by Social Security, regardless of need. Much of the federal aid to education benefited the children of the middle class. In addition, Johnson successfully pressed for expansion of the national park system, for legislation to improve the quality of the air and water, for increased land-use planning, and, at the insistence of his wife, Lady Bird Johnson, for the Highway Beautification Act of 1965. That year also saw the creation of the National Endowment for the Arts to support the performing and creative arts, and the National Endowment for the Humanities, which encouraged efforts to understand and interpret the nation's cultural and historical heritage.

The War on Poverty

Although Johnson's programs offered something for every constituency in the Democratic coalition, he always insisted that the top priority of his Great Society was "an end to poverty in our time." The problem of poverty was very real. Poor people made up about a fourth of the American population; three-fourths of the poor were white. The poor in the United States were isolated farmers and miners in Appalachia, blacks mired in urban ghettos, Hispanics in migrant labor camps and urban barrios, native Americans on reservations, women raising families on their own, and the abandoned and destitute elderly. As Michael Harrington had pointed out in *The Other America: Poverty in the United States* (1962), the poor were everywhere, but their poverty was curiously invisible in affluent America. Modern technology had "made a longer, healthier, better life possible," Harrington observed, yet it left the poor "on the margin": "They watch the movies and read the magazines of affluent America, and these teach them that they are internal exiles."

New Deal social welfare programs had failed to reach these people. Because unemployment insurance ran out after a few months, it did not protect against extended joblessness. Social Security and other social-insurance programs provided benefits to workers who paid for them through special taxes, but not all workers were covered. Social welfare programs such as Old Age Assistance, Aid to Dependent Children, and Aid to the Blind carried strict restrictions regarding eligibility.

One tactic tried by the Great Society to reduce poverty was expanding long-established social insurance and welfare programs. It broadened Social Security to include waiters and waitresses, domestic servants, farm workers, and hospital employees. Social welfare expenditures increased rapidly, especially for Aid to Families with Dependent Children (AFDC), as did public housing and rent subsidy programs. Food Stamps, begun in 1964 largely to stabilize farm prices, grew into a major program of assistance to low-income families. As in the New Deal, the social welfare system continued to develop in a piecemeal fashion, with no overall direction.

The Office of Economic Opportunity (OEO), established by the omnibus Economic Opportunity Act of 1964, became the Great Society's showcase in the "War on Poverty." Built around the twin strategies of equal opportunity and community action, OEO programs were so numerous and diverse that they recalled the alphabet agencies of the New Deal. Officials at the OEO quickly realized that identifying poverty was one thing; drafting and implementing programs to address it was quite another. Sargent Shriver, who left the Peace Corps to head the new agency, admitted, "It's like we went down to Cape Kennedy (the NASA space center in

Florida) and launched a half dozen rockets at once."

The War on Poverty produced some of the most significant measures of the Johnson administration. Head Start provided free nursery schools designed to prepare disadvantaged preschoolers for kindergarten. The Job Corps and the Neighborhood Youth Corps trained young people. Upward Bound gave low-income teenagers the skills and motivation to plan for college. The Appalachian Regional Development Act, the Metropolitan Area Redevelopment Act, and the Demonstration Cities Act were intended, like foreign aid, to spur development of impoverished areas. Volunteers in Service to America (VISTA), modeled on the Peace Corps, provided technical assistance to the rural and urban poor. The Community Action Program encouraged the poor to organize to demand "maximum feasible participation" in the decisions that affected them. Community Action organizers worked closely with the two thousand lawyers employed by the Legal Services Program to provide the poor with free access to the legal system.

The OEO quickly drew criticism, however. VISTA and Community Action Program agents encouraged poor people to mount militant demands for public services long withheld by unresponsive local governments. Community organizers on the government payroll in Syracuse, New York, for example, formed tenants' rights groups to protest conditions in public housing, conducted voter registration drives to unseat unpopular elected representatives, and even used public funds to bail out activists arrested for protesting at local welfare offices. Legal Services lawyers challenged welfare and housing administrations in class-action suits. Needless to say, such activism upset entrenched political elites. Such mayors as Sam Yorty of Los Angeles and Richard J. Daley of Chicago vociferously resisted OEO guidelines for including poor people in program planning and administration.

Lyndon Johnson's administration put issues of poverty, justice, and access at the center of national political life. But the mixed results suggest the difficulties of promoting fundamental political and economic change through federal initiatives. In the long-term, the War on Poverty did little to reduce poverty or redistribute wealth. Using a definition of poverty as half the median family income, the poverty line in 1963 was set at $3,000. That year, 20 percent of the population lived below the poverty line. In 1976 the median family income had risen to $15,000, but 20 percent of the nation still received less than half that amount. Technological change and economic growth had raised everyone's standard of living, so the poor were better off in an absolute sense. Relatively, however, they remained as far behind the middle class as ever. In effect, the War on Poverty and related social welfare efforts simply provided the nation's poor with about the same share of income they had always received.

Cracks in the New Deal Coalition

The Great Society represented the culmination of the liberal social agenda that had first been advanced during the crisis of the Great Depression. But the implementation of this liberal agenda revealed deep contradictions in the New Deal coalition. This coalition was inherently unstable, torn among its diverse constituencies and their conflicting priorities for the exercise of federal power. These contradictions had been lurking in political life since Franklin Roosevelt and Harry Truman began to expand the power of the federal government, but they surfaced forcefully in the climate fostered by the "politics of expectation."

During the 1960s, Kennedy's brilliant articulation of the aspirations of many Americans, and Johnson's genius at translating these unformed strivings for change into concrete legislative programs, set in motion a remarkable expansion of federal power. Kennedy and Johnson gathered an extraordinarily diverse set of groups into the New Deal coalition—middle-class and poor; white, black, and Hispanic; Protestant, Jewish, and Catholic; urban and rural. As the functions and responsibilities of the government grew, so did demands for further action from this widening cast of politically organized constituencies.

For a brief period between 1964 and 1966, the coalition held together. But inevitably the claims of certain groups—such as the demand of blacks for civil rights and of the urban poor for increased political power—conflicted with the interests of other Democratic supporters, such as white southerners and northern political bosses eager to maintain the status quo. In the end, the New Deal coalition, which had fostered a vast expansion of federal power, could not sustain a consensus over the purposes that such a government ought to serve.

The Great Society was not just a victim of the factionalism of the Democratic coalition. It was also, in the haunting phrase of civil rights leader Martin Luther King, Jr., "shot down on the battlefields of Vietnam." In 1966 the government spent $22 billion on the Vietnam War and only $1.2 billion on the War on Poverty. As Lyndon Johnson turned his full attention to the escalating war, the domestic programs of the Great Society fell by the wayside.

No one realized the trade-off more painfully than Johnson himself. In the crude language that characterized this tough-talking Texan, he posed the dilemma in this way: "If I left the woman I really loved—the Great Society—in order to get involved with that bitch of a war on the other side of the world, then I would lose everything at home. All my programs. All my hopes to feed the hungry and shelter the homeless. All my dreams to provide education and health care to the browns and the blacks and the lame and the poor. But if I left that

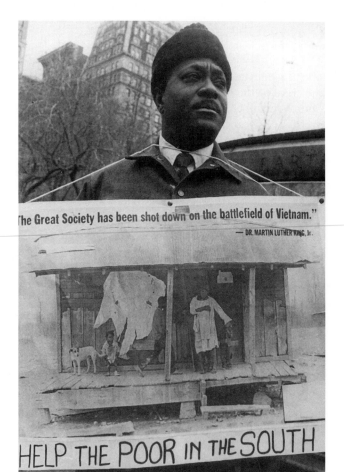

Butter, Not Guns
This placard graphically protested that the Vietnam War diverted money from government social and economic programs aimed at aiding the nation's poor. Many Americans shared this view, and antiwar demonstrations spread across the United States.

war and let the Communists take over South Vietnam, then I would be seen as a coward and my nation would be seen as an appeaser and we would both find it impossible to accomplish anything for anybody anywhere on the entire globe." In the end, his priorities were clear. "Losing the Great Society was a terrible thought, but not so terrible as the thought of being responsible for America's losing a war to the Communists. Nothing could possibly be worse than that."

America and the Vietnam Experience

Vietnam challenged American administrations from Harry Truman to Gerald Ford, and debates about the meanings and lessons of the war still resonate in Ameri-

can life today. American politicians tended to paint the conflict in the starkly ideological terms of the Cold War, but the story is more complicated than simplistic statements about supporting democracy and stopping communism. In postwar foreign relations, Third World concerns became increasingly central to the world order. The United States was in Vietnam not so much to stop the spread of communism as to protect its credibility as the leading noncommunist power in the postwar world order. Ironically, the course of the Vietnam War irrevocably damaged the very American credibility it was supposed to uphold.

The Roots of American Involvement

The roots of U.S. involvement in Vietnam lay in the instability produced by the decolonization of Southeast Asia after World War II. Vietnam had been part of the French colony of Indochina since the late nineteenth century, but was occupied by Japan during World War II. Native resistance to the Japanese was led by the French-educated communist Ho Chi Minh and the Vietnam Independence League, the Vietminh. After the Japanese surrender, Ho proclaimed an independent republic of Vietnam in September 1945. Seven months later the French recognized Vietnam as a "free state" within the French union. Ho and military strategist Vo Nguyen Giap responded by launching attacks to drive the French out completely, thus launching the first phase of the conflict that the Vietminh called the Anti-French War of Resistance.

President Truman came to support the French side in the Indochina war for several reasons. After the Chinese revolution of 1949, the United States was concerned about potential Chinese efforts to sponsor Asian wars of national liberation. Truman also wanted to maintain good relations with France, whose support was crucial to the success of the new NATO alliance. In addition, Indochina played a strategic role in U.S. plans for an integrated Pacific Rim regional economy centered around a reindustrialized Japan, both as a supplier of cheap raw materials and food and as a profitable market for Japanese goods and services.

When the Soviet Union and the new Chinese leaders recognized Ho's government as the legitimate ruler of Vietnam at the beginning of 1950, the United States and Great Britain in turn recognized the French-supported, noncommunist government of Bao Dai. Truman also decided to send supplies to French troops stationed in Vietnam, a policy continued by the Eisenhower administration. By 1954 the United States had sent more than $2 billion worth of military supplies to the French in Vietnam, plus another $703 million in technical and economic assistance, paying nearly 80 percent of the cost of continuing the war.

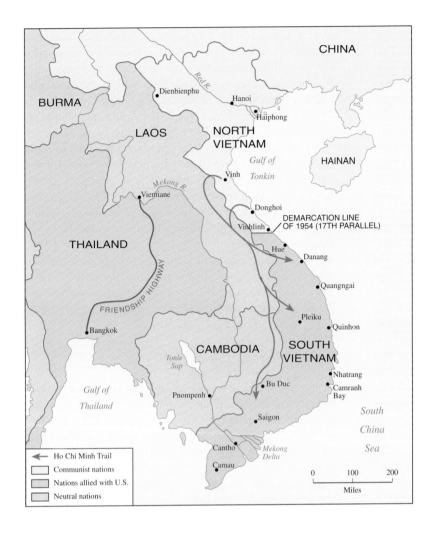

MAP 30.3

The Vietnam War, 1954–1975
The Vietnam War was a guerrilla war, fought in skirmishes and inconclusive encounters rather than decisive battles and major offensives. Supporters of the National Liberation Front filtered into South Vietnam along the Ho Chi Minh trail, which wound through Laos and Cambodia.

Despite these joint French-U.S. efforts, Vietminh forces gained strength in northern Vietnam. By the spring of 1954, they had trapped a large French force at the isolated administrative fortress of Dienbienphu. France asked the United States to launch direct air strikes from nearby carriers to break the siege. Despite the recommendation of several members of the Joint Chiefs of Staff to intervene, Eisenhower refused, and Dienbienphu fell in May 1954 after a fifty-six-day siege.

The dramatic turn of events at Dienbienphu enhanced the negotiating position of the Vietminh at a conference in Geneva just getting underway to discuss the fate of Vietnam. The resulting 1954 Geneva Accords temporarily partitioned Vietnam at the 17th parallel, committed France to withdraw its forces from north of that line within ten months, and forbade both North and South Vietnam from entering into any military alliance with an outside power. A final declaration provided that the two partitioned sectors would hold free elections within two years to choose a unified government for the entire nation. The United States was never an official party to the Geneva Accords, although it agreed to abide by them.

The Eisenhower administration made sure that a pro-American government headed by Ngo Dinh Diem took power in South Vietnam just before the accords were signed. Diem quickly consolidated his power and staged a rigged election in which his ballots were printed on red paper, a Vietnamese symbol of good luck, while his opponent's were green, which stood for misfortune. Diem refused to allow the national elections scheduled for 1956 to take place, mainly because he realized that the popular Ho Chi Minh would easily win in both the north and south. Diem's was just one in a long line of U.S.-backed governments which failed to win the allegiance of the Vietnamese population.

From the perspective of the Vietnamese, the Geneva Accords proved only an interlude between two wars, one to rid the country of French colonial control and a second to reunify Vietnam. (This second goal would not be accomplished until 1975, two years after the final U.S. withdrawal.) By January 1955 the United States had replaced France as the dominant power in South Vietnam. American policymakers now asserted that a noncommunist South Vietnam was vital to the security interests of the United States and they charted American policy accordingly. Said President Eisenhower: "You have a row of dominoes set up, you knock over the first one, and what will happen to the last one is the certainty that it will go over very quickly." Between 1955 and 1961 the Eisenhower administration sent Diem an average of $200 million a year in aid, mostly military. In addition, approximately 675 American military advisers were stationed in Saigon, the capital of South Vietnam.

Inheriting the Vietnam situation from the previous administration, President Kennedy saw Vietnam as an ideal laboratory to try out counterinsurgency tactics. But Kennedy, like all the other American presidents who guided policy, first had to prop up the faltering regime of Ngo Dinh Diem, who remained a highly unpopular leader because of his administration's endemic corruption and ruthless brutality, aloofness from the peasantry, and greedy land policy. Because the Diem regime was so weak, Kennedy increased the number of American military "advisers" (an elastic term which included helicopter units, special forces, minesweeping details, and air reconnaissance pilots) to more than 16,000 by November 1963. As part of the counterinsurgency strategy, he also sent in economic development specialists to win the "hearts and minds" of Vietnamese peasants away from the insurgents while also increasing agricultural production. Kennedy refused, however, to send American combat troops to assist the South Vietnamese. "In the final analysis," he told a journalist in November of 1963, "it is their war."

The American aid did little good. Diem's political inexperience and corruption, combined with his Catholicism in a predominantly Buddhist country, made it impossible for him to create a stable, popular government. He enjoyed much more support from his faraway American backers than he did in his native land. As the situation deteriorated, Diem consistently misled his American allies about South Vietnamese military and social progress. In December 1960 the North Vietnamese Communist party had organized its supporters in South Vietnam into a revolutionary front, the National Liberation Front (NLF). The front's guerrilla forces—called the Vietcong by Diem and his American advisers—made considerable headway against the Diem regime, using the revolutionary tactics of the Chinese leader Mao Zedong to blend into the South Vietnamese civilian population "like fish in the water." But opposition to Diem was far more widespread than just the communists. For example, large segments of the peasantry had been alienated by Diem's strategic hamlet program, which uprooted families and whole villages in a vain attempt to separate them from Ho Chi Minh's sympathizers.

Matters came to a head in late 1963. Militant Buddhists staged a dramatic series of demonstrations against Diem, including several self-immolations that were recorded by American television crews. Kennedy decided that Diem had to be removed. Ambassador Henry Cabot Lodge, Jr., let it be known in Saigon that the United States would support a military coup that had "a good chance of succeeding." On November 1, 1963, Diem was driven from office and assassinated by a faction of the South Vietnamese army.

Kennedy's advisers had given little thought to what would follow Diem's ouster. Before they could formulate any plans, Kennedy himself was assassinated and Lyndon Johnson took his place as president. "I am not going to lose Vietnam," he stated emphatically within weeks of becoming president. "I am not going to be the President who saw Southeast Asia go the way China went." A new phase in the Americanization of the war began. When Johnson assumed the presidency, there were 16,000 American troops in Vietnam. When he left office in January 1969, there were more than 500,000.

Escalation

In the period between Kennedy's assassination in November of 1963 and the summer of 1964, a coalition government headed by General Nguyen Khanh tried, without much success, to build popular support in South Vietnam. American policymakers realized that the Eisenhower-Kennedy policy of military advisers and supplies would probably no longer be enough to save the situation. But the commitment of U.S. forces in an offensive strategy would call for at least tacit congressional support, perhaps even a declaration of war. Originally, Johnson had wanted to wait until after the 1964 election to place this controversial request before Congress, but events gave him the opportunity to win authorization sooner.

The Gulf of Tonkin Resolution. During the summer of 1964, American naval forces had supported several South Vietnamese amphibious attacks on the North Vietnamese coast. The North Vietnamese resisted such attacks, and President Johnson told the nation that on two separate occasions North Vietnamese torpedo boats had fired on American destroyers in international waters in the Gulf of Tonkin. At Johnson's request, in early August Congress authorized him to "take all necessary measures to repel any armed attacks against the forces of the United States and to prevent further aggression." The Gulf of Tonkin resolution passed 88 to 2 in the Senate and 416 to 0 in the House. Only Senators Wayne Morse of Oregon and Ernest Gruening of Alaska opposed it as a "predated declaration of war" that further increased the president's ability to carry out foreign policy without consulting Congress.

Many questions were later raised about the resolution. A draft had been ready for several months awaiting just such an incident. The evidence of a North Vietnamese attack was sketchy at best. As the president admitted soon afterward, "For all I know, our navy was shooting at whales out there." But this trumped-up attack got Johnson what he wanted—the only formal approval of American intervention in Vietnam ever voted by Congress.

During the 1964 presidential campaign, Johnson declared, "We are not going to send American boys nine or ten thousand miles away from home to do what Asian boys ought to be doing for themselves." Yet plans were already under way for a major escalation of the United States effort, the only way, policymakers agreed, that the South Vietnamese government could prevent a Communist takeover. With Congressional support assured and the 1964 election safely over, the Johnson administration began the fateful moves toward the total Americanization of the war. The escalation, which was accomplished during the first several months of 1965, took two forms: the deployment of American ground troops and the initiation of direct U.S. bombing attacks against North Vietnam.

The Arrival of U.S. Ground Troops. The assignment of U.S. ground troops to combat duty in South Vietnam in March of 1965 marked a major turning point in the history of American involvement. Even with the help of numerous American advisers and millions of dollars of supplies, South Vietnamese troops were no longer able to resist the Vietcong. The first U.S. Marines waded ashore at Da Nang on March 8, 1965, ostensibly to protect the large American air base there. Soon they were patroling the countryside and skirmishing with the enemy. At the time the American people were not told that a major change in policy had occurred.

During the next three years, the number of U.S. troops in Vietnam grew dramatically. The war increasingly became an American struggle, fought for American aims. More than 75,000 soldiers were fighting there in June 1965, and 190,000 by the end of that year. In 1966, almost 400,000 American soldiers were stationed in Vietnam, 500,000 in 1967, and 540,000 in 1968. The escalating demands of General William Westmoreland, commander of the U.S. forces in Vietnam, confirmed a prediction made by presidential adviser George Ball in 1961. Ball had warned President Kennedy that if American ground troops were committed to Vietnam, there would be 300,000 there within five years. Kennedy had laughed and said, "George, you're crazier than hell." But as Kennedy observed before his death, requests for troops were like having a drink: "The effect wears off, and you have to take another."

The other major element of the escalation, which occurred simultaneously in March of 1965, concerned bombing attacks against North Vietnam. Retaliatory air strikes against North Vietnamese targets had already been selectively undertaken in February; what was significant about these new plans was that the bombing was not linked to a specific act of provocation, but was an open-ended policy. Such bombing raids, National Security Adviser McGeorge Bundy reasoned, would cripple the North Vietnamese economy and force the communists to the bargaining table. A special target was the Ho Chi Minh trail, an elaborate network of paths, bridges, and shelters that snaked from North Vietnam through Cambodia and Laos into South Vietnam. Some twenty thousand Vietnamese soldiers moved southward along this route each month by 1967, as well as the military hardware and other resources necessary to supply them.

Jungle Warfare in Vietnam
The horror of losing a buddy in war was plain in the faces of these marines as they tried to drag a comrade to safety under fire at the battle of Khe Sanh in 1968. Almost two-thirds of the American soldiers who died in action in Vietnam were twenty-one years old or younger.

Aerial Bombing in Vietnam
The bombs dropped by U.S. forces in an
attempt to root out Vietcong sympathizers inflicted heavy damage on the
countryside and led to civilian deaths.
B-52 bombers dropped most of the
bombs.

Between 1965 and 1968, Operation Rolling Thunder (named for a Protestant hymn) dropped a million
tons of bombs on North Vietnam, 800 tons a day for
three and a half years. Each of these B-52 bombing sorties cost $30,000, a measure of the escalating costs of
the war; already by 1966 the direct costs of the air war
exceeded $1.7 billion. From 1965 to 1973 the United
States dropped three times as many bombs on North
Vietnam, a country roughly the size of Texas, as had
fallen on Europe, Asia, and Africa during World War II.
The several hundred captured pilots downed in the
raids then became pawns in negotiations with the North
Vietnamese over the fate of prisoners of war.

Much to the amazement of American advisers, the
bombing had little effect on the ability of the Vietnamese to wage war. Instead of destroying enemy
morale and bringing the North Vietnamese to the bargaining table, the bombing rekindled Vietnamese nationalism and intensified its will to fight. The flow of
troops and supplies to the south continued unabated.
American leaders could have learned a lesson from
World War II, when extensive bombing of Germany in
1944–1945 had failed to cripple Nazi industrial production. Because North Vietnam had little industry to
destroy, the impact of similar bombing on an agricultural society would predictably be less. The bombing
continued nevertheless.

The massive commitment of troops and airpower
after 1965 threatened to destroy the fragile resources of
this once beautiful country. Taking to the extreme Johnson's call "to leave the footprints of America in Vietnam,"
the campaign of extensive defoliation and military bombardment made it difficult for peasants to practice the
agriculture that provided the economic and cultural

base of Vietnamese society. After one devastating but
not unusual engagement, the commanding U.S. officer
claimed, using the logic of the times, "It became necessary to destroy the town in order to save it." Graffiti on
a plane that dropped defoliants read, "Only you can
prevent forests." (Only later did the devastating human
effect of chemicals such as Agent Orange become clear.)
Meanwhile, American soldiers and dollars flowed into
Saigon and other cities, distorting the local economy, fa-
cilitating corruption and prostitution, and setting off
wild, unmanageable inflation.

Why did the dramatically increased American presence in Vietnam after 1965 make so little difference to
the outcome of the war? Certain advisers, like former
Lieutenant Colonel John Paul Vann, argued that military intervention would do little unless accompanied by
reform of the Saigon government and increased efforts
at pacification in the countryside. Other critics claimed
the war was lost because the United States never committed its full military might to total victory, although
what total victory would have entailed remains in dispute. It is true, however, that no clear, overall military
strategy guided American efforts. Instead, often for domestic reasons, policymakers searched for the illusive
"middle ground" between all-out war and the politically unacceptable alternative of disengagement. This
limited commitment was never enough to ensure victory, however defined.

The determination of the Vietnamese was also a
major factor in the continuation of the war. In the
1940s, Ho Chi Minh had told his French imperialist
foes, "You can kill ten of my men for every one I kill of
yours, but even at those odds, you will lose and I will
win." That same strategy held true twenty years later

against the Americans. The Vietcong were prepared to accept limitless casualties and to fight for as many years as necessary. (Four million Vietnamese on both sides were either killed or wounded in the war, approximately 10 percent of the population.) North Vietnamese strategists astutely realized that the war did not have to be won on the battlefield. They accurately predicted that the United States would be unable to wage an extended war of attrition because American public opinion would eventually limit U.S. participation. Time was on the Vietcong side, although at an enormous cost to both sides.

Vietnam, From the Perspective of Americans Who Fought the War

The average age of the approximately 2.8 million Americans who served in Vietnam was nineteen. These kids were too young to vote or drink, but old enough to fight . . . and die. They served for a variety of reasons. Some responded to the kind of patriotic motives that had led their fathers to fight in World War II or Korea; others joined the army because they had no options at home and wanted to "see the world."

Many served because they were drafted. Until the country shifted to an all-volunteer force in 1973, the draft remained a concrete reminder of the impact of the state on individual lives. As the troop needs intensified, the draft reached deeper into the male population. The casualty figures reflected the increasing role of draftees in Vietnam. In 1965 draftees comprised 16 percent of total battle deaths; this had risen to 34 percent by 1967. By 1969, 62 percent of Army deaths were of draftees. Blacks were drafted, and died, in roughly the same proportion to their draft age population: about 12 to 13 percent.

Many draftees and enlistees initially shared cold war assumptions about the need to fight communism, and a corresponding belief in the superiority of American military strength. Arriving in Vietnam quickly disabused them of simple notions of patriotism or the inevitability of American victory. The first thing they noticed when they got off the plane was the stench—the smell of death, napalm, and human waste in this torrid jungle country. Sometimes they had to sprint from their plane to the safety of the base buildings because of incoming enemy mortar attacks, an augury of the boldness with which enemy forces operated throughout the country.

Unlike World War II soldiers, who served "for the duration," Vietnam soldiers had a tour of duty of exactly one year. For many, it was simply a matter of getting through three hundred and sixty-five days. For the first ninety days or so, they were a "cherry," sexual slang to designate youth and inexperience. Once they neared the end of their tour, soldiers might carry a "short-timer's stick" notched for the remaining days left; as each day passed, they would cut off another notch until left with a small stub. "Grunts" (the ordinary infantrymen) and "bloods" (what black draftees called themselves) were a suspicious lot, however, and they were always afraid of being "wasted" (killed) with only a few days to go. Some soldiers consciously tried not to make close friends, just in case their buddies caught a grenade or triggered a booby trap on a routine patrol.

In "Nam" (soldier's shorthand for Vietnam), days passed in boring menial work, punctuated by flashes of intense fighting. "Most of the time, nothing happened," a soldier recalled, "but when something did, it happened instantaneously and without warning." The pressure of waging war under these conditions drove many soldiers to seek escape with alcohol or cheap and readily available drugs.

The fighting had a certain surreal quality to it. Combat often intensified at night, with incoming and outgoing firepower lighting up the sky while soldiers huddled sleeplessly on watch. There were rarely large-scale battles, only skirmishes; no front lines or territory conquered, just operations during the day in areas that reverted to Vietcong control at night. Although whole units might sometimes be ambushed, casualties more typically came in twos and threes. A former Marine captain recalled:

> You never knew who was the enemy and who was the friend. They all looked alike. They all dressed alike. They were all Vietnamese. Some of them were Vietcong. Here's a woman of twenty-two or twenty-three. She is pregnant, and she tells an interrogator that her husband works in Danang and isn't a Vietcong. But she watches your men walk down a trail and get killed or wounded by a booby trap. She knows the booby trap is there, but she doesn't warn them. Maybe she planted it herself.

He concluded graphically, "It wasn't like the San Francisco Forty-Niners on one side of the field and the Cincinnati Bengals on the other. The enemy was all around you."

American success was measured not in territory gained, but in gruesome "body counts"—the number of enemy soldiers killed—and "kill ratios"—the ratio between enemy losses and American casualties. "If it's dead and Vietnamese, it's VC [Vietcong]" was the rule of thumb in the bush. Casualty figures were often deliberately inflated. As a twenty-four-year-old Special Forces captain recalled, "I went out and killed one VC and liberated a prisoner. Next day the major called me in and told me that I'd killed fourteen VC and liberated six prisoners. You want to see the medal?"

AMERICAN LIVES

John Paul Vann

The divisions over the Vietnam War haunted Arlington National Cemetery on June 16, 1972, when three hundred mourners assembled for the funeral of John Paul Vann. "The soldier of the war in Vietnam," Vann had been killed in a helicopter crash in the Central Highlands the week before. Politicians and military leaders closely associated with the war effort were very much in evidence—General William Westmoreland, CIA Director William Colby, conservative journalist Joseph Alsop, and Secretary of State William Rogers. But so were Daniel Ellsberg, a former Pentagon official who had publicly turned against the war, and Senator Edward Kennedy, another war opponent who had shared Vann's concern about the plight of its refugees. In a time of intense polarization over a war that was still going on, this assemblage of "hawks" and "doves" was highly unusual.

Vann's own family also showed the rifts over Vietnam that day. His wife of twenty-six years, Mary Jane, had requested two pieces of music: the upbeat "Colonel Bogie March" from the film *The Bridge on the River Kwai*, one of her husband's favorites, and the haunting antiwar ballad, "Where Have All the Flowers Gone?," her own expression of opposition to the war. One of Vann's sons, twenty-one-year-old Jesse, hated the war so profoundly that he tore his draft card in two at the funeral, placing half of it on his father's casket. He planned to give the other half to President Richard Nixon at the White House ceremony following the funeral, where his father would be presented posthumously with the Presidential Medal of Freedom. Only at the last moment was Jesse talked out of his act of defiance, agreeing that this was, after all, his father's day, and more than anything else, his father had believed in the war in Vietnam.

Also at the funeral was *New York Times* reporter Neil Sheehan, who decided at that moment to write a biography of Vann, which he finally published sixteen years later, *A Bright Shining Lie*. Sheehan, along with David Halberstam and other reporters, had fallen under

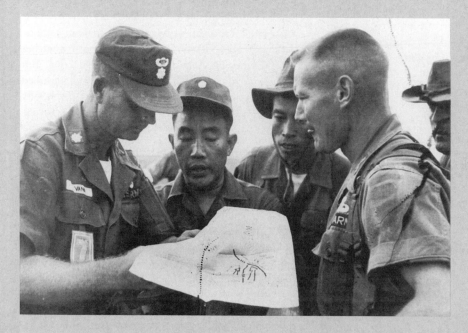

Planning Strategy
Lt. Col. John P. Vann (left) shown here during his tour of duty in Vietnam in 1963 discussing a tactical decision.

Vann's spell during his first tour of duty in Vietnam in 1963, when he seemed like the only American official who was willing to admit that the war was not going well. Sheehan had continued to rely on Vann's outspoken assessments for the rest of the war. "In this war without heroes, this man had been the one compelling figure," concluded Sheehan. "By an obsession, by an unyielding dedication to the war, he had come to personify the American endeavor in Vietnam."

John Paul Vann was an enormously complicated person—a born leader, a visionary, a man who knew no physical fear, but most of all, a true believer in America's mission to share democracy with countries "less fortunate" than ours. His early years were shaped by poverty and lack of opportunity. Born in 1924 to a working-class family in Norfolk, Virginia, he grew up dirt poor during the Great Depression. A colleague later recalled him as a "cocky little red-necked guy with a rural Virginia twang." World War II offered him his ticket out—when he turned eighteen in 1943, he enlisted and made the army his career. He served with distinction in the Korean War and then took assignments in West Germany and the United States. But in 1959 his service record was stained by accusations of the statutory rape of a fifteen-year-old girl. Even though the army eventually dropped the charges, the scandal effectively prevented him from moving up in the military bureaucracy. Neil Sheehan later concluded that Vann's "moral heroism" in speaking out against the conduct of the war to the seeming detriment of his career was rooted in his awareness that he had nothing to lose, although reporters did not know the full story at the time.

In 1963 the thirty-nine-year-old Lieutenant Colonel Vann was sent to Vietnam, where he served as a senior adviser to a South Vietnamese infantry division in the Mekong Delta. At the battle of Ap Bac, he watched his South Vietnamese counterpart purposely refuse to fight the battle the way it had been planned and let the enemy escape. In a moment of epiphany, Vann realized that the rosy reports being fed to Saigon and Washington were false, that Saigon suffered from "an institutionalized unwillingness to fight." After unsuccessful attempts to enlighten his superiors, he leaked his meticulously documented assessments to reporters like Halberstam and Sheehan. His candor won him few friends in the military, and at the end of his tour of duty he was reassigned to the Pentagon. He tried to alert the Joint Chiefs of Staff that the war was not being won, but at the last moment his scheduled briefing was canceled, in large part because the Joint Chiefs did not want to hear his version of the truth. He resigned from the army soon afterward.

Less than two years later, in 1965, Vann was back in Vietnam, just as the major escalation of the war was getting underway. Except for brief trips home, he stayed there until his death. His first position was as a civilian pacification representative for the Agency for International Development, where he worked to win over the peasants to the South Vietnamese side, rather than the National Liberation Front. His honesty and unmatched familiarity with conditions in the countryside led him to conclude that the communists were doing a far better job at appealing to the local population than the corrupt Saigon government: as he wrote to a friend in 1965, "If I were a lad of eighteen faced with the same choice—whether to support the GVN [Government of Vietnam] or the NLF—and a member of a rural community, I would surely choose the NLF." His concern for winning over the local peasantry made him an outspoken opponent of the heavy bombing inflicted on the Vietnamese countryside in an effort to rout out Vietcong sympathizers. He also strongly criticized General Westmoreland's strategy of sending in more American troops to wear down the Vietcong in a war of attrition, arguing that this would be useless without major reforms in the Saigon government.

Despite his role as a gadfly, and even though he was now a civilian, John Paul Vann assumed more and more responsibility in the day-to-day conduct of the war. In 1971 he was given authority over all the U.S. military forces in the Central Highlands, the equivalent of the position of major general. But by then, according to Sheehan, Vann had "lost his compass." He was no longer able to assess realistically the ability or the will of the South Vietnamese to fight without American aid. He continued to insist that the war could be won through pacification and reform in Saigon, despite evidence of growing Vietcong strength. When his helicopter went down at Kontum in 1972, he had almost singlehandedly saved the Central Highlands from a North Vietnamese offensive. Within six months, the United States formally ended its involvement. Two years later, Vietnam was reunited under Communist rule.

John Paul Vann never wavered in his belief that in Vietnam America's cause was just, its intentions good. He had no quarrel with the war itself, just the way it was fought. Vann thought he knew the answers, but Saigon and Washington chose not to listen. His life and death serve as a reminder of the complexities of the Vietnam experience—could it ever really have been "won" and what would "winning" have meant? Neil Sheehan is convinced that Vann "died believing he had won his war."

AMERICAN VOICES

A Vietnam Veteran Remembers *Ron Kovic*

Born on the Fourth of July in 1946, Ron Kovic wanted to be an American hero. He enlisted in the marines and was sent to Vietnam. He came home in a wheelchair and, after a long period of recovery, joined the antiwar movement.

I had been shot. The war had finally caught up with my body. I felt good inside. Finally the war was with me and I had been shot by the enemy. I was getting out of the war and I was going to be a hero. I kept firing my rifle into the tree line and boldly, with my new wound, moved closer to the village, daring them to hit me again. For a moment I felt like running back to the rear with my new million-dollar wound but I decided to keep fighting in the open. A great surge of strength went through me as I yelled for the other men to come out from the trees and join me. I was limping now and the foot was beginning to hurt so much, I finally lay down in almost a kneeling position, still firing into the village, still unable to see anyone. I seemed to be the only one left firing a rifle. Someone came up from behind me, took off my boot and began to bandage my foot. The whole thing was

Ron Kovic

incredibly stupid, we were sitting ducks, but he bandaged my foot and then he took off back into the tree line.

For a few seconds it was silent. I lay down prone and waited for the next bullet to hit me. It was only a matter of time, I thought. I wasn't retreating, I wasn't going back, I was lying right there and blasting everything I had into the pagoda. The rifle was full of sand and it was jamming. I had to pull the bolt back now each time trying to get a round into the

chamber. It was impossible and I started to get up and a loud crack went off next to my right ear as a thirty-caliber slug tore through my right shoulder, blasted through my lung, and smashed my spinal cord to pieces.

I felt that everything from my chest down was completely gone. I waited to die. I threw my hand back and felt my legs still there. I couldn't feel them but they were still there. I was still alive. And for some reason I started believing, I started believing I might not die, I might make it out of there and live and feel and go back home again. I could hardly breathe and was taking short little sucks with the one lung I had left. The blood was rolling off my flak jacket from the hole in my shoulder and I couldn't feel the pain in my foot anymore, I couldn't even feel my body. I was frightened to death. I didn't think about praying, all I could feel was cheated.

All I could feel was the worthlessness of dying right here in this place at this moment for nothing.

Source: Ron Kovic, *Born on the Fourth of July* (New York: McGraw-Hill, 1976), 221–22.

Racism was a fact of everyday life in Vietnam. It was difficult to differentiate between friendly South Vietnamese and Vietcong sympathizers, and many soldiers just lumped them all together as "gooks." A draftee noted of his indoctrination, "The only thing they told us about the Vietcong was they were gooks. They were to be killed. Nobody sits around and gives you their historical and cultural background. They're the enemy. Kill, kill, kill."

Fighting, and surviving, in such conditions took its toll. "War is not killing," recalled one soldier. "Killing is

the easiest part of the whole thing. Sweating twenty-four hours a day, seeing guys drop all around you of heatstroke, not having food, not having water, sleeping only three hours a night for weeks at a time, that's what war is. Survival." Another vet echoed that sentiment: "The hardest thing to come to grips with was the fact that making it through Vietnam—surviving—is probably the only worthwhile part of the experience. It wasn't going over there and saving the world from communism or defending the country." Such cynicism and bitterness was common.

The 15,000 women who served in Vietnam shared many of these experiences. Half of these women were in the military, mainly with the WACS and as nurses; the rest were in civilian service, such as the USO. The nurses, like all medical personnel, had to deal with massive doses of death and mutilation, mainly inflicted on soldiers barely out of their teens. They tried not to get caught up in it emotionally, but as one navy nurse recalled, "it's pretty damn hard not getting involved when you see a nineteen- or twenty-year-old blond kid from the Midwest or California or the East Coast screaming and dying. A piece of my heart would go with each."

After the intensity, and the boredom, of the tour of duty, there remained one last hurdle. Unlike World War II or Korean veterans, who usually came back to this country in groups by a long boat ride, Vietnam veterans could literally be in Saigon one day and the American mainland the next. Soldiers from Vietnam returned home alone, with no deprogramming or counseling. Veterans found this transition enormously disorienting. Once home, they felt embarrassed when they dove under a table at the sound of firecrackers on the Fourth of July or froze when planes flew overhead. Mainly the Vietnam experience was just ignored. Recalled one vet, "Bringing up the Nam was like farting at the dinner table. Everybody looks away embarrassed and acts like nothing happened. Well, pardon me." The psychological tensions of serving in Vietnam, and the abrupt transition back to America, sowed the seeds of the post-traumatic stress disorder. Only in the 1980s did America begin to make its peace with those who had served in America's most unpopular war.

The Consensus Begins to Unravel

Throughout the Kennedy and early Johnson years, there was a broad consensus for the administration's conduct of foreign affairs, as there had been generally throughout the cold war period. Lyndon Johnson sought, and received, public support for the war by linking the fight to cold war principles:

> In the forties and fifties we took our stand in Europe to protect the freedom of those threatened by aggression. . . . Now, the center of attention has shifted to another part of the world where aggression is on the march and the enslavement of free men is its goal. . . . If we allow the Communists to win in Vietnam, it will become easier and more appetizing for them to take over other countries in other parts of the world. We will have to fight again some place else—at what cost no one knows. That is why it is vitally important to every American family that we stop the Communists in South Vietnam.

Note that the needs and desires of the Vietnamese people hardly entered into this formulation.

The Early Antiwar Movement. Although significant public opposition to the war did not surface until 1967, Vietnam became an issue for a small group of Americans well before then. The roots of the emerging antiwar movement date to the 1950s and the issue of atmospheric nuclear testing. Concern over fallout and traces of deadly strontium 90 in milk led to the founding of groups such as SANE (the National Committee for a Sane Nuclear Policy), Physicians for Social Responsibility, and Women's Strike for Peace. These activists opposed the escalating arms race in general and atmospheric testing in particular. Their mobilization played a role in the signing of the 1963 nuclear test-ban treaty between President Kennedy and Soviet Premier Nikita Khrushchev.

Between 1963 and 1965, as the American presence in Vietnam grew, the movement shifted from peace advocacy to opposition to the war. Again, no one organization unified this sentiment, although all were joined by a skepticism about the rationales for the growing American involvement. Critics of intervention argued that the war was morally wrong and antithetical to American ideals; that the goal of attaining an independent, anticommunist South Vietnam was futile; and that American military involvement would not necessarily help the Vietnamese people. At this point, dissenters included liberal activist groups like SANE, older peace or-

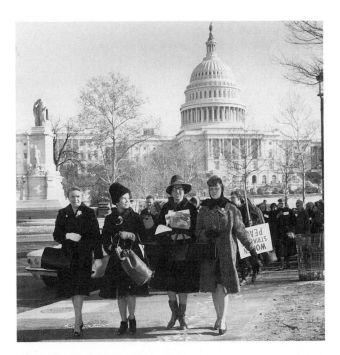

Women March for Peace, 1962
Members of the Women's Strike for Peace set up picket lines at the Capitol in December 1962 to urge an end to atmospheric testing of nuclear weapons by both the United States and the Soviet Union. Such protest groups were forerunners of the broader movement, which opposed the Vietnam War after 1965.

ganizations like the Women's International League for Peace and Freedom, newer ones like Women's Strike for Peace, radical pacifist groups such as the Fellowship for Reconciliation, student groups like Students for a Democratic Society and draft resisters' leagues, and antiwar religious groups. By the mid-1960s, a broad, diffuse movement against the war existed. "The antiwar movement is not a fixed group of people," observed one participant, "it is something that has been happening to America."

Norman Morrison is a symbol of how strongly some Americans felt about Vietnam. In November 1965, Morrison, a thirty-two-year-old Quaker activist, married and the father of an eighteen-month-old daughter, set himself on fire and burned to death near the gates of the Pentagon, barely 50 yards from Defense Secretary Robert McNamara's office. He undertook this protest against the immorality of the war after reading an account by a French priest who had despaired at seeing his Vietnamese parishioners burned by napalm during a bombing attack. Like the priest, Morrison was anguished about his inability to stop the carnage. To his wife of ten years, he left this note: "Know that I love thee but must act for the children of the priest's village."

The Johnson administration paid little heed to the emerging antiwar opposition, dismissing them as "nervous nellies," rebellious children, or communist dupes. Despite calls to "Support Our Boys—Bring Them Home," the president was increasingly adamant that the United States must not back down from its commitment to the South Vietnamese. Thus ensued a two-front offensive: a war for public opinion in America, to parallel the war in Vietnam itself.

The Television War. Television had much to do with shaping American attitudes toward the war. Vietnam was television's first big war; it brought the fighting directly into the nation's living rooms. The escalation in Vietnam coincided with several trends in news broadcasting, notably the expansion of the nightly network newscast from fifteen minutes to half an hour in 1963. By 1967, CBS and NBC were spending $5 million a year to cover the war from their expanded Saigon bureaus. This investment guaranteed that Vietnam appeared on the news every night. Reporters soon learned that combat footage—what they called "shooting bloody"—had a better chance of airing than reports about pacification or political developments. Every night, the newscasts showed American soldiers steadily advancing in the countryside, while reported body counts suggested staggering Vietcong losses against minimal U.S. casualties.

Growing Doubts. Despite the glowing reports that were fed to the American public about the progress of the war, by 1967 many administration officials had pri-

A Televised War

This harrowing scene from Saigon during the Tet offensive in 1968 was broadcast on U.S. network news. The NBC bureau chief described the film in a terse telex message: "A VC OFFICER WAS CAPTURED. THE TROOPS BEAT HIM. THEY BRING HIM TO [Brigadier General Nguyen Ngoc] LOAN WHO IS HEAD OF SOUTH VIETNAMESE NATIONAL POLICE. LOAN PULLS OUT HIS PISTOL, FIRES AT THE HEAD OF THE VC, THE VC FALLS, ZOOM ON HIS HEAD, BLOOD SPRAYING OUT. IF HE HAS IT ALL ITS STARTLING STUFF."

vately reached more pessimistic conclusions. Pentagon analysts estimated that the Vietcong, with only minimal assistance from other Communist powers, could marshal 200,000 guerrillas a year indefinitely. Despite such a prognosis, President Johnson continued to insist that an American victory in Vietnam was vital to U.S. national security and prestige. Journalists, especially those who had spent time in Vietnam, soon commented that the Johnson administration suffered from a "credibility gap."

Economic events also forced Johnson and his advisers on the defensive. In 1966 the federal deficit stood at $9.8 billion. The deficit jumped to $23 billion in 1967, with the Vietnam War costing the taxpayers $27 billion that year. (The total cost of the war from 1965 to 1973 has been estimated at $120 billion.) Although the war was consuming only 3 percent of the gross national product, compared with 48 percent for World War II and 12 percent for the Korean War, Johnson could no longer hide the enormous expense of the war from the American people. But only in the summer of 1967 did he ask for a 10 percent surcharge on individual and corporate income, which Congress delayed approving until 1968. By then the inflationary spiral that plagued the American economy throughout the 1970s was already out of control.

The Tet Offensive

Then came Tet. On January 30, 1968, the Vietcong unleashed a massive, well-coordinated assault on major urban areas in the South. The offensive was timed to coincide with the festive Vietnamese holiday of Tet surrounding the lunar New Year, and perhaps also with the beginning of the 1968 presidential campaign in the United States. Vietcong forces struck thirty-six of the forty-four provincial capitals and five of the six major cities, including an assault on the supposedly impregnable U.S. embassy in Saigon. The United States and the South Vietnamese forces were caught off guard, once again having seriously underestimated the capabilities of their Vietcong foe who had been planning the attack since the previous fall. "Even had I known exactly what was to take place," explained an intelligence officer, "it was so preposterous that I probably would have been unable to sell it to anybody."

American forces recovered quickly and were able to counterattack. In strictly military terms, the Tet offensive was a defeat for the Vietcong—it failed to provoke the collapse of the South Vietnamese government headed since 1967 by Nguyen Van Thieu. But its long-term effect was quite different. As one historian observed, Tet was "probably unique in that the side that lost completely in the tactical sense came away with an overwhelming psychological and hence political victory." In the United States, Tet marked the beginning of a new phase of the war.

Television once again played a major role in shaping American attitudes. The success of the Vietcong made a mockery of official pronouncements that the United States was winning the war. Suddenly, television brought home more disturbing images—the American embassy in Saigon under siege, with a pistol-wielding staff member peering warily from a window; and the Saigon police chief placing a pistol to the head of a Vietcong suspect and executing him on the street. About 20 million viewers watched the latter scene, a symbol of the brutality of the war and the corruption and injustice that characterized the Thieu regime.

The Tet offensive set in motion a major shift in American public opinion about the war. Before Tet, a Gallup poll found that 56 percent of the people considered themselves "hawks" (supporters of the war), while only 28 percent identified themselves as "doves" (opponents); women and blacks consistently opposed the war more than white men did, younger people more than older. By April 1968, three months after the Tet offense, doves outnumbered hawks by 42 to 41 percent. This turnaround did not mean that a majority now supported the peace movement. Many who called themselves doves had simply concluded that the war was unwinnable and that America ought to cut its losses and get out. They opposed the war on pragmatic, rather than moral, grounds. As a housewife told a pollster, "I want to get out but I don't want to give up."

Tet also set in motion changes in the administration's conduct of the war. President Johnson turned down General Westmoreland's request for 206,000 additional troops, a request that would have required the politically explosive course of calling up the reserves. Congressional support was slipping, and even within the administration many advisers had concluded that the war was unwinnable, including the members of the foreign policy establishment dubbed "the Wise Men" (see Chapter 28). On March 31, 1968, Johnson announced a partial bombing halt and a willingness to search for a negotiated end to the war. Then, dramatically, he announced that he would not seek reelection and would devote himself to the search for peace (see Chapter 32). By late May 1968, preliminary peace talks between the United States and North Vietnam had begun in Paris. Johnson's decision to remove himself from the presidential race was a direct result of the lack of consensus at home. His attempts to lead the United States to victory in Vietnam and victory over poverty at home had both ended in stalemate and personal disappointment.

The first months of 1968 thus marked an important turning point in the long history of American involvement in Vietnam. The policy of incremental escalation in force since the 1950s came to an end when Westmoreland's request for more troops was turned down. Furthermore, the evaporating domestic consensus for the war meant that future leaders would have to find a way of disengaging, rather than escalating, the American commitment. But even though a corner had been turned in 1968, there was not yet Robert McNamara's proverbial "light at the end of the tunnel."

The struggle in Vietnam reflected problems characteristic of most new nations in the post-colonial world—nationalist ambitions, religious and cultural conflicts, economic needs, and political turmoil. In reality, Vietnam was too small to play a significant part in the international balance of power; its communism was intensely regional and nationalistic, not expansionist. Yet the Kennedy and Johnson administrations, their predecessors, and Nixon and Ford to follow, allowed their perception of a worldwide communist threat and the need to maintain American credibility to control their actions in Vietnam. By 1968 what Lyndon Johnson had once referred to as "a raggedy-ass little fourth-rate country" had brought the world's most powerful military giant to the bargaining table.

Lyndon Johnson never admitted to the American people the extent of the nation's growing involvement in Vietnam; nor did he confront the true cost of ending poverty through legislative activism. Johnson's attempt to pursue simultaneously the Vietnam War and the Great Society provoked by 1968 a profound crisis from which the Democratic coalition has yet to recover.

Summary

A liberal agenda, especially the commitment to expanding the responsibility of the state for social welfare and economic well-being first begun during the New Deal, shaped political life in the 1960s. The concentration of power in Washington led to a corresponding growth in the responsibilities of the president, whom citizens now invested with rising expectations of leadership. John F. Kennedy stimulated this "politics of expectation," but his expansive vision of presidential leadership was clipped by his limited popular mandate. Lyndon Johnson, building on the wave of public emotion after Kennedy's assassination, used his legislative skills to win enactment of a broad Democratic domestic agenda.

By the late 1960s, however, the controversy over social programs at home and the escalating Vietnam war threatened the liberal consensus.

The same cold war mentality that characterized postwar foreign policy shaped American involvement in Vietnam. The American presence in Vietnam had been increasing gradually since the 1950s, but escalated dramatically after 1965 during the Johnson administration. Despite bombing attacks on North Vietnam and the deployment of half a million U.S. ground troops, the United States and its South Vietnamese allies found themselves no closer to victory. The 1968 Tet offensive and the beginning of peace talks in Paris signaled a major turning point in the war, although America did not officially end its involvement until 1973.

TOPIC FOR RESEARCH

The Vietnam War

In many ways Vietnam became an American war, fought for American aims. You have read about the war from the perspective of policymakers caught up in the Cold War and maintaining American credibility, and from the perspective of the American soldiers sent to "Nam." Yet those with the largest stake in the contest were the Vietnamese people themselves. How does the war look different from the Vietnamese perspective(s)? Who supported the insurgents, and who supported the American-backed governments? What role did religion and agriculture have in shaping loyalties? What is the relation between the kind of nationalistic communism practiced by Ho Chi Minh and Soviet (or Chinese) communism? What meaning would American democracy, however defined, have in a country such as Vietnam?

Several books concentrate on the Vietnamese themselves. An excellent introduction is Frances Fitzgerald, *Fire in the Lake: The Vietnamese and the Americans in Vietnam* (1972), especially Part I. The writings of French journalist Bernard Fall are also insightful, including *The Two Vietnams* (1963), *Vietnam Witness, 1953–1966* (1966), and *Last Reflections on a War* (1967). Marilyn Young, *The Vietnam Wars, 1945–1990* (1991), treats the Vietnamese and American sides with equal weight. Jeffrey P. Kimball, *To Reason Why: The Debate About the Causes of U.S. Involvement in the Vietnam War* (1990), is a collection of speeches and essays on the reasons for U.S. involvement.

BIBLIOGRAPHY

The best general introduction to the politics and social developments of the postwar world is William H. Chafe, *The Unfinished Journey: America Since World War II* (2nd ed., 1991). See also Godfrey Hodgson, *America in Our Time* (1976), and William E. Leuchtenberg, *A Troubled Feast* (1979). Standard overviews of American foreign policy are Stephen Ambrose, *Rise to Globalism* (5th ed., 1988); Walter LaFeber, *America, Russia, and the Cold War* (6th ed., 1990); and Thomas J. McCormick, *America's Half Century: United States Foreign Policy in the Cold War* (1989).

The Politics of Expectation

The best histories of politics of the 1960s are Allen J. Matusow, *The Unraveling of America: A History of Liberalism in the 1960s* (1984); Jim F. Heath, *Decade of Disillusionment: The Kennedy-Johnson Years* (1975); and James L. Sundquist, *Politics and Policy: The Eisenhower, Kennedy, and Johnson Years* (1968).

The indispensable account of the 1960 presidential campaign is Theodore H. White, *The Making of the President—1960* (1961). Arthur M. Schlesinger, Jr., *A Thousand Days* (1965), and Theodore Sorenson, *Kennedy* (1965), offer uncritical but highly readable accounts of the New Frontier. See also Roger Hilsman, another Kennedy aide, *To Move a Nation* (1967); David Burner, *JFK and A New Generation* (1988); and Thomas Brown, *John F. Kennedy: History of an Image* (1988). Critical views appear in David Halberstam, *The Best and the Brightest* (1972); Henry Fairlie, *The Kennedy Promise: The Politics of Expectation* (1973); and Garry Wills, *The Kennedy Imprisonment* (1980). The best account of President Kennedy's assassination is William Manchester's overwritten *The Death of the President* (1967); Anthony Summer, *Conspiracy* (1980), provides a careful review of the ongoing controversy.

For the Supreme Court, useful surveys include Bernard Schwartz, *Super Chief: Earl Warren and the Supreme Court* (1983); Archibald Cox, *The Warren Court* (1968); Alexander Bickel, *The Supreme Court and the Idea of Progress* (1970); and Philip B. Kurland, *Politics, the Constitution, and the Warren Court* (1970). Anthony Lewis, *Gideon's Trumpet* (1964), narrates one of the era's most famous cases, *Gideon v. Wainwright*.

For the foreign policy of the Kennedy years, see Richard Walton, *Cold War and Counterrevolution* (1972). Robert Kennedy, *Thirteen Days* (1969), provides a participant's account of the Cuban missile crisis, which can be supplemented by McGeorge Bundy, *Danger and Survival* (1989). For U.S. relations with the Third World, see Richard Barnet, *Intervention and Revolution* (1968); John L. S. Girling, *America and the Third World* (1980); Samuel Baily, *The United States and the Development of South America, 1945–1975* (1977); Richard Immerman, *The CIA in Guatemala* (1982); and Gabriel Kolko, *Confronting the Third World* (1988). Gerald T. Rice, *The Bold Experiment* (1985), and Karen Schwarz, *What You Can Do for Your Country* (1991), cover the Peace Corps.

Lyndon Johnson's own account of his presidency is *The Vantage Point* (1971). Doris Kearns, *Lyndon Johnson and the American Dream* (1976), and Merle Miller, *Lyndon: An Oral Biography* (1980), are based on extensive conversations with LBJ. Rowland Evans and Robert D. Novak offer a vigorous portrait in *Lyndon B. Johnson: The Exercise of Power* (1966). Robert A. Caro provides a critical interpretation of Johnson's early career in *The Path To Power* (1982) and *Means of Ascent* (1989). Eric F. Goldman, *The Tragedy of Lyndon Johnson* (1969), and George E. Reedy, *The Twilight of the Presidency* (1975), are sympathetic but critical views from former aides. For the 1964 election, see Theodore H. White, *The Making of the President—1964* (1965). Barry M. Goldwater presented his ideas in *The Conscience of a Conservative* (1960), which can be supplemented by Phyllis Schlafly, *A Choice Not an Echo* (1963).

Michael Harrington called attention to poverty in *The Other America* (1962). Charles Murray's conservative viewpoint in *Losing Ground: American Social Policy, 1950–1980* (1983), can be balanced by Michael Katz's liberal perspective in *The Undeserving Poor: From the War on Poverty to the War on Welfare* (1989). Other accounts of poverty include Harry M. Caudill, *Night Comes to the Cumberlands* (1963); J. Wayne Flynt, *Dixie's Forgotten People* (1979); and Susan Estabrook Kennedy, *If All We Did Was to Weep at Home* (1979). Sara A. Levitan describes the war on poverty in *The Great Society's Poor Law* (1969), and, with Robert Taggart, argues that it was quite effective in *The Promise of Greatness* (1976). Charles R. Morris, *A Time of Passion* (1984), offers thoughtful reflections from a former antipoverty administrator. Daniel P. Moynihan criticizes the community action program in *Maximum Feasible Misunderstanding* (1969). Other critical discussions of antipoverty programs include John Donovan, *The Politics of Poverty* (1973), and Richard Cloward and Frances Fox Piven, *Poor People's Movements* (1978). Marvin E. Gettleman and David Mermelstein, eds., *The Great Society Reader* (1965), criticize the prevailing assumptions behind many Johnson initiatives.

Vietnam and the American Experience

For insightful works on the Vietnam War, see the books listed in the Topic for Research. Two other books that provide an excellent introduction to the conflict and the American role in it are Stanley Karnow, *Vietnam: A History* (1983), and George Herring, *America's Longest War* (2nd ed., 1986). A fascinating source to digest is *The Pentagon Papers* (1971). David Halberstam, *The Best and the Brightest* (1972), gives a

deft and biting portrait of the leaders who got the United States into Vietnam. Guenter Lewy offers a controversial defense of the commitment in *America in Vietnam* (1978). James C. Thompson, *Rolling Thunder* (1980), and John Galloway, *The Gulf of Tonkin Resolution* (1970), cover specific topics. The definitive book on the antiwar movement is Charles DeBenedetti, with Charles Chatfield, *An American Ordeal* (1990).

For a sense of what the war felt like to the soldiers who fought it, see Mark Baker, *Nam* (1982), and Ron Kovic, *Born on the Fourth of July* (1976). Wallace Terry, *Bloods* (1984), surveys the experiences of black veterans; Keith Walker, *A Piece of My Heart* (1985), introduces the often forgotten stories of women who served in Vietnam. See also Gloria Emerson, *Winners and Losers* (1976), and Michael Herr, *Dispatches* (1977). Neil Sheehan surveys the entire Vietnam experience through the life of career soldier John Paul Vann in *A Bright Shining Lie* (1988).

TIMELINE

1960	John F. Kennedy elected president
1961	Peace Corps established Bay of Pigs invasion (April 17) U.S. advisers in Vietnam
1962	John Glenn orbits earth Berlin Wall erected (August 15) Cuban missile crisis (October)
1963	Test-ban Treaty Coup ousts Ngo Dinh Diem in Vietnam Kennedy assassinated; Lyndon B. Johnson assumes presidency
1964	Tax cut Civil Rights Act War on Poverty Gulf of Tonkin Resolution (August 5) Johnson elected president
1965	Voting Rights Act Medicare and Medicaid Elementary and Secondary Education Act First U.S. combat troops arrive in Vietnam Beginnings of antiwar movement
1968	Tet offensive begins (January 30) Peace talks open in Paris (November)
1969	U.S. lands first person on the moon

La Huelga

Long live the cause, long live the strike, proclaimed Paul Davis's poster for a 1968 Carnegie
Hall benefit for Cesar Chavez's farm workers'
union, symptomatic of the challenges of protest
movements in the 1960s. (Museum of American
Political Life)

CHAPTER **31** *The Struggles For Equality and Diversity, 1954–1975*

The 1960s are often portrayed as a time of social protest and upheaval. Yet the era of questioning and confrontation was not confined to a single decade. From the early 1950s through the mid-1970s, new issues and movements crowded the national agenda. The struggle of African-Americans for their civil rights gained momentum in the 1950s with early victories against segregation in the South. The youth rebellion and resurgent feminism also had roots in the supposedly complacent 1950s, and the women's movement made its greatest impact on society in the 1970s.

Why did these demands for change occur when they did? Demographic shifts and earlier social changes were partly responsible. The black exodus from the South made civil rights a national, not a sectional, issue. The baby-boom generation swelled the enrollments of the nation's universities, providing recruits for student protest in the 1960s. Changes in women's lives, notably their increased access to education and greater participation in the work force, sparked the revival of feminism.

The civil rights movement was the first protest movement to develop in the postwar period. The tactics it pioneered—legislative and judicial challenges, nonviolent protests, and mobilization of public opinion—would later be adopted by other groups to press their demands. But even at the height of the protest movements, those who demanded change were always outnumbered by those who preferred the status quo. Although such resistance hindered the protestors' achievements, the movements for equality and diversity still had a large impact on American culture. By 1975

society had had its "consciousness raised" (a phrase from the women's movement) about a host of issues and problems that had not been topics of national concern in the two decades after World War II.

The Civil Rights Movement

The civil rights movement was enormously successful in its early days. The breakthroughs were especially dramatic in the South, where segregation, the legal separation of the races that had existed since before the turn of the century, was dismantled. The challenges posed by the civil rights movement to established customs and patterns of authority then rippled through the society in the climate of the "politics of expectation." Observed a northern white professor who participated in the movement, "What started as an identity crisis for Negroes turned out to be an identity crisis for the nation."

The Challenge to Segregation

Legal segregation of the races still governed the southern way of life in the early 1950s. In most states, it was illegal for whites and blacks to eat in the same rooms in restaurants or luncheonettes, use the same waiting rooms or toilet facilities at bus or train stations, or ride in the same taxis. All forms of public transportation were rigidly segregated, either by custom or law. On buses, for example, if whites had filled all the front

945

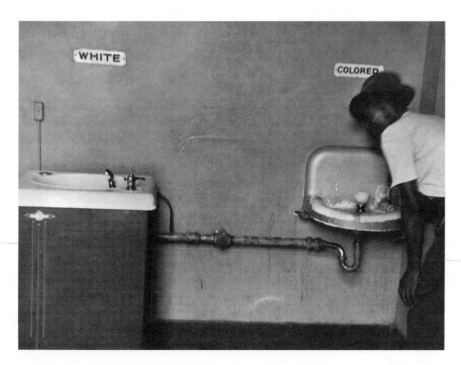

Racial Segregation, North Carolina, 1950
Some pictures are so powerful and shocking they hardly need captions. This is one of them.

seats, blacks were obliged to give up seats in the back until every white had a place. Even drinking fountains were labeled "White" and "Colored."

Usually blacks and whites observed local customs without comment. But there were exceptions. In August 1955, G. H. Mehta, India's ambassador to the United States, walked into a restaurant at the Houston airport. To his indignant surprise, Mehta was told he could not legally be served because he had taken a seat in the "Whites only" section. This incident exposed the southern system to the scrutiny of the world and embarrassed the U.S. government. Within less than a decade these laws would be totally gone.

Leadership in the battle against segregation and racial discrimination came not from the government but from national and community organizations, church groups, and ordinary citizens. Years of patient lobbying by the National Association for the Advancement of Colored People (NAACP) laid the groundwork for the challenge to segregation. Starting in the 1940s, NAACP lawyers such as Thurgood Marshall and William Hastie litigated a series of test cases challenging segregation. Their first victory came in 1944, when the Supreme Court declared that blacks could not be denied the right to vote in party primaries. In 1946 the Court ruled that states could not require segregated seating on interstate buses, and two years later it struck down restrictive residential covenants which prevented the sale of real estate to members of disfavored groups.

Brown v. Board of Education. In 1954, the Supreme Court handed down one of its most far-reaching deci-

sions in a group of challenges to school segregation consolidated as *Brown v. Board of Education of Topeka, Kansas.* The NAACP had filed the Topeka case on behalf of Linda Brown, a black student who attended a segregated school several miles from her home rather than the white elementary school nearby. NAACP Chief Counsel Thurgood Marshall argued that the legal segregation mandated by the Topeka Board of Education was inherently unconstitutional because it stigmatized an entire race and thereby denied it the "equal protection of the laws" guaranteed by the Fourteenth Amendment. In a unanimous decision announced on May 17, 1954, the Supreme Court agreed, overturning the "separate but equal" doctrine of *Plessy v. Ferguson* (see Chapter 19). Speaking for the Court, Chief Justice Earl Warren ruled:

> To separate Negro children . . . solely because of their race generates a feeling of inferiority as to their status in the community that may affect their hearts and minds in a way unlikely ever to be undone. . . . We conclude that in the field of public education the doctrine of "separate but equal" has no place. Separate educational facilities are inherently unequal. . . . Any language in *Plessy v. Ferguson* contrary to these findings is rejected.

Blacks were especially proud that Marshall, a black lawyer, had won such a stunning judicial victory. White reaction was more mixed. White liberals were pleased, but President Eisenhower privately complained that his appointment of Chief Justice Earl Warren was "the biggest damn fool mistake I ever made."

In response to more NAACP suits over the next several years, the Supreme Court used the *Brown* precedent to overturn segregation in city parks, public beaches and golf courses, all forms of interstate and intrastate transportation, and public housing. Meanwhile progress in desegregating schools was frustratingly slow. In a 1955 decision implementing the Kansas decision, known as *Brown II*, the Court declared only that integration should proceed "with all deliberate speed." Many critics would later note that the deliberation was far more evident than the speed. By 1960 less than 1 percent of southern black children were attending desegregated schools. Significant levels of school integration would not be achieved until the 1970s.

Once it became clear that the Court was not going to back down on civil rights, white resistance solidified. In 1956, more than a hundred members of Congress signed a Southern Manifesto denouncing the *Brown* decision as "a clear abuse of judicial power" and encouraging their constituents to defy it. By the end of the year 500,000 southerners had joined White Citizens' Councils dedicated to blocking school integration and other civil rights measures. Some whites revived the old tactics of violence and intimidation, swelling the ranks of the Ku Klux Klan to levels not seen since the 1920s.

So far Eisenhower had accepted the *Brown* decision as the law of the land but had not committed federal power to enforcing it. A crisis in Little Rock, Arkansas, finally forced him to intervene, albeit reluctantly, on the side of desegregation. In September 1957, nine black students attempted to enroll at all-white Central High School after the local school board won a court order to implement a desegregation plan. Governor Orval Faubus called out the National Guard to bar them, despite the court order. Then the mob took over. Every

day a white crowd taunted the poised but obviously terrified black students with such chants as "Go back to the jungle." As the vicious scenes were replayed on television night after night, Eisenhower reluctantly decided to act. He sent 1,000 federal troops to Little Rock and nationalized 10,000 members of the Arkansas National Guard, ordering them to protect the students. Eisenhower thus became the first president since Reconstruction to use federal troops to enforce the rights of blacks. This was the first of many times that white extremism provoked a far more sympathetic response from the federal government toward blacks than would otherwise have occurred.

Nonviolent Protest

The *Brown* decision had shown that the NAACP's strategy of judicial challenge could bring fundamental change. But the magnitude of white resistance to integration had also made it clear that winning in court was not enough. A new strategy was needed to challenge the pervasive racism and segregation that persisted in practice even if no longer in law. Sparked by one tiny but monumental act of defiance, southern black leaders embraced nonviolent protest.

The Montgomery Bus Boycott. On December 1, 1955, Rosa Parks, a seamstress and member of the NAACP in Montgomery, Alabama, refused to give up her seat on a city bus to a white man. She was promptly arrested and charged with violating a local segregation ordinance. "I felt it was just something I had to do," Parks stated simply. Black activist Eldridge Cleaver put her act of resistance in a broader context: "Somewhere in the universe a gear in the machinery had shifted."

Integration in Little Rock
Angry crowds taunted the nine black students who tried to register in 1957 at previously all-white Central High School in Little Rock, Arkansas, with chants such as "Two-four-six-eight, we ain't gonna integrate." The court ordered integration proceeded only after President Eisenhower reluctantly nationalized the Arkansas National Guard.

As the local black community met to discuss the proper response, it turned to the Reverend Martin Luther King, Jr., who had become pastor at Montgomery's Dexter Street Baptist Church the year before. The son of a prominent black minister in Atlanta, King had received a B.A. from Morehouse College and a Ph.D. in theology from Boston University. King embraced the teachings of Mahatma Gandhi, who had organized the brilliant campaigns of passive resistance that led to India's independence from Britain in 1947. Drawing on Gandhian principles, King suggested that blacks boycott Montgomery's bus system until it was integrated.

For the next 381 days, a united black community formed carpools or walked to work. "My feets is tired, but my soul is rested," said one woman. The bus company neared bankruptcy, and downtown stores complained about the loss of business. But not until the Supreme Court ruled in November 1956 that bus segregation was illegal did the city of Montgomery finally comply.

The Montgomery bus boycott catapulted King to national prominence. In 1957 with the Reverend Ralph Abernathy and other southern black clergy he founded the Southern Christian Leadership Conference (SCLC), based in Atlanta. The black church had long been the center of African-American social and cultural life. Now it lent its moral and organizational strength, as well as the voices of its most inspirational preachers, to the emerging civil rights movement. Black churchwomen supplied one of the strongest constituencies, transferring the skills they had honed through years of church work to fighting for racial change. The Southern Christian Leadership Conference joined the NAACP as one of the main spurs for racial justice.

Sit-Ins. The next phase of the nonviolent movement began in Greensboro, North Carolina, on February 1, 1960. Four black students from North Carolina Agricultural and Technical College—Ezell Blair, Jr., Franklin McCain, Joseph McNeill, and David Richmond—took seats at the "Whites only" lunch counter of a local Woolworth store, determined to "sit in" until they were served. When Blair ordered something to eat, "The waitress looked at me as if I were from outer space." The target of their protest demonstrated the capriciousness of southern segregation laws. Blacks could buy toothpaste, underwear, and magazines alongside whites at Woolworth's, but not a sandwich or a cup of coffee.

Although Blair and his fellow protestors were arrested, the sit-in tactic worked. White business owners quickly realized that they would lose business if the disruptions continued. By the end of the year, black activists and a number of white supporters had desegre-

gated lunch counters in 126 cities throughout the South. About 50,000 people participated in sit-ins or other demonstrations, and 3,600 of them were jailed, usually for disturbing the peace. The Student Non-Violent Coordinating Committee (SNCC, pronounced "snick"), an offshoot of the SCLC, organized and coordinated the student sit-ins. Ella Baker, a SCLC administrator and lifelong activist, offered the students moral and tactical support.

Freedom Rides. The success of the upstart SNCC's unorthodox tactics encouraged the Congress of Racial Equality (CORE), an interracial group founded in 1942, to adopt a more confrontational strategy. In 1961, CORE's executive director James Farmer organized a series of "freedom rides" on interstate bus lines throughout the South. Farmer targeted buses, waiting rooms, toilets, and terminal restaurants throughout the deep South to call attention to the continuing illegal segregation of public transportation despite the Supreme Court rulings. Activists, mostly young, both black and white, signed on for the potentially dangerous trips. In Anniston, Alabama, club-wielding Ku Klux Klansmen attacked one of the buses with stones and set it on fire. The freedom riders escaped only moments before the bus exploded. Other riders were brutally beaten in Montgomery and Birmingham, but Alabama governor John Patterson refused to intervene, saying "I cannot guarantee protection for this bunch of rabble rousers."

As film of the beatings and bus burnings appeared on the nightly news, Attorney General Robert Kennedy intervened to protect the freedom riders. He also prodded the Interstate Commerce Commission to tighten regulations against segregation on interstate vehicles and terminal facilities. Faced with potential Justice Department intervention against those who defied the Interstate Commerce Commission rules, most southern communities quietly acceded to the changes. CORE meanwhile learned the lesson that nonviolent protest would succeed if it provoked vicious white resistance and generated lots of publicity. Only when forced to, it appeared, would federal authorities act.

JFK and Civil Rights

The accelerating momentum of the civil rights movement had profound implications for the federal government. The Civil Rights movement was arguably the most important force for change in postwar America, but President John Kennedy initially lacked any great empathy for the black cause. Instead, Kennedy seemed to view civil rights protests as irritating political embar-

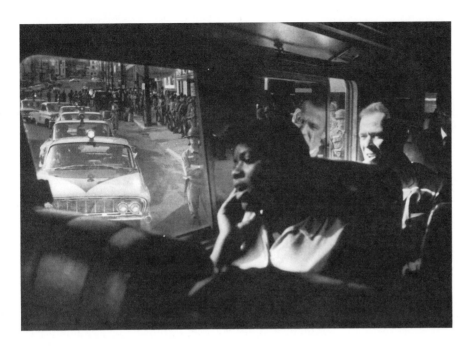

Freedom Riders
Black and white volunteers watch anxiously as they pull into the Montgomery, Alabama, bus station in 1961, while a hostile white crowd gathers outside. Civil rights leader James L. Farmer recalled their determination: "On the bus I noticed . . . boys writing notes and putting them in their pockets, and girls putting them in their brassieres. . . . They were writing names and addresses of next of kin. They really had not expected to live beyond that trip."

rassments that detracted from more important arenas for presidential leadership and action. The Kennedy administration's lack of a response to the emerging civil rights agenda was one of its greatest failures.

Political realities in part dictated Kennedy's reluctance to act, especially tensions within the Democratic coalition. On the one hand, Kennedy needed the votes of southern Democrats to get his programs through Congress, and he did not want to alienate them by embracing the civil rights cause. For the same reason, Kennedy appointed a number of white supremacist judges to the southern bench. On the other hand, blacks had given him strong support in the 1960 election, and Kennedy needed to keep them safely within the coalition. So he reached out to black constituencies with actions such as appointing Thurgood Marshall to the U.S. Circuit Court of Appeals.

But the darkest stain on Kennedy's civil rights record was his acquiescence in the FBI's clandestine surveillance of Martin Luther King, Jr., and the Southern Christian Leadership Conference. In the early 1960s, FBI director J. Edgar Hoover became convinced that the civil rights movement had ties to the Soviet Union. Fears of Communist infiltration found a receptive audience among the cold warriors in the Kennedy White House, and in 1962 Attorney General Robert Kennedy authorized wiretaps on King's Atlanta home and the SCLC headquarters. To its chagrin, the FBI found no evidence of Communist links, but it did uncover evidence of King's extramarital activity, which it then tried unsuccessfully to use to discredit him. Throughout the 1960s the FBI, with the tacit backing of the Kennedy

administration and later Lyndon Johnson's as well, seemed to treat the civil rights movement, in Coretta Scott King's words, "as if it were an alien enemy attack on the United States."

Events in 1963 finally pushed the Kennedy administration to take a stronger stand. In Birmingham, Alabama, Martin Luther King, Jr., and the Reverend Fred Shuttlesworth called for a protest against conditions in what King called "the most segregated city in the United States." In April, thousands of black demonstrators marched downtown to picket Birmingham's department stores. They were met by Eugene ("Bull") Connor, the city's commissioner of public safety, who used snarling dogs, electric cattle prods, and high-pressure fire hoses to break up the crowd; the fire hoses were so strong that they ripped bark from trees and tore bricks from buildings. Television cameras captured the entire scene. "The civil rights movement should thank God for Bull Connor," President Kennedy noted. "He's helped it as much as Abraham Lincoln."

Realizing he could no longer straddle the issue, Kennedy determined to step up the federal role in civil rights. On June 11, 1963, he went on television to promise major civil rights legislation banning discrimination in public accommodations and empowering the Justice Department to seek desegregation on its own authority. Black leaders hailed the speech as a "Second Emancipation Proclamation." But for one person Kennedy's speech came too late. That same night, Medgar Evers, a prominent NAACP activist, was shot in the back and killed in Jackson, Mississippi. The martyred Evers became a spur to further action.

AMERICAN LIVES

Ella Baker

"Who the hell is this old lady here?" asked more than one impudent, and unknowing, newcomer to the offices of the Student Non-Violent Coordinating Committee (SNCC) in Atlanta. Regal, matronly, conservatively dressed in a business suit, and always referred to as "Miss Baker," fifty-seven-year-old Ella Baker did stand out from the black and white college students who flocked to SNCC in the early 1960s. But once activists watched her in action, few doubted that she belonged. Recalled veteran SNCC activist John Lewis, "She was much older in terms of age, but I think in terms of ideas and philosophy and commitment she was one of the youngest persons in the movement."

When Baker used her position as the executive secretary of the Southern Christian Leadership Conference (SCLC) to act as the midwife for the birth of SNCC in 1960, she already had years of experience as an organizer and facilitator of social change, almost all of it be-

hind the scenes. As she recalled, "You didn't see me on television, you didn't see news stories about me. The kind of role that I tried to play was to pick up pieces or put together pieces out of which I hoped organization might come. My theory is, strong people don't need strong leaders." Ella Baker recognized the large, often unheralded roles that women played in the emergence of the civil rights movement: "the movement of the Fifties and the Sixties was carried largely by women, since it came out of church groups. . . . The number of women who carried the movement is much larger than that of the men." Her own life is a prime example.

Ella Baker was born in Norfolk, Virginia, in 1903, and grew up in rural North Carolina on land that her grandparents had originally farmed as slaves. She drew enormous strength from her family, with her mother's community and church work providing a model for her own later activism. Reflecting the importance placed on

Ella Baker
She was a woman of action whose life-long commitment was dedicated to social change.

education by black families, especially for daughters who would need to work even if they married, Baker was sent to Shaw College in Raleigh, North Carolina. Soon after graduating in 1927, she headed north to Harlem, arriving just as the Great Depression dried up opportunities in the promised land of the North. Instead of going to graduate school in sociology as she had hoped, she worked as a journalist, did some political organizing, and was involved in WPA consumer projects. She also was married briefly, and unhappily, to a black minister. In the 1940s she traveled around the country as a field organizer for the National Association for the Advancement of Colored People (NAACP), but she quit that job when she took on the responsibility of raising a seven-year-old niece. Throughout her career, she rarely held regular jobs. "How did I make a living? I haven't. I have eked out existence."

When the SCLC was established in 1957 in the wake of the successful Montgomery bus boycott, Ella Baker was recruited "temporarily" to be its executive secretary. She ended up staying two and a half years. Her organizational skills were very important to the developing movement, but she found herself increasingly restive under King's cautious leadership. In addition, she realized, not for the first time, that her lack of deference to male leadership, her outspoken manner, and her willingness to talk back made black men uncomfortable. She had an especially hard time working with King, who held very traditional ideas about gender roles.

So when the student sit-ins erupted spontaneously in early 1960, Baker watched this development with interest and excitement. She convinced the SCLC to put up $800 toward a conference of student leaders to be held on the campus of her alma mater in Raleigh in April 1960. More than three hundred young people attended, a huge outpouring. At the convention Baker encouraged student leaders to chart an independent role, and not just to become the "youth wings" of established groups like SCLC, the NAACP, or CORE. She did not come right out and say, "Don't let Martin Luther King tell you what to do," recalled Julian Bond, but that was clearly what she meant. The students followed her advice, and SNCC remained independent from existing civil rights organizations. Baker's faith in the students was totally in keeping with her lifelong commitment to grassroots, "group-centered leadership." Probably her greatest dissatisfaction with the SCLC had been how it revolved so completely around Martin Luther King's leadership.

During the turbulent 1960s, Baker offered her organizational skills and material support to SNCC. She never intervened directly in the internal struggles and endless discussions that characterized the group, choosing instead to serve as a facilitator for group consensus and action. She provided not just a bridge across generations, but an incredibly powerful role model of political engagement and activism. This model was especially important to women, both black and white, who drew the lesson that women could be just as effective as organizers and participants as men. The non-hierarchical structure of SNCC, with its emphasis on local leadership and individual initiative, provided an egalitarian climate far more conducive to the utilization of female talent than the society at large. For some women, especially the white volunteers, their experience in SNCC laid the groundwork for the emergence of the women's movement later in the decade.

Voter registration had always been a top priority for SNCC, and in 1964 Ella Baker became involved in an attempt to wrest political power from the regular Democratic party, which remained rigidly all-white in the South. Denied access to the right to vote, SNCC organized an alternative political party—the Mississippi Freedom Democratic party (MFDP). Fannie Lou Hamer became the movement's most visible public orator, but Ella Baker played a crucial behind-the-scenes role. Testifying before the credentials committee at the Democratic convention in Atlantic City that summer, Hamer and Baker led the unsuccessful effort to unseat the all-white Mississippi delegation in favor of the MFDP. When President Johnson and the Democratic leadership offered the MFDP token representation in the delegation, the MFDP rejected this compromise as an insult. Baker was not bitter or discouraged by this outcome, or the many other setbacks she faced in her career. "I keep going because I don't see the productive value of being bitter. What else *do* you do?"

Ella Baker continued her lifelong commitment to participatory democracy and social change long after SNCC had lost its place as the cutting edge of the civil rights movement. She died in 1986 on her eighty-third birthday. At her memorial service, civil rights activist Bernice Johnson Reagon, the founder of the singing group Sweet Honey in the Rock, led the assembled friends in a favorite song that captured the determination and spirituality that shaped Ella Baker's lifelong activism: "Guide my feet while I run this race. . . . for I don't want to run this race in vain."

The March on Washington

To marshall support for Kennedy's bill—and to rouse the conscience of the country at large—civil rights leaders turned to a tactic that A. Phillip Randolph had suggested as early as 1941: a massive march on Washington. Martin Luther King of the SCLC, Roy Wilkins of the NAACP, Whitney Young of the National Urban League, and black socialist Bayard Rustin were the principal organizers. They drew support from a broad coalition, including the National Council of Churches, the National Conference of Catholics for Interracial Justice, the American Jewish Congress, and the AFL–CIO Industrial Union Department.

On August 28, 1963, about 250,000 black and white demonstrators—the largest protest assembled up to that time—gathered at the Lincoln Memorial. Speakers and performers alternately uplifted, challenged, and entertained the crowd. The March on Washington culminated in a memorable speech delivered, indeed preached, by Martin Luther King in the evangelical style of the black church:

> I have a dream that one day on the red hills of Georgia the sons of former slaves and the sons of former slaveowners will be able to sit down together at the table of brotherhood. I have a dream that one day even the state of Mississippi, a desert state sweltering with the heat of injustice and oppression, will be transformed into an oasis of freedom and justice. I have a dream that my four little children will one day live in a nation where they will not be judged by the color of their skin but by the content of their character.

He ended with an invocation from an old Negro spiritual, "Free at last! Free at last! Thank God almighty, we are free at last!"

King's eloquence, and the sight of blacks and whites marching solemnly together, did more than any other event to make black protest acceptable to white Americans. The March on Washington seemed to justify the liberal faith that blacks and whites could work together to promote racial harmony, and it marked the climax of the nonviolent phase of the civil rights movement. It also confirmed King's position, especially for the white liberal community, as the leading speaker for the black cause. His stature was further enhanced when he won the Nobel Peace Prize in 1964.

Despite the impact of the March on Washington on public opinion, even as ardent a civil rights supporter as Senator Hubert Humphrey realized that few congressional votes had been changed by the event. Southern senators continued to block Kennedy's legislation by threatening a filibuster. Even more troubling was a new outbreak of violence by white extremists, determined to

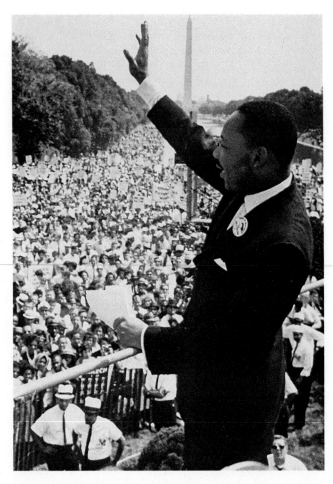

Martin Luther King, Jr.
The Reverend Martin Luther King, Jr. (1929–1968) was one of the most eloquent advocates of the black cause in the 1950s and 1960s. For many, his speech at the 1963 March on Washington was the highpoint of the event.

oppose equality for blacks at all costs. In September a Baptist church in Birmingham was bombed, and four black girls attending Sunday school were killed. Only two months after the Birmingham bombing, President Kennedy was assassinated in Dallas.

Landmark Legislation

Lyndon Johnson promptly turned passage of civil rights legislation into a memorial to his slain predecessor, a slightly ironic twist given Kennedy's lukewarm support for the cause. The Civil Rights Act, finally passed in June 1964, was a landmark in the history of American race relations and one of the greatest achievements of the 1960s. Its keystone, a section known as Title VII,

AMERICAN VOICES

Registering to Vote in Mississippi *Fannie Lou Hamer*

Fannie Lou Hamer was the youngest of twenty children born into a share-cropping family in Montgomery county, Mississippi. When she attempted to register to vote in 1962, she lost her job as a timekeeper on a cotton plantation. In 1964 she led the challenge of the Mississippi Freedom Democratic party to the all-white party regulars in that state.

So then that was in 1962 when the civil rights workers came into this country. Now I didn't know anything about voter registration or nothin' like that, 'cause people had never been told that they could register to vote. . . . So they had a rally. I had gone to church that Sunday, and the minister announced that they were gon' have a mass meeting that Monday night. Well, I didn't know what a mass meeting was, and I was just curious to go to a mass meeting. So I did . . . and they was talkin' about how blacks had a right to register and how they had a right to *vote*. . . . Just listenin' at 'em, I could just see myself votin' people outa office that I know was wrong and didn't do nothin' to help the poor. I said, you know, that's sumpin' I really wanna be involved in, and finally at the end of that rally, I had made up my mind that I was gonna come out here when they said you could go down that Friday [August 31, 1962] to try to register. . . .

He [the registrar] brought a big old book out there, and he gave me the sixteenth section of the Constitution of Mississippi, and that was dealing with de facto laws, and I didn't know nothin' about no de facto laws, didn't know nothin' about any of 'em. I could copy it like it was in the book . . . but after I got through copying it, he told me to give a reasonable interpretation and tell the meaning of that section that I had copied. Well, I flunked out. . . .

Monday, the fourth of December, I went back to Indianola to the circuit clerk's office and I told him who I was and I was there to take that literacy test again.

I said, "Now, you cain't have me fired 'cause I'm already fired, and I won't have to move now, because I'm not livin' in no white man's house." I said, "I'll be here every thirty days until I become a registered voter."

I passed that second test, but it made us become like criminals. We would have to have our lights out before dark. It was cars passing that house all times of the night, driving real slow with guns, and pickups with white mens in it, and they'd pass that house just as slow as they could pass it . . . three guns lined up in the back. . . . Pap couldn't get nothin' to do. . . .

So I started teachin' citizenship class, and I became the supervisor of the citizenship class in this county. So I moved around the county to do citizenship education and later on I become a field secretary for SNCC.

Source: Howell Raines, *My Soul Is Rested* (New York: Putnam, 1977), 249–50, 252.

outlawed discrimination in employment based on race, religion, national origin, or sex. Another section barred discrimination in public accommodations. In addition, the law gave opponents of segregation two powerful new weapons. They could ask the attorney general to withhold federal funds from any state program that was not desegregated. And they could appeal discrimination in public accommodations and employment to the Equal Employment Opportunity Commission, which Kennedy had established soon after assuming office.

The Civil Rights Act had been passed over a southern filibuster, and many white southerners were determined to defy the new law. In particular, they continued to resist efforts to register blacks to vote. When SNCC and CORE had conducted voter registration drives in 1962–1963, blacks who tried to register faced pressure, economic intimidation, and outright violence. For example, when Fannie Lou Hamer participated in a SNCC voter registration campaign in 1962, she was evicted from the farm where she had sharecropped for eighteen years. The FBI agents sent to the South, supposedly to protect the voting rights activists, sided more often with white authorities, and occasionally the Ku Klux Klan, or did nothing at all.

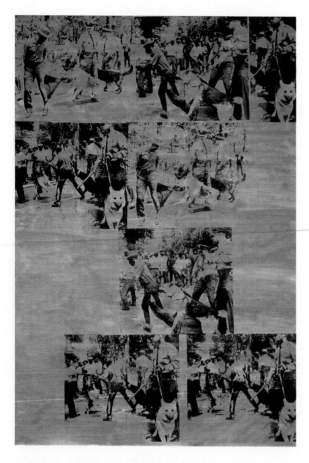

Andy Warhol on Race Relations

Artist Andy Warhol (1928–1987) is forever associated with his pop-art spoofs of consumer culture, such as paintings of Campbell soup cans or Brillo pads, along with his magnetic images of popular icons such as Marilyn Monroe and Elizabeth Taylor. Yet the artist also treated political subjects, such as this provocative (1963) painting *Red Race Riot* depicting violence at a civil rights demonstration. (The Andy Warhol Foundation for the Visual Arts, Inc.)

Freedom Summer. In 1964, with the Civil Rights Act on the brink of passage, black organizations and churches mounted a major registration drive. In that Freedom Summer they recruited several thousand volunteers from across the country, including many idealistic white college students. Violence struck quickly. In June, James Chaney, a CORE volunteer from Mississippi, Andrew Goodman, a student from New York, and Michael Schwerner, a New York social worker, disappeared from Philadelphia, Mississippi, and were presumed murdered. Like many white activists, Goodman and Schwerner were Jewish, a reflection of the large contributions that Jewish groups made to the civil rights movement. As public demand grew for an accounting of their disappearance, Rita Schwerner, Michael's wife, noted, "We all know that this search . . . is because Andrew Goodman and my husband are white. If only Chaney was involved, nothing would have been done."

The three bodies were found several weeks later. Goodman and Schwerner had been killed by a single bullet each, while Chaney had been brutally beaten with a chain and shot several times. An investigation later determined that members of the Ku Klux Klan committed the crime. During Freedom Summer, fifteen civil rights workers were murdered; only 1,600 black voters were registered.

Voting Rights Act of 1965. The need for federal action to support voting rights became even clearer in 1965. In February sheriff's deputies in Marion, Alabama, killed Jimmy Lee Jackson, a black voting-rights advocate, during a voter registration march. In protest, Martin Luther King and other black leaders called for a massive march on Sunday, March 7, from nearby Selma to the state capital, Montgomery, 54 miles away. Governor George Wallace banned the march, disingenuously citing concern for public safety. As soon as the marchers left Selma, mounted state troopers attacked them in broad daylight with tear gas and clubs. The scene was shown on national television later that night; ironically, ABC broke into *Judgment at Nuremberg*, a film about Nazi war crimes, to show the Alabama police attacking American citizens on the Pettus Bridge.

Lyndon Johnson called Bloody Sunday "an American tragedy," and he redoubled his efforts to get Congress to pass his pending voting rights legislation. In a televised speech to a joint session of Congress on March 15, Johnson asserted, "It is wrong—deadly wrong, to deny any of your fellow Americans the right to vote in this country." Then, dramatically and repeatedly, Johnson invoked the best-known slogan of the civil rights movement, "We shall overcome." Watching the speech on television, Martin Luther King was moved to tears.

The Voting Rights Act of 1965, the second legislative landmark of the civil rights movement, marked the high tide of Johnson's Great Society. Passed and signed into law in August, it suspended the literacy tests that most southern states had used to prevent blacks from registering to vote. It also authorized the attorney general to send federal examiners to register voters in any county where less than 50 percent of the voting age population was on the voting lists, thus placing the entire registration and voting process under federal control. Together with the adoption in 1964 of the Twenty-fourth Amendment to the Constitution, which outlawed the federal poll tax, and successful legal challenges to state and local poll taxes, the Voting Rights Act made it possible for millions of blacks to register and vote for the first time. Congress extended the Voting Rights Act in 1970, 1975, and 1982. The results were stunning: in 1960 only 20 percent of eligible blacks were registered. In 1964 the figure had risen to 39 percent, and in 1971 to 62 percent.

Hartman Turnbow, a Mississippi farmer who had risked his life to register to vote in a SNCC-sponsored

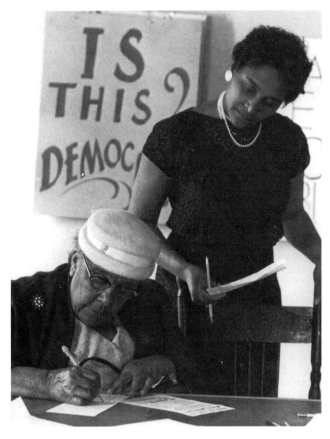

Registering to Vote

Once black citizens could register to vote, they changed the nature of Southern politics, opening new channels of political participation and electoral success. In 1989, there were over 4,440 elected black officials in the South, including 578 in Mississippi alone, a dramatic change in the twenty-five years after the passage of the Voting Rights Act of 1965.

drive during the Freedom Summer of 1964, summed up the momentous changes that had occurred:

> Anybody had a jus told me 'fore it happened that conditions would make this much change between the white and the black in Holmes County here where I live, why I'da just said, "You're lyin'. It won't happen." But it got to workin' just like the citizenship class teacher told us—that if we redish to vote and just stick with it. . . . He said we gon' have difficults, gon' have troubles, folks gon' lose their homes, folks gon' lose their lives, people gon' lose all their money, and just like he said, all of that happened. . . . He hit it kadap on the head, and it's workin' now. It won't never go back where it was.

Rising Militance

Now that the system of legal (*de jure*) segregation had fallen, the civil rights movement turned to a more difficult task: eliminating the *de facto* segregation, enforced by custom, that made blacks second-class citizens throughout the nation. Racial discrimination was less flagrant outside the South, but it was real and pervasive, especially in education, housing, and employment opportunities. While the *Brown* decision outlawed separate but equal schools, it did nothing to change conditions in educational systems where schools were all-black or all-white because of patterns of residential segregation. In the 1960s, 90 percent of Chicago's black students attended predominantly all-black schools. Not until 1973 did federal judges begin to order the desegregation of schools in the rest of the country that had begun in the South two decades earlier.

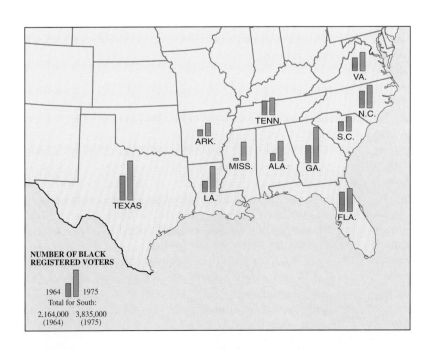

MAP 31.1

Black Voter Registration in the South

After passage of the Voting Rights Act of 1965, black registration in the South increased dramatically. The bars show the number of blacks registered in 1964, before the act was passed, and in 1975, after it had been in effect for ten years. States in the deep South, such as Mississippi, Alabama, and Georgia, had the biggest rises.

As civil rights leaders took on the new target of northern racism, the movement fractured along generational lines. Students who had risked assault to sit in at lunch counters or to register to vote grew impatient with the gradualism of their elders. Many of the freedom riders who had spent months in harsh southern jails found little relevance in Martin Luther King's commitment to nonviolence. Between 1963 and 1965 these activists repudiated the legalistic, nonviolent approach epitomized by the March on Washington and advocated immediate action of a more far-reaching nature. Symbolic of the new militance was their demand to be called blacks or Afro-Americans rather than Negroes, a term they found demeaning because of its historic association with slavery and racism.

Black Separatism. Some younger black activists, eager for confrontation and faster change, even questioned the goal of integration into white society. Black separatism dated back to the nineteenth century, but had been espoused by the Marcus Garvey movement in the 1920s (see Chapter 24). In the 1960s, black separatism was revived by the Nation of Islam, popularly known as the Black Muslims. The Nation of Islam had begun as a small sect in the 1930s, but by the 1960s it had more than 10,000 members, and many more sympathizers. The Black Muslims proselytized very effectively in prisons, urging black inmates to take charge of their lives by adopting a strict code of personal behavior, including the Islamic ban on the use of drugs, alcohol, and tobacco. The Black Muslim ideology was extremely hostile to whites, whom its leader Elijah Muhammad called "blue-eyed devils." Forcefully embracing black nationalism, the Nation of Islam stressed black pride, unity, and self-help. A prominent adherent was the boxer Cassius Clay, who changed his name to Muhammad Ali after his conversion in 1964.

The Black Muslims' most charismatic figure was Malcolm X. Born Malcolm Little in 1925, he converted to the Nation of Islam while serving time in prison for attempted burglary. Taking the name Malcolm X, he portrayed his transformation from petty criminal to minister of Islam as evidence of the redemptive powers of the Black Muslim faith.

A brilliant debater and spellbinding speaker, Malcolm X preached a philosophy quite different from Martin Luther King's. Malcolm advocated militant protest and separatism, although he condoned the use of violence only for self-defense and self-assertion. He was hostile to the traditional civil rights organizations, caustically referring to the 1963 march as the "farce on Washington" and mocking the "angry revolutionists all harmonizing 'We Shall Overcome . . . Suum Day' while tripping and swinging along arm-in-arm with the very people they were supposed to be angrily revolting against."

Malcolm X (1925–1965)
Charismatic, controversial, and caustic, Malcolm X rarely minced words. "Yes, I'm an extremist," he told writer Alex Haley. "The black race here in North America is in extremely bad condition. You show me a black man who isn't an extremist and I'll show you one who needs psychiatric attention!" Director Spike Lee's 1992 film, *Malcolm X,* reignited old controversies, and started some of its own.

In 1963, Malcolm X broke with Elijah Muhammad and the Nation of Islam. The next year he made a pilgrimage to Mecca, the holiest site of traditional Islam, and toured Africa, where he embraced the liberation struggles of all colonial peoples. On February 21, 1965, Malcolm X was assassinated while giving a speech at the Audubon Ballroom in Harlem. Although three Black Muslims were convicted of the murder, so many people opposed Malcolm X that there is a continuing debate over who was responsible for the killing. His autobiography, ghostwritten by Alex Haley and published soon after Malcolm's death, became one of the decade's most influential books.

Black Power. The Black Muslims' demand for cultural and political independence appealed to the young activists of SNCC and CORE, but many balked at the idea of converting to Islam. They wanted a secular black nationalist movement. Abandoning the earlier faith in interracial cooperation, SNCC's Stokely Carmichael christened a new movement in 1966: "We been saying freedom for six years and we ain't got nothing. What we gonna start saying is Black Power!" Soon afterward, Huey Newton and Bobby Seale founded the militant Black Panthers in Oakland, California, the most publicized group advocating Black Power. Newton provocatively told blacks to follow the admonition of China's communist leader Mao Zedong that "political power comes through the barrel of a gun." Only three years after Martin Luther King's "I have a dream" speech, radical black power activists proposed a new agenda: not nonviolence but armed self-defense, not integration but separatism, not working within the system but preparing for revolution.

As a result of this growing militancy, most black organizations went through major identity crises in 1965. By the next year, for all intents and purposes, whites had been kicked out of the civil rights movement. Whites were told they could not understand what it meant to be black; many whites themselves felt guilty about their own complicity in America's institutionalized racism. CORE's decision to bar whites from leadership positions symbolized this shift.

Blacks' new assertiveness alarmed many white Americans. They had been willing to go along with the moderate reforms of the 1950s and early 1960s, but they were wary when blacks started demanding immediate access to higher-paying jobs, better housing in previously white neighborhoods, integrated schools, and increased political power. In 1966, 84 percent of all whites thought blacks were demanding too much change, up from 34 percent just five years earlier.

Summer in the City

A major reason for the eroding white support were the riots that exploded in the nation's cities each summer from 1964 to 1968. The rapid growth of de facto segregation in metropolitan areas provided the backdrop for the riots. Without the education and skills needed for most city jobs, successive generations of blacks moving out of the rural South were unable to find employment that paid an adequate wage. Many were unemployed. Moreover, they were angry at white landlords who owned the substandard housing they were forced to live in; at white shopkeepers who earned money from black trade but would not hire black clerks or salespeople; and at all-white unions—especially in the construction industry—that controlled access to skilled jobs. Young adults especially were painfully aware of their exclusion from the dominant consumer culture. Stimulated by television coverage of southern blacks who had challenged whites and gotten results, young urban blacks expressed their grievances with their own brand of "direct action." Their parents and adult neighbors often supported them in spirit.

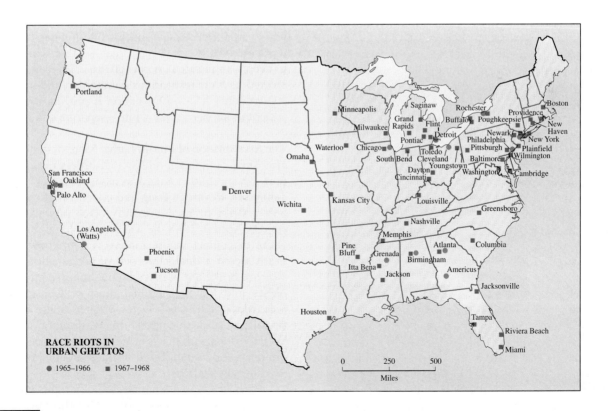

MAP 31.2

Racial Unrest in America's Cities, 1965–1968
American cities suffered four "long hot summers" of rioting in the mid-1960s. In 1967, the worst year, riots broke out in cities throughout the United States, including the South and West. Major riots usually did not occur in the same city two years in a row.

The first "long hot summer" began in July 1964 in New York City, when police shot a black criminal suspect in Harlem. Angry youths looted and rioted for a week. The volatile issue of police brutality would set off riots in a number of cities later that year, and in the years to come. In August rioting spread to several cities in New Jersey, as well as Philadelphia and Chicago.

Racial turmoil worsened the following summer. Thirty-four blacks died in a riot in the Watts section of Los Angeles, where 60 percent of the adult population was on relief. Ironically, Watts erupted only five days after President Johnson hailed passage of the Voting Rights Act of 1965 as the next great step toward racial equality. For many young urban blacks, however, the legal gains of the civil rights movement and the deferred promises of underfunded Great Society programs were irrelevant to their daily experiences of poverty and economic exploitation. Instead of "We shall overcome," Watts rioters shouted the frightening refrain, "Burn, baby, burn." "We won!" shouted a twenty-year-old unemployed rioter to onlooker Martin Luther King. How can we have won, King countered, when the community lay in ruins? "We won because we made the whole world pay attention to us," the rioter replied. "We made them come."

Watts in Flames
The nation's worst racial disturbance since the Detroit race riot of 1943 began in the Watts section of Los Angeles on August 11, 1965. An altercation broke out when white police officers stopped two blacks for a minor traffic violation. Thirty-four persons died in the Watts riot.

The riots of 1967 were the most serious of all. Rioting began in the spring in several southern cities, increased in number in June, and engulfed twenty-two cities in July and August. Large-scale disturbances hit Toledo, Ohio; Grand Rapids, Michigan; Plainfield, New Jersey; and Milwaukee, Wisconsin. Violent riots in Newark and Detroit produced widespread destruction and loss of life. Forty-three people were killed in Detroit alone, nearly all of them black, and at least a fourth of the city was burned, with $50 million worth of property destroyed. Federal paratroopers, some just back from service in Vietnam, were sent in to restore order, and Mayor Jerome Cavanaugh compared devastated Detroit to war-ravaged Berlin in 1945. As with most of the riots, the arson and looting were directed at white-owned stores and property, but there was little physical violence against white people. Almost all the reported sniping turned out to involve wild shooting by the police.

The riots finally provoked a response from the federal government. On July 29, 1967, President Lyndon Johnson appointed a special commission under Governor Otto Kerner of Illinois to investigate the reasons for the rioting. The final report of the National Advisory Commission on Civil Disorders, released in March 1968, detailed the patterns of inequality and racism embedded in urban life. It also issued a warning: "What white Americans have never fully understood—but what the Negro can never forget—is that white society is deeply implicated in the ghetto. White institutions created it, white institutions maintain it, and white society condones it. . . . Our nation is moving toward two societies, one black, one white—separate and unequal."

The Assassination of Martin Luther King. Barely a month after the Commission on Civil Disorders released its report, Martin Luther King was assassinated in Memphis, Tennessee. Reverend King had gone to that city to support a strike by predominantly black sanitation workers. On April 4, 1968, he was shot by James Earl Ray, a white ex-convict whose motive was unknown. King's death set off a final cataclysm of urban rioting. Major violence broke out in more than a hundred cities. As violence and looting engulfed most of Chicago's West Side, Mayor Richard J. Daley ordered police to "shoot to kill" suspected snipers. In Washington, National Guard troops with machine guns protected the Capitol; on television, it appeared framed by the fires from neighboring ghettoes.

With King's assassination, the civil rights movement lost the black leader most able to stir the conscience of white America. At the time of his death, he was only thirty-nine years old. During the last years of his life, King had moved toward a more comprehensive view of the structural problems of poverty and racism faced by blacks in contemporary America. In 1966 he had confronted the issue of residential segregation in a losing campaign for open housing in Chicago. He spoke out eloquently against the Vietnam War. In 1968 he was planning a poor people's campaign to raise issues of economic injustice and inequality.

King's death robbed the country of the one leader who could mediate between an increasingly fragmented black community and an ever more resistant white world. By the 1970s black Americans were too diverse economically and too divided politically to constitute a unified civil rights movement any longer. And the political climate had become too conservative to support further change.

The Legacy of the Civil Rights Movement. The 1950s and 1960s brought permanent, indeed revolutionary, changes in American race relations. Jim Crow segregation was overturned in less than a decade, and federal legislation granted black Americans their basic civil rights. The enfranchisement of African-Americans in southern states ended the political control there by a lily-white Democratic party, and candidates who had once been ardent segregationists now courted the black vote. In time Martin Luther King's greatness was recognized even in the South; in 1986 his birthday became a national holiday.

The Spreading Demand for Equal Rights

The civil rights movement inspired other groups, such as Hispanics and native Americans, to organize to press their claims. Until 1960 few Hispanic-Americans had participated in politics. Poverty, uncertain legal status, and language barriers kept them politically silent. This situation began to change when the Mexican-American Political Association (MAPA) mobilized support for John F. Kennedy in 1960, probably providing a margin of the victory in the closely contested states of Texas, New Mexico, and Illinois. In return, Kennedy appointed several Hispanic-American leaders to posts in Washington, and his administration paid increased attention to Hispanic issues.

Chicano activism. Younger Hispanics quickly grew impatient with MAPA, however. More radical and more inclined to celebrate cultural achievements and traditions, the younger leaders pursued increasingly diverse goals. The *barrios* of Los Angeles and other western cities produced the militant Brown Berets, who modeled themselves on the Black Panthers. In 1969, a new term, *Chicano*, was coined to replace Mexican-American. This revolution in consciousness also produced a political party, *La Raza Unida* (the united race), to promote Hispanic interests and candidates in public life.

Chicano strategists also pursued economic objectives. Working in the fields around Delano, California, labor leader Cesar Chavez organized the United Farm Workers, the first successful union to represent migrant workers. A 1965 grape pickers' strike and a nationwide boycott of table grapes brought Chavez and his union national publicity. Quietly advocating their cause, they won the support of the AFL–CIO and Senator Robert F. Kennedy of New York, and Chavez was soon receiving almost as much media attention as Martin Luther King, Jr. In 1968, Chavez undertook a twenty-five-day fast to protest the increasing strife and violence in the fields. Victory came in 1970, when California grape growers signed contracts recognizing the United Farm Workers.

Cesar Chavez

Mexican-American labor leader Cesar Chavez addresses a rally in Guadalupe, California. Chavez won national attention in 1965 during a strike of migrant farm workers, most of them Mexican-Americans, against California grape growers. Drawing on tactics from the civil rights movement, Chavez called for nonviolent action and effectively mobilized support from white liberals who boycotted non-union table grapes.

Asserting Rights for Native Americans. American Indians also found a model in the civil rights movement. Native Americans, who numbered nearly 800,000 in the 1960s, were an exceedingly diverse group, divided by language and tribal history, region, personal experience, and degree of integration into mainstream American life. But they shared certain things, such as an unemployment rate ten times the national average. Native Americans suffered the worst poverty, the most inadequate housing, the highest disease rates, and the least access to education of any group in the United States.

As early as World War II, the National Council of American Indians had lobbied for improvement. But now some Indian groups became more assertive. In 1961 representatives of sixty-seven tribes issued a Declaration of Indian Purpose that foreshadowed much of the later civil rights activism. During the War on Poverty, Indian groups successfully lobbied the Johnson administration to channel antipoverty funds into Indian communities. Paralleling the progression from liberal reform to more radical change seen in the civil rights movement, younger native Americans challenged the accommodationist approach of their elders. Like blacks and Hispanics, they proposed a new name for themselves—native Americans—and organized protests and demonstrations to build support for their cause. In 1968 several Chipewyan from Minnesota organized the militant American Indian Movement (AIM), which drew its strength from the third of the Indian population who lived in "red ghettoes" in cities throughout the West.

AIM consciously modeled itself on the black power movement, and for a few years its tactics attracted considerable public attention. In November 1969, AIM seized the deserted federal penitentiary on Alcatraz Island in San Francisco Bay, offering the government $24 worth of trinkets to pay for it. (This was supposedly what the Dutch had paid the local inhabitants for Manhattan Island in 1626.) The Indian occupation of Alcatraz lasted until the summer of 1971. In November 1972, a thousand protesters occupied the headquarters of the Federal Bureau of Indian Affairs in Washington, D.C., to many Indians a hated symbol of the inconsistent federal policy on behalf of tribal welfare. In February 1973, two hundred Sioux organized by AIM leaders began a seventy-one-day occupation of the tiny village of Wounded Knee, South Dakota, the site of the army

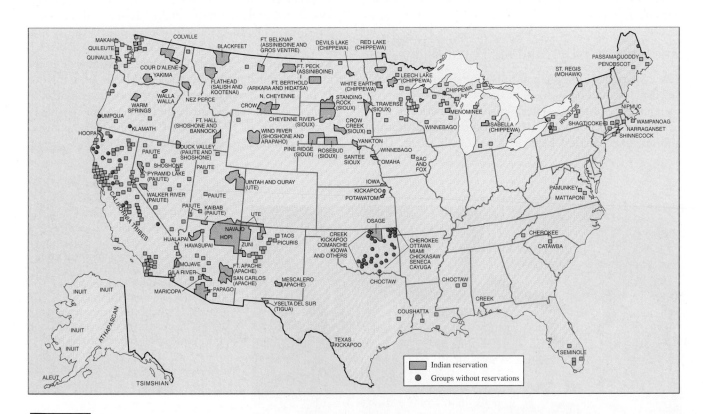

MAP 31.3

American Indian Reservations

Although native Americans have been able to preserve small enclaves in the northeastern states, most Indian reservations are in the West. In the 1990s various Indian tribes continue to press land claims against the federal and state governments.

Wounded Knee Revisited

In 1973 members of the American Indian Movement staged a 71-day protest at
Wounded Knee, South Dakota, the site of the 1890 massacre of two hundred Sioux
by U.S. soldiers. The takeover was sparked by the murder of a local Sioux by a group
of whites, but quickly expanded to include demands for basic reforms in federal Indian policy and tribal governance.

massacre of Sioux in 1890 (see Chapter 17). They were protesting the light sentences given a group of white men convicted of killing a Sioux in 1972. The protesters took eleven hostages and occupied several buildings to dramatize their cause. But when a gun battle with the FBI left one protester dead and another wounded, the siege collapsed.

These militant confrontations captured media attention, but often alienated public opinion. More effective in rousing white sympathy were a number of books published by a new generation of native American writers. *Custer Died for Your Sins* (1969), by Vine Deloria, Jr., a Sioux, N. Scott Momaday's Pulitzer Prize-winning novel *House Made of Dawn* (1968), and Dee Brown's best-selling *Bury My Heart at Wounded Knee* (1971) gave whites a better understanding of Indian history and concerns. As the nation marked the quincentenary of Columbus's arrival in 1492, historians continued to reconsider the meaning of that first encounter between native Americans and Europeans.

Other Voices. Civil rights, which began as a demand for the rights of black people, also spurred some predominantly white groups to claim justice, equality, and new identities. Americans of Polish, Italian, Greek, and Slavic descent, most of them working-class and Catholic, proudly embraced a new ethnic awareness modeled on black pride. George Wiley organized poor people, mostly women on welfare, into the National Welfare Rights Organization. Calling welfare a right, not a privilege, activists staged sit-ins at government offices to demand better treatment and higher benefits.

Homosexual men and women also banded together to protest legal and social discrimination based on sexual preference. The gay liberation movement was born in 1969 with the "Stonewall Riot" in New York City, when patrons of a gay bar in Greenwich Village fought back against police harassment. The assertion of gay pride that followed the Stonewall incident would probably not have occurred without the example of the civil rights movement. Adapting the model of the earlier movement, activists took the new name of gay rather than homosexual, founded advocacy groups, newspapers, and political organizations to challenge discrimination and prejudice, and provided emotional support for those who "came out" and publicly affirmed their homosexual identity. Models for increased political activism and heightened group identity represented one of the most important legacies of the African-American struggle to the rest of American society.

The Challenge of Youth

"There is everywhere protest, revaluation, attack on the Establishment," asserted social critic Paul Goodman at the end of the 1960s. Novelist Norman Mailer agreed. "We're in a time that's divorced from the past. . . . There's utterly no tradition anymore." The African-American drive for equality had ignited the challenge to established institutions. American youth joined in. New concerns roused young people, especially those from the white middle class, to mount colorful and sometimes shocking challenges to authority and traditional values. Vietnam would be the defining political issue of their generation.

Student Activism

The 1960s witnessed the first active student movement since the 1930s. The idealism of Kennedy's New Frontier raised students' expectations of what they and their society could accomplish. Then the civil rights movement exposed white youths to the brutality of race relations in the South and taught college students new protest tactics such as marches, sit-ins, and mass confrontations. In addition, the escalation of the Vietnam War in 1965 offered a compelling political cause to rally around, especially as the draft affected more college-age males.

The depression-scarred generation who came of age in the 1930s had been unable to afford higher education, but its children—the baby boomers—flocked to colleges and universities in the postwar period. In addition, many soldiers who had served during World War II and Korea used the benefits of the GI Bill to finance higher education that probably would have been out of their reach otherwise. In 1940, when only 15 percent of all college-age youth attended college, graduating was a major sign of upward social mobility for most minority and ethnic groups. In 1960, the year of John Kennedy's election, 40 percent of the college-age population was in college. In 1963, the year of his assassination, the proportion had reached almost 50 percent.

During the 1950s most students reflected the practical career-oriented values of their society. Engineering and business administration (for men) and home economics and teaching (for women) were the most popular courses of study, and students took little part in politics. Some critics suggested that students, responding to the repressive atmosphere of McCarthyism, had become a "silent generation." Even so, many young people felt dissatisfied in the 1950s. A vague awareness of the existence of poverty and the looming threat of nuclear war caused many to question the materialism of American society. J. D. Salinger's novel *Catcher in the Rye* (1951), which chronicled Holden Caulfield's quiet revulsion at the hypocrisy of his family, neighbors, and schoolmates, became a bestseller.

Early Stirrings. Student dissatisfaction began to coalesce in the early 1960s. In June 1962, forty students from Big Ten and Ivy League universities met at a United Auto Workers conference center in Port Huron, Michigan, to found the Students for a Democratic Society (SDS). Their manifesto, written by Tom Hayden, a University of Michigan student, drew heavily on the writing of radical Columbia sociologist C. Wright Mills. It expressed hostility toward bureaucracy, rejected cold war ideology, emphasized community participatory politics, and designated students as the major force for change in society. SDSers referred to their movement as the "New Left," to distinguish themselves from the "Old Left" Communists of the 1930s. SDS consciously adopted the activist tactics pioneered by SNCC and devoted much of its early attention to grass-roots organizing in the nation's cities and on campus.

The first student protests broke out at the University of California at Berkeley. In the fall of 1964 the university administration banned political activity near the Telegraph Avenue entrance to the campus, where student groups had traditionally distributed leaflets and recruited volunteers. In response, all the major student organizations, ranging from SNCC and SDS to the conservative Youth for Goldwater, formed a coalition to protest what they considered an abridgment of free speech. The Free Speech Movement organized a sit-in at the main administration building and persuaded the university to drop the ban.

The Free Speech Movement owed a strong debt to the civil rights movement. Berkeley had sent more volunteers to Freedom Summer in Mississippi in 1964 than any other campus, and the students had been radicalized by the experience. Free Speech leader Mario Savio spoke for many of them:

> Last summer I went to Mississippi to join the struggle there for civil rights. This fall I am engaged in another phase of the same struggle, this time in Berkeley. The two battlefields may seem quite different to some observers, but this is not the case. The same rights are at stake in both places—the right to participate as citizens in a democratic society and to struggle against the same enemy. In Mississippi an autocratic and powerful minority rules, through organized violence, to suppress the vast, virtually powerless majority. In California, the privileged minority manipulates the university bureaucracy to suppress the students' political expression.

On a deeper level, Berkeley students were challenging the university because it had grown too big, too impersonal, and too insulated from the major social issues of the day. The largest universities, like the largest corporations, had grown the fastest in the postwar era. In 1940, only two campuses had as many as 20,000 students. By 1969, thirty-nine were at least that large. Many students objected that they were treated as impersonally as a computer punch card in these "multiversities." "I am a student," one slogan ran, "Please do not fold, spindle, or mutilate." Emboldened by the Berkeley experience, students at institutions across the country were soon protesting everything from dress codes to course requirements, tenure decisions, and academic grading systems.

Students also protested the universities' complicity in the problems of the ghettoes that surrounded many urban campuses. Columbia, for example, was a major property owner in Harlem, which bordered on its campus. In 1968, Columbia announced plans to build a new gymnasium, displacing local stores and housing. Chanting "Gym Crow Must Go," students tore down the fence at the construction site and took over several Columbia buildings, including the office of President Grayson Kirk. (Photographs of protesters sampling Kirk's cigars and sherry did little to build public support.) At Berkeley, students and administrators clashed in 1969 over a parcel of vacant land near campus that a coalition of students and residents had turned into a "People's Park." When the university asserted its rights to the land, a violent confrontation broke out and an onlooker was killed. At both Columbia and Berkeley, the administration decided to use city police officers to break up the demonstrations; the brutality of the police radicalized far more students than had originally supported the protests. As campus disturbances spread, and more and more university buildings were blocked, occupied, or picketed, classes had to be canceled and academic life temporarily came to a halt.

Although black students participated in many of the protests, student movements increasingly split along racial lines, reflecting the separatism that affected the civil rights movement by the mid-1960s. Strongly inspired by the black power movement, black students at predominantly black institutions like Howard University and at mainly white universities demanded more courses in African-American history and culture. University administrators were open to such demands as a way to ease campus unrest, and many universities established separate Afro-American or Black Studies departments in the late 1960s and early 1970s. Black protestors also won university support for separate dormitories and cultural centers, a protest against the racism black students claimed pervaded university life on predominantly white campuses.

The Antiwar Movement. But no issue provoked more impassioned and sustained protest than the Vietnam War. In March 1965, several months after the Free Speech confrontation at Berkeley, President Johnson dramatically escalated the Vietnam War by committing American ground troops and bombing North Vietnam.

In response, faculty members and student activists at the University of Michigan organized a *teach-in* against the war. In marathon sessions they debated the political, diplomatic, and moral facets of U.S. involvement in Vietnam. Teach-ins quickly spread to other universities, as students turned their full attention to protesting the Vietnam war.

A strong spur to activism was a change in the Selective Service System. In the past, students could use deferments for college, graduate school, teaching, and parenthood to avoid the draft until they reached the cut-off age of twenty-six. But in response to criticisms about the unfairness of this system, the Selective Service System gradually phased out deferments. In January 1966 automatic student deferments were abolished altogether.

Young men's options were limited. Some enlisted in the National Guard or reserves to avoid being sent to Vietnam. Some reluctant draftees sought out sympathetic doctors to give them medical or psychiatric excuses or help them flunk the induction physical. Some filed for conscientious objector status, fulfilling their military commitment through alternative service in the United States or noncombatant duty in Vietnam. Several thousand ignored the induction notice entirely, risking prosecution for draft evasion. The Resistance, started at Berkeley and Stanford and widely recognized by its Omega symbol, provided support to draft resisters, but thousands left the country altogether (Canada and Sweden were the most popular destinations). Opponents of the war burned their draft cards in public acts of civil disobedience, closed down induction centers with mass protests, and on a few occasions broke into Selective Service offices to destroy or mutilate files.

As antiwar and draft protests increased after 1965, students realized that their own universities were deeply implicated in the war effort. In some cases as much as 60 percent of a university's research budget came from government contracts, especially from the Defense Department. Protesters blocked campus recruitment by the Dow Chemical Company because it produced the napalm used to burn Vietnamese villages and Agent Orange, which defoliated South Vietnam's forests. Arguing that universities should not train students for war, protesters demanded that the Reserve Officer Training Corps (ROTC) be removed from campus. ROTC was one of the main targets of the student protests at Columbia in 1968 and Harvard in 1969.

Mass Protests. Mass demonstrations against the war consumed much of the energy of the student movement in the late 1960s. Students became part of the much larger antiwar movement of peace activists, housewives, religious leaders, and a few elected officials. On October 15, 1969, millions joined a one-day "moratorium" on business as usual to demonstrate against the war. On November 15, 1969, hundreds of thousands of people mobilized in Washington to call for an end to the fighting in Vietnam.

The most extensive outbreak of student unrest came in the spring of 1970, after President Richard M. Nixon ordered American troops to invade Cambodia. Student leaders organized a national student strike in protest. At Kent State University outside Cleveland, panicky National Guardsmen fired into a crowd of students at a noontime antiwar rally on May 4. Four people were killed and eleven wounded. Only two of those killed, Jeffrey Miller and Alison Krause, had been at the demonstration; William Shroeder and Sandra Scheur were passing by on their way to class. Soon after, two black students were killed at Jackson State College in Mississippi. More than 450 colleges closed down on strike, and 80 percent of all American college campuses experienced some kind of protest.

In June 1970, immediately after the Kent State slayings, a Gallup poll reported that campus unrest was the main issue troubling Americans. But after 1970 the universities basically stayed calm. Student strikes in the spring of 1971 and 1972 never approached the intensity of the earlier demonstrations. Students had effectively challenged many aspects of university control over their lives, but their broader attack on American society had

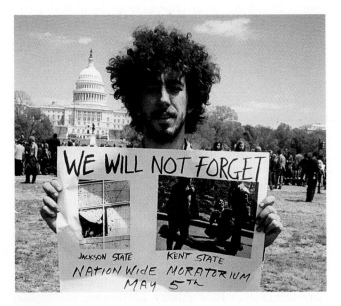

Kent State

The shootings by National Guardsmen of four students at Kent State University in Ohio on May 4, 1970, set off campus demonstrations and protests throughout the country. The protestor shown here holds a placard memorializing the slain students, as well as the two black students killed soon after at Jackson State College in Mississippi. The president of Columbia University called May 1970 "the most disastrous month . . . in the history of American higher education."

been less successful. They returned to the classroom, somewhat cynical, burned out, and no longer confident they could change the world.

The Rise of the Counterculture

Alongside student activism and protest, new forms of cultural expression emerged among the nation's young. In an amazingly short period of time, youth's clothing and hair styles changed radically. At Berkeley's Free Speech demonstrations in 1964, young men wore coats and ties, women skirts and sweaters. At the antiwar protests just three or four years later, youth defiantly dressed in a unisex fashion that featured ragged blue jeans, tie-dyed T-shirts, beads, and other adornments. Unorthodox clothes and long, unkempt hair identified a new phenomenon of American youth culture, the *hippie*. The uncomprehending older generation often had a simple response: "Get a haircut."

The Beats. The forerunners of the hippies were members of the Beat Generation of the 1950s. In the post-McCarthy climate of conformity, rebellion in the 1950s was more likely to take artistic than political forms. "Beats" such as poet Allen Ginsberg and writer Jack Kerouac were among the first to articulate the personal alienation that was at the heart of much of the rebelliousness of the 1960s. Kerouac's *On the Road* (1957), the tale of a group of drifters hitchhiking across the country, became the bible of the Beat Generation. Beats popularized beards for men, black tights for women, and sandals for both sexes. They experimented with sex and drugs and helped revive interest in folk music.

Popular Music. Throughout the 1960s, as one journalist noted, "popular music coincided uncannily with changing political moods." Folk singer Pete Seeger, free at last from the McCarthy-era blacklist, set the tone for the era's political idealism with such songs as the antiwar ballad "Where Have All the Flowers Gone?" In 1963, the year of the Birmingham demonstrations and President Kennedy's assassination, Bob Dylan's "Blowin' in the Wind" reflected the impatience of people whose liberalism was turning sour.

Early in 1964, the Beatles, four working-class youths from Liverpool, England, burst onto the American scene. Like Elvis Presley eight years earlier, they thrust their way into the national consciousness by a series of television appearances on the "Ed Sullivan Show." The Beatles's music, by turns lyrical and driving, was phenomenally successful, spawning a commercial and cultural phenomenon called Beatlemania. The more rebellious, angrier music of other British groups, notably the Rolling Stones, found a broad audience shortly afterward.

Sgt. Pepper's Lonely Hearts Club Band
The colorful collage on the cover of this 1967 Beatles's album allowed fans to debate (occasionally under the influence of marijuana or LSD) the symbolism of those chosen. Can you identify Mae West, Karl Marx, Bob Dylan, Albert Einstein, Lenny Bruce, Marilyn Monroe, as well as the "Fab Four" in their various disguises? (©Apple Corps Ltd.)

Drug Culture. Drugs were almost as important as rock music in the youth culture of the 1960s. Drugs were hardly new to the American scene: many jazz musicians from the 1920s on had used heroin and cocaine, and the Beats had experimented with mind-altering drugs in San Francisco. Now widespread recreational use of drugs extended beyond artistic and jazz circles.

Marijuana was the preferred drug among college students, but stronger drugs also gained popularity. The hallucinogen lysergic acid diethylamide, popularly known as LSD or "acid," was one of the most potent. It was popularized in California by writer Ken Kesey and his Merry Pranksters, who conducted "acid tests" (public "happenings" where tabs of LSD were distributed) in 1965 and 1966. San Francisco bands such as the Grateful Dead and the Jefferson Airplane, guitarist Jimi Hendrix, and Britain's Pink Floyd developed a style of music known as "acid rock." Even the Beatles, whose early songs had simply stated "I Want to Hold Your Hand" and "Please Please Me," now recorded tunes like "Lucy in the Sky with Diamonds," whose "tangerine trees and marmalade skies" celebrated the new drug-induced consciousness.

For a brief time, adherents of the *counterculture*— so named because it challenged so many established values—believed a new age was dawning. "The closest Western Civilization has come to uniting since the Congress of Vienna in 1815 was the week the *Sgt. Pepper* album was released," gushed a rock critic in 1968 about the newest Beatles's release. Others pointed to the "age of Aquarius" trumpeted in the 1968 Broadway rock musical *Hair*. In 1967, the "world's first Human Be-In" drew 20,000 people to Golden Gate Park in San Francisco. Allen Ginsberg "purified" the site with a Buddhist ritual, political activists embraced "drug freaks," and LSD advocate Timothy Leary, a former Harvard psychology instructor, urged the gathering to "turn on to the scene, tune in to what is happening, and drop out."

Hippies. "Tune in, turn on, drop out" and "Make love, not war" became catchwords for youthful alienation. By the summer of 1967, San Francisco's Haight-Ashbury, New York's East Village, Chicago's Uptown, and similar hippie neighborhoods in other large cities were crowded with young people, as well as swarms of reporters and busloads of tourists who gawked at the so-called flower children. The faith in instant love and peace quickly began to turn sour, however, as dropouts, drifters, and teenage runaways tried to cope with bad drug trips, venereal disease, loneliness, and violence. In 1967, seventeen murders and more than a hundred rapes were reported in Haight-Ashbury alone.

Another way to drop out was to join a commune. Many communes were located in isolated areas such as the mountains between Santa Cruz and San Francisco, the wide open spaces of New Mexico, or the rural solitude of Vermont, out of the watchful eye of mainstream America (and local drug enforcement agents). Communes, following in the utopian tradition, provided an economic and sexual alternative to nuclear families. They also promised a return to the land, as members banded together to grow their own food, bake their own bread, and reject the materialism and commercialism of American life. But the communes of the 1960s did not just look backward. Their advocacy of organic farming—growing food without chemicals or pesticides—anticipated the environmental concerns that would emerge in the 1970s and 1980s (see Chapter 32).

Meanwhile, the appeal of rock music and drugs continued to spread. In August 1969, four hundred thousand young people journeyed to Bethel, New York, to attend the Woodstock Music Festival. Despite torrential rain, people "got high" on music, drugs, and sex. The successful festival gave its name to the "Woodstock generation" of the late 1960s.

By 1970 the youth culture had revolutionized lifestyles and cultural expression. Even as political activism and rebellion waned, their spirit was absorbed and marketed by the consumer culture. The crowds at Woodstock and other rock festivals revealed the size of the youth market, and corporate entrepreneurs rushed to cash in on it.

The alternative values of the 1960s soon filtered into the dominant culture. *The Village Voice* and *Rolling Stone* outgrew their beginnings as underground publications and became respected voices of American journalism. Symbols of cultural defiance were coopted and homogenized by the mass culture. The ragged "bell bottoms" of the 1960s became the expensive designer jeans of the 1970s. The unkempt hair and beards of male hippies emboldened some middle-aged executives to sport a moustache or allow their hair to cover their ears. The "Afro" hairstyle, once worn only by radical black activists, was now favored by blacks and whites of both sexes who let their hair go natural. Women's fashion picked up the theme of personal liberation with the miniskirt, an innovation that had arrived from England in the mid-1960s. Women also found greater acceptance for wearing pants in public, even on the job. Many of these cultural changes continue to influence American life today.

Flower Children

Yale law professor Charles A. Reich celebrated the new freedom of youth in his best-selling book, *The Greening of America* (1970). Reich described a new consciousness that had "emerged out of the wasteland of the Corporate State, like flowers pushing up through the concrete pavement." Counterculture hippies were also called flower children.

The Revival of Feminism

In 1960, feminism was a dead issue. The words *sexism* and *Ms.* had not been coined. There were no rape crisis centers, women's health collectives, or battered women's shelters. Not a single university offered a course in women's studies, and women's sports programs were small and underfunded. At least ten thousand women a year lost their lives in illegal back-alley abortions.

All that changed during the next fifteen years. The women's movement rivaled the civil rights movement in the success it achieved in a short period of time. By the mid-1970s, however, feminism had provoked a backlash, and its progress too had stalled.

Women's Changing Lives

Social movements do not just spring up when leaders announce a set of demands. Leaders arise only when there is a constituency ready to be mobilized. Preconditions for feminism lay in the changing social and demographic bases of women's lives, especially increased labor force participation, greater access to higher education, the declining birthrate, and changing patterns of marriage.

The most important factor was the dramatic rise in women's participation in the work force during the postwar years. In 1950 almost one-third of women were employed, and one-quarter of them were married. By 1970, 42.6 percent of women were working, and four out of ten working women were married. Especially significant was the growth in the number of working women with preschool children—up from 12 percent in 1950 to 30 percent in 1970. Working mothers had become both socially accepted and economically necessary.

Women also benefited from increased access to education. Immediately after World War II the percentage of women college students had declined: the GI Bill gave men a temporary advantage in access to higher education, and many college women dropped out of school to marry and raise families at the height of the baby boom. By 1960, however, the percentage of women students had climbed to 35 percent, and by 1970 to 41 percent.

The meaning of marriage was changing too. The baby boom only temporarily interrupted the century-long decline in the birthrate. The introduction of the birth control pill, first marketed in 1960, and the intrauterine device (IUD) helped women control their fertility, as did the legalization of abortion in the 1970s. Women had fewer children and, because of increased life expectancy (75 years in 1970, up from 54 years in 1920), spent fewer years of their lives involved primarily in childcare. At the same time, the divorce rate, which had risen slowly through the twentieth century, shot up. It doubled from 15 per thousand marriages in 1960 to 32 per thousand in 1975. Women could no longer assume that their marriages would last until "death do us part."

As a result of these changes, traditional gender expectations were dramatically undercut. To be female in America now usually included work and marriage, often childrearing and a career, and possibly bringing up children as a single parent after a divorce. These changing social realities created a major constituency for the revival of feminism in the 1960s.

Paths to Feminism

During the 1960s, two distinct movements renewed the national interest in women's concerns. The *women's rights* branch of the new feminism, led by the National Organization for Women (NOW), consisted of older,

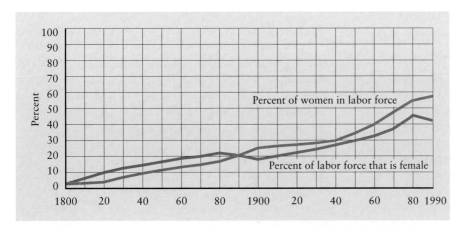

FIGURE 31.1

Women in the Labor Force, 1800–1990

Over the past two centuries, women have steadily increased their participation in the labor force. Paid employment outside the home is now part of the life cycle for most women.

Joanie Caucus, Modern Woman

The character of Joanie Caucus in Garry Trudeau's popular comic strip, *Doonesbury,* provided a running commentary on women's changing lives in the 1960s and 1970s. Caucus, a former housewife, ran away from her husband and family to a commune and then tried to raise the consciousness of the children at the day care center where she worked. Here she applies to law school. After graduation, she became a legislative aide to a female member of Congress, remarried, and had a child in her forties. (Doonesbury, By Garry Trudeau. Copyright, 1974, G. B. Trudeau. Reprinted with permission of Universal Press Syndicate. All rights reserved.)

politically active professional women who sought political change by working through the system. The *women's liberation* branch, on the other hand, attracted primarily younger women—especially recent college graduates who had been active in civil rights, the New Left, and the antiwar movement. Their vision of feminism was more radical and confrontational: mirroring the separatism of black power advocates, they were initially quite hostile to men.

Women's Rights. In 1961, President Kennedy established a Presidential Commission on the Status of Women, an attempt to counter criticism about his administration's poor record on women's issues. Eleanor Roosevelt served as honorary head of the commission. The group's 1963 report documented the employment and educational discrimination faced by women, but its impact extended beyond its rather conservative recommendations. The presidential commission, and the state commissions that were its offshoots, set up a rudimen-

tary nationwide network of women in public life who were concerned about feminist issues.

One spark that ignited the revival of feminism was Betty Friedan's bestselling book, *The Feminine Mystique,* published in 1963. This book, a pointed indictment of the trap of women's suburban domesticity, grew out of her own experiences as a housewife in the 1950s. Friedan called it "the problem that has no name":

> As she made the beds, shopped for groceries, matched slipcover material, ate peanut butter sandwiches with her children, chauffeured Cub Scouts and Brownies, lay beside her husband at night—she was afraid to ask even of herself the silent question—"Is this all?"

Women responded enthusiastically to Friedan's story, especially the white, college-educated, middle-class women whose backgrounds resembled the author's. Friedan's book sold three million copies, and many more women read excerpts in major women's magazines. *The Feminine Mystique* gave women a vocabulary for their dissatisfaction and introduced many women to the powerful ideas of modern feminism.

Legislative Change. Like so many constituencies in postwar America, women's rights activists looked to the federal government for action. In 1963, as recommended by the Presidential Commission on the Status of Women, Congress passed the Equal Pay Act, which directed that men and women be paid the same wages for doing the same job.

Even more important was the Civil Rights Act of 1964, which had as great an impact on women as it did on blacks and other minorities. The key provision, Title VII, barred discrimination in employment on the basis of race, color, religion, national origin, or sex. The category of sex was added by a conservative representative, Howard Smith of Virginia. He did this not out of concern for women's equality—he called it "my little amendment"—but to make the civil rights bill so controversial as to kill it completely. His strategy backfired. Title VII eventually became a powerful legal tool in the fight against sex discrimination.

The National Organization for Women. Dissatisfied that the Equal Employment Opportunity Commission had avoided implementation of Title VII, Friedan and others founded the National Organization for Women in 1966. NOW, modeling itself after groups like the NAACP, aimed to be a civil rights organization for women. "The purpose of NOW," its statement of purpose declared, "is to take action to bring women into full participation in the mainstream of American society now, exercising all the privileges and responsibilities thereof in truly equal partnership with men." Friedan served as NOW's first president, and its membership grew from 1,000 in 1967 to 15,000 in 1971. Men made up a fourth of NOW's early membership. It is still the largest feminist organization in the United States.

Women's Liberation. Women's liberationists came to feminism by a different path. White women had made up about half the students who went South with SNCC in the 1964 Freedom Summer voter-registration project. While in Mississippi, they received conflicting messages. College women developed self-confidence and organizational skills and found role models in the black women and older southern white women who were prominent in the civil rights movement, such as Ella Baker, Anne Braden, and Virginia Foster Durr. Yet women volunteers also found that they were expected to do all the cleaning and cooking at the Freedom Houses where SNCC volunteers lived. "We didn't come down here to work as a maid this summer," one complained.

Intensely committed to civil rights, and lacking a feminist vocabulary to express their concerns, Freedom Summer volunteers raised their objections only tentatively. When they did, they compared women's position with that of blacks. "Assumptions of male superiority are as widespread and deeply rooted and every much as crippling to the woman as the assumptions of white superiority are to the Negro," they argued. Both black and white men in the movement laughed off these attempts to raise feminist issues. Stokely Carmichael made one of the most notorious retorts: "The only position for women in SNCC is prone."

Black power militancy made white women unwelcome in the civil rights movement after 1965. But when they transferred their energies to student and antiwar groups, they found the New Left equally male-dominated and unsupportive. Once again, women were expected to take notes or serve coffee, while men monopolized the leadership roles. As the New Left focused increasingly on draft resistance as a strategy to oppose the war, women found themselves treated primarily as sex objects. "Girls say yes to guys who say no," went a popular slogan. Women who tried to raise feminist issues at conventions were shouted off the platform with such jeers as "Move on, little girl, we have more important issues to talk about here than women's liberation." The "little girl" who received this taunt was Shulamith Firestone, whose *The Dialectic of Sex* (1971) was an early text of the women's movement.

Around 1967 groups of radical women realized that they needed their own movement. The contradictions between the New Left's commitment to egalitarianism and women's actual treatment by male leaders became so striking that women felt they had no other choice. This process occurred independently in five or six cities, including Chicago, San Francisco, and New York. In contrast to women's rights groups like NOW, which had traditional organizational structures and dues-paying members, radical women participated in loose collectives with shifting memberships that often lacked any coordinating structure at all.

The women's liberation movement (or "women's lib," as it was dubbed by the somewhat hostile media) went public when it staged a protest at the 1968 Miss America pageant. The demonstration included a "freedom trash can," into which women were encouraged to throw false eyelashes, hair curlers, brassieres, and girdles—all considered symbols of female oppression. The media quickly labeled the radical feminists "bra burners." The derisive name stuck, although no brassieres were actually burned.

A technique of more lasting impact was *consciousness raising*, group sessions in which women shared common experiences about being female. Swapping stories about being passed over for promotion, needing a husband's signature on a credit card application, or enduring the humiliation of whistles and leers while simply walking down the street helped participants to realize that their individual problems were part of wider patterns of oppression. (The women's movement called this moment of epiphany "click.") The slogan "The personal is political" became a watchword of the early radical feminists.

The High Tide of Feminism

Before 1969 most women learned about the feminist movement through word of mouth. After that, media attention brought women's issues to a much broader audience than could ever have been reached by NOW or the women's liberation collectives. A flood of new converts broke down the barriers between the two branches of the movement. Feminism's potential as a mass movement was demonstrated on August 26, 1970, when thousands of women throughout the country marched to celebrate the fiftieth anniversary of the Nineteenth Amendment.

The distinction between women's rights and women's liberation also began to blur because of the growing convergence of interests. Radical women learned that key feminist goals—child care, equal pay, abortion rights—could best be achieved in the political arena. At the same time, more traditional political activists developed a broader view of women's oppression, including tentative support for divisive issues like lesbianism and abortion. Feminists were beginning to think of themselves as part of a broad, growing, and increasingly influential social movement. "It's not a movement," said journalist Sally Kempton, "it's a state of mind." Robin Morgan's best-selling book, *Sisterhood is Powerful* (1970), similarly reflected feminist optimism. Only later did the movement grapple with the fact that perhaps as many issues divided women—race, class, age, sexual preference—as unified them.

AMERICAN VOICES

The Politics of Housework *Pat Mainardi*

The slogan "the personal is political" brought feminism into many aspects of daily life. Nowhere were disputes more heated than over housework, traditionally considered women's work. Painter Pat Mainardi, a member of the radical feminist group Redstockings, describes the ongoing debate with her husband over who would do what, a dialogue repeated in many households.

"I don't mind sharing the housework, but I don't do it very well. We should each do the things we're best at."

Meaning: Unfortunately I'm no good at things like washing dishes or cooking. What I do best is a little light carpentry, changing light bulbs, moving furniture (*how often do you move furniture?*)

Also Meaning: Historically the lower classes (black men and us) have had hundreds of years experience doing menial jobs. It would be a waste of manpower to train someone else to do them now.

Also Meaning: I don't like the dull stupid boring jobs, so you should do them.

"I don't mind sharing the work, but you'll have to show me how to do it."

Meaning: I ask a lot of questions and you'll have to show me everything everytime I do it because I don't remember so good. Also don't try to sit down and read while I'm doing my jobs because I'm going to annoy the hell out of you until it's easier to do them yourself.

"We used to be so happy!" (Said whenever it was his turn to do something.)

Meaning: I used to be so happy.

Meaning: Life without housework is bliss. (*No quarrel here. Perfect agreement.*)

"We have different standards, and why should I have to work to your standards. That's unfair."

Meaning: If I begin to get bugged by the dirt and crap I will say "This place sure is a sty" or "How can anyone live like this?" and wait for your reaction. I know that all women have a sore called "Guilt over a messy house" or "Household work is ultimately my responsibility." I know that men have caused that sore—if anyone visits and the place *is* a sty, they're not going to leave and say, "He sure is a lousy housekeeper." You'll take the rap in any case. I can outwait you.

Also Meaning: I can provoke innumerable scenes over the housework issue. Eventually doing all the housework yourself will be less painful to you than trying to get me to do half. Or I'll suggest we get a maid. She will do my share of the work. You will do yours. It's women's work.

"I've got nothing against sharing the housework, but you can't make me do it on your schedule."

Meaning: Passive resistance. I'll do it when I damned well please, if at all. If my job is doing dishes, it's easier to do them once a week. If taking out laundry, once a month. If washing the floors, once a year. If you don't like it, do it yourself oftener, and then I won't do it at all.

"I *hate* it more than you. You don't mind it so much."

Meaning: Housework is garbage work. It's the worst crap I've ever done. It's degrading and humiliating for someone of *my* intelligence to do it. But for someone of *your* intelligence . . .

"Housework is too trivial to even talk about."

Meaning: It's even more trivial to do. Housework is beneath my status. My purpose in life is to deal with matters of significance. Yours is to deal with matters of insignificance. You should do the housework.

"This problem of housework is not a man-woman problem! In any relationship between two people one is going to have a stronger personality and dominate."

Meaning: That stronger personality had better be *me*.

"In animal societies, wolves, for example, the top animal is usually a male even where he is not chosen for brute strength but on the basis of cunning and intelligence. Isn't that interesting?"

Meaning: I have historical, psychological, anthropological, and biological justification for keeping you down. How can you ask the top wolf to be equal?

"Women's liberation isn't really a political movement."

Meaning: The Revolution is coming too close to home.

Also Meaning: I am only interested in how *I* am oppressed, not how I oppress others. Therefore the [Vietnam] war, the draft, and the university are political. Women's liberation is not.

"Man's accomplishments have always depended on getting help from other people, mostly women. What great man would have accomplished what he did if he had to do his own housework?"

Meaning: Oppression is built into the System and I, as the white American male receive the benefits of this System. I don't want to give them up.

Postscript

Participatory democracy begins at home.

Source: Pat Mainardi, "The Politics of Housework," in Robin Morgan, ed., *Sisterhood is Powerful: An Anthology of Writings from the Women's Liberation Movement* (New York: Random House, 1970), 503–6.

Significant progress in the battle for women's equality occurred in the early 1970s. The media made new terms such as "sexism" and "male chauvinism" part of the national vocabulary. Many colleges across the country started women's studies programs. Former all-male bastions, including Yale, Princeton, and the U.S. Military Academy, admitted women undergraduates for the first time; women's colleges like Vassar and Sarah Lawrence admitted men. Gloria Steinem and other journalists founded *Ms.* magazine in 1972. The proportion of women in graduate and professional schools rose.

Women were increasingly visible in politics and public life. The National Women's Political Caucus, founded in 1971, actively promoted the election of women to public office. Bella Abzug, Elizabeth Holtzman, Shirley Chisholm, Patricia Schroeder, and Geraldine Ferraro served in Congress; Ella Grasso won election as Connecticut's governor in 1974, and Dixie Lee Ray as Washington's in 1976. Twenty thousand women came to Houston in November 1977 for the first National Women's Conference, part of the observance of the United Nations' International Women's Year. Their "National Plan of Action" represented a hard-won consensus on topics ranging from violence against women to homemakers' rights, the needs of older women, health, and, most controversially, reproductive freedom.

The women's movement achieved passage of significant federal legislation. The Equal Credit Opportunity Act of 1974 made it possible for women to get credit, including charge cards and mortgages, in their own names and based on their (not their husband's) incomes. Congress authorized child-care deductions for working parents and employment benefits for married female federal employees. In many cases, federal policies on civil rights were simply extended to include women as well as men. Title IX of the Educational Amendments Act of 1972 broadened the coverage of the 1964 Civil Rights Act to educational institutions; it prohibited colleges and universities that received federal funds from discriminating on the basis of sex. By requiring schools to fund sports programs for women at a comparable level to men, Title IX increased women's access to sports dramatically.

Supreme Court Victories. The Supreme Court also advanced the cause of women's rights, although not always as a result of pressure from the women's movement. In several rulings, the Court read a right of privacy into the Ninth and Fourteenth amendments' concept of personal liberty to give women more control over their reproductive lives. In 1965, the case of *Griswold v. Connecticut* overturned state laws against the sale of contraceptive devices to married adults; in 1972, *Baird v. Eisenstadt* extended this protection to single persons. In 1973, *Roe v. Wade* struck down Texas and Georgia statutes that allowed abortions only if the mother's life was in danger. According to this 7–2 decision, states could no longer outlaw abortions during the first trimester, or three months, of pregnancy. Rather than addressing the issue in feminist terms, such as women's right to control their bodies, the justices interpreted abortion as a medical issue, basing their decision on the confidentiality of the doctor-patient relationship as well as the right of privacy. *Roe v. Wade* nationalized the liberalization of state abortion laws that had begun in New York in 1970.

Running for Women's Rights

Feminists including Bella Abzug (in hat) and Betty Friedan (far right), join runners who carried a torch from Seneca Falls, New York, site of the first women's rights convention in 1848, to Houston for the 1977 National Women's Conference. Funded by Congress in honor of International Women's Year, the conference brought together two thousand delegates and twenty thousand observers who adopted a National Plan of Action for women's rights.

The Equal Rights Amendment. In the 1970s the women's movement increasingly united around the proposed Equal Rights Amendment to the Constitution (ERA), which stated in its entirety, "Equality of Rights under the law shall not be denied or abridged by the United States or any State on the basis of sex." The ERA, first introduced in Congress in 1923 by the National Woman's party, was dusted off by modern feminists. In 1970 the measure passed the House but died in the Senate. In the 1971–1972 session, it passed both houses and was submitted to the states for ratification. Thirty-four states quickly passed the ERA between 1972 and 1974. Then the momentum stopped, confirming the pattern that once a constitutional amendment becomes controversial, its chances for success plummet. Only Indiana ratified after that point, leaving the amendment three states short of the necessary three-fourths majority. Most of the non-ratifying states were in the South; Illinois also held out, despite spirited campaigns there by ERA supporters. Congress extended the deadline for ratification until June 30, 1982, but the Equal Rights Amendment still fell short.

Stalemate

The fate of the ERA suggested that, by the mid-1970s, the momentum of the women's movement was beginning to slow or even stop. Although 63 percent of women told the Harris poll in 1975 that they favored "efforts to strengthen and change women's status in society," a growing minority of men and women expressed concern over what seemed to be revolutionary changes in women's roles. A new conservatism was influencing political and social life by the mid-1970s, spearheaded by the Moral Majority and other organizations whose members belonged largely to evangelical Protestant groups (see Chapter 32). Especially disturbing to these conservatives were changes in attitudes that seemed to denigrate women who chose to stay home as full-time housewives.

Phyllis Schlafly, long active in conservative causes—she had written *A Choice, Not an Echo*, a best-seller extolling Barry Goldwater in 1963—led the antifeminist backlash. Despite her law degree and active career while raising five children, Schlafly advocated traditional

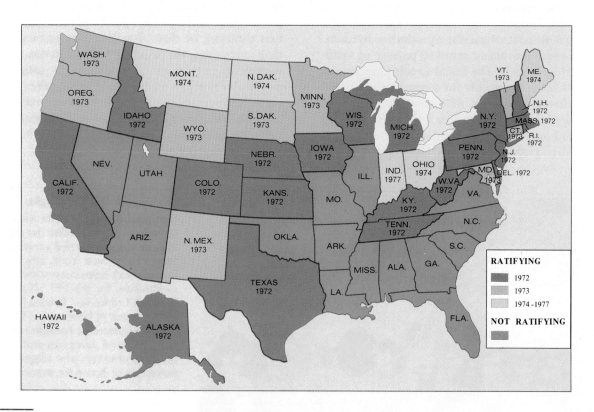

MAP 31.4

States Ratifying the Equal Rights Amendment

The Equal Rights Amendment quickly won state support in 1972 and 1973, but then it stalled. ERAmerica, a coalition of women's groups formed in 1976, lobbied extensively, particularly in Florida, North Carolina, and Illinois, but it failed to sway the conservative legislatures in those states. Efforts to revive the ERA in the 1980s were also unsuccessful.

roles for women. As she told audiences, "A man's first significant purchase is a diamond for his bride, and the major financial investment of his life is a home for her to live in." She baited feminists by opening her speeches, "I'd like to thank my husband for letting me be here tonight."

Schlafly's STOP ERA organization claimed the amendment would create an unnatural "unisex society," cause women to be drafted, legalize homosexual marriages, and prohibit separate toilets for men and women. (These charges have no basis in the language of the amendment.) Grass roots evangelical networks mobilized conservative women, who then showed up at state houses with home-baked bread and apple pies, symbols of their traditional domestic roles. The message that women would lose more than they would gain if the ERA passed found favor among many men and women, especially those deeply troubled by the rapid pace of social change.

Like the civil rights movement before it, the women's movement also found that choices were harder, and causes less clear-cut, as the 1970s progressed. Affirmative action guidelines, instituted by the Labor Department in 1968 to ensure nondiscriminatory hiring through quotas and preferential treatment to blacks and women, proved more politically unpopular than Title VII (see Chapter 32). Similarly, *comparable worth*, the doctrine that people with jobs involving similar levels of skill or responsibility, such as secretaries and maintenance workers, should be paid the same wages, was far more problematic than equal pay for equal work.

Abortion Controversy. But no issue could match the controversy that raged over abortion. The legalization of abortion in 1973 sparked a powerful Right to Life movement. Foes of abortion believed that the rights of a fetus took precedence over the right of the mother to choose whether to terminate her pregnancy. Therefore, they attempted to circumvent and overturn the *Roe v. Wade* decision. In 1976, Representative Henry Hyde of Illinois sponsored an amendment to deny Medicaid funds for abortions for poor women. Passed over a presidential veto, the amendment was upheld by the Supreme Court in 1980.

Although feminists had been forced on the defensive by the mid-1970s, women's lives showed no signs of returning to the patterns of 1950 or even of 1970. Pervasive changes were here to stay. So, too, were the victories won by blacks, Hispanics, native Americans, and gay people, incomplete though they may have been. American society had been permanently altered by the twenty-year struggle for equality.

★

Summary

Between 1954 and 1975, a series of social movements challenged the American status quo. The civil rights movement triggered the process, and its attacks on legalized segregation in the South expanded into challenges to institutionalized racism throughout the country. The tactics and ideology developed in the civil rights movement encouraged other groups, including Hispanics, native Americans, poor people, homosexuals, and women, to demand equality as well. Many were college students, who also challenged the policies of their universities and American participation in the Vietnam War.

All the protest movements had their roots in structural and demographic changes and shifting cultural values. Black migration from the South because of the transformation of agriculture made civil rights a national, not just a regional, problem. The postwar baby boom led to a rapid expansion of higher education. More women took jobs outside the home, faced rising divorce rates, and acquired better access to education.

The protest movements followed a similar progression. At first, efforts centered on the political or judicial front. These early successes led to heightened expectations, but the next stage—changing people's attitudes and gaining social and economic justice—proved more difficult. By the mid-1970s, the civil rights and women's movements each produced a backlash from those who thought change had gone far enough, but not before lasting alterations had been made in American society.

TOPIC FOR RESEARCH

The Life and Legacy of Malcolm X

Malcolm X (1925–1965) remains a controversial figures more than twenty-five years after his death. Was he a symbol of black pride and self-reliance, or was he a hatemonger? Which was more relevant to the 1960s—Malcolm X's message of self-defense and defiance or Martin Luther King's calls for integration and nonviolence?

Since advocates and detractors have variously distorted Malcolm's views over the years, the best way to understand his philosophy is to read his own speeches and writings. The place to begin this investigation of Malcolm X is through Alex Haley, *The Autobiography of Malcolm X* (1965). For his collected writings and speeches, see George Breitman, ed., *Malcolm X Speaks* (1965) and *Malcolm X: By Any Means Necessary* (1970). See also Bruce Perry, ed., *Malcolm X: The Last Speeches* (1989). What were the main tenets of Malcolm's philosophy? Did they change over time? Was his message better suited to northern urban residents than southern blacks?

In addition, you may wish to examine some broader questions: What was his impact on the civil rights movement, and what is his legacy today? Studies of Malcolm X's life include Peter Louis Goldman, *The Death and Life of Malcolm X* (1973), George Breitman, *The Last Year of Malcolm X: The Evolution of a Revolutionary* (1967), and John Henrik Clarke, ed., *Malcolm X: The Man and His Times* (1965). A full listing of secondary sources on Malcolm X's life is Timothy V. Johnson, *Malcolm X: A Comprehensive Annotated Bibliography* (1986).

BIBLIOGRAPHY

William H. Chafe, *The Unfinished Journey* (2nd ed., 1991), provides the best overview of the entire postwar period. Four strong surveys of the 1960s are Todd Gitlin, *The Sixties: Years of Hope, Days of Rage* (1987); Allen J. Matusow, *The Unraveling of America* (1984); William L. O'Neill, *Coming Apart* (1971); and Milton Viorst, *Fire in the Streets* (1979). For additional general material on the period, see Godfrey Hodgson, *America in Our Time* (1976), and Todd Gitlin, *The Whole World is Watching* (1980).

The Civil Rights Movement

Robert Weisbrot, *Freedom Bound* (1990), and Harvard Sitkoff, *The Struggle for Black Equality* (1981), offer comprehensive overviews. Richard Kluger, *Simple Justice* (1975), and Mark Tushnet, *The NAACP's Legal Strategy Against Segregated Education* (1987), analyze the *Brown* decision and its context, while Anthony Lewis, *Portrait of a Decade* (1964), covers southern reaction to the decision. J. Harvey Wilkinson III continues the story of the Supreme Court and integration through the 1970s in *From Brown to Bakke* (1979). Jules Tygiel, *Baseball's Great Experiment: Jackie Robinson and His Legacy* (1983), surveys integration on the field.

Histories of the major civil rights organizations include Clayborne Carson's study of SNCC, *In Struggle* (1981), and August Meier and Elliot Rudwick, *CORE* (1973). Mary Aickin Rothschild, *A Case of Black and White* (1982), describes northern volunteers during the Freedom Summer; Mary King, *Freedom Song* (1987), is a compelling personal memoir about SNCC. Victor Navasky, *Kennedy Justice* (1971), is extremely critical of President Kennedy's civil rights

record; Carl Brauer, *John F. Kennedy and the Second Reconstruction* (1977), is more sympathetic. William H. Chafe, *Civilities and Civil Rights* (1980), is a superb case study of the impact of civil rights on Greensboro, North Carolina, from the 1950s through the 1970s.

Major texts of the civil rights movement include Stokely Carmichael and Charles Hamilton, *Black Power* (1967); James Baldwin, *The Fire Next Time* (1963); and Eldridge Cleaver, *Soul on Ice* (1968). Anne Moody, *Coming of Age in Mississippi* (1968), is a moving autobiography; Howell Raines, *My Soul is Rested* (1977), and Henry Hampton and Steve Fayer, *Voices of Freedom* (1990), are fine oral histories. Joanne Grant, *Black Protest* (1968), and August Meier and Elliot Rudwick, *Black Protest in the Sixties* (1970), are good anthologies of basic texts.

The material on Martin Luther King, Jr., is extensive and continues to grow. King tells his own story in *Stride Toward Freedom* (1958) and *Why We Can't Wait* (1964). Biographies of King include David Garrow, *Bearing the Cross* (1986); Taylor Branch, *Parting the Waters: America in the King Years, 1954–1963* (1988); Stephen Oates, *Let the Trumpet Sound* (1982); and David Lewis, *King* (1970). David Garrow, *The FBI and Martin Luther King, Jr.* (1981), chronicles the FBI surveillance of the civil rights movement.

Record of the National Advisory Commission on Civil Disorders (1968) analyzes the decade's major race riots. See also Joe R. Feagin and Harlan Hahn, *Ghetto Revolts* (1973), and Robert Fogelson, *Violence as Protest* (1971). Robert Conot, *Rivers of Blood, Years of Darkness* (1968), studies the Watts riot.

Stan Steiner, *La Raza* (1970), and Matt Meier and Feliciano Rivera, *The Chicanos* (1972), document early Hispanic political activity. Vine DeLoria, Jr., *Behind the Trail of Broken Treaties* (1974) and *Custer Died for Your Sins* (1969), convey the new Indian assertiveness. See also Stan Steiner, *The New Indians* (1968); Helen Hertzberg, *The Search for an American Indian Movement* (1971); and Wilcomb Washburn, *Red Man's Land, White Man's Law* (1971). John D'Emilio, *Sexual Politics, Sexual Communities* (1983), describes the emergence of gay identity between 1940 and 1970.

The Challenge of Youth

The student activism of the 1960s drew its share of scholarly chroniclers. See Kenneth Keniston, *The Uncommitted* (1965) and *Young Radicals* (1969); Daniel Bell and Irving Kristol, *Confrontation* (1969); Nathan Glazer, *Remembering the Answers* (1970); and Philip Slater, *The Pursuit of Loneliness* (1970). On student revolt, see W. J. Rorabaugh, *Berkeley at War* (1968); Seymour Lipset and Sheldon Wolin, eds., *The Berkeley Student Revolt* (1965); and Jerry Avorn, *Up Against the Ivy Wall* (1968). John P. Diggins, *The American Left in the Twentieth Century* (1973), and Irwin Unger, *The Movement: A History of the American New Left* (1974), provide general background. Kirkpatrick Sale, *SDS* (1973), can be supplemented by James Miller, *Democracy is in the Streets* (1987), which covers the years from the Port Huron Statement to the siege of Chicago in 1968. Lawrence Baskir and William A. Straus, *The Draft, the War, and the Vietnam Generation* (1978), explain who was drafted and why. For the antiwar movement, see Charles DeBenedetti, with Charles Chatfield, *An American Ordeal* (1990), and Nancy Zaroulis and Gerald

Sullivan, *Who Spoke Up? American Protest Against the War in Vietnam, 1963–1975* (1984).

Morris Dickstein, *Gates of Eden* (1977), is an excellent account of cultural developments in the 1960s. Todd Gitlin, *The Sixties*, also treats the counterculture extensively. Other sources include Theodore Roszak, *The Making of a Counter-Culture* (1969), and Charles Reich, *The Greening of America* (1970). Joyce Maynard, *Looking Back* (1973), provides a "chronicle of growing up old" in the 1960s. Todd Gitlin, *The Whole World is Watching* (1980), discusses the impact of the mass media on the New Left. Gerald Howard, ed., *The Sixties* (1982), is a good anthology of the decade's art, politics, and culture. Philip Norman, *Shout! The Beatles in Their Generation* (1981), and Jon Weiner, *Come Together: John Lennon in His Times* (1984), cover developments in popular music. Joan Didion, *Slouching Toward Bethlehem* (1968) and *The White Album* (1979), explore some of the darker sides of the hippie phenomenon.

For background on the Beat Generation of the 1950s, start with Ann Charters, *Kerouac* (1973); Dennis McNally, *Desolate Angel* (1979); and Jane Kramer, *Allen Ginsberg in America* (1969). John Tytell, *Naked Angels* (1976), covers the lives and literature of the Beat Generation. Tom Wolfe's *Electric Kool-Aid Acid Test* (1965) describes the antics of Beat survivors Ken Kesey and his Merry Pranksters in the 1960s.

The Revival of Feminism

Jo Freeman, *The Politics of Women's Liberation* (1975); Barbara Deckard, *The Women's Movement* (1975); and Judith Hole and Ellen Levine, *The Rebirth of Feminism* (1971), chronicle the revival of feminism in the 1960s and 1970s. Alice Echols, *Daring to Be Bad* (1989) traces radical feminism from 1967 to 1975. Gayle Graham Yates, *What Women Want* (1975), concentrates on feminist ideology, while William H. Chafe, *Women and Equality* (1977), draws comparisons between feminism and civil rights. Sara Evans, *Personal Politics* (1979), traces the roots of feminism in the civil rights movement and the New Left. General histories of women's postwar activism include Cynthia Harrison, *On Account of Sex: The Politics of Women's Issues, 1945–1968* (1988); Leila J. Rupp and Verta Taylor, *Survival in the Doldrums: The American Women's Rights Movement, 1945 to the 1960s* (1987); and Susan M. Hartmann, *From Margin to Mainstream* (1989).

Material on women's changing lives is found in Alice Kessler-Harris, *Out to Work* (1982); Carl Degler, *At Odds: Women and the Family in America from the Revolution to the Present* (1980); and Valerie Kincaid Oppenheimer, *The Female Labor Force in the United States* (1970). Ethel Klein, *Gender Politics* (1984), links demographic change with the revival of feminism. Phyllis Schlafly, *The Power of the Positive Woman* (1978); Andrea Dworkin, *Right Wing Women* (1983); and Rebecca E. Klatch, *Women of the New Right* (1987), present the ideas of antifeminist women that gained force in the 1970s. Mary Berry, *Why ERA Failed* (1986), and Jane J. Mansbridge, *Why We Lost the ERA* (1986), offer two perspectives on the demise of the Equal Rights Amendment. For the controversy over abortion, see Marion Faux, *Roe v. Wade* (1988), and Kristin Luker, *Abortion and the Politics of Motherhood* (1984).

TIMELINE

1954	*Brown v. Board of Education of Topeka, Kansas*
1955–1956	Montgomery bus boycott
1957	Southern Christian Leadership Conference (SCLC) founded
1960	Greensboro, North Carolina, sit-ins Birth control pill becomes available
1961	Presidential Commission on the Status of Women Freedom Rides
1962	Students for a Democratic Society (SDS) founded
1963	Betty Friedan's *The Feminine Mystique* March on Washington
1964	Civil Rights Act Free Speech Movement at Berkeley
1965	Voting Rights Act
1966	National Organization for Women (NOW) founded Stokely Carmichael proclaims Black Power
1967	Height of race riots in northern cities Hippie counterculture
1968	Martin Luther King, Jr., assassinated Robert F. Kennedy assassinated Women's liberation movement
1969	Vietnam moratorium Woodstock festival American Indian Movement (AIM) seizes Alcatraz Stonewall riot leads to gay liberation movement
1970	Kent State killings
1972	Congress passes Equal Rights Amendment
1973	*Roe v. Wade* legalizes abortion

In addition to the works of Betty Friedan, Robin Morgan, and Shulamith Firestone mentioned in the chapter, see Kate Millett, *Sexual Politics* (1970); Germaine Greer, *The Female Eunuch* (1972); and Susan Brownmiller, *Against Our Will: Men, Women, and Rape* (1975). Sara Ruddick and Pamela Daniels, eds., *Working It Out* (1977), chronicle the struggles of twenty-three women to find personal and professional fulfillment during a period of rapid change in women's lives.

Our Fragile Environment

NASA photographs from space captured both the
beauty and the fragility of the planet Earth.

32 *A More Conservative Era,*
1968–1980

In many ways, the years between 1963 and 1968 were distinct. The civil rights movement spurred the nation to debate the political issues of the day in terms of morality, justice, fairness, and equality. In the tumultuous year of 1968, the political system and social fabric seemed to unravel at an alarming pace. The events of 1968 ushered in an era of political, social, and cultural conservatism, which would dominate American life through the 1970s and 1980s. Richard Nixon won election as president in 1968 and again in 1972 by capitalizing on this shifting mood. But in 1974 the Watergate scandal forced Nixon from office, adding to the crisis of confidence that had been set in motion by the Vietnam War and the upheavals of the 1960s.

In the years after Nixon's resignation, the United States faced new challenges in national life. Economically, Americans found themselves in a period of limited growth, declining productivity, and runaway inflation, exacerbated by a dramatic rise in the price of imported oil after 1973. Internationally, the prolonged American withdrawal from Vietnam and increasing instability in the Middle East shared attention with continuing tense relations with the Soviet Union, as both superpowers engaged in an escalating nuclear arms race that threatened the fragile international peace.

Even after the election of Richard Nixon in 1968, activism continued, although civil rights was no longer the driving force. The women's movement made important gains in the early 1970s, and the birth of a new environmental movement was celebrated on Earth Day, April 22, 1970. Ironically, this was just two weeks

before the killings of four students at Kent State in the last gasp of antiwar demonstrations. The ghost of Vietnam would hover over much of the 1970s.

The Watershed Year: 1968

Many historians point to 1968 as a watershed for America, "the pivotal dividing line of the postwar years." In the first half of the year, the pace of change seemed out of control, with events taking on special significance because it was a presidential election year. Yet by the time of the election in November, the tide had shifted decisively away from the previous period of protest and challenge.

A Year of Shocks

The first traumatic event of 1968 was the Tet offensive of January 30, a surprise Vietcong attack on major installations throughout South Vietnam, including the U.S. embassy in Saigon. Although U.S. forces repulsed the attack, the Vietcong's demonstrated strength mocked American claims that the enemy was being defeated. President Johnson's political stock fell accordingly. The war had "come home," affecting domestic politics, and especially the Democratic party, in a way that none of Johnson's advisers had anticipated.

At the urging of liberal antiwar activist Allard Lowenstein, Senator Eugene J. McCarthy of Minnesota had already entered the Democratic primaries as an alternative to Lyndon Johnson. (Lowenstein had first approached New York senator Robert Kennedy, whose instincts told him to run but whose advisers said he should wait until 1972.) A core of student activists "came clean for Gene," that is, they cut their hair and put away their blue jeans to avoid alienating voters. When the Tet offensive revealed how badly things were going in Vietnam, support for the war eroded further. Although President Johnson won the New Hampshire primary in early March, McCarthy received a stunning 42.2 percent of the vote. McCarthy's vote reflected profound dissatisfaction with the course of the war, including, ironically, those who believed Johnson was not hawkish enough. Sensing the president's vulnerability, Robert Kennedy changed his mind and entered the race. Johnson realized his political support was evaporating, and, in the midst of an otherwise mundane televised address on March 31, he stunned the nation by announcing he would not seek reelection. Johnson vowed to devote his remaining months in office to the search for peace in Vietnam. Johnson's vague pledge had little effect on the fighting, however, and protesters redoubled their efforts to stop the war.

Just five days after Johnson's withdrawal, Martin Luther King, Jr., was assassinated in Memphis, provoking urban riots across the country that left forty-three people dead. Soon after, a major student confrontation erupted at Columbia University, ending only when police violently removed protesters from the administration buildings they had occupied. Student unrest seemed likely to become a worldwide phenomenon in May, when a massive strike by students and labor unions toppled the French government.

Then came the final, and for many, the most painful tragedy of the year. As Robert Kennedy celebrated his California primary victory over Eugene McCarthy on June 5, 1968, he was assassinated by Sirhan Sirhan, a young Palestinian thought to oppose Kennedy's pro-Israel stand. Once again, the nation went through the ritual of burying a Kennedy. In two strokes—the assassinations of Martin Luther King and Robert Kennedy—liberalism had been, in the words of student leader Tom Hayden, "decapitated."

Robert Kennedy's assassination shattered the dreams of many who hoped that social change could be achieved through the political system. Kennedy's death also had major implications for the Democratic party, because only he had seemed able to mobilize a constituency broader than just the antiwar movement. In his brief but dramatic campaign, Robert Kennedy had excited, indeed energized, the traditional components of the New Deal coalition, including blue-collar workers and black voters, in a way that the more cerebral Eugene McCarthy never did. So widespread was Kennedy's appeal that election-day exit polls in Indiana

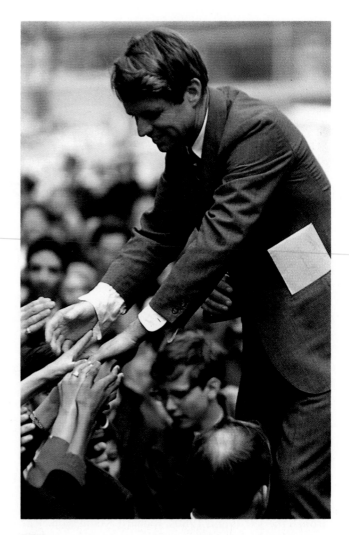

RFK

Bobby Kennedy inspired strong passions during his 1968 campaign. Followers often tore off his cufflinks as they tried to touch him or shake his hand.

found that many voters who had supported him in the primary actually voted for conservative candidate George Wallace in November.

The Democratic party, which was still reeling from Johnson's withdrawal when Kennedy was assassinated, never fully recovered. McCarthy proceeded listlessly through the rest of his campaign. Senator George S. McGovern of South Dakota entered the Democratic race in an effort to keep the Kennedy forces together. Meanwhile, Vice-President Hubert H. Humphrey lined up pledges from the traditional Democratic constituencies—unions, city machines, and state political organizations. The Democrats thus found themselves on the verge of nominating, not an antiwar candidate, but a public figure closely associated with Johnson's war policies. The stage was set for the Democratic National Convention in Chicago in August.

Chicago, 1968
Protesters gather in Chicago's Grant Park during the 1968 Democratic convention.
The large structure in the background is the Conrad Hilton Hotel, where most of the
delegates were staying.

Turmoil and Political Backlash

The Democrats had experienced disastrous conventions in the past, as in the 103-ballot meeting in 1924, but the 1968 convention hit a new low. Most of the drama occurred not in the convention hall but outside, on the streets of Chicago. Protesters led by Jerry Rubin and Abbie Hoffman, who the year before had tried to "levitate" the Pentagon as a way of ending the war, descended on Chicago, calling themselves the Youth International Party, or Yippies. With theatrics geared for maximum media exposure, they announced a platform that included an end to the war, the legalization of marijuana, and the abolition of money. To mock the "pigs" who ruled America, they nominated a live pig for president, which was promptly confiscated by the Chicago humane society. Their stunts diverted attention from the more serious, and far more numerous, antiwar activists who had come to Chicago as convention delegates or volunteers to take a stand against the Democrats' war policy.

Old-line Democratic mayor Richard J. Daley grew increasingly angry at the way the protesters were mocking *his* city and disrupting *his* convention. He called out the police and gave them broad discretion to break up the demonstrations. Several nights of skirmishes between protesters and police culminated on the evening that the names of candidates were put in nomination. In what an official report later described as a "police riot," the police dispersed protesters, who never numbered more than ten thousand, with mace, tear gas, and clubs.

The tear gas was so strong that it wafted into the air conditioning ducts of the Conrad Hilton hotel, where most delegates were staying.

While protesters chanted, "The whole world is watching!" the television networks ran film of the riot in the midst of the nominating speeches. In one memorable exchange, Senator Abraham Ribicoff of Connecticut interrupted his nominating speech for Senator McGovern to interject, "With George McGovern we wouldn't have Gestapo tactics on the streets of Chicago." The cameras panned to Mayor Daley, livid with rage and clearly mouthing obscenities.

Television coverage of the riots was hardly excessive—about 32 minutes on CBS and less than 14 minutes on NBC—but it cemented an impression of the Democrats as the party of disorder. The Democrats dispiritedly gave the nomination to Hubert H. Humphrey, who chose Senator Edmund S. Muskie of Maine as his running mate. The convention approved a middle-of-the-road, pro-administration platform that endorsed the policy of continuing the fighting in Vietnam while exploring diplomatic means to end the conflict.

One result of the Democratic convention was the beginning of a backlash against protest. The general public did not differentiate between the antics of the small group of Yippies who wanted to shut the system down and the actions of a far greater number of antiwar activists who were still trying to work within the system. Polls showed overwhelming support for Mayor Daley and the police over the demonstrators. After 1968 the New Left splintered into factions, its energy

★

AMERICAN VOICES

The Siege of Chicago *Steve Lerner*

Steve Lerner published his account in *The Village Voice* of the altercation between protesters and the Chicago police during the Democratic convention in August 1968. The scene: Lincoln Park on Chicago's North Side, where many of the protesters hung out. The time: around midnight.

Around midnight on Tuesday some four hundred clergy, concerned local citizens, and other respectable gentry joined the Yippies, members of Students for a Democratic Society, and the National Mobilization Committee to fight for the privilege of remaining in the park. Sporting armbands decorated with a black cross and chanting pacifist hymns, the men of God exhorted their radical congregation to lay down their bricks and join in a nonviolent vigil.

Having foreseen that they could only wage a symbolic war with "little caesar Daley," several enterprising clergymen brought with them an enormous wooden cross which they erected in the midst of the demonstrators under a street lamp. Three of them assumed heroic poses around the cross, more reminiscent of the Marines raising the flag over Iwo Jima than any Christ-like tableau they may have had in mind.

During the half-hour interlude between the arrival of the clergy and the police attack, a fascinating debate over the relative merits of strict nonviolence versus armed self-defense raged between the clergy and the militants. While the clergy was reminded that their members were "over thirty, the opiate of the people, and totally irrelevant," the younger generation was warned that "by calling the police pigs and fighting with them you become as bad as they are." Although the conflict was never resolved, everyone more or less decided to do his own thing. By then the demonstrators, some eight hundred strong, began to feel the phalanx of police which encircled the park moving in; even the most militant forgot his quibbles with "the liberal-religious sellout" and began to huddle together around the cross.

When the police announced that the demonstrators had five minutes to move out before the park was cleared, everyone went into his individual kind of panic. One boy sitting near me unwrapped a cheese sandwich and began to stuff it into his face without bothering to chew. A girl standing at the periphery of the circle who had been alone all evening walked up to a helmented boy with a mustache and ground herself into him. People all over the park were shyly introducing themselves to each other as if they didn't want to die alone. "My name is Mike Stevenson from Detroit; what got you into this?" I heard someone asking behind me. Others became increasingly involved in the details of survival: rubbing Vaseline on their face to keep the Mace from burning their skin, buttoning their jackets, wetting their handkerchief and tying it over their nose and mouth. "If it's gas, remember, breathe through your mouth, don't run, don't pant, and . . . don't rub your eyes," someone thoughtfully announced over the speaker. A boy in the center of the circle got up, stepped over his seated friends, and made his way toward the woods. "Don't leave now," several voices called in panic. The boy explained that he was just going to take a leak.

It happened all in an instant. The night which had been filled with darkness and whispers exploded in a fiery scream. Huge tear-gas canisters came crashing through the branches, snapping them, and bursting in the center of the gathering. From where I lay, groveling in the grass, I could see ministers retreating with the cross, carrying it like a fallen comrade. Another volley shook me to my feet. Gas was everywhere. People were running, screaming, tearing through the trees. Something hit the tree next to me, I was on the ground again, someone was pulling me to my feet, two boys were lifting a big branch off a girl who lay squirming hysterically. I couldn't see. Someone grabbed onto me and asked me to lead them out of the park. We walked along, hands outstretched, bumping into people and trees, tears streaming from our eyes and mucus smeared across our faces. I flashed First World War doughboys caught in no-man's-land during a mustard gas attack. I felt sure I was going to die. I heard others choking around me. And then everything cleared.

Source: Steve Lerner account from *The Village Voice*, excerpted in Norman Mailer, *Miami and the Siege of Chicago: An Informal History of the Republican and Democratic Conventions of 1968* (New American Library, 1968), 151–52.

Hard Hats
Many construction workers (and the unions they belonged to) were vocal supporters of the Vietnam War. Sometimes hard hats clashed with long-haired protesters during antiwar marches and sidewalk demonstrations.

spent. One radical faction broke off from SDS to form the Weathermen (taking their name from a Bob Dylan song). A tiny band of self-styled revolutionaries, who embraced violence and bombings as tactics to bring about change, most were soon forced underground to avoid arrest. Broad-based antiwar protests continued, however, until at least 1970.

Conservative Backlash. Events in Chicago in August 1968 also strengthened support for proponents of "law and order," which became the catch phrase of the next several years. Many Americans were fed up with protest and dissent. Governor George C. Wallace of Alabama, a third-party candidate, skillfully exploited the public's growing hostility by making student protests and urban riots his chief campaign issues. He also spoke out against school desegregation and forced busing. Early polls showed that Wallace would receive as much as 20 percent of the vote, possibly enough to deadlock the electoral college and send the election to the House of Representatives.

Richard Nixon, even more than George Wallace, tapped the growing conservative mood of the electorate. After his unsuccessful presidential campaign in 1960 and his failure in the California gubernatorial race in 1962, Nixon engineered an amazing political comeback. In 1968 the "new" Nixon easily beat back primary challenges from three governors—Ronald Reagan of California, George Romney of Michigan, and Nelson Rockefeller of New York—to win the Republican nomination. He chose Maryland governor Spiro Agnew as his running mate to attract southern voters who opposed Democratic civil rights legislation, especially potential Wallace supporters. (One of Agnew's

more memorable quotes was, "If you've seen one city slum, you've seen them all.") In the campaign, Nixon pledged to represent the "quiet voice" of the "great majority of Americans, the forgotten Americans, the non-shouters, the nondemonstrators." He declared, "The first civil right of every American is to be free from domestic violence."

Despite the Democratic debacle in Chicago, the election was close. Humphrey rallied in the last weeks of the campaign by gingerly disassociating himself from Johnson's war policies. Nixon countered by declaring that he had a "secret plan" to end the war. Nixon received 43.4 percent of the vote to Humphrey's 42.7 percent, defeating him by a scant 510,000 votes out of the 73 million cast. Wallace finished with 13.5 percent of the popular vote, becoming the most successful third-party candidate since Progressive Robert M. La Follette in 1924. Nixon's "southern strategy," his carefully crafted inroad into the once solidly Democratic South, certainly contributed to his victory. Yet Nixon owed his election more to the split in the Democratic coalition than to the emergence of a new Republican majority.

A Changing Mood. The closeness of the 1968 election suggested how polarized American society had become over the events of the 1960s. Nixon appealed to what came to be known as the *silent majority.* According to social scientists Ben J. Wattenberg and Richard Scammon in their influential book *The Real Majority* (1970), the typical American was a forty-seven-year-old machinist's wife from Dayton, Ohio, and this was what she was concerned about:

To know that the lady in Dayton is afraid to walk the streets alone at night, to know that she has a mixed

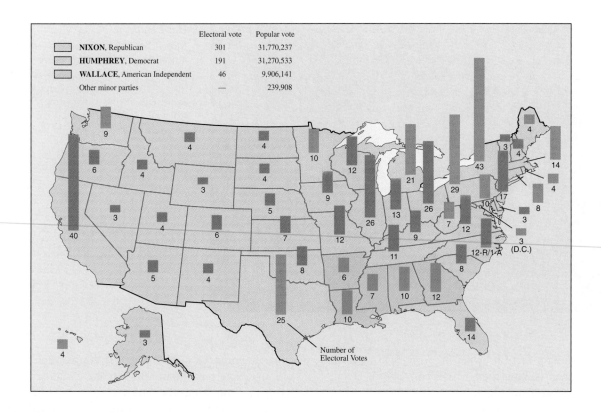

MAP 32.1

The Election of 1968

As late as mid-September, third-party candidate George C. Wallace of Alabama had the support of 21 percent of the voters. But in November he received only 13.5 percent of the vote, winning five states and showing that the South was no longer solidly Democratic. Republican Richard M. Nixon defeated Hubert H. Humphrey with only 43.4 percent of the popular vote.

view about blacks and civil rights because before moving to the suburbs she lived in a neighborhood that became all black, to know that her brother-in-law is a policeman, to know that she does not have the money to move if her new neighborhood deteriorates, to know that she is deeply distressed that her son is going to a community junior college where LSD was found on campus—to know all this is the beginning of contemporary political wisdom.

But while political appeals after 1968 were targeted more to voters who were (in the words of Wattenberg and Scammon) "unblack, unpoor, and unyoung," protest and controversy would remain part of the political process until the divisive issue of the Vietnam War was resolved.

The Nixon Years

The figure and personality of Richard Nixon dominated, indeed haunted, the landscape of postwar American political history. Columnist Meg Greenfield defined the "Nixon Generation" in 1972:

At regular intervals now, ever since the first vote in 1952, our generation has either been supporting or opposing Richard Nixon. The psychological implications of this fact are staggering. . . . What distinguishes us as a group from those who came before and those who have come after is that we are too young to remember a time when Richard Nixon was not on the political scene, and too old reasonably to expect that we shall live to see one.

What Greenfield could not have predicted when she wrote those words was that less than two years later, Nixon would be forced from office in order to avoid impeachment. But then too, who would have predicted Nixon's remarkable political resiliency, as he resurfaced in the 1980s as an influential author, television pundit, elder statesman, and unofficial adviser to Democratic and Republican presidents alike?

Domestic Agendas

Richard Nixon had waited eight years for his chance at the presidency, and he wanted to leave his mark on history. He anticipated ending his two terms in 1976 with a triumphant celebration of the nation's bicentennial.

Before the Watergate scandal brought his administration to an untimely end, Nixon had served his entire first term and part of the second. In that time, he counted both accomplishments and setbacks.

Richard Nixon proclaimed an ideological commitment to a *new federalism*, pledging to "reverse the flow of power and resources from the states and communities to Washington and start power and resources flowing back . . . to the people." One important innovation was the 1972 program of *revenue sharing*, whereby a portion of federal monies were turned back to the states to be spent as states saw fit. At the same time, however, the Nixon administration expanded the regulatory apparatus of the modern state. The Environmental Protection Agency (EPA) was set up in 1970 to coordinate the growing federal responsibilities for environmental action. The Occupational Safety and Health Administration (OSHA) and the Consumer Product Safety Commission were established in 1972 out of growing concern for the health and safety of workers and consumers.

Social Programs. In other areas Nixon worked to scale down government programs that had grown dramatically during the two previous Democratic administrations. Most Great Society programs received reduced funding and the Office of Economic Opportunity was totally dismantled in 1971. The administration claimed to support civil rights, but was embarrassed by a leaked 1970 memo by presidential adviser Daniel Patrick Moynihan, a Democrat who had joined the Nixon White House, which suggested that "the issue of race could benefit from a period of benign neglect." Nixon also vetoed a 1971 bill to establish a comprehensive national child care system because it would commit "the vast moral authority of the national government to communal approaches to child rearing, over against the family centered approach."

Despite these attacks on Democratic social programs, the administration put forward its own poverty program in an ambitious attempt to overhaul the jerry-built social welfare system dating from the New Deal. Following the advice of urban expert Moynihan, Nixon in 1969 proposed a Family Assistance Plan, which would guarantee a family of four an income of $1,600 a year, plus $860 in food stamps. One attraction of a guaranteed annual income was simplicity: it would eliminate the multiple layers of bureaucrats (caseworkers, local and state officials, and federal employees) who administered the burgeoning Aid to Families with Dependent Children program (AFDC), the largest welfare program by the 1960s. But the bill floundered in the Senate: conservatives attacked it for putting the federal government too deeply into the welfare business, while liberals and social welfare activists opposed it for not going far enough. No serious attempt at welfare reform has come as close to passage since.

The Supreme Court. The Nixon administration showed its commitment to conservative social values in its appointments to the Supreme Court. One of Nixon's first acts was to nominate hard-line conservative Warren Burger to replace retired Chief Justice Earl Warren in the spring of 1969. When another vacancy occurred later that year, Nixon attempted to appoint a conservative southern judge as a way of cementing his political support in that region. But two nominees in succession, Clement F. Haynsworth and G. Harrold Carswell, failed to win Senate confirmation. Haynsworth, a federal Circuit Court judge from South Carolina, was turned down after revelations that he had sat on cases in which he had a financial interest. Carswell failed, in part, because he had participated in a white segregationists' scheme in Tallahassee, Florida, to buy a public golf course to prevent its integration. Eventually, Nixon would name three more Supreme Court justices: Harry Blackmun, Lewis F. Powell, Jr., and William Rehnquist.

Conservative judges did not always give Nixon the conservative decisions he wanted. Despite attempts by the Justice Department to halt further desegregation, the Court ruled in *Swann v. Charlotte-Mecklenburg Board of Education* (1971) in favor of forced busing to achieve racial balance. The *Furman v. Georgia* decision (1972) contained strict guidelines restricting the implementation of capital punishment, although it did not rule the death penalty unconstitutional. And, in the controversial 1973 case of *Roe v. Wade,* the Court struck down Texas and Georgia laws that had prohibited abortion.

Foreign Policy

Some of Richard Nixon's most stunning first-term initiatives came in the realm of foreign policy. Paradoxes abound here. At the same time that he was prosecuting the war in Vietnam, ostensibly to halt the spread of communism, he was laying the groundwork for détente with the Soviet Union and China. As a lifelong anti-Communist crusader, Nixon had greater political maneuverability to reach out to these two Communist superpowers than a Democratic president. After all, no one could accuse Richard Nixon of being soft on communism. National Security Adviser Henry Kissinger, a former Harvard government professor, influenced the president's thinking in this direction. Like Nixon, Kissinger had a huge ego, and both wanted to leave their mark on history. Foreign policy gave them that chance.

Since the Chinese revolution of 1949, the United States had refused to recognize the government of the People's Republic of China, instead giving unconditional support to the Nationalist Chinese government that had set itself up in Taiwan. Nixon moved away from that policy, reasoning that the United States could profitably exploit the growing rift between the People's Republic of China and the Soviet Union. He sent Kissinger on a secret mission to Beijing in the summer of 1971 and in July told a startled world that he would visit the People's Republic in the near future. He did so in February 1972, walking along the Great Wall and toasting Chinese leaders in Beijing. Nixon's visit set the stage for the formal establishment of diplomatic relations, which took place in 1979.

In a similar spirit of détente, Nixon journeyed to Moscow in May of 1972 to sign SALT I, a treaty resulting from Strategic Arms Limitations Talks between the United States and the Soviet Union. (Both trips were timed to give him maximum television publicity in an election year.) Although President Nixon boasted that the SALT agreement was a dramatic step toward stopping the arms race, what the accords really did was limit production and deployment of intercontinental ballistic missiles (ICBMs) and antiballistic missile systems (ABMs), leaving untouched other equally destructive systems of nuclear warfare. Yet the treaty was also a recognition that the United States could no longer afford the massive military spending that would have been necessary to regain the nuclear and military superiority of the immediate postwar years. By the early 1970s, factors such as inflation, the decline in American hegemony over the world system, and domestic dissent were all limiting and reshaping American options in international relations.

Nixon's War

Vietnam, long Lyndon Johnson's war, also became Richard Nixon's. Fifteen thousand Americans would lose their lives in Vietnam during Nixon's presidency. Yet Nixon operated within political parameters that differed fundamentally from Johnson's. Realizing that the public would not support major sacrifices to win the war, Nixon and Kissinger searched for a way out. A new plan to reduce American troop involvement, called "Vietnamization," delegated most of the ground fighting to South Vietnamese troops. When Nixon took office, more than 543,000 American soldiers were serving in Vietnam; by the end of 1970, there were 334,000, and two years later 24,200. American casualties, and the political liabilities they generated, fell correspondingly. But the slaughter in Vietnam continued. As Ambassador to Vietnam Ellsworth Bunker noted cynically, it was just a matter of changing "the color of the bodies."

The companion policy to troop withdrawal was a dramatic increase in American bombing raids over North Vietnam. Expanded air support was an attempt to strengthen Nguyen Van Thieu's faltering South Vietnamese government while the gradual process of Vietnamization went into effect. The escalation of the air war was virtually concealed from the American public, who believed that the war was winding down, based on the much-publicized troop withdrawals.

Hanoi Devastated

The North Vietnamese capital of Hanoi sustained heavy damage from bombing raids by American B-52s. The most devastating raids occurred during the "Christmas bombing" in December 1972, just weeks before the Paris Peace Accords were signed.

In March 1969, Nixon went further and ordered secret bombing raids on neutral Cambodia, through which the Vietnamese transported supplies and reinforcements. To keep Congress ignorant about these sorties, accurate information about the raids was fed into one Defense Department computer, while data omitting the Cambodia targets were fed into another. The faulty projections from the second computer were the ones given to Congress. The secret war culminated in an April 30, 1970, "incursion" by American ground forces into Cambodia to destroy enemy troop havens there. The invasion of Cambodia triggered widespread protests and led to the Kent State killings on May 4 (see Chapter 31). No matter how much the United States escalated its activity, however, the Vietnamese fought on.

The War at Home. Like Lyndon Johnson, who by 1968 had become so unpopular that his appearance caused protests everywhere except on military bases, Richard Nixon seemed to inspire domestic conflict. To discredit critics, he denounced student demonstrators as "bums" and stated that "North Vietnam cannot defeat or humiliate the United States. Only Americans can do that." Vice-President Spiro Agnew added emphasis, attacking dissidents as "ideological eunuchs" and "nattering nabobs of negativism." Nixon staunchly insisted he would not be swayed by the mounting protests against the war. When close to half a million protesters marched on Washington in November 1969, the president barricaded himself in the White House and watched football games on television.

By 1970 dissatisfaction with the war had spread widely throughout society. Even American troops in Vietnam showed mounting opposition to their mission. They fought on, but many sewed peace symbols on their uniforms. A number of overbearing junior officers were "fragged"—that is, killed or wounded by a fragmentation grenade thrown by their own soldiers. A group called Vietnam Veterans Against the War turned in their combat medals at mass demonstrations at the U.S. Capitol.

My Lai. The Vietnam War was brought home forcefully to the American people in 1971, when Lieutenant William L. Calley was court-martialed for atrocities committed in the Vietnamese village of My Lai in March 1968. Calley had commanded a platoon on a routine search and destroy mission. Retaliating for casualties sustained by their buddies on an earlier engagement, the soldiers apparently murdered 350 Vietnamese villagers. The incident came to light because one member of the platoon refused to go along with a military cover-up; investigative reporter Seymour Hersh of the *New York Times* broke the story. In the court martial proceedings, a jury of six soldiers who had served in

Vietnam sentenced Calley to life imprisonment for his part in the massacre. Yet conservatives called Calley a hero rather than a villain, and after President Nixon's intervention, his sentence was reduced to three years' house arrest.

The 1972 Election

The Democratic party, still divided over Vietnam and civil rights, would have had a difficult time countering Nixon at the end of his first term under any circumstances. Disarray within the party in 1972 made their task even harder. Following the 1968 national convention, the party had changed its way of selecting delegates and candidates, pledging to include "minority groups, young people and women in reasonable relationship to their presence in the population." The ratification of the Twenty-sixth Amendment in 1971, lowering the national voting age to eighteen, increased the impact of this procedural change.

The McGovern Campaign. South Dakota senator George McGovern reaped the greatest benefit from the new Democratic guidelines. By 1972 he was supported by an army of antiwar activists, who blitzed the precinct-level caucuses and won delegate commitments far beyond his voter support. In the past, an alliance of party bosses and union leaders would almost certainly have rejected an upstart candidate like McGovern. But few old-line party leaders qualified as delegates to the nominating convention under the changed rules. Typical of the new Democratic look, black leader Jesse Jackson replaced Mayor Richard Daley of Chicago as the head of the Illinois delegation.

McGovern's campaign against Nixon was an unrelieved disaster. Surprised to learn that his running mate, Senator Thomas F. Eagleton of Missouri, had undergone electroshock therapy for depression some years earlier, McGovern first supported him "1,000 percent," then abruptly insisted that he leave the ticket. Sargent Shriver, a brother-in-law of John and Robert Kennedy, was prevailed upon to join the ticket at the last minute. George McGovern was far too liberal for many traditional Democrats, who rejected his ill-defined proposals for welfare reform, did not rally around his calls for unilateral withdrawal from Vietnam, and ignored his charges that the Nixon administration had corruptly abused its power.

Nixon's campaign took full advantage of McGovern's weaknesses. Although the president had failed to end the war, his Vietnamization policy had reduced weekly American combat deaths from three hundred in 1968 to almost none in 1972. Just a few days before the election, Henry Kissinger returned from negotiations with the North Vietnamese in Paris and announced, somewhat disingenuously, that "peace is at hand." These initiatives robbed the Democrats of their greatest appeal—their antiwar stance. In addition, the improving economy helped the Republicans.

Nixon won handily, receiving nearly 61 percent of the popular vote and carrying every state except Massachusetts and the District of Columbia. (After the Watergate scandal gathered momentum, Bay State bumper stickers would proclaim, "Don't Blame Me—I'm from Massachusetts.") The threat of a conservative third-party challenge had ended abruptly the previous May, when George Wallace was shot and paralyzed from the waist down by an assailant in a suburban Maryland shopping mall. McGovern's vote demonstrated large cracks in the traditional Democratic coalition: he received only 18 percent of the southern white Protestant vote and 38 percent of the big-city Catholic vote. Only African-Americans, Jews, and low-income voters remained loyal to the Democratic cause. Yet Nixon failed to kindle strong Republican loyalties in the electorate. Only 55.7 percent of eligible voters bothered to go to the polls, and Democrats maintained their control of both houses of Congress.

American Withdrawal From Vietnam

Following his second election victory, Nixon moved to end American involvement in Vietnam. In a final destructive demonstration of American military strength for the benefit of South Vietnamese president Thieu, homefront hawks, and the Third World in general, he initiated the "Christmas bombings." From December 17 to December 30, 1972, American planes subjected North Vietnamese civilian and military targets to the most devastating bombing of the entire war. Then, on January 27, 1973, a ceasefire was signed in Paris by representatives of the United States, North and South Vietnam, and the Vietcong; it differed little from the proposal of the previous October. The Paris Peace Accords failed to deliver Nixon's often-repeated promise of peace with honor. Basically, they mandated the unilateral withdrawal of American troops in exchange for the return of American prisoners of war held in North Vietnam. For most Americans, that amount of face saving was enough.

The public outpouring of emotion that greeted the six hundred returning prisoners contrasted sharply with public indifference to ordinary Vietnam veterans. Advocates for Vietnam veterans would later charge that they experienced higher than average rates of divorce, suicide, and unemployment, as well as recurring physical and psychological problems that came to be associated with post-Vietnam trauma syndrome. For many Vietnam veterans, the war never ended.

The 1973 Peace Accords did not resolve the civil war that had raged in Vietnam for almost three decades. Without massive U.S. military and economic aid, and with Vietcong guerrillas operating freely throughout the countryside, it was only a matter of time before the South Vietnamese government of General Nguyen Van Thieu fell to the more disciplined and popular Communist forces. In April 1975 a North Vietnamese offensive reunited the country. On television, horrified American viewers watched South Vietnamese officials and soldiers struggle with American embassy personnel for space on the last helicopters that flew out of Saigon before the Vietcong entered the city. (As a testimonial to its founding leader, who had died in 1969, the Vietnamese government renamed it Ho Chi Minh City.) Strife still engulfs Vietnam and its neighbors Laos, Cambodia, and Thailand. The epitaph that journalist David Halberstam coined for American participation in the war applies to Southeast Asia itself: "No light at the end of the tunnel, only greater darkness."

Watergate

Watergate, the great constitutional crisis of the early 1970s, was a direct result of Richard Nixon's secretive style of governing and his obsession with opposition to the Vietnam War at home. Many Americans saw Watergate as only the evil deeds of one person (Richard Nixon) and one unlawful act (the obstruction of justice following a break-in). But Watergate was not just an isolated incident; it was part of a broad pattern of illegality and misuse of power that grew out of the era—and the war—that preceded it.

The new administration had begun to stretch the boundaries of the law under the guise of national security just four months into Nixon's first term. In the spring of 1969, after the *New York Times* reported the secret bombing of Cambodia, the White House arranged for the FBI to investigate the source of the story. Without seeking any judicial warrants, the FBI secretly (and illegally) taped phone conversations of several low-level staffers on the National Security Council, as well as five newspeople. The source was never found.

Over the next several years, the Nixon administration would repeatedly invoke supposed domestic threats to national security to conceal its actions. In 1970 the White House asked Tom Huston, a former army intelligence officer, to draw up an extensive plan for secret domestic counterintelligence—such as opening mail, tapping phones, and arranging break-ins—by the FBI, CIA, and Justice Department. President Nixon approved the scheme, only to have it blocked by FBI Director J. Edgar Hoover, who refused to cooperate with other government agencies in activities he interpreted as being exclusively within the scope of the FBI.

The Pentagon Papers. White House paranoia was next aroused in June 1971, when Daniel Ellsberg, a former Defense Department analyst who had grown disillusioned with the war, leaked the so-called Pentagon Papers to the *New York Times*. The Pentagon Papers were classified Defense Department documents commissioned by Secretary of Defense Robert McNamara in 1967 and completed eighteen months later. The report detailed so many American blunders and misjudgments that McNamara had commented on first reading it, "You know, they could hang people for what is in there." The Nixon administration unsuccessfully attempted to block publication of the Pentagon Papers, increasing Ellsberg's stature as a hero to the antiwar movement. In an effort to discredit Ellsberg, White House underlings burglarized his psychiatrist's office to look for damaging information.

In preparation for the 1972 campaign, the White House had established a clandestine intelligence group of its own, led by former CIA agents G. Gordon Liddy and Howard Hunt. Known as the "plumbers" because they were supposed to plug leaks of government information, they relied on such tactics as using the Internal Revenue Service and other agencies to harass opponents of the administration named on an "enemies list" drawn up by presidential counsel John Dean. A major target of the "plumbers" was the Democrats, whose primary frontrunner Edmund Muskie in 1972 was the beneficiary of several "dirty tricks." For example, New Hampshire primary voters were awakened in the middle of the night by callers from the "Harlem for Muskie" committee; posters appeared in Florida saying "Help Muskie in Busing More Children Now."

The Break-in. These secret and questionable activities led to the break-in that triggered the Watergate scandal. In the early morning of June 17, 1972, an alert security guard noticed something amiss at the door to the headquarters of the Democratic National Committee at the Watergate apartment complex in Washington. Five men carrying cameras and wiretapping equipment were arrested; two accomplices were apprehended soon after. Two of the accused men had worked as security consultants in the White House; a third had held a responsible position on the Committee to Re-Elect the President (aptly known as CREEP); the remaining four, all from Miami, had been involved in CIA-linked anti-Castro activities. Nixon's press secretary, Ronald Ziegler, archly dismissed the break-in as a "third-rate burglary attempt." Nixon himself stated categorically that "no one in the White House staff, no one in this administration, presently employed, was involved in this bizarre incident." The cover-up had begun.

It would later be revealed that six days after the break-in, the president ordered his chief of staff, H. R. Haldeman, to instruct the CIA to tell the FBI not to probe too deeply into connections between the White House and the burglars. This action constituted an obstruction of justice. Nixon apparently feared that the Watergate burglary would lead to an investigation of the dubious fundraising methods and political sabotage used by his re-election committee.

Trial and Investigations. The Watergate burglars were convicted and sent to jail in January 1973. White House counsel John Dean tried to buy their continued silence with $400,000 in hush money and hints of presidential pardons. But, prodded by the presiding judge, John Sirica, several of the convicted burglars began to talk. Two tenacious investigative reporters at the *Washington Post*, Carl Bernstein and Bob Woodward, kept the story alive. In February the Senate voted 70–0 to establish a select committee to investigate the scandal. Dean started to get nervous, and in March 1973 he warned Nixon, referring to the cover-up, that "there is a cancer within, close to the presidency, that is growing." On April 30, Nixon accepted the resignations of Haldeman and chief domestic adviser John Ehrlichman. He also fired Dean. As evidence mounted linking the scandal directly to the White House, press secretary Ziegler declared that all previous statements on Watergate were "inoperative."

Watergate Hearings
Some of the most damaging testimony against President Richard Nixon came from the former White House counsel, John Dean, shown here testifying before the Senate Watergate Committee in June 1973. Revelations from a secret taping system in the Oval Office later confirmed Dean's nearly total recall of conversations he had had with the president.

AMERICAN LIVES

Woodward and Bernstein, Investigative Reporters

★

"Woodstein"—that is how they were referred to around the newsroom of the *Washington Post*. Bob Woodward and Carl Bernstein, the two young reporters who broke the Watergate story, were definitely an odd couple. Woodward was a neatly dressed, Yale man who liked classical music and voted Republican; Bernstein was a rumpled Jewish college dropout who liked rock music and was definitely left-of-center in his political views. At times, the "kids" (as they were also called in the newsroom) seemed like a case of the Establishment versus the Counterculture, and not a likely combination for a Pulitzer Prize-winning series that eventually brought down the Nixon presidency.

In June 1972, when the Watergate break-in occurred, Bob Woodward had been at the *Washington Post* for only nine months, assigned to the not-so-prestigious metropolitan desk, where his most recent stories had been about restaurant health violations and police corruption. Born in 1943 in an affluent Chicago suburb, he had graduated from Yale in 1965 and then spent five years in the navy. He worked for a local Maryland paper for a year before wangling a position at the *Post*. His first day on the job he made over a hundred phone calls looking for a story. Ideologically, Woodward was no muckraker—he was always more interested in finding out the facts than changing the status quo.

Carl Bernstein was the shaggy-haired free spirit to Woodward's buttoned-down patrician. Born in 1944 in Washington, D.C., he began working for the *Washington Star* at age sixteen, rising from copy boy to reporter by 1965, and along the way dropping out of the University of Maryland after three years. Bernstein joined the staff of the *Washington Post* in 1966, where he covered Virginia politics. Permanently rumpled and with more than a trace of arrogance (a trait he shared with Woodward), Bernstein was notorious for his irregular hours and his barely concealed contempt for routine stories. He was also infamous for his penchant for high living, even when he did not have the money to pay for it. At the time Watergate broke, he was twenty-eight years old, a year younger than (and light years away from) his new partner in investigative journalism.

"Woodstein"

When Carl Bernstein (left) anb Bob Woodward (right) began their investigation of the Watergate break-in, they were referred to as "Woodstein" around the newsroom. Their story won them a Pulitzer Prize for investigative reporting in March 1973.

When a tip came into the metropolitan desk of the *Post* on the morning of June 17, 1972, about a break-in at the Watergate headquarters of the Democratic National Committee, the story was assigned to city reporter Woodward rather than to one of the the more seasoned regulars who covered national politics for the capital's most influential paper. After all, the break-in was just local news. But this local story had some intriguing aspects, like the links of one of the burglars to the Central Intelligence Agency, and soon Carl Bernstein was snooping around too. Without really knowing where this was going, both Woodward and Bernstein found themselves working on the story fulltime; in six weeks, they were sharing a byline.

What followed was months of tough, boring, frustrating investigative journalism. Recalled Bernstein, "We knocked on doors, we talked to people at the bottom, which is to say secretaries and file clerks rather than starting at the top . . . and there was nothing glamorous about it." Slowly the case inched forward. Most of their sources pointed to the White House, especially to Nixon's re-election campaign. Eventually, of course, the tracks would lead directly to the Oval Office.

The *Washington Post* was the only major newspaper to devote significant resources to the story at first, and it made sure that the stories were airtight. Any significant facts had to be verified by at least two independent sources, and a senior editor had to approve each story before it appeared. As a result, only once did the *Post* have to back down from a story. Throughout, Bernstein and Woodward had the complete support of the newspaper brass, all the way up to executive editor Ben Bradlee and publisher Katherine Graham.

The two reporters might have been stymied more than once were it were not for the help of a highly placed confidential source nicknamed Deep Throat (from a pornographic movie popular at the time). This source rarely provided new information but was willing to corroborate things that Bernstein and Woodward had uncovered. In the cloak and dagger style that shaped much of the investigation, if Woodward wanted to meet with Deep Throat, he would move a flower pot with a red flag to the rear of his apartment balcony, a signal to meet at 2 A.M. in an underground garage. If Deep Throat wanted to meet Woodward, he would send a message via the copy of the *New York Times* delivered to Woodward's apartment, where, on the lower corner of page 20, clock hands would show the time of the designated rendezvous. To this day, the identity of Deep Throat remains a mystery.

The Watergate story entered a new phase in March 1973, when convicted burglar James McCord sent a letter to Judge John Sirica confirming what Woodward and Bernstein had patiently been proving over the last nine months—that the White House had been involved in the original break-in. Now all the major newspapers began covering the story more aggressively, and the *Post* lost its prime role in pursuing the scandal.

Watergate changed the lives of the two "cub" reporters. In March 1973 the *Washington Post* won a Pulitzer Prize for their investigative reporting on the Watergate story. Bernstein and Woodward received a $55,000 advance to write a book about their investigation (at the time, their combined salaries totalled only $30,000) and actor Robert Redford acquired the movie rights. *All the President's Men* was published in June 1974, and instantly made the bestseller list. The book, which was written in the third person like a fast-paced

Woodward and Bernstein?
Robert Redford and Dustin Hoffman starred in the screen version of Woodward and Bernstein's book *All the President's Men*. In fact, their performances were so believable that many people mistook the actors for the reporters.

detective story ("Bernstein and Woodward called the White House. . . ."), came out just as the nation was moving into the final stage of the Watergate saga—the impeachment hearings. Bernstein and Woodward later took a leave of absence to write a second book, *The Final Days,* which covered the last summer of the Nixon presidency. That book was published in 1976, about the time that the movie of *All the President's Men* premiered, starring Robert Redford as Bob Woodward and Dustin Hoffman as Carl Bernstein. So convincing was the movie version that in many people's minds, Redford and Hoffman *are* Woodward and Bernstein.

Watergate set off, in Carl Bernstein's words, "an orgy of self-congratulation" about the power and importance of an independent press. Yet Watergate was less a victory for freedom of the press than a testament to the tenacity of two investigative journalists, who stuck with a story the rest of the media dismissed as a "caper." Bernstein and Woodward, now approaching fifty, are senior and respected journalists. Bob Woodward is the author of bestselling books on the Supreme Court and the CIA and has been the assistant managing editor of the *Washington Post* since 1981. Carl Bernstein is a correspondent for *Time* magazine, having formerly worked for ABC News. Neither reporter ever dreamed that when they set out to investigate a seemingly innocuous break-in they would help to topple a presidency. But that is precisely what Bob Woodward and Carl Bernstein did.

In May the Senate Watergate committee, chaired by Senator Sam Ervin of North Carolina, began a summer of nationally televised hearings. In five days of riveting testimony in late June, John Dean implicated President Nixon in the cover-up. Even more startling testimony from aide Alexander Butterfield revealed that Nixon had a secret taping system in the Oval Office. "I was hoping you fellows wouldn't ask me about that," Butterfield sheepishly told the committee. Until the existence of the tapes was disclosed, it had been Dean's word against Nixon's; now it appeared possible to find out what had actually been said. The president steadfastly "stonewalled," citing executive privilege and national security as he refused to release the tapes. When a lower federal court held in October that he had to give selected tapes to a special prosecutor, Nixon released heavily edited transcripts whose most frequent phrase seemed to be "expletive deleted," a phrase necessitated by the repeated profanity picked up on the tapes. Senate Republican leader Hugh Scott called these edited transcripts "deplorable, disgusting, shabby, immoral." Most suspicious was an eighteen-minute gap in the tape of a crucial meeting between Nixon, Haldeman, and Ehrlichman on June 20, 1972, three days after the break-in.

The Final Days. The Watergate affair moved into its final phase in the summer of 1974, when a committee of the House of Representatives convened impeachment hearings. On July 30, seven Republicans joined the Democratic majority to vote three articles of impeachment against Richard Nixon: obstruction of justice, abuse of power, and acting in a way subversive to the Constitution. Two days later the Supreme Court ruled unanimously that Nixon had no right to claim executive privilege as justification for refusing to turn over additional tapes requested by the special prosecutor. Under duress, Nixon released the unexpurgated tapes on August 5, which contained shocking evidence (the so-called "smoking gun") that he had indeed ordered the cover-up as early as six days after the break-in. In effect, the president had been lying to the American people ever since. Senator Barry Goldwater gravely informed the president that no more than fifteen senators still supported him. Facing certain conviction in a Senate trial, on August 9, 1974, Nixon became the first U.S. president to resign.

The transfer of power to Vice-President Gerald Ford went remarkably smoothly. In 1973 Ford had replaced Spiro Agnew, who had been forced to resign after being indicted for allegedly accepting kickbacks on construction contracts while governor of Maryland and vice-president. In the wake of the assassinations of John Kennedy, Robert Kennedy, and Martin Luther King, Jr., as well as the first resignation of an incumbent vice-president, the idea of substituting leaders was no nov-

Nixon Resigns
On August 9, 1974, Richard M. Nixon became the first American president to resign. He is shown here minutes after turning over the presidency to Gerald R. Ford. He retired to his home in San Clemente, California, refusing to admit guilt for what had happened.

elty. The public had greater difficulty a month later in accepting President Ford's "full, free, and absolute" pardon of Nixon, on the grounds of sparing the country the agony of rehashing Watergate.

The Aftermath. In response to the abuses of the Nixon administration and the Vietnam era, Congress adopted several reforms to contain the power of what historian Arthur M. Schlesinger, Jr., named "the imperial presidency." The War Powers Act of 1973 required the president to report any use of military force—such as had occurred in Korea, Vietnam, and Cambodia—to Congress within forty-eight hours and directed that hostilities must cease within sixty days unless Congress declared war. The 1974 Congressional Budget and Impoundment Control Act restricted the president's authority to impound federal funds (that is, refuse to spend money appropriated by Congress for programs opposed by the White House.) The Fair Campaign Practices Act of 1974 limited campaign contributions and demanded stricter accounting of campaign expenditures. A strengthened Freedom of Information Act in 1974 gave citizens greater access to files that federal government agencies had amassed on them.

In the aftermath of Watergate, twenty-five members of the Nixon administration went to prison, including Nixon's closest advisers, H. R. Haldeman, John Ehrlichman, and Attorney General John Mitchell. Richard Nixon retired to his estate in San Clemente, California. He refused to admit guilt for what had happened, conceding only that Watergate represented an error of judgment.

Lowered Expectations and New Challenges

In 1973 the European economist E. F. Schumacher published *Small Is Beautiful*, a book whose message was well-timed for the 1970s. Schumacher challenged the "bigger is better" philosophy that had fueled the West's industrial growth and was posing a growing threat to the Third World. He was especially outspoken about the dangers of the dramatic world thirst for oil. "Less is more" became the watchword of the developing environmental movement, as the United States began to grapple with living in a world where resources were limited and American economic domination was no longer as secure as in the immediate postwar period.

The Hydrocarbon Age

"Without oil," Interior Secretary Harold Ickes had noted back in 1933, "American Civilization as we know it could not exist." That continues to be true to this day, when not only the United States but the entire modern world lives in a *hydrocarbon age,* totally dependent on petroleum and its byproducts. Oil supplanted coal as the main energy source for the industrial world, because it was cheaper, cleaner, and more abundant. Between 1949 and 1972, world energy consumption more than tripled, and the demand for oil increased by more than five and a half times. Access to oil, especially at the low prices that prevailed in the 1950s and 1960s, fostered rapid economic growth and rising standards of living throughout most of the world, and especially in the United States. Imported oil literally fueled the dramatic growth of the Japanese and Western European economies to positions of world dominance.

Until well into the twentieth century, the United States was both the world's leading producer and consumer of oil. During World War II, America still produced two-thirds of the world's oil, but its share of world production fell to only 22 percent in 1972, even though domestic production continued to rise. By the late 1960s the United States was buying more and more oil on the world market to keep up with shrinking domestic reserves and growing demand. Daily imports rose from 3.2 million barrels in 1970 to 6.2 million by the summer of 1973.

America imported oil primarily from the Middle East, where production increased a stupendous *1,500* percent in the twenty-five years after World War II. Oil had first been discovered in the region in 1908, when a vast "elephant" (oil industry jargon for a giant field) was uncovered in Persia (later Iran). Initially all Persian Gulf oil was extracted under a *concession* system—a foreign oil company or consortium would contract with a sovereign to explore for, own, and produce oil in a given territory, paying a rental fee in return. These arrangements proved enormously profitable to European and, after World War II, American oil companies.

With the postwar rise of nationalism and end of colonialism, Persian Gulf nations found the concession system demeaning. But rather than nationalizing their oil fields—and losing access to Western technology and equipment—most oil-rich countries renegotiated their agreements. The foreign companies still extracted the oil, but they recognized that it belonged to the exporting countries and split the profits accordingly. For example, a consortium of Western companies, including Jersey, Socony, Texaco, Standard of California, Gulf, and Shell, negotiated for access to Iran's oil on a 50–50 profit-sharing basis in 1947.

In 1960 oil-exporting countries in the Third World formed OPEC (Organization of Petroleum Exporting Countries) in an attempt to exercise more control over the world oil market. Five of the founding countries, the Middle Eastern states of Saudi Arabia, Kuwait, Iran, and Iraq, plus Venezuela, were the source of more than 80 percent of the world's crude oil exports. In 1960 the oil industry was in the middle of a twenty-year period of surplus capacity, and prices stayed low. In the early 1970s, however, the balance shifted. Several trends—a sharp increase in worldwide demand, the end of excess capacity, political instability in the Middle East, the shift of the United States from a net exporter to net importer of oil—came together to set up what would soon be OPEC's "golden age."

The year 1973 was the turning point. Between 1973 and 1975, OPEC deliberately raised the price of a barrel of oil from $3 to $12. At the end of the decade it peaked at $34 a barrel. Because the United States now depended heavily on Middle Eastern oil, the price rise set off furious inflation.

Also in 1973, OPEC instituted an oil embargo, showing that oil could be used as a weapon in global politics. On October 6, 1973, Egyptian and Syrian forces had coordinated a surprise invasion of Israel on Yom Kippur, the holiest day in Judaism. At first, American policymakers held back their support of Israel for fear of jeopardizing relations with the oil-producing countries, which supported the invaders. But the initial attack was so devastating that the United States reversed its stand and quickly sent enough supplies and military equipment to enable the Israelis to regain most of their lost territory in a few weeks. A ceasefire soon ended the fighting, but the international repercussions were just beginning. In retaliation against the United States, Western Europe, and Japan, which had all aided Israel in the Yom Kippur War, OPEC halted all exports to those countries. The embargo lasted until 1974.

The United States scrambled to meet its domestic energy needs. Americans were forced to curtail their driving or spend long hours in line at the pumps; gas prices climbed 40 percent in a matter of months. A national speed limit of 55 mph was instituted to conserve fuel. Drivers wanted to buy more fuel-efficient cars, but the U.S. automobile industry had nothing to offer except the "gas guzzlers" that had been built to run on cheap gasoline. Soon the domestic auto industry was in a recession, as Americans bought cheaper, more fuel-efficient foreign cars, primarily those manufactured in Japan and West Germany. Since the United States owed much of its twentieth-century prosperity to the automobile (one in six jobs was tied directly or indirectly to the industry in the 1970s), this downturn had profound implications for the American economy.

The energy crisis of the mid-1970s was an enormous shock to the American psyche. Suddenly Americans felt like hostages to economic forces beyond their control. As OPEC's oil ministers set even higher oil prices at their annual meetings, they seemed to be able to determine whether Western economies grew or stagnated. Despite extensive public education about energy conservation and a second gas shortage in 1979, it was impossible to wean the nation from foreign oil. In 1970 the United States imported $4 billion of foreign oil; the figure would grow to $90 billion by 1980. Inflation caused only part of the rise. Americans were using even more foreign oil after the energy crisis than before, testimony to the enormous thirst of modern industrial and consumer societies for petroleum.

The Environmental Movement

The energy crisis of the 1970s interacted with a growing awareness of environmental issues, which had been building since the 1960s. Along with the women's

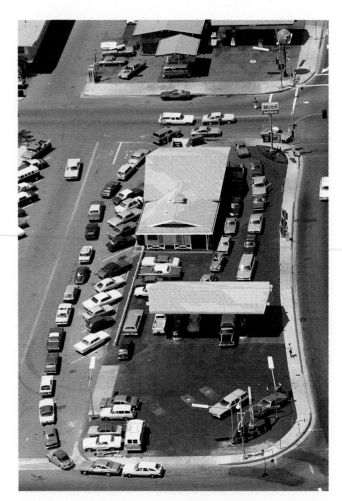

No Gas
During the energy crisis of 1973–1974, American motorists faced widespread gasoline shortages for the first time since World War II. Although gas was not rationed, gas stations were closed on Sundays, air travel was cut by 10 percent, and a national speed limit of 55 miles per hour was imposed.

movement, the environmental movement had its greatest impact after 1970.

Emphasis on the environment and ecology did not originate in the postwar period, of course. John Muir and the Sierra Club had led the fight for the creation of the national park system in the late nineteenth century (see Chapter 17). This earlier conservation movement had advocated resource management and balancing open space and recreational needs against development. The post-1945 environmental movement operated in a different social and political context. Protecting nature in its pristine state became an inherent goal: activists talked about the "rights of nature," just as they did about the rights of women or blacks. Furthermore, there was a new awareness of the possible exhaustion of the earth's resources. Since America had always consumed vast quantities of natural resources, accepting the idea that there were "limits to growth" was revolutionary and troubling.

In some ways the environmental movement built on the activism of the 1960s. Protest tactics developed in the civil rights and antiwar movements were used to mobilize mass support for specific issues or legislation. Many 1960s radicals evolved into 1970s environmental activists. For example, the search for alternative technologies (especially solar power) could be a political statement against a corporate structure that seemed increasingly inhospitable to human-scale technology, and humans as well. Above all, the environmental movement was characterized by its grass-roots nature.

In other ways environmental activism represented something new—the mobilization of a broad mainstream constituency of people concerned about the air they breathed, the food they ate, and their desire to find recreation in undeveloped wilderness. Concern for environmental quality and ecological values can be seen as an offshoot of the advanced consumer economy that defined the postwar period. Now that most Americans had bought the basic necessities, and then some, they wanted an even higher standard of living, one that included a healthy environment and corresponding lifestyles. This desire led to new demands on the state—citizens expected the federal government to take responsibility for environmental issues. Governmental activism on consumer issues and the environment joined the welfare and warfare states of the post-1945 years.

The birth of the modern environmental movement is often dated to the 1962 publication of Rachel Carson's *The Silent Spring*, a powerful analysis of the impact of pesticides, especially DDT, on the food chain. Citizen awareness of the fragility of the environment spurred both federal action and grass-roots involvement. Federal legislation in 1965, 1967, and 1970 covered water and air pollution; the 1970 Clean Air Act set standards for auto emissions to reduce smog and air pollution that still have not been met.

Environmental activists were also concerned about protecting wildlife, and they lobbied successfully for the Endangered Animals Act of 1964, widened to the Endangered Species Act of 1973. These acts gave species like snail darters, moths, and owls certain rights, which had to be balanced against human plans for development or recreation. Also important after 1970 were interagency provisions for an Environmental Impact Statement (EIS), an assessment of the consequences of changing use patterns on a particular ecological area. The EIS soon became a useful tool for citizens' groups trying to block unwanted development by private industry or government.

Early issues that galvanized public opinion included a huge oil spill in January 1969 off the coast of Santa Barbara, California; the environmental impact of such projects as the Alaska pipeline and a proposed airport in the Florida Everglades; and the harmful effects to the earth's atmosphere (ozone layer) caused by supersonic air transport. Environmentalism became a mass movement on the first Earth Day, April 22, 1970, when 20 million citizens gathered across the country to show their support for their endangered planet.

The environmental movement raised public awareness of the dangers inherent in the chemicals and petrochemical byproducts in American consumer goods, especially in foods and their packaging materials. Another concern was the careless dumping of toxic and radioactive wastes. The ironically named Love Canal housing development, near Niagara Falls, New York, had been built over an underground chemical waste disposal site. Residents noticed that trees turned black and sparks escaped from the pavement; even graver was the abnormally high rate of illness, miscarriages, and birth defects experienced by Love Canal families. In 1980 a state of emergency was declared, and the New York State government paid homeowners to relocate. Soon horror stories appeared about other poorly maintained waste-disposal sites across the country. "We just don't know how many potential Love Canals there are," admitted one federal official. "There are ticking time bombs all over."

One of the worst offenders was the federal government itself. In the cold war rush to produce bombs and weapons for national security, nuclear weapons plants carelessly released or dumped billions of gallons of radioactive waste into the environment. For example, the uranium processing plant built in 1954 at Fernald, Ohio, dumped liquid wastes into open-air waste-storage pits, which then leaked into regional waterways. At the Hanford Nuclear Reservation near Richland, Washington, plutonium waste and toxic chemicals contaminated the soil and seeped into the Columbia River. Outside of Denver, the Rocky Flats Plant and the Rocky Mountain Arsenal stored dangerous concentrations of plutonium, pesticide, and nerve gas wastes. Cleaning up the environmental morass resulting from forty years of reckless production will require one of the largest engineering projects ever undertaken.

Nuclear Energy. Nuclear energy also became a cause for citizen action in the 1970s, pitting environmental concerns against the need for alternative energy sources. In response to the energy crisis, some politicians and utility companies promoted the expansion of nuclear power to reduce American reliance on foreign oil. Forty-two nuclear power plants were in operation by January 1974 and more than a hundred others were planned. Construction of nuclear power plants and reactors, which generally went unchallenged in the 1950s and 1960s, now drew protests from community activists concerned about such issues as inadequate disaster evacuation plans and disposal of radioactive waste. At a reactor construction site in Seabrook, New Hampshire, the Clamshell Alliance staged protests reminiscent of the antiwar demonstrations of the previous decade.

Longstanding public fears about nuclear safety seemed to be confirmed in March 1979. At Three Mile Island, near Harrisburg, Pennsylvania, a nuclear plant came critically close to a meltdown of its central core reactor. (Fears were exacerbated by eerie similarities to *The China Syndrome*, a recently released movie starring Jane Fonda.) A hundred thousand residents were evacuated as a precaution. A prompt shutdown brought the problem under control before any radioactive material was released into the environment. As a member of the panel investigating the accident admitted, "We were damn lucky."

Three Mile Island made Americans reassess the future of nuclear power. Cost overruns, faulty construction, and waste disposal problems raised doubts that nuclear power was a viable solution to energy needs. Trying to think and act ecologically, Americans faced a difficult balancing act if they wanted to maintain the high level of consumer affluence they had grown accustomed to.

Three Mile Island
On March 30, 1979, the Three Mile Island nuclear power plant near Harrisburg, Pennsylvania, came close to suffering a dangerous meltdown of its central core reactor. The accident, caused in part by the failure of safety systems and by human error, helped undermine American faith in nuclear technology.

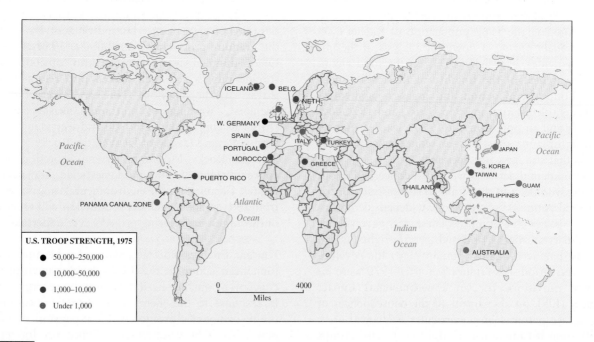

MAP 32.2

U.S. Troops Around the World, 1975
After its withdrawal from Vietnam, the United States maintained a substantial military presence around the world, especially in cold war troublespots in Europe and Asia. While the large military establishment provided millions of jobs for Americans, it also posed a continuing drain on the U.S. treasury.

Economic Trends

In retrospect, the 1970s marked the end of the *Pax Americana,* the overwhelming superiority the United States enjoyed in the world economy during the postwar era. The oil embargo of 1973–1974 and the energy crisis demonstrated that the domestic economy was vulnerable to world developments. The dollar was no longer the world's strongest currency. In 1971 the Bretton Woods system, set up at the United Nations monetary conference in 1944 (see Chapter 29), collapsed. The dollar now fluctuated in relation to the price of an ounce of gold, which increased from its former set price of $35 to as much as $800 on the international money market during the 1970s. Also in 1971, the United States posted its first balance of trade deficit in almost a century. Competition from the reviving economies of West Germany and Japan reduced demand for American goods worldwide. The U.S. share of world trade, which had declined by 16 percent between 1960 and 1970, dropped another 25 percent during the 1970s.

The more generalized prosperity of the postwar period also ended in the 1970s. The energy crisis merely speeded up a shift that was already underway. Overall economic growth as measured by the gross national product of the United States averaged 4.1 percent per year in the 1960s, but only 2.9 percent per year in the 1970s. Tellingly, all the real growth occurred before 1973. From 1973 to 1979 workers saw virtually no real income gain—instead of experiencing a rising standard of living, they found themselves worse off. By the early 1980s discretionary income per worker had declined 18 percent since 1973. Furthermore, the average price of a single-family house more than doubled during the 1970s, making home ownership inaccessible to wider segments of the working and middle class, including the baby boom generation that had now entered adulthood. By 1980, nine Western European countries had surpassed the United States in per capita GNP.

Deindustrialization. By the 1970s the industrial base of the United States had entered what would become a prolonged period of decline. Economists Barry Bluestone and Bennett Harrison estimate that the United States lost between 32 and 38 million jobs in the 1970s as a direct result of *deindustrialization,* "the widespread, systematic disinvestment in the nation's productive capacity." Instead of capital being invested in basic industries, it began to be diverted to speculation, to mergers and acquisitions, and to foreign investment. This was encouraged by policies that reduced taxes for corporations that could offset foreign expenses against their domestic profits. By the end of the 1970s, the hundred largest multinational corporations and banks earned more than a third of their overall profits abroad. For some corporations the proportion was much higher: in 1979, 94 percent of Ford's profits came from overseas operations, as did 83 percent of banking giant Citicorp's profits in 1977.

The most dramatic consequences of deindustrialization were found in the older industrial regions referred to as the Rust Belt. Nightly newscasts were full of stories of the closings of unprofitable plants. Corporations relocated overseas to take advantage of cheaper labor and production costs, or they dispersed their manufacturing functions into geographically disparate locations. The dominant images of mid-twentieth century American industry—huge factories such as Ford's River Rouge outside Detroit, the General Electric plant in Lynn, Massachusetts, or the U.S. Steel compound in Gary, Indiana—were becoming relics of a past stage of industrial development.

When a community's major employer closed up shop and left town, the effect was devastating. In 1977 the Lykes Corporation shut down the Campbell Works of the Youngstown Sheet and Tube Company, laying off 4,100 Ohio steelworkers. Two years later the community was still reeling. A third of the displaced workers, too old to retrain for new positions, had been forced to take early retirement, at half their previous salary. Ten percent had moved, and another 15 percent were still looking for work, their unemployment compensation long since exhausted. Of the 40 percent who were the "success stories" (those that found other jobs), many took huge wage cuts. A former rigger was selling women's shoes for $2.37 an hour. *Fortune* magazine tried to make Youngstown's story upbeat, titling it "Youngstown Bounces Back," but its cheerful conclusions belied the economic reality. The caption of a photograph of an unemployed steelworker sitting at a piano read, "Crane operator Ozie Williams, thirty-two, has a lot of time to practice his music." The impact of such plant closings rippled through communities across the heartland of America.

Challenges for Labor. The changed economic conditions that fostered foreign investment and plant closings posed enormous challenges for the labor movement. In labor's heyday during the 1940s and 1950s, American managers had learned grudgingly to cooperate with unions. With profits high, there was room for accommodation. But in the profit squeeze of the 1970s, industry was less willing to treat labor as a partner in making economic decisions. Union leaders might learn about a plant closing on the news at the same time as ordinary workers and the general public. Priorities of union leaders shifted to holding on to gains already won. But labor's bargaining position was increasingly vulnerable, given the resources and international mobility of multinational conglomerates. As employers turned to a cheaper workforce abroad, labor's prospects for regaining its earlier strength at home were dim.

Lifestyles and Social Trends

The Seventies as a decade defies easy generalization. Journalist Tom Wolfe labeled it the "Me Decade" for its widespread obsession with lifestyles and personal well-being. Historian Christopher Lasch referred derisively to its "culture of narcissism." Yet those labels hardly do justice to a decade in which the women's movement had its greatest impact, nor do they explain the broad-based activism of the environmental movement. Furthermore, such characterizations do not suggest the growing conservatism in social and political life. In fact, all these trends coexisted in a decade where, in the words of a popular history of the 1970s, "it seemed like nothing happened."

Turning Inward. In part due to the continuing influence of the counterculture, the 1970s featured a growing emphasis on personal fulfillment. One manifestation was the fitness craze. Millions of Americans, with the health-conscious baby boomers leading the way, began jogging, riding ten-speed bicycles, or working out on Nautilus machines. Jim Fixx's *Complete Book of Running* (1977) spurred the running boom—and the success of such athletic shoe companies as Nike and Adidas. (Reebok would be the success story of the 1980s.) The

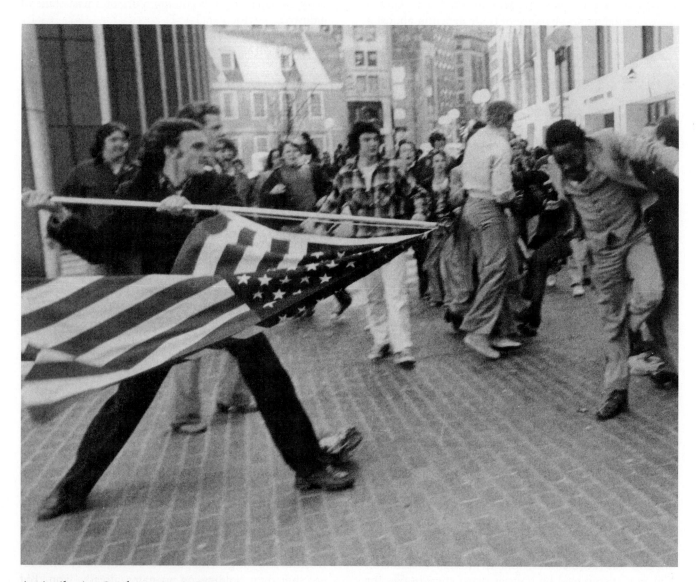

An Antibusing Confrontation in Boston
Tensions over court-ordered busing still ran high in Boston in 1976. When a black lawyer tried to cross the city hall plaza during an antibusing demonstration, he became another victim of Boston's climate of racial hate and violence. This photograph by Stanley Forman for the *Boston Herald American*, showing protesters trying to impale the man with a flagstaff, won a Pulitzer Prize.

nation's emphasis on health and fitness interacted with the heightened environmental awareness to spur demands for pesticide-free foods. Health foods soon became a multimillion-dollar business.

Another legacy of the counterculture was the *human potential* movement, which took the form of a variety of self-help and spiritual approaches. Some people joined encounter sessions—nicknamed "T-groups" for "sensitivity training"—in order to "get in touch with their feelings." Many couples attended marriage-renewal conferences. Other people turned to yoga, Zen Buddhism, Transcendental Meditation (TM), est (Erhard Seminars Training), and Gestalt movements in a quest for self. Numerous young adults joined religious cults, such as Hare Krishna, the Church of Scientology, or the Unification Church of the Reverend Sun Myung Moon (his followers were called "Moonies"); their parents often claimed that their children had been brainwashed to adopt a rigidly communal life and hired "deprogrammers" to rescue them. When hundreds of the predominantly African-American followers of the Reverend Jim Jones, a messianic cult leader, ritualistically committed suicide by drinking fruit punch laced with cyanide at the People's Temple in Guyana in 1978, the potential for excess in such cults was exposed.

The interest in religious cults and paths to inner awareness paralleled a major revival in mainstream religious denominations, which had been building since the 1950s. Much of this religious fervor occurred in evangelical Christian denominations, led by such charismatic preachers as Billy Graham, who learned to use the media, especially television, to spread the gospel. Soon evangelical groups set up their own school systems, newspapers, and broadcasting networks.

By the 1970s, 70 million Americans, almost a third of the population, were affiliated with Christian churches that fostered a "born-again" experience. President Jimmy Carter proudly proclaimed his direct personal relationship with Jesus Christ, as did singers Pat Boone and Johnny Cash, former Watergate convicts Jeb Magruder and Charles Colson, and black power activist Eldridge Cleaver. Religion entered public life when leaders like the Reverend Jerry Falwell, the founder of the Moral Majority, tried to inject their opinions on sensitive issues such as abortion, busing, school prayer, and censorship into politics.

Busing. The most disruptive social issue of the 1970s was the forced busing of children to achieve school integration. Following its 1954 ruling in *Brown v. Board of Education of Topeka,* the Supreme Court had called for desegregation "with all deliberate speed," but progress was limited before 1970. In the 1970s, however, the courts and the Justice Department pushed for more action, beginning in the South, which grudgingly complied, and then in the rest of the country. In 1971 the Supreme Court upheld a federal judge's order requiring the Charlotte-Mecklenburg, North Carolina, school system to transport students from neighborhood to more distant schools in order to integrate the citywide school system. In 1974 the Supreme Court rejected combining the schools of a city and its suburbs to achieve racial balance, but specified that cities with their deeply ingrained patterns of residential segregation must use busing within city boundaries to integrate their classrooms.

These court decisions provoked controversy and violence, with some of the worst occurring in Boston in 1974–1975. The strongly Irish Catholic working-class neighborhood of South Boston responded to the arrival of black students from the Roxbury section with mob scenes reminiscent of Little Rock in 1957. Only armed riot police kept South Boston High School open. Many white parents in Boston, and in other cities threatened by court-ordered busing, transferred their children to private schools; the resulting "white flight" increased the racial imbalance that busing was intended to solve. By the late 1970s the federal courts were backing away from their earlier insistence on busing to achieve racial balance.

Affirmative Action. Almost as divisive as busing was the implementation of *affirmative action* procedures and targets to achieve racial and sexual balance. First put forward by the Department of Labor in 1968, affirmative action was refined by a series of Supreme Court and lower court rulings that identified acceptable procedures for expanding the access of minority-group members to education and jobs. But whites, especially white men, soon raised the cry of "reverse discrimination," claiming they had been passed over in favor of less qualified minorities or women. In 1978 a white man named Allan Bakke sued the University of California Medical School at Davis for rejecting him while admitting minority candidates with lesser qualifications. The Supreme Court ruling in *Bakke v. University of California* was inconclusive: by a 5 to 4 margin, the Court proclaimed that the medical school's absolute quota was illegal and ordered Bakke admitted. At the same time, also by a 5 to 4 margin, it ruled that racial factors could properly be considered in making hiring or admission decisions, thus upholding the principle of affirmative action.

On balance the *Bakke* decision was a setback to the struggle for economic and racial equality that had concerned the nation throughout the 1960s. The often vociferous public opposition to busing, affirmative action, and the Equal Rights Amendment, along with the rapidly growing antiabortion "right to life" movement, constituted a broad backlash against the social changes of the previous decade. Signaling a new conservatism in the social order, many citizens said no to the use of federal power to encourage further change.

Busing in Boston *Phyllis Ellison*

Nowhere in the North was busing a more divisive issue than in Boston in 1974–1975. Phyllis Ellison was one of fifty-six black students from the predominantly black neighborhoods of Columbia Point and Roxbury assigned to South Boston High School. Here she describes incidents from her sophomore year, including the day that a white student was stabbed by a black student during a melee at the school. The student's wound was not fatal, but the incident led to heightened resistance and recrimination.

I remember my first day going on the bus to South Boston High School. I wasn't afraid because I felt important. I didn't know what to expect, what was waiting for me up the hill. We had police escorts. I think there was three motorcycle cops and then two police cruisers in front of the bus, and so I felt really important at that time, not knowing what was on the other side of the hill.

Well, when we started up the hill you could hear people saying, "Niggers go home." There were signs, they

had made a sign saying, "Black people stay out. We don't want any niggers in our school." And there were people on the corners holding bananas like we were apes, monkeys. "Monkeys get out, get them out of our neighborhood. We don't want you in our schools." So at that time it did frighten me somewhat, but I was more determined then to get inside South Boston High School, because of the people that were outside.

When I got off the bus, first of all I felt important, because of the news media that was there. [Television reporter] Natalie Jacobson out in front of your school getting the story on your school. So I felt really important going through the metal detectors and making sure that no one could come into the school armed. I felt like this was a big deal to me, to attend South Boston High School.

I felt like I was making history, because that was the first year of desegregation and all the controversies and conflicts at that time. I felt that the black students there were making history. . . .

On a normal day there would be anywhere between ten and fifteen fights. You could walk down the corridor and a black person would bump into a white person or vice versa. That would be one fight. And they'd try to separate us, because at that time there was so much tension in the school that one fight could just have the school dismissed for the entire day because it would just lead to another and another and another.

You can't imagine how tense it was inside the classroom. A teacher was almost afraid to say the wrong thing, because they knew that that would excite the whole class, a disturbance in the classroom. The black students sat on one side of the classes. The white students sat on the other side of the classes. The teachers didn't want to assign seating because there may be some problems in the classrooms. So the teachers basically let the students sit where they wanted to sit. In the lunchrooms, the black students sat on one side. The white students sat on the other side. And the ladies' room. It was the same thing. The black

Post-Watergate Politics: Failed Leadership

In the wake of Watergate, many citizens had become cynical about the federal government and politicians in general. "Don't vote. It only encourages them," read one bumper sticker during the 1976 presidential campaign. "The lesser of two evils is still evil," proclaimed another. Political leaders proved unable to deal with the rising inflation, stagnant growth, and declining productivity that plagued the U.S. economy in the 1970s. The fall of Saigon in 1975 reminded Americans of the failure of the Vietnam policy. The world was changing,

and Americans had to grapple with the unsettling idea that perhaps the United States was no longer the all-powerful country it had been for much of the postwar era. As Americans approached the 1980 election, this growing sense of impotence erupted in fury over the Iranian hostage crisis.

Ford's Caretaker Presidency

Gerald Ford, the former congressman from Michigan who had become vice-president after Spiro Agnew's resignation, was unable to establish his legitimacy as president during the two years he held the office. His pardon students went to the right of the ladies' room; the white students went to the left of the ladies' room. So really, it was separate, I mean, we attended the same school, but we really never did anything together. Gym classes. If the blacks wanted to play basketball, the whites wanted to play volleyball. So we never played together. They would play volleyball. We would play basketball. . . .

I remember the day Michael Faith got stabbed vividly, because I was in the principal's office and all of a sudden you heard a lot of commotion and you heard kids screaming and yelling and saying, "He's dead, he's dead. That black nigger killed him. He's dead, he's dead." And then the principal running out of the office. There was a lot of commotion and screaming, yelling, hollering, "Get the niggers at Southie." I was really afraid. And the principal came back into the office and said, Call the ambulance and tell all the black students that were in the office to stay there. A police officer was in there and they were trying to get the white students out of the build-

ing, because they had just gone on a rampage and they were just going to hurt the first black student that they saw. Anyone that was caught in the corridor that day would be hurt. Once that happened, it probably took about fifteen, twenty minutes for the police officers to get all the white students out. The black students were locked in their rooms and all the white students were let go out of their classrooms. I remember us going into a room, and outside you just saw a crowd of people, I mean, just so many people, I can't even count. They just looked like little bumblebees or something, there was that many. And that Louise Day Hicks was on top of the stairs saying, Let the niggers go back to Roxbury. Send them back to Roxbury. And the crowd booing her. I remember the police cars coming up the street, attempting to, and people turning over the police cars, and I was just amazed that they could do something like that. The police tried to get horses up. They wouldn't let the horses get up. They stoned the horses. They stoned the cars. And I thought that day that we

would never get out of South Boston High School. . . .

If I had it to do all over again, for the civil rights part of it, I would do it over, because I felt like my rights were being violated by the white people of South Boston telling me that I could not go to South Boston High School. As for as my education, I think I could have gotten a better education if I didn't spend so much time out of school with the fighting and the violence and being dismissed from school at least once or twice a week. We were allowed to go home early because there was just so much tension inside of the school that if we didn't, someone may be killed or really seriously injured. I think that I could have gotten a better education if I'd spent more time in school than out of school at that time.

Source: Henry Hampton and Steve Fayer, *Voices of Freedom: An Oral History of the Civil Rights Movement from the 1950s Through the 1980s* (New York: Bantam, 1990), 600–1, 610, 612–13, 618.

of Nixon a month after becoming president hurt his credibility as a political leader. Distrust toward politicians spilled onto his choice for vice-president, Nelson A. Rockefeller, the former governor of New York, whose extensive family financial holdings were subjected to acrimonious Senate hearings before he finally won confirmation. Rockefeller's moderate brand of Republicanism also put him out of step with the more hard-line conservatives in the party.

Ford's biggest problem as president was the economy, reeling with inflation set in motion by the Vietnam War and worsened by the OPEC price rises and the growing trade deficit. The 1974 inflation rate soared to almost 12 percent. In an attempt to curtail prices, the

Federal Reserve tightened the money supply and drove up interest rates. In 1975 the economy entered its deepest downturn since the Great Depression, but the government refused to increase spending or cut taxes, generally acknowledged by economists as spurs to recovery. Production declined more than 10 percent, and nearly 9 percent of the work force was unemployed. The 1975 recession temporarily reduced the inflation rate to less than 5 percent, but it soon rose again. Ford's call to "Whip Inflation Now," complete with much-mocked "WIN" buttons, only served to draw attention to his inability to influence broader economic trends.

In foreign policy, Ford was equally lacking in presidential leadership. He maintained Nixon's initiatives to-

FIGURE 32.1

The Consumer Price Index, 1960–1990

The annual inflation rate peaked in 1980, the last year of Carter's presidency. *Source: U.S. Statistical Abstract, 1991.*

ward détente by asking Henry Kissinger to stay on as secretary of state, a position he had held since 1973. Ford met with Soviet leaders at Vladivostok to begin hammering out details of a hoped-for SALT II (Strategic Arms Limitation Talks) agreement, but there was little concrete progress on arms control. Ford and Kissinger also continued Nixon's policy of increasing American support for the Shah of Iran, failing to notice that the Shah's policy of rapid modernization was provoking bitter opposition and anti-Western sentiment among Iran's growing Muslim fundamentalist population.

After the paranoia and abuses of the Nixon era, Ford's personal style and candor were refreshing. But he failed to demonstrate the assurance and competence needed in a time of mounting economic and international problems. "Gerald Ford is an awfully nice man who isn't up to the presidency," the *New Republic* concluded, and the voters agreed.

The Outsider as President

Only in the skewed political atmosphere of post-Watergate America could the Democrats have chosen their 1976 nominee, James E. Carter, Jr. "Jimmy Who?" the media scoffed at first about this engineer and former entrepreneur in agricultural commodities from Plains, Georgia, popularly portrayed as a peanut farmer. But they soon changed their tune as Carter won key primaries, giving his candidacy momentum and credibility. Carter played up his role as a Washington outsider (his previous political experience had been as governor of Georgia, and before that as state senator), and pledged to restore morality to government. "I will never lie to you," he piously told voters.

The 1976 presidential campaign was one of the blandest in years. On the Republican side, President Ford staved off a conservative challenge from Governor Ronald Reagan of California; then he dumped Vice-President Nelson Rockefeller in favor of hard-line conservative Senator Robert J. Dole of Kansas. Carter chose as his running-mate Senator Walter F. Mondale of

Minnesota, who had ties to the traditional Democratic constituencies of labor, liberals, blacks, and big-city machines. Avoiding issues and controversy, Carter won the election with 50 percent of the popular vote to Ford's 48 percent.

Jimmy Carter immediately tried to set a different tone for his administration. On Inauguration Day he renounced formal wear in favor of a business suit; instead of riding in a limousine, he and his wife, Rosalynn, walked from the Capitol to the White House. Throughout his term he relied heavily on symbolic gestures—dressing in an informal cardigan sweater for fireside chats to the nation, carrying his own luggage on and off planes, holding town meetings, and staying in the homes of ordinary citizens. Carter's homespun approach soon wore thin as people looked for substance behind the symbols. "If the Carter administration were a television show," quipped columnist Russell Baker, "it would have been canceled months ago."

Domestic Leadership. Part technocrat, part preacher, Carter failed to develop an effective style of domestic leadership, a task made even more difficult by the post-Watergate climate of cynicism and apathy. His campaign as an outsider had distanced him from traditional sources of power in Washington, and he did little to heal the breach. Well into the term, Carter's chief domestic aide, Hamilton Jordan, had never introduced himself to Thomas ("Tip") O'Neill, the Speaker of the House of Representatives and the most powerful Democrat on Capitol Hill. Shying away from established Democratic leaders, Carter turned to advisers and friends who had worked with him in Georgia, none of whom had national experience. When his budget director Bert Lance was questioned about financial irregularities at his Atlanta bank, the case undercut Carter's pledges to restore integrity and morality in government.

The nemesis of inflation was Carter's major domestic challenge. When he took office the nation was just coming out of the severe 1975 recession. To speed recovery, Carter called for increased government spending and lower taxes. When these actions provoked renewed inflation, he reversed himself, calling for spending cuts and a delay in the tax reductions. This zigzag fiscal policy eroded both business and consumer confidence. Unemployment hovered between 6 and 7 percent, and inflation rose from 6.5 percent in 1977 to the "double-digit" level of 12.4 percent in 1980. As the Federal Reserve Board raised rates to counter inflation, interest rates briefly topped 20 percent in 1980, a historic high. A deep recession finally broke the inflationary spiral in 1982, two years after Carter left office.

Among its domestic initiatives, the Carter presidency reformed the civil service system and created the separate cabinet-level departments of Energy and Education. It also oversaw the deregulation of the airline, trucking, and railroad industries. Carter supported gradual decontrol of oil and natural gas prices as a spur to domestic production and conservation. But his attempt to provide leadership during the energy crisis failed. He called efforts for energy conservation "the moral equivalent of war" (borrowing a phrase from the nineteenth-century philosopher William James). A hostile media, unable to find the specifics, wickedly reduced the phrase to "MEOW." By the summer of 1979, when gas lines once again reminded Americans of their dependence on foreign oil, Carter's approval rating was only 26 percent, lower even than Richard Nixon's at the height of the Watergate scandal.

Foreign Policy and Diplomacy. Jimmy Carter's commitment to human rights was the centerpiece of his new direction in foreign affairs. He criticized the suppression of dissent in the Soviet Union—especially as it affected the right of Jewish citizens to emigrate—and he withdrew economic and military aid from Argentina, Uruguay, Ethiopia, and other non-Communist countries that violated human rights. He also established an Office of Human Rights within the State Department. But he could not change the internal policies of longtime U.S. allies and serious human rights violators, such as the Philippines, South Korea, and South Africa.

President Carter did achieve a stunning success in the Middle East, a complex arena of international instability. Relations between Egypt and Israel had remained tense since the 1973 Yom Kippur War. In November 1975, Israel's prime minister, Menachem Begin, moved to break the ice by inviting the Egyptian president Anwar Sadat to Israel to discuss the possibility of peace. Sadat came in 1977, but the talks stalled. President Carter broke the stalemate in 1978 by inviting Begin and Sadat to Camp David, the presidential retreat in the Maryland mountains. Two weeks of discussions and Carter's promise of significant additional foreign aid for Egypt persuaded Sadat and Begin to agree on a "framework for peace." The framework included Israel's return of the Sinai peninsula, which it had occupied since

A Framework for Peace
President Jimmy Carter's greatest foreign policy achievement was the personal diplomacy he exerted to persuade President Anwar Sadat of Egypt (left) and Prime Minister Menachem Begin of Israel (right) to sign a peace treaty in 1978.

1967; the transfer of Sinai territory took place from 1979 to 1982.

In Latin America, Carter's most important contribution was resolution of the lingering dispute over control of the Panama Canal. In a treaty signed on September 7, 1977, the United States agreed to turn over control of the canal to Panama on December 31, 1999. In return, the United States retained the right to send its ships through the canal in case of war, even though the canal itself was declared neutral territory. Despite conservatives' outcry that the United States was giving away more than it got, the Senate narrowly approved the treaty.

Carter had campaigned to free the United States from its "inordinate fear of Communism," but relationships with the Soviet Union soon became tense. Recriminations surrounding the SALT II arms limitation talks were a major cause. By the time that Carter met Soviet leader Leonid Brezhnev in Vienna in July 1979 to sign the accords, the president had ordered the construction of a new category of ballistic missiles (Pershing II) and the Soviets had forged ahead with new SS-20 missiles. The SALT II treaty of 1979 was therefore already seriously behind the current technology and did little to stop the escalating arms race.

Ratification of the SALT II treaty was soon tabled

indefinitely, as part of the Carter administration's response to the Soviet Union's invasion of Afghanistan in December 1979. Carter called this the most serious threat to world peace since World War II, largely because he feared that the Soviet move was a stepping stone toward the rich Middle Eastern oil supplies. In retaliation, the United States curtailed grain sales to the U.S.S.R. and boycotted the 1980 summer Olympic games in Moscow. (The Soviets returned the gesture, boycotting the 1984 summer games in Los Angeles.) When Carter left office in 1980, relations with the Soviet Union were worse than when he came in.

The Iranian Hostage Crisis

The most serious foreign policy problem of the Carter administration occurred in Iran. Ever since the CIA had helped install Muhammad Riza Pahlavi on the throne in 1953, the United States had counted on his regime as a steady pillar (or more accurately, a heavy-handed police officer) in the troubled Middle East. The Shah was a major customer for American arms, using "petrodollars" from the sale of oil to the United States to purchase close to $20 billion worth of weapons between 1972 and 1979. (These arms sales were large enough to have a positive impact on the U.S. balance of payments deficit.) President Carter had visited Iran in late 1977 and declared it "an island of stability in one of the more troubled areas of the world." With this personal endorsement, the human rights advocate Carter overlooked the repressive tactics of Iran's CIA-trained secret police, SAVAK. For American policymakers, access to oil reserves and support for the Shah's consistently anti-Communist stance outweighed all other considerations.

Early in 1979, a revolution led by a fundamentalist Muslim leader, the Ayatollah Ruhollah Khomeini, overturned the Shah's government and drove him into exile. The United States had ignored warning signals that the Shah's efforts to westernize Iran had offended fundamentalist Islamic leaders; the CIA had also downplayed the extent to which hatred of the United States had helped to coalesce opposition to the Shah. Once the mullahs (religious leaders) were in power, the United States seemed unsure how to deal with the new Iranian officials, who denounced the Soviet Union and the United States with equal ferocity.

In late October 1979, the Carter administration made a controversial decision to admit the deposed Shah, who was suffering from incurable cancer, into the United States for medical treatment. Iran's new leaders had warned that such an action would provoke retaliation, but foreign policy leaders like Henry Kissinger and David Rockefeller argued that the United States owed this gesture to the Shah both for humanitarian reasons and in return for his years of support for American policy. In response, on November 4, 1979, fundamentalist Muslim students under Khomeini's direction seized the U.S. embassy in Teheran, taking American hostages in a flagrant violation of the principle of diplomatic immunity. After the release of nineteen hostages, primarily women, black marines, and those suffering from serious illness, fifty-two remained in captivity. The hostage-takers demanded that the Shah be returned to Iran for trial and punishment. The United States refused. President Carter suspended arms sales to Iran, froze Iranian assets in American banks, and threatened to deport Iranian students studying in the country, but no more hostages were released.

For the next fourteen months, the Iranian hostage

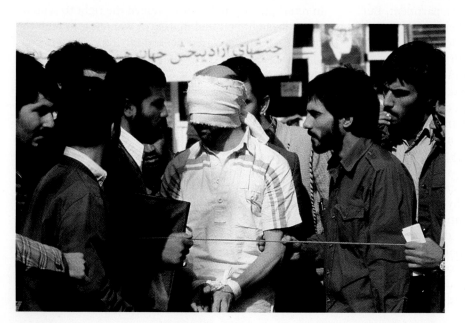

American Hostages in Iran
Images of blindfolded, handcuffed, American hostages seized by Iranian militants at the American Embassy in Teheran in November 1979 shocked Americans and created a foreign policy crisis that eventually cost Jimmy Carter the presidency.

crisis paralyzed the presidency of Jimmy Carter. Each night humiliating pictures of blindfolded hostages appeared on television newscasts. (Media-conscious Iranian students conveniently printed their anti-American placards in English.) The late night television news program, *Nightline*, featuring journalist Ted Koppel, originated as "America Held Hostage," a nightly update on the news from Iran which provided an unexpected way for ABC to compete with Johnny Carson's *Tonight Show*.

In many ways, Carter's insistence that the safe return of the hostages was his top priority actually enhanced their value to their captors. But amid mounting calls for strong American action, Carter could do little to win their release until a stable Iranian government was willing to negotiate. An attempt to mount a military rescue of the hostages failed miserably in April 1980, six months into the crisis, when helicopter equipment failures in the desert meant the rescue literally never got off the ground. Secretary of State Cyrus Vance resigned in protest over the attempt, claiming it would have endangered the lives of the hostages further. The abortive rescue mission reinforced the view of Carter as bumbling and ineffective.

The White House took on an embattled tone. President Carter decided not to enter the presidential primary elections underway in 1980, claiming that he wanted to devote all his energy to the safe return of the hostages. This "above politics" stance did help Carter beat back a challenge from Massachusetts senator Edward Kennedy for the Democratic nomination, but it worked to his detriment during the general presidential campaign against Republican challenger Ronald Reagan. In a scenario reminiscent of the 1932 election, Carter played the part of the embattled, defensive Hoover, while Reagan took the upbeat, decisive Roosevelt role. Candidate Reagan continually harped on the hostage stalemate, calling the Iranians "barbarians" and "common criminals" and hinting that he would take strong action to wrest their return. This rhetorical stance played a definite role in Reagan's decisive electoral victory in November 1980.

In all, the hostages spent 444 days in captivity. They were released at precisely the moment when Jimmy Carter turned over the presidency to Ronald Reagan on January 20, 1981. The hostages returned home to an ecstatic patriotic welcome, a reflection of American frustration over their long ordeal.

While most Americans continued to maintain that "We're Number One," the hostage crisis in Iran came to symbolize the loss of America's power to control world affairs. Its psychological impact was magnified because it came at the end of the decade that had witnessed Watergate, the American defeat in Vietnam, and the OPEC embargo. To a large extent, this decline in influence was magnified by the unusual predominance the United States had enjoyed after World War II, a dominance that could not realistically have been expected to last forever. The return to economic and political power of Japan and Western Europe, the control of vital oil resources by Middle Eastern countries, and the industrialization of some Third World nations had widened the cast of international actors. Still, many Americans were unable to accept anything less than the economic and political supremacy of the postwar years. Ronald Reagan rode their frustrations to victory in 1980.

Summary

The year 1968 saw an unprecedented level of domestic unrest, including the assassinations of Martin Luther King, Jr., and Robert F. Kennedy and major protests at the Democratic convention in Chicago. Richard Nixon was elected president by promising to restore quieter times. However, the nation continued to debate the value of American involvement in Vietnam, which did not end until the signing of the Paris Peace Accords in January 1973. Meanwhile, the Nixon administration took part in a series of illegal and questionable acts in connection with the president's campaign for reelection in 1972. The resulting Watergate scandal led to Nixon's resignation in 1974. Vice-President Gerald Ford became president, but he lost the 1976 election to Jimmy Carter of Georgia, who campaigned as an outsider.

During the rest of the decade, the United States struggled with economic problems including high inflation, skyrocketing energy costs, and a diminished position in world trade. Many citizens became cynical about national leadership in the wake of Watergate. The environmental movement promoted the vision that "small is beautiful," and many citizens sought federal action to promote clean air and water. A new, more conservative social mood limited further progress of the civil rights and women's movements; this mood injected values drawn from evangelical religion into political life. The end of the decade was dominated by the Iranian hostage crisis, as Islamic fundamentalists held fifty-two hostages at the U.S. embassy in Teheran for 444 days. The hostage crisis virtually paralyzed Carter's presidency, helping Ronald Reagan win election in 1980.

TOPIC FOR RESEARCH

The Alaska Pipeline and the Environment

In 1968 an "elephant" was found near Prudhoe Bay, Alaska, on the Arctic coast, that was twice as large as any oil field in North America. In 1977 completion of the 800-mile Trans-Alaska pipeline linked Prudhoe Bay to the port of Valdez at a cost of $7.7 billion. The delay in construction of the pipeline was due to extensive litigation that pitted oil companies against environmentalists. Environmental concerns included the impact of the pipeline on Alaskan wildlife and the risk of oil tanker accidents at Valdez in Prince William Sound.

Research the pros and cons of building the pipeline. What were the arguments on both sides? What strategies were pursued? What finally tipped the balance? In light of the *Exxon Valdez* accident in 1989 (which, as environmentalists had feared, saturated Prince William Sound with oil), were the earlier predictions of environmentalists accurate? Why had they failed to get their message across?

The best introduction to oil issues is Daniel Yergin, *The Prize* (1991). The public debate can be traced through newspapers and magazines in the 1970s, as well as the government hearings on the issue. Other sources include Potter Wickware, *Crazy Money: Nine Months on the Trans-Alaska Pipeline* (1979); Ed McGarth, *Inside the Alaska Pipeline* (1977); Robert Douglas Mead, *Journeys Down the Line: Building the Trans-Alaska Pipeline* (1978); and Mim Dixon, *What Happened to Fairbanks? The Effects of the Trans-Alaska Pipeline on the Community of Fairbanks* (1978).

BIBLIOGRAPHY

The Watershed Year

Material on 1968 as a turning point in postwar America can be found in various sources. See David Caute, *The Year of the Barricades* (1968); David Farber, *Chicago '68* (1988); and Lewis Chester, Godfrey Hodgson, and Bruce Page, *An American Melodrama* (1970). Norman Mailer provides his contemporary view on the conventions in *Miami and the Siege of Chicago* (1968). William H. Chafe's overview of the postwar period, *An Unfinished Journey* (2nd edition, 1991), gives a central role to developments in that year.

Kevin Phillips, *The Emerging Republican Majority* (1969), and Richard Scammon and Ben J. Wattenberg, *The Real Majority* (1970), describe the voters whom Richard Nixon tried to reach. Theodore H. White, *The Making of the President—1968* (1969) and *The Making of the President—1972* (1973), cover the election campaigns.

The Nixon Years

Jonathan Schell, *The Time of Illusion* (1976), offers an insightful discussion of the Nixon administration. Herbert Parmet, *Richard Nixon and His America* (1990), and Stephen Ambrose, *Nixon* (1987), are two of many biographies of this complicated political character. Kim McQuaid, *The Anxious Years: America in the Vietnam-Watergate Era* (1989), is an overview of the period. See also William Safire, *Before the Fall* (1975); Leonard Silk, *Nixonomics* (1972); and Garry Wills, *Nixon Agonistes* (1971).

Robert S. Litwak, *Détente and the Nixon Doctrine* (1984), and Tad Szulc, *The Illusion of Peace* (1978), are overviews of Nixon's foreign policy. Stanley Karnow, *Vietnam: A History* (1983), describes events through the fall of Saigon in 1975; Marilyn Young continues the story in *The Vietnam Wars, 1945–1990* (1991). William Shawcross, *Sideshow: Kissinger, Nixon, and the Destruction of Cambodia* (1979), is strongly critical of U.S. policy. Robert Jay Lifton, *Home from the War* (1973); Paul Starr, *The Discarded Army* (1973); and Lawrence Baskir and William A. Strauss, *Chance and Circumstance* (1978), discuss the problems of returning Vietnam veterans. Ron Kovic, *Born on the Fourth of July* (1976), is a moving personal memoir.

Stanley Kutler, *The Wars of Watergate* (1990); Anthony Lukas, *Nightmare: The Underside of the Nixon Years* (1976); and Theodore H. White, *Breach of Faith* (1975), are comprehensive accounts of the Watergate scandal. Also of interest are the books by the *Washington Post* journalists who broke the story, Carl Bernstein and Bob Woodward, *All the President's Men* (1974) and *The Final Days* (1976). John Dean, *Blind Ambition* (1976), is the best account by a participant; see also H. R. Haldeman, *The Ends of Power* (1978), and Richard M. Nixon, *RN: The Memoirs of Richard Nixon* (1978). Richard M. Cohen and Jules Witcover, *A Heartbeat Away* (1974), describes Spiro Agnew's fall from power. Arthur M. Schlesinger, Jr., *The Imperial Presidency* (1973), analyzes changes in the institution that provided a backdrop for the Watergate affair.

Lowered Expectations and New Challenges

Peter Carroll, *It Seemed Like Nothing Happened* (1982), provides a historian's view of the 1970s. General introductions to economic developments of the decade are in Barry Bluestone and Bennett Harrison, *The Deindustrialization of America* (1982); Richard J. Barnet and Ronald E. Muller, *Global Reach* (1974); Richard J. Barnet, *The Lean Years* (1980); John P. Hoerr, *And the Wolf Finally Came: The Decline of the Steel Industry* (1988); Robert Calleo, *The Imperious Economy* (1982); and Gardner Means et al., *The Roots of Inflation* (1975). John M. Blair, *The Control of Oil* (1976), and J. C. Hurewitz, ed., *Oil, the Arab-Israeli Dispute, and the Industrial World* (1976), treat OPEC developments.

Barry Commoner, *The Closing Circle* (1971) and *The Poverty of Power* (1976), and Robert Heilbroner, *An Inquiry into the Human Prospect* (1974), cogently assess the origins of the energy crisis and the prospects for the future. See also Lester C. Thurow, *The Zero-Sum Society* (1980), and Robert Stobaugh and Daniel Yergin, *Energy Future* (1980). For a general overview of the environmental movement, see Samuel P. Hays, *Beauty, Health, and Permanence: Environmental Politics in the United States, 1955–1985* (1987). Roderick Nash provides a history of environmental ethics in *The Rights of Nature* (1989). Influential books in shaping public awareness of ecological issues included Paul R. Ehrlich, *The Population Bomb* (1968); Frances Moore Lappe, *Diet for a Small Planet* (1971); and Philip Slater, *Earthwalk* (1974).

Much of the material on post-Watergate politics has been provided by journalists rather than historians. Richard Reeves, *A Ford, Not a Lincoln* (1975); J. F. ter Horst, *Gerald Ford and the Future of the Presidency* (1974); and John Osborne, *White House Watch: The Ford Years* (1977), cover the Ford presidency. See also A. James Reichley, *Conservatives in an Age of Change: The Nixon and Ford Administrations* (1981). Jules Witcover, *Marathon* (1977), describes the pursuit of the presidency in 1976, while Theodore H. White, *America in Search of Itself* (1982), looks more broadly at public life between 1954 and 1980.

Portraits of the Carter presidency, generally unfavorable, are found in Robert Shogan, *Promises to Keep* (1977); Haynes Johnson, *In the Absence of Power* (1980); and Clark Mollenhoff, *The President Who Failed* (1980). See also Erwin Hargrove, *Jimmy Carter as President* (1989), and Charles Jones, *The Trusteeship Presidency* (1988). James Wooten, *Dasher* (1978), and Betty Glad, *Jimmy Carter: From Plains to the White House* (1980), are competent biographies. See also Jimmy Carter's own campaign manifesto, *Why Not the Best?* (1975), and his presidential memoirs, *Keeping Faith* (1982). Rosalynn Carter contributes her perspective in *First Lady from Plains* (1984). James Fallows, *National Defense* (1981), is an incisive overview of defense developments. See also A. Glenn Mower, Jr., *Human Rights and American Foreign Policy: The Carter and Reagan Experiences* (1987). Stephen Ambrose, *The Rise to Globalism* (5th ed., 1988), includes a summary of the Iranian hostage crisis.

Stanley Aronowitz, *False Promises* (1973); Richard Krickus, *Pursuing the American Dream* (1976); and Michael Novak, *The Rise of the Unmeltable Ethnics* (1977), describe the concerns of the white ethnic middleclass. J. Anthony Lukas, *Common Ground* (1985), tells the story of the Boston busing crisis through the lives of three families in a compelling narrative. Nathan Glazer, *Affirmative Discrimination* (1975); Thomas Sowell, *Race and Economics* (1975); and Allan P. Sindler, *Bakke, Defunis, and Minority Admissions* (1978), treat the controversial topic of affirmative action.

Tom Wolfe gave the decade its name in "The Me Decade and the Third Great Awakening," *New York Magazine* (August 23, 1976). Influential books included Christopher Lasch, *The Culture of Narcissism: American Life in an Age of Diminishing Expectations* (1978), and Gail Sheehy, *Passages* (1976). Alan Crawford, *Thunder on the Right* (1980), surveys the new conservatism, as does Peter Steinfels, *The Neo-Conservatives* (1979). John Woodridge, *The Evangelicals* (1975), and Marshall Frady, *Billy Graham* (1979), analyze the rise of evangelical religion; James Reston, Jr., *Our Father Who Art in Hell* (1981), tells the story of Reverend Jim Jones and the Guyana tragedy. Carol Felsenthal's biography of Phyllis Schlafly, *The Sweetheart of the Silent Majority* (1981), shows how the Moral Majority identified feminism as a target.

TIMELINE

1968	Tet offensive Robert Kennedy assassinated Democratic convention marred by street violence in Chicago Nixon elected president
1970	U.S. troops invade Cambodia; renewed antiwar demonstrations Earth Day first observed Environmental Protection Agency established
1971	Pentagon Papers published Collapse of Bretton Woods system
1972	Watergate break-in Nixon reelected
1973–1974	Arab oil embargo
1973	Paris Peace Accords Spiro Agnew resigns; Gerald R. Ford appointed vice-president War Powers Act
1974	Nixon resigns; Ford becomes president
1974–1975	Busing controversy in Boston
1975	Recession Fall of Saigon
1976	Jimmy Carter elected president
1978	Camp David accords between Israel and Egypt *Bakke v. University of California* limits affirmative action
1979	Hostages seized at American embassy in Teheran, Iran Three Mile Island nuclear accident Formal recognition of People's Republic of China U.S.S.R. invades Afghanistan
1980	Ronald W. Reagan elected president

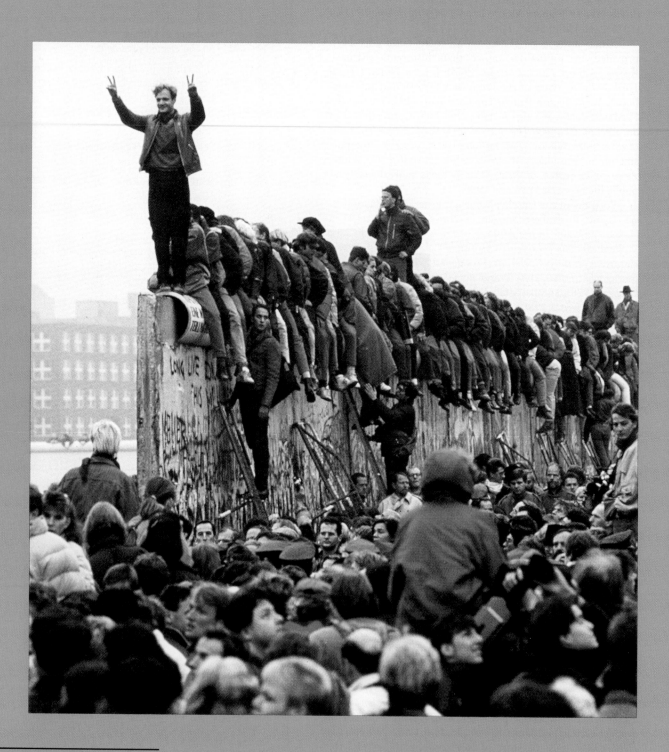

The Wall Comes Tumbling Down

The destruction of the Berlin Wall in November 1989
symbolized the end of the Cold War.

CHAPTER **33** *Toward a New World Order, 1980 to the Present*

In the 1920s, Americans were drawn into a national web of shared experience. In the 1980s, an international web linked Americans with the rest of the world. Political choices made in Washington, such as incurring huge budget deficits to maintain American defense and domestic spending while cutting taxes, had international economic implications. Similarly, decisions made in Tokyo, Hong Kong, Bonn, or Brussels affected what kind of consumer products Americans could buy, what the prime rate would be, and even whether American workers kept their jobs. More than ever, events in the United States and the rest of the world were inextricably intertwined.

A Coca-Cola executive captured why American corporations increasingly had to think in global terms. "Willie Sutton used to say he robbed banks because that's where the money is. Well, we are increasingly global because 95 percent of the world's consumers are outside this country. It's that simple." But not all American companies found it easy to adapt and compete in these new conditions. Lee Iaccoca, head of the Chrysler Corporation, which struggled throughout the 1980s to stay ahead of foreign competitors, often complained that international trade was an uneven football field on which United States industries had to play uphill. But the fact of the matter was that for the first time since the end of World War II, the field no longer tilted in America's favor.

The United States now shares dominance with other nations in an interconnected global economy that is constantly affected by changing international political realities. Most dramatically, the collapse of commu-

nism in Eastern Europe and the Soviet Union ended the Cold War, which had shaped American foreign and domestic policy for four decades. But the "new world order" that will replace the old economic and political relationships among nations is still emerging.

The Reagan Presidency

After 1968 the New Deal Democratic coalition that had dominated national politics since Franklin Roosevelt slowly but steadily declined. At the same time, the Republican party underwent a conservative rebirth that translated into electoral success. In 1989, when Vice-President George Bush succeeded Ronald Reagan, the Republicans had won five out of the last six presidential contests. The Democrats, on the other hand, continued to find more electoral success in Congress and in state government.

Ronald Reagan and the Conservative Agenda

Ronald Reagan's path to the presidency holds clues both to the resurgence of the Republican party and its core values. Born in 1911 in Tampico, Illinois, Reagan won a modest reputation as a Hollywood actor, then served as a corporate spokesperson on television for General Electric. During this time his political philosophy shifted from New Deal Democrat to conservative

Republican. After endorsing Barry Goldwater in 1964, Reagan decided to enter politics. He was twice elected governor of California, serving from 1966 to 1974. This positioned him well to try for the presidency in 1976, although he lost the nomination to Gerald Ford. During the 1980 primary season, he handily dispatched his opponents, including former U.N. ambassador and CIA director George Bush, whom he then chose as his running mate. In the general election, Reagan and Bush roundly defeated incumbent president Jimmy Carter as well as an independent candidate, Representative John B. Anderson of Illinois. The Republican landslide also gave the party control of the Senate for the first time since 1954, although the Democrats maintained their hold on the House.

One key to the Republican resurgence of the 1970s and 1980s was money. As the party of the well-to-do and the business community, Republicans were supported by financial resources that far exceeded those available to the Democrats, whose main support came from organized labor. Political action committees, or PACs, collected large sums for conservative candidates. The Republicans' financial superiority enabled them to make sophisticated and highly effective use of television to address voters directly.

Another key was a realignment of the electorate. The core of the Republican party that elected Ronald Reagan remained the upper-middle-class white Protestant voters who supported balanced budgets, disliked government activism, feared crime and communism, and believed in a strong national defense. These values were the essence of postwar conservatism. Now new groups gravitated toward the Republican vision, often for reasons of economic self-interest: southern whites disaffected by big government and blacks' civil rights gains; formerly urban ethnic group members who had moved to the suburbs; blue-collar workers, especially Catholics; young voters who identified as conservatives; and voters in the Sunbelt, a region traditionally more conservative than the Midwest or East. When California's Proposition 13, calling for sharp cuts in property taxes, was approved in a 1978 referendum, it suggested that voters were more concerned about their bank balances than with supporting public education or government services.

Perhaps the most significant constituency energizing the Republican party was the New Right, whose emphasis on traditional values and fundamentalist Christian morality dovetailed well with conservative Republican ideology. The New Right was particularly

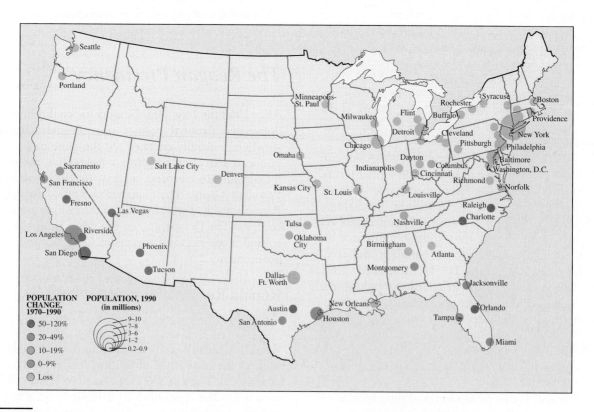

MAP 33.1

The Growth of the Sunbelt, 1970–1990

The Sunbelt states of the South and West were the key to the Republican resurgence in the 1980s. While older industrial cities like New York, Chicago, Philadelphia, and Detroit lost population, newer metropolises—Phoenix, Houston, and San Diego—grew spectacularly.

upset by the rapid social changes underway since the 1960s, especially those viewed as undermining traditional family and gender roles. Jimmy Carter, a southerner and a devout evangelical Protestant, had captured much of this vote in 1976, but four years later New Right voters were more comfortable in the Republican party. Their concerns formed the basis for the party's platform, which called for a constitutional ban on abortion, voluntary prayer in the public schools, and a mandatory death penalty for certain crimes; it also demanded an end to forced busing and, for the first time in forty years, opposed the Equal Rights Amendment, reflecting the New Right's strongly felt belief that women belonged at home with their families.

The Reagan Style

When sixty-nine-year-old Ronald Wilson Reagan took office in January 1981, he became the oldest man ever to serve as president. (He was actually six years older than John F. Kennedy would have been, had he lived.) He showed his remarkable physical stamina just months into office when he survived an assassination attempt outside a Washington, D.C., hotel. Just as robust was his personal popularity, which remained high throughout his two terms. He became known as the "Great Communicator" for his ability to establish rapport with the American people through the medium of television.

During his long acting career and his stint in state government, Reagan developed a somewhat removed leadership style. Once, when asked what kind of governor he would be, he replied, "I don't know, I've never played a governor." Many observers found him better at general platitudes and encouragement than details: "We have a great task ahead of us," Reagan would say, but never state what that task was.

To maintain his hands-off style of governance, he depended on the support and advice of his appointees. Among his closest personal advisers were Chief of Staff James Baker, presidential counselor Edwin Meese, and Secretary of the Treasury Donald Regan, who became chief of staff in 1985 when Baker switched to the Treasury post. Reagan also relied heavily on his wife Nancy, who was fiercely protective of both his image and his schedule, even to the point of consulting an astrologer before planning major White House events.

Reaganomics

Buoyed by his electoral mandate and the conservative resurgence, Ronald Reagan seized the chance to redefine the nation's priorities. Ever since the New Deal, the public had generally assumed that the nation's social and economic problems could best be solved by ex-

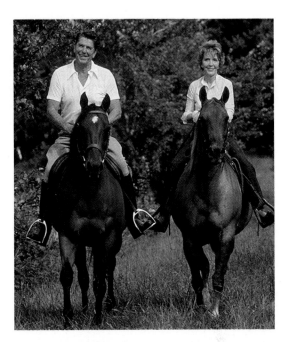

Back Home on the Ranch
Like many members of the Hollywood community, Nancy and Ronald Reagan preferred the southern California lifestyle to the frenetic rhythms of Washington and New York. Here they ride horseback at their California ranch.

panding federal action. The election of Ronald Reagan ended almost half a century of activism. "Government is not the solution to our problem," he declared. "Government is the problem."

Reagan first moved to reshape the nation's fiscal and tax policies. The term *Reaganomics* came to stand for the tax cuts and domestic budget reductions enacted in 1981 and 1982 and the supply-side economic theory behind them. According to this theory, excessive taxation siphoned off capital that should be invested to stimulate economic growth. Tax cuts would give businesses and individuals more money to invest, investments would cause the economy to expand, and total tax revenues would be greater—despite the lower rates. Government expenditures would be trimmed by shrinking government benefits, especially entitlement programs begun during the New Deal. And the federal budget deficit would go down. That, at least, was the theory. Critics charged that conservatives deliberately cut taxes to mandate reductions in federal funding for social programs they abhorred.

The first part of this economic policy—tax cuts—was enacted in the Economic Recovery Tax Act of 1981, arguably the most significant legislation of the Reagan years. Building on a proposal originally developed by Senator William Roth of Delaware and Representative Jack Kemp of New York, this across-the-board tax cut reduced basic personal income tax rates 25 percent over three years. It also introduced the indexing of tax brackets, which kept tax rates constant when incomes rose solely because of inflation. According to budget director David Stockman, the tax cut was to be linked with large cutbacks in expenditures, especially in human services. Congressional resistance kept programs such as Social Security and Medicare intact, but more than half of Reagan's proposed cuts were enacted. If all had gone according to Stockman's plan, the budget should have been balanced by 1984. This did not happen. Despite what seemed like wrenching cuts in federal programs, the drop in revenues from the tax cuts was far steeper than the amount pruned from the budget. Deficits began to balloon alarmingly.

Another contribution to the deficit was the $1.7 trillion, five-year defense buildup advocated by the president and his Defense secretary, Caspar Weinberger. This huge increase fulfilled Republican campaign pledges to "make America Number One again" militarily. Especially favored was development of such equipment as the B-1 bomber, which Carter had canceled, and the MX mobile missile. Reagan's most ambitious, and controversial, weapons plan was the 1983 Strategic Defense Initiative (SDI), popularly known as "Star Wars" from the movie of the same name. SDI would be a satellite and laser shield to detect and intercept incoming missiles before they could strike. Reagan supporters claimed SDI would render nuclear war obsolete, but scientists doubted its feasibility.

Limiting Government. The Reagan administration also moved to abolish or reduce government regulations affecting the workplace, health care, consumer protection, and the environment. Reaganomics claimed such regulations were not only inefficient but also impeded productivity because of the high cost of compliance. (Much of the slack, and the cost, was transferred to the states.) Reagan's appointees to such formerly activist regulatory agencies as the National Labor Relations Board and the Environmental Protection Agency lessened the impact of existing regulations by scaling back budget requests, not spending allocated funds, or delaying action on pending cases.

Meanwhile, the Federal Reserve Board used monetary policy to combat the still troubling problem of inflation, which had been high since the mid-1970s. By raising the interest rate for corporate borrowers, the Federal Reserve did reduce inflation from 12.4 percent in 1980 to 4 percent in 1982. But tightening the money supply in this way also reduced business investment, contributing to a severe recession in 1981–1982. Slack industrial growth raised the unemployment rate to 10.7 percent, the highest since the Great Depression; thousands of workers were laid off, especially in the Midwest. The automobile and steel industries, already facing challenges from foreign competitors using newer

and more efficient technologies as well as lower-paid workers, were particularly hard hit. Due to the severe cutbacks in entitlement programs under Reagan, only 45 percent of those who lost their jobs received unemployment compensation, compared with 75 percent at the height of the harsh 1975 recession.

It was a relatively brief recession: the economy began growing again in early 1983. For the rest of the decade inflation stayed low, aided by a worldwide drop in energy costs, and the Reagan administration presided over the longest peacetime economic expansion in American history. But in many ways this sense of economic well-being was an illusion, "an illusion based on borrowed time and borrowed money," as the federal budget deficit continued to mount.

Foreign Relations

In foreign relations, Ronald Reagan's first-term break with postwar traditions was less dramatic than in domestic social policy. Détente had collapsed late in the Carter administration over the Soviet Union's invasion of Afghanistan, and Reagan entered the presidency with a confrontational approach to the Soviet Union, including a strong commitment to stopping Communist expansion in developing nations. Giving voice to the beliefs of Republican hardliners, Reagan articulated some of the harshest anti-Soviet rhetoric heard in the United States since the 1950s. In March 1983 he called the Soviet Union an "evil empire" that was "the focus of evil in the modern world."

The Middle East continued to challenge policymakers, always mindful of America's dependence on the region for oil. Reagan's hopes for peace in the Middle East were thwarted when Israeli troops invaded southern Lebanon in 1982, intending to dislodge the Palestine Liberation Organization from its bases there. The Israelis overran much of Lebanon, and the Lebanese government disintegrated into warring factions. Reagan ordered a contingent of marines to Lebanon to help keep the peace, but instead they became a highly vulnerable target in the turmoil of Lebanon's civil war. The tragic result was the death of 241 American soldiers when an explosive-laden car rammed into their Beirut barracks in October 1983. The marines were soon withdrawn, although a number of American hostages remained in captivity in Beirut. (The last American hostages would not be released until 1991, after the Persian Gulf War.)

The Reagan administration devoted its most concerted attention to Central America. Halting what was seen as the spread of communism in the region became practically an obsession. In El Salvador, the United States supported a repressive right-wing regime that was fighting against leftists. In 1983 Reagan ordered

U.S. Marines to invade the tiny Caribbean island of Grenada, claiming that its Cuban-supported Communist regime was a threat to other states in the region. Reporters were kept uninformed about the military operation until it was over. The Grenada invasion, which featured the rescue of several dozen American medical students trapped on the island, occurred just days after the Lebanon bombing and helped shift public attention to a foreign policy "victory" rather than the Middle East policy failures.

Nicaragua's Sandinista government proved the most troubling to Reagan's foreign policy advisers. The Sandinistas, guerrillas who had overthrown the right-wing President Anastasio Somoza in 1979, were leftists but not Communists, although they were friendly with Marxist leaders such as Cuba's Fidel Castro. In 1981 the United States suspended aid to Nicaragua, charging that the Sandinista government, along with Cuba and the Soviet Union, was supplying arms to the rebels in El Salvador, a charge denied by the Sandinistas. At the same time, the CIA began to provide extensive support to Nicaragua's opposition forces, known as the "Contras" or counterrevolutionaries. Reagan called the Contras "freedom fighters," but Congress was not convinced. In 1984 it added the Boland Amendment banning military support to the Contras to a defense appropriations bill.

Reagan's Second Term

The 1984 Election. In 1984 the Democrats nominated Walter Mondale, Carter's vice-president and a former Minnesota senator, to run against Ronald Reagan. Mondale symbolized the New Deal coalition. He had been a protégé of Hubert Humphrey, with strong ties to labor unions, minority groups, and party leaders. He appealed to many women voters by selecting Representative Geraldine Ferraro of New York as his running mate, the first woman on a major party ticket. But the 1984 election was not even close. Reagan campaigned on the theme of "It's Morning in America," suggesting that a new day of prosperity was dawning. Voters gave him another landslide victory—59 percent of the popular vote. Reagan carried the entire country except Minnesota and the District of Columbia. He did especially well among young (eighteen- to twenty-one-year-old) voters, receiving 62 percent of their support.

After a string of administrations that had ended in discord (Johnson and Vietnam), disgrace (Nixon and Watergate), or frustration (Carter and Iran), many people responded warmly to Reagan's strong and confident leadership. Reagan was a convincing performer, and voters believed him when he said he could solve America's problems. Reagan's enormous personal popularity recalled Dwight Eisenhower's appeal in the 1950s. Also like Eisenhower, his coattails were short: Democrats maintained control of the House and picked up two seats in the Senate; they would regain control of the Senate in 1986.

Tax Reform. In its second term the Reagan administration continued to pursue its conservative agenda. The 1986 Tax Reform Act was the most sweeping overhaul of the tax code in history, but it was not designed to reduce the deficits accumulated since the 1981 tax cut. The 1986 act was *revenue-neutral* (that is, it did not change the amount of taxes raised, just how they were raised). It resulted from an unlikely alliance: liberal Democrats who wanted to close loopholes that allowed some wealthy individuals and corporations to avoid paying taxes altogether, joined supply-side Republicans who wanted so much to lower rates that they went along with the reforms, such as removing low-income taxpayers from the rolls. The act closed loopholes worth $300 billion over five years, balancing them with lower tax rates. It also raised corporate taxes by $120 billion over five years, the largest increase ever.

The Iran-Contra Affair. Reagan's second term was marred by a major scandal in 1986. Foreign newspapers broke the story that the administration had negotiated an arms-for-hostages deal with the revolutionary government of Iran, the same government Reagan had denounced at the height of the 1980 hostage crisis. Despite objections from Secretary of State George Shultz and Defense secretary Weinberger, but at the instigation of CIA director William Casey and National Security Advisor Robert McFarlane, the United States

A First for the Nation
Geraldine Ferraro, Walter Mondale's running mate in 1984, was the first woman nominated by a major party to its national ticket. Despite her presence, a majority of women voted for Reagan in the 1984 Republican landslide.

secretly sold arms to Iran, which was locked in a costly and lengthy war with neighboring Iraq. The intent was to gain Iran's help in freeing American hostages believed held by pro-Iranian forces in Lebanon. (Only one hostage was released.) These arm sales generated large profits, some of which, in the most controversial aspect of what became known as the Iran-Contra affair, were diverted as military aid for the Contras in Nicaragua. This diversion was both illegal (contravening the Boland Amendment) and unconstitutional (bypassing the sole right of Congress to appropriate funds).

The arms-for-hostages deal had been discussed at the highest levels of government, but the diversion of funds to the Contras seems to have been the brainstorm of Marine Lieutenant Colonel Oliver North, who was on assignment to the National Security Council. After the press picked up the story, North destroyed many incriminating documents, but he missed a key memo that linked the White House to the plan. Congress investigated the mounting scandal in 1986 and 1987; in their testimony, John Poindexter, the new National Security Advisor, North, and others provided details of the covert actions, but all insisted that the president knew nothing of the diversion. (William Casey, who died of a brain tumor in 1987, never testified.) Ronald Reagan's defense remained simple and consistent: "I don't remember."

The full story of the illegal arms operation may never be known. The scandal bore many similarities to Watergate, including the possibility that the president acted illegally, but there were no significant calls for Reagan's impeachment. The Democratic Congress was

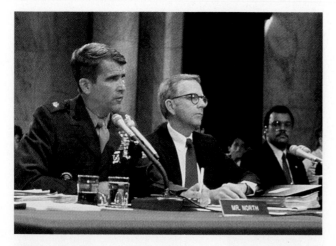

Oliver North

North's uncompromising stance before the congressional committee investigating the Iran-Contra affair made him a popular speaker before conservative audiences, especially those that shared his deep anti-Communist convictions. Indicted and tried for perjury and obstruction of justice, his conviction was overturned in 1990.

not keen to attack a president whose popularity remained remarkably high, nor were investigators able to shake the stonewalling by key presidential aides. Reagan's ability to weather "Iran-Contragate" further testified to what Representative Patricia Schroeder of Colorado, a leading Democratic critic in Congress, dubbed his "Teflon presidency"—bad news didn't stick; it just rolled off.

The Return of Détente. The most significant foreign policy development in Reagan's second term was a reduction in tensions with the Soviet Union. This process was set in motion by the ascent to power in 1985 of Soviet leader Mikhail Gorbachev. That same year, Gorbachev and Reagan met in Geneva, the first superpower summit meeting since 1979. They met again the following year in Reykjavik, Iceland. In 1987 the United States and the Soviet Union agreed to eliminate their short-range missiles based in Europe, the first time an existing category of weapons had been scrapped and the most significant postwar disarmament decision since the 1972 SALT I agreement. Although a fourth Reagan-Gorbachev summit in Moscow in mid-1988 produced no further nuclear arms cuts, it did demonstrate cordial relations between the two superpowers. When the Soviets announced soon after that they were withdrawing from Afghanistan, prospects for cooperation appeared even brighter.

Reagan Legacies

Ronald Reagan came into the presidency promising to dismantle an intrusive federal bureaucracy, reduce federal entitlements programs, give free-market forces more scope in the modern economy, and stand up to the Soviet menace. The so-called Reagan Revolution proved to be more a "Reagan revision." Although he changed the priorities of the national government and attempted to curb its expansion, he failed to reduce its size or scope. When he left office, government functions remained much as he found them. Defense spending had increased considerably; Social Security and most poverty programs were still in operation, although the latter at reduced levels. And events had brought the Soviet Union and the United States closer together.

One of Reagan's most enduring legacies was his conservative judicial appointments, the area where the New Right had its greatest impact on his administration. In 1981, Reagan nominated Sandra Day O'Connor to the Supreme Court, the first woman ever to serve; he later appointed two other conservatives, Antonin Scalia and Anthony Kennedy. Justice William Rehnquist, a noted conservative who had been appointed by Nixon, was elevated to chief justice in 1986. But when the Reagan administration tried to nominate federal judge Robert Bork in 1987, the Senate refused to confirm him because of Bork's outspoken opposition to judicial activism, with its potential threat to the protection of individual liberties.

Ironically, for a president who promised to balance the budget by 1984, Reagan's greatest legacy was the federal debt, which tripled during his two terms from the combined effect of vastly increased military spending, substantial tax reductions for high-income taxpayers, and Congress's refusal to approve the deep cuts in domestic programs requested by Reagan. There had been federal deficits before, but never on this scale. In 1989 the national debt stood at $2.8 trillion, more than $11,000 for every American citizen. Interest payments on the borrowed money, $216 billion by 1988, were the fastest growing item in the federal budget; by the year 2000, the accumulating interest was expected to consume one-quarter of the entire federal budget.

Trade with other nations was also running at a deficit, which peaked at $171 billion in 1987. Exports had been falling since the 1970s, as American products encountered increasing competition in world markets. The high exchange rate for dollars in the early 1980s made U.S. goods more expensive for buyers with other currencies, while foreign-made goods became more affordable in the United States. The decline in the value of the dollar in the late 1980s helped reduce the trade deficit to $95 billion in 1990.

The budget and trade deficits contributed to a major shift in 1985: for the first time since 1915, the United States was a debtor, not a creditor, nation. Since then, with phenomenal speed, the United States has accumulated the world's largest foreign debt.

These twin deficits have major economic and political ramifications. With so great a chronic budget deficit, money is channeled to servicing the debt rather than being invested to increase productivity; interest rates soar as the government competes with private-sector borrowers for the limited amount of investment capital. With less money to develop new products or purchase efficient modern equipment, American producers lose sales to those offering newer and better products at lower prices. An influx of foreign funds, especially after 1985, filled part of the investment gap and helped to keep interest rates low. But the growing debt to foreign lenders and trading partners meant that more dollars left the country as returns on foreign investment.

The political system was unable to address this mounting economic crisis. On the one hand, members of Congress were unwilling to cut programs their constituents depended on for services or jobs. Fearing unemployment in the military-industrial complex and lobbied by military leaders and defense contractors, they also hesitated to reduce the military budget, although it grew less dramatically after mid-decade. On the other hand, few politicians could buck the popular

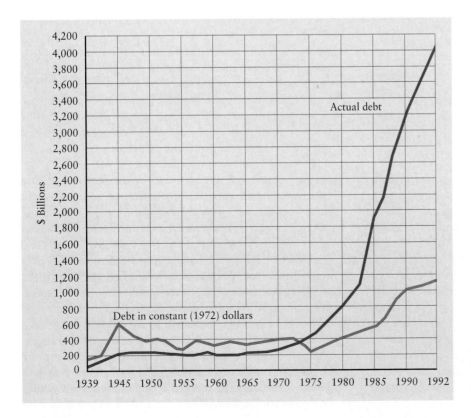

FIGURE 33.1

The Escalating Federal Debt, 1939-1992

The federal debt, which soared during World War II, remained relatively stable until the huge deficits of the 1980s.

Source: *U.S. Statistical Abstract, 1991; Economic Report of the President* (Feb. 1992).

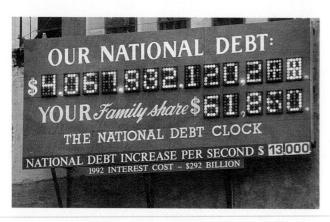

The National Debt
A "clock" in Times Square in New York City kept track of the mounting national debt. A 1990 tax hike slowed the rate of increase in the debt but did nothing to reduce the debt itself.

resistance to new taxes. In 1985, Congress passed the Gramm-Rudman Balanced Budget and Emergency Deficit Reduction Control Act, which tried to achieve a balanced budget by 1991 by mandating specific cuts that would automatically be instituted if deficit reduction targets were not met.

The budget deficit peaked at $221 billion in 1986, and then dropped slightly before leveling off, but the damage had been done. Ever since, both political parties have found it difficult to reverse the consequences of Reaganomics. A huge deficit remains, which, along with the interest needed to service it, will affect all political, economic, and social initiatives throughout the 1990s, and probably into the twenty-first century.

The Best of Times, The Worst of Times

The 1980s was a decade of stark contrasts: the billionaire Donald Trump (a tower, an airline, a casino, a best-selling book, even a board game) and a homeless person, living on the street and begging for change. In the 1980s the gap between poor and rich widened, largely because Reagan's policies reduced spending on social programs for poor people while putting tax-cut money in the pockets of the wealthy. Wage earners were on a treadmill, often working harder just to stay even financially. The population became even more diverse, as more immigrants entered the United States than at any time since the 1920s. Popular culture and technology increasingly reflected global trends, and AIDS touched off a medical crisis that transcended national boundaries.

The Second Gilded Age

Wealth, ostentation, and an unabashed glorification of material success set the tone for much of the 1980s. Corporate leaders such as Chrysler's Lee Iacocca or real estate developer Donald Trump, whose best-selling autobiographies detailed "the art of the deal," became popular icons.

Much of the action took place on Wall Street, which promoted unlimited riches and opportunities reminiscent of the bull market of the 1920s. Instead of investing venture capital to start new companies or increase the productivity of existing ones, investment bankers devised ways to make money through *paper entrepreneurship*. In these innovative and intricate financial arrangements—especially leveraged buyouts and managerial buybacks—existing corporations assumed heavy debt loads to acquire other companies or buy back their own stock. (These debt loads, manageable in the still-expanding economy of the 1980s, led to downsizing and bankruptcy as profits began to shrink in 1990 and beyond.) Most of these deals were initiated by the investment banking departments of established brokerage firms such as Shearson Lehman or Drexel Burnham Lambert, which made extraordinary profits. So did many corporate executives. Middle-level managers and assembly-line workers, however, might find themselves out of a job as the companies they worked for were taken over or restructured.

Much of this activity was fueled by *junk bonds*. Corporations and governments routinely sell bonds to investors to raise capital for various purposes, promising to pay interest and repay principal over a fixed period of time. The likelihood that the seller will make good on this promise depends on its stability and assets. Junk bonds were issued by relatively unstable corporations. To compensate bond buyers (lenders) for the higher risk, the sellers promised to return higher rates of interest than traditional—and safer—investments. Until the 1980s, few investors would buy such volatile, high-risk bonds, but they became central to many of the mergers, leveraged buyouts, and buybacks that restructured corporate America. So much in demand were these new paper investments that "junk bond king" Michael Milken of Drexel Burnham Lambert received $550 million compensation in 1987 alone.

As the 1980s went on, corporate deal-making and acquisition frenzy reached new heights. In 1985 there were eighteen separate deals for $1 billion or more, most financed by junk bonds. Capital Cities Communication bought ABC, General Electric bought RCA, and Philip Morris acquired General Foods. The tobacco company R. J. Reynolds bought Nabisco, becoming the largest consumer product company in the United States. Three years later the merged RJR Nabisco itself would be acquired for $25 billion, in a Wall Street deal that

Lifestyles of the Rich and Famous
Trump Tower in midtown Manhattan (named for its flamboyant developer, Donald Trump, a.k.a. "the Donald") catered to the super rich, the just plain wealthy, and the rest of us, who gawked at its ostentatious displays of conspicuous consumption.

came to symbolize the rapaciousness and greed of such corporate takeovers.

In 1986 financier Ivan Boesky told graduates of the University of California's business school at Berkeley, "I think greed is healthy. You can be greedy and still feel good about yourself." But there was something disturbing about young Wall Street traders making $200,000 or more a year, or executives voting themselves million-dollar *golden parachutes* (severance pay deals negotiated just before corporate restructuring or takeovers cost them their jobs). It turned out that some of the financial activities of the 1980s were illegal as well as unseemly: soon Boesky was jailed for *insider trading* (making advantageous trades based on information not yet made public) and Michael Milken for securities fraud. By decade's end the most excessive aspects of the "casino society" had run their course, although the long-term impact was just beginning to emerge.

That the rich had indeed been getting richer in the Reagan years was confirmed by Congressional Budget Office statistics, which showed that the richest *1 percent* of American families reaped most of the gains of the decade's prosperity. The country's wealthiest 666,000 families accounted for 60 percent of the growth in average after-tax income of all American families between 1977 and 1989—and 77 percent of the rise in average pre-tax income. The top quintile (fifth) saw a 29 percent increase in pre-tax income over that

period. Economists debate the causes for the shift, with some stressing reduced tax rates for the wealthy and others pointing to factors like higher returns on capital gains and the explosion of executive pay. But the trend was clear—increasing concentration of riches at the top and growing inequality, the first significant widening of the gap since the 1920s.

The Struggling Middle Class

The Michelob beer slogan, "You can have it all," summed up the lifestyles of the fast-track, young, definitely upwardly mobile segment of society that the media dubbed "Yuppies" (young urban professionals). The Yuppies, with their BMWs, Perrier water, expense account lunches, and aggressive networking, captured the attention of advertisers and marketing directors because of their high disposable incomes and propensity to spend conspicuously. Yuppies were sometimes confused with the whole baby-boom generation, but this affluent set constituted only 5 percent of their age group. Far more baby boomers were confronting the realization that they would not necessarily do better than their parents, a startling slap to a generation raised in the affluence and optimism of the 1950s and 1960s.

Despite the apparent economic booms in the mid-1970s and throughout the 1980s, real income has stagnated since the early 1970s. The typical family saw only a 4 percent rise in pretax income between 1977 and 1989, while households in the bottom 40 percent saw their incomes decline in constant dollars. The federal tax cuts of the Reagan years did less to help middle-income taxpayers, who often saw their overall tax liability rise, as state and local taxes and payroll deductions for Social Security and other benefits increased steadily. (The surplus revenue accumulated for Social Security, which collects more than it currently pays out, was used in part to finance the deficit.) Soon many lower-income wage earners were paying more into Social Security than for federal income taxes.

In part, the stagnation in personal income was linked to broad trends, such as deindustrialization and the shift to a service economy (see Chapter 32), which decreased the number of blue-collar and white-collar jobs. Between 1954 and 1982, half of the 10,000 factories in Chicago shut down, a loss of 400,000 jobs. In their place were service jobs in supermarkets, fast-food outlets, check-cashing establishments, and the like, most at the low end of the pay scale. A hamburger flipper at Burger King or a security guard at a downtown office building did not earn enough to support a family. As a result, many households became dependent on two incomes. Some 70 percent of female baby boomers were in the workforce, compared to 30 percent of their mothers at that age. Some households became "three-income families," with one worker holding down a second job. Many also relied heavily on high levels of consumer debt (borrowing and buying on credit).

For certain occupations, a two-tiered compensation system appeared. To cut costs, and undercut the power of labor unions, companies hired new workers at lower wages than senior workers performing similar jobs. This strategy, along with overly stressful working conditions and other issues, led to the 1981 walkout of three-quarters of the nation's air controllers, who supervise takeoffs and landings at airports. In response, President Reagan fired all the strikers and destroyed their union, the Professional Air Traffic Controllers Organization (PATCO). Reagan's get-tough stance signaled the business community that it was okay to be anti-union. The labor movement, also facing dwindling membership due to the loss of blue-collar jobs, struggled to maintain its influence in the unfavorable economic climate of the 1980s.

Poverty in the 1980s

Here is a snapshot of poverty in America at the end of the 1980s: in 1989 about 31.5 million Americans, or 12.8 percent of the population, were classified by federal standards as poor, that is, their income was below $12,675 for a family of four. Many of the poor were employed, but at low wages. American poverty had racial variations: 10 percent of whites were poor, compared to 26 percent of Hispanics and 30 percent of blacks. Poverty was most common among families headed by women, who were often disadvantaged in the job market by their lack of skills, need for part-time jobs, or the scarcity of affordable child care. Nearly 40 percent of America's poor were children under eighteen, half of whom lived in female-headed households; one child in five, and two-thirds of all black children, would receive Aid to Families with Dependent Children (AFDC) payments at some point. By contrast, the elderly, who used to be among the poorer segments of the population, were relatively better off, thanks in part to Social Security and Medicare.

In many cities, Americans who did not have a roof over their heads at night became increasingly visible on the streets. Of course, there had been homeless people before. Called tramps or bums, they were usually white, middle-aged alcoholics. The 1980s homeless were far more diverse. Some were former mental patients who had been released as part of the 1960s movement toward deinstitutionalization. Some were drug addicts. Others ended up on the streets when loss of a job or cutbacks in social service and disability benefits reduced their ability to pay rent or a mortgage installment. Some were employed but earned too little for both food and rent. Men predominated, but there were growing num-

The Homeless
The majority of homeless people on the nation's streets and sidewalks were men, but the number of homeless women and children has increased. Their needs for health care, housing, and education put demands on already stretched city budgets.

bers of homeless women and children, their shifting locations and disrupted lives a challenge to urban school systems.

This problem was exacerbated by the lack of low-cost housing in the nation's cities. Urban renewal projects often demolished dilapidated but still liveable housing, replacing it with civic complexes and shiny office projects. SRO (single-room occupancy) rooming houses, which had provided cheap temporary or long-term housing for the poor, were often demolished as well. Construction of subsidized public housing failed to keep pace with the growing need for affordable apartments in urban America.

The Two Worlds of Black America

Until the 1960s, African-American neighborhoods had a mix of middle-class professionals, working-class members, and the poor. The civil rights revolution and affirmative action programs opened many doors for blacks to leave inner-city neighborhoods: armed with an improved education, a number of African-Americans secured business and professional jobs and were able to afford to move to suburban neighborhoods no longer closed by segregation. As upwardly mobile blacks moved out, so did black-owned businesses and the extensive family networks that had given stability to the community. Inner-city ghettoes deteriorated so badly after the 1960s in part because so many of their inhabitants found better lives elsewhere. They also deteriorated because of federal inaction. The peak of federal attention to urban areas occurred between 1964 and 1972; since then, but especially under Reaganomics, inner-city problems have been a low priority.

By the 1980s joblessness was a way of life, two-parent households scarce, and social contacts outside of the neighborhood rare for ghetto inhabitants. At the heart of the problem was the inability to find productive work. Unemployment rates rose as high as 60 percent, in part for demographic reasons: inner cities had a far larger proportion of young people than the general population, due to a higher birthrate and overall younger age of childbearing. Cities had too few entry-level jobs, and most of the inner cities' unemployed lacked the training to qualify for better-paying jobs.

Social scientists use the term *underclass* to describe people in the inner cities, often minorities, who lack resources to escape poverty and are cut off from mainstream society. Noted one social scientist, "venturing outside the neighborhood is like going to Mars." In the 1980s, conditions for young black men in urban areas became so bad that one sociologist called them "an endangered species." Black men were much more likely to be high school dropouts, unemployed, addicted to alcohol or drugs, or in prison than any other group. Especially disturbing was the homicide rate for black men, six times that for white men, and so high that the life expectancy of African-American men and women has been declining since 1986.

The struggles of black teenage mothers run on a parallel track. With so many black men unemployed or absent from the community, many black women do not marry, instead bearing and raising children on their own. In 1965, 26 percent of all black children were born out of wedlock. In 1989 this figure reached 66 percent. Most unmarried first-time mothers were teenagers, and virtually all dropped out of school while pregnant, leaving them unskilled and therefore unemployable, which contributed to the ongoing poverty of female-headed households.

By the 1980s the historical tide of black migration from the South that had begun in World War I was receding. Southern blacks who learned of the poor job prospects were less likely to seek new lives in urban areas; quite the contrary, anyone who could was leaving the inner cities, usually for a more stable neighborhood or to the suburbs. Some blacks were even making a re-

verse migration back to the South. Compared to living in a crime-ridden and dilapidated northern housing project, conditions in the post-civil rights South seemed attractive. From the Mississippi Delta to Chicago and back to Mississippi, all in one lifetime—what could say more about how the "promised land" of migration had failed?

In April 1992 the frustration and anger of impoverished black Americans erupted in five days of riots in Los Angeles, the worst civil disorders since the 1960s. The rioting was set off by the acquittal on all but one charge of four white Los Angeles police officers accused of using excessive force when arresting a black motorist, Rodney King, on March 3, 1991. The predominantly white jury was not swayed by a graphic 81-second amateur video of the arrest, which showed the officers kicking, clubbing, and beating King. The video, which was shown repeatedly on television, brought renewed attention to the issue of police brutality and the harassment of minorities. Three months later, the officers were indicted on federal charges of violating King's civil rights.

The violence in South-Central Los Angeles took sixty lives and caused $850 million in damage. A shaken Rodney King went on television to plead, "Can we all get along?" But when the fires were finally extinguished and order restored, the conditions in the central cities, as well as the racism that contributed to and perpetuated them, remained.

To Live and Die in L.A.
The images from South-Central Los Angeles in the wake of the 1992 riots looked eerily similar to those from Watts in 1965. The underlying causes were similar as well—police brutality, racism, and frustration about lack of jobs and opportunity.

Toward a Pluralistic Society

The 1990 census counted 246.9 million Americans. By far the most dramatic shift since the 1980 census was the changing racial composition of the United States. In 1990 one in four Americans had African, Asian, Hispanic, or American Indian ancestry, up from one in five just ten years earlier. In retrospect, the 1980s may emerge as a watershed decade in the emergence of the United States as a fully pluralistic society.

In the 1980s over 7 million immigrants entered the country, accounting for more than a third of the population growth in that decade. LAX and JFK, the Los Angeles and New York airports, were the main points of entry, not Ellis Island, which, after decades of abandonment and decay, was turned into a museum and tourist attraction. In the first major immigration legislation since 1965, the 1986 Immigration Reform and Control Act (Simpson-Mazzoli) attempted to establish a fair entry process. It also granted legal status to some illegal aliens, primarily Mexicans and other Latinos, who had entered the United States before 1982. Revisions to the law in 1990 expanded the number of immigrants allowed to enter, and gave priority to skilled workers and reunifying families.

Hispanic Immigration. A major component of the new immigration was from Latin America and the Caribbean. The terms *Hispanic* or *Latino*, which cover various Spanish-speaking groups from Mexico, Cuba, Puerto Rico, El Salvador, and other Latin American countries, represent a variety of distinctive heritages. Hispanics are the second largest minority group after blacks, and the second fastest growing, after Asians. Western states like California, Texas, and New Mexico, which border on Mexico, originally contained the most Hispanic immigrants, but in the postwar period Latinos from Puerto Rico, and Central and South America increasingly settled on the East Coast. Hispanics now live in urban areas throughout the country, making up one-tenth of the populations of Florida and New York, for example.

Asian-Americans. Asia was the other major source of immigration. The major components of this migration, which increased almost 108 percent from 1980 to 1990, were Chinese, Filipino, Vietnamese, Laotian, Cambodian, Korean, Pakistani, and Asian Indian. California had more Asian-Americans, almost 10 percent of the population, than any other state. Chinese-Americans are still the dominant Asian group in the United States, followed by Filipinos.

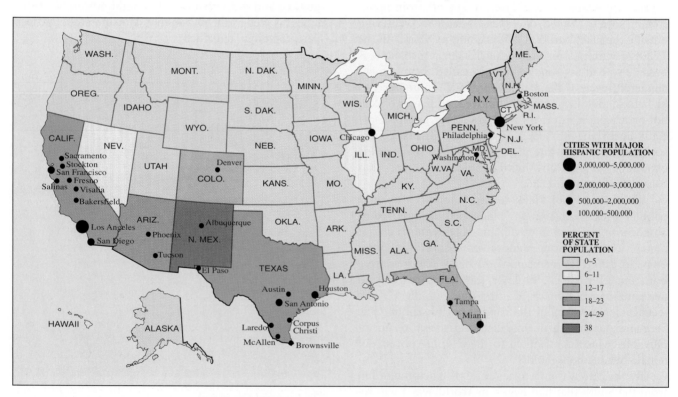

MAP 33.2

American Hispanic Population, 1990

The Hispanic population of the United States is concentrated in California, New York, Texas, Florida, and Illinois, mainly in urban areas. Hispanic Americans are the second largest minority group, after African-Americans.

AMERICAN VOICES

L.A. Journal *Rubén Martínez*

Rubén Martínez, born and raised in Los Angeles to Mexican and Salvadoran parents, describes himself as a member of the generation "that arrived too late for Che Guevara and too early for the fall of the Berlin Wall." Here he compares daily life in Los Angeles with San Salvador's state of siege.

June 1991

Was that a shotgun? In answer, a series of pops . . . a small automatic? I crouch by the window, look into the hazy balmy night. Mute buildings. Now, from afar, another sound begins, like the whine of a mosquito in the darkness of a stifling room in the tropics. The whine becomes a roar that rattles the windows. A shaft of light pours down from the sky. Sirens shriek in the distance. They come closer . . . closer: patrol cars race up the avenue.

I am not in San Salvador, I tell myself. Those are not soldiers down there, bursting through doors to ransack the apartments of high school kids who participated in a protest march . . . Y is okay, she works for a human rights organization in Los Angeles, she's not FMLN in San Salvador anymore, this is Los Angeles, not San Salvador, this is 1991, not 1979, this is gang strife, not civil war. I don't believe myself. Images past and present merge: It is 1979 and 1991 and San Salvador and Los Angeles and gang strife and civil war all at once.

When the helicopters thud-thud-thud-thud fades away, I light a cigarette. Did the bullets find their mark in a rival gangster, a three-year-old's skull? I wait for the ambulance's siren, but the neighborhood remains quiet. The bullets found nothing but the night, as though the night itself were both target and victim of the desperate rage that led the finger to pull on the trigger.

I return to my post next to the computer, in my Echo Park apartment (my latest stop in search of a home) whose living room holds my altar. Amidst votive candles and before a crucifix, I've gathered together objects from the living and the dead: a wallet-sized photo of Y, her stare questioning me across the distance of our latest— and final?—separation; on a cassette sleeve, a photo of Mexico City kids who look like a cross between Irish idealists U2 and the street toughs of *Los Olvidados*; a black-and-white snapshot of a graffiti artist cradling his brutally scarred arm, result of an evening when the bullets did find their mark; a brittle, yellowed leaf from Palm Sunday at La Placita, where Father Luis Olivares showered the thousands of Mexicanos and Centroamericanos surrounding him with holy water; the embossed card that says that one Fidel Castro Ruz, *Presidente del Consejo de Estado y del Gobierno de la República de Cuba*, requests my presence at a reception; a rather ugly postcard entitled "La Frontera, Tijuana, BC," that shows an antiseptic-clean highway on one side and a labyrinth of dusty paths on the other . . . shards of my identity . . . .

This jumble of objects is as close as I get to "home." As close as I get, because my home is L.A. and L.A. is an anti-home; that's why I've left it so many times, and returned just as many. Taking to the road, I've crossed and recrossed the border heading south and north—trying to put things back into place the way they were before . . . before what? The civil war? My grandfather's heart attacks? The gangland massacres? My father's alcoholism, the Latin American dictatorships, my first failed love, the treaty of Guadalupe Hidalgo?

I turn off the overhead light so that the candle flame transforms the shadow of the crucifix on the wall into a pair of wavering, reaching arms. I gaze upon the photos of my late grandparents. This is my history, I tell myself. "This is my home," I whisper, looking out through the window again at the avenues of Echo Park, which are now as deserted and tense as any in San Salvador during a state of siege. . . .

Source: Rubén Martínez, The Other Side: Fault Lines, Guerilla Saints, and the True Heart of Rock 'n' Roll (Verso: London and New York, 1992), 165–66.

Much of this immigration was traceable to the upheavals in Southeast Asia. More than 700,000 Indochinese refugees came in the decade after American involvement in Vietnam ended in 1975. The first of these refugees were highly educated, and after a few years they generally achieved economic success. Many of the later refugees, however, who came with less education and fewer skills, struggled for a foothold in new Indochinese neighborhoods that developed in places such as Arlington, Virginia, or Lowell, Massachusetts. When the Cambodian population in that former textile town increased from 3,500 in 1985 to 20,000 just three years later, local resources were strained, and the school system struggled to find bilingual teachers fluent in Khmer, the Cambodian language.

Asian-Americans are often referred to as a "model minority" for the educational and professional success achieved by many of their members. Yet this label masks their enormous diversity. They have also been subjected to racial slurs and blatant discrimination, often because people feared their success. Informal quotas, especially in college admissions, recall the similar expressions of anti-Semitism as late as the 1950s.

Ethnic Diversity. The new immigration has already affected the social, economic, and cultural landscape of the country. Thriving ethnic enclaves are one example: Little Saigon in Orange County, California; Little Havana in Miami; Koreatown in Los Angeles. Tens of thousands of Soviet Jews fleeing religious and political persecution created "Little Odessa" in Brooklyn, New York. At least 300 periodicals serve immigrant readers—*Nguoi Viet* in California, *La Voz de Houston* in Texas, and *Korea Times* in Queens, New York. Koreans have purchased and revitalized corner grocery stores in New York City, Los Angeles, and Washington, D.C. People from the Indian subcontinent manage small hotel chains in California, and Vietnamese now dominate the Gulf of Mexico shrimp fishing industry in Texas.

Occasionally, these newcomers have been the victims of racial altercations and conflicts. In 1982, Chinese-American Vincent Chin was beaten to death in a Detroit bar by two unemployed autoworkers, who apparently thought he was Japanese and thus a symbol of the foreign competition they believed had cost them their jobs. Several states have passed referendums to make English the official state language, a slap at the increasing use of bilingual documents, particularly to aid Spanish-speakers. Blacks have boycotted Korean-owned grocery stores, expressing the tensions between blacks still trapped in the nation's inner cities and more recent arrivals struggling to get ahead, and often succeeding. In the 1992 riots in Los Angeles, black protesters particularly targeted Korean-owned stores for arson and looting.

In contradiction to widespread fear that immigrants will strain resources and take jobs from American-born workers, economists generally believe that immigrants give more than they take. They provide a fresh source of predominantly youthful and highly motivated workers, who either take jobs that are not wanted by other people or move into new jobs in the growing service sector. They also create jobs to meet their own needs, such as *bodegas* in Hispanic neighborhoods, or travel agencies to facilitate family visits to and from the former homeland. To show good will toward the communities in which they set up small businesses, Koreans and other immigrant entrepreneurs may hire local workers and join neighborhood organizations.

Mainstream advertisers and producers are only now beginning to tap the huge consumer market represented by this increasingly multiracial society. For example, the major cosmetics companies have begun to sell cosmetics for darker complexions, a market previously monopolized by black-run companies. The process works the other way as well, as ethnic products, especially foods, enter the national market. New food treats such as stir-fry cooking, tacos, pita pockets, jalapeño peppers, and tofu have enriched the American palate, and the diversity of American life.

Health Care Costs and the Challenge of AIDS

The United States spends more on health care than any other country, and yet many citizens feel the health-care system is in crisis. By the late 1980s, nearly 12 percent of the gross national product went to health care, and the percentage was climbing, mainly due to what one journalist has called "the medical technology arms race." More and more, newspapers covered medical breakthroughs the way they did sports or local politics.

The United States is the only major industrialized country that does not provide national health insurance, in part because of the New Deal's decision not to push for a federal health care program in the 1930s. Instead, health care is financed primarily through group medical insurance provided by employers. This system has proven inadequate on several counts. With their employment-based benefits vulnerable to layoffs and corporate takeovers, workers avoided changing jobs because they or their families feared losing their medical coverage, a situation referred to by economists as "job lock." Spiraling medical costs (double the rate of inflation since 1970) and rising premiums stretched employ-

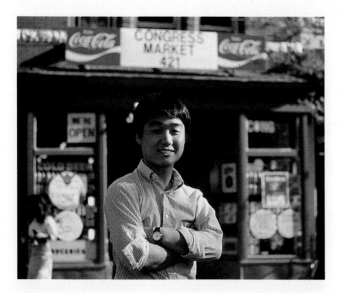

New Immigrants
In the 1980s many Korean immigrants got their start by opening small grocery stores in urban neighborhoods. Their success sometimes led to conflict with other racial groups, such as blacks and Hispanics, who were often their customers as well as competitors.

ers' ability to pay; a growing number of companies, often small businesses, fail to provide any health insurance to their workers. From the business perspective, health care was devouring profits just when those profits were shrinking in a competitive global economy.

About 35 million Americans, more than one-sixth of the population, had no health insurance in 1990, and many feared being bankrupted by a medical emergency or illness. Especially at risk were workers who had been unemployed for extended periods of time and individuals with preexisting medical conditions that made them ineligible for coverage. Rising costs put private health insurance out of the reach of many individuals. Only the very poorest Americans qualify for Medicaid, which despite vast expenditures fails to provide adequate medical services, especially for more cost-effective preventive care.

As medical costs escalated in the 1980s, health care became a political issue. Federal, state, and local governments now pay more than 40 percent of the nation's $600 billion yearly tab for health care. Economists fear that if costs are not brought under control, health spending will adversely affect national prosperity. Yet neither politicians nor medical administrators have found ways to reduce the costs of sophisticated, and ever more expensive, new medical equipments and procedures and a system that provides little incentive to control costs, since insurers and the government pay most of the bills. The goals are clear—universal access, reasonable cost, and top-quality care—but the means remain elusive.

AIDS. The AIDS epidemic, one of the most pressing medical and social issues of our times, and one with vast political implications as well, exemplifies the problems afflicting the American health-care system. Acquired Immune Deficiency Syndrome (AIDS) was first recognized in 1981. Its cause was soon identified as the human immunodeficiency virus (HIV), which weakens the immune system, causing infected persons to succumb to secondary infections such as pneumonia or the skin cancer known as Kaposi's Sarcoma. (HIV is transmitted through the exchange of infected body fluids, such as semen and blood.) Already about 18 million people worldwide are affected; most will experience lengthy debilitating illness and eventual death. By the year 2000, researchers project, more than 24 million people will have died from AIDS.

Initially, little organized action or government funding was directed to AIDS research or treatment, and critics charged that this reflected conservative antipathy toward homosexual men, who were the disease's earliest victims. AIDS began to gain public attention only when it became clear that heterosexuals, such as hemophiliacs who received the virus through blood transfusions, were affected as well. The October 1985 announcement of the death from AIDS of film star

Rock Hudson, who had hidden his sexual orientation to maintain his Hollywood career, finally broke through the barriers of public apathy.

Many members of the gay community organized early on, but others were slow to respond to the implications of AIDS. Throughout the 1970s, the gay community's increased visibility and political clout, especially in New York and San Francisco, had been accompanied by a pattern of high-risk sexual practices that contributed to the spread of HIV infection. When it became clear that the disease was being transmitted through frequent casual sexual contacts, some were quick to advocate "safe-sex" practices, such as the use of condoms, which succeeded in slowing the spread of AIDS; others, however, balked at relinquishing their hard-won sexual freedoms.

After mid-decade, AIDS cases increased among heterosexuals, especially intravenous drug addicts and their sexual partners, as well as bisexuals. Especially tragic was the transmission of AIDS to infants by infected mothers. The marginal status of these new victims, often members of the urban underclass, did not command attention from the federal health establishment. The controversial advocacy group, ACT-UP (AIDS Coalition to Unleash Power), has found dramatic ways to confront drug manufacturers, politicians, and others in an effort to gain attention and funding. Caring for AIDS patients will put an even greater financial strain on the American health care system.

A few drugs such as AZT have been developed to delay the onset and reduce the severity of symptoms. There are blood tests to screen blood for transfusions and detect the HIV virus in infected individuals. But no cure or vaccine is in sight. The barriers are as much political and bureaucratic as medical. Many non-urban Americans see the AIDS epidemic as one more expres-

ACT UP

This poster *Untitled*, 1989 by artist Keith Haring for the group ACT UP (AIDS Coalition to Unleash Power) tries to mobilize public action against the deadly disease, which would later claim Haring's life. (© Estate of Keith Haring)

sion of big-city decay. Federal red tape, and prohibitive expense, have limited the distribution of AZT and other medications. Already more Americans have died of AIDS than were killed in the Korean and Vietnam wars combined. The toll, in the United States and throughout the world, continues to rise.

Popular Culture and Popular Technology

Image was everything in the 1980s, or so commentators said, pointing to rock stars Michael Jackson and Madonna, and even to President Ronald Reagan. One strong influence on the images of the decade was MTV, which premiered in 1981. With its creative choreography, flashy colors, and rapid cuts, it seemed a perfect fit to the short attention spans of the TV generation raised on shows such as "Sesame Street." The MTV style soon showed up in mainstream advertising, network television shows like "Miami Vice," and even political campaigns. The national newspaper *USA Today*, which debuted in 1982, adapted the style, featuring flashy graphics, color photographs, and short, easy-to-read articles. Soon more staid newspapers followed suit.

New technology shaped television, especially with satellite transmission and live "mini-cam" broadcasting. Also new was the increased availability of cable channels. In the 1950s, Americans had only three networks to choose from; public television did not debut until 1967. By the end of the 1980s, such upstarts as Ted Turner's all-news CNN (Cable News Network), ESPN's all-sports channel, and the Fox network were challenging the major networks for viewers and profits.

Media, communications, and entertainment were big business, increasingly drawn into global financial networks and markets. Corporate mergers and takeovers reshaped these industries, as ownership of several entertainment conglomerates and major Hollywood studios passed into foreign, often Japanese, hands. In 1987, Sony acquired Columbia Pictures and CBS Records; in 1990 the consumer electronics firm Matsushita agreed to acquire MCA Inc., a large entertainment company, whose subsidiaries included theme parks, Universal Studios, recordings, and a talent agency. As manufacturers of "hardware" such as stereo components and VCRs, these investors saw a competitive advantage if they also produced "software" such as recordings and films to be used with that technology. This strategy reflected a widespread business belief, evident in the 1989 merger of Time Inc. and Warner Communications, that sheer size enhanced competitive ability in a global economy. Japanese companies acquired U.S. ones not from a desire to take over the American entertainment industry, but because certain American companies wanted to sell and others failed to bid. As Sony chairman Akio Morita put it, "If you don't want Japan to buy it, then don't sell it."

Technology also entered, and reshaped, the home. The 1980s saw the introduction of compact disc players, cellular phones, personal computers, and fax (facsimile) machines. By the end of the decade the vast majority of Americans had one or more of the new electronic toys. In 1990, for example, more than half of American households had a videocassette recorder (VCR). At first Hollywood feared decreasing box office admissions, but soon found that VCR's created a large new market for recent films, as well as for home videos. Video was everywhere—stores, elevators, airplanes, tennis courts, operating rooms. With the introduction of camcorders, the family photo album was supplanted by the video of the high school graduation, marriage, or birth. Personal computers, led by Apple's Macintosh and IBM's PC, enabled individual users to do everything from desktop publishing to tracking their investments, balancing checkbooks, and writing textbooks. Computers also made it possible to run a business from home or, with a fax machine and a telephone, to work at home and still be connected to an office.

The implications of this technology and communications revolution are staggering. When Federal Express and the U.S. Postal Service first introduced overnight deliveries, business practices changed, as people expected a response the next day instead of a week later. Then fax machines made possible instant communication with every corner of the world; now people expect a response the very same day. With cellular phones, business executives and sales representatives no longer fear being out of touch, whether driving on the freeway, flying across the country, or just walking down the street. Only a few voices questioned the stress and intensification that came with this new information technology. Most learned to live with it, and soon felt they could not live without it.

The End of the Eighties

The trends that characterize a decade are not always confined neatly to a ten-year period, and some of the images associated with the 1980s began to wane several years before the decade ended. The slipping popularity of television shows about the rich and fashionable, such as "Dallas" and "Dynasty," suggested a shift in values. Tom Wolfe's exposé of the moral bankruptcy of Wall Street, *The Bonfire of the Vanities* (1987), seemed remarkably prescient when the stock market fell 508 points on Black Monday, October 19, 1987. After the crash, some 15,000 Wall Street employees lost their jobs, and the investment firm Drexel Burnham Lambert declared bankruptcy. In the wake of the convictions of Ivan Boesky and Michael Milken, the world of investment banking suddenly seemed less appealing. Within a few years, Donald Trump's financial empire was on the verge of bankruptcy.

NEW TECHNOLOGY *The Electronic Office*

The 1980s witnessed an explosion in office and communications technology, as the early, bulky mainframe computers were replaced by more compact and efficient models.

The big breakthrough came from the upstart Apple Computer Company. Two young tinkerers and hobbyists, Steve Jobs and Steve Wozniak, operating from a bedroom and garage in Palo Alto, California, and using the $1,300 proceeds from the sale of an old Volkswagen, built the first easy-to-use, small, inexpensive computer. They achieved a runaway engineering and marketing success in 1977, when they offered the Apple II personal computer for only $1,195.

Belatedly, other companies scrambled to get into the market. IBM, already a leader in producing tabulating machines and mainframe computers for business and government, offered its first personal computer, the IBM PC, in the summer of 1981. Competition between IBM, Apple, and other low-cost models kept prices affordable, and by 1990 a quarter of American homes had at least one personal computer. But its greatest impact was on business. More than any other technological advance, the personal computer created the electronic office of today. Even the smallest business could keep all its records, do all its correspondence and billing, and run its own direct-mail advertising campaigns from a single desktop machine.

Personal computers' ability to store massive amounts of data increased every year. Small file boxes of floppy disks can now hold a decade's worth of business records, while optical disks can hold not only as many words as an encyclopedia but pictures and sounds as well. Optical disks are at the heart of CD-ROM (Compact Disk–Read Only Memory) multimedia systems, in which text, graphics, animation, video, music, and voice can be linked into one presentation. Many architects, engineers, and designers now use computer-aided design (CAD) software, which shows drawings in three dimensions on the screen, to design buildings, automobiles, clothing, and other products on their desktop computers.

Computers rely on *digital* technology, essentially a vast array of on-off switches. Today there are a host of other digital devices—modems, laser printers, cellular telephones, and fax machines—and all are able to be linked by wired and wireless communications. Fiber-optic cables, microwave relays, and satellites can transmit massive quantities of information to and from almost

The electronic office of today has simplified arduous tasks. Here six people work on a car design using computer imaging in this "Capture Lab."

any place on earth, and even from space. Business people and scholars can readily study enormous databases of information, such as periodicals, specialized reference works, and government statistics, or they can get the latest financial information from the world's stock markets. The very structure of the office is changing, as people are able to work at home and "telecommute" via computer and fax machine. But there are perils in such easy exchanges of information, too. In particular, concerns have grown about protecting sensitive electronic files, such as credit and medical records and corporate financial data, from unauthorized users.

Computers have replaced much tedious work, as well as many unskilled workers who performed drudge jobs. They have created new jobs that require more education and new skills, and spawned entire new industries. Overall there has been a gain in number of jobs, productivity, and economic growth—despite the loss of low-skill, entry-level jobs. The electronic office of today and the workplace of the future belong to those who come prepared—prepared with current skills, and prepared to retrain as often as necessary during a career lifetime that is certain to see ever more technological change and challenge.

By the late 1980s, a new social mood was becoming evident. Jay McInerney's Yuppie classic, *Bright Lights, Big City* (1984), was transformed into a 1988 movie version only after "laser surgery" (as one studio executive put it) cut down the drug use in the plot. What caused the turnaround? Cocaine, the "drug of choice" for fast trackers, was not as harmless as many had believed. The appearance in mid-decade of crack, a highly addictive form of cocaine, took a deadly toll, especially in the inner cities where it led to an increase in drug-related violence.

The declining appeal of drugs ("Just say 'no,'" Nancy Reagan told the country) was part of adults' general rejection of chemicals and other stimulants, such as cigarettes and alcohol. (Drug use declined among teenagers as well, while smoking and drinking increased.) Widespread bans on smoking in public areas reduced cigarette smoking to an outdoor activity practiced furtively during breaks from work or classes. Fearing melanoma and clogged arteries, Americans also avoided excessive suntanning and high cholesterol. A "new prohibitionism" attacked alcohol consumption, causing wineries and distilleries to worry how to maintain consumption while allaying public fears. The "designated driver" was one solution; label warnings against alcohol consumption by pregnant women was another.

In sexual matters, Americans seemed to be saying "no" to the casual experimentation of the preceding decades. Here the AIDS crisis was central. Campaigns promoting safe sex and the fear of sexually transmitted diseases made many people more cautious about whom they slept with, and how often. Hedonism was out, monogamy—and even celibacy—was in.

Also at the end of the eighties came sexual scandals involving several New Right religious leaders who had been influential in the early Reagan years. First to fall from grace was the PTL (Praise the Lord) television empire of Jim and Tammy Bakker. Reverend Bakker lost his pulpit in March 1987 and ultimately went to jail after admitting he had paid a secretary $265,000 from PTL funds to keep quiet about a sexual relationship. The next year, Reverend Jimmy Swaggart of the Assemblies of God confessed his sin of patronizing prostitutes. While these scandals focused attention on the personal and financial excesses of some television preachers, evangelical religion continued strong.

Beyond the Cold War

"Jack, smile. We won." That's how General Colin Powell, head of the Joint Chiefs of Staff, greeted a glum U.S. NATO commander who remained preoccupied with the Soviet threat in Europe even as it receded and crumbled. The end of the Cold War removed the Soviet Union as America's main ideological enemy, but new post-Cold War challenges quickly appeared. During the Persian Gulf crisis in 1990, President George Bush called for a "new world order . . . in which nations recognize the shared responsibility for freedom and injustice." As events abroad progressed dramatically, especially the end of Soviet hegemony in Eastern Europe in 1989 and the collapse of communism within the Soviet Union itself in 1991, the United States grappled with the implications of this new world order.

The Bush Administration

George Herbert Walker Bush, the first sitting vice-president since Martin Van Buren in 1836 to be elected to the presidency, was no clone of Ronald Reagan. He lacked Reagan's abiding conservativism; in fact, many wondered if he had any ideological vision at all. In the 1988 campaign, Bush promised a "kinder, gentler administration," and announced his intention to go down in history as the education and environment president. Yet the deficit inherited from the Reagan years, along with Bush's own preference for foreign affairs, kept him from articulating a clear domestic agenda.

The 1988 Election. Bush won the Republican nomination by beating back challenges from Senate minority leader Robert Dole, television evangelist Pat Robertson, and tax-cutting representative Jack Kemp. In one of several controversial moves of his candidacy, Bush chose the young conservative Indiana senator Dan Quayle for vice-president. Even many Republicans questioned Quayle's qualifications to assume the duties of president, while Democrats, noting his hawkish views on defense, charged him with hypocrisy for having avoided service in Vietnam by joining the Indiana National Guard.

The early Democratic front runner, Colorado senator Gary Hart, was forced out of the race in early 1988 because of a sex scandal. Another senator, Al Gore of Tennessee, failed to inspire voters with his pro-environment message and withdrew after the New York and Pennsylvania primaries. The remaining primaries became a contest between Massachusetts governor Michael Dukakis and the charismatic civil rights leader Jesse Jackson. Audiences responded enthusiastically to Jackson's populist vision of a "Rainbow Coalition," but he was unable to convince enough Democrats that an African-American candidate could win. Dukakis, a somewhat bland figure known for a technocratic approach to state government, won the nomination. For his vice-president, Dukakis passed over Jackson in favor of Senator Lloyd Bentsen of Texas.

The 1988 campaign had a harsh cast to it, with negative commercials and brief televised *sound bites* replacing discussion of the issues. The sound bite, "Read My

Lips: No New Taxes," became the Republican campaign mantra. The Republicans portrayed the Democrats as liberals (the "L" word) who were unpatriotic, big spenders, soft on crime, and too generous to minorities. A television ad criticizing Massachusetts' prison furlough program pandered to racist fears by including a mug shot of Willie Horton, a black convicted murderer who had committed another murder while on parole. Forced on the defensive, Dukakis failed to mount an effective campaign. Bush carried thirty-eight states, winning the popular vote 54 to 46 percent. Only 50 percent of eligible voters went to the polls.

The Savings and Loan Crisis. The new Bush administration was almost immediately confronted by a major and embarrassing banking scandal. Its roots lay in decisions made during the Reagan administration and before, but its full impact hit only after Bush took office.

Savings and loan associations (S & L's), also called "thrifts," invest their depositors' savings in home mortgages. Since 1934 deposits in S & L's have been insured by the Federal Savings and Loan Insurance Corporation (FSLIC), which is distinct from the Federal Deposit Insurance Corporation (FDIC) established in 1933 to insure accounts in commercial banks. When S & L's complained in 1982 that high inflation and soaring interest rates were reducing their profits, Reagan's deregulation program permitted the thrifts to invest in commercial real estate and businesses. Such investments were more risky than home mortgages, and lack of supervision from Washington encouraged many speculative, and some fraudulent, deals.

For most of the 1980s the real estate market was booming, and so the loans and investments were profitable. But when construction and the Southwest oil boom slowed, and stock prices on Wall Street tumbled sharply in 1987, saving and loan associations losses mounted and the value of their assets plummeted. When the banks lost their depositors' funds, the government had to make good its guarantees to individual depositors. To recoup some of the massive losses, the federal government took over the insolvent banks, and, in 1989, set up a temporary agency to regulate the industry and sell the banks' remaining assets, primarily defaulted real estate. The total bill to American taxpayers is projected at $200 billion.

What was to blame? Reagan's commitment to diminished government regulation and a bullish business climate encouraged high-risk deals. Congress was lax in supervising the banking industry, on which lawmakers depended heavily for campaign contributions. The media had difficulty explaining this dry and technical issue to readers and viewers. Moreover, the public found it hard to grasp the size of the bailout. Only occasionally was there a live "villain" such as Charles Keating, whose failed Lincoln Savings and Loan in California alone added $2.5 billion to the bailout cost.

Economic Agendas. In his 1990 message to Congress, budget director Richard Darman compared the federal budget to Sesame Street's Cookie Monster for its "excessive tendencies towards consumption." The 1985 Gramm-Rudman Act mandated automatic cuts if budget targets were not met in 1991. Facing the prospect of a halt to non-essential government services and layoffs of thousands of government employees, the Congress struggled to produce a deficit-reduction plan. This compromise combined cuts with increased taxes and fees—recognition that the Reagan legacy of lower taxes and higher levels of spending was no longer tenable. Bush was forced, by inevitable circumstances, to break his "no new taxes" campaign promise.

The federal government can run up deficits, but state and local governments cannot. By the early 1990s, they were in bad fiscal shape. Reagan's new federalism had made states and localities responsible for formerly federal programs, but at the same time had cut back on grants to them for housing, education, transportation, public works, and social services. Social problems increased, but funding for services declined. Federal-state programs such as Medicaid, whose costs soared in the 1970s and 1980s due to inflation and higher demand, ate up increasingly large parts of state budgets, as did spending for welfare, education, and prisons. State and local governments could balance their budgets only by finding new sources of revenue (thus risking taxpayer revolts) or by reducing spending and services. Fiscal conditions were especially bad in the Northeast, but California and several other states also faced severe shortfalls.

Recession. A recession began in 1990, further eroding state and local tax revenues. In 1991 unemployment approached 7 percent nationwide; industrial and white-collar layoffs spread, and in many American families someone had either already lost a job or feared it might happen soon. Poverty increased sharply, and incomes declined: according to the Census Bureau, 2.1 million more Americans lived in poverty in 1990 than in 1989. Bankruptcies increased; so did defaults on mortgage payments. Unemployment grew as state and local governments laid off workers to save money, even as they faced greater demands for social services and unemployment compensation. The United States had had eight recessions since World War II, and in each case the economy rebounded within six to sixteen months. But in the early 1990s recovery was slowed by the massive federal debt, overburdened state and local governments, and decreasing consumer confidence.

Supreme Court Conservatism. During the Bush administration, the Supreme Court continued its transformation from liberal activism to a far more conservative stance. Former Supreme Court justice William Brennan used to tell his clerks, "Five votes can do anything

A Woman of Conscience
Accusations by University of Oklahoma professor Anita Hill
that Supreme Court nominee Clarence Thomas had sexually
harassed her sparked fierce political debate. Many felt that if
there had been more women in the Senate, Professor Hill's
charges would have been treated more seriously, and this
played a role in many campaigns in the 1992 election.

around here," and under the leadership of Chief Justice
William Rehnquist, the Court, often by 5–4 margins,
chipped away at the Warren Court legacy in such areas
as individual liberties and the rights of criminal defendants. The conservative shift was especially felt on the
issue of abortion. The 1989 *Webster v. Reproductive
Health Services* decision permitted states to restrict
abortion, and the next year, in *Rust v. Sullivan*, the
Court upheld a federal regulation which forbade personnel at federally funded health clinics from discussing
abortion with their clients. In 1992, in *Planned Parenthood v. Casey*, another 5–4 decision upheld provisions
of a Pennsylvania law mandating a 24-hour waiting period and informed-consent requirements. Yet the Court
also reaffirmed what it called the "essential holding" of
Roe v. Wade: that women have a constitutional right to
abortion.

In Bush's rush to secure a conservative Court,
presumed opposition to abortion became one of the
"litmus tests" for potential nominees. David Souter, a
little-known federal judge from New Hampshire, won
confirmation easily in 1990. Clarence Thomas, a black
conservative with little judicial experience who opposed
affirmative action, had a much harder time in 1991, es-

pecially after former staff member Anita Hill accused
him of sexually harassing her. After widely watched
(and widely debated) televised testimony by both
Thomas and Hill before the all-male Senate Judiciary
Committee, the Senate confirmed Thomas by a narrow
margin. In the wake of the hearings, national polls confirmed the pervasiveness of sexual harassment on the
job: four out of ten women said they had been the object of unwanted sexual advances from men at work.

The Collapse of Communism

The image of young East and West Germans dancing on
the Berlin Wall on November 9, 1989, symbolized the
end of the Cold War. The breaching of this border between the two Germanies culminated in their reunification just one year later. During 1989, communism's grip
on Eastern Europe loosened, then let go completely in a
series of mostly nonviolent "velvet revolutions." For
years, American policymakers had warned about the
"domino" effect of countries falling to communism.
Now the domino effect was unexpectedly working in
the opposite way. Soon the Soviet Union also succumbed to the forces of change.

As modern technology and communications
brought Soviet bloc states into contact with the rest of
the world, the Iron Curtain became increasingly vulnerable. While the people of Eastern Europe experienced
severe food, housing, and fuel shortages, as well as political repression, they saw televised scenes of prosperity
and freedom from the outside world, images which
state-controlled media could not counter. When Poland
started to stir with workers' strikes led by the Solidarity
union, its messages of freedom were spread to the rest
of the Communist bloc by shortwave radios, television,
and telephones. By the end of 1989, Poland had elected
a non-Communist government headed by Solidarity
founder and leader Lech Walesa, and hardline regimes
in East Germany, Bulgaria, Czechoslovakia, and Romania had been toppled. The democratic movements in
these countries quickly demanded and won guarantees
of multiparty elections and more democratic governance. More than anything else, the swiftness of these
changes and their generally peaceful course startled
politicians and diplomats.

The background for the dramatic upheavals in
Eastern Europe lay in the changes set in motion by Soviet president Mikhail Gorbachev, who came to power
in 1985. His policies of *glasnost* (openness) and *pere-
stroika* (economic restructuring) signaled a willingness
to tolerate significant changes in the Soviet bloc and in
Soviet relationships with the rest of the world. The new
openness within the U.S.S.R. exposed severe problems.
The economy was sluggish, the standard of living poor,
and rates of growth had been declining since the 1960s;
agricultural production was so low that the Soviet

AMERICAN VOICES

A Third-Wave Feminist *Laurie Ouellette*

Laurie Ouellette, born in 1966 and educated at the University of Minnesota, represents the generation of women who benefited from the changes set in motion by the revival of feminism but are confused about what feminism means. She considers herself a feminist, but calls on the movement to broaden its vision.

As a member of the first generation of women to benefit from the gains of the '70s women's movement without participating in its struggles, I grew up on the sidelines of feminism—too young to take part in those moments, debates, and events that would define the women's movement but old enough to experience firsthand the societal changes it had wrought.

Ironically, it is due to the modest success of feminism that many young women like myself were raised with an illusion of equality. Like most women my age, I never really thought much about feminism while I was growing up. Looking back, though, I believe it has always influenced me. Growing up with divorced parents, especially a father who was ambivalent about parental responsibilities, probably has much to do with this fact. I was only five when my parents separated in 1971, and I couldn't possibly have imagined or understood the ERA marches or the triumphal result of *Roe v. Wade* that would make history in just a few short years. Certainly I couldn't have defined the word *feminism*. Still, watching my mother struggle emotionally and financially as a single parent made the concept of gender injustice painfully clear, teaching

me a lesson that would follow me always.

It was at the University of Minnesota that I first took an interest in feminist classics like *The Feminine Mystique, Sisterhood Is Powerful,* and *Sexual Politics.* They expressed the anger of an earlier generation that simultaneously captivated me and excluded me. Reading them so long after the excitement of their publication made my own consciousness-raising seem anticlimactic. Like many of my white middle-class friends, I believed that we wouldn't have to worry about issues like discrimination, oppression, and getting stuck in the housewife role. We wondered why we should join forces with a battle for women's equality that the media repeatedly declared was already "won."

My experiences after college made me think again about feminism. A public television internship where I was expected to perform menial secretarial tasks while my male (and, I might add, less experienced) co-interns worked on interesting and challenging projects shocked me into realizing the difficulties facing women in the workplace. Likewise, living in an inner-city neighborhood and being involved in community issues there showed me the dire need for feminism in the lives of the poor women, elderly women, and women of color who were my neighbors. Watching these women, many of them single mothers, struggle daily to find shelter, child care, and food made me realize that they had not been touched at all by the women's movement gains of the '70s. . . .

While the feminist movement of

the '70s focused primarily on getting women into high-paying, powerful occupations and combating sexual discrimination on the job, these issues—while still critical—are not the only goals of feminism. My 24-year-old sister stands out as an example of other routes that feminism must move toward. Whereas I have focused my energies on attending graduate school and working toward a professional career, she has chosen to forfeit similar plans, for now, in favor of marrying young, moving to the country, and raising a family. Does she signify a regression into the homemaker role of the 1950s? On the contrary. For her, issues such as getting midwifery legalized and insured, providing information about breast-feeding to rural mothers, countering the male-dominated medical establishment by using and recommending natural and alternative healing methods, and raising her own daughter with positive gender esteem are central to a feminist agenda.

Only by recognizing and helping to provide choices—both lifestyle and reproductive—for women of all races, economic levels, and ages, as well as supporting all women in their struggles to make those choices, will the women of my generation, the first to be raised in the shadow of feminism and witness its successes and failures, be able to build a successful third wave of the feminist movement.

Source: Laurie Ouellette, "Our Turn Now: Reflections of a 26-Year-Old Feminist," *Utne Reader* (July-August, 1992), 118–20.

Union had to import grain. In addition, the costs of maintaining a vast military and political empire drained the resources of the state.

Gorbachev established strong personal rapport with both presidents Reagan and Bush, and raised enor-

mous expectations worldwide about the possibilities of change within the U.S.S.R. But the Soviet leader soon found it was easier to call for the dismantling of the old system than to build something new. In addition, conflicts among the Soviet republics, some of which were

Gorbachev and Bush
The leaders of the two superpowers, shown here at a press conference during the Malta summit in December 1989 developed a warm personal relationship. Some later felt that Bush delayed reacting to changes in the Soviet Union out of loyalty to his friend.

eager to apply the lessons of Eastern Europe and gain their own independence, threatened the unity of the country. As Gorbachev moved to allow a rudimentary market economy and reduce price subsidies on some basic goods, he was attacked by hardliners who wanted to maintain the status quo and by reformers who wanted to move at once to a totally free market.

The dramatic, and generally peaceful, transfer of power in Eastern Europe, and the hesitant steps toward change within the Soviet Union, encouraged Chinese students in 1989 to undertake their own democratic movement. In June they staged a peaceful protest in central Beijing, only to be violently suppressed when Chinese leader Deng Xiaoping ordered a massive military attack. Troops killed dozens of protesting students who

were camped out in Tiananmen Square and literally crushed the dissent. This harsh crackdown, broadcast live to the rest of the world, put China increasingly out of step with the political and economic loosening taking place everywhere else in the Communist world. George Bush and the rest of the world's leaders took no action against China, however.

In 1990, Soviet president Mikhail Gorbachev was awarded the Nobel Peace Prize for his efforts to restructure the Soviet Union, his introduction of quasi-democratic elections, the withdrawal of Soviet troops from Afghanistan, and his tacit support for the "velvet revolutions" that swept Communist regimes from power in Eastern Europe. But he was more popular outside the Soviet Union than at home. Symbolizing this discrepancy, Gorbachev did not travel to Stockholm to receive the Nobel Prize because events in his country were moving toward a crisis.

On August 19, 1991, while Gorbachev was vacationing at his summer home in the Crimea, officials in his own government attempted to oust him. The precipitating factor was the imminent signing of a Union Treaty that would have given limited autonomy to the fifteen Soviet republics and increased power to the republics' recently elected leaders. The plotters—officials of the Communist party, bureaucrats and overlords of the central economy, and leaders of the internal police force and KGB—stood to lose the most from decentralization. But by August 21, the coup had failed and the grip of the Communist party over the Soviet Union was broken. The Baltic republics of Latvia, Estonia, and Lithuania declared their independence, which was soon recognized by the United States and the rest of the world.

Why did the coup fail? The bland collective behind it had little appeal compared to the new generation of popularly elected leaders, and was unwilling or unable to use brutal force to consolidate its power. The coup's planning was also very disorganized, almost haphazard: "We knew the Communists couldn't do anything right," went one popular joke in Moscow. For example, the

A Defiant Boris Yeltsin
This image of Russian premier Boris Yeltsin defying Soviet authorities in August 1991 was broadcast worldwide and helped to turn the momentum against the coup. The impact of this gesture of individual defiance shows how telecommunications can affect political events.

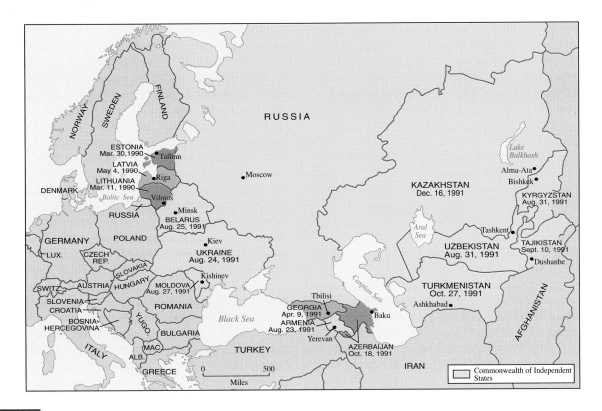

MAP 33.3

The Collapse of Communism in Eastern Europe and the Soviet Union
The end of the Soviet empire in Eastern Europe and the collapse of communism in the
Soviet Union itself dramatically changed the borders of Europe and Central Asia. West
and East Germany reunited, while the nations of Czechoslovakia and Yugoslavia,
created by the 1919 Versailles treaty, divided into smaller states. The old Soviet Union
produced fifteen new countries, of which twelve remained loosely bound in the Confederation of Independent States (CIS).

plotters had ordered 250,000 pairs of handcuffs and
preprinted blank arrest forms, but made no effort to detain the charismatic Boris N. Yeltsin, elected president
of the Russian republic in 1989 and a leader of the
movement for reform. When news of the coup attempt
reached Moscow, Yeltsin defiantly mounted a Soviet
tank to urge citizens to resist. Television coverage of this
dramatic act, carried live throughout the U.S.S.R. and,
indeed the world, solidified resistance. As in Eastern Europe two years earlier, instantaneous global communications fostered political and economic change.

The collapse of the coup left Gorbachev and Yeltsin
uneasily co-leading what remained of the U.S.S.R., but
its days were numbered. The twelve remaining Soviet
republics struggled to find a way to cooperate in some
kind of loose confederation, since none, not even the
Russian republic, was strong enough to go it alone. In
December 1991 the Union of Soviet Socialist Republics
formally dissolved itself to make way for the Commonwealth of Independent States (CIS). Boris Yeltsin remained president of the largest and most populous
Russian republic; Gorbachev was out of a job.

The breakup of the Soviet Union, which was hastened by the needs of long-suppressed ethnic and religious minorities within the republics, sharpened the
focus on ethnic conflict as a threat to international stability. Events within the Soviet Union paralleled the
struggle between Kurds and Shiite Muslims in Iran, the
ethnic and religious disputes in India, the takeover of
Ethiopia by secessionist rebels from Eritrea, and especially the deep internal divisions in former Soviet satellites such as Yugoslavia, which split into several states
in 1991 and soon erupted into a violent civil war.

Economic issues were an even greater challenge.
The end of Soviet domination over Eastern Europe and
the dissolution of the union revealed that the Soviet
economy was in more of a shambles than had been realized. Conversion from state-controlled production to a
free-market economy would not be easy. Leaders of
Russia and former Eastern bloc states turned eagerly to
the West for economic aid, hoping for something similar to the Marshall Plan that had rebuilt Europe after
World War II. Western leaders responded hesitantly,
seeking signs of political stability from the CIS.

The dissolution of the Soviet Union left only one military superpower, the United States. With the end of the Cold War went much of the justification for maintaining permanent mobilization. Americans talked about how the country might spend the *peace dividend*, money that could be saved out of the military budget. Intellectuals, ordinary citizens, and politicians alike faced adjustment to a new climate where communism as a political and ideological force was dead. Nikita Khruschev had told the United States in 1956, "We will bury you." Now the tombstone read, "The Soviet Union, 1917–1991."

War in the Persian Gulf

Even as events in Eastern Europe and the Soviet Union were reshaping Cold War polarities, new challenges were arising in the Middle East. On August 2, 1990, Iraq invaded Kuwait. Saddam Hussein's brutal conquest of his oil-rich neighbor caught American policymakers by surprise, but within days President Bush articulated the position that eventually led to war: "This will not stand, this aggression against Kuwait." Bush orchestrated broad international support for a United Nations Security Council resolution condemning Iraq, calling for its withdrawal, and imposing an embargo and trade sanctions; for emphasis, the United Nations dispatched a multinational force of 150,000 troops to the area. The United Nations was finally working the way its Dumbarton Oaks planners had hoped in 1945, in large part because superpower tensions had abated with the end of the Cold War.

When Saddam Hussein showed no signs of complying with the U.N. resolution, Bush prodded the United Nations to create a legal framework for an international military offensive against the man he repeatedly called "the butcher of Baghdad." On November 29 the Security Council voted to use force if Iraq did not withdraw by January 15. A massive multinational build-up continued; eventually troops, supplies, and pledges of financial support came from thirty-seven countries, including several Arab states but not the Soviet Union. In early January, Congress debated whether to allow sanctions more time to work, then narrowly voted authorization for war. On January 16, President Bush announced to the nation, "the liberation of Kuwait has begun."

The United States commitment of 540,000 troops matched the height of the Vietnam mobilization in 1968. But this was a new, all-volunteer military, which included thousands of reservists called up from their civilian jobs. African-Americans and minorities, many of whom had been attracted to military service by benefits such as education and health care, made up a third of the force. Women, approximately 10 percent of the troops, were a far greater presence than in Vietnam.

Although they served in support, not direct combat, positions, women would be among the relatively few casualties and POWs, raising questions about whether they should continue to be barred from combat when they were at risk anyway.

The 42-day war was a resounding success for the coalition forces, which, as in the Korean War, were predominantly American. The new post-Vietnam military was symbolized by General Colin Powell, head of the Chiefs of Staff, and General H. Norman Schwartzkopf, commander of first-stage Operation Desert Shield, renamed Desert Storm when the fighting began. Their air-land strategy involved a month of air strikes on Iraq designed to crush communications, destroy existing armaments, and pummel the morale of the Iraqi troops, followed by a ground offensive against Iraqi bases in Kuwait. As reported in daily Pentagon press briefings (about the only access to information the media was allowed), the laser-based technology and computerized weaponry seemed like a video game. Critics charged that such military jargon as "attriting" rather than killing enemy forces or "collateral damage" for destruction of civilian facilities sanitized the war's brutality. The ground phase of the war was finally launched on February 23; within days, thousands of Iraqi troops surrendered and the fighting quickly ended.

The rapid success of the ground war produced a euphoric reaction at home, a blizzard of yellow ribbons in support of the troops, and relief at the amazingly low U.S. casualties (145 Americans killed in action). The performance of American troops became for many a banishment of the ghost of Vietnam, the anti-military

Women at War
Women played key, and visible, roles in the Persian Gulf War, comprising approximately 10 percent of the American troops. Increasing numbers of women are choosing to make a career out of the military, despite widespread reports of sexual harassment and other forms of discrimination.

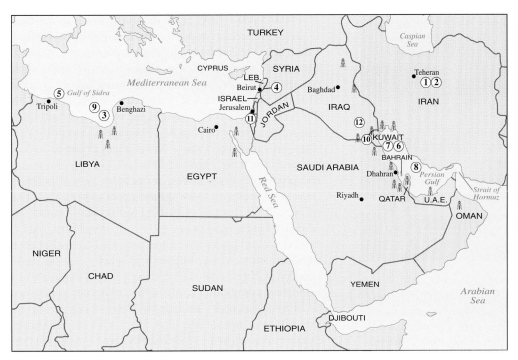

MAP 33.4

U.S. Involvement in the Middle East, 1980–1992

The United States has long played an active role in the Middle East, pursuing the twin goals of protecting Israel's security and assuring a reliable supply of low-cost oil from the Persian Gulf states. By far the largest intervention came in 1991, when, under United Nations auspices, President Bush sent 540,000 American troops to liberate Kuwait from Iraq.

malaise resulting from the prolonged, inconclusive, and politically divisive war of two decades earlier. "By God, we've kicked the Vietnam Syndrome once and for all," gloated George Bush.

One of the biggest winners was the president himself, whose approval rating approached 90 percent. Appearing to act from strong, unequivocal beliefs, Bush made the brutality of the Iraqi aggression the main issue, rather than the need to maintain a steady supply of oil at reasonable prices. Bush profited from the support that often accompanies swift presidential action, such as Reagan's invasion of Grenada in 1983 or his own deployment of troops to Panama in December of 1989 to capture its president, suspected drug dealer Manuel Noriega.

Ironically, at war's end, very little had changed, except that Kuwait was liberated and Iraq no longer was an immediate military threat to its neighbors. Saddam Hussein was still in power. The war had been devastating for Iraqi civilians and as the fighting finished, Bush called on them to "take matters into their own hands" and force Saddam Hussein to "step aside." But when Iraq's minority Kurdish and Shiite rebels rose up against Saddam, only to be brutally repressed by Iraqi forces,

the United States refused support. Perhaps as many as two million refugees fled over the border to Turkey or Iran, where, homeless and starving, they set up makeshift encampments. The United States offered only humanitarian aid.

Once the cheering stopped, doubts surfaced. Why wasn't George Bush providing the leadership on domestic issues that he had brought to the coalition against Saddam Hussein? If America could apply itself so purposefully to war, why couldn't it do the same for the problems of its inner cities, unemployment, the environment, or finding a cure for AIDS? Would the war help end the recession? Observed one consumer, "The country is feeling good about the war, I'm feeling good about it, but I still can't afford a new car."

The Spread of Environmentalism

The Persian Gulf War was the first conflict in modern history to stir public concern about environmental issues while it was being fought. In a deliberate act of sabotage before surrendering, the Iraqis opened Kuwait's oil storage tanks, letting a huge spill foul large

Kuwait Oil Fires
The fires in Kuwaiti oil fields set during the Persian Gulf War caused intense respiratory distress and heavy localized environmental damage, but their longterm effect on the global environment seem not to be as devastating as originally feared.

areas of the Persian Gulf. The spill, between four and ten times larger than that from the oil tanker *Exxon Valdez* off Alaska in 1989, damaged the gulf's delicate ecological balance and threatened to contaminate the desalination plants so essential to this arid region. The Iraqis also deliberately set fires in Kuwait's oil wells while retreating. The heavy acrid smoke from the fires blocked sunlight and caused pollution and respiratory distress over a wide area.

Be Kind to Your Mother (Earth)
The annual celebrations on Earth Day—April 22—began in 1970. Simple things that ordinary citizens can do to save the earth include stopping junk mail, recycling cans and bottles, carpooling, taking shorter showers, and recharging batteries rather than throwing them away.

The Persian Gulf crisis demonstrated the ongoing U.S. dependence on imported oil, recalling the OPEC oil embargo in 1973–1974 and the gas shortages of 1979. Americans were startled to learn that in 1990 their country depended as much on imported oil (42 percent of total consumption) as before the earlier crisis. This dependence had been encouraged by Reagan administration policies, which took advantage of a world oversupply of oil in the 1980s. When prices dropped to $12 a barrel, there was little incentive to conserve, develop alternative energy sources, or achieve self-sufficiency. By relying solely on free-market forces to keep the price of oil down, Reagan's shortsighted policy ignored the Middle East's enormous political instability. As it turned out, oil prices rose during the Gulf crisis but then subsided somewhat. But it was clear that a more lengthy disruption of the industrial world's single most important commodity could have had disastrous effects.

Environmental awareness had been growing steadily even before the Gulf War, both in the United States and worldwide (the so-called *greens* or *green politics*). A major impetus was the meltdown in a reactor at the Chernobyl nuclear energy plant in the Soviet Ukraine in 1986, the world's worst nuclear power accident to date. Chernobyl released a 50-ton cloud of radioactive dust into the air (ten times the fallout at Hiroshima), which soon spread throughout Europe. The accident raised grave questions about the safety of nuclear reactors worldwide.

Increasingly, environmental problems crossed national boundaries and demanded international action. Three pressing issues were the depletion of the ozone layer, acid rain, and global warming. Scientists have detected a gap in the ozone shield that protects the earth from the sun's ultraviolet rays, caused by the release of chlorofluorocarbons or CFCs (industrial chemicals used in refrigeration, air conditioning, and some aerosol products) into the atmosphere. Acid rain, which is caused by the release into the air of sulfur dioxide and oxides of nitrogen as byproducts of industrial processes, damages the water supply, plants, and stone structures. Global warming, or the "greenhouse effect," is believed to result from the widespread burning of fossil fuels or tropical rain forests, which releases carbon dioxide. This traps heat from the sun in the lower atmosphere (the equivalent of a "dirty window over the Earth"), which can gradually cause temperatures on earth to increase. A rise of between 2 and 5 degrees could produce such devastating effects as drought and the melting of polar and glacial ice, with a corresponding rise in sea level and flooding of low-lying coastal regions, including many of the world's most populated cities.

An important precedent for international action on environmental issues was the 1987 Montreal protocol, where thirty-four nations agreed to limit ozone-damaging chlorofluorocarbons over a period of time. In June 1992 a major environmental Earth Summit in Rio de Janeiro adopted a treaty on global warming. President Bush attended the conference and signed the treaty, but he refused to commit the United States to specific goals and timetables.

According to polls, more than three-quarters of Americans consider themselves environmentalists. The twentieth anniversary of Earth Day on April 22, 1990, drew millions worldwide to activities designed to encourage recycling, conservation, and more careful use of natural resources. Unfortunately, little progress had been made since the first Earth Day in 1970. Moving away from the convenience of a fuel-guzzling, "throw-away" society to one that conserves and recycles has been slow and halting.

The 1992 Election

With the end of the Cold War, domestic affairs returned to their more normal place at the center of American politics. As the election campaign of 1992 got underway, the economy, not the environment, was *the* overriding issue, as the recession that began in 1990 showed few signs of abating. As businesses failed and unemployment grew, the administration continued to respond with supply-side rhetoric and additional cuts in interest rates, hoping that this would lead to new investment and "trickle down" to create new jobs. Only it didn't.

It was a very disaffected nation that pondered a large field of Democratic contenders as the primary season began. Bill Clinton, long-time governor of Arkansas, one of the nation's poorest states, emerged as the front runner, surviving charges of marital infidelity and draft-dodging to win the Democratic nomination in July. For his running mate he chose Al Gore, a second-term senator from Tennessee who at age forty-four was a year and a half younger than Clinton, making them the first baby boom national ticket.

President Bush easily won renomination by facing down a primary challenge from conservative columnist Pat Buchanan to win renomination. But to solidify support with the New Right, Vice-President Dan Quayle spoke out strongly for family values and other conservative social agendas. Bush responded to criticism that he lacked a vision for domestic affairs by blaming the Democratic Congress for thwarting all his initiatives.

In the midst of the primary season, the television talk shows launched a third-party challenger, Texas billionaire H. Ross Perot, who more than any other candidate capitalized on voters' desire for change. On the last day of the Democratic convention, Perot dropped out almost as suddenly as he had entered. He then just as suddenly reentered the race less than five weeks before the election, adding a well-financed wildcard in this most unusual of election years.

Besides the state of the economy, the election focused attention on issues that had come to the fore in the preceding year. Women ran for office in unprecedented numbers, many galvanized by the insensitivity of the all-male, all-white Senate Judiciary Committee to Professor Anita Hill's charges of sexual harassment against Supreme Court nominee Clarence Thomas. "They just don't get it" became a rallying cry. Meanwhile, attacks on Hillary Rodham Clinton, a practicing lawyer and the wife of the Democratic candidate, suggested an uneasiness about women's roles in public life.

The Democrats, having learned something from the last three campaigns, mounted an aggressive, effective campaign that focused on Clinton's plans to solve domestic problems, especially education, health care, and revitalizing the economy, while Gore added expertise on defense and environmental issues. Opinion polls fluctuated through the fall, especially because it was hard to measure the impact of independent candidate Ross Perot. On election day, Clinton scored a decisive victory, winning 43 percent of the popular vote to Bush's

Clinton/Gore

Baby boomers Bill Clinton and Al Gore celebrated their 1992 victory to the strains of rock music. Billing themselves as representing a "new generation of leadership," they campaigned in dramatic new ways—appearing on MTV and the Arsenio Hall show, holding talk-show-style town meetings, and going on bus tours to out-of-the way locales all over the country.

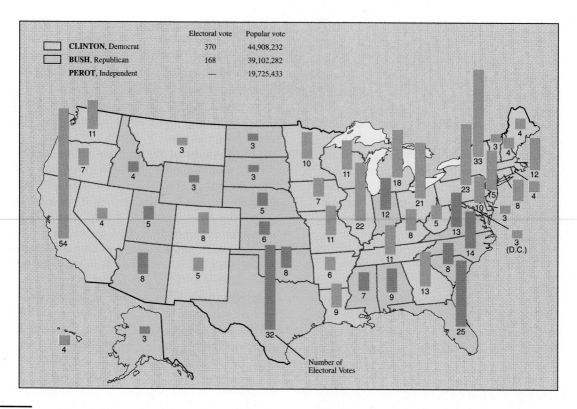

MAP 33.5

The Election of 1992

The first national election since the end of the Cold War was dominated by concern over the ailing economy. The first-ever all-southerner Democratic ticket of Bill Clinton and Al Gore won broad support across the country, cutting into the Republican strongholds of the South and West. Independent candidate H. Ross Perot won no electoral votes but polled an impressive 19 percent of the popular vote.

38 percent and Perot's 19 percent. The results in the electoral college were even more lopsided, with Clinton winning 370 votes to Bush's 168. Although Perot did not win a single state, his popular vote was the highest for an independent candidate since Theodore Roosevelt in 1912. The Democrats retained control of both houses of Congress, ending twelve years of divided government. And the number of women in Congress increased dramatically: forty-seven in the House of Representatives (up from twenty-eight) and an all-time high of six in the Senate, including Illinois Democrat Carol Moseley Braun, the first African-American woman elected to that body. Perhaps most important of all, voter turnout was up dramatically, suggesting a new engagement in the political process on the part of American citizens, as well as hope in Bill Clinton's promise of change.

The New World Order

In 1941, Henry Luce, the publisher of *Life* magazine, confidently predicted the beginning of an "American

century" when World War II ended. As we approach the year 2000, it seems likely that the twenty-first century will be known not as an American century but as a "global century." Economically, power will be shared among multiple players, a sharp contrast to the immediate postwar period when the U.S. dominated the world economy. Militarily, superpower conflict will no longer be a threat, although smaller ethnic and religious conflicts will periodically rock international stability.

The new world order will be characterized by interdependent capitalist market economies organized around four major trading blocks. The first, North America, will be dominated by the United States and include Canada, Mexico, and the developing Central American countries. The second will be Russia and the other nations of the former Soviet Union and Eastern European bloc. The third, the Pacific Rim, will center on Japan, but also include China, South Korea, Hong Kong, Singapore, and Taiwan. The fourth will be the newly revitalized European Community (EC), with a strong Germany at its heart.

The early twenty-first century will likely be most favorable to the Pacific Rim and EC countries, already emerging as strong contenders in global markets as the United States no longer predominates and the CIS lags far behind. The strongest individual economies will likely continue to be those of Japan and Germany, who as the defeated enemies of World War II were kept out of the expensive arms race that absorbed the two superpowers from 1945 to 1991. Historians may later conclude that the United States and the former Soviet Union fell victim to "imperial overstretch," concentrating their resources on a vast military establishment while consumer-oriented production fell behind in the face of foreign competition. It would be a great irony if the United States "won" the Cold War only to have jeopardized its status as a world economic leader in the resulting peace.

The *Pax Americana* lasted from the end of World War II through the 1970s. That the United States no longer dominates the world does not mean that the country is on an inevitable decline toward obscurity and powerlessness. In the 1990s the world appears to be returning to a situation in which power, both economic and military, is dispersed among a number of key players, of which the United States still is one of the most important. This emerging new world order will shape the future of the United States and the globe in the twenty-first century and beyond.

Summary

Ronald Reagan's administration advocated a smaller role for the federal government in domestic programs and the restoration of American prestige abroad. Reagan remained enormously popular throughout his two terms, but left huge budget deficits to his successor, Vice-President George Bush. Reagan's economic policies, notably deregulation and tax cuts, added to the concentration of wealth in the 1980s. As Wall Street boomed, more Americans fell into poverty, and middle-income households struggled to stay afloat.

American society in the 1980s continued to be defined by diversity. Increased immigration, notably from Asia and Latin American countries, changed the demographic balance of many areas, especially the cities, and the postwar trend of population growth in the South, West, and metropolitan areas continued. The economy shifted toward the service sector, and traditional smokestack industries declined.

The most dramatic change of the decade was the end of the Cold War, which had been the guiding principle of American foreign policy since the end of World War II. The dramatic collapse of communism within the Soviet Union itself further complicated the old truisms. The post-Cold War future seemed to promise a fragile world peace, vulnerable to regional and ethnic conflicts, and an increasingly global economy, with the United States playing a leading role, but not dominating, as it did in the *Pax Americana* of the immediate postwar world.

TOPIC FOR RESEARCH

Feminism in the 1980s

In a widely read 1991 book, journalist Susan Faludi described a powerful backlash against the gains American women had won in the 1960s and 1970s. The media consistently held the women's movement responsible for every ill afflicting modern women—from infertility to eating disorders to rising divorce rates to the "man shortage." According to Faludi, the message that the women's movement was women's own worst enemy and that women were unhappy precisely because they had achieved equality was a myth. Instead, Faludi traced many of American women's problems to the fact that they do not have *enough* equality.

Use Faludi's thesis as a starting point for an assessment of the women's movement and women's lives in the 1980s and 1990s. Is there a backlash against women? How are women portrayed in the media and popular culture, especially in television, film, popular music, and advertising? Why is feminism often unappealing to younger women: have we moved into a postfeminist era? What do current debates about reproductive rights, sexual harassment, pay equity, the "glass ceiling," and the "mommy track" tell us about how much equality American women have actually achieved?

In addition to Susan Faludi, *Backlash: The Undeclared War Against American Women* (1991), see Naomi Wolf, *The Beauty Myth* (1991), and Marilyn French, *The War Against Women* (1992). Arlie Hochschild, *The Second Shift* (1989), challenges the notion that women can "do it all." Gloria Steinem's revealing memoir, *Revolution from Within* (1992), identifies self-esteem as the key to personal and political change.

BIBLIOGRAPHY

Few historians have turned their attention yet to the period since 1980, leaving the field to journalists, economists, and political scientists. For the stuff that history is made of, the Bureau of the Census offers an excellent introduction through the yearly *Statistical Abstract of the United States* (110th edition, 1990). Synthetic essays on important issues are also offered in the Congressional Quarterly's *Editorial Research Reports*. Indexes to newspapers and periodicals point toward coverage of major events.

The Reagan Presidency

Ronald Reagan has drawn his share of biographers. Historians who have tried their hand include Robert Dallek, *Ronald Reagan: The Politics of Symbolism* (1982), and Michael Rogin, *Ronald Reagan: The Movie* (1987). See also Ronnie Dugger, *On Reagan* (1983), and Lou Cannon, *Reagan* (1982). Nancy Reagan presented her interpretation of the Reagan years in her aptly named *My Turn* (1989), and speechwriter Peggy Noonan offered an insider's view in *What I Saw at the Revolution* (1990). Haynes Johnson, *Sleepwalking Through History* (1991), provides an excellent overview of America in the Reagan years.

On Reaganomics, George Gilder's *Wealth and Poverty* (1981) represents the views held by many in the Reagan administration. See also David Stockman's memoir, *The Triumph of Politics* (1986). John L. Palmer and Isabel Sawhill, eds., *The Reagan Record* (1984), offers a comprehensive assessment of the first term. See also Benjamin Friedman, *Day of Reckoning: The Consequences of American Economic Policy Under Reagan and After* (1988); William Greider, *The Education of David Stockman and Other Americans* (1982); and Robert Lekachman, *Greed Is Not Enough: Reaganomics* (1982). For the effects of deregulation and lax enforcement by government agencies, see Joan Claybrook, *Retreat from Safety: Reagan's Attack on American Health* (1984); Jonathan Lash, *A Season of Spoils: The Story of the Reagan Administration's Attack on the Environment* (1984); and Charles Noble, *Liberalism at Work: The Rise and Fall of OSHA* (1986).

For electoral politics, see Jack W. Germond and Jules Witcover, *Wake Us When It's Over: Presidential Politics of 1984* (1985); Thomas Ferguson and Joel Rogers, *Right Turn: The Decline of the Democrats and the Future of American Politics* (1986); Frances Fox Piven and Richard Cloward, *Why Americans Don't Vote* (1988); and Robert S. McElvaine, *The End of the Conservative Era: Liberalism after Reagan* (1987).

For foreign policy, Stephen Ambrose, *Rise to Globalism* (5th ed., 1988), provides a comprehensive overview of the Reagan years. The Iran-Contra scandal is covered in Jane Hunter et al., *The Iran-Contra Connection* (1987). Other surveys of covert Reagan initiatives are Bob Woodward, *Veil: The Secret Wars of the CIA* (1987), and Steven Emerson, *Secret Warriors: Inside the Covert Military Operations of the Reagan Era* (1988). For relations with the Soviet Union and the arms race, see Strobe Talbott, *Deadly Gambit: The Reagan Administration and the Stalemate in Nuclear Arms Control* (1984) and *The Master of the Game: Paul Nitze and the*

Nuclear Peace (1988), and Seweryn Bialer and Michael Mandelbaum, eds., *Gorbachev's Russia and American Foreign Policy* (1988).

The material on the United States and Central and South America is extensive. Good introductions are Walter LaFeber, *Inevitable Revolutions* (1984); Abraham F. Lowenthal, *Partners in Conflict: The United States and Latin America* (1987); and Kenneth Coleman and George C. Herring, eds., *The Central America Crisis* (1985). On Nicaragua, see E. Bradford Burns, *At War in Nicaragua* (1987); Robert Pastor, *Condemned to Repetition* (1987); and Roy Gutman, *Banana Diplomacy, 1981–1987* (1988). On El Salvador, see Raymond Bonner, *Weakness and Deceit: U.S. Policy in El Salvador* (1984), and Tom Buckley, *Violent Neighbors: El Salvador, Central America and the United States* (1984). Other useful studies include Martin Diskin, ed., *Trouble in Our Backyard* (1984); J. Michael Hogan, *The Panama Canal in American Politics* (1986); and Hugh O'Shaughnessy, *Grenada* (1985).

The Best of Times, The Worst of Times

Kevin Phillips, *The Politics of Rich and Poor* (1989), provides a fairly unflattering view of the excesses of the 1980s. Journalists have chronicled the frenzied atmosphere of Wall Street in works that read like novels. Among the best are Connie Bruck, *The Predators' Ball: The Junk Bond Raiders and the Man Who Staked Them* (1988); Bryan Burroughs and John Helyar, *Barbarians at the Gate: The Fall of RJR Nabisco* (1990); Michael Lewis, *Liar's Poker* (1989); Donna Sammons Carpenter, *The Fall of the House of Hutton* (1989); Jeffrey Birnbaum and Allan S. Murray, *Showdown at Gucci Gulch: Lawmakers, Lobbyists, and the Unlikely Triumph of Tax Reform* (1987); and James B. Stewart, *Den of Thieves* (1991).

Books that address the growing inequality in the decade include Thomas Byrne Edsall, *The New Politics of Inequality* (1984); Leslie W. Dunbar, ed., *Minority Report: What Has Happened to Blacks, Hispanics, American Indians, and Other Minorities in the Eighties* (1984); Frances Fox Piven and Richard Cloward, *The New Class War* (1982); Michael Harrington, *The New American Poverty* (1984); Frank Levy, *Dollars and Dreams: The Changing American Income Distribution* (1987); and Michael Katz, *The Undeserving Poor: From the War on Poverty to the War on Welfare* (1989). For the poor and homeless in the inner cities, see Ken Auletta, *The Underclass* (1982); William J. Wilson, *The Truly Disadvantaged* (1987); Marian Wright Edelman, *Families in Peril* (1987); Jonathan Kozol, *Rachel and Her Children: Homeless Families in America* (1988); and Nicholas Lemann, *The Promised Land* (1989). For the problems of women and children, see Hilda Scott, *Working Your Way to the Bottom: The Feminization of Poverty* (1985); Ruth Sidel, *Women and Children Last* (1986); and Lenore Weitzman, *The Divorce Revolution* (1985). The struggles of contemporary American life are portrayed in Studs Terkel, *The Great Divide* (1988), and Bennett Harrison and Barry Bluestone, *The Great U-Turn: Corporate Restructuring and the Polarizing of America* (1988), which also offers an overview of economic developments in the 1980s.

David Reimers, *Still the Golden Door* (1986), covers immigration policy in the postwar period through the 1980s. See also Nathan Glazer, ed., *Clamor at the Gates: The New Amer-*

ican Immigration (1986); Thomas Muller and Thomas J. Espenshade, *The Fourth Wave: California's Newest Immigrants* (1985); and Al Santoli, *New Americans* (1988). On Hispanics, see Frank Bean and Marta Tienda, *The Hispanic Population of the United States* (1988), and James D. Cockcroft, *Outlaws in the Promised Land* (1986).

Barbara Ehrenreich's collection of essays, *The Worst Years of Our Lives* (1990), covers a variety of political and social topics from the perspective of the left. Randy Shilts, *And the Band Played On: Politics, People, and the AIDS Epidemic* (1987), is a devastating critique of the inaction in the early years of the AIDS epidemic. See also John Langone, *AIDS: The Facts* (1988). Steven Bach, *Final Cut: Dreams and Disaster in the Making of Heaven's Gate* (1985), provides an inside look at Hollywood and the modern studio system. Allan Bloom, *The Closing of the American Mind* (1987), and E. D. Hirsch, *Cultural Literacy* (1988) deal with issues of curriculum, learning, and literacy.

The New World Order

The emergence of a new world order has provoked commentary from economists, journalists, and historians. Paul Kennedy, *The Rise and Fall of the Great Powers* (1987), suggests that the United States, like other empires before it, fell victim to "imperial overstretch." This view has been questioned in such works as Joseph Nye, *Bound to Lead: The Changing Nature of American Power* (1990); Robert Kuttner, *The End of Laissez Faire: National Purpose and the Global Economy after the Cold War* (1991); and Henry R. Nau, *The Myth of America's Decline: Leading the World Economy into the 1990s* (1990). For developments in Eastern Europe, Bernard Gwertzman and Michael T. Kaufman, eds., *The Collapse of Communism* (1990), reviews the events of 1989 through articles published in the *New York Times*. Bob Woodward's treatment of military decision making in *The Commanders* (1991), also provides important background on Operation Desert Storm. H. Norman Schwartzkopf's entertaining autobiography, *It Doesn't Take a Hero* (1992), gives the commanding general's account of the Gulf War.

While there is no general overview of the environmental history in the 1980s and 1990s, many books survey the problems and call for action. The Earth Works Group, *50 Simple Things You Can Do to Save the Earth* (1989), offers a primer on what citizens can do. Barry Commoner, *Making Peace with the Planet* (1990), and the Conservation Foundation, *State of the Environment: An Assessment at Mid-Decade* (1984); and Al Gore, *Earth in the Balance* (1992), are report cards on how well, or poorly, the world is doing on environmental awareness. Daniel Yergin, *The Prize* (1991), chronicles how the commodity of oil dominates modern life, with both economic and environmental consequences. Among the books that try to look to the future are Robert B. Reich, *The Work of Nations: Preparing Ourselves for 21st century Capitalism* (1991), and David Halberstam, *The Next Century* (1991). For discussions of American attitudes toward politics and leaders at the time of the 1992 election, see William Greider, *Who Will Tell the People?* (1992), and E. J. Dionne, *The War Against Public Life: Why Americans Hate Politics* (1991).

TIMELINE

1980	Ronald Reagan elected president
1981	Economic Recovery Tax Act Sandra Day O'Connor nominated to Supreme Court MTV premieres Beginning of AIDS epidemic
1982	Recession
1983	Star Wars proposed
1984	Geraldine Ferraro first woman on major party ticket
1985	Gramm-Rudman Balanced Budget Act United States becomes debtor nation Mikhail Gorbachev takes power in U.S.S.R.
1986	Iran-Contra affair Tax Reform Act Simpson-Mazzoli Immigration Act Chernobyl nuclear disaster
1987	Collapse of stock market
1988	George Bush elected president
1989	Savings and loan crisis *Exxon Valdez* oil spill Political revolutions in Eastern Europe Chinese crackdown at Tiananmen Square *Webster v. Reproductive Health Services*
1990	Recession begins Twentieth anniversary of Earth Day
1990–1991	Persian Gulf crisis
1991	Dissolution of Soviet Union; end of the Cold War
1992	Los Angeles riots Bill Clinton elected president

The Declaration of Independence

The Unanimous Declaration of the Thirteen United States of America

When in the Course of human events, it becomes necessary for one people to dissolve the political bands which have connected them with another, and to assume among the Powers of the earth, the separate and equal station to which the Laws of Nature and of Nature's God entitle them, a decent respect to the opinions of mankind requires that they should declare the causes which impel them to the separation.

We hold these truths to be self-evident, that all men are created equal, that they are endowed by their Creator with certain unalienable rights, that among these are Life, Liberty, and the pursuit of Happiness. That to secure these rights, Governments are instituted among Men, deriving their just powers from the consent of the governed. That whenever any Form of Government becomes destructive of these ends, it is the Right of the People to alter or to abolish it, and to institute new Government, laying its foundation on such principles and organizing its powers in such form, as to them shall seem most likely to effect their Safety and Happiness. Prudence, indeed, will dictate that Governments long established should not be changed for light and transient causes; and accordingly all experience hath shown, that mankind are more disposed to suffer, while evils are sufferable, than to right themselves by abolishing the forms to which they are accustomed. But when a long train of abuses and usurpations, pursuing invariably the same Object evinces a design to reduce them under absolute Despotism, it is their right, it is their duty, to throw off such Government, and to provide new Guards for their future security.—Such has been the patient sufferance of these Colonies; and such is now the necessity which constrains them to alter their former Systems of Government. The history of the present King of Great Britain is a history of repeated injuries and usurpations, all having in direct object the establishment of an absolute Tyranny over these States. To prove this, let Facts be submitted to a candid world.

He has refused his Assent to Laws, the most wholesome and necessary for the public good.

He has forbidden his Governors to pass Laws of immediate and pressing importance, unless suspended in their operation till his Assent should be obtained; and, when so suspended, he has utterly neglected to attend to them.

He has refused to pass other Laws for the accommodation of large districts of people, unless those people would relinquish the right of Representation in the Legislature, a right inestimable to them and formidable to tyrants only.

He has called together legislative bodies at places unusual, uncomfortable, and distant from the depository of their public Records, for the sole purpose of fatiguing them into compliance with his measures.

He has dissolved Representative Houses repeatedly, for opposing with manly firmness his invasions on the rights of the people.

He has refused for a long time, after such dissolutions, to cause others to be elected; whereby the Legislative powers, incapable of Annihilation, have returned to the People at large for their exercise; the State remaining in the mean time exposed to all the dangers of invasion from without and convulsions within.

He has endeavoured to prevent the population of these States; for that purpose obstructing the Laws of Naturalization of Foreigners; refusing to pass others to encourage their migrations hither, and raising the conditions of new Appropriations of Lands.

He has obstructed the Administration of Justice, by refusing his Assent to Laws for establishing Judiciary powers.

He has made Judges dependent on his Will alone, for the tenure of their offices, and the amount and payment of their salaries.

He has erected a multitude of New Offices, and sent hither swarms of Officers to harass our People, and eat out their substance.

He has kept among us, in times of peace, Standing Armies without the Consent of our legislature.

He has combined with others to subject us to a jurisdiction foreign to our constitution, and unacknowledged by our laws; giving his Assent to their Acts of pretended Legislation:

For quartering large bodies of armed troops among us:

For protecting them, by a mock Trial, from Punishment for any Murders which they should commit on the Inhabitants of these States:

For cutting off our Trade with all parts of the world:

For imposing taxes on us without our Consent:

For depriving us of many cases, of the benefits of Trial by jury:

For transporting us beyond Seas to be tried for pretended offences:

For abolishing the free System of English Laws in a neighbouring Province, establishing therein an Arbitrary government, and enlarging its Boundaries so as to render it at once an example and fit instrument for introducing the same absolute rule into these Colonies;

For taking away our Charters, abolishing our most valuable Laws, and altering fundamentally the Forms of our Governments:

For suspending our own Legislatures, and declaring themselves invested with Power to legislate for us in all cases whatsoever.

He has abdicated Government here, by declaring us out of his Protection and waging War against us.

He has plundered our seas, ravaged our Coasts, burnt our towns, and destroyed the lives of our people.

He is at this time transporting large armies of foreign mercenaries to compleat the works of death, desolation, and tyranny, already begun with circumstances of Cruelty & perfidy scarcely paralleled in the most barbarous ages, and totally unworthy the Head of a civilized nation.

He has constrained our fellow Citizens taken Captive on the high Seas to bear Arms against their Country, to become the executioners of their friends and Brethren, or to fall themselves by their Hands.

He has excited domestic insurrections amongst us, and has endeavoured to bring on the inhabitants of our frontiers, the merciless Indian Savages, whose known rule of warfare, is an undistinguished destruction of all ages, sexes, and conditions.

In every stage of these Oppressions We have Petitioned for Redress in the most humble terms: Our repeated Petitions have been answered only by repeated injury. A Prince, whose character is thus marked by every act which may define a Tyrant, is unfit to be the ruler of a free people.

Nor have We been wanting in attention to our British brethren. We have warned them from time to time of attempts by their legislature to extend an unwarrantable jurisdiction over us. We have reminded them of the circumstances of our emigration and settlement here. We have appealed to their native justice and magnanimity, and we have conjured them by the ties of our common kindred to disavow these usurpations, which, would inevitably interrupt our connections and correspondence. They too have been deaf to the voice of justice and of consanguinity. We must, therefore, acquiesce in the necessity, which denounces our Separation, and hold them, as we hold the rest of mankind, Enemies in War, in Peace Friends.

We, therefore, the Representatives of the United States of America, in General Congress, Assembled, appealing to the Supreme Judge of the world for the rectitude of our intentions, do, in the Name, and by Authority of the good People of these Colonies, solemnly publish and declare, That these United Colonies are, and of Right ought to be FREE AND INDEPENDENT STATES; that they are Absolved from all Allegiance to the British Crown, and that all political connection between them and the State of Great Britain, is and ought to be totally dissolved; and that as Free and Independent States, they have full Power to levy War, conclude Peace, contract Alliances, establish Commerce, and to do all other Acts and Things which Independent States may of right do. And for the support of this Declaration, with a firm reliance on the Protection of Divine Providence, we mutually pledge to each other our Lives, our Fortunes, and our sacred Honor.

John Hancock

Button Gwinnett	George Wythe	James Wilson	Josiah Bartlett
Lyman Hall	Richard Henry Lee	Geo. Ross	Wm. Whipple
Geo. Walton	Th. Jefferson	Caesar Rodney	Saml. Adams
Wm. Hooper	Benja. Harrison	Geo. Read	John Adams
Joseph Hewes	Thos. Nelson, Jr.	Thos. M'Kean	Robt. Treat Paine
John Penn	Francis Lightfoot Lee	Wm. Floyd	Elbridge Gerry
Edward Rutledge	Carter Braxton	Phil. Livingston	Step. Hopkins
Thos. Heyward, Junr.	Robt. Morris	Frans. Lewis	William Ellery
Thomas Lynch, Junr.	Benjamin Rush	Lewis Morris	Roger Sherman
Arthur Middleton	Benja. Franklin	Richd. Stockton	Sam'el Hunington
Samuel Chase	John Morton	Jno. Witherspoon	Wm. Williams
Wm. Paca	Geo. Clymer	Fras. Hopkinson	Oliver Wolcott
Thos. Stone	Jas. Smith	John Hart	Matthew Thornton
Charles Carroll of Carrollton	Geo. Taylor	Abra. Clark	

The Constitution of the United States of America

We the People of the United States, in Order to form a more perfect Union, establish Justice, insure domestic Tranquility, provide for the common defence, promote the general Welfare, and secure the Blessings of Liberty to ourselves and our Posterity, do ordain and establish this Constitution for the United States of America.

Article I

Section 1 All legislative Powers herein granted shall be vested in a Congress of the United States, which shall consist of a Senate and a House of Representatives.

Section 2 The House of Representatives shall be composed of Members chosen every second Year by the People of the several States, and the Electors in each State shall have the Qualifications requisite for Electors of the most numerous Branch of the State Legislature.

No Person shall be a Representative who shall not have attained to the Age of twenty-five Years, and been seven Years a Citizen of the United States, and who shall not, when elected, be an Inhabitant of that State in which he shall be chosen.

Representatives and direct Taxes shall be apportioned among the several States which may be included within this Union, according to their respective Numbers, *which shall be determined by adding to the whole Number of free Persons, including those bound to Service for a Term of Years, and excluding Indians not taxed, three fifths of all other Persons.** The actual Enumeration shall be made within three Years after the first Meeting of the Congress of the United States, and within every subsequent Term of ten Years, in such Manner as they shall by Law direct. The Number of Representatives shall not exceed one for every thirty Thousand, but each State shall have at Least one Representative; and *until such*

enumeration shall be made, the State of New Hampshire shall be entitled to chuse three, Massachusetts eight, Rhode Island and Providence Plantations one, Connecticut five, New-York six, New Jersey four, Pennsylvania eight, Delaware one, Maryland six, Virginia ten, North Carolina five, South Carolina five, and Georgia three.

When vacancies happen in the Representation from any State, the Executive Authority thereof shall issue Writs of Election to fill such Vacancies.

The House of Representatives shall chuse their Speaker and other Officers; and shall have the sole Power of Impeachment.

Section 3 The Senate of the United States shall be composed of two Senators from each State, *chosen by the Legislature thereof,*† for six Years; and each Senator shall have one Vote.

Immediately after they shall be assembled in Consequence of the first Election, they shall be divided as equally as may be into three Classes. The Seats of the Senators of the first Class shall be vacated at the Expiration of the second Year, of the second Class at the Expiration of the fourth Year, and of the third Class at the Expiration of the sixth Year, so that one-third may be chosen every second Year; *and if Vacancies happen by Resignation, or otherwise, during the Recess of the Legislature of any State, the Executive thereof may make temporary Appointments until the next Meeting of the Legislature, which shall then fill such Vacancies.*‡

No person shall be a Senator who shall not have attained to the Age of thirty Years, and been nine Years a Citizen of the United States, and who shall not, when elected, be an Inhabitant of that State for which he shall be chosen.

The Vice President of the United States shall be President of the Senate, but shall have no Vote, unless they be equally divided.

Note: The Constitution became effective March 4, 1789. Provisions in italics have been changed by constitutional amendment.

*Changed by Section 2 of the Fourteenth Amendment.

†Changed by Section 1 of the Seventeenth Amendment.

‡Changed by Clause 2 of the Seventeenth Amendment.

The Senate shall chuse their other Officers, and also a President pro tempore, in the absence of the Vice President, or when he shall exercise the Office of President of the United States.

The Senate shall have the sole Power to try all Impeachments. When sitting for that Purpose, they shall be on Oath or Affirmation. When the President of the United States is tried, the Chief Justice shall preside: And no Person shall be convicted without the Concurrence of two thirds of the Members present.

Judgment in Cases of Impeachment shall not extend further than to removal from Office, and disqualification to hold and enjoy any Office of honor, Trust or Profit under the United States: but the Party convicted shall nevertheless be liable and subject to Indictment, Trial, Judgment and Punishment, according to Law.

Section 4 The Times, Places and Manner of holding Elections for Senators and Representatives, shall be prescribed in each State by the Legislature thereof; but the Congress may at any time by Law make or alter such Regulations, except as to the Places of Chusing Senators.

The Congress shall assemble at least once in every Year, and such Meeting *shall be on the first Monday in December, unless they shall by Law appoint a different Day.**

Section 5 Each House shall be the Judge of the Elections, Returns and Qualifications of its own Members, and a Majority of each shall constitute a Quorum to do Business; but a smaller number may adjourn from day to day, and may be authorized to compel the Attendance of absent Members, in such Manner, and under such Penalties, as each House may provide.

Each House may determine the Rules of its Proceedings, punish its Members for disorderly Behavior, and, with the Concurrence of two thirds, expel a Member.

Each House shall keep a Journal of its Proceedings, and from time to time publish the same, excepting such Parts as may in their Judgment require Secrecy; and the Yeas and Nays of the Members of either House on any question shall, at the Desire of one-fifth of those Present, be entered on the Journal.

Neither House, during the Session of Congress, shall, without the Consent of the other, adjourn for more than three days, nor to any other Place than that in which the two Houses shall be sitting.

Section 6 The Senators and Representatives shall receive a Compensation for their Services, to be ascertained by Law, and paid out of the Treasury of the United States. They shall in all Cases, except Treason, Felony and Breach of the Peace, be privileged from Arrest during their Attendance at the Session of their respective Houses, and in going to and returning from the same; and for any Speech or Debate in either House, they shall not be questioned in any other Place.

No Senator or Representative shall, during the Time for which he was elected, be appointed to any civil Office under the Authority of the United States, which shall have been created, or the Emoluments whereof shall have been increased, during such time; and no Person holding any Office under the

_____
*Changed by Section 2 of the Twentieth Amendment.

United States, shall be a Member of either House during his Continuance in Office.

Section 7 All Bills for raising Revenue shall originate in the House of Representatives; but the Senate may propose or concur with Amendments as on other Bills.

Every Bill which shall have passed the House of Representatives and the Senate, shall, before it becomes a Law, be presented to the President of the United States; If he approve he shall sign it, but if not he shall return it, with his Objections to that House in which it shall have originated, who shall enter the Objections at large on their Journal, and proceed to reconsider it. If after such Reconsideration two thirds of that House shall agree to pass the Bill, it shall be sent, together with the Objections, to the other House, by which it shall likewise be reconsidered, and if approved by two thirds of that House, it shall become a Law. But in all such Cases the Votes of both Houses shall be determined by Yeas and Nays, and the Names of the Persons voting for and against the Bill shall be entered on the Journal of each House respectively. If any Bill shall not be returned by the President within ten Days (Sundays excepted) after it shall have been presented to him, the Same shall be a Law, in like Manner as if he had signed it, unless the Congress by their Adjournment prevent its Return, in which Case it shall not be a Law.

Every Order, Resolution, or Vote to which the Concurrence of the Senate and the House of Representatives may be necessary (except on a question of Adjournment) shall be presented to the President of the United States; and before the Same shall take Effect, shall be approved by him, or being disapproved by him, shall be repassed by two thirds of the Senate and House of Representatives, according to the Rules and Limitations prescribed in the Case of a Bill.

Section 8 The Congress shall have Power To lay and collect Taxes, Duties, Imposts and Excises, to pay the Debts and provide for the common Defence and general Welfare of the United States; but all Duties, Imposts and Excises shall be uniform throughout the United States;

To borrow money on the credit of the Untied States;

To regulate Commerce with foreign Nations, and among the several States, and with the Indian Tribes;

To establish an uniform Rule of Naturalization, and uniform Laws on the subject of Bankruptcies throughout the United States;

To coin Money, regulate the Value thereof, and of foreign Coin, and fix the Standard of Weights and Measures;

To provide for the Punishment of counterfeiting the Securities and current Coin of the United States;

To establish Post Offices and post Roads;

To promote the Progress of Science and useful Arts, by securing for limited Times to Authors and Inventors the exclusive Right to their respective Writings and Discoveries;

To constitute Tribunals inferior to the supreme Court;

To define and punish Piracies and Felonies committed on the high Seas, and Offenses against the Law of Nations;

To declare War, grant Letters of Marque and Reprisal, and make Rules concerning Captures on Land and Water;

To raise and support Armies, but no Appropriation of Money to that Use shall be for a longer Term than two Years;

To provide and maintain a Navy;

To make Rules for the Government and Regulation of the land and naval Forces;

To provide for calling forth the Militia to execute the Laws of the Union, suppress Insurrections and repel Invasions;

To provide for organizing, arming, and disciplining the Militia, and for governing such Part of them as may be employed in the Service of the United States, reserving to the States respectively, the Appointment of the Officers, and the Authority of training the Militia according to the discipline prescribed by Congress;

To exercise exclusive Legislation in all Cases whatsoever, over such District (not exceeding ten Miles square) as may, by Cession of particular States, and the acceptance of Congress, become the Seat of Government of the United States, and to exercise like Authority over all Places purchased by the Consent of the Legislature of the State in which the Same shall be, for the Erection of Forts, Magazines, Arsenals, dock-Yards, and other needful Buildings;—And

To make all Laws which shall be necessary and proper for carrying into Execution the foregoing Powers, and all other Powers vested by this Constitution in the Government of the United States, or in any Department or Officer thereof.

Section 9 *The Migration or Importation of such Persons as any of the States now existing shall think proper to admit, shall not be prohibited by the Congress prior to the Year one thousand eight hundred and eight but a tax or duty may be imposed on such Importation, not exceeding ten dollars for each Person.*

The privilege of the Writ of Habeas Corpus shall not be suspended, unless when in Cases of Rebellion or Invasion the public Safety may require it.

No Bill of Attainder or ex post facto Law shall be passed.

No capitation, or other direct, Tax shall be laid, unless in Proportion to the Census or Enumeration herein before directed to be taken.*

No Tax or Duty shall be laid on Articles exported from any State.

No Preference shall be given by any Regulation of Commerce or Revenue to the Ports of one State over those of another: nor shall Vessels bound to, or from, one State, be obliged to enter, clear, or pay Duties in another.

No Money shall be drawn from the Treasury, but in Consequence of Appropriations made by law; and a regular Statement and Account of the Receipts and Expenditures of all public Money shall be published from time to time.

No Title of Nobility shall be granted by the United States: And no Person holding any Office of Profit or Trust under them, shall, without the Consent of the Congress, accept of any present, Emolument, Office, or Title, of any kind whatever, from any King, Prince, or foreign State.

Section 10 No State shall enter into any Treaty, Alliance, or Confederation; grant Letters of Marque and Reprisal; coin Money; emit Bills of Credit; make any Thing but gold and silver Coin a Tender in Payment of Debts; pass any Bill of Attainder, ex post facto Law, or Law impairing the Obligation of Contracts, or grant any Title of Nobility.

No State shall, without the Consent of the Congress, lay any Imposts or Duties on Imports or Exports, except what may be absolutely necessary for executing its inspection Laws: and the net Produce of all Duties and Imposts, laid by any State on Imports or Exports, shall be for the Use of the Treasury of the United States; and all such Laws shall be subject to the Revision and Control of the Congress.

No State shall, without the Consent of the Congress, lay any duty of Tonnage, keep Troops, or Ships of War in time of Peace, enter into any Agreement or Compact with another State, or with a foreign Power, or engage in War, unless actually invaded, or in such imminent Danger as will not admit of delay.

Article II

Section 1 The executive Power shall be vested in a President of the United States of America. He shall hold his Office during the Term of four Years, and, together with the Vice President, chosen for the same Term, be elected, as follows:

Each State shall appoint, in such Manner as the Legislature thereof may direct, a Number of Electors, equal to the whole Number of Senators and Representatives to which the State may be entitled in the Congress; but no Senator or Representative, or Person holding an Office of Trust or Profit under the United States, shall be appointed an Elector.

The Electors shall meet in their respective States, and vote by Ballot for two Persons, of whom one at least shall not be an Inhabitant of the same State with themselves. And they shall make a List of all the Persons voted for, and of the Number of Votes for each; which List they shall sign and certify, and transmit sealed to the Seat of the Government of the United States, directed to the President of the Senate. The President of the Senate shall, in the Presence of the Senate and House of Representatives, open all the Certificates, and the Votes shall then be counted. The Person having the greatest Number of Votes shall be the President, if such Number be a Majority of the whole Number of Electors appointed; and if there be more than one who have such Majority, and have an equal Number of Votes, then the House of Representatives shall immediately chuse by Ballot one of them for President; and if no Person have a Majority, then from the five highest on the List the said House shall in like Manner chuse the President. But in chusing the President, the Votes shall be taken by States, the Representation from each State having one Vote; a quorum for this Purpose shall consist of a Member or Members from two thirds of the States, and a Majority of all the States shall be necessary to a Choice. In every Case, after the Choice of the President, the Person having the greatest Number of Votes of the Electors shall be the Vice President. But if there should remain two or more who have equal Votes, the Senate shall chuse from them by Ballot the Vice President.

The Congress may determine the Time of chusing the Electors, and the Day on which they shall give their Votes; which Day shall be the same throughout the United States.

No Person except a natural born Citizen, or a Citizen of the United States, at the time of the Adoption of this Constitution, shall be eligible to the Office of President; neither shall any Person be eligible to that Office who shall not have at-

---

*Changed by the Sixteenth Amendment.

*Superseded by the Twelfth Amendment.

tained to the Age of thirty five Years, and been fourteen Years a Resident within the United States.

In Case of the Removal of the President from Office, or of his Death, Resignation, or Inability to discharge the Powers and Duties of the said Office, the same shall devolve on the Vice President, *and the Congress may by Law provide for the Case of Removal, Death, Resignation, or Inability, both of the President and Vice President, declaring what Officer shall then act as President, and such Officer shall act accordingly, until the Disability be removed, or a President shall be elected.**

The President shall, at stated Times, receive for his Services a Compensation, which shall neither be increased nor diminished during the Period for which he shall have been elected, and he shall not receive within that Period any other Emolument from the United States, or any of them.

Before he enter on the Execution of his Office, he shall take the following Oath or Affirmation:—"I do solemnly swear (or affirm) that I will faithfully execute the Office of President of the United States, and will to the best of my Ability, preserve, protect and defend the Constitution of the United States."

Section 2 The President shall be Commander in Chief of the Army and Navy of the United States, and of the Militia of the several States, when called into the actual Service of the United States; he may require the Opinion, in writing, of the principal Officer in each of the executive Departments, upon any Subject relating to the Duties of their respective Offices, and he shall have Power to Grant Reprieves and Pardons for Offences against the United States, except in Cases of Impeachment.

He shall have Power, by and with the Advice and Consent of the Senate, to make Treaties, provided two thirds of the Senators present concur; and he shall nominate, and by and with the Advice and Consent of the Senate, shall appoint Ambassadors, other public Ministers and Consuls, Judges of the supreme Court, and all other Officers of the United States, whose Appointments are not herein otherwise provided for, and which shall be established by Law: but the Congress may by Law vest the Appointment of such inferior Officers, as they think proper, in the President alone, in the Courts of Law, or in the Heads of Departments.

The President shall have Power to fill up all Vacancies that may happen during the Recess of the Senate, by granting Commissions which shall expire at the End of their next Session.

Section 3 He shall from time to time give to the Congress Information of the State of the Union, and recommend to their Consideration such Measures as he shall judge necessary and expedient; he may, on extraordinary Occasions, convene both Houses, or either of them, and in Case of Disagreement between them, with Respect to the Time of Adjournment, he may adjourn them to such Time as he shall think proper; he shall receive Ambassadors and other public Ministers; he shall take Care that the Laws be faithfully executed, and shall Commission all the Officers of the United States.

Section 4 The President, Vice President and all civil Officers of the United States, shall be removed from Office on Impeachment for, and Conviction of, Treason, Bribery, or other high Crimes and Misdemeanors.

Article III

Section 1 The judicial Power of the United States, shall be vested in one supreme Court, and in such inferior Courts as the Congress may from time to time ordain and establish. The Judges, both of the supreme and inferior Courts, shall hold their Offices during good Behaviour, and shall, at stated Times, receive for their Services a Compensation, which shall not be diminished during their Continuance in Office.

Section 2 The judicial Power shall extend to all Cases, in Law and Equity, arising under this Constitution, the Laws of the United States, and Treaties made, or which shall be made, under their Authority;—to all Cases affecting Ambassadors, other public Ministers and Consuls;—to all Cases of admiralty and maritime Jurisdiction;—to Controversies to which the United States shall be a Party;—to Controversies between two or more States;—*between a State and Citizens of another State;**—between Citizens of different States;—between Citizens of the same State claiming Lands under Grants of different States, and between a State, or the Citizens thereof, and foreign States, Citizens or Subjects.

In all Cases affecting Ambassadors, other public Ministers and Consuls, and those in which a State shall be Party, the supreme Court shall have original Jurisdiction. In all the other Cases before mentioned, the supreme Court shall have appellate Jurisdiction, both as to Law and Fact, with such Exceptions, and under such Regulations as the Congress shall make.

The trial of all Crimes, except in Cases of Impeachment, shall be by Jury; and such Trial shall be held in the State where said Crimes shall have been committed; but when not committed within any State, the Trial shall be at such Place or Places as the Congress may by Law have directed.

Section 3 Treason against the United States, shall consist only in levying War against them, or in adhering to their Enemies, giving them Aid and Comfort. No Person shall be convicted of Treason unless on the Testimony of two Witnesses to the same overt Act, or on Confession in open Court.

The Congress shall have Power to declare the Punishment of Treason, but no Attainder of Treason shall work Corruption of Blood, or Forefeiture except during the Life of the Person attainted.

Article IV

Section 1 Full Faith and Credit shall be given in each State to the public Acts, Records, and judicial Proceedings of every other State. And the Congress may by general Laws prescribe the Manner in which such Acts, Records, and Proceedings shall be proved, and the Effect thereof.

Section 2 The Citizens of each State shall be entitled to all Privileges and Immunities of Citizens in the several States.

---

*Modified by the Twenty-Fifth Amendment.

*Restricted by the Eleventh Amendment.

A Person charged in any State with Treason, Felony, or other Crime, who shall flee from Justice, and be found in another State, shall on demand of the executive Authority of the State from which he fled, be delivered up, to be removed to the State having Jurisdiction of the Crime.

*No Person held to Service or Labour in one State, under the Laws thereof, escaping into another, shall, in Consequence of any Law or Regulation therein, be discharged from such Service or Labour, but shall be delivered up on Claim of the Party to whom such Service or Labour may be due.**

Section 3 New States may be admitted by the Congress into this Union; but no new State shall be formed or erected within the Jurisdiction of any other State; nor any State be formed by the Junction of two or more States, or parts of States, without the Consent of the Legislatures of the States concerned as well as of the Congress.

The Congress shall have Power to dispose of and make all needful Rules and Regulations respecting the Territory or other Property belonging to the United States; and nothing in this Constitution shall be so construed as to Prejudice any Claims of the United States, or of any particular State.

Section 4 The United States shall guarantee to every State in this Union a Republican Form of Government, and shall protect each of them against Invasion; and on Application of the Legislature, or of the Executive (when the Legislature cannot be convened) against domestic Violence.

Article V

The Congress, whenever two thirds of both Houses shall deem it necessary, shall propose Amendments to this Constitution, or, on the Application of the Legislatures of two thirds of the several States, shall call a Convention for proposing Amendments, which, in either Case, shall be valid to all Intents and Purposes, as Part of this Constitution, when ratified by the Legislatures of three fourths of the several States, or by Conventions in three fourths thereof, as the one or the other Mode of Ratification may be proposed by the Congress; Pro-

vided that no Amendment which may be made prior to the Year One thousand eight hundred and eight shall in any Manner affect the first and fourth Clauses in the Ninth Section of the first Article; and that no State, without its Consent, shall be deprived of its equal Suffrage in the Senate.

Article VI

All Debts contracted and Engagements entered into, before the Adoption of this Constitution, shall be as valid against the United States under this Constitution, as under the Confederation.

This Constitution, and the Laws of the United States which shall be made in Pursuance thereof; and all Treaties made, or which shall be made, under the Authority of the United States, shall be the supreme Law of the Land; and the Judges in every State shall be bound thereby, any Thing in the Constitution or Laws of any State to the Contrary notwithstanding.

The Senators and Representatives before mentioned, and the Members of the several State Legislatures, and all executive and judicial Officers, both of the United States and of the several States, shall be bound by Oath or Affirmation, to support this Constitution; but no religious Test shall ever be required as a Qualification to any Office or public Trust under the United States.

Article VII

The Ratification of the Conventions of nine States shall be sufficient for the Establishment of this Constitution between the States so ratifying the Same.

Done in Convention by the Unanimous Consent of the States present the Seventeenth Day of September in the Year of our Lord one thousand seven hundred and Eighty seven and of the Independence of the United States of America the Twelfth. In Witness whereof We have hereunto subscribed our Names.

---

*Superseded by the Twelfth Amendment.

Go. Washington
President and deputy from Virginia

New Hampshire	*New Jersey*	*Delaware*	*North Carolina*
John Langdon	Wil. Livingston	Geo. Read	Wm. Blount
Nicholas Gilman	David Brearley	Gunning Bedford jun	Richd. Dobbs Spaight
	Wm. Paterson	John Dickenson	Hu Williamson
Massachusetts	Jona. Dayton	Richard Bassett	
Nathaniel Gorham		Jaco. Broom	*South Carolina*
Rufus King	*Pennsylvania*		J. Rutledge
	B. Franklin	*Maryland*	Charles Cotesworth Pickney
Connecticut	Thomas Mifflin	James McHenry	Pierce Butler
Wm. Saml. Johnson	Robt. Morris	Dan. of St. Thos. Jenifer	
Roger Sherman	Geo. Clymer	Danl. Carroll	*Georgia*
	Thos. FitzSimons		William Few
New York	Jared Ingersoll	*Virginia*	Abr. Baldwin
Alexander Hamilton	James Wilson	John Blair	
	Gouv. Morris	James Madison, Jr.	

Amendments to the Constitution

Amendment I [1791]*

Congress shall make no law respecting an establishment of religion, or prohibiting the free exercise thereof; or abridging the freedom of speech, or of the press; or the right of the people peaceably to assemble, and to petition the Government for a redress of grievances.

Amendment II [1791]

A well regulated Militia, being necessary to the security of a free State, the right of the people to keep and bear Arms shall not be infringed.

Amendment III [1791]

No Soldier shall, in time of peace, be quartered in any house, without the consent of the Owner, nor in time of war, but in a manner to be prescribed by law.

Amendment IV [1791]

The right of the people to be secure in their persons, houses, papers, and effects, against unreasonable searches and seizures, shall not be violated, and no Warrants shall issue, but upon probable cause, supported by Oath or affirmation, and particularly describing the place to be searched, and the persons or things to be seized.

Amendment V [1791]

No person shall be held to answer for a capital or otherwise infamous crime, unless on a presentment or indictment of a Grand Jury, except in cases arising in the land or naval forces, or in the Militia, when in actual service in time of War or public danger; nor shall any person be subject for the same offence to be twice put in jeopardy of life or limb; nor shall be compelled in any criminal case to be a witness against himself, nor be deprived of life, liberty, or property, without due process of law; nor shall private property be taken for public use, without just compensation.

Amendment VI [1791]

In all criminal prosecutions, the accused shall enjoy the right to a speedy and public trial, by an impartial jury of the State and district wherein the crime shall have been committed, which district shall have been previously ascertained by law, and to be informed of the nature and cause of the accusation; to be confronted with the witnesses against him; to have compulsory process for obtaining witnesses in his favor, and to have the Assistance of Counsel for his defence.

Amendment VII [1791]

In suits at common law, where the value in controversy shall exceed twenty dollars, the right of trial by jury shall be preserved, and no fact tried by a jury, shall be otherwise reexamined in any Court of the United States, than according to the Rules of the common law.

Amendment VIII [1791]

Excessive bail shall not be required, nor excessive fines imposed, nor cruel and unusual punishments inflicted.

Amendment IX [1791]

The enumeration in the Constitution, of certain rights, shall not be construed to deny or disparage others retained by the people.

*The dates in brackets indicate when the amendments were ratified.

Amendment X [1791]

The powers not delegated to the United States by the Constitution, nor prohibited by it to the States, are reserved to the States respectively, or to the people.

Amendment XI [1798]

The Judicial power of the United States shall not be construed to extend to any suit in law or equity, commenced or prosecuted against one of the United States by Citizens of another State, or by Citizens or Subjects of any Foreign State.

Amendment XII [1804]

The Electors shall meet in their respective States and vote by ballot for President and Vice-President, one of whom, at least, shall not be an inhabitant of the same State with themselves; they shall name in their ballots the person voted for as President, and in distinct ballots the person voted for as Vice-President, and they shall make distinct lists of all persons voted for as President, and of all persons voted for as Vice-President, and of the number of votes for each, which lists they shall sign and certify, and transmit sealed to the seat of the government of the United States, directed to the President of the Senate;— The President of the Senate shall, in the presence of the Senate and House of Representatives, open all the certificates and the votes shall then be counted;—The person having the greatest number of votes for President, shall be the President, if such number be a majority of the whole number of Electors appointed; and if no person have such majority, then from the persons having the highest numbers not exceeding three on the list of those voted for as President, the House of Representatives shall choose immediately, by ballot, the President. But in choosing the President, the votes shall be taken by States, the representation from each State having one vote; a quorum for this purpose shall consist of a member or members from two-thirds of the States, and a majority of all the States shall be necessary to a choice. And if the House of Representatives shall not choose a President whenever the right of choice shall devolve upon them, before *the fourth day of March* next following, then the Vice-President shall act as President, as in the case of the death or other constitutional disability of the President.*—The person having the greatest number of votes as Vice-President, shall be the Vice-President, if such number be a majority of the whole number of Electors appointed, and if no person have a majority, then from the two highest numbers on the list, the Senate shall choose the Vice-President; a quorum for the purpose shall consist of two-thirds of the whole number of Senators, and a majority of the whole number shall be necessary to a choice. But no person constitutionally ineligible to the office of President shall be eligible to that of Vice-President of the United States.

Amendment XIII [1865]

Section 1 Neither slavery nor involuntary servitude, except as a punishment for crime whereof the party shall have been duly convicted, shall exist within the United States, or any place subject to their jurisdiction.

*Superseded by Section 3 of the Twentieth Amendment.

Section 2 Congress shall have power to enforce this article by appropriate legislation.

Amendment XIV [1868]

Section 1 All persons born or naturalized in the United States, and subject to the jurisdiction thereof, are citizens of the United States and of the State wherein they reside. No State shall make or enforce any law which shall abridge the privileges or immunities of citizens of the United States; nor shall any State deprive any person of life, liberty, or property, without due process of law; nor deny to any person within its jurisdiction the equal protection of the laws.

Section 2 Representatives shall be apportioned among the several States according to their respective numbers, counting the whole number of persons in each State, excluding Indians not taxed. But when the right to vote at any election for the choice of electors for President and Vice-President of the United States, Representatives in Congress, the Executive and Judicial officers of a State, or the members of the Legislature thereof, is denied to any of the male inhabitants of such State, being twenty-one years of age, and citizens of the United States, or in any way abridged, except for participation in rebellion, or other crime, the basis of representation therein shall be reduced in the proportion which the number of such male citizens shall bear to the whole number of male citizens twenty-one years of age in such State.

Section 3 No person shall be a Senator or Representative in Congress, or elector of President and Vice-President, or hold any office, civil or military, under the United States, or under any State, who, having previously taken an oath, as a member of Congress, or as an officer of the United States, or as a member of any State legislature, or as an executive or judicial officer of any State, to support the Constitution of the United States, shall have engaged in insurrection or rebellion against the same, or given aid or comfort to the enemies thereof. Congress may by a vote of two-thirds of each house, remove such disability.

Section 4 The validity of the public debt of the United States, authorized by law, including debts incurred for payment of pensions and bounties for services in suppressing insurrection or rebellion, shall not be questioned. But neither the United States nor any State shall assume or pay any debt or obligation incurred in aid of insurrection or rebellion against the United States, or any claim for the loss or emancipation of any slave; but all such debts, obligations and claims shall be held illegal and void.

Section 5 The Congress shall have power to enforce, by appropriate legislation, the provisions of this article.

Amendment XV [1870]

Section 1 The right of citizens of the United States to vote shall not be denied or abridged by the United States or by any State on account of race, color, or previous condition of servitude—

Section 2 The Congress shall have power to enforce this article by appropriate legislation.

Amendment XVI [1913]

The Congress shall have power to lay and collect taxes on incomes, from whatever source derived, without apportionment among the several States, and without regard to any census or enumeration.

Amendment XVII [1913]

The Senate of the United States shall be composed of two Senators from each State, elected by the people thereof, for six years; and each Senator shall have one vote. The electors in each State shall have the qualifications requisite for electors of the most numerous branch of the State legislatures.

When vacancies happen in the representation of any State in the Senate, the executive authority of such State shall issue writs of election to fill such vacancies: *Provided,* That the legislature of any State may empower the executive thereof to make temporary appointments until the people fill the vacancies by election as the legislature may direct.

This amendment shall not be so construed as to affect the election or term of any Senator chosen before it becomes valid as part of the Constitution.

Amendment XVIII [1919]

Section 1 After one year from the ratification of this article the manufacture, sale, or transportation of intoxicating liquors within, the importation thereof into, or the exportation thereof from the United States and all territory subject to the jurisdiction thereof for beverage purposes is hereby prohibited.

Section 2 The Congress and the several States shall have concurrent power to enforce this article by appropriate legislation.

Section 3 This article shall be inoperative unless it shall have been ratified as an amendment to the Constitution by the legislatures of the several States, as provided by the Constitution, within seven years from the date of submission hereof to the States by the Congress.*

Amendment XIX [1920]

The right of citizens of the United States to vote shall not be denied or abridged by the United States or by any State on account of sex.

Congress shall have power to enforce this article by appropriate legislation.

Amendment XX [1933]

Section 1 The terms of the President and Vice-President shall end at noon on the 20th day of January, and the terms of Senators and Representatives at noon on the 3d day of January,

*Repealed by Section 1 of the Twenty-First Amendment.

of the years in which such terms would have ended if this article had not been ratified; and the terms of their successors shall then begin.

Section 2 The Congress shall assemble at least once in every year, and such meeting shall begin at noon on the 3d day of January, unless they shall by law appoint a different day.

Section 3 If, at the time fixed for the beginning of the term of the President, the President elect shall have died, the Vice-President elect shall become President. If a President shall not have been chosen before the time fixed for the beginning of his term, or if the President elect shall have failed to qualify, then the Vice-President elect shall act as President until a President shall have qualified; and the Congress may by law provide for the case wherein neither a President elect nor a Vice-President elect shall have qualified, declaring who shall then act as President, or the manner in which one who is to act shall be selected, and such person shall act accordingly until a President or Vice-President shall have qualified.

Section 4 The Congress may by law provide for the case of the death of any of the persons from whom the House of Representatives may choose a President whenever the right of choice shall have devolved upon them, and for the case of the death of any of the persons from whom the Senate may choose a Vice-President whenever the right of choice shall have devolved upon them.

Section 5 Sections 1 and 2 shall take effect on the 15th day of October following the ratification of this article.

Section 6 This article shall be inoperative unless it shall have been ratified as an amendment to the Constitution by the legislavures of three-fourths of the several States within seven years from the date of its submission.

Amendment XXI [1933]

Section 1 The eighteenth article of amendment to the Constitution of the United States is hereby repealed.

Section 2 The transportation or importation into any State, Territory, or possession of the United States for delivery or use therein of intoxicating liquors, in violation of the laws thereof, is hereby prohibited.

Section 3 This article shall be inoperative unless it shall have been ratified as an amendment to the Constitution by conventions in the several States, as provided in the Constitution, within seven years from the date of submission hereof to the States by the Congress.

Amendment XXII [1951]

Section 1 No person shall be elected to the office of President more than twice, and no person who has held the office of President, or acted as President, for more than two years of a term to which some other person was elected President shall be elected to the office of the President more than once. But this Article shall not apply to any person holding the office of

President when this Article was proposed by the Congress, and shall not prevent any person who may be holding the office of President, or acting as President, during the term within which this Article becomes operative from holding the office of President or acting as President during the remainder of such term.

Section 2 This article shall be inoperative unless it shall have been ratified as an amendment to the Constitution by the legislatures of three-fourths of the several States within seven years from the date of its submission to the States by the Congress.

Amendment XXIII [1961]

Section 1 The District constituting the seat of Government of the United States shall appoint in such manner as the Congress may direct:

A number of electors of President and Vice-President equal to the whole number of Senators and Representatives in Congress to which the District would be entitled if it were a State, but in no event more than the least populous State; they shall be in addition to those appointed by the States, but they shall be considered, for the purposes of the election of President and Vice-President, to be electors appointed by a State; and they shall meet in the District and perform such duties as provided by the twelfth article of amendment.

Section 2 The Congress shall have power to enforce this article by appropriate legislation.

Amendment XXIV [1964]

Section 1 The right of citizens of the United States to vote in any primary or other election for President or Vice-President, for electors for President or Vice-President, or for Senator or Representative in Congress, shall not be denied or abridged by the United States or any State by reason of failure to pay any poll tax or other tax.

Section 2 The Congress shall have power to enforce this article by appropriate legislation.

Amendment XXV [1967]

Section 1 In case of the removal of the President from office or of his death or resignation, the Vice-President shall become President.

Section 2 Whenever there is a vacancy in the office of the Vice-President, the President shall nominate a Vice-President who shall take office upon confirmation by a majority vote of both houses of Congress.

Section 3 Whenever the President transmits to the President pro tempore of the Senate and the Speaker of the House of Representatives his written declaration that he is unable to discharge the powers and duties of his office, and until he transmits to them a written declaration to the contrary, such powers and duties shall be discharged by the Vice-President as Acting President.

Section 4 Whenever the Vice-President and a majority of either the principal officers of the executive departments or of such other body as Congress may by law provide, transmit to the President pro tempore of the Senate and the Speaker of the House of Representatives their written declaration that the President is unable to discharge the powers and duties of his office, the Vice-President shall immediately assume the powers and duties of the office as Acting President.

Thereafter, when the President transmits to the President pro tempore of the Senate and the Speaker of the House of Representatives his written declaration that no inability exists, he shall resume the powers and duties of his office unless the Vice-President and a majority of either the principal officers of the executive department or of such other body as Congress may by law provide, transmit within four days to the President pro tempore of the Senate and the Speaker of the House of Representatives their written declaration that the President is unable to discharge the powers and duties of his office. Thereupon Congress shall decide the issue, assembling within forty-eight hours for that purpose if not in session. If the Congress, within twenty-one days after receipt of the latter written declaration, or, if Congress is not in session, within twenty-one days after Congress is required to assemble, determines by two-thirds vote of both Houses that the President is unable to discharge the powers and duties of his office, the Vice-President shall continue to discharge the same as Acting President; otherwise, the President shall resume the powers and duties of his office.

Amendment XXVI [1971]

Section 1 The right of citizens of the United States, who are eighteen years of age or older, to vote shall not be denied or abridged by the United States or by any state on account of age.

Section 2 The Congress shall have power to enforce this article by appropriate legislation.

The American Nation

Admission of States into the Union

	State	Date of Admission		State	Date of Admission
1.	Delaware	December 7, 1787	26.	Michigan	January 26, 1837
2.	Pennsylvania	December 12, 1787	27.	Florida	March 3, 1845
3.	New Jersey	December 18, 1787	28.	Texas	December 29, 1845
4.	Georgia	January 2, 1788	29.	Iowa	December 28, 1846
5.	Connecticut	January 9, 1788	30.	Wisconsin	May 29, 1848
6.	Massachusetts	February 6, 1788	31.	California	September 9, 1850
7.	Maryland	April 28, 1788	32.	Minnesota	May 11, 1858
8.	South Carolina	May 23, 1788	33.	Oregon	February 14, 1859
9.	New Hampshire	June 21, 1788	34.	Kansas	January 29, 1861
10.	Virginia	June 25, 1788	35.	West Virginia	June 20, 1863
11.	New York	July 26, 1788	36.	Nevada	October 31, 1864
12.	North Carolina	November 21, 1789	37.	Nebraska	March 1, 1867
13.	Rhode Island	May 29, 1790	38.	Colorado	August 1, 1876
14.	Vermont	March 4, 1791	39.	North Dakota	November 2, 1889
15.	Kentucky	June 1, 1792	40.	South Dakota	November 2, 1889
16.	Tennessee	June 1, 1796	41.	Montana	November 8, 1889
17.	Ohio	March 1, 1803	42.	Washington	November 11, 1889
18.	Louisiana	April 30, 1812	43.	Idaho	July 3, 1890
19.	Indiana	December 11, 1816	44.	Wyoming	July 10, 1890
20.	Mississippi	December 10, 1817	45.	Utah	January 4, 1896
21.	Illinois	December 3, 1818	46.	Oklahoma	November 16, 1907
22.	Alabama	December 14, 1819	47.	New Mexico	January 6, 1912
23.	Maine	March 15, 1820	48.	Arizona	February 14, 1912
24.	Missouri	August 10, 1821	49.	Alaska	January 3, 1959
25.	Arkansas	June 15, 1836	50.	Hawaii	August 21, 1959

Territorial Expansion

Original states and territories	1783	Puerto Rico	1899
Louisiana Purchase	1803	Guam	1899
Florida	1819	Wake Island	1899
Texas	1845	The Philippines	1899–1946
Oregon	1846	American Samoa	1900
Mexican Cession	1848	Panama Canal Zone	1904–1978
Gadsden Purchase	1853	U.S. Virgin Islands	1917
Midway Islands	1867	Trust Territory of the Pacific Islands	1947
Alaska	1867	(North Mariana Islands, Micronesia, Marshall Islands, and Palau)	
Hawaii	1898		

Presidential Elections

Year	Candidates	Parties	Percent of Popular Vote	Electoral Vote	Percent Voter Participation
1789	**George Washington**	No party designations	*	69	
	John Adams[†]			34	
	Other candidates			35	
1792	**George Washington**	No party designations		132	
	John Adams			77	
	George Clinton			50	
	Other candidates			5	
1796	**John Adams**	Federalist		71	
	Thomas Jefferson	Democratic-Republican		68	
	Thomas Pinckney	Federalist		59	
	Aaron Burr	Democratic-Republican		30	
	Other candidates			48	
1800	**Thomas Jefferson**	Democratic-Republican		73	
	Aaron Burr	Democratic-Republican		73	
	John Adams	Federalist		65	
	Charles C. Pinckney	Federalist		64	
	John Jay	Federalist		1	
1804	**Thomas Jefferson**	Democratic-Republican		162	
	Charles C. Pinckney	Federalist		14	
1808	**James Madison**	Democratic-Republican		122	
	Charles C. Pinckney	Federalist		47	
	George Clinton	Democratic-Republican		6	
1812	**James Madison**	Democratic-Republican		128	
	DeWitt Clinton	Federalist		89	
1816	**James Monroe**	Democratic-Republican		183	
	Rufus King	Federalist		34	
1820	**James Monroe**	Democratic-Republican		231	
	John Quincy Adams	Independent Republican		1	
1824	**John Quincy Adams**	Democratic-Republican	30.5	84	26.9
	Andrew Jackson	Democratic-Republican	43.1	99	
	Henry Clay	Democratic-Republican	13.2	37	
	William H. Crawford	Democratic-Republican	13.1	41	
1828	**Andrew Jackson**	Democratic	56.0	178	57.6
	John Quincy Adams	National Republican	44.0	83	
1832	**Andrew Jackson**	Democratic	54.5	219	55.4
	Henry Clay	National Republican	37.5	49	
	William Wirt	Anti-Masonic	8.0	7	
	John Floyd	Democratic	‡	11	
1836	**Martin Van Buren**	Democratic	50.9	170	57.8
	William H. Harrison	Whig		73	
	Hugh L. White	Whig		26	
	Daniel Webster	Whig	49.1	14	
	W. P. Mangum	Whig		11	
1840	**William H. Harrison**	Whig	53.1	234	80.2
	Martin Van Buren	Democratic	46.9	60	

*Prior to 1824, most presidential electors were chosen by state legislatures rather than by popular vote.

[†]Before the Twelfth Amendment was passed in 1804, the electoral college voted for two presidential candidates; the runner-up became vice-president.

‡Percentages below 2.5 percent have been omitted. Hence the percentage of popular vote may not total 100 percent.

Year	Candidates	Parties	Percent of Popular Vote	Electoral Vote	Percent Voter Participation
1844	**James K. Polk**	Democratic	49.6	170	78.9
	Henry Clay	Whig	48.1	105	
	James G. Birney	Liberty	2.3		
1848	**Zachary Taylor**	Whig	47.4	163	72.7
	Lewis Cass	Democratic	42.5	127	
	Martin Van Buren	Free Soil	10.1		
1852	**Franklin Pierce**	Democratic	50.9	254	69.6
	Winfield Scott	Whig	44.1	42	
	John P. Hale	Free Soil	5.0		
1856	**James Buchanan**	Democratic	45.3	174	78.9
	John C. Frémont	Republican	33.1	114	
	Millard Fillmore	American	21.6	8	
1860	**Abraham Lincoln**	Republican	39.8	180	81.2
	Stephen A. Douglas	Democratic	29.5	12	
	John C. Breckinridge	Democratic	18.1	72	
	John Bell	Constitutional Union	12.6	39	
1864	**Abraham Lincoln**	Republican	55.0	212	73.8
	George B. McClellan	Democratic	45.0	21	
1868	**Ulysses S. Grant**	Republican	52.7	214	78.1
	Horatio Seymour	Democratic	47.3	80	
1872	**Ulysses S. Grant**	Republican	55.6	286	71.3
	Horace Greeley	Democratic	43.9		
1876	**Rutherford B. Hayes**	Republican	48.0	185	81.8
	Samuel J. Tilden	Democratic	51.0	184	
1880	**James A. Garfield**	Republican	48.5	214	79.4
	Winfield S. Hancock	Democratic	48.1	155	
	James B. Weaver	Greenback-Labor	3.4		
1884	**Grover Cleveland**	Democratic	48.5	219	77.5
	James G. Blaine	Republican	48.2	182	
1888	**Benjamin Harrison**	Republican	47.9	233	79.3
	Grover Cleveland	Democratic	48.6	168	
1892	**Grover Cleveland**	Democratic	46.1	277	74.7
	Benjamin Harrison	Republican	43.0	145	
	James B. Weaver	People's	8.5	22	
1896	**William McKinley**	Republican	51.1	271	79.3
	William J. Bryan	Democratic	47.7	176	
1900	**William McKinley**	Republican	51.7	292	73.2
	William J. Bryan	Democratic; Populist	45.5	155	
1904	**Theodore Roosevelt**	Republican	57.4	336	65.2
	Alton B. Parker	Democratic	37.6	140	
	Eugene V. Debs	Socialist	3.0		
1908	**William H. Taft**	Republican	51.6	321	65.4
	William J. Bryan	Democratic	43.1	162	
	Eugene V. Debs	Socialist	2.8		
1912	**Woodrow Wilson**	Democratic	41.9	435	58.8
	Theodore Roosevelt	Progressive	27.4	88	
	William H. Taft	Republican	23.2	8	
	Eugene V. Debs	Socialist	6.0		

Year	Candidates	Parties	Percent of Popular Vote	Electoral Vote	Percent Voter Participation
1916	**Woodrow Wilson**	Democratic	49.4	277	61.6
	Charles E. Hughes	Republican	46.2	254	
	A. L. Benson	Socialist	3.2		
1920	**Warren G. Harding**	Republican	60.4	404	49.2
	James M. Cox	Democratic	34.2	127	
	Eugene V. Debs	Socialist	3.4		
1924	**Calvin Coolidge**	Republican	54.0	382	48.9
	John W. Davis	Democratic	28.8	136	
	Robert M. LaFollette	Progressive	16.6	13	
1928	**Herbert C. Hoover**	Republican	58.2	444	56.9
	Alfred E. Smith	Democratic	40.9	87	
1932	**Franklin D. Roosevelt**	Democratic	57.4	472	56.9
	Herbert C. Hoover	Republican	39.7	59	
1936	**Franklin D. Roosevelt**	Democratic	60.8	523	61.0
	Alfred M. Landon	Republican	36.5	8	
1940	**Franklin D. Roosevelt**	Democratic	54.8	449	62.5
	Wendell L. Willkie	Republican	44.8	82	
1944	**Franklin D. Roosevelt**	Democratic	53.5	432	55.9
	Thomas E. Dewey	Republican	46.0	99	
1948	**Harry S. Truman**	Democratic	49.6	303	53.0
	Thomas E. Dewey	Republican	45.1	189	
1952	**Dwight D. Eisenhower**	Republican	55.1	442	63.3
	Adlai E. Stevenson	Democratic	44.4	89	
1956	**Dwight D. Eisenhower**	Republican	57.6	457	60.6
	Adlai E. Stevenson	Democratice	42.1	73	
1960	**John F. Kennedy**	Democratic	49.7	303	64.0
	Richard M. Nixon	Republican	49.5	219	
1964	**Lyndon B. Johnson**	Democratic	61.1	486	61.7
	Barry M. Goldwater	Republican	38.5	52	
1968	**Richard M. Nixon**	Republican	43.4	301	60.6
	Hubert H. Humphrey	Democratic	42.7	191	
	George C. Wallace	American Independent	13.5	46	
1972	**Richard M. Nixon**	Republican	60.7	520	55.5
	George S. McGovern	Democratic	37.5	17	
1976	**Jimmy Carter**	Democratic	50.1	297	54.3
	Gerald R. Ford	Republican	48.0	240	
1980	**Ronald W. Reagan**	Republican	50.7	489	53.0
	Jimmy Carter	Democratic	41.0	49	
	John B. Anderson	Independent	6.6	0	
1984	**Ronald W. Reagan**	Republican	58.4	525	52.9
	Walter F. Mondale	Democratic	41.6	13	
1988	**George H. W. Bush**	Republican	53.4	426	50.1
	Michael Dukakis	Democratic	45.6	111*	
1992	**Bill Clinton**	Democratic	43.7	370	54.0
	George H. W. Bush	Republican	38.0	168	
	H. Ross Perot	Independent	19.0	0	

*One Dukakis elector cast a vote for Lloyd Bentsen.

Supreme Court Justices

Name	Terms of Service	Appointed by	Name	Terms of Service	Appointed by
John Jay*, N.Y.	1789–1795	Washington	Rufus W. Peckham, N.Y.	1896–1909	Cleveland
James Wilson, Pa.	1789–1798	Washington	Joseph McKenna, Cal.	1898–1925	McKinley
John Rutledge, S.C.	1790–1791	Washington	Oliver W. Holmes, Mass.	1902–1932	T. Roosevelt
William Cushing, Mass.	1790–1810	Washington	William R. Day, Ohio	1903–1922	T. Roosevelt
John Blair, Va.	1790–1796	Washington	William H. Moody, Mass.	1906–1910	T. Roosevelt
James Iredell, N.C.	1790–1799	Washington	Horace H. Lurton, Tenn.	1910–1914	Taft
Thomas Johnson, Md.	1792–1793	Washington	Charles E. Hughes, N.Y.	1910–1916	Taft
William Paterson, N.J.	1793–1806	Washington	**Edward D. White**, La.	1910–1921	Taft
John Rutledge, S.C.	1795	Washington	Willis Van Devanter, Wy.	1911–1937	Taft
Samuel Chase, Md.	1796–1811	Washington	Joseph R. Lamar, Ga.	1911–1916	Taft
Oliver Ellsworth, Conn.	1796–1800	Washington	Mahlon Pitney, N.J.	1912–1922	Taft
Bushrod Washington, Va.	1799–1829	J. Adams	James C. McReynolds, Tenn.	1914–1941	Wilson
Alfred Moore, N.C.	1800–1804	J. Adams	Louis D. Brandeis, Mass.	1916–1939	Wilson
John Marshall, Va.	1801–1835	J. Adams	John H. Clarke, Ohio	1916–1922	Wilson
William Johnson, S.C.	1804–1834	Jefferson	**William H. Taft**, Conn.	1921–1930	Harding
Brockholst Livingston, N.Y.	1807–1823	Jefferson	George Sutherland, Utah	1922–1938	Harding
Thomas Todd, Ky.	1807–1826	Jefferson	Pierce Butler, Minn.	1923–1939	Harding
Gabriel Duvall, Md.	1811–1835	Madison	Edward T. Sanford, Tenn.	1923–1930	Harding
Joseph Story, Mass.	1812–1845	Madison	Harlan F. Stone, N.Y.	1925–1941	Coolidge
Smith Thompson, N.Y.	1823–1843	Monroe	**Charles E. Hughes**, N.Y.	1930–1941	Hoover
Robert Trimble, Ky.	1826–1828	J. Q. Adams	Owen J. Roberts, Penn.	1930–1945	Hoover
John McLean, Ohio	1830–1861	Jackson	Benjamin N. Cardozo, N.Y.	1932–1938	Hoover
Henry Baldwin, Pa.	1830–1844	Jackson	Hugo L. Black, Ala.	1937–1971	F. Roosevelt
James M. Wayne, Ga.	1835–1867	Jackson	Stanley F. Reed, Ky.	1938–1957	F. Roosevelt
Roger B. Taney, Md.	1836–1864	Jackson	Felix Frankfurter, Mass.	1939–1962	F. Roosevelt
Philip P. Barbour, Va.	1836–1841	Jackson	William O. Douglas, Conn.	1939–1975	F. Roosevelt
John Cartron, Tenn.	1837–1865	Van Buren	Frank Murphy, Mich.	1940–1949	F. Roosevelt
John McKinley, Ala.	1838–1852	Van Buren	**Harlan F. Stone**, N.Y.	1941–1946	F. Roosevelt
Peter V. Daniel, Va.	1842–1860	Van Buren	James R. Byrnes, S.C.	1941–1942	F. Roosevelt
Samuel Nelson, N.Y.	1845–1872	Tyler	Robert H. Jackson, N.Y.	1941–1954	F. Roosevelt
Levi Woodbury, N.H.	1845–1851	Polk	Wiley B. Rutledge, Iowa	1943–1949	F. Roosevelt
Robert C. Grier, Pa.	1846–1870	Polk	Harold H. Burton, Ohio	1945–1958	Truman
Benjamin R. Curtis, Mass.	1851–1857	Fillmore	**Frederick M. Vinson**, Ky.	1946–1953	Truman
John A. Campbell, Ala.	1853–1861	Pierce	Tom C. Clark, Texas	1949–1967	Truman
Nathan Clifford, Me.	1858–1881	Buchanan	Sherman Minton, Ind.	1949–1956	Truman
Noah H. Swayne, Ohio	1862–1881	Lincoln	**Earl Warren**, Cal.	1953–1969	Eisenhower
Samuel F. Miller, Iowa	1862–1890	Lincoln	John Marshall Harlan, N.Y.	1955–1971	Eisenhower
David Davis, Ill.	1862–1877	Lincoln	Willaim J. Brennan, Jr., N.J.	1956–1990	Eisenhower
Stephen J. Field, Cal.	1863–1897	Lincoln	Charles E. Whittaker, Mo.	1957–1962	Eisenhower
Salmon P. Chase, Ohio	1864–1873	Lincoln	Potter Stewart, Ohio	1958–1981	Eisenhower
William Strong, Pa.	1870–1880	Grant	Bryon R. White, Colo.	1962–	Kennedy
Joseph P. Bradley, N.J.	1870–1892	Grant	Arthur J. Goldberg, Ill.	1962–1965	Kennedy
Ward Hunt, N.Y.	1873–1882	Grant	Abe Fortas, Tenn.	1965–1969	Johnson
Morrison R. Waite, Ohio	1874–1888	Grant	Thurgood Marshall, Md.	1967–1991	Johnson
John M. Harlan, Ky.	1877–1911	Hayes	**Warren E. Burger**, Minn.	1969–1986	Nixon
William B. Woods, Ga.	1881–1887	Hayes	Harry A. Blackmun, Minn.	1970–	Nixon
Stanley Matthews, Ohio	1881–1889	Garfield	Lewis F. Powell, Jr., Va.	1971–1987	Nixon
Horace Gray, Mass.	1882–1902	Arthur	William H. Rehnquist, Ariz.	1971–1986	Nixon
Samuel Blatchford, N.Y.	1882–1893	Arthur	John Paul Stevens, Ill.	1975–	Ford
Lucius Q. C. Lamar, Miss.	1888–1893	Cleveland	Sandra Day O'Connor, Ariz.	1981–	Reagan
Melville W. Fuller, Ill.	1888–1910	Cleveland	**William H. Rehnquist**, Ariz.	1986–	Reagan
David J. Brewer, Kan.	1890–1910	B. Harrison	Antonin Scalia, Va.	1986–	Reagan
Henry B. Brown, Mich.	1891–1906	B. Harrison	Anthony M. Kennedy, Cal.	1988–	Reagan
George Shiras, Jr., Pa.	1892–1903	B. Harrison	David H. Souter, N.H.	1990	Bush
Howell E. Jackson, Tenn.	1893–1895	B. Harrison	Clarence Thomas, Ga.	1991–	Bush
Edward D. White, La.	1894–1910	Cleveland			

*Chief Justices are printed in bold type.

The American People: A Demographic Survey

A Demographic Profile of the American People

Year	Life Expectancy from Birth		Average Age at First Marriage		Number of Children Under 5 (per 1,000 Women Aged 20–44)	Percent of Women in Paid Employment	Percent of Paid Workers Who Are Female
	White	Black	Male	Female			
1820					1,295	6.2%	7.3%
1830					1,145	6.4	7.4
1840					1,085	8.4	9.6
1850					923	10.1	10.8
1860					929	9.7	10.2
1870					839	13.7	14.8
1880					822	14.7	15.2
1890			26.1	22.0	716	18.2	17.0
1900	47.6	33.0	25.9	21.9	688	21.2	18.1
1910	50.3	35.6	25.1	21.6	643	24.8	20.0
1920	54.9	45.3	24.6	21.2	604	23.9	20.4
1930	61.4	48.1	24.3	21.3	511	24.4	21.9
1940	64.2	53.1	24.3	21.5	429	25.4	24.6
1950	69.1	60.8	22.8	20.3	589	29.1	27.8
1960	70.6	63.6	22.8	20.3	737	34.8	32.3
1970	71.7	65.3	22.5	20.6	530	43.3	38.0
1980	74.4	68.1	24.7	22.0	440	51.5	42.6
1990	76.2	71.4	26.1	23.9	377	57.4	45.2

Source: Historical Statistics of the United States, Colonial Times to 1970 (1975); Statistical Abstract of the United States, 1991.

American Population

Year	Population	Percent Increase	Year	Population	Percent Increase
1610	350	—	1810	7,239,881	36.4
1620	2,300	557.1	1820	9,638,453	33.1
1630	4,600	100.0	1830	12,866,020	33.5
1640	26,600	478.3	1840	17,069,453	32.7
1650	50,400	90.8	1850	23,191,876	35.9
1660	75,100	49.0	1860	31,443,321	35.6
1670	111,900	49.0	1870	39,818,449	26.6
1680	151,500	35.4	1880	50,155,783	26.0
1690	210,400	38.9	1890	62,947,714	25.5
1700	250,900	19.2	1900	75,994,575	20.7
1710	331,700	32.2	1910	91,972,266	21.0
1720	466,200	40.5	1920	105,710,620	14.9
1730	629,400	35.0	1930	122,775,046	16.1
1740	905,600	43.9	1940	131,669,275	7.2
1750	1,170,800	29.3	1950	150,697,361	14.5
1760	1,593,600	36.1	1960	179,323,175	19.0
1770	2,148,100	34.8	1970	203,235,298	13.3
1780	2,780,400	29.4	1980	226,545,805	11.5
1790	3,929,214	41.3	1990	248,709,873	9.8
1800	5,308,483	35.1			

Note: These figures largely ignore the native American population. Census takers never made any effort to count the native American population that lived outside their political jurisdictions and compiled only casual and incomplete enumerations of those living within their jurisdictions until 1890. In that year the federal government attempted a full count of the Indian population: the Census found 125,719 Indians in 1890, compared with only 12,543 in 1870 and 33,985 in 1880.

Source: Historical Statistics of the United States, Colonial Times to 1970 (1975); Statistical Abstract of the United States, 1991.

White/Nonwhite Population

Urban/Rural Population

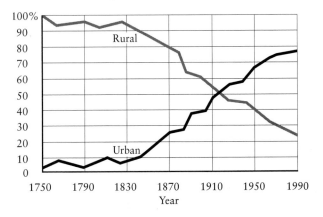

The Ten Largest Cities by Population, 1700–1990

		City	Population				City	Population
1700	1.	Boston	6,700		1910	1.	New York	4,766,883
	2.	New York	4,937*			2.	Chicago	2,185,283
	3.	Philadelphia	4,400†			3.	Philadelphia	1,549,008
						4.	St. Louis	687,029
1790	1.	Philadelphia	42,520			5.	Boston	670,585
	2.	New York	33,131			6.	Cleveland	560,663
	3.	Boston	18,038			7.	Baltimore	558,485
	4.	Charleston, S.C.	16,359			8.	Pittsburgh	533,905
	5.	Baltimore	13,503			9.	Detroit	465,766
	6.	Salem, Mass.	7,921			10.	Buffalo	423,715
	7.	Newport, R.I.	6,716					
	8.	Providence, R.I.	6,380		1930	1.	New York	6,930,446
	9.	Marblehead, Mass.	5,661			2.	Chicago	3,376,438
	10.	Portsmouth, N.H.	4,720			3.	Philadelphia	1,950,961
						4.	Detroit	1,568,662
1830	1.	New York	197,112			5.	Los Angeles	1,238,048
	2.	Philadelphia	161,410			6.	Cleveland	900,429
	3.	Baltimore	80,620			7.	St. Louis	821,960
	4.	Boston	61,392			8.	Baltimore	804,874
	5.	Charleston, S.C.	30,289			9.	Boston	781,188
	6.	New Orleans	29,737			10.	Pittsburgh	669,817
	7.	Cincinnati	24,831					
	8.	Albany, N.Y.	24,209		1950	1.	New York	7,891,957
	9.	Brooklyn, N.Y.	20,535			2.	Chicago	3,620,962
	10.	Washington, D.C.	18,826			3.	Philadelphia	2,071,605
						4.	Los Angeles	1,970,358
1850	1.	New York	515,547			5.	Detroit	1,849,568
	2.	Philadelphia	340,045			6.	Baltimore	949,708
	3.	Baltimore	169,054			7.	Cleveland	914,808
	4.	Boston	136,881			8.	St. Louis	856,796
	5.	New Orleans	116,375			9.	Washington, D.C.	802,178
	6.	Cincinnati	115,435			10.	Boston	801,444
	7.	Brooklyn, N.Y.	96,838					
	8.	St. Louis	77,860		1970	1.	New York	7,895,563
	9.	Albany, N.Y.	50,763			2.	Chicago	3,369,357
	10.	Pittsburgh	46,601			3.	Los Angeles	2,811,801
						4.	Philadelphia	1,949,996
1870	1.	New York	942,292			5.	Detroit	1,514,063
	2.	Philadelphia	674,022			6.	Houston	1,233,535
	3.	Brooklyn, N.Y.	419,921†			7.	Baltimore	905,787
	4.	St. Louis	310,864			8.	Dallas	844,401
	5.	Chicago	298,977			9.	Washington, D.C.	756,668
	6.	Baltimore	267,354			10.	Cleveland	750,879
	7.	Boston	250,526					
	8.	Cincinnati	216,239		1990	1.	New York	7,322,564
	9.	New Orleans	191,418			2.	Los Angeles	3,485,398
	10.	San Francisco	149,473			3.	Chicago	2,783,726
						4.	Houston	1,630,553
						5.	Philadelphia	1,585,577
						6.	San Diego	1,110,549
						7.	Detroit	1,027,974
						8.	Dallas	1,006,877
						9.	Phoenix	983,403
						10.	San Antonio	935,933

*Figure from a census taken in 1698.
†Philadelphia figures include suburbs.
‡Annexed to New York in 1898.
Source: U.S. Census data.

Foreign Origins of the American People

Immigration by Decade

Year	Number	Percent of Total Population	Year	Number	Percent of Total Population
1821–1830	151,824	1.6	1921–1930	4,107,209	3.9
1831–1840	599,125	4.6	1931–1940	528,431	0.4
1841–1850	1,713,251	10.0	1941–1950	1,035,039	0.7
1851–1860	2,598,214	11.2	1951–1960	2,515,479	1.6
1861–1870	2,314,824	7.4	1961–1970	3,321,677	1.8
1871–1880	2,812,191	7.1	1971–1980	4,493,000	2.2
1881–1890	5,246,613	10.5	1981–1990	7,338,000	3.0
1891–1900	3,687,546	5.8	Total	23,338,835	
1901–1910	8,795,386	11.6			
1911–1920	5,735,811	6.2	1821–1990	56,993,620	
Total	33,654,785		Grand Total		

Source: U. S. Bureau of the Census, *Historical Statistics of the United States,*
Colonial Times to 1970 (1975), Part I, pp. 105–106; *Statistical Abstract of the*
United States, 1991.

Regional Origins

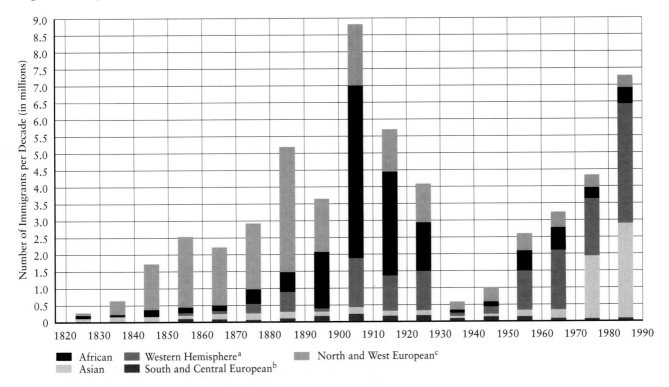

[a] Canada and all countries in South America and Central America.

[b] Italy, Spain, Portugal, Greece, Germany (Austria included, 1938–1945), Poland, Czechoslovakia (since 1920), Yugoslavia (since 1920), Hungary (since 1861), Austria (since 1861, except 1938–1945), former U.S.S.R. (excludes Asian U.S.S.R. between 1931 and 1963), Latvia, Estonia, Lithuania, Finland, Romania, Bulgaria, Turkey (in Europe), and other European countries not classified elsewhere.

[c] Great Britain, Ireland, Norway, Sweden, Denmark, Iceland, Netherlands, Belgium, Luxembourg, Switzerland, France.

Source: Stephan Thernstrom, ed., *Harvard Encyclopedia of American Ethnic Groups* (1980), p. 480; and U.S. Bureau of the Census, *Statistical Abstract of the United States, 1991.*

The Labor Force

(thousands of workers)

Year	Agriculture	Mining	Manufacturing	Construction	Trade	Other Services	Total
1810	1,956	11	75	—	—	288	2,330
1840	3,594	32	500	290	350	894	5,660
1850	4,520	102	1,200	410	530	1,488	8,250
1860	5,880	176	1,530	520	890	2,114	11,110
1870	6,790	180	2,470	780	1,310	1,400	12,930
1880	8,961	280	3,290	900	1,930	2,029	17,390
1890	9,960	440	4,390	1,510	2,960	4,060	23,320
1900	11,680	637	5,895	1,665	3,970	5,223	29,070
1910	11,770	1,068	8,332	1,949	5,320	9,041	37,480
1920	10,790	1,180	11,190	1,233	5,845	11,372	41,610
1930	10,633	1,009	9,884	1,988	8,122	17,194	48,830
1940	9,575	925	11,309	1,876	9,328	23,277	56,290
1950	7,870	901	15,648	3,029	12,152	25,870	65,470
1960	6,015	709	17,145	3,640	14,051	32,500	74,060
1970	3,463	623	19,367	3,588	15,040	36,597	78,678
1980	3,364	1,027	20,285	4,346	20,310	49,971	99,303
1990	3,186	711	19,111	5,136	25,888	63,882	117,914

Source: Stanley Lebergott, "Labor Force and Employment, 1800–1960," *Output, Employment, and Productivity in the United States After 1800* (New York: National Bureau of Economic Research, 1966); U.S. Bureau of Economic Analysis, *Long-Term Economic Growth, 1860–1970* (Washington, D.C., 1973), 260–263; U.S. Bureau of Labor Statistics, *Employment and Earnings* (October–December, 1991).

Changing Labor Patterns

The Aging of the U. S. Population

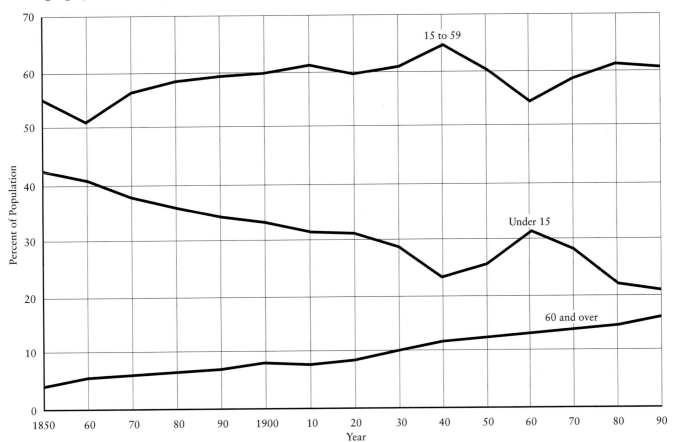

The American Government and Economy

The Growth of the Federal Government

The Federal Government, 1900–1980

Year	Employees (millions)		Year	Receipts and Outlays ($ millions)	
	Civilian	Military		Receipts	Outlays
1900	0.23	0.12	1900	567	521
1910	0.38	0.13	1910	676	694
1920	0.65	0.34	1920	6,649	6,358
1930	0.61	0.25	1930	4,058	3,320
1940	1.04	0.45	1940	6,900	9,600
1950	1.96	1.46	1950	40,900	43,100
1960	2.38	2.47	1960	92,500	92,200
1970	2.98	3.06	1970	193,700	196,600
1980	2.98	2.05	1980	517,112	590,920
1989	2.98	2.13	1990	1,031,462	1,251,850

Source: Statistical Profile of the United States, 1900–1980; Statistical Abstract of the United States, 1991.

Total Federal Debt, 1900–1990

Gross National Product, 1840–1990

*Note: GNP values have not been adjusted for inflation or deflation. GNP is plotted here on a logarithmic scale.
Source: Statistical Abstract of the United States, 1991.

GNP per Capita, 1840–1990

*Note: GNP values have not been adjusted for inflation or deflation. The GNP is plotted here on a logarithmic scale.

Consumer Price Index and Conversion Table

Year	Price Index* (1860 = 100)	Conversion Multiplier†	Year	Price Index	Conversion Multiplier	Year	Price Index	Conversion Multiplier
1700	130	53.3	1800	151	10.4	1900	101	15.5
1710	100	69.3	1810	148	10.6	1910	114	13.7
1720	76	91.3	1820	141	11.1	1920	240	6.5
1730	80	86.7	1830	111	14.1	1930	200	7.8
1740	66	105.1	1840	104	15.1	1940	168	9.3
1750	84	82.6	1850	94	16.6	1950	288	5.4
1760	96	72.3	1860	100	15.6	1960	354	4.4
1770	100	69.3	1870	157	9.9	1970	464	3.4
1780	165	9.5	1880	123	12.7	1980	985	1.6
1790	148	10.6	1890	109	14.3	1990	1563	1.0

* This index estimates how consumer prices changed on the average over ten-year intervals. Such estimates are highly uncertain, particularly when they are used to make comparisons over long periods of time. This is partly because it is extremely difficult to measure how the typical mix of goods (each with its own price) purchased by consumers changes over time.

† To convert £ (pounds Sterling, until 1770) or $ (U.S. dollars, beginning in 1780) from any date in the past to the equivalent in 1990 dollars, multiply the historical price by the appropriate number in this column. For example, £10 Sterling in 1730 would equal about $867 in 1990. (£10 × 86.7 = $867); or $10 in 1870 would equal about $99 in 1990 ($10 × 9.9 = $99).

Source: Adapted from John J. McCusker, "How Much Is That in Real Money? A Historical Price Index for Use as a Deflator of Money Value in the Economy of the United States," *Proceedings of the American Antiquarian Society,* Vol. 101, pt. 2, (1991), 297–390.

Illustration Credits

Chapter 16   **P. 480:** Chicago Historical Society.   **Pp. 482 and 484:** Library of Congress.   **P. 485:** Chicago Historical Society.   **P. 487:** Courtesy of the New-York Historical Society, New York City.   **P. 489:** Library of Congress.   **P. 492:** Collection of Mrs. Nancy W. Livingston and Mrs. Elizabeth Livingston Jaeger. Photograph courtesy of the Los Angeles County Museum of Art.   **P. 493:** The Bettmann Archive.   **P. 495:** Library of Congress.   **P. 496:** *Harper's Weekly,* June 23, 1866. Courtesy of the Newberry Library, Chicago.   **P. 497:** Rutherford B. Hayes Presidential Center, Spiegel Grove, Freemont, OH.   **P. 499:** Brown Brothers.   **P. 500:** Collection Tennessee State Museum. Photograph by Karina McDaniel. Courtesy of the Tennessee State Library & Archives, Nashville.   **P. 506:** Historical Pictures/Stock Montage, Inc.   **P. 508:** *Frank Leslie's Illustrated Newspaper,* September 23, 1876. Courtesy of the Newberry Library, Chicago.

Chapter 17   **P. 514:** Courtesy of the New-York Historical Society, New York City. Bella C. Landauer Collection.   **P. 517:** South Dakota State Historical Society, Pierre.   **P. 518:** Idaho State Historical Society, Boise.   **P. 521:** Culver Pictures.   **P. 522:** Buffalo Bill Historical Center, Cody, WY. Gift of the Coe Foundation.   **P. 523:** Culver Pictures.   **P. 526:** Archives & Manuscript Division of the Oklahoma Historical Society, Oklahoma City.   **P. 528:** Smithsonian Institution Photo No. 3200–b-8.   **P. 530:** The Thomas Gilcrease Institute of American History and Art, Tulsa, OK.   **P. 531:** Bancroft Library, University of California, Berkeley.   **P. 532:** William Hahn, *Market Scene, Sansome Street, San Francisco,* 1872. Oil on canvas, 60" x 96". © 1872 Crocker Collection, Crocker Art Museum, Sacramento, CA.   **P. 535:** Yosemite National Park Research Library, Yosemite National Park, CA.   **P. 536:** Solomon D. Butcher Collection, Nebraska State Historical Society, Lincoln.   **P. 538:** Library of Congress.   **P. 541:** Courtesy of the California Historical Society, San Francisco. FN 29120.   **P. 542:** Library of Congress.

Chapter 18   **P. 546:** Chicago Historical Society.   **P. 549:** Culver Pictures.   **P. 551:** Historical Pictures/Stock Montage, Inc.   **P. 555:** National Museum of American History, Smithsonian Institution Photo No. 89–5099.   **P. 558:** *Harper's Weekly,* Vol. 31, 1887; pp. 158–159. Courtesy of the Newberry Library, Chicago.   **P. 563:** International Museum of Photography at George Eastman House, Rochester, NY.   **P. 565:** The Bettmann Archive.   **P. 566:** Library of

Congress.   **P. 568:** The Bettmann Archive.   **P. 570:** Library of Congress.   **P. 573:** Historical Pictures/Stock Montage, Inc.

Chapter 19   **P. 578:** Museum of American Political Life, University of Hartford, West Hartford, CT. Photograph by Sally Andersen-Bruce.   **P. 580:** Culver Pictures.   **P. 582:** Brown Brothers.   **P. 584:** Museum of American Political Life, University of Hartford, West Hartford, CT. Photograph by Sally Andersen-Bruce.   **P. 586:** The Kansas State Historical Society, Topeka.   **P. 587:** From the Collection of the Newport Historical Society, Newport, RI (P292).   **P. 590:** Brown Brothers.   **P. 593:** Courtesy of the New-York Historical Society, New York City.   **P. 594:** Culver Pictures.   **P. 600:** General Research Division, New York Public Library, Astor, Lenox, and Tilden Foundations.   **P. 602:** Library of Congress.

Chapter 20   **P. 606:** W. Louis Sonntag, Jr., *The Bowery at Night,* 1895, Museum of the City of New York, Gift of Mrs. William B. Miles.   **P. 610:** The Bettmann Archive.   **P. 611:** Museum of the City of New York, Gift of Louis Stearns, 1889–1914.   **P. 614:** Seaver Center for Western History Research, Natural History Museum of Los Angeles County.   **P. 616:** New York Public Library, Astor, Lenox, and Tilden Foundations.   **P. 621:** Culver Pictures.   **P. 622:** Archives of Industrial Society, University Library System, University of Pittsburgh.   **P. 624:** Culver Pictures.   **P. 625:** Historical Pictures/Stock Montage, Inc.   **P. 626:** Brown Brothers.   **P. 627:** The Preservation Society of Newport County, Newport, RI.   **P. 630:** Courtesy of the Cincinnati Historical Society.   **P. 631:** Museum of the City of New York, Byron Collection.   **P. 632:** John Singer Sargent, *Mr. and Mrs. Isaac Newton Phelps Stokes,* 1897. Oil on canvas, 84 $\frac{1}{4}$" x 39 $\frac{3}{4}$". The Metropolitan Museum of Art, New York. Bequest of Edith Minturn Phelps Stokes (Mrs. I.N.), 1938 (38.104).   **P. 634:** The Metropolitan Museum of Art, New York.

Chapter 21   **P. 638:** George Wesley Bellows, *Cliff Dwellers,* 1913. Oil on canvas, 39 $\frac{1}{2}$" x 41 $\frac{1}{2}$". Los Angeles County Museum of Art, Los Angeles County Fund.   **P. 642** (left): Ida M. Tarbell Collection, Reis Library, Allegheny College, Meadville, PA.   **P. 642** (right): Culver Pictures.   **P. 644:** State Historical Society of Wisconsin, Madison.   **P. 647:** Schlesinger Library, Radcliffe College, Cambridge, MA.   **P. 648:** Chicago Historical Society.   **P. 649:** Brown Brothers.   **P. 650:**

The Bettmann Archive. **P. 651:** Brown Brothers. **P. 655:** Courtesy NAACP National Headquarters. **P. 657:** Library of Congress. **P. 658:** Edward Steichen, *J. Pierpont Morgan* (1903), Plate V from the boxed edition de Luxe of the Steichen Supplement to *Camera Work*, April 1906. Published simultaneously with No. XIV, April 1906. Gravure, 8 $\frac{1}{8}$" x 6 $\frac{1}{4}$". Collection, The Museum of Modern Art, New York. Gift of A. Conger Goodyear. **P. 659:** Library of Congress. **P. 662:** Woodrow Wilson—Democratic Nominee For President, *Harper's Weekly*, July 13, 1912. Courtesy of the Newberry Library, Chicago.

Chapter 22 **P. 668:** James G. Tyler, *Battle of Santiago de Cuba,* 1898. Courtesy of the Franklin D. Roosevelt Library, Hyde Park, NY. **P. 672:** Courtesy of the New-York Historical Society, New York City. Bella C. Landauer Collection. **P. 674:** Culver Pictures. **P. 675:** U.S. Naval Historical Center, Washington, DC. **P. 677:** Chicago Historical Society. **P. 681:** Library of Congress. **P. 683** (top): National Archives. **P. 683** (bottom): G. W. Peters, *Harper's Weekly,* April 22, 1899. Courtesy of the Newberry Library, Chicago. **P. 684:** Joseph Keppler, Jr., *His 126th Birthday—Gee, but this is an awful stretch!* From *Puck,* June 29, 1904. Courtesy of the Newberry Library, Chicago. **P. 687:** UPI/Bettmann. **P. 688:** The Pat Hathaway Collection of California Views.

Chapter 23 **P. 696:** The Lester Levy Collection of Sheet Music. Milton S. Eisenhower Library, The Johns Hopkins University, Baltimore, MD. *Oh, How I Hate to Get up in the Morning* © 1918 by Irving Berlin; © renewed 1945 by Irving Berlin; © assigned to Trustees of God Bless America Fund. **P. 699:** Imperial War Museum, London. **P. 700:** Culver Pictures. **Pp. 701 and 702:** UPI/Bettmann. **P. 703:** Library of Congress. **Pp. 706 and 708:** The Bettmann Archive. **P. 709:** UPI/Bettmann. **P. 712:** National Archives. Photograph by M. Rudolph Vetter. **P. 713:** Schlesinger Library, Radcliffe College, Cambridge, MA. **P. 714:** Library of Congress. **P. 715:** Historical Pictures/Stock Montage, Inc. **P. 717:** National Archives. Photograph by M. Rudolph Vetter **P. 720** (all): Chicago Historical Society. Photographs by Jun Fujita.

Chapter 24 **P. 726:** © Mazda, General Electric, courtesy of Baker Library, Dartmouth College, Hanover, NH. Photograph: © 1992 Jeffrey Nintzel. All rights reserved. **P. 728:** The Bettmann Archive. **P. 731:** Charles Sheeler, *Untitled (River Rouge Plant),* 1927, University Art Museum, University of New Mexico, Albuquerque. Gift of Eleanor and Van Deren Coke. **P. 734:** Culver Pictures. **P. 735:** Ruth Kravette, Jericho, NY. **P. 736:** *Portrait of Luisa Ronstadt Espinal,* c. 1921, Arizona Historical Society Library. Gift of Edward Ronstadt, Mexican Heritage Project. **P. 738:** Library of Congress. **P. 739:** Globe Photos. **P. 740:** Photofest. **P. 741:** Courtesy of Christopher Casler. **P. 742:** Kansas City Museum, Kansas City, MO. **P. 743:** George Bellows, *Dempsey and Firpo,* 1924. Oil on canvas, 51" x 63 $\frac{1}{4}$". Whitney Museum of American Art, New York. Purchased with funds from Gertrude Vanderbilt (Whitney. 31.95. Photograph by Geoffrey Clements). **P. 747:** W. A. Swift Collection, Archives and Special Collections, A. M. Bracken Library, Ball State University, Muncie, IN. **P. 749:** Aaron Douglas, *Rise, Shine for Thy Light Has Come,* c. 1930, The Howard University Gallery of Art, Permanent Collection, Washington, DC. **P. 751:** John Sloan, *The Lafayette,* 1928. Oil on canvas, 30 $\frac{1}{2}$" x 36 $\frac{1}{4}$". The Metropolitan Museum of Art, New York. Gift of Friends of John Sloan, 1928 (28.18).

Chapter 25 **P. 756:** Isaac Soyer, *Employment Agency,* 1937. Oil on canvas, 34 $\frac{1}{4}$" x 45". Whitney Museum of American Art, New York. Purchase 37.44. Photograph by Geoffrey Clements. **P. 758:** UPI/Bettmann. **P. 762:** Reginald Marsh, *The Park Bench,* 1933. Tempera on masonite. 24" x 36". Nebraska Art Association Collection, Sheldon Memorial Art Gallery, University of Nebraska, Lincoln. **P. 763:** Franklin D. Roosevelt Library, Hyde Park, NY. **P. 767:** Courtesy of William C. Kluver. **P. 768** (both): Courtesy of Steve

Schapiro. **P. 771** (left): UPI/Bettmann. **P. 771** (right): Schomburg Center for Research in Black Culture, The New York Public Library, Astor, Lenox, and Tilden Foundations. **P. 772:** The Bettmann Archive. **P. 774:** C. David Stone Martin, *Electrification.* Color sketch. Photograph courtesy of the Public Buildings Service, General Services Administration. **P. 775:** The Bettmann Archive. **P. 776:** Ben Shahn, *Years of Dust,* 1936, Library of Congress. **P. 777:** Library of Congress. **P. 778:** University of Texas, The Institute of Texan Cultures, *San Antonio Light* Collection. **P. 780** (top): Brown Brothers. **P. 780** (bottom): FPG International.

Chapter 26 **P. 786:** Library of Congress. **P. 788:** AP/Wide World Photos. **P. 789:** UPI/Bettmann. **P. 791:** Courtesy *Vanity Fair* © 1935 (renewed 1963) by The Condé Nast Publications, Inc. **P. 792:** UPI/Bettmann. **P. 793:** San Francisco Public Library. **P. 794:** Library of Congress. **P. 799:** Brown Brothers. **P. 801:** Franklin D. Roosevelt Library, Hyde Park, NY. **P. 802** (top): Ben Shahn, *Steel Workers Organizing Committee* Poster, 1930s. Library of Congress. **P. 802** (bottom): UPI/Bettmann. **P. 804:** William Gropper, *Construction of a Dam,* 1937. (Mural study, Department of the Interior), National Museum of American Art/Art Resource. **P. 807:** Joseph Binder, *World's Fair* Poster, Collection of The Queens Museum of Art, Queens, NY. Gift of Clara Binder. **P. 808:** O. Louis Guglielmi, *Relief Blues,* c. 1938, National Museum of American Art/Art Resource. **P. 810:** Anthony Velonis, WPA *Macbeth* Poster, Library of Congress. **P. 811:** Margaret Bourke-White, *Life Magazine* © 1936 Time Warner, Inc. **P. 812:** From *Champion,* November 1937. Library of Congress.

Chapter 27 **P. 816:** Library of Congress. **P. 819:** Hugo Jaeger, *Life Magazine* © Time Warner, Inc. **P. 820:** Library of Congress. **P. 822:** UPI/Bettmann. **P. 824:** Courtesy of the Dorothea Lange Collection. The City of Oakland, The Oakland Museum. 1982. **P. 825:** Library of Congress. **P. 826:** National Air and Space Museum, Smithsonian Institution, Washington, DC. **P. 828:** Ben Shahn, *For Full Employment After the War Register Vote,* 1944. Offset lithograph, printed in color, 30" x 39 $\frac{7}{8}$". Collection, The Museum of Modern Art, New York. Gift of the CIO Political Action Committee. **P. 829:** Library of Congress. **P. 830:** Lee Boltin Picture Library. **P. 832:** UPI/Bettmann. **P. 833:** Myron Davis, *Life Magazine* © Time Warner, Inc. **P. 837:** Margaret Bourke-White, *Life Magazine* © Time Warner, Inc. **P. 840:** UPI/Bettmann. **P. 841:** Margaret Bourke-White, *Life Magazine* © Time Warner, Inc. **P. 844:** Frank Scherschel, *Life Magazine* © 1942 Time Warner, Inc. **P. 845:** Franklin D. Roosevelt Library, Hyde Park, NY. (Photographed by U.S. Army Signal Corps.) **P. 846:** UPI/Bettmann.

Chapter 28 **P. 852:** Los Alamos National Laboratory. **P. 854:** FPG International. **P. 856** (left): UPI/Bettmann. **P. 856** (right): AP/Wide World Photos. **P. 858:** UPI/Bettmann. **P. 859:** Fenno Jacobs/Black Star. **P. 863:** UPI/Bettmann. **P. 864:** Wayne Miller/Magnum. **P. 865:** Western History Collections, University of Oklahoma Library, The Helen Gahagan Douglas Collection. **P. 867** (both): UPI/Bettmann. **P. 871:** Robert Phillips/Black Star. **Pp. 873, 874, and 875:** AP/World Wide Photos. **P. 877:** FPG International. **P. 879:** The Bettmann Archive.

Chapter 29 **P. 884:** © 1955 The Curtis Publishing Company. **P. 887:** Tom Wesselmann, *Still Life #24,* 1962, The Nelson-Atkins Museum of Art (Gift of the Guild of the Friends of Art), Kansas City, MO. **P. 888:** FPG International. **P. 889:** Charles Babbage Institute, University of Minnesota. **P. 891:** Ruth Kravette, Jericho, NY. **P. 892:** Photograph by Dan Weiner. Courtesy of Sarah Weiner. **P. 897:** Bern Keating/Black Star. **P. 898:** Levittown Public Library, Levittown, NY. **P. 901:** Globe Photos. **P. 903:** Photograph courtesy of Herbert Gans. Reprinted from Herbert Gans, *The Urban Villagers,* updated and expanded edition, Free Press/Macmillan (© 1962 Free Press; © 1982 Herbert J. Gans). **P. 904:** From the collections of

Henry Ford Museum and Greenfield Village. Courtesy of Franchise Associates, Inc., South Weymouth, MA. **P. 905:** Photofest. **P. 907:** March of Dimes Birth Defects Foundation. **P. 908:** © 1956 BMG Music. **P. 909:** Eve Arnold/Magnum. **P. 911:** Elliott Erwitt/Magnum. **P. 912:** Joe Steinmetz, *Longboat Key, Florida, 1958.* Courtesy of the Carpenter Center for the Visual Arts, Harvard University, Cambridge, MA, and Mrs. Joe Steinmetz.

Chapter 30 **P. 916:** Robert Rauschenberg, *Kite,* 1963. Oil and silkscreen on canvas, 84" x 60". Courtesy of the Sonnabend Collection, NY. © Robert Rauschenberg/VAGA NY. **P. 918:** Hank Walker, *Life Magazine* © Time Warner, Inc. **P. 923:** UPI/Bettmann. **P. 926:** Charles Harbutt/Actuality, Inc. **P. 927:** Dewitt Collection, Museum of American Political Life, University of Hartford, West Hartford, CT. Photograph by Sally Andersen-Bruce. **P. 928:** George Tames/New York Times Pictures. **P. 930:** Michael Abramson/Gamma Liaison. **P. 933:** Robert Ellison, © 1968 *Empire News*/Black Star. **P. 934:** Larry Burrows, *Life Magazine* © Time Warner, Inc. **P. 936:** U.S. Army Photo. U.S. Department of Defense, Still Media Records Center, Washington, DC. **Pp. 938 and 939:** UPI/Bettmann. **P. 940:** AP/World Wide Photos.

Chapter 31 **P. 944:** Museum of American Political Life, University of Hartford, West Hartford, CT. Photograph by Sally Andersen-Bruce. **P. 946:** Elliott Erwitt/Magnum. **P. 947:** AP/Wide World Photos. **P. 949:** Bruce Davidson/Magnum. **P. 950:** Danny Lyon/Magnum. **P. 952:** AP/Wide World Photos. **P. 954:** Andy Warhol, *Red Race Riot,* 1963. Silkscreen ink on synthetic polymer paint on canvas. 137 $\frac{7}{8}$" x 82 $\frac{3}{4}$". The Andy Warhol Foundation for the Visual Arts. **Pp. 955 and 956:** Eve Arnold/Magnum. **P. 958:** Michael Alexander/Black Star. **P. 959:** FPG International. **P. 961:** UPI/Bettmann. **P. 963:** Paul Fusco/Magnum. **P. 964:** Michael Abramson/Black Star. **P. 965:** © Apple Corps Ltd. **P. 966:** Paul Fusco/Magnum. **P. 971:** Steve Northup/*Time.*

Chapter 32 **P. 976:** NASA. **P. 978:** Steve Schapiro/Black Star. **P. 979:** Dennis Brack/Black Star. **P. 981:** Burt Glinn/Magnum. **P. 984:** Marc Riboud/Magnum. **P. 987:** UPI/Bettmann. **P. 988:** R. Mims/Sygma. **P. 989:** Photofest. **P. 990:** Dennis Brack/Black Star. **P. 992:** Tony Korody/Sygma. **P. 994:** Jim Anderson/Black Star. **P. 996:** © Stanley Forman. **P. 1001:** D. B. Owen/Black Star. **P. 1002:** Mingam/Gamma Liaison.

Chapter 33 **P. 1006:** R. Bossu/Sygma. **P. 1009:** Michael Evans/Sygma. **P. 1011:** Tannenbaum/Sygma. **P. 1012:** J. L. Atlan/Sygma. **P. 1014:** John Dolan, hand-coloring by Ann Rhoney. **P. 1015:** Naoki Okamoto/Black Star. **P. 1016:** Thomas Hoepker/Magnum. **P. 1017:** David Butow/Black Star. **P. 1020:** Kay Chernush/The Image Bank. **P. 1021:** © Estate of Keith Haring. **P. 1023:** W. Eastep/The Stock Market. **P. 1026:** Markel/Gamma Liaison. **P. 1028** (top): Reuters/Bettmann. **P. 1028** (bottom): East News/SIPA Press. **P. 1030:** Luc Delahaye/SIPA Press. **P. 1032** (top): S. Compoint/Sygma. **P. 1032** (bottom): Dagmar Fabricius/Gamma Liaison. **P. 1033:** Sobol/SIPA Press.

Index